Sales Composition of Selected Multinational Corporations*

MNC	Total Sales (in millions of $)	U.S. Sales (in millions of $)	U.S. Sales as % of Total	Foreign Sales (in millions of $)	Foreign Sales as % of Total	Europe Sales as % of Total
Alcoa	$10,710	$ 6,383	59.6%	$ 4,327	40.4%	9.3%
Allied Signal	12,343	9,395	76.1	2,948	23.9	14.1
American Brands,	13,781	4,686	37.3	9,095	62.7	61.7
Baxter International	8,100	6,664	82.3	1,436	17.7	12.8
Bristol-Myers Squibb	10,300	7,017	68.1	3,283	31.9	26.0
Chrysler	46,374	30,710	66.2	15,664	33.8	NA
Coca Cola	10,236	3,931	38.4	6,305	61.6	27.4
CPC International	5,781	2,322	40.2	3,459	59.8	36.6
Digital Equipment Corporation	12,942	5,823	45.0	7,119	55.0	40.5
Dow	19,733	9,494	48.1	10,239	51.9	31.8
DuPont	40,047	22,634	56.5	17,413	43.5	32.8
Ford	81,844	48,761	59.6	33,083	40.4	29.0
PepsiCo	17,803	14,047	78.9	3,756	21.1	7.5
Pfizer	6,406	3,473	54.3	2,933	45.7	23.5
Phillip Morris	51,169	36,014	70.4	15,155	29.6	24.3
PPG Industries	6,021	3,958	65.7	2,063	34.3	25.3
Reynolds Metals Company	6,022	4,944	82.1	1,078	17.9	NA
Tenneco	14,511	10,480	72.2	4,031	27.8	21.8
3M	13,021	6,802	52.2	6,219	47.8	28.5
TRW	8,169	5,617	68.8	2,552	31.2	21.7
Union Carbide	7,621	4,846	63.6	2,775	36.4	10.5
USX Corporation	20,659	19,670	95.2	989	4.8	4.0
Warner Lambert	4,687	2,445	52.2	2,242	47.8	23.3
Westinghouse	12,915	11,359	87.9	1,556	12.1	NA
Zenith Electronics	1,410	1,325	93.9	85	6.1	NA

*Data are as of December 31, 1990. Interested readers should obtain annual reports for more specific details.

THIRD EDITION

International Financial Management

THIRD EDITION

International Financial Management

Jeff Madura

Florida Atlantic University

WEST PUBLISHING COMPANY
ST. PAUL   NEW YORK   LOS ANGELES   SAN FRANCISCO

Library of Congress Cataloging-in-Publication Data

Madura, Jeff.
    International financial management / Jeff Madura.— 3rd ed.
        p.   cm.
    Includes bibliographical references and index.
    ISBN 0–314–86272–2
    1. International finance. 2. Foreign exchange problem. 3. Asset
—liability management. 4. Banks and banking, International.
5. International business enterprises—Finance. I. Title.
HG3881.M2765 1992
658.15'99—dc20   91-8112
                                        ∞   CIP

PRODUCTION CREDITS
Artwork   David J. Farr, ImageSmythe, Inc.
Composition   Carlisle Communications, Ltd.
Copyediting   Margaret Jarpey
Cover Design   John Rokusek
Cover Photo   Sydney, Australia by Telegraph Colour Library/FPG International
Text Design   David J. Farr, ImageSmythe, Inc.

To My Parents

CONTENTS IN BRIEF

CONTENTS

Preface xxv

PART ONE

The International Financial Environment 1

CHAPTER 1
Multinational Financial Management: An Overview 3

CHAPTER 4
Exchange Rate Determination 91

CHAPTER 5
Currency Futures and Options 123

PART TWO

Exchange Rate Behavior 151

CHAPTER 6
Government Influence on Exchange Rates 153

CHAPTER 7
International Arbitrage and Interest Rate Parity 179

CHAPTER 8
**Relationships between Inflation, Interest Rates, and
Exchange Rates 201**

PART THREE

Exchange Rate Risk Management 229

CHAPTER 9
Forecasting Exchange Rates 231

CHAPTER 10
Measuring Exposure to Exchange Rate Fluctuations 265

CHAPTER 11
Managing Transaction Exposure 313

CHAPTER 12
Managing Economic Exposure and Translation Exposure 353

PART FOUR

Short-Term Asset and Liability Management 367

CHAPTER 15
International Cash Management 415

PART FIVE

Long-Term Asset and Liability Management 455

CHAPTER 18
Multinational Capital Structure and the Cost of Capital 539

CHAPTER 19
Country Risk Analysis 565

C H A P T E R   20
Long-Term Financing 589

CHAPTER 23

The International Debt Crisis and Bank Assessment of Country Risk 657

PREFACE

The globalization of business is well documented by reviewing annual reports of large and small corporations. This trend has been motivated by the reduction in cross-border barriers, as has recently occurred in Eastern Europe. As markets become more internationally integrated, foreign markets will have more influence on corporate performance. Therefore, an understanding of international financial management is becoming even more critical to a company's success.

INTENDED MARKET

This text presumes an understanding of basic corporate finance. It is suitable for both undergraduate and master's level courses in international financial management. While this third edition is comprehensive, it still maintains its clarity. Some master's courses may attempt to maximize student comprehension by assigning the more difficult questions and problems, as well as the case problems and projects in each chapter. In addition, one or more articles are listed in each chapter as "suggested reading." Students could focus on any particular concept of interest by reviewing the related references at the end of each chapter.

ORGANIZATION OF THE TEXT

This text is organized to first provide a background on the international environment and then to focus on the managerial aspects from a corporate perspective. Part 1 (Chapters 1 to 5) introduces the major markets that serve international business. Part 2 (Chapters 6 to 8) describes relationships between exchange rates and economic variables, and explains the forces that influence these relationships. Part 3 (Chapters 9 to 12) begins the managerial perspective, with a focus on the measurement and management of exchange rate risk. Part 4 (Chapters 13 to 15) concentrates on the corporate management of short-term assets and liabilities. Part 5 (Chapters 16 to 21) describes the management of long-term assets and liabilities. Part 6 (Chapter 22 and 23) describes international financial management from a banker's perspective.

Each chapter in this third edition has been expanded to cover recent developments in international financial management. In addition, two new chapters have been added. Chapter 3 has been added to provide more background on the various financial markets used by multinational corporations. Chapter 18 has been added to cover the capital structure of multinational corporations in detail. Each chapter is self-contained so professors can use classroom time to focus on the more comprehensive concepts and rely on the text to cover the other concepts. Chapters can be rearranged without a loss in continuity.

COVERAGE OF RECENT ISSUES

In addition to the traditional concepts of international financial management, this third edition devotes considerable attention to specific topics that have recently affected corporate performance:

■ New business opportunities in Western Europe, resulting from more standardized regulations across countries.
■ New business opportunities in Eastern Europe and in Russia, resulting from a movement toward free enterprise.
■ Reduced trade barriers of many countries, including the U.S., Canada, and Mexico.
■ The globalization of financial markets.
■ Differences in the cost of capital across countries.
■ The continued U.S. balance of trade deficit—why the weak dollar did not eliminate the trade deficit.
■ The increasing use of currency futures and options contracts to hedge exchange rate movements—how corporations can compare these techniques with alternative methods to determine the optimal hedge.
■ The high degree of government intervention in the foreign exchange markets—why intervention is not always effective.
■ Reaction to monthly balance of trade announcements in the foreign exchange markets.
■ New evidence on the accuracy and bias of exchange rate projections.
■ New techniques for financing international trade.
■ Impact of financing alternatives on the risk of foreign projects.
■ Divestiture analysis and decision-making on foreign projects.
■ Updated tax laws of major countries.

KEY FEATURES

The following features are included in this third edition:

■ Part openers introduce the chapters contained in each part and explain how they are integrated.

■ "In Practice" inserts explain how various techniques are used by practitioners.

■ "Related Research" inserts summarize recent research conducted on the theories and concepts presented.

■ Several new comprehensive questions and problems have been added to the chapters.

■ New to this edition, a case problem has been developed for every chapter. These problems are especially useful for integrating key concepts within each chapter. Some of the case problems also integrate concepts across chapters. Many of the case problems can be completed with the use of a computer spreadsheet (such as Lotus 1-2-3).

■ Projects reinforce concepts and theories.

■ The data bank in the back of the text has been updated to offer students and professors a convenient access to related information. The data bank is also available on disk.

■ Suggested readings are provided for every chapter.

CHANGES IN THIS EDITION

■ A chapter on "International Financial Markets" (Chapter 3) was added to provide a more comprehensive background on the environment surrounding multinational corporations.

■ A chapter on multinational cost of capital and capital structure (Chapter 18) was added to expand the discussion on these topics.

■ Where appropriate, removal of cross-border barriers in Western Europe and the momentum toward free enterprise in Eastern Europe are discussed. Some new end-of-chapter questions force students to apply key concepts in the text to these events.

■ The chapter on "Financing International Trade" (Chapter 13) has incorporated a discussion of all the latest trade financing techniques that are being used.

■ The Appendix to Chapter 16 on international stock diversification has been expanded to incorporate recent findings.

■ The chapter on "Multinational Capital Budgeting" (Chapter 17) has been expanded to cover international acquisitions in more detail.

■ The chapter on "The International Debt Crisis and Bank Assessment of Country Risk" (Chapter 23) now contains a discussion of several recent developments in international lending.

■ Many of the key conceptual relationships discussed are supported by graphs containing the most recent data available.

■ Numerous examples of recent financial strategies by multinational corporations have been added throughout the text.

■ Several new "In Practice" and "Related Research" boxes have been added to incorporate recent developments in international financial management.

■ Challenging end-of-chapter questions and problems have been added to selected chapters.

■ New features of this edition include a challenging case problem at the end of every chapter, an expanded instructor's manual/test bank that contains additional multiple-choice questions (also available on disk), transparency masters, and a disk containing the data bank.

ACKNOWLEDGMENTS

Several people have contributed to the textbook. First, the motivation to write the textbook was primarily due to encouragement by professors Robert L. Conn (Miami University of Ohio), E. Joe Nosari, and William Shrode (Florida State University), Anthony E. Scaperlanda (Northern Illinois University), and Richard A. Zuber (University of North Carolina at Charlotte).

Many of the revisions and expanded sections contained in this third edition are due to comments and suggestions of students who used previous editions. In addition, several professors reviewed various drafts of the text and had a major influence on the contents and organization of the text. They are acknowledged in alphabetical order:

Alan Alford
Northeastern University

H. David Arnold
Auburn University

Robert Aubey
University of Wisconsin

James C. Baker
Kent State University

Gurudutt Baliga
University of Delaware

Bharat B. Bhalla
Fairfield University

Andreas C. Christofi
University of Maryland

W. P. Culbertson
Louisiana State University

Robert Driskill
Ohio State University

Paul Fenton
Bishop's University

Stuart Fletcher
Appalachian State University

Deborah W. Gregory
University of Georgia

Nicholas Gressis
Wright State University

Indra Guertler
Babson College

Ann M. Hackert
Idaho State University

John M. Harris, Jr.
Clemson University

Nathaniel Jackendoff
Temple University

Kurt R. Jesswein
Laredo State University

Manuel L. Jose
Southern Illinois University

Ho-Sang Kang
University of Texas at Dallas

Coleman S. Kendall
Ohio State University

Dara Khambata
American University

Suresh Krishman
The Pennsylvania State University

Boyden E. Lee
New Mexico State University

Carl Luft
DePaul University

K. Christopher Ma
Texas Tech University

Wendell McCulloch, Jr.
California State University—Long
Beach

Carl McGowan
University of Missouri

Edward Omberg
University of Santa Clara

Ali M. Parhizgari
Florida International University

Anne Perry
American University

Frances A. Quinn
Merrimack College

S. Ghon Rhee
University of Rhode Island

Jacobus T. Severiens
Kent State University

Peter Sharp
California State University—
Sacramento

Dilip K. Shome
Virginia Polytechnic Institute
and State University

Joseph Singer
University of Missouri—
Kansas City

Naim Sipra
University of Colorado at Denver

Jacky So
Southern Illinois University
at Edwardsville

Luc Soenen
California Polytechnic
State University

Ahmad Sorhabian
California State Polytechnic
University—Pomona

Stephen G. Timme
Georgia Tech University

Mahmoud S. Wahab
George Washington University

Ralph C. Walter III
Northeastern Illinois
University

Elizabeth Webbink
Rutgers University

Glenda Wong
De Paul University

This third edition also benefited from the input of Mike Dosal (Barnett Bank of Central Florida, Orlando), John Howe (Louisiana State University), John Simms (UNC Greensboro), George Tsetsekos (Drexel University), Alan Tucker (Temple University), and Emilio Zarruk (Florida Atlantic University). I also wish to thank Lucille Ekcroth, Gilda Mann, Raymonde Toland, and Don Toland for their help on various tasks.

The people at West Publishing Company were once again very helpful. Editors Esther Craig and Richard Fenton were helpful in all stages of the book writing process. A special thanks is due to the production editor, Laura Nelson, for her efforts to assure a quality final product.

Finally, I wish to thank my parents, Arthur and Irene Madura, and my wife, Mary, for their moral support. Without their influence, this textbook would not exist.

ABOUT THE AUTHOR

Jeff Madura is presently the SunTrust Bank Professor of Finance at Florida Atlantic University. He has written several textbooks, including *Financial Markets and Institutions*. His research on international finance has been published in numerous journals, including *Journal of Financial and Quantitative Analysis, Journal of Money, Credit and Banking, Journal of Banking and Finance, Applied Financial Economics, Journal of Financial Research*, and *Journal of Financial Services Reasearch*. He received awards for excellence in teaching and research, and has served as a consultant for international banks, securities firms, and other multinational corporations.

The International Financial Environment

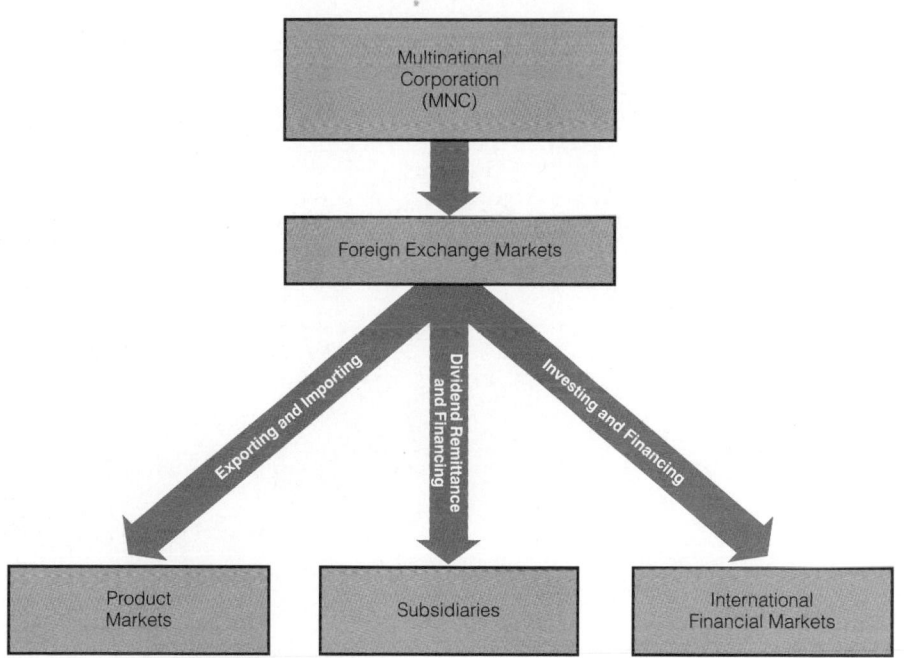

Part 1 (Chapters 1 through 5) provides an overview of the multinational corporation (MNC) and environment in which it operates. Chapter 1 explains the goals of the MNC, along with the motives and risks of international business. Chapter 2 describes the international flow of funds between countries. Chapter 3 describes the international product and financial markets and how these markets facilitate ongoing operations. Chapter 4 explains how exchange rates are determined, while Chapter 5 provides a background on the currency futures and options markets. Managers of MNCs must understand the international environment described in these chapters in order to make proper decisions.

CHAPTER 1

Multinational Financial Management: An Overview

A s businesses grow, so does their awareness of opportunities in foreign markets. Initially, they may merely attempt to export a product to a particular country or import supplies from a foreign manufacturer. Over time, however, many of them recognize additional foreign opportunities and eventually evolve into multinational corporations (MNCs). Some businesses, such as Dow Chemical, Exxon, American Brands, and Colgate-Palmolive, commonly generate more than half their sales in foreign countries. Westinghouse Electric Corporation operates in 16 foreign countries. In 1990 its international revenues exceeded $2 billion. Honeywell has 42 subsidiaries and several other joint-venture projects scattered around the world. Eastman Kodak has subsidiaries in 32 foreign countries. Rockwell International Corp. operates in 26 foreign countries. All of these companies have enjoyed substantial growth as a result of their efforts to capitalize on international business opportunities. As another example, consider CPC International Inc., which operates in 47 different countries and has recently acquired some foreign businesses to strengthen its international position, including Santa Rosa of Italy and Nutrial of France. And perhaps the prime example is the Coca-Cola Company, distributing its products in over 160 countries and using 40 different currencies. In 1990, 80 percent of its total operating income was generated outside the United States.

An understanding of international financial management is crucial to not only the large MNCs with numerous foreign subsidiaries, but also to the small business engaged in exporting or importing. Seventy-eight percent of the 43,300 U.S. firms that export have less than 100 employees. International business is even important to companies that have no intention of engaging in international business, since these companies must recognize how their foreign competitors will be affected by movements in exchange rates, foreign interest rates, labor costs, and inflation. Such economic characteristics can affect the foreign competitors' cost of production and pricing policy.

Companies must also recognize how domestic competitors that obtain foreign supplies or foreign financing will be affected by economic conditions in foreign countries. If these domestic competitors are able to reduce their costs by capitalizing on opportunities in international markets, they may be able to reduce their prices without reducing their profit margin. This could allow them to increase market share at the expense of the purely domestic companies.

Newly appointed chief executive officers (CEOs) of today's MNCs recognize the importance of international business. Many of them, such as the CEOs of Rockwell International Corp., Ford Motor Company, Motorola, and Whirlpool, have been heavily involved in foreign projects and therefore have a more global view than their predecessors. New CEOs will likely be more willing to transfer operations around the globe, which may cause more layoffs in particular countries. George Fisher, the new CEO of Motorola, stated, "We have to differentiate between companies and countries . . . The fact that Motorola and a group of companies like us turn out to be successful doesn't necessarily mean the United States will" (*USA Today*, March 13, 1990, p. 2B). The new CEOs are more focused on gaining a competitive edge, which requires a global perspective.

This chapter discusses the main objective of an MNC and the company decisions that can conflict with it. The chapter then identifies the major factors that motivate international business and discusses how these factors can affect an MNC's size. Finally, it explains the risks incurred by MNCs.

OBJECTIVE OF THE MNC

The commonly accepted objective of an MNC is to maximize shareholder wealth. Developing an objective is necessary since all decisions should contribute to its accomplishment. Thus, if the objective is to maximize earnings in the near future, the firm's policies would be different than if the objective were to maximize shareholder wealth.

Any proposed corporate policy should consider not only potential earnings, but also risks. If the benefits to be derived from a corporate policy outweigh the costs and risks to the extent that the policy will help maximize shareholder wealth, this policy should be implemented. The following quote from CPC International substantiates how international business can maximize shareholder wealth:

> As our international business has grown and strengthened, we have benefited from the fact that the economies and currencies of most foreign countries have also strengthened over the long term, adding to the value of our shareholders' investment.

An MNC should make decisions using the same objective as the purely domestic firm. Yet, there is a much wider range of opportunities for the MNC, causing its decisions to be more complex.

Conflicts Against the MNC Objective

It has often been argued that managers of a firm may make decisions that conflict with the firm's objective to maximize shareholder wealth. For example, a decision to establish a subsidiary in one location versus another may be based on the location's personal appeal to the manager rather than on its potential benefits to shareholders. Decisions to expand may be determined by the desires of managers to make their respective divisions grow in order to receive more responsibility and compensation. If a firm were composed of only one owner who was also the sole manager, a conflict of goals would not occur. However, for corporations with shareholders who differ from their managers, a conflict of goals can exist. This conflict is often referred to as the **agency problem.**

Firms use various strategies to prevent managers from making decisions that do not maximize shareholder value. For example, managers who act according to different goals may be fired, or receive less compensation. The concepts and issues of multinational financial management are explained in this text as if managers act on behalf of the firm's shareholders. Yet, it should be emphasized that due to the size of some MNCs, it is sometimes difficult to determine whether all managers are making decisions based on this single corporate objective. Thus, the agency costs of assuring that managers attempt to maximize shareholder wealth can be larger for MNCs.

Financial managers of an MNC with several subsidiaries may be tempted to make decisions that maximize the value of their respective subsidiaries. This objective will not necessarily coincide with maximizing the value of the overall MNC. While this discrepancy will be discussed in detail later in the text, a simple example can illustrate why a conflict may exist. Consider a subsidiary manager that obtained financing from the parent firm (headquarters) to develop and sell a new product. The manager estimated the costs and benefits of the project from its subsidiary's perspective and determined that the project was feasible. However, the manager neglected to realize that any earnings from this project remitted to the parent would be taxed heavily by the host government. The estimated after-tax benefits received by the parent were more than offset by the cost of financing the project. While the subsidiary's individual value was enhanced, the MNC's overall value was reduced. If financial managers are to maximize the wealth of their MNC's shareholders, they must implement policies that maximize the value of the overall MNC rather than the value of their respective subsidiaries. For many MNCs, major decisions by subsidiary managers must be approved by the parent. However, it is difficult for the parent to monitor all decisions made by subsidiary managers.

Constraints Interfering with the MNC Objective

When financial managers of MNCs attempt to maximize their firm's value, they are confronted with various constraints that can be classified as environmental, regulatory, or ethical in nature.

ENVIRONMENTAL CONSTRAINTS. Each country enforces its own environmental constraints. Some countries may enforce more of these restrictions on subsidiaries whose parent is based in a different country. Building codes, disposal of production waste materials, and pollution controls are examples of the restrictions that force subsidiaries to incur additional costs. Many European countries have recently imposed tougher anti-pollution laws as a result of severe pollution problems.

REGULATORY CONSTRAINTS. Each country also enforces its own regulatory constraints pertaining to taxes, currency convertibility rules, earnings remittance restrictions, and other regulations that can affect cash flows

INTERNATIONAL FINANCIAL MANAGEMENT IN PRACTICE

MNC Perceptions of Agency Costs: A Survey

A recent study surveyed Australian-based MNCs to gain insight into their planning and ownership strategies. The companies surveyed commonly mentioned that the objectives of foreign operations conflicted with corporate objectives. The study concluded that this conflict becomes pronounced as foreign operations grow. The initial establishment of foreign operations is usually narrowly focused and in line with the MNC's overall goals. However, as the foreign operations expand and become diversified, the initial intentions for the foreign operations are forgotten. Managers of these operations become more concerned with the local conditions and attempt to maximize the value of their single entities as if they were independent of the MNC parent. Thus, there is less regard for how the entity can contribute to the overall value of the MNC. An MNC can attempt to prevent this conflict from occurring by rewarding foreign managers according to their contribution to the MNC as a whole.

SOURCE: Boseman, Glenn, "The Australian Multinational-Parent and Subsidiary Relationships," *Management International Review* 26, no. 2 (1986): pp. 43–51.

of a subsidiary established there. Because these regulations can influence cash flows, they must be recognized by financial managers when assessing policies. Also, any change in these regulations may require revision of existing financial policies, so financial managers should not only recognize the regulatory restrictions that exist in a given country but also monitor them for any potential changes over time.

ETHICAL CONSTRAINTS. There is no consensus standard of business conduct that applies to all countries. A business practice that is perceived to be unethical in one country may be totally ethical in another. For example, the U.S.-based MNCs are well aware of common business practices in some less developed countries that would be declared illegal in the United States. Bribes to governments in order to receive special tax breaks or other favors are one example. The MNCs face a dilemma. If they do not participate in such practices, they may be at a competitive disadvantage. Yet, if they do participate, they receive a poor reputation in countries that do not approve such practices. Some U.S.-based MNCs have made the costly choice to restrain from business practices that are legal in certain foreign countries but not legal in the United States. That is, they follow a worldwide code of ethics. This may enhance their worldwide credibility, which can increase global demand for the products they produce.

MOTIVATION FOR INTERNATIONAL BUSINESS

The commonly used explanations for why firms become motivated to expand their business internationally are (1) the theory of comparative advantage,

(2) the imperfect markets theory, and (3) the product cycle theory. The three theories overlap to a degree and can complement each other in developing a rationale for the evolution of international business.

Theory of Comparative Advantage

Multinational business may be conducted by exporting or by direct foreign investment. Both forms of multinational business have generally increased over time. Part of this growth is due to the increasing realization that specialization by countries can increase production efficiency. Some countries, such as Japan and the United States, have a technology advantage, while countries such as Mexico and South Korea have an advantage in the cost of basic labor. Since specialization in some products may result in no production of other products, trade between countries is essential. This is the argument made by the classical **theory of comparative advantage.** Due to comparative advantages, it is understandable why firms are able to penetrate foreign markets.

Imperfect Markets Theory

Countries differ with respect to resources available for the production of goods. Yet, even with such comparative advantages, the volume of international business would be limited if all resources could be easily transferred among countries. If markets were perfect, factors of production (except land) would be mobile and freely transferable. The unrestricted mobility of factors creates equality in costs and returns and removes the comparative cost advantage, the rationale for international trade and investment. However, the real world suffers from **imperfect market** conditions where factors of production are somewhat immobile. There are costs and often restrictions related to the transfer of labor and other resources used for production. There may also be restrictions on funds and other resources transferred among countries. Because markets for the various resources used in production are "imperfect," firms often realize possible advantages offered by another country in terms of its resources. This provides an incentive for firms to seek out foreign opportunities.

Product Cycle Theory

One of the more popular explanations for why firms evolve into MNCs is introduced in the **product cycle theory.** According to this theory, firms become established in the home market as a result of some perceived advantage they would have over existing competitors, such as a need by the market for at least one more supplier of the product. Because information about markets and competition is more readily available at home, a firm is likely to first establish itself in its home country. Foreign demand for the firm's product will initially be accommodated by exporting. As time passes, the firm may feel the only way to retain its advantage over competition in foreign countries is to produce the product in foreign markets, thereby reducing its transportation costs. Over time, the competition in the foreign markets may increase as other producers become more familiar with the firm's product. Thus, the firm may develop strategies to prolong the foreign demand for its product. A

INTERNATIONAL FINANCIAL MANAGEMENT IN PRACTICE

Corporate Views on International Business Education

A recent survey* was conducted to determine corporate perceptions of international business education. According to the survey responses, most companies state that:

■ International awareness is important.
■ International business education is most valuable after related work experience.
■ Their need for executive skills include a background in international business.
■ The combination of an international business background with a foreign language is marketable.

Executives rated international marketing, international finance, and international trade as the three most important international business studies for career progress within their businesses. They were also asked to rate the importance of various skills that were necessary for international positions within their businesses. The most important skills, based on their responses, were communications skills, leadership skills, interpersonal skills, adaptability, and ethical and moral standards.

The authors of the published study conclude that the content of international courses should be structured in consultation with practitioners to assure that the course content is useful. For this reason, they encourage the interchange of ideas between business schools and MNCs.

SOURCE: Beamish, Paul W. and Jonathan L. Calof, "International Business Education: A Corporate View," *Journal of International Business Studies* (Fall 1989): pp. 553–564.

common approach is to attempt differentiating the product so that other competitors cannot offer exactly the same product. These phases of the cycle are illustrated in Exhibit 1.1. As an example, 3M Company uses one new product to penetrate foreign markets. After entering the market, it expands its product line. It now has over $6 billion per year in international sales, about 50 percent of its total sales.

There is more to the product cycle theory than is summarized here. This discussion merely suggests that as a firm matures, it may recognize additional opportunities outside its home country. Whether the firm's foreign business diminishes or expands over time will depend on how successful it is at maintaining some advantage over its competition. The advantage could represent an edge in its production or financing approach that reduces costs. Alternatively, the advantage could reflect an edge in its marketing approach that generates and maintains a strong demand for its product.

INCREASING GLOBALIZATION

Over time, several developments have encouraged globalization of world economies through international trade and investments. These include standardization of products and production processes, closer proximity of nations through improved communication and transportation, and growing

EXHIBIT 1.1 International Product Life Cycle

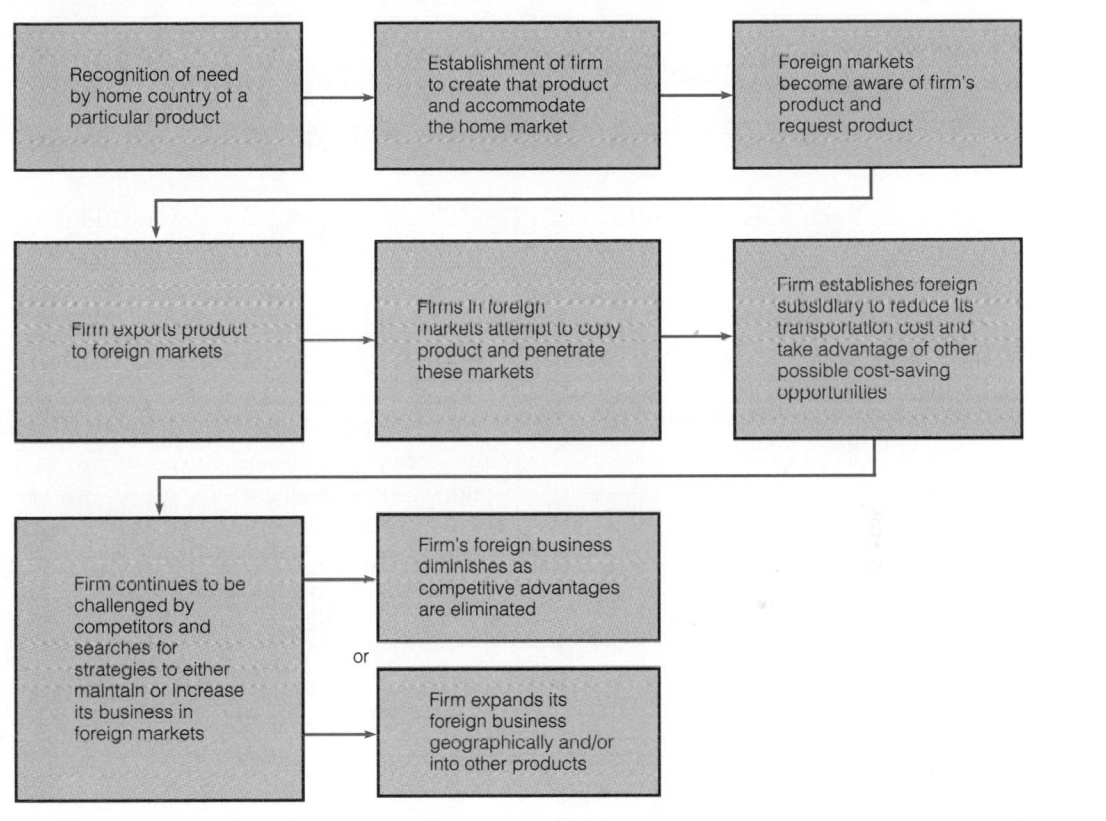

efforts among nations to reduce tariffs and other barriers, thus facilitating movement of goods and services worldwide.

Global integration of goods and services improves the overall efficiency of resource usage. Goods are more likely to be manufactured in those countries that can produce at the lowest cost, and lower costs result in higher real incomes. Furthermore, global integration tends to increase competition, forcing firms to be more efficient.

Several national governments have sold some of their operations to corporations and other investors, allowing for more free enterprise. This so-called **privatization** has already taken place in some Latin American countries such as Brazil and Mexico, and has even begun in Eastern European countries, such as East Germany and Hungary. Privatization allows for greater international business as foreign firms can acquire operations sold by national governments.

The reasons for promoting privatization have varied across countries. Privatization was used in Chile to prevent a few investors from controlling all the shares, and in France to prevent the possible reversal back to a more nationalized economy. In the United Kingdom, privatization was promoted to spread stock ownership across investors, which allows more people to have a direct stake in the success of British industry.

INTERNATIONAL FINANCIAL MANAGEMENT IN PRACTICE

An Expert's View of International Business Education

John H. Dunning, a well-known expert on business and previous president of the Academy of International Business, offered some general comments and suggestions about international business. Some of his main points are summarized below:

■ Since exchange rate movements have become more volatile, effective risk management strategies are needed.

■ The role of governments in influencing costs and benefits of international business has increased. This implies that some attention should be given to government intervention and the assessment of each country's political risk.

■ There has been a surge in the demand for international education, including college courses, conferences, and executive training courses. The supply of qualified instructors has not kept up with demand. Business schools are beginning to respond to the demand by offering more courses. In the United States and Canada, there are relatively few universities that offer major programs in international business. In many European countries, such as France, Sweden, Switzerland, and the United Kingdom, international business programs are more commonly offered.

■ Many business courses attempt to include an international dimension simply by tacking international applications on at the end of the course. This provides less international education than if international applications were infused throughout the course. Courses in some smaller countries such as Hong Kong, Singapore, Sweden, and Switzerland are more internationalized, as these countries recognize their reliance on international business.

SOURCE: Dunning, John H., "The Study of International Business: A Plea for a More Interdisciplinary Approach," *Journal of International Business Studies*, Fall 1989, pp. 411–436.

The primary reason why the market value of a firm may increase in response to privatization is the anticipated improvement in managerial efficiency. The goal of maximizing shareholder wealth is more focused than management of a state-owned business, since the state must consider the economic and social ramifications of any business decision. Also, managers of a privately-owned enterprise are more motivated to assure profitability because their career may depend on it. For these reasons, privatized firms will search for local and global opportunities that could enhance their value. The trend toward privatization will undoubtedly create a more competitive global marketplace.

Another driving force behind the globalization of business is the increasing standardization of products and services across countries. This allows firms to sell their products across countries, without costly product revisions. The previous disparity in product specifications represented an implicit trade barrier because of the extra cost associated with making the product acceptable in particular countries. Standardization greatly reduces the inconvenience of transporting goods and has already resulted in a significant increase in international business.

Growth in International Trade

The international trade as a percentage of GNP is consistently lower for the United States than for other countries. Thus, the U.S. economy may be less sensitive than the economy of other countries to changing economic conditions. While Japan is very dependent on its exports, it has maintained economic growth even when importing countries experience a slowdown. Japan diversifies its exports across numerous countries so that it is not substantially influenced by a single country's economic conditions.

The volume of international trade (exports plus imports) relative to gross national product (GNP) is reported for some major countries in Exhibit 1.2. Note that, as suggested earlier, the international trade volume as a percentage of GNP is generally much larger for Canada and European countries than it is for the United States or Japan. Yet, the importance of trade has increased over time for most countries.

Growth in Direct Foreign Investment

The trends in direct foreign investment per year shown in Exhibit 1.3 provide more evidence of the increase in globalization. Direct foreign investment by U.S. firms was almost $32 billion in 1989. Direct foreign investment by non-U.S. firms in the United States has grown at a higher rate during the 1980s. In 1989 the level was more than double the direct foreign investment by U.S. firms. Direct foreign investment is generally lower in periods when economies are weak, such as the recessions in 1974 and 1983.

Relationship between Globalization and Profitability

A recent study by Daniels and Bracker found that U.S. companies with a higher degree of international business experienced superior profit performance. Since the results could have been somewhat distorted by industry differences, they reassessed the relationship for specific industries. They found that for the majority of industries studied, U.S. companies within that given industry that had a higher degree of international business experienced superior profit performance. While the results cannot be generalized for all firms, it appears that increasing international business may enhance a firm's profitability.

INTERNATIONAL OPPORTUNITIES

Because of possible cost advantages from producing in foreign countries or possible revenue opportunities from demand by foreign markets, the growth potential becomes much greater for firms that consider international business. Exhibit 1.4 illustrates how a firm's growth can be affected by foreign investment and financing opportunities. The hypothetical investment opportunities for both a purely domestic firm and an MNC with similar operating

EXHIBIT 1.2 International Trade as a Percentage of GNP for Major Countries

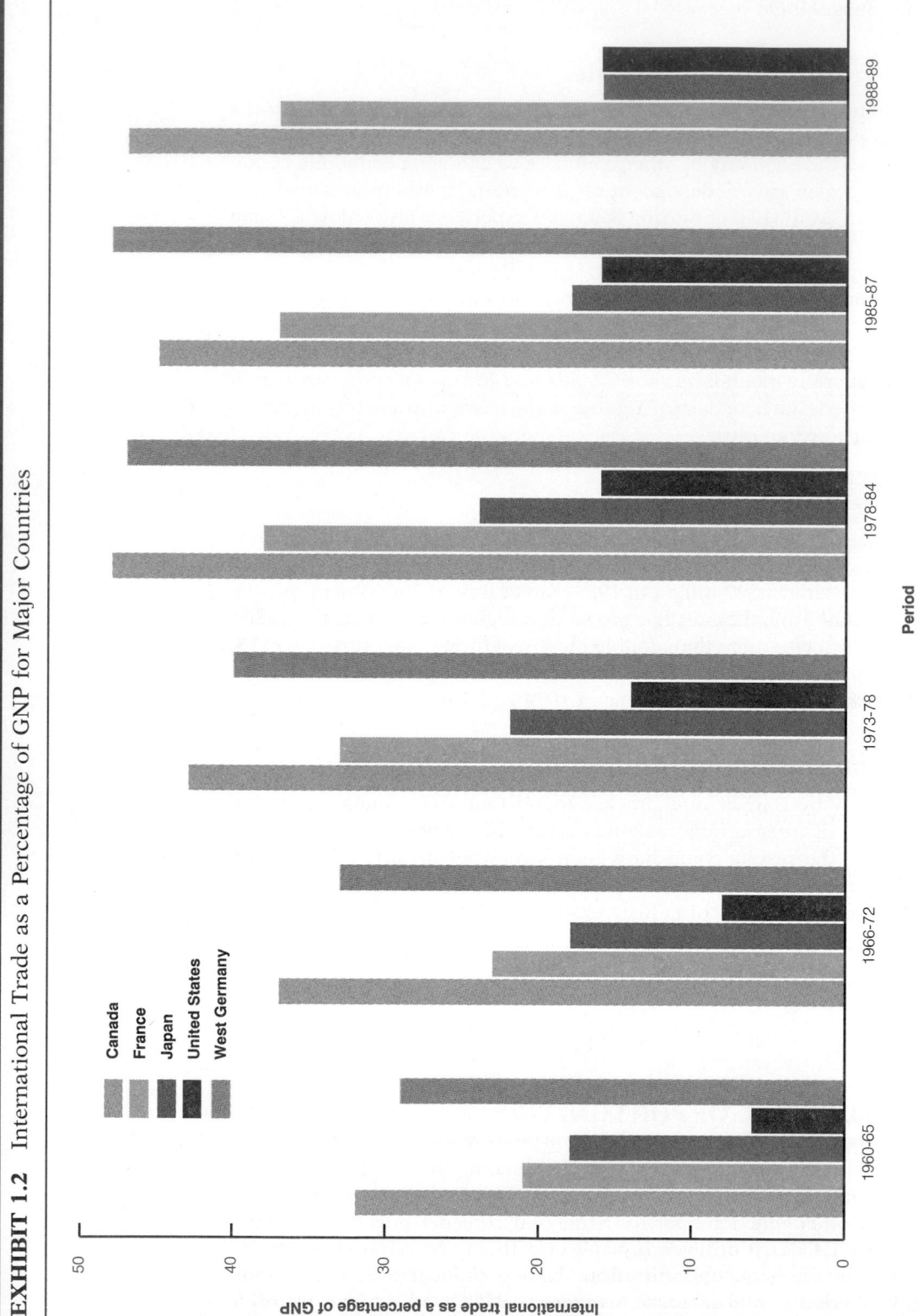

SOURCE: *International Economic Conditions*, Federal Reserve Bank of St. Louis, June 1985, updated by author.

EXHIBIT 1.3 Trends in Direct Foreign Investment

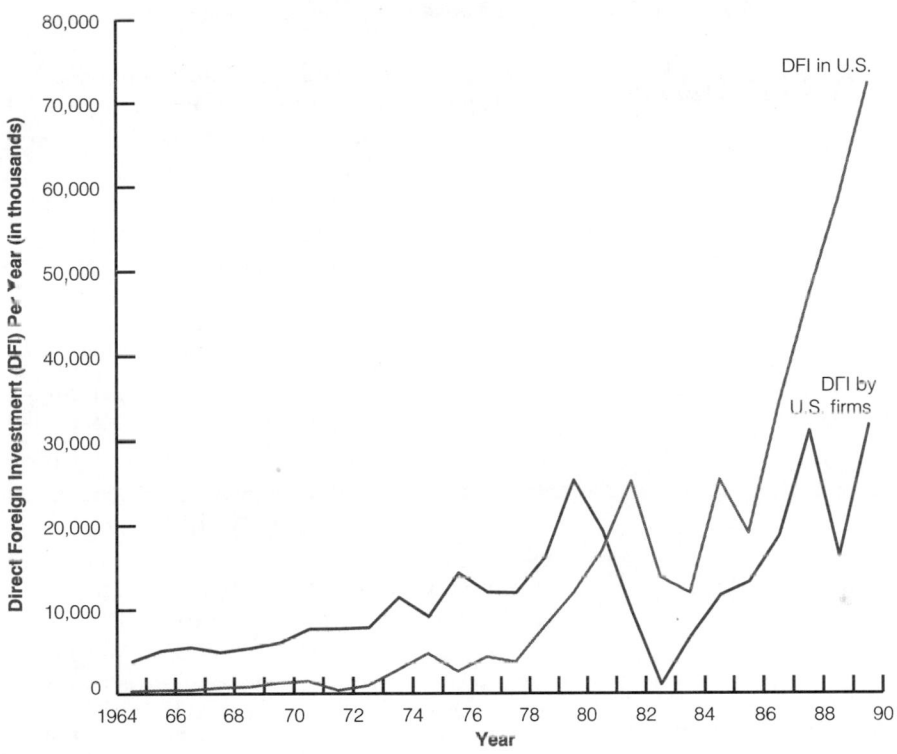

characteristics are shown here. Each horizontal step represents a specific project. Each proposed project is anticipated to generate a marginal return to the firm. The horizontal steps differ in length since project sizes differ. A larger project would represent a greater amount of assets.

Moving from left to right in Exhibit 1.4, the projects are in priority based on marginal return. Assume that these projects are independent of each other and that their expected returns as shown have been adjusted to account for risk. With these assumptions, a firm would select the project with the highest marginal return as most feasible and would undertake this project. Then, it would undertake the proposed project with the next highest marginal return, and so on. The marginal return on projects for the MNC is above that of the purely domestic firm, because of the expanded **opportunity set** of possible projects from which to select.

Exhibit 1.4 also displays cost-of-capital curves for the MNC and purely domestic firm. The cost of capital is shown to increase with asset size for either type of firm. This is based on the premise that creditors or shareholders require a higher rate of return as the firm grows. A growth in asset size requires increased debt, which forces the firm to increase its periodic interest payments to creditors. Consequently, the firm has a greater probability of being unable to meet its debt obligations. To the extent that creditors and shareholders require a higher return for a more highly indebted firm, the cost of capital to the firm rises with its volume of assets. The MNC is shown to

RELATED RESEARCH

Developing a Global Competitive Advantage

An extensive study by Porter offers some interesting insight on the ability of firms to develop a global competitive advantage over other firms in the industry. Some of Porter's key points are listed below.

■ Firms develop competitive advantages through innovation. The advantage is maintained when competitors are slow to respond.
■ Most competitive advantages can be imitated. For example, South Korean firms have successfully created substitutes for color televisions and VCRs produced by Japanese firms. Also, Brazilian firms have created substitutes for casual leather footwear produced by Italian firms.
■ A competitive advantage can be sustained only by continually upgrading it over time. For example, Japanese automobile producers initially penetrated the U.S. and other markets by producing inexpensive cars, using relatively low labor costs at that time to develop a competitive advantage. Since then, they have developed large modern plants to benefit from economies of scale. They have recently focused on customer satisfaction to retain their competitive advantage.

■ Innovation may be more achievable when there is an investment in research and development. Since the rewards from research and development are not immediate, some firms that are short-run oriented will not make the investment and therefore will be less innovative. U.S. companies tend to be somewhat short-run oriented as their shareholders are looking for immediate performance. Conversely, German and Swiss firms tend to be more long-run oriented as their shareholders usually hold on to shares for a long period of time. Commercial banks in these countries invest heavily in stock, whereas U.S. commercial banks cannot invest in stock.
■ Firms should be very selective when engaging in joint ventures for innovation. Alliances tend to be costly because they require the coordination of two separate operations and sets of goals.

The concepts above are applied to countries rather than individual firms. Porter suggests that because competition motivates innovation, the use of government intervention (such as trade barriers or direct subsidies) to protect an industry will discourage innovation. Thus, those countries that are more protected by their governments will be at a competitive disadvantage.

SOURCE: Porter, Michael E., "The Competitive Advantage of Nations," *Harvard Business Review,* March–April 1990, pp. 73–93.

have an advantage in obtaining capital funding at a lower cost than the purely domestic firm. This is due to the larger opportunity set of funding sources around the world from which it has to choose.

Once the marginal cost of financing projects exceeds the marginal return on projects, the firm should not pursue such projects. As shown in Exhibit 1.4, a purely domestic firm will continue to accept projects up to point X. After that point, the marginal cost of additional projects exceeds the expected benefits.

When foreign resources, funds, and potential projects are considered, the firm's volume of feasible projects would be greater. The MNC's projects be-

EXHIBIT 1.4 Cost-Benefit Evaluation for Purely Domestic Firms versus MNCs

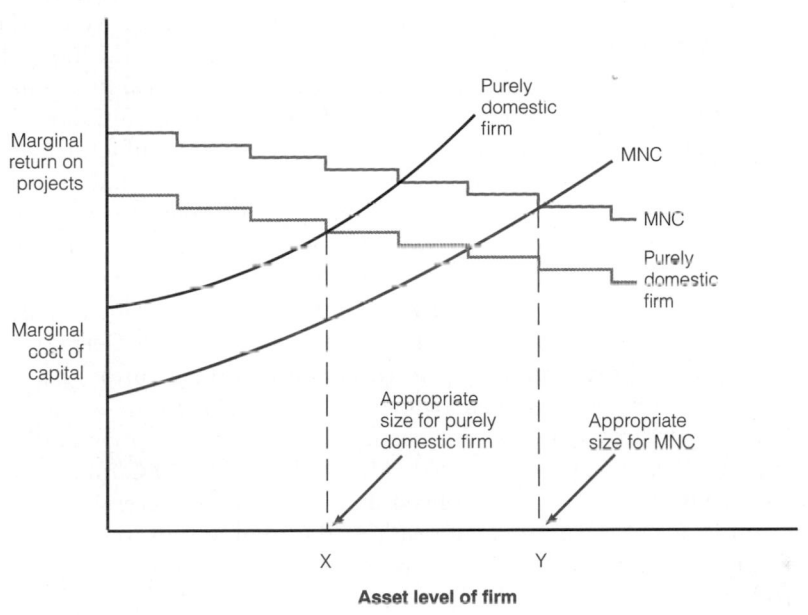

come unacceptable after point Y. This optimal level of assets exceeds that of the purely domestic firm. The difference here is due to cost advantages and opportunities in foreign countries. This comparison illustrates why firms may desire to become internationalized.

There are several limitations to the concept illustrated in Exhibit 1.4. First, there may be some cases where there are no feasible foreign opportunities for a firm. In addition, an argument could be made that foreign projects are riskier than domestic projects and therefore result in a higher cost of capital. Finally, some critics contend that the marginal cost of capital will not rise as more projects are added if the firm diversifies its projects appropriately. Nevertheless, the exhibit offers insight as to why firms expand internationally. Moreover, it illustrates why the optimal size of a given firm will typically be greater if that firm considers foreign opportunities.

New Opportunities in Europe

Over time, economic and political conditions can change, creating new opportunities in international business. A classic example is Europe in the late 1980s and early 1990s. In the late 1980s, industrialized countries in Europe agreed to make regulations more uniform and to remove many taxes on goods traded between these countries. This agreement, affirmed by the Single European Act of 1987, was followed by a series of negotiations among countries to begin phasing in policies that would achieve uniformity by 1992. The act allows firms in a given European country greater access to supplies from firms in other European countries.

Many firms, including European subsidiaries of U.S.-based MNCs, will capitalize on the agreement by attempting to penetrate markets in border countries. Before the Single European Act, some subsidiaries conducted business only in their host country because opportunities in border countries were discouraged by taxes and other barriers. As these barriers were reduced in the late 1980s, firms began to enter new markets. By producing more of the same product and distributing it across European countries, firms may be more able to achieve economies of scale. CPC International announced that it would be able to increase efficiency by streamlining manufacturing operations as a result of the reduction in barriers. Reynolds Metals Company completed the unification of its European operations under the management of their European headquarters in Switzerland to prepare for a more unified Europe. In 1989 another historical event occurred in Europe when the Berlin Wall separating East Germany from West Germany was torn down. This was symbolic of new relations between East Germany and West Germany, and was followed by efforts to reunify the two countries. In addition, it created momentum to encourage free enterprise in all East European countries. As with the Single European Act, this event opened up new opportunities for MNCs. Coca-Cola Company, Reynolds Metals Company, CPC International, and numerous other MNCs announced that they would aggressively pursue expansion in Eastern Europe as a result of the momentum toward free enterprise. In 1990 General Motors began an assembly plant in East Germany for producing automobiles.

INTERNATIONAL BUSINESS RISK

While the advantages of international business discussed up to this point may motivate firms to increase the degree of international business, there are some possible disadvantages that deserve attention as well. Any characteristic of international business that can increase production costs, reduce product demand, or increase risk to the firm is considered a disadvantage. For example, the exchange rates between any two currencies will change over time. Consequently, the number of units of a firm's home currency needed to purchase foreign supplies may change even if the actual price of supplies charged by the foreign producer remains unchanged. In addition, exchange rate fluctuations can affect the foreign demand for the firm's product or the cost of financing with foreign currencies.

For those firms with subsidiaries located in foreign countries, exchange rate fluctuations will affect the value of earnings remitted by the subsidiary to headquarters. Moreover, tax rates imposed by foreign governments can change, or currency restrictions can prohibit the remittance of earnings to headquarters. Finally, the subsidiary's host government may even decide to buy out the subsidiary at whatever value it feels is fair. The risks described here should not prevent a firm from considering expansion of its international business. However, firms that simply evaluate the potential advantages of international business without concern about the risks are more likely to make the wrong decisions.

Some types of risk are **systematic** and cannot be diversified away. For example, a worldwide recession could cause a reduced demand for the firm's products in all countries in which the product is marketed. Other types of risk are nonsystematic and can be diversified away. For example, while a recession in the U.S. could cause a lower U.S. demand for the firm's product, the non-U.S. demand may be unaffected. Diversification across international markets can therefore reduce the impact of adverse conditions unique to the home country.

New Risks in Europe

While the Single European Act of 1987 and the momentum toward free enterprise in Eastern Europe offered new opportunities to MNCs, they also posed new risks. As the Single European Act removes cross-border barriers, it exposes firms to additional competition. Like other historical examples of deregulation, the more efficient firms will benefit at the expense of less efficient firms.

Regarding the momentum for free enterprise in Eastern Europe, firms that enter these markets are subject to the possibility of the momentum reversing back toward socialism in the future. While the potential benefits may outweigh the risk, firms should at least evaluate the risk associated with new opportunities.

SUMMARY

While multinational financial management has been necessary for MNCs for several years, it is not an exact science. There is still much to be learned. Even the smaller companies are now realizing the need to understand international financial management, since international business is not necessarily restricted to the large corporations. If government restrictions do not become excessive, international business should continue to grow. And, accordingly, all the financial management decisions related to an MNC's business, such as financing, working capital management, capital budgeting, and country-risk assessment, should become more critical to their survival and performance.

The first step in multinational financial management is to identify the overall objective of an MNC, since managerial decisions cannot be made until this objective is established. The objective of the MNC, like that of a purely domestic firm, should be to maximize shareholder wealth. While an MNC's criteria for decisions are similar to those of a domestic firm, the set of possible opportunities to achieve its objective is far greater. The additional opportunities may require an assessment of various forms of risk that were not considered when evaluating domestic projects. In general, the MNC has a more complex task due to the larger set of possible strategies to implement and the possible risks of these strategies.

ORGANIZATION OF THE TEXT

The first two sections of this text provide a background on the international financial environment. Part 1 (Chapters 1 through 5) describes the markets that facilitate international trade and finance. Part 2 (Chapters 6 through 8) explains how exchange rates are influenced by governments and currency traders and how exchange rate movements can affect economic variables.

Part 3 (Chapters 9 through 12) describes how MNCs can forecast exchange rates, measure their exposure to exchange rate fluctuations, and manage this exposure.

Part 4 (Chapters 13 through 15) focuses on the management of short-term assets and liabilities. The financing of international trade (Chapter 12) is included in this section, since such financing is normally for a short term.

Part 5 (Chapters 16 through 21) focuses on the management of long-term assets and liabilities. It explains the motives for direct foreign investment (Chapter 16), the evaluation of proposed foreign projects (Chapter 17), the cost of capital used to finance foreign projects (Chapter 18), and the assessment of country risk (Chapter 19). It also explains how MNCs make long-term financing decisions (Chapter 20) and how they implement strategic planning (Chapter 21).

Part 6 (Chapters 22 and 23) focuses on international banking, with some emphasis on the international debt crisis.

QUESTIONS/ PROBLEMS

1. Explain the agency problem of MNCs. Why might agency costs be larger for the MNC as opposed to a smaller firm?

2. Explain how the theory of comparative advantage relates to the need for international business.

3. Explain how the existence of imperfect markets had led to the establishment of subsidiaries in foreign markets.

4. If perfect markets existed, would wages, prices, and interest rates among countries be more similar or less similar than under conditions of imperfect markets? Why?

5. Explain how the product cycle theory relates to the growth of the MNC.

6. How does access to international opportunities affect the size of corporations? Describe a scenario wherein the size of the corporation is not affected by access to international opportunities.

7. What factors cause some firms to become more internationalized than others?

8. What are some potential disadvantages of international business that are often not relevant to domestic business? Briefly state how an MNC can be adversely affected by these disadvantages.

9. Briefly describe the change in the importance of world trade over time. If the trend continues, what does this suggest about the importance of international financial management?

10. As an overall review of this chapter, identify possible reasons for growth in international business. Then, list the various disadvantages that may discourage international business.

11. Describe constraints that interfere with the MNC objective.

12. Describe the trends in the volume of U.S. direct investment abroad over time.

13. The managers of Loyola Corporation recently had a meeting to discuss new opportunities in Europe as a result of the recent integration between European countries. They decided not to penetrate new markets because of

their present focus on expanding market share in the U.S. Financial managers of Loyola Corporation developed forecasts for earnings based on Loyola's 12 percent market share (defined here as its percentage of total European sales) that it presently has in Europe. Is 12 percent an appropriate estimate for next year's European market share? If not, would it likely overestimate or underestimate the actual European market share next year?

14. Would the agency problem be more pronounced for Berkeley Corporation, which has its parent company make most major decisions for its foreign subsidiaries, or Oakland Corporation, which has a decentralized approach?

15. Explain why more standardized product specifications across countries can increase global competition.

16. How can West German subsidiaries of U.S.-based MNCs capitalize on the removal of the Berlin Wall that separated East and West Germany?

17. Describe privatization and explain why it may allow for a greater degree of international business.

18. Describe the Single European Act and explain how it may affect international business by U.S. firms.

Ranger Supply Company
Motivation for International Business

Ranger Supply Company is a large manufacturer and distributor of office supplies. It is based in New York, but sends supplies to firms throughout the U.S. It markets its supplies through periodic mass mailings of catalogues to firms in the U.S. Its clients can make orders over the phone, and Ranger ships the supplies upon demand. Ranger has had very high production efficiency in the past. This is partially attributed to low employee turnover and high morale, as employees are guaranteed job security until retirement.

Ranger already holds a large proportion of the market share in distributing office supplies in the U.S. Its main competition in the U.S. is from one U.S. firm and one Canadian firm. A British firm has a small share of the U.S. market but is at a disadvantage because of its distance. The British firm's marketing and transportation costs in the U.S. market are relatively high.

While Ranger's office supplies are somewhat similar to those of its competitors, it has been able to capture most of the U.S. market because of its high efficiency, which has resulted in low prices charged to the retail stores. It expects a decline in the aggregate demand for office supplies in the U.S. in future years. However, it anticipates strong demand for office supplies in Canada and in Eastern Europe over the next several years. Executives of Ranger began to consider exporting as a method of offsetting the possible decline in domestic demand for its products.

a) Ranger Supply Company plans to either attempt penetrating the Canadian market or the East European market through exporting. What factors deserve to be considered in deciding which market is more feasible?

b) One financial manager was responsible for developing a contingency plan in case whichever market was chosen imposed export barriers over time. This manager proposed that Ranger should establish a subsidiary in the country of concern under such conditions. Is this a reasonable strategy? Are there any obvious reasons why this strategy could fail?

PROJECTS

1. Throughout the semester, you can apply the concepts in the text to the real world by reviewing an annual report of an MNC. Write to the "Investor Relations Department" of an MNC that you are interested in for an annual report so that you can review how that MNC conducts multinational financial management. In general, annual reports do not provide details of managerial decisions, but are still helpful for illustrating concepts in this text. You may wish to select from MNCs in the list in the back of the book if you do not already have a particular MNC in mind.

Many of these MNCs have a toll-free phone number available, so that you can call their "Investor Relations" or "Shareholder's Services" department to request an annual report. Call directory assistance to see if the MNC you are interested in has a toll-free number.

2. Look in a recent annual report of an MNC that interests you. (For addresses, see section in the back of the book.) Summarize any comments made in the annual report about

- the MNC's level of international sales
- the MNC's plans to expand overseas in the future
- the impact of the MNC's foreign business on its recent performance

Does it appear that the MNC has benefited from its international operations? Explain.

SUGGESTED READING

"Global Ethics: Wrestling With the Corporate Conscience," *Business* (July–September 1985), pp. 3–9.

This article explains how the management of an MNC may differ from that of a purely domestic firm.

REFERENCES

Aggarwal, Raj. "Investment Performance of U.S.-Based Multinational Companies: Comments and a Perspective of International Diversification of Real Assets." *Journal of International Business Studies* (Spring–Summer 1980), pp. 98–104.

Aharoni, Yair. "On the Definition of a Multinational Corporation." *Quarterly Review of Economics and Business* (Autumn 1971), pp. 27–37.

Auster, Ellen. "International Corporate Linkages: Dynamic Forms in Changing Environments." *Columbia Journal of World Business* (Summer 1987), pp. 3–6.

Bennett, Thomas, and Craig S. Hakkio. "Europe 1992: Implications for U.S. Firms." *Economic Review, Federal Reserve Bank of Kansas City* (April 1989), pp. 3–17.

Choi, Frederick D. S. "Teaching International Finance: An Accountant's Perspective." *Journal of Financial and Quantitative Analysis* (November 1977), pp. 609–614.

Daniels, J. D., and J. Bracker, "Profit Performance: Do Foreign Operations Make a Difference?" *Management International Review*, no. 1 (1989), pp. 46–56.

Eaker, Mark R. "Teaching International Finance: An Economist's Perspective." *Journal of Financial and Quantitative Analysis* (November 1977), pp. 607–608.

Emerson, Michael. "The Emergence of the New European Economy of 1992." *Business Economics* (October 1989), pp. 5–9.

Findlay, M. Chapman, III, and G. A. Whitmore. "Beyond Shareholder Wealth Maximization." *Financial Management* (Winter 1974), pp. 25–35.

Folks, William R., Jr. "Integrating International Finance into a Unified Business Program." *Journal of Financial and Quantitative Analysis* (November 1977), pp. 599–600.

Haar, Jerry. "A Comparative Analysis of the Profitability Performance of the Largest U.S., European, and Japanese Multinational Enterprises." *Management International Review*, no. 3 (1989), pp. 5–18.

Laczniak, Gene R., and Jacob Naor. "Global Ethics: Wrestling with the Corporate Conscience." *Business* (July–September 1985), pp. 3–9.

Madura, Jeff, and Lawrence C. Rose. "Are Product Specialization and International Diversification Compatible?" *Management International Review*, no. 3 (1987), pp. 37–44.

Porter, Michael E. "The Competitive Advantage of Nations." *Harvard Business Review* (March–April 1990), pp. 73–93.

Rybczynski, T. M. "The European Community and the World Economy." *Business Economics* (October 1989), pp. 24–29.

Schwartz, Peter, and Jerry Saville. "Multinational Business in the 1990s—A Scenario." *Long-Range Planning* (December 1986), pp. 31–37.

Tung, Rosalie L., and Edwin L. Miller. "Managing in the Twenty-first Century: The Need for Global Orientation." *Management International Review*, no. 1 (1990): pp. 5–18.

Vernon, Raymond. "International Investment and International Trade in the Product Life Cycle." *Quarterly Journal of Economics* (May 1966), pp. 190–207.

CHAPTER 2

International Flow of Funds

International business is facilitated by markets that allow for the exchange of foreign currencies and the flow of funds between countries. The transactions arising from international business can cause money flows from one country to another. The balance of payments, a measure of such international money flows, is discussed in this chapter. In addition, factors that influence the balance-of-payments accounts are identified. Finally, the agencies that oversee international transactions are introduced.

BALANCE OF PAYMENTS

The **balance of payments** is a measurement of all transactions between domestic and foreign residents over a specified period of time. The use of the words "all transactions" can be somewhat misleading, since some transactions may be estimated. The recording of transactions is done by **double-entry bookkeeping**. That is, each transaction is recorded as both a credit and a debit. Thus, total credits and debits will be identical for a country's balance of payments in aggregate; however, for any subset of the balance-of-payments statement, there may be a deficit or surplus position.

A balance-of-payments statement can be broken down into various components. Those that receive the most attention are the current account and the capital account.

Current Account

The **current account** is the broadest measure of a country's international trade in goods and services. Its primary component is the **balance of trade**, which is simply the difference between merchandise exports and imports. A deficit in the balance of trade represents a greater value of imported goods than exported goods. Conversely, a surplus reflects a greater value of exported goods than imported goods.

The current account balances of Germany, Japan, and the United States are shown in Exhibit 2.1. Since 1982 the United States has had a negative current account balance while Germany and Japan have had positive balances. The U.S. current account deficit grew to almost $150 billion in 1987 but declined in 1988 and 1989. In 1990, the U.S. deficit was about $99 billion, reaching a six-year low. Much of the U.S. trade deficit has been due to international trade with Japan. Over the period from 1985 to 1990, the trade deficit with Japan has averaged about $50 billion per year.

The **balance on goods and services** adds to the balance of trade the net amount of payments of interest and dividends to foreign investors and from foreign investment, as well as receipts and payments resulting from international tourism and other transactions. The current account adds to the balance on goods and services **unilateral transfers**, which reflect government and private gifts and grants.

As an example of how international transactions affect the current account balance, consider U.S. tourists who spend money in London. These expenditures reflect an outflow of funds from the United States. They will reduce the U.S. current account balance and increase Great Britain's current account balance. Conversely, if British tourists come to Walt Disney World in the United States, their spending represents an inflow of funds into the United States. Thus, the U.S. current account will increase while the current account in Great Britain decreases.

International fund flows also occur to pay for imports and are accounted for when measuring a country's current account. For example, a restaurant based in the United States that imports French wine will be sending funds out of the country to make payment, thereby reducing the U.S. current account. Conversely, a blue jeans manufacturer in the United States exporting jeans to Switzerland will be receiving funds from outside the United States, thereby increasing the U.S. current account.

EXHIBIT 2.1   Current Account Balances

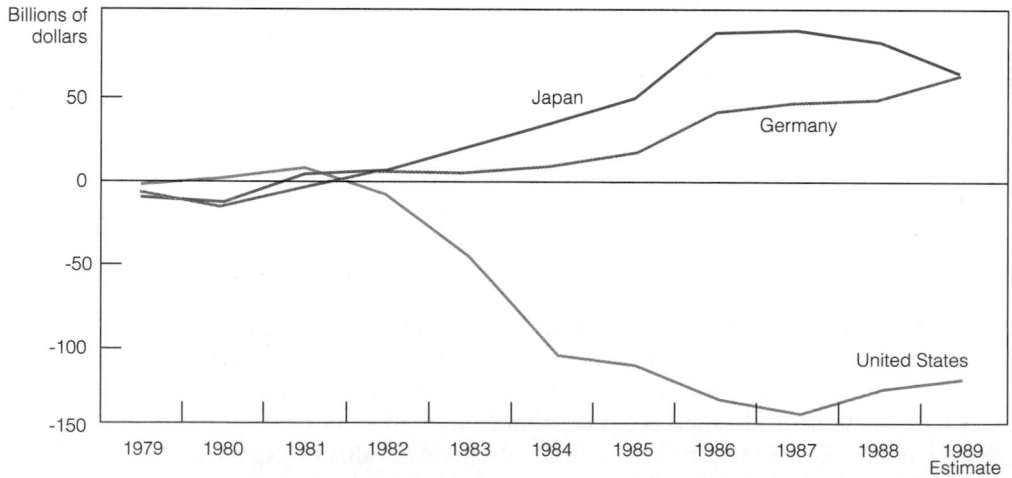

SOURCE: Federal Reserve Bank of New York Annual Report 1989, p. 15.

RECENT CHANGES IN NORTH AMERICAN TRADE. In January 1988, the U.S. and Canada agreed to a free-trade pact, which was initiated in January 1989 and would be completely phased in by 1999. As a result of this agreement, trade barriers on numerous products were reduced. The trade pact was expected to increase competition within various industries. Some firms that had focused exclusively on domestic business were encouraged to consider exporting or importing as the barriers were removed.

In 1990, the U.S. was also negotiating a free-trade pact with Mexico. Canada requested that it be included in the negotiations to complete a three-way agreement. The momentum for completing the pact was slowed because of the slow economies experienced by all three countries in the early 1990s. Industries such as farming, textiles, and steel that were somewhat protected from foreign competition, were generally opposed to the idea of a free-trade pact.

A free-trade pact between all three countries could cause a major increase in international trade within North America. During 1990, trade between the United States and Canada amounted to about $175 billion, while trade between the United States and Mexico was about $57 billion, and trade between Canada and Mexico totaled about $2 billion.

RECENT CHANGES IN EUROPEAN TRADE. Since the Single European Act was implemented to remove explicit and implicit barriers to trade, exports and imports between European countries are expected to rise substantially. The balance of trade of any individual European country relative to other European countries may depend on the severity of barriers that previously existed. For example, a European country that had relatively large barriers imposed on imports will be subject to a large increase in imports. Conversely, another European country that had minor barriers will not experience a change because the opportunities to export to that country had already existed.

The integration among European countries could have a major impact on the balance of trade between European countries and non-European countries. Two possible scenarios are as follows:

SCENARIO 1. "FORTRESS EUROPE"—NO RETALIATION. Some analysts have suggested that while European countries reduce barriers on trade within Europe, they will band together to raise barriers on imports coming from non-European countries. This approach has been referred to as "Fortress Europe", whereby European businesses are protected from exporters outside of Europe. If the European countries believe trade barriers imposed by other countries such as Japan and the United States are excessive, they may impose barriers on goods exported from these countries. For example, European countries banned imports of U.S. meat treated with growth hormones in January 1989. In addition, they imposed floor prices on computer memory chips imported from Japan, after accusing Japan of "dumping" (selling at less than cost) computer memory chips in Europe. If European countries raise barriers, their net exports (value of exports minus value of imports) should increase.

For some European countries, trade barriers on imports from countries outside the European Community (EC) may be reduced. For example, those countries with very strict quotas on Japanese automobile imports may have to conform to a unified EC quota. Italy presently maintains a quota of 3,500 Japanese automobiles, less than 1 percent of its market. The EC quota would likely be in the range of 10 to 11 percent.

If most EC trade barriers outside its community are increased, small and medium-sized companies that export to Europe may be adversely affected. In addition, the removal of barriers between European countries may intensify competition within Europe. This is another reason why exporters to Europe could be at a disadvantage. Exporters that are too small to consider direct foreign investment may be pushed out of the market.

SCENARIO 2. "FORTRESS EUROPE"—RETALIATION. If non-European countries retaliate in response to the "Fortress Europe" approach, then the change in net exports of European countries is less predictable. While imports from non-European countries decline, so would exports to these countries.

In general, the "Fortress Europe" approach may be considered undesirable because it can result in less international trade. However, to the extent that it is simply used as a threat to discourage excessive trade barriers by non-European countries rather than enforced continuously, it may actually encourage free trade.

Another recent event that will affect trade is the momentum for free enterprise in East Germany and other countries in Eastern Europe. Consumers in these countries will have more freedom to purchase imported goods, which should enhance net exports of other European countries in the near future. However, as time passes and private enterprise evolves in Eastern Europe, firms residing there may be able to develop some comparative advantages. Once the West European countries use East European markets to purchase goods as well as sell goods, the change in net exports will be less predictable.

Capital Account

The **capital account** reflects changes in country ownership of long-term and short-term assets. Long-term foreign investment measures all capital investments made between countries, including both direct foreign investment and purchases of securities with maturities exceeding one year. Short-term foreign investment measures flows of funds invested in securities with maturities of less than one year. Because of the short maturity, investors of such securities will often maintain their funds in a given country for only a short time, causing short-term investment flows to be quite volatile over time.

To illustrate the importance of international capital flows, consider that Japanese investors typically purchase between 15 and 30 percent of the 30-year bonds issued by the U.S. Treasury. In addition, Japanese investors are responsible for as much as 25 percent of the volume of stocks traded on the New York Stock Exchange. Some analysts suggest that actions by Japanese investors triggered the two biggest stock market declines in the 1980s. The October 19, 1987, crash began after Japanese investors sold a very large amount of U.S. Treasury bond holdings, precipitating an abrupt increase in interest rates. The October 13, 1989, stock market decline began after two Japanese banks decided not to financially support a proposed $6.75 billion purchase of UAL Corporation by UAL's managers. This event appeared to

EXHIBIT 2.2 Impact of German Reunification on Interest Rates

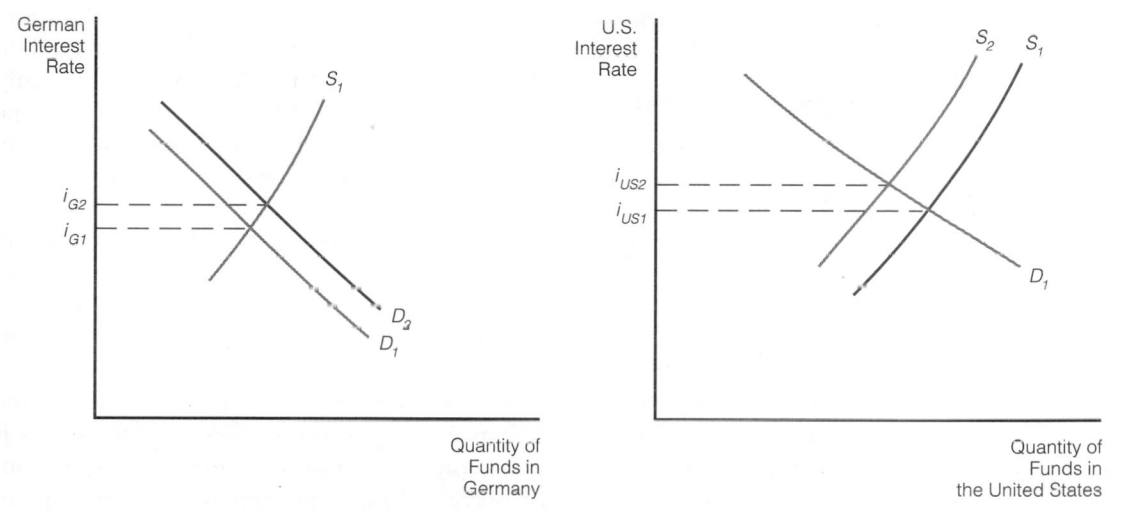

make investors believe that other possible takeovers would not be completed because of insufficient backing by investors.

RECENT CHANGES IN EUROPEAN CAPITAL FLOWS. Capital flows respond to changing regulations over time. When the Single European Act of 1987 was implemented to achieve integration throughout Europe, capital flows were redirected toward European countries to finance the new projects that would be undertaken. The result was less capital channeled to other countries, so that the supply of available funds became less than the demand for funds. Consequently, there was upward pressure on interest rates in those countries.

Capital flows between countries were also affected during the reunification of East and West Germany in late 1989. The encouragement of free enterprise in East Germany caused a substantial increase in the demand for funds there. By February 1990, interest rates in West Germany reached a seven-year high. Capital flows were redirected toward East Germany and West Germany to finance new projects. Consequently, less funds were channeled to the United States and other countries, causing interest rates there to rise (see Exhibit 2.2). Thus, interest rate movements across countries can be highly correlated, as the amounts of flows to and from most countries are influenced by the same factors.

FACTORS AFFECTING THE CURRENT ACCOUNT BALANCE

Because a country's current account balance can significantly affect its economy, it is important to identify and monitor the factors that influence it. The most influential factors are

- Inflation
- National income
- Exchange rates
- Government restrictions

Impact of Inflation

If a country's inflation rate increases relative to the countries with which it trades, its current account would be expected to decrease, other things being equal. Consumers and corporations within the country will most likely purchase more goods overseas (due to high local inflation), while the country's exports to other countries will decline.

Impact of National Income

If a country's income level (national income) increases by a higher percentage than that of other countries, its current account is expected to decrease, other things being equal. As real income levels (adjusted for inflation) rise, so does consumption of goods. A percentage of that increase in consumption will most likely reflect an increased demand for foreign goods. To illustrate the potential impact of national income on the current account balance, consider the July 1989 meeting between major countries in which the United States requested that other countries stimulate their respective economies. This type of policy would increase the foreign demand for U.S. goods, and reduce the U.S. balance of trade deficit. Yet, countries such as Japan and West Germany were more concerned about reducing their inflation and feared that too much economic growth might ignite inflation. Thus, they were not willing to enact stimulative policies, causing the United States to search for other solutions to its large balance of trade deficit. The removal of the Iron Curtain boosted Europe's economy in late 1989 and in 1990, which led to a higher demand for U.S. goods. In fact, the United States experienced a surplus balance of trade with Western Europe over the first four months of 1990, a major improvement from the $1.3 billion deficit in 1989.

Impact of Exchange Rates

If a country's currency begins to rise in value against other currencies, its current account is expected to decrease, other things being equal. Goods exported by the country will become more expensive to the importing countries if its currency strengthens. As a consequence, the demand for such goods will decrease. For example, a tennis racket selling in the United States for $100 would require a payment of 200 German marks by a German importer if the dollar is worth 2 marks. Yet, if the dollar were worth 3 marks, it would take 300 marks to buy that racket, and could discourage German demand for it. This relationship between exchange rates and the current account balance is expected if the traded goods are **price-elastic** (sensitive to price changes).

During the late 1970s, the dollar's value was low. In the early 1980s, its value increased to record highs. This was a primary reason why U.S. trade with nations changed during the early 1980s. The strong dollar encouraged U.S. importing and discouraged foreign demand for U.S. goods.

RELATED RESEARCH

Measuring the Impact of Exchange Rate Movements on International Trade

The responsiveness to exports, imports, or the balance of trade to exchange rates can be measured using regression analysis. (See the appendix for more details on regression analysis.) For example, a recent study analyzed how exchange rates affected U.S. textile imports. The following regression equation was applied:

$$\text{(\% change in U.S. textile imports)}_t = b_0 + b_1 \text{(\% change in real exchange rate of \$)}_{t-1} + b_2 \text{(\% change in real GNP)}_{t-1} + u_t$$

where b_0, b_1, and b_2 represent regression coefficients, t represents the quarter, and u represents an error term.

The real exchange rate of the dollar is a trade-weighted exchange rate adjusted for inflation. The real GNP also adjusts for inflation. Notice that the relationship expressed in the equation is designed to capture the lagged impact of the independent variables on imports. The regression model was applied to quarterly data from 1977 to 1986.

The results of the regression model follow:

$$\text{(\% change in U.S. textile imports)}_t = -29.41 + 1.33 \text{(\% change in real rate of \$)}_{t-1} + 2.91 \text{(\% change in real GNP)}_{t-1}$$

The regression coefficient of 1.33 implies that a 1 percent change in the real exchange rate of the dollar was followed by a 1.33 percent change in U.S. textile imports one quarter later. Furthermore, $b_2 = 2.91$, so that a 1 percent change in GNP was followed by a 2.91 percent change in textile imports one quarter later. Both relationships are statistically significant. The results indicate the likely increase in textile imports that results from a given increase in the inflation-adjusted dollar value and GNP growth.

This analysis could be applied to each industry separately or to all industries consolidated. Furthermore, forecasts of imports in future periods could be developed by applying the regression coefficients to forecasted values of the trade-weighted exchange rate and GNP.

SOURCE: Christine Chmura, "The Effect of Exchange Rate Variation on U.S. Textile and Apparel Imports." *Economic Review*, Federal Reserve Bank of Atlanta, (May–June 1987): pp. 17–22.

The relationship between the **real net exports** (inflation-adjusted exports minus inflation-adjusted imports) and the real (inflation-adjusted) value of the dollar is shown in Exhibit 2.3. As expected, the general inverse relationship between real net exports and the real value of the dollar existed over most of the 1972–1987 period. Yet from 1985 to the beginning of 1987, real net exports decreased even though the dollar depreciated. This contradictory relationship between exchange rates and the trade balance will be explained further.

During a weak-dollar period, many exporters to the United States may offset the higher dollar price to be paid for their goods by reducing the price they charge. For example, assume that office desks imported from West Germany were priced at 500 marks (or DM500). If a mark is worth $.40, a desk

EXHIBIT 2.3   Relationship between the Value of the Dollar and U.S. Real Net Exports

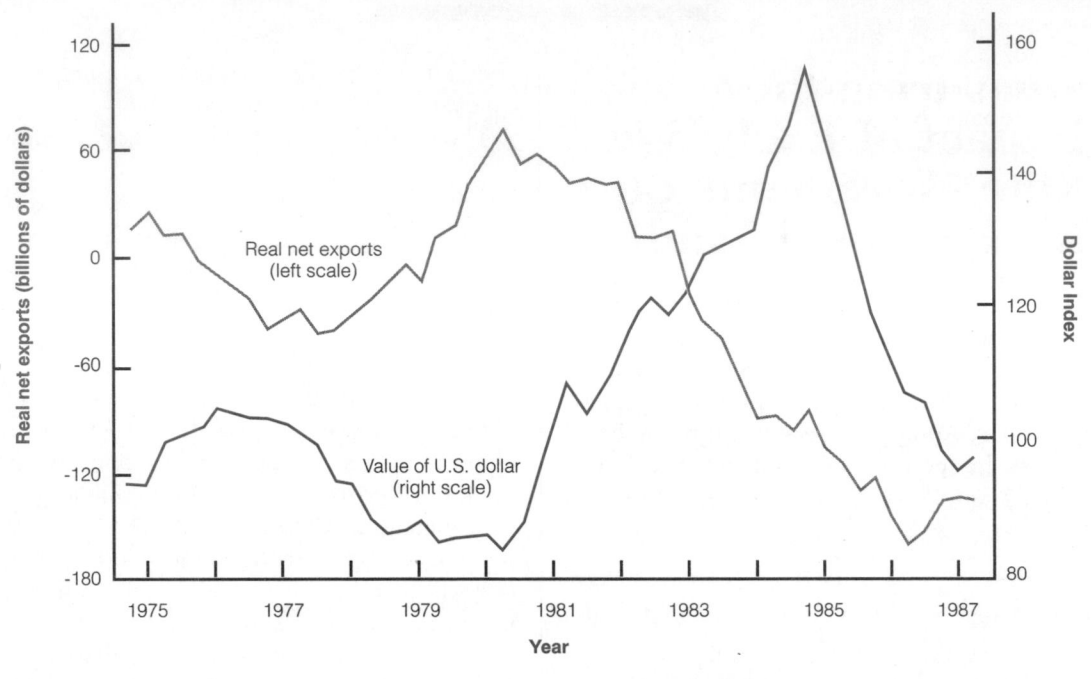

SOURCE: *Economic Review*, Federal Reserve Bank of Kansas City (December 1987): p. 14; and the Board of Governors.

costs a U.S. firm $200. If the mark appreciates (increases in value) by 25 percent to $.50, the desk costs a U.S. firm $250 (computed as DM500 × $.50 per mark). The desk manufacturer may consider reducing the desk price to DM400 for U.S. firms, which would result in a cost of $200. The manufacturer bears the impact of dollar depreciation in this example. The price reduction may not only reduce the manufacturer's profit margin, but in some cases would result in a loss. However, if the dollar's weakness is thought to be short-term, the loss may be worthwhile to maintain market share. Once the dollar strengthens, the manufacturer can adjust the price back to earn previous profit levels. In fact, it may even charge U.S. firms a higher price than DM500 during a strong-dollar period to account for the increased purchasing power of U.S. firms. Its actual price adjustment is somewhat dependent on the competition. If there are several foreign competitors, the price adjustment will depend on the prices charged by competitors to the U.S. customers. If the main competitors are from the United States, the firm exporting to the United States has more flexibility to raise prices during a strong-dollar period, since the dollar's strength will not directly benefit any of these competitors.

As an actual example, consider the case of Fujinon Optical Company, a Japanese exporter, which in 1985 priced its rubber-coated marine binoculars at 93,600 yen (the Japanese currency). At this time, the dollar was worth ¥240 so that U.S. importers could purchase the binoculars for $390 (computed as ¥93,600/¥240 per dollar). By July 1986 the dollar weakened substantially and was worth only ¥156. If the binoculars were still priced at ¥93,600, U.S. importers would need $600 (¥93,600/¥156 per dollar). Fujinon recognized that such a high price could reduce U.S. demand and consequently charged U.S. importers ¥67,080. This translated to $430 (at the exchange rate of ¥156 per dollar) which was 10 percent more than the U.S. importers were paying in the autumn of 1985. Nevertheless, Fujinon's price in terms of yen was about 28 percent lower than its autumn 1985 price.

The prices charged for several other Japanese goods such as shirts, blouses, jeans, handbags, ballpoint pens and records were revised downward in response to the dollar depreciation, by as much as 25 percent. The U.S. Labor Department estimated that from March 1985 through September 1987, just 46 percent of the dollar's average depreciation of 29 percent (against major currencies) was reflected in prices paid by U.S. importers, suggesting that foreign exporters absorbed the remaining 54 percent themselves.

Exhibit 2.4 shows how U.S. import prices have responded to movements in the average exchange rate of the major currencies (relative to the dollar) over time. In the 1970s and early 1980s there was a clear inverse relationship between these two variables. However, when the U.S. dollar began to weaken in 1985, the U.S. import prices increased only slightly—confirmation that non-U.S. exporters compensated U.S. importers for the weak dollar with discounted prices.

When exporters do not compensate U.S. importers for a weaker dollar, there is a greater chance that the importers will search for an alternative source of goods. They may not switch to U.S. firms, however. As the currencies of the major countries appreciated against the dollar from 1986 to 1988,

EXHIBIT 2.4 Relationship between the Dollar's Value and Import Prices

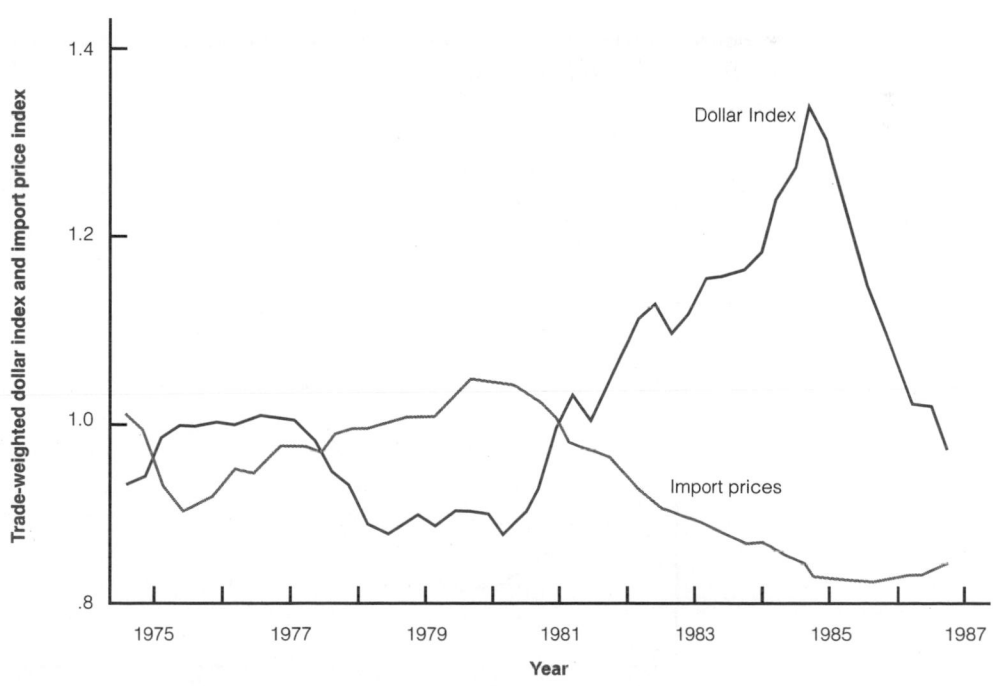

*1980–82 average = 1.0

SOURCE: *Economic Review,* Federal Reserve Bank of Kansas City (July–August 1987): p. 30.

many U.S. importers switched to other countries whose currencies did not appreciate. For example, the currencies of countries such as Singapore, Taiwan, Hong Kong, and South Korea were somewhat stable with respect to the dollar. Consequently, the U.S. trade deficit with these countries grew, more than offsetting any favorable impact on the trade balance with other countries.

Another reason why a weak dollar will not always reduce the U.S. trade deficit is that international trade transactions are prearranged and cannot be immediately adjusted. Thus, non-U.S. importing companies may be attracted to U.S. firms as a result of the weaker dollar, but do not immediately sever their relationships with suppliers from other countries. Over time, they may begin to take advantage of the weaker dollar by purchasing U.S. imports if they believe that the weakness will continue. The lag time between the dollar's weakness and the non-U.S. firm's increased demand for U.S. products has sometimes been estimated to be 18 months or even longer.

There is also a lagged relationship between the value of the dollar and the amount of U.S. imports, for the same reason. U.S. importers will not immediately switch to purchase U.S.-made goods when the dollar weakens. They may have established long-term relations with non-U.S. suppliers, or they may believe that there are no qualified substitutes for these goods in the United States. Given a stable amount of imports purchased and a weaker dollar, the dollar value of imports rises. Therefore, the U.S. balance of trade may actually deteriorate in the short run as a result of dollar depreciation. It only improves once U.S. and non-U.S. importers respond to the change in purchasing power that is caused by the weaker dollar. This represents the so-called **J curve effect**, as illustrated in Exhibit 2.5. The further decline in the trade balance before a reversal creates a trend that can look like the letter J.

EXHIBIT 2.5   Reaction of U.S. Trade Balance to a Weaker Dollar

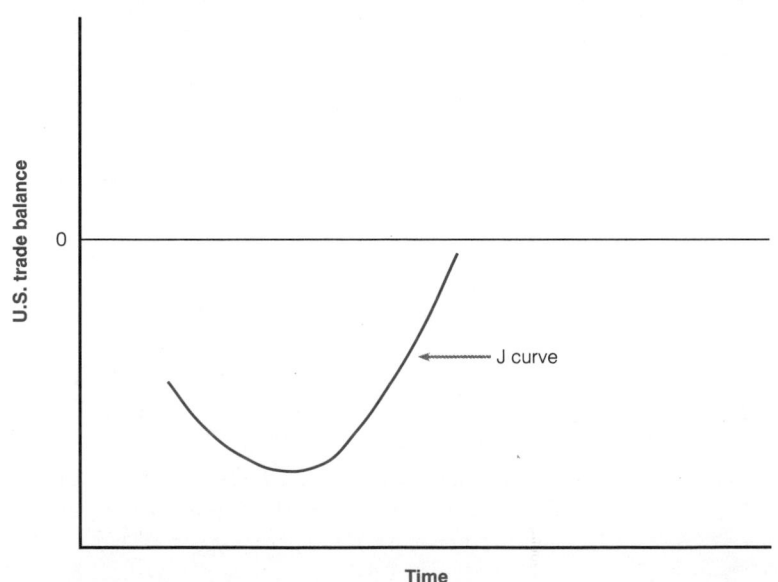

Impact of Government Restrictions

If a country's government imposes a tax on imported goods (often referred to as a **tariff**), the prices of foreign goods to consumers are effectively increased. Tariff rates imposed by the U.S. government are on average lower than those imposed by other governments. However, some industries are more highly protected by tariffs than others. American apparel products and farm products receive substantially more protection against foreign competition as a result of high tariffs on related imports. An increase in the use of tariffs is expected to increase the U.S. current account balance, unless other governments retaliate.

There are significant differences in tariffs among countries. For example, in 1990 the United States charged a tariff of 13.5 cents per case of foreign beer, while Canada charged 24 cents per case, most European countries charged $2.93 per case, and China charged $14.64 per case.

In addition to tariffs, a government can reduce its country's imports by enforcing a **quota**, or a maximum limit that can be imported. Quotas have been commonly applied to a variety of goods imported by the U.S. and other countries.

Trade restrictions may save jobs, but only at a cost. A recent study by the Institute for International Economics estimated the cost per job saved to be $705,000 for the U.S. automobile industry and $1 million for the specialty steel industry. Furthermore, trade restrictions tend to only benefit some industries at the expense of others, as other countries retaliate by imposing their own trade restrictions. In this case, imports by both countries may be reduced so that the current account level might not be much different from where it was before the first round of trade restrictions.

As an example of trade restrictions, the U.S. government enforced quotas on U.S.-imported specialty steel in July 1983 at the request of the U.S. steel industry to help the industry compete against foreign producers. The quotas were imposed on steel imported from European countries. This action is not considered legal based on the **General Agreement on Tariffs and Trade (GATT)** provisions established in 1947. The GATT rules allow for trade restrictions only in retaliation against illegal trade actions of other countries, such as a government that subsidizes exports. The U.S. government-enforced trade restrictions were deemed illegal because they were simply intended to give the U.S. steel industry a competitive edge in its home market. Consequently, the U.S. government was forced to accept restrictions of equal value on U.S. exports. A group of European countries announced shortly thereafter that they would retaliate by imposing tariffs and quotas on U.S. chemicals, plastics, and sporting goods exported to their countries. The U.S. government felt that such retaliatory actions were excessive and considered counter-retaliation on other goods imported by the U.S. from these European countries. In this example, the U.S. steel industry benefited from the U.S. government-enforced trade restrictions, but the chemicals, plastics, and sporting goods industries were adversely affected by the retaliatory actions of the European countries.

Over time, there have been various attempts to reduce trade restrictions. One of the most recent attempts is represented by the **Trade and Tariff Act of 1984** (also referred to as the **Omnibus Act**), enacted in October 1984. This act includes provisions that generally encourage free trade.

RELATED RESEARCH

Are Japanese Trade Barriers Excessive?

Sometimes *implicit* government trade barriers can have a significant impact on international trade. Japan is noted for its implicit barriers, such as extremely stringent product standards on imported products. Some economists argue that these barriers are to blame for the lingering U.S. trade deficit with Japan. Others, however, attribute the deficit to Japan's superior quality and production efficiency.

Japan's economy has substantially benefited since World War II from its participation in international trade. It has had large balance-of-trade surpluses since the early 1980s. Some countries openly criticized Japan for using excessive protectionist policies to maximize exports and limit imports, and Japan reacted to such criticism by reducing its trade barriers to a degree.

A recent study used regression analysis to determine the factors that affect the level of U.S. exports and imports from Japan. (See Appendix 2C for a description of regression analysis.) The analysis found that most of the variation in exports and imports is related to economic variables (such as country prices and incomes) and exchange rates, but not to government trade barriers. This suggests that the imposition of trade barriers has not had a significant impact on the trade balance.

SOURCE: Jeffrey H. Bergstrand. "United States–Japanese Trade: Predictions Using Selected Economic Models." *New England Economic Review,* Federal Reserve Bank of Boston (May–June 1986): pp. 24–37.

During 1989 the members of GATT made further progress on liberalizing world trade by discontinuing farm subsidies. They also agreed to strengthen GATT powers in regulating trade. There was some opposition from special interest groups representing agriculture, textiles, and other industries that prefer more protectionism. In 1990 the United States and Japan reached an agreement in which Japan would reduce its trade restrictions, while the United States would take measures to improve its global competitiveness. The impact of this agreement remains to be seen.

In recent years, the large U.S. balance of trade deficit has encouraged the U.S. government to force other countries to reduce their trade restrictions. For example, in 1988 the U.S. government pressured Taiwan to cut its tariffs. The government of Taiwan must comply with U.S. government requests, since almost half of Taiwan's exports are to the United States. If Taiwan did not cut tariffs, the U.S. government could retaliate on Taiwan's exports. The U.S. government also pressured South Korea to cut its tariffs during 1988.

In some industries, government restrictions on foreign trade will remain. For example, the large U.S. automobile manufacturers have pressured the U.S. government to request that the Japanese government limit auto exports from Japan to the United States. The Japanese government has complied with this request, and has limited auto exports since 1985.

The government also has other ways in which it can influence the current account, beyond imposing restrictions. Its monetary and fiscal policies could affect economic variables such as inflation and income levels, which in turn influence the current account balance. In addition, it may provide subsidies to some firms, which could enhance their export potential. For example, in

INTERNATIONAL FINANCIAL MANAGEMENT IN PRACTICE

Implicit Barriers to Trade: A Survey

In addition to tariffs and quotas, a variety of implicit barriers discourage firms from exporting to foreign countries. A survey found that the most significant ones were

1. Lack of knowledge about marketing products in foreign countries
2. Lack of relevant information about foreign countries
3. Lack of knowledge about foreign business practices
4. Lack of knowledge about export procedures
5. Inability to communicate with foreign customers

The most significant problems for those firms that export were

1. Exchange rate risk
2. Competing with foreign firms
3. Locating distributors in foreign countries
4. Pricing decisions in foreign markets
5. Lack of knowledge about foreign markets

It should be mentioned that this survey was conducted during the strong-dollar period. Exchange rate risk may not have been as critical to existing exporters during a weak-dollar period. Notice that a lack of knowledge underlies many barriers identified by both exporting and nonexporting firms.

SOURCE: Kedia, B. L. and J. Chhokar. "Factors Inhibiting Export Performance of Firms: An Empirical Investigation." *Management International Review,* no. 4 (1986): pp. 33–43.

1991 the French government provided huge subsidies to two of its massive electronics firms. Some European countries criticized this action since it was inconsistent with the recent removals of restrictions and subsidies that had inhibited free trade.

Interaction of Factors

To simplify this discussion, the impact of each economic factor and government restriction has been assessed individually, holding other factors constant. The factors just described interact, so that their simultaneous influence on the balance of trade is complex. For example, as a high U.S. inflation rate reduces the current account, it places downward pressure on the value of the dollar (as discussed in detail in Chapter 4). Since a weaker dollar can improve the current account, it may partially offset the impact of inflation on the current account. Regression analysis is commonly used for assessing the historical impact of one or more factors on the current account (see Appendix 2C for more details).

CORRECTING A BALANCE OF TRADE DEFICIT

By reconsidering some of the factors that affect the balance of trade, it is possible to develop some common methods for correcting a deficit. Any policy that will increase foreign demand for the country's goods and services will improve the balance of trade position. Foreign demand may increase if export prices become more attractive. This can occur when the country's inflation is low or when its currency's value is reduced, thereby making the prices cheaper from a foreign perspective.

A floating exchange rate could possibly correct any international trade imbalances in the following way. A deficit in a country's balance of trade suggests that the country is spending a greater amount of funds on foreign products than it is receiving from them. Because it is selling its currency (to buy foreign goods) in greater volume than the foreign demand for its currency, the value of its currency should decrease. This decrease in value should encourage more foreign demand for its goods in the future. While this theory seems rational, it does not always work in the manner stated. It is possible that, instead, a country's currency will remain stable or appreciate even when it has a balance of trade deficit. Other forces on the currency's value can offset the forces created by the balance of trade deficit. For example, consider a situation where foreign investors are purchasing the currency to invest in the country's securities. This demand for the currency places upward pressure on its value, thereby offsetting the downward pressure caused by the trade imbalance. Consequently, a country cannot always rely on currency movements to correct a trade deficit.

Another possible method of curing the trade deficit is to restrict imports. If a country can increase its export volume while restricting imports to a degree, the trade imbalance should be corrected. However, an improvement in one country's balance of trade (reduced imports) forces deterioration of other countries' balance of trade positions (reduced exports).

IMPACT OF TRADE ON THE INTERNATIONAL DEBT CRISIS

The economic conditions of many **less developed countries** (LDCs) is dependent on the economics of the developed countries to which they export goods. During the early 1980s, most developed countries experienced stagnant growth. The United States and other major countries experienced a recession in 1982. In addition, some of the oil-producing LDCs were forced to sell oil at a much lower world market price than they projected. As a result of the global recession and reduced oil prices, the LDCs experienced a severe decrease in their export volume, which worsened their domestic economy and caused them difficulty in repaying their debt. In the summer of 1982 the international debt crisis began as LDCs could not meet their loan payments. While some other problems may also have helped ignite the international debt crisis, the large trade deficits were a major determinant.

FACTORS AFFECTING THE CAPITAL ACCOUNT BALANCE

As with trade flows, national governments have authority over capital (money) flows that enter the country. A country's government could, for example, impose a special tax on income accrued by local investors who invested in foreign markets. A tax such as this would likely discourage people from sending their funds to foreign markets and could therefore increase the country's capital account. Other countries affected by this tax, however, could retaliate by imposing a similar tax on its local people. The ultimate impact would be a reduction in foreign investing by investors across various countries.

Capital flows are also influenced by capital controls enforced by countries. Over the years, there has been a gradual liberalization of controls on international capital flows. Some countries, such as Canada, West Germany, and the United States, have historically enforced relatively few capital controls. Other countries, such as Finland, Greece, Ireland, Italy, Portugal, Spain, and Sweden, have commonly imposed very restrictive controls on outflows of domestic currency. This imposition is typically designed to deal with a structural weakness in the country's balance of payments position. Countries such as Australia, Denmark, France, and Norway enforced currency outflow restrictions at one time but in recent years have adopted more liberal laws. Some financial intermediaries look forward to the day when other restrictions will be alleviated, so they can compete more fiercely on a global basis. Other, less aggressive financial intermediaries fear the possibility that they will soon face increased competition as global deregulation occurs.

Demographics can also affect the capital account. In the 1980s, the adult population of the United States was very young. In general, young workers demand more capital than they supply to the capital markets. The deficiency has been covered by non-U.S. investment in the U.S. capital markets. As time passes and the average age of the U.S. adult population rises, the capital deficiency will subside and so will the funding by non-U.S. investors.

The anticipated exchange rate movements by investors in securities can also affect the capital account. If a country's home currency is expected to strengthen, foreign investors may be willing to invest in the country's securities to benefit from the currency movement. For example, assume a German investor considers purchasing one-year U.S. Treasury bills, offering a yield of 9 percent. Assume the German investor has DM400,000 available for investment, and that the exchange rate is DM2 per dollar (or $.50 per mark). Assume the investor expects that by the end of the investment period the dollar will strengthen, to be worth 2.5 marks (or $.40 per mark). The investor's initial investment in U.S. Treasury bills is $200,000 (computed as DM400,000 × $.50 per mark), which will accumulate to $218,000 (computed as $200,000 × 1.09) by the end of the year. If the dollar is worth DM2.5 at that time, the investor will receive DM545,000 (computed as $218,000 × DM2.5). Thus, the expected yield to the German investor is

$$\frac{\text{DM545,000} - \text{DM400,000}}{\text{DM400,000}} = 36.25\%$$

While the investor's forecast of the dollar's strength may be inaccurate, this example is simply intended to show why a country's capital account balance may increase if its currency is expected to strengthen. Conversely, a country's capital account balance is expected to decrease if its home currency is expected to weaken, other things being equal.

When attempting to assess why a country's capital account changed or how it will change in the future, all factors must be considered simultaneously. A particular country may experience a reduction in its capital account even when its interest rates are attractive, if its home currency is expected to depreciate.

THE UNITED STATES AS A NET-DEBTOR NATION

The foreign ownership of financial and real assets has consistently increased, providing evidence of increasing globalization. However, the foreign ownership of U.S. assets has grown at a higher rate than U.S. ownership of foreign assets, as shown in Exhibit 2.6. By 1984 foreign ownership of assets in the United States exceeded U.S.-owned assets abroad, making the United States a **net-debtor nation**.

The United States had not been a net-debtor nation since 1914. Its net debt position increased from about $2 billion in 1987 to over $600 billion in 1989. The main reason for the adjustment in the late 1980s was large net-debtor positions with Western Europe and Japan.

A major reason for this change was the growth of the federal budget deficit. A large portion of government financing has been supported with foreign funds. Foreign investors hold more than $300 billion of the U.S. government debt. In addition, U.S. lending to foreign countries has decreased. While the

EXHIBIT 2.6 International Investment Positions, 1970–1989

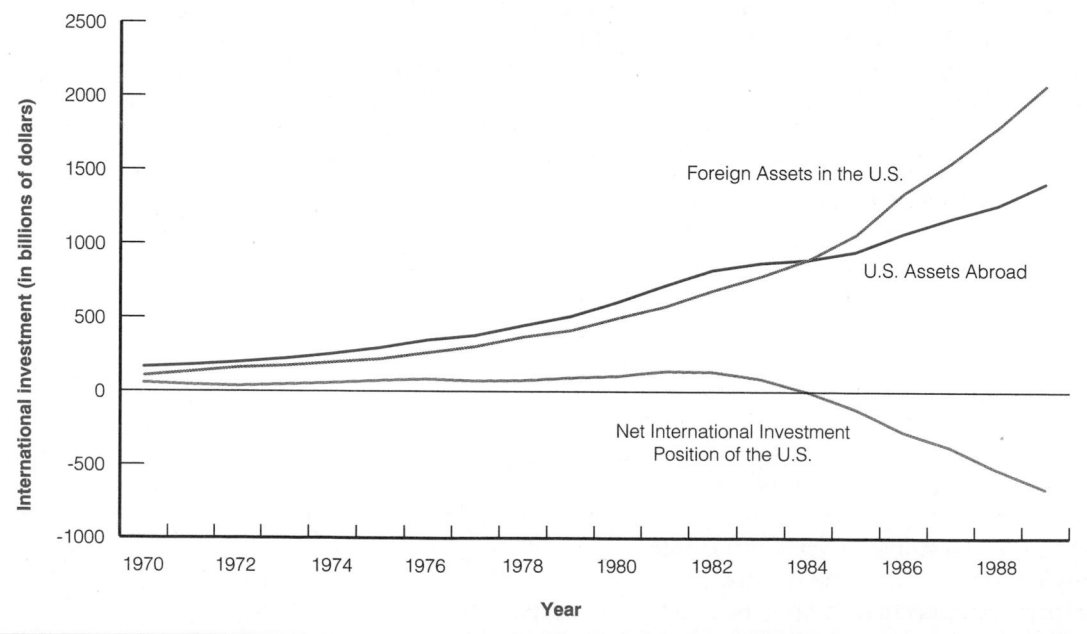

SOURCE: *New England Economic Review,* Federal Reserve Bank of Boston, (September–October 1990): p. 35; and *Survey of Current Business,* various issues.

net-debtor position is sometimes perceived to be unfavorable, it partially reflects more conservative lending practices by U.S. banks in the last few years.

By the end of 1989, the net debt of the United States reached $664 billion. The growth was primarily attributed to increased foreign holdings of government debt, real estate, and businesses.

AGENCIES THAT OVERSEE INTERNATIONAL FLOWS OF FUNDS

A variety of agencies have been established to facilitate international trade and financial transactions. These agencies often represent a collection of nations. A description of some of the more important agencies follows.

International Monetary Fund

The United Nations Monetary and Financial Conference held in Bretton Woods, New Hampshire, in July 1944 was called to develop a structured international monetary system. As a result of this conference, the **International Monetary Fund (IMF)** was formed. The major objectives of the IMF set by the charter are to (1) promote cooperation among countries on international monetary issues, (2) promote stability in exchange rates, (3) provide temporary funds to member countries attempting to correct imbalances of international payments, (4) promote free mobility of capital funds across countries, and (5) promote free trade. It is clear from these objectives that the IMF goals encourage increased internationalization of business.

Before 1973, when exchange rates were maintained within tight boundaries, the IMF concentrated on removing currency exchange restrictions and assuring currency convertibility, with the goal of encouraging international trade. The inception of floating exchange rates in 1973 and the onset of the 1974–1975 recession caused concern by the IMF that countries would attempt reducing their respective currency values to stimulate exports and reduce imports. Thus, the IMF offered financing arrangements to countries experiencing large balance of trade deficits.

During the international debt crisis that erupted in August 1982, the IMF provided financing to many of the countries experiencing debt-repayment difficulties. It worked with each of these countries individually to develop and implement policies that would improve their balance-of-trade positions.

One of the key duties of the IMF is its **compensatory financing facility (CFF),** which attempts to reduce the impact of export instability on country economies. While it is available to all IMF members, it is mainly used by developing countries. A country experiencing financial problems due to reduced export earnings must demonstrate that the reduction is temporary and beyond its control. In addition, it must be willing to work with the IMF in resolving the problem. The IMF may then be willing to provide financing. Requests for CFF financing by developing countries have been particularly high during worldwide recessions, such as in 1982.

Each member country of the IMF is assigned a quota based on a variety of factors reflecting that country's economic status. Members are required by the IMF to pay this assigned quota. The amount of funds that each member can borrow from the IMF is dependent on its particular assigned quota.

The financing by the IMF is measured in **special drawing rights (SDRs).** The SDR is not a currency but simply a unit of account. It is an international reserve asset created by the IMF and allocated to member countries to supplement currency reserves. The SDR's value fluctuates in accordance with the value of five major currencies: (1) U.S. dollar, (2) German mark, (3) French franc, (4) Japanese yen, and (5) British pound. This five-currency composite, designed on January 1, 1981, replaced a more complex 16-currency formula before that time. Each of the five currencies represented by the revised formula was assigned weights (in accordance with their international importance) to determine the SDR value. The U.S. dollar received a 42 percent weight, while the German mark received a 19 percent weight, and remaining currencies each received a 13 percent weight.

World Bank

The **International Bank for Reconstruction and Development (IBRD),** also referred to as the **World Bank,** was established in 1944. Its primary objective is to make loans to countries in order to enhance economic development. Its main source of funds is sale of bonds and other debt instruments to private investors and governments. The philosophy behind the World Bank's objective is profit-oriented. Therefore, loans are not subsidized, but are extended at market rates to governments (and their agencies) that are likely to make repayment.

While the World Bank still concentrates heavily on the partial financing of projects, it has made an effort to encourage economic productivity in recent years. One of its key facilities is the **Structural Adjustment Loan (SAL)** facility established in 1980. The SALs are intended to enhance a country's long-term economic growth. For example, SALs have been provided to Turkey and to some of the LDCs that are attempting to improve their balance of trade.

Because the World Bank provides only a small portion of the financing needed by developing countries, it attempts to spread its funds by entering into **co-financing agreements.** Co-financing is performed in the following ways:

- *Official aid agencies.* Development agencies may join the World Bank in financing development projects in low-income countries.
- *Export credit agencies.* The World Bank co-finances some capital-intensive projects that are also financed through export credit agencies.
- *Commercial banks.* The World Bank has joined with commercial banks to provide financing for private-sector development. In recent years, more than 350 banks from all over the world have participated in co-financing, including Bank of America, Bankers Trust, Chemical Bank, Citibank, and Manufacturers Hanover.

The World Bank has recently established the **Multilateral Investment Guarantee Agency (MIGA),** which offers various forms of political risk insurance. This is an additional means (along with its SALs) by which the

World Bank can encourage the development of international trade and investment.

As one of the largest borrowers in the world, the World Bank's borrowings have amounted to the equivalent of $70 billion. Its loans are well-diversified among numerous currencies and countries. It has received the highest credit rating (AAA) possible.

International Financial Corporation

In 1956 the **International Financial Corporation (IFC)** was established to promote private enterprise within countries. Like the IMF, it is composed of a collection of nations as members. While it aims to enhance economic development, it uses the private rather than government sector to achieve its objectives. It not only provides loans to corporations, but also purchases stock, thereby becoming part owner in some cases rather than just a creditor. The IFC typically provides 10 percent to 15 percent of the necessary funds in the private enterprise projects in which it invests, and the remainder of the project must be financed through other sources. Thus, the IFC acts as a catalyst as opposed to a sole supporter for private enterprise development projects. It traditionally has obtained financing from the World Bank but can borrow within the international financial markets.

In July 1987 the IFC began to offer new loan features. Borrowers willing to accept fixed-rate loans could choose to have their loan rate reset every five years. At the time of reset, they could consider switching to a variable-rate loan and can also switch the currency borrowed. Loans are available in U.S. dollars, German marks, Swiss francs, British pounds, and French francs.

INTERNATIONAL FINANCIAL MANAGEMENT IN PRACTICE

How the IFC Is Promoting Investment in Developing Countries

In 1986 the International Financial Corporation (IFC) used an innovative approach to achieve its objective of promoting investment in developing countries. It created a mutual fund called the Emerging Markets Growth Fund (EMGF). This fund invests in publicly listed shares of companies in developing countries. The EMGF will invest no more than 20 percent of its assets in any one country and no more than 5 percent in any company. The initial creation of the EMGF was to represent about 25 companies, concentrating in nine emerging stock markets. It is anticipated to serve as an attractive investment vehicle for institutional investors such as life insurance companies and pension funds, since it offers them a way to invest in developing countries and provides diversification among several countries.

SOURCE: *Finance and Development* (June 1986): p. 23.

International Development Association

The **International Development Association (IDA)** was created in 1960 with country-development objectives somewhat similar to those of the World Bank. Yet, its loan policy is more appropriate for less prosperous nations. The IDA extends loans at low interest rates to poor nations that cannot qualify for or afford loans from the World Bank.

Bank of International Settlements

The **Bank of International Settlements (BIS)** attempts to facilitate cooperation among countries with regard to international transactions. It also provides assistance to countries experiencing a financial crisis. The BIS is sometimes referred to as the "central bank's central bank" or the "lender of last resort." It played an important role in supporting some of the less developed countries during the international debt crisis in the early and mid-1980s.

Regional Development Agencies

There are several other agencies with more regional (as opposed to global) objectives relating to economic development. These include, for example, the Inter-American Development Bank (focusing on the needs of Latin America), the Asian Development Bank (established to enhance social and economic development in Asia), and the African Development Fund (focusing on development in African countries).

In 1990 the European Bank for Reconstruction and Development was created to help the East European countries adjust from communism to capitalism. Twelve West European countries hold 51 percent interest, while Eastern European countries hold 13.5 percent interest. The United States is the biggest shareholder, holding 10 percent interest. There are 40 member countries in aggregate, including Japan and the Soviet Union.

SUMMARY

The growth and importance of international business is facilitated by international financial markets. Specifically, the foreign exchange market enables firms to exchange currencies. The Eurocurrency, Eurocredit, and Eurobond markets allow for international fund transfers between countries. Agencies have been developed to oversee international financial markets and transactions. The more important agencies include the International Monetary Fund, World Bank, International Financial Corporation, International Development Association, and Bank of International Settlements.

QUESTIONS

1. What is the current account generally made up of?

2. What is the capital account generally made up of?

3. Discuss the trend in the U.S. current account position since 1980. How can you explain the trend?

4. How would a relatively high home inflation rate affect the home country's current account, other things being equal?

5. How would a weakening home currency affect the home country's current account, other things being equal?

6. How can government restrictions affect international payments among countries?

7. Is a negative current account harmful to a country? Discuss.

8. How did the current account position of countries affect the international debt crisis?

9. It is sometimes suggested that a floating exchange rate will adjust to reduce or eliminate any current account deficit. Explain why this adjustment would occur. Why does the exchange rate not always adjust to a current account deficit?

10. What are some of the major objectives of the IMF?

11. From 1985 to 1987 the dollar substantially depreciated but the U.S. demand for particular foreign imports was not significantly affected. Explain why.

12. If a U.S. importer is charged higher prices for its imported supplies, what will influence its decision to switch to a U.S. supplier?

13. From 1986 to 1988 the dollar depreciated against most major currencies but not against the currencies of South Korea and Singapore. Explain why the balance of trade between the United States and these countries would shift in reaction to the dollar's depreciation against major currencies. Would the U.S. balance of trade deficit have been larger or smaller if the dollar depreciated against all countries during this period? Explain.

14. Explain how a country can assess the historical impact of exchange rate movements on its imports. How can we use this information to forecast the expected impact of exchange rate movements on future imports?

15. In 1989 South Korea's export growth stalled. Some South Korean firms suggested that South Korea's primary export problem is the weakness in the Japanese yen. How would you interpret this statement?

16. In 1990, the U.S. balance of trade deficit was about $100 billion, which was the smallest deficit in several years. The relatively small trade deficit was attributed to a strong demand for U.S. exports. (U.S. exports amounted to $389 billion in 1990, the highest level ever). What do you think is the underlying reason for the strong demand for U.S. exports?

17. In recent years there has been considerable momentum to reduce or remove trade barriers in an effort to achieve "free trade". Yet, one disgruntled executive of an exporting firm stated "Free trade is not conceivable; we are always at the mercy of the exchange rate. Any country can use this mechanism to impose implicit trade barriers". What does this statement mean?

18. The Single European Act was expected to promote more cross-border trade within Europe. Yet, there was some concern that firms exporting to Europe would lose business. Why?

19. Explain why events in Japan can influence financial markets in the United States.

20. Explain how the German reunification could affect U.S. interest rates.

Mapleleaf Paper Company
Assessing the Effects of Changing Trade Barriers

Mapleleaf Paper Company is a Canadian firm that produces a particular type of paper that is not produced in the U.S. It focuses most of its sales in the U.S. In the past year for example, 180,000 of its 200,000 rolls of paper were sold to the U.S., with the remaining 20,000 rolls sold in Canada. It has a niche in the U.S., but because there are some substitutes, the U.S. demand for the product is sensitive to any changes in price. In fact, it had estimated that the U.S. demand rises (declines) three percent for every one percent decline (increase) in the price paid by U.S. consumers, other things held constant.

A 12 percent tariff had historically been imposed on the exports to the U.S. Then on January 2, a free-trade agreement between the U.S. and Canada was implemented, eliminating the tariff. Mapleleaf was ecstatic about the news, as it had been lobbying for the free-trade agreement for several years.

The Canadian dollar was worth $.76. Mapleleaf hired a consulting firm to forecast the value of the Canadian dollar in the future. The firm expected the Canadian dollar to be worth about $.86 by the end of the year and then stabilize after that. The expectations of a stronger Canadian dollar were driven by an anticipation that numerous Canadian firms would capitalize on the free-trade agreement more than U.S. firms, which would cause the increase in the U.S. demand for Canadian goods to be much higher than the increase in the Canadian demand for U.S. goods. (However, no other Canadian firms were expected to penetrate the U.S. paper market.) Mapleleaf expected no major changes in the aggregate demand for paper in the U.S. paper industry. It was also confident that its only competition would continue to be two U.S. manufacturers that produce imperfect substitutes of the paper. Its sales in Canada were expected to grow by about 20 percent by the end of the year because of an increase in the overall Canadian demand for paper and then remain level after that. Mapleleaf invoiced its exports in Canadian dollars and planned to maintain its present pricing schedule, since its costs of production were relatively stable. Its U.S. competitors would also continue their pricing schedule. Mapleleaf was confident that the free-trade agreement would be permanent. It immediately began to assess its long-run prospects in the U.S.

a) Based on the information provided, develop a forecast of Mapleleaf's annual production (in rolls) needed to accommodate demand in the future. Since orders for this year have already occurred, focus on the years following this year.

b) Explain the underlying reasons for the change in the demand and the implications of this exercise.

c) Would the general effects on Mapleleaf be similar to the effects on a U.S. paper producer that exports paper to Canada? Explain.

1. Once a month, the U.S. balance of trade figures are announced. Look in *The Wall Street Journal* or other business periodicals to assess this announcement and determine how the U.S. trade deficit has changed. What explanation is given for the change in the trade deficit? Is the change in the trade deficit attributed to a change in the U.S. dollar's value? Explain.

PROJECT

SUGGESTED READINGS

Jack L. Hervey, "Changing U.S. Trade Patterns," *Economic Perspectives*, Federal Reserve Bank of Chicago (March–April 1990), pp. 2–12. This article provides an updated overview on the composition of sources of U.S. imports, and destinations of U.S. exports.

Cletus C. Coughlin, K. Alec Chrystal, and Geoffrey E. Wood, "Protectionist Trade Policies: A Survey of The-

ory, Evidence and Rationale," *Review*, Federal Reserve Bank of St. Louis, (January–February 1988), pp. 12–29. This article provides a background on the gains from free trade and offers some interesting insight on various protectionist issues.

REFERENCES

Baldwin, Robert E. "Determinants of Trade and Foreign Investment: Further Evidence." *Review of Economics and Statistics* (Fall 1979), pp. 40–48.

Bame, Jack J. "Analyzing U.S. International Transactions." *Columbia Journal of World Business* (Fall 1976), pp. 72–84.

Batra, Reveendra N., and Rama Ramachandran. "Multinational Firms and the Theory of International Trade and Invest." *American Economic Review* (June 1980), pp. 278–292.

Bergstrand, Jeffrey H. "United States–Japanese Trade: Predictions Using Selected Economic Models." *New England Economic Review*, Federal Reserve Bank of Boston (May–June 1986), pp. 24–37.

Bernauer, Kenneth. "The Asian Dollar Market." *Economic Review*, Federal Reserve Bank of San Francisco (Winter 1983), pp. 47–63.

Bogdanowicz, Bindert, Christine A. and T. Chris Canavan. "The World Bank and the International Private Sector." *Columbia Journal of World Business* (Fall 1986), pp. 31–35.

Cavusgil, S. Tamer and Jacob Naor. "Firm and Management Characteristics as Discriminators of Export Marketing Activity." *Journal of Business Research* (June 1987), pp. 221–235.

Chmura, Christine. "The Effect of Exchange Rate Variation on U.S. Textile and Apparel Imports." *Economic Review*, Federal Reserve Bank of Richmond (May–June 1987), pp. 17–22.

Clark, Don. "Regulation of International Trade in the United States: The Tokyo Round." *Journal of Business* (April 1987), pp. 297–306.

Coughlin, Cletus C. and Geoffrey E. Wood. "An Introduction to Non-Tariff Barriers to Trade." *Review*, Federal Reserve Bank of St. Louis (January–February 1989), pp. 32–46.

Craig, Gary A. "A Monetary Approach to the Balance of Trade." *American Economic Review* (June 1981), pp. 460–466.

Deppler, Michael C., and Duncan M. Ripley. "The World Trade Model: Merchandise Trade." *International Monetary Fund Staff Papers* (March 1978), pp. 147–206.

Fallon, Padraic, Nigel Adam, and William Ollard. "The Great Deregulation Explosion." *Euromoney* (October 1984), pp. 55–61.

Fieleke, Norman S. "The Terms on Which Nations Trade." *New England Economic Review* (November–December 1989), pp. 3–12.

————. "International Payments Imbalances in the 1980s: An Overview." *New England Economic Review*, Federal Reserve Bank of Boston, (March–April 1989), pp. 4–14.

————. "Europe in 1992." *New England Economic Review*, Federal Reserve Bank of Boston, (May–June 1989), pp. 14–26.

Forrestal, Robert P. "The Rising Tide of Protectionism." *Economic Review*, Federal Bank of Atlanta (March–April 1987), pp. 4–10.

Kravis, Irving B., and Robert E. Lipsey. "Price Behavior in the Light of Balance of Payments Theories." *Journal of International Economics* (May 1978), pp. 193–246.

LaCivita, Charles. "Currency, Trade, and Capital Flows in General Equilibrium." *Journal of Business* (January 1987), pp. 113–135.

Morici, Peter, and Laura L. Megna. *U.S. Economic Policies Affecting Industrial Trade: A Quantitative Assessment* (National Planning Association, 1983).

Obstfeld, Maurice. "Balance-of-Payments Crises and Devaluation." *Journal of Money, Credit, and Banking* (May 1984), pp. 208–217.

Ott, Mack. "Is America Being Sold Out?" *Review*, Federal Reserve Bank of St. Louis (March–April 1989), pp. 47–64.

Rugman, Alan M., and Alain Verbeke. "Multinational Corporate Strategy and the Canada–U.S. Free Trade Assignment. *Management International Review* no. 3 (1990): pp. 253–266.

Rybczynski, T. M. "The Internationalization of Finance and Business." *Business Economics* (July 1988), pp. 14–20.

Salop, Joanne, and Erich Spitaller. "Why Does the Current Account Matter?" *International Monetary Fund Staff Papers* (March 1980), pp. 101–134.

Walter, Norbert. "Implications of EC Financial Integration." *Business Economics* (October 1989), pp. 18–23.

Whitehead, David D. "Moving Toward 1992: A Common Financial Market for Europe?" *Economic Review* Federal Reserve Bank of Atlanta, (November–December 1988), pp. 42–51.

Yavas, Ugur, S. Tamer Cavusgil, and Secil Tuncalp. "Assessments of Selected Foreign Suppliers by Saudi Importers: Implications for Exports." *Journal of Business Research* (June 1987), pp. 237–246.

The Balance of Payments

This appendix is a reprint of a monograph by Norman S. Fieleke in "What Is Balance of Payments," a special study by the Federal Reserve Bank of Boston.

A SHORT DEFINITION

A country's balance of payments is commonly defined as the record of transactions between its residents and foreign residents over a specified period. Each transaction is recorded in accordance with the principles of double-entry bookkeeping, meaning that the amount involved in each transaction is entered on each of the two sides of the balance-of-payments accounts. Consequently, the sums of the two sides of the complete balance-of-payments accounts should always be the same, and in this sense the balance of payments always balances.

However, there is no bookkeeping requirement that the sums of the two sides of a *selected number* of balance-of-payments accounts should be the same, and it happens that the (im)balances shown by certain combinations of accounts are of considerable interest to analysts and government officials. It is these balances that are often referred to as "surpluses" or "deficits" in the balance of payments.

This monograph explains how such measures of balance are derived and interpreted. Full understanding of the derivation requires a grasp of elementary balance-of-payments accounting principles, so these principles are outlined and illustrated in the first two sections.

RECORDING OF TRANSACTIONS: GENERAL PRINCIPLES

The double-entry bookkeeping used in accounting for the balance of payments is similar to that used by business firms in accounting for their financial positions. In ordinary business accounting the amount of each transaction is recorded both as a debit and as a credit, and the sum of all debit entries must, therefore, equal the sum of all credit entries. Furthermore, in business accounting it is recognized that the total value of the assets employed by the firm must be equal to the total value of the claims against the assets, that is, that all assets belong to someone. As is well known, the claims against assets are called the liabilities of the firm. (Assets of the firm not subject to the claims of creditors are, of course, the property of stockholders, so that, broadly speaking, the firm has two classes of liabilities: those due to creditors and those due to stockholders.) By accounting convention, *a debit entry is used to show an increase in assets or a decrease in liabilities, while a credit entry is used to show an increase in liabilities or a decrease in assets.* Since a debit entry is always accompanied by a credit entry, it follows that the value of total assets on the books of a going concern is always equal to the value of total liabilities (including the claims of stockholders).

These elementary principles can be applied to the recording of transactions in the balance of payments. For example, when a foreigner gives up an asset to a resident of this country in return for a promise of future payment, a debit entry is made to show the increase in the stock of assets held by U.S. residents, and a credit entry is made to show the increase in U.S. liabilities to foreigners (i.e., in foreign claims on U.S. residents). Or when a U.S. resident transfers a good to a foreigner, with payment to be made in the future, a debit entry is made to record the increase in one category of U.S. assets (U.S. financial claims on foreigners, i.e., U.S. holdings of foreign IOUs), and a credit entry is made to record the decrease in another category (goods).

These principles are illustrated in greater detail in the following section, which through a series of examples constructs a hypothetical balance-of-payments statement.

RECORDING OF TYPICAL TRANSACTIONS

The balance-of-payments accounts are commonly grouped into three major categories: (1) accounts dealing with goods and services; (2) accounts recording gifts, or unilateral transfers; (3) accounts dealing basically with financial claims (such as bank deposits and stocks and bonds). This section shows how typical transactions in each of these major categories are recorded.

COMMERCIAL EXPORTS: TRANSACTION 1

Suppose that a firm in the United States ships merchandise to an overseas buyer with the understanding that the price of $50 million, including freight, is to be paid within 90 days. In addition, assume that the merchandise is transported on a U.S. ship.

In this case U.S. residents are parting with two things of value, or two assets: merchandise and transportation service. (Transportation service, like other services supplied to foreigners, can be viewed as an asset that is created by U.S. residents, transferred to foreigners, and consumed by foreigners all at the same time.) In return for giving up these two assets, U.S. residents are acquiring a financial asset, namely, a promise from the foreign customer to make payment within 90 days. In accordance with the principles outlined above, the bookkeeping entries required to record these transactions are as follows: (1) a debit of $50 million to the account "U.S. private short-term claims," to show the increase in this kind of asset held by U.S. residents; (2) a credit of $49 million to "Merchandise," and (3) a credit of $1 million to "Transportation," to show the decreases in these assets available to U.S. residents. These figures are entered on lines 21, 2, and 3 in Exhibit 2A.1 and are preceded by the number (1) in parentheses to indicate that they pertain to the first transaction discussed.

EXHIBIT 2A.1 Hypothetical Transactions between U.S. Residents and Foreign Residents *(in millions of dollars)*

Line	Account	Debits	Credits	Excess of Debits (−) or Credits (+)
1	Exports of goods and services		60	+ 60
2	Merchandise		(1) 49	+ 49
3	Transportation		(1) 1	+ 1
4	Income on U.S. investments abroad		(3) 10	+ 10
5	Other			
6	Imports of goods and services	50		− 50
7	Merchandise	(4) 45		− 45
8	Travel	(5) 5		− 5
9	Other			
10	Unilateral transfers	(6) 1		− 1
11	Changes in U.S. claims on foreigners[1]	320	71	−249
12	U.S. official reserve assets			
13	Gold			
14	Special drawing rights	(9)200	(10) 10	− 190
15	Foreign currency balances			
16	Reserve position in IMF			
17	Other U.S. Government claims			
18	U.S. private claims			
19	Direct investments			
20	Other U.S. private "long-term" claims	(7) 60		− 60
21	U.S. private short-term claims	(1) 50(3)10	(2) 50(4)10	
			(6) 1	+ 1
22	Changes in foreign claims on U.S. (i.e., in U.S. liabilities to foreign residents)[2]	85	125	+ 40
23	Foreign official claims[3]	(10) 10	(8) 25	+ 15
24	Foreign private short-term claims	(2) 50(8)25	(4) 35(5)5	
			(7) 60	+ 25
25	Other			
26	Allocations of special drawing rights		(9)200	+200
27	Total	456	456	0
	Memoranda:			
28	Balance on merchandise trade (lines 2 & 7)			+ 4
29	Balance on goods and services (lines 1 & 6)			+ 10
30	Balance on current account (lines 29 & 10)			+ 9
31	Transactions in U.S. official reserve assets and in foreign official assets in the United States (lines 13–16 & 23)			−175

[1]Including U.S. real property abroad.
[2]Including foreign real property in the United States.
[3]Here assumed to exclude U.S. Government liabilities associated with military sales contracts and other transactions arranged with or through foreign official agencies.

PAYMENT FOR COMMERCIAL EXPORTS: TRANSACTION 2

To make payment in dollars for the merchandise he has received from the United States, the foreign customer might purchase from his local bank a demand deposit held by his bank in a U.S. bank, then transfer the deposit to the U.S. exporter. As a result U.S. demand deposit liabilities to foreign residents (i.e., foreign private short-term claims) would be diminished (debited). The payment by the foreign buyer would also cancel his obligation to the U.S. exporter, so that U.S. private short-term claims on foreigners would be reduced (credited). The appropriate entries, preceded by the number (2), are on lines 21 and 24 of the table.

RECEIPT OF INCOME FROM INVESTMENTS ABROAD: TRANSACTION 3

Each year residents of the United States receive billions of dollars in interest and dividends from capital investments in foreign stocks, bonds, and the like. U.S. residents receive these payments in return for allowing foreign residents to use U.S. capital which otherwise could be put to work in the United States.

Suppose that a U.S. firm has a long-standing capital investment in a profitable subsidiary abroad, and that the subsidiary transfers to the U.S. parent (as one of a series of such transfers) some $10 million in dividends in the form of funds held in a foreign bank. The U.S. firm then has a new (or enlarged) demand deposit in a foreign bank, as compensation for allowing its capital (and associated managerial services) to be used by its subsidiary. A debit entry on line 21 shows that U.S. private short-term claims on foreigners have increased, and a credit entry on line 4 reflects the fact that U.S. residents have given up an asset (the services of capital over the period covered) that is valued at $10 million.

COMMERCIAL IMPORTS: TRANSACTION 4

In the balance-of-payments accounts U.S. imports of goods and services have opposite results from U.S. exports. Residents of the United States are acquiring goods and services rather than giving them up, and in return are transferring financial claims to foreigners rather than acquiring them.

To take an illustration, assume that U.S. residents import merchandise valued at $45 million, making payment by transferring $10 million from balances that they hold in foreign banks and $35 million from balances held in U.S. banks. A debit entry on line 7 records the increase in goods available to U.S. residents, while credit entries on lines 21 and 24 record the decrease in U.S. claims on foreigners and the increase in U.S. liabilities.

EXPENDITURES ON TRAVEL ABROAD: TRANSACTION 5

Residents of the United States who tour abroad purchase foreign currency with which to meet their expenses. If U.S. residents transfer balances of $5 million in U.S. banks to foreigners in exchange for foreign currency that they spend traveling abroad, the end result is that the account "Travel" must be debited $5 million to reflect U.S. purchases of this "asset," and "Foreign private short-term claims" must be credited $5 million to show the increase in U.S. demand deposit liabilities. Such expenditures on travel are classified under the general heading of "Imports of goods and services," since the expenditures go to purchase goods and services from foreigners.

GIFTS TO FOREIGN RESIDENTS: TRANSACTION 6

Many residents of this country, some of them recent immigrants, send gifts of money to relatives abroad. If individuals in the United States acquire balances worth $1 million that U.S. banks have held in foreign banks and then transfer these balances to relatives overseas, there must be a credit entry of $1 million showing the decrease in U.S. private short-term claims on foreigners. This transaction differs from the other transactions analyzed in that U.S. residents obtain nothing of material value in return for the asset given up. Yet if the books are to balance, there must be a debit entry of $1 million. The bookkeeping convention followed in such cases is to debit an account called "Unilateral transfers" (line 10). In the official U.S. balance-of-payments presentation, this account is divided into several subsidiary accounts, some of which are used to record grants by the federal government under the foreign aid programs. These foreign aid grants, of course, have been much larger than gifts by private individuals.

LOANS TO BORROWERS ABROAD: TRANSACTION 7

A financial loan by a resident of the United States to a borrower in another country entails the transfer of money by the U.S. resident in exchange for a promise from the borrower to repay at a future time. Suppose that U.S. residents purchase $60 million in long-term bonds issued by Canadian borrowers. Also assume that the bonds are denominated in U.S. dollars, so that payment for them is made by transferring U.S. dollar demand deposits. A debit entry on line 20 records the increase in U.S. holdings of foreign bonds, and a credit entry on line 24 records the increase in demand deposits held by foreigners in U.S. banks.

In principle, direct investment abroad by a U.S. firm could have required the same accounting entries. For the $60 million bond purchase to qualify as a direct investment, the bonds would have to be the obligations of a Canadian firm in which a U.S. party (or affiliated parties) owned at least 10 percent of the voting securities. Typically, however, direct investment abroad by a U.S. firm takes some other form, such as a purchase of foreign equity securities or a simple advance of funds to a foreign subsidiary.

PURCHASES AND SALES OF DOLLAR BALANCES BY FOREIGN CENTRAL BANKS: TRANSACTION 8

At this point it is appropriate to examine the net result of the foregoing seven transactions on the short-term claims of U.S. residents and of foreign residents. As the table shows, these transactions have involved almost the same volume of debits as credits to U.S. private short-term claims on foreigners, with the net result that these claims have been diminished (credited) by $1 million (the figure on line 21 in the last column). By contrast, as shown on line 24, foreign private short-term claims on this country have risen by $50 million (excluding the effects of transaction 8, which remains to be discussed).

It happens that all of this $50 million is in the form of demand deposits, and private foreigners might not wish to retain all of these newly acquired dollar balances. Those who hold demand deposit dollar balances typically do so for purposes such as financing purchases from the United States (or from non-U.S. residents desiring dollars), and there is no guarantee that such motivations will be just strong enough to make the dollar-balance holders exactly satisfied with the $50 million increase in their holdings. For purposes of illustration, assume that foreign residents attempt to sell $40 million of this increase in exchange for balances in their native currencies, but that U.S. residents do not want to trade any of their foreign-currency balances for the proffered dollar balances at the going rates of exchange between the dollar and foreign currencies. In these circumstances the foreign-exchange value of the dollar (the price of the dollar in terms of foreign currencies) will decline.

However, some central banks might hold the view that the foreign-exchange value of their currencies was inappropriately high (i.e., that the foreign-exchange value of the dollar was inappropriately low), in which case they might sell foreign currencies in exchange for dollar balances in order to moderate the decline in the exchange price of the dollar. In the present case, suppose that foreign central banks purchased 25 million in dollar balances from commercial banks within their territories. The U.S. balance-of-payments accounts would register an increase of $25 million in U.S. liabilities held by foreign monetary authorities (line 23) and an equivalent decrease in short-term liabilities held by private foreigners (line 24).

It should be noted that such purchases of dollar balances by foreign central banks supply the commercial banks that sell the dollars with new reserves in their native currencies. In general, these reserves can be used by the banks to expand loans and thus to inflate the money supplies in the countries concerned, if nothing else is changed.

RECEIPT OF ALLOCATION OF SDRs: TRANSACTION 9

Between 1970 and 1972 the International Monetary Fund (IMF) created and distributed the first issue of special drawing rights (SDRs) in order to enlarge the stock of international reserve assets. By international agreement SDRs are to be acceptable in settlement of debts between countries. They are created in limited internationally-agreed amounts and are allocated to participating countries in proportion to their quotas in the IMF. In terms of currency an SDR is defined as a "basket" containing specified quantities of five major currencies—the U.S. dollar, the German mark, the French franc, the Japanese yen, and the U.K. pound.

To illustrate how the receipt of newly created SDRs is treated in the U.S. balance-of-payments accounts, assume that the IMF notified the U.S. authorities that $200 million in new SDRs had been credited to the U.S. account. A debit entry on line 14 would record the increase in this international reserve asset held by the United States. However, this transaction would involve neither a corresponding decrease in other assets nor a corresponding increase in liabilities; so to meet the requirement for an equivalent credit under the system of double-entry bookkeeping, a credit entry of $200 million would be made to a specially created account, "Allocations of special drawing rights" (line 26).

DEALINGS IN SDRs WITH FOREIGN CENTRAL BANKS: TRANSACTION 10

As a result of the foregoing transactions, the dollar holdings of foreign central banks have been enlarged by $25 million (as explained under transaction 8). But for a number of reasons these banks might not wish to hold exactly this additional amount of dollar claims for any length of time. In particular, they might fear a further depreciation of the dollar in the foreign-exchange markets. Whatever the reason, assume that the U.S. authorities wish to cooperate in supporting the foreign-exchange value of the dollar and that they therefore transfer SDRs valued at $10 million to the foreign central bankers in exchange for 10 million in dollar balances. U.S. liabilities held by foreign monetary authorities then decline by $10 million, and U.S.-owned SDRs decline by the same amount. If gold instead of SDRs had been transferred, the credit entry would have been made on line 13 rather than line 14.

STATISTICAL DISCREPANCY

At the beginning of this article it was noted that a country's balance of payments is commonly defined as the record of transactions between its residents and foreign residents over a specified period. Compiling this record presents difficult problems, and errors and omissions in collecting the data are sometimes made.

Take first the matter of coverage. In spite of attempts to gather data on them, some international transactions go unreported. One category of transactions that probably is often substantially underreported is purchases and sales of short-term financial claims; such unreported movements of short-term capital are widely believed to be a major component of total errors and omissions. No attempt is made to collect complete data on certain other transactions, which are estimated by balance-of-payments statisticians. The sample observations on which these estimates are based are sometimes of doubtful reliability, and even the best sampling are estimating techniques will not prevent errors of estimation.

Or take the matter of valuation. While import documentation, for example, may state precise value for the merchandise imported, a different amount may eventually be paid the exporter. The discrepancy can arise for a number of reasons, ranging from default by the importer to incorrect valuation of the merchandise on the import documents.

Because of such problems total *recorded* debits do not equal total *recorded* credits in the actual balance-of-payments accounts in any given year. To provide a specific illustration of how this discrepancy arises, suppose that U.S. export documentation valued an item at $500, while in fact the terms of sale called for payment of only $400 by the foreign importer, who drew down his bank balance in the United States to make the payment. On the basis of the export documentation, balance-of-payments accountants would credit merchandise exports by $500; but when they turned their attention to U.S. short-term liabilities to private foreigners, they would find that U.S. banks had reported a decrease of only $400 (assuming no other transactions). Consequently, recorded credits would mistakenly exceed recorded debits by $100. In fact, of course, the credit entry should have been in the amount of $400.

It is to accommodate such discrepancies that the residual account, "Statistical discrepancy," was created. An excess of credits in all other accounts is offset by an equivalent debit to this account, or an excess of debits in other accounts is offset by an equivalent credit to this account. The account thus serves at least two purposes; it gives the balance-of-payments analyst an indication of the net error in the balance-of-payments statistics, so that he can have some idea of the reliability of the balance-of-payments data, and it provides a means of satisfying the requirement of double-entry bookkeeping that total debits must equal total credits. Of course, there is no need for the account in our hypothetical balance-of-payments table, which displays an equality between total debits and total credits (line 27).

MEASURES OF BALANCE

As noted at the beginning of this monograph, the balances shown by selected combinations of balance-of-payments accounts are of considerable interest to analysts and government officials. Four of these measures are shown on lines 28 and 31 of the table.

The first and simplest of these measures is the balance on merchandise trade, which is derived by computing the net excess of debits or credits in the merchandise accounts. In our hypothetical statement there is a net credit balance or "surplus," of $4 million.

Similarly, by computing the net excess of debits or credits in the goods and services accounts, we obtain the balance on goods and services, which happens to be a credit (an excess of exports over imports) of $10 million. Such a credit balance indicates that the United States transferred more real resources (goods and services) to other countries than it received from them during the period covered by the statement, while a debit balance would indicate the reverse. The balance on goods and services is of interest not only as an approximation of such net transfers of real resources but also because it is defined in roughly the same way as the "net exports of goods and services" that comprise part of the nation's gross national product or expenditure; the main quantitative difference in definition is that interest payments by the U.S. Government to foreign residents are not counted in tallying net exports of goods and services, on the rationale that Government interest is not a payment for services used in the production process, while such interest payments are counted in striking the balance on goods and services.

The third measure, the balance on current account, is the net excess of debits or credits in the accounts for goods, services, and unilateral transfers, that is, the balance on all accounts other than the financial claims, or "capital," accounts. Because total debits must equal total credits in the balance of payments, the balance on the current accounts must equal the balance on the remaining, or capital, accounts. Thus, the current-account balance is an approximation of the change in the net claims of U.S residents on the rest of the world; it is a major component of the change in the country's net international investment position, or "net worth," vis-à-vis the rest of the world.[1]

As a rule, it is much more difficult to interpret the fourth measure, "Transactions in U.S. official reserve assets and in foreign official assets in the United States." From a simple accounting perspective, this balance measures the difference between the change in U.S. official reserves and in foreign official claims on the United States. A debit balance, such as that shown in the statement, indicates that U.S. official reserve assets have risen more (or fallen less) than foreign official claims on this country, while a credit balance would indicate the reverse.

In some circumstances, however, this fourth measure summarizes considerably more information. For example, suppose that there had been no allocation of SDRs (no transaction 9), so that the balance on this fourth measure was a credit of $25 million rather than the debit of $175 million that is shown. From the description of transactions 8 and 10, it is clear that this $25 million credit arose from central bank operations in support of the foreign-exchange value of the dollar. The amount of this credit (support) *along with* any observed decline in the foreign-exchange value of the dollar would then provide a joint indication of the weakness of the dollar in the foreign-exchange markets during the period in question.

Such interpretations require knowledge of the details of transactions like 8 and 10, and the details are often difficult to come by. For example, foreign officials, such as those in some oil-exporting countries, sometimes acquire dollar balances for investment or reserve purposes (rather than as a result of supporting the dollar as in transaction 8). In such cases dollar purchases by foreign central banks testify to the desirability or strength of the dollar in the foreign-exchange markets, rather than to its weakness. Therefore, it is safest to interpret this fourth measure of balance from the simple accounting perspective outlined above.

This measure's first component, "Transactions in U.S. official reserve assets," is worthy of special attention in itself. To illustrate, when foreign central banks acquired $10 million in SDRs in transaction 10, they gave to the U.S. authorities (directly or indirectly) $10 million in U.S. commercial bank balances in return. The Federal Reserve authorities would collect this $10 million by deducting it from the reserve balances member banks hold with the Federal Reserve System, with the result that U.S. commercial banks would have less money to lend.[2] *If* the authorities took no measure to restore such sums to the commercial banks, the reduced lending capacity of the commercial banking system would tend to raise U.S. interest rates and attract more foreign investment into dollar-denominated assets, thereby bolstering the foreign-exchange price of the dollar.

---

1. Other components include allocations of SDRs and accounting adjustments in the value of the assets concerned.
2. Transfers by foreign central banks of their dollar balances from commercial banks to the Federal Reserve Banks would also reduce the lending capacity of the commercial banking system, but such transfers have always been inconsequential.

In fact, of course, the Federal Reserve authorities commonly do act to offset any changes in commercial bank reserves stemming from international transactions unless such changes are in accord with Federal Reserve policy. Moreover, the volume of U.S. official reserve assets can be altered by transactions that lack even an initial impact on commercial bank reserves, such as allocations of SDRs. Therefore, "Transactions in U.S. official reserve assets" also must be interpreted with circumspection.

U.S. Balance of Payments Account

EXHIBIT 2B.1 Transactions Data, 1989–1990 *Not Seasonally Adjusted (In Billions of U.S. Dollars)*

	1989				1990		
	First Quarter	*Second Quarter*	*Third Quarter*	*Fourth Quarter*	*First Quarter*	*Second Quarter*	*Third Quarter*
A. Current Account, excl. Group F...	**−22.94**	**−27.55**	**−31.59**	**−27.96**	**−17.89**	**−20.99**	**−30.05**
Merchandise: exports f.o.b.	88.43	93.52	86.62	91.89	96.28	99.59	92.72
Merchandise: imports f.o.b.	−113.60	−120.35	−118.70	−122.68	−119.81	−120.73	−125.07
Trade balance	−25.17	−26.83	−32.08	−30.79	−23.53	−21.14	−32.35
Other goods, services, and income:							
credit..........................	57.61	60.45	62.43	62.22	61.78	62.88	68.08
Reinvested earnings	*7.14*	*8.18*	*7.65*	*−.56*	*6.65*	*6.12*	*7.38*
Other investment income	*23.58*	*24.54*	*23.28*	*33.74*	*24.76*	*25.29*	*24.39*
Other	*26.89*	*27.73*	*31.50*	*29.04*	*30.37*	*31.47*	*36.31*
Other goods, services, and income:							
debit	−51.76	−58.35	−58.43	−54.58	−52.57	−58.59	−61.71
Reinvested earnings	*2.44*	*−1.82*	*−1.20*	*.68*	*2.14*	*.83*	*1.13*
Other investment income	*−32.84*	*−32.06*	*−30.88*	*−32.74*	*−31.67*	*−32.51*	*−31.76*
Other	*−21.36*	*−24.47*	*−26.35*	*−22.52*	*−23.04*	*−26.91*	*−31.08*
Total: goods, services, and income	−19.32	−24.73	−28.08	−23.15	−14.32	−16.85	−25.98
Private unrequited transfers	−.56	−.25	−.31	−.21	−.50	−.05	−.38
Total, excl. official unrequited transfers	−19.88	−24.98	−28.39	−23.36	−14.82	−16.90	−26.36
Official unrequited transfers	−3.06	−2.57	−3.20	−4.60	−3.07	−4.09	−3.69
Grants (excluding military)	*−2.55*	*−2.05*	*−2.61*	*−3.74*	*−2.41*	*−3.50*	*−3.03*
Other	*−.51*	*−.52*	*−.59*	*−.86*	*−.66*	*−.59*	*−.66*
B. Direct Investment and Other Long-Term Capital, excl. Groups F through H	**26.67**	**13.04**	**11.74**	**36.48**	**−7.38**	**−3.74**	**−12.52**
Direct investment	14.34	6.93	1.77	17.46	−4.67	−.14	−12.59
In United States	*21.34*	*17.06*	*12.37*	*21.46*	*5.54*	*7.23*	*7.63*
Abroad	*−7.00*	*−10.13*	*−10.60*	*−4.00*	*−10.21*	*−7.37*	*−20.22*
Portfolio investment	13.96	6.58	12.50	11.75	−6.71	−8.05	−2.66

EXHIBIT 2B.1   *(Continued)*

| | 1989 | | | | 1990 | | |
	First Quarter	Second Quarter	Third Quarter	Fourth Quarter	First Quarter	Second Quarter	Third Quarter
Other long-term capital							
Resident official sector	.89	.40	.60	.59	−2.05	.58	.21
Disbursements on loans extended .	*−.63*	*−.78*	*−1.72*	*−.74*	*−1.15*	*−1.42*	*−.81*
Repayments on loans extended ...	*1.78*	*.72*	*2.67*	*.93*	*.79*	*.94*	*.88*
Other	*−.26*	*.46*	*−.35*	*.40*	*−1.69*	*1.06*	*.14*
Deposit money banks	−2.52	−.87	−3.13	6.68	6.05	3.87	2.52
Other sectors	—	—	—	—	—	—	—
Total, Groups A plus B	**3.73**	**−14.51**	**−19.85**	**8.52**	**−25.27**	**−24.73**	**−42.57**
C. Other Short-Term Capital, excl.							
Groups F through H	**3.75**	**3.05**	**10.03**	**−.51**	**17.31**	**−9.81**	**22.50**
Resident official sector	1.86	−1.04	.62	.40	1.78	3.03	.33
Deposit money banks	−3.32	−.13	11.70	−.24	1.06	−7.25	20.79
Other sectors	5.21	4.22	−2.29	−.67	14.47	−5.59	1.38
D. Net Errors and Omissions	**−11.49**	**28.98**	**2.46**	**2.63**	**18.97**	**29.79**	**4.90**
Total, Groups A through D	**−4.01**	**17.52**	**−7.36**	**10.64**	**11.01**	**−4.75**	**−15.17**
E. Counterpart Items	**−1.92**	**−1.41**	**1.93**	**2.94**	**−1.47**	**1.34**	**4.45**
Monetization/demonetization of							
gold	.04	.03	.01	−.06	.01	.05	−.02
Allocation/cancellation of SDRs	—	—	—	—	—	—	—
Valuation changes in reserves	−1.96	−1.44	1.92	3.00	−1.48	1.29	4.47
Total, Groups A through E	**−5.92**	**16.11**	**−5.43**	**13.58**	**9.53**	**−3.41**	**−10.72**
F. Exceptional Financing	**—**	**—**	**—**	**—**	**—**	**—**	**—**
Total, Groups A through F	**−5.92**	**16.11**	**−5.43**	**13.58**	**9.53**	**−3.41**	**−10.72**
G. Liabilities Constituting Foreign							
Authorities' Reserves	**8.00**	**−5.44**	**13.35**	**−7.43**	**−7.83**	**4.46**	**13.42**
Total, Groups A through G	**2.08**	**10.67**	**7.92**	**6.15**	**1.70**	**1.05**	**2.70**
H. Total Change in Reserves	**−2.08**	**−10.67**	**−7.92**	**−6.15**	**−1.70**	**−1.05**	**−2.70**
Monetary gold	−.03	−.02	−.01	.05	−.01	−.06	.03
SDRs	.19	.41	−.45	−.46	−.14	−.40	−.18
Reserve position in the Fund	.69	.16	.10	−.26	.32	.28	−.43
Foreign exchange assets	−2.94	−11.22	−7.56	−5.47	−1.87	−.87	−2.12
Other claims	—	—	—	—	—	—	—
Use of Fund credit and loans	—	—	—	—	—	—	—

APPENDIX 2C

Fundamentals of Regression Analysis

Businesses often use **regression analysis** to measure relationships between variables when establishing policies. For example, a firm may measure the historical relationship between its sales and its accounts receivable. It can then forecast the future level of accounts receivable based on a forecast of sales, using the relationship detected. Alternatively, it may measure the sensitivity of its sales to economic growth and interest rates so that it can assess how susceptible its sales are to future changes in these economic variables. In international financial management, regression analysis can be used to measure the sensitivity of a firm's performance (using sales or earnings or stock price as a proxy) to currency movements or economic growth of various countries.

As related to this chapter, regression analysis can be applied to measure the sensitivity of exports to various economic variables. This example will be used to explain the fundamentals of regression analysis. The main steps involved in regression analysis are

1. Specifying the regression model
2. Compiling data
3. Estimating the regression coefficients
4. Interpreting the regression results

SPECIFYING THE REGRESSION MODEL

Assume that your main goal is to determine the relationship between percentage changes in the U.S. exports to West Germany (called *CEXP*) and percentage changes in the value of the German mark (called *CDM*). The percentage change in the exports sent to West Germany is the **dependent variable,** since it is hypothesized to be influenced by another variable. While you are most concerned with how *CDM* affects *CEXP,* the regression model should include any other factors (or so-called **independent variables**) that could also affect *CEXP.* Assume that the percentage change in the German

GNP (called *CGNP*) is also hypothesized to influence *CEXP*. This factor should also be included in the regression model. To simplify the example, assume that *CDM* and *CGNP* are the only factors expected to influence *CEXP*. Also assume that there is a lagged impact of one quarter. In this case, the regression model can be specified as

$$CEXP_t = b_0 + b_1(CDM_{t-1}) + b_2(CGNP_{t-1}) + u_t$$

where

b_0 = a constant
b_1 = regression coefficient that measures the sensitivity of $CEXP_t$ to CDM_{t-1}
b_2 = a regression coefficient that measures the sensitivity of $CEXP_t$ to $CGNP_{t-1}$
u_t = an error term

The t subscript represents the time period. Some models, such as this one, specify a lagged impact of an independent variable on the dependent variable and therefore use a $t - 1$ subscript.

COMPILING THE DATA

Now that the model has been specified, data on the variables must be compiled. Whether a mainframe or personal computer is used, the data is normally input into a data file as follows:

Period (t)	CEXP	CDM	CGNP
1	.03	−.01	.04
2	−.01	.02	−.01
3	−.04	.03	−.02
4	.00	.02	−.01
5	.01	−.02	.02
.	...	...	...
.	...	...	...
.	...	...	...

The column specifying the period is not necessary to run the regression model but is normally included in the data set for convenience.

The difference between the number of observations (periods) and the regression coefficients (including the constant) represents the degrees of freedom. For our example, assume that the data covered 40 quarterly periods. The degrees of freedom for this example is $40 - 3 = 37$. As a rule of thumb, analysts usually try to have at least 30 degrees of freedom when using regression analysis.

Some regression models involve only a single period. For example, if you desired to determine whether there was a relationship between the firm's degree of international sales (as a percentage of total sales) and earnings per share of MNCs, last year's data on these two variables could be gathered for numerous MNCs, and regression analysis could be applied. This example is referred to as **cross-sectional analysis,** whereas our original example is referred to as a **time-series analysis.**

ESTIMATING THE REGRESSION COEFFICIENTS

Once the data has been input into a data file, a regression program can be applied to the data to estimate the **regression coefficients.** There are various packages that can be used on a mainframe computer system. Software packages with regression analysis capabilities are now also available for personal computers. For example, Version 2.01 of Lotus 1–2–3 contains a regression program that can easily be applied to a data file to run regression analysis.

The actual steps conducted to estimate regression coefficients are somewhat complex, which is why computer packages are commonly used. Computation time by the computer is usually a few seconds. For more details on how regression coefficients are estimated, see any econometrics textbook.

INTERPRETING THE REGRESSION RESULTS

Most regression programs provide estimates of the regression coefficients along with additional statistics. For our example, assume that the following information was provided by the regression program:

	Estimated Regression Coefficient	Standard Error of Regression Coefficient	t-statistic
Constant	.002		
CDM_{t-1}	.80	.32	2.50
$CGNP_{t-1}$	.36	.50	.72

Coefficient of determination (R^2) = .33

The independent variable CDM_{t-1} has an estimated regression coefficient of .80, which suggests that a 1 percent increase in CDM is associated with a .8 percent increase in the dependent variable $CEXP$ in the following period. This implies a positive relationship between CDM_{t-1} and $CEXP_t$. The independent variable $CGNP_{t-1}$ has an estimated coefficient of .36, which suggests that a 1 percent increase in $CGNP$ is associated with a .36 percent increase in $CEXP$ one period later.

Many analysts attempt to determine whether a coefficient is statistically different from zero. Regression coefficients may be different from zero simply because of a coincidental relationship between the independent variable of concern and the dependent variable. One can have more confidence that a negative or positive relationship exists by testing the coefficient for significance. A t-test is commonly used for this purpose, as follows:

Test to determine whether CDM_{t-1} affects $CEXP_t$

$$\frac{\text{Calculated}}{t\text{-statistic}} = \frac{\begin{array}{c}\text{Estimated}\\\text{regression coefficient}\\\text{for } CDM_{t-1}\end{array}}{\begin{array}{c}\text{Standard error of}\\\text{the regression coefficient}\end{array}} = \frac{.80}{.32} = 2.50$$

Test to determine whether $CGNP_{t-1}$ affects $CEXP_t$

$$\frac{\text{Calculated}}{t\text{-statistic}} = \frac{\begin{array}{c}\text{Estimated regression}\\\text{coefficient for } CGNP_{t-1}\end{array}}{\begin{array}{c}\text{Standard error of}\\\text{the regression coefficient}\end{array}} = \frac{.36}{.50} = .72$$

The calculated t-statistic is sometimes provided within the regression results. It can be compared to the critical t-statistic to determine whether the coefficient is significant. The critical t-statistic is dependent on the degrees of freedom and confidence level chosen. For our example, assume that there are 37 degrees of freedom and that a 95 confidence level is desired. The critical t-statistic would be 2.02, which can be verified by using a t-table from any statistics book. Based on the regression results, the coefficient of CDM_{t-1} is significantly different from zero, while $CGNP_{t-1}$ is not. This implies that one can be confident of a positive relationship between CDM_{t-1} and $CEXP_t$, but the positive relationship between $CGNP_{t-1}$ and $CEXP_t$ may have occurred simply by chance.

In some particular cases, one may be interested in determining whether the regression coefficient differs significantly from some value other than zero. In these cases, the t-statistic reported in the regression results would not be appropriate. See an econometrics text for more information on this subject.

The regression results indicate the **coefficient of determination** (called R^2) of a regression model, which measures the percentage of variation in the dependent variable that can be explained by the regression model. R^2 can range from 0 to 100 percent. It is unusual for regression models to generate an R^2 of close to 100 percent, since the movement in a given dependent variable is partially random and not associated with movements in independent variables. In our example, R^2 was 33 percent, suggesting that one-third of the variation in $CEXP$ can be explained by movements in CDM_{t-1} and $CGNP_{t-1}$.

Some analysts use regression analysis to forecast. For our example, the regression results could be used along with data for CDM and $CGNP$ to forecast $CEXP$. Assume CDM was 5 percent in the most recent period, while $CGNP$ was -1 percent in the most recent period. The forecast of $CEXP$ in the following period is derived from inserting this information into the regression model as follows:

$$\begin{aligned} CEXP_t &= b_0 + b_1(CDM_{t-1}) + b_2(CGNP_{t-1}) \\ &= .002 + (.80)(.05) + (.36)(-.01) \\ &= .002 + .0400 - .0036 \\ &= .0420 - .0036 \\ &= .0384 \end{aligned}$$

Thus, the *CEXP* is forecasted to be 3.84 percent in the following period. Some analysts might eliminate $CGNP_{t-1}$ from the model because its regression coefficient was not significantly different from zero. This would alter the forecasted value of *CEXP*.

When there is not a lagged relationship between independent variables and the dependent variable, the independent variables must be forecasted in order to derive a forecast of the dependent variable. In this case, an analyst might derive a poor forecast of the dependent variable even when the regression model is properly specified if the forecasts of the independent variables are inaccurate.

As with most statistical techniques, there are some limitations that should be recognized when using regression analysis. These limitations are described in most statistics and econometrics textbooks.

USING LOTUS TO CONDUCT REGRESSION ANALYSIS

Various software packages are available to run regression analysis. The LOTUS version 2.01 is recommended because of its simplicity. The following example illustrates the ease with which regression analysis can be run. Assume that a firm wants to assess the influence of changes in the value of the German mark on changes in its exports to West Germany based on the following data:

Period	Value (in Thousands of Dollars) of Exports to West Germany	Average Exchange Rate of German Mark Over That Period
1	110	$.50
2	125	.54
3	130	.57
4	142	.60
5	129	.55
6	113	.49
7	108	.46
8	103	.42
9	109	.43
10	118	.48
11	125	.49
12	130	.50
13	134	.52
14	138	.50
15	144	.53
16	149	.55
17	156	.58
18	160	.62
19	165	.66
20	170	.67
21	160	.62
22	158	.62
23	155	.61
24	167	.66

Assume the firm applies the following regression model to the data:

$$CEXP = b_0 + b_1 CDM + u$$

where

$$CEXP = \text{percentage change in the firm's export value from one period to the next}$$

$$CDM = \text{percentage change in the average exchange rate from one period to the next}$$

$$u = \text{error term}$$

The first step is to input these three columns into a file using LOTUS. Then the data can be converted into percentage changes. This can be easily performed with a COMPUTE statement in the fourth column (Column D) to derive *CEXP*, and another COMPUTE statement in the fifth column (Column E) to derive *CDM*. These two columns will have a blank first row, since the percentage change cannot be computed without the previous period's data. Many students already know how to use LOTUS to do this. If you do not, ask a friend for a few minutes of help.

Once you have derived *CEXP* and *CDM* from the raw data, you can perform regression analysis as follows. On the main menu, select DATA. This leads to a new menu, in which you should select REGRESSION. Then, select X-RANGE, and identify the range of the independent variable (from D2 to D24 in our example). Then select Y-RANGE, and identify the range of the dependent variable (from E2 to E24 in our example). Then select OUTPUT, and identify the location on the screen where the output of the regression analysis should be displayed. In our example, F1 would be an appropriate location, representing the upper left section of the output. Then, select GO, and within a few seconds, the regression analysis will be complete. For our example, the output is listed below:

Regression Output:		
Constant		0.007950
Std Err of Y Est		0.029114
R Squared		0.783607
No. of Observations		23
Degrees of Freedom		21
X Coefficient(s)	0.867793	
Std Err of Coef.	0.099512	

The estimate of the so-called slope coefficient is about .8678, which suggests that every 1 percent change in the mark's exchange rate is associated with a .8768 percent change (in the same direction) in the firm's exports to West Germany. The *t*-statistic is not shown, but can be estimated to determine whether the slope coefficient is significantly different than zero. Since the standard error of the slope coefficient is .0995, the *t*-statistic is (.8768/.0995) = 8.81. This would imply that there is a significant relationship between *CDM* and *CEXP*. The R-Squared statistic suggests that about 78 percent of the variation in *CEXP* is explained by *CDM*. The correlation between *CEXP* and *CDM* can also be measured by the correlation coefficient, which is the square root of the R-squared statistic.

If you had more than one independent variable, (multiple regression), you should place the independent variables next to each other in the file. Then, for the X-RANGE, identify this block of data. The output for the regression model will display the coefficient and standard error for each of the independent variables. For multiple regression, the R-Squared statistic is interpreted as the percentage of variation in the dependent variation explained by the model as a whole.

Mean

The mean (or average) of a column can be estimated for any variables. In our example, the mean value of *CDM* can be computed by typing the following COMPUTE statement in a blank cell:

$$@AVG(E2..E24)$$

When you type this, the mean of .014 will be displayed.

Variability

The standard deviation of a column can be estimated for any variables. In our example, the standard deviation of *CDM* can be computed by typing the following COMPUTE statement in a blank cell:

$$@STD(E2..E24)$$

When you type this, the standard deviation of .0610 will be displayed. The variance of a column can be estimated by multiplying the cell described above by itself. In our example, the variance of *CDM* (from cell D2 to cell D24) is .0037.

Absolute Value

The absolute value of numbers in the columns can be determined by using @ABS.

Using the "COPY" Command

If you need to repeat a particular type of computation for several different cells, you can use the COPY command that is on the LOTUS menu. You would identify the particular cell in which the computation is performed, and instruct LOTUS to copy that computation over to whatever range of cells you desire. This particular function may take a few minutes of practice, but it is well worth the time.

CHAPTER 3

International Financial Markets

Due to growth in international business over the last 30 years, various international financial markets have been developed. Five widely used international financial markets are the (1) foreign exchange market, (2) Eurocurrency market, (3) Eurocredit market, (4) Eurobond market, and (5) international stock markets. While each market is given attention at various places throughout this text, it is appropriate to introduce them together at the outset. These markets play a role in the majority of international transactions. Each of these markets is discussed in this chapter.

FOREIGN EXCHANGE MARKET

The **foreign exchange market** allows currencies to be exchanged in order to buy products or invest in securities denominated in a foreign currency. If currency could not be exchanged, firms and consumers would be restricted from purchasing foreign goods or investing in foreign securities. The most common type of foreign transaction is for immediate exchange at the so-called **spot rate**. The market in which these transactions occur is known as the **spot market**. From 1944 to 1971, the exchange rate between any two currencies was typically fixed, and governments of countries assisted in preventing exchange rates from changing over time. More specifically, exchange rates were allowed to fluctuate within narrow boundaries: 1 percent in either direction from the initially set rates.

By 1971 the U.S. dollar appeared to be overvalued since the foreign demand for U.S. dollars was substantially less than the supply of dollars for sale (to be exchanged for other currencies). Representatives from the major nations met to discuss how to deal with this dilemma. As a result of this conference, which became known as the **Smithsonian Agreement,** the U.S. dollar was devalued relative to the major currencies. The degree to which the dollar was devalued varied with each foreign currency. Not only was the dollar's value reset, but exchange rates were allowed to fluctuate by 2¼ percent in either direction from the newly set rates. This was the first step in letting market forces (supply and demand) determine the appropriate price of a currency. Although boundaries still existed for exchange rates, they were widened, allowing for the currency values to more freely move toward their appropriate levels.

Even after the Smithsonian Agreement, governments were still having difficulty maintaining exchange rates within the stated boundaries. By March 1973 the more widely traded currencies were allowed to fluctuate in accordance with market forces, and the official boundaries were eliminated.

The average daily foreign exchange trading by banks around the world now exceeds $1 trillion. While there are hundreds of banks in the world that can handle foreign exchange transactions, only 20 or so large banks accommodate 50 percent of the total volume of transactions. The U.S. dollar is not part of every transaction. Foreign currencies can be traded for each other. For example, a French firm may need British pounds to pay for imports from Great Britain. Such a need is quite common and is easily handled in the foreign exchange market. The term "foreign exchange market" should not be thought of as a specific building or location where traders exchange currencies. Requests by companies to exchange one currency for another are normally made by telephone.

Small corporations may request quotes of foreign currencies over the phone from local banks and conduct the trade through mail. If they are not nationally known, they are somewhat restricted from contacting banks outside the local area (since such banks are not aware these firms exist).

Unlike consumers and small firms, large corporations may often find it worthwhile to shop around nationally when they need a foreign currency. Usually, a large bank will offer the best deal to a large corporation, since the transaction amount is often substantial and the corporation may then utilize that bank for other services (loans, etc.).

Bid/Ask Spread of Banks

Commercial banks provide foreign exchange transactions for a fee. At any given point in time their **bid** (buy) quote for a foreign currency will be less than their **ask** (sell) quote. The **bid/ask spread** is intended to cover the costs—including those for employees and computer equipment—involved in accommodating requests to exchange currencies.

To understand how a bid/ask spread could affect you, assume you will have $1,000 and plan to travel from the United States to Great Britain. Assume further that the bank's bid rate for the British pound is $1.52 and its ask rate is $1.60. Before leaving on your trip, you go to this bank to exchange dollars for pounds. Your $1,000 will be converted to 625 pounds, as follows:

$$\frac{\text{Amount of U.S. dollars to be converted}}{\text{Price charged by bank per pound}} = \frac{\$1,000}{\$1.60} = 625 \text{ pounds}$$

Now suppose that because of an emergency you cannot take the trip, and you reconvert the 625 pounds back to U.S. dollars, just after purchasing the pounds. If the exchange rate has not changed, you will receive

INTERNATIONAL FINANCIAL MANAGEMENT IN PRACTICE

How Companies Rank the Importance of Foreign Exchange Characteristics

Along with foreign exchange quotations, the following characteristics of banks are important to customers in need of foreign exchange. These characteristics are listed in order of their importance based on a recent survey.

1. *Competitiveness of quote*. A savings of 1¢ per unit on the order of 1 million units of currency is worth $10,000.

2. *Special relationship with the bank*. The bank may offer cash management services or be willing to make a special effort to obtain even hard-to-find foreign currencies for the corporation.

3. *Speed of execution*. Banks may vary in the efficiency with which they handle a trade that has been ordered. A corporation needing the currency will want a bank that conducts the transaction promptly and properly handles any paperwork.

4. *Advice about current market conditions*. Some banks may provide assessments of foreign economies and relevant activities in the international financial environment that relate to corporate customers.

5. *Forecasting advice*. Some banks may provide forecasts of the future state of foreign economies, the future value of exchange rates, etc.

This lists suggests that a corporation needing a foreign currency should not automatically choose a bank that will sell that currency at the lowest price. Most corporations that often need foreign currencies develop a close relationship with at least one major bank in case they ever need favors from a bank.

SOURCE: John Presland. "Rougher Going in the Forex Market," *Euromoney* (May 1983): pp. 194–97.

$$625 \text{ pounds} \times \frac{\text{(Bank's bid rate of}}{\text{pound, \$1.52)}} = \$950$$

Due to the bid/ask spread, you have $50 (5 percent) less than what you started with. Obviously, the dollar amount of the loss would be larger if you originally converted more than $1,000 for pounds.

The nominal bid/ask spread will look much smaller for currencies worth less than the British pound. For example, the Japanese yen is worth less than a penny. If the bank's bid price for yen is $.007, its ask price may be $.0074. In this case, the nominal bid/ask spread is $.0074 − $.007, or just four-hundredths of a penny. Yet, the bid/ask spread in percentage terms is actually slightly higher for the yen in this example than the pound in the previous example. To prove this, consider a traveler who sells $1,000 for yen at the bank's ask price of $.0074. The traveler receives about ¥135,135 (computed as $1,000/$.0074). If the traveler decides to cancel the trip and converts the yen back to dollars, then, assuming no changes in the exchange rate, the bank would sell these yen back at the bank's bid price of $.007 for a total of about $946 (computed by ¥135,135 × $.007), $54 (or 5.4 percent) less than what the traveler started with. This spread exceeds that of the British pound, which was 5 percent in the previous example. A common way to compute the bid/ask spread in percentage terms follows:

$$\text{Bid/ask spread} = \frac{\text{Ask rate} - \text{Bid rate}}{\text{Ask rate}}$$

Using this formula, the bid/ask spreads are computed in Exhibit 3.1 for both the British pound and the Japanese yen.

Notice that these numbers coincide with those derived earlier. Such spreads are common for so-called "retail" transactions serving consumers. For larger so-called "wholesale" transactions between banks or for large corporations the spread will be much smaller. The spread is normally greater for those currencies that are less frequently traded.

The bid/ask spread as defined here represents the discount in the bid rate as a percentage of the ask rate. An alternative bid/ask spread uses the bid rate as the denominator instead of the ask rate and measures the percentage mark-up of the ask rate above the bid rate. The spread would be slightly higher when using this formula because the bid rate used in the denominator is always less than the ask rate.

In the following discussion and in examples throughout much of the text, the bid/ask spread will be ignored. That is, only one price will be shown for a given currency. This allows one to concentrate on understanding other relevant concepts. These examples depart slightly from reality, because the bid and ask prices are in a sense assumed to be equal. While the ask price will always exceed the bid price by a small amount in reality, the implications from examples should nevertheless hold, even though the bid/ask spreads were not accounted for. In particular examples where the bid/ask spread can contribute significantly to the concept, it will be accounted for.

Foreign Exchange Trading at Banks

A commercial bank's volume of trading in each foreign currency will coincide with the currency's use in international trade and finance. Exhibit 3.2 illustrates the distribution of foreign exchange turnover by banking institutions in the United States. The pie chart illustrates the importance of the Japanese yen and German mark, together comprising more than 54 percent of the total

EXHIBIT 3.1 Computation of the Bid/Ask Spread

Currency	Bid Rate	Ask Rate	$\dfrac{\text{Ask Rate} - \text{Bid Rate}}{\text{Ask Rate}}$ =	Bid/Ask Percentage spread
British pound	$1.52	$1.60	$\dfrac{\$1.60 - \$1.52}{\$1.60}$ =	.05 or 5%
Japanese yen	$ .0070	$ .0074	$\dfrac{\$.0074 - \$.007}{\$.0074}$ =	.054 or 5.4%

EXHIBIT 3.2   Foreign Exchange Turnover Reported by U.S. Banks

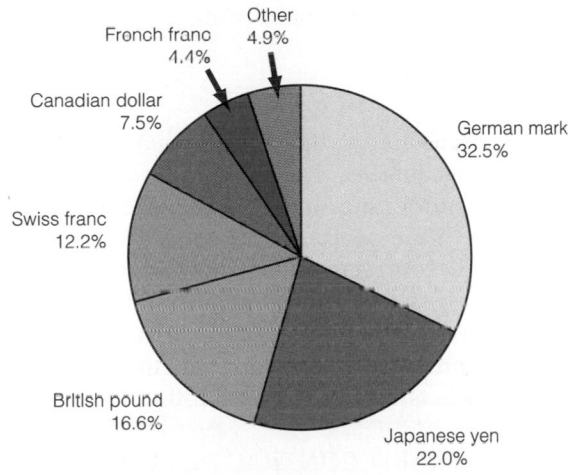

SOURCE: *FRBNY Quarterly Review* (Summer 1984): p. 45.

foreign exchange turnover. The British pound, Swiss franc, and Canadian dollar are also frequently traded. The five currencies listed here make up more than 90 percent of the foreign exchange turnover.

If a bank begins to experience a shortage in a particular foreign currency, it can then purchase that currency from other banks. This trading between banks occurs in what is often referred to as the **interbank market**. Within this market, banks can obtain bid/ask quotes, or they can contact brokers who sometimes act as a middleman, matching one bank desiring to sell a given currency with another bank desiring to buy that currency. About 10 foreign exchange brokerage firms handle much of the interbank transactions.

While foreign exchange trading is conducted only during normal business hours in a given location, these hours vary among locations due to different time zones. Thus, at any given time on a weekday there is a bank open and ready to accommodate foreign exchange requests.

With the newest electronic devices, foreign currency trades are negotiated on computer terminals, and a push of a button confirms the trade. Traders now use electronic trading boards that allow them to instantly register transactions and check their bank's positions in various currencies. Also, by 1988 several U.S. banks had developed night-trading desks. The largest ones, such as Citicorp and Chase Manhattan Corporation, established these night-trading desks to capitalize on foreign exchange movements at night and to accommodate corporate requests for currency trades. Even some medium-sized banks, such as Harris Trust and Savings Bank and First National Bank of Minneapolis, began to use night-trading to accommodate corporate clients.

Exchange Rate Risk at Banks

Because currency values fluctuate over time, a bank holding foreign currencies may gain or lose as a consequence. There are various ways a bank can reduce exposure to this risk. However, some banks do not attempt to hedge their open positions in foreign currencies if they expect the currencies to rise in value over time. Large commercial banks commonly generate foreign exchange earnings of $50 million or more during a given quarter.

Forward Contracts

Up to this point the discussion in this chapter has focused on foreign exchange trading in the spot market. There are also **forward contracts** available which allow for the purchasing or selling of currencies in future periods. When MNCs anticipate future need or future receipt of a foreign currency, they can set up forward contracts to lock in the rate at which they can purchase or sell a particular foreign currency. Virtually all MNCs use forward contracts. As of January 1991, TRW had forward contracts outstanding worth about $140 million to hedge various positions, while CPC International had forward contracts valued at over $200 million.

HOW MNCs USE FORWARD CONTRACTS. Consider a firm that will need 1,000,000 German marks in 90 days to purchase German imports. Assume that it could buy German marks for immediate delivery at the spot rate of $.50 per mark. At this spot rate, the firm would need $500,000 (computed as DM1,000,000 × $.50 per mark). However, it may not have the funds right now to exchange for marks. It could wait 90 days and then exchange dollars for marks at the spot rate existing at that time. Yet, the firm does not know what the spot rate will be at that time. If it rises to $.60 by then, the firm will need $600,000 (computed as DM1,000,000 × $.60 per mark). This represents an additional outlay of $100,000 due simply to the firm waiting 90 days to make payment. Clearly, if the firm knew that the mark value was going to rise to $.60, it would have purchased the marks 90 days earlier just to avoid the additional expense. Even if it did not have the money at the time, it would have been better off borrowing U.S. dollars and using these dollars to buy the marks.

A preferable situation would be for a firm to be able to "lock in" the rate it will pay for marks 90 days from now without having to exchange dollars for marks immediately. This is exactly what the forward contract can do. The forward contract is an agreement between the firm and the bank to exchange currencies at a specified rate (the forward rate) in a specified number of days. The most common forward periods are for 30, 60, 90, 180, and 360 days, although other periods are available. The forward rate of a given currency will typically vary with the length (number of days) of the forward period. In the preceding example, the firm could have set up a 90-day forward contract to lock in the rate at which it would exchange dollars for German marks.

Corporations also use the forward market to lock in the rate at which they can sell foreign currencies. This strategy is used to hedge against the possibility of those currencies depreciating over time. As an example, Sony Corporation invoices some of its exports in dollars. If it expects the dollar to depreciate against the Japanese yen, it sells dollars forward in order to lock in the rate at which it can exchange dollars for yen. It benefited from this strategy in late 1985 and 1986, when the dollar began to weaken.

Just as is the case with spot rates, there is a bid/ask spread on forward rates. For example, a given bank may have set up a contract with one firm where it will sell the firm marks 90 days from now at $.510 per mark. This represents the ask rate. At the same time, it may have agreed to purchase (bid) marks 90 days from now from some other firm at $.505 per mark.

PREMIUM OR DISCOUNT ON THE FORWARD RATE. If the forward rate exceeds the existing spot rate, it contains a premium. If it is less than the existing spot rate, it contains a discount. This premium or discount is normally computed on an annual basis as shown in Exhibit 3.3. For example, assume the forward exchange rates shown in Column 2 of Exhibit 3.3 were quoted for the British pound. Based on those forward rates, the forward discount has been computed for each maturity. The forward discounts can first be computed in decimal form, which is easily converted into percentage form.

Forward rates typically differ from the spot rate for any given currency. If the forward rate were the same as the spot rate, and interest rates of the two countries differed, it would be possible for some investors (under certain assumptions) to use **arbitrage** so as to earn higher returns than would be possible domestically without incurring additional risk. Consequently, the forward rate will usually contain a premium (or discount) that reflects the difference between the home interest rate and the foreign interest rate.

HOW A FORWARD CONTRACT CAN BACKFIRE. While forward contracts are useful to firms that desire to lock in the rate they will need to pay for a foreign currency in the future, the following example illustrates how they can sometimes backfire.

Consider a firm that sets up a 30-day forward contract to buy 1,000,000 marks at $.51 in 30 days. Assume that in 30 days the spot rate is $.47 per mark. If the firm just waited to purchase the marks at the spot rate, it would have paid $470,000 (computed as 1,000,000 marks × $.47 per mark). However, it has already agreed through the forward contract to buy the marks at $.51 per mark or $510,000 for the 1,000,000 marks, and it cannot back out of this contract. Thus, it will need to pay $40,000 more ($510,000 − $470,000) than what it would have paid if it had not requested a forward contract.

Obviously, the firm never would have requested a 30-day forward contract if it had known the spot rate existing 30 days later would be less than the forward rate. On the other hand, at least it knows with certainty the amount

EXHIBIT 3.3   Computation of Forward Rate Premiums or Discounts

Type of Exchange Rate for British Pounds	Value	Maturity	Forward Premium or Discount (Negative Value Implies a Discount)
Spot rate	$1.8632		
30-day forward rate	1.8621	30 days	$\dfrac{\$1.8621 - \$1.8632}{\$1.8632} \times \dfrac{360}{30} = -.71\%$
90-day forward rate	1.8586	90 days	$\dfrac{\$1.8586 - \$1.8632}{\$1.8632} \times \dfrac{360}{90} = -.99\%$
180-day forward rate	1.8526	180 days	$\dfrac{\$1.8526 - \$1.8632}{\$1.8632} \times \dfrac{360}{180} = -1.14\%$

of dollars it will need in 30 days to make payment if it has a forward contract. Some firms attempt to use forward contacts to cover most of their future payments or receipts in foreign currencies. Other firms prefer to use the spot market. Many firms use both markets; their choice of using the forward or spot market is dependent on their forecast of the foreign currency's future spot rate.

TAILOR-MADE FOR MNCs.   The forward contract between a firm and its bank can be tailored to accommodate the needs of the firm. Forward contract periods for two years or even longer are available for widely traded currencies. Some banks offer even five-year forward contracts to some large corporations.

Because forward contracts accommodate large corporations, the forward transaction will often be valued at $1 million or more. Forward contracts are not normally used by consumers or small firms. In some cases, banks may request an initial deposit by the corporation to assure that it will fulfill its obligation. In other cases, the bank may fully trust the corporation and will not require an initial deposit.

Interpreting Foreign Exchange Quotations

Exhibit 3.4 displays foreign currency values as reported on April 8, 1991. In the second column, exchange rates are defined by value in terms of U.S. dollars. Thus, the British pound is valued at $1.7693, the German mark at $.5938, and so on. These quotations disclose only the ask prices for large transactions. Consumers and small corporations would normally have to pay slightly more for any given currency than what is shown here. Of course, the bank's bid prices are slightly less than the figures disclosed here. Since currency values fluctuate continuously throughout the day, the rates reported in any periodical can reflect only one specific time of day. The rates quoted in the second column are sometimes referred to as **direct quotations.** All examples throughout the text involving exchange rates use this method for quoting rates.

The third column, like the second column, displays exchange rates. However, these rates, referred to as **indirect quotations,** are quoted as the number of units of the foreign currency that would equal one U.S. dollar. For example, a currency that was worth $.50 would have a value of 2.00 in Column 3 since it takes two of that currency to equal one U.S. dollar. From Exhibit 3.4, the numbers in Column 3 are the reciprocals of those in Column 2. Notice that the British pound value in Column 2 is (1/$1.7693) or approximately .5652, suggesting that it takes about .5652 pounds to equal one U.S. dollar. The West German mark value in Column 3 is 1.6841, suggesting that it takes 1.6841 marks to equal one U.S. dollar.

The discussion of exchange rate movements can be confusing because some comments refer to direct quotations while other comments refer to indirect quotations. For consistency, direct quotations are used throughout the text unless an example can be clarified with the use of indirect quotations. The direct quotations are easier to link with comments about any foreign currency. For example, the increased value of the German mark is more obvious when using direct quotations, such as from $.50 to $.55.

EXHIBIT 3.4 Foreign Exchange Rate Quotations

Country (currency)	U.S. $ equiv.	Currency per U.S. $
Argentina (Austral)	.0001033	9680.54
Australia (Dollar)	.7851	1.27
Austria (Schilling)	.08432	11.86
Bahrain (Dinar)	2.6528	.3770
Belgium (Franc)	.02891	34.59
Brazil (Cruzeiro)	.00408	245.10
Britain (Pound)	1.7693	.5652
30-Day Forward	1.7601	.5681
90-Day Forward	1.7432	.5736
180-Day Forward	1.7219	.5807
Canada (Dollar)	.8671	1.1533
30-Day Forward	.8646	1.1566
90-Day Forward	.8595	1.1635
180-Day Forward	.8540	1.1710
Colombia (Peso)	.001664	600.96
Denmark (Krone)	.1545	6.4725
France (Franc)	.1755	5.6980
30-Day Forward	.1750	5.7143
90-Day Forward	.1741	5.7438
180-Day Forward	.1727	5.7904
Germany (Mark)	.5938	1.6841
30-Day Forward	.5924	1.6880
90-Day Forward	.5891	1.6975
180-Day Forward	.5850	1.7094
Greece (Drachma)	.005552	180.11
Hong Kong (Dollar)	.1281	7.8064
India (Rupee)	.0514	19.4552
Ireland (Punt)	1.6020	.6242
Israel (Shekel)	.4494	2.2252
Italy (Lira)	.0007996	1250.62
Japan (Yen)	.007331	136.41
30-Day Forward	.007321	136.59
90-Day Forward	.007303	136.93
180-Day Forward	.007291	137.16
Mexico (Peso)	.0003352	2983.29
Netherlands (Guilder)	.5265	1.8993
New Zealand (Dollar)	.5938	1.6841
Norway (Krone)	.1553	6.4391
Pakistan (Rupee)	.0436	22.94
Phillippines (Peso)	.03678	27.19
Portugal (Escudo)	.0069	144.93
Saudi Arabia (Ryal)	.2675	3.7383
Singapore (Dollar)	.5620	1.7794
South Korea (Won)	.0013781	725.63
Spain (Peseta)	.009594	104.23
Sweden (Krona)	.1649	6.0643
Switzerland (Franc)	.7035	1.4215
30-Day Forward	.7026	1.4233
90-Day Forward	.7004	1.4278
180-Day Forward	.6972	1.4343
Taiwan (Dollar)	.0365	27.40
Thailand (Baht)	.0392	25.51
Turkey (Lira)	.0002671	3743.91
Venezuela (Bolivar)	.0182	54.94
SDR	1.3644	.7329
ECU	1.2346	.8090

Notice from Exhibit 3.4 that the forward rates for common maturities are disclosed just below the spot rate for six widely traded currencies. Forward rates for other maturities would have to be obtained directly from a bank. As an example, in Exhibit 3.4, a corporation could lock in the price it would pay for British pounds at $1.7601 for 30 days ahead, $1.7432 for 90 days ahead, and $1.7219 for 180 days ahead. The forward premiums and discounts for those currencies whose forward rates are quoted can be calculated in a manner similar to that illustrated in Exhibit 3.3.

EUROPEAN CURRENCY UNIT (ECU). The ECU was originally established as a unit of account to settle debt obligations between various European governments. Members of the European Economic Community have their currency tied to the ECU. The ECU's value is a weighted average of these currencies. Its value is quoted at the bottom of Exhibit 3.4.

The ECU is now used to denominate some deposits and loans in the Eurocurrency market. Securities denominated in ECUs have been issued in West Germany, Switzerland, France, Belgium, Netherlands, Luxembourg, and the United Kingdom. ECU loans have been provided to both MNCs and governments.

Cross Exchange Rates

Most exchange rate quotation tables express currencies relative to the dollar in a manner similar to Exhibit 3.4. Yet, there are some instances where one is concerned about the exchange rate between two non-dollar currencies. For example, if a British firm needs marks to buy German goods, it is concerned about the German mark value relative to the British pound. The type of rate desired here is known as a **cross exchange rate,** since it reflects the value of one foreign currency relative to another foreign currency. Cross exchange rates can be easily determined with the use of a foreign exchange listing such as that in Exhibit 3.4. The general formula follows.

$$\frac{\text{Value of Currency A relative to Currency B}} = \frac{\text{Dollar value of Currency A}}{\text{Dollar value of Currency B}}$$

Using the example of the British importer of German goods, we need to determine the value of the British pound relative to German marks. Based on the preceding formula and the data in Exhibit 3.4, this is computed as

$$\frac{\text{Value of British pound relative to German mark}} = \frac{\text{(Dollar value of British pound)}}{\text{(Dollar value of German mark)}}$$

$$= 1.7693/.5938$$

$$= \text{about } 2.98$$

Thus, each British pound can buy 2.98 marks. An alternative way of expressing the pound-mark exchange rate is number of pounds necessary to equal one mark. As shown earlier, this figure can be computed by taking the reciprocal: 1/2.98 equals about .356, which suggests that a mark is worth about .356 pounds according to the information provided.

Currency Futures and Options Markets

Some MNCs involved in international trade use the currency futures and options markets to hedge their positions. **Currency futures** contracts specify a standard volume of a particular currency to be exchanged on a specific settlement date. An MNC that desires to hedge payables would buy futures contracts to lock in the price paid for a foreign currency at a future point in time. Conversely, an MNC that desires to hedge receivables would sell futures contracts to lock in the price received in exchange for a foreign currency at a future point in time. Futures contracts are somewhat similar to forward contracts, except that they are sold on an exchange while forward contracts are offered by commercial banks. Additional details on futures contracts, including other differences from forward contracts, are provided in Chapter 5.

Currency options contracts can be classified as calls or puts. A **currency call option** provides the right to buy a specific currency at a specific price (called the **strike price** or **exercise price**) within a specific period of time. It is used to hedge future payables. A **currency put option** provides the right to sell a specific currency at a specific price within a specific period of time. It is used to hedge future receivables.

Currency call and put options can be purchased on an exchange. They offer more flexibility than the forward or futures contracts because they do not require any obligation. That is, the firm can elect not to exercise the option.

Currency options have become a popular means of hedging. Coca-Cola Company has replaced about 30 to 40 percent of its forward contracting with currency options. FMC, a U.S. manufacturer of chemicals and machinery, now emphasizes currency options in place of forward contracts to hedge its foreign sales. A recent study by the Whitney Group found that 85 percent of U.S.-based MNCs use currency options. Additional details about currency options, including other differences from futures and forward contracts, are provided in Chapter 5.

EUROCURRENCY MARKET

Within a given country, financial markets exist in order to most efficiently transfer funds from surplus units (savers) to deficit units (borrowers). These markets are overseen by various regulators that attempt to enhance their safety and efficiency. The primary reason for the existence of financial institutions that make up these financial markets is to provide information and expertise. The surplus units do not typically know who needs to borrow funds at any particular point in time. Furthermore, they often cannot adequately evaluate the credit risk of any potential borrowers, nor establish the documentation necessary when providing loans. Financial institutions specialize in collecting funds from surplus units and then repackaging and transferring the funds to deficit units. The transfer of funds can reflect either a loan by the surplus unit or an investment that would represent partial ownership.

The role of international financial intermediation emerged in the 1960s and 1970s as MNCs expanded their operations. During this period, the **Eurodollar market,** or what is now referred to as the **Eurocurrency market,** grew to accommodate the increasing international business. The Eurodollar market was created as corporations in the U.S. deposited U.S. dollars in European banks. These European banks were willing to accept dollar deposits, since they could then lend dollars to corporate customers based in Europe. Because the U.S. dollar is widely used even by non-U.S. countries as a medium for international trade, there is a consistent need for dollars in Europe. U.S. dollar deposits placed in banks located in Europe and other continents became known as **Eurodollars.** The growth of the Eurodollar market was partially due to U.S. regulations in 1968, which limited foreign lending by U.S. banks. Foreign subsidiaries of U.S.-based MNCs could obtain U.S. dollars from banks in Europe. In addition, ceilings were placed on the interest rates of dollar deposits in the U.S. This motivated the transfer of dollars to the Eurodollar market where such regulations were nonexistent. Furthermore, reserve requirements were nonexistent for Eurodollar deposits. Thus, banks could reduce the spread between what they paid on such deposits and charged on loans, and still make a reasonable profit. This added to the popularity of the Eurodollar market, since banks could offer attractive deposit rates to corporations and governments with excess cash and attractive loan rates to corporations and governments with deficient funds.

The Eurocurrency market is composed of several large banks (sometimes referred to as **Eurobanks**) that accept deposits and provide loans in various currencies. Countries within the **Organization of Petroleum Exporting Countries (OPEC)** also use the Eurocurrency market to deposit a portion of their petroleum revenues. The deposits usually have been denominated in U.S. dollars, since OPEC generally requires payment for oil in dollars. Those dollar deposits by OPEC countries are sometimes referred to as **petrodollars.** The Eurocurrency market has historically recycled the oil revenues from the oil-exporting countries to other countries. That is, oil revenues deposited in the Eurobanks are sometimes lent to those oil-importing countries that are short of cash. As these countries purchase more oil, funds are again transferred to oil-exporting countries, which in turn results in new deposits. This recycling process has been an important source of funds for some countries.

Eurocurrency market transactions normally represent large deposits and loans, often the equivalent of $1 million or more. Large financial transactions such as these can reduce operating expenses for a bank. This is another reason why Eurobanks can offer attractive rates on deposits and loans. Because the deposit and loan size is large, the Eurocurrency market is primarily used by governments and large firms.

When a currency is deposited in or loaned from a Eurobank, it is often described with a "Euro" prefix attached to it. For example, a loan in Swiss francs by a Eurobank is referred to as a "Euro-Swiss franc" loan, while a deposit of Japanese yen in a Eurobank is called a "Euroyen" deposit. One should not become confused by the "Euro" prefix. The interest rate for each Eurocurrency is somewhat representative of that currency's rate in its home country. That is, the Eurodollar loan rate may be just slightly less than a similar dollar loan in the United States, and the Euro-Swiss franc loan rate may be just slightly less than the loan rate for Swiss francs in Switzerland.

However, the rates charged for loans in different foreign currencies vary substantially among currencies, since funds denominated in each currency have their own supply and demand.

The Eurocurrency market can be broadly defined to include banks in Asia that accept deposits and make loans in foreign currencies (mostly dollars). Yet, this market is sometimes referred to separately as the **Asian dollar market.** Most activity takes place in Hong Kong and Singapore. The only significant difference between the Asian market and the Eurocurrency market is location. Like the Eurocurrency market, the Asian dollar market grew to accommodate needs of businesses that were using the U.S. dollar (and some other foreign currencies) as a medium of exchange for international trade. These businesses could not rely on banks in Europe because of the inconvenience of distance and different time zones. In addition, the government of Singapore eliminated its 40 percent withholding tax on interest paid to nonresidents in 1968. In 1973 it reduced its tax on bank profits on Asian dollar **offshore loans** from 40 percent to 10 percent. Other taxes were also reduced or eliminated, thereby encouraging growth in the Asian dollar market. In the mid 1970s, oil-exporting countries added to the growth by establishing large dollar deposits in this market.

The major sources of Asian dollar deposits are MNCs with excess cash and government agencies. The major borrowers in this market are manufacturers.

The major function of banks in the Asian dollar market is to channel funds from depositors to borrowers. Another function is interbank lending and borrowing. Banks participating in this market frequently lend to or borrow from each other. This activity typically results from their primary role as a financial intermediary. Banks that have more qualified loan applicants than they can accommodate use the interbank market to obtain additional funds. Banks in the Asian market commonly borrow or lend to banks in the Eurocurrency market. Dollar loan demand has historically been relatively high at the Hong Kong banks, partially because of their contacts with businesses in South Korea, Taiwan, and the Philippines. Hong Kong banks have often borrowed from Singapore banks through the interbank market in order to obtain sufficient funds.

The potential benefits to a country that allows an offshore banking market to be established include increased employment and higher tax revenues. However, the banks that operate in these markets tend to pull customers away from the local banking markets.

EUROCREDIT MARKET

Loans of one year or longer extended by Eurobanks are commonly called **Eurocredits** or **Eurocredit loans.** Such loans in the **Eurocredit market** have become popular since corporations and government agencies often desire to borrow for a term exceeding one year, and a common maturity for Eurocredit loans is five years.

Because Eurobanks accept short-term deposits and sometimes provide longer-term loans, their asset and liability maturities do not match. This can adversely affect their performance during periods of rising interest rates, since they may have locked in a rate on their Eurocredit loans while their rate paid on short-term deposits is rising over time. To avoid this risk, Eurobanks now commonly use floating-rate Eurocredit loans. The loan rate floats in accordance with the movement of some market interest rate, such as the **London Interbank Offer Rate (LIBOR),** which is the rate commonly charged for loans between Eurobanks. For example, a Eurocredit loan may have a loan rate that adjusts every six months and is set at "LIBOR plus 1 percent." The premium paid above LIBOR will depend on the credit risk of the borrower.

In some cases, a corporation or government agency needs to borrow more funds than any single Eurobank is willing to lend. For this reason, **syndicated Eurocredit loans** have become popular. The banks participating in the syndicate combine funds to create a large loan for the borrower. Since each bank channels only a portion of the total loan to the borrower, no single bank is totally exposed to the risk that the borrower may fail to repay the loan. The risk is spread among the banks within the syndicate.

EUROBOND MARKET

While the Eurocurrency and Eurocredit loans help accommodate short- and medium-term borrowers, international bond markets accommodate the long-term borrower. International bonds are typically classified as either foreign bonds or Eurobonds. A **foreign bond** is issued by a borrower foreign to the country where the bond is placed. For example, a U.S. corporation may issue a bond denominated in German marks, which is sold to investors in West Germany. In some cases, a firm may issue a variety of bonds in various countries. The currency denominating each type of bond is determined by the country where it is sold. Thus, a U.S. corporation may issue mark-denominated bonds that are placed in West Germany, Swiss franc-denominated bonds that are placed in Switzerland, and so on. These foreign bonds are sometimes specifically referred to as **parallel bonds**.

Eurobonds are sold in countries other than the country represented by the currency denominating them. They have been very popular during the last decade as a means of attracting long-term funds.

Eurobonds are underwritten by a multinational syndicate of investment banks and simultaneously placed in many countries, providing a wide spectrum of fund sources to tap. The underwriting process takes place within a stepwise sequence. The multinational managing syndicate sells the bonds to a large underwriting crew. In many cases, a special distribution to regional underwriters is allocated before the bonds finally reach the bond purchasers. One problem with the distribution method is that the second- and third-stage underwriters do not always follow up on their promise to sell the bonds. The managing syndicate is therefore forced to redistribute the unsold bonds or to sell them directly, which creates "digestion" problems in the market and adds to the distribution cost. To avoid such problems, bonds are often distributed in higher volume to the underwriters that fulfilled their commitment in the past at the expense of those that did not. This has helped the Eurobond market maintain its desirability as a bond placement center.

Eurobonds have several distinguishing features. They usually are issued in bearer form, and coupon payments are made yearly. Some Eurobonds carry a **convertibility clause** allowing them to be converted into a specified number of common stock shares. Eurobonds typically have few, if any, protective covenants, which is an advantage to the issuer. Also, call provisions are contained within even the short-maturity Eurobonds. Some Eurobonds, called **floating-rate notes** (FRNs), have a variable-rate provision that adjusts the coupon rate over time according to prevailing market rates.

Various currencies are commonly used to denominate Eurobonds. The U.S. dollar is used the most, denominating 70 to 75 percent of the Eurobonds, and it was even more dominant in earlier years. Non-dollar currencies became more popular during the mid 1980s, when the dollar began to weaken.

Eurobonds have a secondary market. The market makers are in many cases the same underwriters who sell the primary issues. A technological advancement called **Euro-clear** helps to inform all traders about outstanding issues for sale, thus allowing a more active secondary market. The middlemen, or intermediaries, within the secondary market are based in 10 different countries, with those in the United Kingdom dominating the action. They can act not only as brokers, but also as dealers that hold inventories of Eurobonds. Many of these intermediaries, such as Bank of America International, Salomon Brothers, Citicorp International, and Chemical Bank International, are subsidiaries of U.S. parent corporations.

Development and Background of the Eurobond Market

The emergence of the Eurobond market is partially the result of the **Interest Equalization Tax** (IET) imposed by the U.S. government in 1963 in order to discourage U.S. investors from investing in foreign securities. Thus, non-U.S. borrowers that historically sold securities to U.S. investors began to look elsewhere for funds.

During the last decade, corporations from all over the world have begun to attract long-term funds from foreign sources by issuing bonds internationally. This form of borrowing can sometimes escape regulations that would have been imposed on domestically placed bonds, and can also take advantage of lower interest rates often available in foreign countries. However, for an internationally traded bond, the commonly used currency of the issuer often differs from that of the purchaser. Therefore, one of the parties may be exposed to exchange rate risk.

Before 1984, investors that directly purchased U.S.-placed bonds were subject to a 30 percent withholding tax. The issuers of these bonds retained 30 percent of the interest payments to satisfy the withholding tax laws. A variety of tax treaties between the United States and other countries existed, causing this withholding tax to affect investors in some countries more than others. Because of the withholding tax, many U.S. bonds were issued in the Eurobond market through financing subsidiaries in the Netherlands Antilles. A tax treaty allowed interest payments from Antilles subsidiaries of U.S.-based corporations to non-U.S. investors to be exempt from the withholding tax. U.S. firms that used this method of financing were able to sell their bonds at a relatively high price because of the tax exemption. Thus, they obtained funds at a relatively low cost. Some U.S. firms did not use this financing method, since it entailed the cost of their establishing a financing subsidiary in the Netherlands Antilles, and because they knew this method of circumventing the withholding tax might be prohibited by the U.S. government at

RELATED RESEARCH

Cost of Dollar-Denominated Debt: U.S. Market versus Eurobond Market

The following discussion summarizes two related studies on the comparison of borrowing costs in the United States and Eurobond markets.

Research by Kidwell, Marr and Thompson suggested that U.S. firms issue Eurobonds because (1) they can broaden their market, (2) they do not need to disclose as much information (since SEC regulations do not apply to Eurobond sales), and (3) U.S. firms may be able to borrow at a lower interest rate in the Eurobond market (because most Eurobonds are bearer bonds and owners may be able to avoid taxes). With regard to the third reason, the authors compared the yields of dollar-denominated debt issued by public utility companies in the U.S. market versus in the Eurobond market and found no significant difference in yields. This suggests that investors in the Eurobond market value bonds in a manner similar to investors in the U.S. market.

A related study by Finnerty and Nunn examined newly issued Eurobonds and matched them with bonds issued in the

United States that had the same risk rating, industry classification, call feature, maturity, and issue date. The comparisons were classified according to four risk-rating classes: (1) Aaa, (2) Aa, (3) A, and (4) less than A. For the Aaa class, the yields of the matched pairs were not significantly different. For the other three classes, the yields of the Eurobonds were significantly less than the corresponding domestic bonds with which they were matched. The results imply that U.S. companies can reduce their financing costs by issuing dollar-denominated bonds in the Eurobond market rather than the domestic market.

Theory would suggest that in the absence of transaction costs, taxes, or other barriers between the U.S. and Eurobond markets, the yields of comparable bonds should be the same. Any yield differential should be eliminated as companies shift to issuing bonds where yields are lowest. Such actions should cause an adjustment in the supply of bonds issued in the two markets and realign market yields. The existence of a differential in yields of comparable bonds suggests that the bond markets are somewhat segmented.

SOURCE: David S. Kidwell, M. Wayne Marr, and G. Rodney Thompson, "Eurodollar bonds: Alternative Financing for U.S. Companies," *Financial Management* (Winter 1985): pp. 18–27, and J. E. Finnerty and K. P. Nunn, Jr., "The Determinants of Yield Spreads on U.S. and Eurobonds," *Management International Review* (1985/2): pp. 23–33.

some point in the future. Indeed, in July 1984, the U.S. government abolished the withholding tax and allowed U.S. corporations to issue bearer bonds directly to non-U.S. investors. The result was a large increase in the volume of bonds sold by U.S. corporations to non-U.S. investors. In addition, mutual funds containing U.S. securities are accessible to foreign investors. Furthermore, primary dealers of U.S. Treasury notes and bonds have opened offices in London, Tokyo, and other foreign cities to accommodate the foreign demand for these securities.

Eurobond market activity has become more popular each year. U.S. corporate use of this market has generally increased over time, due to the popularity of convertible issues and FRNs. A sizable portion of offerings within the market are energy-related or derived from government agency needs for funds. While ratings are available for most Eurobond issues, there has been a tendency of the purchasers to ignore ratings in favor of a well-known name. This provides an advantage for well-known U.S. firms that have not been assigned the highest rating.

In 1989 all Eurobond issues amounted to $213 billion, which represents about 21 percent of global debt issuance. About one-fourth of the debt issues in the Eurobond market are less than $100 million, while more than one-third of the issues are for more than $300 million.

INTERNATIONAL STOCK MARKETS

New issues of stock are increasingly being floated in international markets for a variety of reasons. Non-U.S. corporations that need large amounts of funds will sometimes issue the stock in the United States due to the liquidity of the new-issues market there. That is, a foreign corporation may be more likely to sell an entire issue of stock in the U.S. market, whereas in other, smaller markets, the entire issue may not necessarily sell. While the volume of new stock issued in the United States by foreign corporations is still somewhat small, it could become much larger over time.

Although the U.S. market offers an advantage for new stock issues due to size, the registration requirements can sometimes cause delays in selling the new issues. For this reason, some U.S. firms have issued new stock in foreign markets in recent years. The existence of various markets for new issues provides a choice for corporations in need of equity. This competition between various new-issues markets should increase the efficiency of new issues.

The locations of the MNC's operations can influence the decision of where to place stock, as the MNC may desire a country where it is likely to generate enough future cash flows to cover dividend payments. The stocks of some U.S.-based MNCs are widely traded on numerous stock exchanges around the world. For example, the stock of Coca-Cola Company is traded on six stock exchanges in the United States, the German exchange in Frankfurt, and four stock exchanges in Switzerland. The stock of TRW Inc. is traded on three stock exchanges in the United States, along with the London and Frankfurt exchanges. CPC International, Allied-Signal, and many other U.S.-based MNCs have their stock listed on more than five different stock exchanges overseas.

A listing of the major stock markets is provided in Exhibit 3.5. Numerous other exchanges are also available. The exhibit shows how the percentage of individual versus institutional ownership of shares varies across stock markets.

Large MNCs have begun to simultaneously float new stock issues in various countries. In some cases, they may even have a different stock-underwriting syndicate in each country. For example, Alcan Aluminum and Bell Canada Enterprise, two Canadian corporations, issued new stock in three separate markets (Canada, Europe, and the United States) using three different underwriting syndicates.

Investment banks underwrite stocks through one or more syndicates across countries. The global distribution of stock can reach a much larger market, so greater quantities of stock can be issued at a given price. Recent

EXHIBIT 3.5   Characteristics of Stock Exchanges

Stock Exchange	Number of Companies Listed	Market Capitalization (in millions of dollars)	Average Daily Volume (in millions of shares)	Trading Hours	Percent of Shares Owned by Individuals	Percent of Shares Owned by Institutions or Funds	Restrictions on Foreign Ownership
Australia	1,506	$ 164,930	102.8	10:15–12:15 2:00–3:15	10%	90%	Only on strategic industries such as uranium.
Belgium	340	50,535	N/A	10:00–3:30	N/A	N/A	
Canada (Montreal)	1,188	368,917	5.36	9:30–4:00	52	48	Some financial institutions are subject to a maximum limit of equity that can be held by nonresidents.
Canada (Toronto)	N/A	N/A	N/A	9:30–4:00	N/A	N/A	*See* Montreal exchange
Canada (Vancouver)	2,334	4,515	14	6:30–1:30	80	20	None
France	888	244,998	N/A	10:00–5:00	30	20	Investors in non-EC countries cannot hold more than 20% of equity without approval
Hong Kong	308	71,697	N/A	10:00–12:30 2:30–3:30	N/A	N/A	None
Italy	211	135,428	N/A	10:00–1:45	N/A	N/A	None
Japan (Osaka)	N/A	2,747,948	118.9	9:00–11:00 1:00–3:00	N/A	N/A	None
Japan (Tokyo)	N/A	3,191,191	1,040	9:00–11:00 1:00–3:00	23.6	72	None
South Korea	N/A	57,007	9.7	9:40–11:40 1:20–3:20	68	29.3	Nonresidents can invest in stocks only through mutual funds and convertible bonds
Mexico	309	N/A	32.9	10:30–1:30	58.33	41.67	N/A
Netherlands	572	91,720	N/A	10:00–4:30	N/A	N/A	None
New Zealand	387	15,208	6.5	9:30–11:00 2:15–3:30	N/A	N/A	Foreigners must have approval for ownership of 24% or more.
Norway	137	13,090	N/A	10:00–3:00	22.5	15	Limits are imposed on foreign ownership of stocks.
Singapore	326	N/A	N/A	10:00–12:30 2:30–4:00	25	75	Restrictions apply for stocks in some industries.
Switzerland (Basel)	483	N/A	N/A	9:10–1:30	N/A	N/A	No restrictions for bearer shares, but ownership of registered shares is normally restricted to residents.
Switzerland (Geneva)	494	100,032	N/A	9:00–1:15	N/A	N/A	*See* Basel exhange.
Switerland (Zurich)	2,914	125,403	N/A	9:30–1:15	10	N/A	*See* Basel exchange.
Taiwan	N/A	92,008	354	9:00–12:00	40.7	50.1	Foreign investors are required to apply for a remittance permit.
United Kingdom	2,656	2,659,707	N/A	9:00–5:00	20	80	None
United States (N.Y.)	1,681	2,400,000	161	9:30–4:00	N/A	N/A	None
West Germany	741	186,601	7,354	11:30–1:30	N/A	N/A	None

SOURCE: *Institutional Investor* (March 1989): pp. 197–204.

RELATED RESEARCH

Shareholder Reaction to Overseas Listings

A recent study assessed how shareholders react to overseas stock listings by U.S.-based MNCs. Five possible reasons for a favorable reaction were cited:

1. Improved relationship between the MNC and foreign government
2. Increased demand for stock as a result of attracting investors in foreign markets
3. Increased access to foreign financial markets as a result of placing stock in these markets
4. Increased ability to use stock for foreign takeovers
5. Increased investor perception as a result of being accepted on foreign stock exchanges

Potential disadvantages of overseas listings were also cited:

1. Listing costs of overseas listings
2. Cost of providing information to foreign financial market participants
3. Costs of complying with foreign disclosure requirements

The authors attempted to determine hwo shareholders reacted to MNCs with new listings. They estimated abnormal returns from 90 trading days before the actual listing to 40 trading days after the listing. They found that the abnormal returns were consistently negative, and in some cases statistically significant.

Some MNCs had a second overseas listing, and others had even a third listing. The authors separately assessed the abnormal returns for a second overseas listing and a third overseas listing. In general, the abnormal returns were significantly negative for both.

Overall, the results suggest that shareholders react unfavorably toward overseas listings. Therefore, the costs involved in overseas listing outweigh the potential benefits. The results in this study are based on a sample; shareholders of any particular MNC may possibly react favorably if the potential benefits to that MNC are more likely to be realized. In addition, if the costs of overseas listing are reduced in the future (if disclosure requirements are standardized globally), shareholder reaction to overseas listings may change.

SOURCE: John S. Howe and Kathryn Kelm, "The Stock Price Impacts of Overseas Listings," *Financial Management* (Autumn 1987): pp. 51–56.

---

research by Saudagaran found that larger MNCs with a greater proportion of international business are more likely to issue and list their stock in foreign markets. This may suggest that MNCs are unwilling to issue and list their stock in a foreign market until they have established a reputation overseas. The placement and listing of the firm's stock may even enhance a firm's reputation overseas.

As a result of recent events, the stock markets have progressed toward a global around-the-clock trading system. The event known as the "Big Bang" allowed for a computerized network (called SEAQ) in London in October 1986 that is somewhat similar to the NASDAQ system in the United States. In addition, the London stock exchange now allows large investment firms in the United States and Japan to trade there. Stocks traded on London, Japanese, and U.S. exchanges almost allow for trading around the clock. There has been a general tendency by MNCs to have their stocks traded on all foreign exchanges.

CORPORATE USE OF INTERNATIONAL FINANCIAL MARKETS

Exhibit 3.6 illustrates the foreign cash flow movements of a typical MNC. These cash flows can be classified into five corporate functions, all of which generally require use of the foreign exchange markets. The spot market, forward market, currency futures market, and currency options market are all classified as foreign exchange markets.

The first function is foreign trade with business clients. Exports generate foreign cash inflows, while imports require cash outflows. A second function is direct foreign investment, or the acquisition of foreign real assets. This function requires cash outflows but generates future inflows through remitted dividends back to the MNC parent or the sale of these foreign assets. A third function is short-term investment in foreign securities. The Eurocurrency market is commonly used for this purpose. A fourth function is short-term financing in the Eurocurrency market. A fifth function is longer-term financing in the Eurocredit, Eurobond, or international stock markets.

The foreign cash flow chart in Exhibit 3.6 can be used to assess a variety of financial policies. For example, the MNC's exposure to any currency's exchange rate movements is dependent on the future cash inflows and outflows

EXHIBIT 3.6 Foreign Cash Flow Chart of an MNC

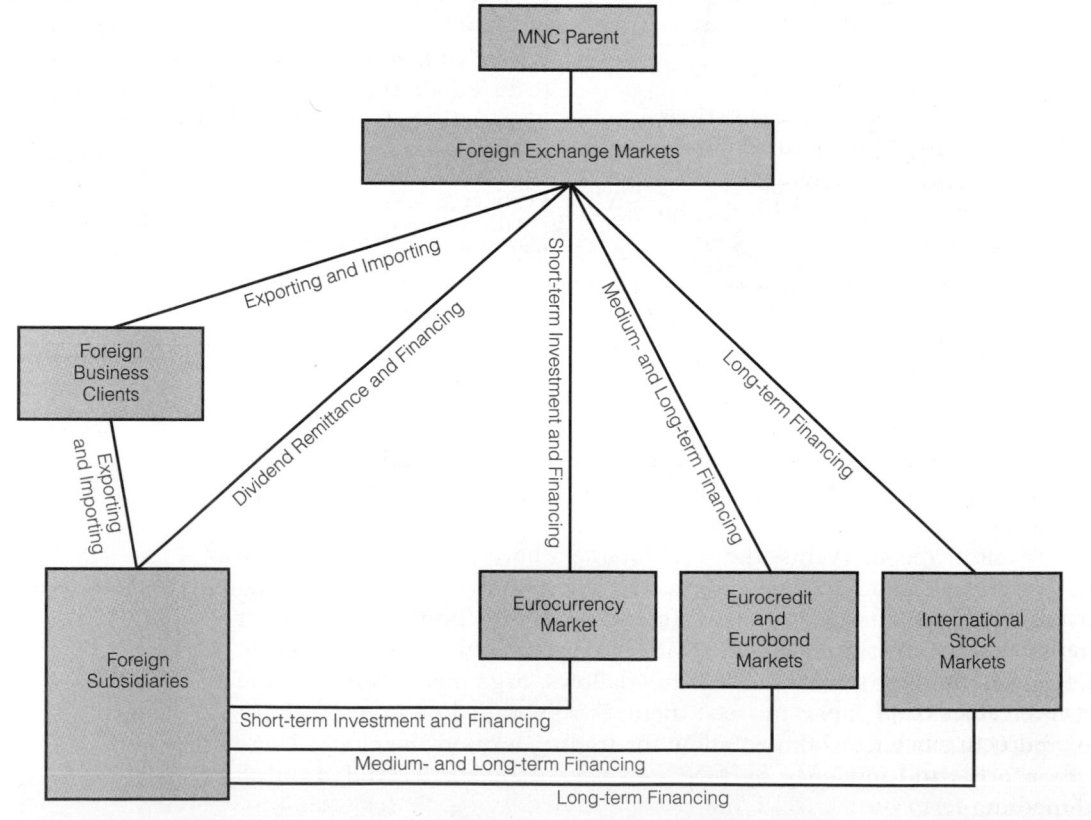

in that currency. The MNC's cost of foreign financing is dependent on the amount of foreign financing received and on the expected future loan repayments. Its return on foreign investment is dependent on the amount of foreign investment and the expected future income to be generated by that investment.

In general, the markets described so far help to link investors with borrowers across the world. This international funds network has allowed for increased efficiency in financial markets. If financial markets were not integrated, funds could not flow efficiently to those firms or governments that need financing. Consequently, potential growth would be more limited in a given country.

DEREGULATION OF INTERNATIONAL FINANCIAL MARKETS

Monetary and regulatory authorities of most major countries have moved toward internationalizing their securities markets in recent years. Consequently, investors have more flexibility to invest in foreign countries, and borrowers have more flexibility to borrow in foreign countries. Some examples of financial deregulation within the international markets follow.

Bundesbank, the West German central bank, has approved the use of floating-rate notes and zero coupon bonds. It also allows foreign-owned underwriters based in West Germany to be the lead manager of security issues. A Frankfurt interbank offer rate is continually updated to price floating-rate notes.

Authorities in the Netherlands recently approved floating-rate securities. Foreign-owned investment banks based in the Netherlands can now act as lead-manager on security underwritings. The Amsterdam interbank offer rate is updated to price floating-rate securities, and trading commissions on the Amsterdam stock exchange have been reduced.

The Japanese government has loosened restrictions on its securities industry, and in 1987 several subsidiaries of non-Japanese banks were permitted to enter. They are allowed to underwrite and trade all securities. Some U.S. commercial banks have established subsidiaries in Japan for this purpose.

The Japanese government has also taken steps to internationalize the yen. There are more opportunities for non-Japanese investors to invest in yen-denominated securities or to borrow yen for conversion into some other currency.

SUMMARY

International financial markets facilitate international business. The foreign exchange market enables firms to obtain or sell foreign currencies. In addition, the currency forward futures and options markets enable firms to hedge their receivables or payables denominated in foreign currencies.

The Eurocurrency market is used by firms that wish to either invest or borrow short-term funds. The Eurocredit market accommodates firms that need medium-term funds, while the Eurobond market facilitates long-term financing. Various currencies are available in these markets, which is especially valuable to MNCs that frequently need to finance foreign projects. The growth and efficiency of these markets has made it easier for MNCs to expand into foreign countries.

QUESTIONS/ PROBLEMS

1. List some of the important characteristics of bank foreign exchange services that MNCs should consider.

2. Assume that a bank's bid price for Canadian dollars is $.7938, while its ask price is $.81. What is the bid/ask percentage spread?

3. Compute the forward discount or premium for the French franc whose 90-day forward rate is $.102 and spot rate is $.10. State whether your answer is a discount or premium.

4. Of what use is a forward contract to an MNC?

5. How can a forward contract backfire?

6. If a dollar is worth 1.7 German marks, what is the dollar value of a mark?

7. Assume a French franc is worth $.17 and a Japanese yen is worth $.008. What is the cross rate of the French franc with respect to yen? That is, how many yen equal a franc?

8. Explain how the Eurocurrency, Eurocredit, and Eurobond markets differ from one another?

9. Briefly describe the historical developments that led to floating exchange rates as of 1973.

10. What is the function of the Eurocurrency market?

11. Briefly describe the reasons for growth in the Eurocurrency market during the last twenty years.

12. Why do interest rates vary among countries?

13. With regard to Eurocredit loans, who are the common borrowers?

14. What is LIBOR, and how is it used in Eurocredit market?

15. Why would a bank desire to participate in syndicated Eurocredit loans?

16. Discuss some reasons for the popularity of the Eurobond market.

17. Compute the forward discount or premium for the British pound whose 180-day forward rate is $1.75 and spot rate is $1.78. State whether your answer is a discount or premium.

18. The Wolfpack Corporation is a U.S. exporter that invoices its exports to the United Kingdom in British pounds. If it expects that the pound will appreciate against the dollar in the future, should it hedge its exports with a forward contract? Explain.

19. Explain why firms may consider issuing stock in foreign markets.

20. Bullet Inc., a U.S. firm, is planning to issue new stock in the United States during this month. The only decision it has left is the specific day in which the stock should be issued. Why do you think this firm monitors results of the Tokyo stock market every morning?

Gretz Tool Company

Using International Financial Markets

Gretz Tool Company is a large U.S.-based multinational corporation with subsidiaries in eight different countries. The parent of Gretz provided an initial cash infusion to establish each subsidiary. However, each subsidiary has had to finance its own growth since then. The parent and subsidiaries of Gretz typically use Citicorp (the largest bank in the U.S., with branches in numerous countries) when possible to facilitate any flow of funds necessary.

a) Explain the various ways in which Citicorp could facilitate Gretz's flow of funds, and identify the type of financial market where that flow of funds occurs. For each type of financing transaction, specify whether Citicorp would serve as the creditor or just an intermediary.

b) The vice-president of Finance for Gretz recently stated how ironic it was that he could not use Citicorp for some financial transactions in the U.S., but that Citicorp could facilitate virtually all financial transactions overseas. What do you think this means?

c) Recently, the French subsidiary called on Citicorp for a medium-term loan and was offered the following alternatives:

Loan Denominated in:	Annualized Rate
French francs	13%
U.S. dollars	11
German marks	10
Japanese yen	8

What characteristics do you think would help the French subsidiary determine which currency to borrow?

PROJECT

1. Look at a recent copy of *The Wall Street Journal,* and fill in the quotes for spot and forward rates in the following table. Also compute the forward rate premiums in this table.

	British pound	Canadian dollar	French franc	Japanese yen	Swiss franc	German mark
	Currency					
Spot rate						
30-day forward rate						
30-day forward premium or discount						
90-day forward rate						

	Currency					
	British pound	Canadian dollar	French franc	Japanese yen	Swiss franc	German mark
90-day forward premium or discount						
180-day forward rate						
180-day forward premium or discount						

REFERENCES

Bernauer, Kenneth. "The Asian Dollar Market." *Economic Review*, Federal Reserve Bank of San Francisco (Winter 1983), pp. 47-63.

Chang, Carolyn W., and Jack S.K. Chang. "Forward and Futures Prices: Evidence from the Foreign Exchange Markets." *Journal of Finance* (September 1990), pp. 1333–1336.

Chrystal, K. Alec. "A Guide to Foreign Exchange Markets." *Review* (March 1984), pp. 5-18.

Cornell, Bradford, and Marc R. Reinganum. "Forward and Futures Prices: Evidence from the Foreign Exchange Markets." *Journal of Finance* (December 1981), pp. 1035-1045.

Fallon, Padraic, Nigel Adam, and William Ollard. "The Great Deregulation Explosion." *Euromoney* (October 1984), pp. 55-61.

Giddy, Ian H. "Why It Doesn't Pay to Make a Habit of Forward Hedging." *Euromoney* (December 1976), pp. 96-100.

_____. "Exchange Risk: Whose View?" *Financial Management* (Summer 1977), pp. 23-33.

Howe, John S., and Jeff Madura. "The Impact of International Listings on Risk: Implications for Capital Market Integration." *Journal of Banking and Finance*. (December 1990), pp. 1133–1142.

Kohlhagen, Steven. "Evidence on the Cost of Forward Cover in a Floating System." *Euromoney* (September 1975), pp. 138-141.

Livingston, Miles. "The Delivery Option on Forward Contracts." *Journal of Financial and Quantitative Analysis* (March 1987), pp. 79-88.

Logue, Dennis E., and George S. Oldfield. "What's So Special About Foreign Exchange Markets?" *Journal of Portfolio Management* (Spring 1977), pp. 19-24.

Walmsley, Julian. "The New York Foreign Exchange Market." *Banker's Magazine* (January-February 1984), pp. 64-69.

CHAPTER 4

Exchange Rate Determination

irms that conduct international business must continuously monitor exchange rates because their cash flows are highly dependent on them. This chapter provides a foundation for understanding how exchange rates are determined. First, the measurement of exchange rate movements is described. Then exchange rate equilibrium is explained, along with a discussion of the factors that influence exchange rate movements. Finally, the manner by which speculators may attempt to capitalize on exchange rate movements is demonstrated.

MEASURING EXCHANGE RATE MOVEMENTS

Foreign exchange rates can change substantially. To illustrate, Exhibit 4.1 shows the value of the British pound over time. The percentage changes from year to year are displayed in the third column. A decline in a currency's value is often referred to as **depreciation.** When the British pound depreciates against the U.S. dollar, this means that the U.S. dollar is strengthening relative to the pound. This increase in a currency value is often referred to as **appreciation.**

Exhibit 4.1 shows that the pound value has experienced cycles. In the 1975–1977 period, the pound was generally depreciating against the dollar. In the 1978–1980 period, it appreciated against the dollar. In the 1981–1985 period, it again depreciated against the dollar. The pound appreciated against the dollar in the 1985–1988 period, but then declined somewhat in 1989 before resuming its climb.

When comparing the spot rates of two specific points in time, we shall refer to the spot rate as of the more recent date as S_t and the spot rate as of the earlier date as S_{t-1}. The percentage change in the value of a foreign currency is computed as

$$\text{Percent } \Delta \text{ in foreign currency value} = \frac{S_t - S_{t-1}}{S_{t-1}}$$

91

EXHIBIT 4.1 Fluctuation of the British Pound Value Over Time

First trading day of July in year:	Approximate spot rate of British pound	Approximate percentage change from year before	Approximate number of pounds one could have purchased with $10,000
1975	$2.180	—	4,587
1976	1.788	−17.9%	5,592
1977	1.720	−3.8	5,814
1978	1.853	7.7	5,397
1979	2.176	17.5	4,595
1980	2.360	8.4	4,237
1981	1.924	−18.5	5,198
1982	1.734	−9.9	5,767
1983	1.527	−11.9	6,549
1984	1.357	−11.1	7,369
1985	1.306	−3.7	7,656
1986	1.530	+17.2	6,536
1987	1.610	+5.2	6,211
1988	1.709	+6.1	5,851
1989	1.550	−9.3	6,452
1990	1.742	+12.4	5,740

A positive percentage change represents appreciation of the foreign currency, while a negative percentage change represents depreciation. For example, from July 1, 1986, to July 1, 1987, the percentage change in the spot rate was

$$\frac{\$1.61 - \$1.53}{\$1.53} = .0523, \text{ or } 5.23\%$$

The positive sign implies appreciation of the pound. Such large percentage changes in a currency as those annual percentage changes disclosed in Exhibit 4.1 would not normally exist on a daily or weekly basis. Yet, rates of change of as much as 5 percent have occurred over a 24-hour period for some currencies.

The fluctuation in values of other currencies will normally differ from those of the British pound. However, most major currencies experienced somewhat similar cycles as the pound.

The value of the dollar is often assessed on television and radio networks relative to several currencies. On some days the dollar will appreciate against some currencies while depreciating against other currencies. This is often described as "the dollar was *mixed* in trading," meaning that the dollar did not move in one direction against all currencies—the results are mixed.

EXCHANGE RATE EQUILIBRIUM

While it is easy to measure the percentage change in the value of a currency, it is more difficult to explain why the value changed, or to forecast how it may change in the future. To achieve either of these objectives, the concept of an **equilibrium exchange rate** must be understood, as well as the factors that affect the equilibrium rate.

Before considering why an exchange rate changes, realize that an exchange rate at a given point in time represents a *price* of a currency. Like any other products sold in markets, the price of a currency is determined by the demand for that currency relative to supply. Thus, for each possible price of a British pound, there would be a corresponding demand for pounds and a corresponding supply of pounds for sale. At any point in time, a currency should exhibit the price at which the demand for that currency is equal to supply—and this represents the equilibrium exchange rate. Of course, conditions can change over time, causing the supply or demand for a given currency to adjust, which would force movement in the currency's price. This topic is more thoroughly discussed in this section.

Demand for a Currency

The British pound is used here to explain exchange rate equilibrium. Exhibit 4.2 shows a hypothetical number of pounds that would be demanded under various possibilities for the exchange rate. At any one point in time there is only one exchange rate. The exhibit shows the quantity of pounds that would be demanded for various exchange rates. The reason for the downward-sloping demand schedule is that U.S. corporations would be encouraged to purchase more British goods when the pound is worth less, since it would take fewer dollars to obtain the desired amount of pounds.

Supply of a Currency for Sale

Up to this point, only the U.S. demand for pounds has been considered, but the British demand for U.S. dollars must also be considered. This can be referred to as a British *supply of pounds for sale,* since pounds are supplied in the foreign exchange market in exchange for U.S. dollars.

EXHIBIT 4.2   Demand Schedule for British Pounds

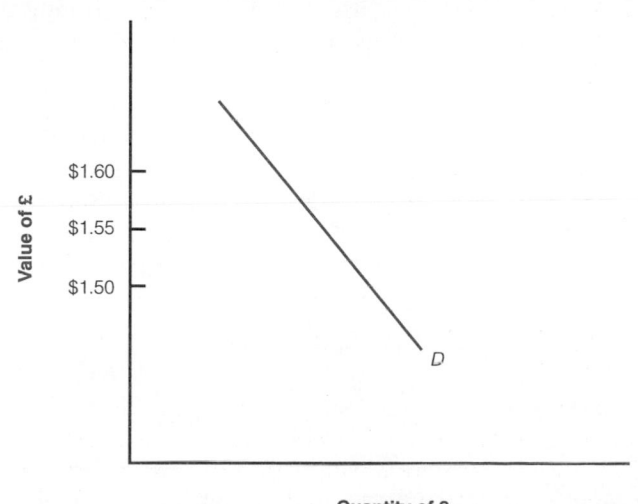

A supply schedule of pounds for sale in the foreign exchange market can be developed in a manner similar to the demand schedule for pounds. Exhibit 4.3 shows the quantity of pounds for sale (supplied to the foreign exchange market in exchange for dollars) corresponding to each possible exchange rate. Notice from the supply schedule in Exhibit 4.3 that there is a positive relationship between the British pound value and the quantity of British pounds for sale (supplied), which can be explained as follows. When the pound is valued high, British consumers and firms are more likely to purchase U.S. goods. Thus, they supply a greater number of pounds to the market, to be exchanged for dollars. Conversely, when the pound is valued low, the supply of pounds for sale is less, reflecting less British desire to obtain U.S. goods.

The demand and supply schedules for British pounds are combined in Exhibit 4.4. At an exchange rate of $1.50, the quantity of pounds demanded would exceed the supply of pounds for sale. Consequently, the banks that provide foreign exchange services would experience a shortage of pounds at that exchange rate. At an exchange rate of $1.60, the quantity of pounds demanded would be less than the supply of pounds for sale. Therefore, banks providing foreign exchange services would experience a surplus of pounds at that exchange rate. According to Exhibit 4.4, the equilibrium exchange rate is presently $1.55, since this rate equates the quantity of pounds demanded to the supply of pounds for sale.

FACTORS THAT INFLUENCE EXCHANGE RATE MOVEMENTS

The equilibrium exchange rate will change over time as supply and demand schedules change. The factors that cause currency supply and demand sched-

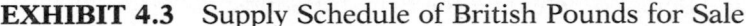

EXHIBIT 4.3 Supply Schedule of British Pounds for Sale

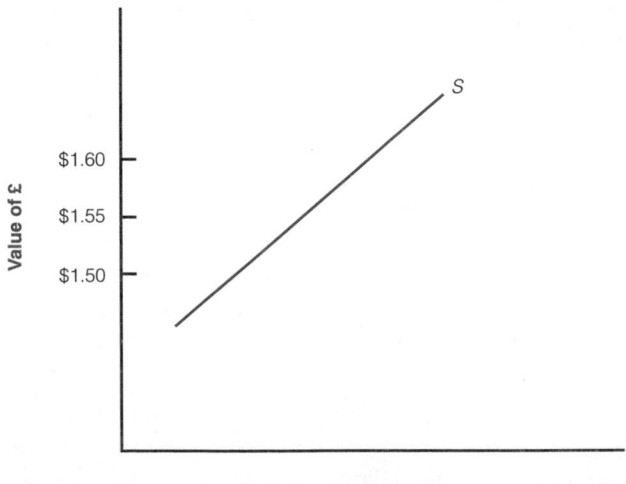

EXHIBIT 4.4   Equilibrium Exchange Rate Determination

ules to change are discussed here by relating each factor's influence to the demand and supply schedules graphically displayed in Exhibit 4.4.

Relative Inflation Rates

What would happen to the demand and supply schedules displayed in Exhibit 4.4 if U.S. inflation suddenly increased substantially while British inflation remained the same? (Assume that both British and U.S. firms sell goods that can serve as substitutes for each other.) The sudden jump in U.S. inflation should cause an increase in the U.S. demand for British goods, and therefore also cause an increase in the U.S. demand for British pounds. In addition, the jump in U.S. inflation should reduce the British desire for U.S. goods and therefore reduce the supply of pounds for sale. These market reactions are illustrated in Exhibit 4.5. At the previous equilibrium exchange rate of $1.55, there would be a shortage of pounds in the foreign exchange market. The increased U.S. demand for pounds and the reduced supply of pounds for sale places upward pressure on the value of the pound. According to Exhibit 4.5, the new equilibrium value is $1.57.

In reality, the actual demand and supply schedules, and therefore the true equilibrium exchange rate, will reflect several factors simultaneously. The point of the preceding example is to logically work through the mechanics of how higher inflation in a country can affect an exchange rate. Each factor is assessed one at a time to determine its separate influence on exchange rates, holding all other factors constant. Then, all factors can be tied together to fully explain why an exchange rate moved the way it did.

As another example, assume there is a sudden and substantial increase in British inflation while U.S. inflation is low. Based on this information, answer the following questions: (1) How is the demand schedule for pounds affected? (2) How is the supply schedule of pounds for sale affected? (3) Will

EXHIBIT 4.5 Impact of Rising U.S. Inflation on the Equilibrium Value of the British Pound

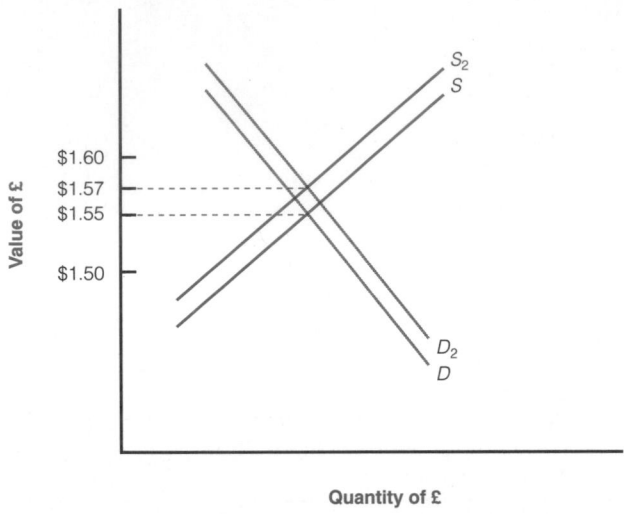

the new equilibrium value of the pound increase, decrease, or remain unchanged? The answers based on the information given are (1) the demand schedule for pounds should shift inward, (2) the supply schedule of pounds for sale should shift outward, and (3) the new equilibrium value of the pound will decrease. Of course, the actual amount by which the pound value will decrease depends on the magnitude of the shifts. There is not enough information to determine the exact magnitude of shifts.

In many cases, the relationship between a particular factor and a currency's value will vary among countries because of other conditions existing at that time. As an example, even though the United Kingdom experienced high inflation during the late 1970s, the British pound appreciated against most currencies during this period as a result of the high foreign demand for pounds to purchase oil discovered in the North Sea.

Relative Interest Rates

A second factor that influences exchange rate movements is relative interest rates. Assume that U.S. interest rates rise while British interest rates remain constant. In this case, U.S. corporations will likely reduce their demand for pounds, since the U.S. rates are now more attractive relative to British rates, and there is less desire for British bank deposits. Since U.S. rates will now look more attractive to British corporations with excess cash, the supply of pounds for sale by British corporations should increase as they establish more bank deposits in the United States. Due to an inward shift in demand for pounds and an outward shift in supply of pounds for sale, the equilibrium exchange rate should decrease. This is graphically represented in Exhibit 4.6. If U.S interest rates decreased relative to British interest rates, we would expect the opposite shifts of those just stated.

EXHIBIT 4.6 Impact of Rising U.S. Interest Rates on the
Equilibrium Value of the British Pound

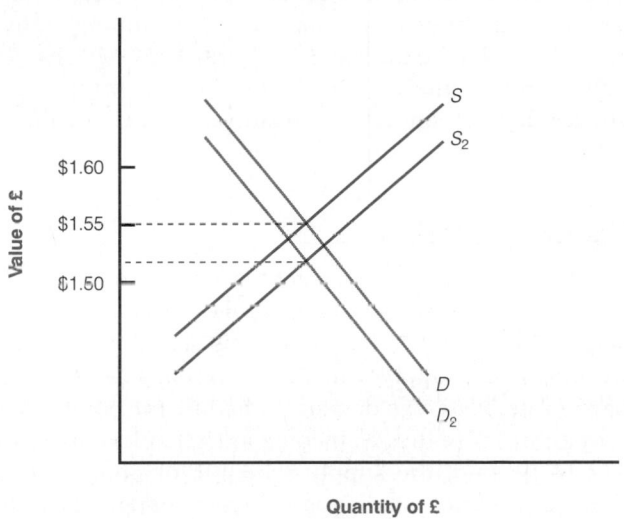

To illustrate how changes in interest rate differentials can affect exchange rates, consider the lifting of the Iron Curtain that separated East and West Germany in November 1989. The reunification of East and West Germany resulted in a strong demand for loanable funds to develop the East German economy, which led to an abrupt increase in German interest rates. Consequently, the gap between U.S. and German interest rates was eliminated, and U.S. investors invested more of their funds into German securities (and other German assets). The flow of funds to Germany caused an increase in the U.S. demand for German marks, placing upward pressure on the mark's value. The mark continued to strengthen, reaching an all-time high in 1991. The strength of the mark was attributed not only to higher German interest rates, but also to a major decline in U.S. interest rates. By 1991, German interest rates had surpassed U.S. interest rates. Many investors attempted to capitalize on the relatively high German interest rates by shifting their funds to Germany. This action placed additional upward pressure on the mark's value.

In some cases, an exchange rate between two countries' currencies can be affected by changes in a third country's interest rate. For example, in early 1987 the Canadian interest rate increased and became more attractive to some Japanese investors than the U.S. rate. This caused Japanese investors to purchase less dollar-denominated securities. That is, the supply of yen to be exchanged for dollars was less than what it would have been without the increase in Canadian interest rates, which placed upward pressure on the value of yen against the U.S. dollar.

REAL INTEREST RATES.   An alternative to the quoted, or nominal, interest rate is the **real interest rate,** which adjusts the nominal interest rate for inflation:

Real interest rate = Nominal interest rate − Inflation rate

The real interest rate is commonly compared among countries to assess exchange rate movements, because it combines nominal interest rates and inflation, both of which influence exchange rates. Other things held constant, one would expect a high correlation between the real interest rate differential and the dollar's value. Exhibit 4.7 compares the real interest rate differential and the value of the dollar (relative to five currencies). This exhibit confirms that a relatively high real interest rate differential (as measured by the U.S. rate minus the average foreign rate) is positively related to the value of the dollar.

Relative Income Levels

A third factor affecting exchange rates is relative income levels. Assume that the U.S. income level substantially rises while the British income level remains unchanged. Consider the impact of this scenario on the (1) demand schedule for pounds, (2) supply schedule of pounds for sale, and (3) equilibrium exchange rate. First, the demand schedule for pounds will shift outward, reflecting an increase in U.S. income and therefore increased demand for British goods. Second, the supply schedule of pounds for sale is not expected to change. Therefore, the equilibrium exchange rate of the pound is expected to rise, as shown in Exhibit 4.8.

Government Controls

A fourth factor affecting exchange rates is government controls. The governments of foreign countries can influence the equilibrium exchange rate in many ways, including (1) the imposition of foreign exchange barriers, (2) the imposition of foreign trade barriers, (3) intervening (buying and selling cur-

EXHIBIT 4.7   Comparison of Real Interest Rate Differentials and the Value of the Dollar

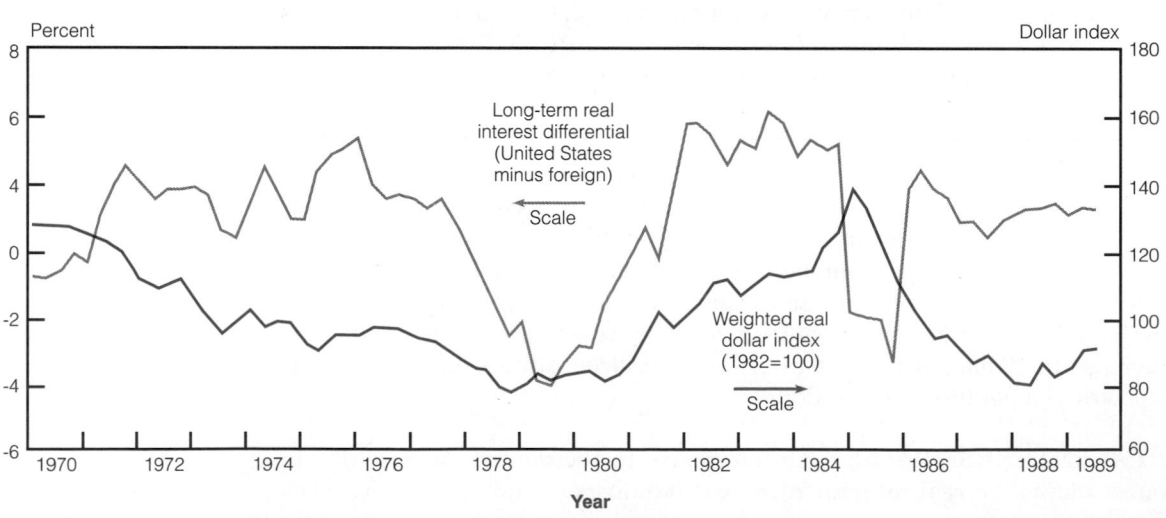

SOURCE: *FRBNY Quarterly Review,* Summer 1990, p. 11.

EXHIBIT 4.8   Impact of Rising U.S. Income Levels on the
Equilibrium Value of the British Pound

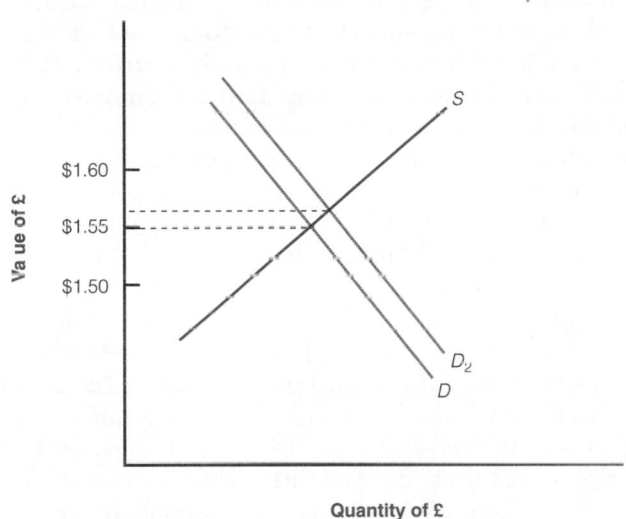

Quantity of £

rencies) in the foreign exchange markets, and (4) affecting macro variables
such as inflation, interest rates, and income levels. Chapter 6 covers these
methods in detail. At this point, one example will be given to illustrate potential governmental influence. Recall the example where U.S. interest rates
rose relative to British interest rates. The expected reaction was an increase
in British supply of pounds for sale to obtain more U.S. dollars (in order to
capitalize on high U.S. money market yields). Yet, if the British government
placed a heavy tax on interest income earned by its people from foreign
investments, this could discourage the exchange of pounds for dollars.

Expectations

A fifth factor affecting exchange rates is market expectations of future exchange rates. Like other financial markets, foreign exchange markets react to
any news that may have a future effect. For example, news of a potential
surge in U.S. inflation may cause currency traders to sell dollars, anticipating
a future decline in the dollar's value. This response places immediate downward pressure on the dollar.

The transactions within the foreign exchange markets facilitate either
trade or financial flows. The trade-related foreign exchange transactions are
generally less responsive to news. However, financial flow transactions are
very responsive to news, since the decisions to hold securities denominated
in a particular currency is often dependent on anticipated changes in currency values. To the extent that news affects anticipated currency movements, it affects the demand for currencies and the supply of currencies for
sale. Because of such speculative transactions, foreign exchange rates can be
very volatile.

Interaction of Factors

Trade-related factors and financial-related factors sometimes interact. For example, a change in the inflation differential may influence the interest rate differential. In addition, foreign investors may evaluate the trade-related factors to forecast their future impact on the dollar and then consider this forecast when deciding whether to purchase U.S. securities. Exhibit 4.9 separates payment flows between countries into trade-related and financial-related flows, and summarizes the factors that affect these flows.

Over a particular period, some factors may place upward pressure on the value of a foreign currency while other factors place downward pressure on the currency's value. For example, assume the simultaneous existence of three scenarios assumed earlier in this chapter: (1) a sudden increase in U.S. inflation, (2) a sudden increase in U.S. national income, (3) a sudden increase in U.S. interest rates. If the British economy were relatively unchanged, the first two scenarios would place upward pressure on the pound while the third would place downward pressure on it. The sensitivity of an exchange rate to these factors is dependent on the volume of international transactions between the two countries. If the two countries engage in a large volume of international trade but very little international capital flows, the first two scenarios would likely be more influential. However, if the two countries engage in a large volume of capital flows, interest rate fluctuations may be most influential.

Assume that Morgan Company, a U.S.-based MNC, desires to forecast the direction of the German mark and Japanese yen, since it commonly purchases supplies from West Germany and Japan. The following one-year projections were developed by financial analysts of Morgan:

Factor	U.S.	West Germany	Japan
Change in interest rates	−1%	−2%	−4%
Change in inflation	+2%	−3%	−6%
Change in national income	+2%	0%	−5%

Assume that the United States and West Germany conduct a large volume of international trade but engage in minimal capital flow transactions. Also assume that the United States and Japan conduct very little international trade but frequently engage in capital flow transactions. What should Mor-

---

EXHIBIT 4.9   Model for Assessing How Factors Affect a Currency's Value

International payment flows that affect the supply and demand for currencies	Factors that influence international payment flows
International trade	Inflation differential Income differential Government restrictions on trade
Financial flows (investment in foreign countries)	Interest rate differential Government restrictions on capital flows

gan expect regarding the future value of the German mark and Japanese yen?

The German mark would be influenced most by trade-related factors because of West Germany's assumed heavy trade with the United States. The expected inflationary and income changes would place upward pressure on the value of the mark. Interest rates are not expected to have much of a direct impact on the mark because of the assumed infrequent capital flow transactions between the United States and West Germany.

The Japanese yen would be most influenced by interest rates because of Japan's assumed heavy capital flow transactions with the United States. The expected interest rate changes would place downward pressure on the yen. The inflationary and income changes are not expected to have much of a direct impact on the yen because of the assumed infrequent trade between the two countries.

An understanding of exchange rate equilibrium does not guarantee accurate forecasts of future exchange rates, since that will depend in part on how the factors that affect exchange rates will change in the future. Even if analysts fully realize how factors influence exchange rates, this does not mean they can predict how those factors will change. The art of forecasting exchange rates is discussed in Chapter 9.

USING AN INDEX TO MEASURE CURRENCY MOVEMENTS

In many cases, analysts measure the dollar's general strength or weakness with an **index.** That is, several currencies are consolidated into a single composite. The weight assigned to each currency is determined by its relative importance in international trade and/or finance. For simplicity, most indexes are based on only the industrialized countries. Exhibit 4.10 shows the

EXHIBIT 4.10 Indexes Used to Measure the Dollar's Value

Currency of	IMF[a] Index	FRB[b] Index
Japan	21.3%	17.4%
Canada	20.3	9.6
West Germany	13.0	19.4
United Kingdom	5.1	11.7
France	10.1	12.1
Italy	7.5	9.3
Belgium/Luxembourg	2.4	6.4
Netherlands	3.2	7.6
Sweden	2.7	3.3
Switzerland	1.7	3.3
Australia	4.9	0.0
All Other Europe	7.9	0.0
	100.0	100.0

[a]These currency weights are from the International Monetary Fund's Multilateral Exchange Rate Model, based on 1977 data.
[b]These weights are from the Federal Reserve Board exchange rate index, based on trade flows in 1983 and 1984.

SOURCE: *Economic Review,* Federal Reserve Bank of Cleveland, (2nd Quarter 1987): p. 9.

Measuring an Exchange Rate's Sensitivity to Economic Factors

Economists frequently assess how various factors have affected exchange rate movements in the past, since the results of such a study may offer insight about the influence of each factor. Regression analysis is commonly used for measuring these relationships. Consider the task of assessing how various factors such as inflation (I), interest rates (i), national income growth (Y) and government-imposed controls by the United Kingdom ($G_{U.K.}$) and the United States ($G_{U.S.}$) affected the value of the British pound over time. The regression model could be specified as

% change in pound value = in period t
$$a_0 + a_1 (I_{U.S.} - I_{U.K.}) + a_2(i_{U.S.} - i_{U.K.,t} + a_3(Y_{U.S.} - Y_{U.K.})_t + a_4 G_{U.K.,t} + a_5 G_{U.S.,t} + \mu_t$$

where a_0 is the intercept, a_1 through a_5 are regression coefficients that measure the responsiveness of the pound's value to a particular variable, and μ_t is an error term. The data for all independent variables must first be compiled. The independent variables $G_{U.K.}$ and $G_{U.S.}$ differ from the others in that they must represent only two possible outcomes: a zero is assigned if government controls are not imposed, a value of 1 is assigned if government controls exist. These variables are sometimes referred to as **dummy variables.** Once data for all variables are compiled, the regression model can be applied to this data to estimate the regression coefficients. Assume the following results from the regression model:

$$a_1 = .83$$
$$a_2 = -.65$$
$$a_3 = .50$$
$$a_4 = 1.3$$
$$a_5 = -.9$$

The regression coefficient $a_1 = .83$, suggesting that a one-unit change in the inflation differential ($I_{U.S.} - I_{U.K.}$) is associated with a .83 percentage change in the pound's value. The positive relationship was expected here because relatively high U.S. inflation places upward pressure on the pound's value. The regression coefficient a_2 suggests a negative relationship between the interest rate differential ($i_{U.S.} - i_{U.K.}$) and the pound's value, while a_3 suggests a positive relationship between the income growth differential ($Y_{U.S.} - Y_{U.K.}$) and the pound's value.

The regression coefficient $a_4 = 1.3$, which suggests that when British-imposed government controls exist, the British pound value is 1.3 percent higher than what it would be if controls did not exist. It was anticipated that the existence of British-imposed import controls would increase the pound value since they reduce the British demand for U.S. goods. The regression coefficient a_5 suggests that when U.S.-imposed import controls exist, the British pound value is .9 percent lower than what it would be if U.S.-mposed import controls did not exist. It was anticipated that the existence of U.S.-imposed import controls would reduce the pound, since they reduce the U.S. demand for British goods.

Once the regression coefficients have been estimated, they can be tested to determine whether they are significantly different from zero. If so, a significant relationship is believed to exist between the independent variable of concern and the dependent variable.

Much of the trading in the foreign exchange markets is of a speculative nature and is not trade-oriented. Therefore, the regression model described here may not totally capture all the independent variables that could affect a currency's value. For example, expectations of higher U.S. inflation could cause the dollar to decline, even if all other data (including a presently low level of inflation) indicate a stronger dollar. The foreign exchange market, like other financial markets, is driven by expectations. Thus, the relationships between each factor and a currency's value may vary over time.

RELATED RESEARCH

Modeling Exchange Rate Movements

A recent study by Frankel offers some interesting insight into exchange rate movements. Frankel states that the high degree of volatility in exchange rate movements should not be surprising because the macroeconomic variables such as inflation and interest rates that influence exchange rate movements are also volatile. Numerous regression models have been used to determine the impact of macroeconomic variables on exchange rate movements. The models have often been disappointing in that the coefficients have the wrong sign or are not significant, and the R-squared value is low. Thus, the empirical results do not strongly support the theories of exchange rate determination. One possible explanation is that the macroeconomic variables do influence exchange rate movements according to theory, but the timing of the impact varies across currencies and over time. Therefore, it is difficult for a regression model to consistently detect the impact of macroeconomic variables on exchange rate movements. In addition, factors other than the macroeconomic variables may be influencing exchange rate movements. Some of these factors, such as implicit trade barriers, are difficult to incorporate in a model, but without them, the model is misspecified, and the true relationship between macroeconomic variables and exchange rate movements is not captured.

SOURCE: Jeffrey Frankel, "Flexible Exchange Rates: Experience Versus Theory," *Journal of Portfolio Management* *(Winter 1989): pp. 45–54.*

---

composition of the two commonly used indexes, which include similar currencies. Yet, the weights assigned to currencies vary among these indexes.

An index is convenient in that it summarizes the movements in the dollar's value. However, analysts using an index should be aware of its composition. For example, an index comprising currencies of the industrialized countries would not be useful for assessing how the dollar's changing value has affected trade with less developed countries (LDCs). During 1986 and 1987 the dollar was depreciating against currencies of the industrialized countries while it was appreciating against LDC currencies.

Historical Review of Exchange Rate Movements

While the dollar's value changes by different magnitudes relative to each foreign currency of concern, its movements with respect to the most widely used foreign currencies are typically in the same direction. From 1977 to 1980, the dollar weakened against most currencies, primarily because of a relatively high U.S. inflation rate. In 1980, U.S. interest rates hit an all-time high that was at least partially due to the high U.S. inflation and growth in the late 1970s. The high interest rates caused a slowdown in the economy. While inflation was lowered, so was total spending. The combination of high U.S. interest rates, a somewhat depressed U.S. economy, and low inflation caused the dollar to strengthen against most currencies. It continued to strengthen throughout the early 1980s and often set all-time high records in 1984 and early 1985.

Movements in the dollar's value with respect to a trade-weighted index since 1983 are illustrated in Exhibit 4.11. The reversal of the dollar in 1985 is quite pronounced. The dollar's value declined consistently from 1985 to the beginning of 1988, when it increased slightly. The decline was partially attributed to the large balance of trade deficit during that period. The dollar's value has been much more stable during the 1988–1990 period than before that period.

SPECULATING ON EXCHANGE RATE MOVEMENTS

Many commercial banks and other types of firms attempt to capitalize on their speculation of exchange rate movements. To illustrate how a bank may attempt to capitalize on the expected change in a currency's value, assume the following:

EXHIBIT 4.11   Movements in the Value of the Dollar

Index, 1980-82 = 1.00

Trade-Weighted Average
Value of the U.S. Dollar

SOURCE: *Economic Trends*, Federal Reserve Bank of Cleveland, June 1990, p. 16.

■ Chicago Bank expects the exchange rate of the German mark (DM) to appreciate from its present level of $.50 to $.52 in 30 days.

■ Chicago Bank is able to borrow $20 million on a short-term basis from other banks.

■ Present short-term interest rates (annualized) in the interbank market are as follows:

Currency	Lending Rate	Borrowing Rate
Dollars	6.72%	7.2%
German marks (DM)	6.48%	6.96%

Because brokers sometimes serve as intermediaries between banks, the lending rate differs from the borrowing rate. Given the information, Chicago Bank could

1. Borrow $20 million.
2. Convert the $20 million to DM40 million (computed as $20,000,000/$.50).
3. Lend the marks at 6.48 percent annualized, which represents a .54 percent return over the 30-day period [computed as 6.48% × (30/360)].
After 30 days, the bank would receive DM40,216,000 [computed as DM40,000,000(1 + .0054)].
4. Use the proceeds of the mark loan repayment (on Day 30) to repay the dollars borrowed. The annual interest on the dollars borrowed is 7.2 percent, or .6 percent over the 30-day period [computed as 7.2% × (30/360)]. The total dollars necessary to repay the loan is therefore $20,120,000 [computed as $20,000,000 × (1 + .006)].

Assuming that the exchange rate on Day 30 is $.52 per mark as anticipated, the number of marks necessary to repay the dollar loan is DM38,692,308 (computed as $20,120,000/$.52 per mark). Given that the bank accumulated DM40,216,000 from its mark loan, it would earn a speculative profit of DM1,523,692, which is the equivalent of $792,320 (given a spot rate of $.52 per mark on Day 30). This speculative profit was earned by the bank without using any funds from deposit accounts, since the funds were borrowed through the interbank market.

If Chicago Bank expected that the mark would depreciate, it could attempt to make a speculative profit by taking positions opposite to those described in the previous example. To illustrate, assume that the bank expects an exchange rate of $.48 for the mark on Day 30. It could borrow marks, convert them to dollars, and lend the dollars out. On Day 30, it could close out these positions. Using the rates quoted in the previous example, and assuming the bank can borrow DM40 million, the following steps could be taken:

1. Borrow DM40 million.
2. Convert the DM40 million to $20 million (computed as DM40,000,000 × $.50).

3. Lend the dollars at 6.72 percent, which represents a .56 percent return over the 30-day period. After 30 days, the bank would receive $20,112,000 [computed as $20,000,000 × (1 + .0056)].

4. Use the proceeds of the dollar loan repayment (on Day 30) to repay the marks borrowed. The annual interest on the marks borrowed is 6.96 percent, or .58% over the 30-day period [computed as 6.96 × (30/360)]. The total marks necessary to repay the loan is therefore DM40,232,000 [computed as DM40,000,000 × (1 + .0056)].

Assuming that the exchange rate on Day 30 is $.48 per mark as anticipated, the number of dollars necessary to repay the mark loan is $19,311,360 (computed as DM40,232,000 × $.48 per mark). Given that the bank accumulated $20,112,000 from its dollar loan, it would earn a speculative profit of $800,640 (computed as $20,112,000 − $19,311,360).

Many U.S. banks correctly speculated on a dollar decline during the October 19, 1987, stock market crash and consequently generated large foreign exchange profits. In that quarter, Bankers Trust New York Corporation earned $337 million in foreign exchange, while Citicorp earned $156 million, and J.P. Morgan earned $89.1 million. Most money center banks continue to take some speculative positions in foreign currencies. In fact, some banks' currency trading profits have averaged over $100 million per quarter in the early 1990s.

The appendix to this chapter illustrates how banks may attempt to speculate in the foreign exchange market. The potential return from foreign currency speculation is high for banks that have large borrowing capacity. Yet, foreign exchange rates are very volatile, and a poor forecast could result in a large loss. One of the most well-known bank failures, Franklin National Bank in 1974, was primarily attributed to massive speculative losses from foreign currency positions.

**QUESTIONS/
PROBLEMS**

1. Assume the spot rate of the British pound is $1.73. The expected spot rate one year from now is assumed to be $1.66. What percentage depreciation does this reflect?

2. Assume the U.S. inflation rate becomes high relative to German inflation. Other things being equal, how should this affect the (a) U.S. demand for German marks, (b) supply of marks for sale, and (c) equilibrium value of the mark?

3. Assume the U.S. interest rates fall relative to British interest rates. Other things being equal, how should this affect the (a) U.S. demand for British pounds, (b) supply of pounds for sale, and (c) equilibrium value of the pound?

4. Assume the U.S. income level rises at a much higher degree than the German income level. Other things being equal, how should this affect the (a) U.S. demand for German marks, (b) supply of marks for sale, and (c) equilibrium value of the mark?

5. Assume the Japanese government relaxes its controls on imports by Japanese companies. Other things being equal, how should this affect the (a) U.S. demand for Japanese yen, (b) supply of yen for sale, and (c) equilibrium value of the yen?

6. What is the expected relationship between the relative real interest rates of two countries and the exchange rate of their currencies?

7. Discuss the historical trend of the dollar's value from the middle 1970s to 1990.

8. Explain why a public forecast by a respected economist about future interest rates could affect the value of the dollar today? Why do some forecasts by well-respected economists have no impact on today's value of the dollar?

9. Assume that substantial capital flows occur between the United States, Country A, and Country B, in all directions. If interest rates in Country A declined, how could this affect the value of Currency A against the dollar? How might this decline in Country A's interest rates possibly affect the value of Currency B against the dollar?

10. Tarheel Company plans to determine how changes in U.S. and German real interest rates will affect the value of the U.S. dollar.
   a) Describe a regression model that could be used to achieve this objective. Also explain the expected sign of the regression coefficient.
   b) If Tarheel Company thought that the existence of a quota in particular historical periods may have affected exchange rates, how may this be accounted for in the regression model?

11. From 1985 through 1987 the dollar weakened against most major currencies. Why do you think the dollar weakened over this period?

12. Blue Demon Bank expects that the French franc (FF) will depreciate against the dollar from its spot rate of $.15 to $.14 in 10 days. The following interbank lending and borrowing rates exist:

	Lending rate	Borrowing rate
U.S. dollar	8.0%	8.3%
French franc	8.5%	8.7%

Assume that Blue Demon Bank has a borrowing capacity of either $10 million or FF70 million in the interbank market, depending on which currency it wants to borrow.
   a) How could Blue Demon Bank attempt to capitalize on its expectations without using deposited funds? Estimate the profits that could be generated from this strategy.
   b) Assume all the preceding information, except assume that Blue Demon Bank expects the French franc to appreciate from its present spot rate of $.15 to $.17 in 30 days. How could it attempt to capitalize on its expectations without using deposited funds? Estimate the profits that could be generated from this strategy.

13. Assume that the United States heavily invests in government and corporate securities of Country K. In addition, residents of Country K heavily invest in the United States. Approximately $10 billion worth of investment transactions occur between these two countries each year. The total dollar value of trade transactions per year is about $8 million. This information is expected to also hold in the future.

Because your firm exports goods to Country K, your job as international cash manager requires you to forecast the value of Country K's currency (the "krank") with respect to the dollar. Explain how each of the following conditions will affect the value of the krank, holding other things equal. Then aggregate all of these impacts to develop an overall forecast of the krank's movement against the dollar.

a) The U.S. inflation has suddenly increased substantially, while Country K's inflation remains low.

b) The U.S. interest rates have increased substantially, while Country K's interest rates remain low. Investors of both countries are attracted to high interest rates.

c) The U.S. income level has increased substantially, while Country K's income level has remained unchanged.

d) The United States is expected to place a small tariff on goods imported from Country K.

e) Combine all expected impacts to develop an overall forecast.

14. Every month, the U.S. trade deficit figures are announced. The foreign exchange traders often react to this announcement and even attempt to forecast the figures before they are announced.

a) Why do you think the trade deficit announcement sometimes has such an impact on foreign exchange trading?

b) In some periods, foreign exchange traders do not respond to a trade deficit announcement, even when the announced deficit is very large. Offer an explanation for such a lack of response.

15. As the barriers are removed to allow free trade and capital flows across European countries, there is much interest in creating a single European currency that would be used by all countries by 1997. The German government stated that a single European currency would only be appropriate if those European countries with relatively high inflation are able to reduce their inflation rates. Why do you think this would be a necessary condition for the implementation of a single European currency?

16. The currencies of some Latin American countries depreciate against the U.S. dollar on a daily basis. What do you think is the major factor that places such severe downward pressure on the value of these currencies? What obvious change in Latin American economic policy is needed to prevent further depreciation of Latin American currencies?

17. As the "Iron Curtain" separating East and West Germany was removed in the fall of 1989, would you have anticipated appreciation or depreciation of the German mark against the dollar? Why?

Bruin Aircraft Inc.
Factors Affecting Exchange Rates

Bruin Aircraft Inc. is a designer and manufacturer of airplane parts. Its production plant is based in California. About one-third of its sales are exports to the United Kingdom. While Bruin invoices its exports in dollars, the demand for its exports is highly sensitive to the value of the British pound. In order to maintain its parts inventory at a proper level, it must forecast the total demand for its parts, which is somewhat dependent on the forecasted value of the pound. The treasurer of Bruin was assigned the task of forecasting the value of the pound (against the dollar) for each of the next five years. He was planning to request from the firm's chief economist forecasts on all the relevant factors that could affect the pound's future exchange rate. He decided to organize his worksheet by separating demand-related factors from supply-related factors, as illustrated by the headings below:

Factors that can affect the value of the pound	Check (√) here if the factor influences the U.S. demand for pounds	Check (√) here if the factor influences the supply of pounds for sale

a) Help the treasurer by identifying the factors in the first column and then checking the second or third (or both) columns. Include any possible government-related factors and be specific (tie your description to the specific case background provided here).

1. Use *The Wall Street Journal* or some other business periodical to obtain the recent spot rate and the spot rate one year ago for major currencies. Compute the percentage change in the currency and offer reasons why the change may have occurred. Use the following table:

PROJECTS

	Currency			
	British pound	*Canadian dollar*	*Japanese yen*	*German mark*
Recent spot rate				
Spot rate one year ago				
Percentage change				
Reason for change				

2. Develop a regression model to test how interest rate and inflation rate differentials influence exchange rate movements. Apply LOTUS version 2.01 (or some other software package) to the appropriate data in the Data Bank in the back of the text to determine whether the hypothesized relationships hold.

SUGGESTED READING

David Y. Wong. "Stabilizing the Dollar: What Are the Alternatives?" *Business Review,* Federal Reserve Bank of Philadelphia (March–April 1989), pp. 13–23. This article reviews historical movements in the value of the dollar and offers explanations for these movements. It illustrates how the fundamental factors discussed in this chapter can influence exchange rates.

REFERENCES

Abdel-Malek, Talaat. "Some Aspects of Exchange Risk Policies Under Floating Rates." *Journal of International Business Studies* (Fall–Winter 1976), pp. 89–97.

Anderson, Gerald H., Nicholas V. Karamouzis, and Peter D. Skaperdas. "A New Effective Exchange Rate Index for the Dollar and Its Implication for U.S. Merchandise Trade." *Economic Review*, Federal Reserve Bank of Cleveland (2d Quarter 1987), pp. 2–22.

Bell, Geoffrey. "The New World of Floating Exchange Rates." *The Journal of Portfolio Management* (Spring 1977), pp. 25–28.

Boyle, Glenn. "International Interest Rates, Exchange Rates, and Stochastic Structure of Supply." *Journal of Finance* (June 1990), pp. 655–672.

Brittain, Bruce. "Tests of Theories of Exchange Rate Determination." *Journal of Finance* (May 1977), pp. 519–529.

Chrystal, K. Alec. "A Guide to Foreign Exchange Markets." *Review* (March 1984), pp. 5–18.

Cornell, Bradford. "Spot Rates, Forward Rates, and Exchange Market Efficiency." *Journal of Financial Economics* (August 1977), pp. 55–65.

_____ . "Determinants of the Bid-Ask Spread on Forward Exchange Contracts Under Floating Exchange Rates." *Journal of International Business Studies* (Fall 1978), pp. 33–41.

Cornell, Bradford, and Marc R. Reinganum. "Forward and Futures Prices: Evidence from the Foreign Exchange Markets." *Journal of Finance* (December 1981), pp. 1035–1045.

Crockett, Andrew. "Determinants of Exchange Rate Movements: A Review." *Finance and Development* (March 1981), pp. 33–37.

Dufey, Gunter. "Corporate Finance and Exchange Rate Variations." *Financial Management* (Summer 1972), pp. 51–57.

Giddy, Ian H. "Why It Doesn't Pay to Make a Habit of Forward Hedging." *Euromoney* (December 1976), pp. 96–100.

_____ . "Exchange Risk: Whose View?" *Financial Management* (Summer 1977), pp. 23–33.

_____ . "Research on the Foreign Exchange Market." *Columbia Journal of World Business* (Winter 1979), pp. 4–6.

Hakkio, Craig S. "Interest Rates and Exchange Rates— What is the Relationship?" *Economic Review*, Federal Reserve Bank of Kansas City, (November 1986), pp. 33–43.

Humpage, Owen F. "Requirements for Eliminating the Trade Deficit." *Economic Commentary*, Federal Reserve Bank of Cleveland, April 1, 1987.

International Letter, Federal Reserve Bank of Chicago, several issues.

Kohlhagen, Steven. "Evidence on the Cost of Forward Cover in a Floating System." *Euromoney* (September 1975), pp. 138–141.

Livingston, Miles. "The Delivery Option on Forward Contracts." *Journal of Financial and Quantitative Analysis* (March 1987), pp. 79–88.

Logue, Dennis E., and George S. Oldfield. "What's So Special About Foreign Exchange Markets?" *Journal of Portfolio Management* (Spring 1977), pp. 19–24.

Marrinan, Jane. "Exchange Rate Determination: Sorting Out Theory and Evidence." *New England Economic Review* (November–December 1989), pp. 39–51.

Officer, Lawrence, H. "The Purchasing Power Parity Theory of Exchange Rates: A Review Article." *IMF Staff Papers* (March 1976), pp. 1–60.

Presland, John. "Rougher Going in the Forex Market." *Euromoney* (May 1983), pp. 194–197.

Stokes, Houston H., and Hugh Neuburger. "Interest Arbitrage, Forward Speculation and the Determination of the Forward Exchange Rate." *Columbia Journal of World Business* (Winter 1979), pp. 86–98.

Walmsley, Julian. "The New York Foreign Exchange Market." *Banker's Magazine* (January–February 1984), pp. 64–69.

Walsh, Carl E. "Interest Rates and Exchange Rates." *FRBSF Weekly Letter*, June 5, 1987.

Woo, Wing Thye. "Some Evidence of Speculative Bubbles in the Foreign Exchange Market." *Journal of Money, Credit, and Banking* (November 1987), pp. 499–514.

Foreign Exchange Trading in the Real World

The following article by David Edwards appeared in the periodical MBA, June–July 1978. It was titled, "The Trading Room: It's Not A Gentlemen's Game." This article illustrates what foreign exchange trading is like in the real world.

Switzerland. The business week began at dinner Sunday night in the Dolder Grand Hotel, overlooking Lake Zurich. Hanas, the Treasurer from the local branch of an American bank, had been asked to dine by the chief traders from the Big Three Swiss banks. The meal, while elegant and copious, drew scant comment from the four of them. Through course after course they gossiped about finance, and politics as it affects finance, guarding their words. Little of importance was revealed until coffee when one of the three chief traders turned to Hanas and informed him that they had each decided to sell a billion dollars during the coming week. The signal had been given. Hanas left his cigar unfinished.

As Hanas rides the trolley along the Bahnhofstrasse on Monday morning, he is indistinguishable from the hordes of watchmakers who ride with him. He knows that if the Big Three are selling dollars, the currency will certainly continue to decline. He was at dinner because he works for an influential bank with branches all over the world and because he is one of the fastest traders in Europe. He will be instrumental in pushing the dollar down. He arrives at work at 7:15 and proceeds to sell $6 million against Swiss francs two time zones backward to Bahrain while the rest of the speculative community finishes breakfast.

England. At 7:30 in Kingston Hill, Jimmy Pritchard boards the London train. He looks much like his neighbors from the stock broker belt. For a minute he even feels like one of them. They wear bowler hats and pin-stripe suits and open the pages of the *Financial Times* as if on cue.

You can tell a currency trader from one of the big American banks by what he reads in the *Financial Times*. Jimmy Pritchard doesn't really read at all. He turns to check Friday's closing price for the dollar in New York (and sees that it was on shaky ground in Singapore), the Federal funds rate, the money supply—one column after another of statistics.

One news item catches his eye. The Federal Reserve in New York has raised the discount rate, pushing up all interest rates in America to make dollar investments more attractive to holders of foreign currencies. "Those bloody fools," he thinks, "do they really think it matters?"

Few of the men on the train know what the numbers mean. Currency traders comprise a tiny fraction of the thousands who work in the City. While brokers and managers spend their days persuading and cajoling, calculating, and projecting, pouring over contracts and shuffling papers, the traders play the fastest game in the world.

Money is a commodity. Traders like Hanas and Jim and their counterparts in other banks manipulate currencies in denominations of millions in transactions that take as little as ten seconds. They are street fighters, accustomed to thinking on their feet, making as many as 50 decisions a day about more money than 100 executives earn in their lifetimes. They have risen through the ranks of international banking to their niches in this esoteric specialty, acquiring hard nerves and a few refined tastes along the way.

When Jimmy arrives in his office adjacent to the trading room, the light for Zurich on his console is already flashing. He picks up the phone.

"Broschnagel took me in last night," Hanas tell him. "The other two have agreed to follow his lead this morning. I called New York this morning and woke Freeman up. It was one o'clock there. Free has agreed. We all follow their lead. I will sell $70 million this morning. Free thought 50 was more appropriate for you."

Jimmy says, "Hanas, I don't know. . . ."

"Look, Jimmy, I'm doing you a favor. When the Big Three move, the market moves. We follow. I'll call Frankfurt. Free wants Fritz to go 50 short also."

"All right, Hanas. Talk to you soon."

"My boys will let you know when we go."

Jimmy looks through the one-way glass at his 25 traders, already as nervous as race horses awaiting the start of the day. They sit at their consoles like NASA engineers monitoring a space shot. They each have perhaps forty direct lines to Europe with automatic dialing machines. Press a button to get a quotation on dollar-mark. Press another to price Norwegian krona against South African Rand.

The light on his intercom flashes.

"Hey, Jim, you've got another American trainee today." Bloody hell. "But this one's a lady. Been telling me how tough it was growing up in Texas and getting her M.B.A. over in France."

Jimmy enters the trading room. Except for the vault, this is the most restricted space in the bank. All around him people are writing, talking, scanning their video screens. Telexes pound out their messages silently under plexiglass cases. Newswires from the United States, Asia, and Europe bring events of the outside world into this soundproof, electronic, command bunker. Television screens give each of the bank's branches' latest price for currency in the currency of the host country. No one deals in those prices, unless trading is slow.

The trainee sits at Jimmy's desk holding a small Fendi purse under her left arm, left hand clutching a stenographer's notebook and a pen. Her right hand is poised to shake with her tutor for the week. . . .

"Hello, miss. I'm Jimmy Pritchard."

She rises, "E. L. Waters."

"What's your real name?" He watches her eyes widen with surprise briefly as she hears him speak. It has happened many times. These American trainees all think that English bankers should speak like Cambridge graduates. Instead they hear the rough strains of East London. It will be a long time before anyone from Oxford or Cambridge replaces this Cockney.

"Emmy Lou," she answers.

"Well, Emmy Lou, how long are you going to be with us?"

"My boss in credit analysis wants me to spend a week here."

Three men have gathered at Jimmy's desk. "Emmy Lou Waters, I'd like you to meet Henry Davids, our chief spot trader, the man who handles our speculative position, buying and selling with other banks. Mark Ricks runs the Eurocurrency deposit and loan operation, lending and borrowing in the interbank market and funding our speculative positions. And Duncan Willis who works with our commercial clients when they need to buy or sell one currency against another." They all shake hands with the newcomer.

Jimmy begins to spit out orders to his lieutenants. "We're going to hit the dollar again today. Henry, you take the lead."

"Right."

"But don't run it all into marks. Spread the book out. Free has given us an additional 50 million limit. Dump 20 million against the mark, 10 against Swiss francs, and 20 against sterling for starters. With the way the dollar is going down today, even the pound will have color in her cheeks by tonight."

Mark says, "There will always be an England."

"Save your energy, because you've got to borrow everything Henry's going to sell today. Borrow through Friday and don't pay more than seven and an eighth."

"My Eurodollar book's 2 billion short right now," Mark says. "Don't forget, last month we lent another billion to other banks for six months at eight. I'm covering the deposits on a day to day basis by having New York take the money in the New York Fed funds market at 7¼ percent. With the way the Fed is raising interest rates, we might lose our shirts on that billion. And everyone's near their limits. We may not be able to cover our positions through the other banks."

"I won't forget." Jimmy glances at the young American who is writing furiously in her notebook. He smiles. By the time she leaves this room she will have learned a whole new language.

He addresses the commercial chief. "Duncan, don't open your mouth before ten. Let Henry kick the hell out of the dollar. Then get your boys to go through the list of multi-nationals. Tell them the dollar might be a little soft. They'll watch the prices start to fall and by noon they'll run into your arms."

Mark says to Emmy Lou, "We do all the work and he has all the fun with our customers."

Jimmy says, "Duncan, we're counting on you to buy back this position for us from your commercials."

The three lieutenants return to their posts.

The trainee says, "I'd like you to define a few terms if you don't mind."

Jimmy wonders where she learned to talk, but before she can raise her notebook to read, one of the telex girls shouts, "I've got a Scandinavian bank on the line. They want to know the opening cable."

Jimmy calls, "How many times do I have to tell you, not until nine." His voice has the indulgent tone of a father, rather than annoyance. He's been at his job too long to lose his temper over anything so small.

Activity in the room is beginning to heat up. Everywhere, telephone consoles are blinking. People are shouting to one another and scribbling on slips of paper. Jimmy excuses himself for a minute and confers with Henry. Emmy Lou begins to write again, picking jargon out of the air at random.

"Marks spot next $2\frac{7}{8}$-$3\frac{1}{6}$ . . . tom. next $2^{15}\!/_{16}$ . . . spot a week 3-$3\frac{1}{4}$ sorry for wide . . . week fixed dollar $6^{15}\!/_{16}$-$7^{1}\!/_{16}$." Only about half the people in the room are speaking English. The rest are using French and German.

Jimmy returns, "I suggest that you don't try to get all the details at once. Just get a feel for the whole. Otherwise your notes will read like cursing in a comic strip."

"May I ask you a few basic questions?"

"Certainly."

She turns back in her notebook to a page where she had carefully written questions the night before.

"Where is the foreign exchange market?"

He smiles at her, again paternally. He has been asked a thousand times.

"The foreign exchange market is not like a stock exchange. The thousands of telephone lines and telexes in this room are connected to others in rooms very much like this in a few banks around the world. We do business with one another. You've probably read about nasty currency speculators in the newspapers. That's us."

"I heard you say before that Mark has to borrow the dollars you are going to sell. How can you sell borrowed money?"

"It's really very simple. Mark borrows say $50 million in the Eurodollar market for four nights. We sell them today against other currencies and then place the pounds, marks, and francs on deposit. On Friday we buy $50 million at a lower price than we sold them for and use the fifty to pay off the interbank deposit. We get to keep the leftover pounds, francs, and marks."

"You mean you make money pushing the dollar down?"

"Exactly. And don't say 'you' when you mean 'we'. You work for this bank too, Emmy Lou."

At 8:59, Henry's men are punching the buttons on their consoles to get quotations from brokers all over Europe. At the stroke of nine, the telexes begin to click furiously, but under their plexiglass casings, the clicking is reduced to a hum. The start of trading is an explosion, and the blast is felt in the sudden surge of energy everywhere in the room. People begin to shout back and forth. Lights on the consoles flash all around.

A Dane on loan to Henry from the Copenhagen branch shouts, "Opening dollar-mark here, 75-85."

Henry yells, "Give 'em five million at 75."

Immediately another trader says, "Dollar-mark now 65-75."

Henry asks, "How many dollars is he paying for at 65?"

"He pays for five."

"$5 million his. Be sure and get the name this time."

Jimmy sits with his pupil. His console is blazing with lights and he leisurely listens in on conversations in different parts of the room. Life at his console is serene compared to the beehive in front of him. He watches with amusement as her uncomprehending eyes stare at the scene below.

"What happened?" she asks.

He explains patiently, "This is a two way market, Emmy Lou. That's why we give two prices—bid and offered. We began selling dollars for marks, receiving 2.1575 marks for each dollar. Henry sold $5 million at that rate in the first transaction of the day. At that moment he could have bought dollars at 2.1585. We always use the last two digits in the price. The prices change very rapidly as you can see, for the next $5 million brought only 2.1565 marks when we sold them."

"Why did Henry say 'be sure and get the name this time'?"

"He was speaking to one of the junior traders. Sometimes they ring off without knowing whom they're dealing with."

"You mean he can sell five million dollars to someone and not know who it is?"

"It's an honest mistake. Embarrassing though to call up a few banks and ask if you've just sold them $5,000,000."

On the flow the frenzy continues and the dollar declines.

A woman shouts from a telex, "Merck, Finck in Munich wants your dollar-mark price."

Henry replies, "It's down further. Tell him 50-65. Sorry for wide."

"He gives you $5 million at 50."

Henry curses under his breath. The low price was intended to discourage anyone from selling dollars to him. "Get every German bank on the line you can."

The Dane says, "Got Deutsche-Duss here."

The junior trader says, "Commerce Hamburg."

"What's it with Dusseldorf?"

"45-55."

"Same in Hamburg."

"Give 'em $10 million apiece."

The Dane yells, "Ten dollars at 45. Done." Into the mouthpiece of the phone he says, "Dusseldorf, where do you want your dollars? Morgan in New York? Done. Pay the marks to our Frankfurt office."

Jimmy explains to Emmy Lou that this is a quiet market that is moving quickly because they have hit it hard. Only $50 million will move the price. He reminds her that his colleagues in Zurich and Frankfurt are selling dollars. He points to the television monitor that he has been watching out of the corner of his eye.

"Look how much the Dollar-Swiss price has fallen. Hanas, our man there, and the Big Three Swiss are pounding the dollar."

She asks, "I heard you tell the others that you wanted them to sell $50 million. It sounds like you must have passed that already. Why don't you just go home now?"

"We have to buy and sell. In order to maintain that $50 million short position, we might have to turn over $700 million today."

"Why do you have to buy dollars if you don't want them?"

"If you get called you have to quote. That's the unwritten rule of this market. There are certain things we can do to discourage others from trying to sell to us like bidding at lower prices, but this is a rapidly moving market and when others see how prices are dropping, they try to dump dollars on us just as we dump on them."

"What happens if you don't buy?"

"Then we don't sell either. No one calls us. No one answers our calls. All this activity comes to a grinding halt."

"The electronic silent treatment."

"Right."

At ten o'clock, Duncan Willis begins his calling. He starts with the assistant treasurer of the largest British chemical company.

"Clive, this is Duncan Willis at the bank. We've seen the dollar soften this morning. I wanted to keep you up to date because your account officers have told us about the size of your dollar exposure. Personally, I think you ought to get out of it, but not right away. We think it might recover a bit."

Across the room, Henry and his traders have just sold another $30 million.

Duncan says, "I'll call you back as soon as we establish the trend for the dollar."

By eleven o'clock, Duncan and his men will have conveyed the same message to every multinational corporation in London.

From the opposite end of the trading room, a short thin man approaches Jimmy's desk. His name is Reggie Carton. Jimmy winces. Carton's two qualifications for his job at the bank are that he speaks proper schoolboy English and that he has had the tenacity to survive fifteen years of trying to become a foreign exchange trader. Now he heads the bank's domestic sterling desk, which funds sterling loans in England and in the former colonies known as sterling protectorates. Like other American banks in London, this one has a tiny sterling deposit base, and no capital at all in England, so in order to make loans in pounds, it is necessary to borrow them from British banks in denominations of one million pounds and up, much as Mark Ricks acquires Eurocurrencies in the interbank market.

Carton looks indignant. "I've got Mr. 80-80 from Athens on the phone," he says. "He wants to borrow another 5 million pounds of domestic sterling for three months in the name of our Bahrain branch. He claims it's to finance sterling trade bills they are holding in Jordan."

"Jimmy, I'm sick and tired of this. You know he doesn't have any commercial business in Jordan. He's turning a loophole in the exchange control laws into a way of life. We're not supposed to let pounds out of England. They are just borrowing sterling from us so they can place it in the Euromarket at higher rates with one of our other branches."

"For Crissakes," Jimmy answers, "Stop being such a moralist. Give it to him. It's no skin off your nose. If he borrows sterling from us at ten percent and places it with Paris at thirteen, it's his business.

"If he gets caught, his knickers are in a twist, not yours. Anyway, when was the last time the Old Lady audited our Jordanian office to find out if we really had the trade bills we claimed?"

Emmy Lou asks, "Who is Mr. 80-80 and who is the old lady?"

Jimmy says, "80-80 is Collins, the treasurer of our Middle East operations. Last year the bank made $80,000,000 in North Africa and the Middle East. The money market operation accounted for 80 percent of that. Every time Collins goes to New York, he can't keep his mouth shut about how much money he's made. The old lady, that's the Bank of England."

Carton becomes more upset. "Jimmy, this is an English branch of an American bank, accountable to British exchange control laws.

"*Oui, monsieur,* now get out of here and don't rip Collins off on the price."

Suddenly, the din among the traders turns into a roar. Henry yells, "Jimmy, we're in trouble and it's getting worse."

Jimmy leaves his seat and hurries to Henry's side.

"It's stopped falling," the spot trader tells him. "It's up 75 points. I don't understand it. I was getting dollars in all morning, and I had trouble getting rid of them faster than they came in. Eight minutes ago, the Scandinavians started buying at 50. It started moving up. Now it's 25 on the next big number. I have Societe Generale in Paris and Commerce Hamburg on the line, both wanting prices for large."

Jimmy looks at the television screen.

"The first thing you'd better do is get a price. Check the London brokers. I'll take care of it. Hand me the phone."

Henry says, "They're paying 25."

Jimmy takes the receiver. "Let me have Soc-Gen first." "Large" for Commerce Hamburg could mean $50 million and up which would move the market, either way, faster than he wanted it to move. By comparison, the Paris bank is small and safe. Commerce Hamburg is a gunslinger. *"Bon-jour, Vingt-cinque—trente-cinque."* He listens for a moment, then releases the button on the phone so that the party on the other end cannot hear what he says. "The son of a bitch wants $10 million at 35. I'll let him have only five. Stall Commerce Hamburg. Tell him anything, but don't give him a price. They're panicking in Paris. *Non, monsieur, cinque million. Trente-cinque."*

One of the traders says, "Now they're paying fifty here in London."

Jimmy sprints the twenty-five yards back to his console. As he runs, he calls out his orders.

"Get me Hanas in Zurich and Fritz in Frankfurt on the same line." When he reaches his desk, the light for Zurich and Frankfurt are already flashing, but before he picks up the phone he says, "Get me our branches in Paris, Amsterdam, Brussels, and Milan in that order."

He picks up the phone. The others are already speaking to one another. Jimmy breaks in, "Cut it short. We're in trouble."

They both say, "I know."

Jimmy says, "Are either of your central banks intervening in the market?"

Fritz answers, "No, it's that maniac in Hamburg. He's taking his profit by turning that $300 million short position he took last week. One of these days I'm going. . . ."

"Cut it out, Fritz."

"It's my market he's playing with."

Hanas asks, "Well, what are we going to do about it?"

Jimmy speaks calmly and with the weight of authority in his tone. "This is what we'll do. We've got to march in step on this before the son of a bitch pushes the dollar up to where it was last week. Do what I say. I'll take the heat from New York if it comes to that. Take him out. Both of you sell him an additional $100 million. I'll drop $100 million here in London. We're all going to go to our daylight limits including the other branches, to set the line. I've got them on the phone now. Stuff him with whatever he needs. He won't know what hit him."

Hanas says, "Jimmy, if it doesn't work, they'll fry you. If it does, the Chairman will have his 15 percent."

"Tell your three friends in Zurich they owe us."

Within 90 seconds, Jimmy has given instructions to the other branches. They all recognize the logic of his tactics instantly.

The traders turn to their posts to unload the $100 million. The atmosphere remains charged. Jimmy sits back in his chair and keeps his eyes on the television screen.

A light blinks on his console. It's his Italian boss, the London treasurer, who sits in another part of the branch.

"Jimmy, how are things going?"

"Fine, Franco. We had a bit of a bother. Nothing we can't handle. Can I help you with something?" He hangs up. He knows his tactics will work. If you gorge the only big buyer, give him more than he needs, he will end up selling too. Hamburg knew better than to do this now.

Twenty minutes later, the dollar resumes its decline.

At 11:30, Duncan taps Jimmy on the shoulder.

"I know you've got problems," says Duncan, "but so do I."

"Anything I can do?"

"I hope so. The treasurer of Pepoco Oil is on line 29, and he's so mad the wire's ready to melt."

"What does he want?"

"To sell dollars and buy Belgian francs because he's got to make a payment in Luxemburg."

"How much?"

"Five million. . . ."

"So what's the problem?"

"He wants last Tuesday's price."

Jimmy folds his arms. A bemused look appears on his face.

Duncan says, "The difference is fifty thousand dollars."

"And if he doesn't get it?"

"He's implying that he'll take all the Sheik's general deposits away and place them with another bank."

Jimmy turns away. "I should have known." Pepoco had good reason to think they could call their shots in this situation. The oil company always took the payments for the Sheik's oil and kept it on deposit until the oil arrived at its destination. Then they turned the principle and the interest it had earned in the intervening four months over to the Sheik. Of course, if they kept 50 million pounds at one bank at rates below market interest, they would expect the bank to do them some favors, and this was a case in point. Jimmy reaches for the phone. He is angry and he grips the receiver so tight that his knuckles turn white, but his voice remains calm.

"I want you to know," he says, "that we are doing this for you at considerable cost to us. We want very much to maintain our relationship. If you absolutely must do this, I am willing to comply. That's what a relationship is all about. Goodbye."

"By the way, Duncan, how are you doing with your commercials?"

"Fine. This morning we shook $30 million loose from the trees at an average price of 35 points under the market. This afternoon we should get another 60. The multinationals are still running."

At 11:50, Jimmy punches the least-used button on his console, the one for his secretary's office. He asks her to make reservations for two at Simpson's on the Strand. She is more than happy to do this, since the only work she has done since last Wednesday is to pass one expense voucher. Jimmy produces little paper. His work disappears into the circuits of the electronic world he inhabits.

Simpson's has been serving . . . London's financial district in baronial elegance for centuries. The doorman in his red uniform greets Jimmy with a cheerful but respectful, "Good morning, sir." . . .

They sit in the largest of several dining rooms, which has about fifty tables. The waiters wear tuxedos. Their pink faces contrast with Jimmy's trading room pallor. The wine steward takes Jimmy's order of a pint of bitter stoically, but he disapproves of the woman's decision not to drink at all.

Emmy Lou asks Jimmy, "How do you feel?"

"Right now I'm three quarters-seven eighths, but after this beer arrives I'll be seven eighths-fifteen sixteenths."

"I assume that means you'll feel better."

"That's right."

"I'm exhausted," she says. "I felt like I was watching you run a war."

"You get used to it." The beer arrives, and Jimmy drinks quietly.

"Don't you feel nervous at all?"

"Today is Monday. The week ends on Friday."

"How much money are you going to make by Friday?" she asks.

"Look at it this way. Our commercial department can make a $100 million loan after six months of negotiations and the bank is lucky to clear one percent a year, or $1 million. If that loan were to an LDC, say Zaire, and it defaults, or its loan is "restructured" as we say now, then the bank must lend $100 million to get back its one percent margin. But this morning I sold $50 million and if the dollar declines two percent by Friday the way I expect it to, by the time I close my position I will make well over $1 million. That's in one week. And to that the money we earn in the normal course of trading like the $100,000,000 I sold this morning to take Commerce Hamburg out which I will buy back at lower prices this afternoon. On top of that our commercial foreign exchange department is buying and selling below and above the market levels. The money market, then, is the most profitable sector of international banking."

"What happens when the dollar can't go any lower?"

"If we're lucky, the United States will start selling the gold reserves from Fort Knox to support it. We'll buy a piece of it. Then we'll start borrowing marks to sell against dollars and turn all our short positions. Then the dollar will rise, but not as fast as it fell."

"How long have you worked for the bank?" she asks.

"Twenty years."

"How long have you been a currency trader?"

"About fifteen."

A man of forty-five with jet black hair and an expensive suit appears at their table. Jimmy rises. The new man is four inches taller than him. His face is lined and sagging.

"Franco Orico, I'd like you to meet Emmy Lou Waters who has been sent to us by Credit Analysis." The Italian shakes her hand. "Emmy Lou, Franco is my boss."

"Very pleased to meet you," Franco says. "And how do you like working for our slow friends in Credit Analysis? Are they still taking six months to approve loans?"

She blushes. "I'm not sure. I'm just a trainee."

"Of course," says Franco. "And tell me, how do you like watching an expert at work?"

"I'm not sure that I understand it all, but I'm impressed."

Franco turns to Jimmy. His lined face becomes taut with concern. "I heard more about this 'bit of a bother' you had during the morning."

"It's over."

"Maybe you are enjoying too much freedom," Franco smiles at Emmy Lou. "Good afternoon, Miss Waters. Jimmy will answer all your questions." He leaves.

Jimmy sits down again. He is angry and afraid that it shows. Five days a week he turns over seven hundred million dollars plus another billion in Eurocurrencies, shaving a bit here, scraping there, massaging the market— last year his Group accounted for $45 million profit—all for the bank. Then one day something happens, something he cannot foresee, and he handles it like a master, but does anyone tip his hat? Does anyone even say thanks? No. Instead, he is humiliated in front of a trainee.

Jimmy says, "You know, Franco used to work for Bardolo. You've probably never heard of Bardolo but he's the one who helped Sindon kill one of your New York City banks a few years ago, in 1974, the last time the dollar took a real beating."

"The last time?" . . . "This has happened before?" . . .

Jimmy takes a long drink from his beer. . . . He knows what she is thinking, that he is responsible for debasing her precious dollar.

"Why are you selling the dollar? I want to know. I work for this bank too."

"Because everyone else is selling it except for that bloody fool in Hamburg."

"But why? Is it because of America's balance of trade deficit?"

"No, that's just part of the rationalization we give the press when it falls." She is clearly startled. He continues, "Last spring we began watching the dollar. We know the United States was building up a large deficit. But the commercials, particularly the oil companies, weren't selling dollars, and we couldn't understand it. We didn't know at the time that the Saudi petrodollars were being recycled into the United States Treasury. We started to sell in anticipation of commercial selling. We got out of the dollar before they did, which caused the commercials to run after us. We bought their dollars cheaper than we had sold ours, which allowed us to double up and sell them again. For the past six months, the dollar's decline has been making head-lines. People are wringing their hands. It's the best streak we've had since 1974."

"But wasn't there a $30 billion deficit last year?"

Jimmy drinks, then says, "Maybe Americans are buying more oil than they should be. However, your own Commerce Department announced last month that foreign holdings of U.S. government securities increased over $20 billion last year, most of it from O.P.E.C. In other words, the Saudis put back every-thing they took. And to that West Germany's recent agreement with the United Sates to support the dollar to the tune of $20 billion, and suddenly there is no trade deficit. And still the dollar has been going down. Now we say that fear of U.S. inflation is the reason for the dollar's continued weakness."

"That's ridiculous. You're creating the inflation in the U.S. Every time the dollar goes down it costs more to import goods and that inflation doesn't wait for the production cycle. It's immediate. I read the paper! The new chairman of our Federal Reserve Board said the dollar's decline since December has added ¾ of 1 percent to our cost of living!"

"Now wait a minute. That's the way it is. We both work for the bank. You want those first-class plane tickets and subsidized apartments on Park Avenue in New York and Park Lane in London. Stop making judgments about where they come from. I know plenty of people like you who went to business school because life hadn't kept its promises. . . . You wanted something better. Now, Miss Waters, you've got it. So leave your moral baggage outside the door of my trading room."

He leans back in his seat and finishes the last of his bitter. . . . [Emmy Lou] seems not angry, but chastened. She will serve the bank well, once she is convinced that's where all her loyalties belong.

"There's a saying in England," Jimmy tells her. "A cockney is someone born within the sound of the great bell of Bow Church. That's home for me."

"Where is it?"

"About a mile from here." The food arrives. Jimmy pulls his linen napkin into his lap. "But when I set foot in the bank, for the first, I was as far from the Bells of Bow as you are from Texas."

After lunch Jimmy broke up an argument between Henry and a junior trader. Henry had sold $10 million to a bank in Geneva over the phone. The trader wrote up the deal as a purchase. Luckily someone found the mistake before the entries were passed by the booking section.

Later, the Bahrain branch placed $40 million with London for six months at 8 percent and then took a deposit of $40 million back from the London branch for a week at 7 percent.

Jimmy called Athens, headquarters for the Middle East, and complained about Bahrain's irresponsibility. Bahrain would be making a profit of 1 percent on $40 million. London would lose 1 percent. The man in Athens said he would be more careful in the future, something he promised Jimmy an average of once a week, year in and year out.

The afternoon ended on a positive note. New York panicked. At three o'clock in London, it is nine a.m. in New York. Everyone had heard on the Today Show and Good Morning America of the pounding the greenback had taken in Europe. When the New York banks opened for business, they all sold, pushing the dollar lower. Henry's traders bought back all the dollars they had sold in the morning. Jimmy had made $1,235,000 and the week had just begun. On Tuesday the foreign exchange profit would disappear into "interest earned through a series of swaps," lowering the cost of funding his loan portfolio.

On the train going home, Jimmy looked at the men around him. Many of them were dozing. He wondered what they had been doing all day that could possibly have induced this exhaustion. Some were reading of scandal in the afternoon tabloid while others read paperback books. At the front of the car, a spirited game of bridge was being played. The sound of the bidding penetrated the rhythmic pounding of the train as it rolled forward. Cards and all other forms of gambling had always bored Jimmy, but horse racing especially bored him. It takes a horse two minutes to make a circuit of the track.

The rest were talking to one another. Jimmy thought about the years he had spent in the trading room, and he realized that he had never had a conversation on the train going home. What would he say to people? "Had a hard day at the office. Commerce Hamburg almost cost me a million at 11 this morning, but I fixed them at 11:01. Then at 11:02. . . ."

Had anyone taken the trouble to compare, they would have seen that while Jimmy dressed like the rest, they differed in some particulars. Jimmy's shoes were more worn that those of his neighbors. His shirt was from Marks and Spencer, not from Turnbull and Asser. The fact was that Jimmy had never developed expensive tastes. But how many of them could run the trading room? You think differently when you spend five days a week running as if your life depended on it. In general, it was not a gentleman's game.

CHAPTER 5

Currency Futures
and Options

This chapter is devoted entirely to the currency futures market and currency options market, often used by speculators interested in trading currencies simply to achieve profits, but also used by firms to cover their foreign currency positions. Since firms commonly use currency futures and options, it is important to understand the background of these markets and how they can help achieve corporate goals. In addition, this chapter discusses the factors that influence the prices of currency futures and options.

CURRENCY FUTURES MARKET

In 1919 the Chicago Mercantile Exchange (CME) was established as a commodity futures exchange to meet the needs of farmers and users of agricultural goods. In 1972 the CME established the International Monetary Market (IMM) division, which allows for futures in some short-term securities, gold, and foreign currencies.

Currency Futures Contracts versus Forward Contracts

Currency futures are contracts specifying a standard volume of a particular currency to be exchanged on a specific settlement date. They are similar to forward contracts in that they allow one to lock in the price to be paid for a given currency at a future point in time. Yet, their characteristics differ from forward rates. They are traded face to face, unlike forward contracts, which are negotiated over the telephone. Face-to-face transactions require a trading floor, which is provided by the International Monetary Market. Here deals are executed by brokers. Contracts have to be standardized, or floor trading would be slowed down considerably as brokers would have to assess contract specifications. Recall that forward contracts, unlike futures contracts, are tailor-made.

The trading volume of currency futures has consistently increased over time; and as growth in international transactions continues, the market should grow as well. Futures contracts are available for seven widely traded currencies at the IMM (see Exhibit 5.1). Typical settlement dates are the third Wednesday in March, June, September, and December.

Since corporations have specialized needs, they normally prefer the forward contracts. Consider a U.S. corporation, which as of January 2 realizes it will need 450,000 marks on February 11 (40 days later). If it attempts to lock in the future purchase price of marks with a futures contract, the closest IMM contract settlement date is the third Wednesday of March. Also, the amount of marks needed (450,000) is more than the standardized amount (125,000) specified in the contracts. The best the firm could do is to buy three mark futures contracts (worth 375,000 marks) or four contracts (worth 500,000 marks) in the IMM. Conversely, the forward market can be tailored to meet the individual needs of the firm. That is, the firm can call a bank and request a forward contract specifying 450,000 marks in 40 days.

Some individual speculators and small firms are not able to set up forward contracts with banks since they have no other working relationship with banks. Also, the normal transaction amount for forward contracts is much larger than individual speculators or small firms may typically desire. Exhibit 5.2 summarizes the comparison of the forward and futures markets.

The price of currency futures will normally be similar to the forward rate for a given currency and settlement date. To understand why, assume that the currency futures price on the pound is $1.50 and that forward contracts for a similar period are available for $1.48. Firms may attempt to purchase forward contracts and simultaneously sell currency futures contracts. If they could exactly match the settlement dates of the two contracts, they could generate guaranteed profits of $.02 per unit. These actions would place downward pressure on the currency futures price. The futures contract and forward contracts of a given currency and settlement date should have the same price, or else guaranteed profits are possible (assuming no transaction costs).

The currency futures price differs from the spot rate, for the same reasons that a forward rate differs from the spot rate. If a currency's spot and futures prices were the same and the currency's interest rate were higher than the U.S. rate, U.S. speculators could lock in a higher return than on U.S. investments. They could purchase the foreign currency at the spot rate, invest the funds at the attractive interest rate, and simultaneously sell currency futures to lock in the exchange rate at which they could reconvert the currency back to dollars. If the spot and futures rates were the same, there would be neither

EXHIBIT 5.1 Currencies Traded on the IMM

Currency	Units per IMM Contract
Australian dollar	100,000
British pound	62,500
Canadian dollar	100,000
French franc	250,000
German mark	125,000
Japanese yen	12,500,000
Swiss franc	125,000

EXHIBIT 5.2 Comparison of the Forward and Futures Markets

	Forward	Futures
Size of contract	Tailored to individual needs.	Standardized.
Delivery date	Tailored to individual needs.	Standardized.
Participants	Banks, brokers, and multinational companies. Public speculation not encouraged.	Banks, brokers and multinational companics. Qualified public speculation encouraged.
Security deposit	None as such, but compensating bank balances or lines of credit required.	Small security deposit required.
Clearing operation	Handling contingent on individual banks and brokers. No separate clearinghouse function.	Handled by exchange clearinghouse. Daily settlements to the market price.
Marketplace	Over the telephone worldwide.	Central exchange floor with worldwide communications.
Regulation	Self-regulating.	Commodity Futures Trading Commission; National Futures Association.
Liquidation	Most settled by actual delivery. Some by offset, at a cost.	Most by offset: very few by delivery.
Transaction costs	Set by "spread" between bank's buy and sell price.	Negotiated brokerage fees, quoted for entry and exit.

SOURCE: Reprinted with the permission of the Chicago Mercantile Exchange.

gain nor loss on the currency conversion. Thus, the higher foreign interest rate would provide a higher yield on this type of investment. The actions of investors to capitalize on this opportunity would place upward pressure on the spot rate and downward pressure on the currency futures price, causing the futures price to fall below the spot rate.

Interpreting Currency Futures Contracts Information

The IMM currency futures prices as of April 8, 1991 are shown in Exhibit 5.3. Prices for upcoming settlement dates are given for some of the currencies for which futures contracts are traded. For example, the price of a German mark June 1991 futures contract is $.5901 per mark. This implies that a firm can buy a futures contract to receive 125,000 marks (the standard amount) for

EXHIBIT 5.3 Currency Futures Contract Prices as of April 8, 1991

Currency	Approximate Closing Price for:	
	June 1991	September 1991
British pound	$1.7491	$1.7284
Canadian dollar	.8608	.8553
German mark	.5901	.5855
Japanese yen	.007309	.007264
Swiss franc	.7011	.6976

$73,762.50 (125,000 marks × $.5901 per mark) on the third Wednesday of June. Assume that a U.S. firm will need German marks on this settlement date. Alternatively, it could wait until that date and purchase marks at the spot rate. Assume the firm expects the mark's spot rate to be $.63 at that date. If its expectations are correct, it would have paid $78,750 (125,000 marks × $.63 per mark) for the 125,000 marks. The purchase of the futures contract would have saved the firm $4,987.50 ($78,750 − $73,762.50). If the firm needed more than 125,000 marks, it could have purchased as many mark futures contracts as necessary.

Closing Out a Futures Position

If a firm holding a currency futures contract decides before settlement date that it no longer wants to maintain such a position, it can close out its position by selling an identical futures contract. The gain or loss to the firm from its previous futures position is dependent on the price of purchasing futures versus selling futures.

The price of a futures contract changes over time in accordance with movements in the spot rate. For example, if the spot rate of a currency increased substantially over a one-month period, the futures price would likely increase by about the same amount. In this case, the purchase and subsequent sale of a futures contract would be profitable. Conversely, a decline in the spot rate over time would correspond with a decline in the currency futures price, meaning that the purchase and subsequent sale of a futures contract would result in a loss. While the purchasers of the futures contract could decide not to close out their position under such conditions, the losses from that position could increase over time.

Selling Currency Futures Contracts

For every buyer of a currency futures contract there must be a seller. In the previous example, a firm or individual could have sold a mark futures contract with a June 1991 settlement date for $.5901 per mark. Sellers of futures contracts are expecting the currency to depreciate by settlement date, when they will fulfill their obligation by delivering the stated amount of currency to the currency futures owner. Alternatively, they could close out their position by purchasing a currency futures contract with a similar settlement date.

Corporate Use of Currency Futures

Corporations that have open positions in foreign currencies can consider the purchase or sale of futures contracts to offset such positions. The ownership of futures contracts locks in the price at which a firm can purchase a currency. For example, assume a U.S. firm orders German goods and upon delivery will need to send 500,000 marks to the German exporter. This amount reflects four German mark futures contracts in the IMM. Thus, the U.S. firm could purchase four futures contracts today, which would lock in the price to be paid for marks at a future settlement date. By holding futures contracts, the firm does not have to worry about the changing spot rate of the mark over time.

Alternatively, a firm may consider selling a futures contract when it plans to receive a currency it will not need (perhaps from exporting products invoiced in the foreign currency preferred by the importer). By selling a futures contract, the firm is locking in the price at which it will be able to sell this currency as of settlement date. Such an action can be appropriate if the firm expects this currency to depreciate against its home currency. The manner by which a firm can use futures contracts to cover, or **hedge,** its currency positions is described more thoroughly in Chapter 11.

Futures contracts on the **European Currency Unit (ECU)** are used by corporations that are exposed to various European currencies. The ECU is a unit of account that represents a portfolio of European currencies. (It is explained further in Chapter 6.) The value of the ECU over time would likely be highly correlated with the currencies to which some U.S. firms are exposed. For example, consider a U.S. firm with subsidiaries in various European countries. Assume that each of the subsidiaries will remit earnings to the U.S. parent in December. The firm is concerned that the dollar may appreciate by then, in which case, the earnings to be remitted will convert to fewer dollars. To hedge this risk, the firm could sell ECU futures so that if the dollar appreciates, the gain on the ECU futures could offset the reduction in dollars received. Some firms may prefer to simply use forward contracts to hedge these future payments to the parent, but forward contracts may not be available for all European currencies. ECU futures can also be used to hedge those internationally traded goods and services that are priced in ECUs.

Speculation with Currency Futures

Currency futures contracts are sometimes purchased by speculators who are simply attempting to capitalize on their expectation of a currency's future movement. If, for example, they expect the British pound will appreciate in the future, they might purchase a futures contract that will lock in the price at which they can buy pounds at a specified settlement date. On settlement date, they can purchase their pounds at the rate specified by the futures contract, and then sell these pounds at the spot rate. If the spot rate has appreciated by this time in accordance with their expectations, they will profit from this strategy.

Currency futures are often sold by speculators who expect that the spot rate of a currency will be less than the rate for which they would be obligated to sell it. For example, assume a mark futures contract specifies a price of $.54 per unit. Also assume speculators expect the spot rate of the mark will be $.50 on the settlement date. They could profit from selling a futures contract as follows. If their expectations are correct, they will be able to purchase 125,000 marks for $62,500 in the spot market as of settlement date. Then, by selling their marks at $.54 per mark as specified by the futures contract, they receive $67,500, and their gain would be $5,000 ($67,500 − $62,500). Of course, expectations are often incorrect. It is because of different expectations that some speculators prefer to purchase a futures contract while other speculators prefer to sell the same contract at a given point in time.

Margin Requirements on Currency Futures

While **forward contracts** represent a personal agreement between a bank and a firm, a **futures contract** is an impersonal agreement between two parties unknown to each other. Yet, there is virtually no possibility of the buyers or sellers not fulfilling their obligations, because the contracts are

RELATED RESEARCH

Speculating with Currency Futures

Results of the following strategy in the currency futures markets were analyzed. In each period, futures on currencies whose prices exhibited *discounts* (where the futures price was less than the spot rate) were purchased. Futures on currencies whose prices exhibited *premiums* (where the futures price exceeded the spot rate per unit) were sold. If the futures price of a currency futures contract was, on average, an unbiased estimator of the spot rate that would exist at the settlement date, this strategy would earn zero profits on average. However, the study revealed large profits on average from this strategy, suggesting that those currencies with futures discounts did not depreciate on average to the degree implied by the futures discount. In addition, those currencies with futures premiums did not appreciate on average to the degree implied by the futures premium.

A second strategy that uses historical exchange rate movements to bet on currency futures was also assessed. A review of historical exchange rate movements suggests that exchange rates tend to move in cycles. This tendency may allow speculators to use recent movements to speculate with currency futures contracts. To determine whether such a system might work, the following simple strategy was applied. At the beginning of each quarter, the movement in a foreign currency was assessed. If the currency appreciated against the dollar in the previous period, this outcome was used as a forecast for the prevailing quarter. Thus, currency futures contracts on this currency were purchased to benefit from this expectation. Conversely, if the currency depreciated against the dollar in the previous period, futures contracts on this currency were sold with the expectation that the currency would continue to depreciate. The results of this strategy were assessed for five different currencies over a period from 1982 through 1987. For the Swiss franc and the Japanese yen, the strategy was profitable about 70 percent of the time. The other currencies did not have as favorable results but still led to profits on average. It should be emphasized that the strategy is risky, as some substantial losses were incurred in various quarters. However, the average gain during profitable quarters exceeded the average loss during loss quarters for all five currencies. Based on the generally favorable results from this simplified strategy, there may be potential for more consistent profits using a more sophisticated strategy.

SOURCE: Lee R. Thomas. "A Winning Strategy for Currency-futures Speculation," *Journal of Portfolio Management* (Fall 1985): 65–69; and Jeff Madura and George Cash, "Investing in Currency Futures Contracts," *Journal of Business and Economic Perspectives,* (Fall 1989): 123–126.

guaranteed by the Chicago Mercantile Exchange (CME). To minimize its risk of such a guarantee, the CME imposes **margin requirements** to cover fluctuations in the value of a contract, meaning that the participant must place a deposit on the contract. Such deposits are not always required for forward contracts due to the more personal nature of the agreement; the bank knows the firm it is dealing with and may trust it to fulfill its obligation.

Transaction Costs of Currency Futures

Brokers that fulfill orders to buy or sell futures contracts charge a transaction or brokerage fee in the form of a bid/ask spread. That is, they buy a futures contract for one price (their "bid" price) and simultaneously sell the contract to someone else for a slightly higher price (their "ask" price). The difference between a bid and ask price on a futures contract may be as little as $7.50. Yet, even this amount is larger in percentage terms than the transaction fees for forward contracts.

CURRENCY OPTIONS MARKET

In late 1982 exchanges in Amsterdam, Montreal, and Philadelphia allowed for trading in standardized foreign currency options. Since that time, options have been offered on the Chicago Mercantile Exchange and the Chicago Board Options Exchange. A **currency option** is an alternative type of contract that can be purchased or sold by speculators and firms. Currency options are presently available for seven currencies on the Philadelphia exchange: (1) British pound, (2) Canadian dollar, (3) German mark, (4) Japanese yen, (5) Swiss franc, (6) French franc, and (7) Australian dollar. The volume of currency represented in each currency option contract on the Philadelphia exchange is half the size of the currency's volume in IMM futures contracts. For example, the German mark option contract represents 62,500 units, which is half the 125,000 units represented by the German mark futures contract.

In addition to the exchanges on which currency options are available, some commercial banks have begun to offer them. In some cases, they are tailored to the specific needs of the firm, rather than standardized. Some financial institutions offer **option look-alikes,** which offer similar characteristics but are not traded at an exchange. Currency options are classified as either **calls** or **puts.** Each is discussed here.

CURRENCY CALL OPTIONS

The owner of a **currency call option** is granted the right to buy a specific currency at a specific price within a specific period of time. The price at which the owner is allowed to buy that currency is known as the **exercise price** or **strike price,** and there are monthly expiration dates for each option.

Call options are desirable when one wishes to lock in the price to be paid for a currency in the future. If the spot rate of the currency rises above the strike price, owners of call options can "exercise" their options by purchasing the currency at the strike price, which will be cheaper than the prevailing spot rate. This strategy is somewhat similar to that used by purchasers of futures contracts, but the futures contracts require an obligation, which the currency option does not. The owner can choose to let the option expire on the expiration date without ever exercising it. Owners of expired call options will have lost the premium they initially paid, but that is the most they can lose.

Interpreting Currency Call Option Information

Exhibit 5.4 reflects the premiums for British pound options that existed as of April 8, 1991. There are three different strike prices listed for the British

EXHIBIT 5.4   Premiums for British Pound Options (on April 8, 1991)

| Exercise (Strike) Price | Cents Per Unit | | | | | |
| | Call Options | | | Put Options | | |
	April	May	June	April	May	June
$1.7750	1.38¢	r	3.64¢	1.65¢	3.68¢	4.75¢
$1.8000	.61¢	1.79¢	r	3.00¢	r	r
$1.8500	.24¢	.91¢	r	r	8.15¢	9.68¢

Note: r implies that contracts were not traded.

pound, implying there were three options available for the British pound. An individual or firm could have purchased a pound option that has a strike price of $1.775, $1.80, or $1.85. Other strike prices were also available but are not shown here.

The second column shows premiums per unit of currency for the various call options based on an April settlement date. For example, the premium for a British pound call option with a strike price of $1.85 and an April settlement date is 0.24 cents per unit. Since the pound option comes in a standardized volume of 31,250 units, this call option is priced at $75 (0.24¢ per unit × 31,250 units.) The third column shows prices per unit of currency for the various call options based on a May settlement date. For example, a British pound call option with a $1.85 strike price and May settlement date is priced at .91 cents per unit or $284 for the 31,250 units in the standard contract at the Philadelphia exchange. The fourth column shows prices per unit of currency for the various options based on a June settlement date. The last three columns in Exhibit 5.4 refer to put options and will be discussed shortly.

Before exploring the mechanics of currency call options, it is important to be able to identify the premium for a particular call option contract if given the (1) currency, (2) strike price, and (3) settlement date. To test your understanding, what is the premium of a May call option with a strike price of $1.80 based on Exhibit 5.4? To answer this question, first identify the premium per unit, which is 1.79 cents. Therefore, this call option would be priced at $559 (computed as 1.79¢ × 31,250 units).

Factors Affecting Call Option Premiums

Premiums of call options vary due to three main factors:

1. *Level of existing spot price relative to strike price.* The higher the spot rate relative to the strike price, the higher will be the option price. This is due to the higher probability of buying the currency at a substantially lower rate than what you could sell it for. To verify the relationship suggested here, review Exhibit 5.4, and notice how the call option price varies with the strike price.

2. *Length of time before the expiration date.* It is generally expected that the spot rate has a greater chance of rising high above the strike price if it has a

longer period of time to do so. A settlement date in June allows two additional months beyond April for the spot rate to move above the strike price. This explains why June option prices exceed April and May option prices given a specific strike price, as verified by Exhibit 5.4.

3. *Potential variability of currency.* The greater the variability of the currency, the higher the probability is that the spot rate will be above the strike price. Thus, more volatile currencies will have higher call option prices. For example, the Canadian dollar is a more stable currency than most other currencies. If all other factors are similar, Canadian call options should be less expensive than call options of other foreign currencies.

Corporate Use of Currency Call Options

Corporations with open positions in foreign currencies can sometimes use currency call options to cover these positions. If, for example, a U.S. firm orders Swiss goods, it may need to send Swiss francs to the Swiss exporter upon delivery. A Swiss franc call option locks in the rate at which a U.S. firm can exchange dollars for Swiss francs. This exchange of currencies at the specified strike price on the call option contract can be executed at any time before the expiration date. In essence, the call option contract has specified the maximum price at which the U.S. firm must pay to obtain these Swiss francs. Yet, if the Swiss franc's value remains below the strike price, the U.S. firm can purchase Swiss francs at the prevailing spot rate when it needs to pay for its imports and can simply let its call option expire.

Sometimes a firm anticipates a possible need for a foreign currency but is not yet certain of that need. Consider a firm that bids on a project required by the German government. If the bid is accepted, the firm will need approximately DM625,000 to purchase German materials and services. However, the firm will not know whether the bid is accepted until three months from now. In this case, it could purchase call options with a three-month expiration date. Ten call option contracts would cover the entire amount of potential exposure. If the bid is accepted, the firm can use the options to purchase the marks needed. If the mark has depreciated over time, the firm will likely let the options expire.

Assume that the exercise price on marks is $.50 and the call option premium is $.02 per unit. The firm would have paid $1,250 per option (since there are 62,500 units per mark option) or $12,500 for the 10 option contracts. With the options, the maximum amount necessary to purchase the DM625,000 is $312,500 (computed as $.50 per mark × DM625,000 marks). Of course, the amount of dollars needed could be less if the mark's spot rate is below the exercise price at the time the marks are purchased.

Even if the project's bid is rejected, the currency call option would be exercised if the mark's spot rate exceeds the exercise price before the option expires. Any gain from exercising may partially or even fully offset the premium paid for the options.

As another example, a U.S. firm involved in a foreign acquisition bid may purchase call options on the currency that would be needed to purchase the foreign company's shares. The call options hedge the U.S. firm against the potential appreciation of the currency that may be needed if the acquisition occurs. If the acquisition does not occur and the spot rate remains below the strike price, the firm could let the call options expire. If the acquisition does not occur and the spot rate exceeds the strike price, the firm could exercise the option and sell the foreign currency in the spot market. This may offset part or all of the premium paid for the option.

These examples suggest that options may be more appropriate than futures or forward contracts for some situations. Chrysler Corporation uses options for about 50 percent of its hedging transactions and forward contracts for the remaining 50 percent. Intel Corporation uses options to hedge its order backlog in semiconductors. If an order is cancelled, it has the flexibility to let the options contract expire. With a forward contract, it would be obligated to fulfill its obligation even though the order was cancelled. When Air Products and Chemicals was hired to perform some projects, it needed capital equipment from West Germany. The purchase of equipment was contingent on whether the firm was hired for the projects. The company used options to hedge this possible future purchase.

Speculating with Currency Call Options

Because this text focuses on multinational financial management, the corporate use of currency options is more important than the speculative use. The use of options for hedging is discussed in detail in Chapter 11. Speculative trading is discussed here in order to provide more of a background on the currency options market.

Individuals may speculate in the currency options market based on their expectation of the future movements in a particular currency. For example, speculators who expect that the Japanese yen will appreciate could purchase Japanese yen call options. Once the spot rate of Japanese yen appreciates, they can exercise their option by purchasing yen at the strike price, then sell the yen at the prevailing spot rate.

Just as is the case with currency futures, for every buyer of a currency call option, there must be a seller. A seller (sometimes called a **writer**) of a call option is obligated to sell a specified currency at a specified price (the strike price) up to a specified expiration date. Speculators may sometimes want to sell a currency call option on a currency that is expected to depreciate in the future. The only way a currency call option will be exercised is if the spot rate is higher than the strike price. Thus, a seller of the currency call option will receive the premium when the option is purchased and can keep the entire amount if the option is not exercised. When it appears that an option will be exercised, there will still be sellers of options. However, such options will sell for high premiums due to the high risk that the option will be exercised at some point.

Just because a call option is exercised, the owner does not necessarily receive profits, nor does the seller incur losses. Suppose that Jim is a speculator who buys a British pound call option with a strike price of $1.40 and a December settlement date. The current spot price as of that date is about $1.39. Jim paid 1.20¢ per unit, or $150 (computed as 12,500 units × 1.20¢ per unit) for the call option. Assume there are no brokerage fees. Just before the settlement date, the spot rate of the British pound reaches $1.41. At this time, Jim exercises the call option and then immediately sells the pounds at the spot rate to a bank. To determine Jim's profit or loss, first compute his revenues from selling the currency, then subtract from this amount the purchase price of pounds when exercising the option, and also subtract the purchase price of the option. The computations follow.

Step 1. Revenues from
selling currency   = $1.41 × 31,250 units = $44,063 per contract
at the existing
spot rate

Step 2. Purchase price
when exercising   = $1.40 × 31,250 units = $43,750 per contract
the option

Step 3. Purchase price
of the option   = $.012 × 31,250 units = $375 per contract
itself

Net profit to the currency call owner	= $44,063 Revenues	− $43,750 Purchase price from exercising the option	− $375 Purchase price of option itself	= − $62 Profit (negative number implies loss)

These computations show that Jim lost money even though he was able to sell the pounds for a higher price than what he paid for them. Before assessing the profit or loss of the seller (let's call her Linda), assume that she did not have British pounds available until Jim exercised the option. It was at that point that Linda purchased the pounds needed to sell to Jim at the strike price.

Linda's revenues come from two sources. She received a premium of 1.20¢ per unit when selling the call option, or $375 ($.012 per unit × 31,250 units) for the contract. She also received $1.40 per unit when selling the currency (as the option was exercised) or $43,750 ($1.40 per unit × 31,250 units). These combined revenues of $44,125 should be weighed against the payments of $44,063 Linda made when buying 31,250 pounds at the spot rate of $1.41. The net profit is $62 ($44,125 − $44,063), which is equal to Jim's loss.

When brokerage fees are ignored, the currency call purchaser's loss will be the seller's gain. The currency call purchaser's expenses represent the seller's revenues, and the purchaser's revenues represent the seller's expenses. Yet, because it is possible for purchasers and sellers of options to close out their positions, the relationship described here will not hold unless both parties begin and close out their positions at the same times.

Break-Even Point on Currency Call Options

The preceding example shows that the purchaser of a currency call option does not automatically profit when exercising an option. Nevertheless, one can at least determine beforehand the spot rate that the currency must reach in order to break even. The purchaser will break even if the revenue from selling the currency at the spot rate equals the payments for (1) the currency (at the strike price) and (2) the option premium. In other words, regardless of the number of units in a contract, a purchaser will break even if the spot rate at which the currency is sold is equal to the strike price plus the option premium. In the previous example, the strike price is $1.40 and the option premium is $.012. Thus, in order for the purchaser to break even, the spot rate existing at the time the call is exercised must be $1.412 ($1.40 + $.012). Of course, speculators would not have purchased the call option if they thought the spot rate would only reach this break-even point without going higher before the expiration date. The computation of the break-even point is useful for a speculator deciding whether to purchase a currency call option.

Net Profit from Speculating on Currency Call Options

The net profit can be computed for a speculative purchaser and seller of a call option given information on the spot rate, option price, and strike price. An example is provided below:

- Call option premium per Swiss franc on May 1 = $.01.
- Option expiration date is September.
- Strike price of Swiss franc option = $.44.

There are 62,500 units in a Swiss franc option. Assume that (1) the call option was exercised in August as the spot rate reached $.49, (2) the purchaser of the call option sells the currency immediately after exercising the call option, and (3) the seller of the currency call option did not have Swiss francs available until the option was about to be exercised.

Given this information, one could determine the net profit (or loss) to the purchaser and seller of the call option in various ways. A common method is to first realize that the purchaser of the option received $.49 per Swiss franc when selling francs. Weigh this amount against the (1) purchase price when exercising the option of $.44 per Swiss franc and (2) option premium of $.01 per Swiss franc. The net profit to the owner of the call option is

$$\$.49 \text{ per unit} - \$.44 \text{ per unit} - \$.01 \text{ per unit} = \$.04 \text{ per unit}$$

Since there are 62,500 units in one Swiss franc option, the net profit to the call owner is $62,500 \times \$.04 = \$2,500$.

Return and Risk of Currency Call Options

To illustrate the return and risk from speculating in foreign currency options, assume the following information:

- Spot rate of British pound = $1.50.
- Premium on the British pound call option = $ .02.
- Exercise price on the British pound call option = $1.50.

Also assume that you expect any of five possible outcomes to occur, as identified in the first column of Exhibit 5.5. This exhibit shows what your profit would be if you invest in currency options. The potential returns are high, but so is the risk.

CURRENCY PUT OPTIONS

The owner of a **currency put option** is granted the right to sell a currency at a specified price (the strike price) within a specified period of time. As with currency call options, the owner of a put option is not obligated to exercise the option. Therefore, the maximum potential loss to the owner of the put

EXHIBIT 5.5 Potential Returns from Investing in Currency Options

Possible Outcome for British Pound	Probability	Nominal Profit per Unit	Profit as a Percent of Investment
$1.45	10%	−$.02	−100%
$1.51	20	−.01	−50
$1.53	40	+.01	+50
$1.55	20	+.03	+150
$1.58	10	+.06	+300

option is the price (or premium) paid for the option contract. In Exhibit 5.4, the fifth, sixth, and seventh columns disclose prices for currency put options. For example, a British pound put option with a strike price of $1.775 and June expiration date can be purchased for 4.75¢ per unit or $1484 (computed as 4.75¢ × 31,250 units) for the contract. The same contract with an April expiration date can be purchased for 3.00¢ per unit or $938 for the contract (computed as 3.00¢ × 31,250 units).

Factors Affecting Currency Put Option Premiums

The three main factors influencing call option premiums also influence put option premiums. First, the spot rate of a currency relative to the strike price is important. The lower the spot rate relative to the strike price, the more valuable will be the put option, since it reflects a higher probability that the put option will be exercised. Recall that just the opposite relationship held for the call option. A second factor influencing the put option premium is the length of time until the expiration date. As with currency call options, the longer the time to expiration, the greater will be the put option price. A longer period offers a higher probability of the currency moving within a range where it would be feasible to exercise the option (whether it's a put or a call). These relationships can be verified in Exhibit 5.4. A third factor that influences the put option premium is the variability of a currency. As with currency call options, the greater the variability, the greater will be the put option premium, again reflecting a higher probability that the option may be exercised.

Corporate Use of Currency Put Options

Corporations with open positions in foreign currencies can use currency put options in some cases to cover these positions. For example, assume a U.S. firm has exported products to Canada and invoiced the products in Canadian dollars (at the request of the Canadian importers). This firm may be concerned that the Canadian dollars it is receiving will depreciate over time. To insulate itself against possible depreciation, it could purchase Canadian dollar put options, which would entitle the firm to sell Canadian dollars at the specified strike price. In essence, the firm would lock in the minimum rate at which it could exchange Canadian dollars for U.S. dollars over a specified period of time. Yet, if the Canadian dollar appreciated over this time period, the firm could let the put options expire and sell the Canadian dollars received at the prevailing spot rate.

Speculating with Currency Put Options

Individuals may speculate with currency put options based on their expectation of the future movements in a particular currency. For example, speculators who expect that the British pound will depreciate could purchase British pound put options, which would entitle them to sell British pounds at a specified strike price. If the pound's spot rate did depreciate as expected, they could then purchase pounds at the spot rate and exercise their put options by selling these pounds at the strike price.

Speculators could also attempt to profit from selling currency put options. The seller of such options is obligated to purchase the specified currency at the strike price from the owner who exercises the put option. Speculators who believe the currency will appreciate (or at least will not depreciate) may consider selling a currency put option. If the currency appreciated over the entire period, the option would not be exercised. This is an ideal situation for put option sellers, since they keep the premiums received when selling the options and bear no cost. However, if the put option is exercised, the seller of the put can lose a substantial amount of funds. For example, assume the strike price of the pound was $1.40 and the pound's spot price declined to $1.30. If the option was exercised at this point, the seller of the option would be obligated to buy the pounds at the strike price of $1.40 per pound, or $43,750 for the 31,250 pounds. If the seller of this put option sold these 31,250 pounds at the existing spot rate of $1.30 per pound, he would receive $40,625. The loss here of $3,125 ($43,750 paid out minus $40,625 received) would more than offset the initial premium received on the sale of the put option.

The seller of the put options could simply refrain from selling the pounds (after being forced to buy them at $1.40 per pound) until the spot rate of the pound rises. However, there is no guarantee that the pound will reverse its direction and begin to appreciate. The seller's net loss could potentially be greater if the pound's spot rate continued to fall unless the pounds were sold immediately.

From the examples related to the put option, whatever an owner of a put option gains, the seller loses, and vice versa. This relationship would hold if brokerage costs did not exist, and if the buyer and seller of options entered and closed their positions at the same time. Brokerage fees for currency options exist, however, and are very similar in magnitude to those of currency futures contracts.

For volatile currencies, one possible speculative strategy is to purchase a **straddle,** which represents both a put option and a call option. This may seem unusual, since owning a put option is appropriate for expectations that the currency will depreciate while owning a call option is appropriate for expectations that the currency will appreciate. However, it is possible that the currency will depreciate (at which time the put is exercised) and then reverse direction and appreciate (allowing for profits when exercising the call). Also, one might anticipate that the currency will be substantially affected by current economic events but be uncertain of what way it will be affected. By purchasing a put option and a call option, one will gain if the currency moves substantially in either direction. If it appreciates, one can exercise the call option and let the put option expire. If it depreciates, one can exercise the put option and let the call option expire. Although two options are purchased and only one is exercised, the gains could more than offset the costs.

An owner of a currency option may simply sell the option to someone else before the expiration date rather than exercising it. The owner can still earn profits, since the option premium changes over time, reflecting the probability that the option can be exercised and the potential profit from exercising it.

Net Profit from Speculating on Currency Put Options

Consider the following example to understand how a put option purchaser's net profit could be computed. Assume that in August you purchase a put option on British pounds with a strike price of $1.40 and expiration date of December. Assume you paid a premium of 1.6¢ per unit, or $500 (31,250 units × $.016), for the put option. Also assume that the spot rate of the pound, which was originally $1.44, depreciates to $1.30 before the settlement date. At this point, you buy 31,250 pounds from a bank and then exercise your put option. You have therefore paid $40,625 (31,250 pounds × $1.30) for the pounds. Then, as you exercised the option, you sold the pounds at a strike price of $1.40 per pound for a total of $43,750 (31,250 pounds × $1.40), $3,125 more than you paid for them. However, keep in mind that you did pay $500 for the put option itself. Thus, your net profit is $3,125 − $500 = $2,625.

One has the right to exercise the currency put option anytime up to the expiration date. An appropriate time to exercise the put option is the point at which pounds can be purchased cheaply (i.e., when the spot rate of the pound is low). Of course, it's difficult to know whether the spot rate will rise or fall in the future. The purchasers of put options would have earned a higher net profit by waiting for the pound to depreciate to its minimum level before the expiration date of the option.

If, in the previous example, the pound's spot rate appreciated over the entire time period the owner held the put option, the owner would not have exercised the put option. This is because the currency is worth more in the spot market than what it could be sold for if the put option is exercised. Thus, the owner of the put option would lose the amount initially paid for the option. Purchasers of both currency puts and calls can lose no more than their initial investment (the premium paid for the options).

DEVELOPING CONTINGENCY GRAPHS FOR OPTIONS

Assume that a British pound call option is available, with an exercise price of $1.50 and a call premium of $.02. The speculative profits to be earned are dependent on the future spot rate of the pound. Assume that the speculator plans to exercise the option on the settlement date (if appropriate at that time) and will immediately sell the pounds received in the spot market. Under these conditions, a **contingency graph** can be created to measure the profit or loss per unit (see the upper left graph Exhibit 5.6). Notice that if the future spot rate is $1.50 or less, the net gain per unit is −$.02 (ignoring transaction costs). This represents the loss of the premium per unit paid for

INTERNATIONAL FINANCIAL MANAGEMENT IN PRACTICE

Executing Currency Option Trades

The way currency option trades are made is perhaps best illustrated by following a typical trade through the Philadelphia Stock Exchange; the other exchanges follow essentially similar procedures. Suppose a customer wants to buy a British pound option with a $1.45 exercise price and June expiration date at the best price available on the market. The trading process begins when the customer calls a broker who is a member of the exchange and places the order. The broker books and clocks the order, then relays it electronically to the broker's booth on the exchange trading floor. The broker's floor trader then walks over to the other pound contract traders standing near the screens on which trades are reported, and shouts out his bid of, say, 1¢. Option price bids are quoted at cents per unit of the underlying currency, and a bid of 1¢ on a 12,500 British pound contract is equal to a premium of $125.

The floor trader's bid would be answered by offers to sell from other traders, at (say) 1.25¢, and 1.15¢. The offers may be coming from three kinds of traders: specialists, market-makers, or floor brokers acting as agents for other customers. **Specialists** are firms designated by the exchange to maintain orderly trading and manage the limit orders for each currency. Some customers give their brokers orders to buy or sell only when prices reach a certain limit (say, "buy at 130.00" or "sell at 150.00"), and the specialist coordinates these orders. **Market-makers** are member firms who buy and sell for their own account, and who must make a bid or offer

on a customer's order if called upon to do so by the specialist. In return for standing ready to trade even when it is not always in their interest to do so, market-makers enjoy reduced margin requirements, and are able to execute trades for their own account faster than traders who must use a broker.

The floor trader takes the lowest offer— in this case 1.15¢, implying a premium of $143.75—and "matches tickets" with the selling trader, confirming the trade in pencil on printed paper slips. The buying trader hands the slips to the specialist, who staples them and gives them to an exchange employee who puts the information into the exchange's computerized reporting system. As soon as the trade is in the exchange's reporting system it is flashed onto the trading floor screens and private wire service screens. By SEC rules, the trade must be reported on the system within 90 seconds of when it occurred. The broker's floor trader then wires confirmation of the trade back to the broker, who advises his customer that the trade has been completed. If the option seller is another customer rather than a market-maker, the seller's order will have followed a similar path through the customer's broker to the exchange floor, with one difference: the seller's broker will have required a margin deposit from its customer to protect the broker, the exchange's clearing corporation, and the option buyer from default.

SOURCE: Brian Gendreau. "New Markets in Foreign Currency Options," Federal Reserve Bank of Philadelphia, *Business Review* (July–August 1984).

the option, as the option would not be exercised. At $1.51, $.01 per unit would be earned from exercising the option, but considering the $.02 premium paid, the net gain is −$.01. At $1.52, $.02 per unit would be earned from exercising the option, which offsets the $.02 premium per unit. This is the break-even point. At any rate above this point, the premium paid will be

EXHIBIT 5.6 Contingency Graphs for Currency Options

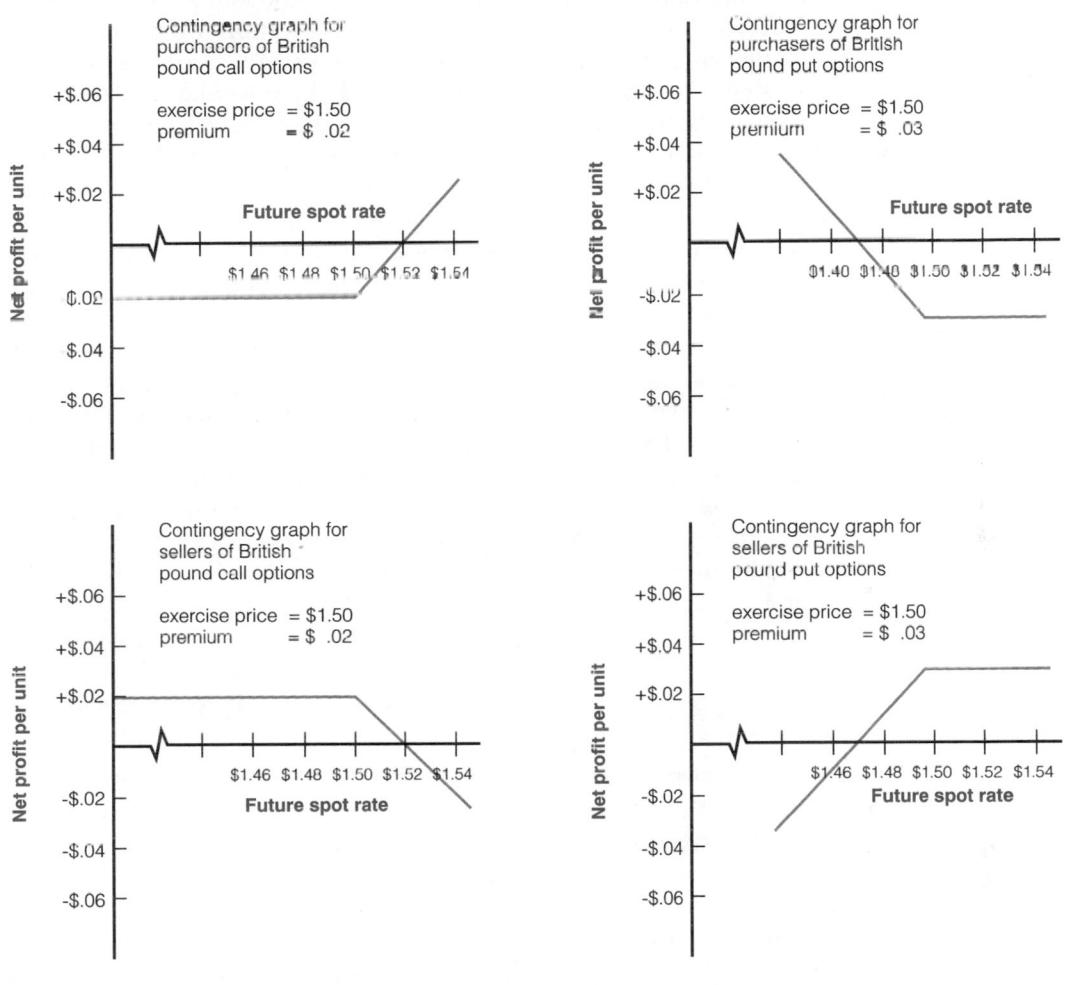

more than offset by the gain from exercising the option, resulting in a positive net gain.

A contingency graph could also be developed for the seller of this call option. The lower left graph shown in Exhibit 5.6 assumes that this seller would purchase the pounds in the spot market just as the option is exercised (ignoring transaction costs). At future spot rates of less than $1.50, the net gain to the seller is the premium of $.02 per unit, as the option would not have been exercised. If the future spot rate is $1.51, the seller would have lost $.01 per unit on the option transaction (paying $1.51 for pounds in the spot market and selling pounds for $1.50 to fulfill the exercise request). Yet, this loss would be more than offset by the premium of $.02 per unit, resulting in a net gain of $.01 per unit. The break-even point is at $1.52, and the net gain to the seller of a call option becomes negative at all rates higher than that point. Notice that the contingency graphs for the buyer and seller of this call option are mirror images of one another in our example.

A contingency graph for a buyer of a put option can also be developed. The upper right graph in Exhibit 5.6 shows the net gains to a buyer of a British pound put option with an exercise price of $1.50 and a premium of $.03 per unit. If the future spot rate is above $1.50, the option will not be exercised. At a future spot rate of $1.48, the put option would be exercised. However, considering the premium of $.03 per unit, there would be a net loss of $.01 per unit. The break-even point in this example is $1.47, since this is the future spot rate that would generate $.03 per unit from exercising the option to offset the $.03 premium. At any future spot rates of less than $1.47, the buyer of the put option would earn a positive net gain.

A contingency graph for the seller of this put option is shown in the lower right graph in Exhibit 5.6. It is the mirror image of the contingency graph for the buyer of a put option.

There are various reasons why an option buyer's net gain will not always represent an option seller's net loss. The buyer may be using call options to hedge a foreign currency, rather than speculate. In this case, the buyer does not evaluate the options position taken by measuring a net gain or loss; the option is simply used for protection. In addition, sellers of call options on a currency where they presently maintain a position would not need to purchase the currency at the time an option is exercised. They could simply liquidate their position in order to provide the currency to the person exercising the option.

COMPARISON OF AMERICAN AND EUROPEAN CURRENCY OPTIONS

The discussion of currency options up to this point has been solely related to American-style options. European-style currency options are also available for speculating and hedging in the foreign exchange market. They are similar to American-style options except that they must be exercised on the expiration date if they are to be exercised at all. Consequently, they do not offer as much flexibility; however, this is not relevant for some situations. For example, firms that purchase options to hedge future foreign currency cash flows will not likely desire to exercise their options before the expiration date anyway. If European-style options are available for the same expiration date as American-style options and can be purchased for a slightly lower premium, some corporations may prefer them for hedging.

EFFICIENCY OF CURRENCY FUTURES AND OPTIONS MARKETS

Speculators may believe that speculation in the currency futures and/or currency options markets can consistently generate abnormally large profits. This would not be possible if such foreign exchange markets were "efficient." In an efficient foreign exchange market, any available contracts would be priced to reflect all relevant information; thus, speculators would not be able to exploit existing information to earn abnormally large profits. Any valuable

INTERNATIONAL FINANCIAL MANAGEMENT IN PRACTICE

Options on Currency Futures

In January 1984 the Chicago Mercantile Exchange introduced a new financial instrument related to foreign exchange and combining the concepts of options and futures. Referred to as **options on futures contracts,** this new instrument reflects options not on the currency itself but on a futures contract representing that currency. The owner of a call option on a futures contract has the right to purchase the standardized futures contract at a given price (the strike price) within a specified period. Recall that the standardized futures contract represents 125,000 German marks to be delivered at a specified settlement date for a specified price. Like the options on currencies discussed in this chapter, options on futures may or may not be exercised; the decision is left to the discretion of the option holder.

Options on futures were originally established for the German mark. They are now also available for British pounds, Canadian dollars, Japanese yen, and Swiss francs. Trading volume in options on currency futures has grown substantially over time.

information would have already caused an adjustment in "sell" or "buy" requests, thereby forcing the contract price to reflect that information.

It is virtually impossible to know with certainty whether the contract prices in foreign exchange markets do contain all relevant information. However, we can at least attempt to determine whether some speculative trading strategies can consistently generate abnormally large profits. Consider a particular speculative strategy in the futures or options market where the return on invested speculative funds is consistently higher than the prevailing rate on risk-free investments such as Treasury bills or insured bank deposits. Does this situation imply these foreign exchange markets are inefficient? Not necessarily. A speculative strategy requires the speculator to incur risk, since the actual results from investing funds in a speculative instrument are uncertain. While a high return (profit as a percent of the amount invested) can sometimes be achieved by speculating in foreign exchange markets, there is considerable risk involved. "Abnormal" profits from a speculative strategy would reflect above-average returns *after* accounting for the risk involved. Individuals who speculate in futures and options markets must believe that they know something the market doesn't. Yet, corporations may use these markets even if they believe in market efficiency. Their positions in currency futures and currency options are usually intended to reduce exposure to fluctuating exchange rates rather than earn a speculative profit.

SUMMARY

Two major instruments within the foreign exchange markets are (1) currency futures contracts and (2) currency options. The two types of contracts are similar in that they are both used by those who have specific expectations about future currency movements. They differ in that purchasers of currency

RELATED RESEARCH

Efficiency of Currency Options, Forwards, and Futures

Due to the popularity of currency options as a speculative tool, much research has been devoted to assessing whether the currency options market is efficient. If currency options are not priced efficiently, excess risk-adjusted returns may be achievable. Recent research by Bodurtha and Courtadon and by Tucker found that when accounting for transaction costs, the currency options market is efficient. This does not prevent speculators from achieving gains, but only suggests that option prices generally reflect all available information.

The forward market, however, was not found to be efficient by research. A study by Kaen, Simos, and Hackey found that the forward rate is a poor forecaster of the future spot rate. A study by Chiang on the forward rates of the British pound, Canadian dollar, French franc, and German mark determined that these rates do not incorporate all relevant information. Bear in mind, though, that the results of such a study tend to vary with the time period and currencies analyzed.

To assess the efficiency of the currency futures market, Thomas developed a trading strategy based on interest rate differentials. This strategy generated a return of about 10.3 percent above the three-month Treasury bill rate on average, suggesting that currency futures are not priced efficiently (if the excess return is assumed to more than compensate for the risk involved).

See the following references for more details on this subject: Bodurtha, James N. Jr., and George R. Courtadon. "Efficiency Tests of the Foreign Currency Options Market." *Journal of Finance* (March 1986): 151–161.
Tucker, Alan L. "Empirical Tests of the Efficiency of the Currency Option Market," *Journal of Financial Research* (Winter 1985): 275–285.
Kaen, Fred R., Erangelos O. Simos, and George A. Hackey. "The Response of Forward Exchange Rates to Interest Rate Forecasting Errors." *Journal of Financial Research* (Winter 1984): 281–290.
Chiang, Thomas. "On the Predictions of the Future Spot Rates." *The Financial Review* (February 1986): 69–83.
Thomas, Lee R. "A Winning Strategy for Currency Futures Speculation." *Journal of Portfolio Management* (Fall 1985): 65–69.

futures are obligated to buy the currency on the settlement date, whereas owners of currency options have the right to buy or sell a currency for a specific price, but are not obligated.

Both types of contracts appeal to individuals and small firms because of their standardized form and relatively small purchase price. It is easy to look at historical data and measure the gains or losses from taking a position in currency futures or options. Yet, it is difficult to project your future gain or loss when taking a new position in currency futures or options. Even the experienced traders have difficulty in achieving consistent profits by taking speculative positions. Speculation in currency futures or options can be very rewarding if your expectations of currency movements do occur. However, if the currency moves against your expectations, speculation can be hazardous to your bank account.

Corporations can use currency futures and/or options to reduce their exposure to exchange rate movements. These instruments can be used in situations where a firm might receive a foreign currency in the future that is expected to weaken over time, or needs to obtain a foreign currency in the future that is expected to strengthen over time.

1. Compare and contrast the forward and futures contracts.

2. How can currency futures be used by corporations?

3. How can currency futures be used by speculators?

4. What is a currency call option?

5. What is a currency put option?

6. When should a firm consider purchasing a call option for hedging?

7. When should a firm consider purchasing a put option for hedging?

8. When should a speculator purchase a call option on German marks?

9. When should a speculator purchase a put option on German marks?

10. List the factors that affect currency call option premiums, and briefly explain the relationship that exists for each.

11. List the factors that affect currency put option premiums, and briefly explain the relationship that exists for each.

12. Assume a speculator purchased a call option on Swiss francs for $.02 per unit. The strike price was $.45, and the spot rate at the time the franc was exercised was $.46. Assume there are 62,500 units in a Swiss franc option. What was the net profit on this option to the speculator?

13. Assume a U.S. speculator purchased a put option on British pounds for $.04 per unit. The strike price was $1.80, and the spot rate at the time the pound was exercised was $1.59. Assume there are 31,250 units in a British pound option. What was the net profit on the option?

14. Assume a U.S. speculator sold a call option on German marks for $.01 per unit. The strike price was $.36, and the spot rate at the time the mark was exercised was $.42. Assume the speculator did not obtain marks until the option was exercised. Also assume there are 62,500 units in a German mark option. What was the net profit to the seller of the call option?

15. Assume a U.S. speculator sold a put option on Canadian dollars for $.03 per unit. The strike price was $.75, and the spot rate at the time the Canadian dollar was exercised was $.72. Assume the speculator immediately sold off the Canadian dollars received when the option was exercised. Also assume there are 50,000 units in a Canadian dollar option. What was the net profit to the seller of the put option?

16. What are the advantages and disadvantages to a corporation that considers currency options rather than a forward contract to hedge against exchange rate fluctuations?

17. Assume that the transactions listed in Column 1 of the following table are anticipated by U.S. firms that have no other foreign transactions. Place an "X" in the table wherever you see a possible way to hedge each of the transactions.

	Forward Contract		Futures Contract		Options Contract	
	Forward Purchase	Forward Sale	Buy Futures	Sell Futures	Purchase a Call	Purchase a Put
a. Georgetown Company plans to purchase German goods denominated in marks.						
b. Harvard Inc. will sell goods to Japan, denominated in yen.						
c. Yale Corporation has a subsidiary in France that will be remitting funds to the U.S. parent.						
d. Brown Inc. needs to pay off existing loans soon that were denominated in French francs.						
e. Princeton Company may purchase a company in Japan in the near future (but the deal may not go through).						

18. Assume that the British pound's spot rate has moved in cycles over time. How might you try to use futures contracts on pounds to capitalize on this tendency? How could you determine whether such a strategy would have been profitable in previous periods?

19. Assume that on November 1 the spot rate of the British pound was $1.58 and the price on a December futures contract was $1.59. Assume that the pound depreciated over November, so that by November 30 it was worth $1.51.

a) What do you think happened to the futures price over the month of November? Why?

b) If you would have known that this would occur, would you have purchased or sold a December futures contract in pounds on November 1? Explain.

20. Assume that a March futures contract on marks was available in January for $.54 per unit. Also assume that forward contracts were available for the same settlement date at a price of $.55 per mark. How could speculators capitalize on this situation, assuming zero transaction costs? How would such speculative activity affect the difference between the forward contract price and the futures price?

21. LSU Corporation purchased German mark call options for speculative purposes. If these options are exercised, LSU will immediately sell the marks in the spot market. Each option was purchased for a premium of $.03 per unit, with an exercise price of $.55. LSU plans to wait until the expiration date before considering whether to exercise the options. Of course, it will exercise the options at that time only if it is feasible to do so. In the following

table, fill in the net profit (or loss) per unit to LSU Corporation based on the listed possible spot rates of the mark that may exist on the expiration date.

Possible spot rate of the mark on the expiration date	Net profit (or loss) per unit to LSU Corporation if that spot rate occurs
$.56	
.58	
.60	
.62	
.65	
.67	

22. Auburn Company purchases Swiss franc put options for speculative purposes. Each option was purchased for a premium of $.02 per unit, with an exercise price of $.66 per unit. Auburn Company would purchase the francs just before it exercises the options (if it is feasible to exercise the options). It plans to wait until the expiration date before considering whether to exercise the options. In the following table, fill in the net profit (or loss) per unit to Auburn Company based on the listed possible spot rates of the franc that may exist on the expiration date.

Possible spot rate of the franc on the expiration date	Net profit (or loss) per unit to Auburn Company if that spot rate occurs
$.56	
.59	
.64	
.67	
.69	
.71	

23. Bama Corporation sold British pound call options for speculative purposes. The option premium was $.06 per unit and the exercise price was $1.58. Bama will purchase the pounds on the day the options are exercised (if the options are exercised) in order to fulfill its obligation. In the following table, fill in the net profit (or loss) to Bama Corporation if the listed spot rate exists at the time the purchaser of the call options considers exercising them.

Possible spot rate at the time the purchaser of call options considers exercising them	Net profit (or loss) per unit to Bama Corporation if that spot rate occurs
$1.53	
1.55	
1.57	
1.60	
1.62	
1.64	
1.68	

24. Bulldog Inc. sold French franc put options at a premium of $.01 per unit, and with an exercise price of $.16 per unit. It has forecasted the French franc's lowest level over the period of concern as shown in the following table. If that level occurs and the put options are exercised at that time, determine the net profit (or loss) per unit to Bulldog Inc.

Possible value of French franc	Net profit (or loss) to Bulldog Inc. if that value occurs
$.12	
.13	
.14	
.15	
.16	

25. A U.S. professional football team plans to play an exhibition game in the United Kingdom next year. Assume all expenses will be paid by the British government, and a check of 1 million pounds will be provided to the team. The team anticipates that the pound will depreciate substantially by the scheduled date of the game. In addition, the National Football League must approve the deal, and approval (or disapproval) will not occur for three months. How could the team hedge its position? What is there to lose by waiting three months to see if the exhibition game is approved before hedging?

Capital Crystal Inc.
Using Currency Futures and Options

Capital Crystal Inc. is a major importer of crystal from Germany. The crystal is sold to prestigious retail stores throughout the U.S. The imports are denominated in German marks (DM). Every year, Capital needs DM500 million. It is presently attempting to determine whether it should use currency futures or currency options to hedge imports three months from now, if it will hedge at all. The spot rate of the mark is $.60. A three month futures contract on the mark is available for $.59 per unit. A call option on the mark is available with a three-month expiration date and an exercise price of $.60. The premium to be paid on the call option is $.01 per unit.

Capital is very confident that the value of the mark will rise to at least $.62 in three months. It has been very accurate in its previous forecasts of the mark's value. The management style of Capital is very risk-averse. Managers receive a bonus at the end of the year if they satisfy minimal performance standards. The bonus is fixed, regardless of how high above the minimum level one's performance is. If performance is below the minimum, there is no bonus, and future advancement within the company is unlikely.

a) As a financial manager of Capital, you have been assigned the task of choosing among three possible strategies: (1) hedge the DM position by purchasing futures, (2) hedge the DM position by purchasing call options, or (3) do not hedge. Offer your recommendation and justify it.

b) Assume the previous information that was provided, except now assume that Capital revised its forecast of the mark to be worth $.57 three months from now. Given this revision, recommend whether Capital should (1) hedge the DM position by purchasing futures, (2) hedge the DM position by purchasing call options, or (3) not hedge. Justify your recommendation.

PROJECTS

1. Using recent quotes from *The Wall Street Journal*, select a currency call option with an expiration date that occurs before the end of your school term. On that date, assume you will either (1) exercise your call option and sell the currency in the spot market or (2) let the option expire. Just before the end of your school term, determine your net profit or loss from this strategy as a percentage of your initial investment (the premium you originally paid).

2. Repeat the preceding project using a currency put instead of a currency call option.

3. Look in a recent issue of *The Wall Street Journal* to find Japanese yen call options. For any single expiration date, assess the relationship between exercise prices and premiums. Explain that relationship.

4. Repeat the preceding project using puts rather than calls.

5. Look in a recent issue of *The Wall Street Journal* and compare the Japanese yen call options that are available with a specific exercise price. Assess the relationship between the remaining time to the expiration date and the premium. Explain the relationship.

6. Repeat the preceding project using puts instead of calls.

SUGGESTED READING

Market Perspectives is a monthly newsletter published by the Chicago Mercantile Exchange, 30 South Wacker Drive, Chicago, Illinois 60606. It offers continued updated information on innovative uses of currency futures and options.

REFERENCES

Adams, Paul and Steve Wyatt. "Biases in Option Prices: Evidence from the Foreign Currency Option Market." *Journal of Banking and Finance* (December 1987), pp. 549–562.

Agmon, Tamir and Rafael Eldon. "Currency Options Cope with Uncertainty." *Euromoney* (May 1983), pp. 227–28.

Biger, Nahum and John Hull. "The Valuation of Currency Options." *Financial Management* (Spring 1983), pp. 24–28.

Bodurtha, James and Georges Courtadon. "Tests of an American Option Pricing Model on the Foreign Currency Options Market." *Journal of Financial Quantitative Analysis* (June 1987), pp. 153–168.

Bodurtha, James N., Jr., and Georges R. Courtadon. "Efficiency Tests of the Foreign Currency Options Market." *Journal of Finance* (March 1986), pp. 151–162.

Carlozzi, Nicholas. "Exchange Rate Volatility: Is Intervention the Answer?" *Business Review*, Federal Reserve Bank of Philadelphia, (November–December 1983), pp. 3–10.

Chrystal, K. Alec. "A Guide to Foreign Exchange Markets." *Review*, Federal Reserve Bank of St. Louis, (March 1984), pp. 5–18.

Doukas, John and Abdul Rahman. "Unit Root Tests: Evidence from the Foreign Exchange Futures Market." *Journal of Financial and Quantitative Analysis* (March 1987), pp. 101–108.

Gendreau, Brian. "New Markets in Foreign Currency Options." *Business Review*, Federal Reserve Bank of Philadelphia, (July–August 1984), pp. 3–12.

Grammatikos, Theoharry. "Intervalling Effects and the Hedging Performance of Foreign Currency Futures." *Financial Review* (February 1986), pp. 21–36.

Goodman, Laurie S. "How to Trade in Currency Options." *Euromoney* (January 1983), pp. 73–74.

Hill, Joanne and Thomas Schneeweis. "The Hedging Effectiveness of Foreign Currency Futures." *Journal of Financial Research* (Spring 1982), pp. 95–104.

Hilliard Jimmy, Jeff Madura, and Alan L. Tucker. "Currency Option Pricing with Stochastic Domestic and Foreign Interest Rates." *Journal of Financial and Quantitative Analysis* forthcoming.

Johnson, Larry J. "Foreign-Currency Options, Ex Ante Exchange-Rate Volatility, and Market Efficiency: An Empirical Test." *Financial Review* (November 1986), pp. 433–450.

Madura, Jeff and E. Theodore Veit. "Use of Currency Options in International Cash Management." *Journal of Cash Management*, (January–February 1986), pp. 42–48.

Maldonado, Rita and Anthony Saunders. "Foreign Exchange Futures and the Law of One Price." *Financial Management* (Spring 1983), pp. 19–23.

Panton, Don B. and Maurice Joy. "Empirical Evidence on International Monetary Market Currency Futures." *Journal of International Business Studies* (Fall 1978), pp. 59–68.

Sender, Henny. "The New Case for Currency Options." *Institutional Investor* (January 1986), pp. 245–247.

Shastri, Kuldeep and Kishore Tandon. "Valuation of American Option on Foreign Currency." *Journal of Banking and Finance* (June 1987), pp. 245–269.

Shastri, Kuldeep, and Kishore Tandon. "Valuation of Foreign Currency Options: Some Empirical Tests." *Journal of Financial and Quantitative Analysis* (June 1986), pp. 145–160.

Shepard, Sidney A. "Forwards, Futures, and Currency Options As Foreign Exchange Risk Protection." *Canadian Banker* (December 1983), pp. 22–25.

Stein, Jerome L., Mark Rzepcznski, and Robert Selvaggio. "A Theoretical Explanation of the Empirical Studies of Futures Markets in Foreign Exchange and Financial Instruments." *Financial Review* (February 1983), pp. 1–32.

Thomas, Lee R. III. "A Winning Strategy for Currency-Futures Speculation." *Journal of Portfolio Management* (Fall 1985), pp. 65–70.

Tucker, Alan L. "Empirical Tests of the Efficiency of the Currency Option Market." *Journal of Financial Research* (Winter 1985), pp. 275–285.

APPENDIX 5

Using Currency Option Pricing Models

Pricing models have been developed to price currency options. Based on information about the option (such as the exercise price and time to maturity) and about the currency (such as its spot rate, standard deviation, and interest rate), pricing models can derive the premium on a currency option. The currency option pricing model of Biger and Hull (1983) is

$$c = e^{-r^*T}S \cdot N(d_1) - e^{-rT}X \cdot N(d_1 - \sigma\sqrt{T})$$

where

$d_1 = \{[\ln(S/X) + (r - r^* + (\sigma^2/2))T]/\sigma\sqrt{T}\}$
c = the price of the currency call option
S = the underlying spot exchange rate
X = the exercise price
r = the U.S. riskless rate of interest
r^* = the foreign riskless rate of interest
σ = the instantaneous standard deviation of the return on a holding of foreign currency
T = the time to option maturity expressed as a fraction of a year
$N(\cdot)$ = the standard normal cumulative distribution function.

This equation is based on the stock option pricing model (OPM) of Black and Scholes (1973), as extended by Merton (1973) for continuous dividends. Since the interest gained on holding a foreign security (r^*) is equivalent to a continuously paid dividend on a stock share, the Merton version of the OPM holds completely. The key transformation in adapting the stock OPM to value currency options is the substitution of exchange rates for stock prices. Thus, the percentage change of exchange rates is assumed to follow a diffusion process with constant mean and variance.

Bodurtha and Courtadon (1987) have tested the predictive ability of the currency option of the pricing model. They compute pricing errors from the model using 3,326 call options for the period of February 28, 1983 to September 21, 1983. The model's average percentage pricing error for all sample call options was −6.90 percent, which is smaller than the corresponding error reported for the dividend-adjusted Black-Scholes stock OPM. Hence, the currency option pricing model has been more accurate than the counterpart stock OPM used by Latane' and Rendleman (1976) and Beckers (1981).

The model developed by Biger and Hull is sometimes referred to as the European model because it does not account for early exercise. Yet, Bodurtha and Courtadon (1987) found that the application of an American currency options pricing model does not improve predictive accuracy. Their average percentage pricing error was −7.07 percent for all sample call options when using the American model.

Shastri and Tandon (1986) employ simulation analysis to demonstrate that the application of an American valuation formula does not systematically alter currency call options valuation. An early exercise, similar to that associated with discontinuous dividend payments on common stocks, should not be an important pricing factor.

Given all other parameters, the currency option pricing model can be used to impute the standard deviation σ. This implied parameter represents the option's market assessment of currency volatility over the life of the option. Such a volatility forecast likely is superior to alternative measures of exchange rate variability [see Scott and Tucker (1990)]. Following a procedure similar to that of Latane' and Rendleman (1976), the implied standard deviation can be determined using an optimization algorithm.

Exchange Rate Behavior

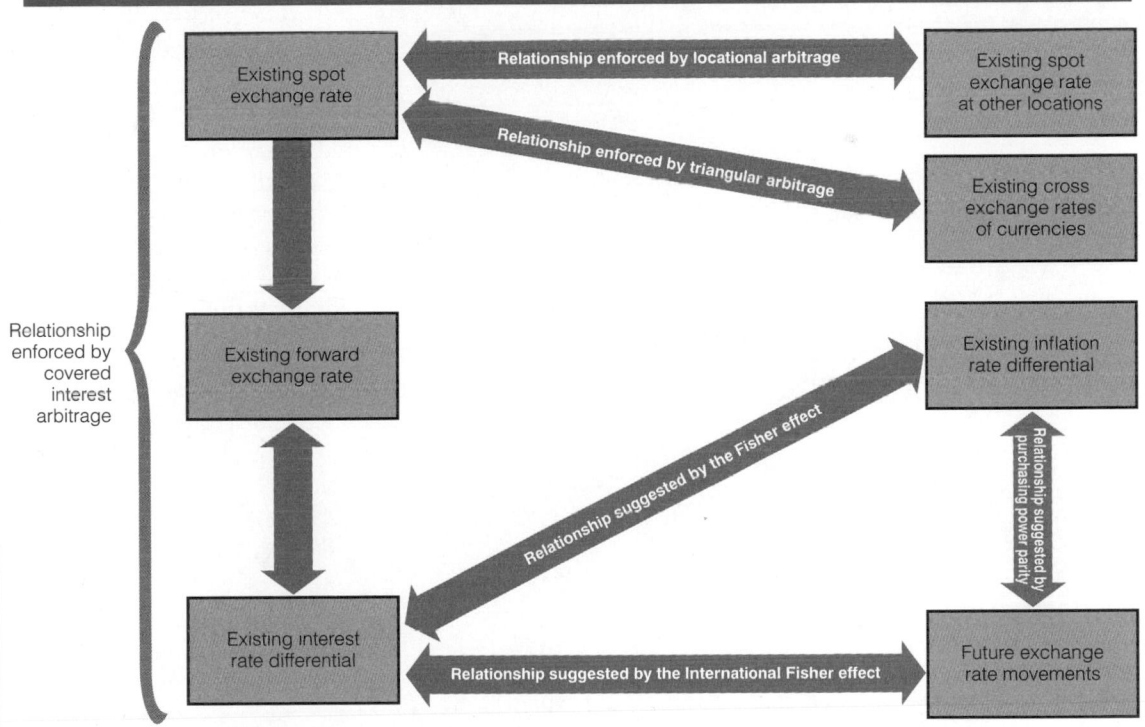

Part 2 (Chapters 6 through 8) focuses on critical relationships pertaining to exchange rates. Chapter 6 explains how governments can influence exchange rate movements and how such movements can affect economic conditions. Chapter 7 demonstrates why exchange rates are similar across locations and explores the relationships among foreign currencies. It also explains how the forward exchange rate is influenced by the differential between interest rates of any two countries. Chapter 8 discusses prominent theories regarding the impact of inflation on exchange rates, and the impact of interest rate movements on exchange rates.

Government Influence on Exchange Rates

This chapter describes the various types of exchange rate systems that have existed in recent years. It also explains how governments can intervene within the foreign exchange markets and affect exchange rates. In addition, the potential impact of fluctuating exchange rates on an economy is presented. The intent of this chapter is to emphasize how government policies can affect exchange rates, and how any change in exchange rates can influence a country's economy and financial markets. Because an MNC's performance is affected by both the economy and exchange rates, the concepts developed in this chapter are critical to managerial decisions by an MNC.

EXCHANGE RATE SYSTEMS

Exchange rate systems can be classified as

- Fixed
- Freely floating
- Managed float
- Pegged

Each of these exchange rate systems is discussed in turn.

Fixed Exchange Rate System

In a **fixed exchange rate** system, exchange rates are either held constant or are allowed to fluctuate only within very narrow boundaries. If an exchange rate begins to move too much, governments can intervene to maintain it within the boundaries. The methods used by governments to control exchange rates are mentioned later in this chapter.

From 1944 to 1971, exchange rates were typically fixed according to a system planned at the Bretton Woods conference (in Bretton Woods, New

Hampshire, 1944), by representatives from various countries. Because this arrangement, known as the **Bretton Woods Agreement,** lasted from 1944 to 1971, that period is sometimes referred to as the Bretton Woods era. Each currency was valued in terms of gold; for example, the U.S. dollar was valued as 1/35 ounce of gold. Since all currencies were valued in terms of gold, their values with respect to each other were fixed. Governments intervened in the foreign exchange markets to ensure that the exchange rate drifted no more than 1 percent above or below the initially set rate.

During the Bretton Woods era, the United States often experienced balance of trade deficits, which may imply that the dollar's value was too strong, since the use of dollars for foreign purchases exceeded the demand by foreign countries for dollar-denominated goods. By 1971 it appeared that some currency values would need to be adjusted in order to restore a more balanced flow of payments between countries. As of December 1971, a conference among representatives of various countries concluded with the **Smithsonian Agreement,** which called for a devaluation of the U.S. dollar by about 8 percent against other currencies. In addition, boundaries for the currency values were expanded to ±2.25 percent of the rates initially set by the agreement. However, international payments imbalances continued, and as of February 1973, the dollar was again devalued. By March 1973 most governments of the major countries were no longer attempting to maintain their home currency value within the boundaries established by the Smithsonian Agreement.

Under a fixed exchange rate environment, the managerial duties of an MNC are less difficult. However, there is still the risk that the government will alter the value of a specific currency. Currency devaluation can boost a country's exports, and therefore productivity (and jobs), since it encourages foreign consumers and firms to purchase goods denominated in that devalued currency. Revaluation (increasing the value) of a currency can increase competition that local firms receive from foreign firms, since foreign currencies can be purchased cheaply. Revaluation is a useful strategy by governments to restrain inflation since it may prevent local firms from substantially raising the prices of their products. Of course, not all currencies can be revalued or devalued simultaneously. If the U.S. dollar is, for example, devalued against other currencies, this implies the other currencies have been revalued against the U.S. dollar.

Freely Floating Exchange Rate System

In a **freely floating exchange rate system,** exchange rate values would be determined by market forces without intervention by various governments. Under such a system, MNCs would need to devote substantial resources to measuring and managing exposure to exchange rate fluctuations. In a fixed exchange rate system, there would be less worry about day-to-day fluctuations in exchange rates.

ADVANTAGES OF A FREELY FLOATING EXCHANGE RATE SYSTEM. From a macro viewpoint, where the stability of the entire world is concerned, a freely floating system could be preferable to a fixed exchange rate system. To illustrate, assume there are only two countries in the world: the United States and Great Britain. These countries trade frequently with each other.

Now assume a fixed exchange rate system. If the United States experiences a much higher inflation rate than Great Britain, we might expect U.S. consumers to buy more goods in Great Britain and British consumers to reduce their imports of U.S. goods (due to the high U.S. prices). This reaction would force U.S. production down and unemployment up. It could also cause higher inflation in Great Britain due to the excessive demand for British goods relative to the supply of British goods produced. In summary, high inflation in the United States could cause high inflation in Great Britain.

The results would not necessarily be the same in a freely floating exchange rate environment. As a consequence of high U.S. inflation, the increased U.S. demand for British goods would place upward pressure on the value of the British pound. As a second consequence of high U.S. inflation, the reduced British demand for U.S. goods would imply a reduced supply of pounds for sale (exchanged into dollars), which would also place upward pressure on the British pound value. The pound would appreciate due to these market forces (it would not be allowed to appreciate under the fixed-rate system). This appreciation would make British goods more expensive to the U.S. consumers—as expensive as U.S. goods even though British producers did not raise their prices. The higher prices would simply be due to the pound's appreciation, requiring a greater number of U.S. dollars to buy the same amount of pounds as before. In Great Britain, the actual price of the goods as measured in British pounds might possibly be unchanged. Even though U.S. prices increased, British consumers would continue to purchase U.S. goods because their pounds could be exchanged for more U.S. dollars (due to the British pound's appreciation against the U.S. dollar).

This discussion indicates that U.S. inflation will have a greater impact on inflation in other countries within a fixed exchange rate system as opposed to a floating exchange rate system. Problems experienced in one country will not necessarily be as contagious to other countries in a freely floating exchange rate environment. In our example, Great Britain was somewhat insulated from the U.S. inflation due to movement in the exchange rate.

Consider a second common economic problem—unemployment. Under a fixed-rate system, high U.S. unemployment will cause a reduction in U.S. income and a decline in U.S. purchases of British goods. Consequently, productivity in Great Britain might decrease and its unemployment rise. Under a floating-rate system, the decline in U.S. purchases of British goods would reflect a reduced U.S. demand for British pounds. Such a shift in demand could cause the pound to depreciate against the dollar (under the fixed-rate system, the pound would not be allowed to depreciate). The depreciation of the pound would make British goods look cheap to U.S. consumers, offsetting the possible reduction in demand for these goods that could result from a lower level of U.S. income. As was true with inflation, a sudden change in unemployment appears to be less influential on a foreign country under a floating-rate system than under a fixed-rate system.

An additional advantage of freely floating rates is that central banks are not required to constantly maintain exchange rates within specified boundaries. Therefore, they are not forced to implement an intervention policy that may have an unfavorable effect on the economy just to control exchange rates. Furthermore, governments can implement policies without concern as to whether the policies will maintain the exchange rates within specified boundaries. Finally, if exchange rates were not allowed to float, investors would invest funds in whatever country had the highest interest rate. This would likely cause governments in countries with low interest rates to restrict investor's funds from leaving the country. Thus, there would be more capital flow restrictions, and financial market efficiency would be reduced.

DISADVANTAGES OF A FREELY FLOATING EXCHANGE RATE SYSTEM.   In the previous examples, Great Britain was somewhat insulated from the problems experienced in the United States due to the freely floating exchange rate system. While this was an advantage in protecting one country (Great Britain), it can be a disadvantage to the country that initially experienced the economic problems. For instance, if the United States experiences high inflation, the dollar may weaken, thereby insulating Great Britain from the inflation as discussed earlier. However, from the U.S. perspective, a weaker U.S. dollar causes import prices to be higher. This can increase the price of U.S. materials and supplies, which will in turn increase U.S. prices of finished goods. In addition, higher foreign prices (from the U.S. perspective) can force U.S. consumers to purchase domestic products. As U.S. producers recognize their foreign competition has been reduced due to the weak dollar, they can more easily raise their prices without losing their customers to foreign competition.

As a second example, consider a situation where the U.S. unemployment rate is increasing. This tends to force the value of the dollar up as the demand for imports decreases. A stronger dollar will then reignite the desire for foreign goods, since they can be purchased cheaply. Yet, such a reaction can actually be detrimental to the United States during periods of high unemployment.

The preceding examples illustrate that a country's problems can sometimes be compounded by freely floating exchange rates. On the other hand, our earlier examples show that in a fixed exchange rate environment a country's problems are more contagious to other countries. Which system is more desirable may depend on a country's political environment, economic conditions, goals, and policies.

Managed-Float Exchange Rate System

The exchange rate system that exists today for some currencies lies somewhere between fixed and freely floating. It resembles the freely floating system in that exchange rates are allowed to fluctuate on a daily basis and official boundaries do not exist. Yet, it is similar to the fixed system in that governments can and sometimes do intervene to prevent their currency from moving too much in a certain direction. This type of system is known as a **managed float,** or "dirty" float (as opposed to a "clean" float where rates float freely without government intervention). The various forms of intervention used by governments to manage exchange rate movements are discussed later in this chapter.

CRITICISM OF A MANAGED-FLOAT SYSTEM.   Some critics suggest that a managed-float system allows a government to manipulate exchange rates in a manner that could benefit its own country at the expense of others. For example, a government may attempt to weaken its currency to stimulate a stagnant economy. The increased aggregate demand for products that results from such a policy may reflect a decreased aggregate demand for products in other countries, as the weakened currency attracts foreign demand. While this criticism is valid, it could apply as well to the fixed exchange rate system, where governments have the power to devalue their currency.

Pegged Exchange Rate System

A variety of exchange rate arrangements exist today. Each involves a policy of "pegging" a currency's value to another currency or to some unit of account. One of the most well-known **pegged exchange rate** arrangements was established by the European Economic Community (EEC) in April 1972, when EEC members determined that their currencies were to be maintained within established limits of each other. This arrangement became known as the **snake.** Market pressure caused some currencies to move outside their established limits. Consequently, some members withdrew from the snake arrangement; it was difficult to maintain, and some currencies were realigned.

Due to continued problems with the snake arrangement, the European Monetary System (EMS) was pushed into operation as of March 1979. The EMS concept is similar to the snake arrangement, but the specific characteristics differ. Under the EMS arrangement, exchange rates of member countries are held together within specified limits and are also tied to the European Currency Unit (ECU). The ECU is not a currency but simply a unit of account. It is a weighted average of exchange rates of the member countries, each weight determined by the member's relative gross national product and activity in intra-European trade. The currencies of these member countries can fluctuate by no more than 2.25 percent (6 percent for Italy) from the initially established par values. To prevent currency values from moving outside their established range, the central banks intervene within the foreign exchange markets. The actual process of central bank intervention is discussed in the following section. The "full" members of the EMS are Belgium, Denmark, France, Germany, Ireland, Italy, Luxembourg, and the Netherlands. Greece, Spain, and the United Kingdom have also signed the EMS Agreement but initially chose not to participate in this exchange rate system.

In October 1990 the United Kingdom agreed to join the exchange rate arrangement of the European Monetary System (EMS). Under the arrangement, the pound would be allowed to move by six percent in either direction from an exchange rate of 2.95 marks per pound.

The central rates of some currencies tied to the ECU have been realigned several times between 1986 and 1991. For example, in April 1986 the French franc was devalued against other currencies with the intention of increasing demand for French exports. In addition, the values of the German mark and Dutch guilder were increased against other currencies tied to the ECU. In January 1990 the Italian lira was devalued against the other currencies.

Each currency tied to the ECU is assigned a so-called **central exchange rate** with respect to the ECU. From these assigned rates, the central exchange rate between any two currencies can be determined. For example, assume that the central rates of the German mark and French franc with respect to the ECU are 6.90 and 2.06, respectively. Given this information, we can determine that the central rate between the German mark (DM) and French franc (FF) is

$$\begin{aligned}\frac{\text{Central rate of FF}}{\text{in units per DM}} &= \frac{\text{Central rate of FF in units per ECU}}{\text{Central rate of DM in units per ECU}}\\ &= \frac{6.90}{2.06}\\ &= 3.35\end{aligned}$$

Alternatively, the central rate of the mark in units per franc could have been determined by inverting the ratio shown here, which equals .298.

Given the central rate of two currencies, the upper and lower limits can be determined by applying the 2.25 percent range above and below the band. For example, the upper and lower limits of the French franc in units per mark is

$$\begin{aligned}\text{FF/DM upper limit} &= \text{Central rate} \times (1 + .0225)\\ &= 3.35 \times 1.0225\\ &= 3.425\end{aligned}$$

$$\begin{aligned}\text{FF/DM lower limit} &= \text{Central rate} \times (1 - .0225)\\ &= 3.35 \times .9775\\ &= 3.275\end{aligned}$$

If the exchange rate between the French franc and the German mark approaches either the lower or upper limit, central banks will intervene to maintain the exchange rate within these limits. If the central banks cannot maintain the exchange rate within the limits, they may realign the central rates of each currency with respect to the ECU.

IMPACT OF EXCHANGE RATE MOVEMENTS ON COUNTRIES WITH PEGGED CURRENCIES. To illustrate how a currency that is pegged to the U.S. dollar can be affected by other exchange rate movements, consider a world of three countries: (1) the United States, (2) a country called FLOAT whose currency fluctuates against the dollar, and (3) a country called PEG whose currency is pegged to the dollar. Assume that FLOAT's currency is presently valued at $.50 while PEG's currency is valued at $1.20. This implies that the cross exchange rate between FLOAT and PEG's currencies is 2.4 units of FLOAT's currency for each unit of PEG's currency (computed as $1.2/$.50 = 2.4). Assume that each country trades with the other two countries, and that some of the products traded are also produced in the other countries. Now assume that over the next six months, FLOAT's currency depreciates against the dollar and is worth only $.40 by the end of this six-month period. The most obvious result would be an increase in the U.S. demand for FLOAT's products, because FLOAT's products can be purchased with fewer dollars. In addition, there would be a decrease in FLOAT's demand for U.S. products, because these products cost more to FLOAT's firms and consumers. Yet, PEG's trade positions will also be affected as follows.

When FLOAT's currency depreciates against the dollar, it also depreciates against PEG's currency, since PEG's currency is pegged to the dollar. In this example, the cross rate would have changed to three units of FLOAT's currency for each unit of PEG's currency (computed as \$1.2/\$.40 = 3). This would cause FLOAT's consumers and firms to reduce their demand for PEG's products, and PEG's consumers and firms to increase their demand for FLOAT's products.

Even though the value of PEG's currency with respect to the U.S. dollar is unchanged, the trade between the U.S. and PEG will be affected. Because U.S. consumers and firms can purchase FLOAT's products with fewer dollars, they will substitute FLOAT's exports for PEG's exports. In addition, PEG's consumers and firms will substitute FLOAT's exports for U.S. exports, because the price they pay for FLOAT's exports has been reduced.

Overall, the depreciation of FLOAT's currency against the dollar (and therefore against PEG's currency) causes an increase in FLOAT's exports to the other two countries and a decrease in FLOAT's demand for imports from those countries. In addition, the volume of trade between the United States and PEG decreases. FLOAT's economy is stimulated by these actions.

The extent of these effects depends on how exporters and importers respond to the changes in purchasing power. If exporting firms in the United States and PEG reduce their prices to compensate for appreciation of their currencies against FLOAT's currency, FLOAT's export volume would not be affected as much. In addition, if reasonable substitutes are not available, the foreign demand for each country's products will not be affected as much by exchange rate movements.

If our example is revised to assume appreciation of FLOAT's currency against the U.S. dollar, the opposite effects would likely occur. The United States and PEG would increase their demand for each other's products and reduce their demand for FLOAT's products. FLOAT would increase demand for U.S. and PEG's products. In general, the economies of the U.S. and PEG would be stimulated by this event.

The validity of this theory can be reinforced with a realistic example. Because the Korean won is essentially pegged to the dollar, while the Japanese yen floats against the dollar, significant adjustments in international trade occurred during the dollar's decline in 1986. Japanese products became more expensive to U.S. importers (except when the Japanese firms would reduce the price to fully compensate for the weak dollar). Consequently, some U.S. importers switched to South Korean manufacturers of autos, steel, and videocassette recorders.

South Korea could be adversely affected during a strong-dollar period. Some U.S. importers may switch back to Japan when the dollar is stronger, since their relative purchasing power for Japanese imports would increase.

Classification of Exchange Rate Arrangements

Exhibit 6.1 categorizes exchange rate arrangements used by various countries. Several small countries peg their currency to the U.S. dollar, while others peg their currency to the French franc or a currency composite. The European countries that peg their currency to the ECU are listed under the heading "Cooperative arrangements."

The Mexican peso has a controlled exchange rate that applies to international trade and a floating market rate that applies to tourism. The floating market rate is influenced by central bank intervention. In November 1987 the

EXHIBIT 6.1 Exchange Rate Arrangements *(As of December 31, 1990)*

Currency Pegged to					Flexibility Limited in Terms of a Single Currency or Group of Currencies		More Flexible		
US Dollar	*French Franc*	*Other Currency*	*SDR*	*Other Composite*	*Single Currency*	*Cooperative Arrangements*	*Adjusted According to a Set of Indicators*	*Other Managed Floating*	*Independently Floating*
Afghanistan	Benin	Bhutan (Indian Rupee)	Burundi	Algeria	Bahrain	Belgium	Chile	China, P.R.	Argentina
Angola	Burkina Faso	Kiribati (Australian Dollar)	Iran, I. R. of	Austria	Qatar	Denmark	Colombia	Costa Rica	Australia
Antigua & Barbuda	Cameroon	Lesotho (South African Rand)	Libya	Bangladesh	Saudi Arabia	France	Madagascar	Ecuador	Bolivia
Bahamas, The	C. African Rep.	Swaziland (South African Rand)	Myanmar	Botswana	United Arab Emirates	Germany	Mozambique	Egypt	Brazil
Barbados	Chad	Tonga (Australian Dollar)	Rwanda	Bulgaria		Ireland	Zambia	Greece	Canada
Belize	Comoros	Yugoslavia (deutsche mark)	Seychelles	Cape Verde		Italy		Guinea	El Salvador
Djibouti	Congo			Cyprus		Luxembourg		Guinea-Bissau	Gambia, The
Dominica	Côte d'Ivoire			Czechoslovakia		Netherlands		Honduras	Ghana
Dominican Rep.	Equatorial Guinea			Fiji		Spain		India	Guatemala
Ethiopia	Gabon			Finland		United Kingdom		Indonesia	Jamaica
Grenada	Mali			Hungary				Korea	Japan
Guyana	Niger			Iceland				Lao P.D. Rep	Lebanon
Haiti	Senegal			Israel				Mauritania	Maldives
Iraq	Togo			Jordan				Mexico	Namibia
Liberia				Kenya				Nicaragua	New Zealand
Oman				Kuwait				Pakistan	Nigeria
Panama				Malawi				Portugal	Paraguay
St. Kitts & Nevis				Malaysia				Singapore	Peru
St. Lucia				Malta				Somalia	Philippines
St. Vincent and the Grenadines				Mauritius				Sri Lanka	Sierra Leone
Sudan				Morocco				Tunisia	South Africa
Suriname				Nepal				Turkey	United States
Syrian Arab Rep.				Norway				Viet Nam	Uruguay
Trinidad and Tobago				Papua New Guinea					Venezuela
Yemen, Republic of				Poland					Zaire
				Romania					
				Sao Tome & Principe					
				Solomon Islands					
				Sweden					
				Tanzania					
				Thailand					
				Uganda					
				Vanuatu					
				Western Samoa					
				Zimbabwe					

SOURCE: *International Financial Statistics* (March 1991).

Mexican central bank removed its support of the Mexican peso, and the peso's value declined by about 25 percent against the dollar in a single day. The exchange rate became so volatile that some banks refused to accept pesos in exchange for dollars.

CONSIDERATION OF A SINGLE EUROPEAN CURRENCY.   One of the issues involved in the efforts to integrate European business is the possibility of a common currency for all European countries. This issue has been temporarily put aside in favor of other goals deadlined for 1992, but it is likely to be revived in the near future. A single currency would encourage additional trade among countries because it would eliminate exchange rate risk, and would also alleviate foreign exchange transaction costs. However, there are some major barriers that could prevent the implementation of a single currency. For example, at what exchange rate would all currencies be cashed in to exchange for the single currency to be used? It would be difficult to reach agreement on this question for each European country's home currency. Also, some economists believe that changing exchange rates serve as a stabilizer for international trade. Thus, the lack of an exchange rate mechanism could possibly cause greater trade imbalances between countries.

An alternative approach would be to let each country continue to use its home currency for domestic purposes, but use a common unit of account, such as the European unit of account (ECU), for international trade. With this approach, the amount of a home currency convertible into the ECU would fluctuate within boundaries. Thus, exchange rate risk would not be eliminated.

GOVERNMENT INTERVENTION IN THE FOREIGN EXCHANGE MARKET

Each country has a government agency that may intervene in the foreign exchange markets to control a currency's value. In the United States, for example, the central bank is the Federal Reserve System (the Fed). Central banks have more duties than intervention in the foreign exchange market. They attempt to control the growth of money supply in their respective countries in a way that will favorably affect economic conditions.

Reasons for Foreign Exchange Intervention

The degree to which the home currency is controlled, or "managed," varies among central banks. Three common reasons for central banks to manage exchange rates are

- Smoothing exchange rate movements
- Establishing implicit exchange rate boundaries
- Reacting to temporary disturbances

If a central bank is concerned that its economy will be affected by abrupt movements in its home currency's value, it may attempt to smooth the currency movements over time. Its actions may keep business cycles less volatile, which is generally perceived favorably by a government. In addition, the smoothing may reduce fears in the financial markets and speculative activity that could cause a freefall in a currency's value.

Some central banks attempt to maintain their home currency rates within some unofficial, or implicit, boundaries. Analysts are commonly quoted in the paper as forecasting that a currency will not fall below or rise above a particular benchmark value because the central bank would intervene to prevent that.

The Federal Reserve periodically intervened between 1983 and 1985 in an attempt to reverse the U.S. dollar's upward momentum and from 1986 through the beginning of 1988 to reverse the dollar's downward momentum. This implies that the Fed may have established implicit boundaries for the dollar. Yet, even if boundaries did exist, they would likely be modified over time. A very weak or strong dollar would be more tolerable in some periods than in others.

In some cases, a central bank may intervene to insulate a currency's value from a temporary disturbance. For example, the news that oil prices will rise could cause expectations of a future decline in the Japanese yen value, since Japan exchanges yen for dollars to purchase oil from oil-exporting countries. Foreign exchange market speculators may exchange yen for dollars in anticipation of this decline. The Japanese government may therefore intervene to offset the immediate downward pressure on the yen caused by such market transactions.

Several studies, such as that by Trehan, have found that government intervention does not have a permanent impact on exchange rate movements. In many cases, intervention is overwhelmed by market forces. Central banks operate on the theory, however, that currency movements would be even more volatile in the absence of intervention.

Direct Intervention

The Fed's direct method of intervention to force dollar depreciation is to exchange dollars for other foreign currencies in the foreign exchange market. This so-called "flooding the market with dollars" places downward pressure on the dollar.

If the Fed desires to strengthen the dollar, it can obtain foreign currencies by engaging in currency swaps with other central banks. It then exchanges the foreign currencies obtained for dollars in the foreign exchange market, thereby placing upward pressure on the dollar.

Direct intervention is usually most effective when there is a coordinated effort among central banks. If all central banks simultaneously attempt to strengthen or weaken the dollar in the manner just described, they can exert greater pressure on the dollar's value.

EXAMPLES OF DIRECT INTERVENTION. Central bank intervention in the foreign exchange markets does not always achieve its objectives. For example, governments of Japan, Switzerland, the United States, and West Germany intervened in the foreign exchange markets in August 1983. Foreign exchange traders estimated that the four governments used between $1 billion and $2 billion of U.S. dollar reserves to purchase currencies such as the German mark, Swiss franc, and Japanese yen. However, the dollar weakened only slightly, and its decline was temporary. It resumed its climb shortly

INTERNATIONAL FINANCIAL MANAGEMENT IN PRACTICE

How to Stabilize the Dollar's Value

In February 1987, central banks of industrial countries agreed to stabilize the value of the U.S. dollar. As a result of this so-called **Louvre agreement** (discussed later in this chapter), the central banks have used a high degree of intervention in the foreign exchange markets. Throughout 1987 and the beginning of 1988, they used their respective home currencies to purchase U.S. dollars in the foreign exchange markets, causing a dramatic increase in their exchange reserves. West Germany's foreign exchange reserves, which averaged about $39 billion during 1980–1985, was $61 billion in October 1987. Japan's foreign exchange reserves, which averaged about $21 billion during 1980–85, was almost $67.5 billion in October 1987.

When the U.S. dollar rose over the summer of 1987, central banks intervened to slow the momentum by selling dollars in exchange for their home currencies. Without this temporary reversal of the U.S. dollar, foreign exchange reserves of central banks would have been even higher. A recent publication by the Federal Reserve Bank of San Francisco[1] suggested that dollar stability requires the following:

1. A coordinated effort among central banks to implement policies that reduce the U.S. balance of trade deficit; this involves a relative decrease in U.S. spending compared to foreign spending, and it can be achieved if more restrictive monetary and fiscal policies are used in the United States.

2. Financial assets in the United States must continue to be attractive to foreign investors to encourage financial flows into the United States and to discourage existing foreign investors from liquidating their current holdings of U.S. financial assets; a more restrictive monetary policy in the United States may be able to maintain U.S. interest rates at higher levels than in West Germany and Japan.

The future stability of the dollar may be tested if foreign economies experience higher inflation than desired. If central banks of foreign countries stimulate their economies as part of the Louvre agreement, they run the risk of igniting inflation. To use more restrictive policies to slow inflation, they will have to disregard the Louvre agreement and may be unable to stabilize the dollar's value.

[1]*FRBSF Weekly Letter*, February 19, 1988.

---

thereafter. In September 1984 the West German central bank sold off $750 million of its U.S. dollar reserves in an effort to weaken the dollar. Again, the effort failed. The high demand for U.S. dollars by corporations, speculators, and so forth was not offset by the central bank sales of U.S. dollar reserves.

In some cases, central bank intervention can have a very strong impact. As an example, in late February 1985 European central banks sold an estimated $1.5 billion in the foreign exchange market, causing the dollar's value to drop by more in one day than in any other day over the previous three and one-half years. However, even in cases like this where the impact of intervention is significant, it may be only temporary. Over a four-day period in late February 1985, the central banks of major countries spent well over $5 billion attempting to force the dollar's value down. Two days later, the dollar's value was about the same as just before the intervention.

In September 1985 the central banks of the United States, West Germany, Great Britain, France, and Japan implemented a coordinated program to weaken the dollar. The foreign exchange markets were flooded with billions of dollars as these central banks exchanged dollars for foreign currencies. This action added momentum to the dollar's fall.

Direct intervention was frequently used in 1986 and 1987 to strengthen the dollar. Yet, the dollar continued to weaken. Perhaps the dollar's decline during 1986 and 1987 would have been even greater if central banks had not intervened.

As the dollar strengthened in the summer of 1989, there was some concern by the industrialized countries that a stronger dollar could adversely affect the world economy. Five central banks intervened on September 14, 1989, precipitating an abrupt 2 percent decline in the dollar's value relative to the British pound and German mark. However, additional central bank intervention in the following month was overwhelmed by market transactions. With the growth in foreign exchange activity, central bank intervention is less effective. The volume of foreign exchange transactions on a single day exceeds the combined values of reserves at all central banks.

NONSTERILIZED VERSUS STERILIZED INTERVENTION.   When the Fed intervenes in the foreign exchange market without adjusting for the change in money supply, it is engaging in **nonsterilized intervention.** For example, if the Fed exchanges dollars for foreign currencies in the foreign exchange markets in an attempt to weaken the dollar, the money supply increases.

If the Fed desires to intervene in the foreign exchange market while retaining the dollar money supply, it uses **sterilized intervention,** achieved by simultaneous transactions in the foreign exchange markets and Treasury securities markets. For example, if the Fed desires to weaken the dollar without affecting the dollar money supply, it (1) exchanges dollars for foreign currencies, and (2) sells some of its existing Treasury securities for dollars. The net effect is an increase in investor's holdings of Treasury securities and a decrease in bank foreign currency balances.

SPECULATING ON DIRECT INTERVENTION.   Some traders in the foreign exchange market attempt to determine when Federal Reserve intervention is occurring, and the extent of the intervention, in order to capitalize on the anticipated results of the intervention effort. Normally, the Federal Reserve attempts to intervene without being noticed. However, dealers at the major banks that trade with the Fed often pass the information to other market participants. Also, when the Fed deals directly with numerous commercial banks, markets are well aware that the Fed is intervening. To hide its strategy, the Fed may pretend to be interested in selling dollars when it is actually buying dollars, or vice versa. It calls commercial banks and obtains both bid and ask quotes on currencies, so that the banks are not sure whether the Fed is considering purchases or sales of these currencies.

Intervention strategies vary among central banks. Some arrange for one large order when they intervene; others arrange several smaller orders, of the equivalent of $5 million to $10 million. Even if traders determine the extent of central bank intervention, they still cannot know with certainty the impact of that intervention on exchange rates.

Indirect Intervention through Government Policy

The Fed can affect the dollar's value indirectly by influencing the factors that affect it. For example, the Fed could attempt to lower interest rates in the United States to discourage foreign investors from investing in U.S. securities, thereby placing downward pressure on the value of the dollar. Or to boost the dollar's value, it could attempt to increase interest rates. It used this strategy in 1987, along with direct intervention in the foreign exchange market.

Recent research by Batten and Thornton has found that some changes in the Fed's discount rate caused a significant reaction in the foreign exchange markets. This suggests that foreign exchange market participants should monitor Fed actions so as to anticipate how those actions will affect the economic variables (such as market interest rates) that influence exchange rates. Just as market participants monitor direct intervention, they also should monitor indirect intervention.

As an example of how the foreign exchange market reacts to the indirect influence of the federal government, the dollar declined substantially on June 2, 1987, when it was announced that Paul Volcker would resign as chairman of the Fed. Volcker was known for his anti-inflationary efforts. Market participants anticipated higher U.S. inflation—and thus possible weakening of the dollar—because of his resignation. These expectations led to large sales of dollars in the foreign exchange market and an immediate decline in the dollar's value.

A good example of indirect intervention to influence exchange rate movements is the effort in Brazil to break the cycle between high inflation and the consistent depreciation in the Brazilian currency (the cruzado). In March 1990 Fernando Collar de Mello was elected president of Brazil. One of his immediate goals was to reduce inflation, which was averaging 70 percent per month. A primary reason for high inflation in Brazil was the lack of competition in some industries. He planned to increase competition with major changes in government policy. First, he planned to dismantle some large state-owned corporations in order to encourage competition in industries such as mining and steel. Second, he planned to reduce restrictions on imports. Third, he planned to reduce inflation by negotiating with businesses to limit wages and prices. He also wanted to reduce money supply growth in Brazil. With such high inflation in Brazil, direct intervention in foreign exchange markets is not likely to have a lasting impact. Therefore, de Mello's efforts to control an underlying cause of the cruzado's depreciation may be more effective.

Indirect Intervention through Government Barriers

A government can also indirectly affect exchange rates by imposing barriers on international trade and finance. For example, if the U.S. government desires to strengthen the dollar, it can impose taxes on any imported goods in order to discourage importing. This action will reduce the U.S. demand for

INTERNATIONAL FINANCIAL MANAGEMENT IN PRACTICE

Exchange Rate Intervention and Conflicts of Interest

In 1991, the Federal Reserve System was faced with an interesting dilemma. The dollar had weakened considerably against most other major currencies. The dollar's weakness was primarily attributed to low U.S. interest rates relative to foreign interest rates. In order to stimulate the sagging U.S. economy, the Federal Reserve had pushed interest rates lower with a loose monetary policy (including a decrease in its discount rate). Meanwhile, Bundesbank (the German central bank) had raised interest rates in Germany to halt any momentum in inflation caused by a strong economy. The changes in interest rates have caused some global investors to shift their investments from the U.S. to Germany. In February 1991, when the dollar reached an all-time low against the mark,

central banks used marks and other currencies to purchase U.S. dollars in the foreign exchange market. This attempt of direct intervention was overwhelmed by market forces resulting from interest rate differentials, which were partially attributed to the central banks. Thus the dollar continued to decline despite the direct intervention. The lesson from this example is that direct intervention in the foreign exchange market cannot usually offset exchange rate movements that are caused by economic conditions. The central banks would have been more successful in boosting the dollar's value if they raised U.S. interest rates and lowered foreign interest rates. Yet this would have conflicted with their initial objectives of stimulating the U.S. economy and slowing German inflation.

foreign currencies and place upward pressure on the dollar's value. As a second possibility, it can place quotas on imported goods to achieve the same result. Third, it can reduce or eliminate any taxes on any interest earned by foreign investors from investments in the United States, which will increase foreign demand for dollars to buy U.S. securities.

Several other barriers could be imposed by the federal government. Any barrier intended to strengthen the home currency would be imposed in order to either (1) induce an increase in the foreign demand for that currency or (2) discourage firms and consumers in the home country from exchanging the home currency for foreign currencies. Barriers to international trade and finance can also be imposed in order to weaken a home currency. For example, the U.S. government could heavily tax interest on U.S. securities purchased by foreign investors, thereby reducing foreign demand for dollar-denominated securities.

RETALIATION AGAINST GOVERNMENT BARRIERS FOR INDIRECT INTERVENTION.   One major problem with imposing barriers is that governments of foreign countries may be disturbed by these barriers and retaliate with their own. For example, consider a situation where the United States and Great Britain trade heavily with each other and both countries are experiencing a recession. The federal government for each country may desire to stimulate its local economy by weakening its home currency and increasing the foreign demand for domestic products. In its attempt to weaken the dollar value against the pound, the U.S. government, may, for example, place a tax on interest earned by British investors from U.S. securities. This action should reduce the British demand for U.S. dollars and therefore reduce the value of the dollar. However, the British government may attempt to prevent the pound from strengthening by imposing a tax on interest earned by U.S. investors on British securities. This action should reduce U.S. demand for pounds and therefore place downward pressure on the pound. Due to the competition between countries to reduce the value of their home currency (or at least prevent it from rising), both countries will probably be worse off. Moreover, barriers may lead to deteriorated relations between the two governments.

A PROPOSAL FOR EXCHANGE RATE TARGET ZONES

In recent years, many economists have criticized the present exchange rate system because of the wide swings in exchange rates of major currencies. Some have suggested that **target zones** be used for these currencies. A **central rate** would be established, with specific boundaries surrounding that rate (similar to the EMS). For example, the mark-dollar exchange rate might have a central rate of $.50 with boundaries of plus and minus 6 percent of that rate, resulting in an upper band of $.53 and a lower band of $.47. Such a target zone is similar to the bands used in the fixed exchange rate system, but a target-zone system would likely allow wider boundaries. Proponents of the target-zone system suggest that it would stabilize international trade patterns by reducing exchange rate volatility.

There are some complications involved in implementing a target-zone system. First, what central rate should be established for each country? Second, how wide should the target zone be? The ideal target zone allows exchange rates to adjust to economic factors without causing wide swings in international trade and fear in financial markets.

Some governments may not agree on the appropriate central rates. For example, the U.S. government would probably prefer that the Japanese yen be assigned a central rate more highly valued than the market rate in order to reduce the U.S. balance of trade deficit with Japan. However, Japan's government may prefer a lower value for the yen. In addition, some governments may prefer a much wider target zone than others.

If target zones were implemented, governments would be responsible for intervening to maintain their currencies within the zones. If the zones were sufficiently wide, government intervention would rarely be necessary; however, such wide zones would basically resemble the exchange rate system as it exists today. Governments tend to intervene when a currency's value moves outside some implicitly acceptable zone.

If the target zones were narrow, governments would be forced to intervene continuously, which in some cases, would interfere with other economic policies. For example, if target zones had existed in the early 1980s, the Federal Reserve would have been forced to intervene in the foreign exchange markets to weaken the dollar, which would have caused inflationary pressure. This strategy would have directly conflicted with the Fed's anti-inflationary policies implemented during this period.

RELATED RESEARCH

Will the Louvre Accord Result in More Stable Exchange Rates?

If the Louvre Accord signed in February 1987 is effective in stabilizing exchange rates, there should be a decline in the volatilities of exchange rates. Recent research has tested for this as follows. First, the variance of each exchange rate's movements was estimated for some major currencies in a period just before the accord and just after the accord. There was no significant difference in these variances.

As a second test, the market's anticipated volatility of each currency was measured before the accord versus after the accord. The implied standard deviation obtained from the currency option pricing model was used as a proxy for the market's anticipated volatility. While there were significant shifts in volatility, the shifts were negative for some currencies and positive for others. Overall, there was no discernible pattern. The results suggest that in general, actual and anticipated exchange rate volatility has not been reduced since the Louvre Accord. It appears that the market believes that coordinated central bank intervention will not stabilize foreign exchange markets.

SOURCE: Alan L. Tucker and Jeff Madura, "Impact of the Louvre on Actual and Anticipated Exchange Rate Volatility," *Journal of International Financial Markets, Institutions and Money*, 1990.

Unless governments could maintain a currency's value within the target zone, this system could not provide stability in international markets. A country experiencing a large balance of trade deficit might intentionally allow its currency to float below the lower boundary in order to stimulate foreign demand for its exports. Wide swings in international trade patterns could result. Furthermore, financial market prices would be more volatile because financial market participants would expect some currencies to move outside of their zones. The result would be a system no different than what exists today.

In February 1987 representatives of the United States, Japan, West Germany, France, Canada, Italy, and the United Kingdom (also known as the **Group of Seven** or **G-7 countries**) signed the Louvre Accord to establish acceptable ranges (not disclosed to the public) for the dollar's value relative to other currencies. There has been no confirmation that central banks will maintain exchange rates within some agreed upon ranges, nor on the length of time these ranges will apply.

IMPACT OF A GOVERNMENT DEFICIT ON EXCHANGE RATES

Up to this point, the chapter has focused on the government's ability to manipulate exchange rates by means of

■ Direct central bank intervention in the foreign exchange markets (the buying or selling of foreign currencies)

■ Government influence on other factors (interest rates, inflation, etc.), which will then influence exchange rates
■ Imposing barriers on foreign trade or investment to affect demand and supply conditions for a particular currency

All of these methods could be employed to intentionally influence exchange rate movements. The government may also unintentionally affect exchange rates. For example, when the budget deficit is large, the Treasury is forced to borrow heavily in financial markets, which places upward pressure on interest rates. Higher interest rates then attract foreign investment in U.S. securities, which increases the demand for dollars and therefore the value of the dollar.

One of the key issues before the 1984 U.S. presidential election was how the federal deficit was "choking" American farm exports and increasing farm imports. The deficit in the early 1980s is thought to be partially responsible for the higher interest rates in the United States relative to some other industrialized countries. The relatively high rates attracted a substantial amount of foreign investment into the United States, and placed upward pressure on the dollar's value. The strong dollar in the early 1980s discouraged foreign consumers from purchasing U.S. farm products and encouraged U.S. consumers to purchase foreign farm products.

From late 1985 through 1987, the dollar weakened even with the continued large U.S. deficit. In 1987, just three years after the government budget deficit was blamed for the strong dollar, it was blamed for the weak dollar. Some economists believed that a high level of government borrowing caused foreign investors to anticipate higher U.S. interest rates and thus sell their holdings of U.S. bonds (assuming that the market values of these bonds would decline once interest rates rose) and reinvest their funds in other countries. This reaction helped bring about the dollar's decline. In addition, the large budget deficit was thought by some economists to reflect lower tax rates on U.S. consumers and firms than appropriate. Consequently, they believe U.S. expenditures are excessive, and a portion of this spending is on foreign goods. This spending placed downward pressure on the dollar's value. Japan criticized the United States for this reason, in response to U.S. criticism that Japan's excessive restrictions on imports caused the dollar to be so weak.

Up to this point the emphasis has been on how the government can affect exchange rates. The following section focuses on how the adjusted exchange rates can affect the local economy.

EXCHANGE RATE ADJUSTMENT AS A GOVERNMENT POLICY TOOL

The federal government of any country can implement its own fiscal and monetary policies to control its economy. In addition, it may attempt to influence the value of its home currency in order to improve its economy, weakening its currency under some conditions and strengthening it under others. In essence, the exchange rate becomes a tool, like tax laws and money supply, by which the government can help achieve its desired economic objectives.

Before discussing when the government should weaken or strengthen its home currency, a review of how the currency's movements affect the economy is necessary. The expected effects of a weak home currency and strong home currency on economic conditions follow.

Influence of a Weak Home Currency on the Economy

A weak home currency can stimulate foreign demand for products. A weak dollar, for example, can substantially boost U.S. exports and U.S. jobs. In addition, it may also reduce U.S. imports.

While a weak currency can reduce unemployment at home, it can lead to higher inflation. For example, in the late 1970s the U.S. dollar was weak, causing U.S. imports from foreign countries to be highly priced. Domestic companies were therefore able to raise their prices since it was difficult for foreign producers to compete. A numerical example can illustrate what was happening. Consider two automobile producers, one from the United States and one from West Germany. Assume that a typical U.S. compact car sells for $10,000, and the typical compact German car of the same quality sells for 30,000 marks. Also, assume the German mark is worth $.333, so that three marks equal roughly one dollar. In this case, U.S. consumers can buy the German car for $10,000. If the German mark value appreciates to $.50 (so that two marks equal a U.S. dollar), it now takes $15,000 to exchange for the same 30,000 marks in order to purchase the German car. The U.S. car producer can more easily raise the price on its automobiles, without losing customers, since U.S. consumers can no longer afford the foreign cars. In the late 1970s, U.S. inflation may have been at least partially attributable to the reduced foreign competition that resulted from a weak U.S. dollar.

U.S. inflation was relatively low during the weak-dollar period of the mid-1980s, possibly because other economic factors such as low oil prices offset any upward pressure on U.S. prices exerted by the weak dollar. This illustrates how the potential inflationary impact of a weak dollar is dependent on other economic conditions.

Influence of a Strong Home Currency on the Economy

A strong home currency can encourage consumers and corporations of that home country to buy goods from other countries. This situation intensifies foreign competition and forces domestic producers to refrain from increasing prices. Therefore, we expect the country's overall inflation rate to be lower if its currency is strengthened, other things being equal.

While a strong currency is a possible cure for high inflation, it may cause higher unemployment due to the attractive foreign prices that result from a strong home currency. Reconsider the automobile example where the U.S. cars were originally priced at $10,000, the German cars were originally priced at 30,000 marks, and the exchange rate was one mark = $.333, or roughly three marks equal one U.S. dollar. Assume the U.S. dollar appreciated to be worth four marks (one mark would equal $.25). In this case, a German car priced at 30,000 marks could be purchased by U.S. consumers for $7,500 (computed as 30,000 marks divided by 4 marks per dollar equals $7,500). This is $2,500 *less* than the amount needed to purchase a U.S. car. While these circumstances will prevent the U.S. car producer from substantially increasing its price, it may also cause the U.S. car producer to impose layoffs, since most consumers would buy the foreign cars. The relatively high

RELATED RESEARCH

Impact of the Changing Dollar Value on Inflation

To empirically assess how the dollar affected any particular economic variable, a statistical model can be developed. For example, to assess how the dollar's value has affected U.S. inflation, the following regression model may be used:

$$\text{Percent change in } CPI_t = \begin{aligned} & a_0 + a_1(\%\triangle MS_{t-1}) \\ & + a_2(\%\triangle GNP_{t-1}) \\ & + a_3(\%\triangle ERI_{t-1}) + \mu_t \end{aligned}$$

where

$$CPI = \text{consumer price index}$$
$$MS = \text{money supply}$$
$$GNP = \text{gross national product}$$
$$ERI = \text{index of various exchange rates of foreign currencies relative to the dollar}$$
$$t = \text{time period}$$
$$a_0, a_1, a_2, a_3 = \text{regression coefficients}$$
$$\mu_t = \text{error term}$$

A suitable proxy for ERI is a trade-weighted index. The actual regression model used would vary among analysts with regard to the independent variables chosen and anticipated lag times. The model described here is simplified in that it specifies only three independent variables.

Applying regression analysis to historical data allows one to assess how U.S. inflation has been affected by changes in the dollar's value (by evaluating the regression coefficient a_3). The other variables were included to form a complete model, which assures more reliable estimates of the relationship between exchange rates and inflation.

Several studies have attempted to empirically measure the impact of exchange rate fluctuations on the price level. The results vary with the currencies and time horizon analyzed, and the type of methodology (see the article by Whitt, Koch, and Rosensweig for a summary of studies). In general, the studies have found that dollar depreciation has had a significant positive impact on the price level. Furthermore, recent research by Whitt, Koch, and Rosensweig[1] found the impact of the dollar's value on inflation is even greater than what many previous studies estimated.

[1] Joseph A. Whitt Jr., Paul D. Koch, and Jeffrey A. Rosensweig. "The Dollar and Prices: An Empirical Analysis," *Economic Review*, Federal Reserve Bank of Atlanta (October 1986): pp. 4–18.

unemployment in the United States during the 1981–1983 period may be partially attributable to the U.S. dollar's strength at that time.

To summarize, a weak currency can reduce unemployment but cause higher inflation, while a strong currency can reduce inflation but cause higher unemployment. The ideal value of the currency depends on the perspective of the country and the officials who are involved with these decisions. The strength or weakness of a currency is just one of many factors that influence a country's economic conditions.

Combining the preceding discussion of how exchange rates affect inflation with the discussion in Chapter 4 on how inflation can affect exchange rates, the dynamics of the exchange rate–inflation relationship are realized. A weak dollar places upward pressure on U.S. inflation, which in turn places further downward pressure on the value of the dollar. A strong dollar places down-

EXHIBIT 6.2 Impact of Government Actions on Exchange Rates

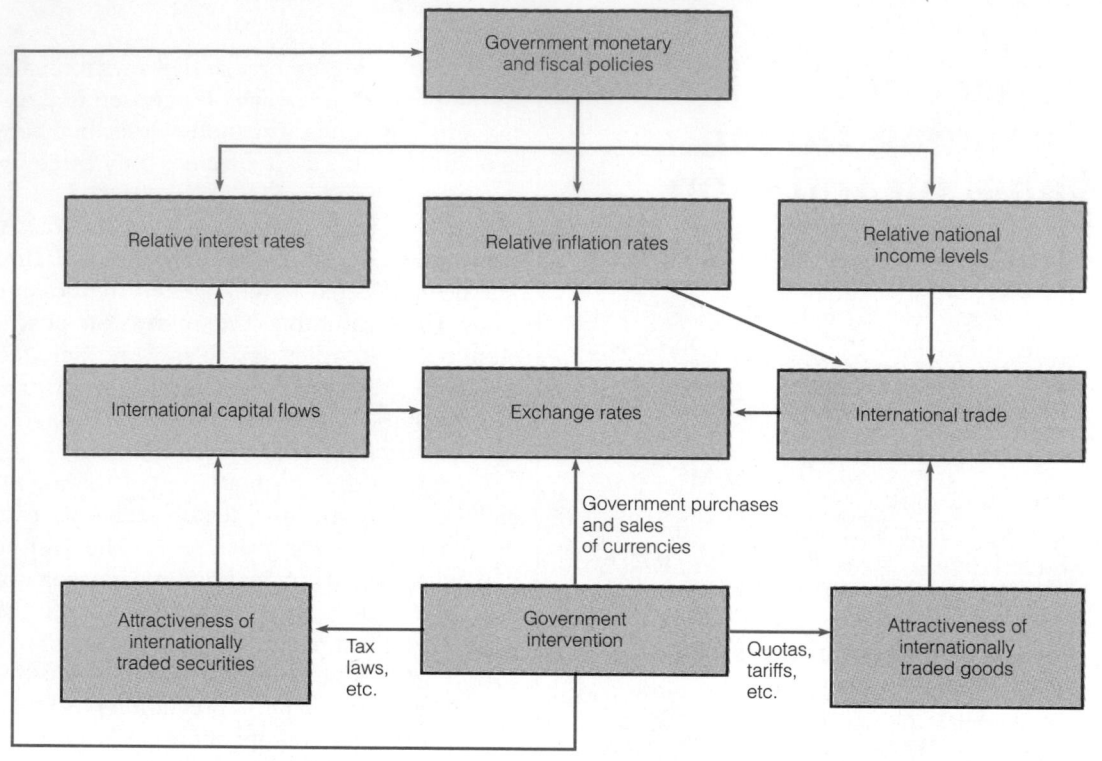

ward pressure on inflation and on U.S. economic growth, which in turn places further upward pressure on the dollar's value.

The interaction between exchange rates, government policies, and economic factors is illustrated in Exhibit 6.2. As already mentioned, factors other than the home currency's strength affect unemployment and/or inflation. Likewise, factors other than the unemployment or inflation level influence a currency's strength. The cycles that have been described here will often be interrupted by these other factors and therefore will not continue indefinitely.

INFLUENCE OF EXCHANGE RATES ON GOVERNMENT POLICY

While governments can affect exchange rates in many ways, exchange rates can also affect government policies. Sometimes governments attempt to guide exchange rates in a manner that will complement existing policies. For example, in the early 1980s the U.S. economy was stagnant, so the Fed effectively implemented a stimulative monetary policy. There was concern that such a policy could reignite inflation, but the strong dollar and low oil prices dampened inflationary pressures. If the dollar had been weak during this period, the Fed might have used a less stimulative monetary policy.

The status of the dollar can also affect fiscal policy. In general, a more stimulative fiscal policy should be used during a strong-dollar period (other things being equal), since a strong dollar curtails inflation. A less stimulative fiscal policy would likely be used during a weak-dollar period, since the weak dollar provides its own stimulus to the U.S. economy.

IMPACT OF THE DOLLAR'S VALUE ON SECURITY PRICES

Financial market participants closely monitor movements in the value of the dollar. Accordingly, dollar movements affect the value of securities traded in these markets. The specific impact is dependent on the type of security traded, but some generalizations can be made about the impact of the dollar on bond and stock prices.

Impact of the Dollar's Value on U.S. Bond Prices

To the extent that fluctuations in the dollar affect interest rates, they affect U.S. bond prices. Other things being equal, expectations of a weaker dollar are likely to increase inflationary expectations. Consequently, the demand for loanable funds increases, the supply of loanable funds decreases, and market interest rates rise. As the yields on existing bonds rise, bond prices decrease. Bondholders expecting dollar depreciation will be less willing to hold U.S. bonds, because the market values of bonds decline if a weaker dollar causes interest rates to increase. The result could be an immediate net sale of bonds, which would place further downward pressure on bond prices.

Impact of the Dollar's Value on Stock Prices

The dollar's value can affect stock prices for a variety of reasons. First, stock prices of U.S. companies may be affected by the actions of foreign investors who use U.S. stocks as a medium to earn speculative currency gains. Foreign investors attempt to purchase U.S. stocks when the dollar is weak and then sell the stocks when the dollar is strong. Thus, the foreign demand for any given U.S. stock may be higher when the dollar is expected to strengthen, other things being equal.

Stock prices are also affected by the impact of the dollar's changing value on cash flows. Stock prices of U.S. firms primarily involved in exporting could be favorably affected by a weak dollar and adversely affected by a strong dollar. Stock prices of U.S. importing firms could be affected in the opposite manner.

Stock prices of U.S. companies may also be affected by exchange rates if stock market participants measure performance by reported earnings. An MNC's consolidated reported earnings would be affected by exchange rate fluctuations even if its cash flows were not affected. A weaker dollar tends to inflate the reported earnings of a U.S.-based MNC's foreign subsidiaries. Some analysts would argue that any effect of exchange rate movements on financial statements is irrelevant unless cash flows are also affected. This issue is discussed in Chapter 10.

Another way the changing value of the dollar can affect stock prices is by influencing expectations of economic factors that influence the firm's performance. For example, if a weak dollar stimulates the U.S. economy, it may enhance a U.S. firm whose sales are dependent on the U.S. economy. A strong dollar could adversely affect such a firm if it dampens U.S. economic growth.

Since inflation affects some firms, a weak dollar value could indirectly affect a firm's stock by placing upward pressure on inflation. A strong dollar would have the opposite indirect impact on a given firm, because it places downward pressure on inflation.

Expectations about the dollar could affect stock prices by influencing interest rates as well. Holding other things equal, expectations of a weak dollar may cause a decrease in capital flows to the United States and therefore place upward pressure on interest rates. As mentioned earlier, a weak dollar may also ignite inflationary fears, thereby placing upward pressure on interest rates. Expectations of a strong dollar may cause a net increase in capital flows to the United States and therefore place downward pressure on interest rates (other things being equal). The expected impact of a given interest rate forecast on U.S. firms will vary because of their different financial characteristics.

In summary, the effect of expectations about the dollar's value on a company's stock value is dependent on

- The degree of exporting or importing conducted
- The composition of export and import markets
- The availability of export or import substitutes
- The degree to which the company hedges its anticipated cash flows against exchange rate movements
- The relative amount of sales and earnings generated by subsidiaries in foreign countries
- The locational composition of subsidiaries
- The company's exposure to economic factors, such as inflation or interest rates

Some companies attempt to insulate the exposure of their stock price to the changing value of the dollar, while other companies purposely remain exposed with the intent to benefit from it.

SUMMARY

The existence of floating exchange rates can better insulate a particular country from problems experienced by other countries. Yet, floating rates complicate financial management practices of a multinational corporation. Future exchange rates become an uncertain rather than known variable in a floating-rate system. Thus, the accuracy of financial projections for all corporate operations depends on the ability to assess future exchange rates.

When a multinational corporation assesses future exchange rates, it needs to consider potential government policies and how these policies (as well as other factors) might affect exchange rates. It is only at this point that the corporation can then assess how the potential movement in exchange rates will affect its financial operations.

Governments can attempt to affect exchange rates in order to influence economic conditions. A weak home currency can stimulate the home country's economy. However, it also tends to place upward pressure on inflation. Conversely, a strong home currency can dampen inflation. Yet, it can lead to higher domestic unemployment.

QUESTIONS

1. Compare and contrast the fixed, freely floating, and managed-float exchange rate systems.

2. What are some advantages and disadvantages of a freely floating exchange rate system versus a fixed exchange rate system?

3. Describe the background of the European Monetary System.

4. How can central banks use direct intervention to change the value of a currency?

5. How can a central bank use indirect intervention to change the value of a currency?

6. How can the U.S. government impose trade barriers to affect the value of the dollar? Why is the effectiveness of this strategy limited?

7. A linkage between the U.S. budget deficit, dollar value, and unemployment level has been proposed in this chapter. Discuss this linkage.

8. What is the impact of a weak home currency on the home economy, other things being equal?

9. What is the impact of a strong home currency on the home economy, other things being equal?

10. Explain the potential feedback effects of a currency's changing value on inflation.

11. Explain why a central bank may desire to smooth exchange rate movements.

12. Explain the Fed's intervention policy in the early 1980s, in 1985, and in 1987.

13. Has the Fed intervened in the foreign exchange markets in the last few months? If so, why? (Use any publicly available information to answer this question.)

14. Why do foreign market participants attempt to monitor the Fed's direct intervention efforts? How does the Fed attempt to hide its intervention actions?

15. Assume that the central rate of the Danish krone is set at 7.85212 units per ECU, and the Dutch guilder is set at 2.31943 units per ECU. What is the central rate of the Danish krone in units per Dutch guilder? Given boundaries of 2.25 percent above and below the central rate, determine the boundaries for the exchange rate between the Danish krone and Dutch guilder.

16. Develop a model that could be used to assess the historical influence of the dollar's value on inflation. Explain how your model estimates the sensitivity of price movements to movements in the dollar's value.

17. Assume the United States trades with Country E and places a strict quota on goods imported by the United States. Country E retaliates by placing a strict quota on goods imported from the United States. What response (increase, decrease, or indeterminate) should we expect in the U.S. demand for Currency E? In the supply of Currency E for sale? In the exchange rate of Currency E against the U.S. dollar? Assume that all other factors remained constant during the period of concern.

18. Assume that the currency of South Korea is tied to the dollar. How would the following trade patterns be affected by the dollar's depreciation against the Japanese yen: (a) South Korean exports to Japan and (b) South Korean exports to the United States. Explain.

19. It is often suggested that expectations of a weak dollar can reduce bond prices, other things being equal. Explain why such a relationship may exist.

20. If you anticipated that the U.S. dollar's value would decline over time, would you prefer to purchase stocks of U.S. companies that (a) were heavily involved in exporting, (b) were heavily involved in importing, or (c) had no international transactions? Explain.

21. The stock price of Hoosier Company is highly positively correlated with the general strength of the U.S. economy. Hoosier conducts no international transactions. However, its stock is significantly affected by the changing value of the dollar. Do you think its stock price movements are positively or negatively related to the dollar's value? Explain.

22. When it was announced on June 2, 1987, that Paul Volcker would resign as chairman of the Federal Reserve, the dollar weakened substantially. Why?

23. It has often been stated that the Fed is more willing to use a stimulative monetary policy on a stagnant economy if the dollar is relatively strong at that time. Why?

24. Explain the meaning of target zones and how they would be implemented. What are their limitations?

25. Explain the difference between sterilized and nonsterilized intervention.

26. Assume there is concern that the United States may experience a recession. Provide recommendations to the Federal Reserve regarding how it should attempt to directly influence the dollar to prevent a recession. How might U.S. exporters react to this policy? (Favorably or unfavorably?) What about U.S. importing firms?

Hull Importing Company
Effects of Pegging the Pound to the ECU

Hull Importing Company is a U.S.-based firm that imports small gift items and sells them to retail gift shops across the U.S. About half of the value of Hull's purchases come from the United Kingdom, while the remaining purchases are from Germany. The imported goods are denominated in the currency of the country where they are produced. Hull normally does not hedge its purchases.

Throughout the 1980s, the German mark (along with other European currencies) was tied to the European Currency Unit through the European Monetary System. The mark's value with respect to the ECU was essentially pegged and could only move within narrow boundaries. Conversely, the United Kingdom had not participated in this arrangement in the 1980s so that the pound's value with respect to the ECU varied substantially.

In previous years, the mark and pound had fluctuated substantially against the dollar (although not by the same degree). Hull's expenses were directly tied to these currency values because all of its products were imported. It had been successful because the imported gift items were somewhat unique and were attractive to U.S. consumers. However, Hull was unable to simply pass on higher costs (due to a weaker dollar) to its consumers, because consumers would switch to different gift items sold at other stores.

a) Hull wanted to assess how the United Kingdom's pegging of the pound to the ECU would affect the variability of its profits over time. Assume that the value of the ECU and the pound have exhibited about the same degree of volatility in their movements against the dollar, although their movements were different. Offer any insight on how Hull's variability of profits may change.

b) Hull used to closely monitor government intervention by Bundesbank (the German central bank) on the value of the mark. Assume that during the 1990s, Bundesbank intervenes to strengthen the mark's value with respect to the dollar by five percent. Would this have a favorable or unfavorable effect on Hull's business? Would this have a larger or smaller effect on Hull's business in the 1990s than in the 1980s (when the pound's value was not tied to the ECU)? Explain.

1. Review *The Wall Street Journal* for the last five days (ignoring the weekend). Summarize any central bank intervention in the table below.

PROJECT

	Identify the central banks that intervened	Was the intervention intended to strengthen or weaken the dollar?	Describe movements of the dollar on that day
One day ago			
Two days ago			
Three days ago			
Four days ago			
Five days ago			

SUGGESTED READING

"Treasury and Federal Reserve Foreign Exchange Operations," is a report contained in issues of the *FRBNY Quarterly Review*. It provides a clear description of information the Federal Reserve considers when deciding whether to intervene in the foreign exchange markets. It also describes recent interventions by the Fed.

REFERENCES

Batten, Dallas S., and Mack Ott. "Five Common Myths About Floating Exchange Rates." *Review*, Federal Reserve Bank of St. Louis (November 1983), pp. 5–15.

Batten, Dallas S., and Mack Ott. "What Can Central Banks Do About the Value of the Dollar?" *Review*, Federal Reserve Bank of St. Louis (May 1984), pp. 16–26.

Batten, Dallas S., and Daniel L. Thornton. "Discount Rate Changes and the Foreign Exchange Market." *Journal of International Money and Finance* (December 1984), pp. 279–92.

Batten, Dallas S., and Daniel L. Thornton. "The Discount Rate, Interest Rates and Foreign Exchange Rates: An Analysis With Daily Data." *Review*, Federal Reserve Bank of St. Louis (February 1985), pp. 22–30.

Bergstrand, Jeffrey H. "Selected Views of Exchange Rate Determination after a Decade of 'Floating,' " *New England Economic Review*, Federal Reserve Bank of Boston (May–June 1983), pp. 14–29.

Burns, Arthur F. "The Need for Order in International Finance." *Columbia Journal of World Business* (Spring 1977), pp. 5–17.

Carlozzi, Nicholas. "Exchange Rate Volatility: Is Intervention the Answer?" *Business Review*, Federal Reserve Bank of Philadelphia (November–December 1983), pp. 3–10.

Friedman Milton, and Robert V. Roosa. "Free versus Fixed Exchange Rates: A Debate." *Journal of Portfolio Management* (Spring 1977), pp. 68–73.

Genberg, Hans. "Effects of Central Bank Intervention in the Foreign Exchange Market." *International Monetary Fund Staff Papers* (September 1981), pp. 451–76.

Glick, Reuven. "ECU, Who?" *FRBSF Weekly Letter*, January 9, 1987.

Humpage, Owen F. "Should We Intervene in Exchange Markets?" *Economic Commentary*, Federal Reserve Bank of Cleveland, February 1, 1987.

Humpage, Owen F. and Nicholas V. Karamouzis. "Target Zones for Exchange Rates?" *Economic Commentary*, Federal Reserve Bank of Cleveland, August 1, 1986.

Kahn, George A. "International Policy Coordination in an Interdependent World." *Economic Review*, Federal Reserve Bank of Kansas City (March 1987), pp. 14–32.

Karamouzis, Nicholas V. "Lessons From the European Monetary System." *Economic Commentary*, Federal Reserve Bank of Cleveland, August 15, 1987.

Madura, Jeff. "Reactions of Foreign Exchange Markets to Discount Rate Adjustments." *Economic Planning* (March–April 1984), pp. 9–11.

McKinnon, Ronald I. "Currency Substitution and Instability in the World Dollar Standard." *American Economic Review* (June 1982), pp. 320–333.

McKinnon, Ronald I. "Dollar Stabilization and American Monetary Policy." *American Economic Review* (May 1980), pp. 382–87.

Miles, Marc A. "The Effects of Devaluation in the Trade Balance and the Balance of Payments: Some New Results." *Journal of Political Economy* (June 1979), pp. 600–620.

Rogoff, Kenneth. "On the Effects of Sterilized Intervention: An Analysis of Weekly Data." *Journal of Monetary Economics* (September 1984), pp. 133–150.

Teck, Alan. "International Business under Floating Rates." *Columbia Journal of World Business* (Fall 1976), pp. 60–71.

Trehan, Bharat. "The September G-5 Meeting and Its Impact." *FRBSF Weekly Letter*, December 13, 1985.

Weber, Warren E. "Do Sterilized Interventions Affect Exchange Rates?" *Quarterly Review*, Federal Bank of Minneapolis (Summer 1986), pp. 14–23.

Westerfield, Janice Moulton. "An Examination of Foreign Exchange Risk Under Fixed and Floating Regimes." *Journal of International Economics* (May 1977), pp. 181–200.

CHAPTER 7

International Arbitrage and Interest Rate Parity

If there are discrepancies within the foreign exchange market, in which quoted prices of currencies vary from what the market prices should be, certain market forces will realign the rates. The mechanics of this realignment take place as a result of international arbitrage. This chapter discusses three different types of international arbitrage. First, **locational arbitrage** can be attempted if foreign exchange rate quotations differ among locations. Second, **triangular arbitrage** can be attempted if a discrepancy among cross exchange rates exists. Finally, **covered interest arbitrage** can be attempted if the differential in interest rates between two countries is not appropriately reflected within the forward rate premium. Each type of arbitrage occurs due to spot or forward exchange rates that are undervalued or overvalued. The act of arbitrage creates market forces that alleviate any discrepancies that previously existed.

This chapter also discusses one of the most popular theories in international finance, **interest rate parity theory,** which specifies a relationship between the interest rate differential of two countries and the forward exchange rate between the home currencies of these countries. The linkage between covered interest arbitrage and interest rate parity is also introduced here. The main purpose of the chapter is to emphasize how arbitrage activities can ensure that spot and forward rates are priced as they should be in the foreign exchange market.

INTERNATIONAL ARBITRAGE

Arbitrage can be loosely defined as capitalizing on a discrepancy in quoted prices. In many cases, there is no investment of funds tied up for any length of time and no risk involved in the strategy. To illustrate, suppose two coin shops buy and sell coins. If Shop A is willing to sell a particular coin for $120, while Shop B is willing to buy that same coin for $130, a person can execute arbitrage by purchasing the coin at Shop A for $120 and selling it to Shop B for $130. The prices at coin shops can vary since demand conditions may vary among shop locations. If two coin shops are not aware of each other's prices, the opportunity for arbitrage may occur.

The act of arbitrage will cause prices to realign. In our example, arbitrage would cause Shop A to raise its price (due to high demand for the coin). At the same time, Shop B would reduce its bid price after receiving a surplus of coins as arbitrage occurs. The type of arbitrage discussed in this chapter is primarily international in scope; it is applied to foreign exchange and international money markets and takes three common forms:

- Locational arbitrage
- Triangular arbitrage
- Covered interest arbitrage

Each form will be discussed in turn.

Locational Arbitrage

Commercial banks providing foreign exchange services will normally quote about the same rates on currencies, so shopping around may not necessarily lead to a more favorable rate. If a particular currency is priced at substantially different rates among banks, reaction by market forces will force realignment in the following manner.

Consider two banks that buy and sell currencies. Initially, we shall ignore the bid/ask spread, and assume that the single rate quoted at Bank A for a British pound is $1.60, while the single rate quoted at Bank B is $1.61. If you had funds available, you could use them to buy pounds at Bank A for $1.60 per pound and then sell pounds at Bank B for $1.61 per pound. Under the condition there is no bid/ask spread and no other costs to conducting this arbitrage strategy, your gain would be $.01 per pound. The gain is risk-free in that you knew as you purchased pounds how much you could sell them for. Also, in this example you did not have to tie your funds up for any length of time. The term **locational arbitrage** implies capitalizing on the differential exchange rates between locations.

Since banks have a bid/ask spread on currencies, we will adjust our example to account for this spread. The information on British pounds at both banks is revised to include the bid/ask spread in Exhibit 7.1. The information in this exhibit shows that you can no longer profit from locational arbitrage. If you buy pounds from Bank A at $1.61 (the bank's ask price) and then sell the pounds at Bank B at their bid price of $1.61, you just break even. The point of this example is to demonstrate that even when the bid prices between two banks or the ask prices between two banks are different, this does

EXHIBIT 7.1   Currency Quotes for Locational-Arbitrage Example

	Bank A	Bank B
Bid price of British pounds	$1.60	$1.61
Ask price of British pounds	$1.61	$1.62

not guarantee that locational arbitrage will be possible. For you to achieve profits from locational arbitrage, the bid price of one bank must be higher than the ask price of another bank.

REALIGNMENT DUE TO LOCATIONAL ARBITRAGE. An example of where locational arbitrage is possible can be helpful in demonstrating how market forces will cause a realignment in the exchange rates of the banks. Examine the quotes for the German mark at two banks as shown in Exhibit 7.2. Information contained in Exhibit 7.2, shows that you can obtain marks from Bank C at the ask price of $.500 and then sell marks to Bank D at the bid price of $.505. This represents one "round-trip" transaction in locational arbitrage. If you started with $10,000 and conducted one round-trip transaction, how many U.S. dollars would you end up with? The $10,000 was initially exchanged for 20,000 marks ($10,000/$.50 per mark) at Bank C. Then the 20,000 marks were sold for $.505 each, for a total of $10,100. Thus, your gain from locational arbitrage was $100. This does not sound like much relative to your investment of $10,000. However, consider that you did not have to tie up your funds. Your round-trip transaction could take place over a telecommunications network within a matter of minutes. Also, if you could use a larger sum of money for the transaction, your gains would be larger. Finally, you could continue to repeat your round-trip transactions until Bank C's ask price is no longer less than Bank D's bid price.

Quoted prices will react to the locational-arbitrage strategy used by investors. Due to the high demand for marks at Bank C (resulting from arbitrage activity), a shortage of marks may soon develop there. As a result of this shortage, Bank C will raise its ask price for marks. The excess supply of marks at Bank D (resulting from sales of marks in exchange for U.S. dollars) will force Bank D to lower its bid price. As the currency prices are adjusted, gains from locational arbitrage will be reduced. Once the ask price of Bank C is not any lower than the bid price of Bank D, locational arbitrage will no longer occur. The time from which locational arbitrage occurred to the time at which prices adjusted may have been just a matter of minutes.

This discussion is not intended to make you believe you could pay for your education through part-time locational arbitrage. There are foreign exchange dealers who have computer terminals, comparing quotes from several banks, that will immediately signal to the dealer any opportunity to employ locational arbitrage. Thus, they will most likely beat you to the profits. The concept of locational arbitrage is relevant in that it explains why prices among banks at different locations will not normally differ by a significant amount. This not only applies to banks on the same street or within the same city, but to all banks across the world.

EXHIBIT 7.2   Currency Quotes for Second Locational-Arbitrage Example

	Bank C	Bank D
Bid price of German marks	$.495	$.505
Ask price of German marks	$.500	$.510

Triangular Arbitrage

Foreign exchange quotations are typically expressed in U.S. dollars, regardless of the country where the quote is provided. Yet, there are many instances where the U.S. dollar is not part of the foreign exchange transaction. **Cross exchange rates** are used to determine the relationship between two non-dollar currencies.

Given two non-dollar currencies called X and Y, the value of X relative to Y is

$$\text{Value of X relative to Y} = \frac{\text{Value of X}}{\text{Value of Y}}$$

For example, if the British pound is worth $1.50, while the German mark is worth $.50, the value of the British pound with respect to the mark is

$$\text{Value of pound with respect to DM} = \$1.50/\$.50 = 3$$

The value of the mark with respect to the pound could also have been determined from the cross exchange rate formula

$$\text{Value of DM with respect to the pound} = \$.50/\$1.50 = .33$$

Notice that the value of a mark with respect to the pound is simply the reciprocal of the value of a pound with respect to the mark. If a quoted cross exchange rate differs from the appropriate cross exchange rate (as determined by the preceding formula), triangular arbitrage is feasible (assuming no transaction costs).

The following example will be simplified by assuming that the bid and ask prices for a bank are the same (i.e., there is no bid/ask spread). Assume that a bank has quoted the British pound at $2.00, the French franc at $.20, and the cross exchange rate at 1 British pound = 11 French francs. Your first task is to use the pound value in U.S. dollars and franc value in U.S. dollars to develop the cross exchange rate that should exist between the pound and franc. The cross-rate formula discussed earlier reveals that the pound should be worth 10 francs. Yet the bank's rate is 1 pound = 11 francs. Thus, this bank is exchanging too many francs for a pound, and is asking for too many francs in exchange for a pound. Based on this information, you could buy pounds with U.S. dollars, convert the pounds to francs, and then sell the francs for U.S. dollars. This action represents **triangular arbitrage.** If you have $10,000, how many dollars will you end up with if you implement this triangular-arbitrage strategy? To answer the question, consider the following steps.

First, determine the number of pounds received for your dollars: $10,000 = 5,000 pounds based on the bank's quote of $2.00 per pound.

Second, determine how many francs you will receive in exchange for pounds: 5,000 pounds = 55,000 francs based on the bank's quote of 11 francs per pound.

Finally, determine how many U.S. dollars you will receive in exchange for the francs: 55,000 francs = $11,000 based on the bank's quote of $.20 per franc (5 francs to the dollar). The triangular-arbitrage strategy generated $11,000, which is $1,000 more than you started with.

Like locational arbitrage, triangular arbitrage does not tie up funds. Also, the strategy is risk-free since there is no uncertainty about the prices at which you will buy and sell the currencies. To make the scenario more realistic, however, consider the information in Exhibit 7.3, which discloses bid and ask rates quoted by a bank. Using Exhibit 7.3, you can determine whether triangular arbitrage is possible by starting with some fictitious amount (say $10,000) of U.S. dollars and figuring out the number of dollars you would end up with after implementing the strategy. The only difference between what is shown in Exhibit 7.3, and the previous example is that bid/ask spreads are now considered.

In the previous example, the triangular-arbitrage strategy suggested exchanging dollars for pounds, pounds for francs, and then francs for dollars. Relate this strategy to the information disclosed in Exhibit 7.3. If you start out with $10,000, that will be converted into 5,000 pounds (based on the bank's ask price of $2.00 per pound). Then the 5,000 pounds are converted into 54,000 francs (based on the bank's bid price for pounds of 10.8 francs per pound, 5,000 pounds × 10.8 = 54,000 francs). Next, the 54,000 francs are converted to $10,800 (based on the bank's bid price of $.200, 54,000 francs × $.200 = $10,800). The profit is $10,800 − $10,000 = $800. Any possible profit opportunities from triangular arbitrage should be only temporary as realignment in exchange rates occur, as explained below.

REALIGNMENT DUE TO TRIANGULAR ARBITRAGE. The realignment that results from the triangular-arbitrage activity is summarized in the second column of Exhibit 7.4. The realignment will likely occur quickly to prevent continued benefits from triangular arbitrage. The discrepancies assumed here are unlikely to occur within a single bank. A more likely case of triangular arbitrage would be three transactions at three separate banks.

Given three currencies, the exchange rate between each pair is displayed in Exhibit 7.5. If any two of these three exchange rates are known, the cross exchange rate of the third pair can be determined. When the actual cross exchange rate differs from the appropriate cross exchange rate, the exchange rates of the currencies are not in equilibrium. Triangular arbitrage would occur to push the exchange rates back into equilibrium.

EXHIBIT 7.3 Currency Quotes for a Triangular-Arbitrage Example

	Quoted Bid Price	Quoted Ask Price
Value of a British pound in U.S. dollars	$1.99	$2.00
Value of a French franc in U.S. dollars	$.200	$.201
Value of a British pound in French francs (FF)	FF10.8	FF11.0

EXHIBIT 7.4   Impact of Triangular-Arbitrage Example

Activity	Impact
1. Participants use dollars to purchase pounds.	Bank increases its ask price of pounds with respect to the dollar.
2. Participants use pounds to purchase French francs.	Bank reduces its bid price of the British pound with respect to the franc; that is, it reduces the number of francs to be exchanged per pound received.
3. Participants use French francs to purchase U.S. dollars.	Bank reduces its bid price of francs with respect to the dollar.

EXHIBIT 7.5   Relationship between Three Currencies

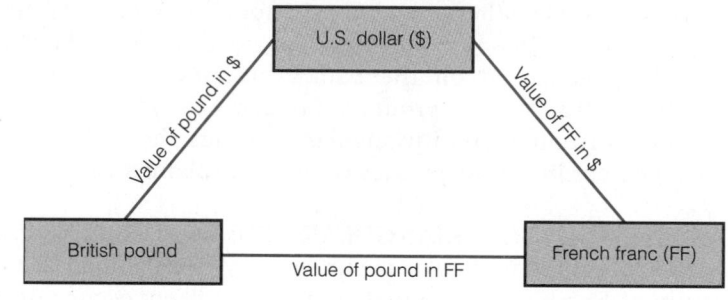

As with locational arbitrage, triangular arbitrage is not normally a strategy that most of us can take advantage of. This is especially true in light of the computer technology available to foreign exchange dealers that can easily detect misalignment in cross exchange rates. The point of this discussion is that because of triangular arbitrage, cross exchange rates are usually aligned correctly. If they are not, triangular arbitrage will take place until the rates are aligned correctly.

Covered Interest Arbitrage

Up to this point two types of arbitrage have been considered. Locational arbitrage forces any particular exchange rate to be similar among banks. Triangular arbitrage forces a quoted cross exchange rate to be appropriately priced. Another arbitrage concept called **covered interest arbitrage** tends to force a relationship between interest rates of two countries and their forward exchange rate premium or discount. Covered interest arbitrage involves investing in a foreign country and covering against exchange rate risk. Some of the literature in international finance specifies that the funds to be invested be borrowed locally. In this case, the investors are not tying up any of their own funds. Other research, however, such as that by Chrystal, does not make this specification. That is, the investors would use their own funds. In this case, the term arbitrage is loosely defined, since there is a positive dollar amount invested over a period of time. Our subsequent discussion is based on this latter meaning of covered interest arbitrage; yet, arbitrage by either interpretation should have a similar impact on currency values and interest rates.

To illustrate how covered interest arbitrage works, assume that you desire to capitalize on relatively high rates of interest in Great Britain, and you have funds available for 90 days. The interest rate is fixed; only the future exchange rate at which you will exchange pounds back to U.S. dollars is uncertain. A forward sale of pounds can be used to guarantee the rate at which you could exchange pounds for dollars at a future point in time. This actual strategy is as follows:

1. On Day 1, convert your U.S. dollars to pounds and set up a 90-day deposit account in a British bank.

2. On Day 1, engage in a forward contract to sell pounds 90 days forward.

3. In 90 days when the deposit matures, convert the pounds to U.S. dollars at the rate that was agreed upon in the forward contract.

The next example uses numbers to illustrate how this would work:

- You have $1,000,000 to invest.
- The current spot rate of the pound is $2.00.
- The 90-day forward rate of the pound is $2.00.
- The 90-day interest rate in the United States is 2 percent.
- The 90-day interest rate in Great Britain is 4 percent.

Based on this information, you could first convert the $1,000,000 to 500,000 pounds and deposit the 500,000 pounds in a British bank, then simultaneously set up a forward contract with a bank to sell it the pounds at $2.00 per pound. By the time the deposit matures, you will have 520,000 pounds. The spot rate of the pound at the time the deposit matures is no longer important, since you have already locked in the rate at which you can sell the pounds through the forward contract. Based on the assumed 90-day forward rate of 1 pound = $2.00, you can convert the 520,000 pounds for $1,040,000. This reflects a 4 percent return over the three-month period, which is 2 percent above the return on a U.S. deposit. In addition, the return on this foreign deposit was locked in, since you knew when you made the deposit exactly how much you would get back for the pounds you accumulated.

Recall that locational and triangular arbitrage did not tie up funds; thus, any profits were achieved almost instantaneously. In the case of covered interest arbitrage, the funds are tied up for a period of time (90 days in our example). This would not be a valuable strategy if it earned 2 percent or less, since you could have earned 2 percent on a domestic deposit. The term arbitrage here suggests that you can guarantee a return on your funds that exceeds the returns you could achieve domestically.

REALIGNMENT DUE TO COVERED INTEREST ARBITRAGE.   As with the other forms of arbitrage, market forces resulting from covered interest arbitrage will cause a market realignment. Once the realignment takes place, excess profits from arbitrage are no longer possible.

EXHIBIT 7.6 Impact of Covered-Interest-Arbitrage Example

Activity	Impact
1. Use dollars to purchase pounds in the spot market.	Upward pressure on the spot rate of the pound.
2. Engage in a forward contract to sell pounds forward.	Downward pressure on the forward rate of the pound.
3. Funds from the U.S. are invested in Great Britain.	Possible upward pressure on U.S. interest rates and downward pressure on British interest rates.

In the preceding discussion, four variables (pound spot rate, British interest rate, U.S. interest rate, and pound forward rate) could be affected by covered interest arbitrage. It is difficult to forecast the exact magnitude of each change. Yet, it should be clear that each change is reducing the excess return that was initially achieved from covered interest arbitrage.

The impact of covered interest arbitrage on the exchange rates and interest rates is summarized in Exhibit 7.6. If we assume no adjustment in interest rates, covered interest arbitrage would be feasible until the forward rate of the pound was sufficiently below the spot rate to offset the interest rate advantage. Given that the British interest rate is 2 percent above the U.S. interest rate, U.S. investors could benefit from covered interest arbitrage until the forward rate was about 2 percent less than the spot rate.

If interest rates change in response to the flow of funds into Great Britain, the interest rate differential would be reduced. Consequently, it would take a smaller differential between the spot and forward rate of the pound to offset the interest rate differential.

Assume that the exchange rates and interest rates changed as shown in Exhibit 7.7. With these new rates, covered interest arbitrage no longer provides a return to U.S. investors that is higher than the prevailing U.S. interest rate. This can be shown by computing the return earned from covered interest arbitrage, as follows (assume an initial investment of $1,000,000):

1. Convert $1,000,000 to pounds:

$$\$1,000,000/\$2.01 = £497,512$$

EXHIBIT 7.7 Adjustments in Exchange Rates and Interest Rates Due to Covered Interest Arbitrage

	Original Value	Value After Being Affected by Covered Interest Arbitrage
British pound spot rate in U.S. dollars	$2.00	$2.01
British pound 90-day forward rate in U.S. dollars	2.00	1.99
U.S. interest rate for 90 days	2%	2.47%
British interest rate for 90 days	4%	3.50%

2. Accumulated pounds over 90 days at 3.5 percent:

$$£497,512 \times 1.035 = £514,925$$

3. Reconvert pounds to dollars (at the forward rate of $1.99) after 90 days:

$$£514,925 \times \$1.99 = \$1,024,701$$

4. Yield earned from covered interest arbitrage:

$$(\$1,024,701 - \$1,000,000)/\$1,000,000 = .0247, \text{ or } 2.47\%$$

This example has shown that those individuals who initially conduct covered interest arbitrage cause exchange rates and interest rates to move in such a way that future attempts at covered interest arbitrage provide a return that is no better than what is possible domestically. At some point in the future, there may again be opportunities for excess profits through covered interest arbitrage. But as they are realized, the transactions from arbitrage will again affect exchange rates and interest rates such that further attempts at arbitrage are not feasible. Due to the market forces from covered interest arbitrage, a relationship between the forward rate premium and interest rate differentials should exist. This relationship is discussed in the following section.

INTEREST RATE PARITY

Once market forces cause the interest rates and exchange rates to be such that covered interest arbitrage is no longer feasible, we are in an equilibrium state referred to as **interest rate parity (IRP).** In equilibrium, the forward rate differs from the spot rate by a sufficient amount to offset the interest rate differential between two currencies. In our previous example, the U.S. investor receives a higher interest rate from the foreign investment, but there is an offsetting effect due to the investor paying more per unit of foreign currency (at the spot rate) than what is received per unit when the currency is sold forward (at the forward rate). Recall that when the forward rate is less than the spot rate, this implies the forward rate exhibits a discount.

The relationship between a forward premium (or discount) of a foreign currency and the interest rates representing these currencies according to IRP can be determined as follows. Consider a U.S. investor who attempts covered interest arbitrage. The return to a U.S. investor from using covered interest arbitrage can be determined given

■ The amount of the home currency (U.S. dollars in our example) initially invested (A_h)
■ The spot rate (S_j) when the foreign currency was purchased
■ The interest rate on the foreign deposit (i_j)
■ The forward rate at which the foreign currency will be converted back to U.S. dollars (F_j). The amount of the home currency received at the end of the deposit period due to such a strategy (called A_n) is

$$A_n = (A_h/S_j)(1 + i_j)F_j$$

Since F_j is simply S_j times one plus the forward premium (called p), we can rewrite this equation as

$$A_n = (A_h/S_j)(1 + i_j)[S_j(1 + p)]$$
$$= A_h(1 + i_j)(1 + p)$$

The rate of return from this investment (called r_j) is:

$$r_j = \frac{A_n - A_h}{A_h}$$

$$= \frac{[A_h(1 + i_j)(1 + p)] - A_h}{A_h}$$

$$= (1 + i_j)(1 + p) - 1$$

If interest rate parity exists, then the rate of return achieved from covered interest arbitrage (r_j) should be equal to the rate available in the home country. Set the rate that can be achieved from using covered interest arbitrage to the rate that can be achieved from an investment in the home country (the return on a home investment is simply the home interest rate called i_h):

$$r_j = i_h$$

By substituting into the formula how r_j is determined, we obtain

$$(1 + i_j)(1 + p) - 1 = i_h$$

By rearranging terms, we can find out what the forward premium of the foreign currency should be under conditions of interest rate parity:

$$(1 + i_j)(1 + p) - 1 = i_h$$

$$(1 + i_j)(1 + p) = (1 + i_h)$$

$$(1 + p) = \frac{(1 + i_h)}{(1 + i_j)}$$

$$p = \frac{(1 + i_h)}{(1 + i_j)} - 1$$

As an example, assume that the French franc exhibits a six-month interest rate of 6 percent, while the U.S. dollar exhibits a six-month interest rate of 5 percent. From a U.S. investor's perspective, the U.S. dollar is the home currency. According to IRP, the forward rate premium of the franc with respect to the U.S. dollar should be

$$p = \frac{(1 + .05)}{(1 + .06)} - 1$$

$$= -.0094, \text{ or } -.94\% \text{ (not annualized)}$$

Thus, the franc should exhibit a forward discount of about .94 percent. This implies that U.S. investors would receive .94 percent less when selling francs six months from now (based on a forward sale) than what they pay for francs today at the spot rate. Such a discount would offset the interest rate advantage of the franc. If the French franc's spot rate was $.10, a forward discount of .94 percent means that the six-month forward rate is

$$
\begin{aligned}
F_j &= S_j(1 + p) \\
&= \$.10(1 - .0094) \\
&= \$.09906
\end{aligned}
$$

The following numerical example will confirm that if interest rate parity exists, covered interest arbitrage will not be feasible. Use the previous information on the spot rate and six-month forward rate of the franc, as well as the French interest rate, to determine a U.S. investor's return from using covered interest arbitrage. Assume the investor begins with $1,000,000 to invest.

Step 1. On the first day, the U.S. investor converts $1,000,000 into francs at $.10 per franc:

$1,000,000/$.10 per franc = 10,000,000 francs

Step 2. On the first day, the U.S. investor also sells francs six months forward. The number of francs to be sold forward is the anticipated accumulation of francs over the six-month period, which is estimated as

10,000,000 francs × (1 + 6%) = 10,600,000 francs

Step 3. After six months, the U.S. investor withdraws the initial deposit of francs along with the accumulated interest amounting to 10,600,000 francs. The investor converts the francs into dollars in accordance with the forward contract agreed upon six months earlier. The forward rate was $.09906, so the number of U.S. dollars received from the conversion is

10,600,000 francs × ($.09906 per franc) = $1,050,036

Results. The act of covered interest arbitrage achieved a return of about 5 percent here. Rounding the forward discount at .94 percent caused the slight deviation from the 5 percent return.

The results suggest that using covered interest arbitrage generated a return that is about what the U.S. investors would have received anyway if they had simply invested their funds domestically. This confirms that covered interest arbitrage is not worthwhile if interest rate parity exists.

The relationship between the forward premium (or discount) and the interest rate differential according to interest rate parity is simplified in an approximated form as follows:

$$
p = \frac{F_j - S_j}{S_j} \approx i_h - i_j
$$

where

$$p = \text{forward premium (or discount)}$$
$$F_j = \text{forward rate}$$
$$S_j = \text{spot rate}$$
$$i_h = \text{home interest rate}$$
$$i_j = \text{foreign interest rate}$$

The variables in this equation are not annualized. In our example, the U.S. (home) interest rate was less than the foreign interest rate, so the forward rate contains a discount (the forward rate is less than the spot rate). The larger the degree by which the foreign interest rate exceeds the home interest rate, the larger will be the forward discount of the foreign currency specified by the IRP formula.

If the foreign interest rate is less than the home interest rate, the interest rate parity relationship suggests that the forward rate should exhibit a premium. There may be reason for investors to attempt covered interest arbitrage even if the home interest rate is more than the foreign interest rate. Consider a situation where the foreign interest rate is just slightly less than the home rate. In this case, interest rate parity would exist if the forward rate were just slightly larger than spot rate (exhibiting a slight premium). Then, what U.S. investors gained from the forward rate premium will be offset by the slightly lower interest rate. However, if the forward rate exhibited a large premium, the U.S. investor could achieve a higher return through covered interest arbitrage than what was possible domestically.

Graphic Analysis of Interest Rate Parity

We can examine the interest rate differential that exists and compare it to the forward premium (or discount) with the aid of a graph as shown in Exhibit 7.8. One could plot all the possible points that represent interest rate parity by using the approximation expressed earlier and plugging in numbers. For example, if the foreign interest rate (i_j) exceeds the home interest rate (i_h) by 1 percent ($i_h - i_j = -1\%$), then the forward rate should exhibit a discount of 1 percent. This is represented by point A on the graph. If the foreign interest rate exceeds the home rate by 2 percent, then the forward rate should exhibit a discount of 2 percent, as represented by point B on the graph, and so on. For cases where the foreign interest rate is less than the home interest rate, the forward rate should exhibit a premium approximately equal to that differential. For example, if the home interest rate exceeds the foreign rate by 1 percent ($i_h - i_j = 1\%$), then the forward premium should be 1 percent, as represented by point C. If the home interest rate exceeds the foreign rate by 2 percent ($i_h - i_j = 2\%$), then the forward premium should be 2 percent, as represented by point D, and so on. Any points lying on the diagonal line cutting the intersection of axes represent interest rate parity. For this reason, that diagonal line is referred to as the **interest rate parity (IRP) line.**

An individual or corporation could at any time examine all currencies to compare forward rate premiums (or discounts) to interest rate differentials. From a U.S. perspective, interest rates in Switzerland and Japan are typically lower than the home interest rates. Consequently, the forward rate of these currencies (Swiss franc and Japanese yen) will usually exhibit a premium.

Thus, we would expect these currencies to be represented by points such as
C or D or even above D along the diagonal line of Exhibit 7.8. Conversely,
countries such as Great Britain and France often have higher interest rates
than the United States, and their forward rates often exhibit a discount. Thus,
we would expect these currencies to be represented by points such as A or B.

Exhibit 7.8 can be used whether or not you annualize the rates, as long as
you are consistent. That is, if you annualize the interest rates to determine
the interest rate differential, you should also annualize the forward premium
or discount.

What if a three-month deposit represented by a foreign currency offers an
annualized interest rate of 10 percent versus an annualized interest rate of 7
percent in the home country? Such a scenario is represented on the graph by
$i_h - i_j - -3\%$. Also assume that the foreign currency exhibits an annualized
forward discount of 1 percent. The combined interest rate differential and
forward discount information can be represented by point X on the graph.
Since point X is not on the IRP line, we should expect that covered interest
arbitrage is beneficial for some investors. The investor attains 3 percent more
for the foreign deposit, and this advantage is only partially offset by the 1
percent forward discount.

Assume the annualized interest rate for the foreign currency is 5 percent
relative to 7 percent for the home country. The interest rate differential expressed on the graph is $i_h - i_j = 2\%$. However, assume the forward premium
of the foreign currency is 4 percent (point Y in Exhibit 7.8). Thus, what the
investor loses on the lower interest rate from the foreign investment is more
than made up by the high forward premium.

Shift to the left side of the IRP line. Take point Z, for example. This represents a foreign interest rate that exceeds the home interest rate by 1 per-

EXHIBIT 7.8   Illustration of Interest Rate Parity

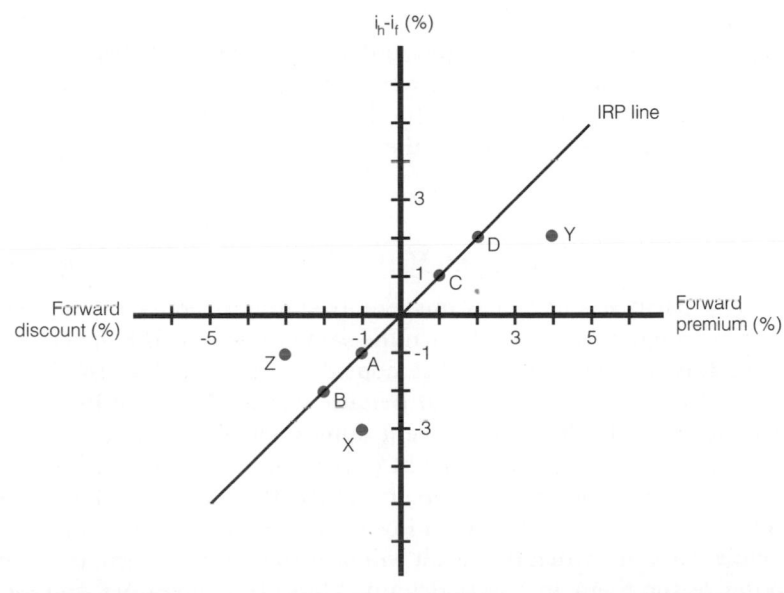

cent, while the forward rate exhibits a 3 percent discount. This point, like all points to the left on the interest rate parity line, represents a situation where a U.S. investor would achieve a lower return on a foreign investment than what is available domestically. The reason for this lower return is normally because either (1) the advantage of the foreign interest rate relative to the U.S. interest rate is more than offset by the forward rate discount (which reflects point Z), or (2) the degree by which the home interest rate exceeds the foreign rate more than offsets the forward rate premium.

However, for points such as these, covered interest arbitrage is feasible from the perspective of the foreign investors. Consider British investors in Great Britain where the interest rate is 1 percent higher than the U.S. interest rate, and the forward rate (with respect to the dollar) contains a 3 percent discount (as represented by point Z). British investors would sell their foreign currency in exchange for dollars, invest in dollar-denominated securities, and engage in a forward contract to purchase pounds forward. While they earn 1 percent less on a U.S. investment, they are able to purchase their home currency for 3 percent less than what they initially sold it for. This type of activity will place downward pressure on the spot rate of the pound and upward pressure on the pound's forward rate, until covered interest arbitrage is no longer feasible.

How to Test Whether Interest Rate Parity Exists

An investor or firm can plot all realistic points for various currencies on a graph such as Exhibit 7.8 to determine whether gains from covered interest arbitrage can be achieved. The location of the points provides an indication of whether covered interest arbitrage is worthwhile. For points to the right of the IRP line, investors in the home country should consider using covered interest arbitrage, since a return higher than the home interest rate (i_h) is achievable. Of course, as investors and firms take advantage of such opportunities, there will be a tendency for the point to move toward the IRP line. Covered interest arbitrage should continue until the IRP relationship holds.

The points to the left of the IRP line are not suitable for covered interest arbitrage by home-country investors but are suitable for foreign investors. Foreign investors would conduct covered interest arbitrage by purchasing and depositing the home currency (dollars in our example) while simultaneously selling dollars forward for the date at which the U.S. deposit matures.

Interpretation of Interest Rate Parity

Interest rate parity is sometimes mistakenly summarized as follows: "If IRP exists, then foreign investors will earn the same returns as U.S. investors." To prove that this statement is incorrect, consider two countries—the U.S. with a 10 percent interest rate, and Great Britain with a 14 percent interest rate. U.S. investors could achieve 10 percent domestically or attempt to use covered interest arbitrage. If they attempt covered interest arbitrage while IRP exists, then the result will be a 10 percent return, the same as that possible for them in the United States. If British investors attempt covered interest arbitrage while IRP exists, then the result will be a 14 percent return, the same as that possible for them in Great Britain. Thus, U.S. investors and British investors do *not* achieve the same nominal return here, even though IRP exists. An appropriate summary explanation of interest rate parity is that if interest rate parity exists, investors cannot use covered interest arbitrage to achieve higher returns than those achievable in their home country.

Does Interest Rate Parity Hold?

To correctly determine whether IRP holds, it is necessary to compare the forward rate (or discount) and interest rate quotations that occur at the same time. If the forward rate and interest rate quotations do not reflect the same time of day, then results could be somewhat distorted. Due to limitations in access to data, it is difficult to get quotations that reflect the same point in time. Consequently, the testing of whether IRP holds is subject to some error. Yet, that should not discourage attempts to determine whether IRP exists. Empirical examination of IRP has been conducted by Aliber, Branson, Frenkel and Levich, Stokes and Neuburger, and others. The actual relationship between the forward rate premium and interest rate differentials generally supports IRP. While there are deviations, they are often not large enough to make covered interest arbitrage worthwhile, as will now be discussed in more detail.

Other Considerations When Assessing Interest Rate Parity

If IRP does not hold, there is still the possibility that covered interest arbitrage is not worthwhile. This is due to potential costs that arise from foreign investments but not from domestic investments. Such costs could include transaction costs, currency restrictions, and differential tax laws.

If investors wish to account for transaction costs, the actual point reflecting the interest rate differential and forward rate premium must be further from the IRP line to make covered interest arbitrage worthwhile. Exhibit 7.9 identifies the areas that reflect potential for covered interest arbitrage *after* accounting for transaction costs. Notice the band surrounding the IRP line. For points not on the IRP line but within this band, covered interest arbitrage is not worthwhile (because the excess return is offset by costs). For points to the right (or below) the band, investors residing in the home country could gain through covered interest arbitrage. For points to the left (or above) the band, foreign investors could gain through covered interest arbitrage.

Even if covered interest arbitrage appears feasible after accounting for transaction costs, the act of investing funds overseas is subject to political risk. While the forward contract locks in the rate at which the foreign funds should be reconverted, there is no guarantee that funds will be allowed to be reconverted. A crisis in the foreign country could cause its government to restrict any exchange of the local currency for other currencies. In this case, the investor would be unable to use these funds until the foreign government eliminated the restriction. Investors may also perceive a slight default risk on foreign investments such as foreign Treasury bills, since they might not be assured that the foreign government will guarantee full repayment of interest and principal upon default.

Firms and investors recognize the impact that taxes may have on income. Because tax laws vary among countries, investors and firms that set up deposits in other countries must be aware of the existing tax laws. It is possible

EXHIBIT 7.9 Potential for Covered Interest Arbitrage When Considering Transaction Costs

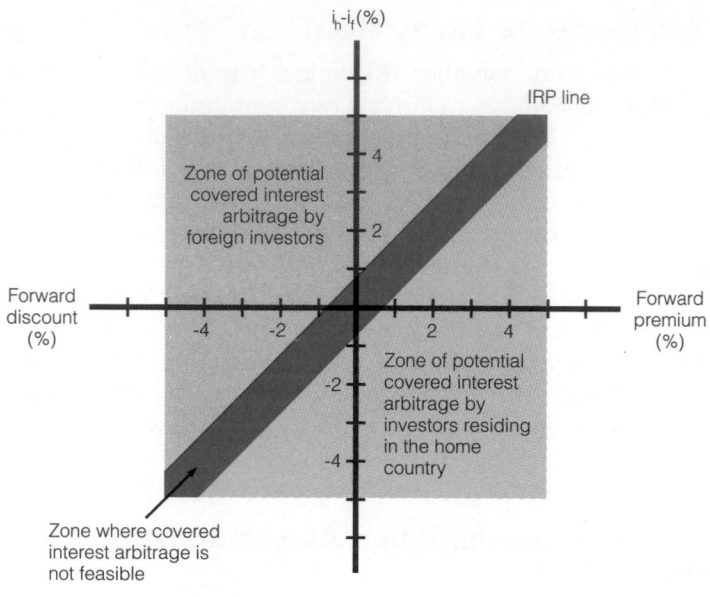

that covered interest arbitrage could be feasible when considering before-tax returns but not necessarily when considering after-tax returns. Such a scenario would be due to differential tax rates.

If IRP does not hold, the possibility of covered interest arbitrage deserves consideration. However, the existence of transaction costs, potential currency restrictions, and differences in national tax laws could remove any abnormal returns possible from covered interest arbitrage. Thus, covered interest arbitrage is not automatically feasible when IRP does not hold. Covered interest arbitrage should be attempted only if abnormal returns remain after considering transaction costs, potential currency restrictions, and taxes.

CORRELATION BETWEEN SPOT AND FORWARD RATE MOVEMENTS

Because of interest rate parity, a foreign currency's forward rate will normally move in tandem with the spot rate. This correlation of movement depends on interest rate movements, as shown in Exhibit 7.10. Currency A's spot rate (S_A) and forward rate (F_A) are shown, along with a comparison of the U.S. interest rate ($i_{U.S.}$) and Country A's interest rate (i_A). From time t_0 to t_1, i_A exceeds $i_{U.S.}$, and F_A is therefore less than S_A by approximately that interest rate differential. The size of the interest rate differential declines over this period, causing the discount on F_A to decline along with it. At time t_1, the interest rates of the two countries are equal, so that F_A is equal to S_A. From time t_1 to t_2, i_A is below $i_{U.S.}$, causing F_A to be above S_A. At the beginning of

EXHIBIT 7.10 Relationship between Interest Rate Differentials and Forward Rate Premiums Over Time

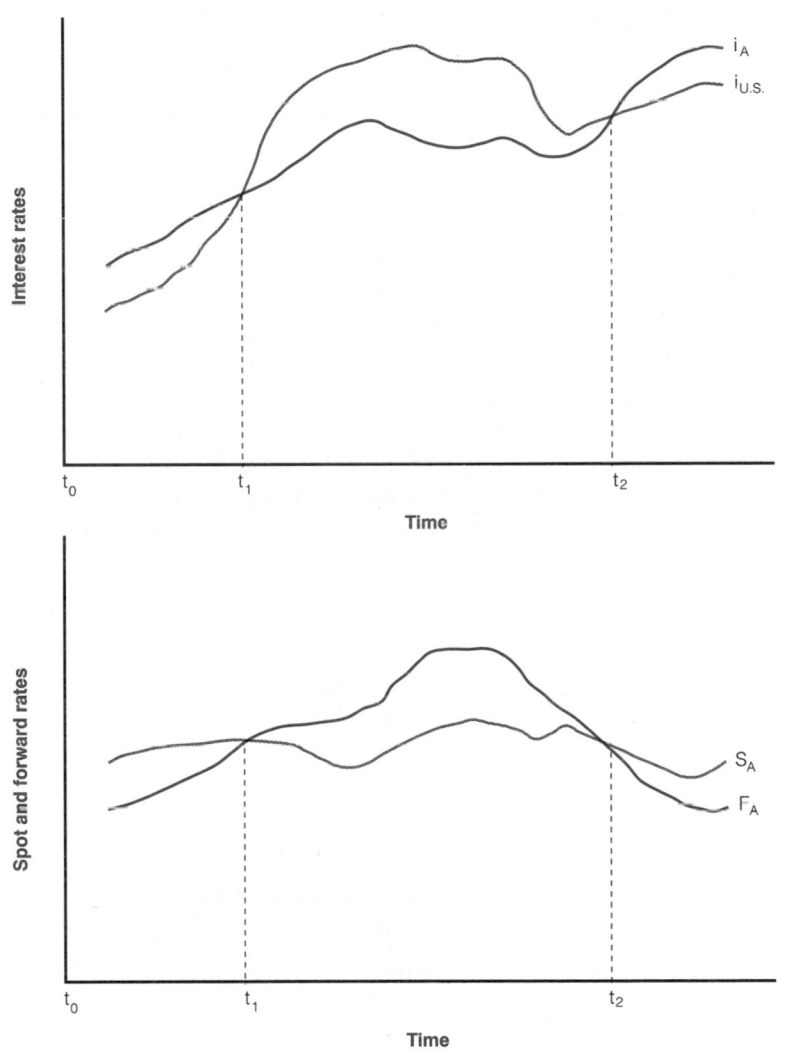

this period, the premium on F_A rises because the differential between $i_{U.S.}$ and i_A becomes larger. As time t_2 approaches, the interest rate differential narrows until $i_A = i_{U.S.}$ at time t_2, causing F_A to equal S_A. After time t_2, i_A exceeds $i_{U.S.}$, forcing F_A to fall below S_A.

International arbitrage is the act of capitalizing on a discrepancy in exchange rates. The profit to be earned from such an act is without risk. Three forms of international arbitrage were mentioned in this chapter. First, locational arbitrage may occur if foreign exchange quotations differ among banks. The

SUMMARY

act of locational arbitrage should force the foreign exchange quotations of banks to become realigned, and locational arbitrage will no longer be possible.

Second, triangular arbitrage is related to cross exchange rates. A cross exchange rate between two currencies is determined by the values of these two currencies with respect to a third currency. If the actual cross exchange rate of these two currencies differs from the rate that should exist, triangular arbitrage is possible. The act of triangular arbitrage should force cross exchange rates to become realigned and triangular arbitrage will no longer be possible.

Third, covered interest arbitrage is based on the relationship between the forward rate premium and the interest rate differential. The size of the premium or discount exhibited by the forward rate of a currency is dependent on the differential between the interest rates of the two countries of concern. In general terms, the forward rate of the foreign currency will contain a discount (premium) if its interest rate is higher (lower) than the U.S. interest rate. Interest rate parity (IRP) provides a more exact relationship between the interest rate differential and forward premium (or discount). If the actual relationship between the interest rate differential and the forward premium deviates substantially from the expected relationship stated by interest rate parity, then covered interest arbitrage is possible. This type of arbitrage represents a foreign short-term investment in a foreign currency covered by a forward sale of that foreign currency in the future. In this manner, the investor is not exposed to fluctuation in the foreign currency's value.

The various forms of international arbitrage help illustrate why foreign exchange rates are usually aligned as they should be. Market forces resulting from arbitrage will help to maintain spot and forward exchange rates at their appropriate levels.

QUESTIONS/ PROBLEMS

1. Explain the concept of locational arbitrage and the scenario necessary for it to be plausible.

2. Assume the following information:

	Bank X	Bank Y
Bid price of Swiss francs	$.401	$.398
Ask price of Swiss francs	$.404	$.400

Given this information, is locational arbitrage possible? If so, explain the steps that would reflect locational arbitrage, and compute the profit from this arbitrage if you had $1,000,000 to use.

3. Based on the information in the previous question, what market forces would occur to eliminate any further possibilities of locational arbitrage?

4. Explain the concept of triangular arbitrage and the scenario necessary for it to be plausible.

5. Assume the following information for a particular bank:

	Quoted Price
Value of Canadian dollar in U.S. dollars	$.90
Value of German mark in U.S. dollars	$.30
Value of Canadian dollar in German marks	DM3.02

Given this information, is triangular arbitrage possible? If so, explain the steps that would reflect triangular arbitrage, and compute the profit from this strategy if you had $1,000,000 to use.

6. Based on the information in the previous question, what market forces would occur to eliminate any further possibilities of triangular arbitrage?

7. Explain the concept of covered interest arbitrage and the scenario necessary for it to be plausible.

8. Assume the following information:

Spot rate of Canadian dollar	= $.80
90-day forward rate of Canadian dollar	= $.79
90-day Canadian interest rate	= 4%
90-day U.S. interest rate	= 2.5%

Given this information, what would be the yield (percentage return) to a U.S. investor who used covered interest arbitrage? (Assume the investor invests $1,000,000.)

9. Based on the information in the previous question, what market forces would occur to eliminate any further possibilities of covered interest arbitrage?

10. Assume the following information:

Spot rate of the French franc	= $.100
180-day forward rate of the French franc	= $.098
180-day French interest rate	= 6%
180-day U.S. interest rate	= 5%

Given this information, is covered interest arbitrage worthwhile for French investors? Explain your answer.

11. Explain the concept of interest rate parity. Provide a rationale for why interest rate parity may exist.

12. Describe a method for testing whether interest rate parity exists.

13. Why are transaction costs, currency restrictions, and differential tax laws important when evaluating whether covered interest arbitrage can be beneficial?

14. Assume that the existing U.S. one-year interest rate is 10 percent and the Canadian one-year interest rate is 11 percent. Also assume that interest rate parity exists. Should the forward rate of the Canadian dollar exhibit a discount or premium? If U.S. investors attempted covered interest arbitrage, what would be their return? If Canadian investors attempted covered interest arbitrage, what would be their return?

15. Why would investors consider covered interest arbitrage in a foreign country where the interest rate is lower than their home interest rate?

16. Consider investors that invest in either U.S. or British one-year Treasury bills. Assume zero transactions costs and no taxes.

   a) If interest rate parity exists, then the return by U.S. investors who use covered interest arbitrage would be the same as the return of U.S. investors who invest in U.S. Treasury bills. Is this statement true or false? If false, correct the statement.

   b) If interest rate parity exists, then the return by British investors who use covered interest arbitrage would be the same as the return of British investors who invest in British Treasury bills. Is this statement true or false? If false, correct the statement.

17. Assume that the Swiss forward rate presently exhibits a premium of 6 percent, and that interest rate parity exists. How will this premium change if U.S. interest rates decrease, in order for interest rate parity to be maintained. Why might we expect the premium to change?

18. In the early 1980s the forward rate premiums of several currencies were higher than they are now. What does this imply about interest rate differentials between the United States and foreign countries today compared to the early 1980s.

19. If the relationship that is specified by interest rate parity does not exist at any period, but does exist on average, then covered interest arbitrage should not be considered by U.S. firms. Do you agree or disagree with this statement? Explain.

20. The one-year Swiss interest rate is 6 percent. The one-year U.S. interest rate is 10 percent. The spot rate of the Swiss franc is $.50. The forward rate of the Swiss franc is $.54. Is covered interest arbitrage feasible for U.S. investors? Is it feasible for Swiss investors? Explain why each of these possible opportunities for covered interest arbitrage is or is not feasible.

21. Assume that the one-year U.S. interest rate is 11 percent, while the one-year interest rate in a specific less developed country (LDC) is 40 percent. Assume that a U.S. bank is willing to purchase the currency of that country from you one year from now at a discount of 13 percent. Would covered interest arbitrage be worth considering? Is there any reason why you should not attempt covered interest arbitrage in this situation? (Ignore tax effects.)

22. Why do you think currencies of countries with high inflation rates tend to have forward discounts?

23. In 1989 and 1990 the West German economy was expected to expand significantly in response to European integration and the potential reunification with East Germany. How might these conditions affect the forward discount of the German mark?

Zuber Inc.
Using Covered Interest Arbitrage

Zuber Inc. is a U.S.-based MNC that has been aggressively pursuing business in Eastern Europe since the Iron Curtain was lifted in 1989. One of the Eastern Bloc countries allowed for its currency's value to be market-determined. The spot rate of the currency is $.40. The country also began to allow investments by foreign investors, as a method of attracting funds to help build its economy. Its interest rate on one-year securities issued by the federal government is 14 percent, which is substantially higher than the nine percent rate presently offered on one-year U.S. Treasury securities.

A local bank began to create a forward market for the local currency. This bank was recently privatized and was trying to make a name for itself in international business. The bank quoted a one-year forward rate of $.39.

As an employee in Zuber's international money market division, you have been asked to assess the possibility of investing short-term funds in this country. You are in charge of investing $10 million over the next year. Your objective is to earn the highest return possible, while maintaining safety (since the funds will be needed by the firm next year).

Since the exchange rate has just become market-determined, there is a high probability that the currency's value will be very volatile for several years as it seeks out its true equilibrium value. The expected value of the currency in one year is $.40, but there is a high degree of uncertainty about this. The actual value in one year may be as much as 40 percent above or below this expected value.

a) Would you be willing to invest the funds in this country without covering your position? Explain.

b) Suggest how you could attempt covered interest arbitrage. What is the expected return from using covered interest arbitrage?

c) What risks are involved in using covered interest arbitrage here?

d) If you had to choose between investing your funds in U.S. Treasury bills at 9 percent or using covered interest arbitrage, what would be your choice? Defend your answer.

PROJECTS

1. Look up the spot rate and 180-day forward rate of the British pound in a recent issue of *The Wall Street Journal*. Also, look up (in the "Money Rates" section) U.S. and British 180-day interest rates. Assume these rates were applicable for investors and reflected investments with equal risk. Determine whether a U.S. investor would benefit from utilizing covered interest arbitrage.

2. Using a recent issue of *The Wall Street Journal*, fill in the first three blanks that follow this question. Using those three exchange rates, determine the cross exchange rates and fill in the next three blanks. (Assume that cross exchange rates are properly aligned so that triangular arbitrage is not profitable.)

Spot rate of British pound relative to the dollar	=	$_____
Spot rate of Swiss franc relative to the dollar	=	$_____
Spot rate of the Japanese yen relative to the dollar	=	$_____
Spot rate of the British pound relative to the Swiss franc	=	SF_____
Spot rate of the British pound relative to the Japanese yen	=	¥_____
Spot rate of the Swiss franc relative to the Japanese yen	=	¥_____

3. Determine whether covered interest arbitrage would have been profitable from a U.S. perspective, using the Data Bank in the back of this text on a country of your choice. Assess several historical points in time.

SUGGESTED READING

Daniel L. Thornton. "Tests of Covered Interest Rate Parity." *Review,* Federal Reserve Bank of St. Louis (July–August 1989), pp. 55–66. This somewhat tech-nical article empirically tests the interest rate parity theory and offers interesting implications.

REFERENCES

Adler, Michael, and Bernard Dumas. "International Portfolio Choice and Corporation Finance: A Synthesis." *Journal of Finance* (June 1983), pp. 925–984.

Aliber, Robert Z. "The Interest Rate Parity Theorem: A Reinterpretation." *Journal of Political Economy* (December 1973), pp. 1451–1459.

Branson, William H. "The Minimum Covered Interest Differential Needed for International Arbitrage Activity." *Journal of Political Economy* (December 1979), pp. 1029–1034.

Brittain, Bruce. "Tests of Theories of Exchange Rate Determination." *Journal of Finance* (May 1977), pp. 519–529.

Chrystal, K. Alec. "A Guide to Foreign Exchange Markets." *Review* (March 1984), pp. 5–18.

Cornell, Bradford. "Spot Rates, Forward Rates, and Market Dynamics." *Journal of Political Economy* (December 1976), pp. 1161–1176.

Dooley, Michael P., and Peter Isard. "Capital Controls, Political Risks, and Deviations from Interest-Rate Parity." *Journal of Political Economy* (April 1980), pp. 370–384.

Frenkel, Jacob A., and Richard M. Levich. "Transaction Costs and Interest Arbitrage: Tranquil Versus Turbulent Periods." *Journal of Political Economy* (December 1977), pp. 1209–1226.

————. "Covered-Interest Arbitrage and Unexploited Profits Reply." *Journal of Political Economy* (April 1979), pp. 418–422.

Geweke, J., and E. Feige. "Some Joint Tests of the Efficiency of Markets for Forward Foreign Exchange." *Review of Economics and Statistics* (October 1979), pp. 334–341.

Giddy, Ian H. "An Integrated Theory of Exchange Rate Equilibrium." *Journal of Financial and Quantitative Analysis* (December 1976), pp. 883–92.

————. "Exchange Risk: Whose View?" *Financial Management* (Summer 1977), pp. 23–33.

Solnik, Bruno. "International Parity Conditions and Exchange Risk: A Review." *Journal of Banking and Finance* (August 1978), pp. 281–293.

Stokes, Houston H., and Hugh Neuburger. "Interest Arbitrage, Forward Speculation and the Determination of the Forward Exchange Rate." *Columbia Journal of World Business* (Winter 1979), pp. 86–98.

CHAPTER 8

Relationships between Inflation, Interest Rates, and Exchange Rates

This chapter describes theories of how exchange rates respond to changes in inflation rates and interest rates. First, purchasing power parity, a prominent theory of international finance, is used to explain how exchange rates react to changes in inflation rates of countries. The rationale for this theory is presented, along with a graphic analysis and a method for testing the theory. In addition, the theoretical relationship between inflation rates and exchange rates as suggested by purchasing power parity is compared with the actual relationship that has existed. This comparison provides evidence on whether the theory holds in reality.

After the discussion of how inflation rate differentials between countries can affect exchange rates, this chapter examines the impact of interest rate differentials between countries on exchange rates. In particular, the international Fisher effect is applied to specify the expected relationship. The discussion is supplemented with a graphic analysis, and actual data are used to show whether this theory proves true in reality.

Finally, this chapter integrates these two theories with interest rate parity theory (from the previous chapter) to show how they are related, but carry different implications. Because each of these theories refers to a different relationship, there is no conflict among them. All three theories could possibly hold true in reality at the same time. The relationships discussed here provide insight for corporations that forecast future exchange rates.

PURCHASING POWER PARITY (PPP)

In Chapter 4, the expected impact of relative inflation rates on exchange rates was discussed. Recall from this discussion that when one country's inflation rate rises relative to another, the demand for its currency declines as its exports decline (due to its higher prices). In addition, consumers and firms in the country with higher inflation tend to increase their importing. Both of these forces place downward pressure on the currency of the high-inflation country. Inflation rates often vary among countries, causing international trade patterns to adjust accordingly and influencing exchange rates.

One of the most popular and controversial theories in international finance is the **purchasing power parity (PPP) theory,** which focuses on the inflation–exchange rate relationship. There are various forms of PPP theory. The **absolute form,** also called the "law of one price," suggests that prices of similar products of two different countries should be equal when measured in a common currency. If a discrepancy in prices as measured by a common currency exists, the demand should shift so that these prices should converge. For example, if the same product is produced by the United States and the United Kingdom, and the price in the United Kingdom is lower when measured in a common currency, the demand for that product should increase in the United Kingdom while it declines in the United States. Consequently, the actual price charged in each country may be affected and/or the exchange rate may adjust. Both forces would cause the prices of the products to be similar when measured in a common currency. Realistically, the existence of transportation costs, tariffs, and quotas may prevent the absolute form of PPP. If transportation costs were high in this example, the demand for the products might not shift in the manner suggested. Thus, the discrepancy in prices would continue.

The **relative form** of PPP is an alternative version that accounts for the possibility of market imperfections such as transportation costs, tariffs, and quotas. This version acknowledges that because of these market imperfections, prices of similar products of different countries will not necessarily be the same when measured in a common currency. However, it states that the rate of change in the prices of products should be somewhat similar when measured in a common currency, as long as the transportation costs and trade barriers are unchanged. To illustrate the relative form of PPP, assume that two countries initially have zero inflation. Also assume that the current exchange rate between the two country's currencies is in equilibrium. As time passes, both countries may experience inflation; for PPP to hold, the exchange rate should adjust to offset the differential in the inflation rates of the two countries. If this occurs, the prices of goods in either country should appear similar to consumers. That is, consumers should note little difference in their purchasing power in the two countries.

Assume that the price indexes of your home country (h) and a foreign country (f) are equal. Now assume that over time, the home country experiences an inflation rate of I_h, while the foreign country experiences an inflation rate of I_f. Due to inflation, the price index of goods in the consumer's home country (P_h) becomes

$$P_h(1 + I_h)$$

The price index of the foreign country (P_f) will also change due to inflation in that country:

$$P_f(1 + I_f)$$

If $I_h > I_f$, and the exchange rate between the currencies of the two countries does not change, then your purchasing power on foreign goods is greater than on home goods. In this case, PPP does not exist. If $I_h < I_f$, and the exchange rate between the currencies of the two countries does not change, then your purchasing power on home goods is greater than on foreign goods. In this case also, PPP would not exist.

The theory of PPP suggests that the exchange rate would not remain constant, but would adjust to maintain the parity in purchasing power. If inflation occurs and the exchange rate of the foreign currency changes, the foreign price index from the home consumer's perspective becomes

$$P_f(1 + I_f)(1 + e_f)$$

where e_f represents the percentage change in the value of the foreign currency. According to PPP theory, the percentage change in the foreign currency (e_f) should change to maintain parity in the new price indexes of the two countries. We can solve for e_f under conditions of PPP by setting the formula for the new price index of the foreign country equal to the formula for the new price index of the home country, as follows:

$$P_f(1 + I_f)(1 + e_f) = P_h(1 + I_h)$$

Solving for e_f, we obtain

$$(1 + e_f) = \frac{P_h(1 + I_h)}{P_f(1 + I_f)}$$

$$e_f = \frac{P_h(1 + I_h)}{P_f(1 + I_f)} - 1$$

. Since P_h equals P_f (because price indexes were initially assumed equal in both countries), they cancel, leaving

$$e_f = \frac{(1 + I_h)}{(1 + I_f)} - 1$$

This formula reflects the relationship between relative inflation rates and the exchange rate according to PPP. Notice that if $I_h > I_f$, e_f should be positive. This implies that the foreign currency will appreciate when the home country's inflation exceeds the foreign country's inflation. Conversely, if $I_h < I_f$, then e_f should be negative. This implies that the foreign currency will depreciate when the foreign country's inflation exceeds the home country's inflation.

As a numerical example, assume that the exchange rate is in equilibrium initially. Then the home currency experiences a 5 percent inflation rate, while the foreign country experiences a 3 percent inflation rate. According to PPP, the foreign currency will adjust as shown:

$$e_f = \frac{1 + I_h}{1 + I_f} - 1$$

$$= \frac{1 + .05}{1 + .03} - 1$$

$$= .0194, \text{ or } 1.94\%$$

The implications are that the foreign currency should appreciate by 1.94 percent in response to the higher inflation of the home country relative to the foreign country. If this exchange rate change does occur, the price index of the foreign country will be as high as that in the home country from the perspective of consumers in the home country. Even though the inflation is lower in the foreign country, appreciation of the foreign currency pushes the foreign country's price index up from the perspective of consumers in the home country. When considering the exchange rate effect, price indexes of both countries rose by 5 percent from the home country perspective. Thus, the purchasing power on foreign goods is equal to that on the home goods.

As a second example, again assume that the exchange rate is in equilibrium initially. Then the home country experiences a 4 percent inflation rate, while the foreign country experiences a 7 percent inflation rate. According to PPP, the foreign currency will adjust as shown:

$$e_f = \frac{(1 + I_h)}{(1 + I_f)} - 1$$

$$= \frac{1 + .04}{1 + .07} - 1$$

$$= -.028, \text{ or } -2.8\%$$

The implications are that the foreign currency should depreciate by 2.8 percent in response to the higher inflation of the foreign country relative to the home country. If this exchange rate does occur, the price index of the home country will be as high as that in the foreign country. Even though the inflation is lower in the home country, the depreciation of the foreign currency places downward pressure on the foreign country's price index from the perspective of the consumers in the home country. When considering the exchange rate impact, price indexes of both countries rose by 4 percent. Thus, PPP would still exist due to the adjustment in the exchange rate.

A more simplified but less precise relationship based on PPP is

$$e_f = I_h - I_f$$

That is, the exchange rate percentage change should be approximately equal to the differential in inflation rates between two countries. To illustrate the use of this simplified formula, consider two countries, the United States and Great Britain, which trade extensively with each other. Assume an equilibrium state where the exchange rate of the British pound is initially worth $2.00. Now assume that the United States experiences a 9 percent inflation rate, while Great Britain experiences a 5 percent inflation rate. Under these conditions, PPP theory would suggest that the British pound should appreciate by approximately 4 percent, the differential in inflation rates.

Rationale behind the Purchasing Power Parity Theory

If two countries produce products that are substitutes for each other, the demand for products should adjust as inflation rates differ. In our previous example, prices increased in the United States by 9 percent versus 5 percent in Great Britain. This should initially cause U.S. consumers to increase imports from Great Britain and British consumers to lower their demand for the U.S. goods (since prices of British goods increased by a lower rate). Such forces place upward pressure on the British pound value. The shifting in consumption from the United States to Great Britain will continue until the British pound value has appreciated to an extent whereby (1) the prices paid for British goods by U.S. consumers are no lower than in the United States, and (2) the prices paid for U.S. goods by British consumers are no higher than in Great Britain. The level of appreciation in the pound needed to achieve this new equilibrium situation is approximately 4 percent, as will be verified here.

Given British inflation of 5 percent and the pound's appreciation of 4 percent, U.S. consumers would be paying about 9 percent more for the British goods than what they paid in the initial equilibrium state. This is equal to the 9 percent increase in prices of U.S. goods from the U.S. inflation. Consider a situation where the pound appreciated by only 1 percent. In this case, the increased price of British goods to U.S. consumers would be approximately 6 percent (5 percent inflation and 1 percent appreciation in the British pound), which is less than the 9 percent increase in the price of U.S. goods to U.S. consumers. Thus, we would expect U.S. consumers to continue to shift their consumption to British goods. Purchasing power parity suggests that the increasing U.S. consumption of British goods by U.S. consumers would persist until the pound appreciated by about 4 percent. Any level of appreciation less than this would represent more attractive British prices relative to U.S. prices from the U.S. consumer's viewpoint.

From the British consumer's point of view, the U.S. goods would have initially increased by 4 percent more than British goods. Thus, British consumers would continue to reduce imports from the United States until the pound appreciated enough to make U.S. goods no more expensive than British goods. Once the pound appreciated by 4 percent, this would partially offset the increase in U.S. prices of 9 percent from the British consumer's perspective. To be more precise, the net effect is that the prices of U.S. goods would increase approximately 5 percent to British consumers (9 percent inflation minus the 4 percent savings to British consumers due to the pound's 4 percent appreciation).

Using Purchasing Power Parity to Assess Future Currency Movements

The new value of the spot exchange rate of a given currency (called $S_{j,t+1}$) would be a function of the initial spot rate that existed in equilibrium (called S_j) and the inflation differential, as shown here:

$$S_{j,t+1} = S_j\left[1 + \frac{(1 + I_h)}{(1 + I_f)} - 1\right]$$

$$= \frac{S_j(1 + I_h)}{(1 + I_f)}$$

The approximate version is

$$S_{j,t+1} = S_j[1 + (I_h - I_f)]$$

From our previous example, recall that the pound was assigned an initial value of $2.00. Then the 4 percent inflation differential occurred, which, according to PPP theory, would cause the approximate adjustment:

$$S_{j,\,t+1} = S_j[1 + (.09 - .05)]$$
$$= \$2.00(1.04)$$
$$= \$2.08$$

To test your understanding, consider a second example. Assume that France and the United States trade extensively with each other and that both countries produce somewhat similar products. Assume that initially the equilibrium value of the French franc (FF) is $.20. Then, assume that the U.S. experiences 1 percent inflation while France experiences 6 percent inflation. According to PPP theory, the spot rate of the franc will adjust as follows:

$$S_{j,\,t+1} = S_j[1 + (.01 - .06)]$$
$$= \$.20[1 + (-.05)]$$
$$= \$.19$$

Graphic Analysis of Purchasing Power Parity

Using PPP theory, we should be able to assess the potential impact of inflation on exchange rates. Exhibit 8.1 is a graphic representation of PPP theory. The points on the exhibit suggest that given the inflation differential between the home and the foreign country of X percent, the foreign currency should

EXHIBIT 8.1   Illustration of Purchasing Power Parity

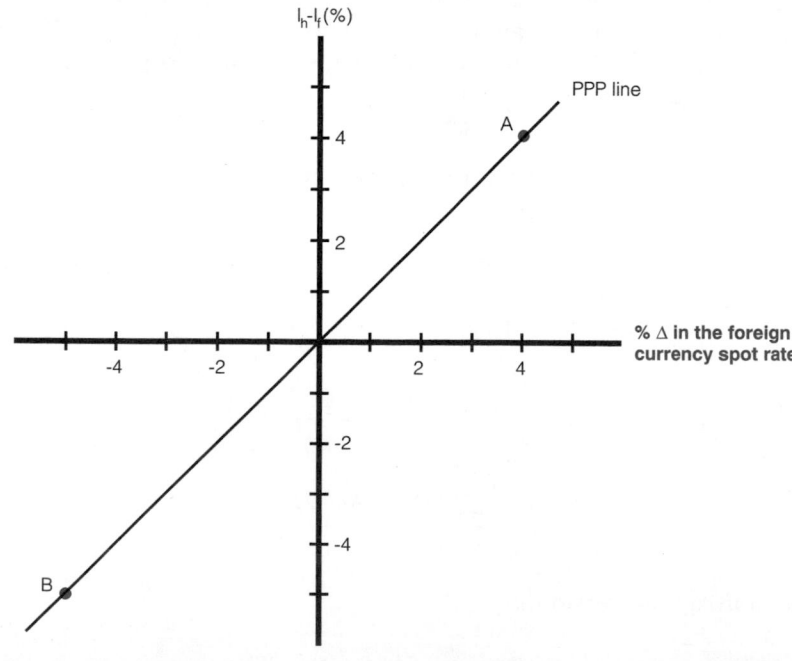

adjust by X percent due to that inflation differential. The diagonal line connecting all these points together is known as the **PPP line.** Point A represents our example where U.S. (to be considered as the home country here) and British inflation rates were assumed to be 9 percent and 5 percent, respectively, so that $I_h - I_f = 4\%$. Recall that this led to the anticipated appreciation in the British pound of 4 percent as illustrated by point A. Point B reflects the example where the U.S. and French inflation rates were assumed to be 1 percent and 6 percent, respectively, so that $I_h - I_f = -5\%$. Recall that this led to anticipated depreciation of the French franc by 5 percent as illustrated by point B. If the exchange rate does respond to inflation differentials according to PPP theory, the actual points should lie on or close to the PPP line.

Exhibit 8.2 identifies areas of purchasing power disparity. Assume an initial equilibrium situation, then a change in the inflation rates of the two countries. If the exchange rate does not move as PPP theory would suggest, there is a disparity in the purchasing power of the two countries.

Point C in Exhibit 8.2 represents home inflation (I_h) in excess of foreign inflation (I_f) by 4 percent. Yet, the foreign currency appreciated only by 1 percent in response to this inflation differential. Consequently, purchasing power disparity exists. The home consumer's purchasing power on foreign goods has become more favorable relative to the purchasing power on the home country's goods. The PPP theory would suggest that such a disparity in purchasing power should exist only in the short run. Over time, as the home country consumers take advantage of the disparity by purchasing more for-

EXHIBIT 8.2 Identifying Disparity in Purchasing Power

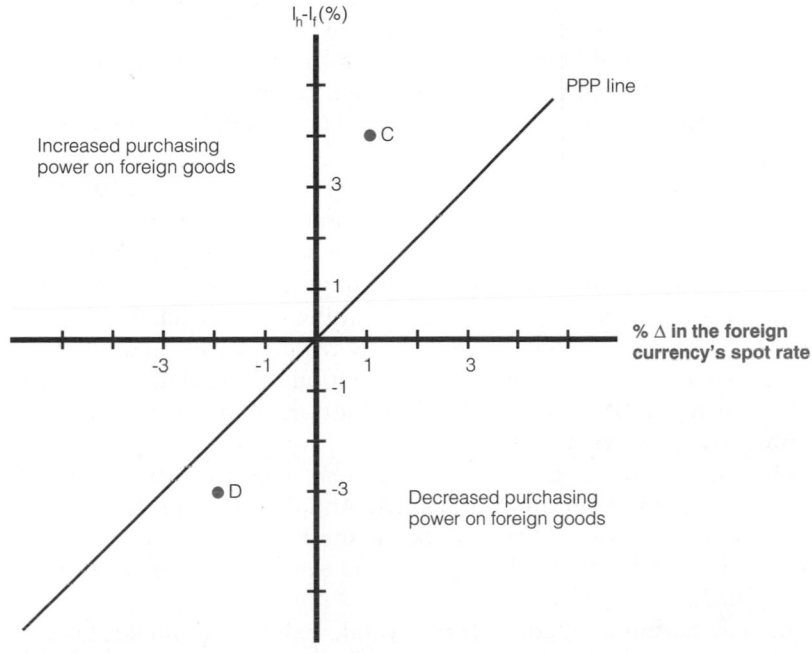

eign goods, upward pressure on the foreign currency's value will cause point C to move toward the PPP line. All points to the left of (or above) the PPP line represent more favorable purchasing power on foreign goods than on home goods.

Point D in Exhibit 8.2 represents home inflation below foreign inflation by 3 percent. Yet, the foreign currency has depreciated by only 2 percent. Again, purchasing power disparity exists. The purchasing power on foreign goods has become less favorable relative to the purchasing power on the home country's goods. The PPP theory would suggest that the foreign currency in this example should have depreciated by 3 percent to fully offset the 3 percent inflation differential. Since the foreign currency did not weaken to this extent, the home country consumers may discontinue their purchasing of goods in the foreign country, causing the foreign currency to weaken to the extent anticipated by PPP theory. If so, point D would move toward the PPP line. All points to the right of (or below) the PPP line represent more favorable purchasing power on home country goods than on foreign goods.

Testing the Validity of the Purchasing Power Parity Theory

The PPP theory not only provides an explanation of how relative inflation rates between two countries can influence an exchange rate, but it also provides information that could be used to forecast exchange rates. Substantial research has been conducted to examine whether PPP exists. The results of these tests will be discussed shortly. But first, how would you go about testing whether PPP exists? One simple method would be to choose two countries (say, the United States and a foreign country) and compare their differential in inflation rates to the percentage change in the foreign currency's value during several time periods. We could plot on a graph similar to Exhibit 8.2 each point representing the inflation differential and exchange rate percentage change for each specific time period, and then determine whether these points closely resemble the PPP line as drawn in Exhibit 8.2. If the points deviate significantly from the PPP line, then the percentage change in the foreign currency is not being influenced by the inflation differential in the manner PPP theory suggests.

As an alternative test of PPP, several foreign countries could be compared with the home country over a given time period. Each foreign country would exhibit an inflation differential relative to the home country, which could be compared to the exchange rate change during the period of concern. Thus, a point could be plotted on a graph such as Exhibit 8.2 for each foreign country analyzed. If the points deviate significantly from the PPP line, then the exchange rates are not responding to the inflation differentials in accordance with PPP theory. PPP theory can be tested for any countries on which inflation information is available.

Much research has been conducted to test whether PPP exists. Recent studies by Mishkin, Adler and Dumas, and Abuaf and Jorion found evidence of significant deviations from PPP, persisting for lengthy periods. Another related study by Adler and Lehman provided evidence against PPP even over the long run.

To further examine whether PPP is valid, Exhibit 8.3 illustrates relative inflation rates over time. The inflation differential shown in the exhibit is

EXHIBIT 8.3   Comparison of Average Annual Inflation Differentials and Exchange Rate Movements for Four Major Countries

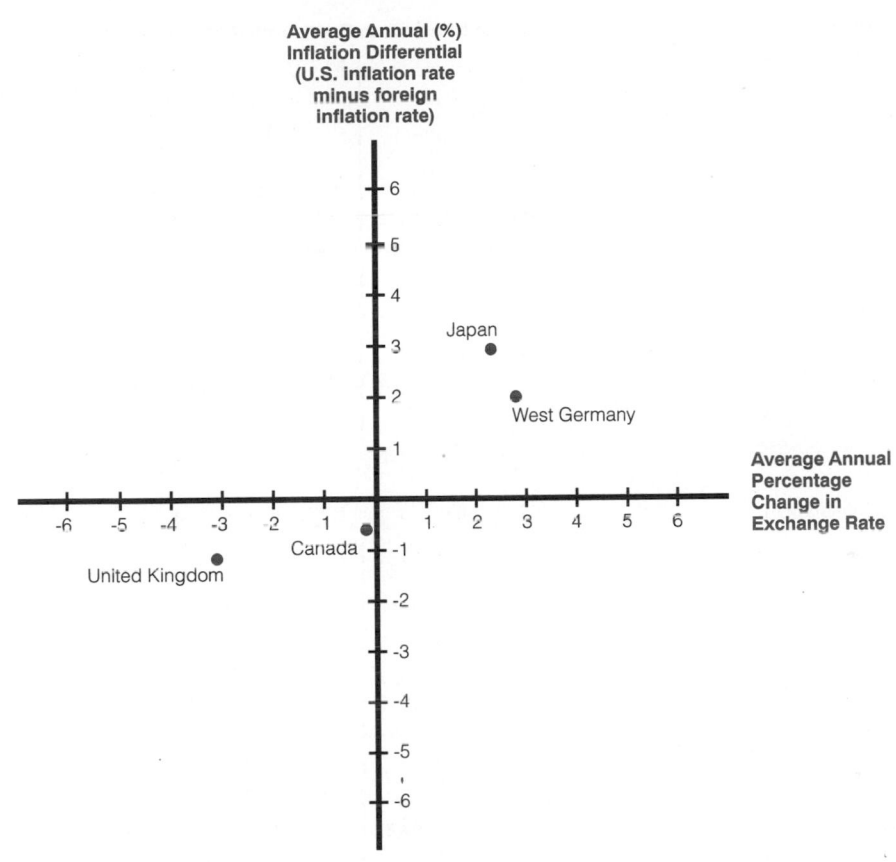

measured as the U.S. inflation rate minus the foreign inflation rate. The differential in inflation between the United States and each foreign country is represented on the vertical axis of Exhibit 8.3. In addition, the mean annual exchange rate percentage change of each foreign currency (relative to the U.S. dollar) is represented on the horizontal axis. If PPP existed during the period examined, the points plotted on the graph should be near an imaginary 45-degree line, which would split the axes (like the PPP line shown in Exhibit 8.2). The points for Canada, Japan and West Germany generally reflect PPP while the points for the United Kingdom deviate further from the imaginary PPP line.

Further assessment of the relationship between inflation differentials and exchange rates is shown in Exhibit 8.4. This is based on annual data from 1981 to 1990. The annual inflation rates during this period were identified for Canada, Japan, the United Kingdom, the United States, and West Germany and used to measure the differential between U.S. inflation and each country's inflation. The inflation differentials and exchange rate percentage changes are plotted for all years. A separate graph is used for each currency.

EXHIBIT 8.4 Comparison of Annual Inflation Differentials and Exchange Rate Movements for Four Major Countries

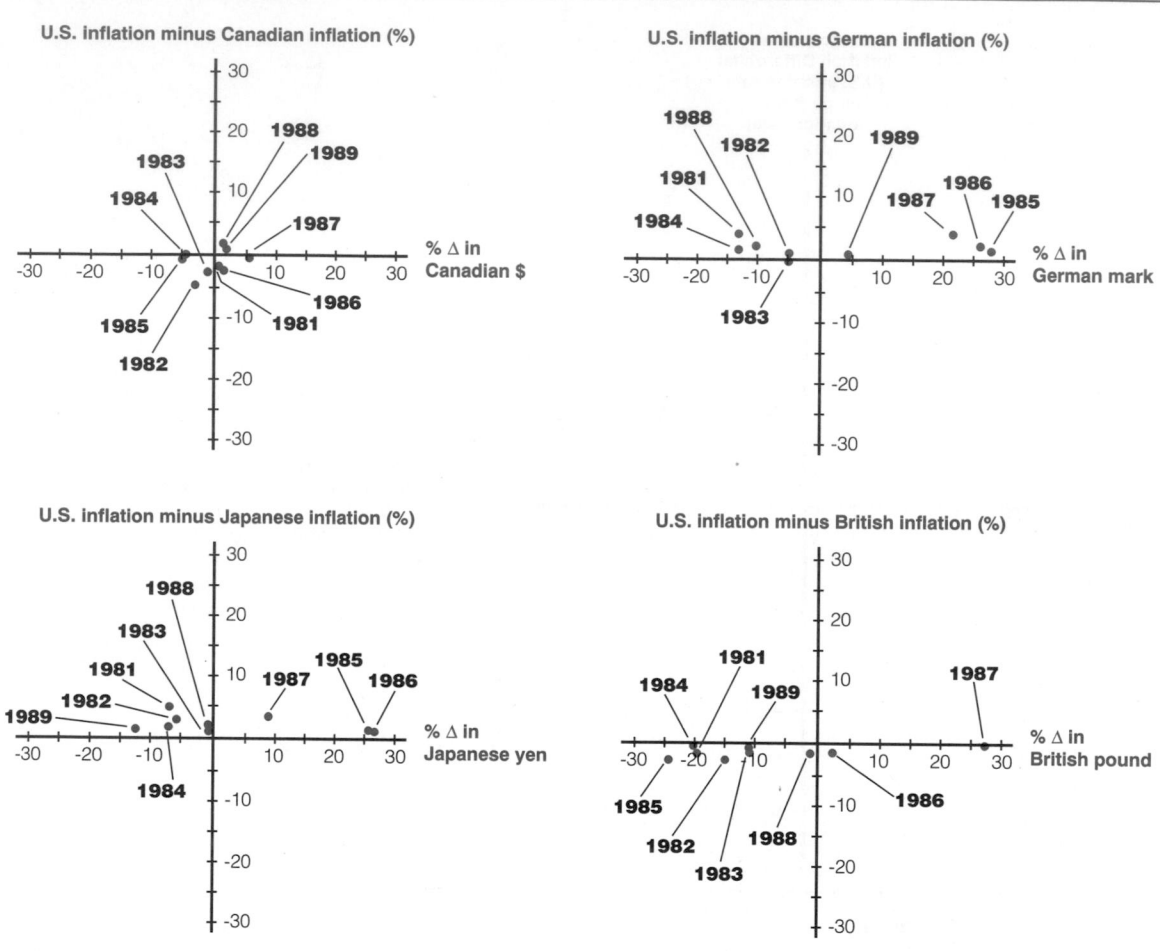

While the results for each graph are different, some general comments apply to all graphs. The percentage change in exchange rates typically was much more volatile than the inflation differential. Thus, the exchange rate movements are changing to a greater degree than would be anticipated by PPP theory. In some years, even the direction of a currency would not have been anticipated by PPP theory. The results in Exhibit 8.4 suggest that the relationship between an inflation differential and exchange rate movements often becomes distorted. This short-run assessment is less supportive of PPP theory than the long-run assessment provided in Exhibit 8.3.

Consider the case of Zenith Electronics Corporation, which has some of its TVs and VCRs produced in Mexico. If Mexican wages rise with Mexican inflation, and if purchasing power parity holds, any excess of an increase in Mexican wage rates above the increase in U.S. wage rates should be offset by a weakened peso. Thus, dollar amounts paid for these products sent to the United States should be unaffected by the wage rate. However, in 1990 the rise in Mexican wages exceeded the degree of peso devaluation, which increased production costs by $16 million. Since purchasing power parity does not consistently hold, firms cannot presume that any inflationary effects will be offset by exchange rate effects.

Monitoring "Real" Exchange Rates to Test the Purchasing Power Parity Theory

If PPP did exist, a currency's quoted or so-called "nominal" exchange rate with respect to all other currencies should move in line with its country's differential in inflation relative to those other countries. A currency's "real" exchange rate is the quoted exchange rate adjusted for its country's inflation relative to inflation in other countries. The real exchange rate is an indicator of the purchasing power when converting the home currency into the foreign currency. The purchasing power reflects the value of foreign goods that can be purchased. For a given currency f, the real exchange rate (S^*) can be defined as

$$S^*_f = \frac{S_f}{P_f/P_{U.S.}}$$

where:

S_f = spot exchange rate of the foreign currency relative to the dollar
$P_{U.S.}$ = U.S. price level
P_f = foreign price level

Real exchange rates can be monitored to test the PPP theory. If an exchange rate adjusts to the inflation differential in accordance with PPP, the real exchange rate remains the same. If PPP holds, real exchange rates should be somewhat stable over time.

Exhibit 8.5 shows the exchange rate trends of major foreign currencies against the dollar. It also illustrates the trend in the foreign currency's real (effective) exchange rate index (relative to several major currencies), using 1980 as the base year. (The real exchange rate index was assigned a value of 100 in the base year.) An increase in the currency's real exchange rate represents an increase in purchasing power, and a decrease represents a decrease in purchasing power. As an example, the German mark (in the upper left graph) declined substantially until 1985 and appreciated since 1985. However, its real exchange rate was not as volatile. The real exchange rates of all other foreign currencies were more volatile. Overall, the instability of real exchange rates suggests that inflation differentials are rarely offset by exchange rate movements in the manner implied by PPP theory.

Why Purchasing Power Parity Does Not Consistently Hold

Two of the most commonly proposed reasons for why PPP does not consistently hold follow:

1. *Other influential factors.* Exchange rates are affected by other factors in addition to the inflation differential. Recall that differentials in interest rate and income levels as well as government controls are important. To illustrate, assume the French inflation rate was 5 percent above the U.S. inflation rate.

EXHIBIT 8.5 Real Exchange Rates Over Time (*a measure of each currency's purchasing power*)

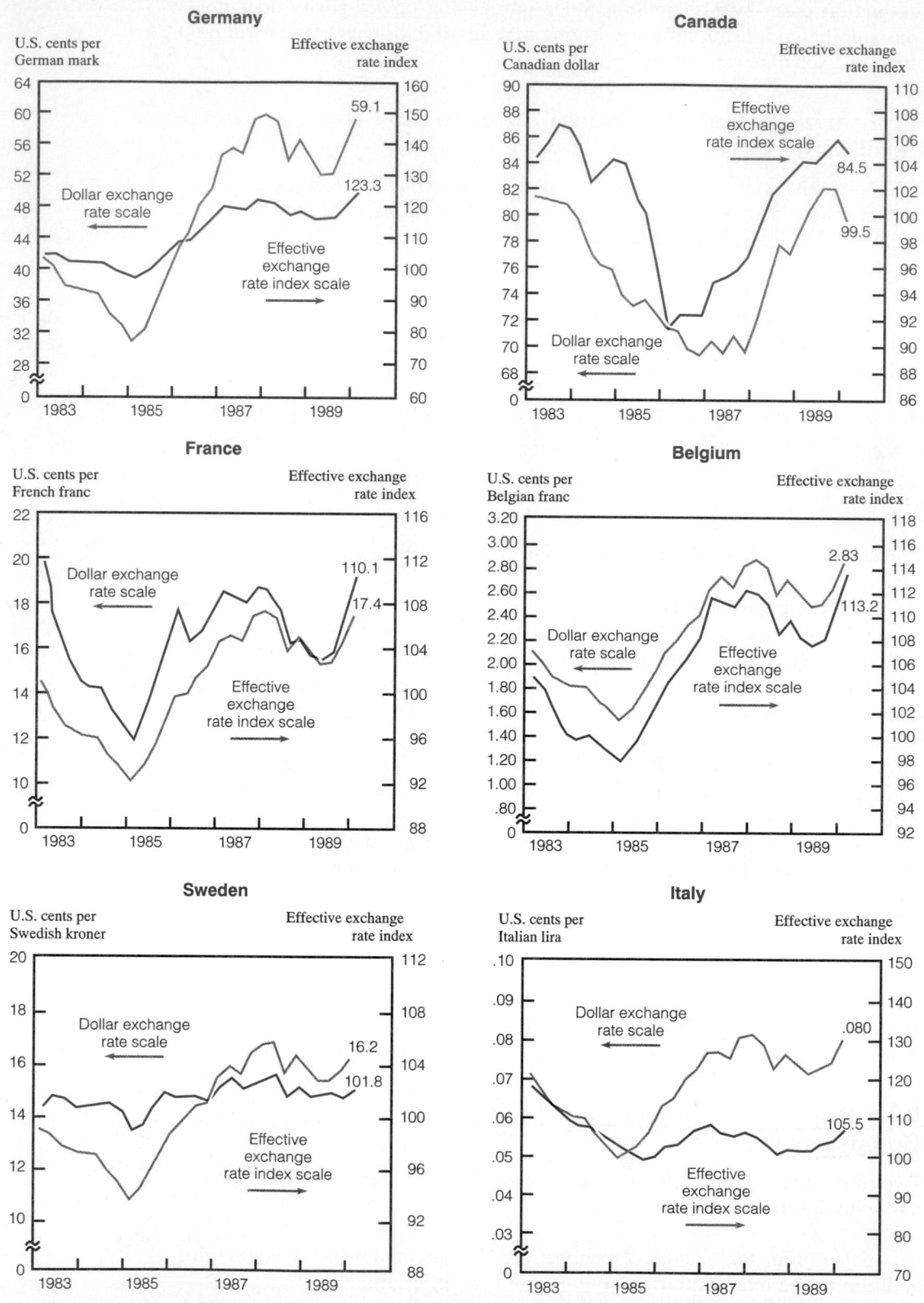

SOURCE: Federal Reserve Bank of St. Louis.

RELATED RESEARCH

Statistical Test of PPP

A somewhat simplified statistical test of purchasing power parity could be developed by applying regression analysis to historical exchange rates and inflation differentials. To illustrate, let's focus on one particular exchange rate. The quarterly percentage changes in the foreign currency value (e_f) can be regressed against the inflation differential that existed at the beginning of the quarter, as shown here:

$$e_f = a_0 + a_1\left[\frac{(1 + I_{U.S.})}{(1 + I_f)} - 1\right] + \mu$$

where a_0 is a constant, a_1 is the slope coefficient, and μ is an error term. Regression analysis would be applied to quarterly data to determine the regression coefficients. The hypothesized values of a_0 and a_1 are 0 and 1.0, respectively. These coefficients imply that for a given inflation differential, there is an equal offsetting percentage change in the exchange rate, on average. The appropriate t-test for each regression coefficient requires a comparison to the hypothesized value, and division by the standard error (s.e.) of the coefficient, as follows:

Test for $a_0 = 0$:　　　Test for $a_1 = 1$

$$t = \frac{a_0 - 0}{\text{s.e. of } a_0} \qquad t = \frac{a_1 - 1}{\text{s.e. of } a_1}$$

The t-table would then be used to find the critical t-value. If either t-test finds that the coefficients differ significantly from what is expected, the relationship between the inflation differential and the exchange rate differs from that stated by PPP theory. It should be mentioned that the appropriate lag time between the inflation differential and exchange rate is subject to controversy. See the related references at the end of this chapter for a more comprehensive explanation of tests on PPP theory.

From this information, PPP theory would suggest the French franc should depreciate by 5 percent against the U.S. dollar. Yet, if the government of France imposed trade barriers on U.S. exports, French consumers and firms could not adjust their spending in reaction to the inflation differential. Therefore, the exchange rate would not adjust.

2. *No substitutes for traded goods*. The idea behind PPP theory is that as soon as the prices become relatively higher in one country, the other country will discontinue importing and shift to domestic purchases instead of importing. This shift influences the exchange rate. However, what if substitute goods are not available domestically? For example, if French inflation increases by 5 percent more than U.S. inflation, U.S. consumers may not necessarily find suitable substitute goods at home. Thus, they may continue to buy the highly priced French goods and the French franc may *not* depreciate as it was originally expected to.

Limitation in Testing Whether Purchasing Power Parity Holds

A limitation of testing PPP is that the results will vary with the base period used. For example, if 1978 is used as a base period, most subsequent periods will show a relatively overvalued dollar; whereas, if 1984 is used, the dollar may appear undervalued in subsequent periods.

The base period chosen should reflect an equilibrium position, since subsequent periods are evaluated in comparison to it. Unfortunately, it is difficult to choose such a base period. In fact, one of the main reasons for abolishing fixed exchange rates was the difficulty in identifying an appropriate equilibrium exchange rate.

INTERNATIONAL FISHER EFFECT

Along with PPP theory, another major theory in international finance is the **international Fisher effect (IFE)** theory. It uses interest rate rather than inflation rate differentials to explain why exchange rates change over time, but it is closely related to the PPP theory because interest rates are often highly correlated with inflation rates. Therefore, interest rate differentials between countries may be the result of inflation rate differentials.

In the previous chapter, it was shown that if interest parity exists, an investor's return from covered interest arbitrage is no higher than the domestic yield. Under this condition, a firm with excess short-term cash may still consider foreign investments, but must be willing to leave the foreign currency position open (uncovered). Whether this strategy provides a higher yield than that available domestically depends on what happens to the value of that currency. For example, consider a U.S. corporation that can attain a 10 percent rate on a U.S. bank deposit versus 12 percent on a British bank deposit. To invest in the British deposit, the U.S. firm must initially exchange its dollars for pounds. Then, when the deposit matures, the firm will receive pounds and will most likely need to convert those pounds back to dollars. If the pound depreciates substantially over the time the U.S. firm holds the British deposit, the yield on this deposit would be less than the yield on a U.S. deposit.

Related to the firm's decision of whether to invest in foreign securities is the international Fisher effect (IFE) theory, which suggests that given two countries, the currency in the country with the higher interest rate will depreciate by the amount of the interest rate differential. That is, the nominal interest rate (i) should consist of a real rate of return and anticipated inflation. The nominal interest rate would also incorporate the *default risk* of an investment. The following examples will focus on investments that are risk-free, so that default risk will not have to be accounted for.

Assume that investors in the United States expect a 6 percent rate of inflation over one year, and require a real return of 2 percent over one year; the nominal interest rate on one-year Treasury securities would be 8 percent. If investors in all countries required the same real rate of return for one year, then the differential in nominal interest rates among any two countries would represent their respective inflation differentials. For example, assume that the nominal interest rate is 8 percent in the United States and 5 percent in Japan. If investors in both countries require a real return of 2 percent, then the differential in expected inflation is 3 percent (6 percent in the United States versus 3 percent in Japan). According to PPP theory, the Japanese yen would be expected to appreciate by the expected inflation differential of 3 percent. If the exchange rate changes as expected, Japanese investors that attempt to capitalize on the higher U.S. interest rate would earn a return similar to what they could have earned in their own country. While the U.S. interest rate is 3 percent higher, the Japanese investors would have repurchased their yen for 3 percent more than they sold yen.

To reinforce the concept, assume that the nominal interest rate in France is 13 percent. Given that investors in France also require a real return of 2 percent, the expected inflation rate in France must be 11 percent. According to PPP theory, the French franc is expected to depreciate by approximately 5 percent against the dollar (since the French inflation rate is 5 percent higher). Therefore, U.S. investors would not benefit from investing in France because the 5 percent interest rate differential would be offset by investing in a currency that would be worth 5 percent less by the end of the period. U.S. investors would earn 8 percent on the French investment, which is the same as what they could earn in the United States.

Given this information, the expected inflation differential between France and Japan is 8 percent. According to PPP theory, this inflation differential suggests that the French franc should depreciate by 8 percent against the yen. Therefore, even though Japanese investors would earn an additional 8 percent interest on a French investment, the franc would be valued at 8 percent less by the end of the period. Under these conditions, the Japanese investors would earn a return of 5 percent, which is the same as what they would earn on an investment in Japan. These possible investment opportunities along with some others are summarized in Exhibit 8.6. Note that wherever investors of a given country invest their funds, the expected nominal return is the same.

The precise relationship between the interest rate differential of two countries and the expected exchange rate change according to IFE can be derived as follows. First, the actual return to investors who invest in money market

EXHIBIT 8.6 Illustration of the International Fisher Effect (IFE) from Various Investor Perspectives

Investors residing in	Attempt to invest in	Expected inflation differential (home inflation minus foreign inflation)	Expected percentage change in currency needed by investors	Nominal interest rate to be earned	Return to investors after considering exchange rate adjustment	Inflation anticipated in home country	Real return earned by investors
Japan	Japan			5%	5%	3%	2%
	U.S.	3%− 6% = −3%	−3%	8	5	3	2
	France	3%−11% = −8%	−8	13	5	3	2
U.S.	Japan	6%− 3% = 3%	3	5	8	6	2
	U.S.			8	8	6	2
	France	6%−11% = −5	−5	13	8	6	2
France	Japan	11%− 3% = 8%	8	5	13	11	2
	U.S.	11%− 6% = 5%	5	8	13	11	2
	France			13	13	11	2

securities (such as short-term bank deposits) in their home country is simply the interest rate offered on those securities. However, the actual return to investors who invest in foreign money market security depends on not only the foreign interest rate (i_f), but also the percent change in the value of the foreign currency (e_f) denominating the security. The formula for the actual or so-called "effective" (exchange rate adjusted) return on a foreign bank deposit (or any money market security) is

$$r = (1 + i_f)(1 + e_f) - 1$$

According to the IFE, the effective return on a home investment should on average be equal to the effective return on a foreign investment. That is,

$$r = i_h$$

where r is the effective return on the foreign deposit and i_h is the interest rate on the home deposit. We can determine the degree by which the foreign currency must change in order to make investments in both countries generate similar returns. Take the previous formula for what determines r, and set it equal to i_h as follows:

$$r = i_h$$
$$(1 + i_f)(1 + e_f) - 1 = i_h$$

Now solve for e_f:

$$(1 + i_f)(1 + e_f) = (1 + i_h)$$

$$(1 + e_f) = \frac{(1 + i_h)}{(1 + i_f)}$$

$$e_f = \frac{(1 + i_h)}{(1 + i_f)} - 1$$

As verified here, the IFE theory contends that when $i_h > i_f$, e_f will be positive. That is, the foreign currency will appreciate when the foreign interest rate is less than the home interest rate. This appreciation will improve the foreign return to investors from the home country, making returns on foreign securities similar to returns on home securities. Conversely, when $i_f > i_h$, e_f will be negative. That is, the foreign currency will depreciate when the foreign interest rate exceeds the home interest rate. This depreciation will reduce the return on foreign securities from the perspective of investors in the home country, making returns on foreign securities no higher than returns on home securities.

As a numerical example, assume that the interest rate on a one-year insured home bank deposit is 11 percent and the interest rate on a one-year insured foreign bank deposit is 12 percent. For the actual returns of these two investments to be similar from the perspective of investors in the home country, the foreign currency would have to change over the investment horizon by the following percentage:

$$e_f = \frac{(1 + i_h)}{(1 + i_f)} - 1$$

$$= \frac{(1 + .11)}{(1 + .12)} - 1$$

$$= -.0089, \text{ or } -.89\%$$

The implications are that the foreign currency denominating the foreign deposit would need to depreciate by .89 percent in order to make the actual return on the foreign deposit equal to 11 percent from the perspective of investors in the home country. This would then make the return on the foreign investment equal to the return on a domestic investment. A more simplified but less precise rule of the IFE is

$$e_f = i_h - i_f$$

That is, the exchange rate percentage change over the investment horizon will equal the interest rate differential between two countries. For example, if the British rate on six-month deposits were 2 percent above the U.S. rate, the British pound would depreciate by approximately 2 percent over six months according to IFE. If this occurred, U.S. investors would earn about the same return on British deposits as they would on U.S. deposits. Thus, there would be no advantage to the foreign investments even though they exhibited a higher interest rate than domestic investments.

Graphic Analysis of the International Fisher Effect

Exhibit 8.7 displays the set of points that conform to the argument behind IFE theory. For example, point E reflects a situation where the foreign interest exceeded the home interest rate by three percentage points. Yet, the foreign currency depreciated by 3 percent to offset its interest rate advantage. Thus, an investor setting up a deposit in the foreign country would have achieved a return similar to what was possible domestically. Point F represents a home interest rate 2 percent above the foreign interest rate. If investors from the home country establish a foreign deposit, they are at a disadvantage regarding the foreign interest rate. However, IFE theory suggests the currency should appreciate by 2 percent to offset the interest rate disadvantage.

Point F in Exhibit 8.7 can also illustrate the IFE from a foreign investor's perspective. The home interest would appear attractive to the foreign investor. However, IFE theory suggests the foreign currency will appreciate by 2 percent, which, from the foreign investor's perspective, implies the home country's currency denominating the investment instruments would depreciate to offset the interest rate advantage.

All the points along the so-called **IFE line** in Exhibit 8.7 reflect the exchange rate adjusting to offset the differential in interest rates. This means an investor will end up achieving the same yield (adjusted for exchange rate fluctuations) whether investing at home or in a foreign country.

To be precise, IFE theory does not suggest this relationship will exist over each time period. The point of IFE theory is that if a corporation periodically makes foreign investments to take advantage of higher foreign interest rates,

EXHIBIT 8.7 Illustration of IFE Line *(when exchange rate changes perfectly offset interest rate differentials)*

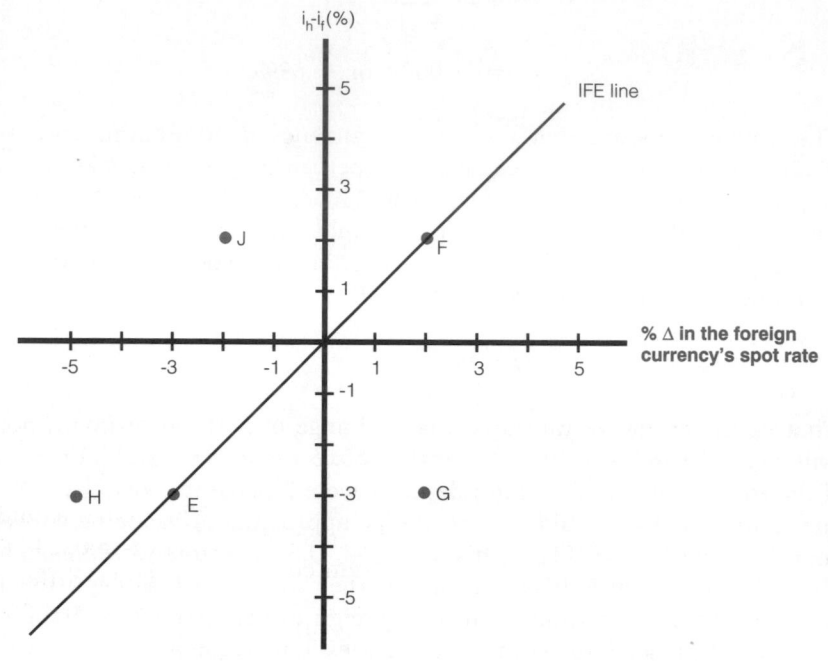

it will achieve a yield that is sometimes above and sometimes below the domestic yield. Periodic investment by a U.S. corporation that attempts to capitalize on the higher interest rates would on the average, therefore, achieve a similar yield if it simply made domestic deposits periodically.

Points below the IFE line generally reflect the higher returns from investing in foreign deposits. For example, point G in Exhibit 8.7 represents the foreign interest rate exceeding the home interest rate by 3 percent. In addition, the foreign currency appreciated by 2 percent. The combination of the higher foreign interest rate plus the appreciation of the foreign currency will cause the foreign yield to be higher than what was possible domestically. If actual data were compiled and plotted, and the vast majority of points were below the IFE line, this would suggest that investors of the home country could have consistently increased their investment returns by establishing foreign bank deposits. Such results refute the IFE theory.

Points above the IFE line generally reflect lower returns from foreign deposits than the returns that are possible domestically. For example, point H reflects a foreign interest rate that is 3 percent above the home interest rate. Yet, point H suggests that the exchange rate of the foreign currency depreciated by 5 percent to more than offset its interest rate advantage.

As another example, point J represents a situation where an investor of the home country is hampered in two ways by investing in a foreign deposit. First, the foreign interest rate is less than the home interest rate. Second, the foreign currency depreciated during the time the foreign deposit was held. If actual data were compiled and plotted, and the vast majority of points were

RELATED RESEARCH

Statistical Test of IFE

A somewhat simplified statistical test of the international Fisher effect can be developed by applying regression analysis to historical exchange rates and the nominal interest rate differential. The percentage changes in the foreign currency value (E_f) can be regressed against the nominal interest rate differential that existed at the beginning of the quarter:

$$E_f = a_0 + a_1 \left[\frac{1 + i_{U.S.}}{1 + i_f} - 1 \right] + \mu$$

where a_0 is a constant, a_1 is the slope coefficient, and μ is an error term. Regression analysis would determine the regression coefficients. The hypothesized values of a_0 and a_1 are 0 and 1.0, respectively. These coefficients imply that a given differential in nominal interest rates is offset on average by an equal percentage change in the exchange rate.

The appropriate t-test for each regression coefficient requires a comparison to the hypothesized value and then division by the standard error (s.e.) of the coefficients, as follows:

Test for $a_0 = 0$

$$t = \frac{a_0 - 0}{\text{s.e. of } a_0}$$

Test for $a_1 = 1$

$$t = \frac{a_1 - 1}{\text{s.e. of } a_1}$$

The t-table would then be used to find the critical t-value. If either t-test finds that the coefficients differ significantly from what was hypothesized, the IFE is refuted.

---

above the IFE line, this would suggest that investors of the home country would have received consistently lower returns from foreign investments as opposed to investments in the home country. Such results refute the IFE theory.

If the actual points (one for each period) of interest rates and exchange rate changes were plotted over time on a graph such as Exhibit 8.7, we could determine whether the points were systematically below the IFE line (suggesting higher returns from foreign investing), above the line (suggesting lower returns from foreign investing), or evenly scattered on both sides (suggesting a balance of higher returns from foreign investing in some periods, and lower foreign returns in other periods).

Exhibit 8.8 is an example of a set of points that tend to support the IFE theory. The implications are that returns from short-term foreign investments are on the average about equal to the returns that are possible domestically. Notice that each individual point reflects a change in the exchange rate that does not exactly offset the interest rate differential. In some cases, the exchange rate change did not fully offset the interest rate differential. In other cases, the exchange rate change more than offset the interest rate differential. Overall, the results balanced out such that the interest rate differentials were *on the average* offset by changes in the exchange rates. Thus, foreign investments generated yields that were on the average equal to those of domestic investments.

If foreign yields are expected to be about equal to domestic yields, a U.S. firm would most probably prefer the domestic investments, because the yield

EXHIBIT 8.8 Illustration of IFE Concept *(when exchange rate changes offset interest rate differentials on average)*

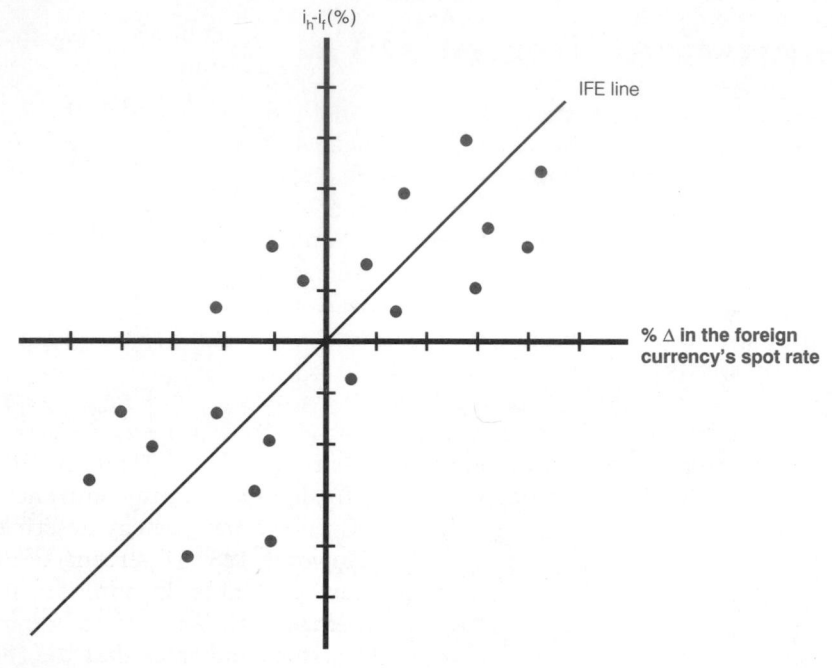

on domestic short-term securities (such as bank deposits) is known in advance. However, the yield to be attained from foreign short-term securities is uncertain due to the uncertainty of the spot exchange rate that will exist when the security matures. Investors generally prefer an investment in which the return is known over an investment whose return is uncertain, assuming that all other features of the investments are similar.

Does the International Fisher Effect Hold?

Whether the IFE holds in reality depends on the particular time period examined. From 1974 to 1977, the U.S. interest rates were generally lower than foreign interest rates. As IFE theory would predict, these foreign currencies weakened during this period. In 1978–1979, the U.S. interest rates were generally higher than foreign interest rates, and the foreign currency values strengthened during this period (again supporting IFE theory to an extent). However, during the 1980–1984 period, the foreign currencies consistently weakened far beyond what would have been anticipated according to IFE theory. Furthermore, during the 1985–1987 period foreign currencies strengthened to a much greater degree than suggested by the interest differential. While the IFE theory may hold during some time frames, there is evidence that it does not consistently hold.

If the IFE holds, then a strategy of borrowing in one country and investing the funds in another country should not provide a positive return on average.

The reason is that exchange rates should adjust to offset interest rate differentials on the average. Research by Madura and Nosari simulated a speculative strategy whereby the currency with the lowest quoted interest rate was borrowed by a U.S. speculator and converted and invested in the currency exhibiting the highest interest rate. At the end of the investment period, the funds were withdrawn and loan repayment was made. This strategy was continued periodically over time. If the IFE held for these periods, the **spread** (difference between return on the investment and cost of borrowing) should have been zero on average (in the absence of transaction costs). The trend of spreads during the various periods is illustrated in Exhibit 8.9, showing that the spread was usually positive.

The process described here was repeated from the perspective of speculative investors in seven other major countries. Regardless of the perspective, the spread was found to be significantly above zero, on average. These results refute the IFE theory.

A related study by Thomas tested the IFE theory by examining the results of (1) purchasing currency futures contracts of currencies with high interest rates that contained a discount (relative to the spot rate) and (2) selling futures on currencies with low interest rates that contained a premium. If the high-interest-rate currencies depreciate and the low-interest-rate currencies appreciate to the extent suggested by the IFE theory, the strategy described here would not generate significant profits. However, 123 (57 percent) of the 216 transactions created by this strategy were profitable. In addition, the average gain was much higher than the average loss. The rate of return averaged 77 percent on an annual basis. This study indicates that the IFE does not hold—which is not to say that all MNCs should immediately place all excess cash in high-interest-rate currencies. There is significant risk in such a strategy, as verified by the existence of losses generated in some periods of the study.

EXHIBIT 8.9 Assessing Speculative Spreads to Determine Whether the IFE Holds

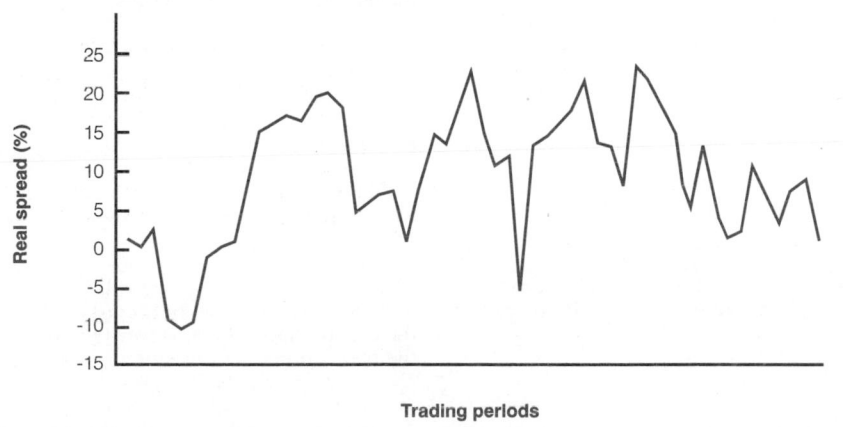

SOURCE: Akron Business and Economic Review (Winter 1984), p. 51.

Why the International Fisher Effect Does Not Always Hold

Earlier in the chapter, it was mentioned that purchasing power parity has not held over certain periods. Since the international Fisher effect is based on purchasing power parity, it does not consistently hold either. Because there are factors other than inflation that affect exchange rates, the exchange rates do not adjust in accordance with the inflation differential. Assume a nominal interest rate in a foreign country that is 3 percent above the U.S. rate because expected inflation in that country is 3 percent above expected U.S. inflation. Even if these nominal rates properly reflect inflationary expectations, the exchange rate of the foreign currency will react to other factors in addition to the inflation differential. If these other factors place upward pressure on the foreign currency's value, they will offset the downward pressure placed by the inflation differential. Consequently, foreign investments will achieve higher returns for the U.S. investors than domestic investments.

COMPARISON OF IRP, PPP, and IFE THEORIES

At this point, it may be helpful to compare three related theories of international finance: (1) interest rate parity (IRP), discussed in the previous chapter, (2) purchasing power parity (PPP), and (3) the international Fisher effect (IFE). Exhibit 8.10 summarizes the main theme of each theory. Note that all

EXHIBIT 8.10 Comparison of IRP, PPP, and IFE Theories

Theory	Key Variables of Theory		Summary of Theory
Interest rate parity (IRP)	Forward rate premium (or discount)	Interest rate differential	The forward rate of one currency with respect to another will contain a premium (or discount) that is determined by the differential in interest rates between the two countries. As a result, covered interest arbitrage will provide a return that is no higher than a domestic return.
Purchasing power parity (PPP)	Percentage change in spot exchange rate	Inflation rate differential	The spot rate of one currency with respect to another will change in reaction to the differential in inflation rates between the two countries. Consequently, the purchasing power for consumers when purchasing goods in their own country will be similar to the purchasing power when importing goods from the foreign country.
International Fisher effect (IFE)	Percentage change in spot exchange rate	Interest rate differential	The spot rate of one currency with respect to another will change in accordance with the differential in interest rates between the two countries. Consequently, the return on uncovered foreign money market securities will on average be no higher than the return on domestic money market securities from the perspective of investors in the home country.

three theories relate to the determination of exchange rates. Yet, they differ in their implications. The theory of IRP focuses on why the forward rate differs from the spot rate and the degree of difference that should exist. This relates to a specific point in time. Conversely, PPP theory and IFE theory focus on how a currency's spot rate will change over time. While PPP theory suggests that the spot rate will change in accordance with inflation differentials, IFE theory suggests that it will change in accordance with interest rate differentials. PPP is nevertheless related to IFE because inflation differentials influence the nominal interest rate differentials between two countries.

With regard to determinants of exchange rates, inflation is often thought to be one of the most important. Purchasing power parity (PPP) theory specifies a precise relationship between relative inflation rates of two countries and their exchange rate. In inexact terms, PPP theory suggests that the equilibrium exchange rate will adjust by the same magnitude as the differential in inflation rates between two countries. While PPP continues to be a valuable concept, there is evidence of sizable deviations from the theory in the real world.

Interest rate differentials between countries represent another important determinant of exchange rates. The theory, known as the international Fisher effect (IFE), specifies a precise relationship between relative interest rates of two countries and their exchange rates. It suggests that an investor who periodically invests in foreign interest-bearing securities will on average achieve a return similar to what was possible domestically. This implies that the exchange rate of the country with high interest rates will depreciate to offset the interest rate advantage achieved by foreign investments. However, there is evidence that during some periods the IFE does not hold. Thus, investment in foreign short-term securities may achieve a higher return than what is possible domestically. If a firm attempts achieving this higher return, however, it does incur the risk that the currency denominating the foreign security might depreciate against the investor's home currency during the investment period. In this case, the foreign security could generate a lower return than domestic securities, even if it exhibits a higher interest rate.

1. Explain the theory of purchasing power parity (PPP). Based on this theory, what is the general forecast of the values of currencies in highly inflated countries?

2. Explain the rationale behind purchasing power parity theory.

3. Explain how you could determine whether purchasing power parity exists.

4. Relate the existence of purchasing power parity to "real" (effective) exchange rates.

5. Provide reasons why purchasing power parity does not hold.

6. Describe a limitation in testing whether purchasing power parity holds.

7. Explain the international Fisher effect (IFE). What are the implications of IFE to firms with excess cash that consistently invest in foreign Treasury bills?

8. What is the rationale for the existence of the international Fisher effect?

9. Assume U.S. interest rates are generally above foreign interest rates. What does this suggest about the future strength or weakness of the dollar based on the international Fisher effect? Explain.

10. Compare and contrast interest rate parity (discussed in the previous chapter), purchasing power parity (PPP), and the international Fisher effect (IFE).

11. One assumption made in developing the international Fisher effect is that all investors in all countries require the same real return. What does this mean?

12. How could you use regression analysis to determine whether the relationship specified by purchasing power parity (PPP) existed on average. Specify the model, and describe how you would assess the regression results to determine if there was a *significant* difference from the relationship suggested by PPP.

13. Describe a statistical test for the international Fisher effect.

14. If investors in the United States and Canada required the same real return, and the nominal rate of interest were 2 percent higher in Canada, what would this imply about expectations of U.S. inflation and Canadian inflation? What do these inflationary expectations suggest about future exchange rates?

15. Some countries with high inflation rates tend to have high interest rates. Why?

16. Currencies of some Latin American countries such as Brazil and Argentina consistently weaken against most other currencies. What concept in this chapter would explain this occurrence?

17. Japan has typically had lower inflation than the United States. How would one expect this to affect the Japanese yen's value? Why has this expected relationship not always occurred?

18. Assume that the nominal interest rate in Mexico is 48 percent and the interest rate in the United States is 8 percent for one-year securities that are free from default risk. What would the Fisher effect suggest about the differential in expected inflation in these two countries? Using this information and the purchasing power parity theory, describe the expected nominal return to U.S. investors who invest in Mexico.

19. Shouldn't the international Fisher effect discourage investors from attempting to capitalize on higher foreign interest rates? Why do some investors continue to invest overseas, even when they have no other transactions overseas?

20. Assume that the inflation rate in France is expected to increase substantially. How would this affect French nominal interest rates and the French

exchange rate? If the international Fisher effect holds, how would the nominal return to U.S. investors who invest in France be affected by the higher inflation in France? Explain.

21. How is it possible for purchasing power parity to hold, but not the international Fisher effect?

22. Explain the rationale for the international Fisher effect not holding when one assesses historical data.

23. Assume that the spot exchange rate of the British pound is $1.73. How would this spot rate adjust according to purchasing power parity if Great Britain experiences an inflation rate of 7 percent while the United States experiences an inflation rate of 2 percent? (You can use the approximate formula to answer this question.)

24. Assume the spot exchange rate of the Swiss franc is $.70. The one-year interest rate is 11 percent in the United States and 7 percent in Switzerland. What would be the spot rate in one year according to the international Fisher effect? (You can use the approximate formula to answer this question.)

25. As of today, assume the following information was available:

	U.S.	France
Real rate of interest required by investors	2%	2%
Nominal interest rate	11%	15%
Spot rate rate	_____	$.20
One-year forward rate	_____	$.19

a) Use the forward rate to forecast the percentage change in the French franc over the next year.
b) Use the differential in expected inflation to forecast the percentage change in the French franc over the next year.
c) Use the spot rate to forecast percentage change in the French franc over the next year.

26. During February 1990, interest rates of the German mark rose to their highest level in seven years. The increase was mostly attributed to the strong demand for funds in West Germany as a result of the reunification effort with East Germany. Explain how the forward premium of the German mark would likely be affected by this event. How would the forecast of the percentage change in the mark be affected by the increased German interest rates according to the international Fisher effect?

27. Would PPP be more likely to hold between the United States and Hungary if trade barriers were removed or if Hungary's currency was allowed to float? Explain.

28. Would IFE be more likely to hold between the United States and Romania if trade barriers were removed or if Romania's currency was allowed to float? Explain.

Flame Fixtures Inc.

Business Application of Purchasing Power Parity

Flame Fixtures Inc. is a small U.S. business in Arizona that produces and sells lamp fixtures. Its costs and its revenues have been very stable over time. Its profits have been adequate, but Flame was searching for means of increasing profits in the future. It has recently been negotiating with a Mexican firm called Coron' Company to purchase some of the necessary parts. Every three months Coron' Company would send a specified amount of parts with the bill invoiced in Mexican pesos. Having the parts produced by Coron' was expected to save about 20 percent on production costs. Coron' would only be willing to work out a deal if it was assured that it would receive orders every three months of a minimum specified amount over the next ten years. Flame was required to use its assets to serve as collateral in case it did not fulfill its obligation.

The price of the parts would change over time in response to the costs of production. Flame recognized that the cost to Coron' would increase substantially over time as a result of the very high inflation rate in Mexico. Therefore, the price charged in pesos would likely rise substantially every three months. However, Flame felt that because of the concept of purchasing power parity (PPP), its dollar payments to Coron' would be very stable. According to PPP, if Mexican inflation was much higher than U.S. inflation, the peso would weaken against the dollar by that difference. Since Flame did not have much liquidity, it could experience a severe cash shortage if its expenses were much higher than anticipated.

The demand for Flame's product has been very stable, and is expected to continue that way. Since the U.S. inflation rate was expected to be very low, Flame would likely continue pricing its lamps at today's prices (in dollars). It believes that by saving 20 percent on production costs, it will substantially increase its profits. It is about ready to sign a contract with Coron' Company.

a) Describe a scenario that could allow Flame to save even more than 20 percent on production costs.

b) Describe a scenario that could allow Flame to actually incur higher production costs than if it simply had the parts produced in the U.S.

c) Do you think that Flame will experience stable dollar outflow payments to Coron' over time? Explain. (Assume that the amount of parts ordered is constant over time).

d) Do you think that Flame's risk changes at all as a result of its new relationship with Coron' Company? Explain.

PROJECTS

1. Use the "Money Rates" section of a recent issue of *The Wall Street Journal* to determine U.S. and British interest rates. Using this information, determine the expected percentage change in the pound's spot rate over the next year according to the international Fisher effect.

2. Use data from the Data Bank in the back of this text to determine whether a U.S. investor could have earned a higher return (on average) on

consecutive investments in the United Kingdom than in the U.S. Assess several historical periods. What do your results imply about the international Fisher effect?

SUGGESTED READING

Jeffrey Frankel. "Flexible Exchange Rates: Experience Versus Theory." *Journal of Portfolio Management* (Winter 1989), pp. 45–54. This article provides an overview of the behavior of exchange rate movements, including a discussion about whether purchasing power parity holds.

REFERENCES

Abuaf, Niso, and Philippe Jorion. "Purchasing Power in the Long Run." *Journal of Finance* (March 1990), pp. 157–174.

Adler, Michael, and Bernard Dumas. "International Portfolio Choice and Corporate Finance: A Synthesis." *Journal of Finance* (June 1983), pp. 925–984.

Adler, Michael, and Bruce Lehmann. "Deviations from Purchasing Power Parity in the Long Run." *Journal of Finance* (December 1983), pp. 1471–1487.

Brittain, Bruce. "Tests of Theories of Exchange Rate Determination." *Journal of Finance* (May 1977), pp. 519–529.

Cornell, Bradford. "Inflation, Relative Price Changes, and Exchange Risk." *Financial Management* (Autumn 1980), pp. 30–34.

_____. "Relative Price Changes and Deviations from Purchasing Power Parity." *Journal of Banking and Finance* (September 1979), pp. 263–279.

_____. "Spot Rates, Forward Rates, and Market Dynamics." *Journal of Political Economy* (December 1976), pp. 1161–1176.

Cumby, Robert E., and Maurice Obstfeld. "A Note on Exchange-Rate Expectations and Nominal Interest Differentials: A Test of the Fisher Hypothesis." *Journal of Finance* (June 1981), pp. 697–703.

Dornbusch, Rudiger. "Expectations and Exchange Rate Dynamics." *Journal of Political Economy* (December 1976), pp. 1161–1176.

_____. "Flexible Exchange Rates and Interdependence." *International Monetary Fund Staff Papers* (March 1983), pp. 3–38.

Eun, C. S. "Global Purchasing Power View of Exchange Risk." *Journal of Financial and Quantitative Analysis* (December 1981), pp. 639–650.

Fama, Eugene F. "Efficient Capital Markets: A Review of Theory and Empirical Work." *The Journal of Finance* (May 1970), pp. 383–417.

Frankel, Jeffrey. "Flexible Exchange Rates: Experience Versus Theory." *Journal of Portfolio Management* (Winter 1989), pp. 45–54.

Frenkel, Jacob A. "Purchasing Power Parity: Doctrinal Perspective and Evidence from the 1920s." *Journal of International Economics* (May 1978), pp. 169–192.

_____. "Flexible Exchange Rates, Prices, and the Role of News: Lessons from the 1970s." *Journal of Political Economy* (August 1981), pp. 665–705.

Galliott, Henry J. "Purchasing Power Parity as an Explanation of Long-Term Changes in Exchange Rates." *Journal of Money, Credit, and Banking* (August 1970), pp. 348–357.

Genberg, H. "Purchasing Power Parity Under Fixed and Flexible Rates." *Journal of International Economics* (May 1978), pp. 247–276.

Geweke, J., and E. Feige. "Some Joint Tests of the Efficiency of Markets for Forward Foreign Exchange." *Review of Economics and Statistics* (October 1979), pp. 334–341.

Giddy, Ian H. "An Integrated Theory of Exchange Rate Equilibrium." *Journal of Financial and Quantitative Analysis* (December 1976), pp. 883–892.

———. "Exchange Risk: Whose View?" *Financial Management* (Summer 1977), pp. 23–33.

Hakkio, Craig S., "Interest Rates and Exchange Rates—What Is the Relationship?" *Economic Review,* Federal Reserve Bank of Kansas City (November 1986), pp. 33–43.

Huang, Roger. "Risk and Parity in Purchasing Power." *Journal of Money, Credit, and Banking* (August 1990), pp. 338–356.

Kahn, George A., "Inflation and Disinflation: A Comparison across Countries." *Economic Review,* Federal Reserve Bank of Kansas City, (February 1985), pp. 23–42.

Kane, Alex, Leonard Rosenthal, and Greta Ljung. "Tests of the Fisher Hypothesis with International Data: Theory and Evidence." *Journal of Finance* (May 1983), pp. 539–551.

Kim, Yoonbai. "Purchasing Power in the Long Run: A Cointegration Approach." *Journal of Money, Credit, and Banking* (November 1990), pp. 491–503.

Koveos, Peter, and Bruce Seifert, "Purchasing Power Parity and Black Markets." *Financial Management* (Autumn 1985), pp. 40–46.

Kravis, Irving B., and Robert E. Lipsey. "Price Behavior in the Light of Balance of Payments Theories." *Journal of International Economics* (May 1978), pp. 193–246.

Krugman, Paul R. "Purchasing Power Parity and Exchange Rates." *Journal of International Economics* (August 1978), pp. 397–407.

Madura, Jeff, and E. Joe Nosari. "Speculative Trading in the Eurocurrency Market." *Akron Business and Economic Review* (Winter 1984), pp. 48–52.

Manzur, Meher. "An International Comparison of Prices and Exchange Rates: A New Test of Purchasing Power Parity." *Journal of International Money and Finance* (March 1990), pp. 75–91.

Mishkin, Frederic S., "Are Real Interest Rates Equal across Countries? An Empirical Investigation of International Parity Conditions." *Journal of Finance* (December 1984), pp. 1345–1357.

Officer, Lawrence H. "The Purchasing Power Parity Theory of Exchange Rates: A Review Article." *International Monetary Fund Staff Papers* (March 1976), pp. 1–60.

Rogalski, Richard, and Joseph D. Vinso. "Price Level Variations as Predictors of Flexible Exchange Rates." *Journal of International Business Studies* (Spring–Summer 1977), pp. 71–81.

Solnik, Bruno. "International Parity Conditions and Exchange Risk: A Review." *Journal of Banking and Finance* (August 1978), pp. 281–293.

Thomas, Lee R., "A Winning Strategy for Currency-futures Speculation." *Journal of Portfolio Management* (Fall 1985), pp. 65–69.

Thornton, Daniel L. "Tests of Covered Interest Rate Parity." *Review,* Federal Reserve Bank of St. Louis. (July–August 1989), pp. 55–66.

Whitt, Joseph A., Jr. "Purchasing-Power Parity and Exchange Rates in the Long Run." *Economic Review,* Federal Reserve Bank of Atlanta (July–August 1989), pp. 18–32.

Whitt, Joseph A. Jr., Paul D. Koch, and Jeffrey A. Rosensweig, "The Dollar and Prices: An Empirical Analysis," *Economic Review,* Federal Reserve Bank of Atlanta (October 1986), pp. 4–18.

Wolff, Christian, "Forward Foreign Exchange Rates, Expected Spot Rates, and Premia: A Signal-Extraction Approach," *Journal of Finance* (June 1987), pp. 395–406.

PART THREE

Exchange Rate Risk Management

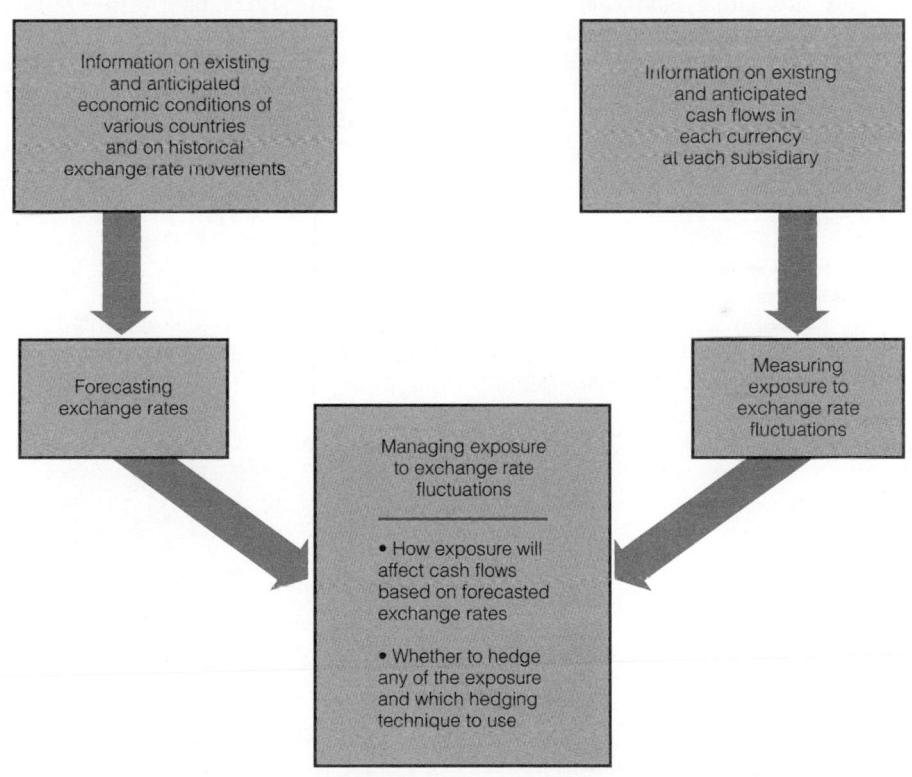

Part 3 (Chapters 9 through 12) explains the various functions involved in managing exposure to exchange rate risk. Chapter 9 describes various methods used to forecast exchange rates and explains how to assess forecasting performance. Chapter 10 demonstrates how to measure exposure to exchange rate movements. Given a firm's exposure and forecasts of future exchange rates, Chapters 11 and 12 explain how to hedge that exposure.

Forecasting Exchange Rates

The quality of an MNC's corporate decisions depends on the accuracy of exchange rate projections. This chapter first emphasizes why forecasts of exchange rates are critical for multinational financial management. Then, particular forecasting techniques and services are discussed, along with some evidence of their recent performance. Finally, a practical method for evaluating the accuracy of exchange rate forecasts is demonstrated.

WHY MULTINATIONAL FIRMS FORECAST EXCHANGE RATES

Virtually every operation of an MNC can be influenced by changes in exchange rates. Several corporate functions for which exchange rate forecasts are necessary follow:

1. *Hedging decision.* MNCs are constantly confronted with the decision of whether to hedge future payables and receivables in foreign currencies. Whether a firm hedges may be determined by its forecasts of foreign currency values. As a simple example, consider a firm in the United States that plans to pay for steel imported from France in 90 days. If the forecasted value of the French franc in 90 days is sufficiently below the 90-day forward rate, the MNC may decide not to hedge.

2. *Short-term financing decision.* When large corporations borrow, they have access to several different currencies. The currency they borrow would ideally (1) exhibit a low interest rate and (2) weaken in value over the financing period. If, for example, a U.S. firm borrowed Swiss francs, and the Swiss franc depreciated against the U.S. dollar over the financing period, the firm could pay back the loan with fewer dollars (when converting those dollars in exchange for the amount of francs owed). This financing decision should therefore be influenced by exchange rate forecasts of any currencies available for financing.

3. *Short-term investment decision.* Corporations sometimes have a substantial amount of excess cash available for a short term. Large deposits can

be established in several currencies. The ideal currency for deposits would (1) exhibit a high interest rate and (2) strengthen in value over the investment period. Consider, for example, a U.S. corporation that had excess cash deposited into a British bank account, and assume the British pound appreciated against the dollar by the end of the deposit period. As the British pounds are withdrawn and exchanged for U.S. dollars, more dollars will be received due to the pound's appreciation against the dollar. Exchange rate forecasts of the currencies denominating available deposit accounts should therefore be considered when determining where to invest the short-term cash.

4. *Capital budgeting decision.* When an MNC attempts to determine whether to establish a subsidiary in a given country, a capital budgeting analysis is conducted. Forecasts of the future cash flows used within the capital budgeting process will be dependent on future currency values. This dependency can be due to (1) future inflows or outflows denominated in foreign currencies that will require conversion to the home currency and/or (2) the influence of future exchange rates on demand for the corporation's products. There are several additional ways by which exchange rates can affect the estimated cash flows, but the main point here is that accurate forecasts of currency values will improve the estimates of the cash flows, and therefore enhance the MNC's decision-making abilities.

5. *Long-term financing decision.* Corporations that issue bonds to secure long-term funds may consider denominating the bonds in foreign currencies. As with short-term financing, corporations would prefer the currency borrowed (denominating the debt) to depreciate over time against the currency they are receiving from sales. To estimate the cost from issuing bonds denominated in a foreign currency, forecasts of exchange rates are required.

6. *Earnings assessment.* When earnings of an MNC are reported, subsidiary earnings are consolidated and translated into the currency representing the parent firm's home country. For example, consider an MNC with its home office in the United States and subsidiaries in Switzerland and Great Britain. The Swiss subsidiary's earnings in Swiss francs must be measured by translation to U.S. dollars. The British subsidiary's earnings in pounds must also be measured by translation to U.S. dollars. "Translation" does not suggest that the earnings are physically converted to U.S. dollars. It is simply a recording process to periodically report consolidated earnings in a single currency. Using the scenario just described, appreciation of the Swiss franc will boost the Swiss subsidiary's earnings when reported (translated) in U.S. dollars. Forecasts of exchange rates thus play an important role in the overall forecast of an MNC's consolidated earnings.

The need for accurate exchange rate projections should now be clear. The following section describes forecasting methods available.

FORECASTING TECHNIQUES

The numerous methods available for forecasting exchange rates can be categorized into four general groups: (1) technical, (2) fundamental, (3) market-based, and (4) mixed.

Technical Forecasting

Technical forecasting involves use of historical exchange rate data to predict future values. It is sometimes conducted in a "judgmental" manner, without statistical analysis. For example, the fact that a given currency has increased in value over four consecutive days may provide an indication of how the currency will move tomorrow. Often, however, statistical analysis is applied in technical forecasting. For example, a computer program can be developed to detect particular historical trends. (See Exhibit 9.1.)

There are also several **time series models** that examine moving averages and thus allow a forecaster to develop some rule, such as, "The currency tends to decline in value after a rise in the moving average over three consecutive periods." Normally, consultants who use such a method will not disclose their particular rule for forecasting. If they did, their potential clients might apply the rules themselves rather than pay for the consultant's advice.

Technical forecasting of exchange rates is similar to its application on the stock market. If the pattern of currency values over time appears random, then technical forecasting is not appropriate. Unless historical trends in exchange rate movements can be identified, examination of past movements will not be useful for indicating future movements.

Technical forecasting models have helped some speculators in the foreign exchange market at various times. However, a model that worked well in one particular period will not necessarily work well in another. With the abundance of technical models existing today, some are bound to generate speculative profits in any given period. But none has proven consistently profitable.

Many foreign exchange participants argue that even if a particular technical forecasting model is shown to lead consistently to speculative profits, it will no longer be useful once other participants begin to use it. The trading based on its recommendation would push the currency value to a new position immediately. Speculators using technical exchange rate forecasting often incur large transaction costs due to frequent trading. In addition, it can be time-consuming to monitor currency movements in the search for any systematic pattern. Furthermore, speculators need sufficient capital to absorb losses that may occur.

From the corporate point of view, use of technical forecasting may be limited in that it typically focuses on the near future, which is not that helpful

EXHIBIT 9.1 Application of Technical and Fundamental Analysis to Forecast Exchange Rates

Forecasting Techniques	Judgmental Use of This Forecasting Technique	Statistical Use of This Forecasting Technique
1. Technical forecasting	Examining a historical series of exchange rates to determine whether some non-random pattern exists, and making a projection based on this pattern.	Using a computer program to detect non-random patterns, or to compute moving averages, etc.
2. Fundamental forecasting	Comparing economic factors in a general manner (such as one country's inflation rate being higher than another country's) to determine how a currency's value will change in the future.	Using a statistical model such as regression analysis to (1) determine how factors have affected exchange rates and (2) use this information to develop forecasts of currency values based on the current values of these factors.

INTERNATIONAL FINANCIAL MANAGEMENT IN PRACTICE

Using Exchange Rate Movements in January as a Signal

An understanding of factors that affect exchange rates can enable firms or individuals to forecast future exchange rates. However, there is one other indicator that has been very accurate even though it is not fundamentally sound. The movement in the dollar's value during January tends to signal the trend for the remaining eleven months of each year.

In seven years over the 1981–1990 period, the dollar's value rose against a trade-weighted index of other currencies by more than one percent in January. In each of those years, the dollar rose further over the remaining eleven months of the year. In the other four years, the dollar declined (or rose by less than one percent) in January. In each of those years, the dollar's value declined against other currencies. Thus, the month of January served as a reasonable indicator for the remainder of the year. There does not appear to be any fundamental reason for the accurate signal provided by the results in January. However, the consistent accuracy in signalling the direction of the dollar may be enough of a reason for some firms or individuals to monitor the month of January. Of course, there is no guarantee that the results in January will continue to reflect the dollar's direction over the rest of the year. Many foreign exchange traders would dismiss the historical relationship as a coincidence and would focus on other fundamental factors instead.

for developing corporate policies. Also, it rarely provides point estimates or a range of possible future values, as pointed out by Goodman. Because technical analysis will not typically estimate future exchange rates in precise terms, it is not, by itself, an adequate forecasting tool for corporate treasurers of MNCs.

Fundamental Forecasting

Fundamental forecasting is based on fundamental relationships between economic variables and exchange rates. Given current values of these variables along with their historical impact on a currency's value, corporations can develop exchange rate projections. For example, high inflation in a given country can lead to depreciation in the currency representing that country. Of course, all other factors that may influence exchange rates should also be considered.

From a "judgmental" perspective, a forecast may arise simply from a subjective assessment of the degree to which general movements in economic variables in one country are expected to affect exchange rates. From a statistical perspective, a forecast would be based on quantitatively measured impacts of factors on exchange rates. While some of the full-blown fundamental models are beyond the scope of this text, a simplified discussion follows.

The focus here is on only two of the many factors that affect currency values. Before identifying them, consider the corporate objective to forecast the percentage change (rate of appreciation or depreciation) in the British pound with respect to the U.S. dollar during the next quarter. For simplicity, assume the firm's forecast for the British pound is dependent on only two factors that affect the pound's value:

1. Inflation in the United States relative to inflation in Great Britain.
2. Income growth in the United States relative to income growth in Great Britain (measured as a percentage change).

The first step is to determine how these variables have affected the percentage change in the pound value based on historical data. This is commonly achieved with regression analysis. First, quarterly data can be compiled for the inflation and income growth levels of both Great Britain and the United States. The dependent variable is the quarterly percentage change in the British pound value (called *BP*). The independent (influential) variables may be set up as follows:

1. Previous quarterly percentage change in the inflation differential (U.S. inflation rate minus British inflation rate), referred to as *INF*
2. Previous quarterly percentage change in the income growth differential (U.S. income growth minus British income growth), referred to as *INC*

The regression equation can be defined as

$$BP = b_0 + b_1 \, INF + b_2 \, INC + \mu$$

where b_0 is a constant, b_1 measures the sensitivity of *BP* to changes in *INF*, b_2 measures the sensitivity of *BP* to changes in *INC*, and μ represents an error term. A set of historical data would be needed to obtain previous values of *BP*, *INF*, and *INC*. Using this data set, regression analysis will generate the values of the regression coefficients (b_0, b_1, and b_2). That is, regression analysis determines the direction and degree to which *BP* is affected by each independent variable. The coefficient b_1 will exhibit a positive sign if, when *INF* changes, *BP* changes in the same direction (other things held constant). A negative sign indicates that *BP* and *INF* move in opposite directions. In the equation given, b_1 is expected to exhibit a positive sign, because when inflation in the United States relative to Great Britain increases, this exerts upward pressure on the pound value.

The regression coefficient b_2 (which measures the impact of *INC* on *BP*) is expected to be positive, since when U.S. income growth exceeds British income growth, there is upward pressure on the pound's value. These relationships have already been thoroughly discussed in Chapter 4.

Once regression analysis is employed to generate values of the coefficients, these coefficients can be used to forecast. To illustrate, assume the following values: $b_0 = .002$, $b_1 = .8$, and $b_2 = 1.0$. The coefficients can be interpreted as follows. For a one-unit percentage change in the inflation differential, the pound is expected to change by .8 percent in the same direction, other things held constant. For a one-unit percentage change in the income differential, the British pound is expected to change by 1.0 percent in the same direction, other things held constant. To develop forecasts, assume the most recent quarterly percentage change in *INF* (the inflation differential) is 4 percent and in *INC* (the income growth differential) is 2 percent. Using this information along with our estimated regression coefficients, the forecast for *BP* is:

$$BP = b_0 + b_1\,INF + b_2\,INC$$
$$= .002 + .8(4\%) + 1(2\%)$$
$$= .2\% + 3.2\% + 2\%$$
$$= 5.4\%$$

Thus, given the current figures for inflation rates and income growth, the pound should appreciate by 5.4 percent during the next quarter.

This example is simplified to illustrate how fundamental analysis can be implemented for forecasting. A full-blown model may include many more than two factors. Yet, the application would still be somewhat similar. For example, a 20-factor regression model would be expressed as

$$BP = b_0 + b_1 x_1 + b_2 x_2 + \ldots b_{20} x_{20} + \mu$$

where b_0 is the constant, b_1 through b_{20} are regression coefficients and x_1 through x_{20} represent the 20 factors, and μ is an error term. A large time series database (perhaps 50 or more periods) would be necessary to warrant any confidence in the relationships detected by such a model.

EXAMPLE OF FUNDAMENTAL FORECASTING. When a regression model is used for forecasting, and the values of the influential factors have a lagged impact on exchange rates, the actual value of those factors can be used as input for the forecast. For example, if the inflation differential has a lagged impact on exchange rates, the inflation differential in the previous period may be used to forecast the percentage change in the exchange rate over the future period. However, some factors may have an instantaneous influence on exchange rates. Since these factors are not known, forecasts must be used. Firms recognize that poor forecasts of these factors can cause poor forecasts of the exchange rate movements, so they may attempt to account for the uncertainty by using **sensitivity analysis,** where more than one possible outcome is considered for the factors exhibiting uncertainty.

To illustrate how sensitivity analysis can be applied to forecasting exchange rate movements, assume that Phoenix Corporation develops a regression model to forecast the percentage change in the German mark's value. Our example will be simplified by assuming that the real interest rate differential and the inflation differential are the only factors that affect exchange rate movements, as shown in this regression model:

$$e_t = a_0 + a_1 INT_t + a_2 INF_{t-1} + \mu$$

where

$$e_t = \text{percentage change in the exchange rate over period } t$$
$$INT_t = \text{real interest rate differential over period } t$$
$$INF_{t-1} = \text{inflation differential in the previous period}$$

a_0, a_1, a_2 = regression coefficients

μ = error term

Historical data would be used to determine values for e_t, along with values for INT_t and INF_{t-1} for several periods (preferably 30 or more periods would be used to build the database). The length of each historical period (quarterly, monthly, etc.) should match the length of the period for which the forecast is needed. The historical data needed per period for the German mark model are (1) percentage change in mark value, (2) U.S. real interest rate minus German real interest rate, and (3) U.S. inflation rate in the previous period minus German inflation rate in the previous period. Assume that regression analysis has provided the following estimates for the regression coefficients:

Regression Coefficient	Estimate
a_0	.001
a_1	$-.7$
a_2	.6

The negative sign of a_1 suggests a negative relationship between INT_t and the mark's movements, while the positive sign of a_2 suggests a positive relationship between INF_{t-1} and the mark's movements.

To forecast the mark's percentage change over the upcoming period, INT_t and INF_{t-1} must be estimated. Assume that INF_{t-1} was 1 percent. However, INT_t is not known at the beginning of the period and must therefore be forecasted. Assume that Phoenix Corporation has developed the following probability distribution for INT_t:

Probability	Possible Outcome
20%	-3%
50%	-4%
30%	-5%
100%	

A separate forecast of the percentage change in e_t can be developed from each possible outcome of INT_t, as follows:

Forecast of INT	Forecast of Percent Change in ER_t	Probability
-3%	$.1\% + (-.7)(-3\%) + .6(1\%) = 2.8\%$	20%
-4%	$.1\% + (-.7)(-4\%) + .6(1\%) = 3.5\%$	50%
-5%	$.1\% + (-.7)(-5\%) + .6(1\%) = 4.2\%$	30%

If other currencies were to be forecasted, the probability distributions of their movements over the upcoming period could also be developed in a similar manner. For example, the percentage change in the Japanese yen could be forecasted by regressing historical percentage changes in the yen's value against (1) the differential between U.S. real interest rates and Japanese real interest rates, and (2) the differential between the U.S. inflation in the previous period and Japanese inflation in the previous period. The regression coefficients estimated by regression analysis for the yen model will differ from those for the mark model. The estimated coefficients could then be used along with estimates for the interest rate differential and inflation rate differential to develop a forecast of the percentage change in the yen. Sensitivity analysis could be used by reforecasting the yen's percentage change based on alternative estimates of the interest rate differential.

LIMITATIONS OF FUNDAMENTAL FORECASTING.   While fundamental forecasting accounts for the expected fundamental relationships between factors and currency values, the following limitations exist:

- Uncertain timing of impact
- Forecasts needed for factors with instantaneous impact
- Omission of other relevant factors from model
- Change in sensitivity of currency movements to each factor over time

Each of these factors will be discussed.

First, the precise timing of the impact of some factors on a currency's value is not known. It is possible that the impact of inflation on exchange rates will not completely occur until two, three, or four quarters later. The regression model would need to be adjusted accordingly.

A second limitation (as mentioned earlier) is related to those factors that exhibit an immediate impact on exchange rates. Their inclusion in a fundamental forecasting model would be useful only if forecasts could be obtained for them. Forecasts of these factors should be developed for a period that corresponds to the period in which a forecast for exchange rates is necessary. In this case, the accuracy of the exchange rate forecasts will be somewhat dependent on the forecasting accuracy of these factors. Even if firms knew exactly how movements in these factors affect exchange rates, their exchange rate projections could be inaccurate if they cannot predict the values of the factors.

A third limitation is that there are many other factors that deserve consideration in the fundamental forecasting process. Although regression analysis can sometimes include as many independent variables as is necessary to account for all factors that influence exchange rates, there are always factors that cannot be easily quantified or assessed in any way. For example, what if large German exporting firms experienced an unanticipated labor strike causing shortages? This would reduce the availability of German goods for U.S. consumers, and therefore reduce U.S. demand for German marks. Such an event, which places downward pressure on the German mark value, is not normally incorporated into the forecasting model.

A fourth limitation with the fundamental model is that coefficients derived from the regression analysis will not necessarily remain constant over time. In the previous example, the coefficient for *INF* was .6, suggesting that for a one-unit change in *INF*, the mark will appreciate by .6 percent. Yet, if the German or U.S. governments impose new trade barriers, or eliminate existing barriers, the impact of the inflation differential on trade (and therefore on the mark's exchange rate) may be affected.

These limitations of fundamental forecasting are discussed to emphasize that even the most sophisticated forecasting techniques (fundamental or otherwise) are not going to consistently provide accurate forecasts. MNCs that use forecasting techniques must allow for some margin of error, and recognize the possibility of error when implementing corporate policies.

USE OF PPP FOR FUNDAMENTAL FORECASTING.   Recall that the theory of purchasing power parity (PPP) specifies the fundamental relationship between the inflation differential and the exchange rate. In simple terms, PPP states that the currency of the relatively inflated country will depreciate by an amount that reflects that country's inflation differential. If this theory were accurate in reality, there would not be a need to even consider alternative forecasting techniques. However, using the inflation differential of two countries to forecast their exchange rate is not always accurate. Problems arise because (1) the timing of the impact of inflation fluctuations on changing trade patterns, and therefore on exchange rates, is not known with certainty, (2) data used to measure relative prices of two countries may be somewhat inaccurate, (3) barriers to trade can disrupt the trade patterns that would have emerged in accordance with PPP theory, and (4) other factors such as the interest rate differential between countries can also affect exchange rates. For these reasons, the inflation differential by itself is not sufficient to most accurately forecast exchange rate movements. Yet, it should be included in any fundamental forecasting model.

Market-Based Forecasting

The process of developing forecasts from market indicators, known as **market-based forecasting,** is usually based on (1) the spot rate or (2) the forward rate. To clarify why the spot rate can serve as a market-based forecast, assume the British pound is expected to appreciate against the dollar in the very near future. This would encourage speculators to buy the pound with U.S. dollars today in anticipation of its appreciation, and these purchases could force the pound's value up immediately. Conversely, if the pound is expected to depreciate against the dollar, speculators would sell off pounds now hoping to purchase them back at a lower price after they decline in value. Such action could force the pound to depreciate immediately. Thus, the current value of the pound should reflect the expectation of the pound's value in the very near future. Corporations can use the spot rate to forecast, since it represents the market's expectation of the spot rate in the near future.

Alternatively, the forward rate can serve as a forecast of the future spot rate. Assume the 30-day forward rate of the British pound is $1.40, and the general expectation of speculators is that the future spot rate of the pound will be $1.45 in 30 days. If speculators expect the future spot rate to be $1.45, and the prevailing forward rate is $1.40, they could buy pounds 30 days forward at $1.40 and then sell them when received (in 30 days) at the spot rate existing then. If their forecast is correct, they earn $.05 ($1.45 − $1.40) per pound. If a large number of speculators implement this strategy, the substantial demand to buy pounds forward will cause the forward rate to increase until this speculative demand stops. Perhaps this speculative demand will terminate when the forward rate reaches $1.45, since at this rate, no profits would be expected by implementing the strategy described. This example shows that the forward rate should move toward the market's general expectation of the future spot rate. In this sense, the forward rate serves as a market-based forecast, since it reflects the market's expectation of the spot rate at the end of the forward horizon (30 days from now in the example above).

While the focus of this chapter is on corporate forecasting rather than speculation, it is the speculation that helps to push the forward rate to the level that reflects the general expectation of the future spot rate. If corporations are convinced the forward rate is a reliable indicator of the future spot rate, they can simply monitor this publicly quoted rate to develop exchange rate projections.

While forward rates are sometimes available for two to five years, such rates are rarely quoted. However, the quoted interest rates on risk-free instruments of various countries can be used to determine what the forward rate would be under conditions of interest rate parity. For example, assume that the U.S. five-year interest rate is 10 percent, annualized, while the British five-year interest rate is 13 percent. The five-year compounded return on investments in each of these countries is computed as follows:

Country	Five-year compounded return
U.S.	$(1.10)^5 - 1 = 61\%$
U.K.	$(1.13)^5 - 1 = 84\%$

Thus, the appropriate five-year forward rate premium (or discount) of the British pound would be

$$p = \frac{(1 + i_{\text{U.S.}})}{(1 + i_{\text{U.K.}})} - 1$$

$$= \frac{1.61}{1.84} - 1$$

$$= -.125, \text{ or } -12.5\%$$

The results of our computation suggest that the five-year forward rate of the pound should contain a 12.5 percent discount. That is, the spot rate of the pound is expected to depreciate by 12.5 percent over the five-year period when the forward rate is used to forecast.

Mixed Forecasting

Because no single forecasting technique has been found consistently superior to the others, some MNCs may prefer to use a combination of forecasting techniques. This method is referred to as **mixed forecasting.** Various forecasts for a particular currency value could be developed using several forecasting techniques. Each of the techniques used could be assigned weights in such a way that the weights total to 100 percent, with the techniques thought to be more reliable being assigned higher weights. The actual forecast of the currency by the MNC would be a weighted average of the various forecasts developed. In addition, the MNC might even wish to assess the degree of uncertainty by measuring the range of forecasts generated by them.

FORECASTING SERVICES

Thousands of firms around the world need projections of currency movements, and the need has become more pronounced since the advent of floating exchange rates in the early 1970s. Moreover, the high volatility of currency values in the 1980s reinforced the importance of forecasting with accuracy. In contrast, when a fixed exchange rate system was in place, before the early 1970s, currency values were stable, and there was little room for forecasting error.

The corporate need to forecast currency values has prompted the emergence of several consulting firms, including Business International, Conti Currency, Predex, and Wharton Econometric Forecasting Associates. In addition, some large investment banks such as Goldman Sachs and commercial banks such as Citibank, Chemical Bank, and Chase Manhattan Bank offer forecasting services. The techniques used to predict future currency values vary among consulting services, but, in general, they use at least two different types of analysis to generate separate forecasts, and then a weighted average of the forecasts is produced.

Some forecasting services, such as Capital Techniques, FX Concepts, and Preview Economics, focus on technical forecasting, while other services, such as Corporate Treasury Consultants Ltd. and WEFA focus on fundamental forecasting. Many services, such as Chemical Bank, Forexia Ltd., and Henley Centre for Forecasting, use both technical and fundamental forecasting. In some cases, the technical forecasting techniques are emphasized by the forecasting firms for short-term forecasts, while fundamental techniques are emphasized for long-run forecasts.

Forecasts are even provided for currencies that are not widely traded. Firms provide forecasts on any currency for time horizons of interest to their clients, ranging from one day to ten years from now. In addition, some firms will offer advice on international cash management, assessment of exposure to exchange rate risk, and hedging. Many of the firms provide their clients with forecasts and recommendations monthly, or even weekly, for an annual fee.

In addition to a forecast of exchange rates, other commonly provided services include an overall forecast of factors that influence currencies, an assessment of the current and anticipated climate of foreign exchange regulations, and cash management. The fees charged to MNCs vary among consulting firms, and the annual fees for some forecasting services that have recently been quoted in magazines can be misleading, since one firm that appears relatively inexpensive may not conduct a thorough forecasting analysis. Fees ranging from between $15,000 and $25,000 are quite common, although an MNC may end up paying much more or less depending on the amount of work required.

Recently, most forecasting services have been inaccurate regarding currency values. Keep in mind that due to the recent volatility in foreign exchange markets, it is quite difficult to forecast currency values. One way for a corporation to determine whether a forecasting service is valuable is to compare the accuracy of its forecasts to that of alternative publicly available and free forecasts. The forward rate serves as a benchmark for comparison here since it is quoted in many newspapers and magazines. A study by Richard Levich compared the forecasts of several currency forecasting

INTERNATIONAL FINANCIAL MANAGEMENT IN PRACTICE

Using Trade Deficit Announcements to Forecast Exchange Rates

Some foreign exchange market participants speculate according to the dollar's expected movements over the next few days or weeks, since their speculative positions may last only that long. They are less concerned about long-term relationships between economic factors and exchange rates than they are about how the market may react on any given day to news. In the late 1980s and early 1990s, monthly trade deficit announcements were closely monitored by speculators. The announcements carried an implicit forecast of future exchange rates that was used by speculators to take positions, as described below.

In October 1987 the August trade deficit of $15.68 billion was announced. Foreign exchange market participants were expecting more favorable news and reacted to the announcement by switching from dollars to other currencies. Their actions caused an immediate decline in the dollar's value. Within seconds of the trade report, the dollar de-clined against the German mark by .5 percent. Even though the trade deficit news had already occurred, it created forecasts about future trade, and therefore modified forecasts of the dollar's value.

In January 1988 the announced November trade deficit was lower than anticipated, causing forecasts of a stronger dollar. The reaction by foreign exchange market partici-pants caused the dollar to strengthen imme-diately. In February 1988 the announced December trade deficit was lower than antic-ipated, and a similar market reaction occurred.

In the early months of 1991, trade deficit announcements revealed a smaller trade def-icit for the U.S. than anticipated. The dollar strengthened immediately in response to the possible signals provided by these announce-ments. Each month, a new monthly trade deficit is announced, and new implicit fore-casts of the dollar's value are created. Each implicit forecast lasts only until the next trade deficit announcement.

services regarding nine different currencies to the forward rate. Only 5 per-cent of the forecasts (when considering all forecasting firms and all curren-cies forecasted) for one month ahead were more accurate than the forward rate, while only 14 percent of forecasts for three months ahead were more accurate. These results are frustrating to the corporations that have paid $25,000 per year or more for expert opinions. Perhaps some corporate clients of these consulting firms believe the fee is worth it even when the forecasting performance is poor if other services (such as cash management) are in-cluded in the package. It is also possible that a corporate treasurer, in rec-ognition of the potential for error in forecasting exchange rates, may prefer to pay a consulting firm for its forecasts. Then the treasurer is not (in a sense) directly responsible for corporate problems that result from inaccurate cur-rency forecasts. Not all MNCs hire consulting firms to do their forecasting. For example, Kodak, Inc., previously used a service, but became dissatisfied with it and has now developed its own forecasting system.

While the performance of the forecasting services has been relatively poor, it may improve in the future. Floating rates have been in existence only since the early 1970s, so it is likely that the forecasting services will improve their performance as they gain more experience.

FURTHER EXAMINATION OF THE FORWARD RATE AS A PREDICTOR

Recall that as a market-based forecast, the forward rate should equal the market's expectation of the spot rate that will exist at the end of the forward period. If it does not, some speculators will trade forward contracts to capitalize on the situation. This speculative tendency should force the forward rate to approach the expected spot rate in the future. If all corporations accepted this reasoning as a basis for the forward rate being an accurate predictor, however, none would be paying for forecasts generated by consulting firms.

One reason firms might not accept the forward rate as a predictor is because of a second market force. Recall that according to interest rate parity, the forward premium (or **discount**) is determined by the interest rate differential. If, for example, the 30-day interest rate of the British pound is above the 30-day U.S. interest rate, we expect the forward rate on the pound to exhibit a discount. The size of the discount would be such that U.S. investors could not achieve abnormal returns from using covered interest arbitrage (convert dollars to pounds, invest pounds in a British 30-day account, and simultaneously sell pounds 30 days forward in exchange for dollars). Based on this information, consider that the forward rates of some currencies, such as the German mark, Japanese yen, and Swiss franc (with respect to the dollar), are usually above their current spot rates. That is, they almost always exhibit a forward premium (since their interest rates are typically below the U.S. rates). If we use the forward rate as a forecast of the future spot rate, we are advised by the forward rate that the mark, yen, and franc are almost always expected to appreciate (whenever their forward rate is above the existing spot rate). Even when all other factors are suggesting the Swiss franc, for example, will depreciate, the forward rate implies the Swiss franc will appreciate. This provides some justification for corporations to doubt the accuracy of the forward rate as a predictor of the spot rate.

The preceding argument provides support for corporations that look for an alternative to the forward rate when predicting currency movements. As mentioned earlier, corporations are often no better off when they do hire forecasting services, since these forecasts are typically less accurate than the forward rate as a predictor. Even with these results, it is not yet clear whether the forward rate is an accurate predictor. What if the forecasting services in the cases studied were so bad that the forward rate was superior simply by default (that is, it was not as poor as the services)? In the next section, data are examined to investigate the forecasting accuracy of the forward rate. From this analysis, a useful method to evaluate forecasting performance is disclosed.

HOW TO EVALUATE EXCHANGE RATE FORECASTING PERFORMANCE

An MNC should not only develop exchange rate projections, but should also monitor its forecasting performance over time. This will indicate whether the

MNC is providing reasonable forecasts, or if it should revise its forecasting method.

To illustrate how forecasting performance can be evaluated, the 90-day forward rates of the British pound are shown quarterly from January 1974 through 1990 in the second column of Exhibit 9.2. The spot rate that occurs (is realized) 90 days later is disclosed in the third column. The nominal difference between the forecast based on the forward rate and what actually occurs is provided in Column 4. The absolute value of the error is provided in Column 5. This absolute error term is then expressed in percentage terms (as a percentage of the realized value) in Column 6.

A multinational corporation that forecasts exchange rates must monitor its performance over time to determine whether the forecasting procedure is satisfactory. For this purpose, a measurement of the forecast error is required. There are various ways to compute forecast errors. Only one possible measurement will be discussed here and is defined as follows:

$$\begin{array}{c}\text{Absolute} \\ \text{forecast error} \\ \text{as a percentage of} \\ \text{the realized value}\end{array} = \frac{\left|\begin{array}{cc}\text{Forecasted} & \text{Realized} \\ \text{value} & \text{value}\end{array}\right|}{\begin{array}{c}\text{Realized} \\ \text{value}\end{array}}$$

This is how the error term shown in Column 6 of Exhibit 9.2 was computed. The error is computed using an absolute value, since this avoids a possible offsetting effect when determining the mean forecast error. For example, consider a simplified example where the forecast error is .05 in the first period and − .05 in the second period (if the absolute value is not taken). The mean error here over the two periods is zero. Yet, that is misleading since the forecast was not perfectly accurate in either period. The absolute value avoids such a misrepresentation.

When measuring forecast performance of different currencies, it is often useful to adjust for their relative size so forecasting ability can be compared among currencies. As an example, consider the following forecasted and realized values by a U.S. firm during one period:

	Forecasted Value	Realized Value
British pound	$1.35	$1.50
French franc	.12	.10

In this case, the difference between the forecasted value and realized value is $.15 for the pound compared to $.02 for the franc. This does not necessarily imply that the forecast of the franc is more accurate. When considering the size of what is forecasted (dividing the difference by the realized value), one can see that the British pound was predicted with more accuracy on a percentage basis. With the data given, the forecasting error (as defined earlier) of the British pound is

$$\frac{|\$1.35 - \$1.50|}{\$1.50} = \frac{\$ .15}{\$1.50} = .10, \text{ or } 10\%$$

EXHIBIT 9.2 Computation of Forecast Errors for the British Pound

First Trading Day In:	90-Day Forward Rate of the British Pound (Expressed in U.S. Dollars)	Spot Rate of the British Pound (Expressed in U.S. Dollars) Realized 90 Days Later	Nominal Forecast Error	Absolute Forecast Error	Absolute Forecast Error as a Percentage of the Realized Value
Weak £ Cycle					
January 1974	$2.3225	$2.3940	−$ .0715	$.0715	2.99%
April 1974	2.3365	2.3910	−.0545	.0545	2.28
July 1974	2.3745	2.3375	.0370	.0370	1.58
October 1974	2.3195	2.3362	.0167	.0167	.71
January 1975	2.2847	2.4067	−.1220	.1220	5.00
April 1975	2.3764	2.1800	.1964	.1964	9.01
July 1975	2.1675	2.0434	.1241	.1241	6.07
October 1975	2.0267	2.0242	.0025	.0025	.12
January 1976	1.9993	1.9163	.0830	.0830	4.33
April 1976	1.8961	1.7883	.1078	.1078	6.03
Strong £ Cycle					
July 1976	1.7516	1.6690	.0826	.0826	4.95
October 1976	1.6240	1.7025	−.0785	.0785	4.61
January 1977	1.6594	1.7201	−.0607	.0607	3.52
April 1977	1.7028	1.7200	−.0172	.0172	1.00
July 1977	1.7068	1.7479	−.0411	.0411	2.35
October 1977	1.7501	1.9200	−.1699	.1699	8.84
January 1978	1.9232	1.8650	.0582	.0582	3.12
April 1978	1.8647	1.8530	.0117	.0117	.63
July 1978	1.8400	1.9746	−.1346	.1346	6.82
October 1978	1.9574	2.0435	−.0861	.0861	4.21
January 1979	2.0399	2.0695	−.0296	.0296	1.43
April 1979	2.0629	2.1765	−.1136	.1136	5.22
July 1979	2.1585	2.1990	−.0405	.0405	1.84
October 1979	2.1923	2.2145	.0222	.0222	1.00
January 1980	2.2025	2.1580	.0445	.0445	2.06
April 1980	2.1680	2.3600	−.1920	.1920	8.14
July 1980	2.3190	2.3860	−.0670	.0670	2.81
October 1980	2.3761	2.3950	−.0189	.0189	.79
January 1981	2.4160	2.2370	.1790	.1790	8.00
April 1981	2.2504	1.9240	.3264	.3264	16.96
July 1981	1.9505	1.8060	.1445	.1445	8.00
October 1981	1.8112	1.9280	−.1168	.1168	6.06

Continued

In comparison, the forecast error of the French franc is

$$\frac{|.12 - .10|}{.10} = \frac{.02}{.10} = .20, \text{ or } 20\%$$

Thus, the French franc was predicted with less accuracy.

Consider a U.S. corporation that needed to purchase 100,000 British pounds every quarter to pay for imports. Assume it has forecasted its cash outflows (in U.S. dollars) to equal 100,000 pounds × forward rate (since the forward rate serves as a forecast of the spot rate that will exist in 90 days). In January 1974 the nominal error term was −$.0715 (see Column 4, Exhibit 9.2). Thus, the forecast for U.S. dollars needed to exchange for 100,000

EXHIBIT 9.2 Computation of Forecast Errors for the British Pound *(continued)*

First Trading Day In:	90-Day Forward Rate of the British Pound (Expressed in U.S. Dollars)	Spot Rate of the British Pound (Expressed in U.S. Dollars) Realized 90 Days Later	Nominal Forecast Error	Absolute Forecast Error	Absolute Forecast Error as a Percentage of the Realized Value
Weak £ Cycle					
January 1982	$1.9195	$1.7850	$ .1345	$.1345	7.53%
April 1982	1.7940	1.7340	.0600	.0600	3.46
July 1982	1.7474	1.6950	.0524	.0524	3.09
October 1982	1.7001	1.6200	.0801	.0801	4.94
January 1983	1.6165	1.4840	.1325	.1325	8.93
April 1983	1.4810	1.5275	−.0465	.0465	3.04
July 1983	1.5281	1.4995	.0286	.0286	1.91
October 1983	1.4999	1.4525	.0474	.0474	3.26
January 1984	1.4552	1.4390	.0162	.0162	1.12
April 1984	1.4457	1.3570	.0887	.0887	6.54
July 1984	1.3660	1.2345	.1315	.1315	10.65
Strong £ Cycle					
October 1984	1.2372	1.1592	−.0034	.0034	.29
January 1985	1.1558	1.2080	−.0522	.0522	4.32
April 1985	1.2923	1.3062	−.0139	.0139	1.06
July 1985	1.2800	1.4010	−.1210	.1210	7.47
October 1985	1.3890	1.4445	−.0555	.0555	3.84
January 1986	1.4315	1.4853	−.0538	.0538	3.62
April 1986	1.4719	1.5303	−.0584	.0584	3.81
July 1986	1.5195	1.4500	.0695	.0695	4.79
October 1986	1.4326	1.4745	−.0419	.0419	2.84
January 1987	1.4568	1.6050	−.1482	.1482	9.23
April 1987	1.5922	1.6100	−.0178	.0178	1.10
July 1987	1.6019	1.6297	−.0278	.0278	1.70
October 1987	1.6215	1.8715	−.2500	.2500	13.35
January 1988	1.8640	1.8867	−.0227	.0227	1.20
Weak £ Cycle					
April 1988	1.8704	1.7093	.1611	.1611	9.42
July 1988	1.7007	1.6855	.0152	.0152	.90
October 1988	1.6720	1.8095	−.1375	.1375	7.60
January 1989	1.7932	1.6888	.1044	.1044	6.18
April 1989	1.6787	1.5502	.1285	.1285	8.29
Strong £ Cycle					
October 1989	1.5331	1.6252	−.0921	.0921	5.67
January 1990	1.6041	1.6055	−.0014	.0014	.09
April 1990	1.6221	1.6428	−.0207	.0207	1.26
July 1990	1.7207	1.7418	−.0211	.0211	1.21
October 1990	1.8511	1.9255	−.0744	.0744	3.86

pounds would have been $7,150 less than what was actually needed. Scan Column 4 of Exhibit 9.2 using this example to see how far off the firm was in its forecasts of dollars needed to make payment. This should help illustrate how cash flow projections of corporations can be inaccurate due to inaccurate exchange rate projections.

Forecast Accuracy Over Time

Has there been any improvement in forecasting in recent years? The answer depends on the method used to develop forecasts. With regard to the forward rate as a predictor, the magnitude of the absolute errors is shown in Column 5 of Exhibit 9.2 and plotted in Exhibit 9.3. The size of the errors changes over time. However, there does not appear to be a consistent movement toward larger or smaller errors.

The year 1981 stands out as a period in which forecasts were worse than ever. Recall that U.S. interest rates were extremely high at the time, which attracted foreign (including British) demand for U.S. dollars to buy U.S. securities. Consequently, the British pound depreciated to such a degree that the 90-day forecasts based on the forward rate were off by as much as $.32 per pound.

This discussion is intended to emphasize how inaccurate even the most respected forecast methods can be. A firm could react to such results by hedging every foreign currency position so that it would not have to worry as much about forecasting exchange rates. However, there can be an opportu-

EXHIBIT 9.3   Absolute Forecast Errors over Time for the British Pound *(using the forward rate to forecast)*

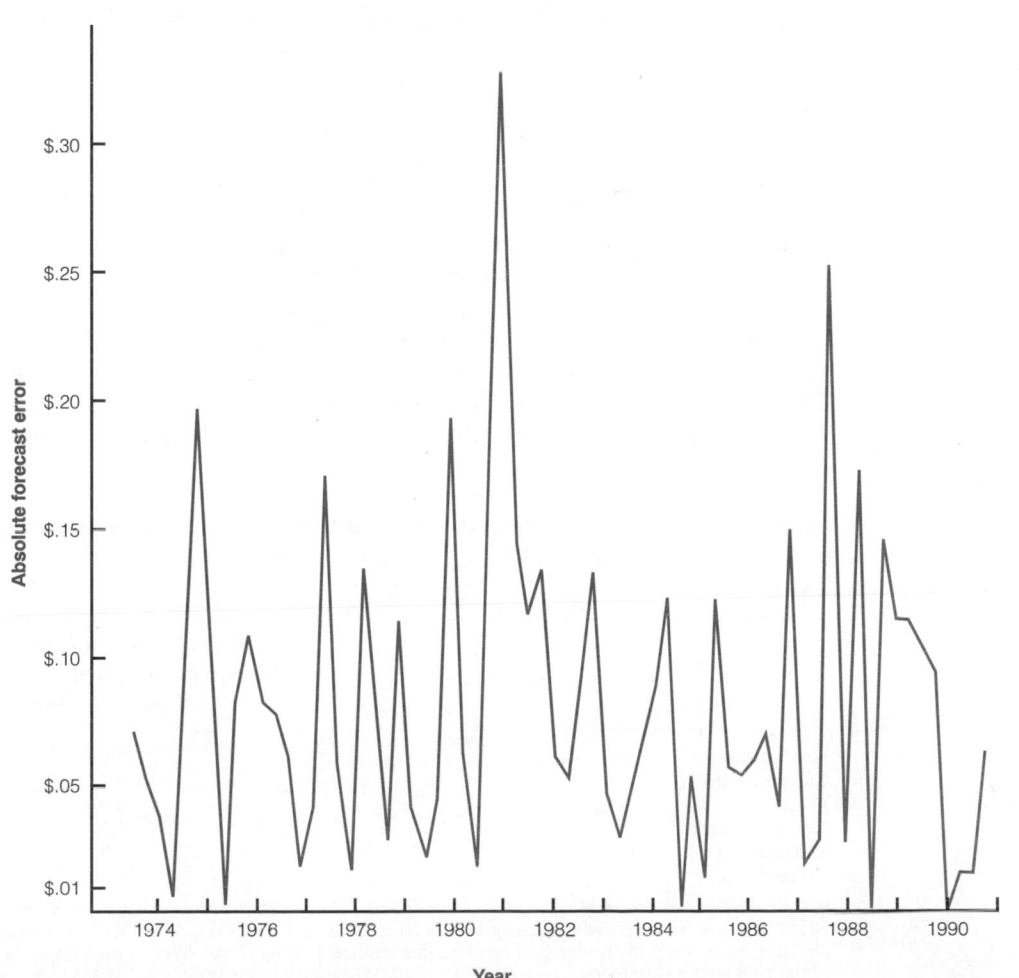

nity cost to hedging. For example, assume that in April 1981 a firm realized the need to obtain 100,000 pounds in 90 days. The 90-day forward rate at that time was approximately $2.25. If the firm hedged, it would pay $225,000 ($2.25 per pound × 100,000 pounds) for the pounds. However, if it did not hedge, it would need only about $192,000 (based on the realized spot rate of approximately $1.92 per pound), $33,000 less than the hedging cost.

The forecasting analysis discussed here has concentrated on the British pound. Data for other major currencies are available in the data bank near the end of the text so one can evaluate forecasting performance for these currencies using the method that has been described.

Forecast Accuracy among Currencies

The ability to forecast currency values may vary with the currency of concern. For example, Exhibit 9.4 discloses the mean forecast errors of six major currencies. These errors are derived when using the forward rate to forecast. The Canadian dollar stands out as the currency most accurately predicted. Its mean error is roughly one-third of the mean errors of the other currencies. This is important information, since a financial manager of a U.S. firm can feel more confident about the number of dollars to be received (or needed) on Canadian transactions. Conversely, it appears much more difficult to forecast the future value of the Swiss franc.

Search for Forecast Bias

Exhibit 9.2 is used to develop a graphical time series of nominal forecast errors in Exhibit 9.5. This exhibit shows how to detect trends in forecast bias. Negative errors over time represent underestimating, while positive errors represent overestimating. If the errors are consistently positive or negative over time, then a bias in the forecasting procedure does exist. In this example, it appears that a bias did exist in six distinct periods. From January 1974 through April 1976, the forecast errors were generally positive. From July 1976 through October 1981, the errors were generally negative. From January 1982 through July 1984, the errors were typically positive. Then, from

EXHIBIT 9.4 Comparison of Forecasting Errors among Six Currencies

Currency	Mean Absolute Forecast Error as a Percentage of the Realized Value
British pound	5.6%
Canadian dollar	2.0
French franc	6.9
German mark	6.0
Japanese yen	6.3
Swiss franc	7.5

NOTE: The results are based on quarterly data from January 1981 to July 1984. While the mean absolute error would likely change over time, the relative ranking of the errors would typically remain somewhat stationary.

EXHIBIT 9.5 Comparison of Forecasted and Realized Spot Rates over Time for the British Pound *(using the forward rate to forecast)*

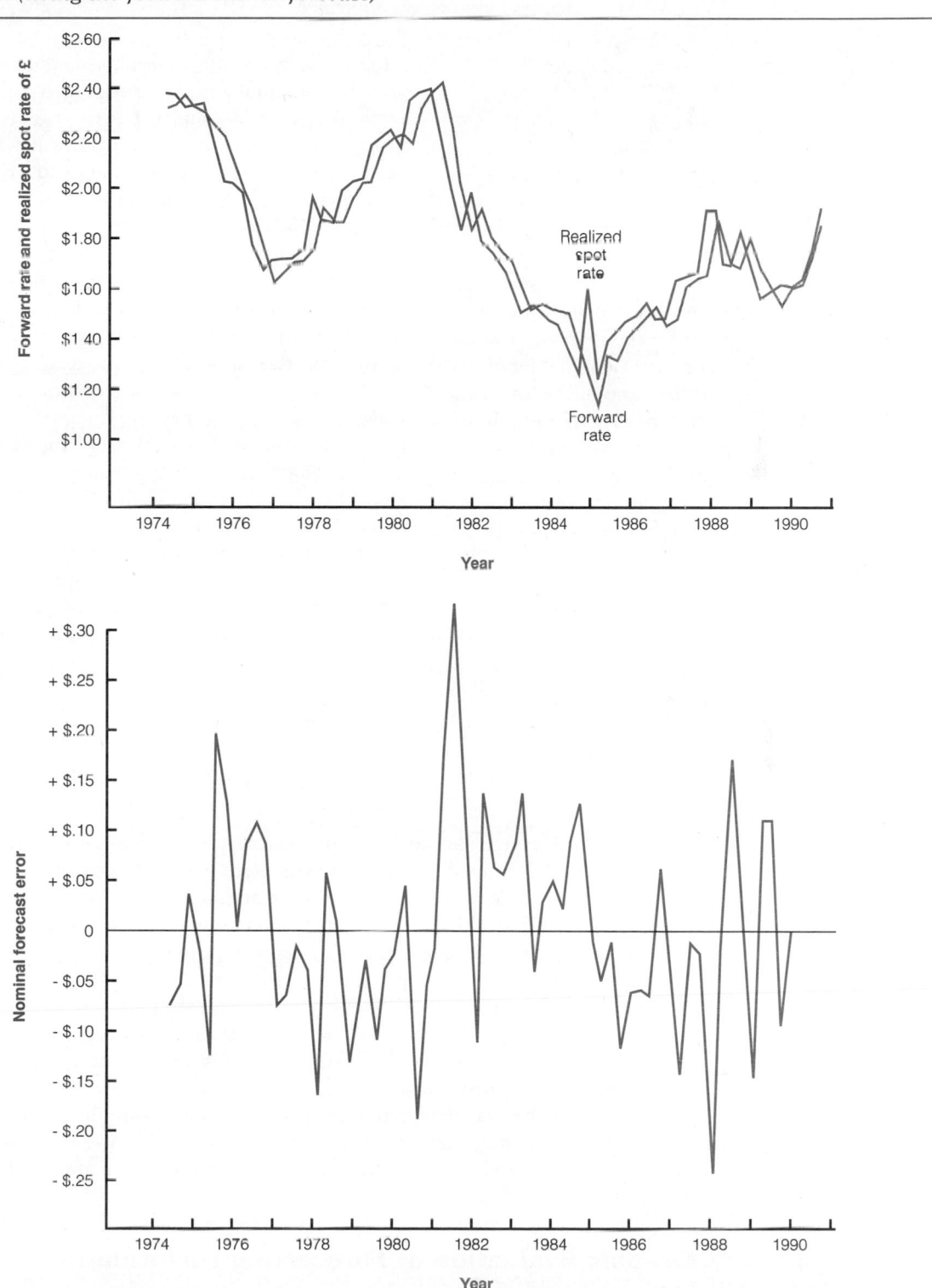

Statistical Test of Forecast Bias

If the forward rate is an unbiased predictor of the future spot rate, this implies that alternative forecasts cannot consistently outperform the forward rate as a predictor. If the forward rate is unbiased, it fully reflects all available information about the future spot rate. Any forecast errors would be the result of events that could not have been anticipated from existing information at the time of the forecast. A conventional method of testing for a forecast bias is to apply the following regression model to historical data:

$$s_t = a_0 + a_1 F_{t-1} + \mu_t$$

where

$$
\begin{aligned}
s_t &= \text{spot rate at time } t \\
F_{t-1} &= \text{forward rate at time } t-1 \\
\mu_t &= \text{error term} \\
a_0 &= \text{intercept} \\
a_1 &= \text{regression coefficient}
\end{aligned}
$$

If the forward rate is unbiased, the intercept should equal zero and the regression coefficient a_1 should equal 1.0. If $a_0 = 0$ and a_1 is significantly less than 1.0, this implies that the forward rate is systematically overestimating the spot rate. For example, if $a_0 = 0$ and $a_1 = .90$, the future spot rate is estimated to be 90 percent of the forecast generated by the forward rate. Conversely, if $a_0 = 0$ and a_1 is significantly greater than 1.0, this implies that the forward rate is systematically underestimating the spot rate. For example, if $a = 0$ and $a_1 = 1.1$, the future spot rate is estimated to be 1.1 times the forecast generated by the forward rate. When a bias is detected and anticipated to persist in the future, future forecasts may incorporate the bias detected. Using the example where $a_1 = 1.1$, future forecasts of the spot rate may incorporate this information by multiplying the forward rate times 1.1 to create a forecast of the future spot rate.

October 1984 through January 1988, the errors were typically negative. From April 1988 through April 1989, the errors were generally positive, but a reversal in the pound's value caused negative errors in the following five quarters. During the first, third, and fifth periods identified above, the pound was strengthening, while in the other periods, the pound was weakening. This implies that during a strong-pound period, the forecasts underestimate, while in a weak-pound period, the forecasts overestimate.

By detecting a bias, an MNC may be able to revise its forecast to adjust for the bias so it can improve its forecasting accuracy. For example, if the errors are consistently positive, an MNC could adjust today's forward rate downward to reflect the bias detected. Over time, the forecasting bias can change (from underestimating to overestimating, or vice versa). Any adjustment to the forward rate used as a forecast would need to reflect the anticipated bias for the period of concern.

Graphic Evaluation of Forecasting Performance

Performance from forecasting can be examined with the use of a graph that compares forecasted values with the realized values for various time periods.

As a hypothetical example, consider the corporate exchange rate projections for Currency Q with respect to the U.S. dollar in Exhibit 9.6.

The predicted and realized exchange rate values in Exhibit 9.6 can be compared graphically as shown in Exhibit 9.7. For example, in period 1, the predicted value of Currency Q was $.20 and the realized value was $.16. This point is illustrated in Exhibit 9.7 and designated with a "1."

The 45-degree line in Exhibit 9.7 represents perfect forecasts. To clarify, consider a case where the realized value turned out to be exactly what was

EXHIBIT 9.6 Hypothetical Forecasting Evaluation

Period	Predicted Value of Currency Q for End of Period	Realized Value of Currency Q as of End of Period
1	$.20	$.16
2	.18	.14
3	.24	.16
4	.26	.22
5	.30	.28
6	.22	.26
7	.16	.14
8	.14	.10

EXHIBIT 9.7 Comparison of Forecasted and Realized Spot Rates

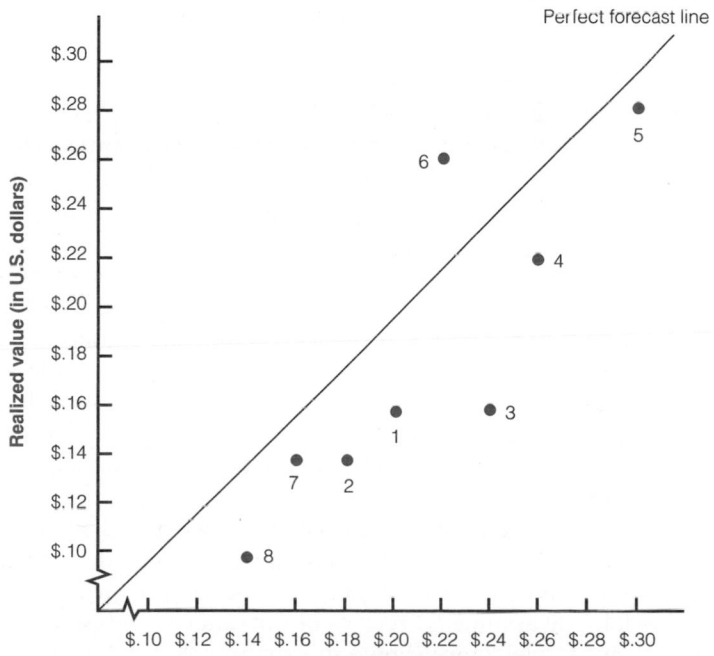

predicted over several periods. All points would be located on that 45-degree line in Exhibit 9.7. For this reason, the line is referred to as the **perfect forecast line.** While in our example the forecasts were not perfectly accurate, the perfect forecast line can still be useful for assessing forecasting performance. The closer the points reflecting the eight periods are vertically to the 45-degree line, the better is the forecast. The vertical distance between each point and the 45-degree line is the forecast error. For example, the 45-degree line is $.04 above the point representing period 1. This implies the forecast for period 1 was $.04 above the realized value. All points below the 45-degree line reflect overestimation by the forecasts. In Exhibit 9.7, seven of the eight points are in this range. Thus, it appears the forecasts tend to be *upward biased* (typically above the realized value).

All points above the 45-degree line reflect underestimation by the forecasts. In Exhibit 9.7, only one of the eight points is in this range. None of the eight points is on the 45-degree line. This means that Currency Q was not predicted with perfect accuracy in any of the eight periods.

If points appear to be scattered evenly on both sides of the 45-degree line, then the forecasts are said to be *unbiased*, since they are not consistently above or below the realized values. It is possible to find unbiased inaccurate forecasts. Such results are discouraging to a corporation, since it may not know how to improve its forecasts if no bias is detected.

Whether evaluating the size of forecast errors or attempting to search for a bias, more reliable results are obtained when examining a large number of periods. Only eight periods were evaluated here in order to provide a simplified example.

The forecast evaluation procedure described here is applied to the British pound and shown in Exhibit 9.8. All forecasts shown in Exhibit 9.2 are plotted in Exhibit 9.8. In general, there is no obvious bias when evaluating all forecasts together. However, separating the entire period into subperiods, (as shown in Exhibit 9.9), reveals a forecast bias.

COMPARISON OF FORECASTING TECHNIQUES

When an MNC evaluates its forecasting performance, it must realize that errors will commonly occur. To at least minimize the errors, it may desire to compare forecasting errors of various available methods. This can be done by plotting the points relating to both methods on a graph similar to Exhibit 9.7. The points pertaining to each method could be distinguished by a particular mark or color. The performance of the two methods could be evaluated by comparing distances of points from the 45-degree line. In some cases, neither forecasting method may stand out as superior when compared graphically. If so, a more precise comparison can be conducted by computing the forecast errors for all periods for each method, and then comparing these errors.

As an example, the data from Exhibit 9.6 will be used as one set of forecasts assumed to be developed by a U.S. firm for Currency Q's value. Assume the firm also had a second forecast for each period based on an alternative forecasting model. The assumed forecasts of Currency Q, using what shall be called Model 1 and Model 2, are shown in Columns 2 and 3, respectively, of Exhibit 9.10 along with the realized value of Currency Q in column 4.

EXHIBIT 9.8 Graphic Comparison of Forecasted and Realized Spot Rates for the British Pound *(using the forward rate as the forecast)*

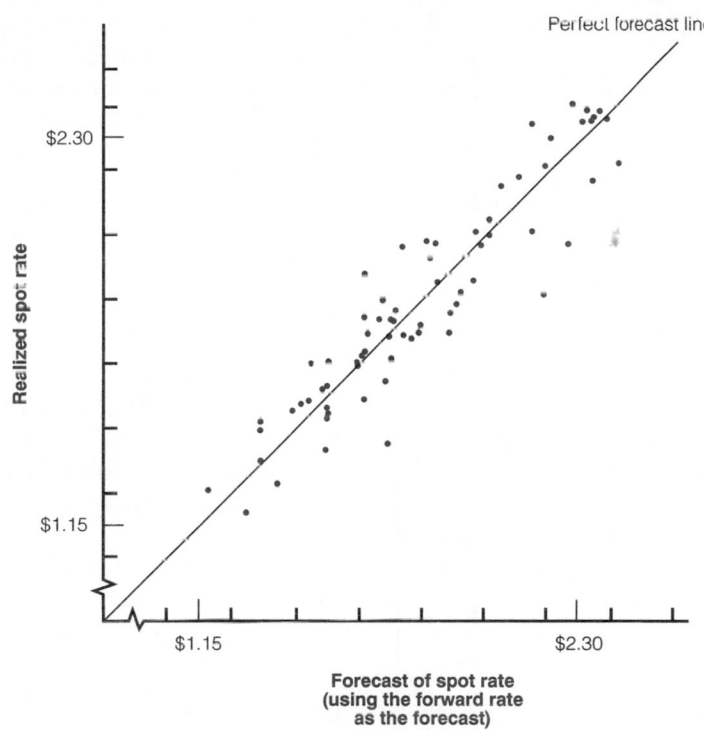

Perfect forecast line

Realized spot rate

$2.30

$1.15

$1.15

$2.30

**Forecast of spot rate
(using the forward rate
as the forecast)**

The absolute forecast errors of forecasting with Model 1 and Model 2 are shown in Columns 5 and 6, respectively. Notice that Model 1 outperformed Model 2 in six of the eight periods. The mean absolute forecast error when using Model 1 was $.04, meaning that forecasts with Model 1 were off by $.04 on the average. While Model 1 is not perfectly accurate, it did a better job than Model 2, whose mean absolute forecast error was $.07. Overall, predictions with Model 1 were on the average $.03 closer to the realized value.

For an MNC to do a complete comparison of performance among forecasting techniques, it should evaluate as many periods as possible. Only eight periods were used in our example, since that is enough to illustrate how to compare forecasting performance. If the MNC has a large number of periods to evaluate, it could statistically test for significant differences in forecasting errors using a *t*-test or a nonparametric test. Results from such a test would determine whether there was a significant difference in the accuracy of the forecasting techniques.

FORECASTING PERFORMANCE AND MARKET EFFICIENCY

If the foreign exchange rate market is **weak-form efficient,** then historical and current exchange rate information would not be useful for forecasting

EXHIBIT 9.9 Graphic Comparison of Forecasted and Realized Spot Rates in Different Subperiods for the British Pound *(using the forward rate as the forecast)*

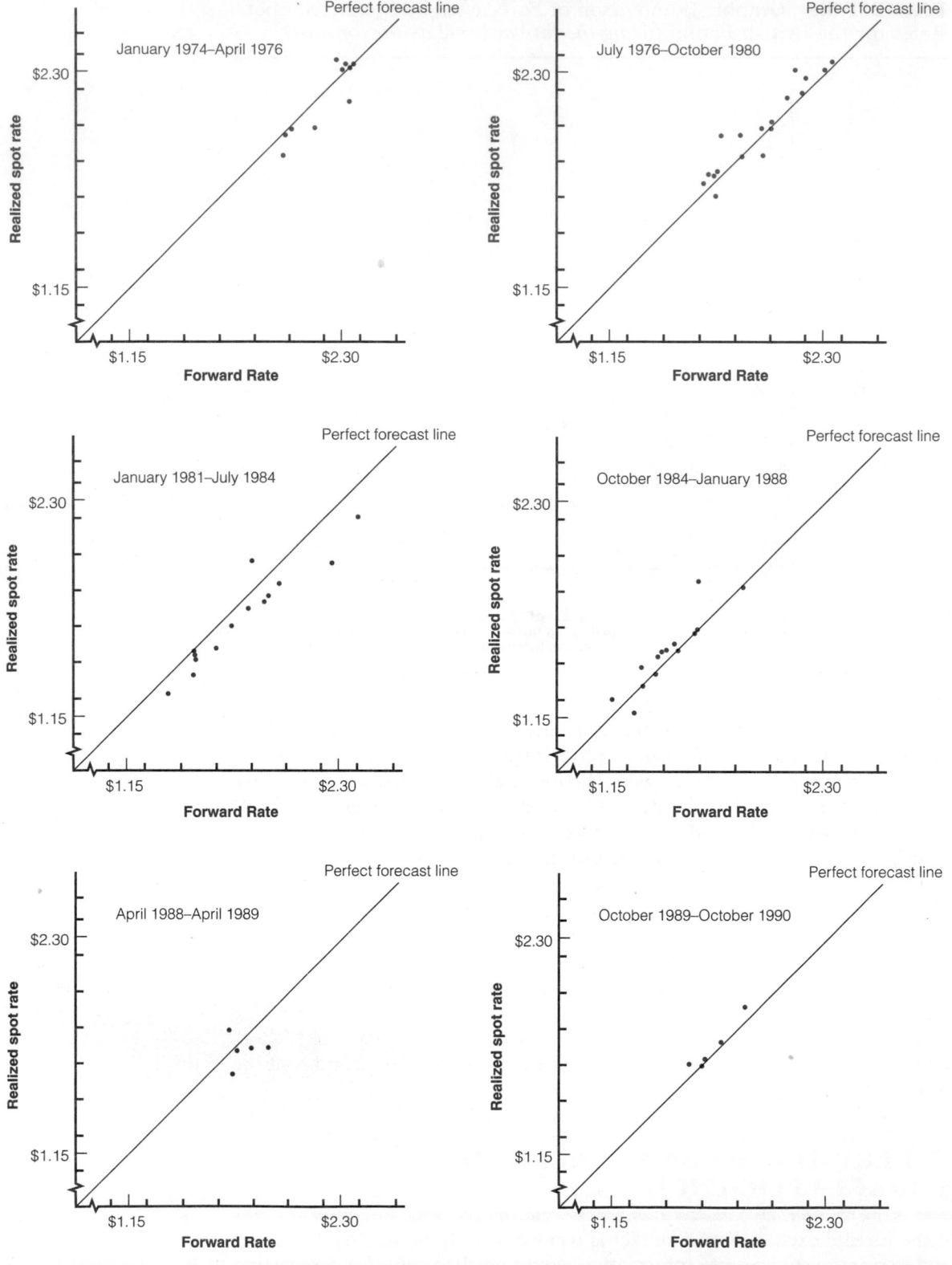

EXHIBIT 9.10 Comparison of Forecasting Techniques

(1)	(2)	(3)	(4)	(5)	(6)	(7) = (5) − (6)
Period	Predicted value of Currency Q by Model 1	Predicted value of Currency Q by Model 2	Realized value of Currency Q	Absolute forecast error using Model 1	Absolute forecast error using Model 2	Difference in absolute forecast errors (Model 1 − Model 2)
1	$.20	$.24	$.16	$.04	$.08	− $.04
2	.18	.20	.14	.04	.06	− .02
3	.24	.20	.16	.08	.04	.04
4	.26	.20	.22	.04	.02	.02
5	.30	.18	.28	.02	.10	.08
6	.22	.32	.26	.04	.06	− .02
7	.16	.20	.14	.02	.06	− .04
8	.14	.24	.10	.04	.14	− .10
				Sum = .32	Sum = .56	Sum = − .24
				Mean = .04	Mean = .07	Mean = − .03

exchange rate movements, since today's exchange rates would reflect all of this information. If the foreign exchange market is **semistrong-form efficient,** then *all* relevant public information would already be reflected in today's exchange rates. If today's exchange rates fully reflected any historical trends in exchange rate movements, but not other public information on expected interest rate movements, the foreign exchange market would be weak-form efficient, but not semi-strong form efficient. Much research has tested the efficient-market hypothesis for foreign exchange markets. Research by Giddy and Dufey, Levich, Logue and Sweeney, Cornell and Dietrich, and Rogalski and Vinso suggest that foreign exchange markets appear to be weak-form efficient and semistrong-form efficient.

If foreign exchange markets are **strong-form efficient,** then all relevant public *and* private information would already be reflected in today's exchange rates. This form of efficiency cannot be tested, since private information is not available.

Even though foreign exchange markets are generally found to be at least semistrong-form efficient, forecasts of exchange rates by MNCs may still be worthwhile. Their goal is not necessarily to earn speculative profits, but to use reasonable exchange rate forecasts to implement policies. When MNCs assess proposed policies, they usually prefer to develop their own forecasts of exchange rates over time rather than simply use market-based rates as a forecast of future rates. MNCs are often interested in more than a point estimate of an exchange rate one year, three years, or five years from now. They prefer to determine a variety of scenarios and assess how exchange rates may change for each scenario. Even if today's forward exchange rate properly reflects all available information, it does not indicate to the MNC the possible deviation of the realized future exchange rate from what is expected. MNCs need to determine the range of various possible exchange rate movements in order to assess the degree to which their operating performance could be affected.

SUMMARY

Multinational corporations need exchange rate forecasts for the following reasons:

- Hedging decision
- Short-term financing decision
- Short-term investment decision
- Capital budgeting decision
- Long-term financing decision
- Earnings assessment

The most common forecasting techniques can be classified as (1) technical, (2) fundamental, (3) market-based, and (4) mixed. Unfortunately, these techniques have generally performed rather poorly in recent years. Yet, due to the high variability in exchange rates, it should not be surprising that forecasts will not always be accurate. Also, floating rates have been in existence only since the early 1970s, which has not allowed for much time to improve forecasting ability by experience.

A commonly asked question is whether it is worth it for the multinational corporation to buy forecasting services. The answer depends on what the corporation expects from these services. If it is solely interested in accuracy of the forecasts, the services have not been worthwhile in recent years, as evidenced by the fact that a free publicly available forecast (the forward rate) typically outperformed the forecasting services during a recent time period. Yet, one must consider that some forecasting services provide advice on international cash management and other corporate functions that may in itself be worth the fee. In addition, some multinational corporate treasurers may feel a forecasting service is worthwhile simply because they aren't forced to develop highly error-prone forecasts themselves.

In many cases, an MNC is not so concerned with developing a perfect forecast, since this is often an impossible task. Instead, the MNC may concentrate on estimating whether or not a forecast will be above or below some critical level. Its corporate policy decision may be dependent on this type of assessment. Thus, if the MNC can at least correctly assess whether a currency value will be above or below some critical level, it can be more assured of making the correct corporate policy decisions.

QUESTIONS/ PROBLEMS

1. Explain corporate motives for forecasting exchange rates.

2. Explain the technical technique for forecasting exchange rates.

3. Explain the fundamental technique for forecasting exchange rates.

4. Explain the market-based technique for forecasting exchange rates.

5. Explain the mixed technique for forecasting exchange rates.

6. What are some limitations of using technical forecasting to predict exchange rates?

7. What are some limitations of using a fundamental technique to forecast exchange rates?

8. What is the rationale for using market-based forecasts?

9. Explain how to assess the performance of forecasting exchange rates.

10. Explain how to detect a bias in forecasting exchange rates.

11. You are hired as a consultant to assess a firm's ability to forecast. The firm has developed a point forecast for two different currencies. It wants to determine which currency was forecast with greater accuracy. The information is provided.

Period	Yen Forecast	Actual Yen Value	Pound Forecast	Actual Pound Value
1	$.0050	$.0051	$1.50	$1.51
2	.0048	.0052	1.53	1.50
3	.0053	.0052	1.55	1.58
4	.0055	.0056	1.49	1.52

12. You are hired as a consultant to determine whether there is a bias from forecasting the percentage change in the Dutch guilder (DG). A set of 200 data points were used to develop the following regression equation.

$$\text{Actual percent change in the DG over period } t = a_0 + a_1 \binom{\text{Forecasted percent change}}{\text{in the DG over period } t}$$

The regression results are as follows:

Coefficient	Standard error
$a_0 = .006$	.011
$a_1 = .800$	.05

Based on these results, is there a bias in the forecast? Verify your conclusion. If there is a bias, explain whether it is an overestimate or underestimate.

13. Syracuse Corporation believes that future real interest rate movements will affect exchange rates and has applied regression analysis to historical data in order to assess the relationship. It will use the regression coefficient derived from this analysis along with forecasted real interest rate movements in order to predict exchange rates in the future. Explain at least three limitations of this method.

14. Lexington Company is a U.S.-based MNC with subsidiaries in most major countries. Each subsidiary is responsible for forecasting the future exchange rate of its local currency, relative to the U.S. dollar. Comment on this policy. How might Lexington Company assure consistent forecasts among the different subsidiaries? (See the appendix to this chapter.)

15. Assume that the following regression model was applied to historical quarterly data:

$$e_t = a_0 + a_1 INT_t + a_2 INF_{t-1} + \mu_t$$

where

$$e_t = \text{percentage change in exchange rate of the franc in period } t$$

$$INT_t = \text{average real interest rate differential (U.S. interest rate minus French interest rate) over period } t$$

$$INF_{t-1} = \text{inflation differential (U.S. inflation rate minus French inflation rate) in the previous period}$$

$$a_0, a_1, a_2 = \text{regression coefficients}$$

$$\mu_t = \text{error term}$$

Assume that the regression coefficients were estimated as follows:

$$a_0 = 0.0$$
$$a_1 = .9$$
$$a_2 = .8$$

Also assume that the inflation differential in the most recent period was 3 percent. The real interest rate differential in the upcoming period is forecasted as follows:

Interest Rate Differential	Probability
0%	30%
1	60
2	10

If Stillwater Inc. uses this information to forecast the French franc's exchange rate, what will be the probability distribution of the franc's percentage change over the upcoming period?

16. Assume that the four-year annualized interest rate in the United States is 9 percent and the four-year interest rate in Switzerland is 6 percent. Assume interest rate parity holds for a four-year horizon. Assume that the spot rate of the Swiss franc is $.60. If the forward rate is used to forecast exchange rates, what would be the forecast for the Swiss franc's spot rate in four years? What percentage appreciation or depreciation does this forecast imply over the four-year period?

17. Assume that foreign exchange markets were found to be weak-form efficient. Does this suggest anything about utilizing technical analysis to speculate in the foreign exchange markets?

18. If MNCs believed that foreign exchange markets are strong-form efficient, why would they develop their own forecasts of future exchange rates? Why wouldn't they simply use today's quoted rates as indicators about future rates? After all, today's quoted rates should reflect all relevant information.

19. Most foreign currencies appreciated substantially against the dollar during the 1985–1987 period. Would market-based forecasts have overestimated or underestimated the realized values over this period? Explain.

20. The director of currency forecasting at Champaign-Urbana Corporation made the statement, "The most critical task of forecasting exchange rates is not to derive a point estimate of a future exchange rate, but to assess how wrong our estimate might be." What does this statement mean?

21. Assume that in the 1990s, some countries in East Europe allow the exchange rates of their currencies to fluctuate against the dollar. Would the fundamental technique based on historical relationships be useful for forecasting future exchange rates of these currencies? Explain.

22. Royce Company is a U.S. firm with future receivables one year from now in Canadian dollars and British pounds. Its pound receivables are known with certainty, while its estimated Canadian dollar receivables are subject to a two percent error in either direction. The dollar values of both types of receivables are similar. There is no chance of default by the customers involved. The treasurer of Royce stated that the estimate of dollar cash flows to be generated from the British pound receivables is subject to greater uncertainty than that of the Canadian dollar receivables. Explain the rationale for such a statement.

23. In the early months of 1991, most major currencies declined substantially against the dollar. Do you think the 30-day forward rates of major currencies were unbiased predictors of their respective future spot rates over these months? Explain.

24. Assume that you obtain a quote for a one-year forward rate on the Mexican peso. Over the next year, the peso depreciates by 12 percent. Do you think the forward rate overestimated the spot rate one year ahead in this example? Explain.

25. The treasurer of Glencoe Inc. detected a forecast bias when using the 30-day forward rate to forecast future spot rates over various periods. He believed he could use such information to determine whether imports ordered every week should be hedged (payment is made 30 days after each order.)   The president of Glencoe stated that in the long run, the forward rate is unbiased and suggested that the treasurer should not waste time trying to "beat the forward rate", but should just hedge all orders. Who is correct?

Whaler Publishing Company
Forecasting Exchange Rates

Whaler Publishing Co. specializes in producing textbooks in the United States and marketing these books in foreign universities where the English language is used. Its sales are invoiced in the currency of the country where the textbooks are sold. The expected revenues from textbooks sold to university book stores are disclosed next:

University Book Stores In:	Local Currency	Today's Spot Exchange Rate	Expected Revenues from Book Stores This Year
Australia	Australian Dollars (A$)	$ .7671	A$38,000,000
Canada	Canadian Dollars (C$)	.8625	C$35,000,000
New Zealand	New Zealand Dollars (N$)	.5985	N$33,000,000
United Kingdom	Pounds (£)	1.9382	£34,000,000

Whaler is comfortable with the estimated foreign currency revenues in each country. However, it is very uncertain about the U.S. dollar revenues to be received from each country. At this time (which is the beginning of year 16), Whaler is using today's spot rate as its best guess of the exchange rate at which the revenues from each country will be converted into U.S. dollars at the end of this year (which implies a zero percentage change in the value of each currency). Yet, it recognizes the potential error associated with this type of forecast. Therefore it desires to derive the annual percentage change in the exchange rate over each of the last fifteen years for each currency to derive a standard deviation in the percentage change of each foreign currency. By assuming the percentage changes in exchange rates are normally distributed, it plans to develop two ranges of forecasts for the annual percentage change in each currency: (1) one standard deviation in each direction from its best guess to develop a 68 percent confidence interval, and (2) two standard deviations in each direction from its best guess to develop a 95 percent confidence interval. These confidence intervals can then be applied to today's spot rates to develop confidence intervals for the future spot rate one year from today.

The exchange rates at the beginning of each of the last 16 years for each currency (with respect to the U.S. dollar) are shown next:

Beginning of Year	Australian $	Canadian $	New Zealand $	British Pound
1	$1.2571	$.9839	$1.0437	$2.0235
2	1.0864	.9908	.9500	1.7024
3	1.1414	.9137	1.0197	1.9060
4	1.1505	.8432	1.0666	2.0345
5	1.1055	.8561	.9862	2.2240
6	1.1807	.8370	.9623	2.3850
7	1.1279	.8432	.8244	1.9080
8	.9806	.8137	.7325	1.6145
9	.9020	.8038	.6546	1.4506
10	.8278	.7570	.4776	1.1565
11	.6809	.7153	.4985	1.4445
12	.6648	.7241	.5235	1.4745
13	.7225	.8130	.6575	1.8715
14	.8555	.8382	.6283	1.8095
15	.7831	.8518	.5876	1.5772
16	.7671	.8625	.5985	1.9382

By developing ranges for the annual percentage change in each exchange rate, it will be able to develop ranges for exchange rates and for dollar revenues associated with each country. Complete this assignment for Whaler Publishing Company, and also rank the currencies in terms of uncertainty (degree of volatility). Since the exchange rate data provided are real, the analysis will indicate (1) how volatile currencies can be, (2) how much more volatile some currencies are than others, and (3) how estimated revenues can be subject to a high degree of uncertainty as a result of uncertain exchange rates. [If you use a spreadsheet to do this case, you may want to retain it since the case in the following chapter is an extension of this case.]

1. Assess the forecasting accuracy of the forward rate using a currency of your choice and the Data Bank in the back of this text. Use a procedure similar to that used within this chapter on the British pound. Is the forward rate of your currency more accurate than the forward rate of the pound (based on results shown in this chapter)? Did your forward rate exhibit an upward or downward bias in any periods? Explain.

PROJECT

SUGGESTED READING

Walter Wasserfallen. "The Behavior of Flexible Exchange Rates: Evidence and Implications." *Journal of Portfolio Management* (September–October 1988), pp. 36–44. This article assesses the performance of forecasting exchange rates based on historical trends.

REFERENCES

Bilson, John F. "The Speculative Efficiency Hypothesis." *Journal of Business* (July 1982), pp. 435–451.

Chiang, Thomas C. "On the Predictors of the Future Spot Rates—A Multi-Currency Analysis." *The Financial Review* (February 1986), pp. 69–83.

Cornell, Bradford. "Spot Rates, Forward Rates and Exchange Market Efficiency." *Journal of Financial Economics* (August 1977), pp. 55–66.

Cornell, Bradford, and J. Kimball Dietrich. "The Efficiency of the Market for Foreign Exchange Under Floating Exchange Rates." *Review of Economics and Statistics* (February 1978), pp. 111–120.

Dufey, Gunter, and Ian Giddy. "Forecasting Exchange Rates in a Floating World." *Euromoney* (November 1975), pp. 28–35.

_____ . "International Financial Planning: The Use of Market-Based Forecasts." *California Management Review* (Fall 1978), pp. 69–81.

Dufey, Gunter, and Rolf Mirus. "Forecasting Foreign Exchange Rates: A Pedagogical Note." *Columbia Journal of World Business* (Summer 1981), pp. 53–61.

Fama, Eugene F. "Forward Rates as Predictors of Future Spot Rates," *Journal of Financial Economics* (October 1976), pp. 361–377.

_____ . "Forward and Spot Exchange Rates." *Journal of Monetary Economics* (November 1984), pp. 320–338.

Finnerty, J. E., J. Owers, and F. J. Creran. "Foreign Exchange Forecasting and Leading Economic Indicators: The U.S.–Canadian Experience." *Management International Review* (1987), no. 2, pp. 59–70.

Folks, William R., Jr., and Stanley R. Stansell. "The Use of Discriminant Analysis in Forecasting Exchange Rate Movements." *Journal of International Business Studies* (Spring 1975), pp. 35–40.

Frankel, Jeffrey. "Tests of Rational Expectations in the Forward Exchange Market." *Southern Economic Journal* (April 1980), pp. 1083–1001.

Giddy, Ian H., and Gunter Dufey. "The Random Behavior of Flexible Exchange Rates: Implications for Forecasting." *Journal of International Business Studies* (Spring 1975), pp. 1–32.

Goodman, Stephen H. "Foreign Exchange Rate Forecasting Techniques: Implications for Business and Policy." *Journal of Finance* (May 1979), pp. 415–427.

————. "No Better Than the Toss of a Coin." *Euromoney* (December 1978), pp. 75–85.

————. "Two Technical Analysts Are Even Better Than One." *Euromoney* (August 1982), pp. 85–97.

Goodman, Stephen, and Richard Jaycobs. "How the Current Forecaster Services Rate." *Euromoney* (August 1983), pp. 132–193.

Hansen, Lars Peter, and Robert J. Hodrick. "Forward Exchange Rates as Optimal Predictors of Future Spot Rates: An Econometric Analysis." *Journal of Political Economy* (October 1980), pp. 829–853.

Levich, Richard M. "How the Rise of the Dollar Took Forecasters by Surprise." *Euromoney* (August 1982), pp. 98–111.

————. "Are Forward Exchange Rates Unbiased Predictors of Future Spot Rates?" *Columbia Journal of World Business* (Winter 1979), pp. 49–61.

————. "Currency Forecasters Lose Their Way." *Euromoney* (August 1983), pp. 140–148.

Logue, Dennis E. and Richard J. Sweeney. "White Noise in Imperfect Markets: The Case of the Franc-Dollar Exchange Rate." *The Journal of Finance* (June 1977), pp. 761–768.

Longworth, David. "Testing the Efficiency of the Canadian U.S. Exchange Market Under the Assumption of a No Risk Premium." *Journal of Finance* (March 1981), pp. 43–49.

McFarland, James W., R. Richardson Pettit, and San Sung. "The Distribution of Foreign Exchange Price Changes: Trading Day Effects and Risk Measurement." *Journal of Finance* (June 1982), pp. 693–715.

Madura, Jeff. "Detecting Bias in Forward Exchange Rates." *Journal of Business Forecasting* (Fall 1983), pp. 19–20.

Ott, Mack and Paul T. W. M. Veugelers. "Forward Exchange Rates in Efficient Markets: The Effects of News and Changes in Monetary Policy Regimes." *Review*, Federal Reserve Bank of St. Louis (June–July 1986), pp. 5–15.

Retkwa, Rosalyn. "The Forex Party is Over." *Euromoney* (April 1983), pp. 44–45.

Rogalski, Richard J. and Vinso, Joseph D. "Price Level Variations as Predictors of Flexible Exchange Rates." *Journal of International Business Studies* (Spring–Summer 1977), pp. 71–82.

Rosenberg, Michael R. "Is Technical Analysis Right for Currency Forecasting?" *Euromoney* (July 1981), pp. 125–130.

Sweeney, Richard J. "Beating the Foreign Exchange Market," *Journal of Finance* (March 1986), pp. 163–182.

Wolff, Christian. "Exchange Rates, Innovations, and Forecasting." *Journal of International Money and Finance* (March 1988), pp. 49–62.

Developing Consistent Forecasts with the Use of Currency Betas

Because many exchange rate movements are highly correlated, MNCs must be careful to maintain consistency as they forecast future exchange rates. For example, consider an MNC that forecasts substantial appreciation of the French franc against the dollar and depreciation of the German mark against the dollar. These forecasts are conflicting, because both exchange rates tend to move in the same direction against the dollar. Although MNCs cannot always achieve accurate forecasts, they can at least assure consistent forecasts by accounting for the relationships between exchange rates. One method of accounting for these relationships is to estimate **currency betas,** which measure the responsiveness of a particular currency to a market index of foreign currencies. The beta can be estimated by applying the following regression model to historical data:

$$e_{j,t} = a_0 + a_1 (e_{m,t}) + \mu_t$$

where

$$e_{j,t} = \text{percentage change in the exchange}$$
$$\text{rate over period } t,$$
$$e_{m,t} = \text{percentage change in the market exchange}$$
$$\text{rate over period } t$$
$$\mu_t = \text{error term}$$
$$a_0 = \text{intercept}$$
$$a_1 = \text{regression coefficient}$$

The regression coefficient provides an estimate of a currency's beta. For example, if $a_1 = 1.2$, this implies that the exchange rate changes by 1.2 times the percentage change in the market index. If the MNC estimates currency betas for all currencies of concern, it implicitly controls for the relationships among all of these currencies.

Based on a general forecast of the market index, it can derive forecasts of any individual currency by applying the appropriate beta. For example, assume that the German mark had a beta of 1.1, while the Swiss franc had a beta of 1.2. Also assume that the market index was expected to appreciate against the dollar by 4 percent over the following quarter. The German mark would therefore be expected to appreciate by 4.4 percent (1.1 times 4 percent), while the Swiss franc would be expected to appreciate by 4.8 percent (1.2 times 4 percent). Because both currencies have positive betas, their forecasted movements based on a forecast of the market must be in the same direction. The Swiss franc's higher beta implies that the franc is more volatile, or more sensitive to changes in the market index than the mark. (The intercept was ignored in the preceding examples, assuming that it was negligible).

To determine betas of various currencies, regression analysis was applied to quarterly exchange rate movements from January 1972 through December 1987. The market index was defined here as an equal weighted index of the following currencies: (1) British pound, (2) Dutch guilder, (3) French franc, (4) German mark, (5) Japanese yen, and (6) Swiss franc. (A firm should use whatever index it provides forecasts for in the regression analysis.) The results of the regression analysis follow:

Currency	Estimated beta
British pound	.69
Dutch guilder	1.12
French franc	1.01
German mark	1.12
Japanese yen	.84
Swiss franc	1.22

The sensitivity to market movements varies among currencies, sometimes by a substantial degree. Yet, all of the currencies move in the same direction against the U.S. dollar.

Even if an MNC decides to develop forecasts of each of these currencies in some other manner, it should at least consider the positive correlation between the currencies that is implied here. If some of these currencies are forecasted to appreciate against the dollar while others are forecasted to depreciate, the models used to develop the forecasts should be rechecked.

CHAPTER 10

Measuring Exposure to Exchange Rate Fluctuations

Exchange rate risk represents the risk that a company's performance will be affected by exchange rate movements. This chapter first addresses the relevance of exchange rate risk. Then it identifies the main forms of exposure to exchange rate fluctuations and discusses how a company's performance may be affected by each form.

IS EXCHANGE RATE RISK RELEVANT?

Some critics may suggest that a firm's exposure to exchange rate risk is not relevant and that firms therefore need not measure or manage their exposure. One argument for exchange rate irrelevance is that, according to purchasing power parity (PPP) theory, exchange rate movements should be matched by price movements. For example, consider the case of Office Import Company, a U.S. importer of office supplies that distributes these supplies throughout the country. Assume that Office Import Company presently competes against several U.S. companies that produce their own office supplies. If the dollar depreciates, Office Import Company will need more dollars to cover its import payments. Yet, according to PPP, a decline in the dollar would be associated with relatively high inflation in the United States. Thus, while the local competitors would not be affected by the dollar's decline, their cost of producing supplies would increase as a result of inflation. And although Office Import Company would be adversely affected by the dollar's decline, it would avoid the higher production costs in the United States. It may therefore be argued that this offsetting effect makes exchange rate risk irrelevant. However, PPP does not necessarily hold. It is quite possible that the exchange rate will not change in accordance with the inflation differential between the two countries. Since a perfect offsetting effect is unlikely, the firm's competitive capabilities may indeed be influenced by exchange rate movements.

A second argument for exchange rate irrelevance is that investors in MNCs could hedge this risk on their own. For example, if investors in Office Import Company are aware that performance may be affected by exchange rate fluctuations, they may choose to take positions (in futures contracts or options contracts) to offset any adverse impact of dollar depreciation on Office Import Company. The reason is that exchange rate risk is not relevant to corporations because shareholders can deal with this risk individually. However, this argument assumes that investors have complete information on corporate exposure to exchange rate fluctuations as well as the capabilities to correctly insulate their individual exposure. To the extent that investors prefer that corporations perform the hedging for them, exchange rate exposure is relevant to corporations. Furthermore, the firm's cost of financing may be reduced if its cash flow stream is perceived to be less volatile. Since exchange rate risk can increase cash flow volatility, it may also affect the cost of financing, which is still another reason why exchange rate risk is relevant to corporations.

Multinational corporations (MNCs) strive to generate a high level of earnings while maintaining their risk at a tolerable degree. The risk of an MNC reflects uncertainty about its future cash flows. A firm cannot always accurately predict future net cash flows. For those firms that have cash inflows and outflows denominated in various foreign currencies, the net cash flows in terms of their home currency is even more difficult to predict, due to potential exchange rate fluctuations.

As mentioned in the previous chapter, exchange rates cannot be forecasted with perfect accuracy, but the firm can at least measure its exposure to exchange rate fluctuations. If the firm is highly exposed to exchange rate fluctuations, it can consider techniques to reduce its exposure. Such techniques are identified in the following chapter. Before choosing among them, the firm should first measure its degree of exposure.

Exposure to exchange rate fluctuations comes in three forms:

- Transaction exposure
- Economic exposure
- Translation exposure

Each type of exposure will be discussed in turn.

TRANSACTION EXPOSURE

The value of a firm's cash inflows received in various currencies will be affected by respective exchange rates of these currencies when converted into the currency desired. Similarly, the value of a firm's cash outflows in various currencies will be dependent on the respective exchange rates of these currencies. The degree to which the value of future cash transactions can be affected by exchange rate fluctuations is referred to as **transaction exposure.**

Because of the high variability in exchange rates, transaction risk is critical to an MNC. Two steps are involved in measuring transaction exposure: (1) determine the projected net amount of inflows or outflows in each foreign currency and (2) determine the overall risk of exposure to those currencies. Each of these steps is discussed in turn.

Transaction Exposure to "Net" Cash Flows

Measurement of transaction exposure requires projections of the consolidated net amount of currency inflows or outflows for all subsidiaries categorized by currency. Subsidiary X may have net inflows of 500,000 pounds, while Subsidiary Y may have net outflows of 600,000 pounds. The consolidated net inflows here would be −100,000 pounds. If the pound depreciates before the individual cash flows take place, this will have an unfavorable impact on Subsidiary X, since the pounds will be worth less when converted to the desired currency. However, the pound's depreciation will have a favorable impact on Subsidiary Y, since it will not need as much of its currency to make payments denominated in pounds. The net effect of the pound's depreciation on the MNC is minor, since there is an offsetting effect. The net effect could be substantial, though, if most subsidiaries had future inflows of British pounds. Estimating the consolidated net cash inflows is a useful first step when assessing an MNC's exposure, since it helps to determine the MNC's overall position in each currency.

Some MNCs use a noncentralized approach in which each subsidiary assesses and manages its individual exposure to exchange rate risk. Such a strategy may be used if individual subsidiaries are allowed to manage cash flows independently of the parent or other subsidiaries. While this allows each subsidiary important responsibilities, it can cause redundancy in hedging. For example, consider an MNC that has two subsidiaries in West Germany. One subsidiary receives 20 million British pounds each month as a result of exports sent to Great Britain. The other subsidiary pays 20 million pounds per month to purchase supplies from a British firm. Assume the subsidiaries act independently to hedge their exposure, and that the local bank that serves both subsidiaries has a bid/ask spread of about 1 percent on its forward rates. Thus, it provides German marks in exchange for pounds with one subsidiary and sells these pounds to the other subsidiary in exchange for marks for 1 percent more. The spread on 20 million pounds represents 200,000 pounds per month, or 2.4 million pounds per year. If the MNC's exposure management were centralized, it would realize that the individual subsidiary exposures offset each other, so that hedging is not necessary. Therefore, the transaction fee paid to the bank could be avoided.

Consider a U.S.-based MNC called Miami Company that estimates its consolidated cash flows as shown in Exhibit 10.1. for one period ahead. All estimated inflows and outflows for a currency are combined to determine the "net" position in that currency. Any offsetting positions in a currency are of no concern, since they do not contribute to transaction exposure of the entire

EXHIBIT 10.1 Consolidated Net Cash Flow Assessment of Miami Company

Currency	Total Inflow	Total Outflow	Net Inflow or Outflow	Current Exchange Rate	Net Inflow or Outflow as Measured in U.S. Dollars
Canadian dollar (C$)	C$2,000,000	C$6,000,000	C$4,000,000 (outflow)	$.80	$3,200,000 (outflow)
German mark (DM)	DM10,000,000	DM12,000,000	DM2,000,000 (outflow)	$.50	$1,000,000 (outflow)
French franc (FF)	FF100,000,000	FF60,000,000	FF40,000,000 (inflow)	$.10	$4,000,000 (inflow)
Swiss franc (SF)	SF1,000,000	SF6,000,000	SF5,000,000 (outflow)	$.60	$3,000,000 (outflow)

MNC. The largest open (non-offset) currency position in Exhibit 10.1 is in French francs from the U.S.-based MNC's perspective. Its net cash flow position shows a net inflow of 40 million units.

Assume that Miami Company uses the information in Exhibit 10.1 to develop a range of possible exchange rates that may exist at the end of the period. Applying the range of possible exchange rates to the number of units of each currency to be received or needed one period ahead, the MNC could determine a possible range of its local currency (the U.S. dollar in our example) inflows or outflows related to each foreign currency. Exhibit 10.2 illustrates how this can be done. The first row of the exhibit shows an expected net outflow of 4 million Canadian dollars, as was given earlier. Based on the possible exchange rate of the Canadian dollar ranging from $.79 to $.81, the range of possible net inflows or outflows is $3,160,000 at the low end (computed as C$4 million × $.79 per unit) and $3,240,000 at the high end (computed as C$4 million × $.81 per unit). This range of possible net inflows or outflows expressed in the MNC parent's local currency is displayed in the last column of Exhibit 10.2. Notice from that column that the range of possible U.S. dollar outflows needed to obtain Swiss francs is actually larger than the range of possible U.S. dollar outflows needed to obtain Canadian dollars. This occurs because the range of possible exchange rates for the Swiss franc was wider than for the Canadian dollar. The main point of this comparison is that a firm's transaction exposure in any foreign currency is not based merely on the size of its open position in that currency. It is also based on the range of possible exchange rates that may occur for each foreign currency.

In the preceding example, the net inflows or outflows in each foreign currency were provided, but the exchange rates at the end of the period were assumed uncertain. In reality, the net inflows or outflows in each foreign currency would also be uncertain. Thus, the MNC might develop a range of possible net inflows and outflows of each currency instead of a point estimate. If so, the second column of Exhibit 10.2 would show a range. At this point, the measurement of exposure in each currency becomes more complex. Some methods, though, such as sensitivity analysis or simulation, could

EXHIBIT 10.2 Estimating the Range of Net Inflows or Outflows in Each Currency for Miami Company

Currency	Net Inflow or Outflow	Range of Possible Exchange Rates at End of Period	Range of Possible Net Inflows or Outflows in U.S. Dollars (Based on Range of Possible Exchange Rates)
Canadian dollar (C$)	C$4,000,000 (outflow)	$.79 to $.81	$3,160,000 to $3,240,000 (outflow)
German mark (DM)	DM2,000,000 (outflow)	$.48 to $.52	$960,000 to $1,040,000 (outflow)
French franc (FF)	FF40,000,000 (inflow)	$.09 to $.11	$3,600,000 to $4,400,000 (inflow)
Swiss franc (SF)	SF5,000,000 (outflow)	$.56 to $.64	$2,800,000 to $3,200,000 (outflow)

be used to generate a range of estimates for exposure in each currency based on the given ranges of the possible net inflows or outflows in each currency as well as the possible exchange rates.

In the previous example, the net cash flow situation was assessed for only one period. This period could reflect a month, a quarter, or a year. MNCs may desire to assess their transaction exposure during several periods. To do this, the same methods described earlier could be applied to each period. The further into the future the MNC attempts to measure transaction exposure, the less accurate will be the measurement. This is due to greater uncertainty about inflows or outflows in each foreign currency as well as future exchange rates over periods further into the future. The net exposure identified in Exhibits 10.1 and 10.2 will be assessed after discussing currency variability and correlations.

Transaction Exposure Based on Currency Variability

In the previous example, the ranges of projected exchange rates for the end of the period were given without any explanation as to how they were derived. Each MNC may have its own method for developing exchange rate projections. Some methods were described in the previous chapter. While it is sometimes impossible to predict future currency values with much accuracy, an MNC can evaluate historical data in order to at least assess the potential degree of movement for each currency.

The standard deviation statistic serves as one possible way to measure the degree of movement for each particular currency. To demonstrate the use of such information, consider a U.S.-based MNC trying to assess currency movements. It could evaluate the historical variability in each foreign currency based on the standard deviation statistics. The second column of Exhibit 10.3 displays the standard deviation of eight foreign currencies (based on quarterly data) during the 1974–1989 period. From this exhibit, it appears that some currencies fluctuate much more than others. For example, the German mark exhibits a standard deviation of about 6 percent, which is almost three times that of the Canadian dollar. Other currencies such as the British pound and French franc exhibit more than double the variability of the Canadian dollar. Based on this information, a U.S.-based MNC may feel that an open asset or liability position in Canadian dollars is not as worri-

EXHIBIT 10.3 Standard Deviations of Exchange Rate Movements

Currency	Time Period:		
	1974–1989	*1974–1980*	*1981–1989*
Belgian franc	.0652	.0558	.0737
British pound	.0511	.0444	.0569
Canadian dollar	.0217	.0210	.0225
French franc	.0560	.0475	.0633
German mark	.0584	.0564	.0611
Japanese yen	.0640	.0621	.0669
Italian lira	.0543	.0507	.0583
Swiss franc	.0710	.0777	.0643

some as an open position in other currencies. That is, the potential for these other currencies to deviate far from their projected future values is greater than for the Canadian dollar (from the U.S. firm's perspective). Yet, there is more to consider than the currency's standard deviation when assessing transaction exposure, as will be discussed shortly.

Currency Variability over Time

The variability of a currency will not necessarily remain consistent from one time period to another. Columns 3 and 4 in Exhibit 10.3 illustrate how standard deviations can change over time. All currencies except the Swiss franc were more volatile against the dollar in the 1981–1989 period than in the 1974–1980 period.

Recognizing that the variability of each currency changes over time is important. These changes imply that the MNC's assessment of a currency's variability will not be perfect when a previous time period is used as the indicator for the future. However, the MNC can benefit from information such as that in Exhibit 10.3 if it is used wisely. While the MNC may not be able to predict a currency's future variability with perfect accuracy, it can identify currencies whose values are *most likely* to be stable or highly variable in the future. For example, the Canadian dollar's variability has changed in each period. Nevertheless, it's a safe bet the Canadian dollar will continue to exhibit lower variability than any of the other currencies in the future. Thus, the U.S.-based MNC would be less concerned with open positions in the Canadian dollar relative to most other foreign currencies, even though it's not sure what the Canadian dollar's variability will be in the future.

Transaction Exposure Based on Currency Correlations

While the preceding analysis can help an MNC measure its transaction exposure, currency correlations must also be assessed. Consider two U.S.-based MNCs (called American MNC and National MNC) that have consolidated the net inflows or outflows for all currencies of all subsidiaries. Assume American MNC is exposed to a large volume of Canadian-dollar future inflows and National MNC to a large volume of German-mark future inflows and French-franc future outflows. Which MNC is more exposed to transaction risk? It may seem that National MNC is more exposed, since its exposure is to two currencies that fluctuate to a high degree against the U.S. dollar. American MNC may appear to be less exposed, since the Canadian dollar is quite stable. This reasoning ignores the important concept of currency correlations, which will now be discussed.

Assume for the moment the German mark and the French franc values relative to the U.S. dollar are highly positively correlated. This means that when the mark is appreciating against the U.S. dollar, so will the French franc, and by about the same degree. Also, if one of these currencies is depreciating against the U.S. dollar, the other currency is following a similar pattern. Relate this information to National MNC, which had future inflows in marks and future outflows in French francs. If these currencies simultaneously depreciate against the U.S. dollar, the mark inflows will be worth less when converted to U.S. dollars, and it will take fewer U.S. dollars to pay for the outflows denominated in French francs. Two highly correlated currencies

---

RELATED RESEARCH

Exchange Rate Volatility Before versus After the 1987 Stock Market Crash

The October 1987 stock market crash has caused many investors to reevaluate the risk of investing in the stock market. Since the same alleged determinants of the stock market crash (such as concerns about the U.S. federal budget deficit and the U.S. balance of trade deficit) can also influence exchange rate movements, the risk perception of various currencies may have been affected as well. Recent research assessed the variance of daily exchange rate movements over 112 days before the crash and over 112 days after the crash for six major currencies. For all six currencies, the variance had more than quadrupled in the post-crash period. This major shock to the foreign exchange markets did not receive much attention because actual exchange rates did not "crash," but simply became much more volatile on a daily basis. Nevertheless, this is critical to corporations that are continually exposed to exchange rate risk.

The substantial increase in the variance of exchange rate movements could have been a temporary response to the stock market crash, as investors began to shift funds across global stock markets in search of a safe market. This may have led to the higher exchange rate volatility. As time passes, we will be able to determine whether the higher volatility is here to stay. If so, many companies would likely hedge a larger proportion of their exposure to exchange rate risk.

SOURCE: Jeff Madura, and Alan L. Tucker, "Intertemporal Shifts in Actual and Anticipated Exchange Rate Risk," *Journal of Global Business*, (Summer 1990): 5–10.

---

act almost as if they are two of the same currency. The transaction exposure to inflows of one currency and outflows of the other currency are then offset. Normally, currencies do not move exactly in tandem over time. Yet, even if the currencies move in the same direction to a degree, a partial offsetting effect will take place when one currency represents an inflow while the other currency represents an outflow.

When the MNC has two or more inflow currencies, it can still benefit from assessing correlations. Consider these inflows as a portfolio. The lower the correlations are in this case, the lower will be the overall variability of the portfolio of cash inflows. From a U.S. MNC's perspective, variability provides a measure of the potential degree to which the portfolio's dollar value may fluctuate. This reflects the uncertainty about what the portfolio will be worth. MNCs would normally prefer to have a cash inflow portfolio that exhibits low variability, since there is less chance the value of such a portfolio will substantially deviate from what was expected. A portfolio of currencies with low (or negative) correlations can reduce portfolio variability, because all the currencies would not all be moving in the same direction at about the same magnitude (as they would be if they were highly correlated). Thus, there is an offsetting effect, making the overall movement of the portfolio over time more stable. A similar methodology could be used by the MNC to assess the various consolidated net outflow currencies (or the portfolio of cash outflows).

The correlations among currency movements can be measured by their *correlation coefficients*, which indicate the degree to which two currencies move in relation to each other. Thus, MNCs could use such information when deciding their degree of transaction exposure. The extreme case is perfect positive correlation, which is represented by a correlation coefficient equal to 1.00. Correlations can also be negative, reflecting an inverse relationship between individual movements, the extreme case being −1.00. The correlation coefficients (based on quarterly data) for currency pairs in three different periods are illustrated in Exhibit 10.4. First consider the top number in each cell, which represents the 1974–1989 period. It is clear that some currency pairs exhibit a much higher correlation than others. For example, the German mark/French franc correlation is .89 and the German mark/Swiss franc correlation is .85. At the other extreme, the Canadian dollar/Italian lira correlation is −.03. Currency correlations are generally positive, which implies currencies tend to move in the same direction against the U.S. dollar (though by different degrees). The positive correlation may not always occur on a day-to-day basis, but it appears to hold during longer periods of time for most

EXHIBIT 10.4 Correlations Among Exchange Rate Movements*

	German mark (DM)	Belgian franc (BF)	British pound (BP)	Japanese yen (JY)	Italian lira (IL)	French franc (FF)	Swiss franc (SF)	Canadian dollar (C$)
German mark (DM)	1.00 1.00 1.00							
Belgian franc (BF)	.87 .97 .81	1.0 1.0 1.0						
British pound (BP)	.60 .52 .65	.51 .55 .48	1.0 1.0 1.0					
Japanese yen (JY)	.66 .47 .82	.60 .45 .72	.44 .29 .56	1.0 1.0 1.0				
Italian lira (IL)	.74 .56 .89	.76 .58 .88	.51 .52 .52	.59 .36 .76	1.0 1.0 1.0			
French franc (FF)	.89 .81 .95	.81 .80 .81	.60 .53 .63	.68 .51 .81	.83 .78 .88	1.0 1.0 1.0		
Swiss franc (SF)	.85 .82 .90	.73 .78 .73	.54 .47 .61	.69 .53 .88	.67 .56 .82	.78 .72 .86	1.0 1.0 1.0	
Canadian dollar (C$)	.08 .06 .11	.06 −.01 .11	.06 −.09 .19	.05 −.17 .24	−.03 −.16 .07	.06 −.11 .13	.11 −.04 .31	1.0 1.0 1.0

*The top number in each cell represents the entire 1974–1989 period, while the middle number in each cell represents an early subperiod (1974–1980), and the lower number represents the more recent subperiod (1981–1989).

currencies. This is especially true of European currency movements against the dollar.

Currency Correlations over Time

Notice from Exhibit 10.4 that correlations are not constant over time. Therefore, the MNC cannot use previous correlations to predict future correlations with perfect accuracy. There are some pairs of currencies whose co-movements are somewhat stable over time, however, so the correlations disclosed in Exhibit 10.4 can provide valuable information for MNCs. For example, the European currencies are consistently highly correlated with each other. At the other extreme, the Canadian dollar consistently appears to move almost independently of the other currencies based on its continued low correlations with them.

The actual movements of some major currencies against the U.S. dollar are shown in Exhibit 10.5. In this exhibit, it is clear that the Swiss and German currencies are highly correlated. In fact, all European currencies shown here tend to move in tandem. The characteristics of currencies illustrated by Exhibit 10.5 support the information provided earlier on currency correlations.

Using Currency Correlations to Assess Transaction Exposure

When reviewing currency correlations, the MNC needs to assess whether there are consolidated net *inflows* or *outflows* in these currencies. Recall that high positive correlation between two currencies could actually reduce exposure when one of the currencies is an inflow and the other currency is an outflow. However, if both currencies represent future cash inflows, then the exposure is high.

To illustrate how MNCs would assess exposure based on currency movements, consider the historical exchange rate fluctuations as shown in Exhibit 10.6 for Currencies X, Y, and Z. Assume you are treasurer of a U.S.-based MNC when examining these scenarios.

Scenario 1. Assume you expect as of one year from now to need $10 million for the purchase of Currency X and another $20 million to purchase Currency Y. You also expect to receive about $30 million when converting inflows of Currency Z one year from now. There is transaction risk for each currency, since future values of each currency are uncertain. This may cause errors in your projections of dollars needed and dollars received. There is much transaction exposure in this scenario, considering all currencies simultaneously.

Exhibit 10.6 suggests Currencies X and Y are highly correlated with each other, but negatively correlated with Currency Z. If Currencies X and Y appreciate against the dollar, more dollars will be needed to purchase them. If they appreciate against the U.S. dollar, Currency Z will likely depreciate against the dollar, based on its historical co-movements with Currencies X and Y. Since Currency Z is to be received by the MNC in the future, this cash inflow will convert to fewer U.S. dollars if it does depreciate. Thus, the MNC could possibly end up receiving fewer dollars and paying out more dollars than it currently expects.

Scenario 2. Assume you expect as of one year from now to need $10 million for the purchase of Currency X and another $20 million to purchase Cur-

EXHIBIT 10.5 Movements of Major Currencies against the Dollar

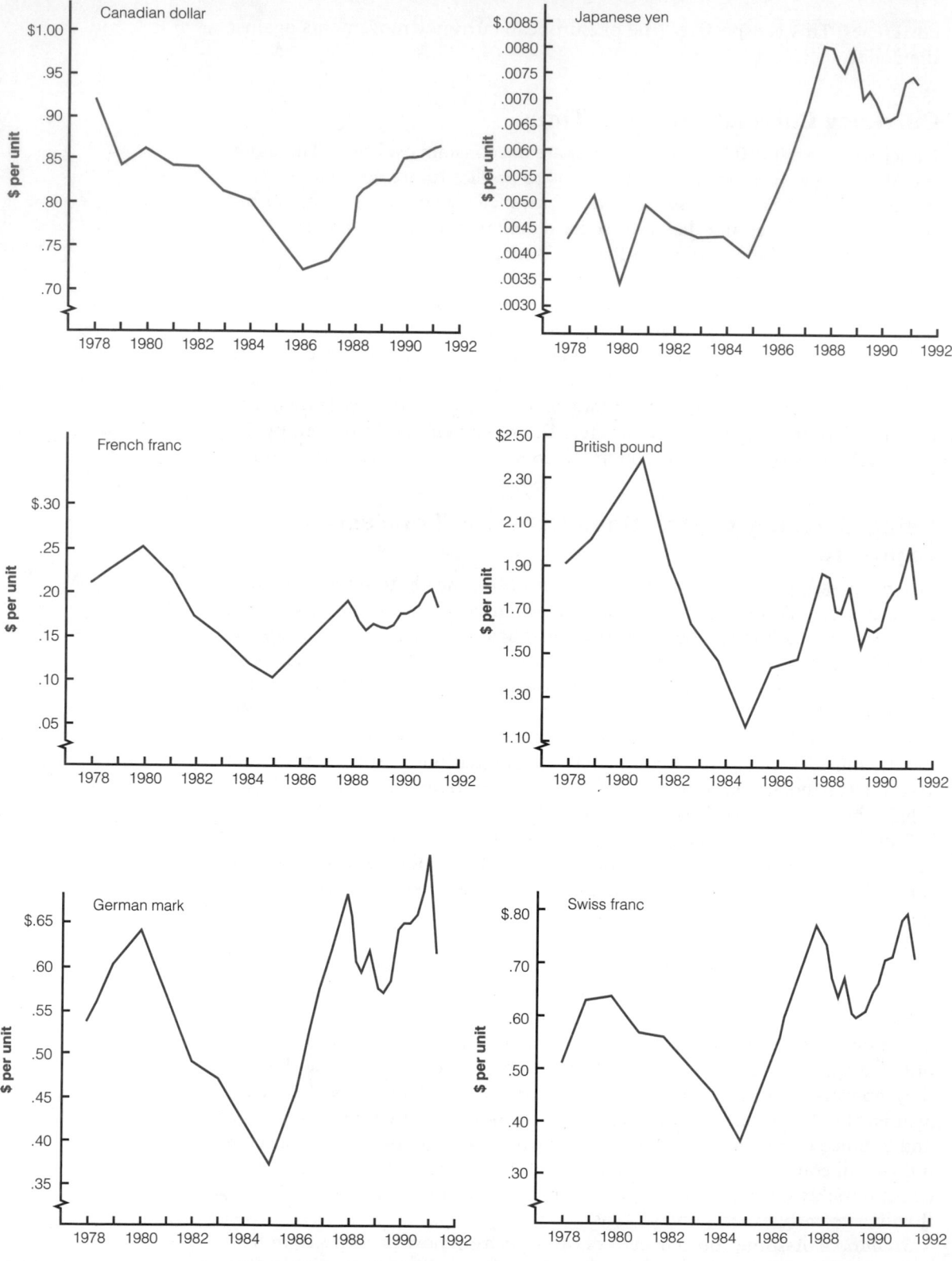

EXHIBIT 10.6 Illustration of Currency Movements for Case Scenarios

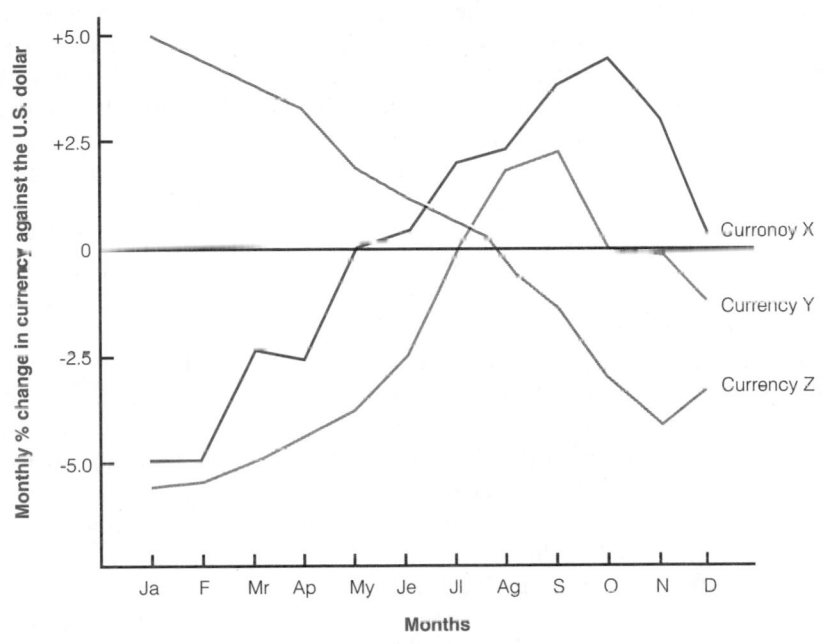

rency Y (same as in Scenario 1). Also, assume you expect to need another $30 million to purchase Currency Z one year from now. Finally, assume you have no projected inflows in foreign currencies. There is not much transaction risk in this scenario when you consider all currencies simultaneously. Based on the correlations that appear to exist as seen in Exhibit 10.6, the changes in values of Currencies X and Y will be somewhat offset by opposite movements in Currency Z. For example, if Currencies X and Y appreciate by 20 percent, the MNC will need $36 million instead of $30 million to buy these currencies. Yet, Currency Z will likely depreciate under this situation. A perfect offset would occur if Currency Z depreciated by 20 percent so that it would take only $24 million to purchase the necessary amount of Currency Z. Then, the additional $6 million needed to purchase Currencies X and Y would be offset by the $6 million saved due to depreciation of Currency Z. A perfect offset is not likely to occur, but the point here is to be able to detect positions that could somewhat offset each other.

In summary, the first step when assessing transaction exposure is to determine the size of the position in each currency (i.e., number of units of each foreign currency position). The second step is to determine how that individual currency position could affect the firm. This is accomplished by assessing the standard deviations and correlations of the currencies. Even if a particular currency is perceived as risky, its impact on the firm's overall variability will not be severe if the firm has taken just a minor position in that currency. For this reason, both of these steps must be considered simultaneously when developing an overall assessment of the firm's transaction risk.

Assessing Transaction Exposure: An Example

The concept of currency correlations can be applied to our earlier example of Miami Company's transaction exposure, displayed in Exhibit 10.1. If European currencies such as the German mark, French franc, and Swiss franc are highly correlated, then these individual currency exposures would offset each other to a degree. Miami Company anticipates cash inflows in French francs equivalent to $4 million, and cash outflows in German marks and Swiss francs with a combined equivalent of $4 million. Thus, if a weak-dollar cycle occurs, it will be adversely affected by its exposure to German marks and Swiss francs, but favorably affected by its French franc exposure. During a strong-dollar cycle, it will be adversely affected by the French franc exposure, but favorably affected by the German mark and Swiss franc exposure. Under these conditions, the only exposure of concern to the firm would be the Canadian dollar. Since the firm has an outflow position in Canadian dollars, it could be adversely affected if the Canadian dollar appreciates against the U.S. dollar. Yet, because the Canadian dollar is somewhat stable with respect to the U.S. dollar over time, the risk of substantial appreciation of the Canadian dollar is low. In general, the overall transaction exposure of the firm to possible changes in exchange rates is low, because of the offsetting effects of the European currencies and the stability of the Canadian dollar.

To test your ability of assessing transaction exposure, consider the exposure of Boston Company to exchange rate fluctuations. Boston's transaction exposure is summarized in Exhibit 10.7. Notice that the only difference between Boston Company and Miami Company is that Boston's French franc exposure represents a cash outflow rather than an inflow, and its Canadian dollar exposure represents a cash inflow rather than an outflow. Assume as before that the European currencies are now highly correlated. Boston Company would be adversely affected by a weak-dollar cycle, since it will need more dollars to make payment on each currency position. There is no offsetting effect as there was for Miami Company, since the Canadian dollar is the only inflow currency, and it does not move in tandem with the European currencies. It should be recognized that Boston Company is more likely to benefit from a strong-dollar cycle, since it will need less dollars to make payment on each currency position (and its inflows in Canadian dollars will not likely be affected much by the dollar's strength). Whether Boston Company decides to hedge its exposure will depend on its forecasts of exchange rates.

EXHIBIT 10.7 Transaction Exposure of Boston Company

Currency	Net Inflow or Outflow
Canadian dollar	C$4 million (inflow)
German mark	DM2 million (outflow)
French franc	FF40 million (outflow)
Swiss franc	SF5 million (outflow)

ECONOMIC EXPOSURE

The degree to which a firm's present value of future cash flows can be influenced by exchange rate fluctuations is referred to as **economic exposure** to exchange rates. Transaction exposure is a subset of economic exposure. However, the influence of exchange rate fluctuations on a firm's cash flows is not always due to transaction of currencies. This will become clear shortly. Some of the more common variables representing an MNC's cash flows subject to economic exposure are listed in the first column of Exhibit 10.8. They are categorized by inflows and outflows. The second column of Exhibit 10.8 suggests how each of these variables may be affected by appreciation of the firm's local currency, while the third column suggests how each variable is affected by depreciation of the firm's local currency. A discussion of the impact of local currency appreciation on each variable follows.

Economic Exposure to Local Currency Appreciation

The following discussion of economic exposure to local currency appreciation is related to Column 2 in Exhibit 10.8. With regard to the firm's cash inflows, its local sales (within the firm's country) are expected to decrease as a result of appreciation in the local currency. This is due to the increased foreign competition as local customers could obtain foreign substitute products cheaply with their strengthened currency. The extent of reduced local sales would depend on the degree of foreign competition within the local market.

Cash inflows from exports denominated in the local currency would likely be reduced as a result of appreciation in the local currency. The reason is that foreign importers would need more of their own currency to pay for these

EXHIBIT 10.8   Economic Exposure to Exchange Rate Fluctuations

Variables That Influence the Firm's Local Currency Inflows	Impact of Local Currency Appreciation on Variables	Impact of Local Currency Depreciation on Variables
Local sales (relative to foreign competition in local markets)	Decrease	Increase
Firm's exports denominated in local currency	Decrease	Increase
Firm's exports denominated in foreign currency	Decrease	Increase
Interest received from foreign investments	Decrease	Increase
Variables That Influence the Firm's Local Currency Outflows		
Firm's imported supplies denominated in local currency	No Change	No Change
Firm's imported supplies denominated in foreign currency	Decrease	Increase
Interest owed on foreign funds borrowed	Decrease	Increase

products. Exports denominated in the foreign currency would also likely cause reduced cash inflows, but for a different reason. Demand for the firm's product by foreign importers would not change, since they could use their own currency and would not need to obtain the firm's local currency. However, when the firm received the foreign currency inflows, it would convert them to its local currency. If the local currency had appreciated, these inflows would convert to a reduced amount. Finally, any interest or dividends received from foreign investments would convert to a reduced amount of local currency inflows if the local currency had strengthened.

With regard to the firm's cash outflows, the cost of imported supplies denominated in the local currency will not be directly affected by any changes in exchange rates. However, the cost of imported supplies denominated in the foreign currency will be reduced if the local currency appreciates. In addition, any interest to be paid on financing in foreign currencies will be reduced (in terms of the local currency) if the local currency appreciates. This is due to exchange of the strengthened local currency for the foreign currency in order to make interest payments.

Overall, appreciation in the firm's local currency causes a reduction in both cash inflows and outflows. Thus, it is difficult to generalize whether net cash flows will increase or decrease due to the local currency's appreciation. The impact of local currency appreciation on a firm's net cash flows depends on whether the inflow variables are affected more or less than the outflow variables. If, for example, the firm is in the exporting business but obtains its supplies and borrowed funds locally, its inflow variables will be reduced by a greater degree than its outflow variables. In this case, net cash flows will be reduced. Conversely, cash inflows of a firm concentrating its sales locally with little foreign competition will not be severely reduced by appreciation of the local currency. If such a firm obtains supplies and borrowed funds overseas, its outflows will be reduced. Overall, this firm's net cash flows will be enhanced by the appreciation of its local currency.

A prominent example of an MNC's economic exposure is Caterpillar Inc., which has relied heavily on exports for a large portion of its sales. The strengthening of the dollar in the early 1980s increased the price paid by importers for Caterpillar's products. Caterpillar was especially vulnerable to the value of the dollar because its key competitor was Komatsu of Japan, whose exports are denominated in Japanese yen. Since the value of the yen was relatively weak in the early 1980s, many firms switched from Caterpillar to Komatsu. Caterpillar's performance improved substantially in periods when the yen and other foreign currencies strengthened against the dollar.

Economic Exposure to Local Currency Depreciation

If the firm's local currency depreciates (see Column 3 of Exhibit 10.8), the variables will be affected opposite to the way they are influenced by appreciation. Local sales should increase due to reduced foreign competition (since prices denominated in strong foreign currencies would seem high to the local customers). The firm's exports denominated in the local currency would appear cheap to importers, thereby increasing foreign demand for them. Even exports denominated in the foreign currency could increase cash flows since a given amount of foreign currency inflows to the firm would convert to a larger amount of the local currency. In addition, interest or dividends from foreign investments will now convert to more of the local currency.

With regard to cash outflows, imported supplies denominated in the local currency will not be directly affected by any change in exchange rates. However, the cost of imported supplies denominated in the foreign currency will rise, since it takes more of the weakened local currency to obtain the foreign currency needed. Any interest payments paid on financing in foreign currencies will increase.

In general, depreciation of the firm's local currency has caused an increase in both cash inflows and outflows. Because a partial offsetting effect is likely, it is difficult to generalize whether net cash flows will increase or decrease due to the local currency's depreciation. The end result depends on whether inflow variables are affected more than outflow variables. A firm that concentrates on exporting and obtains supplies and borrowed funds locally would likely benefit from a depreciated local currency. This was the case for Caterpillar during the 1985–1988 period, when the dollar weakened substantially against most major currencies. Conversely, a firm that concentrates on local sales, has very little foreign competition, and obtains foreign supplies (denominated in foreign currencies) would likely be hurt by a depreciated local currency.

Indirect Economic Exposure

The impact of a change in the local currency on inflow and outflow variables can sometimes be indirect and therefore different from what was expected. For example, consider a U.S. firm that imports wood from Canada, and assume the imports are denominated in U.S. dollars. If the U.S. dollar depreciates, the U.S. firm is not directly affected, since its payment is in U.S. dollars and it will not need to obtain Canadian dollars. However, the Canadian exporter, upon receipt of the payment in U.S. dollars, may convert them to Canadian dollars. If the U.S. dollar has depreciated, the Canadian exporter will receive less Canadian dollars. To offset this reduction in its inflows, it may charge the U.S. firm higher prices in the future. Such a policy would increase the U.S. firm's cash outflows needed to pay for imports denominated in U.S. dollars. The impact here would be indirect.

Economic Exposure of Domestic Firms

While our focus is on the financial management of MNCs, even purely domestic firms are affected by economic exposure. For example, consider a local steel producer that purchases all of its supplies locally and sells all of its steel locally. Because the firm's transactions are solely in the local currency, it is not subject to transaction exposure. However, if there is foreign competition within the local markets this firm sells to, then it is subject to economic exposure. The economic exposure exists since the firm's cash flows could be affected when exchange rates change. If the exchange rate of the foreign competitor's invoice currency depreciates against the local currency, then customers interested in steel products may shift their purchases toward the foreign steel producer. Consequently, demand for the local firm's steel will likely decrease, and so will net cash inflows. This example illustrates how a firm can be a subject to economic exposure of exchange rate fluctuations without being subject to transaction exposure.

Economic Exposure of MNCs

The degree of economic exposure to exchange rate fluctuations will likely be much greater for a firm involved in international business than for a purely domestic firm. As an example of an MNC's economic exposure, General Corporation arranged to sell software to Mexican customers in the early 1980s. However, the Mexican peso was devalued by 40 percent against the dollar, substantially increasing the Mexican customer's purchase price. Consequently, sales by General Corporation to Mexico declined. As another example, DuPont Company suffered a similar setback due to the dollar's strength during 1983. The treasurer of DuPont estimated the 1983 losses to be as high as $100 million as a result of the dollar's strength in that year. The losses were not solely due to the weak foreign currency cash flows being converted to U.S. dollars. They also represented lost dollar inflow payments that would have occurred if the U.S. dollar had not been so expensive from the perspective of potential importers of U.S. products.

While the U.S. dollar's strength in 1983 hurt DuPont, it exerted a favorable impact on Bayer, West Germany's largest chemical company. Due to the strong dollar, U.S. competitors could not penetrate the West German market (since the price of the U.S.-exported goods would be expensive in terms of German marks). In addition, 1983 sales by Bayer in other countries were high, primarily due to the German mark's low value. Consequently, Bayer achieved record sales during 1983.

DuPont Company and many other U.S.-based MNCs benefited from the weaker dollar in the 1985–1988 period, and also during 1990. Their dollar amount of exports increased substantially in response to a weaker dollar. DuPont's performance is very sensitive to exchange rates because its export business is valued at over $3 billion.

The impact of the U.S. dollar's movements varies across U.S.-based MNCs because of their differences in operating characteristics. Even those U.S.-based MNCs that can be classified as heavy exporters may be affected differently, depending on how their competitors react to the changing value of the dollar. A U.S. exporter whose foreign competitors are willing to reduce their profit margin during a weak-dollar period may not necessarily increase its export sales.

While economic exposure can force either a favorable or unfavorable impact on a company, it is critical for the company to assess the potential degree of exposure that exists and then determine whether it should attempt to insulate itself against this exposure.

Measuring Economic Exposure

Assessing the economic exposure of an MNC is difficult due to the complex interaction of fund flows into, out of, and within the MNC. Consider an MNC with subsidiaries around the world that attempts to identify its economic exposure. Each subsidiary will be affected differently by fluctuations in currencies. Subsidiaries in different countries will have different local curren-

INTERNATIONAL FINANCIAL MANAGEMENT IN PRACTICE

Impact of a Weak Dollar on European Business

To understand the potential impact of the dollar's value on corporate performance, consider the effects of the weak dollar on European firms. Volvo, Volkswagen, Jaguar, Airbus, Air France, Daimler Benz, and other European firms experienced a significant decline in U.S. demand because they were priced out of the U.S. market when the dollar weakened. Jaguar experienced losses of about $100 million in 1990, as its exports declined in response to the weak dollar. Since Jaguar normally receives about 40 percent of its revenues from exports to the U.S., its performance was very sensitive to the weakening of the dollar. During the beginning of 1991 when the British pound was worth almost $2, Jaguar's exports to the United States had declined by about 66 percent. Airbus was also adversely affected by the weak dollar. It receives dollars for its work contracts while its expenses are in French francs. The dollar revenues when converted to francs were diminished by the exchange rate.

Some European governments are attempting to cushion the exchange rate effects on

firms. For example, the French government provided Air France with capital. The German government provided subsidies to Daimler Benz.

The weak dollar not only concerns European exporters, but also European firms that may compete with U.S. exporters in the European markets. Some of these firms prefer that trade barriers be imposed on U.S. firms. Consequently, the momentum for free trade was slowed.

The desire for free trade is somewhat dependent on the exchange rate. When the dollar was stronger in the early 1980s, some U.S. firms desired that trade barriers be enforced to prevent excessive foreign competition. As the dollar weakened considerably by the 1990s, the European firms used the same argument. Some firms that are either involved in international trade or compete with foreign exporters would identify the exchange rate as the most critical factor affecting their performance.

cies. The overall impact of a given currency's fluctuation on all of the subsidiaries is extremely complex.

SENSITIVITY OF REVENUES AND COSTS TO POSSIBLE EXCHANGE RATE MOVEMENTS. One method of measuring an MNC's economic exposure is to classify the cash flows into different income-statement items and subjectively predict each income-statement item based on a forecast of exchange rates. Then an alternative exchange rate scenario can be considered and the forecasts for the income-statement items revised. By reviewing how the earnings forecast in the income statement changed in response to alternative exchange rate scenarios, the firm can assess the influence of currency movements on earnings and cash flows. If the firm's costs and revenues are affected by a similar degree, it will be somewhat insulated from exchange rate movements.

To illustrate this procedure, consider Madison Inc., which is a U.S.-based company that conducts a portion of its business in Canada. Its U.S. sales are denominated in U.S. dollars, while its Canadian sales are denominated in Canadian dollars. Its pro forma income statement for next year is shown in Exhibit 10.9. The income-statement items are segmented into the U.S. (in Column 2) and Canada (Column 3). Assume that Madison Inc. desires to assess how its income-statement items would be affected by three possible exchange rate scenarios for the Canadian dollar over the period of concern: (1) $.75, (2) $.80, and (3) $.85. These scenarios are separately analyzed in the second, third, and fourth columns of Exhibit 10.10.

If the U.S. sales are unaffected by the possible exchange rates, the impact of exchange rates on all income-statement items can be assessed from the information contained in Exhibit 10.9. However, to make the example more realistic, assume that Madison's sales in the United States are higher when the Canadian dollar (C$) is stronger, since Canadian competitors will be priced out of the U.S. market. To be specific, assume the following forecasts for U.S. sales corresponding to each possible exchange rate scenario:

Possible Exchange Rate of C$	Forecasted U.S. Sales (in Millions)
$.75	$300
.80	304
.85	307

The impact of an exchange rate on local sales for any firm would depend on the foreign competition of concern. Historical data could be used to assess how local sales had been affected by exchange rates in the past. For our example, the impact of the exchange rate on local sales is given, so there is no need to assess historical data.

Given this information, Madison Inc. can determine how its pro forma statement would be affected by each exchange rate scenario, as shown in Exhibit 10.10. The assumed impact of exchange rates on U.S. sales is shown in Row 1. Row 2 shows the amount of U.S. dollars to be received as a result of Canadian sales (after converting the forecasted C$4 million of Canadian sales into U.S. dollars). Row 3 represents the estimated U.S. dollars to be received from total

EXHIBIT 10.9 Revenue and Cost Estimates: Madison Inc. *(in millions of U.S. dollars and Canadian dollars)*

	U.S. Business	Canadian Business
Sales	$304	C$ 4
Cost of goods sold	$ 50	C$200
Gross profit	$254	−C$196
Operating expenses		
Fixed	$ 30	—
Variable	$ 30.72	—
Total	$ 60.72	—
Earnings before interest and taxes	$193.28	−C$196
Interest expense	$ 3	C$ 10
Earnings before taxes	$190.28	−C$206

EXHIBIT 10.10 Impact of Possible Exchange Rate Movements on Earnings *(in millions)*

	C$ = $.75	C$ = $.80	C$ = $.85
Sales			
(1) U.S.	$300	$304	$307
(2) Canadian	C$4 = $ 3	C$4 = $ 3.2	C$4 = $ 3.4
(3) Total	$303	$307.2	$310.4
Cost of goods sold			
(4) U.S.	$ 50	$ 50	$ 50
(5) Canadian	C$200 = $150	C$200 = $160	C$200 = $170
(6) Total	$200	$210	$220
(7) Gross profit	$103	$ 97.2	90.4
Operating expenses			
(8) U.S.: Fixed	$ 30	$ 30	$ 30
(9) U.S.: Variable (10% of total sales)	$ 30.3	$ 30.72	$ 31.04
(10) Total	$ 60.3	$ 60.72	$ 61.04
(11) Earnings before interest and taxes (EBIT)	$42.7	$36.48	$29.36
Interest expense			
(12) U.S.	$ 3	$ 3	$ 3
(13) Canadian	C$10 = $ 7.5	C$10 = $ 8	C$10 = $ 8.5
(14) Total	$10.5	$ 11	$ 11.5
(15) Earnings before taxes	$32.2	$ 25.48	$ 17.86

sales, which is determined by combining Rows 1 and 2. Row 4 shows the cost of goods sold in the U.S. Row 5 converts the estimated C$200 million cost of goods sold into U.S. dollars for each exchange rate scenario. Row 6 measures the estimated U.S. dollars needed to cover the total cost of goods sold, which is determined by combining Rows 4 and 5. Row 7 estimates the gross profit in U.S. dollars, as measured by Row 3 minus Row 6. Rows 8 through 10 show estimated operating expenses, and Row 11 subtracts total operating expenses from gross profit to determine earnings before interest and taxes (EBIT). Row 12 estimates the interest expenses paid in the United States, while Row 13 estimates the U.S. dollars needed to make interest payments in Canada. Row 14 combines Rows 12 and 13 to estimate total U.S. dollars needed to make all interest payments. Row 15 shows earnings before taxes, estimated by subtracting Row 14 from Row 11.

The effect of exchange rates on Madison's revenues and costs can now be reviewed. Exhibit 10.10 illustrates how both U.S. sales and the dollar value of Canadian sales would increase as a result of a stronger Canadian dollar. Because Madison's Canadian cost of goods sold exposure (C$200 million) is much greater than its Canadian sales exposure (C$4 million), there is a negative overall impact of a strong Canadian dollar on gross profit. The total U.S. dollars needed to make interest payments is also higher when the Canadian dollar is stronger. In general, Madison Inc. would be adversely affected by a stronger Canadian dollar. It would be favorably affected by a weaker Canadian dollar, since the reduced value of total revenues is more than offset by the reduced cost of goods sold and interest expenses.

A general conclusion from our example is that firms with more (less) foreign costs than foreign revenues will be unfavorably (favorably) affected by a stronger foreign currency. Yet, the precise anticipated impact can be determined only by utilizing the procedure described here, or some alternative procedure. Our example was based on a one-period time horizon. If firms have developed forecasts of sales, expenses, and exchange rates for several periods ahead, they can assess their economic exposure over time. Their economic exposure will be affected by any change in operating characteristics over time.

Another possible method of assessing the firm's economic exposure to currency movements is to apply regression analysis to historical cash flow and exchange rate data as follows:

$$PCF_t = a_0 + a_1 \, PER_t + \mu_t$$

where

$$PCF_t = \text{percentage change in inflation-adjusted}$$
cash flows measured in the firm's home currency over period t

PER_t
$$= \text{percentage change in the exchange rate}$$
of the currency over period t
$$\mu_t = \text{random error term}$$
$$a_0 = \text{intercept}$$
$$a_1 = \text{slope coefficient}$$

The regression coefficient a_1, estimated by regression analysis, would indicate the sensitivity of PCF_t to PER_t. If the firm anticipated no major adjustments in its operating structure, it would expect the sensitivity detected from regression analysis to be somewhat similar in the future.

The preceding regression model may be revised to handle more complex situations. For example, if additional currencies were to be assessed, they could be included in the model as additional independent variables. Each currency's impact would be measured by the estimate of its respective regression coefficient. If an MNC were influenced by numerous currencies and were more concerned with its overall sensitivity to currency movements rather than a single currency's impact, it could consolidate the currencies into an *index* (or *composite*) as follows:

$$PCF_t = b_0 + b_1 PERI_t + \mu_t$$

where $PERI_t$ represents the percentage change in a composite of currencies over period t, and the weight assigned to each currency is based on the proportion of total foreign cash flows attributable to that currency.

If currency movements had a lagged impact on cash flows, this could also be captured in a regression model by including lagged variables. For example, if the firm expected that $PERI_t$ had not only an instantaneous impact but also a one-period lagged impact, it could use the following regression model:

$$PCF_t = b_0 + b_1 PERI_t + b_2 PERI_{t-1} + \mu_t$$

The estimated regression coefficient b_2 would indicate the sensitivity of cash flows over a given period to movements in the currency composite over the previous period.

Some MNCs may prefer to use their stock prices as a proxy for the firm's value, and then assess how their stock price changes in response to currency movements. Regression analysis could also be applied to this situation, by replacing PCF_t with the percentage change in stock price in the models specified here.

Some researchers, including Adler and Dumas, suggest the use of regression analysis for this purpose. By assigning stock returns as the dependent variable, regression analysis can indicate how firm value is sensitive to exchange rate fluctuations. The specifics of the regression model are provided in Appendix 10A.

Would appreciation of a foreign currency improve or lower an MNC's stock price? There is no simple answer to this question. It would depend on the specifics of the MNC, as was discussed earlier in this chapter. Because there are several ways in which exchange rate fluctuations can affect a firm, it is not possible to form a general hypothesis. However, it is possible to estimate the economic exposure of any individual MNC to exchange rate fluctuations based on historical data. Unless this firm drastically changes its operating strategies, the exposure detected should be an indicator of the firm's future exposure.

Some companies may assess the impact of exchange rates on particular corporate characteristics, such as earnings, exports, or sales. For example, Toyota Motor Corporation has measured the sensitivity of exports to the yen exchange rate (relative to the U.S. dollar). Consequently, the firm can forecast the expected impact of a forecasted yen value on future exports.

TRANSLATION EXPOSURE

The exposure of the MNC's consolidated financial statements to exchange rate fluctuations is known as **accounting** or **translation exposure.** For example, if the assets or liabilities of the MNC's subsidiaries are translated at something other than historical rates, the balance sheet will be affected by fluctuations in currency values over time. In addition, subsidiary earnings translated into the reporting currency on the consolidated income statement are subject to changing exchange rates. The importance of translation exposure is questioned in the following section. Then the determinants of translation exposure are identified. Finally, a description of the current accounting rule's impact on translation exposure is provided, and some examples of translation exposure are offered.

Does Translation Exposure Matter?

Translation of financial statements for consolidated reporting purposes does not affect an MNC's cash flows. For this reason, some analysts suggest that translation exposure is not relevant. Other analysts argue that because consolidated financial statements are representative of an MNC's performance, translation exposure is relevant. In the middle 1970s, a survey found that most firms identified translation exposure to be more important than transaction exposure. By 1977 a repeat of the survey found transaction exposure to be perceived as more important. This attitude appears to hold today. Each company has its own opinion as to whether it should attempt to hedge translation exposure. As an example, Kodak, Inc., does not spend much time hedging translation exposure but is more concerned with transaction exposure.

MNCs not concerned with translation exposure could argue that the subsidiary earnings do not actually have to be converted into the parent's currency. Therefore, if the subsidiary's local currency is currently weak, the earnings could be retained rather than converted and sent to the parent. The earnings could be reinvested in the subsidiary's country if feasible opportunities existed. Because the subsidiary's earnings do not necessarily have to be exchanged for the parent's currency, the translation of a weakened subsidiary currency might distort the true performance of the subsidiary. If financial analysts recognize this distortion, they will not automatically assign a poor evaluation to MNCs whose consolidated earnings are reduced due to weakened subsidiary currencies.

Because all firms are not convinced that translation exposure is irrelevant, it is important to understand what influences a firm's degree of exposure to translation gains and losses. This topic is discussed in the following section.

Determinants of Translation Exposure

Translation exposure is dependent on

- The degree of foreign involvement by foreign subsidiaries
- The locations of foreign subsidiaries
- The accounting methods used

The greater the percentage of an MNC's business conducted by its foreign subsidiaries, the larger will be the percentage of a given financial statement item that is susceptible to translation exposure. For example, the foreign involvement of some MNCs may be mostly in the form of exporting. These MNCs don't have much of their business conducted by foreign subsidiaries. Thus, the consolidated financial statement will not be substantially affected by exchange rate fluctuations (although such firms may exhibit a high degree of transaction and economic exposure).

The locations of the subsidiaries can also influence the degree of translation exposure, since the financial statement items of each subsidiary are typically measured by that country's home currency. For example, consider the reporting situation of a U.S. MNC with a German subsidiary. The German subsidiary's assets, liabilities, earnings, etc., are measured in German marks. The MNC must develop consolidated quarterly financial statements that require translation of the German subsidiary figures into U.S. dollar terms. If the subsidiaries are located in countries such as Canada, where the currency is somewhat stable against the U.S. dollar, then translation risk would be less.

Finally, the MNC's degree of accounting exposure can be greatly affected by the accounting procedures it uses to translate when consolidating financial statement data. Under the Financial Accounting Standards Board No. 52 (FASB-52) adopted in December 1981, the consolidated accounting rules for U.S.-based MNCs changed dramatically. Listed are some of the more important points of FASB-52:

1. The functional currency of an entity is the currency of the economic environment in which the entity operates.

2. The current exchange rate as of the reporting date is used to translate the assets and liabilities of a foreign entity from its functional currency into the reporting currency.

Shareholder Reaction to FASB No. 52

As shown in this chapter, a firm's income statement based on FASB No. 52 may differ from one based on FASB No. 8. The Financial Accounting Standards Board replaced FASB No. 8 with FASB No. 52 in order to improve guidelines for translating foreign subsidiary operations. A recent study assessed shareholder reaction to the announcement of the change in translation guidelines.[1] This study used the event study methodology.

The MNCs surveyed generated more than 30 percent of their corporate earnings from foreign operations. The authors looked for an increase in abnormal stock returns of these MNCs after different announcements that signaled the potential revision of translation guidelines. While the authors assessed 11 different announcement dates, their analysis focused on two of those dates: (1) the initial exposure draft date (August 28, 1980) and (2) the announcement date on which FASB No. 52 was adopted by the Financial Accounting Standards Board (December 8, 1981). The abnormal returns of the MNCs were measured from five trading days before each announcement date to five trading days after each announcement date. The abnormal returns were not significantly different from zero on any days, which implies that shareholders did not expect the revised translation guidelines to affect the value of MNCs.

[1]See T. Dessa Garlicki, Frank J. Fabozzi, and Robert Fonfeder, "The Impact of Earnings under FASB 52 on Equity Returns." *Financial Management* (Autumn 1987), pp. 36–44.

3. The weighted average exchange rate is used to translate revenue, expenses, and gains and losses of a foreign entity from its functional currency into the reporting currency.

4. Translated income gains or losses due to changes in foreign currency values are not recognized in current net income but are reported as a second component of stockholder's equity; an exception to this rule is a foreign entity located in a country with high inflation.

5. Realized income gains or losses due to foreign currency transactions are recorded in current net income, although there are some exceptions.

FASB-52 versus FASB-8

The provisions of FASB No. 52 differ from FASB No. 8 (used before December 1981) in various ways. First, FASB-8 was based on the **monetary/nonmonetary approach** when translating financial statements for consolidation purposes. That is, current exchange rates (as of the reporting date) were used to measure monetary assets and liabilities, while historic exchange rates were used to measure nonmonetary items. Inventory and fixed assets are examples of nonmonetary items. The values of nonmonetary items were translated at the exchange rate in effect at the date of purchase. Because some items were being measured at historical rates while other items were measured at current rates, the consolidated accounting statements could become distorted. Since FASB-52 requires all assets and liabilities to be measured at current exchange rates, such a distortion should no longer occur. Thus, translation exposure should be reduced due to the elimination of this distortion.

A second difference between FASB-8 and FASB-52 is the way translation gains and losses are recorded. Under FASB-8, they were included in the reported net income. Under FASB-52, they are included not in the income statement, but instead in shareholder's equity in a **cumulative translation adjustment (CTA) account.** This is expected to reduce the variability of consolidated net income, since only realized changes in net income will be recorded in the income statement.

To illustrate the difference between FASB-8 and FASB-52 as related to translation exposure, consider the following situation for a company called SUB, which has been in operation for one year. SUB is a subsidiary of a U.S.-based MNC. The financial statements for this company are disclosed in Exhibit 10.11. The financial statements are translated according to FASB-8 and FASB-52.

Notice that the assets of SUB are translated to a greater amount under FASB-8 than under FASB-52. This is due to the translation of inventory and fixed assets at the historical rate under FASB-8 versus the current rate under FASB-52. If the functional currency (the local currency used by SUB) had appreciated over time, the total assets would have been valued higher under FASB-52, since all assets would have been translated at the higher current rate.

EXHIBIT 10.11 Translation of a Subsidiary's Financial Statements under FASB-8 and FASB-52 Rules *(figures are in thousands)*

Assets	Value in Functional Currency	FASB-8 Translation Rates	Translation to U.S. Dollars Under FASB-8	FASB-52 Translation Rates	Translation to U.S. Dollars Under FASB-52	
Cash	4,000	Current; $1.50	6,000	Current; $1.50	$ 6,000	
Inventory	6,000	Historical; $1.80	10,800	Current; $1.50	9,000	
Fixed assets	10,000	Historical; $1.90	19,000	Current; $1.50	15,000	
Total Assets	20,000		35,800		$30,000	
Liabilities and equity						
Accounts payable	2,000	Current; $1.50	3,000	Current; $1.50	3,000	−3,100 (cumulative translation account) +5,100 (accumulated earnings)
Long-term debt	10,000	Current; $1.50	15,000	Current; $1.50	15,000	
Common stock	5,000	Historical; $2.00	10,000	Historical; $2.00	10,000	
Retained earnings	3,000	Forced	7,800	Forced	2,000 →	
Total liab. and equity	20,000		35,800		$30,000	
Income Statement						
Sales	12,000	Weighted avg.; $1.70	20,400	Weighted avg.; $1.70	20,400	
− Cost of sales	8,000	Historical; $1.80	14,400	Weighted avg.; $1.70	13,600	
Gross profit	4,000		6,000		6,800	
− Operating expenses	1,000	Weighted avg.; $1.70	1,700	Weighted avg.; $1.70	1,700	
Operating profit	3,000		4,300		5,100	
Gain on translation			3,500			
Net income	3,000		7,800		5,100	

The liabilities are translated to the same amount for FASB-8 as FASB-52. This similarity occurs because both reporting rules use the current rate to translate liabilities.

Stockholder's equity is translated to a larger amount under FASB-8 relative to FASB-52. Even though common stock is translated at the historical rate under both reporting rules, retained earnings is a plug figure dependent on the difference between assets and the sum of liabilities plus common stock. Since assets were larger for FASB-8, the amount of retained earnings is forced to be larger.

The gross income translated to U.S. dollars is lower under FASB-8 than FASB-52 due to FASB-8 using the historical rate to translate cost of sales. A functional currency that was strong when the costs of sales were incurred but weakens by the time the financial statements are disclosed, will show a relatively low gross income (since revenues would be translated at the low current rate). If the functional currency had appreciated against the dollar from the time costs were incurred to the time of financial statement disclosure, the gross income would have been relatively high. Under FASB-52, sales and cost of sales are translated using a weighted average of exchange rates over the reporting period. Thus, even if most costs were incurred when the functional currency was strong against the dollar, and most sales were generated later when the functional currency was weak, the net income will not be distorted (since cost of sales will not be translated at the historical exchange rate).

When operating expenses are deducted from gross income to determine net income, they are translated at the weighted average exchange rate under both FASB-8 and FASB-52. However, because of the difference in computing translated gross income, the reported net income in U.S. dollars by SUB will vary among the two accounting rules.

Since this is SUB's first year in operation and no cash dividends were paid, the retained earnings account is equal to net income under FASB-8. The difference between this net income figure of $7.8 million and the operating profit of $4.3 million is the translation gain of $3.5 million. Under FASB-52, the translation gain or loss is not incorporated within the income statement. Instead, it is included as a component of retained earnings. Exhibit 10.11 shows that the retained earnings account under FASB-52 was divided into *accumulated earnings* (as determined by the income statement) and the *cumulative translation account* (which measures the translation gain or loss). Since retained earnings are forced to be $2 million, and accumulated earnings are translated at $5.1 million, the cumulative translation account is the residual of −$3.1 million.

The translation of costs into the reporting currency according to the historical exchange rate can be misleading. If the subsidiary used its local currency when incurring the costs, the fact that its currency was strong against the dollar at that time did not affect the actual cost to the subsidiary. In addition, the inclusion of translation gains and losses in the income statement can be misleading, since these gains and losses were not actually realized. These distortions to translated net income due to FASB-8 rules have been alleviated by FASB-52 with its use of the weighted average exchange rate during the reporting period for both revenues and expenses, and its omission of translation gains and losses from the income statement. Although MNCs will always be faced with translation gains and losses due to the sometimes wide fluctuations in exchange rates, FASB-52 appears to help present a more accurate picture of the true financial position and results of operations by foreign subsidiaries.

Although FASB-52 should reduce an MNC's exposure to translation risk, it cannot totally eliminate it. Recall that the stockholder's equity account is increased due to a translation gain or reduced due to a translation loss. Thus, financial ratios such as return on equity (net income/equity) and leverage (debt/equity) are influenced by translation gains and losses.

Even under FASB-52, year-to-year consolidated earnings are subject to exchange rate fluctuations. For example, consider a British subsidiary of a U.S.-based MNC that, as of December 1980, reported local earnings of 5 million pounds. Assume that four years later, as of December 1984, reported local annual earnings were 6 million pounds. When these earnings were consolidated along with other subsidiary earnings, they were translated into the parent's reporting currency (U.S. dollars in our example). The weighted average exchange rate of the British pound over Year 1 is assumed to be $2.40 and as of Year 2 is assumed to be $1.15. The translated earnings for each reporting period in U.S. dollars are determined as follows:

Reporting Date	Assumed Local Earnings of British Subsidiary	Weighted Average Exchange Rate of Pound as of the Reporting Date	Translated U.S. Dollar Earnings of British Subsidiary
Year 1	5 million pounds	$2.40	$12.0 million
Year 2	6 million pounds	$1.15	$ 6.9 million

Notice that even though local earnings increased by 1 million pounds at the British subsidiary, consolidated MNC dollar earnings translated from the British subsidiary decreased by over $5 million. The discrepancy here is due to the change in the weighted average of the British pound exchange rate from $2.40 to $1.15. It is possible that financial analysts may give the MNC a poor evaluation due to its British subsidiary's reduced earnings (when measured in dollars) during the four-year period. Yet, the drop in earnings is not the fault of the British subsidiary, but rather due to a weakened British pound that makes its year 2 earnings look small (when measured in U.S. dollars). The exchange rates in this example have occurred from reality. In early 1980 the pound was worth $2.40, while by late 1984 it had weakened to about $1.15. By 1988, the pound's exchange rate rose to about $1.80, which substantially increased the dollar value of a given amount of British pound earnings, relative to the 1984 value. By 1990, the pound's value declined to about $1.60, causing a reduction in the translated dollar amount of a given level of pound earnings. But by 1991, the pound rose to $1.93. The sharp movements in exchange rates can cause reported earnings to be very volatile.

Consider a U.S.-based MNC with subsidiaries concentrated in Europe. The functional currencies for reporting purposes will likely be highly correlated. Consequently, during a strong-dollar cycle, all functional currencies are likely to weaken against the dollar by about the same degree, and the impact on reported earnings could be substantial. If an MNC's functional currencies are not highly correlated, reported consolidated earnings are likely to be less sensitive to exchange rate movements, since some of the functional currency values may move in opposite directions or by smaller degrees than others.

Examples of Translation Exposure

Consolidated earnings of Black & Decker were substantially reduced by the dollar's strength in 1983 and 1984. More than a third of its assets and sales are overseas. The earnings in foreign countries appeared small due to the reduced values of the foreign currencies when foreign earnings were translated into U.S. dollars. As another example, International Business Machines (IBM) announced in February 1985 that its first-quarter 1985 earnings would be flat, due partially to the dollar's strength. Furthermore, if the dollar had not strengthened during 1984, IBM's earnings would have increased by 32.4 percent in 1984 from the previous year. However, due to the dollar's strength in 1984, the consolidated earnings were up by only 19.6 percent. Eastman Kodak Company estimated that its reported 1984 earnings would have been $.60 per share higher if the dollar had not strengthened during the 1984 period.

Conversely, some non-U.S. companies with subsidiaries in the United States showed large earnings increases during the 1983–1985 period due to the dollar's strength. Their dollar earnings are translated into their home currency for consolidated income statement reporting. In particular, many British-owned MNCs showed large income gains due to their subsidiary presence in the U.S.

The earnings of numerous U.S.-based MNCs were favorably affected by the weakened dollar over the 1985–1988 period. The boost in earnings was primarily attributed to the foreign subsidiary earnings that were translated into dollars at a higher exchange rate.

In 1989 some non-U.S. currencies depreciated against the dollar, reducing the reported sales and profits of many U.S.-based MNCs. For example, CPC International stated that its reported non-U.S. sales were $50 million less as a result of weaker foreign currencies in 1989. However, in 1990 most currencies appreciated against the dollar, thereby boosting the consolidated profits of U.S.-based MNCs. But in the first quarter of 1991, these currencies depreciated substantially against the dollar, deflating the quarterly consolidated profits of IBM and numerous other U.S.-based MNCs. The effect of translation exposure on consolidated earnings can be documented by reviewing the annual reports of MNCs.

An MNC must face three forms of exposure: (1) transaction exposure, (2) economic exposure, and (3) translation exposure. The determinants of the firm's degree of exchange rate exposure are summarized in Exhibit 10.12. Once an MNC measures its various forms of exposure, it needs to determine whether and how to reduce or eliminate that exposure. This is discussed in the next two chapters.

SUMMARY

EXHIBIT 10.12 Comparison of Exchange Rate Exposure

Type of Exchange Rate Exposure	Determinants of Degree of Exposure
Transaction exposure	■ Future net receivable or net payable position in each foreign currency ■ Potential degree of movement in each foreign currency's value ■ Correlation of currency's movement with other foreign currencies that the MNC has a position in
Economic exposure	■ All of the above, plus: ■ Impact of foreign currency fluctuations on cash flows denominated in the home currency
Translation exposure	■ Degree of business conducted in each foreign subsidiary ■ Potential degree of movement in the value of each functional currency with respect to the reporting currency ■ Correlations of exchange rate movements of functional currencies

QUESTIONS/ PROBLEMS

1. Why would an MNC consider examining only its "net" cash flows in each currency when assessing its transaction exposure?

2. Your employer, a large MNC, has asked you to assess its transaction exposure. Its projected cash flows are as follows for the next year:

Currency	Total Inflow	Total Outflow	Current Exchange Rate in U.S. Dollars
French francs (FF)	FF4million	FF2million	$ .15
British pounds (£)	£2million	£1million	$1.50
German marks (DM)	DM3million	DM4million	$ .30

Provide your assessment as to your firm's degree of economic exposure (as to whether the exposure is high or low). Substantiate your answer. Use any background data available to you in order to answer your question.

3. What factors affect a currency's degree of transaction exposure? For each factor, explain the desirable characteristics that would reduce transaction exposure.

4. Are currency correlations perfectly stable over time? What does your answer imply about using past data on correlations as an indicator for the future?

5. If a firm has net receivables in several currencies that are highly correlated with each other, what does this imply about the firm's overall degree of transaction exposure?

6. Compare and contrast transaction exposure versus economic exposure.

7. How should appreciation of a firm's home currency generally affect its cash inflows? Why?

8. How should depreciation of a firm's home currency generally affect its cash outflows? Why?

9. Assume that Firm Z is in the exporting business and that it obtains its supplies and borrows funds locally. How would depreciation of this firm's local currency likely affect its net cash flows? Why?

10. Why are even the cash flows of a purely domestic firm exposed to exchange rate fluctuations?

11. Assume an MNC hires you as a consultant to assess its degree of economic exposure to exchange rate fluctuations. How would you handle this task? Be specific.

12. a) In using regression analysis to assess a firm's degree of economic exposure to exchange rate movements, what is the use of breaking the database into subperiods? (See Appendix 10A.)
b) Assume the regression coefficients based on assessing economic exposure were much higher in this second subperiod than in the first subperiod. What does this tell you about the firm's degree of economic exposure over time? Why might such results occur? (See Appendix 10A.)

13. a) Present an argument for why translation exposure is relevant to an MNC.
b) Present an argument for why translation exposure is not relevant to an MNC.

14. What factors affect the firm's degree of translation exposure? Explain how each factor influences translation exposure.

15. How have MNCs changed over time (based on surveys) with respect to their attitude about the importance of transaction exposure versus translation exposure?

16. How does FASB-52 differ from FASB-8?

17. Consider a period in which the U.S. dollar weakens against most foreign currencies. How will this affect the reported earnings of a U.S.-based MNC with subsidiaries all over the world?

18. Consider a period in which the U.S. dollar strengthens against most foreign currencies. How will this affect the reported earnings of a U.S.-based MNC with subsidiaries all over the world?

19. Walt Disney World built an amusement park in France that opened in 1992. How do you think this project will affect their overall economic exposure to exchange rate movements? Explain.

20. Using the cost and revenue information for DeKalb Inc. on page 294, determine how the costs, revenues, and earnings items would be affected by three possible exchange rate scenarios: (1) DM = $.50, (2) DM − $.55, (3) DM = $.60. (Assume U.S. sales will be unaffected by the exchange rate). Assume that DM earnings will be remitted to the U.S. at the end of the period.

21. Aggie Company produces chemicals. It is a major exporter to West Germany, where its main competition is from other U.S. exporters. All of these companies invoice the products in U.S. dollars. Is Aggie's transaction expo-

Revenue and Cost Estimates: DeKalb Company
(in millions of U.S. dollars and German marks)

	U.S. Business	German Business
Sales	$ 800	DM 800
Cost of goods sold	$ 500	DM 100
Gross profit	$ 300	DM 700
Operating expenses	$ 300	
Earnings before interest and taxes	0	DM 700
Interest expenses	$ 100	0
Earnings before taxes	–$ 100	DM 700

sure likely to be significantly affected if the mark strengthens or weakens? Explain. If the mark weakened for several years, can you think of any change that might occur within the global chemicals market?

22. Longhorn Company produces hospital equipment. Most of its revenues are in the United States. About half of its expenses require outflows in German marks (to pay for German materials). Most of Longhorn's competition is from U.S. firms that have no international business at all. How would Longhorn Company be affected if the mark strengthens?

23. Lubbock Inc. produces furniture and has no international business. Its major competitors import most of their furniture from Switzerland, then sell it out of retail stores in the United States. How would Lubbock Inc. be affected if the Swiss franc strengthens over time?

24. Sooner Company is a U.S. wholesale company that imports expensive high-quality luggage and sells it to retail stores around the United States. Its main competitors also import high-quality luggage and sell it to retail stores. None of these competitors hedge their exposure to exchange rate movements. The treasurer of Sooner Company told the board of directors that the firm's performance would be more volatile over time if it hedged its exchange rate exposure. How could a firm's cash flows be more stable as a result of such high exposure to exchange rate fluctuations?

25. Boulder Inc. exports chairs to West Germany (invoiced in U.S. dollars) and competes against local West German companies. If purchasing power parity exists, why would Boulder not benefit from a stronger mark?

26. Toyota Motor Corporation measures the sensitivity of exports to the yen exchange rate (relative to the U.S. dollar). Explain how regression analysis could be used for such a task. Identify the expected sign of the regression coefficient if Toyota primarily exported to the United States. If Toyota established plants in the United States, how might the regression coefficient on the exchange rate variable change?

27. How can a U.S. company use regression analysis to assess its economic exposure to fluctuations in the British pound?

28. Cornhusker Company is an exporter of products to France. It wants to know how its stock price is affected by changes in the franc's exchange rate.

It believes that the impact may occur with a lag of one to three quarters. How could regression analysis be used to assess the impact?

29. Vegas Corporation is a U.S. firm that exports most of its products to West Germany. It had historically invoiced its products in German marks to accommodate the importers. However, it was adversely affected during the first quarter of 1989, when the mark weakened against the dollar. Since Vegas did not hedge, its mark receivables were converted into a relatively small amount of dollars. After a few more years of continual concern about possible exchange rate movements, Vegas called its customers and requested that they pay for future orders with dollars instead of marks. At this time, the mark was valued at $.51. The customers decided to oblige, since the number of marks to be converted to dollars when importing the goods from Vegas was still slightly less than the number of marks that would be needed to buy the product from a German manufacturer. Based on this situation, has transaction exposure changed for Vegas Corporation? Has economic exposure changed? Explain.

30. Saab, the Swedish automobile manufacturer, purchases many of its components from Germany. It exports many of its automobiles to the United States. During 1990, the Swedish kronor depreciated against the German mark and appreciated against the U.S. dollar. Holding other factors constant, how would Saab's performance be affected by these currency movements?

31. A German company called Bonz Company has heavy exposure in French francs as a result of importing French supplies denominated in French francs. Stark Company, also German, has heavy exposure in Canadian dollars as a result of importing Canadian supplies denominated in Canadian dollars. Both firms receive German mark cash flows on all their products sold. Neither firm hedges payments on the imports. Assume that the values of imported supplies ordered by the firms are about the same. Also assume that other characteristics of the firms are similar. Which firm will likely experience more volatile profit streams over time? Why?

Whaler Publishing Company
Measuring Exposure to Exchange Rate Risk

Recall the situation of Whaler Publishing Company from the previous chapter. Whaler needed to develop confidence intervals of four exchange rates in order to derive confidence intervals for U.S. dollar cash flows to be received from four different countries. Each interval was isolated on a particular country. The intervals could not be combined because of the possibility that the exchange rates are positively correlated over time. Assume that Whaler would like to estimate the range of its aggregate dollar cash flows to be generated from other countries. Whaler plans to simulate how the expected currency cash flows would convert to U.S. dollars using each of the previous years as a possible scenario (recall that exchange rate data were provided in the original case in Chapter 9). Specifically, Whaler will determine the annual percentage change in the spot rate of each currency for a given year. Then it will apply that percentage to the respective existing spot rates to determine a possible spot rate in one year for each currency. Recall that today's spot rates are assumed as follows:

Australian dollar	= $ .7671
Canadian dollar	= $ .8625
New Zealand dollar	= $ .5985
United Kingdom pound	= $1.9382

Once the spot rate is forecasted for one year ahead for each currency, the U.S. dollar revenues received from each country can be forecasted. This process can be repeated, using each of the previous years as a possible future scenario. There will be 15 possible scenarios, or 15 forecasts of the aggregate U.S. dollar cash flows. Each of these scenarios is expected to have an equal probability of occurring. By assuming that these cash flows are normally distributed, Whaler desires to develop 68% and 95% confidence intervals surrounding the "expected value" of the aggregate level of U.S. dollar cash flows to be received in one year.

a) Perform these tasks for Whaler in order to determine these confidence intervals on the aggregate level of U.S. dollar cash flows to be received. The methodology described above is used by Whaler rather than simply combining results of individual countries (from the previous chapter) since exchange rate movements may be correlated.

b) Review the annual percentage changes in the four exchange rates. Do they appear to be positively correlated? Estimate the correlation coefficient between exchange rate movements either with a calculator or a spreadsheet package (you may wish to run simple regressions to derive the R^2 statistic; the correlation coefficient is the square root of the R^2 statistic). Based on this analysis, you can fill out the correlation coefficient matrix below:

	A$	C$	N$	£
A$	1.00			
C$		1.00		
N$			1.00	
£				1.00

Would aggregate dollar cash flows to be received by Whaler be more risky than if the exchange rate movements were completely independent? Explain.

c) One executive of Whaler suggested that a more efficient way of deriving the confidence intervals would be to simply use the exchange rates instead of the percentage changes as the scenarios and derive U.S. dollar cash flow estimates directly from them. Do you think this method would be as accurate as the method now used by Whaler? Explain.

PROJECTS

1. Select an MNC and assess the sensitivity of its stock returns to particular exchange rate movements using the procedure described in Appendix A. Several software packages have a regression package that can perform regression analysis, including LOTUS, version 2.01.

2. Review the annual report of an MNC, and summarize how the MNC was affected by recent changes in the U.S. dollar's value. Explain why the MNC was favorably or unfavorably affected by the dollar's recent movement. Summarize the MNC's translation exposure and the effect of the dollar's recent movements on consolidated earnings.

3. Estimate the correlation coefficient between the German mark and French franc over the period of 1988–1990. This can be accomplished by applying regression analysis to the percentage changes in the two currencies. The data for this project is in the Data Bank in the back of the text. The correlation coefficient is the square root of the R^2 statistic. Based on your analysis, would a U.S. firm with periodic cash outflows in both currencies be highly exposed to exchange rate risk? What if the firm had periodic outflows in one currency and periodic inflows in the other? See Appendix 2C for a discussion of using LOTUS to run regression analysis.

4. Using the Data Bank in the back of the text, estimate the standard deviation of
   a) percentage changes in the British pound over the 1984–1990 period.
   b) percentage changes in the German mark over the 1984–1990 period.
   c) percentage changes in the Japanese yen over the 1984–1990 period.
   d) percentage changes in an equally weighted portfolio of these three currencies; that is, the percentage change in the portfolio is equal to $(1/3 \times \%\Delta$ in pound$) + (1/3 \times \%\Delta$ in mark$) + (1/3 \times \%\Delta$ in yen$)$.

Compare the standard deviation of the portfolio to that of the individual currencies. Explain why the portfolio's standard deviation is lower. See Appendix 10C for related information, and see Appendix 2C for using LOTUS to compute the standard deviation.

SUGGESTED READINGS

Donald R. Lessard and John B. Lightstone. "Volatile Exchange Rates Can Put Operations at Risk." *Harvard Business Review*, (July–August 1986), pp. 107–114. This article illustrates the difficulties involved in assessing exposure to exchange rate risk.

Robert S. Eckley. "Caterpillar's Ordeal: Foreign Competition in Capital Goods." *Business Horizons* (March–April 1989), pp. 80–86. This article offers a good case example of how exchange rate movements can influence the revenues of an MNC.

REFERENCES

Adler, Michael, and Bernard Dumas. "Exposure to Currency Risk: Definition and Measurement." *Financial Management* 13, no. 2 (Summer 1984), pp. 41–50.

_____."Should Exposure Management Depend on Translation Accounting Methods?" *Euromoney* (June 1981), pp. 132–138.

Aggarwal, Raj. "FASB No. 8 and Reported Results of Multinational Operations: Hazard for Managers and Investors." *Journal of Accounting, Auditing, and Finance* (Spring 1978), pp. 197–216.

Anvari, M. "Efficient Scheduling of Cross-Border Cash Transfers." *Financial Management* (Summer 1986), pp. 40–49.

Beaver, William, and Mark Wolfson. "Foreign Currency Translation Gains and Losses: What Effect Do They Have and What Do They Mean." *Financial Analysts Journal* (March–April 1984), pp. 28–36.

Choi, Jongmoo Jay. "A Model of Firm Valuation with Exchange Exposure." *Journal of International Business Studies* (Summer 1986), pp. 153–160.

Flood, Eugene, Jr., and Donald R. Lessard. "On the Measurement of Operating Exposure to Exchange Rates: A Conceptual Approach." *Financial Management* (Spring 1986), pp. 25–36.

George, Abraham M. "Cash Flow Versus Accounting Exposure to Currency Risk." *California Management Review* (Summer 1978), pp. 50–55.

Giddy, Ian H. "Exchange Risk: Whose View?" *Financial Management* (Summer 1977), pp. 23–33.

Hekman, Christine R. "Measuring Foreign Exchange Exposure: A Practical Theory and Its Applications." *Financial Analysts Journal* (September–October 1983), pp. 59–65.

Jacque, Laurent L. "Management of Foreign Exchange Risk: A Review Article." *Journal of International Business Studies* (Spring–Summer 1981), pp. 81–99.

Jorion, Philippe. "The Exchange Rate Exposure of U.S. Multinationals." *Journal of Business* (July 1990), pp. 331–346.

Kennedy, John Whitcomb. "Risk Assessment for U.S. Affiliates Based in Less Developed Countries." *Columbia Journal of World Business* (Summer 1984), pp. 76–79.

Kwok, Chuck C. Y. "Examining Event Study Methodologies in Foreign Exchange Markets." *Journal of International Business Studies* (Second Quarter 1990), pp. 189–224.

Lessard, Donald R., and John B. Lighthouse. "Volatile Exchange Rates Can Put Operations at Risk." *Harvard Business Review* (July–August 1986), pp. 107–114.

Luehrman, Timothy A. "The Exchange Rate Exposure of a Global Competitor." *Journal of International Business Studies* (Second Quarter 1990), pp. 225–242.

Madura, Jeff. "Empirical Measurement of Systematic Exchange Rate Risk." *Journal of Portfolio Management* (Summer 1983), pp. 43–46.

_____."Assessment of Exchange Rate Risk from Various Country Perspectives." *International Review of Economics and Business* (July 1990), pp. 655–666.

Madura, Jeff, and E. Joe Nosari. "Utilizing Currency Portfolios to Mitigate Exchange Rate Risk." *Columbia Journal of World Business* (Spring 1984), pp. 96–99.

Makin, John H. "Portfolio Theory and the Problem of Foreign Exchange Risk." *The Journal of Finance* 33, no. 3 (May 1978), pp. 517–534.

Maskus, Keith E. "Exchange Rate Risk and U.S. Trade: A Sectoral Analysis." *Economic Review,* Federal Reserve Bank of Kansas City (March 1986), pp. 16–28.

Prindl, Andreas R. *Foreign Exchange Risk.* (London, John Wiley & Sons, 1976).

Reier, Sharon. "Life With FAS No. 52." *Institutional Investor* (November 1983), pp. 223–225.

Rodriguez, Rita M. "FASB No. 8: What Has It Done for Us?" *Financial Analysts Journal* (March–April 1977), pp. 40–47.

_____. "Management of Foreign Exchange Risk in U.S. MNCs." *Sloan Management Review* (September 1978), pp. 31–49.

Soenen, Luc. *Foreign Exchange Exposure Management—A Portfolio Approach.* The Hague/Boston: Martinus Nijhoff Publishing Company, (1979).

Soenen, Luc. "The Optimal Currency Cocktail—A Tool for Strategic Foreign Exchange Management." *Management International Review* 25, no. 2 (1985), pp. 12–22.

Srinivasulu, S. L. "Classifying Foreign Exchange Exposure." *Financial Executive* (February 1983), pp. 36–44.

Westerfield, Janice M. "How U.S. Multinationals Manage Currency Risk." *Business Review* (March–April 1980), pp. 19–27.

Wurst, Charles M., and Raymond H. Alleman. "Translation Adjustments for a Strong Dollar." *Financial Executive* (June 1984), pp. 38–41.

APPENDIX 10A

Measuring Economic Exposure to Exchange Rate Fluctuations: An Example

To provide an actual example of an MNC's economic exposure to exchange rate fluctuations, quarterly data on a company's (name withheld) stock and on several currencies were compiled for an eight-year period. Regression analysis was then conducted to determine how the percentage change in a company's stock price was affected by fluctuations in each exchange rate. The stock price represents firm value and should reflect shareholder's assessment of future cash flow.

Regression analysis was conducted separately for each currency as follows:

$$r_{s,t} = a_0 + a_1 USI_t + a_2 e_t + \mu_t$$

where r_s reflects the percentage change in the stock price of the company, USI_t is the percentage change in an index of U.S. stocks, e_t is the percentage change in a particular currency's value, a_0, a_1, and a_2 are regression coefficients, and μ_t is an error term. The index of U.S. stocks is included in the analysis, since it is thought to exert a major influence on any particular U.S. stock. Thus, the regression analysis is set up to determine whether e has any impact on r_s above and beyond the influence of USI. The regression model will generate values for a_0, a_1 and a_2. The regression coefficient a_2 will suggest how movements in the currency of concern affects the company's value. Regression analysis can then be repeated to analyze the impact of each currency on the company's value.

The individual impact of four different currencies on the company's stock value is provided in Exhibit 10A.1. The data set was split into two equal subperiods. Results are shown for each subperiod. The data were segmented so we could assess whether the impact of an individual currency on the company has changed over time. Four separate regressions were run for each subperiod to assess the sensitivity of a U.S.-based MNC's stock returns to each of the four currencies. Notice from Exhibit 10A.1 that a_2 was typically negative. This implies that as the value of the currency appreciates against the U.S. dollar, the company stock value falls, and vice versa. The larger the

EXHIBIT 10A.1   Sensitivity of a Company's Stock Value to Currency Movements Based on Regression Analysis

Currency	Regression Coefficient a_2: Earlier Subperiod	Regression Coefficient a_2: More Recent Subperiod
Canadian dollar	-.81	-.06
French franc	.05	.05
German mark	-.73	-.01
Swiss franc	-.26	-.27

size of the regression coefficient, the greater the sensitivity of the firm's value to movements in the foreign currency.

From Exhibit 10A.1, it appears that movements in the Canadian dollar and German mark exerted the most influence on the company value in the earlier subperiod. In the more recent subperiod, the Swiss-franc movements were most influential, although the size of the regression coefficient did not differ substantially among the four currencies. While the regression coefficients were generally negative for these currencies, they may be positive when applied to some other companies.

The MNC could repeat the regression analysis for a more recent time period so as to determine whether its firm value is becoming more sensitive to exchange rate fluctuations. It would do this by comparing the regression coefficients based on the recent subperiod with those derived in the earlier subperiod for each currency. If the coefficients increase in size, then the MNC's degree of economic exposure to exchange rate fluctuations has increased, and vice versa.

The impact of each currency has been weaker in the recent subperiod in the exhibit. For example, the Canadian dollar's a_2 coefficient was $-.81$ in the earlier subperiod, which implies a 1 percent change in the Canadian dollar will cause an .81 percent change (in the opposite direction) in the company's value. However, in the more recent subperiod, the coefficient a_2 is $-.06$, suggesting that a 1 percent change in the Canadian dollar will cause a .06 percent change (in the opposite direction) in the company's value. This reflects a weaker impact than in the earlier subperiod. Because there are so many variables that may influence the movements in a company's stock, it is difficult to perfectly disentangle the individual impacts of each variable. Yet the regression analysis applied to separate subperiods at least indicates whether the company has become more or less exposed to an individual currency's movements.

A company may become more exposed or sensitive to an individual currency's movements over time for several reasons, including

- Reduction in hedging
- Greater involvement in the country represented by that currency
- Increased use of that currency to purchase goods

The opposite pattern for these factors could reduce exposure to an individual currency. The regression analysis discussed earlier could help determine whether a particular corporate policy has increased or reduced the MNC's economic exposure.

A suggested exercise to become more familiar with this method is to pick an MNC and replicate the procedure described here. Your results would indicate (1) how sensitive a company is to a currency's movements, (2) the direction of the impact (positive or negative), and (3) whether the MNC is becoming more or less sensitive to movements of a particular currency over time.

It is possible that currencies have a lagged impact on the MNC's stock returns. A regression model could capture this impact if it included exchange rate movements in previous periods. For example, if an MNC was exposed only to the British pound and desired to assess the instantaneous impact of the pound as well as the impact of the pound's previous movements, it could use this model:

$$r_{s,t} = a_0 + a_1 USI_t + a_2 e_t + a_3 e_{t-1} + a_4 e_{t-2} + \mu_t$$

where

$$e_t = \text{percentage change in British pound over period } t$$
$$e_{t-1} = \text{percentage change in pound in the previous period } (t-1)$$
$$e_{t-2} = \text{percentage change in pound two periods earlier } (t-2)$$
$$\mu_t = \text{error term}$$

The regression coefficients a_3 and a_4 would indicate the lagged impact of movements in the British pound on stock returns.

Measuring Economic Exposure to a Country's Economic Conditions

Regression analysis can be used to assess the sensitivity of a company's performance to economic conditions. First, a measure of the economy's condition is needed for each country. Two possible measures are gross national product and national income, but these variables do not indicate the anticipated future condition of the economy. The stock price index for each country, on the other hand, not only reflects the current conditions but also expectations about the future.

To assess the exposure of an MNC to country economies, regression analysis can set the MNC's firm value as a function of the stock indexes for all countries of concern. In general, we would expect the regression coefficients to be positive, since the MNC's value should increase if the stock index of a particular country increases (since a higher stock index reflects favorable economic conditions). For some countries, the regression coefficient may be close to zero, implying the MNC is hardly exposed to the economic conditions of foreign countries. Information such as this can identify those countries whose economies are more influential on the MNC's value. Using stock indexes, the regression equation can be written as

$$r_{s,t} = c_0 + c_1 HI_t + c_2 FI_t + \mu_t$$

where r_s is the return of the company's stock, HI_t is the return on the country's home stock index, FI_t is the return on the foreign stock index, and μ_t is an error term. The coefficient c_0 is a constant, while c_1 and c_2 are regression coefficients measuring the sensitivity of r_s to HI and FI respectively. Regression analysis in the form described here was conducted for a specific U.S.-based MNC and the results of the analysis are displayed in Exhibit 10B.1.

The regression analysis was run separately for four different foreign countries to determine the separate impact of each country. In addition, the time period was split into two subperiods to determine whether the influence of any country had changed over time. From Exhibit 10B.1, the German economy appears to have the greatest influence on the MNC of concern. This statement holds for either subperiod. In the more recent subperiod, for ex-

EXHIBIT 10B.1 Sensitivity of a Company's Stock Value To Country Economies Based on Regression Analysis

Stock Index of:	Regression Coefficient in Earlier Subperiod	Regression Coefficient in More Recent Subperiod
Canada	.5	.7
France	.1	.1
Germany	.9	1.4
Switzerland	.3	.8

ample, a 1 percent change in the German index coincided with a 1.4 percent change (in the same direction) in the company's stock price. The French economy appears to have a relatively minor influence on this MNC's value.

With regard to the sensitivity of the company to foreign economies over time, the MNC appears to be generally more sensitive in the more recent time period than in the earlier time period. The only exception is its sensitivity to the French economy that remained stable over time. Increased sensitivity to foreign economies over time could be due to a greater amount of business in these countries.

A more thorough evaluation of an MNC's sensitivity to foreign economies could be achieved by including all relevant country indexes within one *multiple regression equation*. For example, the regression equation including the U.S. stock index plus all foreign country indexes previously examined, is shown here:

$$r_{s,t} = d_0 + d_1 USI_t + d_2 CANI_t + d_3 FRANI_t + d_4 GERI_t + d_5 SWITI_t + \mu_t$$

where $r_{s,t}$ is the MNC's stock return, while *USI, CANI, FRANI, GERI,* and *SWITI* are stock index returns on the countries. The coefficient d_0 is a constant, while d_1, d_2, d_3, d_4 and d_5 are regression coefficients, each measuring the sensitivity of r_s to a particular country stock index. This regression equation could be applied to two separate subperiods to determine if the individual country impact changed over time. The results here would not necessarily conform to the results stated in Exhibit 10B.1, since this regression equation examines the *simultaneous* influence of all country index returns on the MNC's stock returns.

A suggested exercise to become more familiar with assessing an MNC's sensitivity to foreign economies is to replicate the procedure just described for a particular MNC in which you are interested. Your analysis would indicate

■ How sensitive the MNC is to changes in each foreign economy
■ The direction of the impact
■ Whether the MNC is becoming more or less sensitive to the foreign economies

If the MNC believes a stock index is not an accurate indication of each country's economic condition, it could use an alternative proxy (such as GNP).

Once the MNC has determined its sensitivity to economic conditions in other countries, it should then review its projected business involvement in these countries. The degree of exposure detected from previous data and the projections of business involvement in the country of concern should be considered simultaneously when evaluating the MNC's potential exposure to economic conditions of that particular country.

Estimating the Variability of a Currency Portfolio

To illustrate how the variability of foreign currency cash flows is affected by correlations, consider a simplified example where an MNC has only two foreign currencies. Fifty percent of the MNC's funds are expected to come from Currency A and the remaining funds from Currency B. Assume that over an annual period, the standard deviation of exchange rate movements is 4 percent for Currency A and 4 percent for Currency B. Also assume that these two currencies are perfectly positively correlated, so that their correlation coefficient is 1.00. The standard deviation of this two-currency portfolio (σ_p) can be determined from the following equation:

$$\sigma_p = \sqrt{W_A^2\sigma_A^2 + W_B^2\sigma_B^2 + 2W_AW_B\sigma_A\sigma_B CORR_{AB}}$$

where

W_A = percentage of funds to be received from receivables in Currency A

W_B = percentage of funds to be received from receivables in Currency B

σ_A = standard deviation of exchange rate movements for Currency A

σ_B = standard deviation of exchange rate movements for Currency B

$CORR_{AB}$ = correlation coefficient of exchange rate movements between Currencies A and B

Using the information provided, the variability of the combined (portfolio) cash flows of Currencies A and B can be estimated as

$$\sigma_P = \sqrt{.5^2(.04)^2 + .5^2(.04)^2 + 2(.5)(.5)(.04)(.04)(1.0)}$$
$$= \sqrt{.0004 + .0004 + .0008}$$
$$= \sqrt{.0016}$$
$$= .04, \text{ or } 4\%$$

Notice that the standard deviation in the portfolio is as high as the standard deviation of either individual currency. The diversification between these two currencies did not reduce variability because the currency movements are perfectly positively correlated. Diversification between currencies with a low correlation could substantially reduce the variability of the portfolio of inflow currencies. For example, if the two currencies had a correlation coefficient of .2, the portfolio variability (assuming 50 percent weight to each currency) would be

$$\sigma_P = \sqrt{.5^2(.04)^2 + .5^2(.04)^2 + 2.(.5)(.5)(.04)(.04)(0.2)}$$
$$= \sqrt{.0004 + .0004 + .00016}$$
$$= \sqrt{.00096}$$
$$= \text{about } .031, \text{ or } 3.1\%$$

A negative correlation coefficient between Currencies A and B would have reduced the portfolio variability to even a greater degree. For example, consider an extreme example in which Currencies A and B are perfectly negatively correlated, as represented by a correlation coefficient of -1.00. The portfolio variability (assuming 50 percent weight to each currency) would be

$$\sigma_P = \sqrt{.5^2(.04)^2 + .5^2(.04)^2 + 2(.5)(.5)(.04)(.04)(-1.0)}$$
$$= \sqrt{.0004 + .0004 + (-.0008)}$$
$$= \sqrt{0}$$
$$= 0$$

The portfolio's exchange rate movements against the dollar would be stable because of the offsetting effects between Currencies A and B, if they are perfectly negatively correlated. Such a situation would normally be favorably perceived by an MNC since the home currency value of the portfolio of foreign currencies could be virtually insulated from movements in these currencies.

It is unlikely that the MNC will be able to structure its foreign cash flows so that it is totally insulated against exchange rate movements. However, the examples given here demonstrate that a set of foreign currency cash inflows is less volatile if the pairwise correlations are low. The cash flows would also be less volatile if the standard deviations of the individual currencies are lower. This can be verified by assuming a standard deviation of less than 4 percent for each currency in the preceding examples and recomputing the portfolio's standard deviation.

Assessment of Exchange Rate Risk from Various Country Perspectives*

Exchange rate risk has generally been measured using the dollar as the home currency. This appendix assesses currency risk from several different perspectives, in order to offer insight on exchange rate risk for parents and subsidiaries in various countries. For example, consider a German subsidiary of a decentralized U.S. multinational corporation that has been instructed to hedge its own risk. Its main concern is how exchange rates of its currency positions may move against the mark. Its only concern about currency fluctuations against the dollar would relate to the portion of cash flows that were to be remitted to the U.S. parent. This portion may be quite small in relation to its overall cash flows. If its day-to-day business operations require marks, its risk is that the currencies representing long positions (such as future receivables) depreciate against the mark or that currencies representing short positions (such as future payables) appreciate against the mark.

Most hedging techniques are designed to cover short-term exposure but do not adequately insulate companies against long-term exposure. An assessment of the variability and covariability of exchange rate movements can be used to determine the firm's long-run exposure to its portfolio of foreign cash flows.

The variability and covariability (as measured by correlation coefficients) are disclosed and discussed for each of four perspectives. Each table represents a separate perspective. The top of each cell in the matrix represents the correlation coefficient for the entire period (1974 to 1989), the middle of the cell represents the earlier subperiod (1974–1980) and the bottom of the cell represents the more recent subperiod (1981–1989). The righthand column of the table discloses standard deviations of each currency's movements against the base currency for each of the three periods. Each perspective is discussed in turn to reflect the risk assessment of subsidiaries based in that particular country.

---

*Much of this appendix was drawn from the article, "Assessment of Exchange Rate Risk from Various Country Perspectives," by Jeff Madura, *International Review of Economics and Business*, July 1990, pp. 655–666. Reprinted with permission.

British Perspective (See Exhibit 10D.1)

The Belgian franc and Italian lira are clearly the most volatile currencies from a British subsidiary's perspective. The U.S. dollar was less volatile than any other currency against the British pound. Four of the eight currencies exhibited increased volatility over time, while the other four currencies exhibited less volatility. In general, currencies are much more volatile against the pound than they are against the dollar.

Correlations between the Belgian franc, Canadian dollar, Italian lira, and U.S. dollar were generally high. Yet, there were several currency pairs that exhibited low or negative correlations. Sixteen of the 28 correlations (57 percent) increased over time, while one correlation remained stable.

German Perspective (See Exhibit 10D.2)

Similar to the British perspective, the Belgian franc and Italian lira exhibited the most volatility from a German subsidiary's perspective. The French

EXHIBIT 10D.1 British Perspective

	Correlation Coefficients								Standard Deviation
	C$	FF	DM	JY	SF	BF	IL	U.S.$	
Canadian dollar (C$)	1.0* 1.0** 1.0***								.0556 .0509 .0593
French franc (FF)	.34 .41 .31	1.0 1.0 1.0							.0492 .0464 .0527
German mark (DM)	.34 .35 .33	.85 .76 .93	1.0 1.0 1.0						.0511 .0521 .0510
Japanese yen (JY)	.38 .35 .39	.65 .57 .74	.63 .50 .76	1.0 1.0 1.0					.0673 .0637 .0605
Swiss franc (SF)	.28 .16 .43	.72 .65 .81	.80 .77 .86	.63 .49 .85	1.0 1.0 1.0				.0621 .0692 .0556
Belgian franc (BF)	.76 .75 .76	−.07 .01 −.13	−.14 −.23 −.09	.08 .19 −.03	−.12 −.24 −.02	1.0 1.0 1.0			.1053 .0886 .1195
Italian lira (IL)	.81 .80 .82	−.05 −.03 −.10	0.10 .09 −.07	.14 .25 .03	−.03 −.06 .00	.90 .80 .96	1.0 1.0 1.0		.0991 .0902 .1083
U.S.$	.92 .90 .93	.37 .44 .32	.35 .33 .36	.40 .45 .36	.26 .17 .37	.83 .83 .83	.85 .82 .88	1.0 1.0 1.0	.0525 .0447 .0591

*Top of each cell: 1974–1989.
**Middle of each cell: 1974–1980.
***Bottom of each cell: 1981–1989.

ASSESSMENT OF EXCHANGE RATE RISK FROM VARIOUS COUNTRY PERSPECTIVES

EXHIBIT 10D.2   German Perspective

	Correlation Coefficient								Standard Deviation
	C$	FF	JY	SF	BP	BF	IL	U.S.$	
Canadian dollar (C$)	1.0*								.0605
	1.0**								.0592
	1.0***								.0622
French franc (FF)	.27	1.0							.0266
	.45	1.0							.0324
	.05	1.0							.0197
Japanese yen (JY)	.32	.33	1.0						.0502
	.35	.42	1.0						.0607
	.29	.14	1.0						.0382
Swiss franc (SF)	.04	.11	.29	1.0					.0365
	−.16	.1	.17	1.0					.0433
	.34	.09	.59	1.0					.0288
British pound (BP)	.52	.32	.25	.04	1.0				.0488
	.60	.47	.34	−.04	1.0				.0506
	.47	.08	.14	.14	1.0				.0477
Belgian franc (BF)	.90	.24	.31	.01	.53	1.0			.1223
	.94	.50	.46	−.11	.66	1.0			.1146
	.87	−.05	.13	.18	.44	1.0			.1307
Italian lira (IL)	.89	.08	.27	−.04	.47	.93	1.0		.1099
	.87	.19	.35	−.20	.50	.88	1.0		.1013
	.91	−.05	.18	.16	.45	.97	1.0		.1193
U.S.$	.94	.30	.34	−.01	.55	.96	.93	1.0	.0585
	.94	.52	.45	−.13	.68	.99	.88	1.0	.0571
	.93	.02	.20	.18	.45	.94	.97	1.0	.0607

*Top of each cell: 1974–1989.
**Middle of each cell: 1974–1980.
***Bottom of each cell: 1981–1989.

franc and Swiss franc are clearly the most stable currencies, followed by the British pound and U.S. dollar. Three of the eight currencies experienced a higher degree of volatility over time while the volatility of the other five currencies decreased.

While the correlations between the Belgian franc, Canadian dollar, Italian lira, and U.S. dollar were generally high, most other correlations were much lower. Eighteen of the 28 correlations (64 percent) decreased over time, suggesting greater risk reduction from diversifying long positions across currencies.

French Perspective (See Exhibit 10D.3)

From a French perspective, the German mark exhibited the lowest level of volatility. At the other extreme, the volatility (as measured by standard deviation) of the Belgian franc and Italian lira more than tripled that level. Six of the eight currencies experienced an increase in volatility over time against the French franc.

EXHIBIT 10D.3   French Perspective

	Correlation Coefficient								Standard Deviation
	C$	DM	JY	SF	BP	BF	IL	U.S.$	
Canadian dollar (C$)	1.0*								.0598
	1.0**								.0536
	1.0***								.0650
German mark (DM)	.18	1.0							.0277
	.11	1.0							.0334
	.26	1.0							.0210
Japanese yen (JY)	.29	.24	1.0						.0489
	.21	.15	1.0						.0557
	.35	.38	1.0						.0414
Swiss franc (SF)	.09	.54	.35	1.0					.0441
	−.14	.55	.21	1.0					.0527
	.41	.52	.67	1.0					.0346
British pound (BP)	.49	.22	.21	.13	1.0				.0477
	.48	.16	.20	.02	1.0				.0450
	.51	.33	.25	.29	1.0				.0510
Belgian franc (BF)	.88	−.02	.24	−.03	.48	1.0			.1198
	.87	−.24	.27	−.29	.49	1.0			.1027
	.88	.21	.21	.25	.48	1.0			.1349
Italian lira (IL)	.91	.18	.29	.05	.48	.92	1.0		.1129
	.89	.15	.33	−.11	.46	.85	1.0		.1023
	.92	.22	.25	.24	.50	.97	1.0		.1237
U.S.$	.93	.17	.30	.05	.52	.95	.95	1.0	.0573
	.92	.06	.31	−.15	.57	.94	.92	1.0	.0491
	.94	.31	.29	.29	.50	.95	.97	1.0	.0644

*Top of each cell: 1974–1989.
**Middle of each cell: 1974–1980.
***Bottom of each cell: 1981–1989.

Once again, the correlations among the Belgian franc, Canadian dollar, Italian lira, and U.S. dollar were high. The British pound's correlation with several currencies was moderately high. Twenty-two of the correlations (78.5 percent) increased over time.

Japanese Perspective (See Exhibit 10D.4)

Once again, the Belgian franc and Italian lira are most volatile. The other currencies exhibited a somewhat similar degree of volatility. Six of the eight currencies experienced a decrease in volatility over time.

The correlations among the Belgian franc, Canadian dollar, Italian lira, and U.S. dollar are very high. In addition, correlations are moderately high among the British pound, French franc, German mark, and Swiss franc. Seventeen of the 28 correlations decreased over time.

When considering the general decrease in currency volatilities and correlations detected here, exchange rate risk of currency portfolios has generally declined over time from a Japanese perspective. When comparing the corre-

ASSESSMENT OF EXCHANGE RATE RISK FROM VARIOUS COUNTRY PERSPECTIVES

EXHIBIT 10D.4 Japanese Perspective

	Correlation Coefficients								Standard Deviation
	C$	FF	DM	SF	BP	BF	IL	U.S.$	
Canadian dollar (C$)	1.0*								.0639
	1.0**								.0674
	1.0***								.0616
French franc (FF)	.49	1.0							.0482
	.65	1.0							.0554
	.29	1.0							.0399
German mark (DM)	.47	.85	1.0						.0497
	.57	.85	1.0						.6000
	.32	.87	1.0						.0378
Swiss franc (SF)	.31	.64	.74	1.0					.0528
	.32	.66	.77	1.0					.0680
	.37	.61	.68	1.0					.0310
British pound (BP)	.62	.65	.62	.44	1.0				.0592
	.72	.74	.67	.47	1.0				.0634
	.52	.49	.53	.39	1.0				.0551
Belgian franc (BF)	.83	.18	.11	.02	.45	1.0			.1156
	.81	.28	.08	−.07	.50	1.0			.1007
	.87	.11	.17	.20	.45	1.0			.1299
Italian lira (IL)	.85	.17	.20	.06	.44	.92	1.0		.1058
	.82	.25	.26	.03	.46	.85	1.0		.0961
	.89	.09	.15	.13	.44	.97	1.0		.1162
U.S.$	.94	.51	.48	.29	.65	.89	.89	1.0	.0616
	.96	.66	.56	.31	.76	.86	.83	1.0	.0606
	.93	.34	.40	.31	.55	.92	.94	1.0	.0636

*Top of each cell: 1974–1989.
**Middle of each cell: 1974–1980.
***Bottom of each cell: 1981–1989.

lations among perspectives, it appears that the potential currency diversification benefits are greater for British or German subsidiaries than for Japanese subsidiaries.

Comparison of Perspectives

A summary of the perspectives analyzed is provided in Exhibit 10D.5. The U.S. perspective (which was assessed in the chapter, Exhibits 10.3 and 10.4) is exposed to the least risk, based on the mean standard deviations of currency movements against the U.S. dollar and the mean correlation coefficient of currency pairs against the U.S. dollar. The correlations of foreign currencies were clearly lower for the French perspective than any other perspective. A comparison of the equal-weighted currency portfolio's variability among perspectives is provided in column 4. The standard deviation of the equal-weighted portfolio is lower for the U.S. perspective than any other perspective.

EXHIBIT 10D.5 Comparison of Perspectives

Perspective	Mean Standard Deviation	Mean Correlation Coefficient	Standard Deviation of Equally-Weighted Foreign Currency Portfolio	Percentage of Currencies Exhibiting Increasing Volatility	Percentage of Currency Pairs Exhibiting Increasing Correlation
U.S.	.0552	.5264	.0452	87.5%	82.1%
British	.0673	.4246	.0470	50.0	57.1
German	.0642	.4293	.0500	37.5	64.3
French	.0648	.3925	.0495	75.0	78.5
Japanese	.0696	.5254	.0542	25.0	60.7

The risk characteristics of the Japanese perspective appear to be the highest. Foreign currencies are more volatile against the yen on average than against any other currency. In addition, the foreign currency correlations are higher on average when the yen serves as the base currency. When assessing risk characteristics over time (see columns 5 and 6), exchange rate risk appears to be increasing the most for the U.S. and French perspectives. At the other extreme, the exchange rate variability for 75 percent of the currencies declined over time from the Japanese perspective. However, about 61 percent of the currency pairs exhibited increasing correlation over time against the yen. The change in risk over time for the British and German perspectives was less favorable than the Japanese perspective but more favorable than the U.S. and French perspectives.

When using the analysis here to assess risk, keep in mind that the degree of risk can be more precisely estimated by accounting for the firm's positions in foreign currency. A firm with net inflows in some currencies and net outflows in the other could be favorably affected by increasing correlations.

Overall, the results suggest that risk can vary significantly among country perspectives. Thus, some subsidiaries of decentralized MNCs may face a greater challenge of hedging exchange rate risk than others, even if their operations and cash flow streams are somewhat similar. Furthermore, the degree of risk incurred by multinational corporations is dependent on, among other factors, the location of the parent.

CHAPTER 11

Managing Transaction Exposure

Recall from the previous chapter that there are three forms by which a multinational corporation (MNC) is exposed to exchange rate fluctuations: (1) transaction exposure, (2) economic exposure, and (3) translation exposure. If the degree of exposure is thought to be significant, the MNC may desire to eliminate it, or **hedge.** This chapter identifies commonly used hedging techniques, and illustrates how each technique can hedge transaction exposure. In some cases, hedging may not be possible, and then some alternative techniques can be used to at least reduce transaction exposure. This chapter explains these techniques as well. The following chapter explains how the other two forms of exposure (economic and translation exposure) can be managed.

TRANSACTION EXPOSURE

Transaction exposure exists when the future cash transactions of a firm are affected by exchange rate fluctuations. For example, a U.S. firm that purchases German goods may need marks to buy the goods. While it may know exactly how many marks it will need, it doesn't know how many dollars will be needed to exchange for those marks. This uncertainty occurs because the exchange rate between marks and dollars fluctuates over time. MNCs often desire to avoid transaction exposure since they would prefer to know the amount of their currency needed for future purchases.

The example just cited is from the perspective of a U.S.-based MNC that needs a foreign currency to make payment. Its future payables are exposed to exchange rate fluctuations. Also consider a U.S.-based MNC that will be receiving a foreign currency for which it will have no use. Its future receivables are exposed since it is uncertain of the dollars it will obtain when exchanging the foreign currency received.

If transaction exposure does exist, the firm faces three major tasks. First, it must identify the degree of transaction exposure. Second, it must decide whether to hedge this exposure. Finally, if it decides to hedge part or all of the exposure, it must choose among the various hedging techniques available. Each of these tasks is discussed in turn.

Identifying Net Transaction Exposure

Before the MNC makes any decisions related to hedging, it should identify the individual **net transaction exposure** on a currency-by-currency basis. The term "net" here refers to the consolidation of all expected inflows and outflows for a particular time and currency. The management at each subsidiary would play a vital role in the process of reporting its expected inflows and outflows. Then a centralized group would consolidate subsidiary reports in order to identify, for the MNC as a whole, the expected net positions in each foreign currency during several upcoming periods. The MNC can identify its exposure by reviewing this consolidation of subsidiary positions. For example, one subsidiary may have net receivables in German marks three months from now, while a different subsidiary may have net payables in marks. If the mark appreciates, this will be favorable to the first subsidiary and unfavorable to the second subsidiary. However, the impact on the MNC as a whole is at least partially offset. Each subsidiary may desire to hedge its net currency position in order to avoid the possible adverse impacts on its performance due to fluctuation in the currency's value. However, the overall performance of the MNC could already be insulated by the offsetting positions between subsidiaries. Therefore, hedging the position of each individual subsidiary may not be necessary.

To determine the net exposure in each currency over all subsidiaries, the MNC should first identify each subsidiary's position in all currencies. Exhibit 11.1 shows an example of an MNC that has four subsidiaries and deals in four currencies. Review the position in Currency 1 from Exhibit 11.1. Two subsidiaries have net inflows in Currency 1, while the other two subsidiaries have net outflows in Currency 1. On a consolidated basis, the MNC has an expected net inflow of 20,000 units in Currency 1. Each currency's consolidated net inflows have been computed by accounting for all subsidiary positions.

It may be difficult for management of an individual subsidiary to be comfortable with remaining exposed to currency fluctuations. But the goal in

EXHIBIT 11.1   Example of Net Exposure of Currencies for Each Subsidiary as of a Particular Point in Time

| Subsidiary | Net Position in Each Particular Currency Measured in the Parent Currency (in 1,000s of units): | | | |
	Currency 1	Currency 2	Currency 3	Currency 4
London	+100	−60	−80	− 30
Munich	− 50	−30	+50	− 20
Paris	− 60	−50	+70	+100
Toronto	+ 30	+70	−10	− 50
Consolidated net exposure for each currency	+ 20	−70	+30	+ 0

multinational financial management is to maximize the value of the overall multinational corporation, not any particular subsidiary. The role of subsidiary management is still important, even if currency exposure is managed by the parent. It involves reporting current and projected financial data, as well as assessing the economic environment and potential trends. Because subsidiary management is local to the subsidiary, it may perform these duties better than the centralized management group at the headquarters.

The view that consolidated net positions in cash flows are more important than each individual subsidiary's net positions is disputed by some. Critics claim that when a subsidiary requests a loan locally, the creditors will evaluate the individual subsidiary rather than the MNC as a whole. In this case, a large unhedged foreign currency position in a particular subsidiary could be perceived as a risk by creditors. In the event that this open (unhedged) position increases the risk of the subsidiary, the creditors may either deny the loan request or charge a higher loan rate. In this case, the creditors are more interested in the subsidiary's financial data than the overall exposure and performance of the MNC.

If the subsidiary hedges a position to reduce its individual risk, this action may actually increase the overall exposure of the MNC. There may be an offsetting effect here when the MNC is viewed as a whole. If one subsidiary desires to hedge its position (in order to reduce its individual exposure and earn a better evaluation by local creditors), then there is no longer an offsetting effect for the MNC as a whole. The other subsidiary would now need to hedge its position for the MNC to avoid exposure. Hedging by both subsidiaries could eliminate the exchange rate exposure, but transaction costs are incurred. Appropriate communication among subsidiaries along with a centralized currency exposure management division can sometimes avoid such costs. For a centralized approach to be successful, an adequate reporting system by each subsidiary is necessary.

As an example of this issue, consider Eastman Kodak Company's implementation of a centralized currency management approach. At one time, it billed its subsidiaries in U.S. dollars when it provided them with supplies. This forced subsidiary managers to deal with currency exposure. Kodak now bills subsidiaries in their local currencies. The rationale for a change in strategies was to shift the foreign exchange exposure from subsidiaries to the parent company. Because the parent was reorganized to concentrate its resources and expert personnel, it centralized the currency exposure management. The parent now receives foreign currencies from its subsidiaries overseas and converts them to U.S. dollars. It can maintain the currencies as foreign deposits if it believes such currencies will strengthen against the U.S. dollar in the near future.

As another example, Borg-Warner Corporation has set up a central clearinghouse system that also reflects a centralized management approach. Thus, its assessment and management of currency exposure is conducted on the entire portfolio of all subsidiaries rather than on each subsidiary individually.

As a final example of centralized management, Fiat, the Italian auto manufacturer, has implemented such a system to monitor 421 subsidiaries dispersed among 55 countries. A key to its success is a comprehensive reporting system that keeps track of its aggregate cash flows in each currency. The net inflow or outflow position for each currency can then be assessed as to whether and how the position should be balanced out.

These examples support the centralized approach to hedging, in which net transaction exposure in each currency must be identified. Then, the firm can assess the degree of net exposure in each currency by using the techniques described in the previous chapter. For example, it can determine whether any of the net inflow currencies is highly correlated with the net outflow currencies. If so, it may not consider hedging for these currencies, since an offsetting effect should occur. There will likely be some net currency positions that are not offsetting, and the MNC must decide whether to hedge these positions. A discussion of this issue follows.

Is Hedging Worthwhile?

Before MNCs take the time to consider various techniques for hedging, they may question whether hedging is worthwhile. Consider the firm that is deciding whether to hedge its periodic future payables denominated in a foreign currency. The forward contract is a common hedging device against this foreign currency position. If the spot rate in the future exceeds today's forward rate, then the MNC will save money by hedging its net payables (as opposed to no hedge). If the spot rate in the future is less than today's forward rate, then the MNC will lose money by hedging its net payables. A forward rate that serves as an unbiased forecast of the future spot rate will underestimate and overestimate the future spot rate with equal frequency. In this case, periodic hedging with the forward rate will be more costly in some periods and less costly in other periods. On the average, it will not reduce the MNC's costs. Thus, it could be argued that hedging is not worthwhile.

In response to this argument, some MNCs may pick and choose those situations where they expect the currency to move in a direction that will make hedging feasible. That is, they may hedge future payables if they foresee appreciation in the currency denominating the payables. In addition, they may hedge future receivables if they foresee depreciation in the currency denominating the receivables. For other cases, they could leave the position open. Some MNCs may desire to hedge all foreign currency positions. This does not necessarily mean they expect hedging to always save or earn the MNC more money. In fact, such MNCs may even believe that hedging will on the average result in the same cash inflows or outflows as no hedge. Yet, they may prefer knowing what their future cash inflows or outflows in terms of their home currency will be in each period, since this could enhance corporate planning. A hedge would allow the firm to know the future cash flows (in terms of the home currency) that will result from any foreign transactions that have already been negotiated.

Adjusting the Invoice Policy to Manage Transaction Exposure

Under some circumstances, the U.S. firm may be able to modify its pricing policy to hedge against transaction exposure. That is, the firm may be able to invoice (price) its exports in the same currency that will be needed to pay for imports. For example, assume the firm has continual payables in Swiss francs, perhaps because a Swiss exporter sends goods to the U.S. firm under the condition that the goods be invoiced in Swiss francs. Consequently, the

U.S. firm is now exposed to fluctuations in the value of the Swiss franc. Assume the U.S. firm exports products (invoiced in U.S. dollars) to other corporations in Switzerland. It could modify its invoicing policy from U.S. dollars to Swiss francs in order to match its future payables in Swiss francs. In this way, the Swiss-franc receivables from these exports can be used to pay off the U.S. firm's future payables in Swiss francs.

It would be difficult, if not impossible, to (1) invoice the precise amount of exports in Swiss francs in order to exactly match the Swiss-franc payables and (2) perfectly match the timing of inflows and outflows. Because the matching of assets and liabilities in foreign currencies does have its limitations, it will not completely hedge all of the firm's exposed positions in foreign currencies. Therefore, other hedging techniques deserve consideration.

TECHNIQUES TO ELIMINATE TRANSACTION EXPOSURE

If the MNC decides to hedge part or all of its transaction exposure, it may select from the following hedging techniques:

- Futures contract hedge
- Forward contract hedge
- Money market hedge
- Currency option hedge

Each of these hedging techniques is discussed in turn, with examples provided. After all techniques have been discussed, a comprehensive example illustrates how all the techniques can be compared to determine the appropriate technique to hedge a particular position.

Futures Contract Hedge

Currency futures can be used by firms that desire to hedge transaction exposure. The concept of a futures contract hedge is very similar to that of forward contracts (to be discussed shortly), except that forward contracts are common for large transactions whereas futures contracts may be more appropriate for firms that prefer to hedge in smaller amounts.

A firm that buys a currency futures contract is entitled to receive a specified amount of a specified currency for a stated price on a specified date. To hedge payment on future payables in a foreign currency, the firm may desire to purchase a currency futures contract representing the currency it will need in the near future. By holding this contract, it locks in the amount of its home currency needed to make payment on the payables.

While currency futures can reduce the firm's transaction exposure, they sometimes backfire on the firm. If the firm was hedging payables, the locked-in futures price for the currency could end up being higher than the future spot rate of the currency (if the currency depreciated over time). If the firm expected the currency's value to depreciate by the time it would need to make payment, it would not purchase a currency futures contract.

A firm that sells a currency futures contract is entitled to sell a specified amount of specified currency for a stated price on a specified date. To hedge the home currency value of future receivables in a foreign currency, the firm may desire to sell a currency futures contract representing the currency it shall be receiving. This way the firm knows how much of its home currency it will receive after converting the foreign currency receivables into its home currency. By locking in the exchange rate at which it will be able to exchange the foreign currency for its home currency, it insulates the value of its future receivables from the fluctuations in the foreign currency's spot rate over time.

As with the purchase of currency futures, a sale of currency futures can backfire. In our example where the firm is hedging future receivables, the locked-in currency futures price at which the firm will sell the foreign currency may end up being lower than the spot rate of the currency (if the foreign currency appreciated over time). Nonetheless, due to the uncertainty of future currency values, the firm may be more comfortable with hedging than remaining exposed to exchange rate fluctuations.

Forward Contract Hedge

Forward contracts are commonly used by large corporations that desire to hedge. To use the forward contract hedge, the MNC purchases that currency denominating the payables forward. For example, if a U.S.-based MNC must pay a Swiss supplier 100,000 francs in 30 days, it can request from a bank a forward contract to accommodate this future payment. The bank agrees to provide the Swiss francs to the MNC in 30 days in exchange for U.S. dollars. The forward contract will specify the exchange rate at which the currencies will be exchanged. This exchange rate reflects the so-called 30-day forward rate. The MNC hedges its position by locking in the rate it will pay for Swiss francs in 30 days. Thus, it now knows the number of dollars it will need to exchange for francs.

If the U.S.-based MNC expects receivables in Swiss francs in 30 days, it would like to lock in the rate at which it can sell these francs for dollars. In this case, a request for a forward sale of Swiss francs is appropriate. Many MNCs commonly implement the forward hedging technique. For example, Du Pont Company often has the equivalent of $300 million to $500 million of forward contracts at any one time to cover open currency positions. Its forward sale contracts are designed to sell incoming foreign currencies at a specified rate, while its forward purchase contracts are designed to lock in a price for foreign currencies needed in the future. Numerous U.S. companies used forward contracts to hedge payables in foreign currencies during the 1985–1990 period.

In 1989 Zenith Electronics Corporation hedged the purchases of components imported from Japan. However, the Japanese yen weakened over this period, causing the purchase price in dollars to be higher with the hedge than it would have been without the hedge.

Forward contracts are commonly used by non-U.S. companies as well. For example, Waterford Crystal Company of Ireland used forward contracts to hedge its dollar receivables when it was concerned that the dollar might weaken. During the mid 1980s, Waterford's receivables were converted to 48 million Irish pounds as a result of a forward contract. Since the dollar declined over this period, receivables would have been worth only 37 million pounds if it had not hedged. Sony Corporation used forward contracts to cover some of its dollar receivables during the dollar's downturn since 1985.

Forward Contract Hedge versus No Hedge

The decision as to whether to hedge a position with a forward contract or remain unhedged can be made by comparing the known result from hedging to the possible results from remaining unhedged. To illustrate, assume that a U.S. firm will need 100,000 British pounds in 90 days to pay for British imports. Assume that today's 90-day forward rate of the British pound is $1.40. To assess the future value of the British pound, the firm may develop a probability distribution as shown in Exhibit 11.2. This is graphically illustrated in Exhibit 11.3, which breaks down the probability distribution. Both exhibits can be used to determine the probability that a forward hedge will be more costly than no hedge. This is achieved by estimating the real cost of hedging payables (RCH_p), as shown here:

$$RCH_p = NCH_p - NC_p$$

where

NCH_p = nominal cost of hedging payables
NC_p = nominal cost of payables without hedging

The RCH_p is estimated for each scenario in Column 5 of Exhibit 11.2. While NCH_p is certain, NC_p is uncertain, causing RCH_p to be uncertain.

While the firm doesn't know RCH_p in advance, it can at least use the information in Exhibits 11.2 and 11.3 to decide whether a hedge is feasible. First, it could estimate the expected value of the RCH_p. This expected value is determined by

$$\text{Expected value of } RCH_p = \Sigma P_i RCH_{p,i}$$

EXHIBIT 11.2   Feasibility Analysis for Hedging

Possible Spot Rate of British Pound in 90 Days	Probability	Nominal Cost of Hedging 100,000 British Pounds	Amount of U.S. Dollars Needed to Buy 100,000 British Pounds if Firm Remains Unhedged	Real Cost of Hedging 100,000 British Pounds
$1.30	5%	$140,000	$1.30 × £100,000 = $130,000	$10,000
$1.32	10	$140,000	$1.32 × £100,000 = $132,000	$ 8,000
$1.34	15	$140,000	$1.34 × £100,000 = $134,000	$ 6,000
$1.36	20	$140,000	$1.36 × £100,000 = $136,000	$ 4,000
$1.38	20	$140,000	$1.38 × £100,000 = $138,000	$ 2,000
$1.40	15	$140,000	$1.40 × £100,000 = $140,000	$ 0
$1.42	10	$140,000	$1.42 × £100,000 = $142,000	−$ 2,000
$1.45	5	$140,000	$1.45 × £100,000 = $145,000	−$ 5,000

EXHIBIT 11.3 Comparison of Costs of Hedging versus No Hedge

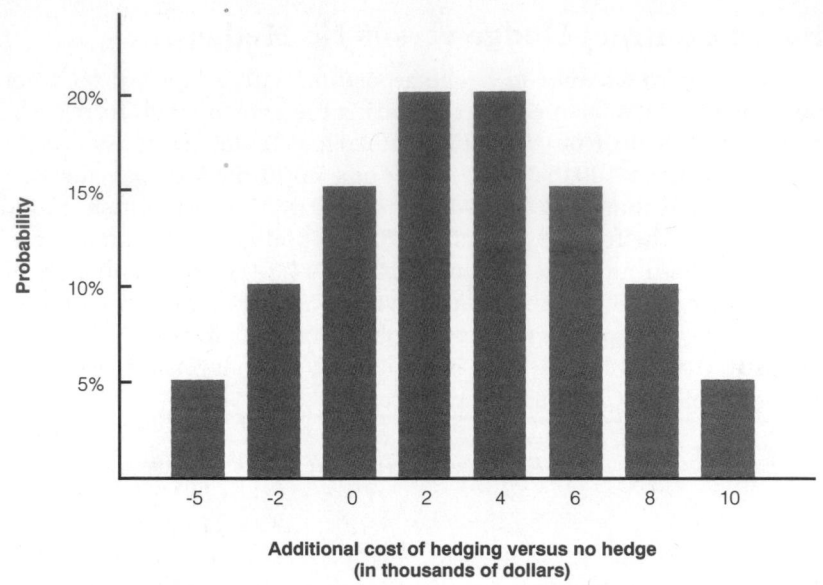

Additional cost of hedging versus no hedge
(in thousands of dollars)

where P_i represents the probability that the ith outcome will occur. In our example, the expected value of the RCH_p can be computed as

$$
\begin{aligned}
E\ (RCH_p) &= \Sigma P_i\ RCH_{p,i} \\
&= 5\%(10{,}000) + 10\%(8{,}000) + 15\%(6{,}000) \\
&\quad + 20\%(4{,}000) + 20\%(2{,}000) + 15\%(0) \\
&\quad + 10\%(-2{,}000) + 5\%(-5{,}000) \\[6pt]
&= \$500 + \$800 + \$900 \\
&\quad + \$800 + \$400 + 0 \\
&\quad - \$200 - \$250 \\[6pt]
&= \$2{,}950
\end{aligned}
$$

While this expected value is useful in assessing RCH_p, it does not clearly indicate the overall probability that hedging will be more costly. Such additional information could be determined by reviewing Exhibits 11.2 or 11.3. The data indicate there is a 15 percent chance that the RCH_p will be negative (that the nominal cost of hedging will be lower than remaining unhedged). Some firms may be more comfortable hedging, since this way they will know the exact amount of U.S. dollars needed for future purchases. Other firms may be willing to remain unhedged if the projected unhedged cost will most likely be less than the nominal cost of hedging. In our example, the probability of incurring a lower cost when remaining unhedged is 85 percent. The hedge versus no-hedge decision will be based on the firm's degree of risk aversion. Firms with a greater desire to avoid risk would be expected to hedge their open positions in foreign currencies more often than firms that are less concerned with risk.

If the forward rate is an accurate predictor of the future spot rate, the RCH_p will be zero. Because the forward rate often underestimates or overestimates the future spot rate, RCH_p differs from zero. If, however, the forward rate is an unbiased predictor of the future spot rate, RCH_p will be zero on average, as the differences between the forward rate and future spot rate will offset each other over time. If a firm believes that the forward rate is an unbiased predictor of the future spot rate, it will consider hedging its payables, since the forecasted RCH_p is zero, and the transaction exposure can be eliminated.

For firms with exposure in receivables, the real cost of hedging receivables (RCH_r) can be estimated as

$$RCH_r = NR_r - NRH_r$$

where

$$NR_r = \text{nominal home currency revenues}$$
$$\text{received without hedging}$$
$$NRH_r = \text{nominal home currency revenues}$$
$$\text{received from hedging}$$

The preceding equation is structured so that the real cost of hedging receivables is positive when hedging results in lower revenues than not hedging. This allows for consistency between RCH_p and RCH_r, since a negative (positive) value of either implies that hedging had a more (less) favorable result than not hedging.

As with payable positions, firms can determine whether to hedge receivable positions by first developing a probability distribution for the future spot rate, and then using it to develop a probability distribution of RCH_r. If the RCH_r is likely to be negative, hedging would be preferred. If the RCH_r is likely to be positive, the firm would need to evaluate whether the potential benefits from remaining unhedged are worth the risk. If the forward rate is believed to be an unbiased predictor of the future spot rate, firms would consider hedging their receivables position at an expected real cost of zero (ignoring transaction costs).

The RCH has been defined here in terms of the MNC's home currency (U.S. dollars in our example). It can also be expressed as a percentage of the nominal hedged amount. This may be a useful measurement when comparing the RCH for various currencies. For example, if a U.S. firm were hedging various currencies in different amounts, a comparison of the dollar amount of RCH among currencies would be distorted by the dollar amount of payables or receivables hedged. For this reason, RCHs for each currency should be measured as a percentage of their respective hedged amounts if they are to be compared.

The RCH cannot be determined until the payables or receivables period is over. Firms should be pleased when they hedge if the RCH turns out to be very low or especially if it is negative. Conservative firms, however, may feel hedging is worthwhile even if the RCH turns out to be high.

The real cost of hedging British pounds over time (from a U.S. firm's perspective) is displayed in Exhibit 11.4. The top graph shows the real cost of hedging payables, while the lower graph shows the real cost of hedging receivables. Ninety-day periods were used to measure the real costs of hedging.

EXHIBIT 11.4   Real Cost of Hedging British Pounds over Time

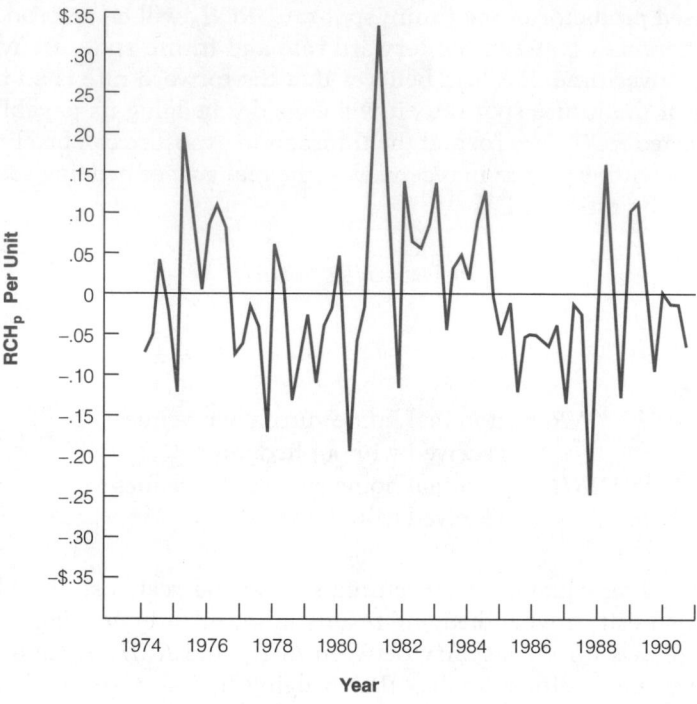

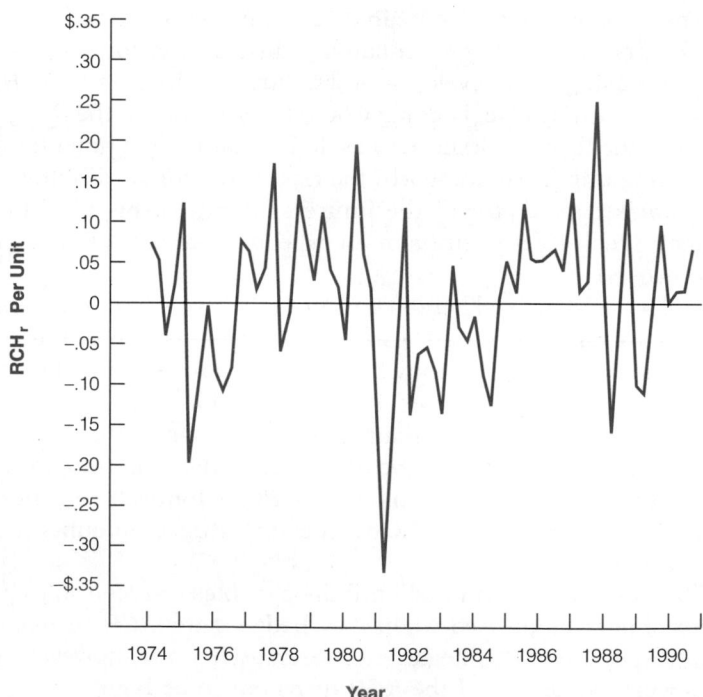

INTERNATIONAL FINANCIAL MANAGEMENT IN PRACTICE

How Interest Rate Movements Can Affect the Cost of Hedging

Interest rate movements and the forces behind interest rate parity can have an indirect impact on the costs of hedging imports or exports. The unification of East and West Germany in late 1989 placed upward pressure on German interest rates, ultimately causing these rates to rise above U.S interest rates. Consequently, the forces behind interest rate parity caused the forward rate on the German mark to be less than the spot rate. (If it was not, covered interest arbitrage would be possible). This was a marked change from the 1980s when the mark's forward rate consistently exhibited a premium. The shift from a forward premium to a discount was beneficial to U.S. firms that consistently hedge their mark payables, while it adversely affected U.S. firms that consistently hedge their mark receivables. However, one must also consider that the same force (rising German interest rates relative to U.S. interest rates) that caused a forward discount on the mark also placed upward pressure on the spot rate of the mark in the early 1990s. Thus, even though U.S. importers could now buy marks forward at a discount, the discount from a very high spot rate still made the hedged payables seem expensive. Conversely, U.S. firms sold marks forward at a discount to hedge mark receivables. But, the dollar value of receivables was still substantial because of the mark's strength in the early 1990s.

The costs were measured on a per-unit basis. The real cost of hedging pound payables (shown in the top graph of Exhibit 11.4) was high in the early 1980s, since the pound was weakening over this period. Thus, the existing spot rate at the time payables were due was typically below the forward rate available at the beginning of each corresponding 90-day period. The real cost of hedging pound payables was commonly negative in the late 1970s and late 1980s, since the pound was strengthening over these periods.

The real cost of hedging receivables is measured in the bottom graph of Exhibit 11.4. Since transaction costs were ignored when measuring the real costs of hedging in Exhibit 11.4, the real cost of hedging receivables is the exact opposite of the real cost of hedging payables.

Money Market Hedge

A **money market hedge** involves taking a money market position to cover a future payables or receivables position. The money market hedge on payables will be discussed separately from receivables.

MONEY MARKET HEDGE ON PAYABLES. First, a simplified money market hedge will be illustrated in which the firm has excess cash. Then, the second example will show how a firm can use a money market hedge to hedge payables, even if it does not have excess cash.

If a firm has excess cash, it can create a short-term deposit in the foreign currency that it will need in the future. For example, if a U.S. firm needs

SF1,000,000 in 30 days and it could earn 6 percent annualized (.5 percent for 30 days) on a Swiss security over this period, the amount needed to purchase a Swiss one-month security is

$$\text{Deposit amount to hedge SF payables} = \frac{\text{SF1,000,000}}{1 + .005}$$

$$= \text{SF995,025}$$

Assuming that the franc's spot rate is $.65, $646,766 would be needed to purchase the Swiss securities (computed as SF995,025 × $.65). In 30 days, the security would mature and provide SF1,000,000 to the U.S. firm, which could then be used to cover its payables. Regardless of how the Swiss exchange rate changes over this period, the U.S. firm's Swiss investment will be able to cover the payables position.

In many cases, firms would prefer to hedge payables without using their cash balances. A money market hedge can still be used in this situation, but it requires two money market positions: (1) borrowed funds in the home currency, and (2) a short-term investment in the foreign currency. To illustrate, reconsider the previous example where SF1,000,000 is needed in 30 days. Recall that $646,766 is needed to obtain the investment of SF995,025, which in turn will accumulate to the SF1,000,000 needed in 30 days. If the U.S. firm has no excess cash, it can borrow $646,766 from a U.S. bank, and exchange those dollars for francs in order to purchase the Swiss security.

Because the Swiss investment will cover the future payables position, the U.S. firm needs to be concerned only about the dollars owed back on the loan in 30 days. The firm's money market hedge used to hedge payables can be summarized as follows:

STEP 1. Borrow $646,766 from a U.S. bank; assume a .7 percent interest rate over the 30-day loan period.

STEP 2. Convert the $646,766 to SF995,025, given the exchange rate of $.65 per franc.

STEP 3. Use the francs to purchase a Swiss security that offers .5 percent over one month.

STEP 4. Repay the U.S. loan in 30 days, plus interest; the amount owed is $651,293 (computed as $646,766 × 1.007).

Consider a U.S. firm that plans to implement either a forward contract hedge or a money market hedge to cover its future payables. Which of these two hedging techniques would be most appropriate for the MNC? The answer can be determined by comparing the payment dictated by the forward contract to the loan repayment made on borrowed funds when using the money market hedge. The forward hedge and money market hedge are directly comparable, as long as the firm's cash balances are not used in the money market hedge. Thus, a firm can determine which hedge is preferable before implementing a hedge. Of course, it cannot determine whether either hedge will outperform an unhedged strategy until the period of concern has elapsed.

MONEY MARKET HEDGE ON RECEIVABLES. Consider a U.S. firm that expects to receive DM400,000 in 90 days. A simplified money market hedge could be implemented if the firm needed to borrow U.S. funds for 90 days anyway. Instead of borrowing dollars, it could borrow marks and convert them into dollars for use. Assuming an annualized interest rate of 8 percent, or 2 percent over the 90-day period, the amount of marks to be borrowed to hedge the future receivables would be

$$\text{Borrowed amount to hedge DM receivables} = \frac{\text{DM400,000}}{1 + .02}$$

$$= \text{DM392,157}$$

If the firm borrows DM392,157 and converts those marks to dollars, then the receivables can be used to pay off the mark loan in 90 days. Meanwhile, the proceeds of the loan can be used for whatever purpose the firm desires.

In some cases, the firm may not need to borrow funds for a 90-day period. In these situations, a money market hedge could still be used to hedge receivables by taking two positions in the money markets: (1) borrow the foreign currency representing future receivables, and (2) invest in the home currency. To illustrate, reconsider the previous example of DM400,000 in receivables. Even if the U.S. firm did not have a use for the DM392,157 borrowed, it could invest them in a 90-day U.S. security. Assuming that a mark is worth $.55, the marks borrowed could be converted to $215,686. Assuming an annualized U.S. interest rate of 7.2 percent (1.8 percent over 90 days) on 90-day securities, the U.S. investment will be worth $219,568 (computed as $215,686 × 1.018) in 90 days. Since the receivables can cover the existing loan, the firm will have $219,568 as a result of enacting the money market hedge.

The results of the money market hedge in the previous example could be compared to the results of a forward hedge in order to determine which type of hedge is preferable. Since the results of either hedge are known beforehand, the firm can implement the one that is more feasible. As with hedging payables, the firm will not know whether the chosen hedge on receivables will outperform an unhedged strategy until the period of concern has elapsed.

Implications of Interest Rate Parity for Comparing the Forward Hedge and Money Market Hedge

If interest rate parity exists, and transaction costs do not exist, the forward rate hedge will yield the same results as the money market hedge. This is because the forward premium on the forward rate would reflect the interest rate differential between the two currencies. The hedging of future payables with a forward purchase would be similar to borrowing at the home interest rate and investing at the foreign interest rate. The hedging of future receivables with a forward sale would be similar to borrowing at the foreign interest rate and investing at the home interest rate. Even if the forward premium generally reflects the interest rate differential between countries, the existence of transaction costs may cause the results of a forward hedge to differ from the money market hedge.

Currency Option Hedge

Firms recognize that hedging techniques such as the forward hedge and money market hedge can backfire when a payables currency depreciates or a receivables currency appreciates over the hedged period. In these situations, an unhedged strategy would likely outperform the forward hedge or money market hedge. The ideal type of hedge would insulate the firm against adverse exchange rate movements but allow the firm to benefit from favorable exchange rate movements. Currency options exhibit these attributes. However, firms must assess whether the advantages of a currency option hedge are worth the price (premium) paid for it. Details on currency options were provided in Chapter 5. The following discussion illustrates how they can be used in hedging.

HEDGING PAYABLES WITH CURRENCY CALL OPTIONS.   As stated in Chapter 5, a currency call option provides the right to buy a specified amount of a particular currency at a specified price (the exercise price) within a given period of time. Yet, unlike a futures or forward contract, the currency call option *does not obligate* its owner to buy the currency at that price. To illustrate, consider a firm that has payables in British pounds. If the spot rate of the pound remains lower than the exercise price throughout the life of the option, the firm that needs pounds could let the option expire and simply purchase them at the existing spot rate. On the other hand, if the spot rate of the pound appreciates over time, the call option allows the firm to purchase pounds at the exercise price. That is, the firm owning a call option has locked in a maximum price (the exercise price) to pay for the currency. It also has the flexibility, though, to let the option expire and obtain the currency at the existing spot rate when the currency is to be sent for payment.

Consider Clemson Corporation, which has payables of 100,000 British pounds 90 days from now. Assume there is a call option available with an exercise price of $1.60. Clemson doesn't have to exercise its call option if it can obtain pounds at a lower spot rate. Assume that the option premium is $.04 per unit. For options that cover the 100,000 units, the total premium is $4,000 (100,000 × $.04).

Assume that Clemson expects that the spot rate of the pound to be either $1.58, $1.62, or $1.66 when the payables are due. The effect on each of these scenarios on Clemson's cost of payables is shown in Exhibit 11.5. The first two columns simply identify the scenario to be analyzed. The third column shows the premium per unit paid on the option, which is the same regardless of the spot rate that occurs when payables are due. The fourth column shows the amount that Clemson would pay per pound for the payables under each scenario, assuming that it owns call options. If Scenario 1 occurs, Clemson will let the options expire and purchase pounds in the spot market for $1.58 each. If Scenarios 2 or 3 occur, Clemson will exercise the options and therefore purchase pounds for $1.60 per unit. The fifth column is the sum of the third and fourth columns, as it determines the amount paid per unit when including the premium paid on the call option. The sixth column converts the fifth column into a total dollar cost, based on the 100,000 pounds hedged.

HEDGING RECEIVABLES WITH CURRENCY PUT OPTIONS.   Like currency call options, currency put options can also be a valuable hedging

EXHIBIT 11.5 Use of Currency Call Options for Hedging British Pound Payables *(exercise price = $1.60; premium = $.04)*

(1)	(2)	(3)	(4)	(5) = (4) + (3)	(6)
Scenario	Spot Rate When Payables Are Due	Premium per Unit Paid on Call Options	Amount Paid per Unit When Owning Call Options	Total Amount Paid per Unit (including the Premium) When Owning Call Options	Dollar Amount Paid for 100,000 Pounds When Owning Call Options
1	$1.58	$.04	$1.58	$1.62	$162,000
2	1.62	.04	1.60	1.64	164,000
3	1.66	.04	1.60	1.64	164,000

device. The currency put option provides the right to sell a specified amount of a particular currency at a specified price (the exercise price) within a given period of time. It could be used by firms to hedge future receivables in foreign currencies, since it guarantees a certain price (the exercise price) at which the future receivables can be sold. The currency put option *does not obligate* its owner to sell the currency at a specified price. If the existing spot rate of the foreign currency is above the exercise price when the firm receives the foreign currency, the firm can sell the currency received at the spot rate and let the put option expire. The application of put options for hedging will now be discussed.

Assume that Knoxville Inc. expects to receive DM600,000 in about 90 days. If Knoxville is concerned about the possibility of the mark depreciating against the dollar, it could purchase put options to cover its receivables. Assume that the mark put options considered here have an exercise price of $.50 and a premium of $.03 per unit. Also assume that Knoxville anticipates the spot rate in 90 days to be either $.44, $.46, or $.51. The amount to be received as a result of owning currency put options is shown in Exhibit 11.6. Columns 2 through 5 are on a per unit basis. Column 6 is determined by multiplying the per unit amount received in Column 5 by 600,000 units.

EXHIBIT 11.6 Use of Currency Put Options for Hedging German Mark Receivables *(exercise price = $.50; premium = $.03)*

(1)	(2)	(3)	(4)	(5) = (4) − (3)	(6)
Scenario	Spot Rate When Payment on Receivables Is Received	Premium Per Unit on Put Options	Amount Received per Unit When Owning Put Options	Net Amount Received per Unit (after Accounting for Premium Paid)	Dollar Amount Received from Hedging DM600,000 Receivables with Put Options
1	$ .44	$.03	$.50	$.47	$282,000
2	.46	.03	.50	.47	282,000
3	.51	.03	.51	.48	288,000

Jaguar, the British automobile manufacturer, used currency put options to hedge future Canadian dollar inflows. It was uncertain how many cars it would sell in Canada, so it did not want to be committed to sell a specified amount of Canadian dollars (as would have been required with a forward contract). The currency put option gave Jaguar more flexibility since if it did not receive much revenue in Canadian dollars, it could let the put options expire.

Comparison of Hedging Techniques

The first step for a firm is to determine its degree of transaction exposure in each currency. Then, it should evaluate the hedging techniques that are available. Each of the hedging techniques is briefly summarized in Exhibit 11.7.

The firm must determine (1) whether to hedge and (2) which technique to use if it does hedge. With regard to the futures contract, forward contract, and the money market hedge, it can estimate the funds (denominated in its home currency) that it will need for future payables, or the funds it shall receive after converting foreign currency receivables. Thus, it can compare the costs or revenues and determine which of these hedging techniques is appropriate. However, the cash flow associated with the currency option hedge cannot be determined with certainty, because the costs of purchasing payables or the revenues generated from receivables are not known ahead of time. These costs or revenues will be known only when we know the spot rate that exists at the time the payables or receivables are due. Of course, by that time the firm would already have decided on a hedging device.

Those corporate managers responsible for the decision on whether to hedge short-term positions in foreign currencies often have varied opinions. For example, Eastman Kodak Company and Merck & Co. use a partial hedging approach, whereas Seagram Company essentially uses a full hedging approach. A partial hedging approach allows currency positions to remain

EXHIBIT 11.7 Review of Techniques for Hedging Transaction Exposure

Hedging Technique	To Hedge Payables	To Hedge Receivables
1. Futures contract hedge	Purchase a currency futures contract (or contracts) representing the currency and amount related to the payables.	Sell a currency futures contract (or contracts) representing the currency and amount related to the receivables.
2. Forward contract hedge	Purchase a forward contract representing the currency and amount related to the payables.	Sell a forward contract representing the currency and amount related to the receivables.
3. Money market hedge	Borrow local currency and convert to currency denominating payables. Invest these funds until they are needed to cover the payables.	Borrow the currency denominating the receivables, and convert it to the local currency and invest it. Then pay off the loan with cash inflows from the receivables.
4. Currency option hedge	Purchase a currency call option (or options) representing the currency and amount related to the payables.	Purchase a currency put option (or options) representing the currency and amount related to the receivables.

open if they are anticipated to be worth more (or cost less) when unhedged as compared to being hedged. A full hedging approach is based on a more passive philosophy that firms cannot consistently outperform the market in guessing whether hedging will be more or less costly than not hedging. Thus, virtually all open currency positions (at least on a net basis) shall be hedged. The question of whether to hedge should be given serious consideration by corporate treasurers, since the firm's profitability can be significantly affected by this decision. If the firm decides to hedge, all hedging techniques should be evaluated, since all techniques will not necessarily generate the same results.

To reinforce an understanding of the hedging techniques, a comprehensive example follows. Assume that Fresno Corporation will need 200,000 pounds (£) in 180 days. It considers either (1) a forward hedge, (2) a money market hedge, (3) an option hedge, or (4) remaining unhedged. Its analysts develop the following information, which can be used to assess the alternative solutions:

- Spot rate of pound as of today = $1.50.
- 180-day forward rate of pound as of today = $1.47.
- Interest rates are as follows:

	U.K.	U.S.
180-day deposit rate	4.5%	4.5%
180-day borrowing rate	5.0%	5.0%

- A call option on pounds that expires in 180 days has an exercise price of $1.48 and a premium of $.03.
- A put option on pounds that expires in 180 days has an exercise price of $1.49 and a premium of $.02.
- Fresno Corporation forecasted the future spot rate in 180 days as follows:

Possible Outcome	Probability
$1.43	20%
$1.46	70%
$1.52	10%

Each alternative solution to the existing problem is assessed in Exhibit 11.8. Now these solutions will be compared to determine the best one.

Each of the alternative solutions has been analyzed to estimate the nominal dollar cost of paying for the payables denominated in pounds. The cost is known with certainty for the forward rate hedge and money market hedge. However, the cost when using either the call option or when remaining unhedged is dependent on the spot rate 180 days from now. The costs of the four alternatives are also compared with the use of probability distributions as shown in Exhibit 11.9. A review of this exhibit shows that the forward hedge is superior to the money market hedge, since the dollar cost is definitely less. A comparison of the forward hedge to the call option hedge shows that there is an 80 percent chance that the call option hedge will be more expensive. Thus, the forward hedge appears to be the optimal hedge.

EXHIBIT 11.8 Comparison of Hedging Alternatives for Fresno Corporation

Forward Hedge
Purchase pounds 180 days forward

$$\text{Dollars needed in 180 days} = \text{Payables in £} \times \text{Forward rate of £}$$
$$= £200,000 \times \$1.47$$
$$= \$294,000$$

Money Market Hedge
Borrow $, Convert to £, Invest £, Repay $ loan in 180 days

$$\frac{\text{Amount of £}}{\text{to be invested}} = \frac{£200,000}{(1 + .045)}$$
$$= £191,388$$

$$\left\{ \begin{array}{l} \text{Amount of \$} \\ \text{needed to convert} \\ \text{into £ for deposit} \end{array} \right\} = £191,388 \times \$1.50$$
$$= \$287,081$$

$$\begin{array}{c} \text{Interest and principal owed} \\ \text{on \$ loan} \\ \text{after 180 days} \end{array} = \$287,081 \times (1 + .05)$$
$$= \$301,435$$

Call Option
Purchase call option (the following computations assume that the option is to be exercised on the day pounds are needed, or not at all). (Exercise price = $1.48; premium = $.03.)

Possible Spot Rate in 180 days	Premium per Unit Paid for Option	Exercise Option?	Total Price (Including Option Premium) Paid per Unit	Total Price Paid for £200,000	Probability
$1.43	$.03	No	$1.46	$292,000	20%
$1.46	$.03	No	$1.49	$298,000	70%
$1.52	$.03	Yes	$1.51	$302,000	10%

Remain Unhedged
Purchase £200,000 in the spot market 180 days from now.

Future Spot Rate Expected in 180 Days	Dollars Needed to Purchase £200,000	Probability
$1.43	$286,000	20%
$1.46	$292,000	70
$1.52	$304,000	10

EXHIBIT 11.9 Nominal Dollar Cost of Pound-Denominated Payables

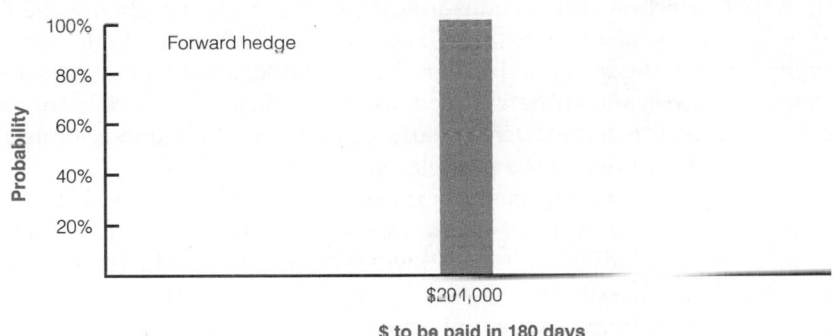

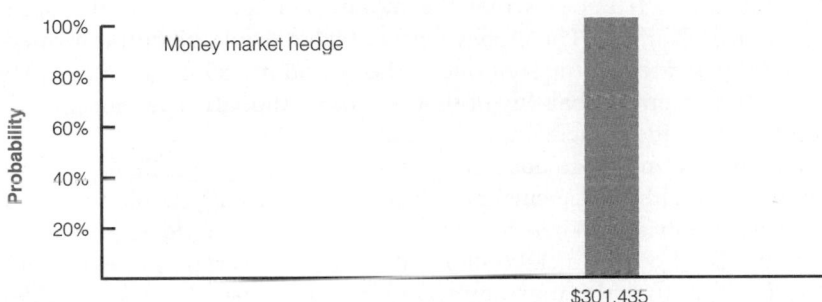

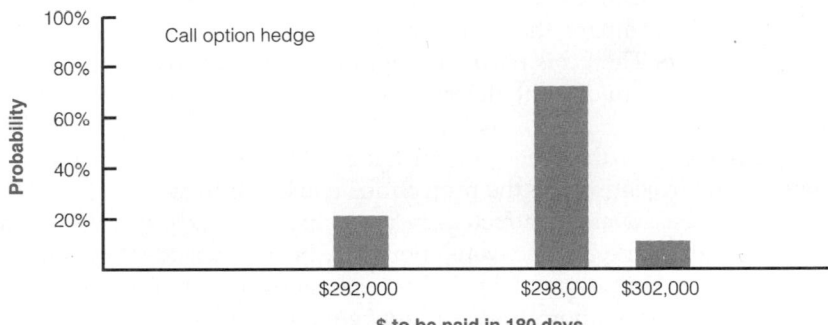

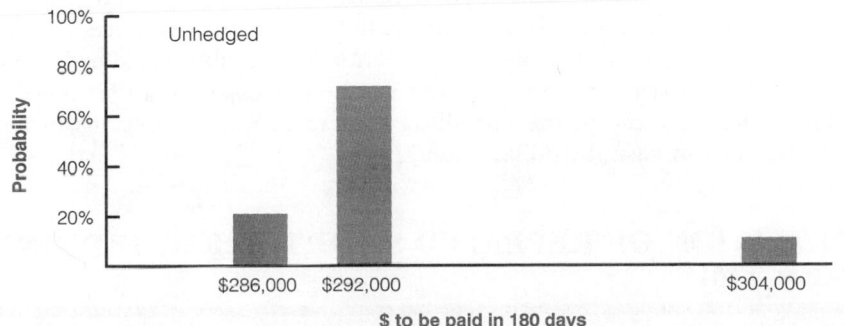

The probability distribution of outcomes for the no-hedge strategy appears to be more favorable than that of the forward hedge. Fresno Corporation is likely to perform best if it remains unhedged, but it should choose the forward hedge if it prefers to hedge. If Fresno does not hedge, it should periodically reassess the hedging decision. For example, after 60 days it should repeat the analysis shown here, based on the applicable spot rate, forward rate, interest rates, call option information, and forecasts of the spot rate 120 days into the future (when the payables are due).

A similar analysis of transaction exposure could be conducted if a firm desired to hedge receivables. For example, assume that Gator Corporation anticipates no payables in pounds, but will receive £300,000 in 180 days. The same information on the spot, forward, and options prices is used to compare hedging techniques and an unhedged strategy in Exhibit 11.10.

The dollars to be received from each of the four alternatives are compared in Exhibit 11.11. It appears that the money market hedge is the optimal hedge for this example. The money market hedge would be outperformed by the no-hedge strategy if the spot rate of the pound in 180 days is $1.52. There is only a 10 percent probability of that outcome, though. Therefore, the firm would likely decide to hedge its receivables position.

While this example included the assessment of one particular currency option, several alternative currency options are normally available with different exercise prices. When hedging payables, firms could reduce the premium paid by choosing a call option with a higher exercise price. Of course, the trade-off is that the maximum amount to be paid for the payables is higher. Similarly, firms hedging receivables could reduce the premium paid by choosing a put option with a lower exercise price. In this case, the trade-off is that the minimum amount to be received for the receivables is lower. Firms generally compare the available options first to determine which is most appropriate. Then this particular option can be compared to the other hedging techniques in order to determine which technique (if any) should be used.

It should be clear that the optimal hedging technique is dependent on exchange rate projections. If the projections cause the firm to believe that it will definitely be adversely affected by its transaction exposure, a forward hedge or money market hedge would normally be appropriate. Conversely, if the firm believes that it may benefit from its exposure, the currency option hedge would be more appropriate (if any hedge is used at all). As a realistic example of choosing among hedging techniques, consider the case of The Merck & Co., with worldwide sales of over $6 billion. It has recently used put options to hedge its receivables denominated in foreign currencies, because it did not want to forgo the potential benefits if the dollar weakened. Under this type of scenario, the option would not be exercised, as the receivables would be worth more at the prevailing spot rate. Yet, the options provide insurance just in case the dollar strengthens.

LIMITATION OF REPEATED SHORT-TERM HEDGING OVER TIME

While the hedging techniques described in this chapter can be useful, they have limited effectiveness for the long term. To illustrate, consider a U.S. importer that specializes in importing particular Japanese stereos in one

EXHIBIT 11.10 Comparison of Hedging Alternatives for Gator Corporation

Forward Hedge
Sell pounds 180 days forward

$$\text{Dollars to be received in 180 days} = \text{Receivables in £} \times \text{Forward rate of £}$$
$$= £300,000 \times \$1.47$$
$$= \$441,000$$

Money Market Hedge
Borrow £, convert to $, invest $, use receivables to pay off loan in 180 days

$$\text{Amount of £ Borrowed} = \frac{£300,000}{(1 + .05)}$$
$$= £285,714$$
$$\begin{array}{l}\text{\$ received}\\\text{from converting £}\end{array} = £285,714 \times \$1.50 \text{ per £}$$
$$= \$428,571$$
$$\begin{array}{l}\text{\$ accumulated}\\\text{after 180 days}\end{array} = \$428,571 \times (1 + .045)$$
$$= \$447,857$$

Put Option Hedge
Purchase put option (assume the options are to be exercised on the day pounds are to be received, or not at all).
(Exercise price = $1.49; premium = $.02.)

Possible Spot Rate in 180 days	Premium per Unit Paid for Option	Exercise Option?	Total Dollars Received per Unit (After Accounting for the Premium)	Total Dollars Received from Converting £300,000	Probability
$1.43	$.02	Yes	$1.47	$441,000	20%
1.46	.02	Yes	1.47	441,000	70
1.52	.02	No	1.50	450,000	10

Remain Unhedged

Possible Spot Rate in 180 Days	Total Dollars Received from Converting £300,000	Probability
$1.43	$429,000	20%
1.46	438,000	70
1.52	456,000	10

EXHIBIT 11.11 Dollars Received from Pound-Denominated Receivables

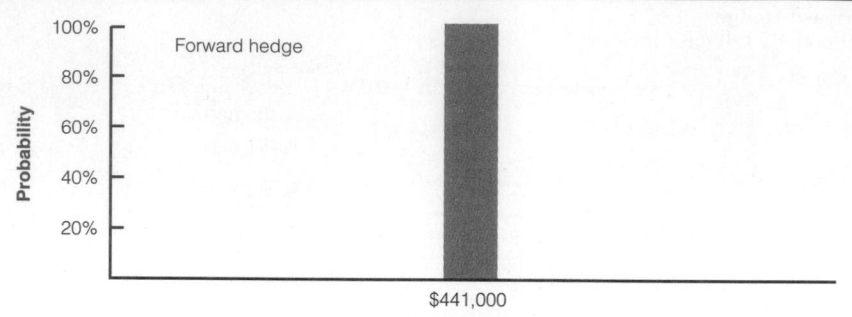

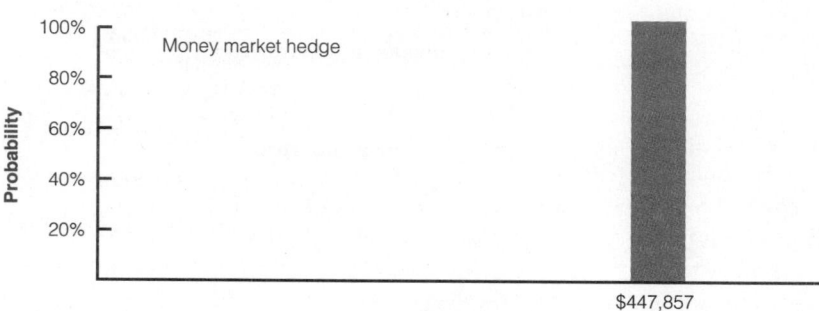

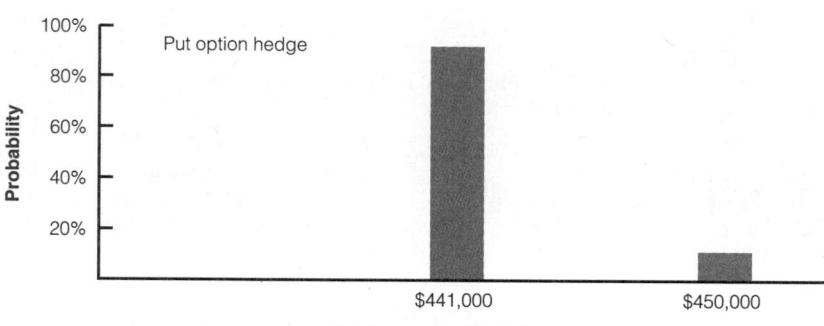

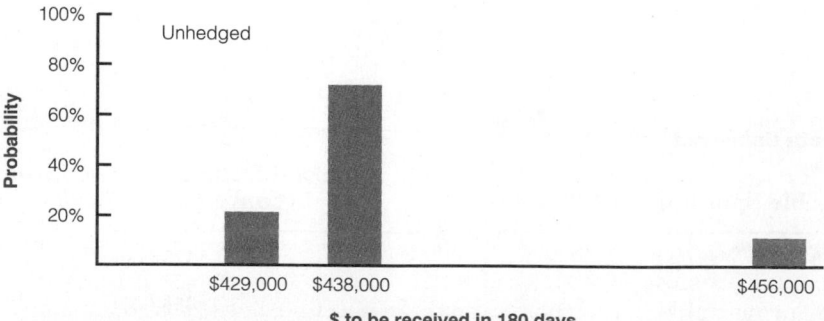

RELATED RESEARCH

Hedging Performance of Currency Options versus Forwards

A recent study simulated a process of hedging a position in each of five major currencies over each quarter from April 1983 through October 1987. The objective was to compare the effectiveness of hedging with currency options versus forward contracts in each quarter. The study was first conducted from the perspective of a U.S. importing firm, followed by a U.S. exporting firm. From the importer's perspective, the results were mixed. In some quarters, the importer would have been better off with currency call options, while in other quarters the forward purchase would have been preferable. Of course, the superiority of one technique over another would not have been determined until after the periods were over. On average, there was no significant difference in the amount paid for imports when hedging with currency call options versus forward purchases. This result held for each of the five currencies. From the U.S. exporter's perspective, there was on average no significant difference between using currency put options or forward sales to hedge receivables for four of the currencies. For the Japanese yen, the dollar value of the

receivables was significantly higher when using put options rather than forward sales.

A comparison was also conducted between currency options and an unhedged strategy. From an importer's perspective, there was no significant difference on average between the amount paid using currency call options versus using an unhedged strategy. One exception was the German mark, in which the unhedged strategy was superior.

From an exporter's perspective, there was no significant difference on average between the amount received when hedging with currency put options versus using an unhedged strategy. One exception was the British pound, in which the unhedged strategy was superior.

Overall, currency options generally performed about as well as forward contracts or the unhedged strategy, and they may alleviate any concerns managers have about exchange rate movements. Furthermore, they offer the opportunity to benefit if exchange rates move in a favorable direction. While the results of this study cannot be applied to the future, they suggest that currency options should be given serious consideration.

SOURCE: Jeff Madura, "Hedging With American Currency Options A Five-Year Appraisal," *Journal of Business and Economic Perspectives*, Spring 1990, pp. 35–38.

large shipment per year and then sells them to retail stores throughout the year. Assume that today's exchange rate of the Japanese yen is $.005, and that the stereos are worth ¥60,000, or $300. Further assume that the forward rate of the yen generally exhibits a premium of 2 percent. Exhibit 11.12 shows the dollar/yen exchange rate to be paid by the importer over time. As the spot rate changes, the forward rate will often change by a similar amount. Thus, if thespot rate increases by 10 percent over the year, the forward rate may increase by about the same amount, and the importer will pay 10 percent more for next year's shipment of stereos (assuming no change in the yen price quoted by the Japanese exporter). The use of a one-year forward contract during a strong-yen cycle is preferable to no hedge in this case but will still result in subsequent increases in prices paid by the importer each year. This illustrates that the use of short-term hedging techniques do not com-

EXHIBIT 11.12   Illustration of Repeated Hedging of Foreign Payables When the Foreign Currency is Appreciating

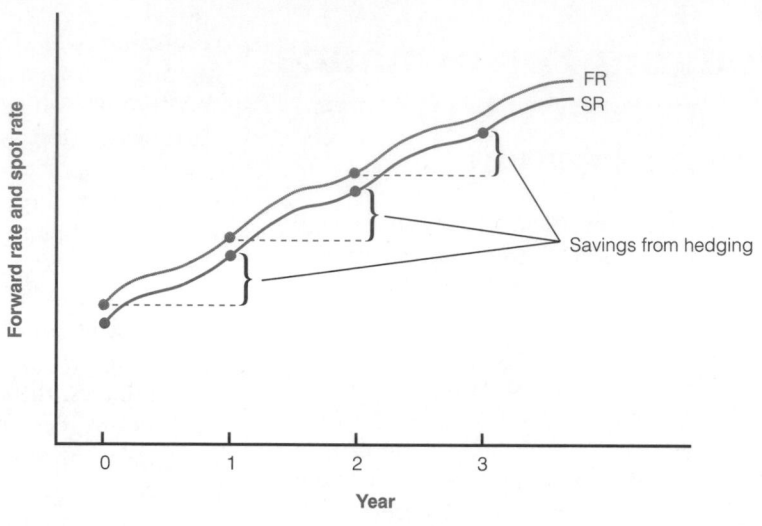

pletely insulate a firm from exchange rate exposure, even if they are repeatedly used over time.

If the hedging techniques could be applied to longer-term periods, they could more effectively insulate the firm from exchange rate risk over the long run. To illustrate, the stereo importer could, as of Time 0, create a hedge for shipments to arrive at the end of each of the next several years. The forward rate for each hedge would be based on the spot rate as of today, as shown in Exhibit 11.13. During a strong-yen cycle, such a strategy would save a substantial amount of funds. However, the limitation of this strategy is that the amount of yen to be hedged further into the future is more uncertain, since the shipment size will be dependent on economic conditions or other factors at that time. If a recession occurs, the importer may reduce the amount of stereos ordered, but the amount of yen to be received by the importer is dictated by the forward contract that was created. If the stereo manufacturer goes bankrupt, or simply experiences stockouts, the importer is still obligated to purchase the yen, even if a shipment is not forthcoming.

HEDGING LONG-TERM TRANSACTION EXPOSURE

Some MNCs are certain of having cash flows denominated in foreign currencies for several years, and attempt to use long-term hedging. For example, in 1988 the Walt Disney Company hedged its Japanese yen cash flows that would be remitted to the United States (from the Japanese theme park) for the next 20 years. Since the hedging techniques discussed so far are generally for short-term purposes, other techniques are necesssary for long-term hedging.

For firms that can accurately estimate foreign currency payables or receivables that will occur several years from now, there are three commonly used techniques to hedge such long-term transaction exposure:

EXHIBIT 11.13   Long-term Hedging of Payables When the Foreign Currency is Appreciating

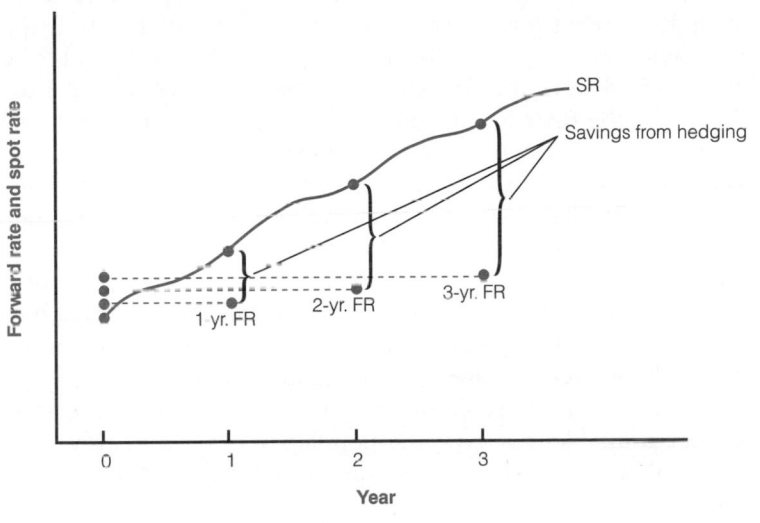

- Long-term forward contract
- Currency swap
- Parallel loan

Each technique is discussed in turn.

Long-Term Forward Contract

Until recently, **long-term forward contracts,** or **long forwards,** were seldom used. Today the long forward is quite popular. Most large international banks will routinely quote forward rates for terms up to five years for British pounds, Canadian dollars, German marks, and Swiss francs. Long forwards are especially attractive to firms that have set up fixed-price exporting or importing contracts over a long period of time and want to protect their cash flow from exchange rate fluctuations.

Like short-term forward contracts, the long forward can be tailored to accommodate the specific needs of the firm. Maturities of up to 10 years or more can sometimes be set up for the major currencies. Because a bank is trusting that a firm will fulfill its long-term obligation specified in the forward contract, it will consider only very creditworthy customers.

Currency Swap

A **currency swap** is a second technique for hedging long-term transaction exposure to exchange rate fluctuations. It can take many forms. One type of currency swap accommodates two firms that have different long-term needs. Consider a U.S. firm, hired to build an oil pipeline in Great Britain, that expects to receive payment in British pounds in five years when the job is completed. At the same time, a British firm is hired by a U.S. bank for a long-term consulting project. Assume that payment to this British firm will be in U.S. dollars and that much of the payment will occur in five years. The U.S. firm will be receiving British pounds in five years and a British firm will be receiving U.S. dollars in five years. These two firms could arrange a currency swap that allows for an exchange of pounds for dollars in five years at some negotiated exchange rate. In this way, the U.S. firm could lock in the number of U.S. dollars the British pound payment will convert to in five years. Likewise, the British firm could lock in the number of British pounds the U.S. dollar payment will convert to in five years.

To create a currency swap, firms need to find other firms that can accommodate their needs. There are brokers employed by large banks and investment firms that act as middlemen for swaps. They are notified by those corporations that want to eliminate transaction exposure to specific currencies at certain future dates. Using this information, they can match up firms when the one firm needs the currency the other firm wants to dispose of (and vice versa). The brokers receive a fee for their service.

Currency swaps have been commonly used. Now that long-term forward contracts are available, however, the popularity of currency swaps may diminish due to the more extensive documentation required on swap arrangements.

Over time, the currency-swap obligation may become undesirable to one of the parties involved. Using our previous example, if the British pound appreciates substantially over time, the U.S. company that agreed to swap pounds for dollars will be worse off than if it had been able to obtain its dollars in the spot market. Of course, it did not know this when it engaged in a swap agreement. The swap agreement may require periodic payments from one party to the other to account for exchange rate movements, so as to reduce the possibility of one party not fulfilling its obligation by the time the swap is supposed to occur.

Parallel Loan

A **parallel loan** (or **back-to-back loan**) involves an exchange of currencies between two parties, with a promise to re-exchange currencies at a specified exchange rate and future date. It represents two swaps of currencies, one swap at the inception of the loan contract and another swap at the specified future date. A parallel loan is interpreted by accountants as a loan and is therefore recorded on financial statements.

TECHNIQUES TO REDUCE TRANSACTION EXPOSURE

Sometimes a firm is not able to completely eliminate its transaction exposure. For example, a firm cannot always accurately forecast the sales (representing inflow payments) on products and/or the purchases (representing outflow payments) on supplies denominated in foreign currencies. Thus, it does not know the precise amount to hedge for each foreign currency. In addition, projected costs of the hedging techniques may seem too high to be worthwhile. Finally, there is also the possibility that the currencies a firm is exposed to cannot be hedged, perhaps due to the nonexistence of a forward market or currency options market for such currencies. Even the money market hedge may not be possible if there are barriers to foreign investing or borrowing in the home country of that currency. Also, the swap arrangement may be difficult to set up if the currency is not widely traded, since there would not be an active market for swaps in that currency.

When a perfect hedge is not available (or is too expensive) to eliminate transaction exposure, the firm should consider methods to at least reduce exposure. Such methods include

- Leading and lagging
- Cross-hedging
- Currency diversification

Each method is discussed in turn.

Leading and Lagging

The act of **leading and lagging** represents an adjustment in the timing of payment request or disbursement to reflect expectations about future currency movements. For example, consider a multinational corporation based in the United States that has subsidiaries dispersed around the world. The focus here will be on a subsidiary in Great Britain that purchases some of its supplies from a subsidiary in West Germany. Assume these supplies are denominated in German marks. If the British subsidiary expects the pound will soon depreciate against the mark, it may attempt to accelerate the timing of its payment before the pound depreciates. This strategy is referred to as **leading.**

As a second possibility, consider a scenario where the British subsidiary expects the pound will soon appreciate against the mark. In this case, the British subsidiary may attempt to stall its payment until after the pound appreciates. In this way it could use fewer pounds to obtain the marks needed for payment. This strategy is referred to as **lagging.** General Electric and other well-known MNCs commonly use leading and lagging strategies in countries that allow them.

Some country governments limit the length of time involved on leading and lagging strategies, so that the flow of funds into or out of a country is not disrupted. Consequently, a multinational corporation must be aware of government restrictions of any countries in which it conducts business before using these strategies.

Cross-hedging

Cross-hedging is a common method to reduce transaction exposure when the currency cannot be hedged. Assume a U.S. firm has payables in Currency X 90 days from now. Because it is worried that Currency X may appreciate against the U.S. dollar, it may desire to hedge this position. If forward contracts and the other hedging techniques are not possible for this currency, the firm may consider cross-hedging, in which case it needs to first identify a currency that can be hedged and is highly correlated with Currency X. It could then set up a 90-day forward contract on this currency. If two currencies are highly correlated relative to the U.S. dollar (that is, they move in a

RELATED RESEARCH

Reducing Exchange Rate Risk through Diversification

A recent study by Soenen provides insight on the potential reduction in exchange rate risk (as measured by variance) attributed to diversification. First, the average variance of monthly percentage changes in exchange rates was estimated for each currency (with respect to the U.S. dollar). Then the average variance of randomly selected two-currency, equally weighted currency portfolios was estimated. The procedure was replicated for other portfolios containing more currencies. The objective was to determine the degree to which risk could be reduced on average by adding additional currencies to the portfolio. In general, one would expect that a more diversified portfolio of currencies should exhibit less risk. However, to the extent that the movements of most currencies against the dollar are positively correlated, the benefits from diversification may be limited after some point. The results are disclosed in the next column. The results suggest that diver-

Number of Currencies in Portfolio	Average Variance	Average Percentage Risk Reduction Relative to a Single Foreign Currency
1	10.360%	-
2	8.536	17.6%
4	7.099	31.5
6	6.993	32.5
8	6.700	35.3
10	6.680	35.5
12	6.600	36.3

sification can effectively reduce risk. However, once the portfolio contains four to six currencies, adding more currencies has a negligible effect on variance. The implications are that while firms can reduce the risk by diversifying among currencies, diversification beyond some small number of currencies will not necessarily reduce risk any further. Results would vary with the particular currencies chosen, though.

SOURCE: Luc A. Soenen, "Risk Diversification Characteristics of Currency Cocktails," *Journal of Economics and Business*, (May 1989), pp. 177–189.

similar direction against the U.S. dollar), then the exchange rate between these two currencies should be somewhat stable over time. When purchasing the one currency 90 days forward, the U.S. firm can then exchange that currency for Currency X. The effectiveness of this strategy depends on the degree to which these two currencies are positively correlated. The stronger the positive correlation, the more effective will be the cross-hedging strategy.

To illustrate a second use of cross-hedging, consider a U.S. firm that has net inflows denominated in German marks and net outflows denominated in Swiss francs. Because these two currencies often move in tandem against the U.S. dollar, a cross-hedge exists. If by chance the mark depreciates, the U.S. firm will obtain fewer dollars when exchanging those marks received. Of course, the Swiss franc would probably also have depreciated (though not necessarily by the same degree) against the dollar. Thus, fewer dollars will be needed to obtain francs when sending outflow payments. Regardless of whether these currencies depreciate or appreciate against the U.S. dollar, the

U.S. firm in this example will be somewhat insulated from the exchange rate fluctuations if the two currencies are highly positively correlated.

Currency Diversification

A third method for reducing transaction exposure is currency diversification. Consider a multinational firm based in the U.S. that is heavily involved in exporting and importing and has more inflows in each foreign currency than outflows. In this case, the MNC will be hurt by a strong dollar since the foreign currencies received would not be worth as many dollars. If all the inflows are denominated in one or a few foreign currencies, substantial depreciation of one of these currencies would severely affect the *dollar value* of the firm's inflows. However, substantial depreciation in one foreign currency would not be as damaging if that currency was only one of several to which the firm was exposed. This is because the single currency would represent only a small portion of total inflows and would therefore not severely affect the dollar value of the total inflows.

The dollar value of future inflows in foreign currencies will be more stable if the foreign currencies received are *not* highly positively correlated. The reason is that lower positive correlations or negative correlations can reduce the variability of the dollar value of all foreign currency inflows. If the foreign currencies were highly correlated with each other, diversifying among them would not be a very effective way to reduce risk. If one of the currencies had substantially depreciated, the others would have as well, given that all these currencies move in tandem.

When a firm desires to hedge its transaction exposure, it may use one or more of the following hedging techniques:

SUMMARY

- Futures contract hedge
- Forward contract hedge
- Money market hedge
- Currency option hedge

Once the optimal hedging technique is determined, the firm can determine whether that technique is preferable to an unhedged strategy. The preferred hedging technique and the decision of whether to hedge are dependent on the forecast of the future spot rate.

The aforementioned hedging techniques are generally for short-term positions. Firms that desire to hedge a long-term position commonly consider the following techniques for hedging:

- Long-term forward hedge
- Currency swap
- Parallel loan

Hedging techniques are not available for all currencies. Even if the firm cannot eliminate transaction exposure, there are ways to at least reduce the exposure, including

- Leading and lagging
- Cross-hedging
- Currency diversification

The effectiveness of these strategies varies with the manner by which the firm is exposed.

This entire chapter focused solely on the management of transaction exposure. The management of economic exposure and translation exposure are explained in the following chapter.

QUESTIONS/ PROBLEMS

Quincy Corporation estimates the following cash flows in 90 days at its subsidiaries as follows:

	Net Position in Each Currency Measured in the Parent's Currency		
Subsidiary	*Currency 1*	*Currency 2*	*Currency 3*
B	+100	−40	−10
C	−180	+200	−40

Determine the consolidated net exposure of the MNC to each currency.

2. Assume that Stevens Point Company has net receivables of 100,000 Swiss francs in 90 days. The spot rate of the franc is $.50, and the Swiss interest rate is 2 percent over 90 days. Suggest how the U.S. firm could implement a money market hedge. Be precise.

3. Assume that Vermont Company has net payables of 200,000 French francs in 180 days. The French interest rate is 7 percent over 180 days, and the spot rate of the French franc is $.10. Suggest how the U.S. firm could implement a money market hedge. Be precise.

4. Assume that Citadel Company purchases some goods in West Germany that are denominated in marks. It also sells goods denominated in U.S. dollars to some German firms. At the end of each month, it has a large net payables position in German marks. How can this U.S. firm use an invoicing strategy to reduce this transaction exposure? List any limitations on the effectiveness of this strategy.

5. Explain how a U.S. corporation could hedge net receivables in British pounds with futures contracts.

6. Explain how a U.S. corporation could hedge net payables in Japanese yen with futures contracts.

7. Explain how a U.S. corporation could hedge net receivables in French francs with a forward contract.

8. Explain how a U.S. corporation could hedge payables in Canadian dollars with a forward contract.

9. Assume that Loras Corporation, needs 100,000 Swiss francs 180 days from now. It is trying to determine whether or not to hedge this position. It has developed the following probability distribution for the Swiss franc:

Possible Value of Swiss Franc in 180 days	Probability
$.40	5%
.45	10
.48	30
.50	30
.53	20
.55	5

The 180-day forward rate of the Swiss franc is $.52. The spot rate of the Swiss franc is $.49. Develop a table showing a feasibility analysis for hedging. That is, determine the possible differences in the costs of hedging versus no hedge. What is the probability that hedging will be more costly to the firm than no hedge for this U.S. firm?

10. Using the information in Question 9, what is the expected value of the additional cost of hedging?

11. If hedging is expected to be more costly than no hedge, why would a firm even consider hedging?

12. Assume that Suffolk Company negotiated a forward contract to purchase 200,000 British pounds in 90 days. The 90-day forward rate was $1.40 per British pound. The pounds to be purchased were to be used to purchase British supplies. On the day the pounds were delivered in accordance with the forward contract, the spot rate of the British pound was $1.44. What was the real cost of hedging the payables for this U.S. firm?

13. Repeat Question 12, except assume that the spot rate of the British pound was $1.34 on the day the pounds were delivered in accordance with the forward contract. What was the real cost of hedging the payables in this example?

14. Assume that Bentley Company negotiated a forward contract to sell 100,000 Canadian dollars in one year. The one-year forward rate on the Canadian dollar was $.80. This strategy was designed to hedge receivables in Canadian dollars. On the day the Canadian dollars were to be sold off in accordance with the forward contract, the spot rate of the Canadian dollar was $.83. What was the real cost of hedging receivables for this U.S. firm?

15. Repeat Question 14, except assume that the spot rate of the Canadian dollar was $.75 on the day the Canadian dollars were to be sold off in accordance with the forward contract. What was the real cost of hedging receivables in this example?

16. Assume the following information:

90-day U.S. interest rate	4%
90-day German interest rate	3%
90-day forward rate of German mark	$.400
Spot rate of German mark	$.404

Assume that Santa Barbara Company in the United States will need 300,000 marks in 90 days. It wishes to hedge this payables position. Would it be better off using a forward hedge or a money market hedge? Substantiate your answer with estimated costs for each type of hedge.

17. Assume the following information:

180-day U.S. interest rate	8%
180-day British interest rate	9%
180-day forward rate of British pound	$1.50
Spot rate of British pound	$1.48

Assume that Riverside Corporation from the United States will receive 400,000 pounds in 180 days. Would it be better off using a forward hedge or a money market hedge? Substantiate your answer with estimated revenues for each type of hedge.

18. Why would a firm consider hedging net payables or net receivables with currency options rather than forward contracts? What are the disadvantages of hedging with currency options as opposed to forward contracts?

19. Relate the use of currency options to hedging net payables and receivables. That is, when should currency puts be purchased, and when should currency calls be purchased?

20. Can an MNC determine whether currency options will be more or less expensive than a forward hedge when considering both hedging techniques to cover net payables? Why or why not?

21. How can a firm hedge long-term currency positions? Elaborate on each method.

22. Under what conditions would an MNC's subsidiary consider use of a "leading" strategy to reduce transaction exposure?

23. Under what conditions would an MNC's subsidiary consider use of a "lagging" strategy to reduce transaction exposure?

24. Explain how cross-hedging can be used by a firm to reduce transaction exposure.

25. Explain how currency diversification can be used by a firm to reduce transaction exposure.

26. a) Assume that Carbondale Company expects to receive SF500,000 in one year. The existing spot rate of the Swiss franc is $.60. The one-year forward rate of the Swiss franc is $.62. Carbondale created a probability distribution for the future spot rate in one year as follows:

Future Spot Rate	Probability
$.61	20%
.63	50
.67	30

Assume that one-year put options on francs are available, with an exercise price of $.63 and a premium of $.04 per unit. One-year call options on francs are available with an exercise price of $.60 and a premium of $.03 per unit. Assume the following money market rates:

	U.S.	Switzerland
Deposit rate	8%	5%
Borrowing rate	9	6

Given this information, determine whether a forward hedge, money market hedge, or a currency options hedge would be most appropriate. Then compare the most appropriate hedge to an unhedged strategy, and decide whether Carbondale should hedge its receivables position.

b) Assume that Baton Rouge Inc. expects to need SF1 million in one year. Using any relevant information in part a, determine whether a forward hedge, money market hedge, or a currency options hedge would be most appropriate. Then compare the most appropriate hedge to an unhedged strategy, and decide whether Baton Rouge should hedge its payables position.

27. SMU Corporation has future receivables on DM4,000,000 in one year. It must decide whether to use options or a money market hedge (MMH) to hedge this position. Use any of the following information to make the decision. Verify your answer by determining the estimate (or probability distribution) of dollar revenues to be received in one year for each type of hedge.

Spot rate of DM	$.54
One-year call option	exercise price = $.50; premium = $.07
One-year put option	exercise price = $.52; premium = $.03

	U.S.	Germany
One-year deposit rates	9%	6%
One-year borrowing rates	11	8

	Rate	Probability
Forecasted spot rate of DM	$.50	20%
	.51	50
	.53	30

28. As treasurer of Tucson Corporation, you must decide how to hedge (if at all) future receivables of 250,000 marks 90 days from now. Put options are available for a premium of $.03 per unit and an exercise price of $.49 per mark. The forecasted spot rate of the mark in 90 days follows:

Future Spot Rate	Probability
$.44	30%
.40	50
.38	20

Given that you hedge your position with options, create a probability distribution for dollars to be received in 90 days.

29. As treasurer of Tempe Corporation, you are confronted with the following problem. Assume the one-year forward rate of the British pound is $1.59. You plan to receive 1 million pounds in one year. There is a one-year put option available. It has an exercise price of $1.61. The spot rate as of today is $1.62, and the option premium is $.04 per unit. Your forecast of the percentage change in the spot rate was determined from the following regression model:

$$e_t = a_0 + a_1 \, DINF_{t-1} + a_2 \, DINT_t + \mu$$

where

$$
\begin{aligned}
e_t &= \text{percentage change in British pound} \\
&\quad \text{value over period } t \\
DINF_{t-1} &= \text{differential in inflation} \\
&\quad \text{between the United States and the} \\
&\quad \text{United Kingdom in period } t-1 \\
DINT_t &= \text{average differential between the} \\
&\quad \text{United States interest rate and} \\
&\quad \text{British interest rate over period } t \\
a_0, a_1, \text{ and } a_2 &= \text{regression coefficients} \\
\mu &= \text{error term}
\end{aligned}
$$

The regression model was applied to historical annual data, and the regression coefficients were estimated as follows:

$$
\begin{aligned}
a_0 &= 0 \\
a_1 &= 1.1 \\
a_2 &= .6
\end{aligned}
$$

Assume last year's inflation rates were 3 percent for the United States and 8 percent for the United Kingdom. Also assume that the interest rate differential $(DINT)_t$ is forecasted as follows for this year:

Forecast of $DINT_t$	Probability
1%	40%
2	50
3	10

Using any of the available information, decide whether the treasurer should choose the forward hedge or a put option hedge. Show your work.

30. Would a U.S. firm's real cost of hedging Swiss franc payables every 90 days have been positive, negative, or about zero on average over the 1985–1987 time period? What does this imply about the forward rate as an unbiased predictor of the future spot rate? Explain.

31. If interest rate parity exists, would a forward hedge be more favorable, equally favorable, or less favorable than a money market hedge on French franc payables? Explain.

32. Would a U.S. firm's real cost of hedging Japanese yen receivables have been positive, negative, or about zero on average over the 1985–1987 time period? Explain.

33. If you are a U.S. importer of German goods, and you believe that today's forward rate of the mark is a very accurate estimate of the future spot rate, do you think German mark call options would be a more appropriate hedge than the forward hedge? Explain.

34. You are an exporter of goods to the United Kingdom, and you believe that today's forward rate of the British pound substantially underestimates the future spot rate. Company policy requires you to hedge your British pound receivables in some way. Would a forward hedge or put option hedge be more appropriate? Explain.

35. Explain how a French firm can use the forward market to hedge periodic purchases of U.S. goods denominated in U.S. dollars.

36. Explain how a German firm can use the forward market to hedge periodic sales of goods sold to the U.S. that are invoiced in dollars.

37. Explain how a French firm can use the forward market to hedge periodic purchases of Japanese goods denominated in yen.

38. Cornell Company purchases computer chips on a monthly basis from a Japanese supplier that are denominated in yen. To hedge its exchange rate risk, this U.S. firm negotiates a three-month forward contract three months before the next order will arrive. In other words, Cornell is always covered for the next three monthly shipments. Because Cornell consistently hedges in this manner, it is not concerned with exchange rate movements. Is Cornell insulated from exchange rate movements? Explain.

39. Malibu Inc. is a U.S. company that imports British goods. It plans to use call options to hedge payables of £100,000 in 90 days. Three call options are available with an expiration date 90 days from now. Fill in the number of dollars needed to pay for the payables (including the option premium paid) for each option available under each possible scenario.

Scenario	Spot Rate of Pound 90 Days from Now	Exercise Price = $1.74; Premium = $.06	Exercise Price = $1.76; Premium = $.05	Exercise Price = $1.79; Premium = $.03
1	$1.65			
2	1.70			
3	1.75			
4	1.80			
5	1.85			

If each of the five scenarios had an equal probability of occurrence, which option would you choose? Explain.

Blackhawk Company
Forecasting Exchange Rates and the Hedging Decision

This case is intended to illustrate how forecasting exchange rates and hedging decisions are related. Blackhawk Company plans to purchase DM800,000 one quarter from now to pay for imports. As Treasurer of Blackhawk, you are responsible for determining whether and how to hedge this payables position. Several tasks will need to be completed for you to make these decisions. The entire analysis can be performed using LOTUS.

Your first goal is to assess three different models for forecasting the value of DM at the end of the quarter (also called the future spot rate, or FSR):

- Using the forward rate (FR) at the beginning of the quarter
- Using the spot rate (SR) at the beginning of the quarter
- Estimating the historical influence of the inflation differential during each quarter on the percentage change in the DM (which leads to a forecast of the FSR of the DM).

The historical data to be used for this analysis are provided in the following table.

Quarter	Spot Rate of DM at the Beginning of the Quarter	90-Day Forward Rate of DM at the Beginning of the Quarter	Spot Rate of DM at End of Quarter	Last Quarter's Inflation Differential	Percentage Change in DM Over Quarter
1	$.3177	$.3250	$.3233	−.05%	1.76%
2	.3233	.3272	.3267	−.46	1.05
3	.3267	.3285	.3746	.66	14.66
4	.3746	.3778	.4063	.94	8.46
5	.4063	.4093	.4315	.58	6.20
6	.4315	.4344	.4548	.23	5.40
7	.4548	.4572	.4949	.02	8.82
8	.4949	.4966	.5153	1.26	4.12
9	.5153	.5169	.5540	.86	7.51
10	.5540	.5574	.5465	.54	−1.35
11	.5465	.5510	.5440	1.00	−.46
12	.5440	.5488	.6309	1.09	15.97
13	.6309	.6365	.6027	.78	−4.47
14	.6027	.6081	.5409	.23	−10.25
15	.5491	.5538	.5320	.71	−3.11
16	.5320	.5365	.5617	1.18	5.58
17	.5617	.5667	.5283	.70	−5.95
18	.5283	.5334	.5122	−.31	−3.05
19	.5122	.5149	.5352	.62	4.49
20	.5352	.5372	.5890	.87	10.05
21(Now)	.5890	.5878	to be forecasted	.28	to be forecasted

a) Use regression analysis to determine whether the forward rate is an unbiased estimator of the spot rate at the end of the quarter.

b) Use the simplified approach of assessing the signs of forecast errors over time. Do you detect any bias when using the FR to forecast? Explain.

c) Determine the average absolute forecast error when using the forward rate to forecast.

d) Determine whether the spot rate of the DM at the beginning of the quarter is an unbiased estimator of the spot rate at the end of the quarter using regression analysis.

e) Use the simplified approach of assessing the signs of forecast errors over time. Do you detect any bias when using the SR to forecast? Explain.

f) Determine the average absolute forecast error when using the spot rate to forecast. Was the spot rate or the forward rate a more accurate forecast of the FSR? Explain.

g) Use the following regression model to determine the relationship between the inflation differential (called DIFF, and defined as the U.S. inflation minus German inflation) and the percentage change in the DM (called PDM):

$$PDM = b_0 + b_1 \, DIFF$$

Once you have determined the coefficients b_0 and b_1, use them to forecast PDM based on a forecast of 2% for DIFF in the upcoming quarter. Then apply your forecast for PDM to the prevailing spot rate (which is \$.589) to derive the expected FSR of the DM.

h) Blackhawk plans to develop a probability distribution for the FSR. First, it will assign a 40 percent probability to the forecast of FSR derived from regression analysis in the previous question. Second, it will assign a 40 percent probability to the forecast of FSR based on either the forward rate or spot rate (whichever was more accurate according to your earlier analysis). Third, it will assign a 20 percent probability to the forecast of FSR based on either the forward rate or spot rate (whichever was less accurate according to your earlier analysis).
Fill in the table that follows:

Probability	FSR
40	
40	
20	

i) Assuming that Blackhawk does not hedge, fill in the following table.

Probability	Forecasted Dollar Amount Needed to Pay for Imports in 90 Days
40	
40	
20	

j) Based on the probability distribution for the FSR, use the table that follows to determine the probability distribution for the real cost of hedging if a forward contract is used for hedging (recall that the prevailing 90-day forward rate is \$.5878).

Probability	Forecasted Dollar Amount Needed if Hedged With a Forward Contract	Forecasted Amount Needed if Unhedged	Forecasted Real Cost of Hedging Payables
40			
40			
20			

k) If Blackhawk hedges its position, it will use either a 90-day forward rate, a money market hedge, or a call option. The following data is available at the time of its decision.

- Spot rate   = $.589
- 90-Day forward rate   = $.5878
- 90-Day U.S. borrowing rate   =   2.5%
- 90-Day U.S. investing rate   =   2.3%
- 90-Day German borrowing rate   =   2.4%
- 90-Day German investing rate   =   2.1%
- Call option on DM has a premium of $.01 per unit
- Call option on DM has an exercise price of $.60

Determine the probability distribution of dollars needed for a call option if used (include the premium paid) by filling out the table below:

Probability	FSR	Dollars Needed to Pay for Payables
40%		
40		
20		

l) Compare the forward hedge to the money market hedge. Which is superior? Why?

m) Compare either the forward hedge or the money market hedge (whichever is better) to the call option hedge. If you hedge, which technique would you use? Why?

n) Compare whatever hedge you believe is the best to an unhedged strategy. Would you hedge or remain unhedged? Explain.

PROJECTS

1. Assume that your company needed 100,000 units of a foreign currency every quarter to purchase foreign supplies. Use the Data Bank in the back of the text to determine the real cost of hedging with that currency. (Choose a currency.) Identify periods in which the real cost of hedging was typically positive. Was the dollar strengthening or weakening in those periods? Explain. (This exercise could easily be set up on a spreadsheet first to reduce your computational time).

2. Repeat the preceding project, except assume that you will receive 100,000 units of a foreign currency every quarter.

SUGGESTED READING

Judy C. Lewent and A. John Kearney. "Identifying, Measuring, and Hedging Currency Risk at Merck." *Journal of Applied Corporate Finance* (Winter 1990), pp. 19–28. This article clearly illustrates how fore-casting exchange rates, measuring exposure, and the hedging decision are interrelated at The Merck & Co., a huge pharmaceutical MNC with annual sales of over $6 billion.

REFERENCES

Boothe, Robert, and Jeff Madura. "Reducing Exposure to Exchange Rate Risk: A Case Study." *Long-Range Planning* (June 1985), pp. 98–101.

"By Trading Currencies, Kodak's Eric Nelson Saves the Firm Millions." *The Wall Street Journal*, March 5, 1985.

Calderon-Rossell, Jorge R. "Covering Foreign Exchange Risks of Single Transactions: A Framework for Analysis." *Financial Management* (Autumn 1979), pp. 78–85.

Chrystal, K. Alec. "A Guide to Foreign Exchange Markets," *Review*, Federal Reserve Bank of St. Louis (March 1984), pp. 5–18.

Dufey, Gunter, and S. L. Srinivasulu. "The Case for Corporate Management of Foreign Exchange Risk." *Financial Management* (Winter 1983), pp. 54–62.

Eaker, Mark R. "The Numeraire Problem and Foreign Exchange Risk." *Journal of Finance* (May 1981), pp. 419–426.

Fieleke, Norman S. "The 1971 Flotation of the Mark and the Hedging of Commercial Transactions Between the United States and Germany." *Journal of International Business Studies* (Spring 1973), pp. 43–59.

Giddy, Ian H. "Exchange Risk: Whose View?" *Financial Management* (Summer 1977), pp. 23–33.

Gull, Don S. "Composite Foreign Exchange Risk." *The Columbia Journal of World Business* (Fall 1975), pp. 51–69.

Hammer, Jerry A., "Hedging Performance and Hedging Objectives: Tests of New Performance Measures in the Foreign Currency Market", *Journal of Financial Research* (Winter 1990), pp. 307–324.

Hekman, Christine R. "Measuring Foreign Exchange Exposure: A Practical Theory and Its Application." *Financial Analysts Journal* (September–October 1983), pp. 59–65.

Imai, Yutaka. "Exchange Rate Risk Protection in International Business." *Journal of Financial and Quantitative Analysis* (September 1975), pp. 447–456.

Jacque, Laurent L. "Management of Foreign Exchange Risk: A Review Article." *Journal of International Business Studies* (Spring–Summer 1981), pp. 81–99.

Johnson, R. Stafford, and Richard A. Zuber. "Currency Cocktail Diversification and the Reduction of Exchange Rate Risk." *Atlantic Economic Journal* (September 1980), p. 67.

Kaufold, Howard, and Michael Smirlock. "Managing Corporate Exchange and Interest Rate Exposure." *Financial Management* (Autumn 1986), pp. 64–72.

Kohlhagen, Steven W. "A Model of Optimal Foreign Exchange Hedging without Exchange Rate Projections." *Journal of International Business Studies* (Fall 1978), pp. 9–19.

Kwok, Chuck. "Hedging Foreign Exchange Exposures: Independent vs. Integrative Approaches," *Journal of International Business Studies* (Summer 1987), pp. 33–52.

Lessard, Donald R., and John B. Lightstone. "Volatile Exchange Rates Can Put Operations at Risk." *Harvard Business Review* (July–August 1986), pp. 107–114.

Logue, Dennis E., and George S. Oldfield. "Managing Foreign Assets When Foreign Exchange Markets Are Efficient." *Financial Management* (Summer 1977), pp. 16–22.

Madura, Jeff. "Assessment of Exchange Rate Risk from Various Country Perspectives." *International Review of Economics and Business*, (July 1990), pp. 655–666.

Madura, Jeff. "Empirical Measurement of Exchange Rate Betas." *The Journal of Portfolio Management* (Summer 1983), pp. 43–45.

_____ . "Hedging With American Currency Options: A Five-Year Appraisal." *Journal of Business and Economic Perspectives*, (Spring 1990), pp. 35–38.

_____ . "The Real Costs of Hedging in the Forward Exchange Market: An Empirical Investigation." *Management International Review*, no. 2 (1984), pp. 24–27.

Madura, Jeff, and Richard Fosberg. "Intertemporal Exchange Rate Risk: Implications for Corporate Exposure." *International Review of Economics and Business* (October–November 1988), pp. 1053–1060.

Madura, Jeff, and E. Joe Nosari. "Utilizing Currency Portfolios to Mitigate Exchange Rate Risk." *Columbia Journal of World Business* (Spring 1984), pp. 96–99.

Madura, Jeff, and L. A. Soenen. "Asymmetric Risk Aversion and the Real Costs of Hedging in the Foreign Exchange Market." *European Journal of Accounting and Finance* (July–August 1985), pp. 304–309.

Madura, Jeff, and E. Theodore Veit. "Use of Currency Options for International Cash Management." *Journal of Cash Management* (January–February 1986), pp. 42–48.

Makin, John H. "Portfolio Theory and the Problem of Foreign Exchange Risk." *The Journal of Finance* 33 (May 1978), pp. 517–534.

Rodriguez, Rita M. "Corporate Exchange Risk Management: Theme and Aberrations." *Journal of Finance* (May 1981), pp. 427–439.

_____ . "Management of Foreign Exchange Risk in U.S. Multinationals." *Sloan Management Review* (Spring 1978), pp. 31–49.

Serfass, William D., Jr. "You Can't Outguess the Foreign Exchange Market." *Harvard Business Review* (March–April, 1976), pp. 134–137.

Shapiro, Alan C., and Rutenberg, David P. "Managing Exchange Risks in a Floating World." *Financial Management* (Summer 1976), pp. 48–58.

Soenen, L. A., and E. F. Van Winkel, "The Real Costs of Hedging in the Forward Exchange Market," *Management International Review*, no. 1 (1982), pp. 53–59.

Srinivasulu, S. L. "Currency Denomination of Debt: Lessons from Rolls-Royce and Laker Airways." *Business Horizons* (September–October 1983), pp. 19–23.

Stanley, Marjorie T., and Stanley B. Block. "Portfolio Diversification of Foreign Exchange Risk: An Empirical Study," *Management International Review*, no. 1, (1980), pp. 83–92.

Swanson, Peggy, and Stephen Caples. "Hedging Foreign Exchange Risk Using Forward Foreign Exchange Markets: An Extension." *Journal of International Business Studies*, (Spring 1987), pp. 75–82.

Westerfield, Janice M. "How U.S. Multinationals Manage Currency Risk." *Business Review* (March–April 1980), pp. 19–27.

Yang, James G.S. "Managing Multinational Exchange Risks." *Management Accounting* (February 1986), pp. 45–52.

CHAPTER 12

Managing Economic Exposure and Translation Exposure

This chapter explains how economic exposure and translation exposure can be managed. Because the characteristics of these types of exposure differ from those of transaction exposure, the techniques used to manage the exposure also differ. In general, it is more difficult to effectively hedge economic or translation exposure than transaction exposure for reasons explained in this chapter.

MANAGING ECONOMIC EXPOSURE

From a U.S. firm's perspective, transaction exposure represents only the exchange rate risk when converting net foreign cash inflows to U.S. dollars, or when purchasing foreign currencies to send outflow payments. Economic exposure represents any impact of exchange rate fluctuations on a firm's future cash flows. For example, a stronger dollar may encourage U.S. purchases of foreign goods rather than of U.S. goods. Thus, a U.S. firm's cash flows can be affected by exchange rate movements in ways not directly associated with its foreign transactions.

Example of Managing Economic Exposure

To illustrate how economic exposure can be managed, reconsider the case of Madison Inc. discussed in Chapter 10. Madison's economic exposure to exchange rate movements can be assessed by determining the sensitivity of expenses and revenues to various possible exchange rate scenarios. The original revenue and expense information from Exhibit 10.10 of Chapter 10 is restated in Exhibit 12.1. The U.S. revenues are assumed to be sensitive to different exchange rate scenarios because of the foreign competition. Canadian sales are anticipated to be C$4 million, regardless of the exchange rate scenario. Yet, the dollar amount received from these sales would depend on the scenario. The cost of goods sold attributable to U.S. orders is assumed to be $50 million, and insensitive to exchange rate movements. The cost of

EXHIBIT 12.1 Original Impact of Exchange Rate Movements on Earnings: Madison Inc. *(in millions)*

	C$ = $.75		C$ = $.80		C$ = $.85	
Sales						
(1) U.S.		$300		$304		$307
(2) Canadian	C$4 =	$ 3	C$4 =	$ 3.2	C$4 =	$ 3.4
(3) Total		$303		$307.2		$310.4
Cost of goods sold						
(4) U.S.		$ 50		$ 50		$ 50
(5) Canadian	C$200 =	$150	C$200 =	$160	C$200 =	$170
(6) Total		$200		$210		$220
(7) Gross profit		$103		$ 97.2		90.4
Operating expenses						
(8) U.S.: Fixed		$ 30		$ 30		$ 30
(9) U.S.: Variable (10% of total sales)		$ 30.3		$ 30.72		$ 31.04
(10) Total		$ 60.3		$ 60.72		$ 61.04
(11) Earnings before interest and taxes		$ 42.7		$ 36.48		$ 29.36
Interest expense						
(12) U.S.		$ 3		$ 3		$ 3
(13) Canadian	C$10 =	$ 7.5	C$10 =	$ 8	C$10 =	$ 8.5
(14) Total		$ 10.5		$ 11		$ 11.5
(15) Earnings before taxes		$ 32.2		$ 25.48		$ 17.86

goods sold attributable to Canadian orders is assumed to be C$200 million. The U.S. dollar amount of this cost varies with the exchange rate scenario. The gross profit shown in Exhibit 12.1 is determined by subtracting the total dollar value of cost of goods sold from total dollar value of sales.

Operating expenses are separated into fixed and variable. The fixed expenses are $30 million per year, while the projected variable expenses are dictated by projected sales. The earnings before interest and taxes are determined by the total U.S. dollar amount of gross profit minus total U.S. dollar amount of operating expenses. The interest owed to U.S. banks is insensitive to the exchange rate scenario. However, the projected dollars needed to pay interest on existing Canadian loans varies with the exchange rate scenario. Earnings before taxes is estimated by subtracting total interest expenses from earnings before interest and taxes.

Exhibit 12.1 enabled Madison to assess how its income statement items would be affected by different exchange rate movements. A stronger Canadian dollar results in an increase in Madison's U.S. sales and in the dollar revenues earned from Canadian sales. However, it also increases Madison's cost of materials purchased from Canada and its amount of dollars needed to pay interest on loans from Canadian banks. The higher expenses more than offset the higher revenues in the strong Canadian dollar scenario. Thus, the amount of Madison's earnings before taxes is inversely related to the strength of the Canadian dollar.

If the Canadian dollar strengthens consistently over the long run, Madison's cost of goods sold and interest expenses will likely rise at a higher rate than U.S. dollar revenues. Consequently, it may wish to enact some policies to create a more balanced impact of Canadian dollar movements on its revenues and expenses. At the present time, its high exposure to exchange rate movements is due to its expenses being more susceptible than its revenues to the changing value of the Canadian dollar. A policy to either increase Canadian sales or reduce orders of Canadian materials would provide more balance.

Effect of Restructured Operations on Economic Exposure

Assume that Madison decides to create more balance by increasing Canadian sales. It believes that it can achieve Canadian sales of C$20 million if it spends $2 million more on advertising (which is part of its fixed operating expenses). The increased sales will also require an additional expenditure of $10 million on materials from U.S. suppliers. In addition, it plans to reduce its reliance on Canadian suppliers and increase its reliance on U.S. suppliers. This strategy is expected to reduce the cost of goods sold attributable to Canadian suppliers by C$100 million and increase the cost of goods sold attributable to U.S. suppliers by $80 million (not including the $10 million increase resulting from increased sales to the Canadian market). Furthermore, it plans to borrow additional funds in the United States and retire some existing loans from Canadian banks. The result will be an additional interest expense of $4 million to U.S. banks and a reduction of C$5 million owed to Canadian banks. The anticipated impact of these strategies on the projected income statement is shown in Exhibit 12.2. For each of the three exchange rate scenarios, the initial projections are in the left column while the revised projections (as a result of the proposed strategy) are in the right column.

Each of the revised estimates of the income statement items will be explained. First, the projected total sales increased in response to intentions of penetrating the Canadian market. Second, the U.S. cost of goods sold is now $90 million higher than before, resulting from a $10 million increase to accommodate increased Canadian sales, and an $80 million increase due to the shift from Canadian suppliers to U.S. suppliers. The Canadian cost of goods sold decreased from C$200 million to C$100 million as a result of this shift. The revised fixed operating expenses of $32 million include the increase in advertising expenses necessary to penetrate the Canadian market. The variable operating expenses were revised because of revised estimates for total sales. The interest expenses were revised because of the increased loans from the U.S. banks and reduced loans from Canadian banks.

If Madison increases its Canadian dollar inflows and reduces its Canadian dollar outflows as proposed, its revenues and expenses will be affected by Canadian dollar movements in a somewhat similar manner. Thus, its performance would be less susceptible to movements in the Canadian dollar. Exhibit 12.3 illustrates the sensitivity of Madison's earnings before taxes to the three exchange rate scenarios (derived from Exhibit 12.2). The reduced sensitivity of Madison's proposed restructured operations to exchange rate movements is obvious.

The way a firm restructures its operations to reduce economic exposure to exchange rate risk depends on the form of exposure. For Madison Inc., future expenses were more sensitive than future revenues to the possible values of

EXHIBIT 12.2 Comparing the Impact of Possible Exchange Rate Movements on Earnings under Two Alternative Operational Structures *(in millions)*

	Exchange Rate Scenario C$ = $.75		Exchange Rate Scenario C$ = $.80		Exchange Rate Scenario C$ = $.85	
	Original Operational Structure	*Proposed Operational Structure*	*Original Operational Structure*	*Proposed Operational Structure*	*Original Operational Structure*	*Proposed Operational Structure*
Sales						
U.S.	$300	$300	$304	$304	$307	$307
Canadian	C$4 = $ 3	C$20 = $ 15	C$4 = $ 3.2	C$20 = $ 16	C$4 = $ 3.4	C$20 = $ 17
Total	$303	$315	$307.2	$320	$310.4	$324
Cost of goods sold						
U.S.	$ 50	$140	$ 50	$140	$ 50	$140
Canadian	C$200 = $150	C$100 = $ 75	C$200 = $160	C$100 = $ 80	C$200 = $170	C$100 = $ 85
Total	$200	$215	$210	$220	$220	$225
Gross profit	103	100	$ 97.2	$100	$ 90.4	$ 99
Operating expenses						
U.S.: Fixed	$ 30	$ 32	$ 30	$ 32	$ 30	$ 32
U.S.: Variable (10% of total sales)	$ 30.3	$ 31.5	$ 30.72	$ 32	$ 31.04	$ 32.4
Total	$ 60.3	$ 63.5	$ 60.72	$ 64	$ 61.04	$ 64.4
Earnings before interest and taxes	$ 42.7	$ 36.5	$ 36.48	$ 36	$ 29.36	$ 34.6
Interest expense						
U.S.	$ 3	$ 7	$ 3	$ 7	$ 3	$ 7
Canadian	C$10 = $ 7.5	C$5 = $ 3.75	C$10 = $ 8	C$5 = $ 4	C$10 = $ 8.5	C$5 = $ 4.25
Total	$ 10.5	$ 10.75	$ 11	$ 11	$ 11.5	$ 11.25
Earnings before taxes	$ 32.2	$ 25.75	$ 25.48	$ 25	$ 17.86	$ 23.35

EXHIBIT 12.3 Economic Exposure Based on the Original and Proposed Operating Structures

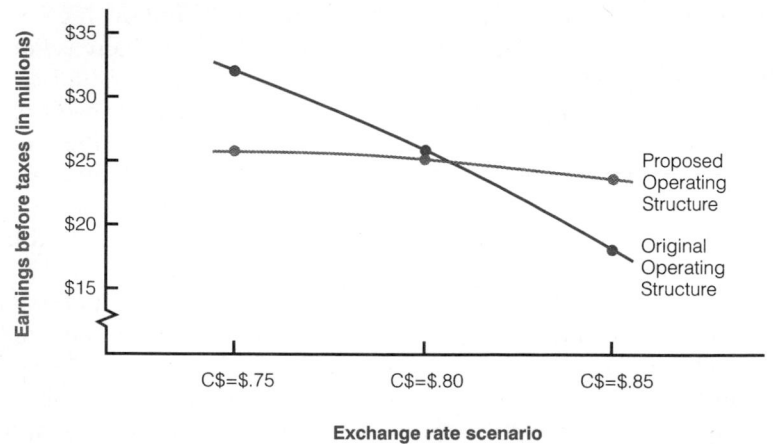

a foreign currency. Therefore, economic exposure could be reduced by increasing the sensitivity of revenues and reducing the sensitivity of expenses to exchange rate movements. Firms that have a greater amount of exchange rate-sensitive revenues than expenses, however, would reduce economic exposure by decreasing the amount of exchange rate-sensitive revenues, or by increasing the amount of exchange rate-sensitive expenses.

It should be mentioned that some revenues or expenses may be more exchange rate-sensitive than others. Therefore, simply matching the amount of exchange rate-sensitive revenues to the amount of exchange rate-sensitive expenses may not completely insulate a firm from exchange rate risk. The firm can best evaluate a proposed restructuring of operations by forecasting various income-statement items for various possible exchange rate scenarios (as shown in Exhibit 12.2) and then assessing the sensitivity of earnings to these different scenarios.

Determining the sensitivity of earnings before taxes to alternative exchange rate scenarios could also be expedited by computer. A spreadsheet similar to Exhibit 12.2 could be created. Forecasts could be input by the analyst for items such as sales, cost of goods sold, and fixed operating expenses. The remaining items could be defined by formula, so that they could be estimated by computer after forecasts of the other items are input. For example, the exchange rate forecast influences projections of (1) dollars received from Canadian sales, (2) cost of goods sold attributable to purchases of Canadian materials, and (3) amount of dollars needed to cover the Canadian interest payments. The firm could revise the input in accordance with proposed restructured operations, in order to determine how economic exposure would be affected. A computerized spreadsheet would allow the analyst to assess several possible operational structures.

Recall that Madison Inc. assessed one alternative operational structure where it increased foreign Canadian sales by C$16 million, reduced its purchases of Canadian materials by C$100 million, and reduced its interest owed to Canadian banks by C$5 million. If it had computerized the spreadsheet, it could have easily assessed the impact of alternative strategies such as increasing Canadian sales by other amounts and/or reducing the Canadian expenses by other amounts. This would have offered Madison more information about its economic exposure under various operational structures and would therefore have enabled it to devise the operational structure that would reduce economic exposure to the degree desired.

The previous discussion entails assessing economic exposure under various scenarios and therefore is closely related to Chapter 10. However, the reason for assessing the different scenarios is to identify an operational structure that can reduce economic exposure to a tolerable level. If the sensitivity of earnings to possible exchange rate movements is tolerable under the existing operational structure, then the operations do not need to be restructured.

When deciding how to restructure operations to reduce economic exposure, one must address the following questions:

■ Should the firm attempt to increase or reduce sales in new or existing foreign markets?
■ Should the firm increase or reduce its dependency on foreign suppliers?

INTERNATIONAL FINANCIAL MANAGEMENT IN PRACTICE

Hedging "Soft" Currencies

Firms that recently capitalized on the free enterprise in Eastern Europe have a peculiar type of exposure to exchange rate risk. The "soft" currencies of the Eastern Europe countries are not convertible into so-called "hard" currencies that are traded around the world. Firms are using a variety of strategies to deal with this problem. For example, Digital Equipment Corp. opened a sales office in Hungary. Since most of its customers there are from Western Europe, it requires payment in hard currencies.

In April 1990, Pepsi Co. reached an agreement with the Soviet Union to double its production of Pepsi and to build Pizza Huts in Moscow. The deal is valued at about $3 billion. Rather than accept the Soviet currency (rubles), which are not convertible into dollars or any other widely traded currency, Pepsi Co. will receive ten ships (mostly oil tankers) and vodka made in the Soviet Union.

Even if the ruble becomes convertible someday, it is expected to be devalued with respect to other currencies over time. Thus, the cash flows to Pepsi Co. would be reduced by devaluation, especially if conversion of all rubles were not allowed until after the devaluation. While Pepsi Co. has avoided exchange rate risk, its future cash flows from this deal are still uncertain. How much can ten ships and vodka be sold for in the United States? However, even though the ultimate cash flows to Pepsi Co. from this deal are not known, there is less uncertainty than if the company had accepted rubles.

In 1991, Gillette Company negotiated to exchange rubles for dollars on a Soviet joint venture. This was a major achievement, since the Soviet Union normally has not allowed such an exchange. The exchange rate for this deal has been set at six rubles per dollar.

■ Should the firm establish or eliminate production facilities in foreign markets?
■ Should the firm increase or reduce its level of debt denominated in foreign currencies?

Each of these four questions reflects a different part of the firm's income statement. This first relates to foreign cash inflows and the remaining ones to foreign cash outflows. Some of the more common solutions to balancing a foreign currency's inflows and outflows are summarized in Exhibit 12.4. Any restructuring of operations that can reduce the periodic balance between a foreign currency's inflows and outflows can reduce the firm's economic exposure to that currency's movements.

MNCs that have production and marketing facilities in various countries may be able to shift their allocation of operations in order to reduce any adverse impact of economic exposure. For example, consider a U.S.-based MNC that produces products in the United States, France, and Great Britain and sells these products to several countries. If the German mark strengthens against many currencies, the MNC may boost production in Great Britain, expecting a decline in demand for the German subsidiary's products. The MNC parent may even request that some machinery be transported from

EXHIBIT 12.4 How to Restructure Operations to Balance the Impact of Currency Movements on Cash Inflows and Outflows

Type of Operation	When a Foreign Currency Has a Greater Impact on Cash Inflows	When a Foreign Currency Has a Greater Impact on Cash Outflows
Sales in foreign currency units	Reduce foreign sales	Increase foreign sales
Reliance on foreign supplies	Increase foreign supply orders	Reduce foreign supply orders
Proportion of debt structure representing foreign debt	Restructure debt to increase debt payments in foreign currency	Restructure debt to reduce debt payments in foreign currency

West Germany to Great Britain and allocate more marketing funds to the British subsidiary at the expense of the German subsidiary. This type of strategy may forgo economies of scale that could be achieved if production were concentrated at one particular subsidiary while other subsidiaries focused on warehousing and distribution.

MANAGING TRANSLATION EXPOSURE

The distortion in consolidated income under Financial Accounting Standards Board No. 8 (FASB-8) rules resulting from volatile exchange rates led to proposals for revised accounting standards. As of December 1981, FASB No. 52 was adopted. FASB-52 requires the current exchange rate as of the reporting date to be used to translate the assets and liabilities of a foreign entity from its functional currency to the reporting currency. In addition, the weighted average exchange rate is used to translate revenue, expenses, and gains and losses of a foreign entity from its functional currency into the reporting currency. Translated income gains or losses due to changes in foreign currency values are not recognized in the current net income (except in the case of highly inflated countries), but are reported as a second component of stockholder's equity. This ruling is a dramatic departure from FASB-8, which included translation gains and losses in the income statement. While FASB-52 may be an improvement over FASB-8, the MNC is still subject to translation exposure.

Translation exposure results from an MNC translating each subsidiary's financial data to its home currency for consolidated financial statements. It is not cash flow but consolidated financial data that are exposed here. Because cash flow is not affected, some people would argue that it is not necessary to hedge or even reduce accounting exposure. Still, some firms are concerned with translation exposure because of its potential impact on reported consolidated earnings.

Some MNCs attempt to hedge their translation exposure by matching foreign liabilities with foreign assets. For example, Phillip Morris uses foreign financing to match their level of foreign assets.

To reduce translation exposure, a firm could use the same techniques employed to cover transaction exposure. Consider a U.S.-based MNC that has

INTERNATIONAL FINANCIAL MANAGEMENT IN PRACTICE

Economic Exposure of Laker Airways

To illustrate the importance of hedging economic exposure, consider the case of Laker Airways, a British Airline.[1] Laker generated about half of its revenues in dollars and half in British pounds. However, a large proportion of its expenses (such as fuel, oil, and debt payments) were denominated in dollars. As the dollar strengthened in 1981, Laker needed larger amounts of pounds to cover the dollar-denominated expenses.

In January 1981, Laker borrowed $131 million from a group of U.S. and European banks. The debt was denominated in U.S. dollars and therefore required debt repayments in U.S. dollars. By borrowing U.S. dollars in 1981, Laker further increased its degree of economic exposure. As the dollar continued to strengthen, the firm's revenues could not adequately cover its dollar-denominated expenses. Consequently, Laker Airways went bankrupt. It might have survived if it had reduced its economic exposure, either by reducing its dollar-denominated expenses or by increasing its dollar-denominated revenues.

[1]See S. L. Srinivasulu, "Currency Denomination of Debt: Lessons from Rolls-Royce and Laker Airways," *Business Horizons* (September–October 1983), pp. 19–23.

just one subsidiary located in Great Britain. Assume the British subsidiary as of the beginning of its fiscal year forecasts earnings at 20 million British pounds. Assume this subsidiary plans to reinvest the entire amount of earnings in Great Britain and does not plan to remit any earnings back to the parent in the United States. While there is no foreseeable transaction exposure from the future earnings (since the pounds will remain in Great Britain), translation exposure does exist for the MNC.

Based on FASB-52, the British earnings would be translated at the weighted average value of the pound over the course of the fiscal year. If the British pound is currently worth $1.50, and if its value was constant during the fiscal year, the forecasted translation of British earnings into U.S. dollars would be $30 million (computed as 20 million pounds × $1.50 per pound). Of course, the pound's value will not remain constant. Therefore, the translated subsidiary earnings will differ from $30 million.

The MNC may be concerned that the translated value of British earnings will be reduced if the pound's average value decreases during the year. To prevent this translation exposure, it could implement a forward hedge as follows. Recall that the expected earnings is 20 million pounds as of the start of the fiscal year. Assume the forward rate at that time is $1.50, the same as the spot rate. The MNC could sell 20 million pounds forward.

At the end of the fiscal year, the MNC could buy 20 million pounds at the spot rate and fulfill its forward contract obligation to sell 20 million pounds. If the pound depreciates during the fiscal year, then the MNC will be able to purchase pounds at the end of the fiscal year at a cheaper rate than it could sell them for ($1.50 per pound) to fulfill the forward contract. Thus, it will have generated income that could offset the translation loss. The translation loss is based on the pound depreciating during the year.

The precise level of income generated by the forward contract will depend on the spot rate of the pound at the end of the fiscal year. Under conditions where the pound depreciates, the translation loss will be somewhat offset by the gain generated from the forward contract position. This example illustrates how translation exposure can be reduced. However, there are limitations to such a strategy, addressed in the following section.

Limitations of Hedging Translation Exposure

There are several limitations on hedging translation exposure. First, a subsidiary's forecasted earnings for the end of the year are not guaranteed. In our example, British earnings were projected to be 20 million pounds. If the actual earnings turned out to be much higher, the translation loss in the previous example would likely exceed the gain generated from the forward contract strategy.

A second limitation is that forward contracts are not available for all currencies. Thus, an MNC with subsidiaries in some smaller countries may not be able to obtain forward contracts for the currencies of concern. It might, however, be able to implement a money market hedge against the translation exposure as follows.

The MNC could borrow the functional currency representing the subsidiary, convert the borrowed currency into its local currency, and use it to purchase a one-year money market instrument. At the end of one year, it could then cash in its money market instrument and purchase the subsidiary's currency. If the subsidiary's currency depreciates substantially during the one-year period, it can be purchased at a much lower rate than at the start of the year when it was borrowed. Income generated from this strategy would at least partially offset the translation loss resulting from the subsidiary's currency depreciating.

This strategy would be useful only if foreign exchange controls do not exist. Even then, the strategy is limited (as was the forward contract strategy) in that the projected subsidiary earnings are uncertain. Consequently, a perfect hedge (full coverage) on translation exposure is nearly impossible.

A third limitation is that the forward-rate gain or loss reflects the difference between the forward rate and future spot rate, whereas the translation gain or loss reflects the average exchange rate over the period of concern. In addition, the translation losses are not tax deductible, whereas gains on forward contracts used to hedge translation exposure are taxed.

The fourth and most critical limitation with a hedging strategy (forward or money market hedge) on translation exposure is that the MNC may be increasing its transaction exposure. For example, consider a situation where the subsidiary's currency appreciates during the fiscal year, resulting in a translation gain. If the MNC enacts a hedge strategy at the start of the fiscal year, this strategy will generate a transaction loss that will somewhat offset the translation gain. Some MNCs may not be comfortable with this offsetting effect. The translation gain is simply a paper gain; that is, the reported dollar value of earnings is higher due to the subsidiary currency's appreciation. Yet, the parent does not receive any more income due to this appreciation if the subsidiary reinvests the earnings. The MNC parent's net cash flow is not affected. Conversely, the loss resulting from a hedge strategy is a *real* loss. That is, the net cash flow to the parent will be reduced due to this loss. In this example, the MNC reduced its translation exposure at the expense of increasing its transaction exposure.

The main point of the preceding discussion is that if the MNC does desire to reduce translation exposure, the methods available to achieve this objective are limited in their effectiveness. In addition, MNCs must recognize the possibility of increasing their transaction exposure due to reducing their translation exposure. Under these conditions, MNCs concerned about translation exposure may decide not to hedge, since the benefits (reduced translation exposure) may be outweighed by the costs (increased transaction exposure).

Perhaps the best way for MNCs to deal with translation exposure is to clarify how their consolidated earnings were affected by exchange rate movements. In this way, shareholders and potential investors will be more aware of the translation effect. An unusually low level of consolidated earnings may not discourage shareholders and potential investors if it is attributed to translation of subsidiary earnings at low exchange rates.

Recall from Chapter 10 that some MNCs do not consider hedging translation exposure because they do not perceive this exposure to be relevant. For example, Phillips Petroleum has stated in its annual report that translation exposure is not hedged because translation effects do not influence cash flows. Many other MNCs follow a similar policy.

SUMMARY

Economic exposure can be managed by balancing the sensitivity of revenues and expenses to exchange rate fluctuations. To accomplish this, however, the firm must first recognize how its revenues and expenses are affected by exchange rate fluctuations. For some firms, revenues are more susceptible. These firms are most concerned that their home currency will appreciate against foreign currencies, since the unfavorable effects on revenues will more than offset the favorable effect on expenses. Conversely, firms whose expenses are more exchange rate-sensitive than revenues are most concerned that their home currency will depreciate against foreign currencies. When firms reduce their economic exposure, they reduce not only these unfavorable effects, but also the favorable effects if the home currency value moves in the opposite direction.

Translation exposure can be reduced by creating a short position in the foreign currency used to measure a subsidiary's income. If the foreign currency depreciates against the home currency, the adverse impact on the consolidated income statement can be offset by the gain on a short position in that currency. If the foreign currency appreciates over the time period of concern, there will be a loss on the short position that is offset by a favorable effect on the reported consolidated earnings. However, many MNCs would not be satisfied with a "paper gain" that offsets a "cash loss."

QUESTIONS/ PROBLEMS

1. St. Paul Company does business in the United States and West Germany. It is attempting to assess its economic exposure and has compiled the following information.

a) Its U.S. sales are somewhat affected by the German mark's value, because it faces competition from German exporters. It forecasts the U.S. sales based on the following three exchange rates scenarios.

Exchange Rate of Mark	Revenue from U.S. Business (in millions)
DM = $.48	$100
DM = .50	105
DM = .54	110

b) Its German mark revenues on sales to West Germany invoiced in marks are expected to be DM600 million.

c) Its anticipated cost of goods sold is estimated at $200 million from the purchase of U.S. materials and DM100 million from the purchase of German materials.

d) Fixed operating expenses are estimated at $30 million.

e) Variable operating expenses are estimated at 20 percent of total sales (after including German sales, translated to a dollar amount).

f) Interest expense is estimated at $20 million on existing U.S. loans, and the company has no existing German loans.

Create a forecasted income statement for St. Paul Company under each of the three exchange rate scenarios. Explain how St. Paul's projected earnings before taxes are affected by possible exchange rate movements. Explain how it can restructure its operations to reduce the sensitivity of its earnings to exchange rate movements, without reducing its volume of business in West Germany.

2. Baltimore Inc. is a U.S.-based MNC that obtains 10 percent of its supplies from European manufacturers. Sixty percent of its revenues are in Europe, where its product is invoiced in European currencies. Explain how Baltimore Inc. could attempt to reduce its economic exposure to exchange rate fluctuations.

3. UVA Company is a U.S.-based MNC that obtains 40 percent of its foreign supplies from Switzerland. It also borrows Swiss francs from Swiss banks and converts the francs to dollars to support U.S. operations. It presently receives about 10 percent of its revenues from Swiss customers. Its sales to Swiss customers are denominated in francs. Explain how UVA Company can reduce its economic exposure to exchange rate fluctuations.

4. Albany Corporation is a U.S.-based MNC that has a large government contract with West Germany. The contract will continue for several years and generate more than half of Albany's total sales volume. The West German government pays Albany in German marks. About 10 percent of Albany's operating expenses are in German marks; all other expenses are in U.S. dollars. Explain how Albany Company can reduce its economic exposure to exchange rate fluctuations.

5. When an MNC restructures its operations to reduce its economic exposure, it may sometimes forego economies of scale. Explain.

6. Explain how a U.S.-based MNC's consolidated earnings are affected if the dollar weakened against most foreign currencies.

7. Explain how a firm can hedge its translation exposure.

8. Explain some limitations of hedging translation exposure.

9. Would a more established MNC or a less established MNC be more capable of effectively hedging its given level of translation exposure. Why?

10. If U.S.-based MNCs are concerned with how shareholders' react to changes in consolidated earnings, but prefer not to hedge their translation exposure, how can they attempt to reduce shareholder reaction to a decline in consolidated earnings that results from a strengthened dollar?

11. Carlton Company and Palmer Inc. are U.S.-based MNCs with subsidiaries in Germany that distribute medical supplies (produced in the United States) to customers throughout Europe. Both subsidiaries purchase the products at cost and sell the products at 90 percent mark-up. The other operating costs of the subsidiary are very low. Carlton Company has a research and development center in the United States which focuses on improving its medical technology. Palmer Inc. has a similar center that is based in France. The parent of each firm subsidizes its respective research and development center on an annual basis. Which firm is subject to a higher degree of economic exposure? Explain.

12. Nelson Company is a U.S. firm with annual export sales of about DM800 million. Its main competitor is Mez Company, also based in the United States, with a subsidiary in Germany that generates about DM800 million in annual sales. Any earnings generated by the subsidiary are reinvested to support its operations. Based on the information provided, which firm is subject to a higher degree of translation exposure? Explain.

Madison, Inc.

Assessing Economic Exposure

The situation for Madison, Inc. was described in this chapter to illustrate how alternative operational structures could affect economic exposure to exchange rate movements. Ken Moore, the vice-president of finance at Madison, Inc., was seriously considering a shift to the proposed operational structure described in the text. He was determined to stabilize the earnings before taxes and believed that the proposed approach would achieve this objective. The firm expected that the Canadian dollar would consistently depreciate over the next several years. Over time, it has been very accurate in its forecasts. Moore paid little attention to the forecasts, stating that regardless of how the Canadian dollar changed, future earnings would be more stable under the proposed operational structure. He also was constantly reminded of how the strengthened Canadian dollar from 1986 to 1991 had adversely affected the firm's earnings. In fact, he was somewhat concerned that he might even lose his job if the adverse effects from economic exposure continued throughout the 1990s.

    a) Would a revised operational structure at this time be in the best interests of the shareholders? Would it be in the best interests of the vice-president?

    b) How could a revised operational structure possibly be feasible from the vice-president's perspective but not from the shareholder's perspective?

Explain how the firm might be able to assure that the vice-president make decisions related to economic exposure that were in the best interests of the shareholders.

1. Many annual reports of MNCs indicate where their operations are located. Use this information to suggest how the MNC could restructure its operations (without reducing its foreign business) to reduce exposure. Refer back to the chapter for an example. Your analysis may need to be more generalized than the example used in the chapter because you will not have specific details.

PROJECT

SUGGESTED READING

Eugene Flood, Jr., and Donald R. Lessard. "On the Measurement of Operating Exposure to Exchange Rates: A Conceptual Approach." (Spring 1986), pp. 25–36. This article offers valuable insight on an MNC's economic exposure to exchange rate risk.

REFERENCES

Boothe, Robert, and Jeff Madura. "Reducing Exposure to Exchange Rate Risk: A Case Study." *Long-Range Planning* (June 1985), pp. 98–101.

Calderon-Rossell, Jorge R. "Covering Foreign Exchange Risks of Single Transactions: A Framework for Analysis." *Financial Management* (Autumn 1979), pp. 78–85.

Eaker, Mark R. "The Numeraire Problem and Foreign Exchange Risk." *Journal of Finance* (May 1981), pp. 419–426.

Giddy, Ian H. "Exchange Risk: Whose View?" *Financial Management* (Summer 1977), pp. 23–33.

Hekman, Christine R. "Measuring Foreign Exchange Exposure: A Practical Theory and Its Application." *Financial Analysts Journal* (September–October 1983), pp. 59–65.

Imai, Yutaka. "Exchange Rate Risk Protection in International Business." *Journal of Financial and Quantitative Analysis* (September 1975), pp. 447–456.

Jacque, Laurent L. "Management of Foreign Exchange Risk: A Review Article." *Journal of International Business Studies* (Spring–Summer 1981), pp. 81–99.

Kaufold, Howard, and Michael Smirlock. "Managing Corporate Exchange and Interest Rate Exposure." *Financial Management* (Autumn 1986), pp. 64–72.

Kohlhagen, Steven W. "A Model of Optimal Foreign Exchange Hedging Without Exchange Rate Projections." *Journal of International Business Studies* (Fall 1978), pp. 9–19.

Logue, Dennis E., and George S. Oldfield. "Managing Foreign Assets When Foreign Exchange Markets Are Efficient." *Financial Management* (Summer 1977), pp. 16–22.

Madura, Jeff. "Empirical Measurement of Exchange Rate Betas." *The Journal of Portfolio Management* (Summer 1983), pp. 43–45.

———. "The Real Costs of Hedging in the Forward Exchange Market: An Empirical Investigation." *Management International Review*, no. 2 (1984), pp. 24–27.

Madura, Jeff. "Is Long-term Hedging Worthwhile?" *Journal of Financial and Strategic Decisions*, forthcoming.

Madura, Jeff. "Assessment of Exchange Rate Risk from Various Country Perspectives." *International Review of Economics and Business*, (July 1990), pp. 655–666.

Madura, Jeff, and E. Joe Nosari. "Utilizing Currency Portfolios to Mitigate Exchange Rate Risk." *Columbia Journal of World Business* (Spring 1984), pp. 96–99.

Madura, Jeff, and L.A. Soenen. "Asymmetric Risk Aversion and the Real Costs of Hedging in the Foreign Exchange Market." *European Journal of Accounting and Finance* (July–August 1985), pp. 304–309.

Madura, Jeff, and Alan L. Tucker, "Intertemporal Shifts in Actual and Anticipated Exchange Rate Volatility." *Journal of Global Business*, (Summer 1990), pp. 5–10.

Madura, Jeff, and E. Theodore Veit. "Use of Currency Options for International Cash Management." *Journal of Cash Management* (January–February 1986), pp. 42–48.

Makin, John H. "Portfolio Theory and the Problem of Foreign Exchange Risk." *The Journal of Finance* 33 (May 1978), pp. 517–534.

Rodriguez, Rita M. "Corporate Exchange Risk Management: Theme and Aberrations." *Journal of Finance* (May 1981), pp. 427–439.

Rodriguez, Rita M. "Management of Foreign Exchange Risk in U.S. Multinationals." *Sloan Management Review* (Spring 1978), pp. 31–49.

Shapiro, Alan C., and Rutenberg, David P. "Managing Exchange Risks in a Floating World." *Financial Management* (Summer 1976), pp. 48–58.

Soenen, L. A., and E. F. Van Winkel, "The Real Costs of Hedging in the Forward Exchange Market," *Management International Review*, no. 1 (1982), pp. 53–59.

Srinivasulu, S. L. "Currency Denomination of Debt: Lessons from Rolls-Royce and Laker Airways." *Business Horizons* (September–October 1983), pp. 19–23.

Stanley, Marjorie T., and Stanley B. Block. "Portfolio Diversification of Foreign Exchange Risk: An Empirical Study," *Management International Review*, no. 1 (1980), pp. 83–92.

Westerfield, Janice M. "How U.S. Multinationals Manage Currency Risk," *Business Review* (March–April 1980), pp. 19–27.

Yang, James G. S. "Managing Multinational Exchange Risks." *Management Accounting* (February 1986), pp. 45–52.

PART FOUR

Short-Term Asset and Liability Management

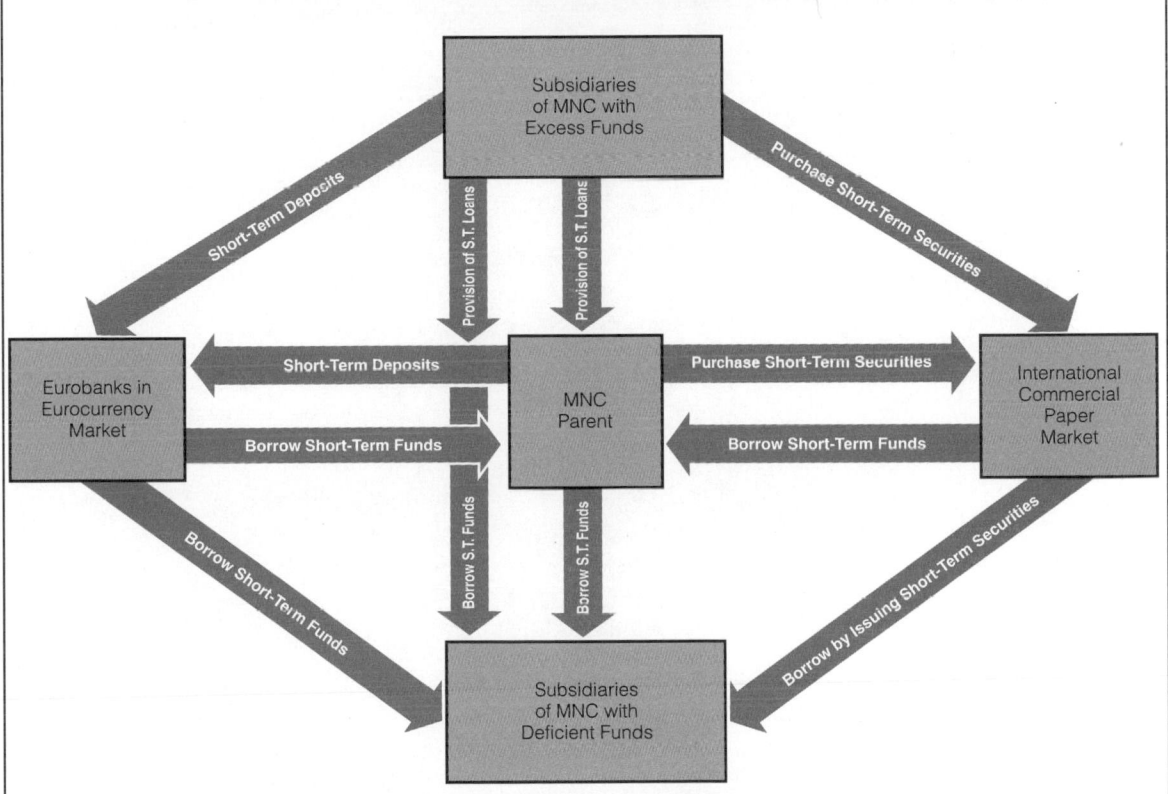

Part 4 (Chapters 13 through 15) focuses on the MNC's management of short-term assets and liabilities. Chapter 13 describes methods by which MNCs can finance their international trade. Chapter 14 identifies sources of short-term funds and explains the criteria used by MNCs to make their short-term financing decisions. Chapter 15 describes how MNCs optimize their cash flow and explains the criteria used to make their short-term investment decisions.

Financing
International
Trade

The international trade activities of MNCs have grown in importance over time. This trend is attributed primarily to the various ways in which the commercial banks can finance and facilitate international trade. While banks also finance domestic trade, their role in financing international trade is more critical due to the additional complications involved. First, the exporter might question the importer's ability to make payment. Second, even if the importer is creditworthy, the government might impose exchange controls that prevent payment to the exporter. Third, the importer might not trust that the exporter will ship the goods ordered. Fourth, even if the exporter does ship the goods, trade barriers or time lags in international transportation might delay arrival time.

Overall, information on each party involved is sometimes scarce. In addition, time delays on either transportation or payment are common and hard to overcome due to the distance between parties. Commercial banks can resolve these complications with various financing methods that are described throughout the chapter.

TERMS OF PAYMENT FOR INTERNATIONAL TRADE

In any international trade transaction, credit is provided by either the supplier (exporter), buyer (importer), one or more financial institutions, or any combination of these. The supplier may have sufficient cash flow to fund the entire trade cycle, beginning with the production of the product until payment is eventually made by the buyer. This is known as **supplier credit.** In some cases, the exporter may require bank financing to augment its cash flow. On the other hand, the supplier may not desire to provide financing, in which case the buyer will have to finance the transaction itself, either internally or externally with its bank. Banks on both sides of the transaction can thus play an integral part in trade financing.

In general, five basic methods of payment are used to settle international transactions, each varying in the degree of risk to the exporter and importer (Exhibit 13.1):

EXHIBIT 13.1   Comparison of Payment Methods

Method	Usual Time of Payment	Goods Available to Buyers	Risk to Exporter	Risk to Importer
Cash in advance	Before shipment	After payment	None	Relies completely on exporter to ship goods as ordered
Letter of credit	When shipment is made	After payment	Very little or none, depending on credit terms	Assured shipment made, but relies on exporter to ship goods described in documents
Sight draft; documents against payment	On presentation of draft to buyer	After payment	If draft unpaid, must dispose of goods	Same as above unless importer can inspect goods before payment
Time draft; documents against acceptance	On maturity of drafts	Before payment	Relies on buyer to pay drafts	Same as above
Consignment	At time of sale by buyer	Before payment	Allows importer to sell inventory before paying exporter	None; improves cash flow of buyer
Open account	As agreed	Before payment	Relies completely on buyer to pay account as agreed	None

- Prepayment
- Letters of credit
- Drafts (sight/time)
- Consignment
- Open account

Prepayment

Under the **prepayment** method, the exporter will not ship the goods until the buyer has remitted payment to the exporter. Payment is usually made in the form of an international wire transfer to the exporter's bank account or bank draft. This method affords the supplier the greatest degree of protection, and it is normally requested of first-time buyers whose creditworthiness is unknown or countries in financial difficulty. Most buyers, however, are not willing to bear all the risk by prepaying an order.

Letters of Credit (L/C)

A **letter of credit (L/C)** is an instrument issued by a bank on behalf of the buyer (importer) promising to pay the exporter (beneficiary) upon presentation of shipping documents in compliance with the terms stipulated therein. In effect, the bank is substituting its credit for that of the buyer. This method is a compromise between seller and buyer because it affords certain advantages to both parties. The exporter is assured of receiving payment from the issuing bank as long as it presents documents in accordance with the L/C. It is important to point out that the issuing bank is obligated to honor drawings under the L/C regardless of the buyer's ability or willingness to pay. On the other hand, the importer does not have to pay for the goods until shipment has been made and documents are presented in good order. However, the importer still must rely upon the exporter to ship the goods as described in the documents, since the L/C does not guarantee that the goods purchased will be those invoiced and shipped. A fundamental premise of L/C transactions is that banks deal in documents, not merchandise. Therefore, payment is made by the bank based upon its examination of the documents, not upon receipt of the merchandise or upon examination of the goods. Letters of credit will be described in greater detail later in this chapter.

Drafts

A **draft** (or **bill of exchange**) is an unconditional promise drawn by one party, usually the exporter, on the buyer, instructing the buyer to pay the face amount of the draft upon presentation. The draft represents the seller's formal demand for payment from the buyer. A draft affords the supplier less protection than an L/C since the banks are not obligated to honor payments on the buyer's behalf.

Most trade transactions handled on a draft basis are processed through banking channels. In banking terminology, they are known as **documentary collections.** In a documentary collection transaction, banks on both ends act as intermediaries in the processing of shipping documents and the collection of payment. If shipment is made under a sight draft, the exporter is paid once shipment has been made and the draft is presented to the buyer for payment. The buyer's bank will not release the shipping documents to the buyer until the buyer has paid the draft. This is also known as **documents against payment.** It is a practice that provides the exporter with some protection, since the banks will release the shipping documents only according to the exporter's instructions. The buyer needs the shipping documents to pick up merchandise. The importer does not have to pay for the merchandise until the draft has been presented.

If a shipment is made under a time draft, the exporter provides instructions to the buyer's bank to release documents against acceptance (signing) of the draft. This method of payment is sometimes referred to as **documents against acceptance.** By accepting the draft, the importer is promising to pay the exporter at the specified future date. This accepted draft is also known as a **trade acceptance,** which is different than a banker's acceptance. In this type of transaction, the buyer is able to obtain the merchandise prior to paying for it. It is the buyer's responsibility to honor that draft at maturity. In this case, the seller is providing the financing and is dependent upon the buyer's financial integrity to pay the draft at maturity. Shipping on a time draft basis provides some added comfort in that banks at both ends are used as collection agents. In addition, a draft serves as a binding financial obligation in case the exporter wishes to pursue litigation on uncollected receivables. The added risk is that if the buyer fails to pay the draft at maturity, the bank is not obligated to honor payment. The exporter is assuming all the risk and must analyze the buyer accordingly.

Consignment

Under a **consignment** arrangement, the exporter ships the goods to the importer while still retaining actual title to the merchandise. The importer has access to the inventory but does not have to pay for the goods until they have been sold to a third party. The exporter is trusting the importer to remit payment for the goods sold at that time. If the importer fails to pay, the exporter has limited recourse, since there is no draft involved and the goods have already been sold. As a result of the high risk, the consignment method is seldom used except by affiliated and subsidiary companies trading with the parent company.

Open Account

The opposite of prepayment is the **open-account** transaction in which the exporter ships the merchandise and expects the buyer to remit payment according to the agreed upon terms. The exporter is relying fully upon the financial creditworthiness, integrity, and reputation of the buyer. As might be expected, this method is used when seller and buyer have a great deal of experience with each other and mutual trust. Despite the risks involved, open-account transactions are expanding, particularly with the industrialized nations.

TRADE FINANCE TECHNIQUES

As mentioned in the section under "Terms of Payment for International Trade," banks on both sides of the transaction play a critical role in financing international trade. Some of the more popular methods of financing international trade include

- Accounts receivable financing
- Factoring
- Letters of credit
- Banker's acceptance
- Short-term bank loans
- Forfaiting
- Countertrade

Each of these methods is described in turn.

Accounts Receivable Financing

In some cases, the exporter of goods may be willing to ship goods to the importer without an assurance of payment from a bank. This could take the form of an open-account shipment or a time draft. Prior to shipment, the exporter should have conducted its own credit check on the importer to determine creditworthiness. If the exporter is willing to wait for payment, it is extending credit to the buyer. If it were not for the exporter's acceptance of such an arrangement, the importer would either have to use its own cash or obtain bank financing to provide payment to the exporter before shipment.

If the exporter needs funds immediately but the importer wants terms, the exporter may require financing from a bank. In what is referred to as **accounts receivable financing,** the bank will provide a loan to the exporter secured by an assignment of the account receivable. Most banks establish advance ratios ranging from 60 percent to 80 percent of the invoiced amount. It is important to note that the bank's loan is made to the exporter based on its creditworthiness. In the event the buyer fails to pay the exporter for whatever reason, the exporter is still responsible to repay the bank. This is unlike **factoring** (discussed next), where the bank purchases the receivable without recourse to the exporter. The bank's debtor is the foreign buyer. This type of financing involves additional risks from other factors, such as government restrictions and exchange controls, that may prevent the buyer from paying the exporter. As a result, the loan rate is often higher than domestic accounts receivable financing. The length of a financing term is usually one to six months. If lenders are not satisfied with the credit risk of the account receivable, they may require export credit insurance to strengthen the value of the collateral. The Foreign Credit Insurance Association (FCIA) offers a variety of credit insurance programs designed to protect the exporters or lenders against the risk of nonpayment by the foreign buyer. These programs are described later in this chapter.

Factoring

When an exporter ships goods before receiving payment, the accounts receivable balance increases. Unless the exporter has received a loan from a bank, it is initially financing the transaction, and it must monitor the collections of receivables. Since there is a danger that the buyer will never pay at all, the exporting firm may consider selling the accounts receivable to a third party, known as a **factor.** In this type of financing, the exporter sells the account receivable without recourse. The factor then assumes all administrative responsibilities involved in collecting from the buyer and the associated credit exposure. As one would expect, the factor performs its own credit approval process on the foreign buyer before purchasing the receivable. For providing this service, the factor usually purchases the receivable at a discount and also receives a flat processing fee.

Factoring provides several benefits to the exporter. First, by selling the accounts receivable, the exporter does not have to worry about the administrative duties involved in maintaining and monitoring an accounts receivable accounting ledger. Second, the factor assumes the credit exposure to the buyer, so the exporter does not have to maintain personnel to assess the creditworthiness of foreign buyers. (As mentioned, in consideration for assuming this credit risk, the factor normally purchases the invoice at less than face value.) Finally, the sale of the receivable to the factor provides immediate payment and improves the exporter's cash flow.

Since it is the importer who must be creditworthy from a factor's point of view, **crossborder factoring** is often used. This involves a network of factors in various countries who assess credit risk. The exporter's factor contacts a correspondent factor in the buyer's country to assess the importer's creditworthiness and handle the collections of the receivable. Factoring services are usually provided by the factoring subsidiaries of commercial banks, commercial finance companies, and other specialized finance houses.

Letters of Credit (L/C)

Introduced earlier, the letter of credit (L/C) is one of the oldest forms of trade finance still in existence. Because of the protection and benefits it accords to both the exporter and importer, it is a critical component of many international trade transactions. The L/C is an undertaking by a bank to make payments on behalf of a specified party to a beneficiary under specified conditions. The beneficiary (exporter) is paid upon presentation of the required documents in compliance with the terms of the L/C. The L/C process normally involves two banks, the exporter's bank and the importer's bank. The issuing bank is substituting its credit for that of the importer. It has essentially guaranteed payment to the exporter, provided the exporter complies with the terms and conditions of the L/C.

It is important to mention that the L/C does not guarantee that the buyer will receive what was ordered. Banks deal in documents only, not merchandise. The bank's decision to pay is based upon an examination of documents, not receipt of or inspection of the merchandise. Therefore the buyer must trust the seller to ship the goods in accordance with L/C and buyer's purchase order.

Sometimes the exporter is uncomfortable with the issuing bank's promise to pay since the bank is located in a foreign country. Even if the issuing bank is well-known worldwide, the exporter may be concerned that the foreign government might impose exchange controls or other restrictions that would prevent payment by the issuing bank. For this reason, the exporter may request a local bank to confirm the L/C and thus assure that all the responsibilities of the issuing bank will be met. The confirming bank is obligated to honor drawings made by the exporter in compliance with the L/C regardless of the issuing bank's ability to make that payment. Consequently, the confirming bank is trusting that the foreign bank issuing the L/C is sound. The exporter, however, need worry only about the credibility of the confirming bank.

Trade-related letters of credit are known as **commercial L/Cs** or **import/ export letters of credit.** There are basically two types: revocable and irrevocable. **A revocable L/C** can be cancelled at any time without prior notification to the beneficiary, and it is seldom used. An **irrevocable L/C** (see Exhibit 13.2) cannot be cancelled or amended without the beneficiary's approval. It obligates the issuing bank to honor all valid drawings. Letters of credit are normally governed by the provisions contained in the "Uniform Customs and Practice for Documentary Credits," published by the International Chamber of Commerce.

The bank issuing the L/C makes payments once the required documentation has been presented in accordance with the payment terms. The importer must pay the issuing bank the amount of the L/C plus accrued fees associated with obtaining the L/C. The importer will usually have an account established at the issuing bank to be drawn upon for payment so that the issuing bank does not tie up its own funds. However, if the importer does not have sufficient funds in his account, the issuing bank is still obligated to honor all valid drawings against the L/C. This is why the bank's decision to issue an L/C on behalf of an importer involves an analysis of the buyer's creditworthiness and is analogous to making a loan. The documentary credit procedure is described in the flowchart in Exhibit 13.3.

In what is commonly referred to as a *refinancing of a sight L/C,* the bank arranges to fund a loan to pay out the L/C instead of charging the importer's

---

EXHIBIT 13.2   Example of an Irrevocable Letter of Credit

                                                                Name of issuing bank

                                                                Address of issuing bank

Name of exporter

Address of exporter

Gentlemen:

We establish our irrevocable letter of credit:
for the account of (importer name),
in the amount of (value of exports),
expiring (date),
available by your draft at (time period) days sight, and accompanied by:
    (any invoices, packing lists, bills of lading, etc., that need to be presented
    with the letter of credit)
Insurance provided by (exporter or importer)
covering shipment of (merchandise description)
From: (port of shipment)
To: (port of arrival)

                                                        (Authorized Signature)

EXHIBIT 13.3   Documentary Credit Procedure

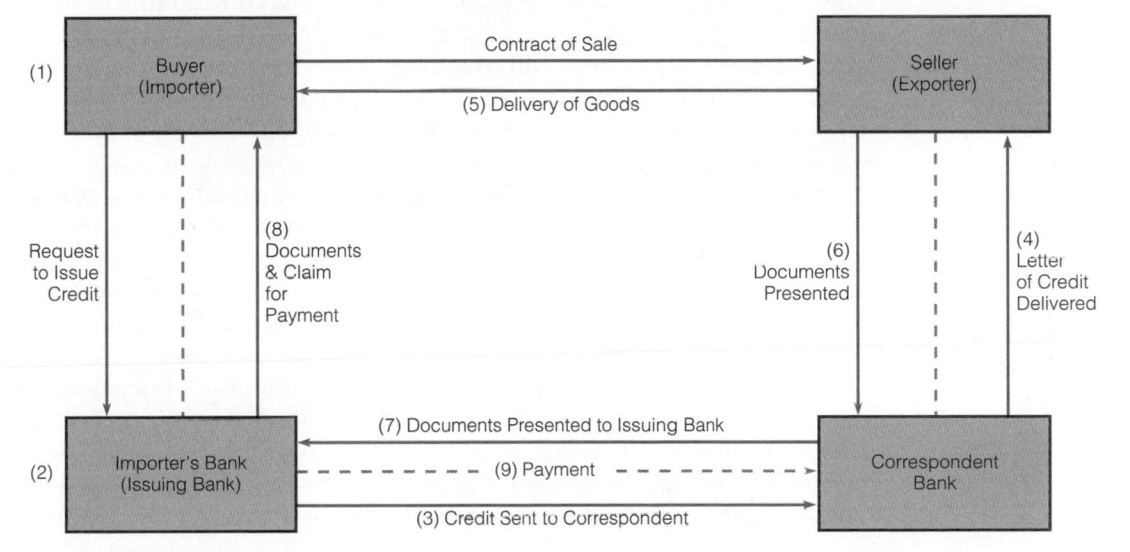

account immediately. The importer is responsible for repaying the bank both principal and interest at maturity. This is just another method of providing extended payment terms to a buyer when the exporter insists upon payment at sight.

The bank issuing the L/C, makes payment to the beneficiary (exporter) upon presentation of documents that meet the conditions stipulated in the L/C. Letters of credit are either payable at sight (upon presentation of documents) or time (at a specified future date). The typical documentation required under an L/C includes a draft (sight or time), commercial invoice, and bill of lading. Depending upon the agreement, product, or country, other documents (such as a certificate of origin, inspection certificate, packing list, or insurance certificate) might be required. The three most common L/C documents are as follows.

DRAFT.   Also known as a **bill of exchange,** a draft (introduced earlier) is an unconditional promise drawn by one party, usually the exporter, on the importer or importer's bank (drawee), requesting the drawee to pay the face amount of the draft at sight or at a specified future date. If the draft is drawn at sight, it is payable upon presentation of documents. If it is payable at a specified future date (a time draft), and it is accepted by the importer, it is known as a **trade acceptance. A banker's acceptance** is a time draft drawn on and accepted by a bank. When presented under a letter of credit, the draft represents the exporter's formal demand for payment. The time period, or **tenor,** of most time drafts is usually anywhere from 30 to 180 days.

BILL OF LADING.   The key document in an international shipment under an L/C is the **bill of lading (B/L).** It serves as a receipt for shipment, a summary of freight charges, and most importantly, conveys title to the merchandise. If the merchandise is to be shipped by boat, the carrier will issue what is known as an **ocean bill of lading.** When the merchandise is shipped by air, the carrier will issue an **airway bill.** The carrier presents the L/C to the exporter (shipper), who in turn presents it to the bank along with the other required documents.

A significant feature of a B/L is its negotiability. A straight B/L is consigned directly to the importer or consignee. Since it does not represent title to the merchandise, the consignee (importer) does not need it to pick up the merchandise. However, when a B/L is made out to order, it is said to be in negotiable form. The exporter would normally endorse the B/L to the bank once payment is received from the bank.

The bank would not endorse the B/L over to the importer until payment has been made. The importer needs the original B/L to pick up the merchandise. With a **negotiable B/L,** title passes to the holder of the endorsed B/L. Because a negotiable B/L grants title to the holder, banks can take the merchandise as collateral. Some of the usual provisions contained within a B/L include

- A description of the merchandise
- Identification marks on the merchandise
- Evidence of loading (receiving) ports
- Names of the exporter (shipper)
- Name of the importer or consignee

- Status of freight charges (prepaid or collect)
- Date of shipment

COMMERCIAL INVOICE.   The exporter's (seller's) description of the merchandise being sold to the buyer is the **commercial invoice,** which normally contains the following information:

- Name and address of seller
- Name and address of buyer
- Date
- Terms of payment
- Price, including freight, handling, and insurance if applicable
- Quantity, weight, packaging, etc.
- Shipping information

Under an L/C shipment, the description of the merchandise outlined in the invoice must correspond exactly to that contained in the L/C.

VARIATIONS OF THE L/C.   There are several variations of the L/C that are useful in financing trade. A **standby L/C** can be used to guarantee invoice payments to a supplier. It promises to pay the beneficiary if the buyer fails to pay as agreed. It is a performance-related instrument used extensively in the United States in lieu of bid bonds, performance bonds, and other contractual obligations. In an international or domestic trade transaction the seller would agree to ship to the buyer on standard open-account terms as long as the buyer provides a standby L/C for a specified amount and term. As long as the buyer pays the seller as agreed, the standby L/C is never funded. However, if the buyer fails to pay, the exporter may present documents under the L/C and request payment from the bank. The buyer's bank is essentially guaranteeing that the buyer will make payment to the seller.

A **transferable L/C** is a variation of the standard commercial L/C that allows the first beneficiary to transfer all or a part of the original L/C to a third party. This type of L/C is used extensively by brokers, or middlemen, who are not the actual suppliers. For example, the broker asks the foreign buyer to issue an L/C for $100,000 in his favor. The L/C must contain a clause stating the L/C is transferable. The broker has located a supplier who will provide the product for $80,000. However, the end supplier has requested payment in advance from the broker. With a transferable L/C, the broker can transfer $80,000 of the original L/C to the end supplier under the same terms and conditions, except for the amount, the latest shipment date, the invoice, and period of concern. When the end supplier ships the product, it presents its documents to the bank. When the bank pays the L/C, $80,000 is paid to the end supplier and $20,000 goes to the broker. In effect, the broker has utilized the credit of the buyer to finance the entire transaction.

An **assignment of proceeds** under an L/C is another method of financing a transaction involving a middleman. The original beneficiary of the L/C may pledge or assign, to the end supplier, the proceeds under an L/C. The end supplier has the assurance from the bank that if and when documents are presented in compliance, with the terms of the L/C, the bank will pay the end supplier according to the assignment instructions. This assignment is valid only if the beneficiary (middleman) presents documents that comply with the L/C. The end supplier must recognize that the issuing bank is under no obligation to pay the end supplier if the original beneficiary never ships the goods, or fails to comply with the terms of the L/C.

Banker's Acceptance

Introduced earlier, a **banker's acceptance** (shown in Exhibit 13.4) is a bill of exchange, or time draft, drawn on and accepted by a bank. It is the accepting bank's obligation to pay the holder of the draft at maturity. According to the Federal Reserve, banker's acceptances are considered either eligible or ineligible, depending upon whether or not they meet established criteria. To be eligible for discount at the Fed, they must meet both maturity and transaction requirements. The tenor of the acceptance must normally be within six months, or nine months in some cases. In addition, the acceptance must meet one of the following underlying transaction requirements: import or export, domestic shipment or storage of goods, pre-export financing, or creation of dollar exchange. The financing is available to either the importer or exporter.

The first step in the creation of a banker's acceptance is for the importer to order goods from the exporter. The importer then requests its local bank to issue an L/C on its behalf. The L/C will allow the exporter to draw a time draft on the bank in payment for the exported goods. The exporter presents the time draft along with shipping documents to its local bank, and the exporter's bank sends the time draft along with the shipping documents to the importer's bank. The importer's bank accepts the draft, thereby creating the banker's acceptance. If the exporter does not want to wait until the specified date to receive payment, it can request that the banker's acceptance be sold in the money market. In this case, the funds received from the sale of a banker's acceptance are less than if the exporter waits to receive payment. Such a discount reflects the time value of money.

A money market investor may be willing to buy the banker's acceptance at a discount and hold it until payment is due. This investor will then receive full

---

EXHIBIT 13.4 Banker's Acceptance

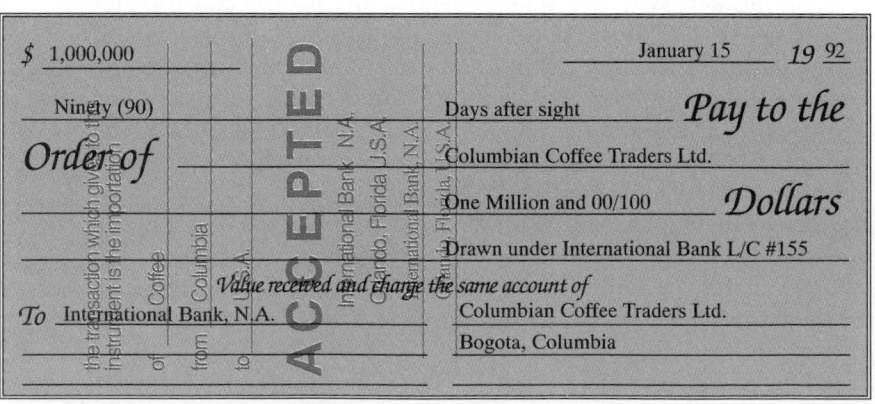

payment, because the banker's acceptance represents a future claim on funds of the bank represented by the acceptance. The bank will make full payment at the date specified, since it expects to receive this amount plus an additional fee from the importer.

If the exporter holds the acceptance until maturity, it provides the financing for the importer, as it does with accounts receivable financing. In this case, the key difference between use of a banker's acceptance and accounts receivable financing is that a banker's acceptance guarantees payment to the exporter by a bank. However, if the exporter sells the banker's acceptance in the secondary market, it is no longer providing the financing for the importer. The holder of the banker's acceptance is financing instead.

A banker's acceptance can be beneficial to the exporter, importer, and issuing bank. The exporter does not need to worry about the credit risk of the importer and can therefore penetrate new foreign markets without concern about the credit risk of potential customers. In addition, there is little exposure to political risk or to exchange controls imposed by a government. Banks are normally allowed to meet their payment commitments even under the existence of controls. Yet, an importer may have greater difficulty in making payment to the exporter if controls are imposed. Without a banker's acceptance, an exporter might not receive payment, even if the importer is willing to pay, due to exchange controls. Finally, the exporter can sell the banker's acceptance at a discount before payment is due and thus obtain funds up front from the issuing bank (or the ultimate holder of the acceptance if the bank sells it in the money market).

The importer benefits from a banker's acceptance in that it has greater access to foreign markets when purchasing supplies and other products. Without banker's acceptances, exporters may be unwilling to accept the credit risk of importers. Due to the documents presented along with the acceptance, the importer is assured that goods have been shipped. Even though the importer did not pay in advance, this assurance is valuable since the importer may need to know if and when supplies and other products will arrive. Finally, because the banker's acceptance allows the importer to pay at a later date, the importer's payment is financed until the maturity date of the banker's acceptance. Without an acceptance, the importer would likely be forced to pay in advance, thereby tying funds up.

The bank accepting the drafts benefits in that it earns a commission for creating an acceptance. The commission that the bank charges the customer reflects the perceived creditworthiness of the customer. The interest rate charged the customer, which is commonly referred to as the **all-in rate,** consists of the discount rate plus the acceptance commission. In general, the all-in rate for acceptance financing is lower than prime-based borrowings, as shown in the following comparison:

	Loan	Acceptance
Amount:	$1,000,000	$1,000,000
Term:	180 Days	180 Days
Rate:	Prime + 1.5%	BA Rate + 1.5%
	10.0% + 1.5% = 11.5%	7.60% + 1.5% = 9.10%
Interest Cost:	$57,500	$45,500

In this example, the interest savings for a six month period is $12,000. Since the banker's acceptance is a marketable instrument with an active secondary market, the rates on acceptances usually fall between that of short-term Treasury bills and commercial paper. Investors are usually willing to purchase acceptances as an investment because of their yield, safety, and liquidity. When a bank creates, accepts, and sells the acceptance, it is actually using the investor's money to finance the bank's customer. As a result, the bank has created an asset at one price, sold it at another, and retained a commission (spread) as its fee.

Banker's acceptance financing can also be arranged through the refinancing of a sight letter of credit. In this case, the exporter (beneficiary) of the letter of credit may insist upon payment at sight. So that the importer can obtain terms, the bank arranges to finance the payment of the sight letter of credit under a separate acceptance-financing agreement. The importer (borrower) simply draws drafts upon the bank, which in turn accepts and discounts the drafts. Proceeds are used to pay the exporter. At maturity, the importer is responsible for repayment to the bank.

Acceptance financing can also be arranged without the use of a letter of credit under a separate acceptance agreement. Similar to a regular loan agreement, it stipulates the terms and conditions under which the bank is prepared to finance the borrower using acceptances instead of promissory notes. As long as the acceptances meet one of the underlying transaction requirements, the bank and borrower can utilize banker's acceptances as an alternative financing mechanism. The life cycle of a banker's acceptance is illustrated in Exhibit 13.5.

Exhibit 13.6 illustrates the U.S.-dollar value of outstanding banker's acceptances in the United States. Over time, their popularity has risen, primarily due to the increase in international trade.

Short-Term Bank Loans

As just explained, a banker's acceptance can allow an exporter to receive funds immediately, yet allow an importer to delay its payment until a future date. The bank may even provide short-term loans beyond the banker's acceptance period. In the case of an importer, the purchase from overseas usually represents the acquisition of inventory. The loan finances the working capital cycle that begins with the purchase of inventory and continues with the sale of the goods, creation of an account receivable, and conversion to cash. With an exporter, the short-term loan might finance the manufacture of the merchandise destined for export (pre-export financing) or the time period from when the sale is made until payment is received from the buyer. For example, the firm may have imported foreign beer, which it plans to distribute to grocery and liquor stores. The bank can provide not only a letter of credit for trade finance, but can also finance the importer's cost from the time of distribution and collection of payment.

Forfaiting

Because capital goods are often quite expensive, an importer may not be able to make payment on the goods within a short time period. Thus, longer-term financing may be required here. The exporter could be able to provide fi-

EXHIBIT 13.5 Life Cycle of a Typical Banker's Acceptance

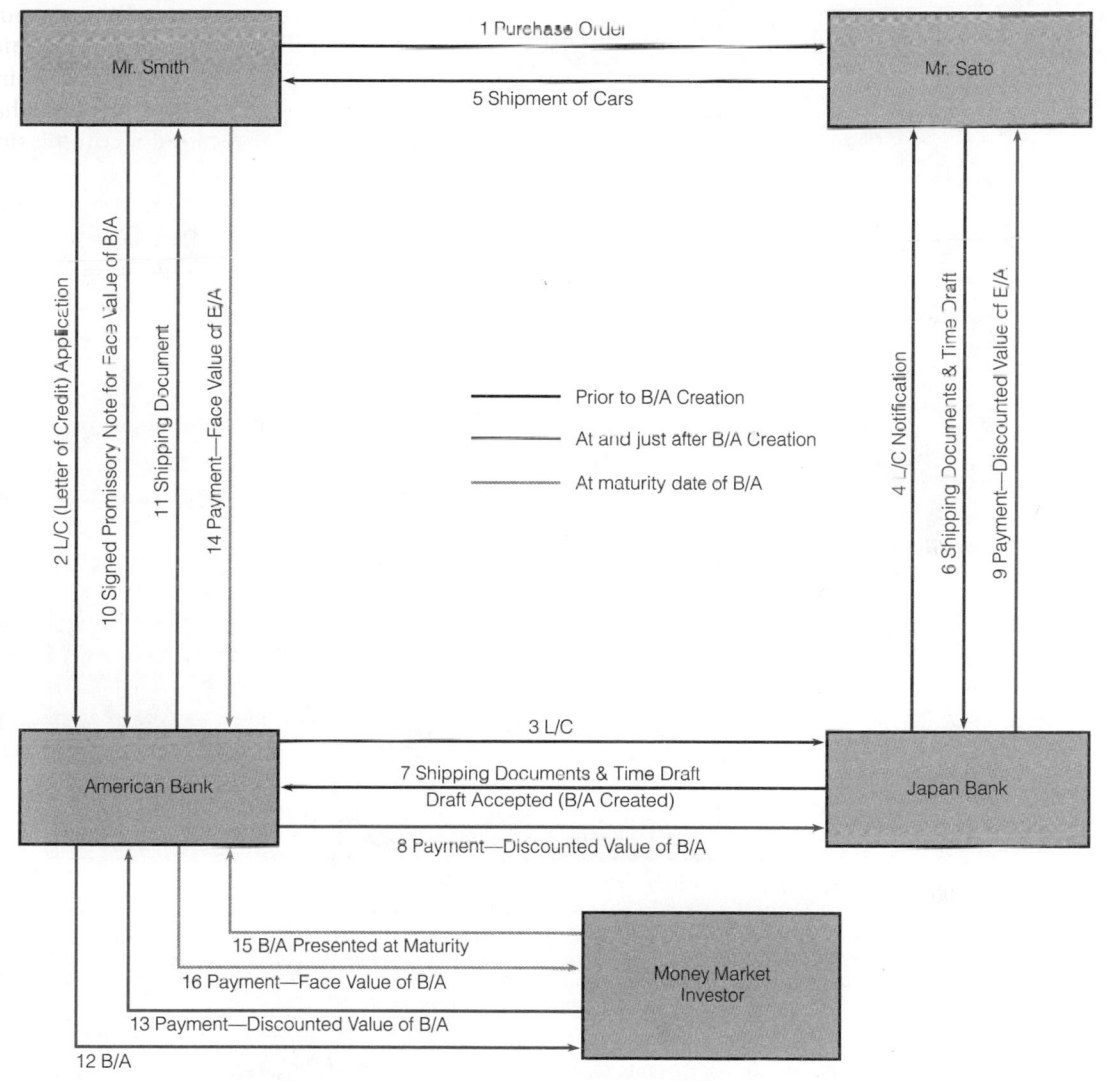

SOURCE: *Instruments of the Money Market*, Sixth Edition, Federal Reserve Bank of Richmond, p. 127.

nancing for the importer but may not desire to do so, since the financing may extend over several years. In this case, a type of trade finance known as **forfaiting** could be used. Forfaiting refers to the purchase of financial obligations, such as bills of exchange or promissory notes, without recourse to the original holder, usually the exporter. In a forfait transaction, the importer would issue a promissory note in favor of the exporter to pay for the imported capital goods. The term generally ranges from three to seven years. The exporter would then sell the notes, without recourse, to the forfaiting bank. In some respects, this is similar to factoring in that the forfaiter (or factor) assumes responsibility for the collection of payment from the buyer and the

EXHIBIT 13.6 Banker's Acceptance Volume (by transaction type)

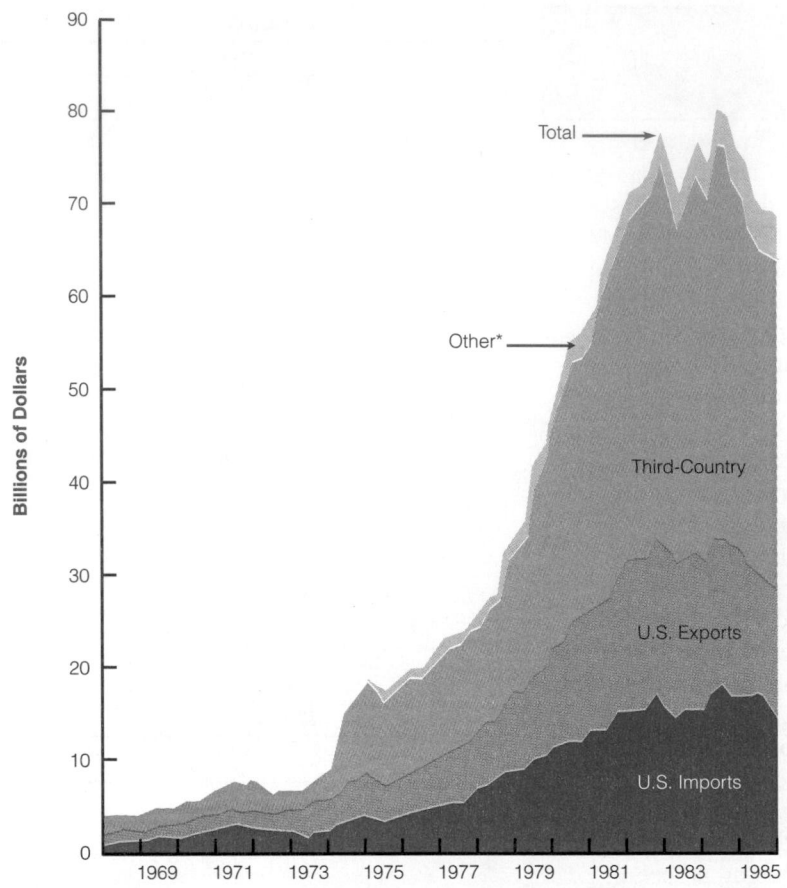

*Includes domestic shipment, domestic storage, and dollar exchange acceptances.
SOURCE: Federal Reserve Bank of New York; and *Instruments of the Money Market,* Sixth Edition, Federal Reserve Bank of Richmond, p. 129.

underlying credit risk and country risk. Since the forfaiting bank assumes the risk of nonpayment, it should assess the creditworthiness of the importer as if it were extending a medium-term loan. Forfait transactions are normally collateralized by a bank guarantee or letter of credit issued by the importer's bank for the term of the transaction. Since financial information is usually difficult to obtain on the importer, the forfaiting bank places a great deal of reliance on the bank guarantee as the collateral in the event the buyer fails to pay as agreed. It is this guarantee backing up the transaction that has fostered the growth of the forfait market, particularly in Europe, as a practical means of trade finance.

Forfaiting transactions usually are in excess of $500,000 and can be denominated in most currencies. For some larger transactions, more than one bank may be involved. In this case, a syndicate is formed wherein each participant assumes a proportionate share of the underlying risk and profit.

A forfaiting firm may decide to sell the promissory notes of the importer to other financial institutions willing to purchase them. However, the forfaiting firm is still responsible for payment on the notes in the event the importer is unable to pay.

Countertrade

The term **countertrade** denotes all types of foreign trade transactions in which the sale of goods to one country is linked to the purchase or exchange of goods from that same country. Some types of countertrade, such as barter, have been in existence for thousands of years. However, only recently has countertrade gained popularity and importance. The growth in various types of countertrade has been fueled by large balance of payments disequilibrium, foreign currency shortages, the LDC debt problem, and stagnant worldwide demand. As a result, many multinationals have been confronted with countertrade opportunities, particularly in Asia, Latin America, and Eastern Europe. The most common types of countertrade include barter, compensation, and counterpurchase.

Barter represents the exchange of goods between two parties without the use of any currency as a medium of exchange. Most barter arrangements are one-time transactions governed by one contract. An example would be the exchange of 100 tons of wheat from Canada for 20 tons of shrimp from Ecuador.

In a **compensation** arrangement, the delivery of goods to one party is compensated for by buying back a certain amount of product from that same party. The transaction is governed by one contract, and the value of the goods is expressed in monetary terms. The buy-back arrangement could be for a fraction of the original sale (**partial compensation**) or more than 100 percent of the original sale (**full compensation**). An example of compensation would be the sale of phosphate from Morocco to France in exchange for purchasing a certain percentage of fertilizer. In some countries, this is also referred to as an industrial cooperation arrangement. Such arrangements often involve the construction of large projects, such as power plants, in exchange for purchasing the project's output over an extended period of time. For example, a hydroelectric plant was sold by Brazil to Argentina in exchange for Brazil purchasing a percentage of the plant's output over a long-term contract.

The term **counterpurchase** denotes the exchange of goods between two parties under two distinct contracts expressed in monetary terms. Delivery and payment of both goods are technically separate transactions. An example would be the sale of televisions by Lucky-Goldstar in Korea to Yugoslavia in exchange for Lucky-Goldstar marketing Yugo cars in Korea.

The countertrade market is still developing. The primary participants are governments and multinationals, with assistance provided by specialists in the field such as attorneys, financial institutions, and trading companies. The transactions are usually very complex and large. Many variations of countertrade exist, and the terminology used by the various market participants is still forming. Nonetheless, despite the economic inefficiencies of countertrade, it is a type of trade the experienced exporter must be prepared to consider.

AGENCIES THAT MOTIVATE INTERNATIONAL TRADE

Due to the inherent risks of international trade, insurance against various forms of risk is desirable. Some agencies provide insurance, or combine it with various loan-support programs or guarantees.

The prominent agencies providing this service in the United States are

- Export-Import Bank of the U.S. (Eximbank)
- Foreign Credit Insurance Association (FCIA)
- Private Export Funding Corporation (PEFCO)
- Overseas Private Investment Corporation (OPIC)

Each of these agencies is described in turn.

Export-Import Bank of the United States

Eximbank was established in 1934 with the original intention to facilitate Soviet-American trade. Its mission today is to finance and facilitate the export of American goods and services and maintain the competitiveness of American companies in overseas markets. It operates as an independent agency of the U.S. government and, as such, carries the full faith and credit of the United States. In over 50 years, Eximbank has supported over $190 billion in U.S. exports.

The programs of Eximbank are designed to meet three board objectives: (1) by assuming the underlying credit and country risk, encourage private lenders to finance export trade, (2) provide direct loans to foreign buyers when private lenders are unwilling to do so, and (3) help U.S. exporters meet subsidized foreign competition.

The programs can be categorized into four major groups: (1) working capital, (2) guarantees, (3) direct loans, and (4) intermediary loans. The Working Capital Guarantee Program allows exporters to obtain short-term loans from commercial banks for the manufacture, processing, or sale of goods destined for export. The banks are usually more willing to provide financing since Eximbank guarantees up to 90 percent of the principal and a portion of the interest should the exporter default. The loans are fully collateralized and require that guarantee fees be paid to Eximbank. Eximbank's guarantee protects the lender against the risk of default by the exporter. It does not protect the exporter against the risk of nonpayment by the buyer.

The Guarantee programs provide medium-term protection (one to seven years) against the risk of nonpayment by the foreign buyer due to political and commercial factors. Under the Guarantee programs, the bank extends a loan to the foreign buyer to purchase U.S. goods. The Eximbank guarantees repayment of principal up to 85% of the export value and a portion of interest. The guarantee fees are determined by the country, type of borrower, and term of the loan.

Under the Direct Loan Program, Eximbank offers a fixed-rate, long-term loan direct to the foreign buyer to purchase U.S. goods that are facing officially subsidized foreign competition. Large-scale projects and capital equipment, such as power plants or airplanes, are eligible for direct loan financing. The transaction size is usually over $10 million with repayment terms beyond seven years. The rates are generally below market and must coincide with the established OECD guidelines. The Intermediary Loan Program enables commercial banks to provide fixed-rate, medium-term loans to foreign buyers by assuring the lenders of fixed-rate funds. Eximbank lends the funds to the commercial bank at the applicable OECD rate, and the bank in turn lends the money to the foreign buyer at a specified rate over its cost of funds.

Intermediary loans provided by Eximbank are usually under $10 million with repayment terms of less than seven years. The commercial bank must still repay Eximbank even if the foreign borrower defaults. If the bank wants to protect itself from the risk of nonpayment by the foreign buyer, it must utilize one of the other guarantee or insurance programs.

Foreign Credit Insurance Association (FCIA)

FCIA, in cooperation with Eximbank, offers a broad range of short-term and medium-term insurance policies to protect exporters and lenders from the risk of nonpayment due to commercial and political reasons. Originally formed in 1961, FCIA used to consist of a group of private insurance companies that assumed the underlying commercial risk. However, as a result of heavy losses sustained in the early 1980s, many of the private insurers pulled out of the market. As a result, Eximbank now underwrites and assumes all the underlying commercial and political risk. Many FCIA policies have been recently revised and improved.

A variety of insurance policies is available to exporters and banks. Basically, all the policies provide credit protection against the risk of nonpayment by foreign buyers. If the foreign buyer fails to pay the exporter, because of commercial reasons such as cash flow problems or insolvency, FCIA usually reimburses the exporter for up to 90 percent of the invoice amount. If the loss is due to political factors such as foreign exchange controls or war, FCIA will reimburse the exporter for 100 percent of the invoice amount. FCIA usually requires the exporter to retain a portion of the commercial risk, but not the political risk, since this is not within the exporter's control. Certain restrictions may apply to particular countries, depending upon FCIA's experience and existing economic or political conditions.

The **New-Export Policy** provides enhanced coverage to the novice exporter. In addition to providing 95 percent coverage on commercial risk defaults, the policy offers lower premiums and no first loss deductible. Certain policy restrictions apply regarding the exporter's size and export sales. The **Umbrella Policy** operates in a slightly different fashion. The policy itself is issued to an "administrator," such as a bank, trading company, insurance broker, or government agency. Eligible exporters may then insure their shipments under the administrator's policy. The primary benefit for the exporter is that the administrator handles all the reporting requirements and administrative work.

The **Multi-Buyer Policy** is used primarily by the experienced exporters. It provides comprehensive credit risk coverage on export sales to many different buyers, on both a short- and medium-term basis. Premiums are based on the exporter's sales profile, credit history, losses, terms of payment, country, and other factors. Based upon the exporter's experience and the buyer's creditworthiness, FCIA may grant the exporter authority to preapprove specific transactions up to a certain limit. The **Single-Buyer Policy** allows the exporter to selectively insure certain transactions on a short-term or medium-term basis.

FCIA insurance serves as a marketing tool, enabling the exporter to seek new buyers and new markets. By having insurance protection, the exporter is able to offer more competitive payment terms. Instead of insisting upon a letter of credit as payment, the exporter can offer open-account terms to the buyer. Before approving a particular foreign buyer for coverage, FCIA requires that the exporter obtain certain financial information on the buyer. FCIA charges insurance premiums based on the type of buyer, country, and terms of payment. Another attractive feature of an FCIA policy is that the exporter can usually obtain financing from a bank with the insured receivables serving as collateral. The insured exporter may assign its rights under the policy to the lending bank.

FCIA also offers several policies available to banks. The recently created **bank letter of credit policy** enables banks to confirm letters of credit issued by foreign banks supporting U.S. exports. Without this insurance, some banks would not be willing to assume the underlying commercial and political risk associated with confirming a letter of credit. The banks are insured anywhere from 90 percent of the financial amount up to 100 percent, depending upon the type of buyer and coverage selected. The premium is based upon the type of buyer, repayment term, and country. The **buyer credit policy** permits banks to extend loans to foreign borrowers to purchase U.S. goods, usually on payment terms from six months to five years. The coverage and premiums are similar to the other policies. The **lease insurance policy** provides insurance coverage to banks, leasing companies, or manufacturers that participate in the leasing of U.S.-manufactured equipment to foreign entities.

Private Export Funding Corporation (PEFCO)

PEFCO, a private corporation, is owned by a consortium of commercial banks and industrial companies. In cooperation with Eximbank, PEFCO provides medium- and long-term fixed-rate financing to foreign buyers. Eximbank guarantees all export loans made by PEFCO. Most PEFCO loans are to finance large projects and as a result have very long terms (5 to 25 years). Since commercial banks usually do not extend such long terms, PEFCO fills a void in the market. PEFCO raises its funds in the capital markets through the issuance of long-term bonds. These bonds are readily marketable since they are in effect secured by Eximbank guaranteed loans.

Overseas Private Investment Corporation (OPIC)

OPIC, formed in 1971, is a self-sustaining federal agency responsible for insuring direct U.S. investments in foreign countries against the risks of currency inconvertibility, expropriation, and other political risks. Through the direct loan or guaranty program, OPIC will provide medium- to long-term financing to U.S. investors undertaking an overseas venture. In addition to the general insurance and finance programs, OPIC offers specific types of coverage for exporters bidding on or performing foreign contracts. American

CHAPTER 13

FINANCING INTERNATIONAL TRADE

387

contractors can insure themselves against contractual disputes and even the wrongful calling of standby letters of credit.

Other Considerations

Beyond the insurance and financing, there are U.S. tax provisions that encourage international trade. Beginning in 1985, the Foreign Sales Corporation (FSC) replaced the Domestic International Sales Corporation (DISC) as the primary tax vehicle to promote U.S. exports. DISC provided a U.S. exporter with a tax deferral on a percentage of its income generated through export sales. The new FSC rules allow for the exporter to receive up to a 15 percent tax exemption on income earned through the FSC. However, the FSC must be incorporated offshore and meet certain procedural and administrative requirements.

SUMMARY

International trade involves complications not normally existing for domestic trade. These complications revolve around the lack of information among trading firms, the geographical distance between them, and differences in the economic conditions of the various countries. Time delays related to the transporting of goods and payment are common, and various techniques for financing international trade are used to resolve them. Commercial banks are largely involved in facilitating and financing international trade through use of these techniques.

As international trade has grown over time, banking institutions have recognized the potential for generating business related to this trade. As a result, the competition for servicing international trade has become intense. This is a primary reason why so many methods of financing international trade exist today. The future promises additional innovative trade financing techniques as knowledge about the industry increases.

QUESTIONS

1. How can a banker's acceptance be beneficial to (1) an exporter, (2) an importer, and (3) a bank?

2. Why would an exporter provide financing for an importer? Is there much risk in this activity? Explain.

3. What is the role of a factor within the international trade transactions? How can a factor aid an exporter?

4. What is the role today of the Export-Import Bank of the United States?

5. What are bills of lading, and how do they facilitate international trade transactions?

6. What is forfaiting? Specify the type of traded goods for which forfaiting is applied?

7. Briefly describe the role of PEFCO.

8. Briefly describe the role of the FCIA.

9. Describe how the desirability for foreign trade would be affected if banks did not provide trade-related services?

10. What is countertrade?

11. Briefly describe the Working Capital Guarantee Program administered by the Export-Import Bank.

12. Describe the Direct Loan Program that is administered by the Export-Import Bank.

13. Describe the New-Export Policy.

14. Describe the role of the Overseas Private Investment Corporation (OPIC).

15. In this chapter, numerous forms of government insurance and guaranty programs were described. What motivates a government to establish so many programs?

Ryco Chemical Company
Using Countertrade

Ryco Chemical Company produces a wide variety of chemical products that are sold to manufacturing firms. Some of the chemicals used in its production are imported from Concellos Chemical Company in Brazil. Concellos uses some chemicals in its production that are produced by Ryco (although Concellos has historically purchased these chemicals from another U.S. chemical company rather than from Ryco). The Brazilian cruzeiro depreciated continuously against the dollar so that Concellos' cost of obtaining chemicals is always rising. Concellos would probably pay two times as much for these chemicals this year because of the weak cruzeiro. It would likely attempt to pass on most of its higher costs to its customers in the form of higher prices. However, it may not always be able to pass on higher costs from a weak cruzeiro, because its competitors make all their chemicals locally and their costs are directly tied to Brazil's inflation. Its competitors sell all their goods locally. This year, Concellos planned to charge Ryco a price in cruzeiros that was substantially above last year's price.

Representatives from Ryco were flying to Brazil to discuss its trade problems with Concellos. Specifically, Ryco wants to avoid its exposure to the high inflation rate in Brazil. This adverse effect is somewhat offset by the consistent decline in the value of the cruzeiro, allowing Ryco to obtain more cruzeiros with a given amount of dollars every year. However, the offset is not perfect and Ryco wants to create a better hedge against Brazilian inflation.

a) Describe a countertrade strategy that could reduce Ryco's exposure to Brazilian inflation.
b) Would Concellos be willing to consider this strategy? Is there any favorable effect on Concellos that may motivate Concellos to accept the strategy?
c) Assume that countertrade is agreed upon by both parties. Why would the cost of obtaining imports still rise over time for Concellos? Would Concellos earn lower profits as a result?

REFERENCES

Barovick, Dick. "U.S. Banks Plunge Into Export Trading." *Euromoney* (January 1984), pp. 128–130.

Belton, Austin, J. "A New Weapon in the Battle for Trade." *Euromoney* (February 1984), 123–129.

Brendt, Hans. "Zurich Looks Good to the German Exporter." *Euromoney* (January 1984), pp. 124–126.

Bowen, David. "Learning to be Safe, Not Sorry." *Euromoney* (January 1985), pp. 133–139.

_____. "Mixed Opinions Divide Consensus." *Euromoney* (January 1985), pp. 141–142.

Cook, Timothy, ed. *Instruments of the Money Market.* Federal Reserve Bank of Richmond, 1986.

Easton, Dick. "Forfaiting is Not for the Ponderous Banker." *Euromoney* (January 1984), pp. 122–123.

Gmur, Charles J. "Trade Financing." *Euromoney* (1986).

Guide to Documentary Credit Operations. International Chamber of Commerce Publishing, (1985).

Hennart, Jean-Francois, "Some Empirical Dimensions of Countertrade," *Journal of International Business Studies* (Second Quarter, 1990), pp. 243–270.

Welt, Leo. "Why Latin America is Wary of Barter." *Euromoney* (January 1984), pp. 132–134.

CHAPTER 14

Short-Term Financing

All firms make short-term financing decisions periodically. Because MNCs have access to additional sources of funds, their short-term financing decisions are more complex than those of other companies. This chapter discusses those decisions, which can be summarized by two questions: First, should an MNC parent or subsidiary in need of funds borrow internally or from some other source? Second, should the MNC obtain a loan denominated in its home currency or some foreign currency? This second decision is analyzed in detail, since it can greatly influence the performance of the firm.

SOURCES OF SHORT-TERM FINANCING

MNC parents and their subsidiaries typically use various methods of obtaining short-term funds. One method increasingly used in recent years is the issuing of **Euronotes,** or unsecured debt securities. The interest rates on these notes are based on LIBOR (the interest rate which Eurobanks charge on interbank loans). They typically have maturities of one, three, or six months. Some MNCs continually roll them over as a form of intermediate-term financing. Commercial banks underwrite the notes for MNCs, and some commercial banks purchase them for their own investment portfolios.

In addition to Euronotes, MNCs also issue **Euro-commercial paper** to obtain short-term financing. Dealers issue this paper for MNCs without the backing of an underwriting syndicate, so a selling price is not guaranteed to the issuers. Maturities can be tailored to the investor's preferences. Dealers make a secondary market by offering to repurchase Euro-commercial paper before maturity.

Another popular source of short-term funds by MNCs, direct loans from Eurobanks, is typically utilized to maintain a relationship with Eurobanks. If other sources of short-term funds become unavailable, MNCs will rely more heavily on direct loans from Eurobanks. Most MNCs maintain credit arrangements with various banks around the world. For example, Westinghouse has credit arrangements with 110 foreign and domestic banks.

INTERNAL FINANCING BY MNCs

Before an MNC's parent or subsidiary in need of funds searches for outside funding, it should determine whether there are any available internal funds. That is, it should check other subsidiaries' cash flow positions. If, for example, earnings have been high at particular subsidiaries and a portion of funds generated is simply invested locally in money market securities, the parent may request these funds from the subsidiaries. This is especially feasible during periods when the cost of obtaining funds in the parent's home country is relatively high. In 1980, for example, high interest rates in the United States encouraged MNC parents needing funds to request that subsidiaries remit earnings as quickly as possible. Travenol Laboratories Inc. is a case in point. It received $76 million from its Puerto Rican subsidiary.

If subsidiary earnings are not available, parents could consider borrowing from their overseas subsidiaries. For example, Thetford Corporation of the United States borrowed $1.6 million from its subsidiaries in Great Britain and the Netherlands during 1980 when U.S. interest rates were at their peak. Thetford paid an average interest rate of 13 percent on these funds, substantially lower than the 18.5 percent interest rate it was paying on local loans from U.S. banks. Exchange rate risk exists when funds from overseas are borrowed, since the firm must later obtain the foreign currency borrowed to pay back foreign loans. However, some companies are willing to take the risk when the foreign interest rates are much lower than domestic interest rates.

Parents of MNCs can also attempt to be financed by subsidiaries through increasing their mark-up on supplies they send to the subsidiaries. In this case, the funds given to the parent by the subsidiary will never be returned. This method of supporting the parent can sometimes be more feasible than the previously discussed methods if it avoids restrictions or taxes enforced by national governments (discussed more thoroughly in Chapter 15). Yet, this method itself may be restricted or limited by host governments where subsidiaries are located.

WHY MNCs CONSIDER FOREIGN FINANCING

Regardless of whether an MNC parent or subsidiary decides to obtain financing from subsidiaries or from some other source, it also must decide which currency to borrow. Even if it needs its home currency, it may prefer to borrow a foreign currency. Reasons for this preference follow.

Foreign Financing to Offset Foreign Receivables

Large firms may finance in a foreign currency to offset a net receivables position in that foreign currency. For example, consider a U.S. firm that has net receivables denominated in German marks. If it needs short-term funds, it could borrow marks and convert them to U.S. dollars for whatever reason it needs funds. Then, the net receivables in marks will be used to pay off the loan. In this example, financing in a foreign currency reduces the firm's exposure to fluctuating exchange rates. This strategy is especially appealing if the interest rate of the foreign currency is low.

Foreign Financing to Reduce Costs

Even when an MNC parent or subsidiary is not attempting to cover foreign net receivables, it may still consider borrowing foreign currencies if the interest rates on such currencies are attractive. Financing in foreign currencies is common as a result of the development of the Eurocurrency market. The cost of financing can vary with the currency borrowed in the Eurocurrency market. A Eurocurrency loan may offer a slightly lower rate than a loan in the same currency through the home country. Therefore, a U.S.-based MNC, for example, may be able to obtain a lower rate when borrowing U.S. dollars in the Eurocurrency market as opposed to a local bank. Yet, the U.S. MNC may also consider financing in a foreign currency through the Eurocurrency market, even if it needs U.S. dollars. Assume the Eurodollar financing rate is 12 percent, while the Euro-Swiss franc financing rate is 8 percent. The U.S. MNC could borrow Swiss francs and immediately convert those francs to dollars for use. Once the loan repayment is due, the U.S. firm would need to obtain Swiss francs in order to pay off the loan. If the Swiss franc value in terms of U.S. dollars has not changed from the time the loan was given until the loan was repaid, the U.S. firm will pay 8 percent on that loan.

Exhibit 14.1 illustrates how interest rates differ among currencies. The Swiss interest rate is typically lowest, while British, Canadian, and U.S. interest rates are often much higher. In some periods, there is a 7 percent differential between the highest and lowest interest rates. Based on Exhibit 14.1, it should not be surprising that some U.S. or British-based MNCs consider financing in Swiss francs, Japanese yen, or German marks.

DETERMINATION OF THE EFFECTIVE FINANCING RATE

In reality, the value of the currency borrowed will most likely change with respect to the borrower's local currency over time. The actual cost of financing by the debtor firm will depend on (1) the interest rate charged by the bank that provided the loan and (2) the movement in the borrowed currency's value over the life of the loan. Thus, the actual or "effective" financing rate may differ from the quoted interest rate. This point is illustrated in the following example.

A U.S. firm is given a one-year loan of 1,000,000 Swiss francs at the quoted interest rate of 8 percent. When the U.S. firm receives the loan, it converts the Swiss francs to U.S. dollars to pay a supplier for materials. The exchange rate at that time is $.50 per Swiss franc, so the 1,000,000 Swiss francs are converted to $500,000 (computed as 1,000,000 francs × $.50 per franc = $500,000). One year later, the U.S. firm pays back the loan of 1,000,000 Swiss francs plus interest of 80,000 Swiss francs (interest computed as 8% × 1,000,000 Swiss francs.) Thus, the total amount of Swiss francs (SF) needed by the U.S. firm is SF1,000,000 + SF80,000 = SF1,080,000 francs. Assume the Swiss franc appreciates from $.50 to $.60 by the time the loan is to be repaid. The firm will need to convert $648,000 (computed as 1,080,000 francs × $.60 per franc) to the necessary number of francs for loan repayment.

To compute the effective financing rate, first determine the number of dollars beyond the amount borrowed that were paid back. Then divide by the number

EXHIBIT 14.1   Short-Term Interest Rates for Various Countries

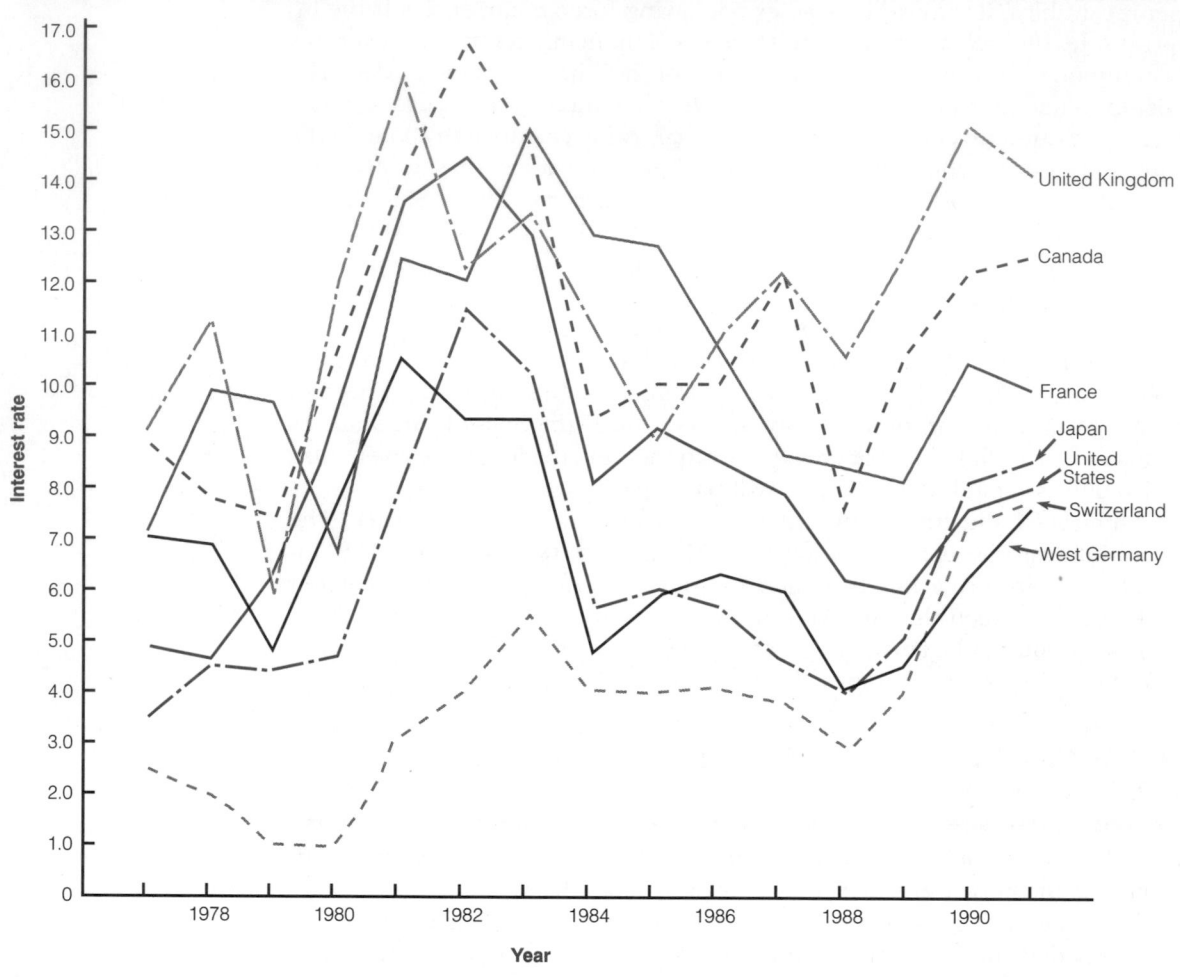

SOURCE: *International Economic Conditions*, Federal Reserve Bank of St. Louis.

of dollars borrowed (after converting the francs to dollars). Given that the firm borrowed the equivalent of $500,000 and paid back $648,000 for the loan, the effective financing rate in this case is $148,000/$500,000 = 29.6%. If the exchange rate remained constant throughout the life of the loan, the total loan repayment would have been $540,000, representing an effective rate of $40,000/$500,000 = 8%. Since the Swiss franc appreciated substantially in our example, the effective financing rate was very high. If the U.S. firm had anticipated the Swiss franc's substantial appreciation, it would not have borrowed the francs.

The effective financing rate (called r_f) is derived as follows:

$$r_f = (1 + i_f)\left[1 + \frac{(S_{f,t+1} - S_f)}{(S_f)}\right] - 1$$

where i_f represents the financing rate of the foreign currency, and S_f and $S_{f,t+1}$ represent the spot rate of the foreign currency at the beginning and end of the financing period, respectively. Since the terms in parentheses reflect the percentage change in the foreign currency's spot rate (denoted as e_f), the preceding equation can be rewritten as

$$r_f = (1 + i_f)(1 + e_f) - 1$$

In our example, e_f reflects the percentage change in the Swiss franc (against the U.S. dollar) from the day francs were borrowed until the day they were paid back by the U.S. firm. The Swiss franc appreciated from $.50 to $.60, or by 20 percent over the life of the loan. With this information and the quoted interest rate of 8 percent, the effective financing rate on Swiss francs by the U.S. firm can be computed as

$$
\begin{aligned}
r_f &= (1 + i_f)(1 + e_f) - 1 \\
&= (1 + .08)(1 + .20) - 1 \\
&= .296 \text{ or } 29.6\%
\end{aligned}
$$

which is the same rate determined from the alternative computational approach.

To test your understanding of financing in a foreign currency, consider a second example for the U.S. firm. Based on a quoted interest rate of 8 percent for the Swiss franc, and depreciation in the franc from $.50 (on the day funds were borrowed) to $.45 (on the day of loan repayment), what is the effective financing rate of a one-year loan from the viewpoint of a U.S. firm? The answer can be determined by first computing the percentage change in the Swiss franc's value: ($.45 − $.50)/$.50 = −10%. Next, the quoted interest rate (i_f) of 8%, and the percentage change in the Swiss franc (e_f) of −10% can be inserted into the formula for the effective financing rate (r_f):

$$
\begin{aligned}
r_f &= (1 + .08)[1 + (- .10)] - 1 \\
&= [(1.08)(.9)] - 1 \\
&= -.028 \text{ or } -2.8\%
\end{aligned}
$$

A *negative* effective financing rate implies the U.S. firm actually paid fewer dollars in total loan repayment than the amount of dollars borrowed. Such a result can occur if the Swiss franc depreciates substantially over the life of the loan. This does not imply a loan will be basically "free" anytime the currency borrowed depreciates over the life of the loan. Yet, depreciation of any amount will cause the effective financing rate to be less than the quoted interest rate, as can be substantiated by reviewing the formula for the effective financing rate.

The examples provided so far suggest that a firm should not simply consider the quoted interest rates of foreign currencies when choosing which currency to borrow. The expected rate of appreciation or depreciation should also be considered.

CONSIDERATIONS WHEN FINANCING IN FOREIGN CURRENCIES

There are various criteria an MNC must consider in its international financing decision, including

- Interest rate parity
- The forward rate as a forecasting tool
- Exchange rate forecasts

These criteria can influence the MNC's decision of which currency or currencies to borrow. Each is discussed in turn.

Interest Rate Parity as a Criterion for the Financing Decision

Recall that covered interest arbitrage was described in Chapter 7 as a foreign short-term investment with a simultaneous forward sale of the foreign currency denominating the foreign investment. From a financing perspective, covered interest arbitrage could be conducted as follows. First, borrow a foreign currency and convert that currency to the home currency for use. Also, simultaneously purchase the foreign currency forward to lock in the exchange rate of the currency needed to pay off the loan. If the foreign currency's interest rate is low, this may appear to be a feasible strategy. However, such a currency will normally exhibit a forward premium that reflects the differential between its interest rate and the home interest rate.

This can be shown by recognizing that the financing firm would no longer be affected by the percentage change in exchange rates, but instead by the percentage difference between the spot rate at which the foreign currency was converted to the local currency and the forward rate at which the foreign currency was repurchased. The difference reflects the forward premium (unannualized). The unannualized forward premium (p) can substitute for e_f in the equation introduced earlier to determine the effective financing rate when covering in the forward market under conditions of interest rate parity:

$$r_f = (1 + i_f)(1 + p) - 1$$

If interest rate parity exists, it was shown in Chapter 7 that

$$p = \frac{(1 + i_h)}{(1 + i_f)} - 1$$

where i_h represents the home currency. When this equation is used to reflect financing rates, we can substitute the formula for p to determine the effective financing rate of a foreign currency under conditions of interest rate parity:

$$r_f = (1 + i_f)(1 + p) - 1$$

$$= (1 + i_f)\left[1 + \frac{(1 + i_h)}{(1 + i_f)} - 1\right] - 1$$

$$= i_h$$

Thus, if interest rate parity exists, the attempt of covered interest arbitrage to finance with a low interest rate currency will result in an effective financing rate similar to the domestic rate.

Exhibit 14.2 summarizes the implications of a variety of scenarios relating to interest rate parity. Even if interest rate parity exists, financing with a foreign currency may still be feasible, but it would have to be conducted on an uncovered basis (without use of the forward market). That is, foreign financing may result in a lower financing cost than domestic financing, but it cannot be guaranteed (unless the firm has receivables in that same currency).

The Forward Rate as a Criterion for the Financing Decision

Assume the forward rate (F_f) of the foreign currency borrowed was used by firms as a predictor of the spot rate that would exist at the end of the financing period. The expected effective financing rate from borrowing a foreign currency would be forecasted by substituting F_f for $S_{f,t+1}$ in the following equation:

EXHIBIT 14.2 Interest Rate Parity and Implications for Short-Term Financing

Scenario	Implications
1. Interest rate parity holds.	Foreign financing and a simultaneous hedge of that position in the forward market will result in financing costs similar to domestic financing.
2. Interest rate parity holds, and the forward rate is an accurate forecast of the future spot rate.	Uncovered foreign financing will result in financing costs similar to domestic financing.
3. Interest rate parity holds, and the forward rate is expected to overestimate the future spot rate.	Uncovered foreign financing is expected to result in lower financing costs than domestic financing.
4. Interest rate parity holds, and the forward rate is expected to underestimate the future spot rate.	Uncovered foreign financing is expected to result in higher financing costs than domestic financing.
5. Interest rate parity does not hold; the forward premium (discount) exceeds (is less than) the interest rate differential.	Foreign financing with a simultaneous hedge of that position in the forward market results in higher financing costs than domestic financing.
6. Interest rate parity does not hold; the forward premium (discount) is less than (exceeds) the interest rate differential.	Foreign financing with a simultaneous hedge of that position in the forward market results in lower financing costs than domestic financing.

$$r_f = (1 + i_f) \left[1 + \frac{(S_{f,t+1} - S_{f,t})}{S_{f,t}} \right] - 1$$

$$r_f = (1 + i_f) \left[1 + \frac{(F_f - S_{f,t})}{S_{f,t}} \right] - 1$$

As already shown, the right side of this equation is equal to the home currency financing rate if interest rate parity exists. If the forward rate is an accurate estimator of the future spot rate, $S_{f,t+1}$, the foreign financing rate would be similar to the home financing rate.

When interest rate parity exists here, the forward rate can be used as a break-even point to assess the financing decision. When a firm is financing with the foreign currency (and not covering the foreign currency position), the effective financing rate will be less than the domestic rate if the future spot rate of the foreign currency (spot rate at the time of loan repayment) is less than the forward rate (at the time the loan is granted). Conversely, the effective financing rate in a foreign loan will be greater than the domestic rate if the future spot rate of the foreign currency turns out to be greater than that forward rate.

If the forward rate is an unbiased predictor of the future spot rate, then the effective financing rate of a foreign currency would on average be equal to the domestic financing rate. In this case, firms that consistently borrowed foreign currencies would not achieve lower financing costs. While the effective financing rate in some periods may turn out to be lower than the domestic rate, it would be higher in other periods, causing an offsetting effect. Firms that believe the forward rate is an unbiased predictor of the future spot rate would prefer borrowing their home currency, where the financing rate is known with certainty and is not expected to be any higher on average than foreign financing.

The fact that some firms utilize foreign financing suggests that they believe reduced financing costs can be achieved. To assess this issue, the effective financing rates of the Swiss franc (a currency with a low interest rate) and the U.S. dollar are compared from the perspective of a U.S. firm. Because the U.S. dollar represents the local currency in this comparison, the U.S. interest rate is the effective financing rate for financing with dollars. The 12-year period from 1975 to 1987 is used to compare financing rates. The data are segmented into 12 annual periods.

Results of the comparison are shown in Exhibit 14.3. The fourth column measures the effective financing rate for the Swiss franc (based on information provided in Columns 2 and 3), while the fifth column shows the U.S. rate. The sixth column represents the difference. A positive difference suggests a lower U.S. financing rate while a negative difference suggests a lower effective financing rate of the Swiss franc.

The borrowing of Swiss francs was most advantageous from 1980 through 1984. During these years, the franc depreciated substantially, so that the effective financing rate on francs was usually negative from a U.S. firm's perspective. The difference between Swiss-franc and U.S.-dollar financing rates during these years ranged from 14 percent to 34.5 percent. As an extreme example, the Swiss franc's effective financing rate was −24.9 percent in 1984, versus 9.6 percent for dollars, causing a difference of 34.5 percent.

EXHIBIT 14.3   Comparison of Financing with Swiss Francs versus Dollars

Financing Date	One-Year Foreign (Swiss) Interest Rate	Percentage Change in Exchange Rate of SF Over One-Year Period	Effective Financing Rate of SF	One-Year U.S. Interest Rate	Differ- ence
1/75	4.0%	−3.1%	.8%	5.8%	5.0%
1/76	2.0	7.0	9.1	5.0	4.1
1/77	3.5	22.5	26.8	5.3	21.5
1/78	2.0	23.4	25.8	7.2	18.6
1/79	3.0	2.6	5.7	10.0	−4.3
1/80	4.0	−10.3	−6.7	11.6	−18.3
1/81	2.3	−2.1	.1	14.1	−14.0
1/82	2.9	−9.9	−7.3	10.7	−18.0
1/83	1.3	−8.5	−7.3	8.6	−15.9
1/84	1.8	−26.2	−24.9	9.6	−34.5
1/85	3.3	24.5	28.6	7.5	21.1
1/86	3.8	27.9	32.8	6.0	26.8
1/87	3.2	24.8	28.8	5.8	23.0
1/88	3.2	−15.0	−12.3	6.0	−18.3
1/89	4.0	−2.7	1.2	7.7	−6.5
1/90	7.4	18.0	26.7	7.7	19.0

NOTE: The Swiss interest rate and the U.S. interest rate may not be directly comparable since they represent different money market rates. Yet, the impact of exchange rates on the differential between financing costs would be somewhat similar to that shown in this table, even if interest rates were not directly comparable.

A U.S. firm that borrowed francs rather than dollars to obtain a $1,000,000 loan would therefore have reduced financing costs by $345,000 (34.5% × $1,000,000).

The results of borrowing francs have not always been so favorable. In the mid 1980s, the franc appreciated, causing its effective financing rate (from a U.S. perspective) to be high. Therefore, U.S. firms that borrowed francs during this time incurred much higher financing costs than if they had borrowed dollars.

Exhibit 14.3 demonstrates the potential savings in financing costs that can be achieved if the foreign currency depreciates against the firm's home currency. It also demonstrates how the foreign financing could backfire if the firm's expectations are incorrect and the foreign currency appreciates over the financing period.

Exchange Rate Forecasts as a Criterion for the Financing Decision

While the forecasting capabilities of firms are somewhat limited, some firms may make decisions based on cycles in currency movements. Column 3 in Exhibit 14.3 shows that the franc's movements generally continued in one direction for a few years before reversing direction. Firms may use the recent movements as a forecast of future movements to determine whether they should borrow a foreign currency. This strategy would have been successful on average if utilized in the past. It will be successful in the future if currency movements continue to move in one direction for long periods of time.

Once the firm develops a forecast for the exchange rate's percentage change over the financing period (e_f), it can use this forecast along with the foreign interest rate to forecast the effective financing rate of a foreign currency. The forecasted rate can then be compared to the domestic financing rate. For example, assume a U.S. firm needs funds for one year, and is aware that the one-year interest rate in U.S. dollars is 12 percent and the interest rate from borrowing Swiss francs is 8 percent. Assume the U.S. firm forecasts that the Swiss franc will appreciate from its current rate of \$.45 to \$.459, or by 2 percent over the next year. The expected value for e_f (written as $E(e_f)$) will therefore be 2 percent. Thus, the expected effective financing rate $[E(r_f)]$ would be

$$E(r_f) = (1 + i_f)[1 + E(e_f)] - 1$$
$$= (1 + .08)(1 + .02) - 1$$
$$= .1016, \text{ or } 10.16\%$$

In this example, financing in Swiss francs is expected to be less expensive than financing in U.S. dollars. However, the value for e_f is forecasted and therefore is not known with certainty. Thus, there is no guarantee that foreign financing will truly be less costly. In recognition that e_f is not known, the U.S. firm may attempt to at least determine what value of e_f would make the effective rate from foreign financing the same as domestic financing. To determine this value, begin with the effective financing rate formula and solve e_f as shown:

$$r_f = (1 + i_f)(1 + e_f) - 1$$
$$(1 + r_f) = (1 + i_f)(1 + e_f)$$
$$\frac{(1 + r_f)}{(1 + i_f)} = (1 + e_f)$$
$$\frac{(1 + r_f)}{(1 + i_f)} - 1 = e_f$$

Since the U.S. financing rate was 12 percent in our previous example, that is the rate that would be plugged in for r_f. We can also plug in 8 percent for i_f so the break-even value of e_f would be

$$e_f = \frac{(1 + r_f)}{(1 + i_f)} - 1$$

$$= \frac{(1 + .12)}{(1 + .08)} - 1$$

$$= .037037, \text{ or } 3.7037\%$$

This suggests the Swiss franc must appreciate by about 3.7 percent to make the Swiss-franc loan as costly as a loan in U.S. dollars. Any lesser degree of appreciation would make the Swiss-franc loan less costly. The U.S. firm can use this information when determining whether to borrow U.S. dollars or Swiss francs. If it expects the Swiss franc to appreciate by more than 3.7 percent over the loan life, it should prefer borrowing in U.S. dollars. If it expects the Swiss franc to appreciate by less than 3.7 percent, or to depreciate, its decision is more complex. If the potential savings from financing with the foreign currency outweighs the risk involved, then the firm should choose that route. The final decision here will be influenced by the firm's degree of risk aversion.

To gain more insight in the financing decision, the firm may wish to develop a probability distribution for the percentage change in value for a particular foreign currency over the financing horizon. As discussed in Chapter 9, even expert forecasts are not always accurate. Thus, it is sometimes useful to develop a probability distribution when forecasting instead of relying on a single point estimate. Using the probability distribution of possible percentage changes in the currency's value, along with the currency's interest rate, the firm can determine the probability distribution of the possible effective financing rates for the currency. Then, it can compare this distribution to the known financing rate of the home currency in order to make its financing decision. An example follows.

Assume a U.S. firm is deciding whether to borrow Swiss francs for one year. It finds that the quoted interest rate for the Swiss franc is 8 percent, and the quoted rate of a U.S. dollar is 15 percent. The firm then develops a probability distribution for the Swiss franc's possible percentage change in value over the life of the loan. The probability distribution is displayed in Exhibit 14.4. The first row in Exhibit 14.4 shows there is a 5 percent probability of a 6 percent depreciation in the Swiss franc over the loan life. If the Swiss franc does depreciate by 6 percent, the effective financing rate would be 1.52 percent. This implies there is a 5 percent probability of the U.S. firm incurring a 1.52 percent effective financing rate on its loan. The second row shows there is a 10 percent probability of a 4 percent depreciation in the Swiss franc over the loan life. If the Swiss franc does depreciate by 4 percent, the effective financing rate would be 3.68 percent. This implies there is a 10 percent probability of the U.S. firm incurring a 3.68 percent effective financing rate on its loan. For each possible percentage change in the Swiss franc's

EXHIBIT 14.4 Analysis of Financing with a Foreign Currency

Possible Rate of Change in the Swiss Franc Over the Life of the Loan (e_f)	Probability of Occurrence	Effective Financing Rate If This Rate of Change in the Swiss Franc Does Occur (r_f)	
−6%	5%	$(1.08)[1 + (−6\%)] − 1 =$	1.52%
−4	10	$(1.08)[1 + (−4\%)] − 1 =$	3.68
−1	15	$(1.08)[1 + (−1\%)] − 1 =$	6.92
+1	20	$(1.08)[1 + (1\%)] − 1 \quad =$	9.08
+4	20	$(1.08)[1 + (4\%)] − 1 \quad =$	12.32
+6	15	$(1.08)[1 + (6\%)] − 1 \quad =$	14.48
+8	10	$(1.08)[1 + (8\%)] − 1 \quad =$	16.64
+10	5	$(1.08)[1 + (10\%)] − 1 =$	18.80
	100%		

value, there is a corresponding effective financing rate. We can associate each possible effective financing rate (Column 3) with a probability of that occurring (Column 2). From these two columns we can attain an expected value for the effective financing rate of the Swiss franc. An expected value of the effective financing rate is determined by multiplying each possible effective financing rate by its associated probability. Based on the information in Exhibit 14.4, the expected value of the effective financing rate, referred to as $E(r_f)$, is computed:

$$
\begin{aligned}
E(r_f) = {} & 5\%(1.52\%) + 10\%(3.68\%) + 15\%(6.92\%) + 20\%(9.08\%) \\
& + 20\%(12.32\%) + 15\%(14.48\%) \\
& + 10\%(16.64\%) + 5\%(18.80\%) \\[8pt]
= {} & .076\% + .368\% + 1.038\% + 1.816\% \\
& + 2.464\% + 2.172\% + 1.664\% + .94\% \\[8pt]
= {} & 10.538\%
\end{aligned}
$$

It has been determined that the expected value of the effective financing rate for borrowing Swiss francs is 10.538 percent. Given this information, should the U.S. firm borrow Swiss francs or U.S. dollars? The answer may depend on what the interest rate is for a U.S.-dollar loan. Recall that it is assumed to be 15 percent. If you are the treasurer of the U.S. firm, are you going to borrow U.S. dollars (and pay 15 percent interest) or borrow Swiss francs (with an expected value of 10.538 percent for the effective financing rate)? You may choose to borrow U.S. dollars, since you desire knowing with certainty the rate you will pay for your loan. However, you may be willing to borrow Swiss francs if you feel the potential reduction in financing costs from a Swiss franc loan outweighs the risk involved. What is the risk in this case? Using Exhibit 14.4, you can see that the risk reflects the 5 percent chance (probability) that the effective financing rate on Swiss francs will be 18.8 percent or the 10 percent chance that the effective financing rate on Swiss francs will be 16.64 percent. Either of these possibilities represents a greater expense to the U.S. firm than would have been incurred if it had borrowed U.S. dollars. For this reason, some of the more conservative firms may choose to avoid the uncertainty by simply borrowing U.S. dollars. Other firms may be willing to borrow francs and tolerate the risk.

To further assess the decision of which currency to borrow, the information in Columns 2 and 3 of Exhibit 14.4 is used to develop a probability distribution in Exhibit 14.5. This exhibit illustrates the probability of each possible effective financing rate that may occur if the U.S. firm borrows Swiss francs. Notice that the U.S. interest rate (15 percent) is included in Exhibit 14.5 for comparison purposes. There is no distribution of probabilities for the U.S. rate since the rate of 15 percent is known with certainty (no exchange rate risk exists). There is a 15 percent probability that the U.S. rate will be less than the effective rate on Swiss francs and an 85 percent chance that the U.S. rate will be greater than the effective rate on Swiss francs. This information can lead the firm to its financing decision.

Some firms incur much higher financing costs because they have subsidiaries in inflationary countries where interest rates are relatively high. For

EXHIBIT 14.5 Probability Distribution of the Effective
Financing Rate

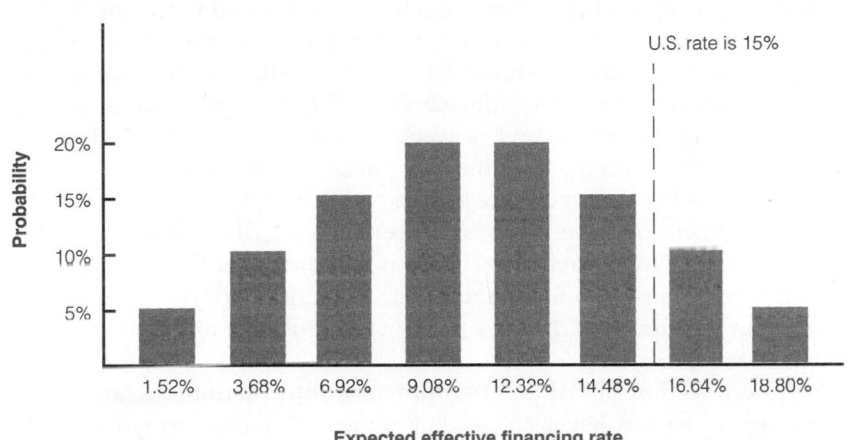

example, Dow Chemical Company had the equivalent of $221 million in short-term borrowings during 1986, with a weighted average annual interest rate of 18.2 percent. Dow Chemical could have attempted to reduce its financing costs by borrowing currencies with low interest rates. However, the firm's subsidiaries' local currencies generally depreciated against other currencies. Therefore, the effective financing rate of borrowing such low–interest rate currencies could backfire.

FINANCING WITH A PORTFOLIO OF CURRENCIES

Recent research by Eaker and Lenowitz has found that foreign financing can result in significantly lower financing costs. Yet, the variance in financing costs over time is higher when financing in foreign currencies, reflecting the risk of such a financing strategy. MNCs may be able to achieve lower financing costs without excessive risk by financing with a portfolio of foreign currencies, as demonstrated here.

Assume a U.S. firm needs to borrow $100,000 for one year and obtains the following interest rate quotes:

> Interest rate for a one-year loan in U.S. dollars = 15%.
> Interest rate for a one-year loan in Swiss francs = 8%.
> Interest rate for a one-year loan in Japanese yen = 9%.

Due to relatively low quotes for a loan in Swiss francs or Japanese yen, the U.S. firm may desire to borrow in a foreign currency. If the U.S. firm decides to use foreign financing, it has three choices based on the information given: (1) borrow only Swiss francs, (2) borrow only Japanese yen, and (3) borrow a mixture or portfolio of francs and yen. Assume the U.S. firm has established possible percentage changes in the spot rate from the time the loan would begin until loan repayment for both the Swiss franc and Japanese yen, as shown in Column 2 of Exhibit 14.6. For each possible percentage change that might occur, a probability of that occurrence is disclosed in the third column. Based on the assumed interest rate of 8 percent for the Swiss franc, the effective financing rate is computed for each possible percentage change in the Swiss franc's spot rate over the loan life. There is a 30 percent chance the Swiss franc will appreciate by 1 percent over the loan life. If the Swiss franc appreciates by 1 percent, the effective financing rate will be 9.08 percent. Thus, there is a 30 percent chance that the effective financing rate will be 9.08 percent. Furthermore, there is a 50 percent chance that the effective financing rate will be 11.24 percent and a 20 percent chance that it will be 17.72 percent. Given that the U.S. loan rate is 15 percent, there is only a 20 percent chance that the financing in Swiss francs will result in a higher financing cost than domestic financing.

The lower section of Exhibit 14.6 provides information on Japanese yen. For example, the yen has a 35 percent chance of depreciating by 1 percent over the loan life, and so on. Based on the assumed 9 percent interest rate and the exchange rate fluctuation forecasts, there is a 35 percent chance that the effective financing rate will be 7.91 percent, a 40 percent chance that it will be 12.27 percent, and a 25 percent chance that it will be 16.63 percent. Given the 15 percent rate on U.S. dollar financing, there is a 25 percent chance that financing in Japanese yen will be more costly than domestic financing. Before examining the third possible foreign financing strategy (the portfolio approach), determine the expected value of the effective financing rate for each foreign currency by itself. This is accomplished by totaling the products of each possible effective financing rate and its associated probability as follows:

Currency	Computation of Expected Value of Effective Financing Rate
Swiss francs	(30%) (9.08%) + 50% (11.24%) + 20% (17.72%) = 11.888%
Japanese yen	(35%) (7.91%) + 40% (12.27%) + 25% (16.63%) = 11.834%

EXHIBIT 14.6   Development of Possible Effective Financing Rates

Currency	Possible Percentage Change in the Spot Rate Over the Loan Life	Probability of That Percentage Change in the Spot Rate Occurring	Computation of Effective Financing Rate Based on That Percentage Change in the Spot Rate
Swiss franc	1%	30%	$(1.08)\,[1 + (.01)] - 1 = .0908$, or 9.08%
Swiss franc	3	50	$(1.08)\,[1 + (.03)] - 1 = .1124$, or 11.24%
Swiss franc	9	20	$(1.08)\,[1 + (.09)] - 1 = .1772$, or 17.72%
		100%	
Japanese yen	−1%	35%	$(1.09)\,[1 + (-.01)] - 1 = .0791$, or 7.91%
Japanese yen	3	40	$(1.09)\,[1 + (-.03)] - 1 = .1227$, or 12.27%
Japanese yen	7	25	$(1.09)\,[1 + (.07)] - 1 = .1663$, or 16.63%
		100%	

The expected financing costs of the two currencies are almost the same. The individual degree of risk (that the costs of financing will turn out to be higher than domestic financing) is about the same for each currency. If the U.S. firm does choose to finance with only one of these foreign currencies, it is difficult to pinpoint (based on our analysis) which currency is more appropriate. Now, consider the third and final foreign financing strategy—the portfolio approach.

Using the information in Exhibit 14.6, one can see three possibilities for the Swiss franc's effective financing rate. The same holds true for the Japanese yen. If a U.S. firm borrows half of its needed funds in each of the foreign currencies, then there will be nine possibilities for this portfolio's effective financing rate, as shown in Exhibit 14.7. The first two columns list all possible joint effective financing rates. The third column computes the joint probability of that occurrence. The fourth column shows the computation of the portfolio's effective financing rate based on the possible rates disclosed for the individual currencies shown in the first two columns.

An examination of the top row will help to clarify the table. This row suggests that one possible outcome from borrowing both Swiss francs and Japanese yen is that they will exhibit effective financing rates of 9.08 percent and 7.91 percent, respectively. The probability of the Swiss franc rate occurring is 30 percent, while the probability of the Japanese yen rate occurring is 35 percent. Recall that these percentages were given in Exhibit 14.6. The joint probability that both of these rates will occur simultaneously is (30%) (35%) = 10.5%. Assuming that half (50%) of the funds needed are to be borrowed from each currency, the portfolio's effective financing rate will be .5(9.08%) + .5(7.91%) = 8.495% (if those individual effective financing rates occur for each currency).

A similar procedure was used to develop the remaining eight rows in Exhibit 14.7. From this table, there is a 10.5 percent chance that the portfolio's effective financing rate will be 8.495 percent, a 12 percent chance that it will be 10.675 percent, and so on.

EXHIBIT 14.7 Analysis of Financing with Two Foreign Currencies

(1) (2) Possible Joint Effective Financing Rates		(3) Computation of Joint Probability	(4) Computation of Effective Financing Rate of Portfolio (50% of Total Funds Borrowed in Each Currency)
Swiss Franc	Japanese Yen		
9.08%	7.91%	(30%) (35%) = 10.5%	.5 (9.08%) + .5 (7.91%) = 8.495%
9.08	12.27	(30%) (40%) = 12.0	.5 (9.08%) + .5(12.27%) = 10.675
9.08	16.63	(30%) (25%) = 7.5	.5 (9.08%) + .5(16.63%) = 12.885
11.24	7.91	(50%) (35%) = 17.5	.5(11.24%) + .5 (7.91%) = 9.575
11.24	12.27	(50%) (40%) = 20.0	.5(11.24%) + .5(12.27%) = 11.755
11.24	16.63	(50%) (25%) = 12.5	.5(11.24%) + .5(16.63%) = 13.935
17.72	7.91	(20%) (35%) = 7.0	.5(17.72%) + .5 (7.91%) = 12.815
17.72	12.27	(20%) (40%) = 8.0	.5(17.72%) + .5(12.27%) = 14.995
17.72	16.63	(20%) (25%) = 5.0	.5(17.72%) + .5(16.63%) = 17.175
		100.0%	

Recall that financing solely in Swiss francs had a 20 percent chance of being more costly than domestic financing, while financing solely in Japanese yen had a 25 percent chance of being more costly. The analysis in Exhibit 14.7 suggests that financing in a portfolio (50 percent financing in Swiss francs with the remaining 50 percent financed in Japanese yen) has only a 5 percent chance of being more costly than domestic financing. These results will be explained.

When both currencies are borrowed in our example, the only way the portfolio will exhibit a higher effective financing rate than the domestic rate is for *both* currencies to experience their maximum possible level of appreciation (which is 9 percent for the Swiss franc and 7 percent for the Japanese yen). If only one does, the severity of its appreciation will be somewhat offset by the other currency not appreciating by such a large extent. The probability of maximum appreciation is 20 percent for the Swiss franc and 25 percent for the Japanese yen. The joint probability of both of these events occurring simultaneously is $(20\%)(25\%) = 5\%$. This is an advantage of financing in a portfolio of foreign currencies. In our example, the U.S. firm has a 95 percent chance of attaining lower costs with the foreign portfolio than with domestic financing.

The expected value of the effective financing rate for the portfolio can be determined by multiplying the percentage financed in each currency by the respective expected value of its individual effective financing rate. Recall that the expected value was 11.888 percent for the Swiss franc and 11.834 percent for the Japanese yen. Thus, for a portfolio representing 50 percent of funds borrowed in each currency, the expected value of the effective financing rate is $.5(11.888\%) + .5(11.834\%) = 11.861\%$. Based on an overall comparison, the portfolio's expected value of the effective financing rate is very similar to that from financing solely in either foreign currency. However, the risk (of incurring a higher effective financing rate than the domestic rate) when financing with the portfolio is substantially less.

In our example, the computation of joint probabilities requires the assumption that the movements in the two currencies are independent. If movements of the two currencies were actually highly positively correlated, then financing in a portfolio of currencies would not be as beneficial as demonstrated, since there is a strong likelihood of both currencies experiencing a high level of appreciation simultaneously. If the two currencies are not highly correlated, we would not expect them to simultaneously appreciate to such a degree. Thus, the chances that the portfolio's effective financing rate will exceed the U.S. rate are reduced when the currencies included in the portfolio are not highly positively correlated.

The previous example included two currencies in the portfolio. Financing with a more diversified portfolio of additional currencies that exhibit low interest rates may even increase the probability of foreign financing being less costly than domestic financing, since several currencies are not likely to move in tandem and therefore simultaneously appreciate to offset the advantage of their low interest rate. Again, the degree to which these currencies are correlated with each other is important here. If all currencies are highly positively correlated with each other, financing with such a portfolio would not be much different than financing with a single foreign currency. The correlations between currencies can be measured with the use of correlation coefficients, which were computed from historical data for several major currencies in Chapter 10.

Repeated Financing with a Currency Portfolio

A firm that repeatedly finances in a currency portfolio would normally prefer to compose a financing package that exhibits a somewhat predictable effective financing rate on a periodic basis. The more volatile a portfolio's effective financing rate over time, the more uncertainty (risk) there is about the effective financing rate that will exist in any period. The degree of volatility depends on the standard deviations and paired correlations of effective financing rates of the individual currencies within the portfolio.

We can use the portfolio variance as a measurement for degree of volatility. The variance of a two-currency portfolio's effective financing rate [$VAR(r_p)$] over time is computed as

$$VAR(r_p) = w^2_A\sigma^2_A + w^2_B\sigma^2_B + 2w_Aw_B\sigma_A\sigma_BCORR_{AB}$$

where w_A and w_B represent the percentage of total funds financed from Currencies A and B respectively, σ^2_A and σ^2_A represent the individual variances of each currency's effective financing rate over time, and $CORR_{AB}$ reflects the correlation coefficient of the two currencies' effective financing rates. Since the percentage exchange rate change plays an important role in influencing the effective financing rate, it should not be surprising that $CORR_{AB}$ is strongly affected by the correlation between the exchange rate fluctuations of the two currencies. A low correlation between currency fluctuations may force $CORR_{AB}$ to be low.

To illustrate how the variance in a portfolio's effective financing rate is related to characteristics of the component currencies, assume the following information based on historical information of several three-month periods:

Mean effective financing rate of Canadian dollar for three months = 3%.
Mean effective financing rate of Swiss franc for three months = 2%.
Standard deviation of Canadian dollar's effective financing rate = .04.
Standard deviation of Swiss franc's effective financing rate = .09.
Correlation coefficient of effective financing rates of these two currencies = .10.

Given this information, the mean effective rate on a portfolio (r_p) of funds financed 50 percent by Canadian dollars and 50 percent by Swiss francs is determined by totaling the weighted individual effective financing rates:

$$
\begin{aligned}
r_p &= w_Ar_A + w_Br_B \\
&= .5(.03) + .5(.02) \\
&= .015 + .01 \\
&= .025 \ or \ 2.5\%
\end{aligned}
$$

The variance of this portfolio's effective financing rate over time is

$$
\begin{aligned}
VAR(r_p) &= .5^2(.04)^2 + .5^2(.09)^2 + 2(.5)(.5)(.04)(.09)(.10) \\
&= .25(.0016) + .25(.0081) + .00018 \\
&= .0004 + .002025 + .00018 \\
&= .002605
\end{aligned}
$$

The preceding example suggests how an MNC can use historical data to determine the mean effective financing rate and variance of a two-currency portfolio. Thus, it can compare various financing packages to see which package would have been most appropriate. The MNC may be more interested in estimating the mean return and variability for repeated financing in a particular portfolio in the future. There is no guarantee that past data will be indicative of the future. Yet, if the individual variability and paired correlations are somewhat stable over time, the historical variability of the portfolio's effective financing rate should be a reasonable forecast.

This analysis is not restricted to just two currencies. The mean effective financing rate for a currency portfolio of any size will be determined by totaling the products of percentage of funds financed in each currency times its respective individual effective financing rate. Solving the variance of a portfolio's effective financing rate becomes more complex as more currencies are added to the portfolio, but computer software packages are commonly applied to more easily determine the solution.

SUMMARY

The decision of which currency or currencies to borrow for short-term financing is easier when the firm has future receivables denominated in foreign currencies that exhibit low interest rates. Such currencies should be borrowed, and the future incoming payments representing the receivables can be used to pay off the short-term loans. If the firm does not have future receivables in low-interest rate currencies, the decision becomes more complex. The effective financing rate of any foreign currency is unknown due to the uncertain fluctuation of that currency's value against the firm's local currency over the loan life. To make the financing decision of which currency (or currencies) to borrow, one can forecast the effective financing rate of all possible currencies by estimating each currency's percentage appreciation or depreciation against the local currency. The accuracy of the forecasted effective financing rate is substantially influenced by the accuracy of the forecasted percentage change in the currency's value. And since exchange rate forecasts are often inaccurate, the financing decision should not be based solely on them.

Additional insight into the financing decision can be achieved by computing the break-even exchange rate percentage change at which a foreign currency's effective financing rate would equal the rate from financing in the local currency. If the actual exchange rate percentage change is any less than this break-even point, financing in the foreign currency would be less costly than in the local currency. Conversely, if the actual exchange rate change turns out to be greater than this break-even point, financing in a foreign currency would be more costly than in the local currency. Again, the debtor firm is limited in that it does not know what the exchange rate percentage change will be. Still, it is easier to guess whether the change will be greater or less than the break-even point than to guess the percentage change itself.

To further assess the financing decision, the debtor firm could develop a probability distribution of exchange rate fluctuations. From this information a probability distribution of effective financing rates could be created to determine the probability that the effective financing rate for a particular foreign currency will be greater than the local financing rate.

To reduce the risk (uncertainty) from foreign financing, a firm should consider borrowing a portfolio of currencies. While individual currencies can exhibit volatile fluctuations in their effective financing rates, a currency portfolio's effective financing rate is normally more stable due to differences in individual currency movements. Since not all currencies move in tandem, the portfolio value will not be changing to the degree of the individual currency values. It is possible for a firm to substantially reduce its risk when financing with a portfolio of currencies rather than a single foreign currency. The degree by which the debtor firm can reduce risk from financing with a portfolio will be increased if the component currencies exhibit relatively low (or negative) correlations with each other.

QUESTIONS/ PROBLEMS

1. Explain why an MNC parent would consider financing from its subsidiaries.

2. Discuss the use of specifying a break-even point when financing in a foreign currency.

3. Discuss the development of a probability distribution of effective financing rates when financing in a foreign currency. How is this distribution developed?

4. Once the probability distribution of effective financing rates from financing in a foreign currency is developed, how can it be used in deciding whether to finance in the foreign currency or home currency?

5. How can a firm finance in a foreign currency and not necessarily be exposed to exchange rate risk?

6. Explain how a firm's degree of risk aversion enters into its decision on whether to finance in a foreign currency or a local currency. What motivates the firm to even consider financing in a foreign currency?

7. Assume a U.S.-based MNC needs $3 million for a six-month period. Within six months, it will generate enough U.S. dollars to pay off the loan. It is considering three options: (1) borrowing U.S. dollars at a rate of 6 percent, (2) borrowing Swiss francs at a rate of 3 percent, or (3) borrowing German marks at a rate of 4 percent. The MNC has forecasted that the Swiss franc will appreciate by 1 percent and that the German mark will appreciate by 3 percent. What is the expected "effective" financing rate for each of the three options? Which option appears to be most feasible? Why might the MNC not necessarily choose the option reflecting the lowest effective financing rate?

8. How is it possible for a firm to incur a negative effective financing rate?

9. If interest rate parity did not hold, what strategy should a U.S. firm consider when it needs short-term financing? Assume a U.S. firm needs dollars. It borrows German marks at a lower interest rate than what it would have paid on borrowed dollars. If interest parity exists and if the forward rate of the mark is a reliable predictor of the future spot rate, what does this suggest about the feasibility of such a strategy? If the MNC expects the current spot rate to be a more reliable predictor of the future spot rate, what does this suggest about the feasibility of such a strategy?

10. A firm needs local currency. Assume the local one-year loan rate is 15 percent, while a foreign one-year loan rate is 7 percent. By how much must the foreign currency appreciate to cause the foreign loan to be more costly than a local loan?

11. A U.S.-based MNC decides to borrow Japanese yen for one year. The interest rate on the borrowed yen is 8 percent. The MNC has developed the following probability distribution for the yen's degree of fluctuation against the dollar:

Possible Degree of Fluctuation of Yen against the Dollar	Percentage Probability
−4%	20%
−1	30
0	10
3	40

Given this information, what is the expected value of the effective financing rate of the Japanese yen from the U.S. corporation's perspective?

12. Assume that interest rate parity exists. If a firm believed that the forward rate was an unbiased predictor of the future spot rate, would it expect to achieve lower financing costs by consistently borrowing a foreign currency with a low interest rate?

13. Assume a U.S. firm considers obtaining 40 percent of its one-year financing in Canadian dollars and 60 percent in Swiss francs. The forecasts of appreciation in the Canadian dollar and Swiss franc for the next year are as follows:

Currency	Possible Percentage Change in the Spot Rate Over the Loan Life	Probability of That Percentage Change in the Spot Rate Occurring
Canadian dollar	4%	70%
Canadian dollar	7	30
Swiss franc	6	50
Swiss franc	9	50

The interest rate on the Canadian dollar is 9 percent, and the interest rate on the Swiss franc is 7 percent. Develop the possible effective financing rates of the overall portfolio and the probability of each possibility based on the use of joint probabilities.

14. Why might a corporation attempt to borrow a portfolio of foreign currencies even when it needs to make payments in its local currency?

15. Does borrowing a portfolio of currencies offer any possible advantages beyond the borrowing of a single foreign currency?

16. If a firm borrows a portfolio of currencies, what characteristics of the currencies will affect the potential variability of the portfolio's effective financing rate? What characteristics would be desirable from a borrowing firm's perspective?

17. Boca Inc. needs $4 million for one year. It presently has no business in West Germany but plans to borrow marks from a German bank, because the German interest rate is three percentage points lower than the U.S. rate. Assume that interest rate parity exists; also assume that Boca believes the one-year forward rate of the mark exceeds the future spot rate one year from now. Would the expected effective financing rate be higher, lower, or the same as financing with dollars? Explain.

18. Jacksonville Corporation is a U.S.-based firm that needs $600,000. It has no business in Switzerland but is considering one-year financing with Swiss francs, because the annual interest rate would be 5 percent versus 9 percent in the United States. The spot rate of the Swiss franc is presently $.62, while the forward rate is $.6436.

   a) Can Jacksonville benefit from borrowing Swiss francs and simultaneously purchasing francs one year forward to avoid exchange rate risk? Explain.

   b) Assume that Jacksonville does not cover its exposure and uses the forward rate to forecast the future spot rate. Determine the expected effective financing rate. Should Jacksonville finance with Swiss francs? Explain.

   c) Assume that Jacksonville does not cover its exposure and expects that the Swiss franc will appreciate by either 5 percent, 3 percent, or by 2 percent, with an equal probability of each occurrence. Use this information to determine the probability distribution of the effective financing rate. Should Jacksonville finance with Swiss francs? Explain.

19. Assume that the U.S. interest rate is 7 percent and the Swiss interest rate is 4 percent. Assume that the Swiss franc's forward rate has a premium of 4 percent. Is the following statement true? "Interest rate parity does not hold; therefore U.S. firms could lock in a lower financing cost by borrowing Swiss francs and purchasing francs forward for one year." Explain your answer.

20. Orlando Inc. is a U.S.-based MNC with a subsidiary in Mexico. Its Mexican subsidiary needs a one-year loan of 10 million pesos for operating expenses. Since the Mexican interest rate is 70 percent, it is considering borrowing dollars, which it would convert to pesos to cover the operating expenses. By how much would the dollar have to appreciate against the peso to cause such a strategy to backfire? (The one-year U.S. interest rate is 9%.)

21. Assume the following information. Raleigh Corporation needs to borrow funds for one year to finance an expenditure in the United States. The following interest rates are available:

	Borrowing Rate
U.S.	10%
Swiss	6%
Japan	5%

The future spot rate (in one year) of the Swiss franc and Japanese yen are as follows:

	Swiss Franc		Japanese Yen	
Probability	Percentage Change in Spot Rate	Probability	Percentage Change in Spot Rate	
10%	5%	20%	6%	
90%	2%	80%	1%	

If Raleigh Corporation borrows a portfolio, 50 percent of funds from francs and 50 percent of funds from yen, determine the probability distribution of the effective financing rate of the portfolio. What is the probability that Raleigh will incur a higher effective financing rate from borrowing this portfolio than if it had borrowed dollars?

Flyer Company
Composing the Optimal Currency Portfolio for Financing

As treasurer for Flyer Company, you must develop a strategy for short-term financing. The firm, based in the United States, presently has no transactions exposure to currency movements. Assume the following data as of today:

Currency	Spot Exchange Rate	Annualized Interest Rate on a Three-Month Loan
Australian dollar	$ .75	13.00
British Pound	1.70	12.5
Canadian Dollar	.86	11.0
French franc	.17	11.5
German mark	.60	7.0
Italian lira	.0008	12.0
Japanese yen	.006	8.0
Swedish krona	.16	9.0
Swiss franc	.71	6.0
U.S. dollar	1.00	9.0

Your forecasting department has provided you with the following forecasts of the spot rates three months from now:

	Strong $ Scenario	Somewhat Stable $ Scenario	Weak $ Scenario
Australian dollar	$ .66	$ .76	$ .85
British pound	1.58	1.73	1.83
Canadian dollar	.85	.85	.91
French franc	.14	.173	.18
German mark	.53	.59	.63

	Strong $ Scenario	Somewhat Stable $ Scenario	Weak $ Scenario
Italian lira	.00073	.00079	.00086
Japanese yen	.0055	.0062	.0072
Swedish krona	.15	.155	.17
Swiss franc	.62	.69	.78
U.S. dollar	1.00	1.00	1.00

The probability of the strong dollar scenario is 30 percent, the probability of the somewhat stable dollar scenario is 40 percent and the probability of the weak dollar scenario is 30 percent. Based on the information provided, prescribe the composition of the portfolio that would achieve the minimum expected effective financing rate based on each of the following risk preferences:

1. Risk neutral	Focus on minimizing the expected value of your effective financing rate, without any constraints.
2. Balanced	Borrow no more than 25 percent in any foreign currency.
3. Conservative	Borrow at least 60 percent U.S. dollars and no more than 10 percent of the funds from any individual foreign currency.
4. Ultra-conservative	Do not create any exposure to exchange rate risk.

Fill out the following table:

Risk Preference	Forecasted Effective Financing Rate of Portfolio Based on a:			Expected Value of Effective Financing Rate
	Strong $ Scenario	Stable $ Scenario	Weak $ Scenario	
Risk neutral portfolio				
Balanced portfolio				
Conservative portfolio				
Ultra-conservative portfolio				

Which portfolio would you prescribe for your firm? Why?

PROJECT

1. Use the interest rate and exchange rate data from the Data Bank in the back of the text to determine a U.S. firm's effective financing rate when borrowing German marks on a quarterly basis. Identify the periods in which this strategy would have resulted in very low effective financing rates. Was the dollar strengthening or weakening in those periods? (A computer spreadsheet could easily be created to reduce your computational time.)

SUGGESTED READING

M. R. Eaker and J. Lenowitz. "Multinational Borrowing Decisions and the Empirical Exchange Rate Evidence." *Management International Review*, no. 1 (1986), pp. 24–32. This article examines the ability of MNCs to reduce financing costs by borrowing foreign currencies. The results and implications are very interesting.

REFERENCES

Biger, Nahum. "Exchange Risk Implications of International Portfolio Diversification." *Journal of International Business Studies* (Fall 1979), pp. 64–74.

de Faro, Clovis, and James V. Jucker. "The Impact of Inflation and Devaluation on the Selection of an International Borrowing Source." *Journal of International Business Studies* (Fall 1973), pp. 97–104.

Eaker, M. R., and J. Lenowitz. "Multinational Borrowing Decisions and the Empirical Exchange Rate Evidence." *Management International Review*, no. 1 (1986), pp. 24–32.

Finney, Malcolm, and Nigel Meade. "A Practical Approach to Corporate Borrowing and Exchange Rate Risk." *Euromoney* (October 1978), pp. 191–197.

Folks, William R. "Optimal Foreign Borrowing Strategies with Operations in Forward Exchange Markets." *Journal of Financial and Quantitative Analysis* (June 1978), pp. 245–254.

Jucker, James V., and Clovis de Faro, "The Selection of International Borrowing Sources." *Journal of Financial and Quantitative Analysis* (September 1975), pp. 381–407.

Levy, Haim. "Optimal Portfolio of Foreign Currencies with Borrowing and Lending." *Journal of Money, Credit, and Banking* (August 1981), pp. 325–341.

Madura, Jeff. "Borrowing Abroad: How to Choose Best Mix of Foreign Currencies." *Journal of Business Forecasting* (Winter 1982–83), pp. 9–11.

_____. "Model for Financing in International Money Markets," *International Review of Economics and Business* (October–November 1986), pp. 1049–1056.

_____. "Development and Evaluation of International Financing Models," *Management International Review* 25, no. 4 (1985), pp. 17–27.

Madura, Jeff, and E. Joe Nosari. "Optimal Portfolio of Foreign Currencies with Borrowing and Lending." *Journal of Money, Credit, and Banking* (November 1982), p. 531.

Mirus, Rolf. "The Impact of Inflation and Devaluation on the Selection of an International Borrowing Source: A Note." *Journal of International Business Studies* (Spring/Summer 1978), pp. 125–128.

Severn, Alan K., and David R. Meinster. "The Use of Multicurrency Financing by the Financial Manager." *Financial Management* (Winter 1978), pp. 45–53.

"U.S. Business Starts to Repatriate Its Cash." *Business Week* (March 31, 1980), p. 83.

CHAPTER 15

International Cash Management

The term **cash management** can be broadly defined to mean optimization of cash flows and investment of excess cash. From an international perspective, cash management is very complex because of different laws among countries that pertain to cross-border cash transfers. In addition, exchange rate fluctuations can affect the value of cross-border cash transfers. This chapter begins with a description of the cash flow cycle for a subsidiary and then the parent. Next, it explains how an MNC can optimize its cash flows and identifies common complications in doing so. Finally, it explains how MNCs determine where to invest excess cash.

CASH FLOW ANALYSIS: SUBSIDIARY PERSPECTIVE

The management of working capital (such as inventory, accounts receivable, and cash) has a direct influence on the amount and timing of cash flow. Working capital management and the management of cash flow are integrated. They are discussed here first before focusing on cash management. Exhibit 15.1 is used to complement the discussion.

Begin with outflow payments by the subsidiary to purchase raw materials or supplies. The subsidiary will normally have a more difficult time forecasting future outflow payments if its purchases are international rather than domestic because of exchange rate fluctuations. In addition, the possibility exists of substantially higher payments due to appreciation of the invoice currency. Consequently, the firm may wish to maintain a large inventory of supplies and raw materials so that it can cut down on purchases if the invoice currency appreciates and instead draw from its inventory. Still another possibility is that imported goods from another country could be restricted by the importer's government (through quotas, etc.). In this event, a larger inventory would give a firm more time to search for alternative sources of supplies or raw materials. A subsidiary with domestic supply sources would not experience such a problem and therefore would not need as large an inventory.

Outflow payments for supplies will be influenced by future sales. If the sales volume is substantially influenced by exchange rate fluctuations, its

EXHIBIT 15.1   Cash Flow from a Subsidiary's Perspective

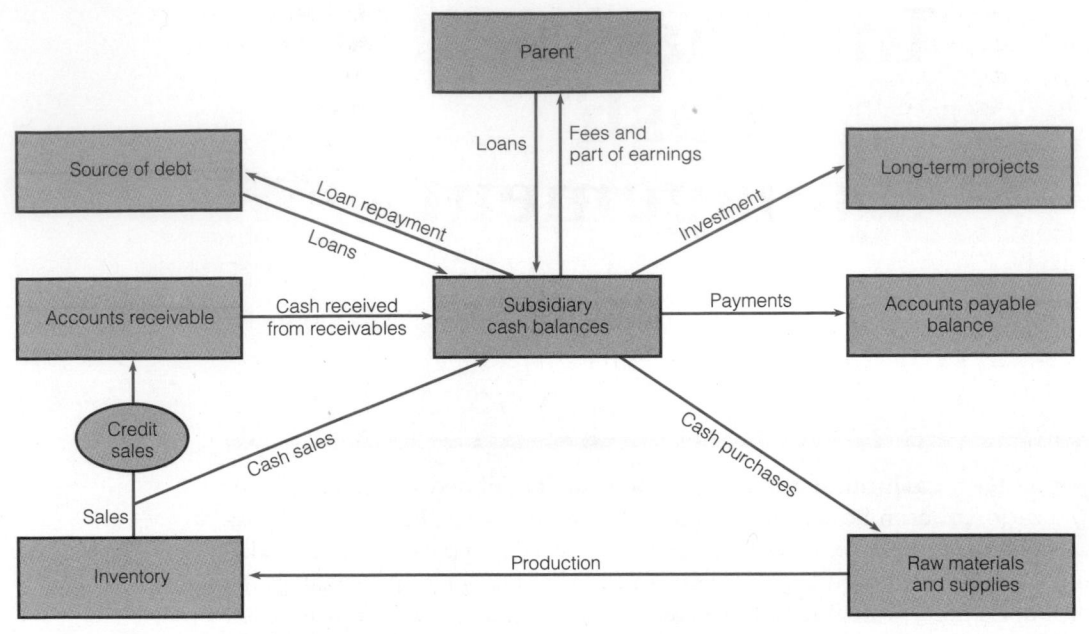

future level becomes more uncertain, which makes outflow payments for supplies more uncertain. Such uncertainty may force the subsidiary to maintain larger cash balances in order to cover any unexpected increase in supply requirements.

Subsidiaries use their raw materials and/or supplies in their production process. If their finished goods are exported overseas, the sales volume may be more volatile than if the goods were sold only domestically. This could be due to the fluctuating exchange rate of the invoice currency. Demand for these finished goods by importers would most likely decrease if the invoice currency appreciates. The sales volume of exports is also susceptible to business cycles of the importing countries. If the goods were sold domestically, the exchange rate fluctuations would not have a direct impact on sales, although they would still have an indirect impact, since they influence prices paid by local customers for imports from foreign competitors.

Sales can often be increased when relaxing credit standards. However, it is important to focus on cash inflows due to sales rather than sales itself. Looser credit standards may cause a slowdown in cash inflows from the point of sales, which could offset the benefits of increased sales. In any case, the point to be made here is that accounts receivable management is an important part of the subsidiary's working capital management because of its potential impact on cash inflows.

The subsidiary may be expected to periodically send dividend payments and other fees to the parent. These fees could represent royalties or charges for overhead costs incurred by the parent that benefit the subsidiary. An example is research and development costs incurred by the parent, which would improve the quality of goods produced by the subsidiary. Whatever the reason, payments by the subsidiary to the parent are often necessary. When dividend payments and fees are often known in advance and denominated in the subsidiary's currency, forecasting cash flows is easier for the subsidiary. The level of dividends paid by subsidiaries to the parent is dependent on liquidity needs, potential uses of funds at various subsidiary locations, expected movements in the currencies of subsidiaries, and host-country government regulations.

After accounting for all outflow and inflow payments, the subsidiary will either find itself with excess or deficient cash. Thus, it will periodically need to either invest its excess cash or borrow to cover its cash deficiencies. If it anticipates a cash deficiency, short-term financing is necessary, as was described in the previous chapter. If it anticipates excess cash, it must determine how the excess cash should be used. Investing in foreign currencies can sometimes be attractive, but exchange rate risk makes the effective yield uncertain. This issue is discussed later in this chapter.

Liquidity management is a crucial component of a subsidiary's working capital management. Subsidiaries commonly have access to numerous lines of credit and overdraft facilities in various currencies. Therefore, they may maintain adequate liquidity without substantial cash balances. While liquidity is important for the overall MNC, it cannot be properly measured by liquidity ratios. Potential access to funds is more relevant than cash on hand.

CASH FLOW ANALYSIS: CENTRALIZED PERSPECTIVE

Each subsidiary should manage its working capital by simultaneously considering all of the points discussed thus far. Often, though, each subsidiary is more concerned with its own operations than with the overall operations of the MNC. Thus, a **centralized cash management** group may need to monitor, and possibly manage, the parent-subsidiary and inter-subsidiary cash flows. This role is critical since it can often benefit individual subsidiaries in need of funds or overly exposed to exchange rate risk. As an example, Kraft's treasury department is centralized to manage liquidity, funding, and foreign exchange requirements of its global operations.

Exhibit 15.2 may be helpful throughout our discussion of cash flow management. It is a simplified cash flow diagram for an MNC with two subsidiaries in different countries. While each MNC may handle its payments in a different manner, Exhibit 15.2 is based on simplified assumptions that will help illustrate some key concepts of multinational cash management. The exhibit reflects the assumption that the two subsidiaries periodically send fees and dividends to the parent and often send excess cash to the parent (where the centralized cash management process is assumed to take place). These cash flows represent the incoming cash to the parent from the subsidiaries. The parent's cash outflows to the subsidiaries include loans and the return of cash previously invested by the subsidiaries. The subsidiaries also have cash flows between themselves due to purchasing of supplies from each other.

While each subsidiary is managing its working capital, there is a need to monitor and manage the cash flows between the parent and subsidiaries, as

EXHIBIT 15.2   Cash Flow of the Overall MNC

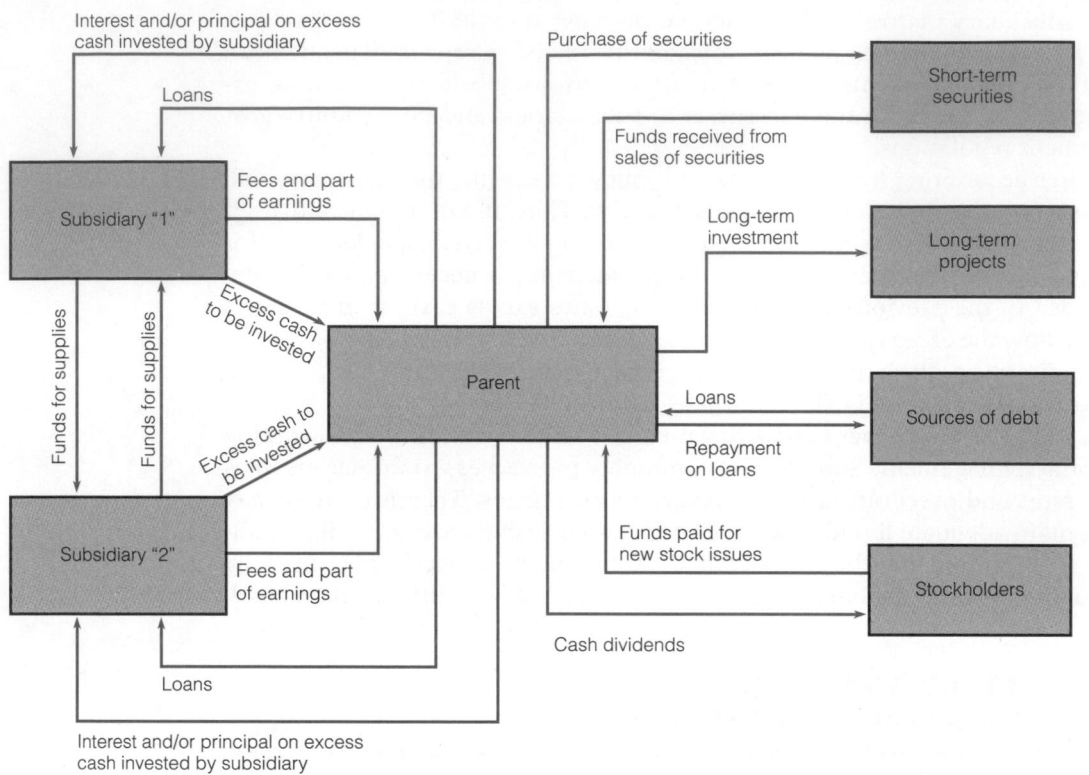

well as between the individual subsidiaries. This task of international cash management should be delegated to a centralized cash management group. International cash management can be segmented into two functions: (1) optimizing cash flow movements and (2) investing excess cash. The first function is based on conventional objectives to accelerate cash inflows, slow cash outflows, and minimize costs associated with cash flow. The second function is based on using available funds to best cover future net outflows if necessary, generating high returns on the funds, and maintaining risk (uncertainty about future returns) at a tolerable level. Perhaps no single strategy of international cash management can best satisfy all of these objectives simultaneously. This is what makes international cash management so challenging. First, techniques available to optimize cash flows will be discussed, followed by a discussion of how to invest excess cash.

TECHNIQUES TO OPTIMIZE CASH FLOWS

Cash inflows can be optimized by:

- accelerating cash inflows
- using **netting** (defined later) to minimize currency conversion costs

- minimizing the tax on cash flow
- managing blocked funds
- implementing inter-subsidiary cash transfers

Each of these tasks is discussed in turn.

Accelerating Cash Inflows

The first goal in international cash management is to accelerate cash inflows, since the quicker the inflows are received, the quicker they can be invested or used for other purposes. Several managerial practices are advocated for this endeavor, some of which may be implemented by the individual subsidiaries. First, a corporation may establish **lockboxes** around the world, which are post office box numbers to which customers are instructed to send payment. When set up in appropriate locations, a lockbox can help reduce mailing time (**mail float**). The processing of incoming checks at a lockbox is normally taken care of by a bank on a daily basis. A second method for accelerating cash inflows is the **preauthorized payment**, which allows a corporation to charge a customer's bank account up to some limit. Both the preauthorized payment and lockboxes are even used in a domestic setting. Because international transactions may have a relatively long mailing time, these methods to accelerate cash inflows can be quite valuable for an MNC.

Using Netting to Minimize Currency Conversion Costs

Another technique for optimizing cash flow movements, **netting**, can be implemented with the joint effort of subsidiaries or by the centralized cash management group. This technique optimizes cash flow by reducing the administrative and transaction costs that result from currency conversion. Consider an MNC with two subsidiaries located in different countries. Any time one subsidiary purchases goods from a second subsidiary, it may need a foreign currency to make payment. The second subsidiary may do the same when purchasing goods from the first subsidiary. Both subsidiaries could avoid (or at least reduce) the transaction costs of currency conversion if they netted out the payments—that is, if they accounted for all of their transactions over a given period to determine one net payment.

Any firm, whether domestic or multinational, can reduce administrative costs by netting out payments between different branches or subsidiaries. Yet, the MNC can benefit to a greater degree than a domestic firm. To illustrate, consider Firm A with 20 manufacturing plants, all within the United States, each specializing in producing various components. There is considerable inter-plant purchasing of components. Also consider Firm B, which is in the same business and is the same size as Firm A but has its 20 manufacturing plants scattered throughout the world. Both firms could benefit from a netting system whereby only net payments are made at the end of each period, since administrative costs would be reduced. Firm A, however, does not require conversion of currencies. Therefore, its benefits from netting are more limited than the benefits realized by Firm B, the MNC.

Over time, the use of netting has become increasingly popular. Its key benefits are as follows. First, it reduces the number of cross-border transactions between subsidiaries, thereby reducing the overall administrative cost of such cash transfers. Second, it reduces the need for foreign exchange conversion, since transactions occur less frequently, thereby reducing the transaction costs associated with foreign exchange conversion. Third, the process of netting forces tight control over information on transactions between subsidiaries. Thus, there is a more coordinated effort among all subsidiaries to accurately report and settle their various accounts. Finally, cash flow forecasting is easier since only net cash transfers are made at the end of each period rather than individual cash transfers throughout the period. Improved cash flow forecasting can enhance financing and investment decisions.

A **bilateral netting system** involves transactions between two units, such as between the parent and a subsidiary or between two subsidiaries. A **multilateral netting system** usually involves a more complex interchange among the parent and several subsidiaries. For most large MNCs, a multilateral netting system would be necessary to effectively reduce administrative and currency conversion costs. Such a system is normally centralized, so that all necessary information is consolidated. From the consolidated cash flow information, net cash flow positions for each pair of units (subsidiaries, or whatever) is determined, and the actual reconciliation at the end of each period can be dictated. The centralized group may even maintain inventories of various currencies so currency conversion for the end-of-period net payments can be completed without significant transaction costs.

Exhibit 15.3 is an example of an inter-subsidiary payments matrix that totals each subsidiary's individual payments against each other subsidiary. For example the first row implies the Canadian subsidiary owes the French subsidiary the equivalent of $40,000, the Canadian subsidiary owes the British subsidiary the equivalent of $80,000, and so on. During this same period, these subsidiaries also received goods from the Canadian subsidiary for which payment is due. In the second column (under Canada), the table suggests the French subsidiary owes the Canadian subsidiary the equivalent of $60,000, the British subsidiary owes the Canadian subsidiary the equivalent of $90,000, and so on.

Since subsidiaries owe each other, currency conversion costs can be reduced by requiring that only the net payment be extended. Using the inter-subsidiary table, the schedule of net payments is determined as shown in

EXHIBIT 15.3 Inter-Subsidiary Payments Matrix

Payments Owed by Subsidiary Located In:	U.S. Dollar Value (in Thousands) of Payments Owed to Subsidiary Located in:						
	Canada	France	Great Britain	Japan	Switzerland	U.S.	W. Germany
Canada	—	40	80	90	20	40	60
France	60	—	40	30	60	50	30
Great Britain	90	20	—	20	10	0	40
Japan	100	30	50	—	20	30	10
Switzerland	10	50	30	10	—	50	70
U.S.	10	60	20	20	20	—	40
West Germany	40	30	0	60	40	70	—

Exhibit 15.4. Since the Canadian subsidiary owes the French subsidiary the equivalent of $40,000, but is owed the equivalent of $60,000 by the French subsidiary, the net payment required is from the French subsidiary to the Canadian subsidiary amounting to the equivalent of $20,000. Exhibits 15.3 and 15.4 convert all figures to U.S. dollar equivalents to allow for consolidating payments in both directions so the net payment could be determined.

There can be some limitations to multilateral netting due to foreign exchange controls. Although the major industrialized countries typically do not impose such controls on netting, some other countries do. For a third class of countries, netting is prohibited. Thus, an MNC with subsidiaries around the world may be able to implement the multilateral netting system only over some of its subsidiaries. Obviously, this will limit the degree to which the netting system can reduce administration and transaction cost.

Minimizing Tax on Cash Flow

To further optimize cash flows, the MNC must consider the tax consequences of altering its cash flow. If, for example, the host-country government of a particular subsidiary places a high withholding tax on subsidiary earnings remitted to the parent, the parent of the MNC may instruct the subsidiary to temporarily refrain from remitting earnings and to reinvest them in that host country instead. If the high withholding tax appears permanent, the MNC's parent may charge higher royalty or overhead payments for its task of overseeing the subsidiary's operations. To the extent this charge reflects a cost to the subsidiary's reported earnings, taxes paid by the subsidiary may be reduced. As an alternative approach, the MNC may instruct the subsidiary to set up a research and development division that will benefit subsidiaries elsewhere. The main purpose behind this strategy is to search for a way to efficiently use the funds abroad if the funds cannot be sent to the parent without excessive taxation.

Another possible strategy to deal with such high taxation is to adjust the **transfer pricing** policy. To illustrate, suppose that Oakland Corporation has established two subsidiaries to capitalize on low production costs. One of these subsidiaries, (called Hitax Sub) is located in a country whose government charges a 50 percent tax rate on before-tax earnings. Hitax Sub pro-

EXHIBIT 15.4 Netting Schedule

Net Payments to be Made by Subsidiary Located In:	Net U.S. Dollar Value (in Thousands) of Payments Owed to Subsidiary Located in:						
	Canada	France	Great Britain	Japan	Switzerland	U.S.	W. Germany
Canada	–	0	0	0	10	30	20
France	20	–	20	0	10	0	0
Great Britain	10	0	–	0	0	0	40
Japan	10	0	30	–	10	10	0
Switzerland	0	0	20	0	–	30	30
U.S.	0	10	20	0	0	–	0
West Germany	0	0	0	50	0	30	–

INTERNATIONAL FINANCIAL MANAGEMENT IN PRACTICE

Characteristics of Multinational Netting Systems

Numerous MNCs such as Monsanto and Baxter Laboratories use netting procedures to substantially reduce transaction costs. Results of a recent survey of MNCs by Srinivasan and Kim revealed the following:

■ About 82 percent of the respondents net their intra-company payments.

■ The most popular type of netting is multilateral netting.

■ About 86 percent of the firms that net payments between subsidiaries do so on a monthly basis. Some firms used a bimonthly basis.

■ Most respondents that use netting systems develop the netting schedule by forecasting actual cash flows to and from subsidiaries. Only a small percentage of respondents use a mathematical model to determine the net payments, but most respondents use internally created computer programs to facilitate their analysis.

■ Some of the MNCs had built-in safety mechanisms to change data right up to the settlement day. Some of the MNCs that did not have safety mechanisms stated that the forecasted information is normally reliable, so safety mechanisms are not necessary.

Overall, the results suggest that netting is a commonly used tool to reduce currency conversion costs and that the specific netting procedure varies among MNCs.

SOURCE: Venkat Srinivasan and Yong H. Kim, "Payments Netting in International Cash Management: A Network Optimization Approach," *Journal of International Business Studies* (Summer 1986), pp. 1–20.

duces partially finished products and sends them to the other subsidiary (called Lotax Sub), where the final assembly takes place. The host government of Lotax Sub charges a 20 percent tax on before-tax earnings. To simplify the example, assume that no dividends are to be remitted to the parent in the near future. Given this information, pro forma income statements would be as shown in the top part of Exhibit 15.5 for Hitax Sub (Column 2), Lotax Sub (Column 3), and the consolidated subsidiaries (Column 4). The income statement items are reported in U.S. dollars to more easily illustrate how a revised transfer pricing policy can affect earnings.

The sales level shown for Hitax Sub matches the cost of goods sold for Lotax Sub, implying that all Hitax Sub sales are to Lotax Sub. The additional expenses incurred by Lotax Sub to complete the product are classified as operating expenses.

Notice from Exhibit 15.5 that both subsidiaries have the same earnings before taxes. Yet, because of the differences in tax rates, Hitax Sub will earn an after-tax income of $7.5 million less than Lotax Sub. If Oakland Corporation could revise its transfer pricing, its consolidated earnings after taxes would be increased. To illustrate, suppose that the price of products sent from Hitax Sub to Lotax Sub is reduced, causing the sales of Hitax Sub to decline from $100 million to $80 million. This would also reduce the cost of goods sold of Lotax Sub by $20 million. The revised pro forma income statement resulting from the change in the transfer pricing policy is shown in the

EXHIBIT 15.5 Impact of Transfer Pricing Adjustment on Pro Forma Earnings and Taxes: Oakland Corporation (*in thousands*)

	Original Estimates		
	Hitax Sub	*Lotax Sub*	*Consolidated*
Sales	$100,000	$150,000	$250,000
Less: cost of good sold	50,000	100,000	150,000
Gross profit	50,000	50,000	100,000
Less: operating expenses	20,000	20,000	40,000
Earnings before interest and taxes	30,000	30,000	60,000
Interest expense	5,000	5,000	10,000
Earnings before taxes	25,000	25,000	50,000
Taxes (50% for Hitax and 20% for Lotax)	12,500	5,000	17,500
Earnings after taxes	12,500	20,000	32,500

	Revised Estimates Based on Adjusting Transfer Pricing Policy		
	Hitax Sub	*Lotax Sub*	*Consolidated*
Sales	$ 80,000	$150,000	$230,000
Less: cost of good sold	50,000	80,000	130,000
Gross profit	30,000	70,000	100,000
Less: operating expenses	20,000	20,000	40,000
Earnings before interest and taxes	10,000	50,000	60,000
Interest expense	5,000	5,000	10,000
Earnings before taxes	5,000	45,000	50,000
Taxes (50% for Hitax and 20% for Lotax)	2,500	9,000	11,500
Earnings after taxes	2,500	36,000	38,500

bottom part of Exhibit 15.5. The difference in forecasted earnings before taxes between the two subsidiaries is now $40 million, although the consolidated amount has not changed. Because earnings have been shifted from Hitax Sub to Lotax Sub, the consolidated tax payments are reduced to $11.5 million from the original estimate of $17.5 million. Thus, the after-tax earnings are now forecasted to be $6 million less than originally expected.

It should be mentioned that there are some limitations to such an adjustment in the transfer pricing policy, since host governments may enforce laws that restrict such practices when the intent is to avoid taxes.

Financing strategies may also be used to deal with high taxation. For example, the parent of Oakland Corporation may provide only minimal financial support to Hitax Sub, thereby forcing it to borrow and incur annual interest expenses. Debt becomes a more attractive source of funds when the tax rates are high. In fact, the parent may attempt to have Hitax Sub borrow more funds than needed and channel funds to subsidiaries in other countries. Hitax Sub would receive the largest tax benefit from borrowing because of the high tax rate. This strategy represents one more way in which the high-tax subsidiary subsidizes other subsidiaries. Such a strategy reduces that subsidiary's profits but increases cash flow for the MNC overall. Some host

INTERNATIONAL FINANCIAL MANAGEMENT IN PRACTICE

What Factors Affect an MNC's Transfer Pricing Decision?

A recent study by Tang attempted to determine which factors were most important to an MNC's transfer pricing decision. A survey of 80 companies yielded the following information:

■ The overall profit to the company was the most important factor affecting the transfer pricing decision. Most respondents were in agreement as to the importance of this factor.

■ Other factors that had a strong influence in the transfer pricing decision were (1) the competitive position of subsidiaries in foreign countries, (2) the performance evaluation of subsidiaries, (3) restrictions imposed by host governments on remitted earnings,

(4) the need for cash by foreign subsidiaries, (5) the interests of local partners in foreign subsidiaries, and (6) rules and requirements of financial reporting for foreign subsidiaries.

■ Some other, less influential factors were (1) rates of inflation in foreign countries, (2) the volume of interdivisional transfer, (3) the risk of expropriation in foreign countries, and (4) domestic government requirements on direct foreign investments.

For more information, see the article from which this brief summary was drawn.

SOURCE: Roger Y. W. Tang, "Environmental Variables of Multinational Transfer Pricing: A U.K. Perspective," *Journal of Business, Finance, and Accounting* (Summer 1982), pp. 179–189.

---

country governments may attempt to prevent MNCs from implementing such a strategy.

Another method of reducing taxes is through the establishment of a **reinvoicing center**. The main objective is to shift profits to subsidiaries where tax rates are low. Title to goods passes through the reinvoicing center, but the goods do not. The invoice is normally denominated in the currency of the exporting subsidiary. The reinvoicing centers serve as a centralized payments facility, and subsidiaries are charged a fee for using the facility. This arrangement essentially shifts profits from other subsidiaries to the reinvoicing center and therefore reduces overall taxes incurred by the MNC.

Managing Blocked Funds

Cash flows can also be affected by a host government's blockage of funds, which might occur if the government requires all funds to remain within the country in order to create jobs and reduce unemployment. To deal with funds blockage, the MNC may implement the same strategies used in the case of high host country government taxation. To make efficient use of these funds, the subsidiary may be instructed by the MNC to set up a research and development division, which incurs costs and possibly generates revenues for other subsidiaries.

Another strategy is to use transfer pricing in a manner that will increase the expenses incurred by the subsidiary. A host-country government is likely to be more lenient on funds sent to cover expenses than on earnings remitted to the parent.

When subsidiaries are restricted from transferring funds to the parent, the parent may instruct the subsidiary to obtain financing from a local bank rather than from the parent. By borrowing through a local intermediary, the subsidiary is assured that its earnings can be distributed to pay off previous financing. If the earnings were to be sent to the parent, the host government could enforce a blockage of funds.

As an example of managing blocked funds, subsidiaries of a U.S. MNC based in the Philippines were prevented from exchanging their Philippine pesos into U.S. dollars to send these dollars home. To deal with such restrictions, one general manager reportedly loaded pesos into his luggage and took them to Hong Kong, where he converted them into U.S. dollars. A better way of dealing with such restrictions is to find a use of the currency within the host country. For example, in the case of the Philippine government restriction, one company held its corporate meeting in Manila so it could use the pesos to pay the expenses of the meeting (hotel, food, etc.) in pesos. This approach is somewhat similar to sending the funds to the parent, since it is likely the parent would have paid the expenses of the corporate meeting had it been held in the parent's country.

Inter-subsidiary Cash Transfers

Proper management of cash flows can also be beneficial to a subsidiary in need of funds. Assume Short Sub needs funds, while Long Sub has excess funds. Also assume that Short Sub periodically purchases some of its supplies from Long Sub. In this case, Long Sub could provide financing by allowing Short Sub to *lag* (delay) on its payments. Or, if Long Sub purchases suppliers from Short Sub, it could provide financing by paying for its supplies earlier than necessary. This technique is often called **leading**. The leading or lagging strategy can avoid the need to borrow and therefore reduce the amount of debt reported on the balance sheet. Some host governments prohibit the practice by requiring that payments between subsidiaries occur at the time at which goods are transferred. An MNC would need to be aware of any existing laws that restricted use of this strategy.

COMMON COMPLICATIONS IN OPTIMIZING CASH FLOW

Most complications encountered in optimizing cash flow can be classified into five categories:

- Company-related characteristics
- Government restrictions
- Characteristics of banking systems
- Perceived irrelevance of cash flow optimization
- Distortion of subsidiary performance

Each complication is discussed in turn.

INTERNATIONAL FINANCIAL MANAGEMENT IN PRACTICE

Optimizing Subsidiary-Parent Cash Flows: A Survey

A recent survey of chief financial officers of the U.S.-based MNCs that have subsidiaries in Latin America produced some interesting results:

■ About 67 percent of the firms utilize inter-subsidiary financing.
■ Only 7 percent of the firms provide financing to the parent by a subsidiary.
■ About 67 percent of the firms use leading and lagging strategies.
■ About 80 percent of the firms prefer loans to equity funding for financing subsidiary development. The author presumed the reason to be that subsidiaries are not restricted from using funds to cover debt repayment, whereas they are sometimes restricted from remitting funds back to the parent.

■ About 53 percent of the firms transfer parts to subsidiaries for partial or complete assembly. Of these firms, 57 percent use an arm's-length transfer pricing policy. Other firms that have partial assembly performed by subsidiaries use a "cost-plus" or other type of method for determining transfer pricing.

These results are not necessarily representative of all U.S.-based MNCs, since the survey focused on MNCs with Latin American subsidiaries. Nevertheless, the results suggest that some of the techniques mentioned in this chapter for optimizing cash flow are commonly utilized.

SOURCE: R. Grosse, "Financial Transfers in the MNE: The Latin America Case," *Management International Review* 26 (1986), pp. 33–44.

Company-Related Characteristics

In some cases, optimizing cash flow can become complicated due to characteristics of the MNC. For example, if one of the subsidiaries delays payments to other subsidiaries for supplies received, the other subsidiaries may be forced to borrow until the payments arrive. A centralized approach that monitors all inter-subsidiary payments should be able to minimize such problems.

Government Restrictions

The existence of government restrictions can disrupt a cash flow optimization policy. For example, some governments prohibit the use of a netting system, as noted earlier. In addition, some countries will periodically prevent cash from leaving the country, thereby preventing net payments from being made. These problems can arise even for MNCs that do not experience any company-related problems.

Characteristics of Banking Systems

The ability of banks to facilitate cash transfers for MNCs will vary among countries. Banks in the United States are advanced in this field, but banks in some other countries do not offer services needed by MNCs. For example,

MNCs prefer some form of a zero-balance account where excess funds can be used to make payments but earn interest until they are used. In addition, some MNCs benefit from the use of lockboxes. Such services will not be available in some countries. In addition, there may be insufficient updating on the MNC's bank account information, or fees for banking services may not be broken down in a detailed manner. Without full use of banking resources and information, international cash management is limited in its effectiveness. In addition, an MNC with subsidiaries in, say, eight different countries will typically be dealing with eight different banking systems. Much progress has been made in foreign banking systems in recent years. As time passes, and a more uniform global banking system emerges, such problems may be alleviated.

Perceived Irrelevance of Cash Flow Optimization

The effectiveness of a cash flow optimization strategy can be dampened by its perceived irrelevance in non-U.S. countries. While the cash flow optimization practice in the United States has progressed significantly during the last 30 years, it still has much room for improvement in non-U.S. countries. Research by Finnerty suggests that there is a lack of awareness by non-U.S. countries of the importance in accelerating cash inflows. Finnerty recommends that an MNC's resources be allocated toward educating subsidiaries of the non-U.S. countries about the expenses incurred from an ineffective cash management system.

Distortion of Subsidiary Performance

The various techniques that can be used by an MNC to optimize cash flow will often distort the profits of each individual subsidiary. For example, a change in the transfer pricing policy or inter-subsidiary cash transfer could have been beneficial to the MNC overall. Yet, from the perspective of individual subsidiaries, earnings of one subsidiary may increase at the expense of another subsidiary. While the executives of a subsidiary may recognize the overall benefits to the MNC, they may worry that their jobs will be at stake due to the distorted earnings reports. That is, one subsidiary's reported earnings will look worse than they really are. The low earnings may be totally due to transfer pricing policies or leading and lagging strategies designed to deal with high taxes, currency blockage, etc. The parent, in its evaluation of performance of individual subsidiaries, must take into account such policies that were implemented. If these policies are ignored, executives will be more concerned with maximizing earnings of their individual subsidiaries without concern for the overall MNC. This would lead to a goal conflict between the subsidiary executives and the owners (shareholders) of the MNC. The shareholder's goal is to maximize the value of the firm. If the executives make decisions that maximize their subsidiary earnings rather than shareholder wealth, then their philosophy will restrict the MNC from fully satisfying its owners. To ensure there is no goal conflict, each subsidiary's performance should not be based on individual earnings, but instead on its contribution to the overall value of the MNC. Thus, executives will be rewarded based on how their decisions affect the overall value of the MNC.

If a subsidiary exists as part of the MNC that is not wholly owned by the parent, the goal conflict will be more pronounced. The minority owners of the subsidiary would prefer that this particular subsidiary do what is best for itself rather than for the overall MNC. Such a conflict can sometimes make management of an MNC's cash flow quite complicated.

The centralized cash management division of an MNC cannot always accurately forecast events that affect parent-subsidiary or inter-subsidiary cash flows. It should, however, be ready to react to any event by considering (1) any potential adverse impact on cash flows and (2) how to avoid such an adverse impact. If the cash flow situation between the parent and subsidiaries results in a cash squeeze on the parent, it should have sources of funds (credit lines) available. On the other hand, if it has excess cash after considering all outflow payments, it must consider where to invest funds. This decision is thoroughly examined here.

INVESTING EXCESS CASH

Along with optimizing cash flow, the other key function of international cash management is investing excess cash. International money markets have grown to accommodate corporate investment of excess cash, one of the key markets being the Eurocurrency market. The dollar volume of deposits has more than doubled since 1980. Eurodollar deposits commonly offer MNCs a slightly higher yield than bank deposits in the United States. Many MNCs utilize the Eurocurrency market as a temporary use of funds. For example, Westinghouse maintains over $400 million in Eurodollar deposits. Many MNCs also establish deposits in non-dollar currencies in the Eurocurrency market. While deposits still dominate the market, the relative importance of non-dollar currencies has increased over time.

In addition to the Eurocurrency market, MNCs can also purchase foreign Treasury bills and commercial paper. Improved telecommunications systems have increased access to these securities in foreign markets and allow for a greater degree of integration among money markets in various countries.

There are several aspects of short-term investing that deserve consideration by the MNC. First, should the excess cash of each subsidiary remain separated or be pooled together? Second, how can the MNC determine the effective yield expected from each possible alternative? Third, what does interest rate parity suggest about short-term investing? Fourth, how can the quoted forward rate be used to evaluate the short-term investment decision? Fifth, how can forecasted exchange rates influence the short-term investment decision? Finally, is it worthwhile to diversify investments among currencies? Each of these questions is discussed in turn.

Centralized Cash Management

An MNC's short-term investing policy can either maintain separate investments for all subsidiaries or employ a centralized approach. Recall that the function of optimizing cash flow could be improved by a centralized approach, since all subsidiary cash positions could be monitored simultaneously. With regard to the investing function, centralization allows for more efficient usage of funds, and possibly higher returns. The term *centralized* implies that excess cash at each subsidiary is pooled together until it is needed by that particular subsidiary. To understand the advantages of such a system, consider that the rates paid on short-term investments such as bank deposits are often higher for larger denominations. Thus, if two subsidiaries have excess cash of $50,000 each for one month, the rates on their individual bank deposits may be lower than the rate they could obtain if they pooled the funds into a single $100,000 bank deposit. In this manner, the centralized (pooling) approach generates a higher rate of return on excess cash.

The centralized approach can also improve the efficiency of working capital management by reducing the MNC's overall financing costs. To illustrate, suppose that Subsidiary A has excess cash during the next month of $50,000, while Subsidiary B needs to borrow $50,000 for one month. If cash management is not centralized, Subsidiary A may use the $50,000 to purchase a one-month bank certificate earning, say, 10 percent (on an annualized basis). At the same time, Subsidiary B may borrow from a bank for one month at a rate of, say, 12 percent. The bank must charge a higher rate on loans than it offers on deposits. With a centralized approach, Subsidiary B could borrow Subsidiary A's excess funds, thereby reducing its financing costs. This approach is limited since the excess cash of one subsidiary may be denominated in a currency different than that needed by the other subsidiary. While the cash transfer is still possible, the chance of exchange rate fluctuations could discourage it.

The pooling of invested funds and matching of subsidiaries with excess funds may result in excessive transaction costs. For example, consider an MNC whose subsidiaries are transacting in several different currencies. A fully centralized approach would require all excess funds to be pooled and converted to a single currency for investment purposes. In this case, the advantage of pooling may be offset by the transaction costs incurred when converting to a single currency. Centralized cash management could still be valuable, though. The short-term cash available in each currency could be pooled together so there would be a separate pool for each currency. The excess cash of subsidiaries in a particular currency could still be used to satisfy other subsidiary deficiencies in that currency. In this way, funds could be transferred from one subsidiary to another without incurring transaction costs that banks charge for exchanging currencies. This strategy would be especially feasible if all subsidiary deposits were deposited in branches of a single bank, so that funds could easily be transferred among subsidiaries.

Our discussion of using excess cash has emphasized two suggestions: (1) pool together short-term cash denominated in a particular currency whenever possible in order to get the highest return on short-term bank deposits with a given maturity, and (2) attempt to accommodate short-term financing needs of subsidiaries with excess funds available at other subsidiaries whenever possible. We have not yet discussed where to invest the remaining short-term funds denominated in each currency after accommodating any subsidiary financing needs. This is a major issue in international cash management, since the return on short-term investments will often vary substantially among alternatives. Because the funds here are available for a short period of time, bank deposits and government securities are common investments by MNCs. The quoted yields of these investments will depend on the currency denominating the investment. In the Eurocurrency market, where short-term deposits and loans are denominated in a variety of currencies, a bank will often offer a much higher rate on a deposit denominated in British pounds than a deposit denominated in, say, German marks. Exhibit 15.6 illustrates

EXHIBIT 15.6 Interest Rates among Currencies

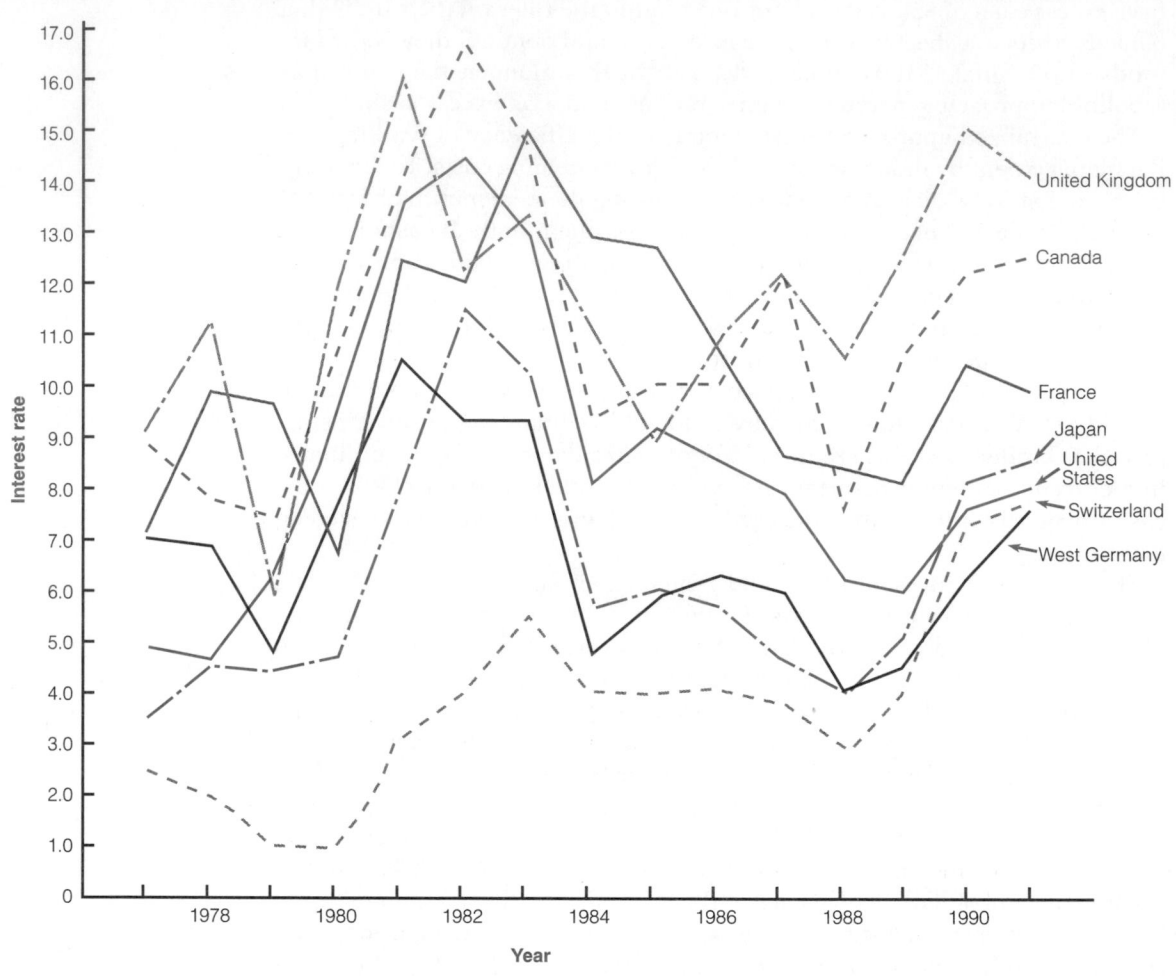

the differential in interest rates among currencies over time. Notice that in some periods, the magnitude of the differential amounts to eight or more percentage points. The difference illustrated here does not imply that short-term funds should automatically be placed in the high-interest rate currencies. If these currencies depreciated against the firm's home currency, the **effective yield** (yield adjusted for the exchange rate change) may actually be relatively low.

Some firms may prefer simply to invest in a security denominated in the currency it shall need when the investment matures. While such an approach can guarantee the yield to be earned as the investment is made, it may not be as lucrative as investments in alternative currencies.

When a firm has excess cash available, its first concern is whether to cover any payables positions in foreign currencies. If the firm has future cash outflows in foreign currencies expected to appreciate, it may desire to cover such positions by creating a short-term deposit in that currency. The maturity of the deposit would ideally coincide with the date at which the funds are needed.

Determining the Effective Yield from Foreign Investing

The interest rates on deposits at a Eurobank vary with the currency denominating the deposit. Therefore, it is worth surveying the various alternatives before making a deposit. The firm could set up a deposit denominated in the currency reflecting the highest interest rate, and then convert the funds to whatever currency it will need when the deposit matures. However, this strategy will not necessarily be feasible, since the currency denominating the deposit may depreciate over the life of the deposit. If it does, the advantage of a higher interest rate may be more than offset by the degree of depreciation in the currency representing the deposit. It is the deposit's **effective yield**, not its interest rate, that is most important to the cash manager. The effective yield of a bank deposit considers both the interest rate as well as the rate of appreciation (or depreciation) of the currency denominating the deposit and can therefore be much different than the quoted interest rate on a deposit denominated in a foreign currency ("foreign" here refers to a currency that differs from the currency the firm will need when the deposit is withdrawn). An example follows to illustrate this point.

Assume a large U.S. corporation with $1,000,000 in excess cash creates a three-month deposit in French francs at 6 percent (not annualized). The exchange rate of the French franc at the time of the deposit is $.20. The U.S. dollars are first converted to 5,000,000 French francs (since $1,000,00/$.20 per franc = 5,000,000 francs), then deposited in a Eurobank. Three months later, the Eurobank will pay the U.S. corporation a total of 5,300,000 francs (the initially deposited 5,000,000 francs plus interest of 6% × 5,000,000 francs = 300,000 francs). Assume the U.S. corporation has no use for francs and only chose a French franc deposit because of its attractive interest rate. Also assume the exchange rate of the French franc is $.19 as the deposit is withdrawn. The 5,300,000 francs convert to $1,007,000 (computed by 5,300,000 francs × $.19 per franc). The yield on the short-term investment is

$$\frac{\$1,007,000 - \$1,000,000}{\$1,000,000} = .007, \text{ or } .7\%$$

This example demonstrates how the yield on a short-term foreign deposit can be influenced by a change in the exchange rate. If the U.S. corporation decided to set up a Eurodollar deposit instead, it would have earned more than .7 percent. In addition, it would not have been exposed to exchange rate fluctuations if it planned to use the proceeds to cover expenses in the United States. However, the results of a foreign deposit would not always be unfavorable as in our example. If the franc appreciated from $.20 to $.21 over the life of the deposit, then the 5,300,000 francs received from the Eurobank as the deposit matures would be worth $1,113,000. In this case, the effective yield on the three-month deposit to the U.S. corporation would be

$$\frac{\$1,113,000 - \$1,000,000}{\$1,000,000} = .113, \text{ or } 11.3\%$$

This high effective yield over just three months for the U.S. corporation is due to both the high interest rate on the deposit and the appreciation of the franc against the U.S. dollar. The examples provided here illustrate how appreciation of a currency denominating the foreign deposit over the deposit period will force the effective yield to be above the quoted interest rate. Conversely, depreciation will create the opposite effect.

The preceding computation of the effective yield on foreign deposits was conducted in a logical manner. A quicker method is shown below:

$$r_d = (1 + i_d)(1 + e_d) - 1$$

where r_d is the effective yield on the foreign deposit, i_d is the quoted deposit rate, and e_d is the percentage change (from the day of deposit to the day of withdrawal) in the value of the currency representing the foreign deposit. In our example, e_d represents the percentage change in the French franc (against the U.S. dollar) from the date francs were purchased (and deposited) until the day they were withdrawn (and converted back to U.S. dollars). In our first example, the French franc depreciated from $.20 to $.19, or by 5 percent over the life of the deposit. Using this information as well as the quoted deposit rate of 6 percent, we find that the effective yield to the U.S. firm on this deposit denominated in French francs is

$$\begin{aligned} r_d &= (1 + i_d)(1 + e_d) - 1 \\ &= (1 + .06)[1 + (-.05)] - 1 \\ &= .007, \text{ or } .7\% \end{aligned}$$

which is the same rate we computed from the alternative approach.

To test your ability to use the formula for the effective yield, apply it to our revised example, where the French franc appreciated from $.20 to $.21, or by 5 percent. Based on the quoted interest rate of 6 percent, and the appreciation of 5 percent, the effective yield is

$$\begin{aligned} r_d &= (1 + i_d)(1 + e_d) - 1 \\ &= (1 + .06)(1 + .05) - 1 \\ &= .113, \text{ or } 11.3\% \end{aligned}$$

which is the same rate we computed earlier for this revised example.

The effective yield could be negative if the currency denominating the deposit depreciates to an extent that more than offsets the interest accrued from the deposit. For example, if a U.S. corporation sets up a foreign deposit that has a quoted interest rate of 5 percent, and the currency depreciates against the dollar by 7 percent, the effective yield is

$$\begin{aligned} r_d &= (1 + .05)[1 + (-.07)] - 1 \\ &= -.0235, \text{ or } -2.35\% \end{aligned}$$

The result here suggests the firm would end up with 2.35 percent fewer funds than it initially deposited.

Up to this point, only bank deposits have been considered. There may also be other short-term foreign securities available. Any available securities denominated in a particular currency should have somewhat similar yields. As with bank deposits, the effective yield on all other securities denominated in a foreign currency is influenced by the fluctuation of that foreign currency's exchange rate. Our discussion will continue with a focus on bank deposits for short-term foreign investment. Yet, the implications of our discussion can be applied to other short-term securities as well.

Interest Rate Parity as a Criterion for the Investing Decision

Recall that covered interest arbitrage was described in Chapter 7 as a foreign short-term investment with a simultaneous forward sale of the foreign currency denominating the foreign investment. One might think a foreign currency with a high interest rate would be an ideal candidate for covered interest arbitrage. However, such a currency will normally exhibit a forward discount that reflects the differential between its interest rate and the investor's home interest rate. This relationship is based on the theory of interest rate parity as was discussed in Chapter 7. Investors cannot lock in a higher return when attempting covered interest arbitrage if interest rate parity exists.

Even if interest rate parity does exist, short-term foreign investing may still be feasible, but would have to be conducted on an uncovered basis (without use of the forward market). That is, short-term foreign investing may result in a higher effective yield than domestic investing, but it cannot be guaranteed.

The Forward Rate as a Criterion for the Investing Decision

If interest rate parity exists, the forward rate can still be a useful indicator to the U.S. firm's investment decision. Consider the following information:

One-year U.S. interest rate = 12%.
One-year French interest rate = 15%.
Spot rate of French franc = $.20.
One-year forward rate of French franc = $.1948.
Amount of excess funds available at U.S. firm = $400,000.

The U.S. firm may first consider using covered interest arbitrage by investing in French francs and covering the position. This would result in the purchasing of 2,000,000 francs (computed as $400,000/$.20 per franc). At the end of one year, the U.S. firm will receive 2,300,000 francs (computed as 2,000,00 francs × 1.15). It can lock in the number of U.S. dollars received when converting those francs back to dollars by selling francs one year forward. At the forward rate of $.1948, this would amount to $448,040 (2,300,000 francs × $.1948 per franc). The effective yield here would be

$$\frac{\$448,040 - \$400,000}{\$400,000} = .12, \text{ or } 12\%$$

This is no more lucrative for the U.S. firm than simply investing in the United States.

Now consider a second possibility where the U.S. firm does not cover in the forward market. Assume the actual spot rate at the time the deposit matures turns out to be $.1948. This is the same exchange rate that the U.S. firm could have negotiated in the forward market when the deposit was created. We know from the previous example that at this exchange rate, the investment will yield about 12 percent, the same as the yield on a U.S. investment.

If the franc's actual spot rate after one year turns out to be more than $.1948, the total U.S. dollars received from the investment will be more than $448,040, and the effective yield will be more than 12 percent (and therefore more rewarding than a U.S. investment). If the actual spot rate after one year turns out to be less than $.1948, the total U.S. dollars received will be less than $448,040, and the effective yield will be less than 12 percent (and therefore less rewarding than the U.S. investment). This example demonstrates that if interest rate parity exists, we can use the forward rate as a break-even point to assess the short-term investment decision. When investing in the foreign currency (and not covering the foreign currency position), the effective yield will be more than the domestic yield if the spot rate of the foreign currency after one year is more than the forward rate at the time the investment is undertaken. Conversely, the yield of a foreign investment will be lower than the domestic yield if the spot rate of the foreign currency after one year turns out to be less than the forward rate at the time the investment is undertaken.

RELATIONSHIP WITH THE INTERNATIONAL FISHER EFFECT. When interest rate parity exists, MNCs that use the forward rate as a predictor of the future spot rate would expect the yield on foreign deposits to equal U.S. deposits. While the forward rate is not necessarily an accurate predictor, it could still be a reasonable forecasting tool if it provides unbiased forecasts of the future spot rate. Being unbiased suggests that it would underestimate or overestimate the future spot rate with equal frequency. Thus, the effective yield on foreign deposits would be equal to the domestic yield on average. MNCs that consistently invest in foreign short-term securities would earn a yield similar on average to what they could have earned on domestic securities.

Our discussion here is closely related to the international Fisher effect (IFE) discussed in Chapter 8. Recall that the international Fisher effect suggested that the exchange rate of a foreign currency was expected to change by an amount reflecting the differential between its interest rate and the U.S. interest rate. If interest rate parity exists, the forward premium or discount reflects that interest rate differential and represents the expected percentage change in the currency's value when the forward rate is used as a predictor of the future spot rate. The IFE suggests that firms cannot consistently earn higher short-term yields on foreign securities than on domestic securities, since the exchange rate is expected to adjust to the interest rate differential on average. If interest rate parity holds and the forward rate is an unbiased predictor of the future spot rate, we could expect the IFE to hold.

The IFE may appear to hold for some currencies and not for others. To determine whether IFE holds, compare the effective yield from investing in a foreign currency with that of domestic investing. If the effective yields of the two alternatives' costs appear to be similar over time on average, then the results would support the IFE. Whether or not an analysis would support or refute IFE depends not only on the foreign currency evaluated, but also on the time periods.

Exhibit 15.7 compares the interest rate differentials to exchange rate move-ments for various foreign currencies. If the exchange rate movements exactly offset the interest rate differentials, the effective yield on foreign investments would be similar to the U.S. yields. In this case, the points would run along the 45-degree line that cuts through the origin. Exhibit 15.7 shows that the points often deviate substantially from the 45-degree line. For many periods, the points are not even in the same quadrant as expected, meaning that either (1) a foreign currency had a higher interest rate than the U.S. rate and appreciated over the period, or (2) a foreign currency had a lower interest rate than the U.S. rate and depreciated.

While Exhibit 15.7 confirms that effective yields on foreign investments will not always match the U.S. yield, this does not mean that U.S. firms will automatically benefit from investing in foreign money market instruments. Points below the 45-degree line represent higher yields from foreign invest-

EXHIBIT 15.7   Comparison of Interest Rate Differentials and Exchange Rate Movements

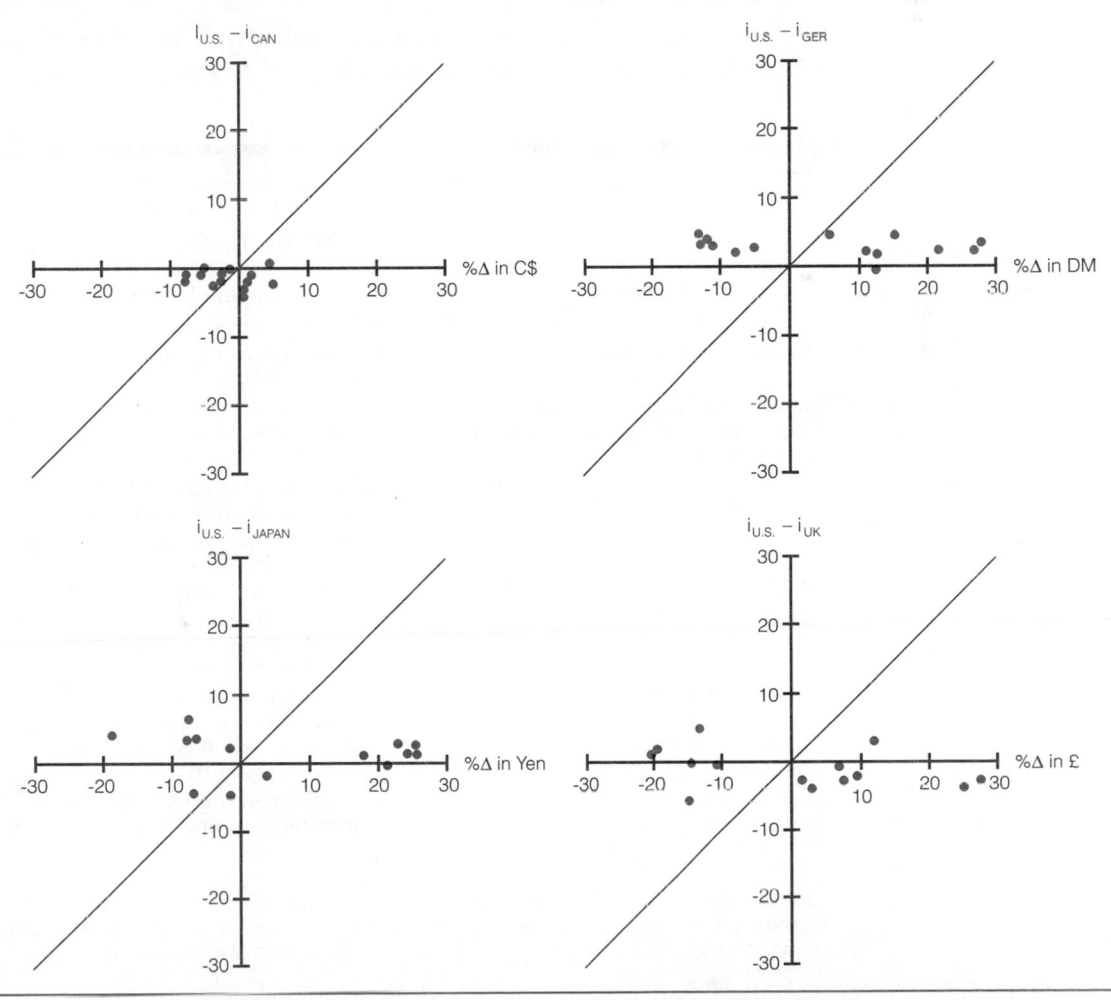

ments while points above it represent lower yields. The points are somewhat scattered on both sides of the line for all currencies. If U.S. firms could accurately forecast future exchange rates, they would be able to benefit from short-term investing in periods when foreign currencies are strengthening and avoid these markets when the foreign currencies are weakening. While U.S. firms have only limited forecasting capabilities, they might consider monitoring exchange rate cycles when making their decisions. Foreign currency values have historically moved in a particular direction for at least two years before reversing direction. Firms that invest for one-month periods could possibly use historical movements to develop expectations about the future. This strategy would have been successful for firms in the past. It will be successful in the future if exchange cycles continue for long periods of time.

The key implications of interest rate parity and the forward rate as a predictor of future spot rates for foreign investing are summarized in Exhibit 15.8. This exhibit explains the conditions necessary for investment in foreign short-term securities to be feasible.

Exchange Rate Forecasts as a Criterion for the Investing Decision

While MNCs do not know how a currency's value will change over the investment horizon, they can use the formula for the effective yield (r_d) pro-

---

EXHIBIT 15.8 Considerations When Investing Excess Cash

Scenario	Implications for Investing in Foreign Money Markets
1. Interest rate parity exists.	Covered interest arbitrage is not worthwhile.
2. Interest rate parity exists, and the forward rate is an accurate forecast of the future spot rate.	An uncovered investment in a foreign security is not worthwhile.
3. Interest rate parity exists, and the forward rate is an unbiased forecast of the future spot rate.	An uncovered investment in a foreign security will on average earn an effective yield similar to an investment in a domestic security.
4. Interest rate parity exists, and the forward rate is expected to overestimate the future spot rate.	An uncovered investment in a foreign security is expected to earn a lower effective yield than an investment in a domestic security.
5. Interest rate parity exists, and the forward rate is expected to underestimate the future spot rate.	An uncovered investment in a foreign security is expected to earn a higher effective yield than an investment in a domestic security.
6. Interest rate parity does not exist; the forward premium (discount) exceeds (is less than) the interest rate differential.	Covered interest arbitrage is feasible for investors residing in the home country.
7. Interest rate parity does not exist; the forward premium (discount) is less than (exceeds) the interest rate differential.	Covered interest arbitrage is feasible for foreign investors but not for investors residing in the home country.

vided earlier in this chapter and plug in their forecast for the percentage change in the foreign currency's exchange rate (e_d). Since the interest rate of the foreign currency deposit (i_d) is known, the effective yield can be forecasted given a forecast of e_d. This projected effective yield on a foreign deposit can then be compared with the yield when investing in the firm's local currency. For example, assume a U.S. firm has funds available for one year. It is aware that the one-year interest rate on a U.S. dollar deposit is 11 percent and the interest rate on a French franc deposit is 14 percent. Assume the U.S. firm forecasts the French franc will depreciate from its current rate of $.1600 to $.1584, or a 1 percent decrease. The expected value for e_d [$E(e_d)$] will therefore be −1 percent. Thus, the expected effective yield [$E(r_d)$] on a French franc denominated deposit is

$$E(r_d) = (1 + i_d)[1 + E(e_d)] - 1$$
$$= (1 + 14\%)[1 + (-1\%)] - 1$$
$$= 12.86\%$$

In this example, investing in a French franc deposit is expected to be more rewarding than investing in a U.S. dollar deposit. Keep in mind that the value for e_d is forecasted and therefore is not known with certainty. Thus, there is no guarantee that foreign investing will truly be more lucrative.

In recognition that e_d is not known, the U.S. firm may attempt to at least determine what value of e_d would make the effective yield from foreign investing the same as investing in a U.S. dollar deposit. To determine this value, begin with the effective yield formula and solve for e_d, as follows:

$$r_d = (1 + i_d)(1 + e_d) - 1$$
$$(1 + r_d) = (1 + i_d)(1 + e_d)$$

$$\frac{(1 + r_d)}{(1 + i_d)} = (1 + e_d)$$

$$\frac{(1 + r_d)}{(1 + i_d)} - 1 = e_d$$

Since the U.S. deposit rate was 11 percent in our previous example, that is the rate that would be plugged in for r_d. We can also plug in 14 percent for i_d so the break-even value of e_d would be

$$e_d = \frac{(1 + r_d)}{(1 + i_d)} - 1$$

$$= \frac{(1 + 11\%)}{(1 + 14\%)} - 1$$

$$= -2.63\%$$

This suggests the French franc must depreciate by about 2.63 percent to make the French-franc deposit generate the same effective yield as a deposit in U.S. dollars. Any lesser degree of depreciation would make the French-franc deposit more rewarding. The U.S. firm can use this information when determining whether to invest in a U.S.-dollar or French-franc deposit. If it expects the French franc to depreciate by more than 2.63 percent over the deposit period, it will prefer borrowing in U.S. dollars. If it expects the French franc to depreciate by less than 2.63 percent, or to appreciate, its decision is more complex. Assuming the potential reward from investing in the foreign currency outweighs the risk involved, then the firm should choose that route. The final decision here will be influenced by the firm's degree of risk aversion.

Since even expert forecasts are not always accurate, it is sometimes useful to develop a probability distribution instead of relying on a single point prediction. An example of how a probability distribution is applied follows.

Assume a U.S. firm is deciding whether to invest in French francs for one year. It finds that the quoted interest rate for the French franc is 14 percent, and the quoted interest rate for a U.S. dollar deposit is 11 percent. The firm then develops a probability distribution for the French franc's possible percentage change in value over the life of the deposit. The probability distribution is displayed in Exhibit 15.9. We see from the first row in the exhibit that there is a 5 percent probability of a 10 percent depreciation in the French franc over the deposit life. If the French franc does depreciate by 10 percent, the effective yield will be 2.60 percent. This implies there is a 5 percent probability of the U.S. firm incurring a 2.60 percent effective yield on its funds. From the second row in the exhibit, we see there is a 10 percent probability of an 8 percent depreciation in the French franc over the deposit period. If the French franc does depreciate by 8 percent, the effective yield will be 4.88 percent, which means there is a 10 percent probability of the U.S. firm generating a 4.88 percent effective yield on this deposit. For each possible percentage change in the French franc's value, there is a corresponding effective yield. We can associate each possible effective yield (Column 3) with a probability of that occurring (Column 2). From these two columns we can attain an *expected value* for the effective yield of the French franc by multiplying each possible effective yield by its associated probability. Based on the

EXHIBIT 15.9   Analysis of Investing in a Foreign Currency

Possible Rate of Change in the French Franc Over the Life of the Investment (e_d)	Probability of Occurrence	Effective Yield if This Rate of Change in the French Franc Does Occur
-10%	5%	$(1.14)[1+(-.10)]-1=.0260$, or 2.60%
-8	10	$(1.14)[1+(-.08)]-1=.0488$, or 4.88
-4	15	$(1.14)[1+(-.04)]-1=.0944$, or 9.44
-2	20	$(1.14)[1+(-.02)]-1=.1172$, or 11.72
$+1$	20	$(1.14)[1+(.01)]-1\ \ =.1514$, or 15.14
$+2$	15	$(1.14)[1+(.02)]-1\ \ =.1628$, or 16.28
$+3$	10	$(1.14)[1+(.03)]-1\ \ =.1742$, or 17.42
$+4$	$\underline{5}$	$(1.14)[1+(.04)]-1\ \ =.1856$, or 18.56
	$\overline{100\%}$	

information in Exhibit 15.9, the expected value of the effective yield, referred to as $E(r_d)$, is computed this way:

$$E(r_d) = 5\%(2.60\%) + 10\%(4.88\%) + 15\%(9.44\%) + 20\%(11.72\%)$$
$$+ 20\%(15.14\%) + 15\%(16.28\%) + 10\%(17.42\%)$$
$$+ 5\%(18.56\%)$$

$$= .13\% + .488\% + 1.416\%$$
$$+ 2.344\% + 3.028\%$$
$$+ 2.442\% + 1.742\% + .928\%$$

$$= 12.518\%$$

We have now determined that the expected value of the effective yield when investing in French francs is approximately 12.5 percent. The decision to invest in French francs or U.S. dollars may depend on what the interest rate is for a U.S. dollar deposit (assumed to be 11 percent).

To further assess the question of which currency to invest in, the information in Columns 2 and 3 from Exhibit 15.9 is used to develop a probability distribution in Exhibit 15.10, which illustrates the probability of each possible effective yield that may occur if the U.S. firm invests in French francs. Notice the U.S. interest rate (11 percent) is known with certainty and is included in Exhibit 15.10 for comparison purposes. A comparison of the French franc's probability distribution against the U.S. interest rate suggests

EXHIBIT 15.10 Probability Distribution of Effective Yields

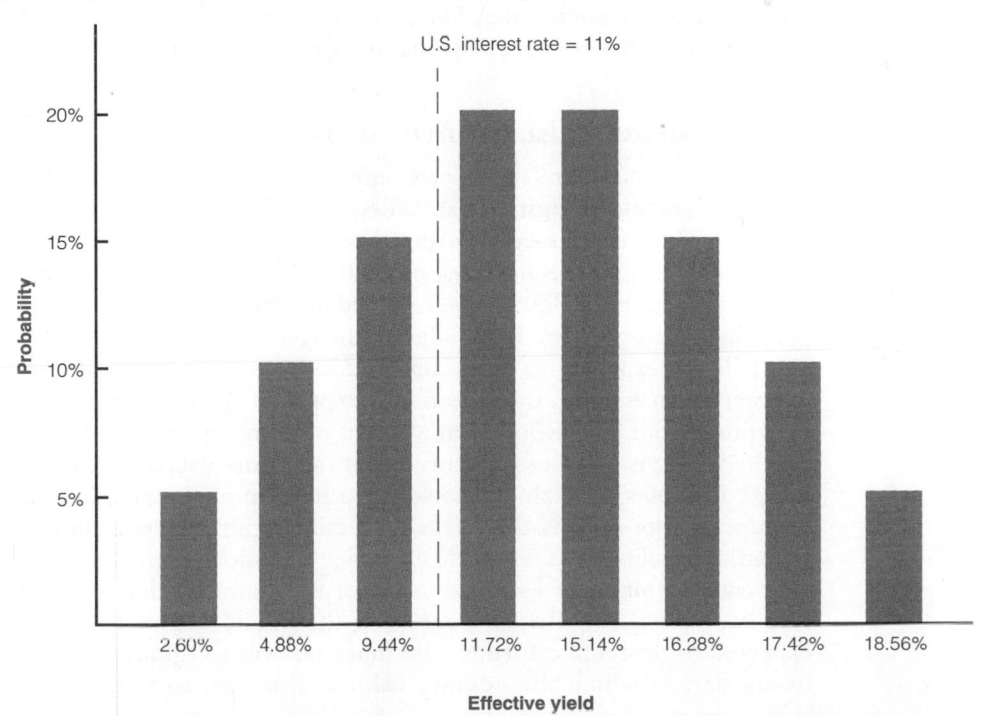

that there is a 30 percent probability of the U.S. rate being more than the effective yield from investing in French francs, and a 70 percent chance of it being less.

If you are the treasurer of the U.S. firm, are you going to invest in U.S. dollars (and earn 11 percent with certainty) or invest in French francs (with an expected value of about 12 percent for the effective yield)? You may choose to invest in a U.S. dollar deposit, since you prefer knowing with certainty the yield you will earn from your investment. Or you may feel the potential reward from the French-franc investment outweighs the risk involved. The risk is the 5 percent chance (probability) that the effective yield on the French franc deposit will be 2.60 percent, or the 10 percent chance the effective yield on the French franc deposit will be 4.88 percent, or the 15 percent chance the effective yield on French francs will be 9.44 percent. Any of these possibilities represent a lower return to the U.S. firm than what would have been earned if it had invested in a U.S. dollar deposit. This explains why some of the more conservative firms choose to avoid the uncertainty and simply choose to invest in U.S. dollars.

Diversifying Cash Across Currencies

Because an MNC is not sure how exchange rates will change over time, it may prefer to diversify cash among securities with different currency denominations. This way it avoids the possibility of incurring substantial losses due to a particular currency's depreciation. Limiting the percentage of excess cash invested in each currency will reduce the MNC's exposure to exchange rate risk. The degree to which a portfolio of investments denominated in various currencies will reduce risk depends on the currency correlations. Ideally, the currencies represented within the portfolio would exhibit low or negative correlations with each other. The potential benefits from investing in a portfolio of currencies is more thoroughly discussed in the appendix.

Using Portfolio Insurance to Hedge Investments

Some commercial banks such as Chase Manhattan Corporation have begun to offer **dynamic hedging** (also called **portfolio insurance**) for firms that invest in short-term securities denominated in foreign currencies. Unlike some other hedging techniques, portfolio insurance does not guarantee the home currency cash flows to be received at a future point in time. It reflects periodic hedging by the bank wherein hedges are applied when the currencies held are expected to depreciate and removed when they are expected to appreciate. In essence, the objective is to protect against downside risk while benefiting from the favorable movement of exchange rates.

When there is more uncertainty about the future exchange rates, a **partial hedge** is applied, which protects only a portion of the positions in foreign currencies. Not only is there less protection against downside risk but the potential benefits from favorable exchange rate movements are also reduced.

Consider a manager assigned to perform dynamic hedging for a U.S. firm that has invested in British pounds. If the pound begins to decline and is expected to depreciate further, the manager will sell pounds forward for a future date at which the pound's value is expected to turn upward. If the

---

RELATED RESEARCH

Composing Efficient Money Market Portfolios

For over two decades, researchers have demonstrated potential gains from international diversification of financial assets. Most of the research has focused on stocks, but a few studies have focused on the investment in money market securities, and these studies are relevant to MNCs, which sometimes have large amounts of short-term cash available to invest. Levy applied a so-called mean-variance model to historical interest rate and exchange rate data. This model was used to identify "efficient" portfolios, defined as having the minimum variance for a given mean return. Levy found that the efficient portfolios dominated the individual currencies. That is, there was an efficient portfolio that could match the return of each individual currency and had less risk than that currency. These results imply that there are possible benefits from an internationally diversified money market portfolio.

Levy applied the model to various country perspectives and demonstrated that the composition of the efficient portfolios vary with the perspective. This is because a currency may have appreciated to different degrees against other currencies, and may have led to higher yields for investors in specific countries.

A related study by Cotner and Seitz found that the composition of efficient portfolios changes over time, which is attributed to changes in the returns from investing in various currencies and changes in the comovements between these returns (which affects the variance, or risk, of the portfolio). Consequently, MNCs may not know the composition of efficient portfolios until the investment period is over. Nevertheless, the study suggests that internationally diversified money market portfolios deserve consideration. Even if an MNC cannot create an efficient portfolio, it may still be able to achieve a more desirable return-risk combination when diversifying its investment among currencies.

SOURCES: Haim Levy, "Optimal Portfolio of Foreign Currencies with Borrowing and Lending," *Journal of Money, Credit, and Banking* (August 1981), pp. 325–341.
John Cotner and Neil Seitz, "A Simplified Approach to Short-Term International Diversification," *Financial Review*, May 1987, pp. 249–266.

---

manager is very confident that the pound will depreciate in the short run, most or all of the position will be hedged. Now assume that the pound begins to appreciate before the forward contract date. Since the contract will preclude the potential benefits from appreciation of the pound, the manager may buy pounds forward to offset the existing forward sale contracts. In this way, the manager has removed the existing hedge. Of course, if the forward rate at the time of the forward purchase exceeds the forward rate that existed at the time of the forward sale, a cost is incurred to remove the hedge.

The manager may decide to only remove part of the hedge, which means offsetting only some of the existing forward sales with forward purchases. With this approach, the position is still partially protected if the pound depreciates further. Overall, the performance from using portfolio insurance is dependent on the manager's ability to forecast the direction of exchange rate movements.

SUMMARY

The international cash management role may be separated into two functions: (1) optimizing cash flow movements and (2) optimizing use of available funds. To optimize cash flow movements, the MNC may consider using preauthorized checks or placement of lockboxes to accelerate inflows. In addition, it may use a netting scheme to minimize float and currency conversion costs.

To optimize use of available funds, the MNC may develop a centralized cash management strategy whereby excess funds at the individual subsidiaries are pooled. This may allow for higher yields due to larger deposits. A centralized approach can also accommodate short-term financing needs of some subsidiaries with excess funds at other subsidiaries.

Once the MNC has used whatever excess funds were needed to cover financing needs, it must determine where to invest the remaining excess funds. Because some foreign currencies may either exhibit a high interest rate or be expected to appreciate, deposits denominated in these currencies can be attractive. Among the factors an MNC should consider are (1) does it have future payables it can cover with a foreign currency deposit, and (2) can covered interest arbitrage lead to a higher return than a domestic deposit? Either situation avoids exposure to exchange rate fluctuations.

As a third consideration, the MNC may be willing to set up a foreign currency deposit and remain uncovered. This may be a worthwhile strategy if the expected effective yield on such a strategy is sufficiently above the return on a domestic deposit to outweigh the exchange rate risk. To forecast the effective yield, a forecast of the exchange rate reflecting the deposit's currency is necessary. For this purpose, the MNC can develop either a point forecast or a probability distribution. Once the exchange rate forecast is used to determine the expected effective yield on the foreign deposit, the MNC can compare its risk and potential reward characteristics with a domestic deposit. Even if several MNCs were faced with the same decision and had a similar assessment, their actual choice might vary since their degrees of risk aversion might vary.

As a final alternative, the MNC should consider investing in a portfolio of foreign currency deposits expected to generate high effective yields. This can often lead to a higher probability that the overall portfolio yield would be more rewarding than a domestic investment, especially if the movements of these currencies are not highly correlated.

QUESTIONS/ PROBLEMS

1. Discuss the general functions involved in international cash management.

2. What is netting, and how can it improve an MNC's performance?

3. How can an MNC implement leading and lagging techniques to help subsidiaries in need of funds?

4. Explain how the MNC's optimization of cash flow can distort the profits of each subsidiary.

5. How can a centralized cash management system be beneficial to the MNC?

6. Why would a firm consider investing short-term funds overseas?

7. Assume a U.S.-based MNC has $2,000,000 in cash available for 90 days. It is considering the use of covered interest arbitrage, since the British 90-day interest rate is higher than the U.S. interest rate. What will determine whether this strategy is feasible?

8. Assume a U.S.-based MNC has $1,000,000 in cash available for 30 days. It can earn 1 percent on a 30-day investment in the U.S. Alternatively, if it converts the dollars to French francs, it can earn $1\frac{1}{2}$ percent on a French deposit. The spot rate of the French franc is $.12. The spot rate 30 days from now is expected to be $.10. Should this firm invest its cash in the U.S. or in France? Substantiate your answer.

9. Assume a U.S.-based MNC has $3,000,000 in cash available for 180 days. It can earn 7 percent on a U.S. Treasury bill or 9 percent on a British Treasury bill. The British investment does require conversion of dollars to British pounds. Assume that interest rate parity holds and that the MNC believes the 180-day forward rate is a reliable predictor of the spot rate to be realized 180 days from now. Would the British investment provide an effective yield that is below, above, or equal to the yield on the U.S. investment? Explain your answer.

10. Repeat Question 9, except assume the firm expects the 180-day forward rate of the pound to substantially overestimate the spot rate to be realized in 180 days.

11. Repeat Question 9, except assume the firm expects the 180-day forward rate of the pound to substantially underestimate the spot rate to be realized in 180 days.

12. Assume the one-year U.S. interest rate is 10 percent, and the one-year Canadian interest rate is 13 percent. If a U.S. firm invests its funds in Canada, what percentage would the Canadian dollar have to depreciate to make its effective yield the same as the U.S. interest rate from the U.S. firm's perspective?

13. A U.S.-based MNC plans to invest its excess cash in France for one year. The one-year French interest rate is 19 percent. The probability of the French franc's percentage change in value during the next year is as follows:

Possible Rate of Change in the French Franc Over the Life of the Investment	Probability of Occurrence
−3%	20%
4	50
10	30

What is the expected value of the effective yield based on this information? Given that the U.S. interest rate for one year is 17 percent, what is the probability that a one-year investment in francs will generate a lower effective yield than if the U.S. firm simply invested domestically?

14. If a U.S. firm believes that the international Fisher effect holds, what are the implications regarding a strategy of continually attempting to generate high returns from investing in currencies with high interest rates?

15. A U.S. firm considers placing 30 percent of its excess funds in a one-year French-franc deposit and the remaining 70 percent of its funds in a one-year Canadian-dollar deposit. The French one-year interest rate is 15 percent, while the Canadian one-year interest rate is 13 percent. The possible percentage changes in the two currencies for the next year are forecasted as follows:

Currency	Possible Percentage Change in the Spot Rate Over the Investment Horizon	Probability of that Percentage Change in the Spot Rate Occurring
French franc	−2%	20%
French franc	1	60
French franc	3	20
Canadian dollar	1	50
Canadian dollar	4	40
Canadian dollar	6	10

Given this information, determine the possible effective yields of the portfolio and the probability associated with each possible portfolio yield. Given a one-year U.S. interest rate of 16 percent, what is the probability that the portfolio's effective yield will be lower than the yield achieved from investing in the United States?

16. Why would a firm consider investing in a portfolio of foreign currencies instead of just a single foreign currency?

17. Tallahassee Company has $2 million in excess cash that it has invested in Mexico at an annual interest rate of 60 percent. The U.S. interest rate is 9 percent. By how much would the Mexican peso have to depreciate to cause such a strategy to backfire?

18. San Antonio Corporation has several subsidiaries in less developed countries that trade goods and supplies with each other. Explain how transfer pricing could be used by San Antonio Corporation to reduce its overall tax payments.

19. Dallas Company has determined that the French interest rate is 16 percent while the U.S. interest rate is 11 percent for one-year Treasury bills. The one-year forward rate of the French franc has a discount of 7 percent. Does interest rate parity exist? Can Dallas Company achieve a higher effective yield by using covered interest arbitrage than by investing in U.S. Treasury bills? Explain.

20. Corpus Company has a subsidiary in Country X that produces computer components and sells them to another subsidiary in Country Y, where the production process is completed. The tax rate in Country X is 50 percent, while the tax rate in Country Y is 20 percent. The pro forma income statements of the Corpus subsidiaries are shown in Exhibit A. Assume that Corpus headquarters adjusts its transfer pricing policy so that sales by Subsidiary X are reduced from $400,000 to $320,000 (this also affects the cost of goods sold at Subsidiary Y by the same amount). Determine the change in total tax payments of the consolidated subsidiaries as a result of this revised transfer pricing policy.

EXHIBIT A   Corpus Company Pro Forma Income Statements for Subsidiaries

	Subsidiary X	Subsidiary Y	Consolidated Subsidiaries
Sales	$400,000	$700,000	$1,100,000
Less: cost of goods sold	220,000	400,000	620,000
Gross profit	180,000	300,000	480,000
Less: operating expenses	80,000	100,000	180,000
Earnings before interest and taxes	100,000	200,000	300,000
Interest expense	10,000	30,000	40,000
Earnings before taxes	90,000	170,000	260,000
Taxes (50% for Sub X and 20% for Sub Y)	45,000	34,000	79,000
Earnings after taxes	45,000	136,000	181,000

Islander Corporation
Composing the Optimal Currency Portfolio for Investing

As treasurer for the Islander Corporation, you must develop a strategy for investing the excess cash that will be available for the next year. The firm, based in the United States, presently has no transactions exposure to foreign currency movements. Assume the following data as of today:

Currency	Spot Exchange Rate	Annualized Interest Rate on a Three-Month Deposit
Australian dollar	.75	13.00
British pound	1.70	12.5
Canadian dollar	.86	11.0
French franc	.17	11.5
German mark	.60	7.0
Italian lira	.0008	12.0
Japanese yen	.006	8.0
Swedish krona	.16	9.0
Swiss franc	.71	6.0
U.S. dollar	1.00	9.0

Your forecasting department has provided you with the following forecasts of the spot rates three months from now:

	Strong $ Scenario	Somewhat Stable $ Scenario	Weak $ Scenario
Australian dollar	$ .66	$ .76	$ .85
British pound	1.58	1.73	1.83
Canadian dollar	.85	.85	.91
French franc	.14	.173	.18
German mark	.53	.59	.63
Italian lira	.00073	.00079	.00086

	Strong $ Scenario	Somewhat Stable $ Scenario	Weak $ Scenario
Japanese yen	.0055	.0062	.0072
Swedish krona	.15	.155	.17
Swiss franc	.62	.69	.78
U.S. dollar	1.00	1.00	1.00

The probability of the strong dollar scenario is 30 percent, the probability of the somewhat stable dollar scenario is 40 percent and the probability of the weak dollar scenario is 30 percent. Based on the information provided, prescribe the composition of the investment portfolio that would maximize the expected value of the effective yield for each of four possible risk preferences:

1. Risk neutral	Focus on maximizing the expected value of your effective yield, without any constraints.
2. Balanced	Invest no more than 25 percent in any foreign currency.
3. Conservative	Invest at least 50 percent of the funds in the U.S. dollar and no more than 10 percent of the funds in any individual foreign currency.
4. Ultra-conservative	Do not create any exposure to exchange rate risk.

Fill out the following table:

	Forecasted Effective Yield of Portfolio for:		
Risk Preference	Strong $ Scenario	Somewhat Stable $ Scenario	Weak $ Scenario
Risk neutral portfolio			
Balanced portfolio			
Conservative portfolio			
Ultra-conservative portfolio			

Which portfolio would you prescribe for your firm? Why? (You may find it helpful to draw bar charts that show the probability distribution of effective yields for each of the portfolios, placing one bar chart above another).

PROJECT

1. Use the interest rate and exchange rate data in the back of the text to determine a U.S. firm's effective (exchange rate-adjusted) yield when investing in British pounds on a quarterly basis. Identify the periods in which this strategy would have resulted in very low effective yields. Was the dollar strengthening or weakening in those periods? (A computerized spreadsheet could easily be created to reduce your computational time.)

REFERENCES

Abdallah, Wagdy M. "How to Motivate and Evaluate Managers with International Transfer Pricing Systems." *Management International Review*, no. 1 (1989), pp. 65–71.

Biger, Nahum. "Exchange Risk Implications of International Portfolio Diversification." *Journal of International Business Studies* 10 (Fall 1979), pp. 64–74.

Bokos, William J., and Anne P. Clinkard. "Multilateral Netting." *Journal of Cash Management* (June–July 1983), pp. 24–34.

Bradley, Frank. "Nature and Significance of International Marketing: A Review." *Journal of Business Research* (June 1987), pp. 205–219.

Cohen, Fred L. "Accelerating Foreign Remittances and Collection." *Cash Flow* (May 1981), pp. 36–40.

Cotner, John, and Neil Seitz. "A Simplified Approach to Short-Term International Diversification." *Financial Review* (May 1987), pp. 249–266.

Cumming, Bruce D. "Understanding and Managing Canadian Availability: A Neglected Cash Management Opportunity." *Journal of Cash Management* (February–March 1983), pp. 26–31.

Dufey, Gunter, and Ian H. Giddy. "Innovation in the International Financial Markets." *Journal of International Business Studies* 12 (Fall 1981), pp. 33–50.

Eaker, M. R., and Catherine Bruno. "Further Evaluation of Financing Costs for Multinational Subsidiaries." *Management International Review* (No. 4, 1983), pp. 26–31.

Finnerty, John P. "What to Expect From an International Cash Management Study." *Cashflow* (October 1981), pp. 39–40.

Giddy, Ian H. "The Public Policy Implications of the Eurocurrency Market." *Columbia Journal of World Business* 14 (Fall 1979), pp. 4–7.

Jacque, Laurent I. "Management of Foreign Exchange Risk: A Review Article." *Journal of International Business Studies* (Spring–Summer 1981), pp. 81–99.

Levy, Haim. "Optimal Portfolio of Foreign Currencies with Borrowing and Lending." *Journal of Money, Credit, and Banking* 13 (August 1981), pp. 326–341.

Levy, Haim, and Marshall Sarnat. "Exchange Rate Risk and the Optimal Diversification of Foreign Currency Holdings." *Journal of Money, Credit, and Banking* (November 1978), pp. 453–463.

Lewis, Karen K. "The Behavior of Eurocurrency Returns Across Different Holding Periods and Monetary Regimes", *Journal of Finance* (September 1990): 1211–1236.

Madura, Jeff. "Model for Financing in International Money Markets." *Review of International Economics and Business* (Summer 1986), pp. 1–9.

Madura, Jeff, and E. Joe Nosari. "Global Money Management: One Approach." *Financial Executive* (June 1984), pp. 42–47.

_____ . "Optimal Portfolio of Foreign Currencies with Borrowing and Lending." *Journal of Money, Credit, and Banking* (November 1982), p. 531.

_____ . "Speculation in International Money Markets." *Atlantic Economic Journal* (July 1983), pp. 87–90.

_____ . "Utilizing Currency Portfolios to Mitigate Exchange Rate Risk." *Columbia Journal of World Business* (Spring 1984), pp. 96–99.

_____ . "Speculative Trading in the Eurocurrency Market." *Akron Business and Economic Review* (Winter 1984), pp. 48–52.

"Multinationals Cut Back in Philippines Because They Can't Sell Pesos for 'Dollars.' " *The Wall Street Journal* (June 11, 1984), p. 2.

Parkinson, Kenneth L. "Dealing with the Problems of International Cash Management." *Journal of Cash Management* (February–March 1983), pp. 16–25.

Samlee, Saeed. "Pricing in Marketing Strategies of U.S. and Foreign Based Companies." *Journal of Business Research* (February 1987), pp. 17–30.

Shapiro, Alan. "Payments Netting in International Cash Management." *Journal of International Business Studies* (Fall 1978), pp. 51–58.

Soenen, L. A. "International Cash Management: A Study of the Practices of U.K.-Based Companies." *Journal of Business Research* (August 1986), pp. 345–354.

Srinivasan, Venkat, and Yong H. Kim. "Payments Netting in International Cash Management: A Network Optimization Approach." *Journal of International Business Studies* (Summer 1986), pp. 1–20.

Swanson, Peggy E. "The International Transmission of Interest Rates." *Journal of Banking and Finance* (December 1988), pp. 563–573.

Swanson, Peggy. "Interrelationships Among Domestic and Euro Currency Deposit Yields: A Focus on the U.S. Dollar." *Financial Review* (February 1988), pp. 81–94.

Swanson, Peggy E., and William S. Y. How. "Portfolio Diversification by Currency Denomination: An Approach to International Cash Management with Implications for Foreign Exchange Markets." *Quarterly Review of Economics and Business* (Spring 1986), pp. 95–103.

Investing in a Portfolio of Currencies

Large financial corporations may consider investing in a portfolio of currencies as illustrated in the following example. Assume a U.S. firm needs to invest $100,000 for one year and obtains these interest rate quotes:

Interest rate for a one-year deposit in U.S. dollars = 11%.
Interest rate for a one-year deposit in French francs = 14%.
Interest rate for a one-year deposit in British pounds = 13%.

Due to relatively high quotes for a deposit in French francs or British pounds, it is understandable why the U.S. firm may desire to invest in a foreign currency. If the U.S. firm decides to use foreign investing, it has three choices based on the information given here:

- Invest in only French francs.
- Invest in only British pounds.
- Invest in a mixture (or portfolio) of francs and pounds.

Assume the U.S. firm has established possible percentage changes in the spot rate from the time the deposit would begin until maturity for both the French franc and British pound, as are shown in Column 2 of Exhibit 15A.1. We shall first discuss the French franc. For each possible percentage change that might occur, a probability of that occurrence is disclosed in the third column. Based on the assumed interest rate of 14 percent for the French franc, the effective yield is computed for each possible percentage change in the French franc's spot rate over the loan life. From Exhibit 15A.1 there is a 20 percent chance the French franc will depreciate by 4 percent during the deposit period. If it does, the effective yield will be 9.44 percent. Thus, there is a 20 percent chance the effective yield will be 9.44 percent. Furthermore, there is a 50 percent chance the effective yield will be 12.86 percent and a 30 percent chance it will be 16.28 percent. Given that the U.S. deposit rate is 11 percent, there is a 20 percent chance that investing in French francs will result in a lower effective yield than a U.S. dollar deposit.

EXHIBIT 15A.1 Development of Possible Effective Yields

Currency	Possible Percentage Change in the Spot Rate Over the Deposit Life	Probability of that Percentage Change in the Spot Rate Occurring	Computation of Effective Yield Based on that Percentage Change in the Spot Rate
French franc	−4%	20%	$(1.14)[1 + (-4\%)] - 1 = 9.44\%$
French franc	−1%	50%	$(1.14)[1 + (-1\%)] - 1 = 12.86\%$
French franc	+2%	30%	$(1.14)[1 + (2\%)] - 1 = 16.28\%$
		100%	
British pound	−3%	30%	$(1.13)[1 + (-3\%)] - 1 = 9.61\%$
British pound	0%	30%	$(1.13)[1 + (0\%)] - 1 = 13.00\%$
British pound	2%	40%	$(1.13)[1 + (2\%)] - 1 = 15.26\%$
		100%	

The lower section of Exhibit 15A.1 provides information on British pounds. We see, for example, that the pound has a 30 percent chance of depreciating by 3 percent during the deposit period, and so on. Based on the 13 percent interest rate for a British pound deposit, there is a 30 percent chance the effective yield will be 9.61 percent, a 40 percent chance it will be 13 percent, and a 30 percent chance it will be 15.26 percent. Keeping in mind the 11 percent rate on a U.S. dollar deposit, there is a 30 percent chance that investing in British pounds will be less rewarding than a U.S. dollar deposit.

Before examining the third possible foreign investing strategy (the portfolio approach) available here, determine the expected value of the effective yield for each foreign currency, summing the products of each possible effective yield and its associated probability as follows:

Currency	Computation of Expected Value of Effective Yield:
French francs	$(20\%)(9.44\%) + 50\%(12.86\%) + 30\%(16.28\%) = 13.202\%$
British pounds	$(30\%)(9.61\%) + 30\%(13.00\%) + 40\%(15.26\%) = 12.887\%$

The expected value of the French franc's yield is slightly higher. In addition, the individual degree of risk (the chance the return on investment will be lower than a U.S. deposit) is higher for the pound. If the U.S. firm does choose to invest in only one of these foreign currencies, it may choose the French franc, since its return and risk characteristics are more favorable. Yet, before making its decision, the firm should consider the possibility of investing in a currency portfolio, as discussed here.

The information in Exhibit 15A.1 shows three possibilities for the French franc's effective yield. The same holds true for the British pound. If a U.S. firm invests half of its available funds in each of the foreign currencies, then there will be nine possibilities for this portfolio's effective yield. These possibilities are shown in Exhibit 15A.2. The first two columns list all possible

EXHIBIT 15A.2   Analysis of Investing in Two Foreign Currencies

Possible Joint Effective Yield		Computation of Joint Probability		Computation of Effective Yield of Portfolio (50% of Total Funds Invested in Each Currency)
French Franc	British Pound			
9.44%	9.61%	(20%)(30%) =	6%	.5 (9.44%) + .5 (9.61%) = 9.525%
9.44	13.00	(20%)(30%) =	6	.5 (9.44%) + .5(13.00%) = 11.22
9.44	15.26	(20%)(40%) =	8	.5 (9.44%) + .5(15.26%) = 12.35
12.86	9.61	(50%)(30%) =	15	.5(12.86%) + .5 (9.61%) = 11.235
12.86	13.00	(50%)(30%) =	15	.5(12.86%) + .5(13.00%) = 12.93
12.86	15.26	(50%)(40%) =	20	.5(12.86%) + .5(15.26%) = 14.06
16.28	9.61	(30%)(30%) =	9	.5(16.28%) + .5 (9.61%) = 12.945
16.28	13.00	(30%)(30%) =	9	.5(16.28%) + .5(13.00%) = 14.64
16.28	15.26	(30%)(40%) =	12	.5(16.28%) + .5(15.26%) = 15.77
			100%	

joint effective yields. The third column computes the joint probability of each possible occurrence. The fourth column shows the computation of the portfolio's effective yield based on the possible rates disclosed for the individual currencies shown in the first two columns. The top row of the table suggests that one possibility of investing in both French francs and British pounds is an effective yield of 9.44 percent and 9.61 percent, respectively. The probability of this French franc effective yield occurring is 20 percent, while the probability of the British pound's effective yield occurring is 30 percent. The joint probability that both of these effective yields will occur simultaneously is (20%) (30%) = 6%. Assuming that half (50%) of the funds available are invested in each currency, the portfolio's effective yields will be .5(9.44%) + .5(9.61%) = 9.525% (if those individual effective yields do occur).

A similar procedure was used to develop the remaining eight rows in Exhibit 15A.2. There is a 6 percent chance the portfolio's effective yield will be 11.22 percent, an 8 percent chance that it will be 12.35 percent, and so on.

Exhibit 15A.2 shows that investing in the portfolio will likely be more rewarding than a U.S. dollar deposit. While there is a 6 percent chance the portfolio's effective yield will be 9.525 percent, all other possible portfolio yields (see column 4) are more than the U.S. deposit rate of 11 percent.

Recall that investing solely in French francs had a 20 percent chance of being less rewarding than the U.S. deposit, while investing solely in British pounds had a 30 percent chance of being more rewarding. The analysis in Exhibit 15A.2 suggests that investing in a portfolio (50 percent invested in French francs with the remaining 50 percent invested in British pounds) has only a 6 percent chance of being less rewarding than domestic investing. These results will be explained.

When an investment is made in both currencies, the only way the portfolio will exhibit a lower yield than the U.S. deposit is when *both* currencies experience their maximum possible level of depreciation (which is 4 percent depreciation for the French franc and 3 percent depreciation for the British pound). If only one of these events occurs, its severity will be somewhat offset by the other currency not depreciating by such a large extent. The probability of maximum depreciation is 20 percent for the French franc and 30 percent for the British pound. The joint probability of both of these events occurring simultaneously is (20%) (30%) = 6%. This is the advantage of investing in a portfolio of foreign currencies. In our example, the U.S. firm has a 94 percent chance of attaining a higher return with the foreign portfolio as opposed to a U.S. deposit.

What is the expected value of the effective yield for the portfolio? It can be determined by multiplying the percentage of funds invested in each currency by its respective expected value of the currency's individual effective yield. Recall that the expected value was 13.202 percent for the French franc and 12.887 percent for the British pound. Thus, for a portfolio representing 50 percent of funds invested in each currency, the expected value of the effective yield is .5(13.202%) + .5(12.887%) = 13.0445%. Based on an overall comparison, the portfolio's expected value of the effective yield is somewhat similar to that from investing solely in either foreign currency. However, the risk (the probability of the effective yield being less than that of the U.S. deposit) when investing in the portfolio is substantially less than that of either individual foreign currency deposit.

In our example, the computation of joint probabilities requires the assumption that the movements in the two currencies are independent. If movements of the two currencies were actually highly correlated, then investing in a portfolio of currencies would not be as beneficial as demonstrated here, because there would be a strong likelihood of both currencies experiencing a high level of depreciation simultaneously. If the two currencies are not highly correlated, they would not be expected to simultaneously depreciate to such a degree.

The previous example included two currencies in the portfolio. Investing in a more diversified portfolio of additional currencies that exhibit high interest rates can even increase the probability that foreign investing will be more rewarding than the U.S. deposit. This is due to the low probability that all currencies will move in tandem and therefore simultaneously depreciate to offset their high interest rate advantage. Again, the degree to which these currencies are correlated with each other is important here. If all currencies were highly positively correlated with each other, investing in such a portfolio would not be much different than investing in a single foreign currency.

REPEATED INVESTING IN A CURRENCY PORTFOLIO

A firm that repeatedly invests in foreign currencies may normally prefer to compose a portfolio package that will exhibit a somewhat predictable effective yield on a periodic basis. The more volatile a portfolio's effective yield over time, the more uncertainty (risk) there is about the yield that portfolio will exhibit in any period. The portfolio's variability depends on the standard deviations and paired correlations of effective yields of the individual currencies within the portfolio.

We can use the portfolio variance as a measurement for degree of volatility. The variance of a two-currency portfolio's effective yield [$VAR(r_p)$] over time is computed as

$$VAR(r_p) = w_A^2 \sigma_A^2 + w_B^2 \sigma_B^2 + 2w_A w_B \sigma_A \sigma_B CORR_{AB}$$

where w_A and w_B represent the percentage of total funds invested in Currencies A and B respectively, σ_A^2 and σ_B^2 represent the individual variances of each currency's effective yield overtime, and $CORR_{AB}$ reflects the correlation coefficient of the two currencies' effective yields. Since the percentage exchange rate change plays an important role in influencing the effective yield, it should not be surprising that $CORR_{AB}$ is strongly affected by the correlation between the exchange rate fluctuations of the two currencies. A low correlation between currency fluctuations can force $CORR_{AB}$ to be low.

To illustrate how the variance in a portfolio's effective yield is related to characteristics of the component currencies, consider the following example. The following information is based on several three-month periods:

Mean effective yield of British pound over 3 months = 4%.
Mean effective yield of French franc over 3 months = 5%.
Standard deviation of British pound's effective yield = .06.
Standard deviation of French franc's effective yield = .10.
Correlation coefficient of effective yields of these two currencies = .20

Given the information above, the mean effective yield on a portfolio (r_p) of funds invested as 50 percent into British pounds and 50 percent into French franc is determined by summing the weighted individual effective yields:

$$r_p = .5(.04) + .5(.05)$$
$$= .02 + .025$$
$$= .045, \text{ or } 4.5\%$$

The variance of this portfolio's effective financing rate over time is

$$VAR(r_p) = .5^2(.06)^2 + .5^2(.10)^2 + 2(.5)(.5)(.06)(.10)(.20)$$
$$= .25(.0036) + .25(.01) + .5(.0012)$$
$$= .0009 + .0025 + .0006$$
$$= .004$$

To test your understanding of this concept, what is the mean effective yield and the variance of a portfolio representing 60 percent of funds invested in British pounds and 40 percent of funds invested in French francs? The answer is provided here so you can check your work:

$$\text{Mean } r_p = .6(.04) + .4(.05)$$
$$= .024 + .02$$
$$= .044, \text{ or } 4.4\%$$
$$VAR(r_p) = .6^2(.06)^2 + .4^2(.10)^2 + 2(.6)(.4)(.06)(.10)(.20)$$
$$= .003472$$

There is a reduction in variance of about 13 percent here relative to our first example. However, the mean effective yield is now lower with this portfolio.

These examples suggest how an MNC can use historical data to determine the mean effective yield and variance of a two-currency portfolio. This way it can compare various currency portfolios to see which portfolio would have been most appropriate. The MNC is typically more interested in estimating the mean return and variability for repeated investing in a particular portfolio in the future. There is no guarantee that past data will be indicative of the future. Yet, if the individual variability and paired correlations are somewhat stable over time, the historical variability of the portfolio's effective yield should be a reasonable forecast of the future portfolio variability.

The analysis presented here need not be restricted to just two currencies. The mean effective yield for a currency portfolio of any size can be determined by summing the products of percentage of funds invested in each currency times its respective effective yield. Solving the variance of a portfolio's effective yield becomes more complex as more currencies are added to the portfolio. However, computer software packages are commonly applied to easily determine the solution.

PART FIVE

Long-Term Asset and Liability Management

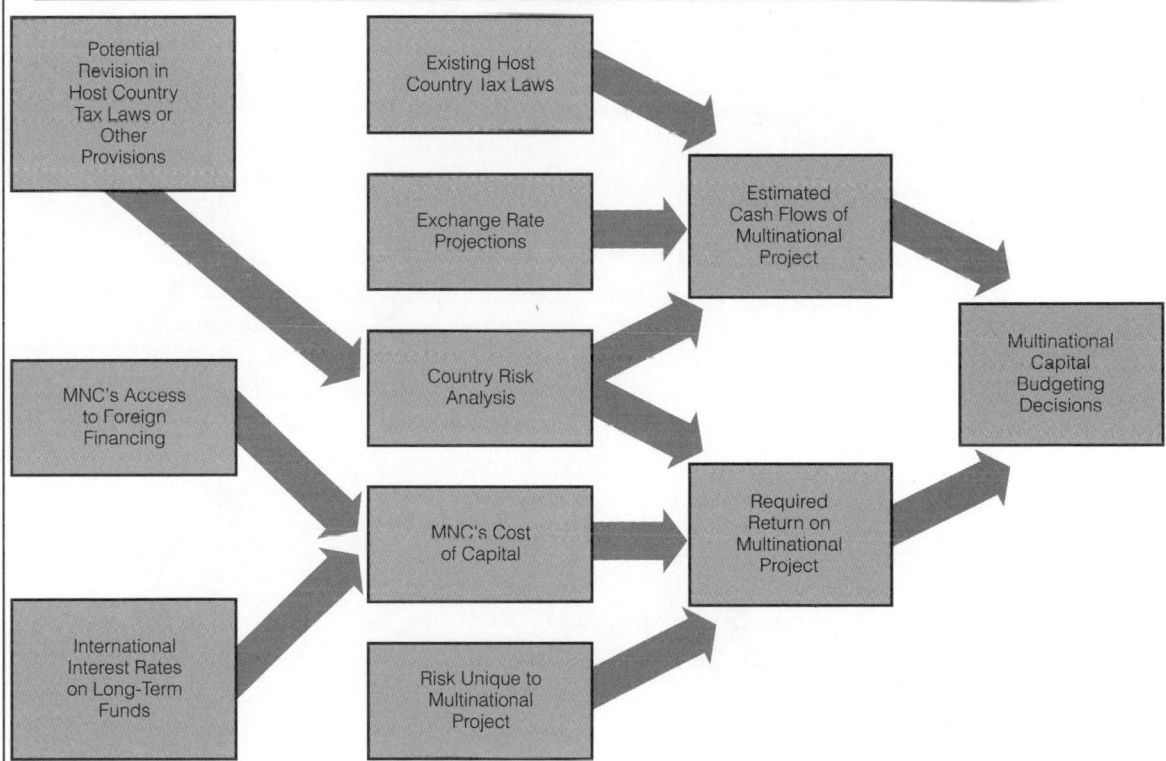

Part 5 (Chapters 16 through 21) focuses on the MNC's management of long-term assets and liabilities. Chapter 16 explains why MNCs are motivated to engage in international business and identifies methods by which MNCs can increase their degree of internationalization. Chapter 17 describes the information MNCs must have in considering multinational projects and demonstrates how the capital budgeting analysis is conducted. Chapter 18 explains the capital structure decision for MNCs, which affects the cost of financing new projects. Chapter 19 explains how MNCs assess country risk, while Chapter 20 describes the MNC's long-term financing decision, and Chapter 21 focuses on multinational tax planning. All chapters in Part 5 are closely related. The capital budgeting decision (Chapter 17) is dependent on the cost of capital (Chapter 18), country risk analysis (Chapter 19), the cost of long-term financing (Chapter 20), and anticipated tax provisions in the host country (Chapter 21).

CHAPTER 16

Direct Foreign Investment

Most large MNCs conduct business around the world. This chapter first identifies motives for increasing international business, then methods of doing so. Next, the relationship between MNC risk and degree of international business is examined. It is shown that MNCs can reduce their risk by increasing their degree of international business. If an MNC attempts to increase its international business through **direct foreign investment** (DFI), it must decide where to establish a new subsidiary. An example of a DFI location decision is provided to demonstrate how the location choice can affect the MNC's risk. Following the example, a graphic analysis illustrates how DFI decisions can affect the risk-return characteristics of the MNC.

CORPORATE MOTIVES FOR INCREASING INTERNATIONAL BUSINESS

A firm seeking to maximize shareholder wealth may find it worthwhile to increase its foreign business. There are several possible motives for a corporation becoming more internationalized. Some of the more popular ones are to

1. Attract new sources of demand.
2. Enter markets where superior profits are possible.
3. Fully benefit from economies of scale.
4. Use foreign factors of production.
5. Use foreign raw materials.
6. Use foreign technology.
7. Exploit monopolistic advantages.
8. Diversify internationally.
9. React to a foreign currency's changing value.
10. React to trade restrictions.
11. Benefit politically.

Each of these motives is discussed in turn:

1. *Attract new sources of demand.* Corporations often reach a stage where growth is limited in their home country. This may be due to intense competition for the product they sell. Even if there is little competition, their market share in their country may already be near its potential peak. Or overall demand for the primary product could be diminished due to changes in consumer tastes. Thus, a possible solution is to consider foreign markets where there is potential demand.

2. *Enter markets where superior profits are possible.* If other corporations within the industry have proven that excessive earnings can be realized in other markets, an MNC may also decide to sell in that market. It may plan to undercut the prevailing, excessively high prices. A common problem with this strategy is that previously established sellers in that market may prevent a new competitor from taking away their business by lowering their prices just as the new competitor attempts to break into this market.

3. *Fully benefit from economies of scale.* The corporation that attempts to sell its primary product in new markets may increase its earnings and shareholder wealth due to **economies of scale** (lower average cost per unit resulting from increased production). Such a motive is more likely for firms that utilize much machinery.

As the Single European Act removed trade barriers, it allowed MNCs to achieve greater economies of scale. For example, Coca-Cola is consolidating its European plants into one control plant in France, as the removal of tariffs between European countries allows it to benefit from economies of scale at one plant without excessive exporting cost. The act also enhances economies of scale by making regulations on television ads, automobile standards, and other products and services uniform across European countries. As a result, Colgate-Palmolive Company, Prime Computer, and other MNCs are manufacturing more homogeneous products that are salable in all European countries, rather than differentiating them to meet country-specific standards.

The actions of MNCs to establish subsidiaries in Taiwan, Hong Kong, and Singapore during the 1980s were primarily driven by the cost advantage of the foreign factors of production. These actions have caused a labor shortage, which resulted in higher labor costs and reduced the cost advantage in these countries.

4. *Use foreign factors of production.* Labor and land costs can vary dramatically among countries. MNCs often attempt to set up production in a location where land and labor are cheap. Due to market imperfections (as discussed in Chapter 1) such as imperfect information, relocation transactions costs, barriers to industry entry by firms, etc., specific labor costs will not necessarily become equal among markets. Thus, it is worthwhile for MNCs to survey markets to determine whether they can benefit from cheaper costs by producing in those markets.

In 1990 the minimum daily wage rate was $4.10 in Mexico versus $30.40 in the United States. Baxter Travenol established manufacturing plants in Mexico and Malaysia to capitalize on lower costs of production (primarily wage rates). Honeywell has some of its joint ventures in countries where production costs are low, such as Korea and India. It also has established subsidiaries in countries where production costs are low, such as Mexico, Malaysia, Hong Kong, and Taiwan.

Japanese companies are increasingly using Mexico and other low-wage countries for production. For example, Sony Corporation recently established a plant in Tijuana. Sanjo Electric maintains a plant in Mexico that produces small refrigerators and electric fans, and sells them to U.S. firms. Matsushita Electrical Industrial Company has a large plant in Tijuana.

Mexico has attracted direct foreign investment because (1) production costs in Mexican plants are low, (2) its government has encouraged direct foreign investment in its country under certain conditions, and (3) the Mexican peso has been weak, allowing foreign firms to establish a plant at a low cost.

Numerous U.S.-based MNCs have subsidiaries in Mexico for similar reasons, including General Electric Company, RCA Corporation, and Zenith Radio Corporation. The growth in such subsidiaries has contributed significantly to Mexico's economy.

5. *Use foreign raw materials.* Due to transportation costs, a corporation attempts to avoid importing raw materials from a given country, especially when it plans to then sell the finished product back to consumers in that foreign country. Under such circumstances, a more feasible solution may be to develop the product in the country where the raw materials are located. Even if the product is to be sold elsewhere, the decision to import may be inappropriate. For example, a U.S. car manufacturer that imports steel from France and then exports cars to West Germany may be better off establishing a manufacturing plant in France or West Germany.

6. *Use foreign technology.* Corporations are increasingly establishing overseas plants or acquiring existing overseas plants to learn about the technology of foreign countries. This technology is then used to improve their production process at all subsidiary plants around the world.

7. *Exploit monopolistic advantages.* Based on industrial organization theory, firms may become internationalized if they possess resources or skills not available to competing firms. If factors of production, information, and products were completely mobile and available without transportation costs, any particular firm would not possess a monopolistic advantage in these markets. That is, factors and product markets would be perfect. Factors of production, information, and products would be transferred wherever a deficiency existed. This would remove the deficiency and force the market prices of a given factor or product to be identical across the world.

In reality, markets are imperfect. There is not complete mobility or accessibility of factor, information, and product markets. Consequently, some countries may possess an advantage over other countries in these markets. Even within a given country, some firms may possess an advantage over other firms in these markets. A common example of monopolistic advantage is technology. If a particular firm possesses advanced technology and has exploited this advantage successfully in local markets, it may attempt to exploit it internationally as well. Technology is not restricted to developing a new product. It can even represent a more efficient production, marketing, or financing process. To the extent the firm has an advantage over competitors, it should be able to benefit from becoming internationalized.

8. *Diversify internationally.* Another reason why firms conduct international business is international diversification. Consider a firm as a portfolio of assets. If all assets of a firm are designed to generate sales of a specific product in one country, the cash flow of the firm would likely be quite unstable, resulting from exposure to changes within its industry or within the economy. The firm may reduce its cash flow variability by diversifying its

product mix. Any decrease in net cash flows due to reduced demand for some of its products may be somewhat offset by an increase in other net cash flows resulting from increased demand for its other products. However, demand for all products produced in a single country are somewhat similarly influenced by the country's economy. This systematic exposure to economic conditions cannot be diversified away, regardless of how many products the firms sells within that single country. The firm can, however, reduce such risk by marketing its product mix among various countries.

The co-movement between country economies can be assessed by measuring their real (inflation-adjusted) growth rates in gross national product (GNP). The GNP growth trends of the United States, Germany, and Japan, are displayed in Exhibit 16.1. It is clear from this exhibit that while the trends are somewhat related, they vary across countries. Since country economies do not move perfectly in tandem over time, net cash flow from sales of products across countries should be more stable than if the products were sold in a single country. By diversifying sales (and possibly even production) internationally, a firm can make its net cash flows less volatile. Thus, the possibility of a liquidity deficiency is less likely. In addition, the firm may enjoy a lower cost of capital as shareholders and creditors assess risk to be lower due to more stable cash flows.

The extent to which international diversification can stabilize an MNC's cash flow is dependent on the potential foreign markets. Consider three neighboring countries in Europe (call them A, B, and C) that trade continuously with each other. The level of economic activity in these three countries may be quite similar at a given point in time, since their substantial trading activity should force a great deal of interdependence between them. Thus, their business cycles should move in tandem. If an MNC concentrated on one

EXHIBIT 16.1 Co-movements in Real GNP Growth Among Countries

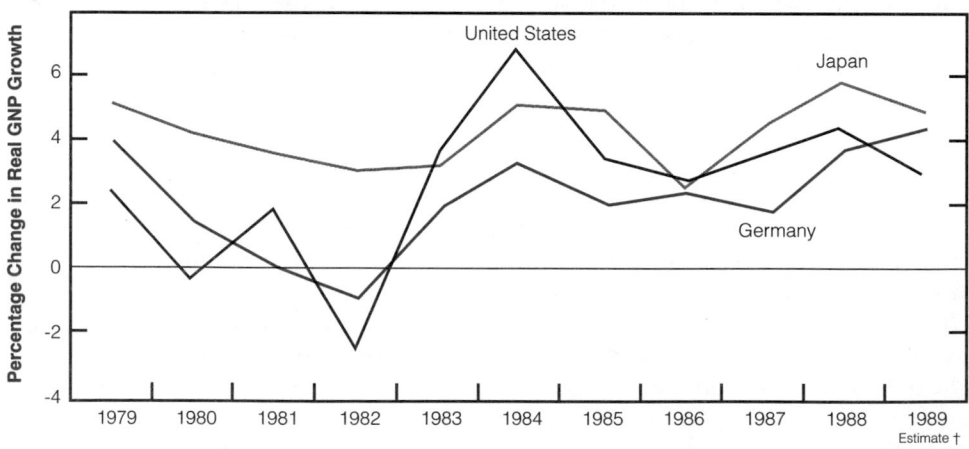

†1989 data for the United States are preliminary.

SOURCES: International Monetary Fund, *World Economic Outlook;* Organization for Economic Cooperation and Development, *OECD Economic Outlook;* U.S. Bureau of Economic Analysis, and *FRBNY Annual Report,* 1989.

product and marketed the product heavily in these three countries, the sales pattern would be similar to that of some other firm that marketed exclusively in only one of these countries. The reason is that diversifying sales among three countries with almost identical business cycle patterns is like not diversifying at all. A preferable diversification strategy would extend the product to countries whose business cycles were not so highly correlated.

As a result of the Single European Act, European economies are likely to become more integrated. Therefore, benefits from diversifying across European countries may be reduced.

9. *React to a foreign currency's changing value.* When a foreign currency is perceived by a firm to be undervalued, the firm may consider direct foreign investment in that country. The initial outlay should be relatively low. If the currency strengthens over time, the earnings remitted to the parent may increase. As an example, Japanese companies substantially increased their DFI in the United States, Taiwan, South Korea, and Southeast Asia in the mid 1980s. This action was taken partially because of the yen's strength at that time, which allowed for a relatively low initial outlay to establish subsidiaries. A related reason for such DFI is to offset the changing demand for a company's exports due to exchange rate fluctuations. For example, in 1986 some U.S. importing firms increased orders from South Korean companies in place of some Japanese companies because of the rising yen value. If these Japanese companies had maintained subsidiaries in South Korea, they might have been able to retain sales to U.S. companies through those subsidiaries.

10. *React to trade restrictions.* In some cases, an MNC uses direct foreign investment as a defensive rather than aggressive strategy. For example, Japanese automobile manufacturers established plants in the United States in anticipation that their exports to the United States would be subject to more stringent trade restrictions. The cost to Japanese companies of manufacturing automobiles in Japan has generally been estimated to be much lower than in the United States, even after considering costs of transporting cars from one country to the other. A key factor distinguishing between locational costs is the substantially higher labor costs for automobile production in the United States. Japanese companies, however, recognized the potential trade barriers that could either limit or prohibit their exports. Since 1980 there have been numerous trade restrictions enforced on automobile imports by the United States.

The possibility of increased trade barriers on firms that export to Europe may encourage additional direct foreign investment in Europe. This possibility motivated Texas Instruments to build a chip production plant in Italy. Hitachi Ltd., Toshiba, IBM, and other multinationals from countries outside Europe are closely assessing these trade barriers so that they can capitalize on them or at least avoid any adverse effects.

11. *Benefit politically.* Some MNCs based in politically unstable countries attempt to expand in other more stable countries. In addition, MNCs based in countries with growing socialism pursue other markets in which they may have greater flexibility to make business decisions. These political motives are especially applicable to MNCs in less developed countries.

While there are several other reasons for increasing internationalization, most will fall under one of these 11 broadly defined motives. All motives are

INTERNATIONAL FINANCIAL MANAGEMENT IN PRACTICE

Investment Opportunities in Europe

A 1989 survey of CEOs from the United States, Canada, Europe, and the Pacific Basin was conducted to get their views on opportunities in Europe as cross-border barriers are eliminated and regulations are standardized across countries. The responses are summarized in Exhibit 15A.

EXHIBIT 15A

Possible Result	Percentage Expecting Result
Easier cross-border transit	94%
Easier labor movement	84
Uniform technical standards	78
More European exports	76
Greater role of U.S. firms in Europe	75
More foreign ownership of European firms	75
Greater role of Japanese firms in Europe	72
Lower consumer prices in Europe	57
Standardized corporate taxes in Europe	56

The CEOs were also asked where in Europe they plan to expand their business. The responses are summarized in Exhibit 15B. Overall, the survey suggests that CEOs expect major changes in Europe, and are planning to capitalize on the new opportunities.

The CEOs were also asked whether a protectionist Europe ("Fortress Europe") will emerge. The responses are summarized in Exhibit 15C.

EXHIBIT 15B

European Country	Percentage Planning to Expand Business into Country
Spain	64%
West Germany	62
France	60
United Kingdom	59
Italy	55
Netherlands	42
Portugal	41
Belgium	38
Ireland	27
Greece	21
Denmark	19
Luxembourg	19

EXHIBIT 15C

	Percentage Expecting a Fortress Europe	Percentage Not Expecting a Fortress Europe
European CEOs	39%	61%
American CEOs	75	25
Japanese CEOs	79	21
Pacific Rim CEOs	87	13

The results suggest a clear difference in opinion between European CEOs and other CEOs. The expectation of a "Fortress Europe" by many non-European CEOs may partially explain their desire to establish a greater presence within Europe.

related to marketing strategy. Yet any given logical motive must be expected to improve one or more financial characteristics that will in turn enhance shareholder wealth.

It should be obvious that while most attempts to increase international business are motivated by some of the factors listed here, there are some corresponding disadvantages as well. For example, the potential cost savings associated with establishing a subsidiary in a less developed country are obvious. However, the expense of establishing the subsidiary, the uncertainty of inflation and exchange rate movements, and the political risk should not be ignored. Decisions to invest in a foreign country must weigh the potential benefits against such costs or additional risks.

Each foreign project is unique in the potential advantages offered. To illustrate, consider the difference in the likely motives behind the following foreign projects:

1. Establishment of distribution centers throughout Europe by a U.S. producer of computer components
2. Establishment of a plant to manufacture and sell advanced agricultural equipment in Latin America

The distribution centers are likely intended to attract new sources of demand, fully benefit from economies of scale (as the components are still produced in the United States), and possibly benefit from potential appreciation in European currencies. Conversely, the establishment of a plant for producing and selling advanced agricultural equipment is likely intended to exploit monopolistic advantages (if the competition is not as advanced), and to capitalize on low-cost foreign factors of production.

Although the opportunities offered by international business are significant, for MNCs to capitalize on these opportunities, they must be able to adjust their strategy to fit their unique situation.

METHODS TO INCREASE INTERNATIONAL BUSINESS

A common method of engaging in international business is direct foreign investment (DFI). However, this method is generally expensive. Also, the investment made to build or purchase a plant in a foreign country is irreversible. If the project fails, the firm may have difficulty in selling the plant. DFI can be the optimal way of entering a foreign market once the firm is confident that it will survive in that foreign market. Until then, there are alternative methods of entering foreign markets that are possibly less risky and involve a smaller initial outlay than DFI.

An MNC's effort to increase international business can sometimes be achieved by **exporting,** so that any increase in production occurs at the existing plants. Exhibit 16.2 summarizes the motives just discussed and offers an example of each motive as related to exporting and direct foreign investment.

Exporting is a safer way to break into a new market since there is less to lose if the strategy fails (as opposed to establishing a subsidiary). The initial cost of producing at home and exporting is low relative to establishing a

EXHIBIT 16.2   Summary of Motives for Increasing International Business

Motive	Example as Related to Exporting	Example as Related to Direct Foreign Investment
1. Attract new sources of demand.	Promote a product in new markets and accommodate orders by exporting.	Establish a subsidiary or acquire a competitor in new markets.
2. Enter new markets where excessive profits are possible.	Promote a product in markets where little competition exists, and undercut the competition's prices; accommodate orders by exporting.	Acquire a competitor that has controlled its local market.
3. Fully benefit from economies of scale.	Firms that specialize in exporting could possibly increase economies of scale by entering new markets; the cost of media marketing relative to sales tends to decrease for higher levels of sales; also, entering new markets will require more production and possibly greater production efficiency.	Establish a subsidiary in a new market that can sell products produced elsewhere; this allows for increased production and possibly greater production efficiency.
4. Use foreign factors of production.	Generally not applicable	Establish a subsidiary in a market that has relatively low costs of labor or land; sell the finished product to countries where the cost of production is higher.
5. Use foreign raw materials.	Generally not applicable	Establish a subsidiary in a market where raw materials are cheap and accessible; sell the finished product to countries where the raw materials are more expensive.
6. Use foreign technology.	Generally not applicable	Participate in a joint venture in order to learn about production process or other operations.
7. Exploit monopolistic advantages.	Export products to areas where production of the products is very expensive or impossible.	Establish a subsidiary in a market where competitors are unable to produce the identical product; sell products in that country.
8. Diversify internationally.	Export to other markets whose business cycles differ from existing export markets.	Establish subsidiaries in markets whose business cycles differ from those where existing subsidiaries are based.
9. React to a foreign currency's changing value.	Export to new markets where the local currency is strong.	Establish a subsidiary in new markets where the local currency is weak but expected to strengthen over time.
10. React to trade restrictions.	Export to new markets where there are no trade restrictions if restrictions are tightened in existing export markets.	Establish a subsidiary in markets where tougher trade restrictions will adversely affect the firm's export volume.
11. Benefit politically.	Export to markets where the government does not control the price of products.	Establish a subsidiary in markets where the government does not control the price of products.

subsidiary. To back out of the new market is therefore much easier when exporting. For example, in 1990 Ford Motor Company decided to penetrate Eastern Europe by exporting rather than establishing a subsidiary there. While exporting is normally a less risky approach, it results in less reliable part replacements, repairs, and refunds for consumers. In addition, shortages of the main product itself may occur due to potential trade restrictions.

Also, exporting expenses over time can become excessive due to high transportation costs and trade taxes imposed by the foreign government. Finally, consumers may prefer locally produced goods, since a subsidiary creates jobs in that country. For these reasons, a corporation may view exporting only as a first step.

If the market shows strong consistent demand, a corporation may decide (after a thorough feasibility study) to initiate direct foreign investment. This decision is determined by the stability of demand, potential competition, and degree of country risk.

An MNC may initiate direct foreign investment by either establishing a new subsidiary or purchasing an existing company in that country. Non-U.S. firms can easily acquire companies in the United States. In Japan and some other countries, though, restrictions impede acquisition activity.

As a compromise between exporting and direct foreign investment, a corporation may consider **licensing.** In this case, a local firm in the host country would produce the goods to the licensing corporation's specifications. As the goods are sold, a portion of the revenues as specified by the agreement would be sent to the licensor.

The advantages of licensing are (1) since exporting is not necessary, transportation costs are avoided, and (2) because a local firm handles production in the host country, direct foreign investment is not necessary. However, there are also some disadvantages of licensing. First, the local firm in the host country may attempt to export the goods to another country, which may reduce sales of the licensing corporation. Second, it is difficult to ensure quality control of the local firm's production process. Third, technology secrets provided to the local firm may leak out to competitive firms in that country. In many cases, licensing is used by firms confronted with high export barriers. It may even take place in countries where subsidiaries exist, as it can allow for further business expansion.

An alternative form of increasing international business is to engage in a **joint venture.** Assume that a U.S. firm has expertise in the construction of contemporary glass office buildings and plans to establish its business in West Germany. Since it is unfamiliar with German building code restrictions, and cultural characteristics, it may consider a joint venture with a German construction firm. The two firms could combine to create a product in West Germany that could not be created by either individual firm. Many MNCs engage in joint ventures. For example, Westinghouse has engaged in joint ventures with foreign firms in various countries, and Toyota and General Motors have been involved in joint ventures. In 1987 Toyota began a joint venture with Volkswagen AG to produce and sell pickup trucks in West Germany. This venture was partially the result of criticism by the European Community about the large volume of Japanese vehicles exported to Europe. The joint venture allowed Toyota to continue business in Europe but also created jobs in Europe as well.

Joint ventures have become a popular method to increase international business. In the late 1980s, they comprised about one-third of all foreign investments by U.S. manufacturing companies. The reduction in barriers throughout Europe has prompted even more joint ventures. For example, General Motors recently agreed to joint ventures with RABA (of Hungary) to build automobiles and engines, with AWE (of East Germany) to produce Opel cars, and with Volga Auto Works (of the Soviet Union) to produce engine control systems. In 1990 Mannesmann, a West German producer of machinery, agreed to joint ventures with 30 different East German firms.

Another popular method of engaging in international business is **franchising**, wherein the firm allows an individual to sell its product in a specific territory. The firm normally receives an initial fee plus periodic royalty payments in return. Pizza Hut and McDonald's have franchises in Europe and in the Soviet Union. Dairy Queen has franchises in the Middle East. Subway Sandwiches and Salads has franchises in Canada and Mexico and plans franchises in France and Korea. The recent relaxation of barriers in Western and Eastern Europe has encouraged numerous openings of franchises, including California Closet Co. and Micro Age Computer Centers Inc. Many U.S. franchises expand first into Canada to develop experience with a foreign country. Expansion into other countries is typically more difficult because of distance and adapting the franchise operations to different cultures. For example, Dairy Queen uses a powdered mix in the Middle East because of a shortage of fresh milk there. Natural Cosmetics franchises must operate in department stores in Taiwan because the real estate prices are too high there to establish separate shops.

A corporation planning to take the plunge and enter new foreign markets should expect to remain for a long enough period of time to more than cover its costs of entering such markets. One of the more common strategies for a corporation to achieve this is to emphasize that its product is different from those of any competitors (**product differentiation.**) Whether this strategy is successful depends on (1) how different the product truly is relative to competitive products and (2) how well the corporation uses marketing skills to make consumers believe the product is unique. An additional strategy is to devote sufficient resources toward research and development so that even if the foreign demand for one product drops, it will be offset by a newly created product. This approach is commonly used by MNCs to maintain their business in foreign markets.

A CLOSER LOOK AT BENEFITS OF INTERNATIONAL DIVERSIFICATION

Earlier in this chapter, international diversification was identified as a method for reducing an MNC's risk. Consequently, it serves as a corporate motive for increasing international business. We shall now focus more closely on the potential benefits to a firm that diversifies its business internationally. First, a numerical example is presented to illustrate how an international project can reduce the firm's risk to a greater degree than a local project. Then the actual relationship between the degree of international business and risk of MNCs is examined.

Numerical Example of Diversification Benefits

Consider a U.S. firm that plans to invest in a new project that shall be located either in the United States or in Great Britain. Once the project is completed, it will constitute 30 percent of the firm's total funds invested in itself. Assume the firm's current investment in its business (the remaining 70 percent) is

RELATED RESEARCH

What Affects Joint Venture Performance?

A recent study by Beamish was based on a survey of MNCs that engaged in joint ventures. The joint ventures were separated into low- and high-performing ventures (after evaluating their performance over time) to determine whether the attitudes of the MNCs with low-performing ventures were any different than those of the high-performing ventures. Some of the more relevant results of the survey are summarized below:

1. MNCs generally did not engage in joint ventures to capitalize on inexpensive labor or to provide access to raw materials.

2. MNCs of the high-performing ventures perceived that the local partner was important for knowledge about current business practices where the venture was to be implemented. However, the perception of MNCs with low-performing ventures was mixed.

3. MNCs of both types of ventures perceived the local partner to be advantageous for avoiding political intervention by the host government.

4. There was no significant association between the degree of capital provided by the MNC parent and the success of the joint venture.

5. The MNCs of high-performing ventures perceived the most important contribution of the local partner to be general knowledge of the local economy, politics, and customs. The MNCs of low-performing ventures did not share this perception.

6. The MNCs of high-performing ventures perceived the contribution of the partners to be more important in general than MNCs of low-performing ventures.

SOURCE: P. W. Beamish, "Joint Ventures in LDCs: Partner Selection and Performance," *Management International Review* no.1, (1987), pp. 23–37.

exclusively in the United States. Characteristics of the proposed project if located in the United States versus Great Britain are forecasted for a five-year period as shown in Exhibit 16.3.

Assume the firm plans to assess the feasibility of each proposed project based on expected return and on risk using a five-year time horizon. Also assume the firm's expected annual after-tax return on investment on its prevailing business is 20 percent and its variability of returns (as measured by standard deviation) is expected to be .10. The firm can assess its expected

EXHIBIT 16.3 Evaluation of Proposed Projects in Alternative Locations

	Characteristics of Proposed Project if Located in the United States	Characteristics of Proposed Project if Located in Great Britain
Mean expected annual return on investment (after taxes)	25%	25%
Standard deviation of expected annual after-tax returns on investment	.09	.11
Correlation of expected annual after-tax returns on investment with after-tax returns of prevailing U.S. business	.80	.02

overall performance based on developing the project in the United States. Then it can repeat the analysis based on developing the business in Great Britain. It is essentially comparing two portfolios. The first portfolio is 70 percent of its total funds invested in its prevailing U.S. business plus the remaining 30 percent of funds invested in a new project located in the United States. The second portfolio again represents 70 percent of the firm's total funds invested in its prevailing business, but the remaining 30 percent of funds are invested in a new project located in Great Britain. Therefore, 70 percent of each portfolio's investment is identical. The difference is reflected in the remaining 30 percent of funds invested.

If the new project is located in the United States, the overall firm's expected after-tax return (R_p) is

$$
R_p = \underset{\substack{\text{Precent of}\\\text{funds}\\\text{invested in}\\\text{prevailing}\\\text{business}}}{(70\%)} \quad \underset{\substack{\text{Expected}\\\text{return on}\\\text{prevailing}\\\text{business}}}{(20\%)} \quad + \quad \underset{\substack{\text{Percent}\\\text{of funds}\\\text{invested}\\\text{in new U.S.}\\\text{project}}}{(30\%)} \quad \underset{\substack{\text{Expected}\\\text{return on}\\\text{new U.S.}\\\text{project}}}{(25\%)} \quad = \quad \underset{\substack{\text{Firm's}\\\text{overall}\\\text{expected}\\\text{return}}}{21.5\%}
$$

This computation is based on weighting the returns according to the percentage of total funds representing each investment. Neglecting the weights would lead to inaccurate estimates of the firm's overall expected return.

If the firm calculates its overall expected return when locating the new project in Great Britain instead of the United States, the results would remain unchanged. This is based on the new project's expected return being the same if located in either country. Therefore, in terms of return, neither new project has an advantage.

With regard to risk, the new project is expected to exhibit slightly less variability in returns during the five-year period if located in the United States (see Exhibit 16.3). Since firms typically prefer more stable returns on their investment, this is an advantage. However, estimating the risk of the individual project without consideration of the overall firm would be a mistake. The expected correlation of the new project's returns with those of the prevailing business must also be considered. Recall from investments theory that portfolio variance is determined by the individual variability of each component as well as their pairwise correlations. The variance of a portfolio (σ_p^2) composed of only two investments (A and B) is computed as

$$
\sigma_p^2 = w_A^2\, \sigma_A^2 + w_B^2\, \sigma_B^2 + 2w_A w_B \sigma_A \sigma_B\ (CORR_{AB})
$$

where w_A and w_B represent the percentage of total funds allocated to Investments A and B, respectively; σ_A and σ_B are the standard deviations of returns on Investments A and B, respectively, and $CORR_{AB}$ is the correlation coefficient of returns between Investments A and B. This equation for portfolio variance can be applied to the problem at hand. The portfolio reflects the overall firm. First, compute the overall firm's variance in returns assuming it locates the new project in the U.S. This variance (σ_p^2) is

$$
\begin{aligned}
\sigma_p^2 &= (.70)^2\, (.10)^2 + (.30)^2\, (.09)^2 + 2(.70)(.30)(.10)(.09)(.80)\\
&= (.49)(.01) + (.09)(.0081) + .003024\\
&= .0049 + .000729 + .003024\\
&= .008653
\end{aligned}
$$

If the firm decided to locate the new project in Great Britain instead of the United States, its overall variability in returns would have been different, because that project differs from the new U.S. project in terms of individual variability in returns and correlation with the prevailing business. The overall variability of the firm's returns based on locating the new project in Great Britain is estimated by variance in the portfolio returns (σ_p^2):

$$
\begin{aligned}
\sigma_p^2 &= (.70)^2 (.10)^2 + (.30)^2 (.11)^2 + 2(.70) (.30) (.10) (.11) (.02) \\
&= (.49) (.01) + (.09) (.0121) + .0000924 \\
&= .0049 + .001089 + .0000924 \\
&= .0060814
\end{aligned}
$$

A comparison of how each of the two proposed projects affects the firm's overall variability in returns shows that the firm would generate more stable returns if the new project was located in Great Britain. The firm's overall variability in returns is expected to be 29.7 percent less if the new project is located in Great Britain rather than in the United States. This percentage was determined as follows:

$$
\text{Reduction in variability} = 1 - \frac{\text{Firm's variance in overall returns if it establishes project in foreign country}}{\text{Firm's variance in overall returns if it establishes project in home country}}
$$

$$
= 1 - \frac{.0060814}{.008653}
$$

$$
= 1 - 70.3\%
$$

$$
= 29.7\%
$$

The reason for the reduced variability when locating in the foreign country is based on the correlation of the new project's expected returns with the expected returns of the prevailing business. If the new project is located in the firm's home country (the United States), this correlation is estimated to be .80. This high correlation implies the new project's performance will closely coincide with the prevailing business performance. Conversely, the correlation between the new project returns if located in Great Britain and the returns from prevailing business is .02. This low correlation suggests the returns of both investments (new project and prevailing business) will not be moving in tandem. Therefore, the variability in returns of the portfolio of these two investments is relatively low.

Because the new project yields similar returns in either location and the firm's overall variability of returns is lower if the project is located in Great Britain, the firm should develop the project there rather than in the United States. The point of the example is if the economic conditions of two countries (such as the United States and Great Britain) are not highly correlated, then a firm may reduce its risk from diversifying its business in both countries rather than concentrating in just one.

Sensitivity of Diversification Benefits to Number of Foreign Projects

By extending the previous example to multiple projects, one can gain further insight on the benefits from international diversification. Consider a set of 60 possible U.S. projects, each of which has expected returns to a firm over the next five years. Assume that the variance of each project's expected returns was estimated, and that the average variance of these 60 projects was also determined. Now consider all possible sets of two projects combined (and equally weighted). If the returns on these projects are not all perfectly positively correlated, the average variance of a typical two-project portfolio will be less than the average variance of individual projects. Similarly, the variance of all possible three-project portfolios (equally weighted) should be even lower. As more projects are added, the portfolio variance should decrease on average. Initially, the average reduction in variance of returns (a measure of risk) associated with the addition of one more project is substantial. However, after some point, the average reduction in variance becomes negligible, meaning that the remaining risk cannot be diversified away by adding more U.S. projects. This is illustrated as the U.S. curve in Exhibit 16.4.

Starting all over, consider a set of 120 projects, the same 60 in the United States and the remaining 60 in various foreign countries. If the procedure just described is applied to this set, the outcome will be similar to the Global curve in Exhibit 16.4 Notice that the degree of risk reduction resulting from adding an additional project was greater for the global set than the U.S. set. For any given number of projects, the global portfolio has less risk. The advantage to the global set is attributed to the lower correlations between returns of projects implemented in different economies.

Even the global curve levels off at some point where further risk reduction from adding projects is negligible. Numerous MNCs have hundreds of for-

EXHIBIT 16.4 Comparison of Benefits from Domestic versus International Diversification

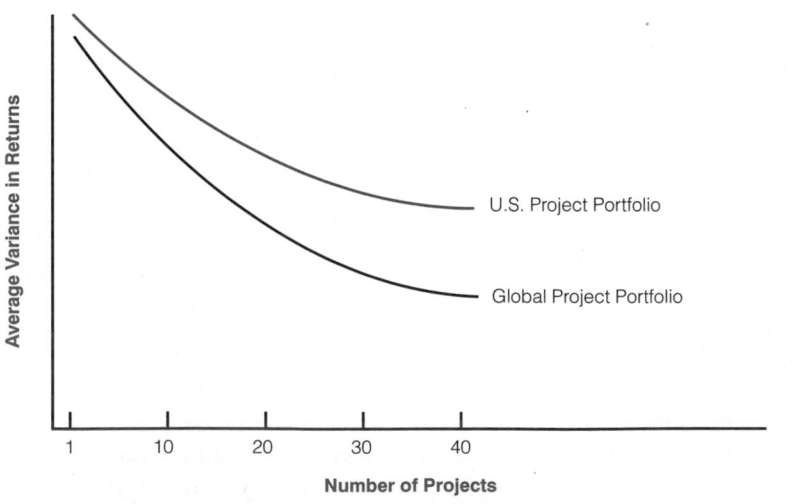

eign projects, which may seem like overkill in reaping benefits from international diversification. Yet, many foreign projects by well-established MNCs are not expected to create further diversification benefits, but are expected to reap other types of benefits.

The exercise described above was applied (with some modifications) to historical returns on stocks by Solnik in 1974, who found additional risk reduction from internationally diversified portfolios. This exercise was updated (with some modifications) by Fosberg and Madura in 1991, who found somewhat similar results. Both studies found that most of the risk reduction occurs within the first 14 or so stocks. It would likely take a larger number of corporate projects to reach a point at which diversification benefits from further investment were negligible. Nevertheless, the degree of diversification benefits from one additional project would still be inversely related to the total number of projects undertaken.

THE DIRECT FOREIGN INVESTMENT DECISION

Like any investor, an MNC with projects positioned around the world is concerned with the risk and return characteristics of the projects. The portfolio of all projects reflects the MNC in aggregate. From a conceptual perspective, the MNC's global strategy of developing projects can be examined using Exhibit 16.5. Each point on the graph reflects a specific project that either has been implemented or is being considered. The return axis may be measured by potential return on assets or return on equity. The risk may be measured by potential fluctuation in the returns generated by each project.

Exhibit 16.5 shows that Project A has the highest expected return of all the projects. While the MNC could devote most of its resources toward this project to attempt to achieve such a high return, its risk is possibly too high by itself. In addition, such a project may not be able to absorb all available

EXHIBIT 16.5   Risk-Return Analysis of International Projects

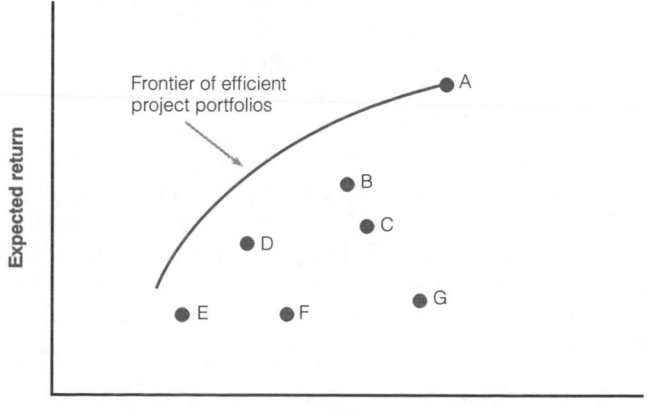

RELATED RESEARCH

Effect of International Involvement on Corporate Risk and Performance

Effect on Risk

Can a firm truly reduce risk by increasing its degree of international business? Certain studies shed considerable light on this question. (See the references for a citation of each study discussed in this section.)

One particular study by Agmon and Lessard examined this issue by assessing the relationship between *betas* (a measure of risk) and the degree of international business among MNCs. First, MNCs were placed into portfolios categorized by their percentage of sales outside the United States Then the betas of each portfolio were computed. The relationship between the foreign sales percentage and beta is shown in the exhibit. The beta was generally lower for portfolios of MNCs that had a high proportion of foreign sales. For example, the portfolio of MNCs with 1 percent to 7 percent of sales outside the United States exhibited a beta value of 1.04. At the other extreme, the portfolio of U.S. MNCs with 42 percent to 62 percent of their sales outside the United States exhibited a beta value of .88. The general reduction in risk (less sensitivity to the U.S. market) of MNCs with a greater percentage of foreign sales substantiates the theory that increased internationalization can reduce risk. Yet, it should be emphasized that even the well-diversified U.S. MNCs are somewhat vulnerable to economic events in the United States.

Overall, these research results suggest MNCs can reduce risk even further by in-

Relationship Between Degree of Foreign Involvement and Risk for MNCs

Portfolio Number	Proportion of Sales Outside the U.S. (%)	Computed Value of Beta as a Measure of Risk
1	1–7	1.04
2	7–10	1.06
3	10–13	.98
4	13–17	.82
5	17–21	.98
6	21–25	.98
7	25–28	.82
8	28–35	.99
9	35–42	.86
10	42–62	.88

SOURCE: These results were drawn from "Investor Recognition of Corporate International Diversification," *Journal of Finance*, September 1977, reprinted with permission of the *Journal of Finance*.1984), p. 98.

creasing their involvement in foreign countries. Any research on this topic is somewhat limited in that the degree of internationalization is measured solely by percentage of foreign sales without accounting for the dispersion of sales among various countries. As an extreme example, consider Firm X, which has 50 percent of its sales in the United States and the remaining 50 percent of its sales dispersed evenly among 10 countries around the world. Also consider a second MNC, Firm Y, in the same industry, which has 40 percent of its total sales in the United States and the remaining 60 percent of its sales in Canada. The degree of internationalization (as defined here) is higher for Firm Y. Yet, Firm X would probably generate more stable cash flows, since Firm Y's cash flows are dependent on two economies that are highly related to each other.

RELATED RESEARCH

The limitation to the definition for degree of internationalization does not necessarily refute the negative relationship detected between foreign involvement and risk. In fact, the relationship might be more pronounced if we had the data available to account not only for percentage of foreign sales but for degree of global dispersion of sales. The point is that international diversification is more effective when marketing a product among several economies rather than in a single foreign market.

Research by Madura and Rose assessed the impact of international diversification *and* the impact of diversity (sales across economies) on an MNC's risk. They found that for MNCs with less than 21 percent of foreign sales, there was an inverse relationship between degree of international business and beta, which supports Agmon and Lessard's findings. For MNCs with a relatively large percent of foreign sales (over 34 percent), they found no relationship.

They also found that higher diversity is associated with higher risk. This result is somewhat surprising, since spreading a business across countries was expected to offer greater diversification benefits than concentrating in a single foreign country. The results may suggest that some MNCs are unable to effectively conduct business in numerous countries, perhaps because of large costs associated with adapting to cultural differences and country-specific regulations. Perhaps today the results would be more favorable in Europe now that regulations have been standardized across countries.

A second test of the relationship between percentage of foreign sales and risk was conducted by Rugman, who used the standard deviation of stock returns rather than the beta as a measure of risk for the firm. His analysis of MNCs found a negative relationship between percentage of foreign sales and

standard deviation of stock returns. The negative relationship suggests that MNCs with a greater degree of foreign business are less risky (their stock price is less volatile), which coincides with the findings just summarized here.

Effect on Performance

Several studies have attempted to assess how a corporation's performance is affected by international involvement. The results have implications as to whether corporations should engage in international business, and whether increased international business can improve performance. However, every study's implications are limited to a particular time period or country's perspective and may not be applicable to a different country or time period. Nevertheless, the studies offer some insight into the relationship between international business and corporate performance.

A study by Sarathy of large Japanese firms attempted to determine how exporting affected corporate performance. It found that firms with greater export concentration had lower shareholder returns over the short run but higher shareholder returns over the medium term. The initial unfavorable result may reflect the significant initial costs of developing an export strategy. This study also found that firms with high growth in exports exhibited a higher degree of profitability.

A recent study by Finnerty, Owers, and Rogers assessed the impact of international joint ventures on an MNC's risk-adjusted stock returns. These returns were evaluated 50 days before and after the announcement to determine how shareholders reacted to such information. The study found no significant impact of the announcement on risk-adjusted stock returns, which implies that the joint ventures were not expected to improve the MNC's value. However, a related

RELATED RESEARCH

study by McConnell and Nantell found that risk-adjusted returns of firms announcing joint ventures increased. This study suggests that shareholders anticipated benefits as a result of the joint venture. The differences in results between the studies might be due to the fact that the joint ventures assessed by McConnell and Nantell were between U.S. firms.

Another way of assessing the impact of a firm's internationalization on performance is to compare risk-adjusted stock returns of MNCs to those of purely domestic firms. Such studies conducted by Hughes, Logue, and Sweeney and by Mikhail and Shawky found that MNCs outperformed domestic firms. However, more recent studies by Brewer and by Fatemi found that MNCs did not outperform domestic firms. The results of such a comparison tend to vary with the time period examined.

capital anyway if its potential market for customers is limited. Thus, the MNC develops a portfolio of projects. By combining Project A with several other projects, the MNC may decrease its expected return. On the other hand, risk could also be reduced substantially. If the MNC appropriately combines projects, its project portfolio may be able to achieve a **risk-return trade-off** exhibited by any of the points on the curve in Exhibit 16.5. This curve represents a frontier of efficient project portfolios that exhibit desirable risk-return characteristics in that no single project could outperform any of these portfolios. The term "efficient" refers to a minimum risk for a given expected return. Project portfolios outperform the individual projects because of the diversification attributes discussed earlier. The lower, or more negative, the correlation in project returns over time, the lower will be the project portfolio risk. As new projects are proposed, the frontier of efficient project portfolios may shift. An MNC is better off if the efficient frontier is further to the left, since this reflects less risk.

Along the frontier of efficient project portfolios, no portfolio can be singled out as "optimal" for all MNCs. This is because MNCs vary in their willingness to accept risk. If the MNC is very conservative and has the choice of any portfolios represented by the frontier in Exhibit 16.5, it will probably prefer one that exhibits low risk (near the bottom of the frontier). Conversely, a more aggressive strategy would be to implement a portfolio of projects that exhibit risk-return characteristics such as those near the top of the frontier.

The actual location of the frontier of efficient project portfolios depends on the business in which the firm is involved. Consider an MNC that sells steel solely to European nations and is considering other related projects. Its frontier of efficient project portfolios would exhibit considerable risk (due to just one product sold to countries whose economies move in tandem). Yet, another MNC that sells a wide range of products to countries all over the world could reduce its project portfolio risk to a greater degree. Therefore, its frontier of efficient project portfolios would be closer to the vertical axis. This comparison is illustrated in Exhibit 16.6. Of course, this comparison assumes the multi-product MNC is knowledgeable about all of its products and the markets to which it sells.

EXHIBIT 16.6 Risk-Return Advantage of a Diversified MNC

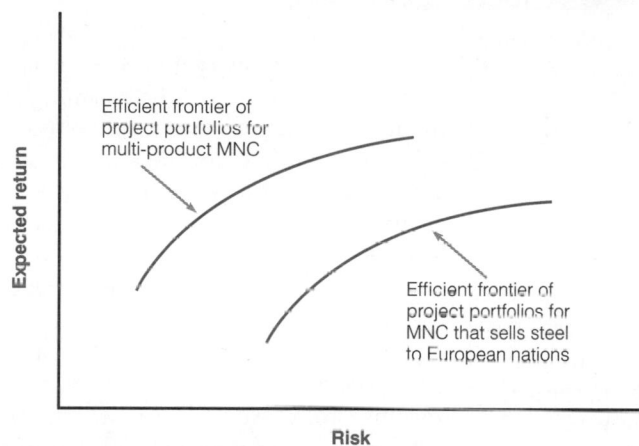

Our discussion suggests that MNCs can achieve more desirable risk-return characteristics from their project portfolios if they sufficiently diversify among products *and* geographical markets. This also relates to the advantage an MNC has over a purely domestic firm with only a local market. The MNC may be able to develop a more efficient portfolio of projects than its domestic counterpart.

Much of the discussion up to this point suggests how direct foreign investment can benefit the MNC. However, these benefits must be compared with the costs and risks involved in order to make the appropriate decisions. The costs include nominal expenses of establishing DFI, and other indirect costs, such as the cost of becoming more familiar with new markets or the need to continually assess political and economic conditions in that country.

There are several types of risk involved in DFI, such as a government takeover or adjusted tax laws over time. Various forms of risk from DFI are discussed in Chapter 19. The point to be made here is that because DFI is a long-term project, conditions will change during the life of DFI that can substantially affect the performance of such an investment. While such conditions are impossible to predict precisely, MNCs can at least attempt to assess the exposure of DFI to these conditions. Then they must decide whether the expected benefits from DFI outweigh the risk. If their answer is affirmative, they should undertake the DFI.

Direct Foreign Investment as an Ongoing Decision

Once DFI takes place, periodic decisions are necessary to determine whether further expansion should take place in that location. In addition, as the project generates earnings, the MNC must decide whether to have the funds remitted to the parent or used by the subsidiary. If the subsidiary has a use for the funds that would be of more value than the parent's use, the subsidiary should retain the funds. Of course, a certain portion of the funds will be needed to maintain operations, but the remaining funds could either be sent to the parent, sent to another subsidiary, or reinvested for expansion purposes.

RELATED RESEARCH

Can MNCs Reduce Risk by Listing Their Stock on Foreign Exchanges?

If a U.S.-based MNC issues stock in a foreign market and lists its stock on the foreign stock exchange, it may be able to reduce its systematic risk (as measured by beta, the sensitivity of its stock returns to the returns of the U.S. market). The reasoning is that firms listed on a given stock exchange may be driven by that market, regardless of the MNC's degree of business in that market. For example, consider a well-known U.S. firm that has its stock listed on the Frankfurt stock exchange. As the prices of stocks traded on this exchange change, some investors search for stocks that have not increased to the same degree. Such stocks may be considered as undervalued temporarily. In fact, the stock of a U.S. firm should not move in unison with the German stocks since the German stock prices should be driven by expectations of the German economy. Yet, if the U.S. firm does some business in Germany, the stock may behave somewhat like that of a German firm. If this stock is somewhat influenced by German-stock market movements, then it cannot be completely driven by U.S. stock market movements, and its beta may decline as a result.

To test whether the stock listing influences a stock's beta, the betas of 68 MNCs whose stocks were listed on foreign stock exchanges were estimated for a four-year period before and after the listing date. The average beta of these firms declined from 1.11 before the listing to .98 after the listing. The sample was partitioned into four groups, based on the specific stock exchange in which the firm's stock was listed. For each of the four stock markets, (France, Germany, Japan, and Switzerland), the average beta of firms declined in the post-listing period. The decline was statistically significant (using a 90 percent confidence level) for firms whose stock was listed on the German stock exchange. The average beta for these firms declined from 1.41 to 1.05. This suggests that some firms may be able to reduce their systematic risk by listing on a foreign stock exchange. The decline in average betas after listing on each of the other foreign stock exchanges was not statistically significant.

SOURCE: Howe, John S., and Jeff Madura. "The Impact of International Listings on Risk: Implications for Capital Market Integration." *Journal of Banking and Finance*, (December 1990), pp. 1133–1142.

The decision of whether the subsidiary should reinvest the earnings should be analyzed on a case-by-case basis. That is, there is no simple guideline to follow. The appropriate decision depends on the economic conditions in the subsidiary's country and parent's country, as well as restrictions imposed by the host-country government. Exhibit 16.7 provides a breakdown of earnings from U.S. DFI in six regions during 1989. The total earnings for each region are divided into "distributed" (sent to parent or elsewhere) versus "reinvested" earnings. Notice how the reinvestment ratio (computed as reinvested earnings divided by total earnings) varies among countries. The ratio is lowest in the developing countries, reflecting fewer opportunities for expansion in these countries.

Exhibit 16.8 provides a breakdown of earnings generated by subsidiaries of non-U.S. MNCs that are located in the United States. Many of these subsid-

EXHIBIT 16.7 Earnings From Direct Foreign Investment Abroad by U.S-Based MNCs: *(in millions of dollars)*

Location	Earnings			Reinvestment Ratio
	Total	*Distributed*	*Reinvested*	
All Areas	55,204	32,788	22,416	.41
Developed countries	40,175	29,628	10,546	.26
Canada	7,290	5,005	2,285	.31
Europe	27,637	21,816	5,821	.21
Other	5,248	2,807	2,441	.47
Developing countries	13,416	10,900	2,515	.19

SOURCE: *Survey of Current Business*, U.S. Department of Commerce (August 1990).

EXHIBIT 16.8 Foreign Direct Investment in the United States: Earnings and Reinvestment *(in millions of dollars)*

Location	Earnings			Reinvestment Ratio
	Total	*Distributed*	*Reinvested*	
All areas	2,589	3,897	−1,308	NA
Canada	−99	847	−946	NA
Europe	3,570	2,133	1,437	.40
Japan	943	594	349	.37
Other	−1,825	322	−2,418	NA

NA = not applicable since the reinvestment was negative.

SOURCE: *Survey of Current Business*, U.S. Department of Commerce (August 1990).

iaries have distributed more than their earnings, perhaps because of agreements with the parents to remit a given amount of funds regardless of the earnings generated. Since subsidiaries recently generated low or even negative earnings, the amount distributed can easily exceed earnings.

Incentives Offered by Host Governments

DFI is sometimes perceived as a cause of and at other times the remedy for national problems. For example, DFI may provide needed employment or technology. However, it may also displace employment by injecting technologies inappropriate to the country's resource base. In addition, locally owned companies may lose business due to the new competition. These effects could lead to proposals for increased protectionism.

The ability of a host government to attract DFI is dependent on the country's markets and resources, as well as government regulations and incentives. Countries such as Singapore and Hong Kong have attracted substantial DFI because they enforce few restrictions.

Some governments offer incentives by reducing production restrictions. For example, in 1989 Mexico reduced its restrictions on automobiles produced there. It had required that Mexican parts make up 65 percent of an automobile produced for the domestic market and 30 percent of one produced for export. This policy was changed to encourage automobile manufacturers from other countries to establish plants in Mexico. Mexico also announced in 1989 that it would allow foreign companies to own 100 percent of their subsidiaries established in Mexico.

Each government must weigh the advantages and disadvantages of DFI in its country. Some types of DFI will be more attractive to some governments than others. The ideal DFI solves problems such as unemployment and lack of technology without taking business away from local firms. An example would be a production plant that uses local labor and produces goods that are not direct substitutes of other locally produced goods. In this case, the plant will not cause a reduction in sales by local firms. A second ideal situation would be a plant that uses local labor and then exports the products (assuming no other local firm exports such products to the same areas).

In most cases, there may be both advantages and disadvantages to a country allowing a given type of DFI into the country. If the advantages appear to outweigh the disadvantages, the government may attempt to provide additional incentives in order to encourage the DFI to take place. Such incentives could include tax breaks on the income earned there, rent-free land and buildings, low-interest loans, subsidized energy, or reduced environmental (pollution, etc.) restrictions. The degree to which a government would offer such incentives depends on the extent to which the MNC's DFI would benefit that country.

As an example of government incentive, consider the recent decision by Allied Research Associates Inc. to build a production facility and office in Belgium. The Belgian government subsidized a large portion of the expenses, offering tax concessions and favorable interest rates on loans to Allied.

SUMMARY

MNCs may increase their degree of international business for one or more of the following reasons:

- Attract new sources of demand.
- Enter markets where superior profits are possible.
- Fully benefit from economies of scale.
- Use foreign factors of production.
- Use foreign raw materials.
- Use foreign technology.
- Exploit monopolistic advantages.
- Diversify internationally.
- React to a foreign currency's changing value.
- React to trade restrictions.
- Benefit politically.

Consider a corporation that, after weighing the advantages against the disadvantages, decides to enter new foreign markets. Multinational decision making does not end here. The next issue of concern is how to enter that foreign market. Three methods were discussed: (1) exporting, (2) direct foreign investment, and (3) licensing. Exporting is often popular during the experimentation stage, since if the firm decides to back out of the market, the cost of doing so is much less than if it had established a foreign subsidiary. However, if the entrance into the foreign market proves to be worthwhile, the firm may decide at some point to set up a foreign subsidiary, since it may be less costly than exporting in the long run.

Even if entrance into a foreign market proves to be successful initially, the firm must develop strategies to sustain its success. This typically involves the use of research and development as well as extensive marketing to emphasize product differentiation.

To successfully compete in foreign markets, marketing concepts such as market analysis of the countries and advertising are clearly important. However, one must not ignore the financial concepts such as risk reduction from international diversification, the capital budgeting decision and cost of capital, country risk, and the overall objective of maximizing shareholder wealth. These concepts are discussed in the next two chapters.

QUESTIONS

1. Why do firms consider increasing their degree of international business? Elaborate on each reason you give.

2. Packer Inc., a U.S. producer of computer diskettes, plans to establish a subsidiary in West Germany in order to penetrate the German market. Executives of Packer believe that the mark's value is relatively strong and will weaken against the dollar over time. If their expectations about the mark value are correct, how will this affect the feasibility of the project? Explain.

3. Bear Company and Viking Inc. are automobile manufacturers that desire to benefit from economies of scale. Bear Company has decided to establish distributorship subsidiaries in various countries, while Viking Inc. has decided to establish manufacturing subsidiaries in various countries. Which firm is more likely to benefit from economies of scale?

4. Raider Chemical Company and Ram Inc. had similar intentions to reduce the volatility of their cash flows. Raider implemented a long-range plan to establish 40 percent of its business in Canada. Ram Inc. implemented a long-range plan to establish 30 percent of its business in Europe and Asia, scattered among 12 different countries. Which company would more effectively reduce cash flow volatility after the plans have been achieved?

5. If the United States placed long-term restrictions on imports, would the amount of direct foreign investment by non-U.S. MNCs in the United States increase, decrease, or be unchanged? Explain.

6. Explain the potential losses to an MNC that initiates an exporting division versus one that initiates direct foreign investment.

7. Why are economies of some less developed countries with strict restrictions on international trade and direct foreign investment somewhat independent from economies of other countries? Why would MNCs desire to enter such countries? If these countries relaxed their restrictions, would their economies continue to be independent of other economies? Explain.

8. Dolphin Inc., a U.S.-based MNC with a German subsidiary, expects that the German mark will appreciate for several years. How might Dolphin Inc. adjust its policy on remitted earnings from the German subsidiary?

9. Bronco Corporation has decided to establish a subsidiary in Taiwan that would produce stereos and sell them in Taiwan. It expects that its cost of producing these stereos will be one-third the cost of producing them in the

United States. Assuming that its production cost estimates are accurate, is Bronco's strategy sensible? Explain.

10. What did the studies mentioned in the chapter reveal about the relationship between degree of international business and risk of MNCs? What do these results imply about the feasibility of increasing international business?

11. What did the chapter suggest about the degree of correlation between country GNPs; were the correlations generally high or low? To the extent that projects are influenced by local economies, do the GNP correlations suggest that international diversification can reduce risk? Why or why not?

12. Once a corporation enters new foreign markets, how does it normally attempt to maintain its international market share?

13. Once an MNC establishes a subsidiary, DFI remains an ongoing decision. What does this statement mean?

14. Why would foreign governments provide MNCs with incentives to undertake DFI there?

15. This chapter concentrated on possible benefits to a firm that increases its international business. What are some risks of international business that may not exist for local business?

16. In 1972 Tandy Corporation established a manufacturing facility in South Korea to produce computer components. One of the attractions was the relatively low cost of labor. In 1989 Tandy closed the facility, as the cost advantage dissipated. Why do you think the relative cost advantage has dissipated in South Korea and other Asian countries such as Hong Kong, Singapore, and Taiwan? (Ignore possible exchange rate effects.)

17. What motives do you think were most important in the decision of Walt Disney Company to build a theme park in France?

Blues Corporation
Capitalizing on the Opening of East European Borders

Blues Corporation has an established reputation in the United States for over fifty years. Executives of Blues Corporation were elated over the reunification between East and West Germany in November 1989. During 1990 and 1991 they developed a strategy for capitalizing on German reunification, which set the stage for various East European countries to open their borders. Most of Blues' business is in the United States. It has a subsidiary in West Germany, which produces goods and exports them to other West European countries. Blues Corporation produces numerous consumer goods that could possibly be produced or marketed in Eastern Europe. The following issues were raised at a recent executive meeting. Offer your comments about each issue.

a) Blues Corporation is considering shifting its European production facility from West Germany to East Germany. There are two key factors motivating this shift. First, the labor cost is much lower in East Germany. Second, there is an existing facility in East Germany presently goverment-owned that is for sale. Blues would like to transform the facility and use its technology to increase the production efficiency. It estimates that it would need only one-fourth of the workers in that facility. What other factors deserve to be considered before making the decision?

b) Blues Corporation expects that it could penetrate the East European markets. It would need to invest considerable funds in promoting its consumer goods in East Europe, since its goods are not well-known in that area. Yet, it believes that this strategy could pay off in the long-run because it could underprice the competition. At the present time, the main competition are government-owned businesses that are perceived to be inefficiently run. The lack of competitive pricing in this market is the primary reason for Blues Corporation to consider marketing their product in Eastern Europe. What other factors deserve to be considered before making a decision?

c) Blues Corporation is presently experiencing a cash squeeze because of a reduced demand for its goods in the United States (although management expects the demand in the United States to increase soon). It is presently near its debt capacity and prefers not to issue stock at this time. The only way Blues Corporation will follow through on purchasing a facility in Eastern Europe or undergoing a heavy promotion program in Eastern Europe is if it can raise funds by divesting a significant amount of its U.S. assets. The market values of its assets are temporarily depressed, but some of the executives think an immediate move is necessary to fully capitalize on the East European market. Would you recommend that Blues Corporation divest some of its U.S. assets? Explain.

Penguin Company
Assessing Global Competition

Penguin Company produces automobile parts that are used by all automobile companies around the world. Its headquarters is in the United States, where it generates about 75 percent of its sales. Its foreign sales are conducted through exporting, as it has no subsidiaries overseas. Its main competition comes from several companies in Hong Kong and a few companies in Taiwan, which produce similar products. These companies dominate most of the non-U.S. markets.

The Hong Kong companies have existed for a long period of time and have traditionally held about 50 percent of market share. In the last few years, their market share has risen. They have strong banking relationships with several major banks and have often successfully engaged in joint venture programs with many different foreign firms. Their manufacturing of the auto parts is performed exclusively in Hong Kong and exported to all major markets.

There are three Taiwan companies which also produce auto parts. These companies are relatively new, although they are growing at a rapid pace.

The specific auto parts produced by these companies could only be duplicated by other companies at great expense. A substantial amount of research and development resources were invested to achieve the technology to mass produce these parts according to automobile manufacturers' specifications. Consequently, there are presently significant barriers to entry in this subset of the auto parts industry.

In recent years, the gain in global market share by the Hong Kong companies has come at the expense of Penguin Company. This year Penguin Company has appealed to the U.S. government that the Hong Kong companies must be selling their product below cost. It is suspected that the Hong Kong government is subsidizing their cost in order to maintain a high level of employment. The Hong Kong companies maintain that it is their work efficiency, not government subsidies, that have allowed them to increase their global market share. Penguin Company is especially concerned because the Hong Kong companies have just begun a major marketing effort to capture a larger portion of the U.S. market. For this reason, Penguin Company continues to pressure the U.S. government to correct this "unfair entrance into the U.S. markets." The Taiwan companies also appear to be more cost-effective than Penguin Company, but they have not penetrated the U.S. market. Their volume of business is not yet large enough to justify a large marketing drive in the United States. The Taiwan companies also do not have the resources to compete against the Hong Kong companies for the U.S. market.

a) Evaluate the situation from the perspective of the U.S. government. That is, define the options the U.S. government has, and evaluate the viability of each option.

b) Evaluate the situation from the perspective of the Hong Kong companies. Should they be willing to spend large sums of money on marketing costs in their effort to gain a large share of the U.S. market? Defend your conclusion. What factors must be considered in their analysis?

c) If the Hong Kong companies decide to continue their marketing drive in the United States, they may consider establishing a production plant in the United States, rather than exporting the products. What factors should be considered when making the decision? That is, what factors would affect the estimated cash inflows and outflows of such a decision? How does the expectation of a weaker U.S. dollar in the future affect the idea of establishing a subsidiary?

d) Evaluate the situation from the perspective of Penguin Company. Besides its appeal to the U.S. government, what other options might it consider in order to survive?

e) Evaluate the situation from the perspective of a global mutual fund portfolio manager whose portfolio is made up mostly of Hong Kong, Taiwan, and U.S. stocks (presently about one-third investment in each group). Is there any reason to consider adjusting the allocation of funds among the three countries discussed here? Explain any relevant events that could affect the stock values of the portfolio, and how you would revise the allocation amount to each country (if at all).

Part of a portfolio manager's job is to continually evaluate the future prospects of existing companies, and to buy or sell stocks based on anticipation. Are there any particular types of companies that could benefit or lose, as a result of any actions that may be taken by the U.S. government,

Penguin Company, or its competitors? Identify these types of companies, and explain how they may benefit or lose. Suggest which companies should be most closely monitored as a result of the situation.

PROJECTS

1. Review recent annual reports of an MNC of your choice and summarize why it increased its international operations over time. Various factors that motivate international business were identified in the chapter. Determine which factors were probably most influential in motivating the MNC's expansion into other countries.

2. Using the Data Bank in the back of the text, estimate the correlation coefficients between stock market returns over the 1984–1990 period. Fill in the table below:

| | Correlation Coefficients | | |
	Canada	*France*	*Japan*
Canada	1.00		
France	?	1.00	
Japan	?	?	1.00

Which stock markets appear to be most integrated? Which stock market is least integrated with the others? (Regression analysis can be used to determine the R^2 for any two sets of stock market returns; the correlation coefficient is the square root of the R^2 statistic. See Appendix 16 for related information about international stock diversification and Appendix 2C for information on how to use LOTUS to conduct regression analysis).

SUGGESTED READINGS

Michael E. Porter. "The Competitive Advantages of Nations." *Harvard Business Review* (March–April 1990), pp. 73–93. This article discusses why firms need to consider direct foreign investment and suggests how they can retain their competitive advantages.

Thomas Bennett and Craig S. Hakkio. "Europe 1992: Implications for U.S. Firms." *Economic Review,* Federal Reserve Bank of Kansas City (April 1989), pp. 3–17. This article provides an overview of how U.S. firms are reacting to reduced regulations across European countries.

REFERENCES

Adler, Michael. "The Cost of Capital and Valuation of a Two Country Firm." *Journal of Finance* (March 1974), pp. 119–132.

———. "Investor Recognition of Corporation International Diversification: Comment." *Journal of Finance* (March 1981), pp. 187–190.

Adler, Michael, and Bernard Dumas. "Optimal International Acquisitions." *Journal of Finance* (March 1975), pp. 1–19.

———. "International Portfolio Choice and Corporation Finance: A Synthesis." *Journal of Finance* (June 1983), pp. 925–984.

Adler, Nancy, John Graham and Theodore Schwarz Gehrke, "Business Negotiations in Canada, Mexico, and the United States," *Journal of Business Research* (October 1987), pp. 411–429.

Aggarwal, R. "Investment Performance of U.S.-Based Multinational Companies: Comments and a Perspective on International Diversification on Real Assets." *Journal of International Business Studies* (Spring–Summer 1980), pp. 98–104.

_____. "Multinationality and Stock Market Valuation: An Empirical Study of U.S. Markets and Companies." *Management International Review* (1979), pp. 5–21.

Agmon, Tamir. "The Relations Among Equity Markets: A Study of Share Price Co-Movements in the U.S., U.K., Germany and Japan." *Journal of Finance* (September 1972), pp. 839–856.

Agmon, Tamir, and Donald Lessard. "Investor Recognition of Corporate International Diversification." *Journal of Finance* (September 1977), pp. 1049–1058.

Arpan, Jeffrey S., and David A. Ricks. "Foreign Direct Investment in the U.S., 1974–1984." *Journal of International Business Studies* (Fall 1986), pp. 149–153.

Avishai, Bernard. "Managing Against Apartheid." *Harvard Business Review* (November–December 1987), pp. 49–56.

Barone, Robert N. "Risk and International Diversification: Another Look." *Financial Review* (Spring 1983), pp. 184–194.

Bergstrom, Gary L. "A New Route to Higher Returns and Lower Risk." *Journal of Portfolio Management* (Fall 1975), pp. 30–38.

Bicksler, James L. "Gains from Portfolio Diversification into Less Developed Countries' Securities: A Comment." *Journal of International Business Studies* (Spring–Summer 1978), pp. 113–115.

Black, Joseph H., Jeff Madura, and Lawrence C. Rose. "Corporate Risk Response to Competing Diversification Stategies: An International Perspective." *Journal of International Finance,* (Fall 1989), pp. 57–72.

Boddewyn, Jean J. "Foreign and Domestic Divestment and Investment Decisions: Like or Unlike?" *Journal of International Business Studies* (Winter 1983), pp. 23–35.

Brewer, H. L. "Investor Benefits from Corporate International Diversification." *Journal of Financial and Quantitative Analysis* 16 (March 1982), pp. 113–126.

Calingaert, Michael. "What Europe 1992 Means for U.S. Business." *Business Economics* (October 1989), pp. 30–36.

Choi, Jongmoo Jay. "Diversification, Exchange Risk, and Corporate International Investment." *Journal of International Business Studies* (Spring 1989), pp. 145–155.

Christelow, Dorothy. "International Joint Ventures: How Important are They?" *Columbia Journal of World Business* (Summer 1987), pp. 7–14.

Cohn, Richard A., and John J. Pringle. "Imperfections in International Financial Markets: Implications for Risk Premia and the Cost of Capital to Firms." *Journal of Finance* (March 1973), pp. 59–65.

Enderwick, Peter. "Multinational Corporate Restructuring and International Competitiveness." *California Management Review* (Fall 1989), pp. 44–60.

Errunza, Vihang R. "Gains from Portfolio Diversification into Less Developed Countries' Securities." *Journal of International Business Studies* (Fall/Winter 1977), pp. 83–99.

Errunza, Vihang R., and L. Senbet. "The Effects of International Operations on the Market Value of the Firm: Theory and Evidence." *Journal of Finance* (May 1981), pp. 401–417.

Essayyad, Musa, and H. K. Wu. "The Performance of U.S. International Mutual Funds." *Quarterly Journal of Business and Economics* (Autumn 1988), pp. 32–46.

Eun, Cheol S., and Bruce G. Resnick. "Estimating the Correlation Structure of International Share Prices." *Journal of Finance* (December 1984), pp. 1311–1324.

_____. "International Corporate Diversification, Market Valuation, and Size-Adjusted Evidence." *Journal of Finance* (July 1984), pp. 727–743.

Fatemi, Ali M. "Shareholder Benefits from Corporate International Diversification." *Journal of Finance* (December 1984), pp. 1325–1344.

Finnerty, J. E., J. E. Owers, and R. C. Rogers. "The Valuation Impact of Joint Ventures." *Management International Review* (1986/2), pp. 14–26.

Finnerty, Joseph, and Thomas Schneeweis. "The Co-Movement of International Asset Returns." *Journal of International Business Studies* (Winter 1979), pp. 66–78.

Fosberg, Richard H., and Jeff Madura. "Risk Reduction Benefits from International Diversification: A Reassessment." *Journal of Multinational Financial Management*, no. 1 (1991), pp. 35–42.

Franko, Lawrence. "New Forms of Investment in Developing Countries by U.S. Companies: A Five Industry Survey." *Columbia Journal of World Business* (Summer 1987), pp. 39–56.

Ghertman, Michel. "Foreign Subsidiary and Parents' Roles During Strategic Investment and Divestment Decisions." *Journal of International Business Studies* (Spring 1988), pp. 47–67.

Grubel, Herbert G. "Internationally Diversified Portfolios: Welfare Gains and Capital Flows." *American Economic Review* (December 1968), pp. 1299–1314.

Grubel, Herbert G., and Kenneth Fadner. "The Interdependence of International Equity Markets." *Journal of Finance* (March 1971), pp. 89–94.

Haney, Richard, and William P. Lloyd. "An Examination of the Stability of the Intertemporal Relationships Among National Stock Market Indices." *Nebraska Journal of Economics and Business* (Spring 1978), pp. 55–65.

Hanink, Dean M. "A Mean-Variance Model of MNF Location Strategy." *Journal of International Business Studies* (Spring 1985), pp. 165–170.

Hergert, Michael, and Deigan Morris. "Trends in International Collaborative Agreements." *Columbia Journal of World Business* (Summer 1987), pp. 15–21.

Hill, Joanne, and Thomas Schneeweis. "International Diversification of Equities and Fixed-Income Securities." *Journal of Financial Research* (Winter 1983), pp. 333–344.

Hisey, Karen B., and Richard E. Caves. "Diversification Strategy and Choice of Country: Diversifying Acquisitions Abroad by U.S. Multinationals, 1978–1980." *Journal of International Business Studies* (Summer 1985), pp. 51–64.

Horn, Bernard. "International Investing Strategies." *American Association of Institutional Investors Journal* (November 1983), pp. 11–19.

Hughes, John S., Dennis E. Logue, and Richard J. Sweeney. "Corporate International Diversification and Market Assigned Measures of Risk and Diversification." *Journal of Financial and Quantitative Analysis* (November 1975), pp. 627–637.

Jacquillat, Bertrand, and Bruno Solnik. "Multinationals Are Poor Tools for Diversification." *Journal of Portfolio Management* (Winter 1978), pp. 8–12.

Kahley, William J. "U.S. and Foreign Direct Investment Patterns." *Economic Review* Federal Reserve Bank of Atlanta (November–December 1989), pp. 42–57.

Kedia, Ben L., and Jagdeep S. Chhokar. "An Empirical Investigation of Export Promotion Programs." *Columbia Journal of World Business* (Winter 1986), pp. 13–20.

Kedia, B. L., and J. Chhokar. "Factors Inhibiting Export Performance of Firms: An Empirical Investigation." *Management International Review* (1986/4), pp. 33–43.

Kim, Wi Saeng, and Esmeralda Lyn. "Foreign Direct Investment Theories, Entry Barriers, and Reverse Investment in U.S. Manufacturing Industries." *Journal of International Business Studies* (Summer 1987), pp. 53–66.

Kim, Wi Saeng, and Esmeralda O. Lyn. "FDI Theories and the Performance of Foreign Multinationals Operating in the U.S." *Journal of International Business Studies* First Quarter (1990), pp. 41–54.

Lee, Insup, and Steve B. Wyatt. "The Effects of International Joint Ventures on Shareholder Wealth." *Financial Review* (November 1990), pp. 641–650.

Lee, W. Y., and K. S. Sachdeva. "The Role of the Multinational Firm in the Integration of Segmented Capital Markets." *Journal of Finance* (May 1977), pp. 479–491.

Lessard, Donald R. "World, Country, and Industry Relationships in Equity Returns: Implications for Risk Reduction through International Diversification." *Financial Analysts Journal* (January–February 1976), pp. 32–38.

Levy, Haim, and Marshall Sarnat. "International Diversification of Investment Portfolios." *American Economic Review* (September 1970), 668–675.

Lloyd, William P. "International Portfolio Diversification of Real Assets: An Inquiry." *Journal of Business Research* (April 1975), pp. 113–119.

Logue, Dennis E. "An Experiment in International Diversification." *Journal of Portfolio Management* (Fall 1982), pp. 22–27.

Madura, Jeff. "Influence of Foreign Markets on Multinational Stocks: Implications for Investors." *Review of International Economics and Business*, forthcoming.

———. "International Portfolio Construction." *Journal of Business Research*, (Spring 1985), pp. 87–95.

Madura, Jeff, and Lawrence C. Rose. "Are Product Specialization and International Diversification Compatible?" *Management International Review* no. 3 (1987), pp. 37–44.

———. "Impact of International Sales Degree and Diversity on Corporate Risk." *International Trade Journal*, (Spring 1989), pp. 261–276.

Madura, Jeff, and Wallace Reiff. "A Hedge Strategy for International Portfolios." *Journal of Portfolio Management* (Fall 1985), pp. 70–74.

Maldonado, Rita, and Anthony Saunders. "International Portfolio Diversification and the Inter-Temporal Stability of International Stock Market Relationships 1957–1978." *Financial Management* (Autumn 1981), pp. 54–63.

McConnell, John J., and Timothy J. Nantell. "Corporate Combinations and Common Stock Returns: The Case of Joint Ventures." *Journal of Finance* (June 1985), pp. 519–536.

Meleka, A. H. "The Changing Role of Multinational Corporations," *Management International Review* (1985/4), pp. 36–45.

Mikhail, A. D., and H. A. Shawky. "Investment Performance of U.S.–Based Multinational Corporations." *Journal of International Business Studies* (Spring–Summer 1979), pp. 53–66.

Mirus, Rolf. "A Note on the Choice Between Licensing and Direct Foreign Investment." *Journal of International Business Studies* (Spring–Summer 1980), pp. 86–91.

Officer, Dennis T., and J. Ronald Hoffmeister. "ADRs: A Substitute for the Real Thing?" *Journal of Portfolio Management* (Winter 1987), pp. 61–65.

Osborn, Richard and C. Christopher Baugh. "New Patterns in the Formation of U.S./Japanese Cooperative Ventures: The Role of Technology." *Columbia Journal of World Business* (Summer 1987), pp. 57–66.

O'Sullivan, P. "Determinants and Impact of Private Direct Foreign Investment in Host Countries," *Management International Review* (1985/4), pp. 28–35.

Perold, Andre F., and Evan C. Schulman. "The Free Lunch in Currency Hedging: Implications for Investment Policy and Performance Standards." *Financial Analysts Journal* (May–June 1988), pp. 45–50.

Rahman, M. Z. "Maximization of Global Interests: Ultimate Motivation for Foreign Investments by Transnational Corporation." *Management International Review* 23 (April 1983), pp. 4–13.

Rao, Ramesh P., and Raj Aggarwal. "Performance of U.S.-based International Mutual Funds." *Akron Business and Economic Review* (Winter 1987), pp. 98–106.

Roll, Richard. "The International Crash of October 1987." *Financial Analysts Journal* (October 1988), pp. 19–35.

Rugman, Alan R. "Foreign Operations and the Stability of U.S. Corporate Earnings: Risk Reduction by International Diversification." *Journal of Finance* (March 1975), pp. 233–234.

———. "International Diversification by Financial and Direct Investment." *Journal of Economics and Business* (Fall 1977), pp. 31–37.

———. *International Diversification and the Multinational Enterprise.* Lexington, MA: Heath, 1979.

———. "A New Theory of the Multinational Enterprise: Internationalization Versus Internalization." *Columbia Journal of World Business* (Spring 1980), pp. 23–29.

Sarathy, R. "Is Exporting Worthwhile? Exploratory Evidence from Japan." *Management International Review* (1986/4), pp. 22–32.

Saunders, Anthony, and Richard S. Woodworth. "Gains from International Portfolio Diversification: U.K. Evidence 1971–75." *Journal of Business Finance and Accounting* (Autumn 1977), pp. 299–309.

Schwartz, Peter, and Jerry Saville. "Multinational Business in the 1990s—A Scenario." *Long-Range Planning* (December 1986), pp. 31–37.

Senchak, Andrew, J., Jr., and W.L. Beedles. "Is Indirect International Diversification Desirable?" *Journal of Portfolio Management* (Winter 1980), pp. 49–57.

Solnik, Bruno H. "Why Not Diversify Internationally Rather Than Domestically." *Financial Analysts Journal* (July/August 1974), pp. 48–54.

Stulz, Rene M. "On the Determinants of Net Foreign Investment." *Journal of Finance* (May 1983), pp. 459–468.

_____. "On the Effects of Barriers to International Investment." *Journal of Finance* (September 1981), pp. 923–934.

Tucker, Alan L. "International Investing: Are ADRs an Alternative?" *AAII Journal* (November 1987), pp. 10–12.

Van Mesdag, Martin. "Winging it in Foreign Markets." *Harvard Business Review* (January–February 1987), pp. 71–74.

Vernon, Raymond. "International Investment and International Trade in the Product Life Cycle." *Quarterly Journal of Economics* (May 1966), pp. 190–207.

Watson, J. "The Stationarity of Inter-Country Correlation Coefficients: A Note." *Journal of Business, Finance, and Accounting* (Spring 1980), pp. 297–303.

Weigand, Robert. "International Investments: Weighing the Incentives." *Harvard Business Review* (July–August 1983), pp. 146–152.

Zeira, Yoram, and Oded Shenkar. "Interactive and Specific Parent Characteristics: Implications for Management and Human Resources in Joint Ventures." *Management International Review* (Special Issue 1990), pp. 7–22.

International Stock Diversification

A substantial amount of research has demonstrated that investors in stocks can benefit by diversifying internationally. The stocks of most firms are highly influenced by the country in which those firms reside (although some firms are more vulnerable to economic conditions than others). When an investor holds stocks representing firms in various countries, the stock portfolio may be somewhat influenced by the economies of these countries, but the economic conditions of any single country should not have too great an impact, since only a subset of the stocks represent firms in that one country.

The disadvantage of holding an internationally diversified security portfolio is that one will not fully benefit from a surge in a single country's stock market. For example, if investors held only 30 percent of funds in U.S. stocks, only this portion would be directly influenced by a surge in the U.S. market. In this case, a portfolio made up solely of U.S. securities would generate higher returns than our diversified example. (Of course, investors do not have the perfect foresight to know which country will experience a surge in its stock market at a particular point in time.) If the Canadian stock market surged, an internationally diversified portfolio would benefit (at least partially) from this event, assuming it contained some Canadian stocks, and the portfolio consisting totally of U.S. stocks would not necessarily benefit.

Because an international portfolio is susceptible to economic swings in *various* countries, the variability in returns will most likely be less than that of a totally domestic portfolio. Since stock markets partially reflect the current and/or forecasted state of each country's economy, they do not move in tandem. Thus, particular stocks of the various markets are not expected to be highly correlated. This contrasts with a purely domestic portfolio where most stocks are often moving in the same direction and by a somewhat similar magnitude.

To assess how country stock markets move relative to one another, correlation coefficients of the stock markets have been computed. Each country's stock index represents a sample of stocks. For the United States, the Standard and Poor's 500 Index was used. The correlation coefficients of stock index returns for nine major countries are displayed in Exhibit 16A.1. Some pairs

EXHIBIT 16A.1 Correlations of Stock Market Movements in Major Countries

	Canada	France	Germany	Japan	Netherlands	Sweden	Switzerland	U.K.
France	.422							
Germany	.296	.383						
Japan	.375	.323	.494					
Netherlands	.410	.471	.582	.640				
Sweden	.428	.249	.448	.279	.504			
Switzerland	.514	.374	.481	.480	.611	.358		
U.K.	.387	.337	.465	.414	.532	.190	.627	
U.S.	.735	.418	.439	.464	.493	.396	.593	.609

of indexes, such as the United States with Canada, and Japan with the Netherlands, exhibit relatively high correlations. For the most part, though, stock index correlations are quite low. Consequently, investors should be able to reduce variability in portfolio returns by diversifying among stocks from several countries.

Investors are often told to diversify their securities among different industries in order to reduce variability in returns. The benefits from such a strategy are limited because corporations in all industries are somewhat similarly affected by the general state of the economy. This so-called *systematic risk* cannot be reduced unless one diversifies investments across nations.

POTENTIAL RISK REDUCTION FOR THE FUTURE

Correlation coefficients and variability levels of the stock markets in our examples are based on past data and therefore may change in the future. Much research has been done to assess how correlations among stock markets have changed over time. A study by Haney and Lloyd found that correlations are generally increasing over time, suggesting that the stock index values are moving more in tandem. Therefore, the variability of portfolios composed of these individual indexes would increase. However, the evidence is not conclusive that correlations are increasing over time. Various studies have found conflicting results. This issue is discussed in more detail here.

Data on country stock index returns have been divided into two subperiods. The correlations between stock indexes for both subperiods have been computed and are displayed in Exhibit 16A.2. The correlations of the earlier subperiod are shown on top of each cell and those of the more recent subperiod in the bottom of each cell. For example, in the upper left corner of the table, the correlation coefficient between the Canadian and French stock market movements was .456 in the earlier subperiod and .029 in the more recent subperiod. The average of all correlation coefficients in the earlier subperiod was .443, as opposed to an average of .655 in the more recent subperiod. Overall, thirty-one of the thirty-six correlations increased over time, which supports some earlier findings by others that stock market correlations are increasing over time. These results suggest that the potential benefits from international stock markets may have been reduced over time.

EXHIBIT 16A.2   Comparison of Stock Market Correlations During Two Subperiods

	Subperiod	Canada	France	Germany	Japan	Netherlands	Sweden	Switzerland	U.K.
France	1*	.456							
	2**	.029							
Germany	1	.262	.376						
	2	.662	.668						
Japan	1	.363	.315	.482					
	2	.677	.700	.786					
Netherlands	1	.362	.475	.559	.628				
	2	.870	.516	.910	.912				
Sweden	1	.393	.270	.488	.293	.530			
	2	.824	.287	.165	.478	.545			
Switzerland	1	.492	.362	.448	.468	.590	.343		
	2	.675	.740	.973	.905	.948	.258		
U.K.	1	.369	.338	.463	.400	.522	.170	.636	
	2	.843	.298	.561	.886	.849	.829	.694	
U.S.	1	.723	.452	.454	.470	.479	.298	.582	.619
	2	.854	.193	.489	.830	.805	.883	.621	.994

*1 = January 1972–December 1977
**2 = January 1978–December 1984

However, this may be offset by the new opportunities that resulted from the opening of additional foreign stock markets.

STOCK MARKET RELATIONSHIPS DURING THE 1987 CRASH

Further evidence on the relationships between stock markets is obtained by assessing market movements during the stock market crash in October 1987. Exhibit 16A.3 shows the stock market movements for four major countries during the crash. While the magnitude of the decline was not exactly the same, all four markets were adversely affected. When institutional investors anticipated a general decline in stocks, they sold some stocks from all markets, rather than just the U.S. market. In addition, the concern about the U.S. economy apparently caused concern about the foreign economies that are influenced by the U.S. economy, causing investors in various countries to react to unfavorable expectations about the U.S. economy.

Many stock markets experienced larger declines in prices than the United States. For example, during the month of October 1987, the U.S. market index declined by about 21 percent, while the West German market index declined by about 23 percent and the United Kingdom index by 26 percent. The stock market indices of Australia and Hong Kong decreased by more than 50 percent over this same month.

Some critics have suggested that the institutional forces in the United States (such as computer-assisted trading, specialists, and concurrent trad-

EXHIBIT 16A.3   Integration Among Foreign Stock Markets During the 1987 Crash

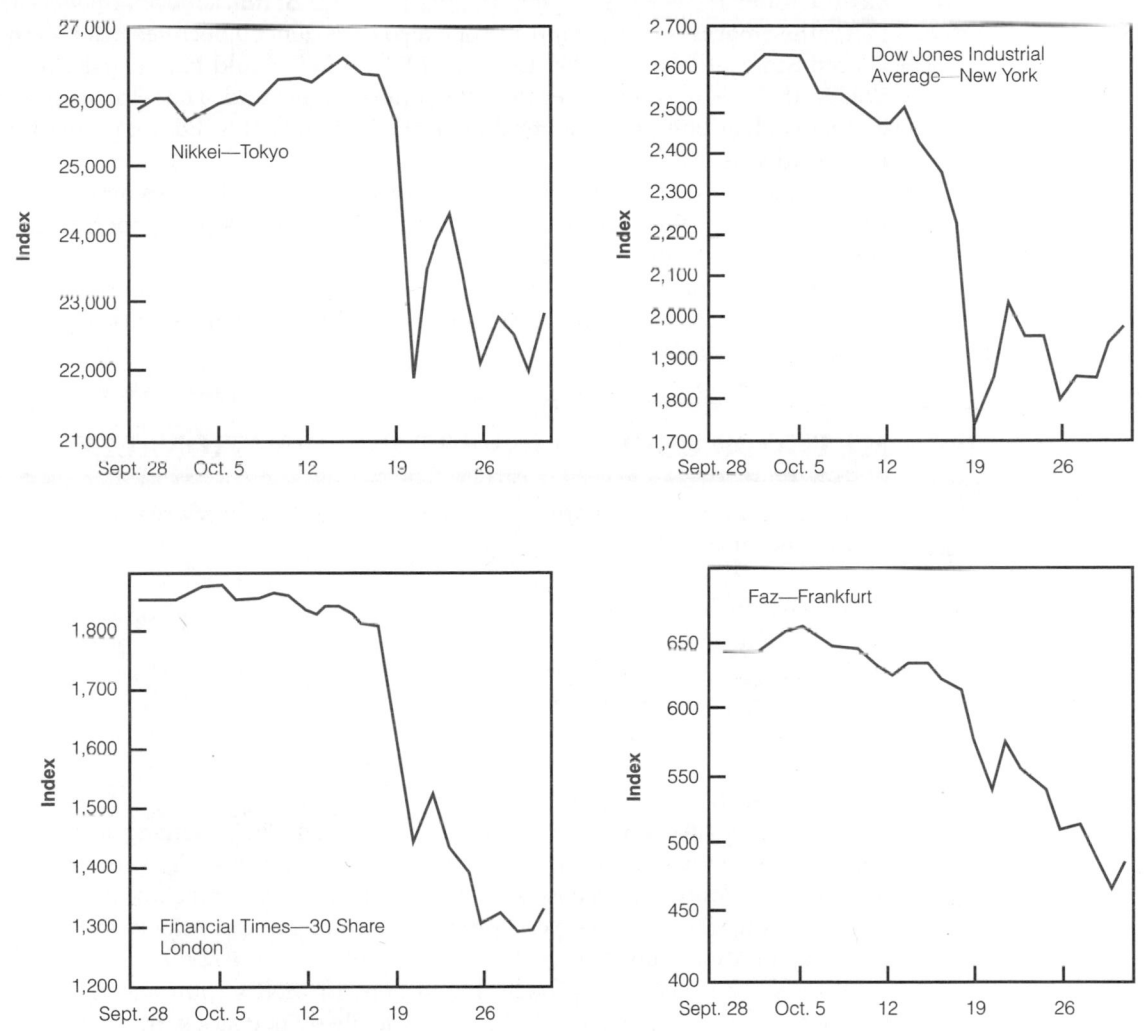

SOURCE OF GRAPHS: *Economic Trends,* Federal Reserve Bank of Cleveland (November 1987), p. 17.

ing in stock-index futures) along with a strong U.S. influence on the world were reasons for a worldwide crash. Yet, a study by Roll shows no evidence that the United States was the sole culprit. Roll shows that during October 1987 country stock-indices became more highly correlated than normal, which was likely due to some underlying factor that was capable of disrupting all markets. If computerized trading did not precipitate the crash, however, it could have exacerbated it. Roll compared the markets in which computerized trading was prevalent during the 1987 crash (Canada, France, Japan, United Kingdom, United States) to other markets. In local-currency terms, the five markets with computerized trading had an average decline of about 21 percent over October 1987, versus a 28 percent average decline for the other markets. This comparison suggests that computerized trading may have even reduced market volatility. Asian markets such as Hong Kong, Malaysia, and Singapore experienced substantial market declines on Black Monday (October 19, 1987) several hours before the U.S. market even opened. In fact, other markets throughout Europe also experienced declines prior to the United States. It appears that the non-U.S. markets could have caused paranoia in the U.S. market rather than the other way around. Thus, institutional factors such as computerized trading in the United States did not precipitate the worldwide crash.

Roll also assessed the possible impact of liquidity on declines across markets in October 1987. He used market capitalization as a proxy for liquidity, since larger markets are generally perceived as more liquid. Roll found no statistical relationship between market capitalization and the magnitude of decline across markets. Therefore, liquidity did not influence market performance during the crash.

METHODS USED TO INVEST INTERNATIONALLY

If investors attempt international stock diversification, there are five common approaches available:

- Foreign stock exchanges
- Investment in MNC stocks
- Foreign stocks on local stock exchanges
- American depository receipts (ADRs)
- International mutual funds (IMFs)

Each approach is discussed in turn.

Foreign securities could be purchased on foreign stock exchanges, but this approach is inefficient because of market imperfections such as unavailable information, transactions costs, and tax differentials among countries. Thus, the remaining four alternative approaches to international stock diversification may be more suitable.

Although the second approach, investment in MNCs (purchasing stock), may actually reflect a purchase of a domestically owned stock, the operations of an MNC represent international diversification. Like a well-managed stock portfolio, an MNC can reduce risk (variability in net cash flows) by diversifying sales not only among industries, but also among countries. In this sense, the MNC as a single firm can achieve stability similar to an internationally diversified stock portfolio.

If investors can diversify themselves, should it matter to them whether a corporation has diversified its sales among countries? To clarify this question, consider an MNC specializing in computers with subsidiaries in the United States, France, Canada, and Belgium. Because the demand for this MNC's product is dependent on these four economies (rather than on one single national economy), its total consolidated sales level is less vulnerable to its home country's economic cycle. Thus, its variability in sales should be less than that of a domestic computer firm located in any one of these countries. Yet, to an investor, the MNC may not necessarily be the preferred corporation to invest in since the purchasing of shares of domestic computer firms residing in various countries would achieve similar diversification benefits as owning shares in the MNC. This portfolio approach is often referred to as **homemade diversification** since the investor constructs it as opposed to it being prepackaged (like the MNC).

Even if investors can construct their own international portfolio, they may find it beneficial to invest in an MNC due to higher than normal transaction costs or taxes and other barriers to purchasing stocks in foreign stock markets. Because of these market imperfections, an investor may not be able to capitalize on the possible advantages of international diversification through homemade diversification. First, they need a list of foreign stocks from which to choose. Local newspapers normally do not provide such a list; and even if they knew of some foreign stocks, current information on their balance sheet and income statement data are not readily available. In addition, any available data would not normally be directly comparable with industry averages, etc., in one's country due to global differences in accounting practices and securities regulations. Even without information barriers, there is the additional brokerage expense of purchasing (and later selling) stocks in foreign stock markets.

If MNC stocks behave like an international portfolio, then they should be sensitive to the stock markets of the various countries in which they operate. A study by Jacquillat and Solnik assessed the sensitivity of MNC returns to various stock market movements during the 1966–1974 period using the following regression model:

$$R_{mnc} = a_o + a_1 R_L + b_1 R_{I,1} + b_2 R_{I,2} + \ldots + b_n R_{I,n} + u$$

where R_{mnc} is the average return on a portfolio of MNCs from the same cuntry, a_o is the intercept, R_L is the return on the local stock market, $R_{I,1}$ through $R_{I,n}$ are returns on foreign stock indices I_1 through I_n, and u is an error term. The regression coefficient a_1 measures the sensitivity of MNC returns to their local stock market, while coefficients b_1 through b_n measure the sensitivity of MNC returns to the various foreign stock markets. The results of the time series regression analysis found that MNCs based in a particular country were typically affected only by the local stock market and were not affected by other stock market movements. This same result occurred for the MNC portfolio of each country.

A recent study by Madura reassessed the sensitivity of MNC returns to various stock markets over the 1974–1987 period. A reassessment was necessary since many MNCs have significantly increased their international operations since the period used by Jacquillat and Solnik to evaluate MNCs. The increased international involvement of MNCs could have caused them to behave more like an internationally diversified stock portfolio. Based on a procedure similar to that of Jacquillat and Solnik, this study again showed that MNC stock returns respond only to the local stock market returns and not to the movements of any other markets. Thus, MNCs are not an effective means to achieve international diversification.

An alternative approach to international diversification is to purchase stocks that represent foreign companies but are sold on the local stock exchange. In the United States, for example, Royal Dutch Shell (of the Netherlands) and Sony (of Japan) stocks are sold on U.S. stock exchanges. Because the number of foreign stocks listed on any local stock exchange is typically quite limited, this method by itself may not be adequate to achieve full benefits of international diversification.

Another approach is to purchase **American depository receipts (ADRs),** which are certificates representing ownership of foreign stocks. There are more than 800 ADRs available in the United States, primarily traded on the Over-the-Counter (OTC) stock exchange. Because most of these ADRs are not actively traded, their prices are typically not reported on a consistent basis. This may change over time, however, as they are becoming increasingly popular.

Officer and Hoffmeister assessed the viability of ADRs as a means of international diversification. They found that while ADR returns were more volatile than U.S. stock returns, combined portfolios of ADRs and U.S. stocks exhibited significantly lower variability than portfolios solely composed of U.S. stocks. Thus, they concluded that ADRs could effectively enable U.S. investors to reduce risk. Related research by Tucker compared the benefits of ADRs to foreign stocks by comparing the marginal benefits from adding ADRs to a U.S. stock portfolio versus adding foreign stocks. The degree of risk reduction with ADRs was quite similar to that of foreign stocks. These results imply that ADRs are an effective means of international diversification, and therefore that investment in ADRs may be an adequate substitute for direct investment in foreign stocks. However, the limited number of ADRs available and the relatively high transaction costs may encourage some investors to use an alternative approach.

A final approach to consider is purchasing shares of **international mutual funds (IMFs),** which are portfolios of stocks from various countries. Several investment firms such as Fidelity, Vanguard, and Merrill Lynch have constructed IMFs for their customers. Like domestic mutual funds, IMFs are popular due to (1) the low minimum investment necessary to participate in the fund, (2) presumed expertise of the portfolio managers, and (3) high degree of diversification achieved by the portfolio's inclusion of several stocks. Yet, an IMF is often thought to be more capable of reducing risk than a purely domestic mutual fund, since it includes foreign securities. An IMF represents a prepackaged portfolio, so investors who use it do not need to construct their own portfolios. While some investors prefer to construct their own portfolios, the existence of numerous IMFs on the market today allows investors to select the one that most closely resembles the type of portfolio they would have constructed on their own. Moreover, there are some investors who feel more comfortable with a professional manager composing the international portfolio.

Research by Essayyad and Wu assessed the performance of 18 international mutual funds over the 1977–1984 period. Fifteen of the 18 IMFs exhibited a higher mean monthly return than the Standard & Poor's (S&P) 500 index. In addition, 16 of the IMFs exhibited a lower coefficient of variation (defined as standard deviation of returns divided by mean return) than the S&P 500 index, suggesting a lower level of risk per unit of return.

To further assess risk, the authors measured the betas of the IMFs, using the S&P 500 index as a proxy for the market. Four of the 18 IMFs had a beta that was not statistically different from zero. For the 18 IMFs, the average percentage of variation in returns explained by market movements was only about 24 percent. This confirms that IMF return patterns differ substantially from U.S. market returns, which is a desirable attribute for portfolio diversification.

A study by Rao and Aggarwal examined the sensitivity of IMF returns to the U.S. market, (with the S&P 500 index as a proxy for the market). Using regression analysis, they found that the betas estimated for IMFs were less than 1.00. Furthermore, the degree of variation in each IMF's returns that could be explained by market movements (as measured by R^2) averaged 30 percent, supporting the findings by Essayyad and Wu. This is significantly below the average R^2 on similar regression applications to domestic mutual funds. IMFs appear to offer U.S. investors some degree of insulation from U.S. market movements, and therefore serve as a useful means of international diversification.

HEDGING EXCHANGE RATE RISK ON FOREIGN STOCK HOLDINGS

The exchange rate risk resulting from foreign stock holdings can be reduced by diversifying among stocks of different countries. For example, a U.S. investor can reduce exchange rate risk by spreading whatever funds are to be used for foreign investments across various non-U.S. countries. If correlations between foreign currency movements (against the U.S. dollar) are low or negative, exchange rate risk can be effectively reduced through diversification.

Many foreign currencies move in tandem against the dollar, especially the European currencies that are pegged to the European Currency Unit (ECU). Because these currencies are essentially fixed relative to one another (within boundaries), they are forced to move by a similar magnitude and direction against the dollar. Thus, if one of these currencies depreciates substantially against the dollar, the others will as well, and all foreign stocks denominated in these currencies will be adversely affected to a similar degree. Investors would achieve more effective diversification of currencies by spreading the foreign investment across continents.

Another method to reduce exchange rate risk is to take short positons in the foreign currencies denominating the foreign stocks. For example, a U.S. investor holding French stocks who expects the stocks to be worth FF1 million one year from now could sell forward contracts (or futures contracts) representing FF1 million. The stocks could be liquidated at that time and the francs could be exchanged for dollars at a locked-in price.

While hedging the exchange rate risk of an international stock portfolio can be effective, it has three limitations. First, the number of foreign currency units to be converted to dollars at the end of the investment horizon is unknown. If the units received from liquidating the foreign stocks are more (less) than the amount hedged, the investor has a net long (short) position in that foreign currency, and the return will be unfavorably affected by its depreciation (appreciation). Nevertheless, while investors may not perform a perfect hedge for this reason, they should normally be able to hedge most of their exchange rate risk.

A second limitation of hedging exchange rate risk is that the investors may decide to retain the foreign stocks beyond the initially planned investment horizon. Of course, they can create another short position after the initial short position is terminated. If they ever decide to liquidate the foreign stocks prior to the forward delivery date, the hedge will be less effective. They could use the proceeds to invest in foreign money market securities denominated in that foreign currency in order to postpone conversion to dollars until the forward delivery date. But this prevents them from using the funds for other opportunities until that delivery date.

A third limitation of hedging is that forward rates for some currencies may not exist or may exhibit a large discount. This limitation generally does not apply to the widely traded currencies.

Some research has been performed on hedging investments in foreign stocks. A study by Madura and Reiff estimated the returns of country stock indices with and without hedging (from a U.S. perspective) in order to determine the degree of risk reduction achievable from hedging. They developed an **efficient frontier** of unhedged portfolios and compared it to an efficient frontier of hedged portfolios. The hedged portfolios generally exhibited about half the variance for a given return level. These results are due to higher variances of unhedged stock index returns, and higher correlations between the unhedged stock index returns.

While the development of ex post efficient portfolios shows potential risk-return levels that could have been achieved, such optimal results are difficult to achieve in reality. A study by Eun and Resnick assessed the performance of hedged and unhedged portfolios on an ex ante basis. That is, only information prior to the decision dates was used to compose the portfolios. Their study found that the hedged portfolios resulted in much lower risk than them unedged portfolios, even on an ex ante basis. The hedged portfolios consistently outperformed unhedged portfolios, suggesting that the benefits of international diversification are best realized by hedging against exchange rate risk.

CHAPTER 17

Multinational Capital Budgeting

MNCs evaluate a direct foreign investment proposal by means of capital budgeting analysis. This chapter explains how multinational capital budgeting can be conducted. First, the issue of whether capital budgeting should be assessed by the parent or subsidiary is addressed. Next, the variables commonly incorporated within a multinational capital budgeting problem are identified. Then, an example is provided to show how a proposed project can be evaluated. This example does not incorporate all the factors that could influence the capital budgeting decision, so other factors are identified and discussed, as well as various methods to account for risk. Because capital budgeting requires an estimated cost of capital, the estimation procedure is also discussed. Factors unique to an MNC versus a purely domestic firm that may affect an MNC's cost of capital are identified.

CAPITAL BUDGETING: SUBSIDIARY VERSUS PARENT PERSPECTIVE

Should capital budgeting for multinational projects be conducted from the viewpoint of the subsidiary that would administer the project or the parent that would most likely finance much of the project? Some would say the subsidiary's perspective should be used, since it will be responsible for administering the project. In addition, since the subsidiary is a subset of the MNC, what is good for the subsidiary would appear to be good for the MNC. This reasoning, however, is not necessarily correct. One could argue that if the parent is financing the project, then it should be evaluating the results from its point of view. The feasibility of the capital budgeting analysis can vary with the perspective, because the net after-tax cash inflows to the subsidiary can differ substantially from those to the parent. Such a difference is due to several factors, some of which are discussed here.

Tax Differentials

Assume the parent considers expanding a subsidiary's marketing department. Also assume the host-country government imposes a very low tax rate

497

on earnings generated by the subsidiary. If the earnings due to the project will someday be remitted to the parent, the MNC would need to consider how the parent's government taxes these earnings. If the parent's government imposes a high tax rate on the remitted funds, the project may be feasible from the subsidiary's point of view, but not from the parent's point of view. Under such a scenario, the parent should not consider financing such a project even though it appears feasible from the subsidiary's perspective.

Restricted Remittances

Consider a potential project to be implemented in a country where the government restricts a percentage of the subsidiary earnings from being sent to the parent. Since the parent may never have access to such funds, the project is not attractive to the parent. Yet, the project may be attractive to the subsidiary. One possible solution to such a problem is to let the subsidiary obtain partial financing for the project within the host country. In this case, the portion of funds not allowed to be sent to the parent can be used to cover the financing costs over time.

Excessive Remittances

Consider a parent that charges its subsidiary very high administrative fees since management is centralized at the headquarters. To the subsidiary, the fees represent an expense. To the parent, the fees represent revenue that may substantially exceed the actual cost of managing the subsidiary. In this case, the project's earnings may appear low from the subsidiary's perspective and high from the parent's perspective. The feasibility of the project would again depend on perspective. In most cases, neglecting the parent's perspective will distort the true value of a foreign project.

Exchange Rate Movements

When earnings are remitted to the parent, they are normally converted from the subsidiary's local currency to the parent's currency. The amount of funds received by the parent is therefore influenced by the existing exchange rate. If the subsidiary project is assessed from the subsidiary's perspective, the cash flows to the subsidiary would not have to be converted to the parent's currency.

Subsidiary versus Parent Perspective: An Example

To illustrate how the capital budgeting analysis may vary among perspectives, consider the following simplified example. Buckeye Corporation, a U.S.-based MNC, has a subsidiary in Mexico that produces and sells farm equipment. Buckeye believes the subsidiary could also develop an equipment-repair business. The following projections and relevant data have been compiled for the analysis:

■ The anticipated initial investment (or initial outlay) is 9.6 billion pesos, which at the existing exchange rate of $.001 per peso, converts to $9.6 million.

■ The business would generate an estimated 5 billion pesos per year for four years.

■ The business will be sold in four years; the host government will acquire the business in four years with no compensation to Buckeye; however, the host government imposes no taxes on income earned by the business. It does impose a withholding tax of 20 percent on any funds remitted to the U.S. parent.

■ The exchange rate of the Mexican peso is forecasted as follows:

End of Year	Value of Mexican peso
1	$.0008
2	$.0006
3	$.0004
4	$.0003

■ The U.S. government will tax any dollar earnings received by the parent from its subsidiary at a 20 percent rate.

■ The required rate of return on the project is 18 percent.

Based on this information, the capital budgeting analysis is conducted as shown in Exhibit 17.1. The top panel is an analysis from the subsidiary's perspective. The present value of the cash flows to be generated is provided, along with the cumulative net present value (NPV). The cumulative NPV is

EXHIBIT 17.1 Capital Budgeting Analysis: Buckeye Corporation (*in thousands*)

	Year 1	Year 2	Year 3	Year 4
Subsidiary Perspective				
Initial investment P9,600,000				
Periodic cash flows	P5,000,000	P5,000,000	P5,000,000	P5,000,000
PV of cash flows (at 18%)	P4,237,288	P3,590,922	P3,043,154	P2,578,944
Cumulative NPV	−P5,362,712	−P1,771,790	P1,271,364	P3,850,308
Parent Perspective				
Initial investment $9,600				
Total cash flows from subsidiary	P5,000,000	P5,000,000	P5,000,000	P5,000,000
Withholding tax if cash flows were remitted to parent (20%)	P1,000,000	P1,000,000	P1,000,000	P1,000,000
Remitted funds after withholding tax	P4,000,000	P4,000,000	P4,000,000	P4,000,000
Exchange rate of Mexican peso	$.0008	$.0006	$.0004	$.0003
Funds to parent	$3,200	$2,400	$1,600	$1,200
Taxes by U.S. government (20%)	$ 640	$ 480	$ 320	$ 240
After-tax funds to parent	$2,560	$1,920	$1,280	$ 960
PV of cash flows (at 18%)	$2,169	$1,379	$ 779	$ 495
Cumulative NPV	−$7,431	−$6,052	−$5,273	−$4,778

useful not only for estimating the project's NPV, but also for determining how long it takes to generate a positive NPV. For projects that may be terminated sooner than planned (due to an unanticipated host government takeover, etc.) there is a desire to achieve a positive NPV as soon as possible. The analysis in Exhibit 17.1 shows that the project has a positive NPV by the end of Year 3.

This same project is analyzed from the parent's perspective in the lower panel of Exhibit 17.1. Now assume that the parent provides the initial investment. The difference in cash flows to the parent occur for three reasons. First, there is a 20 percent withholding tax on any funds remitted to the parent, thereby reducing the amount of pesos to be remitted. Second, the pesos will be converted into dollars before they are remitted to the parent. Because the peso is expected to depreciate, the amount of dollars to be received in each successive year is reduced. Finally, the U.S. government plans to impose a 20 percent tax on the remitted earnings received by the parent, which will reduce the parent cash flows even further (our analysis assumes that all funds remitted represent earnings). From the parent's perspective, the NPV is negative even at the end of the four-year period. Thus, the project should not be undertaken. This conclusion conflicts with the analysis conducted from the subsidiary's perspective.

Some MNCs analyze the feasibility of a project from the subsidiary's perspective, while others use the parent's perspective but most consider both perspectives. If conflicting conclusions are drawn when considering both perspectives, the parent's perspective should be given greater emphasis. This attitude coincides with maximizing wealth of the owners (shareholders) of the firm.

The forthcoming capital budgeting example in this chapter is analyzed from the perspective of the parent. However, keep in mind that some MNCs may decide to use the subsidiary's perspective under some circumstances. If one wished to focus on the subsidiary's perspective, the capital budgeting analysis would still be set up in a similar manner, except that the transfer of funds to the parent and government-imposed taxes on the parent's earnings would be ignored. Throughout this chapter, the parent's perspective is used.

INPUT TO THE CAPITAL BUDGETING DECISION

Regardless of the long-term project to be considered, an MNC will normally require forecasts of the following economic and financial characteristics related to the project:

1. Initial investment
2. Consumer demand
3. Price
4. Variable cost
5. Fixed cost
6. Project lifetime
7. Salvage value
8. Fund-transfer restrictions
9. Tax laws

10. Exchange rates
11. Required rate of return

Each of these characteristics is briefly described in turn.

1. *Initial investment.* The parent's initial investment in a project may reflect the major source of funds to support a particular project. Funds initially invested in a project may include not only whatever is necessary to start the project, but also additional funds such as working capital to support the project over time. Such funds are needed to finance inventory, wages, etc., until the revenues from the project are generated. Because cash inflows will not always be sufficient to cover upcoming cash outflows, working capital is needed throughout a project's lifetime.

2. *Consumer demand.* An accurately forecasted consumer demand for a product is quite valuable when projecting a cash flow schedule. However, future demand is often difficult to forecast. For example, if the project represents a plant in Germany that produces automobiles, the MNC must forecast what percentage of the auto market in Germany it can pull from prevailing auto producers. Once a market share percentage is forecasted, projected demand can be computed with ease. Yet, the forecast of market share is subject to error. Demand forecasts can sometimes be aided by historical data on what market share other MNCs in the industry pulled when they entered this market. However, historical data are not always an accurate indicator of the future. In addition, many projects reflect a first attempt, so there are no predecessors to review as an indicator of the future.

3. *Price.* The price at which the product could be sold can be forecasted using competitive products in the markets as a comparison. However, a long-term capital budgeting analysis requires projections for not only the upcoming period, but for the expected lifetime of the project as well. The future prices will most likely be responsive to the future inflation rate in the host country (where the project is to take place). Yet, the future inflation rate is not known. Thus, future inflation rates must be forecasted in order to develop projections of the product price over time.

4. *Variable cost.* Like the price estimate, variable-cost forecasts can be developed from assessing prevailing comparative costs of the components (such as hourly labor costs, etc.) that make it up. Such costs should normally move in tandem with the future inflation rate of the host country. Even if the variable cost per unit can be accurately predicted, the projected total variable cost (variable cost per unit times quantity produced) may be far off if the demand is inaccurately forecasted.

5. *Fixed cost.* On a periodic basis, the fixed cost may be easier to predict than the variable cost since it is not normally sensitive to changes in demand. It is, however, sensitive to any change in the host country's inflation rate from the point at which the forecast is made until the point at which the fixed costs are incurred.

6. *Project lifetime.* While it is difficult to assess the life of some projects, other projects are designated a specific lifetime at the end of which they will be liquidated. This makes the capital budgeting analysis easier to apply. It should be recognized that the MNC does not always have complete control over the lifetime decision. In some cases, political events may force a liquidation of the project earlier than planned. The probability of such events occurring varies among countries.

7. *Salvage (liquidation) value.* The after-tax salvage value of most projects is difficult to forecast. It will depend on several factors, including the success of the project and the attitude of the host government toward the project. As an extreme possibility, the host government could take over the project without adequately compensating the MNC.

8. *Fund-transfer restrictions.* In some cases, a host government will prevent a subsidiary's earnings from being sent to the parent. This restriction may reflect an attempt to encourage additional local spending, or to avoid excessive sales of the local currency in exchange for some other currency. Since the fund-transfer restrictions prevent cash from coming back to the parent, projected net cash flows from the parent's perspective will be affected by the restrictions. If the parent is aware of these restrictions, it can incorporate them when projecting net cash flows. However, the host government may adjust its fund-transfer restrictions over time, in which case the MNC can only forecast the future fund-transfer restrictions and incorporate these forecasts into the analysis.

9. *Tax laws.* The tax laws of each individual country are complex. Under some circumstances, they allow tax deductions or credits for the MNC due to taxes paid by subsidiaries to their respective host countries. Because after-tax cash flows are necessary for an adequate capital budgeting analysis, tax effects must be accounted for. MNCs can normally handle this task. However, tax laws are not permanent. Because they are changed often, it is difficult to know how they affect a project over time.

10. *Exchange rates.* Any international project will be affected by exchange rate fluctuations during the life of the project, but these movements are often very difficult to forecast. There are methods to hedge against them, though most hedging techniques are used to cover short-term positions. While it is possible to hedge over longer periods (with long-term forward contacts or currency swap arrangements), the MNC has no way of knowing the amount of funds that it should hedge. This is because it is only guessing at its future costs and revenues due to the project. Thus, the MNC may decide not to hedge the projected foreign currency net cash flows. Unfortunately, even if these cash flows are predicted with perfect accuracy, an MNC that does not hedge may improperly estimate the project cash flows to be received by the parent as a result of inaccurate exchange rate forecasts during the life of the project.

11. *Required rate of return.* Once the relevant cash flows of a proposed project are estimated, they can be discounted at the project's required rate of return, which may differ from the MNC's cost of capital because of that particular project's risk. The MNC's cost of capital is discussed in the following chapter.

Additional considerations will be discussed after a simplified multinational capital budgeting example is provided. In the real world, magic numbers aren't provided to MNCs to insert into their computer. The challenge revolves around accurately forecasting the variables relevant to the project evaluation. If garbage (inaccurate forecasts) is input into the computer, the analysis output generated by the computer will also be garbage. Consequently, an MNC may take on a project by mistake. Since such a mistake may be worth millions of dollars, it is understandable why MNCs need to assess the degree of uncertainty for any input that is used in the project evaluation. This is discussed more thoroughly later in the chapter.

MULTINATIONAL CAPITAL BUDGETING: AN EXAMPLE

Capital budgeting for the MNC is necessary for all long-term projects that deserve consideration. The projects may range from a small expansion of a subsidiary division to creation of a new subsidiary. The example that follows reflects the possible development of a new subsidiary. It begins with assumptions that simplify the capital budgeting analysis. Then, additional considerations are discussed in order to emphasize the potential complexity of such an analysis.

The forthcoming example illustrates one of many possible methods available that would achieve the same result. Also, keep in mind that a real-world problem would involve more extenuating circumstances than those shown here.

Example: Background

Spartan Inc., a U.S.-based manufacturer of high-quality tennis rackets, recently considered exporting rackets to Switzerland. However, it anticipates that the Swiss government will prohibit these exports in retaliation for recent trade restrictions placed by the U.S. government on some Swiss exports. Consequently, Spartan is considering the development of a subsidiary in Switzerland that could manufacture and sell the tennis rackets locally. Various departments of Spartan Inc. were asked to supply relevant information for a capital budgeting analysis. In addition, some executives of Spartan Inc. met with government officials of Switzerland regarding the proposed subsidiary. All relevant information follows.

1. *Initial investment.* An estimated 30 million Swiss francs (SF) would be needed for the project. The amount can be divided into SF20 million for the plant and equipment and SF10 million for working capital. The parent will invest SF20 million to entirely finance the plant and equipment. Given the existing spot rate of $.50 per Swiss franc, the dollar amount of the parent's initial investment is $10 million. The SF10 million in working capital is to be borrowed by the subsidiary from a local Swiss bank at an interest rate of 10 percent per year. Interest payments on this loan (of SF1 million) are to be paid by the subsidiary annually, and the principal (SF10 million) will be paid at the end of year 4 when the project is terminated.

2. *Project life.* The project is expected to end in four years. The host government of Switzerland has promised to make a payment to the parent in order to purchase the plant after four years.

3. *Price and demand.* The estimated price and demand schedules during each of the next four years are shown here:

Year	Price per Racket	Demand in Switzerland
1	SF350	60,000 units
2	SF350	60,000 units
3	SF360	100,000 units
4	SF380	100,000 units

4. *Costs*. The variable costs (for materials, labor, etc.) per unit were estimated and consolidated as shown here:

Year	Variable costs (VC) per Racket
1	SF200
2	SF200
3	SF250
4	SF260

The fixed costs, such as overhead expenses to the subsidiary, are estimated to be SF1 million per year.

5. *Exchange rates*. The spot exchange rate of the Swiss franc is $.50. The spot rate is used by Spartan Inc. as its best forecast of the exchange rate that shall exist in the future periods. Thus, the forecasted exchange rate for all future periods is $.50.

6. *Host-country taxes on income earned by the subsidiary*. The Swiss government will allow Spartan Inc. to establish the subsidiary and will impose a 20 percent tax rate on income. In addition, it will impose a 10 percent withholding tax on any funds remitted by the subsidiary to the parent.

7. *U.S. government taxes on income earned by Spartan subsidiary*. The U.S. government will allow a tax credit on taxes paid in Switzerland, so that earnings remitted by the parent will not be taxed by the U.S. government.

8. *Cash flows from Spartan subsidiary to parent*. The Spartan subsidiary plans to send all net cash flow received back to the parent firm at the end of each year. The Swiss government promises no restrictions on the cash flows to be sent back to the parent firm, but does impose a 10 percent withholding tax on any funds sent to the parent, as mentioned earlier.

9. *Depreciation*. The Swiss government will allow Spartan Inc. to depreciate the cost of the plant and equipment over 10 years using the straight-line depreciation method. Since the plant and equipment are initially valued at SF20 million, depreciation expense will be SF2 million per year.

10. *Salvage value*. The Swiss government will send a payment of SF12 million to the parent for the subsidiary at the end of four years. It will also pay Spartan SF10 million for the existing working capital, which Spartan will use to pay off the principal on the loan. Since the salvage value of the subsidiary is expected to equal the book value at the end of Year 4, there should be no capital gain or loss on the sale of the subsidiary.

11. *Required rate of return*. Spartan Inc. requires a 15 percent return on this project.

Example: Analysis

The capital budgeting analysis to determine whether Spartan Inc. should establish the subsidiary is provided in Exhibit 17.2 (review this exhibit as you read on). The first step is to incorporate demand and price estimations in order to forecast total revenue (see Lines 1 through 3). Then, the expenses are summed to forecast total expenses (see Lines 4 through 9). Next, before-tax earnings are computed (in Line 10) by subtracting total expenses from total revenues. Host-government taxes (Line 11) are then

EXHIBIT 17.2   Capital Budgeting Analysis: Spartan Inc.

	Year 0	Year 1	Year 2	Year 3	Year 4
1. Demand		60,000	60,000	100,000	100,000
2. Price per unit		SF350	SF350	SF360	SF380
3. Total revenue = (1) × (2)		SF21,000,000	SF21,000,000	SF36,000,000	SF38,000,000
4. Variable cost per unit		SF200	SF200	SF250	SF260
5. Total variable cost = (1) × (4)		SF12,000,000	SF12,000,000	SF25,000,000	SF26,000,000
6. Fixed cost		SF1,000,000	SF1,000,000	SF1,000,000	SF1,000,000
7. Interest expense on Swiss loan		SF1,000,000	SF1,000,000	SF1,000,000	SF1,000,000
8. Noncash expense (depreciation)		SF2,000,000	SF2,000,000	SF2,000,000	SF2,000,000
9. Total expenses = (5) + (6) + (7) + (8)		SF16,000,000	SF16,000,000	SF29,000,000	SF30,000,000
10. Before-tax earnings of subsidiary = (3) − (9)		SF5,000,000	SF5,000,000	SF7,000,000	SF8,000,000
11. Host government tax (20%)		SF1,000,000	SF1,000,000	SF1,400,000	SF1,600,000
12. After-tax earnings of subsidiary		SF4,000,000	SF4,000,000	SF5,600,000	SF6,400,000
13. Net cash flow to subsidiary = (12) + (8)		SF6,000,000	SF6,000,000	SF7,600,000	SF8,400,000
14. SF remitted by subsidiary (100%)		SF6,000,000	SF6,000,000	SF7,600,000	SF8,400,000
15. Withholding tax imposed on remitted funds (10%)		SF600,000	SF600,000	SF760,000	SF840,000
16. SF remitted after withholding taxes		SF5,400,000	SF5,400,000	SF6,840,000	SF7,560,000
17. Salvage value					SF12,000,000
18. Exchange rate of SF		$.50	$.50	$.50	$.50
19. Cash flows to parent		$2,700,000	$2,700,000	$3,420,000	$9,780,000
20. PV of parent cash flows (15% discount rate)		$2,347,826	$2,041,588	$2,248,706	$5,591,747
21. Initial investment by parent	$10,000,000				
22. Cumulative NPV of cash flows		−$7,652,174	−$5,610,586	−$3,361,880	$2,229,867

deducted from before-tax earnings to determine after-tax earnings (Line 12) for the subsidiary.

The depreciation expense is added to the after-tax subsidiary earnings to compute the net cash flow to the subsidiary (Line 13). All of these funds are to be remitted by the subsidiary, so Line 14 is the same as Line 13. The subsidiary can afford to send all net cash flow to the parent, since its loan from the local bank is providing the working capital to support corporate operations. The funds remitted to the parent are subject to a 10 percent withholding tax (Line 15), so the actual amount of funds to be sent after these taxes is shown in Line 16. The salvage value of the project is shown in Line 17. The funds to be remitted must first be converted into dollars at the exchange rate (Line 18) existing at that time. The parent's cash flow from the subsidiary is shown in Line 19. The periodic funds received from the subsidiary are not subject to U.S. corporate taxes, since it was assumed the taxes paid in Switzerland would represent a credit offsetting taxes owed to the U.S. government.

Although several capital budgeting techniques are available, a commonly used technique is to estimate the cash flows and salvage value to be received by the parent and compute the net present value (NPV) of the project as shown here:

$$NPV = -IO + \sum_{t=1}^{n} \frac{CF_t}{(1 + k)^t} + \frac{SV_n}{(1 + k)^n}$$

where

$\qquad IO$ = initial outlay (investment)
$\qquad CF_t$ = cash flow in period t
$\qquad SV_n$ = salvage value
$\qquad k$ = required rate of return on the project
$\qquad n$ = lifetime of the project (number of periods)

The *present value (PV)* of each period's net cash flow is computed using a 15 percent discount rate (Line 20). The discount rate should reflect the parent's cost of capital with an adjustment for the project's risk. Finally, the cumulative NPV (Line 22) is determined by consolidating the discounted cash flows for each period, and subtracting the initial outlay (in Line 21). For example, as of the end of the Year 2, the cumulative NPV was −$5,610,586. This was determined by consolidating the $2,347,826 in Year 1, the $2,041,588 in Year 2, and subtracting the initial investment of $10,000,000. The critical value in Line 22 is in the last period, since this reflects the NPV of the project.

In our example, the cumulative NPV as of the end of the last period is $2,229,867. Because the NPV is positive, the MNC may accept this project, if the discount rate of 15 percent has fully accounted for the project's risk. However, if the analysis has not yet accounted for risk, the decision may be to reject the project. The manner by which the MNC can account for risk in capital budgeting is discussed shortly.

FACTORS TO CONSIDER IN MULTINATIONAL CAPITAL BUDGETING

The example of Spartan Inc. ignored a variety of factors that may affect the capital budgeting analysis, namely

1. Exchange rate fluctuations
2. Inflation
3. Financing arrangement
4. Blocked funds
5. Remittance provisions
6. Uncertain salvage value
7. Impact of project on prevailing cash flows
8. Government incentives
9. Social costs
10. Threat of expropriation

Each of these factors is discussed in turn.

Exchange Rate Fluctuations

Recall that Spartan Inc. used the Swiss franc's current spot rate ($.50) as a forecast for all future periods of concern. While the company realized that the exchange rate will typically change over time, it did not know whether the franc would strengthen or weaken in the future. While the difficulty in accurately forecasting exchange rates is well known, a multinational capital budgeting analysis could at least incorporate other scenarios for exchange rate movements, such as a pessimistic scenario and an optimistic scenario. From the parent's point of view, appreciation of the franc would be favorable, since the franc inflows would someday be converted to more U.S. dollars. Conversely, depreciation would be unfavorable, since the weakened francs would convert to fewer U.S. dollars over time.

Weak franc and strong-franc scenarios are illustrated in Exhibit 17.3. At the top of the table, the anticipated after-tax franc cash flows are shown for the subsidiary (including salvage value), from Lines 16 and 17 in Exhibit 17.2. The amount of U.S. dollars that these francs convert to depends on the exchange rates existing in the various periods in which they are converted. The number of francs multiplied by the forecasted exchange rate will determine the estimated dollars received by the parent.

Notice from Exhibit 17.3 the differences in cash flow received by the parent in the strong-franc scenario versus the weak-franc scenario. A strong franc is clearly beneficial, as verified by the increased dollar value of earnings received. The large differences in cash flow received by the parent in the different scenarios illustrates the impact of exchange rate expectations on the feasibility of an international project. This explains why a vital part of multinational capital budgeting is forecasting future exchange rates.

The NPV forecasts based on projections for exchange rates are illustrated in Exhibit 17.4. The estimated NPV is highest if the franc is expected to

EXHIBIT 17.3 Capital Budgeting Analysis Using Different Exchange Rate Scenarios: Spartan Inc.

	Year 0	Year 1	Year 2	Year 3	Year 4
SF remitted after withholding taxes (including salvage value)		SF5,400,000	SF5,400,000	SF6,840,000	SF19,560,000
Strong-Franc Scenario					
Exchange rate of SF		$.54	$.57	$.61	$.65
Cash flows to parent		$2,916,000	$3,078,000	$4,172,400	$12,714,000
PV of cash flows (15% discount rate)		$2,535,652	$2,327,410	$2,743,421	$7,269,271
Initial investment by parent	$10,000,000				
Cumulative NPV of cash flows		−$7,464,348	−$5,136,938	−$2,393,517	$4,875,754
Weak-Franc Scenario					
Exchange rate of SF		$.47	$.45	$.40	$.37
Cash flows to parent		$2,538,000	$2,430,000	$2,736,000	$7,237,200
PV of parent cash flows (15% discount rate)		$2,206,957	$1,837,429	$1,798,964	$4,137,893
Initial investment by parent	$10,000,000				
Cumulative NPV of cash flows		−$7,793,043	−$5,955,614	−$4,156,650	−$18,757

EXHIBIT 17.4 Sensitivity of the Project's NPV to Different Exchange Rate Scenarios: Spartan Inc.

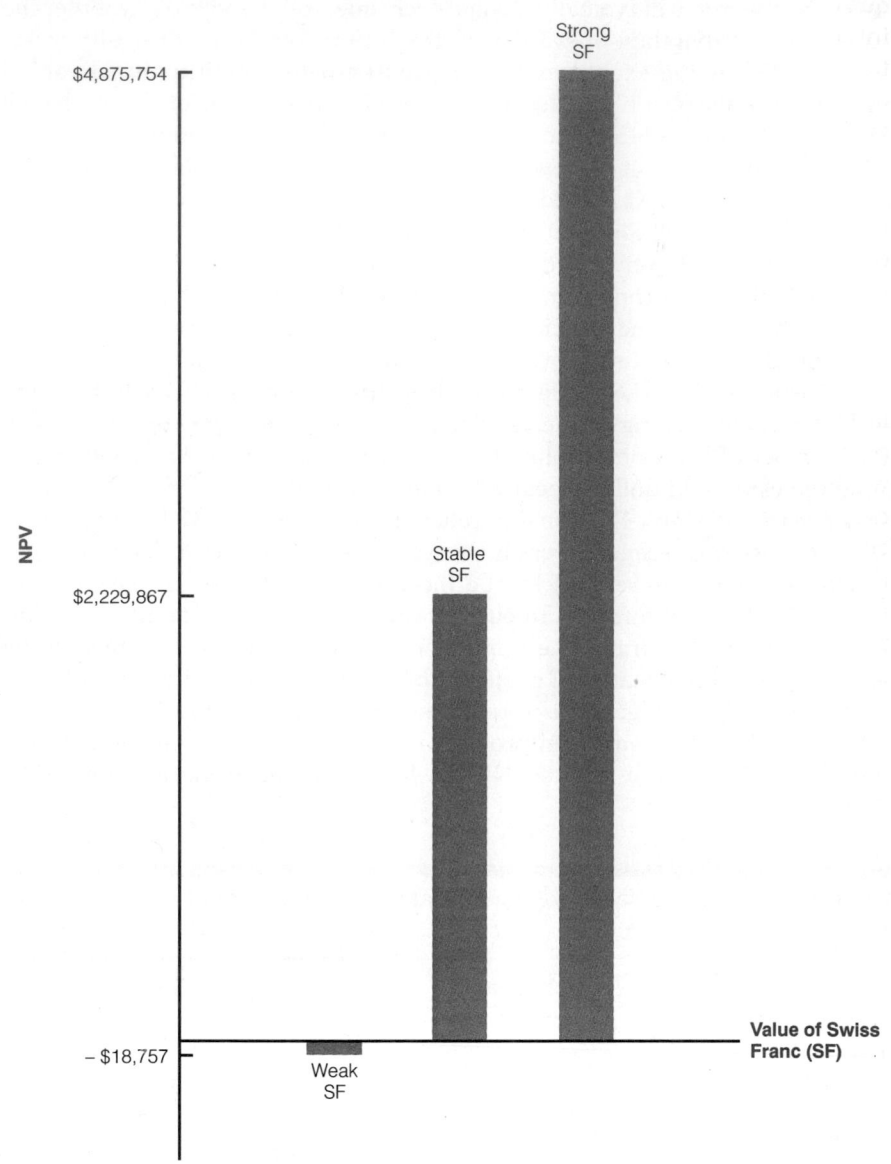

strengthen and lowest if it is expected to weaken. The estimated NPV is negative for the weak-franc scenario but positive for the stable-franc and strong-franc scenarios. Whether this project is truly feasible would depend on the probability distribution of these three scenarios for the franc during the project's lifetime. If there is a high probability that the weak-franc scenario will occur, this project should not be accepted.

Inflation

Our example implicitly considered inflation, since variable cost per unit and product prices were generally rising over time. However, inflation can be quite volatile from year to year in some countries and can therefore strongly influence a project's net cash flows. Inaccurate inflation forecasts could lead to inaccurate net cash flow forecasts. The inflation rate in many less developed countries may be 200 percent or more in any given year. It would be virtually impossible for any subsidiary in these countries to accurately forecast inflation each year.

While both costs and revenues should be affected in the same direction by inflation fluctuations, their magnitudes may be much different from each other. This is especially true when the project involves importing partially manufactured components and selling the finished product locally. The local economy's inflation will most likely have a stronger impact on revenues than costs in such cases.

The joint impact of inflation and exchange rate fluctuations on a subsidiary's net cash flows may produce a partial offsetting effect from the viewpoint of the parent. The exchange rates of highly inflated countries tend to weaken over time. Thus, even if subsidiary earnings are inflated, they will be deflated when converted into the parent's home currency (if the subsidiary's currency did weaken). Such an offsetting effect is not exact or consistent, though. Because inflation is only one of many factors that influence exchange rates, there is no guarantee a currency will depreciate when the local inflation rate is relatively high. Therefore, one cannot ignore the impact of inflation and exchange rates on net cash flows.

Even if relatively high inflation did cause a currency to weaken, the impact on net cash flows of a project would not necessarily be offsetting. Suppose an MNC's subsidiary in a highly inflated country generates highly inflated earnings and invests them in local securities for several years. If and when the inflation subsides and the local currency strengthens, the subsidiary could convert the accumulated earnings to the parent's home currency and send these funds to the parent. This example illustrates why MNCs cannot neglect the impact of inflation and/or exchange rates on cash flows.

Financing Arrangement

The value of a project can be determined by the manner by which it is financed, since the cost of financing may differ among sources. To illustrate, reconsider the example of Spartan Inc., in which the parent provided the funds needed for plant and equipment, while a Swiss bank provided a local loan to cover the SF10 million in working capital. If Spartan Inc. had provided the additional funds for working capital, the loan by the Swiss bank would not have been necessary. This alternative form of financing the project can also be assessed with a capital budgeting analysis. Much of the original analysis still applies; the changes are as follows:

1. Interest expense on the Swiss loan is avoided.
2. The initial investment by the parent is $15 million: $10 million for plant and equipment and $5 million to exchange for SF10 million needed as working capital.

3. Recall that the working capital was to be liquidated for SF10 million at the end of the project to pay off the SF10 million principal on the Swiss loan; if a loan did not exist, the SF10 million could be converted to dollars and sent to the parent when the project is terminated; assume that these funds are not subject to a withholding tax.

The capital budgeting analysis for Spartan Inc. under this revised financing strategy is shown in Exhibit 17.5. This analysis uses our original exchange rate projections of $.50 per Swiss franc for each period. The numbers that were directly affected by the revised financing arrangement are bracketed. Other numbers are also affected indirectly as a result. For example, the subsidiary's after-tax earnings increase as a result of avoiding interest payments. The NPV of the project under this alternative financing arrangement is positive, but less than the original arrangement. Thus, it appears that the original financing arrangement is more feasible for this project.

EXHIBIT 17.5 Capital Budgeting Analysis with an Alternative Financing Arrangement: Spartan Inc.

	Year 0	Year 1	Year 2	Year 3	Year 4
1. Demand		60,000	60,000	100,000	100,000
2. Price per unit		SF350	SF350	SF360	SF380
3. Total revenue = (1) × (2)		SF21,000,000	SF21,000,000	SF36,000,000	SF38,000,000
4. Variable cost per unit		SF200	SF200	SF250	SF260
5. Total variable cost = (1) × (4)		SF12,000,000	SF12,000,000	SF25,000,000	SF26,000,000
6. Fixed cost		SF1,000,000	SF1,000,000	SF1,000,000	SF1,000,000
7. Interest expense on Swiss loan		[SF 0]	[SF 0]	[SF 0]	[SF 0]
8. Noncash expense (depreciation)		SF2,000,000	SF2,000,000	SF2,000,000	SF2,000,000
9. Total expenses = (5) + (6) + (7) + (8)		SF15,000,000	SF15,000,000	SF28,000,000	SF29,000,000
10. Before-tax earnings of subsidiary = (3) − (9)		SF6,000,000	SF6,000,000	SF8,000,000	SF9,000,000
11. Host government tax (20%)		SF1,200,000	SF1,200,000	SF1,600,000	SF1,800,000
12. After-tax earnings of subsidiary		SF4,800,000	SF4,800,000	SF6,400,000	SF7,200,000
13. Net cash flow to subsidiary = (12) + (8)		SF6,800,000	SF6,800,000	SF8,400,000	SF9,200,000
14. SF remitted by subsidiary (100%)		SF6,800,000	SF6,800,000	SF8,400,000	SF9,200,000
15. Withholding tax imposed on remitted funds (10%)		SF680,000	SF680,000	SF840,000	SF920,000
16. SF remitted after withholding taxes		SF6,120,000	SF6,120,000	SF7,560,000	SF8,280,000
17. Salvage value					[SF22,000,000]
18. Exchange rate of SF		$.50	$.50	$.50	$.50
19. Cash flows to parent		$3,060,000	$3,060,000	$3,780,000	$15,140,000
20. PV of parent cash flows (15% discount rate)		$2,660,870	$2,313,780	$2,485,411	$8,656,344
21. Initial investment by parent	[$15,000,000]				
22. Cumulative NPV of cash flows		−$12,339,130	−$10,025,350	−$7,539,939	$1,116,405

The use of a Swiss loan for part of the financing is more feasible because the after-tax rate on the loan is less than the parent's required rate of return on funds provided to the subsidiary. Yet, if local loans had a relatively high interest rate, the use of local financing would not likely be as attractive.

The required rate of return to the parent is assumed to be the same for either financing arrangement. It could possibly differ under certain conditions. For example, if the use of Swiss financing rather than parent financing causes a higher reported degree of financial leverage on the consolidated financial statements, the required return of this financing arrangement could be higher. However, the use of Swiss financing allows a portion of the initial investment to be denominated in the same currency as the project's cash flows. Thus, the potential impact of exchange rate fluctuations on the NPV is reduced, from the parent's perspective. When the entire investment is financed by the parent, the present value of parent cash flows is more sensitive to exchange rate movements.

Blocked Funds

In some cases, the host country may block funds the subsidiary attempts to send to the parent. For example, some countries may require that earnings generated by the subsidiary be reinvested locally for at least three years before they can be remitted. This can possibly affect the accept/reject decision on a project. Reconsider the example of Spartan Inc., assuming that all funds are blocked until the subsidiary is sold. This forces the subsidiary to reinvest those funds until that time. Blocked funds penalize a project if the return on such reinvestment is less than the required rate of return on the project.

Assume that these funds are used to purchase marketable securities, that are expected to yield 5 percent annually, after taxes. A reevaluation of Spartan's cash flows (from Exhibit 17.2) to incorporate the blocked-funds restriction is shown in Exhibit 17.6. The withholding tax is not applied until the funds are remitted to the parent, which is in Year 4. The original exchange rate projections are used here. In addition, the risk of the project is greater, because the parent does not recover any funds until the project is terminated. Thus, all parent cash flows depend on the exchange rate four years from now.

The subsidiary may be able to better utilize blocked funds by repaying the local loan. For example, the SF6 million at the end of Year 1 could be used to reduce the outstanding loan balance rather than invest in marketable securities, assuming that the lending bank allows early repayment. The same is true for the SF6 million at the end of Year 2. The local loan could be paid off early, if permitted by the lending institution.

Remittance Provisions

An MNC parent may force a subsidiary to send a fixed percentage of earnings while retaining the remainder until the project is completed. This action can complicate the forecast of the amount of funds sent to the parent over time because it again requires a forecast of the return that can be earned on the funds that remain with the subsidiary.

EXHIBIT 17.6 Capital Budgeting with Blocked Funds: Spartan Inc.

	Year 0	Year 1	Year 2	Year 3	Year 4
Net cash flow to be remitted by subsidiary (excluding salvage value) before the withholding tax		SF6,000,000	SF6,000,000	SF7,600,000	SF8,400,000
					SF7,980,000
Net cash flow accumulated by reinvesting funds to be remitted					SF6,615,000
					SF6,945,750
					SF29,940,750
Withholding tax (10%)					SF2,994,075
Net cash flow to be remitted after the withholding tax (excluding salvage value)					SF26,946,675
Salvage value					SF12,000,000
Exchange rate					$.50
Cash flows to parent					$19,473,338
PV of parent cash flows (15% discount rate)					$11,133,944
Initial investment by parent	$10,000,000				
Cumulative NPV		−$10,000,000	−$10,000,000	−$10,000,000	$1,133,944

Uncertain Salvage Value

The salvage value of an MNC's project typically has a significant impact on the project's NPV. When the salvage value is uncertain, the MNC may desire to incorporate various possible outcomes for the salvage value and reestimate the NPV based on each possible outcome. It may even desire to estimate the **break-even salvage value,** (also called **break-even terminal value**), which is the salvage value necessary to achieve a zero NPV for the project. If the actual salvage value is expected to equal or exceed the break-even salvage value, the project would be feasible. The break-even salvage value (called SV_n) can be determined by setting NPV equal to zero and rearranging the capital budgeting equation, as follows:

$$NPV = -IO + \sum_{t=1}^{n} \frac{CF_t}{(1 + k)^t} + \frac{SV_n}{(1 + k)^n}$$

$$0 = -IO + \sum_{t=1}^{n} \frac{CF_t}{(1 + k)^t} + \frac{SV_n}{(1 + k)^n}$$

$$\left[IO - \sum_{t=1}^{n} \frac{CF_t}{(1 + k)^t} \right] = \frac{SV_n}{(1 + k)^n}$$

$$\left[IO - \sum_{t=1}^{n} \frac{CF_t}{(1 + k)^t} \right] (1 + k)^n = SV_n$$

To illustrate the use of break-even salvage value, reconsider the Spartan Inc. example and assume that Spartan was not guaranteed a price for the project. The break-even salvage value for that project can be determined by (1) estimating the present value of future cash flows (excluding the salvage value), (2) subtracting the discounted cash flows from the initial outlay, and (3) multiplying the difference times $(1 + k)^n$. Using the original cash flow information from Exhibit 17.2, the present value of cash flows can be determined:

$$\begin{aligned}
\text{PV of parent cash flows} &= \frac{\$2,700,000}{(1.15)^1} + \frac{\$2,700,000}{(1.15)^2} + \frac{\$3,420,000}{(1.15)^3} + \frac{\$3,780,000}{(1.15)^4} \\
&= \$2,347,826 + \$2,041,588 + \$2,248,706 + \$2,161,227 \\
&= \$8,799,347
\end{aligned}$$

Since the present value of parent cash flows (excluding salvage value) is $8,799,347, the project is only feasible if the present value of the salvage value is at least $1,200,653, as shown below:

$$\begin{aligned}
\text{Present value of break-even salvage value} &= \text{Initial outlay} - \text{Present value of cash flows (excluding salvage value)} \\
&= \$10,000,000 - \$8,799,347 \\
&= \$1,200,653
\end{aligned}$$

Given the present value of cash flows and the estimated initial outlay, the break-even salvage value is determined this way:

$$\begin{aligned}
SV_n &= \left[IO - \sum \frac{CF_t}{(1 + k)^t} \right] (1 + k)^n \\
&= [\$10,000,000 - \$8,799,347](1.15)^4 \\
&= \$2,099,950
\end{aligned}$$

Given the original information in Exhibit 17.2, Spartan Inc. would accept the project only if the salvage value was estimated to be at least $2,099,950 (assuming that the project's required rate of return was 15 percent).

Assuming the forecasted exchange rate of $.50 per Swiss franc (2 francs per dollar), the project must sell for more than SF4,199,900 (computed as $2,099,950 divided by $.50) to exhibit a positive NPV (assuming no taxes are paid on this amount). If Spartan did not have a guarantee from the Swiss government, it could assess the probability that the subsidiary would sell for more than the break-even salvage value and then incorporate this assessment in its decision to accept or reject the project.

Impact of Project on Prevailing Cash Flows

In our example, there was no presumed impact of the new project on prevailing cash flows. In reality, however, there may often be an impact. Reconsider the Spartan Inc. example, but assume (1) there is no concern about the Swiss government imposing trade restrictions on imported tennis rackets;

(2) Spartan Inc. still considers establishing a subsidiary in Switzerland because its production costs in Switzerland are expected to be lower than in the United States; and (3) without a subsidiary, Spartan's export business to Switzerland is expected to generate net cash flows of $1 million over the next four years. With a subsidiary, these cash flows would be foregone. The effects of these assumptions are shown in Exhibit 17.7. The previously estimated cash flows to the parent resulting from the subsidiary (drawn from Exhibit 17.2) are restated in Exhibit 17.7. These estimates do not account for foregone cash flows, since the export business is assumed to be prohibited in the future. However, if the export business were allowed to exist, the foregone cash flows attributable to this business would have to be considered, as shown in Exhibit 17.7. The adjusted cash flows to the parent account for the project's impact on prevailing cash flows.

The present value of adjusted cash flows and cumulative NPV are also shown in Exhibit 17.7. The project's NPV is now negative, as a result of the adverse effect on prevailing cash flows. Thus, the project would not be feasible if the exporting business to Switzerland could be established.

It should be mentioned that some foreign projects may have a favorable impact on prevailing cash flows. For example, if a manufacturer of computer components established a foreign subsidiary to manufacture computers, the subsidiary may order the components from the parent. In this case, the sales volume of the parent would increase. The establishment of the subsidiary would increase prevailing cash flows of the parent by the increased amount of revenues attributable to subsidiary orders, minus any expenses involved (on an after-tax basis).

Government Incentives

Some foreign projects proposed by MNCs would have a favorable impact on economic conditions in a host country, and would therefore be encouraged

EXHIBIT 17.7 Capital Budgeting When Prevailing Cash Flows Are Affected: Spartan Inc.

	Year 0	Year 1	Year 2	Year 3	Year 4
Cash flows to parent, ignoring impact on prevailing cash flows		$2,700,000	$2,700,000	$3,420,000	$9,780,000
Impact of project on prevailing cash flows		− $1,000,000	− $1,000,000	− $1,000,000	− $1,000,000
Cash flows to parent, incorporating impact on prevailing cash flows		$1,700,000	$1,700,000	$2,420,000	$8,780,000
PV of cash flows to parent (15% discount rate)		$1,478,261	$1,285,444	$1,591,189	$5,019,994
Initial investment	$10,000,000				
Cumulative NPV		− $8,521,739	− $7,236,295	− $5,645,106	− $625,112

by the host government. Any incentives offered by the host government must be incorporated within the capital budgeting analysis. For example, a low-rate host-government loan or a reduced tax rate offered to the subsidiary would enhance periodic cash flows. If the government subsidized the initial establishment of the subsidiary, the MNC's initial investment would be reduced.

Two types of government incentives may have different impacts on the parent, even if their effect on the subsidiary is similar. Consider a subsidiary in West Germany that has a choice of accepting a low-rate loan, or a tax break, either of which will save the subsidiary DM1 million per year. A tax break in West Germany reduces the tax credit to be granted by the U.S. government on remitted earnings to the parent. Thus, the reduced taxes in West Germany may be offset by higher taxes in the U.S. For this reason, the parent may benefit more from a low-rate loan than from a tax break.

Social Costs

Some projects require *social costs* in addition to the normal operational expenses. For example, Del Monte, a subsidiary of R.J. Reynolds, allocates about $340,000 a year on a social-responsibility program in the Phillipines, providing housing, education, and health care for laborers. Dole, a unit of Castle and Cooke Inc., allocates about $275,000 a year for similar social costs. These costs should be accounted for directly in the periodic cash flow estimates. To ignore them might result in an improper capital budgeting decision.

Threat of Expropriation

There are other forms of country risk that can also be assessed by determining what the project's NPV would be if certain events were to occur. If an MNC anticipates the possibility that the host government will be overthrown, and that all private companies will be acquired by the new government in three years, for example, it should estimate the NPV over that time horizon.

DIVESTITURE ANALYSIS

Even after an MNC's accept/reject decisions are made, they should be reassessed at various times. Some foreign projects that were rejected may become acceptable as a result of a reduction in the MNC's cost of capital, increased host-government incentives, improved economic conditions in the host country, or more favorable projections of exchange rates. Foreign projects that have been implemented must be assessed to determine whether they should be continued or divested.

To illustrate how an MNC might reevaluate a project after it has been implemented, reconsider the example in which Spartan Inc. proposed a Swiss subsidiary. Assume that the project is implemented, and after two years, the spot rate of the Swiss franc is $.46. In addition, forecasts have been revised for the remaining two years of the project, indicating that the Swiss franc should be worth $.44 in Year 3 and $.40 in the project's final year. Because these forecasts have an adverse effect on the project, Spartan Inc.

considers divesting the subsidiary. For simplicity, assume that the original forecasts of the other variables remain unchanged, and that a potential acquirer has offered SF13,000,000 for the subsidiary if the acquirer can assume the existing local loan and retain the existing working capital. Spartan can conduct a divestiture analysis by comparing the after-tax proceeds from the possible sale of the project (in terms of U.S. dollars) to the present value of expected dollar inflows that the project would have generated if it is not sold. This comparison will determine the net present value of the divestiture (NPV_d), as illustrated in Exhibit 17.8. Since the present value of foregone cash flows exceeds the price at which the project could be sold, NPV_d is negative. Thus, the project should not be divested.

Some existing projects that seem profitable when analyzed separately can actually reduce the value of the MNC overall. For example, several U.S.-based corporations had subsidiaries in South Africa in the mid 1980s that appeared to be profitable. Yet, the presence of some of these corporations in South Africa caused reduced cash flows within the United States (due to the boycotting of products, etc.). Numerous U.S. corporations have divested their South African subsidiaries. Some, including Exxon Corporation, General Motors Corporation, IBM, and Fluor Corporation, have sold their South African subsidiaries to employee trusts, where the laborers share in some of the profits and equity. These trusts relieve pressure on the corporations from consumer groups but still allow the corporations to benefit by selling products or technology to them.

Many divestitures occur as a result of a revised assessment of industry or economic conditions. For example, numerous U.S. commercial banks divested foreign subsidiaries when they realized there was not enough business

EXHIBIT 17.8 Divestiture Analysis: Spartan Inc.

	End of Year 2 (Today)	End of Year 3 (One Year from Today)	End of Year 4 (Two Years from Today)
SF remitted after withholding taxes		SF6,840,000	SF19,560,000
Selling price	SF13,000,000		
Exchange rate	$.46	$.44	$.40
Cash flow received from divestiture	$ 5,980,000		
Cash flows foregone due to divestiture		$ 3,009,600	$ 7,824,000
PV of foregone cash flows (15% discount rate)		$ 2,617,044	$ 5,916,068

NPV_d $5,980,000 − ($2,617,044 + $5,916,068)
    = $5,980,000 − $8,533,112
    = − $2,553,112

in the foreign markets to make the investment worthwhile. Warner-Lambert Company divested its Argentina operations in 1989 as economic conditions deteriorated there. Johnson & Johnson divested some of its Latin American subsidiaries in 1990 for the same reason.

INTERNATIONAL ACQUISITIONS

International acquisitions of firms are similar to other international projects in that they require an initial outlay and are expected to generate cash flows whose present value will exceed the initial outlay. Numerous U.S.-based MNCs, including Rockwell International, Ford Motor Co., Scott Paper Co., Borden Inc., and Dow Chemical Co. have recently engaged in international acquisitions. Many more international acquisitions are taking place in Europe now in response to the more uniform standards throughout Western Europe and momentum for free enterprise in Eastern Europe.

Capital budgeting analysis can be used to determine whether a firm should be acquired. The net present value of a company from the acquiring firm's perspective (NPV_a) is

$$NPV_a = -IO_a + \sum_{t=1}^{n} \frac{CF_{a,t}}{(1 + k)^t} + \frac{SV_a}{(1 + k)^n}$$

where

IO_a = initial outlay needed by the acquiring firm to acquire the company

$CF_{a,t}$ = cash flow to be generated by the company for the acquiring firm

k = required rate of return on the acquisition of the company

SV_a = salvage value of the company (expected selling price of the company at a point in the future)

n = time at which the company will be sold.

The capital budgeting analysis of a foreign acquisition must account for the exchange rate of concern. For example, consider a U.S.-based MNC that assesses the acquisition of a foreign company. The dollar initial outlay ($IO_{U.S.}$) needed by the U.S. firm is determined by the acquisition price in foreign currency units IO_f and the spot rate of the foreign currency (S):

$$IO_{U.S.} = IO_f(S)$$

The dollar amount of cash flows to the U.S. firm is determined by the foreign currency cash flows ($CF_{f,t}$) per period remitted to the United States and the spot rate at that time (S_t):

$$CF_{a,t} = (CF_{f,t})S_t$$

This ignores any withholding taxes or blocked-funds restrictions imposed by the host government, or any income taxes imposed by the U.S. government. The dollar amount of salvage value to the U.S. firm is determined by the salvage value in foreign-currency units (SV_f) and the spot rate at that time (period n) when it is converted to dollars (S_n):

$$SV_a = SV_f S_n$$

The net present value of a foreign takeover prospect can be derived by substituting the equalities just described in the previous capital budgeting equation:

$$NPV_a = -IO_a + \sum_{t=1}^{n} \frac{CF_{a,t}}{(1 + k)^t} + \frac{SV_a}{(1 + k)^n}$$

$$= -(IO_f)S + \sum_{t=1}^{n} \frac{(CF_{f,t})S_t}{(1 + k)^t} + \frac{SV_f S_n}{(1 + k)^n}$$

This equation was simplified by ignoring blocked funds and tax considerations.

Factors Considered in International Acquisitions

Several factors must be considered when assessing a possible international acquisition, including

- Exchange rate movements
- Required return of acquiring firms
- Ability to use financial leverage
- Accounting and tax laws
- Country barriers

Each of these factors is discussed.

EXCHANGE RATE MOVEMENTS.   The preceding equation suggests how existing and anticipated exchange rates affect the NPV of a foreign target:

- The lower the existing spot rate (S) is, the lower the price to be paid by the acquiring firm for the company, other things being equal.
- The higher the future spot rates are over each period (S_t), the higher the cash flows received by acquiring firm, other things being equal.
- The higher the spot rate is when the company is sold (S_n), the higher the salvage value from the acquiring firm's perspective, other things equal.

This discussion suggests that the ideal time to purchase a foreign company is when the spot rate of that company's currency is perceived to be very low and is expected to rise over time. Of course, estimates for the foreign initial outlay, foreign cash flows, and foreign salvage value also affect the NPV to be generated by the target. These other factors are also relevant to potential acquiring firms that reside in the same country as the target. Such firms do not, however, need to account for the exchange rates in the manner described above. Consequently, potential acquiring firms from other countries may perceive a company to have a much higher or lower value than local potential acquiring firms. If the company's currency is expected to appreciate (depreciate) against other currencies in the future, potential acquiring firms in other countries would likely value the company higher (lower) today than potential acquirers based in the company's country.

A recent study by Vasconcellos, Madura, and Kish confirmed that international merger activity is influenced by exchange rate movements. After controlling for other factors, the difference between the British acquisitions of U.S. firms and U.S. acquisitions of British firms was positively associated with the strength of the British pound. That is, a relatively strong pound tended to encourage British acquisitions of U.S. firms, but discourage U.S. acquisitions of British firms. A relatively weak pound had the opposite effect.

REQUIRED RETURN OF ACQUIRING FIRMS. Another factor that affects the potential value of an acquisition is the required rate of return for the acquiring firm. Since the cost of capital varies among countries (as explained in the following chapter), so does the required rate of return. Thus, firms in some countries may find acquisitions more attractive than firms in other countries.

ABILITY TO USE FINANCIAL LEVERAGE. Firms commonly finance a portion of international acquisitions with borrowed funds. Firms in some countries have more flexibility to borrow, because investors and creditors in those countries are more receptive to higher degrees of financial leverage (as discussed in the following chapter). Those firms that have greater flexibility to borrow may be more successful in completing international acquisitions. Firms in the United States tend to have less financial leverage than firms in other countries. If the U.S. firms attempted to fund an acquisition with a substantial amount of debt, they might be penalized. Their cost of the debt would increase as creditors commanded a high premium to compensate for the high risk. Consequently, the return required might be too high, so that some international acquisitions are not worthwhile.

ACCOUNTING AND TAX LAWS. Accounting and tax laws can create competitive advantages for acquiring firms in some countries. For example, in most industrialized countries, goodwill (the purchase price of the firm minus the tangible assets) resulting from an acquisition does not affect the acquiring firm's earnings. However, U.S. firms must amortize goodwill against earnings, without any tax deductions. The U.S.-based MNCs are adversely affected because future reported earnings are reduced without any tax benefits. Since share prices of firms are somewhat influenced by earnings, the perceived value of the acquiring firm is adversely affected by the tax provision. Even with this disparity in accounting and tax laws, U.S. firms may benefit from foreign acquisitions. However, foreign firms subject to more favorable accounting and tax provisions may be able to bid higher prices for target firms.

COUNTRY BARRIERS. Explicit and implicit barriers imposed by country governments do not necessarily offer advantages to specific acquiring firms, but instead prevent or discourage the acquisitions of particular targets. For

RELATED RESEARCH

Market Reaction to International Acquisitions

Some MNCs have acquired foreign firms in order to increase the value of their stock. The probable market reaction to foreign acquisitions can be assessed with a so-called event-study methodology. A brief explanation of the event-study methodology follows.

To determine how MNC share prices are affected, a sample of MNCs that acquired foreign firms must first be identified. Then the announcement date of each MNC's policy must be determined. The announcement date is more important than the date on which the policy was actually implemented, because investors would likely react immediately to the announcement if they react at all. Daily stock returns for each MNC in the sample are compiled for a period prior to their respective announcement dates (sometimes weekly observations are used instead). This so-called estimation period is used to estimate each MNC's beta with the following model:

$$R_{j,t} = b_0 + b_1 R_{m,t} + \mu_t$$

where

$R_{j,t}$ = the MNC's return over day t

$R_{m,t}$ = the market return over day t

b_0 = intercept

b_1 = estimated beta of the MNC

μ_t = error term

The length of the estimation period is somewhat subjective, but for our example, assume that it begins 120 days before the announcement date and ends 20 days before the announcement date. Then the expected return of each MNC is determined, based on the regression coefficients and the actual values of the market return. For example, assume that the examination period extended from 19 days before the announcement date until 40 days after the announcement date. The expected return for each observation over this period represents the return on the MNC's stock that should have occurred in the absence of any abnormal reaction by the market. By comparing the actual return to the bank's expected return, we can determine whether any abnormal return ($AR_{j,t}$) occurred for the MNC during observation t:

$$\begin{aligned} AR_{j,t} &= R_{j,t} - E(R_{j,t}) \\ &= R_{j,t} - (b_0 + b_1 R_{m,t}) \end{aligned}$$

The abnormal returns (sometimes called residuals) are estimated for each observation over the examination period. Positive abnormal returns suggest that the actual return is above what would have been expected in the absence of any market reaction and, therefore, that the market reacted favorably. Negative abnormal returns imply that the actual return was less than what would have been expected in the absence of any market reaction and, therefore, that the market reacted unfavorably. In some cases, an abnormal return will occur before the announcement date, which suggests that the market anticipated the news before it was officially announced. Since the examination period usually contains some observations prior to the announcement date, it is possible to detect such an anticipated reaction.

RELATED RESEARCH

The market reaction to an event for a single MNC is not normally considered to be sufficient for making general implications. For this reason, the procedure described here is replicated for all MNCs that had a similar announcement. For each observation within the examination period, the abnormal returns are consolidated among all MNCs to estimate an average abnormal return for the portfolio ($AR_{p,t}$):

$$AR_{p,t} = \sum_{j=1}^{n} AR_{j,t}/n$$

for all n MNCs that were examined. The average abnormal return is estimated over each day of the examination period, with specific emphasis around the announcement date. The abnormal returns starting on the first day of the examination period are accumulated over each successive day to determine cumulative average abnormal returns. Because the average ARs for any given observation could differ from zero by chance, they are tested to determine whether they are statistically significant (different from zero). This test provides greater reliability about any implications that are drawn from the analysis.

While firms expect to benefit from their acquisitions, investors do not always share this expectation. Many studies have found that investors either did not react or reacted negatively in response to announced acquisitions. The investor reaction is assessed by measuring the response of the acquiring firm's share price (after controlling for general market movements) surrounding the announcement. Since most of the studies performed on this topic focused on domestic acquisitions, the implications cannot be applied to international acquisitions. One recent study by Doukas and Travlos assessed the share price reaction of MNCs that engaged in international acquisitions and found that acquisitions in countries where the MNC already had existing operations produced no significant share price reaction, but acquisitions in countries where the MNC had no existing operations produced a significant favorable response. The authors suggest that investors react favorably only when the acquisition allows the MNC to branch into a new market. If the acquisition is in a market where the MNC is already established, no additional benefits are perceived by investors. The authors also determined that the share price reaction was more favorable when the acquisition was in a country that was less developed than the United States. In addition, they found some evidence that the investors reacted more favorably when the firm acquired was in a different industry than the acquiring MNC. This may imply that investors perceive both geographical *and* product diversification benefits from this type of acquisition.

SOURCE: John Doukas and Nickolaos G. Travlos, "The Effect of Corporate Multinationalism on Shareholders' Wealth: Evidence from International Acquisitions," *Journal of Finance* (December 1988), pp. 1161–1175.

example **hostile takeovers** (acquisitions not desired by the target firm) are outlawed or strongly discouraged by governments in most countries. They are tolerated in the United States more than in other countries. Thus, a foreign firm may be able to acquire a U.S. firm through a hostile takeover, but a U.S. firm will probably not be able to acquire non-U.S. firms in this manner.

All countries have one or more agencies that monitor mergers and acquisitions. The acquisition activity in any given country is somewhat influenced by the regulations enforced by these agencies. For example, in France, the Treasury can reject any deal if the acquirer is based outside the European Economic Community. It may also reject a deal if the target is in some closely monitored industries, such as defense or health care. The Monopolies Commission of France also reviews acquisitions to prevent any combined firms from controlling more than 25 percent of an industry or from severely reducing competition.

Acquisitions in Japan are reviewed by the Fair Trade Commission, while acquisitions in West Germany are examined by the Antitrust Authority, and acquisitions in the United Kingdom are reviewed by several regulatory agencies. Acquisitions in the United States are also reviewed by several agencies, including the Securities and Exchange Commission, which regulates the conduct of acquisitions, and the Justice Department and Federal Trade Commission, which analyze the potential impact on competition.

Explicit and implicit barriers to even friendly acquisitions can vary among countries. At one extreme, the U.S. government has allowed even hostile takeovers (unless they violate antitrust laws) while Japan has historically discouraged all acquisitions. While formidable barriers to Japanese markets still remain, some U.S. and European MNCs have acquired Japanese firms. In recent years, U.S.-based MNCs such as Corning Glass Works, Data General, Eastman Kodak, and Motorola have acquired Japanese firms. The Japanese government is more receptive to acquisitions than it was in the past, as long as the Japanese target firm is agreeable.

An implicit barrier to international acquisitions in some countries is the "red tape" involved, such as procedure and documentation requirements. An acquiring firm is subject to a different set of requirements in each country. Therefore, it has been difficult for a firm to become proficient at the process unless it concentrates on international acquisitions within a single foreign country. The current efforts to make regulations uniform across Europe will simplify the paperwork involved in acquisitions of European firms.

Trends in International Acquisitions

Exhibits 17.9 and 17.10 compare the volume and value of cross-border acquisitions involving U.S. firms. While both types of acquisitions have increased over time, U.S. firms are acquired by non-U.S. firms more than they acquire them. The difference is partially attributed to some of the factors just described. U.S. firms that attempt to acquire non-U.S. firms tend to have less flexibility to borrow and are subject to less favorable tax laws and more stringent country barriers. Potential opportunities in the United States may also explain why U.S. firms have been acquired by non-U.S. firms more than they acquire them. However, this trend may change as European firms become the primary targets in response to the more uniform regulations across European countries and the momentum for free enterprise in Eastern Europe.

EXHIBIT 17.9   Trends in International Acquisitions

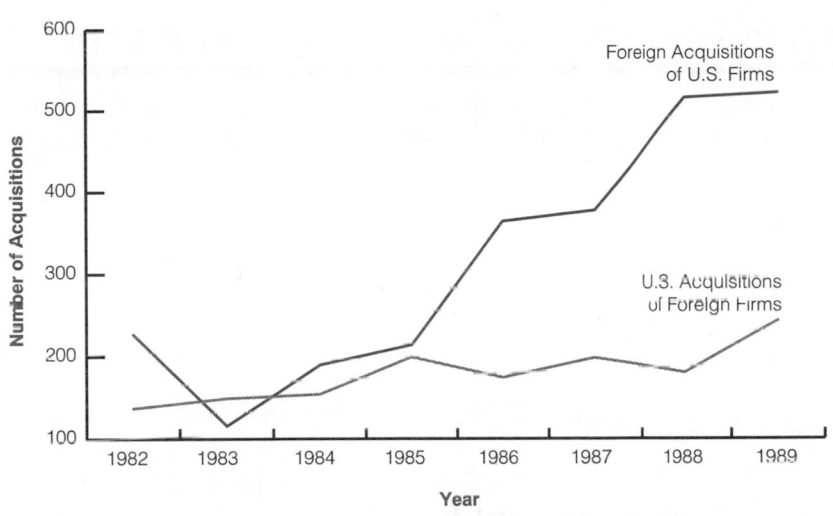

SOURCE: *Mergers & Acquisitions* (May–June 1990).

EXHIBIT 17.10   Value of International Acquisitions

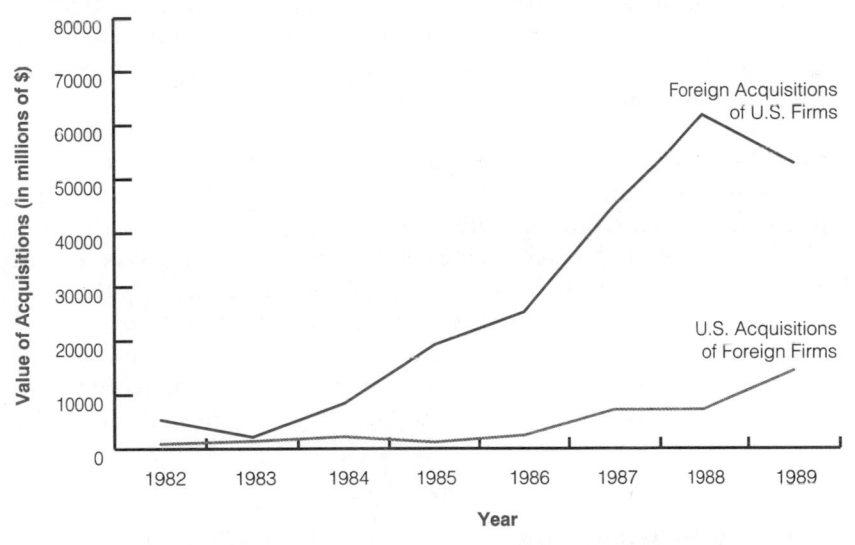

SOURCE: *Mergers & Acquisitions* (May–June) 1990.

Exhibit 17.10 compares the values of U.S. acquisitions of foreign firms to foreign acquisitions of U.S. firms. The value of foreign acquisitions of U.S. firms was consistently higher throughout the 1980s. The difference was especially pronounced in the 1987–1989 period, when the dollar was significantly weaker than in the mid-1980s. In 1989, 158 (30 percent) of the foreign acquisitions of U.S. firms were by British firms. Canadian firms were acquired by U.S. firms more than firms from any other foreign country.

ADJUSTING PROJECT ASSESSMENT FOR RISK

If an MNC is unsure of the projected demand, price per unit, etc., it needs to incorporate an adjustment for this risk. Five common methods used for adjusting the evaluation for risk are:

- Risk-adjusted discount rate
- Certainty equivalents
- Payback period
- Sensitivity analysis
- Simulation

Each method is described in turn.

Risk-Adjusted Discount Rate

The greater the uncertainty about a project's forecasted cash flows, the larger should be the discount rate applied to cash flows, other things being equal. This risk-adjusted discount rate tends to reduce the worth of a project by a degree that reflects the risk the project exhibits. This approach is easy to use, but it is criticized for being somewhat arbitrary. In addition, an equal adjustment to the discount rate over all periods does not reflect differences in the degree of uncertainty from one period to another. If the projected cash flows among periods have different degrees of uncertainty, the risk adjustment of the cash flows should vary also.

Consider a country whose political situation is slowly destabilizing. The probability of blocked funds, expropriation, etc., will increase over time. Thus, cash flows sent to the parent are less certain in the distant future as opposed to the near future. A different discount rate should therefore be applied to each period in accordance with its corresponding risk. Even so, it will be a subjective adjustment that may not accurately reflect the risk.

Despite its subjectivity, the risk-adjusted discount rate is a commonly used technique—perhaps because of the ease with which one can arbitrarily adjust it. In addition, there is no alternative technique that will perfectly adjust for risk, although there are some (discussed next) that in certain cases may better reflect a project's risk.

Certainty Equivalents

Each set of projected cash flows could be multiplied by a **certainty equivalent** (CE) value between zero and 1.00. The assigned value should reflect the degree of uncertainty of the cash flows. If the firm would be just as satisfied obtaining 70 percent of the projected cash flows with certainty, then it would assign the first-period cash flows a CE value of .7. The greater the uncertainty of a given period's cash flows, the less the assigned value would be. If more distant cash flows are less certain than those in the near future, the more distant cash flows could be assigned lower CEs. Because each period's cash flows would be multiplied by CEs (whose values are less than 1.00), the projected cash flows are

INTERNATIONAL FINANCIAL MANAGEMENT IN PRACTICE

Attitudes About the Payback Period for Foreign Projects

A 1989 survey of chief executive officers (CEOs) suggests some differences in attitudes about foreign projects across geographical regions. CEOs were asked what their payback period has been when investing abroad. The average of responses for each group of CEOs is disclosed below:

CEOs from:	Average Payback Period
United States and Canada	4.3 Years
Pacific Rim	5.0
Europe	5.1
Japan	6.6

To assess the attitude about future projects, CEOs were asked if they were willing to accept projects with a longer payback. The percent of respondents in each group that replied yes is disclosed next:

CEOs from:	Percentage of Respondents Willing to Extend Payback Period
United States and Canada	32%
Pacific Rim	42
Europe	49
Japan	63

The comparative responses across groups to the two questions suggest that U.S. CEOs are more short-run oriented than other CEOs, while Japanese CEOs are long-run oriented. The disparity in attitudes may be the result of disparity in shareholder attitudes. U.S. shareholders tend to have a short-run perspective when investing in stocks, while Japanese investors are long-run oriented.

SOURCE: *The Wall Street Journal,* September 22, 1989, p. R1.

reduced to reflect their risk. The degree of reduction is greater for the periods representing greater uncertainty since their CEs will be lower.

Within a single period, some cash flows may be more uncertain than others. For this reason, it may sometimes be appropriate to apply a CE that reflects a weighted average of CEs appropriate for all particular types of cash flow during that period.

The CE approach is valuable in that it can account for the varied degrees of uncertainty of cash flows among periods, or even among the specific projected cash flows within each individual period. Yet, it suffers from a major limitation. There is no precise formula available for assigning a CE value. Cash flows assessed by one firm to deserve a .7 CE value may be assessed by another firm to deserve a .6 CE value. The assigned CE value is an arbitrary decision.

Payback Period

The **payback period** defines an acceptable period during which the initial investment of a project must be recovered. If the accumulated net cash flows

INTERNATIONAL FINANCIAL MANAGEMENT IN PRACTICE

Multinational Capital Budgeting in the Real World

Surveys have been conducted on MNCs to identify how they practice capital budgeting. A brief review of survey results will determine whether actual practice of multinational capital budgeting coincides with the theory described in this chapter. A 1983 survey by Kim, Farragher, and Crick suggests that traditional capital budgeting techniques (such as NPV analysis or internal rate of return) are popular even for international projects. However, it was surprising to find that the payback method is commonly used. Twelve percent of U.S.-based MNCs and 31 percent of the non-U.S. based MNCs use it. Perhaps the payback method is preferred for projects where the probability of a host-government takeover is relatively high. Under such circumstances, recovering the initial outlay as quickly as possible becomes a critical objective. The survey found that more than 90 percent of MNCs adjust foreign projects for their individual levels of risk, although the ways in which they adjust vary.

Another survey by Stanley and Block inquired about the MNCs' estimation of cost of capital within the capital budgeting process. With regard to assessing projects of subsidiaries, the study found that 49 percent of the MNCs used the parent's cost of capital, 32 percent used the subsidiary's cost of capital, and some MNCs used both types. These results suggest that MNCs in some cases are considering the cost of obtaining funds locally rather than considering the MNC parent's cost.

Of those MNCs that consider using foreign funds for financing, 34 percent consider expected changes in the foreign currency value when calculating the cost of foreign debt. This percentage may seem lower than expected. Perhaps firms are unsure about which way exchange rates will move; incorporating exchange rate projections could increase the error in a capital budgeting estimate. Alternatively, some financing in foreign currency can be paid back with foreign earnings received by subsidiaries. In this case there would be less concern about possible exchange rate variations.

during this specified period are expected to be less than the initial investment, the project must be rejected. If they are expected to exceed the initial investment, the project may be given serious consideration. Projects that exhibit greater risk may be assigned a shorter acceptable payback period. For example, a firm considering a project in a historically violent country may require a shorter expected payback period in order to accept the project. The longer the project continues in such a country, the greater the possibility of problems such as a takeover by the government or its people.

The payback method has some limitations, such as not fully accounting for cash flows in all periods and not discounting cash flows to present value. However, it can serve as a criterion to forecast the length of time by which a project will recover its initial investment. If the expected payback period of a project will be longer than the length of acceptable time to be operating in the specific country, the project proposal may be turned down, even if its NPV is

INTERNATIONAL FINANCIAL MANAGEMENT IN PRACTICE

With regard to the perspective from which capital budgeting should be assessed, the survey found that 52 percent of the firms evaluated projects from either the parent's perspective or a combination of parent and subsidiary perspective. The remaining 48 percent of firms evaluated projects specifically from the perspective of the subsidiary involved in the project. It was suggested earlier in the chapter that projects should be viewed from the parent's perspective if shareholders desire to maximize firm value. While 48 percent of the firms in this survey did not follow this procedure, there is an increasing tendency toward consideration of the overall MNC (based on comparison with earlier surveys on multinational capital budgeting). Firms that are not considering the parent's perspective could be criticized, since what is feasible for subsidiaries will not necessarily be feasible for the parent (because currency conversion, parent's country taxes, etc., do not affect cash flow to the subsidiary). Perhaps those subsidiaries that retain most or all of their earnings are not concerned with cash flow from the parent's perspective. Even though the cash may someday be sent back to the parent, such subsidiaries are fully using their net cash inflows. The anticipated time

at which cash will be sent to the parent may be so far ahead (maybe 10 to 25 years in the future), that it would be impossible to accurately forecast values of those variables (such as parent-country taxes and exchange rates) that affect parent cash flows. Consequently, the best the subsidiary can do is assess the project from its own perspective.

Some of the questions within the major surveys discussed here overlapped to a degree. Since their survey sample groups differed, the results do not perfectly coincide. The results reported here are somewhat representative of the surveys.

The main purpose of providing survey results here is to illustrate that there are no unanimous solutions to issues in multinational capital budgeting. The MNCs analyze project characteristics differently. This does not mean that some MNCs are using an incorrect approach. The difference in analysis is most likely due to different backgrounds (industries, locations, etc.) and types of projects. The differences make multinational capital budgeting very challenging, since the appropriate approaches to implement may depend on the specific situation and type of firm involved.

positive. Should the expected payback period be within the acceptable time frame, the project could then be assessed by other means to determine if it is feasible.

While the payback criteria could possibly help screen projects with excessive exposure to forced takeovers, it may not necessarily be able to adjust project valuation for more mild forms of risk. For example, how does one adjust the acceptable payback period for a project whose net cash flows exhibit a moderate degree of uncertainty? Due to this and other previously mentioned limitations, the payback method by itself is not adequate for multinational capital budgeting.

Sensitivity Analysis

Once the MNC has estimated the NPV of a proposed project, it may want to consider alternative estimates to its input variables. For example, demand for the Spartan subsidiary's tennis rackets (in our earlier example) was estimated to be 60,000 in the first two years and 100,000 in the next two years. If demand were 60,000 in all four years, how would that change the NPV results? Alternatively, what if demand were 100,000 in all four years? Use of such *what-if* scenarios is referred to as **sensitivity analysis.** The objective is to determine how sensitive the NPV is to alternative values of the input variables. The estimates of any input variables can be revised to create a new estimate for NPV. If the NPV is consistently positive during these revisions, then the MNC should become more comfortable with the project. If in many cases it is negative, the accept/reject decision for the project becomes more difficult.

The two exchange rate scenarios developed earlier represent a form of sensitivity analysis. The advantage of sensitivity analysis over the use of simple point estimates is that it has less chance of being inaccurate, since it reassesses the project based on various circumstances that may occur. A variety of computer software packages is available to perform sensitivity analysis.

Simulation

Simulation can be used for a variety of tasks, including the generation of a probability distribution for NPV based on a range of possible values for one or more input variables. Simulation is typically performed with the aid of a computer package. To illustrate how it can be applied to multinational capital budgeting, reconsider Spartan Inc., and assume that it expects the exchange rate to depreciate by 3 to 7 percent per year (with an equal probability of all values between this range occurring). Unlike a single point estimate, simulation can consider the entire distribution of possibilities for the franc's exchange rate at the end of each year. It considers all point estimates for the other variables and randomly picks one of the possible values of the franc's depreciation level for each of the four years. Based on this random selection process, the NPV is determined. The procedure just described represents one iteration. Then the process is repeated where the franc's depreciation for each year is again randomly selected (within the range of possibilities assumed earlier). Again, the NPV of the project if these exchange rate fluctuations actually occurred is computed. We now have two iterations. The simulation program may be run for, say, 100 iterations. This means that 100 different possible scenarios are created for the possible exchange rates of the franc during the four-year project period. For example, Iteration no. 1 may have randomly selected a 6 percent depreciation at the end of Year 1; 7 percent at the end of Year 2; 5 percent at the end of Year 3; and 4 percent at the end of Year 4. Iteration no. 2 may have randomly selected a 5 percent depreciation at the end of Year 1; 7 percent at the end of Year 2; etc. Each iteration reflects a different scenario. The NPV of the project based on each scenario is then computed. Thus, simulation generates a distribution of NPVs for the project. The major advantage of simulation is that the MNC can examine the range of possible NPVs that may occur. From the information, it can determine the probability that the NPV will be positive, or greater than a particular level. The greater the uncertainty of the exchange rate, the greater will be the uncertainty of the NPV. The risk of a project will be greater if it involves the transaction of more volatile currencies, other things being equal.

Our example presumed we knew the values of all input variables except the percentage change in the franc. This was intentionally done to show how simulation can be applied. In reality, many or all of the input variables necessary for multinational capital budgeting may be uncertain in the future. Recall that the demand was assumed to be 60,000 in the first year. An MNC can more realistically forecast demand to be within some range (such as between 55,000 and 65,000) for each particular year. The range can vary with each year. Probability distributions could also be developed for all other variables with uncertain future values. Then simulation can be run, accounting for the probability distribution of each input variable. In this case, the simulation program randomly selects one value from the distribution of values for each input variable, and then determines the NPV of the project based on those values. Then it repeats the selection process, each time generating an estimated NPV. The final result is a distribution of possible NPVs that might occur for the project. Of course, only one NPV will actually occur during the life of the project, but we do not know which it will be. Thus, the best we can do is assess the range of possibilities. While a point estimate conveniently forecasts the NPV of a project, this estimate might be wrong. The simulation technique does not put all of its emphasis on any one particular NPV forecast, but instead provides a distribution of the possible outcomes that may occur.

If an MNC is comparing two mutually exclusive projects, simulation can be a useful technique for comparison. It would first require ranges of estimates for the input variables, and from these ranges it would generate a distribution of possible NPVs. Each project would exhibit its own distribution of NPVs. Exhibit 17.11 compares the distribution of NPVs for two projects. In this figure, Project A has a lower mean estimate for NPV than Project B. Yet, Project B has a greater dispersion of possible NPV values. The probability of

---

EXHIBIT 17.11 Comparison of Projects According to Probability Distributions

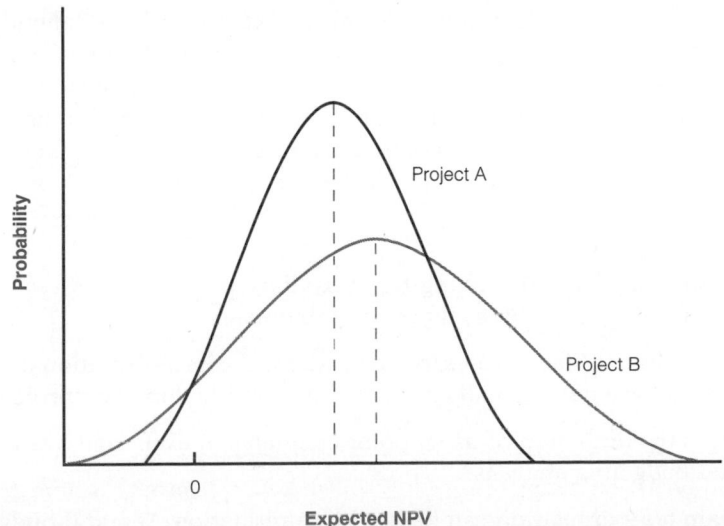

Project B generating a negative NPV is higher than for Project A. Consequently, some MNCs may prefer Project A to Project B even though its mean expected NPV is less. If a point estimate for each input variable were provided instead of a range of estimates, the MNC would not be able to develop a distribution of NPVs. Without this distribution, it might not recognize the higher risk of Project B.

Simulation is difficult to do manually because of the iterations necessary to develop a distribution of NPVs. Yet, computer programs can run 100 iterations and generate results within a matter of seconds. The user of a simulation program must provide the probability distributions for the input variables that will affect the project's NPV. Like any model, the accuracy of results generated by simulation will be determined by the accuracy of the input.

SUMMARY

Several factors influence the multinational capital budgeting decision. Some of the most relevant factors are summarized below:

■ It is normally appropriate for an MNC's parent to assess the project from its perspective rather than a subsidiary's perspective when determining whether the project should be undertaken.
■ A foreign project normally is more beneficial to the parent when the foreign currency appreciates over the life of the project.
■ The impact of exchange rate movements on cash flows to the parent tends to be greater when the parent provides most or all of the investment, and less when the foreign project is financed with debt from the host country.
■ Blocked funds have a greater adverse impact on a foreign project when the investment opportunities in the foreign country are limited.
■ If foreign projects affect prevailing cash flows, this should be accounted for in deciding whether the project is feasible.

An international acquisition is similar to other foreign projects in that it normally involves an initial outlay with expectations of cash flows that will arrive over time. Country-specific regulations on acquisitions need to be considered when estimating future cash flows.

Since most foreign projects involve some uncertainty, the capital budgeting process should attempt to account for the uncertainty. Some of the more common ways to account for uncertainty include the risk-adjusted discount rate, sensitivity analysis, and simulation. Foreign projects tend to have more uncertainty than domestic projects because of country-specific factors that can influence the cash flows of a foreign project.

QUESTIONS/ PROBLEMS

1. Why should capital budgeting for subsidiary projects be assessed from the parent's perspective? Present your arguments.

2. What additional factors deserve consideration in multinational capital budgeting that are not normally relevant for a purely domestic project?

3. What is the limitation of using point estimates of exchange rates within the capital budgeting analysis?

4. Explain how simulation can be used in multinational capital budgeting.

5. Why is simulation applicable to multinational capital budgeting? What can it do that other risk-adjustment techniques cannot?

6. List the various techniques for adjusting risk in multinational capital budgeting. Describe any advantages or disadvantages of each technique.

7. Project X has an NPV estimated by your employees to be $1.2 million. Your employees state in their report that they did not account for risk, but with such a large NPV, the project should be accepted since even a risk-adjusted NPV would likely be positive. You have the final decision as to whether to accept or reject the project. What is your decision?

8. Describe in general terms how future appreciation of the German mark will likely affect the value (from the parent's perspective) of a project established in West Germany today by a U.S.-based MNC. Will the sensitivity of the project value be affected by the percentage of earnings remitted to the parent each year?

9. Repeat Question 8, assuming future depreciation of the German mark.

10. Explain how the financing decision can influence the sensitivity of NPV to exchange rate forecasts.

11. Wolverine Corporation presently has no existing business in West Germany but is considering the establishment of a subsidiary there. The following information has been gathered to assess this project:
■ The initial investment required is DM50 million. Given the existing spot rate of $.50 per mark, the initial investment in dollars is $25 million. In addition to the DM50 million initial investment on plant and equipment, DM20 million is needed for working capital and will be borrowed from a German bank. Wolverine will pay interest only on the loan each year, at an interest rate of 14 percent. The loan principal is to be paid in 10 years.
■ The project will be terminated at the end of Year 3, when the subsidiary will be sold.
■ The price, demand, and variable cost of the product in West Germany are as follows:

Year	Price	Demand	Variable cost
1	DM500	40,000 units	DM30
2	DM511	50,000 units	DM35
3	DM530	60,000 units	DM40

■ The fixed costs, such as overhead expenses, are estimated to be DM6 million per year.
■ The exchange rate of the mark is expected to be $.52 at the end of Year 1, $.54 at the end of Year 2, and $.56 at the end of Year 3.
■ The West German government will impose an income tax of 30 percent on income. In addition, it will impose a withholding tax of 10 percent on earnings remitted by the subsidiary. The U.S. government will allow a tax credit on remitted earnings and will not impose any additional taxes.
■ All cash flows received by the subsidiary are to be sent to the parent at the end of each year. The subsidiary uses its working capital to support ongoing operations.

■ The plant and equipment are depreciated over 10 years using the straight-line depreciation method. Since the plant and equipment are initially valued at DM50 million, the annual depreciation expense is DM5 million.

■ In three years, the subsidiary is to be sold. Wolverine plans to let the acquiring firm assume the existing German loan. The working capital will not be liquidated, but will be used by the acquiring firm. Wolverine expects to receive DM52 million after subtracting capital gains taxes when it sells the subsidiary. Assume that this amount is not subject to a withholding tax.

■ Wolverine requires a 20 percent rate of return on this project.

a) Determine the net present value of this project. Should Wolverine accept this project?

b) Assume that Wolverine also considers an alternate financing arrangement in which it invests an additional $10 million to cover the working capital requirements, and avoids the German loan. If this arrangement is used, the selling price of the subsidiary (after subtracting any capital gains taxes) is expected to be DM18 million higher. Is this alternative financing arrangement more feasible than the original proposed arrangement? Explain.

c) Would the NPV of this project be more sensitive to exchange rate movements if Wolverine used German financing to cover the working capital or invested more of its own funds to cover the working capital? Explain.

d) Assume Wolverine uses the original proposed financing arrangement and that funds are blocked until the subsidiary is sold. The funds to be remitted are reinvested at a rate of 6 percent (after taxes) until the end of Year 3. How is the project's NPV affected?

e) What is the break-even salvage value of this project, if Wolverine Corporation uses the original proposed financing arrangement and funds are not blocked?

f) Assume that Wolverine decides to implement the project, using the original proposed financing arrangement. Also assume that after one year, a German firm offers Wolverine a price of $27 million after taxes for the subsidiary, and that Wolverine's original forecasts for Years 2 and 3 have not changed. Should Wolverine divest the subsidiary? Explain.

12. Huskie Industries, a U.S.-based MNC, considers purchasing a small German manufacturing company that sells products only within West Germany. Huskie has no other existing business in West Germany and no cash flows in German marks. Would the proposed acquisition likely be more feasible if the mark is expected to appreciate or depreciate over the long run? Explain.

13. When Walt Disney World considered establishing a theme park in France, were the forecasted revenues and costs associated with the French park sufficient to assess the feasibility of this project? Were there any other "relevant cash flows" that deserved to be considered?

14. Athens Inc. established a subsidiary in the United Kingdom that was independent of its operations in the United States. The subsidiary's performance was well above what was expected. Consequently, when a British firm approached Athens Inc. about the possibility of acquiring it, Athens' chief financial officer implied that the subsidiary was performing so well that it was not for sale. Comment on this strategy.

15. Lehigh Company established a subsidiary in Switzerland that was performing below the cash flow projections developed before the subsidiary was established. Lehigh anticipated that future cash flows would also be lower than the original cash flow projections. Consequently, Lehigh decided to inform several potential acquiring firms of its plan to sell the subsidiary. Lehigh then received a few bids. Even the highest bid was very low, but Lehigh accepted the offer. It justified its decision by stating that any existing project whose cash flows are not sufficient to recover the initial investment should be divested. Comment on this statement.

16. Flagstaff Corporation is a U.S.-based firm with a subsidiary in Mexico. It plans to reinvest its earnings in Mexico in government securities for the next ten years since the interest rate earned on these securities is so high. Then, after ten years, it will remit all accumulated earnings to the United States. What is a drawback of using this approach? (Assume the securities have no default or interest rate risk.)

17. Colorado Springs Company (based in the United States) plans to divest either its West German or Canadian subsidiary. Assume that if exchange rates stayed constant, the dollar cash flows each of these subsidiaries provided to the parent over time would be somewhat similar. However, the firm expects the German mark to depreciate against the U.S. dollar, and the Canadian dollar to appreciate against the U.S. dollar. The firm can sell either subsidiary for about the same price today. Which one should it sell?

18. San Gabriel Corporation recently considered divesting its Italian subsidiary, and determined that the divestiture was not feasible. The required rate of return on this subsidiary was 17 percent. In the last week its required return on that subsidiary increased to 21 percent. If the sales price of the subsidiary has not changed, explain why the divestiture may now be feasible.

19. Ventura Corporation is a U.S.-based MNC which plans to establish a subsidiary in France. It is very confident that the French franc will appreciate against the dollar over time. The subsidiary will retain only enough revenues to cover expenses and will remit the rest to the parent each year. Would Ventura benefit more from exchange rate effects if its parent provided equity financing for the subsidiary, or if the subsidiary were financed by local banks in France? Explain.

20. Santa Monica Company is a U.S.-based MNC that was considering establishing a consumer products division in West Germany, which would be financed by German banks. It completed its capital budgeting analysis in August 1989. Then, in November 1989, there was evidence of possible reunification between East and West Germany. In response, it increased its expected cash flows by 20 percent and did not adjust the discount rate applied to the project. Why might the discount rate be affected by reunification?

21. Assume a less developed country called LDC removes its barriers to encourage direct foreign investment (DFI) in order to reduce its unemployment rate, presently at 15 percent. Also assume that several MNCs are likely to consider DFI in LDC. The inflation rate in recent years has averaged 4 percent. The hourly wage in LDC for manufacturing is the equivalent of about $5 per hour. As Piedmont Company developed cash flow forecasts to

perform a capital budgeting analysis for a project in LDC, it assumed a wage rate of $5 in Year 1, and applied a 4 percent increase to each of the next ten years. The components produced are to be exported to its headquarters in the United States, where they will be used in the production of computers. Do you think Piedmont will overestimate or underestimate the net present value of this project? Why? (Assume that LDC's currency is tied to the dollar and will remain that way.)

North Star Company
Capital Budgeting

This case is intended to illustrate how the value of an international project is sensitive to various types of input. It also is intended to show how a computer spreadsheet format can facilitate capital budgeting decisions that involve uncertainty.

This case can be performed using LOTUS 1-2-3. The following present value factors may be helpful input in Lotus for discounting cash flows:

Years From Now	Present Value Interest Factor at 18%
1	.8475
2	.7182
3	.6086
4	.5158
5	.4371
6	.3704

For consistency in discussion of this case, you should develop your computer spreadsheet in a somewhat similar format as in the Capital Budgeting chapter with each year representing a column across the top. The use of a computer spreadsheet will significantly reduce the time needed to complete this case.

North Star Company considered establishing a subsidiary to capitalize on the removal of Eastern European border restrictions. The subsidiary would manufacture clothing in West Germany and target the Eastern European countries for most of its business. Its sales would be invoiced in German marks (DM). It has forecasted that the net cash flows to the subsidiary as follows:

Year	Net Cash Flows To Subsidiary
1	DM 8,000,000
2	10,000,000
3	14,000,000
4	16,000,000
5	16,000,000
6	16,000,000

These cash flows do not include financing costs (interest expenses) on any funds borrowed in West Germany. North Star Company also expects to receive DM30 million after taxes as a result of selling the subsidiary at the end of Year 6. Assume there will not be any withholding taxes imposed on this amount.

The exchange rate of the mark is forecasted below based on three possible scenarios of economic conditions:

End of Year	Scenario I: Somewhat Stable Mark	Scenario II: Weak Mark	Scenario III: Strong Mark
1	.50	.49	.52
2	.51	.46	.55
3	.48	.45	.59
4	.50	.43	.64
5	.52	.43	.67
6	.48	.41	.71

The probability of each scenario is shown below:

	Somewhat Stable Mark	Weak Mark	Strong Mark
Probability	60%	30%	10%

Fifty percent of the net cash flows to the subsidiary would be remitted to the parent, while the remaining fifty percent would be reinvested to support ongoing operations at the subsidiary. North Star Company anticipates a 10 percent withholding tax on funds remitted to the United States.

The initial investment (including investment in working capital) by North Star in the subsidiary would be DM40 million. Any investment in working capital (such as accounts receivable, inventory, etc.) is to be assumed by the buyer in Year 6. The expected salvage value has already accounted for this transfer of working capital to the buyer in Year 6. The initial investment could be financed completely by the parent ($20 million converted at the present exchange rate of $.50 per mark to achieve DM40 million). North Star Company will only go forward with its intentions to build the subsidiary if it expects to achieve a return on its capital of 18 percent or more.

The parent is considering an alternative financing arrangement. With this arrangement, the parent would provide $10 million (DM20 million), which means that the subsidiary would need to borrow DM20 million. Under this scenario, the subsidiary would obtain a 20-year loan and pay interest on the loan each year. The after-tax interest payments are DM1.6 million per year. In addition, the forecasted proceeds to be received from selling the subsidiary (after taxes) at the end of 6 years would be DM20 million (the forecast of proceeds is revised downward here because the equity investment of the subsidiary is less; the buyer would be assuming more debt if part of the initial investment in the subsidiary is supported by local bank loans). Assume the parent's required rate of return would still be 18 percent.

a) Which of the two financing arrangements would you recommend for the parent? Assess the forecasted NPV for each exchange rate scenario to compare the two financing arrangements and substantiate your recommendation.

b) In the previous question, an alternative financing arrangement of partial financing by the subsidiary was considered with an assumption that the required rate of return by the parent would not be affected. Is there any reason why the parent's required rate of return may increase when using this financing arrangement? Explain. How would you revise the analysis in the previous question under this situation? (This question requires discussion, not analysis).

c) The political situation regarding the reunification of East and West Germany could influence the net cash flows to the subsidiary. The estimates already provided were based on existing conditions. However, West Germany may consider increasing its withholding tax on all foreign subsidiaries that do much business with East Germany to 20% (from the initial rate of 10%). This extra tax is designed to help fund West Germany's efforts to develop East Germany's economy. Would you recommend that North Star Co. establish the subsidiary even if the withholding tax was 20 percent?

d) Assume that there is some concern about the economic conditions in West Germany which could cause a reduction in the net cash flows to the subsidiary. Explain how LOTUS could be used to re-evaluate the project based on alternative cash flow scenarios. That is, how can this form of country risk be incorporated in the capital budgeting decision? (This question requires discussion, not analysis).

e) Assume that North Star Company did implement the project, investing $10 million of its own funds, with the remainder borrowed by the subsidiary. Two years later, a U.S.-based corporation notifies North Star that it would like to purchase the subsidiary. Assume that the exchange rate forecasts for the somewhat stable scenario are appropriate for years 3 through 6. Also assume that the other information already provided on net cash flows, financing costs, the 10% withholding tax, the salvage value, and the parent's required rate of return is still appropriate. What would be the minimum dollar price (after taxes) that North Star should receive to divest the subsidiary? Substantiate your opinion.

PROJECT

1. Assume that your firm's British subsidiary was able to remit earnings of 400,000 pounds at the end of each year since 1975. Based on the exchange rate at about that time each year, determine the dollar cash flows.

Did this subsidiary contribute more to the parent in 1981–1985 or in 1986–1990? Repeat this analysis for your firm's Canadian subsidiary, which was able to remit C$800,000 at the end of each year since 1975. Was the difference in performance between the two five-year periods greater for the British subsidiary or the Canadian subsidiary? Why? Is the standard deviation of the dollar cash flows higher for the British subsidiary or the Canadian subsidiary? Why? What does this project tell you about the exchange rate risk of a Canadian project versus a British project (from a U.S. perspective)?

REFERENCES

Bavishi, Vinod B. "Capital Budgeting Practices at Multinationals." *Management Accounting* (August 1981), pp. 32–35.

Booth, Laurence D. "Capital Budgeting Frameworks for the Multinational Corporation." *Journal of International Business Studies* (Fall 1982), pp. 114–123.

Collins, J. Markham, and William S. Sekely. "The Relationship of Headquarters Country and Industry Classification to Financial Structure." *Financial Management* (Autumn 1983), pp. 45–51.

Kester, W. Carl. "Capital and Ownership Structure: A Comparison of United States and Japanese Manufacturing Corporations." *Financial Management* (Spring 1986), pp. 5–16.

Kim, Suk H., Edward J. Farragher, and Trevor Crick. "Foreign Capital Budgeting Practices Used by the U.S. and Non-U.S. Multinational Companies." *The Engineering Economist* (Spring 1984), pp. 207–215.

Lessard, Donald R. "Evaluating Foreign Projects: An Adjusted Present Value Approach." In *International Financial Management*, edited by D. R. Lessard. New York: John Wiley & Sons, 1985.

Madura, Jeff, and E. Theodore Veit. "Divestiture Analysis with and without Certainty." *Akron Business and Economic Review* (Winter 1987), pp. 8–17.

Mehra, Rajnish. "On the Financing and Investment Decisions of Multinational Firms in the Presence of Exchange Rate Risk." *Journal of Financial and Quantitative Analysis* (June 1978), pp. 227–244.

Oblak, David J., and Roy J. Helm, Jr. "Survey and Analysis of Capital Budgeting Methods Used by Multinationals." *Financial Management* (Winter 1981), pp. 34–41.

Shapiro, Alan C. "Exchange Rate Changes, Inflation, and the Value of the Multinational Corporation." *The Journal of Finance* (May 1975), pp. 485–507.

_____. "Capital Budgeting for the Multinational Corporation." *Financial Management* (Spring 1978), pp. 7–16.

_____. "Financial Structure and the Cost of Capital in the Multinational Corporation." *Journal of Financial and Quantitative Analysis* (June 1978), pp. 211–226.

Stanley, Margorie T., "Capital Structure and Cost of Capital for the Multinational Firm." *Journal of International Business Studies* (Spring–Summer 1981), pp. 103–120.

Stanley, Marjorie T., and Stanley B. Block. "A Survey of Multinational Capital Budgeting." *Financial Review* (March 1984), pp. 36–54.

_____. "An Empirical Study of Management and Financial Variables Influencing Capital Budgeting Decisions for Multinational Companies in the 1980s." *Management International Review* (November 1983), pp. 61–71.

Srinivasan, Venkat, and Yong H. Kim. "Integrating Corporate Strategy and Multinational Capital Budgeting: An Analytical Framework." *Recent Developments in International Banking and Finance* (1988), pp. 381–397.

Taggart, Robert A. "Capital Budgeting and the Financing Decision." *Financial Management* (Summer 1977), pp. 59–64.

CHAPTER 18

Multinational Capital Structure and the Cost of Capital

The cost of capital has a major impact on the firm's value. Given two firms with similar returns on their investments, the firm with the lower cost of capital will be valued higher because the residual to shareholders is greater. To the extent that a firm's capital structure (proportion of debt versus equity financing) influences its cost of capital, its capital structure decisions can affect its value. This chapter discusses capital structure and the cost of capital from an international perspective. First, capital structure theory is briefly summarized, with a discussion of related decisions peculiar to an MNC. Then reasons are offered for why the capital structure decisions of MNCs may differ from those of domestic firms. The characteristics of an MNC that affect its cost of capital are identified, followed by characteristics of countries that can affect an MNC's cost of capital.

CAPITAL STRUCTURE

The firm's cost of capital (referred to as k_c) can be measured as

$$k_c = \left(\frac{D}{D + E}\right)k_d(1 - t) + \left(\frac{E}{D + E}\right)k_e$$

where D is the amount of the firm's debt, k_d is the before-tax cost of its debt, t is the corporate tax rate, E is the equity of the firm, and k_e is the cost of financing with equity. These ratios reflect the percentage of capital represented by debt and equity respectively. The firm would like to construct the "optimal" capital structure that would represent the combination of debt and equity financing that minimizes the cost of capital (given the investments made or planned by the firm). While much research has attempted to identify the optimal capital structure for firms, there is no consensus. From a practical perspective, there is an advantage to using debt, since interest payments are tax deductible. However, the greater the use of debt, the greater the interest expense, and the higher the probability is that the firm will be unable to meet its expenses. Consequently, the rate of return required by potential new shareholders or creditors will increase to reflect the higher probability of bankruptcy.

The trade-off between debt's advantage (tax deductibility of interest payments) and disadvantage (increased bankruptcy probability) is illustrated in Exhibit 18.1. The firm's cost of capital is shown to initially decrease as the ratio of debt to total capital increases. However, after a point (labeled X in Exhibit 18.1), the cost of capital rises as the ratio of debt to total capital increases. This implies that it is favorable to increase the use of debt financing until the point at which the bankruptcy probability becomes large enough to offset the tax advantage of using debt. To go beyond that point would increase the firm's overall cost of capital.

The optimal capital structure that achieved this minimum cost of capital would vary with each firm's operating characteristics. Firms with more stable cash inflows would be able to handle larger periodic interest payments, and may therefore desire a capital structure with a relatively large proportion of debt.

"Global" versus "Local" Target Capital Structures

An MNC may deviate from its target capital structure in each country where financing is obtained, yet still achieve its target capital structure on a consolidated basis. The following examples of particular foreign country conditions illustrate the motive behind deviating from a local target capital structure while still satisfying a global target capital structure.

First, consider that Country A does not allow MNCs with headquarters elsewhere to list their stock on its local stock exchange. Under these conditions, an MNC would likely decide to borrow funds through bond issuance or bank loans rather than by issuing stock in this country. By being forced to use debt financing here, the MNC may deviate from its target capital structure, which could raise its overall cost of capital. It may offset this concentration in debt by using complete equity financing in some other host country that would allow the firm's stock to be listed on the local exchange.

EXHIBIT 18.1   Searching for the Appropriate Capital Structure

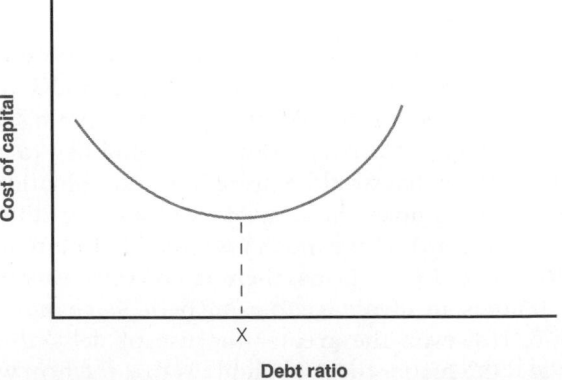

Debt ratio

Consider a second example in which Country B allows the MNC to issue stock there and list its stock on its local exchange. Also assume that the project to be implemented in that country will not generate net cash flows for five years. In this case, equity financing may be more appropriate. The MNC could issue stock, and by paying low or zero dividends, it could avoid any major cash outflows for the next five years. Alternatively, it could consider issuing zero-coupon bonds if the host country's tax laws do not discourage its investors from investing in such bonds.

As a third example, consider an MNC that desires financing in Country C, which is experiencing political turmoil. The use of local bank loans would be most appropriate, since local banks may be able to prevent the MNC's operations in that country from being affected by any political conditions. If the local banks are creditors, it is in their interest to assure that the MNC's operations are sufficiently profitable to repay its loans. These examples illustrate how the MNC's choice of debt versus equity financing may be influenced by country characteristics.

The ideal source of funds for each country will not necessarily sum to match the global target capital structure. However, the parent's mix of debt and equity financing in its own country (where it has the flexibility to use either type) may be adjusted to achieve the global target capital structure.

The strategy of ignoring a "local" target capital structure in favor of a "global" target capital structure is rational as long as it is acceptable by foreign creditors and investors. However, if foreign creditors and investors monitor the local capital structure, they may require a higher rate of return on funds provided to the MNC. For example, the "local" target capital structure for the subsidiary based in Country A (from the earlier example) and Country C is entirely debt (unless some equity investment was provided by the parent). Creditors in these two countries may penalize the MNC for its highly leveraged local capital structure, even though its global capital structure is more balanced, because they believe that the subsidiaries in their respective countries may be unable to meet the high debt repayment levels. Their concern is valid only if the subsidiary would not be rescued by the MNC's parent. If the parent plans to back the subsidiary, it could guarantee debt repayment to the creditors in the foreign countries, which might reduce the risk perception and lower the cost of the debt. Many MNC parents stand ready to financially back their subsidiaries, since if they did not, their other subsidiaries would have difficulty in obtaining future financing.

Wholly versus Partly Owned Subsidiaries

Up to this point, the discussion of capital structure has focused on the optimal mix of debt and equity financing. A related capital structure decision is whether the MNC's subsidiaries should be wholly owned by the parent or just partly owned. A major advantage of a wholly owned subsidiary is that it avoids a conflict of interests. Managers of a wholly owned subsidiary can focus on maximizing the wealth of the MNC shareholders. In the case of a partly owned subsidiary, managers are attempting to simultaneously satisfy majority shareholders of the MNC and outside shareholders of the foreign subsidiary. This results in a conflict of interests.

The conflict of interests is especially pronounced when the managers of a partly owned subsidiary are minority shareholders. These managers may make decisions that can benefit the subsidiary at the expense of the MNC overall. For example, they may use funds for projects that are feasible from their perspective but not from the parent's perspective.

Some countries will allow an MNC to establish a subsidiary there only if the subsidiary can sell shares. An MNC may be willing to tolerate a partly owned subsidiary to meet the host country requirements. In some cases, minority shareholders must maintain a minimum percentage of the capital. Thus, if the subsidiary attempts to expand, it may not be able to accept an equity investment from the parent if the investment causes the minority interest to fall below the minimum level.

One possible advantage of a partly owned subsidiary is that it may open up additional opportunities within the host country. The subsidiary's name may spread as a result of shares placed with minority shareholders in that country. In addition, a minority interest in a subsidiary by local investors may offer some protection against threats of any adverse actions by the host government. Minority shareholders benefit directly from a profitable subsidiary. Therefore, they could pressure their government to refrain from imposing excessive taxes, environmental constraints, or any other provisions that would reduce the profits of the subsidiary.

Capital Structure of MNCs versus Domestic Firms

Should the capital structure of MNCs differ systematically from purely domestic firms? That is, should MNCs carry a greater percentage of capital as compared to purely domestic firms? Or, should they obtain a greater percentage of funds from equity? There is no consensus on this issue since some characteristics of an MNC may favor a debt-intensive capital structure while other characteristics may favor an equity-intensive capital structure. The arguments are as follows.

A debt-intensive capital structure would favor a firm that has stable net cash inflows since it could readily make the interest payments on debt with these cash inflows. Because MNCs are often well diversified geographically, it can be argued they would have more stable cash flows. The thrust of the argument is that diversification reduces the impact of any single event on net cash flows. For MNCs with several subsidiaries, only a small portion of overall subsidiary expenses or sales should be adversely affected by a single event (such as a recession or crisis in any one country). Consequently, an MNC could handle a greater debt burden as a percentage of capital than could a purely domestic firm.

There are other characteristics of an MNC that might cause its cash flow to be more volatile than a purely domestic firm. For example, subsidiary earnings are subject to host-government tax rules that could change over time. Also, a host government could force the local subsidiaries to maintain all earnings within the country. In this event, the funds remitted to the MNC parent could be reduced, thereby destabilizing the net cash flow from the MNC parent's perspective. If the MNC parent does not receive cash inflows from its subsidiaries, it may not be able to make its periodic interest payments to creditors. For this reason, it could be argued that MNCs should generally maintain an equity-intensive capital structure.

A counterargument is that a well-diversified MNC would not be exposed to such a problem. That is, if subsidiaries are scattered around the world, actions by any particular host government will only affect the funds generated by subsidiaries in that government's country. Furthermore, if a portion of the MNC's borrowed funds is from each country where subsidiaries are based, the debt payments could be covered by subsidiaries, even if the host government prohibited funds from being remitted to the parent.

Because MNCs are affected by exchange rate variations, their net cash flows may be more unstable. For example, when the dollar strengthens, a U.S.-based MNC may generally prefer that its subsidiaries retain their earnings by reinvesting them in their respective countries. Foreign earnings will not be worth as much if converted into U.S. dollars while the dollar's value is so high. While the idea of stalling conversion of foreign earnings may seem logical, the MNC parent may need dollar inflows immediately to make its interest payments to creditors. If its capital structure is not debt-intensive, it will have more flexibility in allowing foreign earnings to remain overseas, since it may not need the funds immediately. Thus, an MNC could be better off with its capital structure made up mostly of equity.

Again, a counterargument to this reasoning can be proposed. If an MNC is well diversified among countries, then the subsidiary earnings are in a variety of currencies. Thus, the dollar's strengthening against one or a few currencies will not significantly reduce the total amount of dollars received by the U.S. headquarters after converting foreign earnings from various countries into dollars. The MNC could therefore maintain a debt-intensive capital structure even though it relies on foreign subsidiary earnings to make interest payments on its outstanding debt. This counterargument is dampened by the fact that although currencies do not move by the same magnitude against the U.S. dollar, they do tend to move in the same direction. Consider the 1981–1984 period, when the U.S. dollar strengthened substantially against most major currencies. Consequently, subsidiaries' earnings sent to the U.S. parents could have been greatly reduced (in dollar terms) due to a strong dollar, even if an MNC's operations were well diversified among several countries.

A recent study by Fatemi compared the degree of financial leverage of selected U.S.-based MNCs with at least 25 percent of their sales in foreign countries to a control group of U.S. domestic firms. He found that the MNCs had significantly lower financial leverage than the domestic firms. A related study by Lee and Kwok also found that MNCs had lower financial leverage, but that the results varied significantly among industries.

In summary, the capital structure decision should be made individually by each firm as it considers all characteristics that might affect its ability to make periodic interest payments on outstanding debt. MNCs that generate more stable net cash flows can maintain a larger portion of debt within their capital structure.

Comparison of Capital Structures across Countries

A comparison of debt-to-equity ratios is shown in Exhibit 18.2 for four countries. The debt is measured by its book value while the equity is measured by its market value. From this exhibit, it is clear that firms in Japan and West Germany use a much higher degree of financial leverage (on average) than firms in the United States or the United Kingdom. However, the probability of bankruptcy may generally be lower for MNCs in other countries, since their respective governments may rescue them. There are some situations

EXHIBIT 18.2   Debt-to-Equity Ratios across Countries

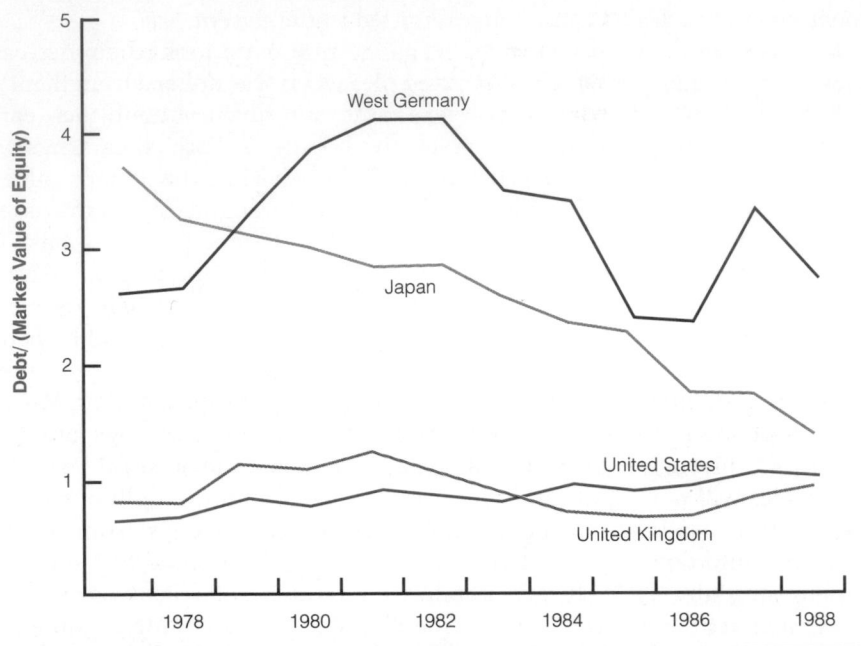

SOURCES: *FRBNY Quarterly Review* (Summer 1989), p. 13, Bank of Japan, Federal Reserve Board, U.K. Central Statistical Office, Organization for Economic Cooperation and Development, Japan Management and Coordination Agency, Tokyo Stock Exchange.

where a high degree of financial leverage is not necessarily perceived as risky. For example, Japanese companies tend to have greater degrees of financial leverage than comparable U.S. companies, but they are not perceived to have excessive risk because of potential backing from their government if they experience financial difficulties. Furthermore, other Japanese firms may offer assistance to a troubled company as well, such as allowing more lenient credit terms or providing favorable pricing. Because Japanese banks are sometimes not only creditors but also owners of a troubled Japanese company, they will attempt to rescue the company rather than force it into bankruptcy.

The higher degree of financial leverage will not necessarily be obvious from Japanese financial statements, because debt is typically reported as "short-term" rather than "long-term." Yet, this debt is commonly rolled over and represents a source of long-term funds.

Once a firm decides on its optimal capital structure, it can continue to maintain the percentage allocated to debt versus equity as it builds its capital to support new projects. However, the actual cost of capital on any new projects will not necessarily be the same as the firm's overall cost of capital, since each new project may exhibit a unique level of risk. For this reason, the firm cannot simply use a discount rate in capital budgeting on new projects that reflects the previous overall cost of capital to the firm. Instead, it must adjust for each new project's risk.

MNC CHARACTERISTICS THAT AFFECT THE COST OF CAPITAL

An MNC should use a discount rate in capital budgeting that reflects its cost of capital adjusted for the proposed project's risk. There are various factors related to an MNC that may affect its cost of capital, including

1. Size of the firm
2. Access to international capital markets
3. International diversification
4. Tax concessions
5. Exchange rate risk
6. Country risk

Each of these factors is discussed in turn.

1. *Size of firm.* MNCs that often borrow substantial amounts of funds may be given preferential treatment by creditors, thereby reducing their cost of capital. Furthermore, their relatively large issues of stocks or bonds allow for reduced flotation costs (as a percentage of the amount of financing). Yet, this is due to their size and not to their internationalized business. That is, a domestic corporation may be given the same treatment if it is large enough. However, a firm's growth is more restricted if it is not willing to operate internationally. Because MNCs may more easily achieve growth, they may be more able to reach the necessary size than purely domestic firms in order to receive preferential treatment from creditors.

2. *Access to international capital markets.* Multinational corporations are normally able to obtain funds through the international capital markets. If funds were completely mobile among countries, there might not be any advantage to such access. But, funds are not completely mobile in a global sense, which suggests the cost of funds can vary among markets. For this reason, the MNC's access to the international capital markets may allow it to attract funds at a lower cost than other domestic firms. In addition, subsidiaries may be able to obtain funds locally at a lower cost than the parent if the prevailing interest rates in the host country are relatively low. Such a form of financing can lower the cost of capital, and will not necessarily increase the MNC's exposure to exchange rate risk, since the revenues generated by the subsidiary will most likely be denominated in the same currency. In this case, the subsidiary is not relying on the parent for financing, although some centralized managerial support from the parent would most likely still exist.

3. *International diversification.* A firm's cost of capital is affected by the probability that it will go bankrupt. If a firm's cash inflows come from sources all over the world, there might be more stability in cash inflows. This reasoning is based on the premise that total sales would not be highly influenced by a single economy. To the extent that individual economies are independent of each other, net cash flows from a portfolio of subsidiaries should exhibit less variability, which may reduce the probability of bankruptcy and therefore reduce the cost of capital.

4. *Tax concessions.* An MNC's net income can be substantially influenced by the tax laws in the locations where it operates. Indeed, it may often choose locations that allow for favorable tax consequences. It may be able to capitalize on tax advantages not available to a purely domestic firm, which could reduce the cost of capital, since creditors and shareholders are most interested in *after-tax* cash flows.

5. *Exchange rate risk.* An MNC's cash flow could be more volatile than that of a domestic firm in the same industry if it is highly exposed to exchange rate risk. As stated earlier, if foreign earnings were remitted to the U.S. parent of an MNC, they would not be worth as much when the U.S. dollar is strong against major currencies. Thus, the capability of making interest payments on outstanding debt is reduced, and the probability of bankruptcy is higher. This could force creditors and shareholders to require a higher return, which increases the MNC's cost of capital.

A purely domestic firm's cash flows would not be directly affected by currency fluctuations. It still may be affected indirectly, though, since the competition from foreign firms may increase or decrease due to these fluctuations. It should be emphasized that exchange rate fluctuations will not always adversely affect cash flow. We can illustrate this by adjusting our previous example to assume a weak U.S. dollar. In this case, remitted foreign earnings would convert to a larger number of dollars and therefore improve the parent's cash flow. Overall, it is thought that a firm more exposed to exchange rate fluctuations would have a wider (more dispersed) distribution of possible cash flows in future periods. Since the cost of capital should reflect that possibility, and since the possibility of bankruptcy would be higher if the cash flow expectations are more uncertain, exposure to exchange rate fluctuations could lead to a higher cost of capital.

6. *Country risk.* An MNC that establishes foreign subsidiaries is subject to the possibility that the host-country government may seize the MNC's subsidiary assets. The probability of such an occurrence is influenced by many factors, including the attitude of the host country government and the industry of concern. If assets are seized and fair compensation is not provided, the probability of the MNC going bankrupt increases. The higher the percentage of an MNC's assets invested in foreign countries, and the higher the overall country risk of operating in these countries, the higher will be the MNC's probability of bankruptcy (and therefore cost of capital), other things being equal. There are other forms of country risk not as critical as a host-government takeover that could affect an MNC subsidiary's cash flows. These less critical types of risk (such as revised tax laws by host-country governments, etc.), are not necessarily incorporated within the cash flow projections, since there is no reason to believe they will arise. Yet, because there is a possibility of these events occurring, the capital budgeting process should incorporate such risk. For example, Exxon has much experience in assessing the feasibility of potential projects in foreign countries. If it detects a radical change in government or tax policy, it adds a premium to the required return of related projects. The size of the premium is determined by financial planners and political analysts.

Six factors that may distinguish between the cost of capital for an MNC versus a domestic firm in a particular industry have been assessed. In general, the first four listed factors (size, access to international capital markets, international diversification, and tax concessions) are favorable to an MNC's cost of capital, while exchange rate risk and country risk are unfavorable. The impact of each of these factors can vary with the specific characteristics of a firm. Thus, it is not possible to say with assurance that the favorable aspects will outweigh the unfavorable aspects, or vice versa.

COUNTRY CHARACTERISTICS THAT AFFECT THE COST OF CAPITAL

A key issue in assessing an MNC's cost of capital is financial market segmentation. If financial markets were completely segmented, the supply and demand conditions for funds in any country would be independent of those in all other countries. In this case, MNC decisions on where to obtain funds could have a significant influence on their cost of capital.

At the other extreme, if financial markets were not segmented in any way, and if all countries used the same currency, the nominal cost of funds would be the same in all countries. In this case, the MNC could not lower its cost of capital by switching its source of funds from one country to another.

In reality, the status of international financial markets is in between these two extremes. Some market imperfections such as tax differentials and foreign exchange controls create barriers between financial markets, so that the cost of funds will not be similar across countries. Thus, MNCs may be able to obtain funds at lower costs. However, exchange rate risk discourages firms from borrowing currencies that differ from the currencies to be received in the future as a result of ongoing operations. Nevertheless, there are ways in which MNCs can attempt to access low-cost funds. They may issue bonds in that country, or they may issue stock there and list their shares on the local stock market. These policies will require future interest payments on debt or dividend payments on the stock that are denominated in the foreign currency. To reduce exchange rate exposure, the MNCs could establish projects in these countries. The future cash flows from the projects could be used to cover interest payments on debt held by creditors or on dividends paid to local shareholders in that country. Essentially, this strategy suggests that the MNC would focus its expansion in countries where the cost of funds is relatively low. Of course, this strategy is rational only if the projects to be undertaken in these countries have a positive net present value.

Country Differences in the Cost of Debt

The cost of debt to a firm is primarily determined by the risk-free interest rate in the currency borrowed and the risk premium required by creditors. The cost of debt for firms in some countries is higher than in others because the corresponding risk-free rate is higher or because the risk premium is higher. Explanations for country differences in the risk-free rate and in the risk premium follow.

DIFFERENCES IN THE RISK-FREE RATE.   The risk-free rate is determined by the interaction of the supply and demand for funds. Any factors that influence the supply and/or demand will affect the risk-free rate. Some of the factors that have such an influence and vary among countries are tax laws, demographics, monetary policies, and economic conditions.

Tax laws in some countries offer more incentives to save than in others, which can influence the supply of savings and therefore interest rates. A country's corporate tax laws related to depreciation and investment tax credits can also affect interest rates through their influence on the corporate demand for funds.

The demographics of a country influence the supply of savings available and the amount of loanable funds demanded. Since demographics differ among countries, so will supply and demand conditions, and therefore nominal interest rates. Countries with younger populations are likely to experience higher interest rates, since younger households tend to save less and borrow more.

The monetary policy implemented by each country's central bank influences the supply of loanable funds and therefore interest rates. Countries that use a loose money policy (high money supply growth) may achieve lower nominal interest rates if they can maintain a low rate of inflation. Some theories suggest that a loose money policy will cause higher interest rates by raising inflationary expectations and the demand for loanable funds. The point here is that regardless of how a monetary policy affects interest rates, each central bank implements its own monetary policy, and this can cause differences in interest rates among countries.

Since economic conditions influence interest rates, they will also cause interest rates to vary across countries. The cost of debt in many less developed countries is much higher than in industrialized countries, primarily because of economic conditions. The high rate of expected inflation causes creditors to require a high risk-free interest rate.

DIFFERENCES IN THE RISK PREMIUM.   The risk premium on debt must be large enough to compensate creditors for the risk that the borrower is unable to meet its payment obligations. This risk can vary among countries because of country differences in economic conditions, relationships between corporations and creditors, government intervention, and degree of financial leverage.

If economic conditions in a particular country tend to be more stable, the risk of a recession is relatively low. Thus, the probability that a firm cannot meet its obligations would be lower, allowing for a lower risk premium.

Relationships between corporations and creditors are closer in some countries than in others. In Japan, creditors stand ready to extend credit in the event of a corporation's financial distress, which reduces the risk of illiquidity. The cost of a Japanese firm's financial problems may be shared in various ways by the firm's management, business customers, and consumers. Since the financial problems are not entirely borne by creditors, there is more motivation for all parties involved to see that the problems are resolved. Thus, there is less likelihood (for a given level of debt) that Japanese firms will go bankrupt, which implies a lower risk premium on the debt of Japanese firms.

Governments in some countries are more willing to intervene and rescue failing firms. For example, in the United Kingdom many firms are partially owned by the government. It may be in the best interests of the government to rescue firms that it partially owns. Even if the government is not a partial owner, it may provide direct subsidies or extend loans to failing firms. In the United States, government rescues are not as well received, since taxpayers prefer not to bear the cost of corporate mismanagement. While there has been some government intervention in the United States to protect particular industries, the probability that a failing firm would be rescued by the government is lower there than in other countries. Therefore, the risk premium on a given level of debt would be higher for U.S. firms than firms of other countries.

Firms in some countries have greater borrowing capacity because their creditors are more willing to tolerate a higher degree of financial leverage. For example, firms in Japan and West Germany have a higher degree of financial leverage than firms in the United States. If all other factors were equal, these high-leverage firms would have to pay a higher risk premium. However, all other factors are not equal. In fact, these firms are allowed to use a higher degree of financial leverage because of their unique relationships with the creditors and governments.

COMPARATIVE COSTS OF DEBT ACROSS COUNTRIES. The cost of debt trends for four countries are displayed in Exhibit 18.3. A comparison of the nominal cost of debt is shown in the top graph. There is some positive correlation between country cost-of-debt levels over time. The nominal cost of debt for firms in each country peaked in 1980, declined sharply in the early 1980s, and then leveled off during the late 1980s. It was consistently higher for firms in the United States and the United Kingdom than for firms in Japan and West Germany. This is mainly because of the higher risk-free rate in the United States and United Kingdom.

The middle graph of Exhibit 18.3 displays the real cost of debt, which is the nominal cost minus the inflation rate of the respective country. Even after inflation is subtracted, the cost of debt is generally higher for firms in the United States and the United Kingdom.

The lower graph of Exhibit 18.3 displays the real cost of debt after adjusting for allowable tax deductions in the respective countries. With these adjustments, the real costs of debt are more similar across countries.

While the middle and lower graphs offer additional insight, the top graph is most critical when assessing investment policies of firms from different countries. Since U.S. and British firms have a higher nominal cost of capital, they will be forced to decline projects that might be feasible for firms in Japan and West Germany. In addition, they may be more likely to divest existing projects because of the high cost associated with funding them. As an example, Lloyds Bank of the United Kingdom decided to sell its U.S. commercial bank operations in 1989. Its reason was that the returns were not adequate, and it could do just as well by investing the funds in British money markets. If the nominal cost of capital for British firms had been lower, Lloyds Bank might have retained this project.

Country Differences in the Cost of Equity

According to McCauley and Zimmer, a country's cost of equity can be estimated by first applying the price/earnings multiple to a given stream of earnings. Then adjustments can be made for the effects of a country's inflation, earnings growth, and other factors. Using some subjective adjustments by McCauley and Zimmer, the cost-of-equity trends for four countries are displayed in Exhibit 18.4. The cost of equity for firms in the United Kingdom

EXHIBIT 18.3 Cost-of-Debt Trends across Countries

The cost of debt is defined as the real after-tax interest rate faced by corporate borrowers. This measure is built up by starting with a weighted average of rates on bank and bond debt adjusted for differing propensities of firms to hold liquid assets,...

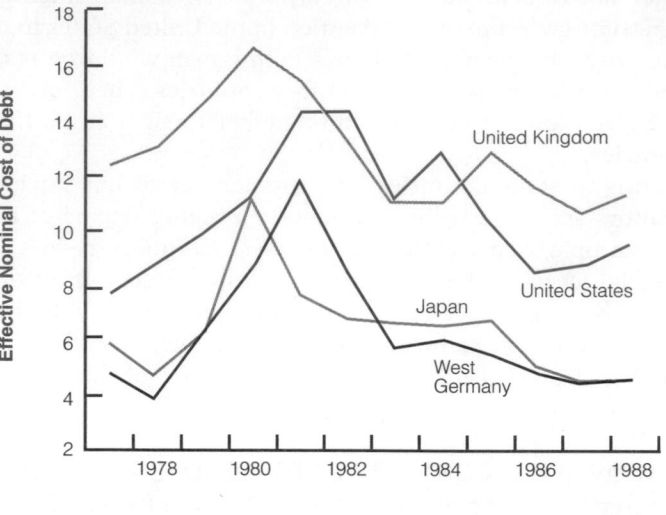

...then subtracting the actual inflation rate to produce a standard real rate of interest measure,...

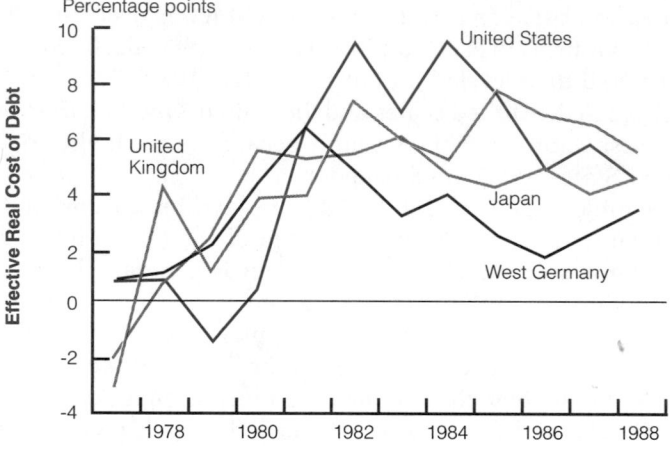

...and, finally, correcting for allowable tax deduction on corporate interest payments to place costs on a real after-tax basis.

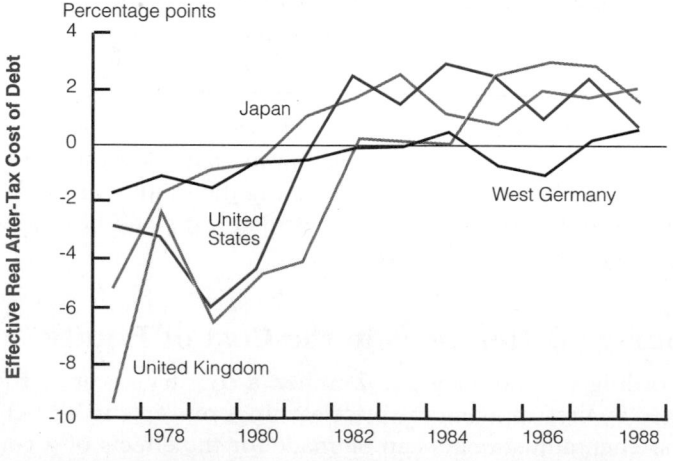

SOURCE: *FRBNY Quarterly Review,* Summer 1989, p. 10. This exhibit incorporates data from the following sources: Federal Reserve Board, U.K. Central Statistical Office, Deutsche Bundesbank, Bank of Japan, Japan Ministry of Finance, International Monetary Fund, Organization for Economic Cooperation and Development, Yamaichi Research Institute, Price Waterhouse, Statistical Office of the European Communities.

EXHIBIT 18.4 Cost-of-Equity Trends across Countries

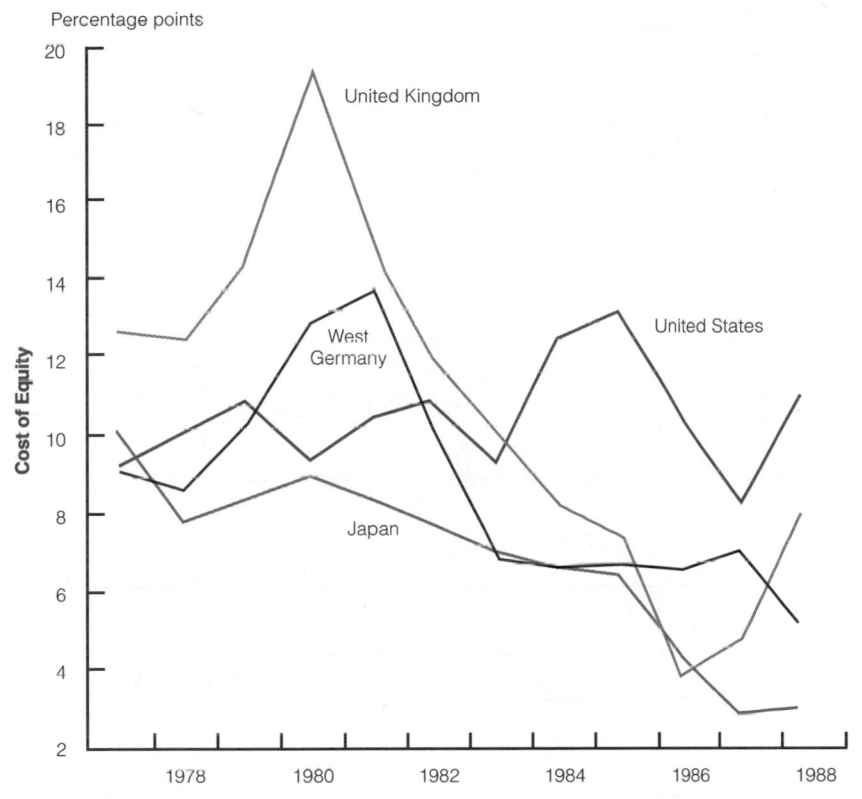

Percentage points

United Kingdom

United States

West Germany

Japan

Cost of Equity

1978   1980   1982   1984   1986   1988

SOURCES: *FRBNY Quarterly Review* (Summer 1989), p. 12; Federal Reserve Bank of New York staff estimates and data from Morgan Stanley Capital International.

was highest until 1983. Since then, the cost of equity for firms in the United States has been higher.

Combining the Costs of Debt and Equity

The costs of debt and equity can be combined to derive an overall cost of capital. The relative proportions of debt and equity used by firms in each country must be applied to reasonably estimate this cost of capital. In addition, another factor that influences a country's cost of capital is the tax value of investment tax credit and depreciation allowances (as explained by Mc-Cauley and Zimmer). After accounting for these tax considerations, the cost of capital for a twenty-year machine in the four countries is displayed in Exhibit 18.5. While there are some problems associated with measuring the cost of equity and the proportions of debt and equity used, the cost of capital shown in the exhibit should be a reasonable estimate for comparison purposes. Note that the cost of capital is consistently lower for firms in Japan and West Germany. This is not surprising, since firms in these countries have a lower cost of debt and equity than firms in the United States and the United Kingdom.

EXHIBIT 18.5   Cost-of-Capital Trends across Countries

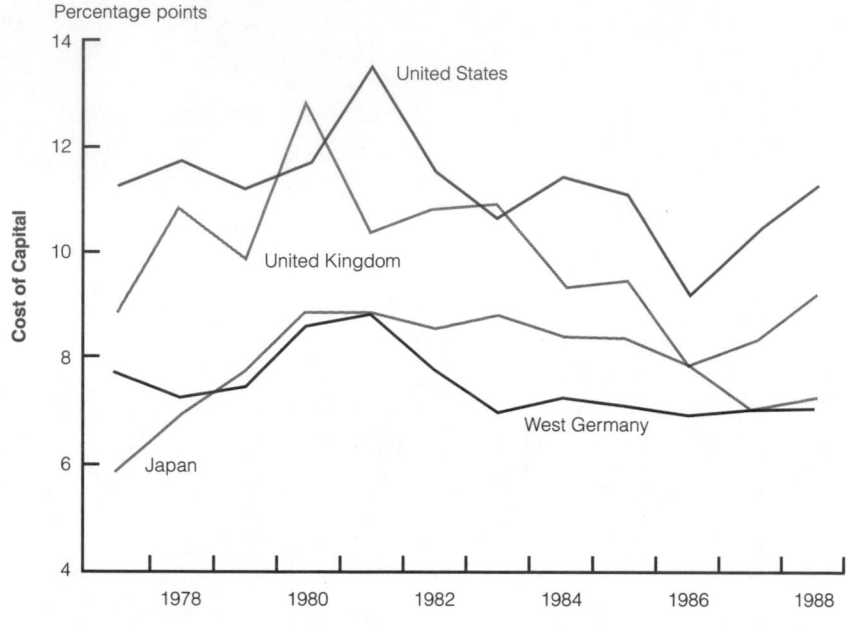

SOURCE: McCauley, Robert N. and Steven A. Zimmer, "Explaining International Differences in the Cost of Capital," Federal Reserve Bank of New York (Summer 1989); Federal Reserve Bank of New York staff estimates.

COST OF CAPITAL COMPARISON USING THE CAPITAL ASSET PRICING MODEL

To assess how required rates of return differ from purely domestic firms, the capital asset pricing model (CAPM) can be applied. It defines the required return (k_e) on a stock as

$$k_e = R_f + B(k_m - R_f)$$

where

$$R_f = \text{risk-free rate of return}$$
$$k_m = \text{market return}$$
$$B = \text{beta of stock}$$

The CAPM suggests that the required return on a firm's stock is a positive function of (1) the risk-free rate of interest, (2) the market rate of return, and (3) the stock's beta. The beta represents the sensitivity of the stock's returns to market returns (a stock index is normally used as a proxy for the market). An MNC has no control over the risk-free rate of interest or over the market returns but may be able to influence its beta. MNCs that increase their amount of foreign sales may be able to reduce their stock's beta and therefore reduce the return required by investors. In this way, they would reduce their cost of capital.

Advocates of the CAPM may suggest that a project's beta could be used to determine the required rate of return for that project. A project's beta represents the sensitivity of the project's cash flow to the firm's overall cash flow. A project whose cash flow is insulated from events that affect the firm's overall cash flow would exhibit a low beta.

For a well diversified MNC with cash flows generated by several projects, each project contains two types of risk: (1) unsystematic variability in cash flows unique to the firm and (2) systematic risk. Capital asset pricing theory suggests that the unsystematic risk of projects can be ignored, since it will be diversified away. However, systematic risk is not diversified away since all projects are similarly affected. The lower a project's beta, the lower is the project's systematic risk, and the lower would be the required rate of return for such a project. If projects of MNCs exhibit lower betas than projects of purely domestic firms, then the required rates of return on MNC projects should be lower. This translates into a lower overall cost of capital.

Capital asset pricing theory would most likely suggest the MNC cost of capital is generally less than that of domestic firms due to the reasoning just presented. It should be emphasized, though, that unsystematic project risk is considered to be relevant by some MNCs. And if it is also considered within the assessment of a project's risk, the required rate of return will not necessarily be less for MNC projects than projects of domestic firms. Thus, the issue remains unsettled.

In summary, we cannot say with certainty whether an MNC will have a lower cost of capital than a purely domestic firm in the same industry. However, we can use the previous discussion to understand why an MNC may attempt to take full advantage of the favorable aspects that reduce its cost of capital, while minimizing exposure to the unfavorable aspects that increase its cost of capital.

SUMMARY

Firms attempt to minimize the cost of the capital they obtain to support their business. MNCs may use "local" target capital structures for foreign subsidiaries that differ from their "global" target capital structure, since the availability of debt and equity financing varies across countries.

One of an MNC's capital structure decisions is whether subsidiaries should be wholly or partly owned by the parent. Wholly owned subsidiaries tend to avoid conflicts of interest, but partly owned subsidiaries may help protect against adverse actions by the host government.

An MNC's cost of capital may be lower than that of a domestic firm in the same industry because of its size advantage, access to international capital markets, ability to stabilize cash flows through international diversification, and tax concessions on foreign operations. However, its cost of capital may be adversely affected by exposure to exchange rate risk and country risk. Those MNCs that can capitalize on the aforementioned advantages while minimizing exposure to exchange rate risk and country risk are more likely to achieve a lower cost of capital.

There are significant differences in the cost of capital across countries. Japan and West Germany tend to have lower costs of capital than the United States and United Kingdom, primarily because their risk-free rates of interest are typically lower. MNCs may more seriously consider establishing projects in countries where the cost of capital is low, since these projects may be more likely to recover their respective costs of capital.

QUESTIONS

1. Create an argument for why an MNC might favor a debt-intensive capital structure.

2. Create an argument for why an MNC might favor an equity-intensive capital structure.

3. Do U.S.-based MNCs in general have a higher or lower degree of financial leverage than U.S. domestic firms (based on recent research)?

4. Describe general differences in the capital structure of firms based in the United States versus firms based in Japan. Offer an explanation for this difference.

5. Why might a firm use a "local" capital structure at a particular subsidiary that differs substantially from its "global" capital structure?

6. Explain how characteristics of MNCs can affect the cost of capital.

7. Explain why managers of a wholly owned subsidiary may be more likely to satisfy the shareholders of the MNC.

8. LaSalle Corporation is a U.S.-based MNC with subsidiaries in various less developed countries where stock markets are not well established. How can LaSalle still attempt to achieve its "global" target capital structure of 50 percent debt and 50 percent equity, even if it plans to use only debt financing for the subsidiaries in these countries.

9. Drexel Company is a U.S.-based company that is establishing a project in a politically unstable country. It is considering two possible sources of financing. Either the parent could provide most of the financing, or the subsidiary could be supported by local loans from banks in that country. Which financing alternative is most appropriate to protect the subsidiary?

10. Charleston Corporation has considered establishing a subsidiary in either West Germany or the United Kingdom. The subsidiary would be mostly financed with loans from the local banks in the host country chosen. It determined that the revenue generated from British subsidiary would be slightly more favorable than the revenue generated by the West German subsidiary, even after considering tax and exchange rate effects. The initial outlay is the same, and both countries appear to be politically stable. Charleston chose to establish the subsidiary in the United Kingdom because of the revenue advantage. Do you agree with its decision? Explain.

11. Fairfield Corporation, a U.S. firm, just established a subsidiary in a less developed country that consistently experiences an annual inflation rate of 80 percent or more. The country does not have a well established stock market, but loans by local banks are available with a 90 percent interest rate. Fairfield has decided to use a strategy in which the subsidiary is financed entirely with funds from the parent. It believes that in this way it can avoid the excessive interest rate in the host country. What is a key disadvantage of using this

strategy that may cause Fairfield to be no better off than if it paid the 90 percent interest rate?

12. Veer Company is a U.S.-based MNC that has most of its operations in Japan. Noticing that the Japanese companies with which it competes use more financial leverage, it has decided to adjust its financial leverage in line with theirs. In this way, it should reap more tax advantages with the heavy emphasis on debt. It believes that the market's perception of its risk will remain unchanged, since its financial leverage is still no higher than that of Japanese competitors. Comment on this.

Sabre Computer Corporation
Cost of Capital

Sabre Computer Corporation is a U.S.-based company that plans to participate in joint ventures in Mexico and in Germany. Each joint venture involves the development of a small subsidiary that helps produce computers. The main contribution of Sabre is the technology and a few key computer components used in the production process. The joint venture in Mexico specifies joint production of computers with a Mexican company owned by the government. The computers have already been ordered by educational institutions and government agencies throughout Mexico. Sabre has a contract to sell all the computers it produces in Mexico to these institutions and agencies at a price that is tied to inflation. Given the very high and volatile inflation levels in Mexico, Sabre wanted to assure that the contracted price would adjust to cover rising costs over time.

The venture will require a temporary transfer of several managers to Mexico, plus the manufacturing of key computer components in a leased Mexican plant. Most of these costs will be incurred in Mexico and will therefore require payment in pesos. Sabre will receive 30 percent of the revenue generated (in pesos) from computer sales. The Mexican partner will receive the remainder.

The joint venture in Germany specifies joint production of personal computers with a German computer manufacturer. The computers will then be marketed to consumers throughout the Eastern Bloc countries in Europe; these countries were generally off limits to computer manufacturers before 1990. Similar types of computers are produced by some competitors, but Sabre believes it can penetrate these markets because its products will be competitively priced. While the economies of the Eastern Bloc countries are expected to be somewhat stagnant, demand for personal computers is reasonably strong. The computers will be priced in marks, and Sabre will receive 30 percent of the revenue generated from sales.

a) Assume Sabre plans to finance most of its investment in the Mexican subsidiary by borrowing Mexican pesos, and to finance most of its investment in the German subsidiary by borrowing German marks. The cost of financing is influenced by the risk-free rate in the respective countries and the risk premium on funds borrowed. Explain how these factors will affect the relative costs of financing each venture. Address this question from the perspective of the subsidiary, not from the perspective of Sabre's parent.

b) Will the joint venture experiencing the higher cost of financing (as determined in the previous question) necessarily experience lower returns to the subsidiary? Explain.

c) The German subsidiary has a high degree of financial leverage. Yet, the parent's capital structure is mostly equity. What will determine whether the creditors of the German subsidiary charge a high risk premium on borrowed funds because of the high degree of financial leverage?

d) One executive of Sabre suggested that since the cost of debt financing by highly leveraged German-owned companies is about 14 percent, its German subsidiary should be able to borrow at about the same interest rate. Do you agree? Explain. (Assume that the chances of the subsidiary experiencing financial problems are the same as these other German-owned firms).

e) There is some concern that the economy in Germany could become inflated. Assess the relative magnitude of an increase in inflation on (1) the cost of funds, (2) the cost of production, and (3) revenue from selling the computers.

SUGGESTED READINGS

William S. Sekely and J. Markham Collins. "Cultural Influences on International Capital Structure." *Journal of International Business Studies* (Spring 1988), pp. 87–100. This article explains capital structure differences across firms in 23 countries.

Robert N. McCauley and Steven A. Zimmer. "Explaining International Differences in the Cost of Capital." *FRBNY Quarterly Review* (Summer 1989), pp. 7–28. This article explains why the cost of funds varies across countries which can explain why MNCs attempt to obtain funds from particular countries.

REFERENCES

Adler, Michael. "The Cost of Capital and Valuation of a Two-Country Firm." *Journal of Finance* (March 1974), pp. 119–132.

Adler, Michael. "International Portfolio Choice and Corporation Finance: A Synthesis." *Journal of Finance* (June 1983), pp. 925–984.

Aggarwal, Raj. "Investment Performance of U.S.-Based Multinational Companies: Comments and a Perspective of International Diversification of Real Assets." *Journal of International Business Studies* (Spring–Summer 1980), pp. 98–104.

Aggarwal, Raj. "International Differences in Capital Structure Norms: An Empirical Study of Large Euro-

pean Companies." *Management International Review*, no. 1 (1981), pp. 75–88.

Alexander, Gordon J., Cheol S. Eun, and S. Janakiramanan. "Asset Pricing and Dual Listing on Foreign Capital Markets: A Note." *Journal of Finance* (March 1987), pp. 151–158.

Alexander, Gordon J., Cheol S. Eun, and S. Janakiramanan. "International Listings and Stock Returns: Some Empirical Evidence." *Journal of Financial and Quantitative Analysis* (June 1988), pp. 135–149.

Buckley, Adrian. "Financing Overseas Subsidiaries." *Accountancy* (August 1987), pp. 73–75.

Cohn, Richard A., and John J. Pringle. "Imperfections in International Financial Markets: Implications for Risk Premia and the Cost of Capital to Firms." *Journal of Finance* (March 1973), pp. 59–66.

Collins, J. Markham, and William S. Sekely. "The Relationship of Headquarters Country and Industry Classification to Financial Structure." *Financial Management* (Autumn 1983), pp. 45–51.

Eaker, Mark R. "Denomination Decisions for Multinational Transactions." *Financial Management* (Autumn 1980), pp. 23–29

Errunza, Vihang R. "Determinants of Financial Structure in the Central American Common Market." *Financial Management* (Autumn 1979), pp. 72–77.

Errunza, Vihang R. "Financing MNC Subsidiaries in Central America." *Journal of International Business Studies* (Fall 1979), pp. 88–93.

Errunza, Vihang, and Lemma W. Senbet. "The Effects of International Operations on the Market Value of the Firm: Theory and Evidence." *Journal of Finance* (May 1981), pp. 401–417.

Errunza, Vihang, and Etienne Losq. "International Asset Pricing Under Mild Segmentation: Theory and Test." *Journal of Finance* (March 1985), pp. 105–124.

Errunza, Vihang. "International Corporate Diversification, Market Valuation and Size-Adjusted Evidence." *Journal of Finance* (July 1984), pp. 727–743.

Eun, Cheol S., and S. Janakiramanan. "A Model of International Asset Pricing with a Constraint on the Foreign Equity Ownership." *Journal of Finance* (September 1986), pp. 897–914.

Fatemi, Ali M. "The Effect of International Diversification on Corporate Financing Policy." *Journal of Business Research* (January 1988), pp. 17–30.

Hodder, James E., and Lemma W. Senbat. "International Capital Market Equilibrium." *Journal of Finance* (December 1990), pp. 1495–1516.

Hodder, James E., and Adrian E. Tschoegi. "Some Aspects of Japanese Corporate Finance." *Journal of Financial and Quantitative Analysis* (June 1985), pp. 173–191.

Howe, John, and Jeff Madura. "The Impact of International Listings on Risk: Implications for Capital Market Integration." *Journal of Banking and Finance* (December 1990), pp. 1133–1142.

Jorion, Philippe, and Eduardo Schwartz. "Integration vs. Segmentation in the Canadian Stock Market." *Journal of Finance* (July 1986), pp. 603–615.

Kornbluth, Jonathan S. H., and Joseph D. Vinso. "Capital Structure and the Financing of the Multinational Corporation: A Fractional Multiobjective Approach." *Journal of Financial and Quantitative Analysis* (June 1982), pp. 147–178.

Kester, W. Carl. "Capital and Ownership Structure: A Comparison of United States and Japanese Manufacturing Corporations." *Financial Management* (Spring 1986), pp. 5–16.

Lee, Kwang Chul, and Chuck C. Y. Kwok. "Multinational Corporations vs. Domestic Corporations: International Environmental Factors and Determinants of Capital Structure." *Journal of International Business Studies* (Summer 1988), pp. 195–217.

McCauley, Robert N., and Steven A. Zimmer. "Explaining International Differences in the Cost of Capital." *FRBNY Quarterly Review* (Summer 1989), pp. 7–28.

Meek, G. K., and S. J. Gray. "Globalization of Stock Markets and Foreign Listing Requirements: Voluntary Disclosures by Continental European Companies Listed on the London Stock Exchange." *Journal of International Business Studies* (Summer 1989): pp. 315–336.

Mehra, Rajnish. "On the Financing and Investment Decisions of Multinational Firms in the Presence of Exchange Rate Risk." *Journal of Financial and Quantitative Analysis* (June 1978), pp. 227–244.

Myers, Stewart C., "The Capital Structure Puzzle." *Journal of Finance* (July 1984), pp. 575–592.

Prakash, Arun J., A. M. Parhizgari, and Gerald W. Perritt. "The Effect of Listing on the Parameters of Characteristic Lines Models." *Journal of Business Finance and Accounting* (Summer 1989), pp. 335–342.

Saudagaran, Shahrokh. "An Empirical Study of Selected Factors Influencing the Decision to List on Foreign Stock Exchanges." *Journal of International Business Studies* (Spring 1988), pp. 101–127.

Sekely, William S., and J. Markham Collins. "Cultural Influences on International Capital Structure." *Jour-

nal of International Business Studies (Spring 1988), pp. 87–100.

Senbet, Lemma W. "International Capital Market Equilibrium and the Multinational Firm Financing and Investment Policies." *Journal of Financial and Quantitative Analysis* (September 1979), pp. 425–450.

Solnik, Bruno H. "Testing International Asset Pricing: Some Pessimistic Views." *Journal of Finance* (May 1977), pp. 503–517.

Stanley, Margorie T. "Capital Structure and Cost of Capital for the Multinational Firm." *Journal of International Business Studies* (Spring–Summer 1981), pp. 103–120.

Stulz, Rene M. "A Model of International Asset Pricing." *Journal of Financial Economics* no. 9 (1981), pp. 383–406.

Stulz, Rene M. "On the Effects of Barriers to International Investment." *Journal of Finance* (September 1981), pp. 923–934.

Taggart, Robert A. "Capital Budgeting and the Financing Decision." *Financial Management* (Summer 1977), pp. 59–64.

Vasconcellos, Geraldo M., Jeff Madura, and Richard J. Kish. "Factors Affecting Cross-Border Acquisitions: Theory and Empirical Evidence." *Global Finance Journal,* forthcoming.

The Capital Structure Puzzle for Multinational Corporations

The controversy surrounding an optimal capital structure has not been completely resolved and perhaps never will be. However, studies have provided insightful explanations that are consistent with corporate behavior. Myers (1984) proposed that firms follow a pecking order in which they prefer to use internal financing in order to avoid issue costs. If internal financing is not sufficient, firms use debt financing first, followed by equity financing. The administrative and underwriting costs associated with debt are less than those of equity. Furthermore, Myers suggests that when managers have more favorable information about a project to be financed, the use of debt will be preferable to external equity.

In what he refers to as the capital structure puzzle, Myers offers a viable explanation for why firms within a single industry can have different capital structures. The objective of this appendix is to extend Myers' theory to a multinational framework. Specifically, the appendix explains how international conditions can cause a multinational corporation (MNC) to either accelerate the shift from one financing method to the next, or to rearrange the pecking order. In this way, factors that can influence an MNC's capital structure are identified.

SIMPLIFIED PECKING ORDER MODEL

To assess the pecking order for an MNC, the following assumptions are used:

- A two-country world
- The MNC's parent is in one country and its wholly-owned subsidiary is in the other.
- The parent presently has the same capital structure as the subsidiary.
- The exchange rate between the currencies of the two countries is fixed.
- The expected cash flows to the headquarters are the same as the subsidiary.
- The corporate tax rates of the two countries are the same.
- There are no withholding taxes in the foreign country.
- The country risk in the foreign country is perceived to be the same as in the home country.

- There are no restrictions on capital flows, causing interest rates to be the same in both countries.
- The MNC has the same degree of recognition in the foreign country as in the home country. It also has its stock traded on exchanges in each country.
- The subsidiary and the parent are separate entities. The parent is not a guarantor for the subsidiary.
- Information is freely available worldwide.

These assumptions are relaxed later in order to reassess the pecking order for more complex situations.

Under the existing conditions, the headquarters behaves as a domestic firm. Using Myer's theory, the headquarters would prefer to use internal funds as a source of capital. If internal funds are not available, external debt financing would be second priority, followed by external equity financing. Since the subsidiary is a separate entity, its characteristics are similar to the headquarters. Therefore, it would share the same pecking order.

GLOBAL CONDITIONS THAT DISRUPT THE PECKING ORDER

The existence of market imperfections can force a rearrangement of financing priorities. In the following discussion, various global conditions that can affect the desirability of a financing choice are identified. Throughout the discussion, it is assumed that the subsidiary periodically remits any earnings beyond what it needs for internal financing to the parent.

Country Risk

If the country risk was higher in the foreign country, the subsidiary may consider a financing strategy that would strengthen its political position. External debt financing in the host country's credit markets would force local banks and other creditors to have a vested interest in the subsidiary's well-being. This type of financing creates an implicit insurance benefit. Alternatively, external stock financing by the subsidiary could allow local investors (including employees who purchase stock) to have a vested interest in the subsidiary, which creates an implicit insurance benefit. Even if internal funds were available, the parent may instruct the subsidiary to remit internal funds and use external funding to create the implicit insurance. This example suggests how external funds can take precedent over internal funds at the subsidiary level. Yet, internal funds remitted to the parent may still be used by the parent before other alternative sources of funds. So it may be argued that the internal funds were still first priority, but only the designated user of the funds (parent versus subsidiary) had changed. However, if the parent had more internal funds than were needed, it may use some of the funds to pay extra dividends. In this case, the use of external financing by the subsidiary was not fully offset by the parent's additional internal financing, and the pecking order was partially rearranged.

Differential Interest Rates

When markets are segmented the cost of capital will be dependent on the country in which the capital is raised. Differential costs of capital can influence the MNC's financing decisions. If interest rates are lower in the host country, the subsidiary may prefer external debt. Any internal funds may be transferred to the parent, especially if the parent does not have enough internal funds to support present needs. Assuming that the subsidiary generates revenues in the local currency, this strategy does not increase exposure to exchange rate risk. Revenues received by the subsidiary can be used to meet its debt obligations. In essence, the subsidiary's external debt financing replaces the parent's debt financing. However subsidiary's access to additional debt may be limited because of its high degree of financial leverage.

If markets are somewhat segmented, and the cost of capital in the subsidiary's country appears too excessive, the parent may use its own funds to support projects implemented by the subsidiary. For example, if interest rates are higher in the host country, the parent may be more willing to provide its own internal funds so that the subsidiary does not need to use external financing. Consequently, the parent's internal funds would be reduced so that it will more quickly resort to external financing.

Exchange Rate Expectations

The external financing by a subsidiary may also be rearranged to capitalize on exchange rate expectations. If the local currency is expected to weaken over time, remitted earnings could be accelerated if the subsidiary issues stock with a low dividend rather than issuing debt. This defers the repayment on funds used, thereby improving the subsidiary's cash flow in the near future and allowing the subsidiary to remit larger amounts to the parent.

If the subsidiary believes its local currency will appreciate against the parent's currency, it may retain more of its internal funds. Consequently, the parent could be forced to use more external financing.

If the parent anticipates that the subsidiary's local currency will appreciate against its own, it may provide an immediate cash infusion to finance growth in the subsidiary. As a result, there is a transfer of internal funds from the parent to the subsidiary, which would possibly cause more external financing by the parent and less financing by the subsidiary. Over time, this strategy should allow the subsidiary to remit larger payments to the parent, which would increase the internal funds available to the parent.

If the parent anticipates that the subsidiary's local currency will depreciate against its own, it may require that the subsidiary obtain any necessary financing in the host country. In this way, the amount of funds to be remitted over time is reduced, minimizing exposure to exchange rate movements. This strategy reduces the internal funds available to the subsidiary, possibly resulting in more external financing by the subsidiary. Since the parent used less of its funds to finance the subsidiary's growth, it would have more internal funds available for its own investment and would need less external financing.

Blocked Funds

If the subsidiary is prevented from remitting funds, the parent will have less internal funds to use for financing. This situation does not disrupt the rank order of financing but may force the parent to use more external financing as its internal funds will be depleted more quickly.

Withholding Taxes

If withholding taxes imposed by the host country on remitted earnings are high, the parent may attempt to transfer explicit or implicit costs to the subsidiary. Thus, the level of earnings generated by the subsidiary would be reduced and the amount of internal funds available to the subsidiary would be reduced as well. This condition may influence the proportion of funds obtained from external sources. The subsidiary may be forced to use more external financing, while the parent should generate more earnings by transferring costs and will have more internal funds available.

Differential Corporate Taxes

If host country corporate income taxes exceed parent country income taxes, the parent may attempt to transfer costs to the subsidiary. Such a transfer pricing policy would ultimately allocate internal funds from the subsidiary to the parent, which forces the subsidiary to use more external financing and may reduce the amount of external financing required by the parent.

Higher host country taxes may also encourage the subsidiary to use heavy debt financing. Given a transfer of costs to the subsidiary, there would be a lack of internal funding anyway for the subsidiary, so that much debt financing might be needed.

Guarantees on Debt

If the parent backs the debt of the subsidiary, the subsidiary's borrowing capacity may be increased, while the borrowing capacity of the parent may be reduced. Therefore, the subsidiary would need less external equity financing.

Consolidating the Global Conditions

The discussion so far has focused on one global condition at a time. These effects of each condition when holding other conditions constant are summarized in Exhibit 18A.1 When the cost of the parent's operations can be fully absorbed by internal funds, the global conditions that cause higher external financing for the subsidiary will result in higher debt ratios for the MNC overall. These conditions are (1) a high level of country risk in the host country, (2) low host country interest rates, and (3) expected strength of the host country currency.

Conversely, the global conditions that cause lower external financing for the subsidiary will result in lower debt ratios for the MNC overall. These conditions are: (1) high interest rates in the host country, (2) expected weakness in the host country currency, (3) blocked funds imposed by the host government, (4) high withholding taxes imposed by the host government, and (5) high corporate taxes imposed by the host government.

IMPLICATIONS OF INCREASED EXTERNAL FINANCING BY THE SUBSIDIARY

When global conditions increase the external financing of the subsidiary, the amount of internal financing needed by the subsidiary is reduced. As these

EXHIBIT 18A.1 Effect of International Conditions on Financing

International Conditions	Amount of External Debt Financing by Subsidiary	Internal Funds Available to Parent	Amount of External Financing by Parent
Higher Country Risk in Host Country	Higher	Higher	Lower
Higher Interest Rates in Host Country	Lower	Lower	Higher
Lower Interest Rates in Host Country	Higher	Higher	Lower
Expected Weakness of Host Country Currency: Causing Accelerated Remittances	Higher	Higher	Lower
Expected Weakness of Host Country Currency: Causing Less Parent Financing of Subsidiary	Higher	Higher	Lower
Expected Strength of Host Country Currency: Causing Deferred Remittances	Lower	Lower	Higher
Expected Strength of Host Country Currency: Causing More Parent Financing of Subsidiary	Lower	Lower	Higher
Blocked Funds Imposed by Host Government	Lower	Lower	Higher
High Withholding Taxes Imposed by Host Government	Higher	Higher	Lower
Higher Corporate Taxes Imposed by Host Government	Higher	Higher	Lower
Parent Guarantees Subsidiary's Debt	Higher	Higher	Lower

extra internal funds are remitted to the parent, the parent will have a larger amount of internal funds for financing before it resorts to external financing. Assuming that the parent's operations absorb all internal funds and require some debt financing, there are offsetting effects on the capital structures of the subsidiary and the parent. The increased use of debt financing subsidiary is offset by the reduced debt financing of the parent. Yet, the cost of capital for the MNC overall could have changed for two reasons. First, the revised composition of debt could affect the interest charged on the debt. Second, it could affect the MNC's overall exposure to exchange rate risk, and therefore influence the risk premium on capital.

There are situations in which the increased use of debt financing of the subsidiary will not be offset by reduced debt financing of the parent. If the parent's operations can be fully financed with internal funds, the parent will not use external financing. In this case, international conditions that encourage increased use of debt financing by the subsidiary will result in a more debt-intensive capital structure for the MNC. Again, the cost of capital to the MNC could be affected by the increased external financing for reasons already mentioned. Yet, an additional reason here is the use of a higher proportion of debt financing.

IMPLICATIONS OF REDUCED EXTERNAL FINANCING BY THE SUBSIDIARY

When global conditions reduce the external financing of the subsidiary, the amount of internal financing needed by the subsidiary is increased. Consequently, it will remit less funds to the parent, reducing the internal funds available to the parent. If the parent's operations absorb all internal funds and require some debt financing, there are offsetting effects on the capital structures of the subsidiary and parent. The reduction in debt financing of the subsidiary is offset by the increased use of debt financing of the parent. The cost of capital may change even if the MNC's capital structure does not, for reasons expressed earlier.

If the parent's operations can be fully financed with internal funds, the parent will not use external financing. Thus, the reduction in external financing of the subsidiary is not offset by increased external financing of the parent, and the MNC's overall capital structure becomes more equity-intensive.

GLOBAL CONDITIONS THAT CAN ENCOURAGE EXTERNAL EQUITY FINANCING

The previous discussion has assumed that the MNC parent's operations could either be absorbed by internal funds or would require some external debt financing. Further steps down the pecking order were not necessary. For an MNC that could not satisfy all funding requirements with external debt financing, external equity financing is next in line. Yet, there are some global conditions that may encourage the MNC to use external equity ahead of debt, which are discussed next.

Agency Costs

If the subsidiary in a host country cannot easily be monitored by investors from the parent's country, agency costs are higher. The subsidiary in a host country may be induced by the parent to issue stock rather than debt in the local market, so that the managers there are monitored to assure maximization of the firm's stock price.

Listing Overseas

An MNC may be more capable of developing a global image if its stock is listed on a foreign stock exchange than if it uses debt financing. External equity financing may be prioritized ahead of debt financing under these circumstances.

If the subsidiary chooses external equity financing instead of debt financing, the MNC's overall capital structure will become more equity-intensive, unless it is offset by the parent's financing mix. The lack of debt financing by the subsidiary could increase the debt capacity of the parent, allowing the parent to borrow funds that the subsidiary did not. Essentially, the increase in external equity financing by the subsidiary could preclude the need for external equity financing by the parent.

Even if the MNC's overall capital structure is not affected by the subsidiary's use of external equity financing, its cost of capital may be affected. If markets are partially segmented, the required rate of return on capital by investors in the host country may differ from investors in the parent's country.

CHAPTER 19

Country Risk
Analysis

ountry risk represents the potentially adverse impact of a country's
environment on the MNC's cash flows. Both bank and non-bank
MNCs commonly evaluate the country risk for each country in which
they do business. However, the assessment approach by banks is often quite
different from that of non-banks. This chapter focuses on the perspective of
non-bank MNCs, who analyze country risk for the following reasons. First,
it can be used as a screening device to avoid countries with excessive risk.
Screening reduces the set of possible countries to consider for proposed
exporting or direct foreign investment opportunities. Research by Nigh
found that events that heighten country risk tend to discourage U.S. direct
foreign investment in that particular country. A second reason for assessing
country risk is that it can be used to monitor countries where the MNC is
presently engaged in international business. If the country risk level of a
particular country begins to increase, the MNC may consider divesting its
subsidiaries located there. A third reason for country risk analysis is to assess
particular forms of risk for a proposed capital budgeting project considered
for a foreign country.

To detect excessive country risk, a simple rating may suffice. However,
when the aim is to measure particular risks of a proposed project, the country
risk rating must be incorporated within the capital budgeting analysis, which
is a task in itself. It is nevertheless essential to fully capture all the potential
risks that may influence the cash flows of a proposed project.

This chapter first provides a brief background on the increasing awareness
of country risk. Next, various political and financial risk factors that constitute country risk are identified. Then, the difference between a macro and
micro assessment of risk is explained, and techniques used to assess country
risk are identified. In addition, a method for comparing country risk ratings
is offered and an example of quantifying country risk is provided. Finally,
methods to protect against host-government takeovers (the extreme form of
country risk) are discussed.

INCREASED AWARENESS OF COUNTRY RISK

In 1976 a division of Consolidated Foods, Inc., searched for an appropriate country in which to expand its manufacturing. The company decided on a location described at the time as a "happy, sleepy country." The location was El Salvador. Within two years of this decision, political turmoil arose whereby a group of leftists held the division's president and about 120 employees hostage until the company agreed to provide wage increases. By 1979 the division was closed. This example illustrates how internal country problems can affect an MNC.

In the 1980s the crises in Iran, Afghanistan, and some Latin American countries made MNCs realize the importance of effective country risk analysis. While MNCs diversify their operations internationally to reduce their exposure to any individual country's problems, they should attempt to reduce risk further by anticipating where country crises are beginning to develop. If the crises are anticipated well in advance, the MNC can avoid further direct foreign investment in that country, and/or withdraw its current operations from that country before the crisis intensifies.

In some cases, a country's problems may even affect firms that are not conducting business there. Consider the effect of the crisis in China in 1989 as an example. During the demonstrations at Tiananmen Square, supplies of styrene (used to produce consumer products) were not allowed in China. An excess global market supply resulted, causing the market price to decline. This had a significant influence on the earnings of companies that produce styrene, including Arco Chemical Company, a large U.S.-based MNC.

POLITICAL RISK FACTORS

An MNC must assess country risk not only in countries where it currently does business, but also where it expects to market exports or establish subsidiaries. Several risk characteristics of a country may significantly affect performance, and the MNC should be concerned about the degree of impact likely for each.

As one might expect, there are many country characteristics related to the political environment that influence an MNC. The extreme form of political risk is the host country taking over a subsidiary. In some cases of expropriation, some compensation (the amount decided by the host country government) is awarded. In other cases, the assets are confiscated and no compensation is provided. Such events can take place peacefully or by force. Some of the more common forms of political risk include:

- "Purchase homemade products" philosophy
- Attitude of people in host country toward the MNC
- Attitude of host government toward the MNC
- Blockage of fund transfers
- War

Each of these characteristics will be examined.

"Purchase Homemade Products" Philosophy

A mild form of political risk (to an exporter) is a philosophy spreading throughout a country to purchase only homemade goods. Even if the exporter decided to set up a subsidiary in the foreign country, this philosophy could prevent its success. All countries tend to exert some pressure on consumers to purchase from locally owned manufacturers. (In the United States, consumers are encouraged to look for the "made in the U.S.A." label.) MNCs that consider entering a foreign market (or have already entered that market) must monitor the general loyalty of consumers toward homemade products. If consumers are very loyal to local products, a joint venture with a local company may be more feasible than an exporting strategy.

Attitude of Public

Sometimes the host government supports the MNC while people of the foreign country do not. For example, the government of the MNC's home country might hire an engineering firm to establish military bases in the foreign country. While the government of the foreign country may welcome this and perceive it as protection, the people in that country may consider it as involvement in a future war. In this case, the host government is friendly toward the subsidiary, but the people may avoid purchasing its goods as a form of protest.

Attitude of Host Government

In the reverse scenario, an automobile manufacturing plant that provides high-quality and low-priced cars might satisfy the local people, but cause pollution. The host government might therefore impose pollution control standards (which affect costs) and additional corporate taxes (which affect after-tax earnings), as well as withholding taxes and fund transfer restrictions (which affect after-tax cash flows sent to the parent).

Some analysts use turnover in government members or philosophy as a proxy for a country's political risk. While this can significantly influence the MNC's future cash flows, it alone does not serve as a suitable representation of political risk. A subsidiary will not necessarily be affected by changing governments. Furthermore, a subsidiary can be affected by adjusted policies of the host government or by a changing attitude toward the subsidiary's home country (and therefore the subsidiary) even when the host government has no risk of being overthrown.

There are various ways in which the host government can make the MNC's operations coincide with its own goals. It may, for example, require the use of local employees for managerial positions at a subsidiary. In addition, it may require social facilities (such as an exercise room, non-smoking areas, etc.), or special environmental controls (air pollution control equipment, etc.). Furthermore, it is not uncommon for a host government to require special permits, impose extra taxes, or subsidize competitors. All of these examples represent political risk in that they reflect a country's political characteristics and could influence an MNC's cash flows.

Blockage of Fund Transfers

Subsidiaries of MNCs often send funds back to the headquarters for loan repayments, purchases of supplies, administrative fees, remitted earnings, or several other possible purposes. In some cases, a host government may block fund transfers, which could force subsidiaries to undertake projects that are not optimal (just to make use of the funds). Alternatively, they could invest the funds in local securities that would provide some return while they are blocked. But, this return might be inferior to other uses of the funds.

War

Some countries tend to engage in constant battles with neighboring countries. This can affect the safety of employees hired by an MNC's subsidiary or by salespeople who attempt to establish export markets for the MNC. In addition, countries consistently plagued with the threat of war typically have volatile business cycles, which make the cash flow generated from such countries more uncertain.

FINANCIAL RISK FACTORS

Along with political factors, financial factors should also be considered when assessing country risk. One of the most obvious financial factors is the current and potential state of the country's economy. An MNC that exports to a country or develops a subsidiary in a country is highly concerned with that country's demand for its products. This demand is, of course, strongly influenced by the country's economy. A recession in the country could severely reduce demand for the MNC's exports or products sold by the MNC's local subsidiary.

In some cases, financial distress in a country can encourage a government to implement policies that could limit the MNC's market penetration there. For example, Ford Motor Company was allowed by the Spanish government to set up production facilities in Spain only if it would abide by certain provisions. These included a limit of Ford's local sales volume to 10 percent of the previous year's local automobile sales. In addition, of the total volume of automobiles produced by Ford in Spain, two-thirds had to be exported. The motivation behind these provisions was creation of jobs for workers in Spain without seriously affecting local competitors. Allowing a subsidiary that primarily exports its product achieved this objective for Spain.

In the preceding example, the MNC (Ford) was aware of the host government's restrictions before establishing a subsidiary. In some cases the rules change after the game has begun. That is, additional host-government restrictions may be enforced after an MNC establishes a foreign subsidiary. For example, during the international debt crisis, many of the less-developed countries were experiencing economic problems, so governments restricted local firms from importing goods from MNCs in an attempt to boost local sales. In addition, some of the MNC's subsidiaries based in these countries were not allowed to import supplies. This restriction affected their production process. Obviously, MNCs must continue to monitor country risk even after establishing a subsidiary.

Because the state of a country's economy is dependent on several financial factors, an MNC should consider all of these factors. Some of the more obvious ones include interest rates, exchange rates, and inflation. Higher interest rates tend to slow the growth of an economy and could reduce demand for the MNC's products. Lower interest rates often stimulate the economy and increase demand for the MNC's products. Exchange rates can strongly influence the demand for the country's exports, which in turn affects the country's production and income level. Inflation can affect the purchasing power of consumers and therefore the consumer's demand for an MNC's goods.

Interest rates, exchange rates, and inflation could also have an impact on each other, which makes the overall assessment of their impact on the economy more complex. Even if we know exactly how these factors influence a country's economy, we are unsure of their future values, so some uncertainty would still remain. As an example, assume that for every percentage point decrease in interest rates in Country X, there would be a 2 percent increase in total production. This can be useful information. However, it is not known with certainty how interest rates will change in the future. A firm may forecast a 3 percent decrease in interest rates, which would lead to a 6 percent increase in total production. Yet, if interest rates actually increased, production may actually decrease. Financial factors that indicate the government's purchasing power are also important in the case where the government serves as a customer of the MNC. For example, a growing budget deficit may force the government to reduce its purchases of goods produced by the MNC and its subsidiaries. A reduction in tax revenues may reduce the government's demand for the MNC's products.

As another example of government intervention, consider the wage-price freeze imposed by Brazil in 1990 and 1991 in order to reduce the inflationary spiral. This action slowed down the economy and affected sales of several subsidiaries of U.S.-based MNCs, including Armco, Inc., Black & Decker Corporation, and Quaker Oats Company.

The discussion up to this point emphasizes that country risk analysis goes far beyond an MNC's estimation of the probability that its subsidiary will be taken over by the local government. It includes an assessment of all factors (political and financial) related to the foreign country that influence the cash flow of the MNC. Also, after assessing country risk, the MNC must decide how to deal with it.

TYPES OF COUNTRY RISK ASSESSMENT

Although there is no consensus as to how country risk can best be assessed, some guidelines have been developed. The first step is to recognize the difference between (1) an overall risk assessment of a country without consideration of the MNC's business and (2) the risk assessment of a country as related to the MNC's type of business. The first type can be referred to as a **macro-assessment** of country risk and the latter type as a **micro-assessment.** Each type is discussed in turn.

Macro-Assessment of Country Risk

A macro-assessment involves consideration of all variables that affect country risk except for those unique to a particular firm or industry. This type of risk is convenient in that it remains the same for a given country, regardless of the firm or industry of concern; however, it excludes relevant information that could improve the accuracy of the assessment. While a macro-assessment of country risk is not ideal for any individual MNC, it serves as a foundation that can then be modified to reflect the particular business in which the MNC is involved.

Any macro-assessment model should consider both political and financial characteristics of the country being assessed. Political factors include the relationship of the host government with the MNC's home-country government, the attitude of the people in the host country toward the MNC's government, the historical stability of the host government, the vulnerability of the host government to political takeovers within the government, and the probability of war in the host country with neighboring countries. Consideration of such political factors will indicate the probability of political events that may affect an MNC and the magnitude of the impact.

The financial factors of a macro-assessment model should include GNP growth, inflation trends, government budget levels (and the government deficit), interest rates, unemployment, the country's reliance on export income, the balance of trade, and foreign exchange controls. The list of financial factors could easily be extended several pages. The factors listed here represent just a subset of the financial factors considered when evaluating the financial strength of a country.

One desirable characteristic of financial factors is that data are available for them. However, databases are limited in that they only reflect historical or current conditions. The MNC is concerned with the future economic conditions. Yet, the future state of the economy may be partially dependent on the current financial data.

There is clearly some degree of subjectivity in identifying each of the relevant political and financial factors for a macro-assessment of country risk. There is also some subjectivity in determining the degree of importance of each factor in contributing to the overall macro-assessment for a particular country. For instance, one assessor may assign a much higher weight (degree of importance) to real GNP growth than another assessor. Finally, there is some subjectivity in predicting the future of these financial factors. Because of the types of subjectivity mentioned here, it is not surprising that the risk assessors often differ in opinion after completing a macro-assessment of country risk.

Micro-Assessment of Country Risk

While a macro-assessment of country risk provides an indication of the country's overall status, it does not assess country risk from the perspective of the particular business of concern. Consider Country Z, which has been assigned a relatively low macro-assessment by most experts, due to its poor financial condition. Also consider two MNCs that are deciding whether to set up a subsidiary in Country Z. One MNC is considering the development of a subsidiary that would produce automobiles, while the other MNC plans to build a subsidiary that would produce military supplies. Country Z's government may be committed to purchasing a given amount of military supplies regardless of how weak the economy is. Thus, the military supply subsidiary may be feasible while the automobile subsidiary may not.

There is always the possibility that Country Z's government will search for a locally owned firm to produce military supplies, since it may desire more confidentiality about what supplies it is ordering. This possibility is an element of country risk, since it is a country characteristic (or attitude) that can affect the feasibility of a project. Yet, this specific characteristic is relevant only to the military supply subsidiary and not to the automobile subsidiary. This example illustrates how an appropriate country risk assessment varies with the firm, industry, and project of concern and therefore why the macro-assessment of country risk has its limitations. A micro-assessment is also necessary when evaluating the country risk as related to a particular project proposed by a particular firm.

One common factor in micro-assessment is the MNC's relationship with the host government. This relationship will not necessarily be the same as with the firm's home government, so a macro-assessment that ignores the unique characteristics of a particular firm may exclude relevant information. For example, it is possible that the host country may react unfavorably to the firm's particular business that would compete with locally owned businesses. Thus, even though the host government may have good relations with the MNC's home country, it might enforce policies that would adversely affect a local subsidiary owned by the MNC.

Another common factor in the micro-assessment of country risk is the people's attitude toward the MNC. Good relations between people of a host country and the MNC's home country do not guarantee that the local consumers of a host country will react favorably to the MNC's subsidiary. For example, if the management team of the subsidiary is hired from the MNC's home country, this could upset the local people in the host country.

In addition to political variables, financial variables are also necessary for micro-assessment of country risk. Micro factors would include the sensitivity of the firm's business to real GNP growth, inflation trends, interest rates, etc. Due to differences in business characteristics, some firms are more susceptible to the host-country's economy than others. Macro factors, on the other hand, simply assess the country's economy without concern for their potential impact on a particular firm.

In summary, the overall assessment of country risk consists of four parts:

1. Macro political risk
2. Macro financial risk
3. Micro political risk
4. Micro financial risk

While these parts can be consolidated to generate a single country-risk rating, it may be useful to keep them separate so an MNC can realize the various ways by which its direct foreign investment or exporting operations are exposed to country risk.

TECHNIQUES TO ASSESS COUNTRY RISK

Once a firm identifies all the macro and micro factors that deserve consideration in the country risk assessment, it may wish to implement a system for evaluating these factors and determining a country risk rating. There are various techniques available to achieve this objective. Some of the more popular techniques are

- Checklist approach
- Delphi technique
- Quantitative analysis
- Inspection visits
- Combination of techniques

Each technique is briefly discussed in turn.

Checklist Approach

A checklist approach involves judgment on all the political and financial factors (both macro and micro) that contribute to a firm's assessment of country risk. Some factors (such as real GNP growth) can be measured from available data, while others (such as probability of entering into a war) must be subjectively measured. The factors should be converted if necessary to some numerical form in which they can be assessed for a particular country. Those factors thought to have a greater influence on country risk should be assigned greater weights. Both the measurement of some factors and the weighting scheme implemented are subjective.

Delphi Technique

The **Delphi technique** involves the collection of independent opinions on country risk without group discussion by the assessors who provided these opinions. The assessors here may be employees of the firm conducting the assessment or outside consultants. The MNC can average these country risk scores in some manner and even assess the degree of disagreement by measuring dispersion of opinions.

Quantitative Analysis

Once the financial and political variables have been measured for a period of time, models for quantitative analysis can attempt to identify the characteristics that influence the level of country risk. Discriminant analysis is a statistical tool commonly used for this purpose. To illustrate, assume there are some countries that historically can be classified as exhibiting tolerable risk while other countries exhibit intolerable risk. Discriminant analysis can examine the financial and political factors of all of these countries and attempt to identify which factors help to distinguish (or discriminate) between a tolerable-risk country and an intolerable-risk country. For example, discriminant analysis may find that real growth in GNP is a crucial variable in explaining why a country is a good or bad risk. This information, along with the information determined for all other factors, can then be used in reassessing countries over time. If real GNP growth and other key variables begin to deteriorate for a particular country, this provides a signal that the country risk is increasing.

Regression analysis may also be used to assess risk, since it can measure the sensitivity of one variable to other variables. For example, a firm could regress a measure of its business activity (such as its percentage increase in sales) against country characteristics (such as real growth in GNP). Results from such an analysis will indicate the susceptibility of a particular business to a country's economy. This is valuable information to incorporate in the overall evaluation of country risk.

While statistical models can quantify the impact of variables on each other, they do have their limitations. For example, discriminant analysis applied to historical data may have found that strong real GNP growth can reduce a country's degree of country risk. But, if the firm cannot predict the real growth in GNP for a country, it may be difficult to predict how a country's risk will change over time. Because the country-risk rating is to be used in assessing possible projects for the future, the ideal rating system would provide an early warning about countries that may cause problems for the firm in the future. Thus, the ideal quantitative techniques would identify characteristics that signal problems well before they actually occur (preferably before the firm's decision to take on a project in that country). At this point in time, such a quantitative model is not known to exist.

Inspection Visits

Inspection visits involve traveling to a country and meeting with government officials, firm executives, and/or consumers. Such meetings will help clarify any uncertain opinions the firm has about a country. Indeed, some variables, such as inter-country relationships, may be difficult to assess without a trip to the host country.

Combination of Techniques

In some cases, it may be most appropriate to implement two or more of the techniques described above. This is common practice since each technique has its own strengths and weaknesses. For example, the inspection visit may provide useful information but does not by itself represent a complete country-risk analysis. Individual evaluations of country risk could be generated by each technique for a particular country and, if significant differences show up, further analysis conducted.

COMPARING RISK RATINGS AMONG COUNTRIES

Some MNCs may evaluate country risk for several countries, perhaps to determine where to establish a subsidiary. One approach for comparing political and financial ratings among countries, advocated by some foreign risk managers, is a **foreign investment risk matrix (FIRM),** which displays the financial (or economic) risk by intervals ranging across the matrix from "acceptable" to "unacceptable." It also displays political risk by intervals ranging from "stable" to "unstable." An example of this matrix is shown in Exhibit 19.1. Each country can be positioned in its appropriate location on the matrix based on its political rating and financial rating.

Some countries, such as Country A in the exhibit, will be acceptable because they have a low degree of political and financial risk. Other countries, such as Country B, have low financial risk but high political risk. For Country C in the exhibit, the converse is true. Still others have a high degree of financial and political risk, such as Country D. A firm that uses this matrix must determine the acceptable and unacceptable zones. Based on the zones

EXHIBIT 19.1   Example of Foreign Investment Risk Matrix

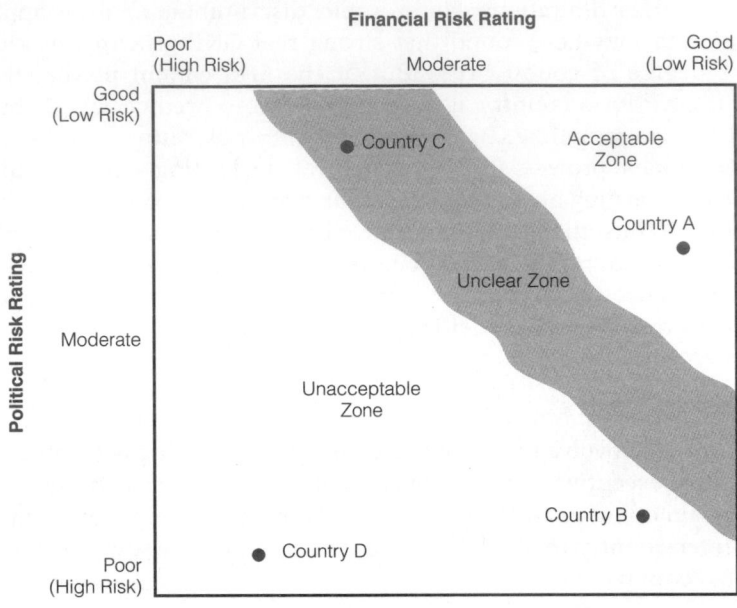

NOTE: This matrix was adapted from a different matrix suggested by Bhalla; see *Euromoney*, June 1983, p. 70.

shown in Exhibit 19.1, Country A is acceptable for implementing projects, while Country B and Country D are unacceptable. Country C is in a so-called "unclear zone," suggesting further evaluation is necessary.

As already mentioned, the importance of political risk versus financial risk varies with the intent of the MNC. Those considering direct foreign investment to attract demand in that country must be highly concerned about financial risk. Those establishing a foreign manufacturing plant to capitalize on cheap production costs, planning to export the goods from there, should be more concerned with political risk.

While the FIRM approach can be useful for an MNC, it does not quantify an overall country-risk rating for any individual country, since its financial and political ratings have not been weighted. An overall rating can be determined once all the components contributing to the assessment have been individually assessed and weighted in terms of importance. An appropriate procedure for quantifying a country's overall risk is described next.

QUANTIFYING COUNTRY RISK: AN EXAMPLE

To develop an overall country risk rating, it is necessary to first construct a separate rating for political and financial risk. As discussed earlier in this chapter, both political risk and financial risk depend on a variety of factors. First, the political factors can be assigned values within some arbitrarily chosen range (such as from 1 to 5, where 5 is the best value—lowest risk).

INTERNATIONAL FINANCIAL MANAGEMENT IN PRACTICE

How Executives Assess Political Risk

A recent survey provided some interesting feedback on how executives perceive the techniques for political risk assessment used by their MNCs. In general, the executives believed that their company's system for assessing political risk was not being used to its fullest potential. Some of their main criticisms are summarized here:

1. *Delay in preparing report.* MNC managers sometimes must make quick decisions on foreign projects, but the political risk assessment may not be completed in time. In some cases, parts of the assessment are outdated by the time the entire assessment is complete.

2. *Assessments are reactive, not proactive.* Many political risk assessments are in response to a proposed project rather than being performed in anticipation that a project proposal may be forthcoming. This causes further delay in the political risk assessment.

3. *Data limitations.* Some of the data on political variables are difficult to quantify. In addition, the assessment of political risk requires information from foreign residents in the country of concern. It is often difficult to obtain relevant information from these residents.

4. *Distorted information.* From the transition of raw data on political variables to a finalized political risk assessment, the data can become distorted. This may occur because some variables are given more or less attention than deserved, or because managers may desire to contrive the data in such a way to support their preconceived opinion.

SOURCE: B. Mascarenhas, and C. Atherton, "Problems in Political Risk Assessment," *Management International Review* no. 3 (1983), pp. 22–32.

Next, these political factors are assigned weights (representing degree of importance), which should add up to 100 percent. The assigned values of the factors times their respective weights can then be summed up to derive a political risk rating.

The process described for deriving the political risk rating can then be repeated to derive the financial risk rating. That is, values can be assigned (from 1 to 5, where 5 is the best value—lowest risk) to all financial factors. The assigned values of the factors times their respective weights can be summed up to derive a financial risk rating.

Once the political and financial ratings have been derived, a country's overall country risk rating as related to a specific project can be determined by assigning weights to the political and financial ratings according to their perceived importance. For example, if the political risk is thought to be much more influential on a particular project than the financial risk, it would receive a higher weight than the financial risk rating (both weights must total to 100 percent). The political and financial ratings multiplied by their respective weights would determine the overall country risk rating for a country as related to a particular project.

As a simplified example, Exhibit 19.2 illustrates Cougar Company's country risk assessment of the hypothetical country Sunland. The company is assessing the establishment of a steel manufacturing plant there. From Exhibit

EXHIBIT 19.2   Determining the Overall Country Risk Rating

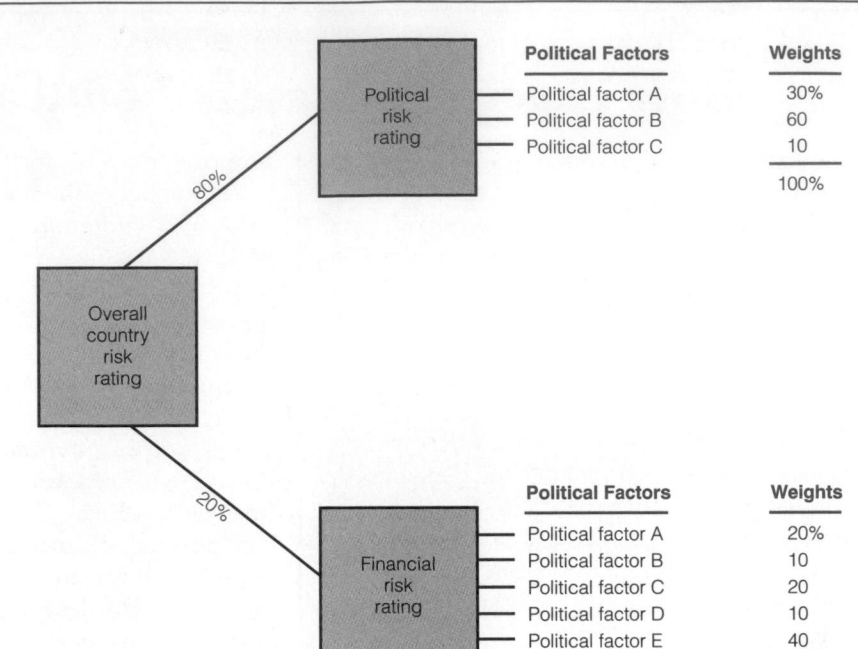

Political Factors	Weights
Political factor A	30%
Political factor B	60
Political factor C	10
	100%

Political Factors	Weights
Political factor A	20%
Political factor B	10
Political factor C	20
Political factor D	10
Political factor E	40
	100%

19.2, there are three political factors and five financial factors that contribute to the overall country risk rating in this example. In a realistic setting, many more factors might be included. Political risk factor A might reflect the degree of political tension within the country, political risk factor B the degree of political tension of the country with its neighboring countries, and so on. Financial risk factor A might reflect potential internal economic growth, and so on.

The number of relevant factors comprising both the political risk and financial risk categories will vary with the country being assessed and the type of corporate operations planned for that country. The assignment of values to the factors, along with the degree of importance (weights) assigned to the factors, will also vary with the country being assessed and type of corporate operations planned for that country.

To complete the example of deriving Sunland's overall country risk as related to Cougar Company's future plans, assume the company has assigned the values and weights to the factors as shown in Exhibit 19.3. In this example, the company generally assigns the financial factors higher ratings than the political factors. The financial condition of the country has therefore been assessed more favorably than the political condition. Political factor B is thought to be most important based on a weighting of 60 percent whereas political factors A and C received the remaining 40 percent weighting. Financial factor E is thought to be very important based on its 40 percent

EXHIBIT 19.3 Derivation of the Overall Country Risk Rating Based on Assumed Information

(1)	(2)	(3)	(4) = (2) × (3)
Political Risk Factors	Rating Assigned by Company to Factor (Within a Range of 1–5)	Weight Assigned by Company to Factor According to Importance	Weighted Value of Factor
Political factor A	4	30 %	1.2
Political factor B	2	60	1.2
Political factor C	3	10	.3
		100 %	2.7 = Political risk rating
Financial Risk Factors			
Financial factor A	5	20 %	1.0
Financial factor B	4	10	.4
Financial factor C	4	20	.8
Financial factor D	5	10	.5
Financial factor E	3	40	1.2
		100 %	3.9 = Financial risk rating

(1)	(2)	(3)	(4) = (2) × (3)
Category	Rating As Determined Above	Weight Assigned by Company to Each Risk Category	Weighted Rating
Political risk	2.7	80%	2.16
Financial risk	3.9	20%	.78
		100%	2.94 = Overall country risk rating

weighting compared to 20 percent weights for factors A and C and 10 percent weights for factors B and D.

The political risk rating is determined by adding the products of assigned ratings (Column 2) and weights (Column 3) of the political risk factors. It equals 2.7, which may appear low based on the individual assigned values. Yet, political factor B carries a 60 percent weight and was assigned a low value, which explains the relatively low political risk rating.

The financial risk rating is computed to be 3.9, which again verifies that the financial condition of the country is better than its political condition. Once the political and financial ratings are determined, the overall country risk rating can be derived (as shown at the bottom of Exhibit 19.3), given the weights assigned to political and financial risk. Column 3 in the lower portion of Exhibit 19.3 suggests the company perceives political risk (receiving an 80 percent weight) to be much more important than financial risk (receiving a 20 percent weight) in this country as related to the proposed project. The overall country risk rating of 2.94 may appear low given the individual category ratings. This is due to the heavy weighting to political risk, which in this example was critical from the firm's perspective. Should Cougar Company establish a steel manufacturing plant in a country that received an overall country risk rating of 2.94 (based on a scale of 1 to 5)? The answer depends on the risk-tolerance of the firm as discussed in the following section.

Before moving on, it should be emphasized that country risk assessors have their own individual procedures for quantifying country risk. The procedure described here is just one of many. Most procedures are similar, though, in that they somehow assign ratings and weights to all individual characteristics relevant to country risk assessment.

DECISION MAKING BASED ON COUNTRY RISK ASSESSMENT

The first step for a firm after developing a country risk rating is to determine whether that rating suggests the risk is tolerable. If the country risk is too high, then the firm does not need to analyze the feasibility of the proposed project any further. Some firms may contend that no risk is too high when considering a project. Their reasoning is that if the potential return is high enough, the project is worth undertaking. However, there are cases where the degree of country risk could be too high regardless of the project's expected return. Consider a proposed development of a subsidiary in Country Z that appears very profitable. If Country Z is often engaged in war, this places a threat on the life of any employees who would be transferred to that subsidiary. In this case, Country Z should be off limits, and the proposed project should not receive further consideration.

If the risk rating of a country is in the tolerable range, any project related to that country deserves further consideration. Capital budgeting analysis would be appropriate to determine whether the project is feasible. The mechanics of capital budgeting from the perspective of an MNC were discussed in the previous chapter.

Incorporating Country Risk in Capital Budgeting

Country risk can be incorporated in the capital budgeting analysis. One approach is to adjust the required rate of return for a particular project according to the country risk rating. The lower the rating, the higher is the perceived risk, and the higher is the discount rate applied to the project's cash flows. This approach is convenient in that one adjustment to the capital budgeting analysis can capture country risk. However, there is no precise formula for adjusting the required rate of return to incorporate country risk. The adjustment is somewhat arbitrary and may therefore cause feasible projects to be rejected or unfeasible projects to be accepted.

Perhaps the most appropriate method for incorporating forms of country risk in a capital budgeting analysis is to estimate how the cash flows would be affected by each form of risk. For example, if there is a 20 percent probability that the host government will temporarily block funds from the subsidiary to the parent, the MNC should estimate the project's net present value (NPV) under these circumstances, realizing that there would be a 20 percent chance that this NPV would occur. (The estimation of a project's NPV when funds are blocked was demonstrated in Chapter 17.)

If there is a chance that the host-government takeover will occur, the foreign project's NPV under these conditions should be estimated. Each possible form of risk has an estimated impact on the foreign project's cash flows and therefore on the project's NPV. By analyzing each possible impact, the MNC can determine the probability distribution of NPVs for the project. Its accept/reject decision on the project would be based on its assessment of the probability that the project will generate a positive NPV, as well as the size of possible NPV outcomes. While this procedure may seem somewhat tedious, it directly incorporates forms of country risk into the cash flow estimates and explicitly illustrates the possible results from implementing the project. The more convenient method of adjusting the discount rate in accordance with the country risk rating does not indicate the probability distribution of possible outcomes. A computer program can expedite the more explicit analysis.

Even after a project is accepted and implemented, country risk must continue to be monitored. For some labor-intensive MNCs where the host country feels it is benefiting from a subsidiary's existence (due to the subsidiary's employment of local people), the chance of expropriation may be low. Yet, there are several other forms of country risk that need to be considered. Decisions regarding subsidiary expansion, fund transfers to the parent, and sources of financing can all be affected by any changes in country risk; and since country risk can change dramatically over time, periodic reassessment is required, especially for the less stable countries.

APPLICATIONS OF COUNTRY RISK ANALYSIS

There are some cases where country risk assessment has enabled MNCs to avoid further involvement and even reduce current involvement in politically tense countries. For example, four months before the fall of the Shah of Iran, a country risk assessor for Gulf Oil anticipated severe political pressure building within Iran. Consequently, Gulf Oil began planning to deal with the subsequent loss of Iranian oil, which at the time amounted to 10 percent of its crude supplies. While dedicating resources to country risk assessment can be well worth the cost, the art of forecasting country crises is far from being perfected.

Whether MNCs hire outside consultants or use in-house staff to perform country risk analysis, they have often been unable to predict major trouble in various countries. For example, the Iranian crisis, Poland's financial crisis, and the economic deterioration of several Latin American countries were generally not detected well in advance. It is understandable that country risk systems are prone to errors. Consider the procedure discussed earlier in this chapter where individual country characteristics are assigned values to rate each characteristic. The values assigned are somewhat arbitrary. In addition, the assigning of weights to reflect the importance of each characteristic is also somewhat arbitrary. Thus, while an overall risk rating of a country can be useful, it cannot always detect upcoming crises.

The general inability of MNCs to predict country crises may also be due to too much reliance on statistics. Quantitative models, while valuable, cannot evaluate subjective data that cannot be quantified. In addition, historical

RELATED RESEARCH

Do MNCs In High-Risk Countries Achieve Higher Returns?

A recent study assessed the relationship between the political risk of a country and the returns on direct foreign investment in that country. Since investors are assumed to be risk-averse, one would hypothesize higher expected returns for investment in riskier countries. The higher return would compensate the investor for the relatively high degree of uncertainty. If the same returns could be achieved in safer countries, one would assume the investors would confine their dealings to those countries. In essence, the expected returns in high-risk countries should contain a risk premium that compensates investors for the high risk.

To test this hypothesis, annual data on political risk ratings and returns on direct foreign investments were compiled for 46 countries over the period of 1972 to 1984. A strong positive risk-return relationship existed during the 1980–1982 period, supporting the hypothesis that firms investing in high-risk countries earn higher returns. However, the strong positive risk-return relationship did not exist in the other ten years. In fact, in some years there was a negative relationship between country risk and return.

In general, the results suggest that firms investing in high-risk countries are not always adequately compensated. That is, they might be able to achieve similar returns on direct foreign investment in less risky countries.

SOURCE: Chase, C. D., J. L. Kuhle, and C. H. Walther, "The Relevance of Political Risk in Direct Foreign Investment," *Management International Review*, no. 3, 1988, pp. 31–38.

---

trends of various country characteristics are not always useful for anticipating an upcoming crisis. Furthermore, warnings by country risk assessors are sometimes ignored by executives higher up in the company's organization.

Due to the exposure to error when assessing country risk, no system has been singled out as optimal. A survey of 193 corporations heavily involved in foreign business found that about half of the corporations have no formal means for making political assessments. This does not mean they neglect to assess political risk, but rather that there is no proven method to use. Some of the assessors' opinions of a country's political risk are based simply on their conversations with other people whom they believe are reliable. While such an approach is quite simplistic, there is no clear-cut evidence that even the most sophisticated technique will more properly assess political risk.

Country Risk Analysis of Eastern Bloc Countries

In order to understand which country characteristics are assessed to measure country risk, consider the following summary of country risk ratings on Eastern Bloc countries offered by *USA Today* in 1990. Hungary was given an A− rating (or grade). This high rating was due to its capable labor force, the recent ease in remitting profits from there, and its government's efforts to promote direct foreign investment. East Germany was given a B + rating, as restrictions on direct foreign investment have been reduced and its economy is more closely tied to West Germany. The Soviet Union was given a B − grade. While it has abundant natural resources, political conflicts and the huge bureaucracy are concerns. Poland was given a C   rating, as its economy is weaker than that of most other Eastern Bloc countries. Romania was also given a C −, as the government has been slow to define precisely how restrictions may be reduced for firms conducting direct foreign investment.

While these ratings may change over time, this assessment summary suggests the more relevant characteristics that influence the ratings of Eastern Bloc countries. Some other important characteristics assessed when measuring country risk in these countries are availability of business, hotels, office space, phone lines, and public transportation.

Country Risk Resulting from the Persian Gulf Crisis

As a result of the Persian Gulf crisis, many MNCs attempted to reassess country risk. Terrorism became a major concern. Various methods were used by MNCs to protect against terrorism. Cross-country travel by executives was reduced, as MNCs used teleconference calls instead. Some MNCs with subsidiaries in Saudi Arabia temporarily closed some of their operations, allowing employees on leave from other countries to return home. Some projects that were being considered for countries that could be subject to terrorist attacks were postponed. Even projects that appeared to be feasible from a financial perspective were postponed because of the potential danger to employees.

In addition to the threat of terrorism, there were numerous other ways in which the Persian Gulf crisis could influence cash flows of MNCs. The effects varied with the characteristics of each MNC. The more obvious effects of the crisis were reduced travel and higher oil prices. The reduction in travel adversely affected airlines, hotels, restaurants, luggage manufacturers, photography-related firms (such as Eastman Kodak Co.), and cruise lines.

The Persian Gulf crisis is a clear example of how country risk can change over time. It would have been difficult to forecast that Iraq was going to invade Kuwait or to forecast the events following the invasion. MNCs recognize that some unpredictable events will unfold that will affect their exposure to country risk. Yet they can at least be prepared to revise their operations in order to reduce their exposure.

REDUCING EXPOSURE TO HOST-GOVERNMENT TAKEOVERS

As mentioned in Chapter 16, there are several possible benefits to direct foreign investment. However, country risk can offset such benefits. If an MNC decides to implement a foreign project, it should then attempt to reduce its exposure to that risk. As mentioned earlier, the most severe country risk is a takeover of some form. The most popular techniques for reducing exposure to a takeover are summarized here:

1. *Short-term profit maximization.* This technique concentrates on recovering cash flow quickly, so that in the event of expropriation, losses are minimized. The firm would also exert only a minimum effort to replace worn-out equipment and machinery at the subsidiary. The effect of this strategy may be somewhat reduced due to possible government restrictions on the amount of earnings a subsidiary is allowed to send to its parent per year.

2. *Unique supplies.* If the subsidiary can bring in supplies from its headquarters (or a sister subsidiary) that cannot be duplicated locally, the host government will not be able to take over and operate the subsidiary without such supplies. Also, the supplies could be cut off by the MNC if the subsidiary is treated unfairly.

3. *Hire local labor.* If local employees of the subsidiary are affected by the host government's takeover, they could pressure their government to avoid such action. However, the government could still let those employees retain their positions after taking over the subsidiary. Thus, this strategy has only limited effectiveness in avoiding or reducing a government takeover.

4. *Borrow local funds.* If the subsidiary borrows funds locally, local banks will be concerned about its future performance. Should there be any reason why a government takeover would reduce the probability that the banks would receive their loan repayments promptly, they may pressure the host government to avoid a takeover. However the host government may guarantee repayment to the banks, so this strategy has only limited effectiveness. Nevertheless, it could still be preferable to a situation where the MNC not only loses the subsidiary but also still owes home-country creditors.

5. *Insurance.* Insurance can be purchased to cover the risk of expropriation. For example, the U.S. government provides insurance through the Overseas Private Investment Corporation (OPIC). The insurance premiums paid by a firm depend on the degree of insurance coverage and the risk associated with the firm. Yet, any insurance policy will typically cover only a portion of the company's total exposure to country risk.

Many home countries of MNCs have investment guarantee programs that insure to some extent the risks of expropriation, wars, or currency blockage. Some guarantee programs have a one-year waiting period or longer before compensation is paid on losses due to expropriation. Also, some insurance policies do not cover all forms of expropriation. Furthermore, to be eligible for such insurance, the subsidiary might be required by the country to concentrate on exporting rather than local sales. Even if a subsidiary qualifies for insurance, there is a cost. Any insurance will typically cover only a portion of the assets and may specify a maximum duration of coverage, such as 15 or 20 years. A subsidiary must weigh the benefits of this insurance against the cost of the policy's premiums and potential losses in excess of coverage. The insurance can be helpful, but it does not by itself prevent losses due to expropriation.

The World Bank recently established an affiliate called the Multilateral Investment Guarantee Agency (MIGA) to provide political insurance for MNCs with direct foreign investment in less developed countries. MIGA offers insurance against expropriation, breach of contract, currency inconvertibility, war, and civil disturbances. It is anticipated that MIGA will also offer information about investment opportunities to MNCs.

INTERNATIONAL FINANCIAL MANAGEMENT IN PRACTICE

Protecting Against Terrorism

One form of political risk is terrorism. In recent years, the threat of terrorism has increased, and MNCs have attempted to protect against it. Some of the terrorism by Middle East groups took place in Europe, where many U.S.-based MNCs have subsidiaries. Numerous U.S.-based MNCs with foreign subsidiaries have attempted to maintain a low profile in foreign countries so that terrorists will not use their subsidiaries to show their hatred for the United States. For example, NCH Corporation, a Texas-based chemical company with about 2,000 employees in Europe, attempts to be perceived as a local business. Philbro-Saloman Inc. has developed contingency plans for evacuating its employees at European offices. U.S.-based MNCs such as Hercules Inc. and General Foods reacted to terrorism events by taking additional security measures to protect their property and employees. Heinz Company considered a proposal to transport European executives to the United States for business meetings rather than transporting U.S. executives to Europe.

6. *Planned divestment.* MNCs can phase out their overseas investment by selling off their assets to local investors or the government in stages over time.

7. *Joint ventures.* MNCs can begin their direct foreign investment through a joint venture agreement with the host government. However, if the host government's ideology changes over time, there is risk that the new government will wish to maintain total control over the investment.

8. *Technological secrets.* If the subsidiary can hide the technology in its production process, a government takeover will be less likely. The only way a takeover would work here is if the MNC is willing to provide the necessary technology, and the MNC would provide such information only under conditions of a friendly takeover where it received adequate compensation.

9. *Use of power.* As a last resort, a subsidiary about to be expropriated could threaten the host government that local labor, etc., will revolt if a takeover occurs, or that the firm will support an opposing political activist group. In all likelihood, the host government would consider these possible retaliatory actions by the firm and would not enforce a takeover if it was worried about such threats. A firm might also attempt to fight the takeover in court. However, MNCs normally do not have much of a chance when fighting a host government in the international judicial system.

The appropriate technique to reduce the probability of a takeover is determined by the level of risk exhibited by the country. An MNC may not believe it is necessary to implement a short-run profit maximization strategy initially. However, if over time tensions build, such a strategy might later be used. Because a country's overall risk rating can change periodically, the firm must continue to monitor country risk. It should also have in mind some critical point at which country risk is deemed sufficiently high to warrant strategies (such as those described here) to reduce the likelihood of a government takeover.

The techniques to reduce the risk of a takeover are discussed here from the perspective of an MNC with direct foreign investment in a particular country. In reality, an MNC normally diversifies its direct foreign investment among many countries and thus attempts to avoid excessive exposure in any particular one.

SUMMARY

Country risk analysis from the perspective of an MNC is composed of several functions. First, the MNC identifies the political and financial variables that contribute to the country risk rating. Second, it assigns a rating to each of these variables. Third, it assesses the importance (or influence) of each variable and consolidates them to generate an overall country risk rating. Fourth, it determines whether the overall country risk rating assigned to the country reflects a tolerable or intolerable risk. If the country risk level is intolerable, the proposed project does not deserve further consideration. If the risk is tolerable, the project does deserve further consideration, and the country risk rating should be incorporated into the capital budgeting analysis to assess the proposed project further. Finally, should the MNC decide to accept the project, it must design its operations to best manage the existing country risk.

Country risk analysis includes not only risk assessment but also management of exposure to country risk. Both tasks are critical to the success of any MNC with a significant volume of foreign business. In some cases, it is more important to be able to cope with the problems as they arise than attempt to forecast problems. This is especially true for those country crises that occur randomly and without prior warning.

QUESTIONS

1. List some forms of country risk other than a takeover of a subsidiary by the host government.

2. Identify common political factors for an MNC to consider when assessing country risk. Briefly elaborate on how each factor can affect the risk to the MNC.

3. Identify common financial factors for an MNC to consider when assessing country risk. Briefly elaborate on how each factor can affect the risk to the MNC.

4. Discuss the use of the foreign investment risk matrix (FIRM) to compare country risk among countries. Why do firms have different acceptable zones when using this matrix?

5. Describe the steps involved in assessing country risk once all relevant information has been gathered.

6. Describe the possible errors involved in assessing country risk. In other words, explain why country risk analysis is not always accurate.

7. Explain an MNC's strategy of diversifying projects internationally in order to maintain a low level of overall country risk.

8. Once a project is accepted, country risk analysis for the foreign country involved is no longer necessary, assuming that no other proposed projects are being evaluated for that country. Do you agree with this statement? Why or why not?

9. If the potential return is high enough, any degree of country risk can be tolerated. Do you agree with this statement? Why or why not?

10. An MNC has decided to call a well-known country risk consultant to conduct a country risk analysis on a small country in which the MNC plans to develop a large subsidiary. The MNC prefers to hire the consultant, since it plans to use its employees for other important corporate functions. The consultant uses a computer program that has assigned weights of importance linked to the various factors. The consultant will evaluate the factors for this small country and insert a rating for each factor into the computer. While the assigned weights to the factors are not adjusted by the computer, the factor ratings are adjusted for each particular country the consultant assesses. Do you think the MNC should use this consultant? Why or why not?

11. Explain the micro-assessment of country risk.

12. How could a country risk assessment be used to adjust a project's required rate of return? How could such an assessment be used to instead adjust a project's estimated cash flows?

13. Explain some methods for reducing exposure to existing country risk while maintaining the same amount of business within a particular country.

14. Why do some subsidiaries maintain a low profile as to where their parent is located?

15. Do you think that a proper country risk analysis can replace a capital budgeting analysis of a project considered for a foreign country? Explain.

16. NYU Corporation considered establishing a subsidiary in Zenland; it performed a country risk analysis to help make the decision. It first retrieved a country risk analysis performed about one year earlier, when it had planned to begin a major exporting business to Zenland firms. Then it updated the analysis by incorporating all current information on the key variables that were used in that analysis such as Zenland's willingness to accept exports, its existing quotas, and existing tariff laws. Is this country risk analysis adequate? Explain.

17. In the early 1990s, MNCs such as Alcoa DuPont, Heinz and IBM donated products and technology to foreign countries where they have subsidiaries. How could these actions reduce some forms of country risk?

King Inc.
Country Risk Analysis

CASE
PROBLEM

King Inc., a U.S. firm, is considering the establishment of a small subsidiary in Bulgaria which would produce food products. All ingredients can be obtained or produced in Bulgaria. The final products to be produced by the subsidiary would be distributed in Bulgaria and other Eastern Bloc countries. King Inc. is very interested in this project since there is little competition in that area. Three high-level managers of King Inc. have been assigned the task of assessing the country risk of Bulgaria. Specifically, the managers were asked to list all characteristics of Bulgaria that could adversely affect the performance of this project. The decision on whether to undertake this project will only be made once this country risk analysis is completed, and accounted for in the capital budgeting analysis. Since King Inc. has focused exclusively on domestic business in the past, it is not accustomed to country risk analysis.

a) What factors related to Bulgaria's government deserve to be considered?

b) What country-related factors can affect the demand for the food products to be produced by King Inc.?

c) What country-related factors can affect the cost of production?

PROJECT

1. Review the 10K annual report of an MNC of your choice. Summarize the forms of country risk that the MNC is exposed to according to the 10K report.

SUGGESTED READINGS

Jean J. Boddewyn. "Political Aspects of MNE Theory." *Journal of International Business Studies* (Fall 1988), pp. 341–363. This article integrates various theories about country risk and how it can influence decisions by MNCs to undertake projects in particular countries.

David A. Schmidt. "Analyzing Political Risk." *Business Horizons* (July–August 1986), pp. 43–50. This article provides a comprehensive description of how MNCs should assess country risk.

REFERENCES

Baliga, B. R. "World-Views and Multinational Corporations' Investments in the Less Developed Countries." *Columbia Journal of World Business* (Summer 1984), pp. 80–84.

Bhalla, Bharat. "How Corporations Should Weigh Up Country Risk." *Euromoney* (June 1983), pp. 66–72.

Boddewyn, Jean J. "Political Aspects of MNE Theory." *Journal of International Business Studies* (Fall 1988), pp. 341–363.

Bradley, David. "Managing Against Expropriation." *Harvard Business Review* (July/August 1977), pp. 75–83.

Brewer, Thomas L. "The Instability of Governments and the Instability of Controls on Funds Transfers by Multinational Enterprises: Implications for Political Risk Analysis." *Journal of International Business Studies* (Winter 1983), pp. 147–157.

Chase, C. D., J. L. Kuhle, and C. H. Walther. "The Relevance of Political Risk in Direct Foreign Investment." *Management International Review,* no. 3 (1988), pp. 31–38.

Davidson, W. H., and D. G. McFetridge. "Recent Directions in International Strategies: Production Rationalization or Portfolio Adjustment?" *Columbia*

Journal of World Business (Summer 1984), pp. 95–101.

Davis, Robert R. "Alternative Techniques for Country Risk Evaluation." *Business Economics* (May 1981), pp. 34–41.

Doz, Yves L., and C. K. Prahalad. "How MNCs Cope with Host Government Intervention." *Harvard Business Review* (March–April 1980), pp. 149–157.

Goldstein, Elizabeth, and Jan Vanous. "Country Risk Analysis: Pitfalls of Comparing the Eastern Bloc Countries with the Rest of the World." *Columbia Journal of World Business* (Winter 1983), pp. 10–16.

Jacque, Laurent L., and Peter Lorange. "Hyperinflation and Global Strategic Management." *Columbia Journal of World Business* (Summer 1984), pp. 68–75.

Kobrin, Stephen J. "Political Risks: A Review and Reconsideration." *Journal of International Business Studies* (Spring–Summer 1979), pp. 67–80.

———. "When Does Political Instability Result in Increased Investment Risk?" *Columbia Journal of World Business* (Fall 1978), pp. 113–122.

———. "Foreign Enterprise and Forced Divestment in LDCs." *International Organization* (Winter 1980), pp. 65–88.

Kobrin, Stephen J., John Basek, Stephen Blank, and Joseph La Palombara. "The Assessment and Evaluation of Noneconomic Environments by American Firms: A Preliminary Report." *Journal of International Business Studies* (Spring–Summer 1980): pp. 32–47.

Leavy, Brian. "Assessing Country Risk for Foreign Investment Decisions." *Long-Range Planning* (June 1984), pp. 141–150.

Lewis, M. "Does Political Instability in Developing Countries Affect Foreign Investment Flow? An Empirical Examination." *Management International Review* 3 (1979): pp. 59–68.

Madura, Jeff. "Credit Risk and the Multinational Corporation." *The Banker's Magazine* (November–December 1983): pp. 69–72.

Mascarenhas, B., and C. Atherton. "Problems in Political Risk Assessment." *Management International Review* (February 1983), pp. 22–32.

Merrill, James. "Country Risk Analysis." *Columbia Journal of World Business* (Spring 1982), pp. 88–91.

Micallef, Joseph V. "Political Risk Assessment." *Columbia Journal of World Business* (Spring 1981), pp. 47–52.

Misawa, Misuru. "Financing Japanese Investments in the U.S.: Case Studies of a Large and a Medium-Sized Firm." *Financial Management* (Winter 1985), pp. 5–12.

Nigh, Douglas "The Effect of Political Events on U.S. Direct Foreign Investment: A Pooled Time-Series Cross-Sectional Analysis." *Journal of International Business Studies* (Spring 1985), pp. 1–17.

Robock, Stefan H. "Political Risk: Identification and Assessment." *Columbia Journal of World Business* (July–August 1971), pp. 6–20.

Rummel, R. J., and David A. Heenan. "How Multinationals Analyze Political Risk." *Harvard Business Review* (January–February 1978), pp. 67–76.

Saini, Krishan G., and Philip S. Bates. "A Survey of the Quantitative Approaches to Country Risk Analysis." *Journal of Banking and Finance* (June 1984), pp. 341–355.

Schmidt, David A. "Analyzing Political Risk." *Business Horizons* (July–August 1986), pp. 43–50.

Simon, Jeffrey. "A Theoretical Perspective on Political Risk." *Journal of International Business Studies* (Winter 1984), pp. 123–143.

Simon, Jeffrey D. "Political Risk Assessment: Past Trends and Future Prospects." *Columbia Journal of World Business* (Fall 1982), pp. 62–71.

Tallman, Stephen B. "Home Country Political Risk and Foreign Direct Investment in the U.S." *Journal of International Business Studies* (Summer 1988), pp. 219–234.

Tavis, Lee A., and Roy L. Crum. "Performance-Based Strategies for MNC Portfolio Balancing." *Columbia Journal of World Business* (Summer 1984), pp. 85–94.

CHAPTER 20

Long-Term Financing

Multinational corporations (MNCs) typically use long-term sources of funds to finance long-term projects. They have access to domestic and foreign sources of funds. It is worthwhile for MNCs to consider all possible forms of financing before making their final decision.

A critical part of the financing decision is the currency of denomination. The influence of exchange rates on the cost of long-term financing is illustrated in this chapter, along with actual data to show how the cost of financing can vary significantly with the currency of denomination. Bonds with floating coupon rates are also discussed to illustrate the uncertainty inherent in the cost of financing. A methodology to assess the costs of borrowing when issuing Eurobonds is suggested. Finally, financing with multiple currencies is discussed.

LONG-TERM FINANCING DECISION

The long-term financing decision of the MNC involves some aspects similar to short-term financing. Recall that the "effective" cost of short-term financing considered both the quoted interest rate and the percentage change in the exchange rate of the currency borrowed over the loan life. Just as currencies exhibit different interest rates on short-term bank loans, bond yields can vary as well among currencies. Exhibit 20.1 illustrates the long-term bond yields for several different countries. The wide differentials in yields at any given point in time are evident. The yields shown in Exhibit 20.1 do not account for exchange rate fluctuations. That is, each yield shown reflects what an investor *within* the country of concern would have earned from bonds denominated in the local currency.

Because Swiss and German bonds sometimes have lower yields, it should not be surprising that U.S. corporations often consider issuing bonds in those countries denominated in Swiss francs or German marks. Since the actual financing cost to a U.S. corporation issuing a foreign currency-denominated bond is affected by that currency's value relative to the U.S. dollar during the financing period, there is no guarantee that the bond would be less costly

EXHIBIT 20.1   Bond Yields Among Countries

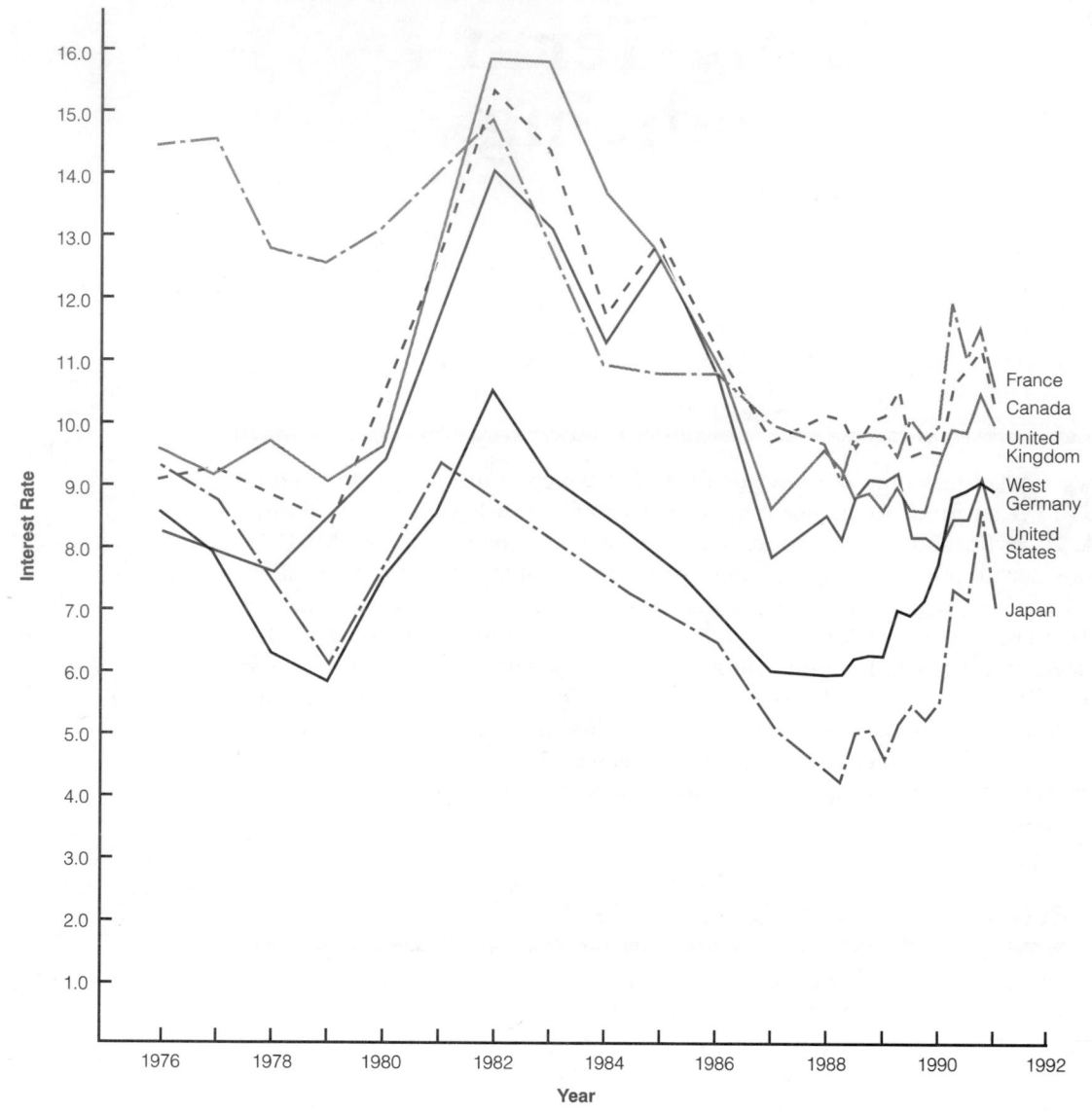

than a U.S. dollar-denominated bond. The borrowing firm must make coupon payments in the currency denominating the bond. If this currency appreciates against the firm's home currency, the funds needed to make coupon payments will increase. For this reason, a firm is not necessarily going to denominate debt in a currency that exhibits a low interest rate.

To make the long-term financing decision, the MNC must (1) determine the amount of funds needed, (2) forecast the price at which it can sell the bond, and (3) forecast periodic exchange rate values for the currency it plans to use for denominating the bond. This information can be used to determine the bond's financing costs, which can be compared with the financing costs the firm would incur using its home currency. Finally, the uncertainty of the actual financing costs to be incurred from foreign financing must be accounted for as well. To illustrate the borrower's analysis of financing with Eurobonds, an example is provided here.

Financing with Bonds Denominated in a Stable Currency

Consider a U.S.-based MNC that needs to borrow $1,000,000 over a three-year period. This reflects a relatively short time period for bond financing but will allow for a more simplified example. Assume the firm believes it can sell dollar denominated bonds at par value if it provides a coupon rate of 14 percent. It also has the alternative of denominating the bonds in German marks to sell in the Eurobond market in which case it would convert its borrowed marks to dollars to use as needed. Then, it would need to obtain marks annually to make the coupon payments. Assume the current exchange rate of the German mark is $.50. The firm would need 2 million marks (computed as $1,000,000/$.50 per mark) to obtain the $1 million it initially needs. The firm believes it can sell the mark-denominated bonds at par value if it provides a coupon rate of 10 percent. No change is expected in the exchange rate in the future, and coupon payments are made on an annual basis. The costs of both financing alternatives are illustrated in Exhibit 20.2. The outflow payment schedule of each financing method is provided here. The outflow payments if the firm finances with dollar-denominated bonds is known. In addition, the number of marks needed at the end of each period is known if the firm finances with a mark-denominated bond. Yet, because the future exchange rate of the mark is uncertain, the number of dollars needed to obtain the necessary marks to each year is uncertain.

If the firm can at least estimate the future exchange rate of the mark, then it can compare the anticipated dollar-outflow payments for both financing alternatives. In this comparison, the first step is to determine the present

EXHIBIT 20.2 Comparison of Financing with U.S. Dollar Bonds versus German Mark Bonds

Financing Alternative	Payment at the End of Year:		
	1	2	3
1.) Denominate bonds in U.S. dollars	$140,000	$140,000	$1,140,000
Present value of financing payments using 14% discount rate	$122,807	$107,725	$769,468
Cumulative present value of financing (using 14% discount rate)	$122,807	$230,532	$1,000,000
2.) Denominate bonds in German marks	DM 200,000	DM 200,000	DM 2,200,000
Dollar outflows assuming no change in exchange rate	$100,000	$100,000	$1,100,000
Approximate present value of financing with marks using 14% discount rate	$87,719	$76,947	$742,469
Approximate cumulative present value of financing (using 14% discount rate)	$87,719	$164,666	$907,135

value of anticipated outflow payments. The present value of dollar-outflow payments for each period is derived in Exhibit 20.2. Adding up these periodic present values will provide the present value of the financing costs for each financing alternative. If the firm finances with dollar-denominated debt, the present value of dollar-outflow payments is $122,807 + $107,725 + $769,468 = $1,000,000. Alternatively, if the firm finances with mark-denominated debt, the present value of anticipated dollar outflow payments is $87,719 + $76,947 + $742,469 = $907,135. Since the firm is financing, it prefers to use the alternative that exhibits a lower present value of financing payments.

In our example, the mark-denominated debt appears to be less costly. However, recall that the cost of this financing is uncertain. It is unrealistic to assume that the mark will remain stable over time. Consequently, some MNCs may choose to issue dollar-denominated debt even though it appears more costly. The potential savings from issuing bonds denominated in a foreign currency must be weighed against the potential risk of such a method. In this example, risk reflects the possibility that the mark will appreciate to a degree that causes the mark-denominated bonds to be more costly than dollar-denominated bonds.

Financing with Bonds Denominated in a Strong Currency

To illustrate the risk involved in financing with a bond denominated in marks, assume the mark appreciated from $.50 to $.55 at the end of Year 1, to $.60 at the end of Year 2, and to $.65 by the end of Year 3. In this case, the payments made by the U.S. firm are displayed in Exhibit 20.3. From a comparison of the dollar outflows in this scenario with the outflows that would have occurred from a dollar-denominated bond, the risk to a firm from denominating a bond in a foreign currency is evident. Of course, the scenario described here will not necessarily occur. Nevertheless, it demonstrates how future outflows related to bond financing can be greater than expected due to unforeseen currency fluctuations. The period of the last payment is particularly crucial for bond financing in foreign currencies. It includes not only the final coupon payment but the principal as well. Normally, exchange rates are more difficult to predict over longer time horizons. Thus, the time at which the principal is to be repaid is so far away that it may be virtually impossible to have a reliable estimate of the exchange rate at that time. For this reason,

EXHIBIT 20.3 Financing with German Marks During a Strong-Mark Period

	End of Year		
	1	*2*	*3*
Payments in German marks	DM 200,000	DM 200,000	DM 2,200,000
Mark exchange rate at time of payment	$.55	$.60	$.65
Payments in U.S. dollars	$110,000	$120,000	$1,430,000
Present value of financing (using 14% discount rate)	$96,491	$92,336	$965,209
Cumulative present value of financing	$96,491	$188,827	$1,154,036

some firms may be uncomfortable issuing bonds denominated in foreign currencies.

Financing with Bonds Denominated in a Weak Currency

Just as an appreciating currency increases the periodic outflow payments of the bond issuer, a depreciating currency will reduce outflow payments. To illustrate, consider the same information provided earlier on a three-year bond denominated in German marks. Also assume the mark depreciates from $.50 to $.45 at the end of Year 1, to $.40 at the end of Year 2, and to $.35 by the end of Year 3. In this case, the payments made by the U.S. firm are shown in Exhibit 20.4. When one compares the dollar outflows in this scenario with the outflows that would have occurred from a dollar-denominated bond (as shown in Exhibit 20.4), the potential savings from foreign financing is evident.

Up to this point, three scenarios have been evaluated: (1) no change in the mark's exchange rate, (2) an appreciating mark, and (3) a depreciating mark. Exhibit 20.5 summarizes the results of the previous scenarios, illustrating how exchange rates can influence the outflow payments from financing with a bond denominated in a foreign currency. Because the numbers in the previous examples were hypothetical, they do not reflect what would have actually occurred for firms in any given period. The discussion that follows provides results more representative of what has occurred in recent years.

BOND FINANCING PERFORMANCE BASED ON ACTUAL DATA

Consider a U.S. firm that as of January 1977 sells bonds at par and makes coupon payments at the end of each year. The bond's term to maturity is assumed to be four years, and the coupon rate is assumed to be fixed over the life of the bond. The initial amount borrowed is assumed to be the equivalent of $50,000,000. The payments made are dependent on the currency denominating the bond. Seven foreign currencies are reviewed here.

After evaluating these bonds, a second four-year period starting in January 1981 is assessed. Then, a three-year period starting in January 1985 is as-

EXHIBIT 20.4 Financing with German Marks During a Weak-Mark Period

	End of Year		
	1	*2*	*3*
Payments in German marks	DM 200,000	DM 200,000	DM 2,200,000
Mark exchange rate at time of payment	$.45	$.40	$.35
Payments in U.S. dollars	$90,000	$80,000	$770,000
Present value of financing (using 14% discount rate)	$78,947	$61,557	$519,728
Cumulative present value of financing	$78,947	$140,504	$660,232

EXHIBIT 20.5 Impact of Currency Fluctuations on Outflow Payments for Mark-Denominated Bonds

	Payment at End of Year:			Cumulative Present Value of Financing Over the 3 Years
	1	*2*	*3*	
Scenario 1: No change in mark value	$100,000	$100,000	$1,100,000	$ 907,135
Scenario 2: Strong mark	$110,000	$120,000	$1,430,000	$1,154,036
Scenario 3: Weak mark	$ 90,000	$ 80,000	$ 770,000	$ 660,232

sessed. To examine each period, exchange rates of the currencies (with respect to the U.S. dollar) are provided on an annual basis. These exchange rates are shown in Exhibit 20.6. These currencies generally appreciated during the first period (from 1977 to January 1981), depreciated during the second period (from January 1981 to January 1985), and appreciated during the third period (from January 1985 to January 1988).

Coupon rates have been estimated using *International Financial Statistics* data for the different currencies and are listed in Exhibit 20.7. They are approximations and actually depend on several factors, including the issuing firm's default risk and the bond's term to maturity. Also, there can be restrictions prohibiting use of a particular currency for bond denomination. Bonds denominated in each currency are examined in Exhibit 20.7 for each period. For each currency, the annual dollar outflows needed to pay bondholders are shown. In the final year of each period, the par value would need to be paid out to the bondholders along with the coupon payment.

A review of Period 1 (the top part of the table) shows that dollar-denominated bonds would have been a less expensive way to borrow. As an extreme example, review the payments necessary for the bonds denominated in British pounds. The coupon payments for pound-denominated bonds are

EXHIBIT 20.6 Exchange Rates of Major Currencies Used to Measure the Cost of Financing in Various Bond Denominations

Date	British Pound	Canadian Dollar	Dutch Guilder	French Franc	German Mark	Japanese Yen	Swiss Franc
1/1/77	$1.7025	$.9916	$.4071	$.2017	$.4240	$.003414	$.4090
1/1/78	1.9200	.9142	.4425	.2128	.4770	.004174	.5032
1/1/79	2.0435	.8435	.5086	.2404	.5510	.005155	.6203
1/1/80	2.2145	.8570	.5284	.2491	.5799	.004767	.6279
1/1/81	2.3950	.8386	.4717	.2208	.5074	.004926	.5618
1/1/82	1.9280	.8429	.4065	.1760	.4459	.004568	.5582
1/1/83	1.6200	.8098	.3802	.1485	.4199	.004271	.4982
1/1/84	1.4525	.8038	.3268	.1200	.3676	.004320	.4587
1/1/85	1.1592	.7576	.2813	.1039	.3175	.003978	.3846
1/1/86	1.4445	.7155	.3608	.1322	.4579	.004988	.4815
1/1/87	1.4745	.7243	.4562	.1549	.4817	.006285	.6161
1/1/88	1.8570	.7678	.5560	.1852	.6266	.008111	.7746

EXHIBIT 20.7 Bond Payment Estimates for Various Currencies Based on Borrowing the Equivalent of $50 Million

Period 1: 1977–1980:

Currency Used to Denominate Bonds	Approximate Coupon Rate as of 1/1/77	Approximate Payments (in Thousands of U.S. Dollars) Made at the End of:			
		1977	1978	1979	1980
British pound	12.73%	$7,178	$7,640	$8,279	$8,954 + $70,338
Canadian dollar	8.70	4,010	3,700	3,759	3,679 + 42,285
Dutch guilder	13.38	7,777	8,358	8,683	7,752 + 57,934
French franc	9.61	5,069	5,727	5,934	5,260 + 54,735
German mark	6.20	3,487	4,029	4,240	3,710 + 59,835
Japanese yen	7.33	4,481	5,534	5,117	5,288 + 72,144
Swiss franc	4.05	2,491	3,071	3,109	2,782 + 68,680
U.S. dollar	7.67	3,835	3,835	3,835	3,835 + 50,000

Period 2: 1981–1984:

Currency Used to Denominate Bonds	Approximate Coupon Rate as of 1/1/81	Approximate Payments (in Thousands of U.S. Dollars) Made at the End of:			
		1981	1982	1983	1984
British pound	14.74%	$5,933	$4,985	$4,470	$3,567 + $24,200
Canadian dollar	15.22	7,649	7,349	7,294	6,875 + 45,171
Dutch guilder	11.55	4,977	4,654	4,001	3,444 + 29,818
French franc	15.66	6,241	5,266	4,255	3,684 + 23,528
German mark	10.40	5,075	4,779	4,184	3,614 + 31,287
Japanese yen	8.66	4,015	3,754	3,797	3,497 + 40,378
Swiss franc	5.57	2,767	2,470	2,274	1,907 + 34,229
U.S. dollar	13.72	6,860	6,860	6,860	6,860 + 50,000

Period 3: 1985–1987:

Currency Used to Denominate Bonds	Approximate Coupon Rate as of 1/1/85	Approximate Payments (in Thousands of U.S. Dollars) Made at the End of:		
		1985	1986	1987
British pound	10.62%	$6,617	$6,754	$8,506 + $80,098
Canadian dollar	11.04	5,213	5,277	5,594 + 50,673
Dutch guilder	7.34	4,707	5,952	7,254 + 98,827
French franc	10.94	6,960	8,155	9,750 + 89,124
German mark	6.90	4,976	5,234	6,809 + 98,677
Japanese yen	6.34	3,975	5,008	6,464 + 101,948
Swiss franc	4.78	2,992	3,829	4,813 + 100,702
U.S. dollar	10.62	5,310	5,310	5,310 + 50,000

often more than twice the required payment for dollar-denominated bonds. By the time par value was paid to bondholders, the pound was very strong. This required more than $70 million to cover payment for par value. Recall that par value was valued at the equivalent of $50,000,000 just four years earlier.

The very high payments resulting from the pound-denominated bond during the 1977–1981 period are due to the strengthening of the pound during this period. If a U.S. firm had expected such currency movements, it would not have even considered issuing bonds denominated in pounds. Of course, it may have mistakenly expected the pound to depreciate during this period. The cost of such a mistake could be devastating to a firm.

Most of the other bonds denominated in foreign currencies would also have been expensive from 1977–1981, although not as expensive as pound-denominated bonds. Only the Canadian dollar bonds would have been preferable to U.S. dollar bonds during this period from the U.S. firm's perspective. This is because the Canadian dollar generally depreciated during this period.

The bonds are reevaluated in the middle section of Exhibit 20.7 for a second four-year period, from 1981–1985. In this period, most currencies weakened against the U.S. dollar. Consequently, most bonds denominated in foreign currencies would have been less expensive sources of financing to a U.S. firm than U.S. dollar-denominated bonds.

The bonds are reevaluated in the lower section of Exhibit 20.7 for a three-year period, 1985–1988. During this period, currencies generally appreciated against the dollar. Consequently, large dollar outflows would have been necessary to cover the payments to bondholders if the bonds had been denominated in a foreign currency.

TECHNIQUES TO EVALUATE BOND DENOMINATION ALTERNATIVES

A firm in need of long-term funds must decide which currency to use in denominating the bond. When considering a foreign currency for which it does not have future cash inflows, it must access the potential strength or weakness of that currency. One approach to assess the feasibility of each currency is to forecast its exchange rate for each period where an outflow payment would be provided to bondholders. Then determine the amount of the home currency needed to cover the payments according to those forecasted exchange rates. Because it is difficult to develop accurate point estimates of exchange rates, this approach can easily lead to poor decisions. Therefore, it is necessary to consider alternative techniques for projecting future exchange rates.

Use of Exchange Rate Probabilities

An alternative approach to project point estimates of future exchange rates is to develop a probability distribution for an exchange rate at each period where payments are made to bondholders. In this case, the *expected value* of the exchange rate can be computed for each period by multiplying each possible exchange rate by its associated probability and totaling the products. Then, the exchange rate's expected value can be used to forecast the cash outflows necessary to pay bondholders over each period. The exchange rate's expected value may vary from one period to another. After developing probability distributions and computing the expected values, one can estimate the present value of financing payments and compare them with the present value of outflow payments related to a bond denominated in the home currency.

Using this approach, a single outflow estimate is derived for each payment period, and a single estimate is derived for the present value of financing costs over the life of the bond. Since this approach does not indicate the range of possible results that may occur, it is difficult to assess the risk of issuing a bond denominated in a foreign currency. In the present context, risk refers to the probability that a bond denominated in a foreign currency is more costly than a bond denominated in the home currency. It is possible to measure such risk through use of simulation, as explained next.

Use of Simulation

A computer simulation model can aid in the long-term financing decision as follows. Consider a U.S. firm that needs $2,000,000 and plans to issue a four-year bond. It is determining whether to denominate the bond in U.S. dollars or British pounds. Assume the pound-denominated bond would exhibit a coupon rate of 10 percent and could be sold at par value. The current exchange rate of the pound is assumed to be $2.00, so if the firm issues pound-denominated bonds, par value of these bonds must equal 1,000,000 pounds. Bondholders would receive 100,000 pounds (10% of par value) at the end of each year during the next four years. At the end of the fourth year, the principal will be paid out along with the final coupon payment. Assume the exchange rate of the pound is expected to be between $1.80 and $2.20 after one year, and is then expected to appreciate each year thereafter by between 10 percent and 20 percent (with an equal probability of any rate within this range occurring).

The U.S. firm can feed the information provided here into a simulation computer program. Then, the program will randomly draw one of the possible values from the exchange rate distribution for the end of each year and determine the outflow payments necessary based on those exchange rates. Consequently, the present value of these financing payments (based on some assumed discount rate) is determined. The procedure described up to this point represents one iteration. Next, the program will repeat the procedure by again randomly drawing one of the possible values from the exchange rate distribution at the end of each year. This will provide a new schedule of outflow payments reflecting those randomly selected exchange rates. The present value of the financing payments for this second iteration is also determined. The simulation program continually repeats this procedure, perhaps 100 times or so (as many times as desired).

For every iteration, a possible scenario of future exchange rates is proposed, which is then used to determine the present value of financing payments if that scenario does occur. Thus, the simulation generates a distribution of present values of financing payments that can then be compared with the known present value of financing costs if the bond was denominated in U.S. dollars (the home currency). Such a comparison will enable a decision on whether the bond to be issued should be denominated in pounds or U.S. dollars.

Using the information provided in this example along with an assumed discount rate of 10 percent, the present value of financing payments from a pound-denominated bond has been estimated using a simulation program. The results are shown in Exhibit 20.8. There is a 90 percent chance the present value of financing payments will be at least $2,545,000 (see below the 90 percent level in the table), an 80 percent chance the present value of financing payments will be at least $2,672,000, and so on. We could compare

EXHIBIT 20.8 Projected Outflow Payments (in U.S. Dollars) if Pound-Denominated Bonds Are Issued (*in thousands of dollars*)

Discounted Outflow Payments to Holders of Pound Denominated Bonds	Probability of Value Being Greater than Indicated:								
	90%	*80%*	*70%*	*60%*	*50%*	*40%*	*30%*	*20%*	*10%*
Strong pound scenario	$2,545	$2,672	$2,745	$2,802	$2,831	$2,880	$2,964	$3,028	$3,096
Moderate pound scenario	$1,803	$1,841	$1,906	$1,960	$2,004	$2,047	$2,089	$2,121	$2,169
Weak pound scenario	$1,222	$1,264	$1,298	$1,334	$1,350	$1,371	$1,399	$1,422	$1,459

this probability distribution of discounted outflow payments with the known discounted payments that would result from issuing a dollar-denominated bond. In this case, the dollar-denominated bond would look more attractive since its discounted outflow payments would be $2,000,000 (if its coupon rate equals 10 percent). While the coupon rates of the two bonds are similar, the pound's anticipated appreciation causes outflow payments in pounds to be expensive.

However, consider a second example where the pound was expected to change by between −5 percent (depreciation) and +5 percent (appreciation) each year. Simulation was applied to this scenario, and the results are shown in Exhibit 20.8. There appears to be about a 50 percent chance that issuing the pound-denominated bond will be more expensive than the dollar-denominated bond (since the figure $2,004,000 under the 50 percent column is close to the $2,000,000 level that reflects discounted outflow payments for the dollar-denominated bond).

As a final example, consider a scenario where the pound is expected to be worth between $1.80 and $2.20 one year from now, and will then depreciate by between 10 percent and 20 percent annually thereafter. The simulation program was applied to this scenario (with the results again shown in Exhibit 20.8). This suggests that based on the given exchange rate projections, financing with pound-denominated bonds will most likely result in discounted outflow payments between $1,222,000 (under the "90%" column) and $1,459,000 (under the "10%" column). Since there is a 10 percent chance the actual value of discounted payments will exceed $1,459,000, this implies a 90 percent chance they will be less than or equal to $1,459,000. Recall that the discounted payments from issuing dollar-denominated bonds amount to $2,000,000. For a weak-pound scenario, financing with pounds should provide favorable results. The simulation program not only confirms such logic, but provides a range of possible outcomes that could occur.

The decision of which currency to use in denominating bonds may vary among firms, even if their results from the simulation technique are the same. This is because firms have different degrees of risk aversion. A very conservative firm may consider a foreign currency to denominate bonds only if there is close to a 100 percent probability that such a strategy could be less costly. A more daring firm may be willing to denominate bonds in a foreign currency if there is even a reasonable chance that such a strategy could be less costly. The simulation results provide a probability that issuing the bond denominated in a foreign currency will be feasible. The results shown in Exhibit 20.8 illustrate how that probability depends on the scenario expected for the foreign currency's value.

FLOATING-RATE EUROBONDS: AN ADDITIONAL RISK TO CONSIDER

Eurobonds are often issued with a floating, rather than fixed, coupon rate. This means the coupon rate will fluctuate over time in accordance with other going interest rates. For example, the coupon rate may somehow be tied to the **London Interbank Offer Rate (LIBOR),** which is a rate at which Euro-banks lend funds to each other. As LIBOR increases, so would the coupon rate of a floating-rate bond. A floating coupon rate can be an advantage to the bond issuer during periods of decreasing interest rates, when otherwise, the firm would be locked in at a higher coupon rate over the life of the bond. It can also be a disadvantage during periods of rising interest rates.

When coupon rates are fixed, the only uncertain variable to be assessed from denominating a bond in a foreign currency is the exchange rate. If the coupon rate is floating, then projections are required for not only exchange rates but for interest rates as well. Recall that simulation can be used to examine the possible outcomes of bond financing based on various possible exchange rate scenarios. It can be used simultaneously to examine outcomes based on various possible changes in the coupon rate over the life of the loan, as the following example illustrates.

Suppose a U.S. firm needs $10 million for five years and considers issuing a U.S. dollar-denominated bond, priced at par, with a fixed coupon rate of 10 percent. As an alternative, it can issue a mark-denominated bond, priced at par, with an initial coupon rate equal to 10 percent, but allowed to float annually. Assume the exchange rate of the mark is expected to depreciate by between 2.5 percent and 7.5 percent annually. The new variable of concern here is the floating coupon rate. Assume the coupon rate of the mark is expected to change by between 0 percent and +2 percent per year, with an equal probability of all points within this range occurring. A simulation program was run using the exchange rate probability distributions along with the coupon rate probability distribution for each period. Both of these variables will have an impact on the amount of dollars the firm will need at the end of each year to pay off the bondholders. Once these payments are estimated, it is possible to estimate the present value of the payments schedule. Each iteration reflects a unique scenario for exchange rates and coupon rates. For each iteration, the present value of the dollar outflows converted to marks for payment to bondholders is estimated. Results of the simulation model applied to the information in this example are displayed in Exhibit 20.9. A discount rate of 10 percent was used to compute present values.

The present value of outflows from issuing a dollar-denominated bond is $10 million and is known with certainty. From Exhibit 20.9, there is a 90 percent chance the mark-denominated bond would require discounted outflows that exceed $9,780,000, an 80 percent chance that discounted outflow payments would exceed $9,870,000 and so on. Since there is a 60 percent chance that discounted outflows would exceed $10,090,000 (see under the "60%" column), this implies there is just over a 60 percent probability the

INTERNATIONAL FINANCIAL MANAGEMENT IN PRACTICE

Corporate Use of the Eurobond Market

Many U.S.-based MNCs utilize the Eurobond market as a source of funds, including Johnson & Johnson, Monsanto, RCA Corporation, Burroughs Corporation, General Electric, Procter & Gamble, Westinghouse, and IBM. Some U.S.-based MNCs use the Eurobond market to issue bonds denominated in non-dollar currencies. While some of these bonds may be exposed to exchange rate risk, others are covered by incoming cash flows in the same currency. As an example, Sperry Corporation issued 10-year bonds in Switzerland. The coupon payments were to be made in Swiss francs. Because Swiss interest rates were lower than U.S. rates, Sperry was reducing its interest payments. While this strategy sometimes backfires on the issuer when the currency denominating the debt strengthens, Sperry had covered against this possibility. Its Swiss subsidiaries used a portion of their dividends that they normally remitted to the parent to make interest payments on the bonds.

Some MNCs utilize a variety of currencies to denominate their currencies. For example, CPC International Inc. recently issued one set of bonds denominated in German marks and another set of bonds denominated in Swiss francs. Dow Chemical has bonds outstanding that are denominated in yen, marks, pounds, and even Kuwaiti dinar. Diversifying among currencies may be aimed at either reducing exchange rate risk (relative to the risk from denominating bonds in a single foreign currency) or at matching the various incoming payments in various currencies.

discounted outflows from issuing a mark-denominated bond will be greater than those from issuing a dollar-denominated bond.

In this example, the mark-denominated bond looks attractive because it is expected to weaken (which would allow fewer dollars to achieve the necessary marks for payment to bondholders). However, because interest rates are expected to increase during this time period, the floating coupon rate could make the mark-denominated bond undesirable. The simulation technique enables the corporation to determine from this information whether mark-denominated bonds should be issued, since it helps quantify the odds that the dollar-denominated bond will be more attractive. Recall that simulation generated an approximate 60 percent probability the dollar-denominated bond would be less expensive to the MNCs. In addition, it generated the range of outcomes that might occur based on the information provided. If the coupon rate had been expected to decrease over time, the results from the simulation

EXHIBIT 20.9 Projections of Discounted Outflow Payments (*in thousands of dollars*) From Issuing a Mark-Denominated Bond

Probability of Value Being Greater Than Indicated:								
90%	*80%*	*70%*	*60%*	*50%*	*40%*	*30%*	*20%*	*10%*
$9,780	$9,870	$9,940	$10,090	$10,170	$10,310	$10,390	$10,450	$10,590

would have been more favorable for the mark-denominated bond than what is shown in Exhibit 20.9.

OFFSETTING EXCHANGE RATE RISK OF DEBT DENOMINATED IN FOREIGN CURRENCIES

Up to this point, bonds denominated in foreign currencies have been evaluated as if the issuing firm had not hedged the exchange rate exposure at all. In reality, some firms may have incoming payments in particular currencies, which could offset upcoming payments related to bond financing. Thus, it may be possible to finance with bonds denominated in a foreign currency that exhibits a lower coupon rate without becoming exposed to exchange rate risk. Yet, it is unlikely that a firm would be able to perfectly match the timing and amount of the outflows in the foreign currency denominating the bond to the inflows in that currency. Therefore, some exposure to exchange rate fluctuations would exist. The exposure can be substantially reduced though, if the firm receives inflows in the particular currency denominating the bond. This can help to stabilize the firm's cash flow. Numerous MNCs, including Allied-Signal Inc. and Coca-Cola Company, issue bonds in some of the foreign currencies that they receive from operations.

Even when a firm does not expect to be receiving foreign currency inflows, it can sometimes issue bonds denominated in foreign currencies to stabilize net cash flows. For example, consider a U.S. firm that often exports products to West Germany with the price denominated in U.S. dollars. If the dollar strengthens, exports become expensive to German purchasers, thereby discouraging their demand for the U.S. products. This would normally reduce cash inflows. However, if a mark-denominated bond was previously issued, a stronger dollar would require fewer dollars to obtain the sufficient number of marks to make coupon payments and this would reduce the cash outflows. Overall, the reduction in both cash inflows and outflows may have no significant impact on net cash flow. If the dollar instead weakened, the outflow payments to cover bond coupon payments would increase. The increased outflow payments would be at least partially offset, however, by increased cash flows due to an increased export business by the U.S. firm (resulting from the weak dollar).

When a bond denominated in a foreign currency has a lower coupon rate than the firm's home currency, the firm may consider issuing bonds denominated in that currency and simultaneously hedging its exchange rate risk through the forward market. Because the forward market can sometimes accommodate requests of five years or longer, such an approach may be possible. The firm could arrange to purchase the foreign currency forward for each time at which payments are required. However, the forward rate for each horizon will most likely be above the spot rate. Consequently, hedging these future outflow payments may not be less costly than the outflow payments needed if a dollar-denominated bond were issued. The relationship implied here is similar to the interest rate parity theory discussed in earlier chapters, except that the point of view in this chapter is long-term rather than short-term.

When financing in bonds, one must assess not only the potential savings from denominating a bond in a foreign currency, but the risk resulting from exchange rate fluctuations as well. Not all foreign currencies exhibit the same risk. From a U.S. borrower's perspective, a bond denominated in Canadian dollars is less risky than a bond denominated in German marks (assuming it has no offsetting position in either of these currencies). This is because the Canadian dollar exhibits less fluctuation against the U.S. dollar over time and therefore is less likely to deviate far from its projected future exchange rate. If all other characteristics of two bonds denominated in different currencies are similar, a U.S. borrower should prefer the bond denominated in the currency that is more stable.

LONG-TERM FINANCING IN MULTIPLE CURRENCIES

Up to this point, discussion has focused on choosing the most feasible currency for a bond. In some cases, the appropriate selection may be not a single currency or bond, but a portfolio of currencies for a borrower. Since the lifetime of bonds is too long to single out any particular currency as being safe, a portfolio of diversified currencies could reduce the risk incurred by the bond issuer. For example, a U.S. firm may denominate bonds in several foreign currencies rather than a single foreign currency so that substantial appreciation of any one particular currency will not drastically increase the dollars necessary to cover the financing payments. To illustrate the potential advantage of bond diversification, consider the example of an MNC based in the U.S. that plans to issue bonds and has considered four alternatives:

1. Issue bonds denominated in U.S. dollars.
2. Issue bonds denominated in Japanese yen.
3. Issue bonds denominated in Swiss francs.
4. Issue some bonds denominated in Japanese yen and some bonds denominated in Swiss francs.

Assume the MNC has no net exposure in either Japanese yen or Swiss francs. Also assume the coupon rate for a U.S. dollar-denominated bond is 14 percent, while for a yen- or franc-denominated bond the coupon rate is 8 percent. It is expected that any of these bonds could be sold at par value.

There is a substantial difference here between the coupon rates of the dollar-denominated bonds versus those denominated in a foreign currency. If the Swiss franc appreciates against the U.S. dollar, the actual financing cost from issuing franc-denominated bonds may be higher than that of the dollar-denominated bonds. If the Japanese yen appreciates substantially against the U.S. dollar, the actual financing cost from issuing yen-denominated bonds may be higher than that of the dollar-denominated bonds. If the exchange rates of the Swiss franc and Japanese yen move in opposite directions against the U.S. dollar, then both types of bonds could not simultaneously be more costly than dollar-denominated bonds, so financing with both type of bonds would almost ensure that the overall financing cost to the U.S. firm will be less than the cost from issuing a dollar-denominated bond.

In reality, there is no guarantee the exchange rates of the Swiss franc and Japanese yen will move in opposite directions. However, if the currency movements are not highly correlated, it is unlikely that both currencies would simultaneously appreciate to an extent that would offset their lower coupon rate advantage. Therefore, financing in bonds denominated in more than one foreign currency can increase the probability that the overall cost of foreign financing will be less than financing with the domestic currency (U.S. dollars in our example). This example involves only two foreign currencies. In reality, a firm may consider several currencies that exhibit lower interest rates and issue a portion of bonds in each of these currencies. Such a strategy can increase the other costs (advertising, printing, etc.) of issuing bonds, but that cost may be offset by a reduction in cash outflows to bondholders.

Currency Cocktail Bonds

There is a method by which a firm can finance in several currencies without issuing various types of bonds (thus avoiding higher transaction costs). It could develop a **currency cocktail bond,** denominated in not one, but a mixture (or "cocktail") of currencies. Within the Eurobond market, a cocktail bond may be preferred over the single-currency bond since it can reduce exchange rate risk. One alternative to this method is homemade diversification, by purchasing separate Eurobond issues, each of which is denominated in a unique currency. But this procedure entails credit checks by the bond purchaser on various bond issuers and necessitates a large pool of investment funds. Also, the transaction costs associated with purchasing small quantities of various Eurobonds are higher than if one type of Eurobond were purchased. These comparisons suggest that a Eurobond may be more marketable if denominated in a currency cocktail rather than a single currency.

A currency cocktail simply reflects a multi-currency unit of account. Several currency cocktails have been developed to denominate international bonds and some have already been used in this manner. Two of the more popular currency cocktails are the **European Currency Unit** (ECU) and **Special Drawing Right** (SDR). The ECU is linked to the weighted currency values of European currencies, and its value changes only when the values of component currencies change. Because the ECU is determined by the values of European currencies, European Monetary System members are the major users.

The ECU has become a popular unit of account for several reasons. It has often been used to price cars, hotel bills, and even to denominate deposits and loans. Because of the common trading among European countries, it reflects a common unit of account to all countries. Since it is made up of currencies, its value will change against any single currency, yet its degree of variability should be low because no single currency has too much influence in its value. Thus, even if one or two of the currencies comprising the ECU change drastically in value, the ECU's value should not be altered to a great degree. The ECU's relative stability also is a desirable characteristic for denominating bonds traded among European countries.

Another popular currency cocktail is the Special Drawing Right (SDR) composite, which was originally devised as an alternative foreign reserve asset but is now used to denominate bonds and bank deposits and to price various services. Its value was defined in terms of gold until 1974, when its formula was specified in terms of 16 currencies. All currencies that were used for at least 1 percent of total world trade were included in the portfolio. The International Monetary Fund (IMF) assigned initial weights to each currency based on the frequency of their use in paying for world exports. The weight assigned to the dollar was adjusted upward to take into account its role as a central bank reserve asset.

On July 1, 1978, the IMF redefined the weights according to the changing importance of the currencies in international trade. Two currencies were replaced in the SDR formula. Then on January 1, 1981, the IMF revised the SDR formula, simplifying it to contain just five major currencies. The delegated weights were based on each currency's relative importance in international trade and finance. The less complex formula has resulted in increased commercial use of the SDR.

Dual Currency Bonds

Before 1971 the majority of international bonds were denominated in U.S. dollars. The riskiness of these bonds was realized by investors after successive devaluations of the dollar. In 1973 floating exchange rates were allowed for most major currencies. Consequently, international bond values were constantly reacting not only to interest rates but also to current exchange rate fluctuations. Bond purchasers became more aware of the inherent risk of holding international bonds and as a result, bond issuers were searching for a way to make their bonds more attractive. Some firms issued **dual currency bonds** having a fixed par value in terms of a single currency and a second fixed par value in terms of a second currency. At maturity, the bondholder could choose among the two par values. Whichever par value could be converted to a greater amount of currency needed by the bondholder would serve as the preferred option.

SUMMARY

A firm in need of funds would prefer bonds denominated in a currency that (1) exhibits a low interest (coupon) rate and (2) has a high probability of depreciating during the life of the bond. While the coupon rate is known in advance, the future exchange rate is not and can only be forecasted. When bonds exhibit floating coupon rates, the future coupon rate is tied to a market interest rate that fluctuates over time. In this case, the feasibility of a bond is evaluated by predicting both future exchange rates and interest rates.

QUESTIONS/ PROBLEMS

1. What factors should be considered by a U.S. firm that plans to issue a floating-rate Eurobond?

2. What is the advantage of using simulation to assess the bond financing position?

3. Explain the difference in the cost of financing with foreign currencies during the 1976–1980 period, the 1981–1984 period and the 1985–1988 period for a U.S. firm.

4. Explain how a U.S.-based MNC issuing bonds denominated in German marks may be able to offset a portion of this exchange rate risk.

5. Is the risk from issuing a floating-rate Eurobond higher or lower than the risk of issuing a fixed-rate Eurobond? Explain.

6. Why is it necessary to compute the present value when assessing the cost of financing for two alternatives?

7. Why would a U.S. firm consider issuing bonds denominated in multiple currencies?

8. Why is the ECU bond popular?

9. When assessing the potential cost of financing with Eurobonds denominated in a foreign currency, what is the most critical point in time at which the exchange rate will have the greatest impact?

10. How would an investing firm differ from a borrowing firm in the features (i.e., interest rate and currency's future exchange rates) it would prefer a floating-rate Eurobond to exhibit?

11. Assume that Seminole Inc. considers issuing a mark-denominated bond at its present coupon rate of 7 percent, even though it has no incoming mark cash flows to cover the bond payments. It is attracted to the low financing rate, since dollar bonds issued in the United States would have a coupon rate of 12 percent. Assume that either type of bond would have a four-year maturity and could be issued at par value. Seminole needs to borrow $10 million. Therefore, it will either issue dollar bonds with a par value of $10 million or mark bonds with a par value of DM20 million. The spot rate of the mark is $.50. Seminole has forecasted the mark's value at the end of each of the next four years, when coupon payments are to be paid:

End of Year	Exchange rate of DM
1	$.52
2	.56
3	.58
4	.53

Determine the present value of bond payments, using a 12 percent discount rate. Should Seminole Corporation issue bonds in dollars or marks? Explain.

12. Why do non-U.S. corporations consider issuing securities in the U.S.?

13. Why do U.S. corporations sometimes issue dollar-denominated bonds in the Eurobond market?

14. If the U.S. government imposes a withholding tax on bonds issued in the United States by foreign corporations, how would this affect costs of borrowing for foreign corporations that plan to issue bonds in the United States? Explain.

15. Assume that Hurricane Inc. is a U.S. company that exports products to Great Britain, invoiced in dollars. It also exports products to West Germany, invoiced in dollars. It presently has no cash outflows in foreign currencies, and it plans to issue bonds in the near future. It could likely issue bonds at par value in (1) dollars with a coupon rate of 12 percent, (2) in marks with a coupon rate of 9 percent, or (3) in pounds with a coupon rate of 15 percent. It expects that the mark and pound will strengthen over time. How could

Hurricane revise its invoicing policy and make its bond denomination decision to achieve low financing costs without excessive exposure to exchange rate fluctuations?

16. Columbia Corporation is a U.S. company with no foreign-currency cash flows. It plans to either issue (1) a bond denominated in German marks with a fixed interest rate or (2) a bond denominated in U.S. dollars with a floating interest rate. It estimates its periodic dollar cash flows for each bond. Which bond do you think would have greater uncertainty surrounding these future dollar cash flows? Explain.

Devil VCR Corporation
Long-Term Financing

Devil VCR Corporation is a U.S.-based company that produces videocassette recorders. It plans a major exporting program in Germany, with a focus on the East German consumers. Three years ago, Devil established a production facility in the United Kingdom, since it sells VCRs there. Devil plans to expand capacity there and will use that facility to produce the VCRs that are to be marketed in East Germany. The VCRs will be sold to distributors in East Germany, invoiced in German marks. The transportation expenses will be substantially less than if the VCRs were built in the United States. If the exporting program is very successful, Devil Corporation will probably build a facility in Germany but plans to wait at least ten years.

Prior to this exporting program, Devil Corporation decided to develop a hedging strategy to hedge any cash flows to the U.S. parent. Its plan is to issue bonds to finance the entire investment in the exporting program. Virtually all expenses associated with this program are denominated in pounds. Yet, the revenue generated by the program is denominated in marks. Any revenue above and beyond expenses is to be remitted to the United States on an annual basis. Aside from the exporting program, the British subsidiary will generate just enough cash flows to cover expenses, and therefore will not be remitting any earnings to the parent. Devil Corporation is considering three different ways to finance the program for ten years:

Issue ten-year mark-denominated bonds at par value; annual coupon rate = 11%.
Issue ten-year pound-denominated bonds at par value; annual coupon rate = 14%.
Issue ten-year U.S. dollar-denominated bonds at par value; annual coupon rate = 11%.

The present exchange rates are 1 pound = $2, $1 = DM 2, and 1 pound = DM 4. The British subsidiary would need 20 million pounds to expand the facility, and two million pounds per year to produce the extra VCRs. The sale of VCR exports is expected to generate DM 25 million per year. Devil can use the forward market if necessary. The forward rates for the next five years are as follows:

End of Year	Pound/$ Forward Rate		DM/$ Forward Rate		Pound/DM Forward Rate	
	Exchanging $ for pounds	Exchanging pounds for $	Exchanging $ for DM	Exchanging DM for $	Exchanging DM for pounds	Exchanging pounds for DM
1	$1.97	$1.95	$.500	$.495	DM 3.94	DM 3.92
2	1.94	1.91	.500	.495	3.82	3.79
3	1.90	1.86	.500	.490	3.80	3.76
4	1.87	1.83	.500	.490	3.74	3.69
5	1.83	1.78	.505	.485	3.66	3.60

a) Assume Devil VCR Corporation would prefer to minimize exchange rate risk if possible. Describe how Devil could issue bonds in a manner that would minimize exchange rate risk.

b) Estimate the earnings to be received by the U.S. parent (in dollars) as a result of the export project over the next five years. Assume Devil VCR Corporation desires to hedge any expected currency transactions when developing your estimates. Also assume no tax effects.

c) Explain why the exporting program will still likely create exchange rate risk (specifically transaction exposure) for Devil VCR Corporation.

1. Review the annual report of an MNC of your choice. Did the MNC issue any bonds denominated in foreign currencies? Does the MNC generate cash flows in that currency that could be used to cover the coupon payments? (Use your opinion if this is not clear from the annual report.) Summarize any statements made regarding the MNC's decision to finance with U.S. dollars versus foreign currencies.

PROJECTS

2. Look at the bond quotations in the section "International Government Bonds" of *The Wall Street Journal*. Compare the yields of Canada, Japan, United Kingdom, and West Germany. Offer some possible explanations for the large differences in bond yields across countries.

SUGGESTED READING

S. L. Srinivasulu. "Currency Denomination of Debt: Lessons from Rolls-Royce and Laker Airways." *Business Horizons* (September–October 1983), pp. 19–23.

This article explains how the debt denomination decision can affect the MNC's performance, with a focus on two MNCs.

REFERENCES

Adler, Michael, and Bernard Dumas. "The Exposure of Long-Term Foreign Currency Bonds." *Journal of Financial and Quantitative Analysis* (November 1980), pp. 973–994.

Aubey, Robert T., and Robert H. Cramer. "The Use of International Currency Cocktails in the Reduction of

Exchange Rate Risk." *Journal of Economics and Business* (Winter 1977), pp. 128–135.

"Coping with Globally Integrated Financial Markets." *Quarterly Review*, Federal Reserve Bank of New York (Winter 1987), p. 1–5.

Elbert, Douglas. "The Globalization of Financial Markets." *The World of Banking* (January–February 1987), pp. 23–25.

Fatemi, Ali. "The Effect of International Diversification on Corporate Financing Policy." *Journal of Business Research* (January 1988), p. 17–30.

Field, Peter, and Lewis James. "The Coming Revolution in Investment Banking." *Euromoney* (March 1980), pp. 7–24.

Finnerty, J. E., and K. P. Nunn Jr. "The Determinants of Yield Spreads on U.S. and Eurobonds" *Management International Review* (1985/2), pp. 23–33.

Finnerty, Joseph E., Thomas Schneeweis, and Shantoram P. Hegde. "Interest Rates in the Eurobond Markets." *Journal of Financial and Quantitative Analysis* (September 1980), pp. 743–755.

Frankel, Jeffrey A. "The Diversifiability of Exchange Risk." *Journal of International Economics* (August 1979), pp. 379–393.

Giddy, I.H. "The Blossoming of the Eurobond Market." *Columbia Journal of World Business* (Winter 1975), pp. 66–76.

Johnson, R. Stafford, Charles W. Hultman, and Richard A. Zuber. "Currency Cocktails and Exchange Rate Stability." *Columbia Journal of World Business* (Winter 1979), pp. 117–126.

Johnson, R. Stafford, and Richard A. Zuber. "Model For Constructing Currency Cocktails." *Business Economics* (May 1979), pp. 9–14.

Kidwell, David S., M. Wayne Marr, and G. Rodney Thompson. "Eurodollar Bonds: Alternative Financing for U.S. Companies." *Financial Management* (Winter 1985), pp. 18–27.

Kramer, Gerald. "Borrowing in the International Capital Markets." *Columbia Journal of World Business* (Spring 1974), pp. 73–77.

Madura, Jeff. "Currency Cocktail Bonds and Exchange Rate Risk." *Investment Analyst* (October 1985), pp. 8–11.

Madura, Jeff, and Ann Marie Whyte. "International Linkage of Credit Risk Among Countries." *International Review of Economics and Business, forthcoming.*

Madura, Jeff, and Richard Fosberg. "The Impact of Financing Sources on Multinational Projects." *Journal of Financial Research* (Spring 1990), pp. 61–69.

Mahajan, Arvind, and Donald R. Fraser. "Dollar Eurobond and U.S. Bond Pricing." *Journal of International Business Studies* (Summer 1986), pp. 22–36.

Muehring, Kevin. "The Looming Battle in International Equities." *Institutional Investor* (October 1986), pp. 318–326.

Pardee, Scott E., "Internationalization of Financial Markets," *Economic Review,* Federal Reserve Bank of Kansas City (February 1987), pp. 3–19.

Park, Y. S. "Currency Swaps as a Long-term International Financing Technique." *Journal of International Business Studies* (Winter 1984), pp. 47–54.

Rhee, S. Ghon, Rosita P. Chang, and Peter E. Koveos. "The Currency-of-Denomination Decision for Debt Financing." *Journal of International Business Studies* (Fall 1985), pp. 143–150.

Robichek, Alexander A., and Mark R. Eaker. "Debt Denomination and Exchange Risk in International Capital Markets." *Financial Management* (Autumn 1976), pp. 11–18.

Shapiro, Alan C. "The Impact of Taxation on the Currency-of-Denomination Decision for Long-Term Foreign Borrowing and Lending." *Journal of International Business Studies* (Summer 1984), pp. 15–25.

Townsend, Charles C. "The Question of Convertibility." *Columbia Journal of World Business* (Spring 1973), pp. 6–8.

"U.S. Companies Reduce Funding Costs By Borrowing in Foreign Currencies." *Wall Street Journal* (February 21, 1985), p. 47.

APPENDIX 20A

Using Swaps to Hedge Risk

When MNCs issue bonds that expose them to interest rate or exchange rate risk, they may use *swaps* to hedge the risk. **Interest rate swaps** can be used to hedge interest rate risk, while **currency swaps** can be used to hedge exchange rate risk.

INTEREST RATE SWAPS

As the popularity of the Eurobond market has increased, so have interest rate swaps, which enable a firm to exchange fixed-rate payments for variable-rate payments. The interest rate swaps are used by bond issuers because they may reconfigure the future bond payments to a more preferable structure. For example, consider two firms that desire to issue bonds:

■ Quality Company is a highly-rated firm that prefers to borrow at a variable interest rate.
■ Risky Company is a low-rated firm that prefers to borrow at a fixed interest rate.

Assume the rates these companies would pay for issuing either variable-rate or fixed-rate Eurobonds are as follows:

	Fixed-rate Bond	Variable-rate Bond
Quality Company	9%	LIBOR + ½%
Risky Company	10½%	LIBOR + 1%

LIBOR, the London interbank offer rate, changes over time. Based on the information given, Quality Company has a comparative advantage when issuing either fixed-rate or variable-rate bonds, but more so with fixed-rate bonds. Quality Company could issue fixed-rate bonds while Risky Company issues variable-rate bonds; then Quality could provide variable-rate payments to Risky in exchange for fixed-rate payments.

Assume that Quality Company negotiates with Risky Company to provide variable-rate payments at LIBOR + ½ percent in exchange for fixed-rate payments of 9½ percent. The interest rate swap arrangement is shown in Exhibit 20A.1. Quality Company benefits since its fixed-rate payments received on the swap exceed the payments owed to bondholders by ½ percent. Its variable-rate payments to Risky Company are the same as what it would have paid if it issued variable-rate bonds. Risky Company is receiving LIBOR + ½ percent on the swap, which is ½ percent less than what it must pay on its variable-rate bonds. Yet, it is making fixed payments of 9½ percent, which is 1 percent less than what it would have paid if it issued fixed-rate bonds. Overall, it saves ½ percent per year of financing costs.

Two limitations of the swap just described are worth mentioning. First, there is a cost of time and resources associated with searching for a suitable swap candidate and negotiating the swap terms. Second, there is a risk to each swap participant that the counter-participant could default on payments. For this reason, financial intermediaries are usually involved in swap agreements. They match up participants and also assume the default risk involved. For their role, they charge a fee, which would reduce the estimated benefits in the previous example, but their involvement is critical to effectively match up swap participants and reduce concern about default risk.

CURRENCY SWAPS

Another swap used to complement bond issues, the **currency swap,** enables firms to exchange currencies at periodic intervals. Consider a U.S. firm called Miller Company that desires to issue a German mark-denominated bond, since it could make payments with mark inflows to be generated from exist-

EXHIBIT 20A.1   Illustration of Interest Rate Swap

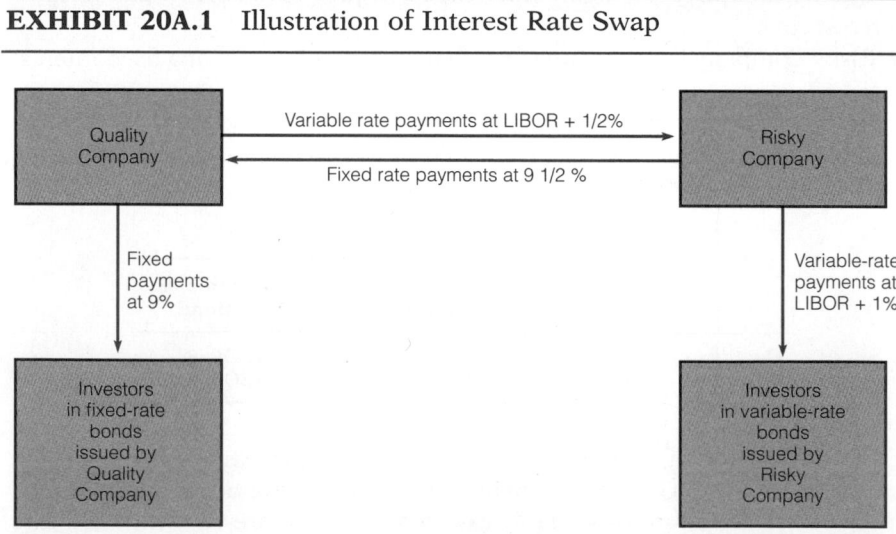

ing operations. However, this firm is not well-known to investors that would consider purchasing mark-denominated bonds. Also, consider a firm called Beck Company that desires to issue dollar-denominated bonds because its inflow payments are mostly in dollars. However, it is not well-known to the investors that would purchase these bonds. If Miller is known within the dollar-denominated market while Beck is known within the mark-denominated market, the following transactions would be appropriate. Miller could issue dollar-denominated bonds while Beck issues mark-denominated bonds. Miller could provide mark payments to Beck in exchange for dollar payments. This swap of currencies would allow the companies to make payments to their respective bondholders without concern about exchange rate risk. This type of currency swap is illustrated in Exhibit 20A.2.

The large commercial banks that serve as financial intermediaries for currency swaps sometimes take positions. That is, they may agree to swap fixed payments for variable payments or swap currencies with a firm, rather than simply search for a suitable swap candidate.

An alternative method by which firms could obtain financing in a foreign currency is the parallel (or back-to-back) loan, which represents simultaneous loans provided by two parties with an agreement to repay at a specified point in the future. For example, assume that the parent of a U.S.-based MNC

EXHIBIT 20A.2 Illustration of Currency Swap

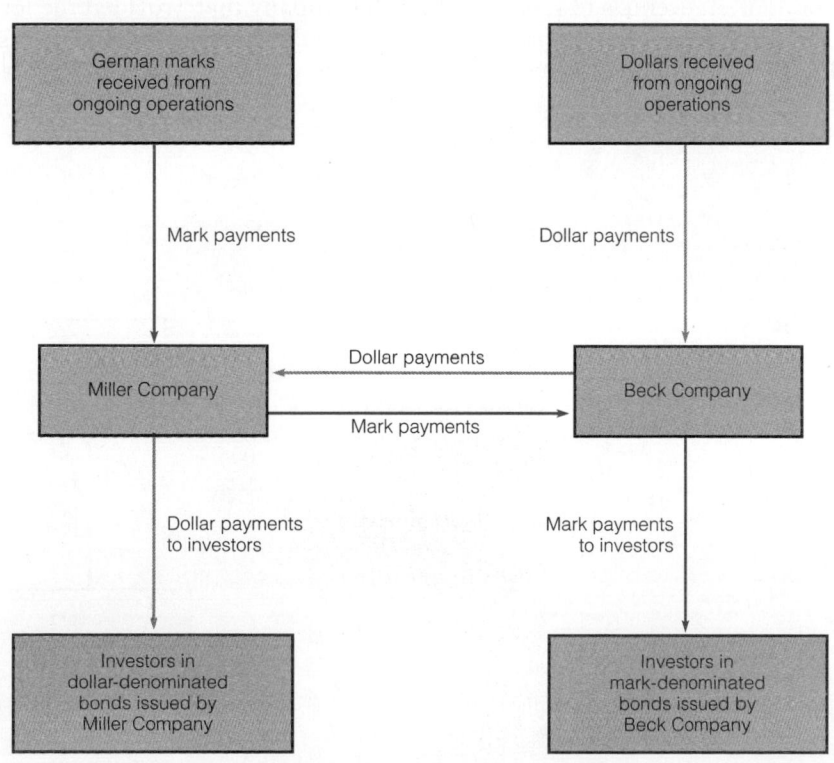

EXHIBIT 20A.3 Illustration of Parallel Loan

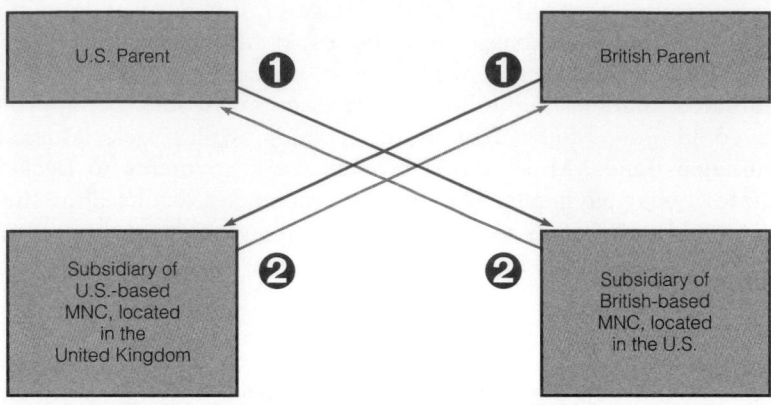

1. Loans are simultaneously provided by parents of MNCs to subsidiary of the other MNC.

2. At a specified time in the future, the loans are repaid in the same currency that was borrowed.

desires to expand its British subsidiary, while the parent of a British-based MNC desires to expand its American subsidiary. The British parent provides pounds to the British subsidiary of the U.S.-based MNC, while the U.S. parent provides dollars to the American subsidiary of the British-based MNC (as shown in Exhibit 20A.3). At the time specified by the loan contract, the loans are repaid. The British subsidiary of the U.S.-based MNC uses pound-denominated revenues to repay the British company that provided the loan. At the same time, the American subsidiary of the British-based MNC uses dollar-denominated revenues to repay the U.S. company that provided the loan.

APPENDIX 20B

Eurobonds as a Long-Term Investment

his chapter has focused on long-term financing, but there are circumstances where MNCs evaluate investment rather than financing opportunities in the Eurobond market. The analysis of Eurobonds from an investor's perspective would be quite similar to a borrower's perspective. Relative interest rates and projected exchange rates will again be influential on the decision. An example follows.

EUROBOND ANALYSIS FROM AN INVESTOR'S PERSPECTIVE

Consider a U.S. firm that has $1,000,000 available for investing over a four-year period. The time horizon is kept relatively short to simplify the example. Assume the investor could purchase four-year U.S. government dollar-denominated bonds at par value with a coupon rate of 13 percent. The firm is also considering four-year bonds issued by the British government and denominated in British pounds, which could be purchased at par value and which exhibit a 15 percent coupon rate. Coupon payments for both bonds are assumed to be paid at the end of each year. The dollar bonds would provide an annual coupon payment of $130,000 (13% x $1,000,000). The initial exchange rate of the British pound is $2.00, so the par value of the bonds denominated in British pounds that could be purchased by the firm (with $1,000,000) is 500,000 pounds. Annual coupon payments from these bonds would amount to 75,000 pounds (15% x 500,000 pounds). However, we do not know the amount of U.S. dollars the British pounds will convert to, since the pound's future exchange rate is unknown. The firm makes the following forecasts for the British pound:

End of Year	Forecast for British Pound
1	$1.95
2	$1.90
3	$1.85
4	$1.80

The investor's task is to choose between receiving the known cash inflows from the dollar-denominated bonds and the uncertain cash flows from the pound-denominated bonds.

The analysis necessary to compare estimated cash flows is provided in Exhibit 20B.1. The first row shows the known dollar cash inflows if dollar-denominated bonds are purchased. The second row shows the known cash inflows in British pounds if pound-denominated bonds are purchased. Just below those figures are the dollar cash inflows that pounds would represent based on the forecasts of the pound's exchange rate.

The known dollar cash flows from the dollar-denominated bonds can be compared with the projected dollar cash flows from the pound-denominated bonds. The present value of known dollar cash inflows from purchasing dollar-denominated bonds is $1,000,000 (using a 13 percent discount rate). The present value of projected dollar cash inflows from purchasing pound-denominated bonds is $971,969. From the perspective of an investing firm, the higher present value of cash inflows from dollar-denominated bonds generates a higher expected return (based on Exhibit 20B.1). In addition, the dollar-denominated bonds are preferable since future cash inflows are known with certainty (no exposure to exchange rate risk). Thus, both return and risk criteria favor the dollar-denominated bond. This example illustrates why choosing a bond simply because it exhibits a higher coupon rate can be a mistake. Even if the bond denominated in a foreign currency is free of default risk, it is risky in the sense that the inflows it provides to the investor are dependent on future exchange rates.

If the firm had anticipated appreciation of the pound against the dollar, the pound-denominated bonds would have been more attractive, since the pounds to be received would convert to a greater number of U.S. dollars. However, there is no guarantee that such exchange rate projections will be accurate. Thus, some conservative U.S. investors would choose the dollar-denominated bonds even when the expected return on the pound-denominated bonds is higher. Other U.S. investors more willing to tolerate the risk would purchase the pound-denominated bonds in an effort to achieve a higher return.

EXHIBIT 20B.1   Comparison of Investing in Bonds Denominated in Dollars versus Pounds

Investment Alternative	Expected Receipts at End of Year:			
	1	*2*	*3*	*4*
1. Purchase dollar-denominated bonds	$130,000	$130,000	$130,000	$1,130,000
2. Purchase pound-denominated bonds—Receipts in pounds	£75,000	£75,000	£75,000	£575,000
Receipts in dollars based on forecasted exchange rate of pound	$146,250	$142,500	$138,750	$1,035,000
Approximate present value of investing in pound-denominated bonds based on forecasted exchange rate of pound (using 13% discount rate)	$129,425	$111,598	$ 96,161	$ 634,785
Approximate cumulative present value of investing (using 13% discount rate) in pound-denominated bonds	$129,425	$241,023	$337,184	$ 971,969

Like borrowers, investors could use a simulation program to assess bonds denominated in a foreign currency. Simulation would provide a probability distribution of possible outcomes rather than just a single point estimate. The main difference is that the investor is attempting to maximize future inflows while the borrower is trying to minimize outflows. With this distinction in mind, simulation can be applied to aid the investing firm's decision in the same manner as described earlier in this chapter for the borrower's decision.

If the investing firm were considering some bonds denominated in foreign currencies that also exhibited floating coupon rates, simulation could be applied to assess the feasibility of such bonds as shown earlier for the borrowing firm. The existence of a floating coupon rate forces the investor to develop probability distributions not only for the exchange rate of concern, but also for the future interest rate of whatever the floating coupon rate is tied to.

The discussion of the investing firm's evaluation of bonds has up to this point presumed that the firm did not have future liabilities in foreign currencies. The firm may have future outflow payments in particular currencies that could offset upcoming inflow payments related to the purchased bonds. Thus, it may be possible to invest in bonds denominated in a foreign currency with a higher coupon rate without becoming exposed to exchange rate risk. Yet, it is unlikely that a firm would be able to perfectly match the timing and amount of the inflow payments in the foreign currency denominating the bond to the outflow payments in that currency. Consequently, some exposure to exchange rate fluctuations would exist.

CHAPTER 21

Global Strategic Planning

A common saying is that in this world, only two things are certain: death and taxes. While taxes will be imposed on earnings, the amount of taxes may depend on the MNC's corporate tax planning. This chapter explains how an MNC's value can be affected by various tax laws and how an MNC can use such information in deciding its corporate policies. Other aspects of centralized corporate planning by MNCs are also reviewed. By necessity, the following discussion of multinational tax planning is in generalities only and is far from complete. An entire textbook would be needed to cover all aspects of this extremely complex area.

INTERNATIONAL TAX CHARACTERISTICS

Tax laws can vary among countries in many ways, but any type of tax causes before-tax cash flows to vary from after-tax cash flows. Since the MNC is most concerned with after-tax cash flows, anticipated taxes must be accounted for.

Each country varies in the way it generates tax revenues. The United States relies on corporate and individual income taxes for federal revenues. Other countries may depend more on the *value-added tax* (VAT) or excise taxes. Since each country has its own philosophy on whom to tax and how much, it is not surprising that among countries corporations may be treated unequally in terms of taxes. Because systems and tax rates are unique to each country, corporations need to compare the various tax provisions of each country. The more important characteristics of a country to be considered within an MNC's international tax assessment are (1) corporate income taxes, (2) withholding taxes, (3) provision for carrybacks and carryforwards, (4) tax treaties, and (5) tax credits. A discussion of each characteristic follows.

Corporate Income Taxes

Each country has its unique corporate income tax laws. The United States, for example, taxes the worldwide income of U.S. "persons"—a term that includes corporations. However, as a general rule, foreign income of a foreign subsidiary of a U.S. company is not taxed until it is transferred to the U.S. parent by payment of dividends or a liquidation distribution. This is the concept of **deferral.** There are statutory exceptions to deferral, such as when a controlled foreign subsidiary earns tax-haven income in excess of a certain percentage of gross earnings or if it invests in U.S. property. Such exceptions to deferral are not important to this discussion and are mentioned only to make the reader aware of their existence.

An MNC planning direct foreign investment in foreign countries must determine how the anticipated earnings from direct foreign investment will be affected. Tax rates vary among countries. In addition, corporate tax rates can differ within a country depending on whether the entity is a domestic corporation. Also, if it is considered to have a permanent establishment in a country, an unregistered foreign corporation may be subject to that country's tax laws on income earned within its borders. Generally, a permanent establishment includes an office or fixed place of business or a specified kind of agency (*independent* agents are normally excluded) through which active and continuous business is conducted. In some cases, the tax can depend on the industry, or on the form of business used (corporation, branch, partnership, etc.).

Withholding Taxes

Various fund outflows from a subsidiary can be subject to withholding taxes by the host country. MNCs interested in direct foreign investment must account for this analysis. While a withholding tax does not affect a subsidiary's cash flows, it can affect after-tax cash flows to the parent (since the government of the host country may tax a portion of the transferred funds). As with corporate tax rates, the withholding tax rate can vary substantially among countries. Even within a country, the withholding tax can vary depending on the purpose of the fund transfer. Dividends, interest, rents, and royalty fees are often paid by a subsidiary to the parent. Each of these fund transfers may be subject to a different withholding tax rate. Withholding taxes can be reduced by income tax treaties (discussed shortly).

Provision for Carrybacks and Carryforwards

Negative earnings from operations can often be carried back or forward to offset earnings in other years. The laws pertaining to these so-called **net operating loss carrybacks and carryforwards** can vary among countries. An MNC generally does not plan to generate negative earnings in foreign countries. Yet, if negative earnings occur, it is desirable to be able to use them to offset other years of positive earnings. Most foreign countries do not allow negative earnings to be carried back. Yet, virtually all countries allow some flexibility in carrying losses forward. For U.S. tax purposes, excess foreign tax credits generated in one year can be carried back two years and then forward for up to five years to offset U.S. tax on foreign source income. In the case of a carryback, an amended U.S. return is filed and a refund of previously paid U.S. tax is requested.

The 1990 tax rates are shown in Exhibit 21.1 for several countries. More information on international tax rates can be drawn from the source of this

EXHIBIT 21.1   Tax Rate Information on Various Countries[a]

	Corporate Income Tax Rate	Capital Gains Tax Rate	Branch Tax Rate	Withholding Tax Rate On:		
				Dividends	Interest	Royalties from Patents, etc.
Argentina	20%	20–36%	36%	20%	14.4%	28.8%
Australia	39	39	39	15	10	10
Bahamas	0	0	0	0	0	0
Belgium	39	19.5	43	5–15	15	0
Canada	44.34	29.56	44.34	10–15	0–15	0–10
China	50	50	50	10	10	10
Denmark	40	40	40	15	0	0
Finland	25	25	25	5–15	0	0
France	37	19	37	5–15	0	5
Germany	50	50	46	10	0	0
Hong Kong	16.5	0	16.5	0	0	1.65
Ireland	43	30–60	43	0	0	0
Italy	36	36	36	5	15	10
Japan	37.5	37.5	37.5	10–15	10	10
Mexico	36	36	36	0	15	15
Netherlands	35	35	35	25	0	0
New Zealand	33	0	38	15	10	10
Norway	50.8	50.8	50.8	15	0	0
Singapore	32	0	32	0	32	32
Spain	35	35	35	25	25	25
Sweden	40	40	40	5	0	0
Taiwan	25	25–35	25	15–35	10–20	10–20
U. Kingdom	35	35	35	0	0	0

[a]The exhibit provides tax rate information on income earned by subsidiaries or on payments made by subsidiaries. The actual tax rate imposed may vary with the subsidiary's home country. There are also many exceptions to the tax rates reported here. This table simply illustrates how tax rates may vary across countries.

SOURCE: *Worldwide Corporate Tax Guide*, 1990 Edition, Ernst & Young International.

information, *Worldwide Corporate Tax Guide,* published by Ernst and Young International. Exhibit 21.1 shows how tax rates can vary among countries.

Tax Treaties

The tax rates discussed so far may give the impression that by the time the parent receives any cash flow from its subsidiaries, there is not much left. Moreover, the parent's government could then tax the remaining earnings, which would reduce the after-tax earnings of the MNC even further. Actually, the severity of taxation is exaggerated here. Countries often establish income tax **treaties** whereby one partner will reduce its taxes by granting a credit for taxes imposed on corporations operating within the other treaty partner's tax jurisdiction. Income tax treaties help avoid corporate exposure to double-taxation. Without such treaties, subsidiary earnings could be taxed by the host country and then again by the parent's country when received by the parent. To the extent that the parent uses some of these earnings to provide cash dividends for shareholders, triple-taxation could result (since the dividend income is also taxed at the shareholder level). Because income tax treaties reduce taxes on earnings generated by MNCs, they help stimulate direct foreign investment. Many foreign projects are perceived as feasible only because of income tax treaties.

Tax Credits

Even without income tax treaties, an MNC may be allowed to credit income and withholding taxes paid in one country against taxes owed by the parent if they meet certain requirements. Like income tax treaties, tax credits help to avoid double-taxation and stimulate direct foreign investment. They also make international tax planning quite complicated. An MNC can benefit substantially from a knowledgeable tax-planning department.

The tax-credit policies can vary among countries (the U.S. is the most complicated), but they generally work like this. Consider a U.S.-based MNC subject to a U.S. tax rate of 34 percent. Assume a foreign subsidiary of this corporation generated earnings taxed at less than 34 percent by the host-country's government. The earnings remitted to the parent from the subsidiary will be subject to an additional amount of U.S. tax to bring the total tax up to 34 percent. From the parent's point of view, the tax on its subsidiary's remitted earnings are 34 percent overall, so it does not matter whether the host country of the subsidiary or the United States receives most of the taxes. From the perspective of the governments of these two countries, however, the allocation of taxes is very important. If subsidiaries of U.S. corporations are established in foreign countries, and if these countries tax income at a rate close to 34 percent, they can generate large tax revenues from income earned by the subsidiaries. The tax revenues received by them is at the expense of the parent's country (the United States in this case).

If the corporate income tax rate in a foreign country is greater than 34 percent, the United States would generally not impose any additional taxes on earnings remitted to a U.S. parent by foreign subsidiaries. In fact, under present law, the U.S. would allow the excess foreign tax to be credited against other taxes owed by the parent due on the same type of income generated by subsidiaries in other lower-tax countries. In a sense, this suggests that some host countries could charge abnormally high corporate income tax rates to foreign subsidiaries and still attract direct foreign investment. If the MNC in our example has subsidiaries located in some countries with low corporate income taxes, the U.S. tax on earnings remitted to the U.S. parent will normally bring up the total tax to 34 percent, as mentioned earlier. Yet, credits against excessive income taxes by high-tax countries on foreign subsidiaries could offset these taxes that would have been paid to the U.S. government. Due to tax credits, therefore, an MNC might consider direct foreign investment in a country with excessive tax rates.

When transfer pricing shifts the tax liability to different subsidiaries, it affects the distribution of tax revenue received by countries. A recent study by the Internal Revenue Service in 1990 found that non-U.S. firms may have avoided about $50 million in taxes over five years. Over a recent ten-year period, more than 50 percent of all non-U.S. firms operating in the United States paid little or no taxes. Ten non-U.S. automobile distributors generated $38 billion in revenue in the United States in 1987 and paid less than 1 percent in taxes to the United States. One non-U.S. electronics distributor paid more than $150 million in U.S. taxes over six years, while another similar firm paid no tax. The difference in tax was attributed to transfer pricing.

USE OF TRANSFER PRICING TO REDUCE TAXES

Once the tax laws of the various countries are fully understood, an MNC should design a network of cash flows that will optimize its value. In some cases, this may cause one subsidiary to gain at the expense of another subsidiary. For example, consider a U.S.-based MNC that has subsidiaries in a high-tax country called HT and in a low-tax country called LT. Assume both subsidiaries plan to retain all of their earnings for future projects. Under this scenario, the United States will not be taxing any of the foreign earnings (since none were remitted to the U.S. parent), and the taxes will be imposed only by the respective country governments of the subsidiaries. The MNC would benefit most if the subsidiary in LT generated the majority of the before-tax earnings. Assume the subsidiaries of these two foreign countries trade goods with each other. The MNC could attempt to devise a transfer pricing strategy whereby the subsidiary in LT charges abnormally high prices when exporting to the subsidiary in HT. Conversely, the subsidiary in HT could export goods to the subsidiary in LT at substantially reduced prices. The transfer pricing schedule suggested here should boost earnings of the LT subsidiary and reduce earnings of the subsidiary located in HT. However, after taxes, there is not an exact offsetting effect, since the tax rates differ among the two countries.

If more earnings can be transferred to the LT subsidiary, then the after-tax earnings from subsidiaries of both countries combined will be higher. This is due to the low tax rate imposed on any earnings at LT. The actual mechanics of international transfer pricing go far beyond the example provided here, and it should be emphasized that such transfer pricing strategies may not be allowed by some countries. The U.S. laws in this area are particularly strict, generally requiring related party transactions to be at arm's length, and can even reach inter-company transactions of foreign subsidiaries of a U.S.-based MNC. Also, the United States has a new "super royalty" rule that requires the income from a transfer of an intangible to be commensurate with the income generated by the intangible. Nevertheless, there are various ways MNCs can justify increasing prices at one subsidiary and reducing them at another.

Earnings may also be shifted from a subsidiary to a parent, or vice versa. Various fees can be implemented for services, research and development, royalties, and administrative duties. Such fees might not be subject to tax by the subsidiary's host country, and could possibly qualify as foreign source income for foreign tax credit purposes (with the potential to use existing excess credits). While the fees may be imposed to shift earnings and minimize tax effects, the actual performance of each subsidiary is distorted. Yet, a centralized MNC approach could account for the transfer pricing strategy implemented when assessing the true performance of each subsidiary.

HOW MNC POLICIES ARE INFLUENCED BY INTERNATIONAL TAX LAWS

Some of the important functions of an MNC that can be affected by tax differentials among countries are

- Short-term financing
- Working capital management

- Capital structure
- Capital budgeting

Consider an MNC's subsidiary that needs to borrow funds and a second subsidiary in a different country that has excess funds. If the second subsidiary is located in a high-tax country, then the MNC's centralized management may request that it provide the loan at a very attractive rate to the subsidiary in need of funds. The lending subsidiary's performance may be reduced, since it could have generated a better return on its funds if it used them elsewhere. The borrowing subsidiary's performance will be enhanced due to the attractive terms of the loan. Without consideration of taxes, the reduced performance of the lending subsidiary would be equal to the increased performance of the borrowing subsidiary, and the MNC as a whole would gain no benefit. Yet, when taxes are considered, the MNC as a whole may indeed benefit from such a strategy, because any shifting of income from subsidiaries in high-tax countries to subsidiaries in low-tax countries can increase the after-tax inflows of the MNC as a whole. If not for the tax advantage, the borrowing subsidiary might have financed from some other source such as a local bank. This example shows how financing decisions can be affected by tax characteristics of countries.

From a working capital management perspective, assume the subsidiary with excess cash wishes to invest that cash for three months. If not for the tax advantage, it would likely invest those funds elsewhere rather than providing the low-rate loan to the other subsidiary. This shows how short-term investing (a role within working capital management) is affected by tax characteristics of countries.

Country tax characteristics can also be influential on the MNC's capital structure policy. Consider an MNC parent that plans to finance a large project for a foreign subsidiary and is considering the issuance of new stock to generate funds. If the subsidiary is based in a high-tax country, the MNC may prefer to have the subsidiary finance the project itself by issuing bonds locally or within the Eurobond market. The interest expenses from bond payments will offset part of the income earned by the subsidiary and reduce taxes. Thus, the decision on how to attract long-term funds can also depend on differences in tax laws among countries.

From a capital budgeting perspective, consider an MNC that desires to establish a manufacturing plant in one of two possibly attractive locations. One location is in a high-tax country and the second location in a low-tax country. While there are obviously many factors to compare among locations, if the tax advantage of establishing the plant in the low-tax country is not offset by any disadvantages, the MNC would choose that site. Even though tax credits can reduce or eliminate the disadvantage exhibited by a high-tax host country, the credits will not necessarily be applied to all income. For example, if a subsidiary retains much of its earnings rather than remitting them to the parent, the tax credits will not be as valuable.

The discussion up to this point has shown how tax differences among countries can influence the more important decisions of the MNC. In all cases, tax differences are not the sole criterion, but they often influence the final corporate policy decision.

For some long-term decisions of the MNC, the current tax characteristics of countries may not be sufficient to determine the tax effects, since tax incentives may be offered in particular circumstances and tax rates can change over time. Consider an MNC that plans to establish a manufacturing plant in Country Y rather than Country X. Assume that while many economic characteristics favor Country X, the current tax rates within Country Y are lower. However, whereas tax rates in Country X have been historically stable and are expected to continue that way, they have been changing every few years in Country Y. In this case, the MNC must assess the future uncertainty of the tax rates. It cannot treat the current tax rate of Country Y as a constant when conducting a capital budgeting analysis. Instead, it must consider possible changes in the tax rates over time, and based on these possibilities, determine whether Country Y's projected tax advantages *over time* sufficiently outweigh the advantages of the Country X location. One approach to account for possible changes in the tax rates is to use sensitivity analysis, which would measure the sensitivity of the net present value (NPV) of after-tax cash flows to various possible tax changes over time. For each tax scenario, a different NPV would be projected. By accounting for each possible tax scenario, the MNC can develop a distribution of possible NPVs that may occur and could then compare these for each country.

An MNC may want to not only account for various possible tax scenarios for a project, but also consider possible scenarios of other important variables as well. The tax rate is only one of several variables relevant to the capital budgeting process whose future values are uncertain. A simulation model can be used to create ranges for each possible variable during each future period. For example, the corporate income tax rate in Country Y may be between 30 percent and 40 percent, the sales in units may be between 6 million and 8 million units and so on. Different ranges could be set for each period when using a full-blown simulation model. Based on the host of possibilities, the simulation program can generate a distribution of possible NPVs that could occur for the project. The procedure could then be replicated for Country X, with ranges set for each variable so that the model could generate possible NPVs. Then the two distributions could be compared. The key point here is that any long-term corporate decisions affected by tax effects should account for any future changes in tax laws that may occur.

An MNC's tax-planning department should be able to determine the tax effects of any corporate decision, provided it has complete information on all cash flows of the MNC, including cash flows among subsidiaries. There are two critical, broadly defined functions involved in tax planning for the MNC. The first is to be aware of all the current tax laws that exist for each country where the MNC does (or plans to do) business. This first function also includes any information that may indicate future changes in tax laws. The second function is to take the information generated from the first function and aid various corporate departments in their centralized decisions. Again, any decisions influenced by taxes must be perceived from the overall MNC's perspective rather than from an individual subsidiary's perspective.

Both of the functions of tax planning for the MNC are obviously very important. The first function requires some perseverance and competence in order to obtain and understand information on current tax provisions among countries. It also requires some insight into how tax provisions may change over time. The second function requires analytical tools and an imagination to fully account for the tax effects on possible corporate policies.

MULTINATIONAL CORPORATE POLICY

An efficient system of multinational corporate policy and planning requires that decisions be made to maximize the MNC as a whole. To achieve this goal, any decision making must avoid two common conflicts that arise. The first is a conflict of interests between a subsidiary's individual goals and the goals of the overall MNC. The second is a conflict of interests between the various corporate departments (financing, investing, etc.) of the MNC.

Subsidiary Versus Centralized Management

An MNC makes some corporate decisions similar to those of a domestic firm, but often the decisions are more complex. Common decisions of MNCs involve:

- Exchange rate forecasts
- Transaction exposure
- Economic exposure
- Translation exposure
- Financing
- Excess cash
- Transfer pricing
- Direct foreign investment
- Capital structure

For many of these decisions, each subsidiary may develop its own assessment of the variables that will influence the outcome of the decision. Virtually all decisions are based on expectations. Thus, projections are needed to assess the feasibility of any proposed project. In many cases, decisions at the subsidiary level may conflict with the best interests of the overall MNC. Based on the presumed goal of MNC to maximize shareholder wealth, such decisions may be inappropriate.

To understand how subsidiary decisions could conflict with what is best for the MNC overall, consider the following examples. With regard to hedging, one subsidiary may hedge its cash inflows of foreign Currency X, while another does not hedge its cash outflows of Currency X. If neither subsidiary hedged, their exposure to fluctuations in Currency X could be offset in aggregate. However, since only one is hedging, the unhedged position of the other is exposed. To avoid exposure, this other subsidiary must also hedge.

Persistent hedging by subsidiaries results in high transaction costs, so hedging should be avoided if it is not necessary. A centralized system can detect individual exposures of each subsidiary, whereas a decision at the subsidiary level may often neglect the positions of other subsidiaries and therefore be inconsistent with maximizing the value of the overall MNC.

As another example, various subsidiaries may make decisions based on their individual exchange rate projections. Given that the exchange rate projections could be the determining factor of a corporate policy, the projections should be consistent among subsidiaries. A centralized system can develop the projections and then distribute them to the subsidiaries. Otherwise, each subsidiary will be using a different basis of reasoning for its policies. In addition, each subsidiary employing its own forecasting team is a waste of resources.

RELATED RESEARCH

Impact of MNC Characteristics on Centralization

A recent study by Gates and Egelhoff attempted to determine why MNCs have different degrees of centralization. They measured centralization as the average level in the organization that needs to approve decisions before they can be implemented. The average was determined from 22 important decisions common to MNCs, including 10 marketing decisions, 5 manufacturing decisions, and 7 financial decisions. Results of the study are summarized here with a focus on financial centralization.

■ Size of foreign operations was negatively related to the degree of financial centralization. This supports the theory that as an MNC grows, it must decentralize so that it does not overload its managers.

■ The size of the MNC was negatively correlated with the degree of financial centralization. The argument used above may explain this result.
■ The extent of outside ownership in foreign subsidiaries was negatively correlated with the degree of financial centralization. The reason may be that foreign subsidiaries with more outside ownership are less legally dependent on the parent, encouraging decentralization.
■ European-based MNCs had less financial centralization than U.S.-based MNCs. Perhaps this results from cultural differences.
■ The age of the MNC was negatively correlated with the degree of financial concentration. The longer the foreign operations have existed, the more decentralized they become.

SOURCE: Stephen R. Gates and William G. Egelhoff, "Centralization in Headquarters-Subsidiary Relationships," *Journal of International Business Studies* (Summer 1986), pp. 71–92.

Many policy decisions of MNCs are based on economic and financial projections, and the centralized management should be largely responsible for these projections. The subsidiaries can assist by providing whatever information is useful for the development of the projections. Several variables need to be forecasted for each country where the MNC conducts business or plans to in the future, including currency exchange rates, inflation rates, interest rates, economic activity (national income, GNP, etc.), balance of trade, trade restrictions, currency restrictions, political problems, technology status, and special industry conditions. The MNC can apply projections of these macro variables to specific policy proposals in order to determine optimal policies for all financial management functions.

Centralization can make efficient use of resources by avoiding redundancy of operations. In addition, it prevents conflicts between subsidiaries with regard to projections. Centralized projections can be used by the subsidiaries to make some decisions on issues that require no other information about other subsidiaries. Other decisions (such as whether to hedge) that benefit from information on other subsidiaries can be made by the centralized management. An argument can be made that taking the decision-making power away from the subsidiaries reduces the control they have on their own performance. This argument has merit. Of course, if a centralized decision is in the best interests of the overall MNC, the subsidiary should abide by that decision even if it does not agree with it.

With a centralized approach, each subsidiary can either gain or lose due to a centralized decision. Therefore, performance evaluation of individual subsidiaries must account for how these decisions affect the subsidiaries. Any reduction in earnings due to centralized decisions should be accounted for. At the same time, earnings at other subsidiaries may have been increased due to centralized decisions. The managers of these subsidiaries should not be more highly rewarded under such circumstances.

Role of Subsidiary Due to Centralization

Because a centralized system places much of the responsibility on the shoulders of a centralized group, the managers of individual subsidiaries would play a more passive role, simply following instructions handed down to them. This could reduce their motivation to increase efficiency at their respective subsidiaries, since each subsidiary's periodic performance would not be as dependent on their decisions. That is, they would no longer receive the credit for superior performance or the blame for poor performance. While this can be a serious problem, the advantages of a centralized system should outweigh any deficiencies. The potential lack of motivation at the subsidiary level due to centralized management could be alleviated if it is properly communicated to subsidiary personnel that the underlying goal is to maximize the value of the overall MNC, not the value of any particular subsidiary.

While the centralized management approach is strongly advocated here, it should be emphasized that the only way such an approach is feasible is if the reward system to personnel is not based on subsidiary performance but instead on how well instructions are followed. Also, some decisions can be made at the subsidiary level as long as they do not have a significant adverse impact on other individual subsidiaries, or on the overall MNC.

Conflict of Interests among Corporate Departments

The conflict of interests discussed thus far was among subsidiaries, or among a subsidiary and its headquarters. Another type of conflict can occur within the centralized management system. Consider the following decisions to be made by the MNC: (1) where to establish direct foreign investment, (2) type of business to engage in, and (3) optimal capital structure. Each of these decisions depends on the other two. Whether direct foreign investment is feasible in a particular location depends on the type of business in which it plans to expand. The capital budgeting analysis to determine whether the investment is feasible will be affected by the cost of capital. The cost of capital can be influenced by the capital structure of the MNC. The optimal capital structure depends on the type of business the MNC is involved in (that is, whether periodic inflow payments in such a business are consistent or erratic). The interdependencies noted here illustrate how policy decisions should not be totally separated from each other. While an MNC may have various departments within the centralized system to make policy decisions, there should be interaction between departments.

Accounting and Control

A primary role in any corporate planning system is the monitoring of previous policy decisions. Ongoing evaluation of previous decisions will help dis-

INTERNATIONAL FINANCIAL MANAGEMENT IN PRACTICE

How MNCs Use Strategic Planning

A recent survey of managers of Australian-based MNCs was conducted to determine managerial attitudes toward organization, planning, and control. Some of the key results of the survey as related to this chapter are summarized below:

■ For 53 percent of the MNCs, area managers were responsible for operations (representing a decentralized system). For about 30 percent of the MNCs, the foreign operations reported to an International Division. For 17 percent of the MNCs, foreign operations reported to the parent.

■ A related characteristic to responsibility is monitoring. For 35 percent of the MNCs, the foreign operations were monitored by the respective subsidiaries, while 47 percent were monitored by the parent. The remaining 18 percent used regional monitoring.

■ Fifty-three percent of the MNCs organized their foreign operations to benefit from synergistic coordination. That is, there were some integrated functions between the subsidiaries.

■ Forty-one percent of the MNCs attempted to maximize their performance from opportunities on a country-by-country basis. Another 41 percent maximized performance on a global basis. The remaining 18 percent did so on a regional basis.

■ Sixty-five percent of the MNCs used political forecasting for their strategic planning. Some political forecasting systems were on a country-by-country basis while others were on a global basis. Thirty-five percent used sociocultural forecasting for their strategic planning. Some MNCs even used both forecasting systems while others used neither.

■ The most preferred form of foreign ownership was wholly owned subsidiaries, followed by majority ownership, and joint ventures with fifty-fifty ownership.

SOURCE: Glenn Boseman, "The Australian Multinational-Parent and Subsidiary Relationships," *Management International Review* no. 2 (1986), pp. 43–51.

tinguish policies that have worked from those that have not. In addition, reasons for the failure of some policies may be detected and thus perhaps similar mistakes are avoided in the future.

To minimize poor decision making, an efficient system of internal accounting control is necessary. The accounting system is largely the responsibility of each subsidiary that must periodically report its status on all aspects of cash flow. For example, a subsidiary may report its actual cash flow in the previous week or month as well as its anticipated cash flow in the upcoming week, month, or quarter. The cash flow figures should be separated into the various foreign currencies. The centralized system can consolidate this information from each subsidiary to identify offsetting positions in particular currencies. Where offsetting positions do not exist, the decision on whether to hedge must be made. Short-term investment and financing decisions may also hinge on the cash flows anticipated by subsidiaries. Thus, it is critical that the subsidiaries provide accurate estimates. Comparison of actual data with their estimates over time will reveal any consistent over- or underestimating of cash flows so that any such bias can be removed in future estimates. This example related to cash flow can be applied to all other financial characteristics reported by subsidiaries.

INTERNATIONAL FINANCIAL MANAGEMENT IN PRACTICE

Management of Foreign Operations by Alcoa, Dow Chemical, IBM, and Westinghouse

A recent article by Naylor explains how strategic planning is implemented by four large U.S.-based MNCs. First, Alcoa has used a decentralized system to manage its foreign operations because of characteristics such as geographic remoteness of the foreign operations and cultural differences. While Alcoa's company managers have some decision-making power, they are expected to keep upper management informed about ongoing performance, conflicts, and goals. Upper management can then compare the information provided by subsidiary managers to avoid any inefficiencies, such as duplication of work by subsidiaries.

The second company, Dow Chemical, is decentralized into six autonomous operating companies headquartered in Brazil, Hong Kong, Canada, Switzerland, and two headquartered in the United States. Dow attempts to assure that any technological improvements or inventions are implemented throughout the world, so as to more easily recover the cost of research and development. Five product vice-presidents monitor and manage Dow's product policies around the world. These vice-presidents assess the capital budgeting requests from each region's managers to assure that the acquisitions of particular assets are not duplicated. Each region provides a periodic income statement so that Dow's upper management can compare regional performance.

IBM, the third company, has five profit centers. The managers of these centers are appointed by the chief executive officer and are assigned financial targets for a five-year period that focus on productivity and profits. Within each profit center there are business units that rely on each other for marketing, manufacturing, and service. IBM also has some business units that focus specifically on the development of a single product.

Finally, Westinghouse has each of its business operations co-managed by the business unit responsible for the operations along with the country manager. In other words, management has a perspective on the specific operations and the specific environment where the operations are located. The business unit manager in charge of a particular operation will therefore interact with country managers of all countries where such operations are located. Country managers make strategic planning decisions related to marketing and distribution of the product. They also can monitor the existing operations within their respective countries to determine whether operations should be integrated in some way. The country managers determine the pricing policies as well, but such policies must be consistent with guidelines for each type of operation.

SOURCE: Thomas H. Naylor, "The International Strategy Matrix," *Columbia Journal of World Business* (Summer 1985), pp. 11–19.

SUMMARY

Varying tax rates among countries can affect common functions of an MNC such as financing and investing. Corporate policies must account for these differences, since the feasibility of a particular policy from a before-tax perspective may differ from an after-tax perspective. All decisions should be based on the assessment from an after-tax perspective.

Because international taxation is such a complex topic, incorporating a discussion of taxes within all of the earlier chapters would likely have taken away from the concepts that were stressed in those chapters. Even in this chapter, the discussion of international taxation just touched the surface. The objective here was not to make the reader an expert in this area, but to emphasize how influential tax characteristics can be on the performance of corporate policies.

One potential conflict of interests that can arise in multinational corporate policy is between the best interests of a subsidiary versus the overall MNC. A subsidiary's decisions that are optimal from its individual perspective could be sub-optimal for the overall MNC. For this reason, a centralized system for multinational corporate planning is advocated. A centralized system not only avoids this conflict of interests, but also allows for the consideration of all other subsidiary conditions simultaneously.

Another conflict of interests can arise between departments. The financing department is worried about minimizing financing costs, while the cash management group desires maximum return, etc. Interaction between these departments can lead to decisions that are best for the MNC, even though each department might have preferred a different policy if it needed only to be concerned with its individual goals.

A centralized approach to multinational financial management requires an efficient accounting system in order to work properly. This involves periodic reporting by each subsidiary to the centralized management on the status of all financial aspects. In addition, the reports should be monitored in order to detect any consistent errors in estimation. Such accounting control can help prevent improper centralized decisions due to inaccurate data.

Perhaps the most obvious lesson is that financial management is often more complex and challenging for MNCs than for domestic companies. While the managerial approach is typically similar for both types of firms, there are often additional variables to be considered in multinational financial management. Those MNCs that best capitalize on the benefits of international business while developing corporate policies to avoid exposure to additional risks will be most successful.

QUESTIONS

1. Discuss how the importance of tax planning at MNCs would change if tax rules were identical among all countries and did not change over time. (Your answer should imply why tax planning is critical to the MNC in reality.)

2. What corporate decisions can be affected when incorporating taxes into the decisions? Briefly elaborate on how each decision is affected by taxes.

3. In what general ways do countries differ with regard to their tax systems?

4. How can tax treaties between countries be beneficial to MNCs?

5. Explain how transfer pricing can be used to reduce the MNC's overall tax liability.

6. Briefly describe the role of tax planning by the MNC. What are the two key functions?

7. Describe the possible conflict of interests between a subsidiary and centralized management?

8. How could an MNC avoid a conflict of interests between a subsidiary and centralized management?

9. Explain why a conflict of interests can often arise among corporate departments at an MNC.

10. How could an MNC avoid conflicts of interests between its various corporate departments?

Redwing Technology Company
Assessing Subsidiary Performance

Redwing Technology Company is a U.S.-based firm that makes a variety of high technology components. Five years ago, it established subsidiaries in Canada, France, and Japan. The earnings generated by each subsidiary as translated (at the average annual exchange rate) in U.S. dollars per year are shown below:

Years Ago	Translated Dollar Value of Annual Earnings in Each Subsidiary (in millions of $)		
	Canada	*France*	*Japan*
5	$20	$21	$30
4	24	24	32
3	28	24	35
2	32	36	41
1	36	42	46

Each subsidiary had an equivalent amount of resources to conduct operations. The wage rates for the labor needed were similar across countries. The inflation rates, economic growth, and degree of competition were somewhat similar across countries. The average exchange rate of the respective currencies over the last five years are disclosed below:

Years Ago	Canadian Dollar	French Franc	Japanese Yen
5	$.84	$.10	$.0040
4	.83	.12	.0043
3	.81	.16	.0046
2	.81	.20	.0055
1	.79	.24	.0064

The earnings generated by each country were reinvested rather than remitted. There were no plans to remit any future earnings either.

A committee of vice-presidents met to determine the performance of each subsidiary in the last five years. The assessment was to be used for (1) determining bonus compensation for the executive in charge of each subsidiary, and (2) determining where additional funds held by the parent should be invested. Since exchange rates of the related currencies were affected by so many different factors, the treasurer acknowledged that there was much uncertainty about their future direction. The treasurer did suggest, however, that last year's average exchange rate would probably serve as at least a reasonable guess of exchange rates in future years. He did not anticipate any of the currencies to experience consistent appreciation or depreciation.

a) Use whatever means you think is appropriate to rank the performance of the executive in charge of each subsidiary. That is, which executive did the best job over the five-year period in your opinion? Justify your opinion.

b) Use whatever means you think is appropriate to determine which subsidiary deserves additional funds from the parent to push for additional growth. (Assume no constraint on potential growth in any country). Where would you recommend the parent's excess funds be invested based on the information available? Justify your opinion.

c) Repeat Question (b), but assume that all earnings generated from the parent's investment would be remitted to the parent every year. Would your recommendation change? Explain.

d) A final task of the committee was to recommend whether any of the subsidiaries should be divested. One vice-president suggested that a review of the earnings translated in dollars shows that the performance of Canadian and French subsidiaries are very highly correlated. The VP concluded that having both of these subsidiaries did not achieve much diversification benefits, and recommended that either the Canadian or French subsidiaries could be sold without forgoing any diversification benefits. Do you agree? Explain.

1. Review the annual report of an MNC of your choice. Based on the annual report, does it appear that the decision making is centralized or decentralized? Elaborate.

PROJECT

SUGGESTED READING

Stephen R. Gates and William G. Egelhoff. "Centralization in Headquarters—Subsidiary Relationships." *Journal of International Business Studies* (Summer 1986), pp. 71–92. This article explains why the degree of centralization varies among MNCs. It discusses how factors influence the centralization decision.

REFERENCES

Adler, Michael, and Bernard Dumas. "Should Exposure Management Depend on Translation Accounting Methods?" *Euromoney* (June 1981), pp. 132–138.

Aggarwal, Raj. "FASB No. 8 and Reported Results of Multinational Operations: Hazard for Managers and Investors." *Journal of Accounting, Auditing and Finance* (Spring 1978), pp. 197–216.

Aggarwal, Raj, and James C. Baker. "Using Foreign Subsidiary Accounting Data: A Dilemma for Multinational Corporations." *Columbia Journal of World Business* (Fall 1975), pp. 83–92.

Banker, Pravin. "You're the Best Judge of Foreign Risks." *Harvard Business Review* (March/April 1983), pp. 157–165.

Barrett, M. Edgar. "Financial Reporting Practices: Disclosure and Comprehensiveness in an International Setting." *Journal of Accounting Research* (Spring 1976), pp. 10–26.

Bartlett, Christopher A., and Sumantra Ghoshal. "Managing Across Borders: New Strategic Requirements." *Sloan Management Review* (Summer 1987), pp. 7–17.

Bavishi, Vinod B., and Harold E. Wyman. "Foreign Operations Disclosures by U.S.-Based Multinational Corporations: Are They Adequate?" *International Journal of Accounting* (Fall 1980), pp. 153–168.

Beaver, William, and Mark Wolfson. "Foreign Currency Translation Gains and Losses: What Effect Do They Have and What Do They Mean?" *Financial Analysts Journal* (March–April 1984), pp. 28–36.

Bettis, Richard A., and William K. Hall. "Strategic Portfolio Management in the Multibusiness Firm." *California Management Review* (Fall 1981), pp. 23–38.

Burns, Jane O. "Transfer Pricing Decisions in U.S. Multinational Corporations." *Journal of International Business Studies* (Fall 1980), pp. 23–39.

Choi, Frederisk D. S. "Diversity in Multinational Accounting." *Financial Executive* (August 1982), pp. 45–49.

Choi, Frederisk D. S., and I. J. Czechowicz. "Assessing Foreign Subsidiary Performance: A Multinational Comparison." *Management International Review* (April 1983), pp. 14–25.

Cowen, Scott S., Lawrence C. Phillips, and Linda Stillabower. "Multinational Transfer Pricing." *Management Accounting* (January 1979), pp. 17–21.

Daniels, John D., and Jeffrey Bracker. "Profit Performance: Do Foreign Operations Make a Difference?" *Management International Reivew*, no. 1 (1989), pp. 46–56.

Dufey, Gunter, and Ian Giddy. "International Financial Planning." *California Management Review* (Fall 1978), pp. 69–81.

Gelinas, A. J. A. "Tax Considerations for U.S. Corporations Using Finance Subsidiaries to Borrow Funds Abroad." *Journal of Corporate Taxation* (Autumn 1980), pp. 230–263.

Giddy, Ian H. "The Demise of the Product Cycle Model in International Business Theory." *Columbia Journal of World Business* (Spring 1978), pp. 90–97.

Godiwalli, Yezdi. "Multinational Planning—Developing a Global Approach." *Long-Range Planning* (April 1986), pp. 110–116.

Hamel, Gary, and C.K. Prahalad. "Do You Really Have a Global Strategy?" *Harvard Business Review* (July–August 1985), pp. 139–148.

Hoffman, Richard C. "The General Management of Foreign Subsidiaries in the U.S.A.: An Exploratory Study." *Management International Review*, no. 2 (1988), pp. 41–55.

Horst, Thomas. "American Taxation of Multinational Firms." *American Economic Review* (June 1977), pp. 376–389.

Hufbauer, G. C. "The Taxation of Export Profits." *National Tax Journal* (March 1975), pp. 43–59.

Jones, Edward H. "Decision-Making Based on Foreign Financial Statements." *Financial Executive* (February 1981), pp. 32–35.

Kim, Seung H., and Stephen W. Miller. "Constituents of International Transfer Pricing Decisions." *Columbia Journal of World Business* (Spring 1979), pp. 69–76.

Kim, Suk H. "On Repealing the Foreign Corrupt Practices Act: Survey and Assessment." *Columbia Journal of World Business* (Fall 1981), pp. 75–80.

Kravis, Irving B., and Robert E. Lipsey. "The Location of Overseas Production and Production for Export by U.S. Multinational Firms." *Journal of International Economics* (May 1982), pp. 201–223.

Kreder, Martina, and Maria Zeller. "Control in German and U.S. Companies." Management International Review, no. 3 (1988), pp. 58–66.

Merville, Larry J., and J. William Petty. "Transfer Pricing for the Multinational Firm." *Accounting Review* (October 1978), pp. 935–951.

Naylor, Thomas H. "The International Strategy Matrix." *Columbia Journal of World Business* (Summer 1985), pp. 11–19.

Rodriguez, Rita M. "Measuring and Controlling Multinationals' Exchange Risk." *Financial Analysts Journal* (November–December 1979), pp. 49–55.

Schneeweis, T. "Determinants of Profitability: An International Perspective." *Management International Review* (February 1983), pp. 15–21.

Schwartz, Peter, and Jerry Saville. "Multinational Business in the 1990s—A Scenario." *Long-Range Planning* (December 1986), pp. 31–37.

Srinivasulu, S. L. "Classifying Foreign Exchange Exposure." *Financial Executive* (February 1983), pp. 36–44.

Tang, Roger L. W., C. K. Walter, and Robert H. Haymond. "Transfer Pricing—Japanese vs. American Style." *Management Accounting* (January 1979), pp. 12–16.

Wurst, Charles M., and Raymond H. Alleman. "Translation Adjustments for a Strong Dollar." *Financial Executive* (June 1984) pp. 34–41.

The International Banking Environment

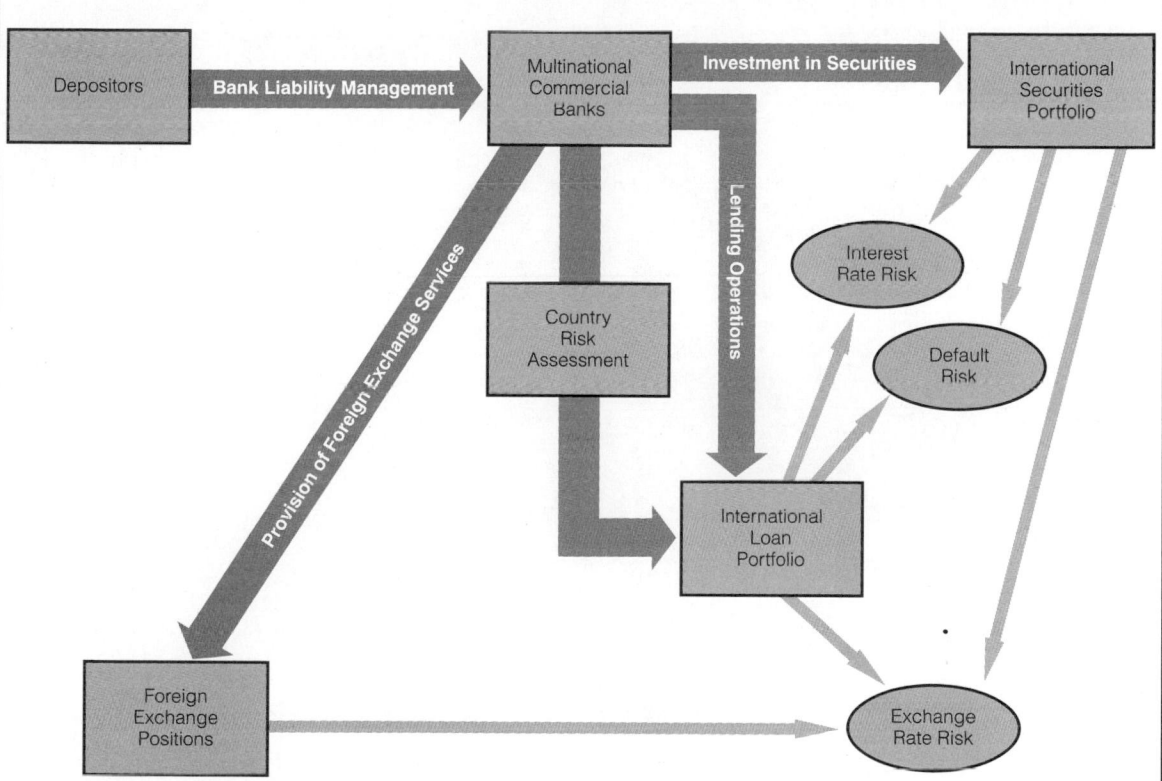

Part 6 (Chapters 22 and 23) provides a background on international banking. Chapter 22 describes the development of international banking and explains the risks incurred by these banks. Chapter 23 concentrates on the risk of nonperforming foreign loans. It describes the events that led to the international debt crisis and explains how banks have attempted to deal with the crisis. It also illustrates how banks use country risk assessment as input to their international lending decisions.

CHAPTER 22

International Banking

Commercial banks play a vital role in facilitating international transactions. They help finance and provide guarantees for international trade. They hold inventories of various currencies so a corporation can obtain the necessary currency to purchase foreign goods or invest in foreign securities. In addition, they offer forward contracts to corporations that desire to lock in the rate at which a currency can be purchased or sold in advance. Commercial banks also provide loans to corporations in various countries. This chapter concentrates on the motives of commercial banks for entering foreign markets, the risks associated with international banking, and the strategies used to cope with these risks.

MOTIVATION FOR INTERNATIONAL BANKING

Large banks have served as primary suppliers of funds to foreign countries. They have found that higher returns can often be achieved, as foreign borrowers are willing to pay higher interest rates in order to obtain funds. In addition, lending to various foreign borrowers is an effective method for banks to diversify their loanable funds. Diversification of loanable funds can be achieved without lending funds overseas. However, if all the firms that borrow from a bank are from the same country, they may all be systematically influenced by the events that occur in that country (such as a recession, etc.). A portfolio of international loans is not expected to be as susceptible to a single economic event as a purely domestic loan portfolio. The argument here reflects benefits of international diversification. This argument has also been used to suggest why an MNC should consider establishing business in several countries. The total sales level of an MNC with globally diversified direct foreign investment is less vulnerable to a particular economic event than a purely domestic firm. The difference between the argument for international diversification from the direct foreign investment perspective as opposed to the banking perspective is the manner by which revenues are generated. In the case of direct foreign investment, revenues are generated from product sales. In the case of international banking, revenues are generated from interest and fees on loans.

Beyond the diversification argument, other motives exist for banks to expand globally. Foreign banking markets may have easy access to entry. Regulations may be more relaxed, as discussed in detail later in this chapter. Economies of scale (lower average cost per unit of output as volume increases) may result from international expansion of banking services. Finally, subsidiaries of MNCs located in foreign markets may request services from the banks which the headquarters uses in the home country. Thus, the establishment of foreign branch banking can further develop relationships already initiated with MNCs. The general growth of international trade and finance calls for banks that have a working knowledge of more than one country. Some banks have devoted resources to become established in various countries and become accustomed to differences in country cultures, politics, and economics. Yet, by providing global banking services, they have differentiated themselves from other regional or national banks. That is, they can provide services to customers that non-global banks are not accustomed to providing—which is one more reason why banks are motivated to expand internationally.

EVOLUTION OF INTERNATIONAL BANKING

The creation and growth of international banking is largely attributed to the growth of international business. However, other characteristics of the banking industry have stimulated its growth as well. The evolution of international banking can be discussed from two aspects: the development of the Eurocurrency market (with movement of U.S. banks to this market) and migration of the non-U.S. banks into the United States.

Development of the Eurocurrency Market

The Eurocurrency market serves as an international banking center where lenders and borrowers from various countries are matched up. The financial intermediaries in this market, often referred to as **Eurobanks,** are located primarily in Europe, and many of the large U.S. banks have branches in Europe that serve as Eurobanks. The liabilities of Eurobanks are mainly time deposits in large amounts and of varied currency denominations. Their assets consist of short-term and medium-term loans to corporations and government agencies.

The creation and growth of the Eurocurrency market is due to several developments during the 1950s and 1960s, when MNCs began to explore new opportunities by entering foreign markets. In addition, international trade became more common. The growth of multinational business encouraged banks to establish branches where subsidiaries of MNCs were located. Banks that had already established relationships with MNC's parents attempted to also develop relationships with their subsidiaries.

Because the U.S. dollar was the primary currency used to denominate internationally traded goods, there was a need for U.S. dollars around the world. This was especially true in Europe, where international trade was quite popular. Banks in Europe welcomed dollar-denominated deposits from corporations with excess cash, since they could lend them to corporations that needed dollars to make payments on imports. The widespread use of these so-called **Eurodollars** contributed to the growth of the Eurocurrency market.

In the early 1960s, funds were being transferred among countries not only to pay for imports, but also to purchase foreign securities. However, the Interest Equalization Tax (IET) imposed on U.S. investors as of 1963 discouraged foreign investments. In addition, the U.S.-based MNCs were asked by the U.S. government to obtain funding for foreign projects from foreign sources. Limitations were placed on U.S. banks regarding their volume of international lending. This government policy, along with the IET, was intended to assure that U.S. funds would be available to finance development within the United States. Due to these policies, both non-U.S. corporations and U.S.-based MNCs in need of funds for projects outside the country were forced to look elsewhere for funds. The Eurocurrency market grew in response to the needs for an international banking arena that could finance business outside the United States.

During the early 1970s, the worldwide demand for oil increased to meet the higher global production of goods and services. As the Organization of Petroleum Exporting Countries (OPEC) exported oil, the oil-importing countries needed to borrow more funds. In addition, the OPEC countries were receiving revenues they desired to invest. Both forces increased the growth of the Eurocurrency market. In fact, the Eurobanks within this market helped recycle the oil payments as they accepted deposits from the cash-rich OPEC countries and converted these funds into loans for the oil-importing countries.

Beyond all the developments described up to this point, the popularity of the Eurocurrency market can also be attributed to the attractive deposit and loan rates offered by Eurobanks due to four characteristics that distinguish them from other commercial banks. First, reserve requirements are not imposed on foreign currency deposits at Eurobanks, allowing them to reduce their spread between the average rate offered on deposits and the average rate charged on loans. Second, interest rate ceilings are not imposed on deposit rates as they were in the United States. Third, the transactions are typically of wholesale rather than retail nature; so each transaction represents a large amount of funds. This characteristic reduces their costs, enabling them to offer attractive rates. Fourth, Eurobank deposits are not insured by a government agency and therefore do not require an insurance premium to be paid by Eurobanks. This again allows the banks to offer attractive rates on their deposits and loans.

Due to these four characteristics, Eurobanks can afford to offer higher interest rates on deposits, and charge lower rates on their loans. Furthermore, the absence of restrictions to entry into the Eurocurrency market assures that rates will remain competitive, since competition between Eurobanks should persist. If collective rate-setting among banks did occur, other banks would enter this market to maintain competition.

During the 1960s, foreign branches of U.S. banks could obtain deposits without holding required reserves. Thus, they could channel funds back to their U.S. offices where loans could be provided. This strategy was discouraged in the early 1970s, as the U.S. government imposed required reserves on any increase in net liabilities of the U.S. offices to their respective foreign branches. Because of the restriction, foreign branches of U.S. banks were forced to provide loans in the foreign markets rather than channel the funds back to the home office, thereby expanding the role of the foreign branches of U.S. banks beyond simple deposit-accepting and into foreign lending. That expanded role is one more reason for the growth of international banking.

Exploration for New Services in International Banking

The primary functions of international banking have been to facilitate foreign trade and provide foreign loans. However, these functions may expand into other areas such as **barter,** where the banks locate firms that can exchange goods with each other. Their primary role here would be to establish a network where they could identify the various products needed or produced by firms in various countries. Banks often explore any potential opportunities for expanding their services in order to distinguish themselves as more of a full-service institution than their competitors.

The largest U.S. banks have divested some foreign operations and are focusing on specific niches in foreign countries. Chase Manhattan is creating a niche in the credit-card business overseas, while Chemical Bank is focusing on mortgage-backed securities and J.P. Morgan is heavily involved in underwriting. Citibank is concentrated in consumer banking and some other services. Many of the super-regional banks in the United States are focusing their growth within the United States.

The most common method for U.S. commercial banks to expand is through establishing **branches,** which are full-service banking offices that can compete directly with other banks located in that area. Commercial banks may also consider establishing **agencies,** which can provide loans but cannot accept deposits or provide trust services.

Migration of Non-U.S. Banks into the United States

As the Eurocurrency market was developing outside the United States, the growth of foreign branches in the United States also continued. One of the key motives for this trend was the development by non-U.S. corporations of subsidiaries within the country. Non-U.S. banks were commonly doing business with these firms in foreign countries. As the non-U.S. firms expanded their business into the United States, so did the non-U.S. banks.

The primary functions of non-U.S. banks within the United States are wholesale- rather than retail-oriented. That is, they emphasize deposits and loans in large denominations rather than the smaller retail transactions. They are mainly located in areas where multinational business is common, such as New York, Los Angeles, San Francisco, and Chicago. Their primary role is to serve the subsidiaries of MNCs whose parents reside in their home country, although they also attempt to serve the headquarters of U.S.-based MNCs. The movement of U.S. banks into the Eurocurrency market and the migration of non-U.S. banks into the United States are the primary reasons for growth in international banking during the last three decades.

In recent years, 8 Japanese banks have been most aggressive in penetrating the U.S. market. They now control about 25 percent of the California market. One major reason for their growth is very competitive corporate loans. They also have been known to provide letters of credit for lower fees than those charged by U.S. banks. Another reason for their growth is a relatively low

---

RELATED RESEARCH

Should Banks Diversify Internationally?

A recent study by Aggarwal and Durnford assessed the impact of international business on risk for commercial banks. Similar studies have been conducted for nonfinancial MNCs, and have generally found an inverse relationship between degree of international business and risk. The results could differ in the banking industry because of the loan repayment problems experienced by less developed countries during the 1980s.

To assess the relationship between degree of international business and risk, the au-

thors compiled data for various proxies. One proxy used for the degree of international business was the ratio of foreign loans to total loans. One proxy used for risk was the bank's beta, which represents systematic risk. Regression analysis was used to measure the relationship between the degree of international business and risk. The authors found a significant inverse relationship, implying that banks may be able to reduce their systematic risk by increasing their degree of international business.

SOURCE: Aggarwal, Raj and Jon Durnford, "Market Assessment of International Banking Activity: A Study of U.S. Bank Holding Companies," *Quarterly Journal of Economics and Business*, (Spring 1989), pp. 58–67.

---

cost of capital, which allows them to take on many ventures that would not be feasible for U.S. banks. Furthermore, the high savings rate of the Japanese allows for substantial growth in deposits in Japan, which may then be channeled to support operations in the United States.

RISKS TO A DEPOSITOR IN THE EUROCURRENCY MARKET

While Eurocurrency deposits typically do offer attractive interest rates, they pose some risks, too. First, there is a possibility that due to political turmoil, Eurocurrency deposits in these banks could be seized by foreign government authorities. Such an event is not likely for depositors who keep their funds in their home country. Second, Eurocurrency deposits are typically not insured. Therefore, if a Eurobank defaults, reimbursement to the depositors is uncertain. Finally, a depositor's assessment of the financial soundness of Eurobanks is more difficult than assessing U.S. banks due to more stringent disclosure requirements in the United States. These risks or inconveniences discourage some corporations from maintaining Eurocurrency deposit balances.

SYNDICATED EUROCURRENCY LOANS

While the Eurocurrency market concentrates on large-volume transactions, there are often times when no single Eurobank is willing to provide the amount of funds needed by a particular corporation or government agency.

In this case, a **syndicate** of Eurobanks may be composed. Each bank within the syndicate participates in the lending. A **lead bank** is responsible for negotiating terms with the borrower. Then the lead bank organizes a group of banks to underwrite the loans. The syndicate of banks is usually formed in about six weeks, or less if the borrower is well known, since the credit evaluation could then be conducted more quickly.

Borrowers who receive a syndicated loan incur various fees besides the interest on the loan. Front-end management fees are paid to represent the costs of organizing the syndicate and underwriting the loan. In addition, a commitment fee of about .25 percent or .50 percent is charged annually on the unused portion of the available credit extended by the syndicate.

Syndicated loans can be denominated in a variety of currencies. The interest rate depends on the currency denominating the loan, the maturity of the loan, and the creditworthiness of the borrower. Interest rates on syndicated loans are commonly adjustable according to movements in LIBOR (London Interbank Offer Rate), and the adjustment may occur every six months or every year.

Syndicated Eurocurrency loans not only reduce the default risk of a large loan to the degree of participation for each individual bank, but they can also add an extra incentive for the borrower to repay the loan. For example, consider a government agency that borrows a substantial amount of funds from a single bank. If the agency is unable to repay the loan, it will likely ruin its relationship with the lending bank. However, other banks may not be as aware of the specifics regarding this loan default. Thus, they may be willing to provide loans to the government in the future. If a government defaults on a loan to a syndicate, however, word will spread among banks quickly, and the government will likely have difficulty in obtaining future loans. Borrowers are therefore strongly encouraged to make prompt loan repayments on syndicated loans. From the perspective of the banks, syndicated Eurocurrency loans increase the probability of prompt repayment.

REGULATION IN THE EUROCURRENCY MARKET

As already mentioned, the popularity of the Eurocurrency market is due largely to its lack of restrictions. Arguments have been made that Eurobanks hold an unfair advantage over other banks and should therefore be subject to the same regulation as other banks. Some pros and cons on regulating the Eurocurrency market follow.

One common reason offered for regulating the Eurocurrency market is that a string of successive bank failures within this market could cause a banking crisis. The Eurocurrency market has become so large that it is vital to the existence of international banking, so some propose that regulation is warranted by its very size and importance. Also, the imposition of reserve requirements by regulators on currency deposits would allow for more control on the growth in money supply, while enforcing deposit insurance along with reserve requirements could better ensure the safety and soundness of the banks within the Eurocurrency market.

Although imposing regulations on the Eurocurrency market could improve its safety, there are some potential adverse consequences. First, recall that the growth in the Eurocurrency market has been primarily due to the absence of regulations. If regulations are imposed, will the Eurocurrency market continue to be as widely used as it is today? The Eurobanks may not be able to attract funds if they are subject to reserve requirements, deposit insurance, etc., since these regulations would force their deposit rates down. Similarly, their loan rates may not be as attractive as they were before the regulations.

Another argument against regulation of the Eurocurrency market is that it would require the cooperation of international regulatory agencies. The responsibility of regulation may be assigned to the home country of the headquarters for each Eurobank or to the country where Eurobanks have been established. Under either alternative, if some governments are not willing to accept their assigned responsibility, Eurobanks under the supervision of these countries would be able to avoid regulations. This would cause a migration of Eurobanks to the regions where regulations are more relaxed.

Regulation in the Eurocurrency market can be effective only if all Eurobanks are regulated to the same degree. Even then, arguments still remain against regulation, particularly the argument that the Eurocurrency market works efficiently because it is not regulated. The discussion in this text is intended to provide arguments for both sides, not suggest the correct position. The reader is left with the duty of deciding whether the pros outweigh the cons, or vice versa. It is quite likely that this issue will be argued for many years to come.

RISKS INCURRED BY A EUROBANK

The risks incurred by a Eurobank are somewhat similar to those of most commercial banks. First, its loans are subject to default risk. Second, it is exposed to exchange rate risk, since its assets may be denominated in a mix of currencies that does not perfectly match its liabilities. Finally, Eurobanks are exposed to interest rate risk since the maturities of their liabilities will not always match the maturities of their assets. Each of these three types of risk will be discussed in turn.

Default Risk of Loans Provided by Eurobanks

The international loan portfolios of Eurobanks may be subject to a high degree of default risk, since Eurobanks may not be able to closely monitor the foreign companies to which they lend. In defense of the Eurobanks, their international loans are typically extended to the prominent corporations around the world as well as governments. This is generally perceived as a plus, since the largest corporations and governments have historically been reliable in paying back their loans. However, the recent international debt crisis has banks wondering whether any loan is safe. Eurobanks attempt to reduce the risk of their loan portfolio by employing effective credit evaluation on loan requests and by maintaining adequate diversification among industries and countries.

Exchange Rate Risk of Eurobanks

Eurobanks are also exposed to currency risk. That is, the currency composition of their assets may differ from that of their liabilities. While this risk may also exist for other commercial banks, it is more pronounced for Eurobanks since they are always accepting foreign deposits and extending foreign loans. To illustrate how currency composition can differ on the asset side from the liability side, consider a firm that wishes to set up a three-month U.S. dollar deposit. At the same time, a German firm requests a three-month loan denominated in German marks from the Eurobank. If the Eurobank does not have marks available, it may take the U.S. dollar deposits and convert those dollars to marks to extend a loan to the firm. In this example, the Eurobank has a liability denominated in U.S. dollars and an asset denominated in German marks. If the mark depreciates against the U.S. dollar, then the loan repayment received by the Eurobank may not be large enough to pay off the U.S. depositor (after the marks received are converted to dollars). To deal with this problem, the Eurobanks will make an effort to match U.S. dollar deposits with U.S. dollar loans, and mark deposits with mark loans. In this way, it will match currencies on the asset and liability side. While such an objective is rational, loan and deposit requests do not always allow for a perfect matching of currencies.

Because a bank cannot always match its currencies borrowed with the currencies denominating loans, its performance will typically be exposed to exchange rate fluctuations. As a simplified example, consider that as of March 1, 1992, Bank A accepts $1 million in three-month U.S. dollar-denominated deposits and then uses the funds to provide a three-month mark-denominated loan amounting to 3 million marks (by first converting the dollars to marks at an exchange rate of $1 = 3 marks). In this case, the bank owes dollars to a depositor in the future, but has no expected future cash inflows in dollars. While it has matched maturities here, it has not matched currencies. This bank is "short" on dollars (since dollar-denominated liabilities exceed dollar-denominated assets) and "long" on marks (since mark-denominated assets exceed mark-denominated liabilities). Now consider Bank B, which as of March 1, 1992, has converted 3 million marks that it received as deposits into $1 million in order to provide a dollar-denominated loan. This bank is short on marks and long on dollars. Assume, for simplicity, that the maturities of the loan and deposit are three months, similar to those of Bank A.

Bank A will receive marks and need to pay out dollars in three months. Bank B will receive dollars and need to pay out marks in three months. Assume that Bank A charges 12 percent annually (3 percent during the three-month loan period) on its mark-denominated loan and pays 8 percent annually (2 percent during the three-month loan period) on its dollar-denominated deposits. Since the exchange rate of the mark with respect to the dollar will not normally remain constant during the three-month period, the profit to the bank is exposed to any change that occurs. To illustrate, assume the dollar is worth 3.10 marks at the end of the three-month period. At that time, the marks would be converted to about $996,774, which does not even cover the amount owed to the depositor. This possibility illustrates the risk to a bank that does not perfectly match currencies on both sides of the balance sheet. Of course, there is a chance the mark will appreciate against the dollar, which would increase the profit generated by Bank A. However, Bank B would be hampered by this occurrence since it is long on dollars and short on marks. If a bank is uncomfortable with its non-offsetting currency positions, it should search for another bank with which it can enact a currency swap. A discussion of the currency swap arrangement follows.

As of March 1, 1992, when both banks became exposed to exchange rate risk, they may have begun to search for a swap candidate. The banks serve as candidates for each other in this example. The swap arrangement could specify that as of June 1, 1992, Bank A will exchange marks to Bank B for dollars according to a specified exchange rate. The actual exchange rate specified within the swap arrangement could be today's spot rate or some other rate agreed upon by both parties. The swap locks in the rate at which Bank A can convert its marks (to be received) to dollars, thereby hedging against the possibility of the mark depreciating over time. In addition, the swap locks in the rate at which Bank B can convert its dollars (to be received) to marks, thereby hedging against the possibility of the dollar depreciating over time.

A swap arrangement will not necessarily provide a perfect hedge, since the timing of the loan and deposit maturities for each bank may not coincide. Or, the amount by which one bank is long on a particular currency may not necessarily match the amount by which the other bank is short on that currency.

Interest Rate Risk of Eurobanks

Eurobanks often face interest rate risk due to a maturity mismatch on their liabilities versus their assets. For example, if the source of funds reflects a shorter term to maturity than the maturity of the loan it extends (with the use of these funds), the bank is subject to interest rate risk. Its spread between average interest earned on its assets and average interest paid out on its liabilities could be reduced during periods of rising interest rates. To insulate itself against this interest rate risk, the bank may arrange a swap with another bank that has mismatched maturities of the opposite type (average liability maturity exceeding average asset maturity). The swap would specify a loan to be provided by the latter bank to the former bank at a specified rate of interest. This effectively insulates the former bank from interest rate risk since it provides a future source of funds at an interest rate specified today. In addition, the latter bank has insulated itself from interest rate risk since it has now locked in the return on its use of funds for a time frame equivalent to the maturity of its fund sources.

As an example, consider Bank X, which as of January 2, 1993, has received a one-month, $1 million deposit and will pay 9 percent annually (.75 percent for the month) on this deposit. Assume it used the $1 million to make a three-month loan at 12 percent annually (3 percent for the three months). If by chance interest rates rise as of one month from now, the deposit rate paid by the bank would need to rise in order to attract more funds. Yet, the return on the $1 million loan given out is locked in for three months. Thus, the margin between interest received on loans versus what the bank pays on deposits will be narrowed. Consider a second bank, called Bank Y, which as of January 2, 1993, received a three-month, $1 million deposit and will pay 9 percent annually (2.25 percent for three months) on this deposit. Assume it used the $1 million to make a one-month loan at 12 percent annually (1 percent over one month). If interest rates decline as of one month from now,

INTERNATIONAL FINANCIAL MANAGEMENT IN PRACTICE

Concerns about International Banking

Gerald Corrigan, president of the Federal Reserve Bank of New York, recently made a speech about international banking and financial markets. Some of his comments that relate directly to this chapter are summarized:

1. There is some concern that the innovative techniques that have been created by financial institutions to reduce risk may actually create risk. (For example, interest rate swaps are often utilized to reduce interest rate risk. But if a financial institution takes a side in a swap rather than simply acting as a middleman, it may increase its risk). Some of these risks are difficult for the market to detect because they are not always visible on financial statements.

2. Globally integrated markets allow more opportunities to market participants. Yet, a shock in one market may now be more likely to affect all other markets.

3. Bank regulations differ among countries. As the competition for services is inter-national in scope, some banks may have an edge because of their local regulations. It may be difficult to limit the risk of a world-wide disaster in the banking system by enforcing laws (such as capital requirements), unless all other countries enforce similar laws.

4. The United States regulates foreign financial institutions within the United States as if they were headquartered here. Yet, some countries use reciprocity rules, so that banks located in a country may be subject to different rules because they come from different countries.

The solutions proposed to some of these concerns are controversial. One is to establish a set of global regulations that all banks must follow. Countries that have benefited from a lack of regulations may be unwilling to support such a proposed solution.

SOURCE: "Coping with Globally Integrated Financial Markets," *FRBNY Quarterly Review* (Winter 1987), pp. 1–5.

the loan rate charged on a new loan by the bank at that time would need to be reduced in order to compete against other banks. Yet, the rate on the $1 million deposit is locked in for three months. Thus, the margin between interest received on loans versus what the bank pays on deposits could be reduced.

Bank X is concerned about a reduced margin if interest rates rise, while Bank Y is concerned about a reduced margin if interest rates fall. The two banks can create a swap to insulate against the existing interest rate risk. In our example, Bank Y could, as of January 2, 1993, arrange to provide Bank X with a future loan of $1 million. This loan rate may be set at, say 10.5 percent annually, and will be provided as of February 2. It will last for two months. The loan between banks occurs on the date at which (1) the funds lent out by Bank Y as of January 2 are repaid and (2) the funds deposited into Bank X as of January 2 are withdrawn.

Based on this example, the results for both banks are as follows. Bank X paid .75 percent over one month to a depositor, and 1.75 percent (10.5 percent annual rate) over two months for the loan from Bank Y. The cost of obtaining funds was therefore 2.50 percent over three months. The return to

Bank X due to its three-month loan was 3 percent. If Bank X had not arranged for a swap, it could not have locked in its cost of obtaining funds and would have faced the possibility of even a negative margin if interest rates increased over time.

Bank Y paid 2.25 percent over three months to a depositor. The return to Bank Y on its funds lent out were 1 percent over the first month, plus 1.75 percent over the next two months. The return amounts to 2.75 percent over three months. If Bank Y had not arranged for a swap, it could not have locked in its return on funds over the three-month period. Thus, it would have faced the possiblity of even a negative margin if interest rates decreased over time.

If both banks had been able to match the maturities of their liabilities to those of their assets, they would not have needed a swap, since fluctuating interest rates would not have affected them. However, only a coincidence would cause the various maturities on liabilities to perfectly match those on assets for a bank. While the bank could actively pursue matched maturities, it might lose prospective customers if it restricted them to limited maturities on deposits or loans.

The use of floating-rate loans has effectively reduced interest rate risk, since the bank's interest received on assets should adjust as the interest paid on liabilities changes. Of course, the adjustment every six months or year still leaves the bank somewhat exposed if its maturities on the liability side are shorter. Thus, the interest rate swap can further reduce exposure to maturity imbalances.

All Risks Combined

In reality, a Eurobank must attempt to manage its default risk, exchange rate risk, and interest rate risk simultaneously. Suppose a Eurobank received most of its deposits in U.S. dollars with short-term maturities. On its asset side, assume that most loans have been long-term in nature, denominated in various European currencies, and focusing on a few selected industries. This Eurobank is exposed to a high degree of default risk, exchange rate risk, and interest rate risk. To reduce some of the risk, it may attempt to enter into currency swaps and interest rate swaps. Yet, it is unlikely to achieve perfect matching of maturities and currencies on its liabilities to its assets. Even if it did, default risk on the loans extended would remain. The discussion here does not imply the risks incurred by Eurobanks are intolerable but simply points out the challenge involved in managing all risks simultaneously.

KEY COMPONENTS OF THE INTERNATIONAL BANKING NETWORK

The growth of international banking has been aided by the establishment of (1) branch banks, (2) Edge Act corporations, and (3) international banking facilities. Each will be discussed in turn.

Branch Banks

A foreign branch bank can provide virtually all of the services its parent provides as long as it abides by host-country regulations. Due to its relationship with its parent, it must also abide by regulations of its parent's home country. Branches of large banks are popular since they are household names internationally and can penetrate different geographical areas. They are convenient to MNCs' subsidiaries that may need local correspondence with banks. Due to branch banking, all subsidiaries of an MNC dispersed around the world can work with one or a few banks.

U.S. banks have commonly set up branches overseas in order to accept deposits and provide loans to foreign customers. Foreign branches of U.S. banks are not subject to the reserve requirements or interest ceilings that exist in the United States. Foreign branches of U.S. banks are concentrated in the United Kingdom, Brazil, Hong Kong, France, Japan, Singapore, and West Germany.

Edge Act Corporations

Due to the International Banking Act of 1978, Edge Act corporations (called **Edges**) have been allowed more flexibility in handling international transactions. Edges are used to establish international banking offices outside the home state. U.S. banks have historically been banned from setting up a branch in a different state (although regulations now allow interstate banking among some states). However, even with the remaining restrictions on interstate banking, a U.S. bank can establish operations in another state through an Edge Act corporation. These operations focus on aiding corporations involved in international trade. Edges are supervised by the U.S. Federal Reserve System.

International Banking Facilities

International banking facilities (IBFs) represent a recent popular innovation in the international banking industry. These are not new physical facilities, but instead a part of the existing bank. Created in the United States in late 1981, IBFs are allowed to accept deposits from or make loans to nonresidents of the United States. Because IBFs are not subject to normal U.S. regulations, they are free from reserve requirements and interest rate ceilings. These advantages are similar to those of institutions located within the Eurocurrency market. The IBFs are subject to some restrictions, though. First, funds borrowed by an IBF from its parent, like funds borrowed from an offshore branch, are subject to reserve requirements. Second, IBF transactions with customers must normally amount to $100,000 or more. This restricts the IBF business to large corporations or government agencies. Finally, IBFs are not allowed to insure certificates of deposit (CDs). This prevents possible competition by IBFs within U.S. money markets.

The preferred locations of IBFs are close to major financial areas. In addition, their choice of location is partially influenced by the state tax laws. As of April 1984, 10 states provided special tax treatment for IBFs, including New York, California, and Illinois (where the key financial centers are located). In particular, Florida offers the most favorable tax treatment to IBFs. It should not be surprising that the bulk of the 500 or so existing IBFs have been established in the four states mentioned above.

The IBFs attract funds largely from foreign banks, foreign government agencies, and other IBFs. Their existence allows greater ability of U.S. banks to provide international banking services. The fact that some banks have replaced their "offshore" banking with IBFs suggests that IBFs may be perceived as a substitute for offshore banking. IBFs sometimes have more tax benefits or lower transaction costs, or even less political risk than offshore banking. It is highly likely that they will continue to become more popular over time as their potential advantages are realized.

BANKING REGULATIONS AMONG COUNTRIES

The United States has a complex regulatory system with the tightest restrictions in the world. In addition, the regulatory process is overseen by four agencies (Federal Reserve Board, Federal Deposit Insurance Corporation, Comptroller of the Currency, and state agencies). Banks in the United States are restricted to a maximum amount loaned to individual borrowers and are forced to write off nonperforming loans. They are also limited to the amount of loans extended to specific countries. In addition, they are not allowed to purchase stock for their asset portfolio or underwrite equities in the U.S.

Canadian banks are regulated by the Office of the Inspector General. Like U.S. banks, they are not allowed to underwrite equities. However, they can purchase stock as long as they do not own more than 10 percent of any Canadian firm. They have no limits on the loan amount to any individual borrower or country. Relative to most countries, Canadian banks enjoy fewer restrictions. The Bank of Canada serves as a lender of last resort to Canadian banks.

French banks are restricted to some extent from non-bank activities. However, they can own stock in non-bank companies. There are limits to the loan amount extended to any individual borrower, but not to any country. The Bank of France serves as a lender of last resort to French banks.

Japanese banks are supervised by the Ministry of Finance and the Bank of Japan. They are restricted from some but not all security underwriting activities. Limits are placed on loans to individual borrowers, although exceptions exist for public and guaranteed loans. Limits are not placed on loans to countries. The Bank of Japan assumes an active role in lending to Japanese banks in need of funds.

The Japanese government has recently allowed some foreign financial institutions to establish subsidiaries there. There were 79 subsidiaries of foreign-owned banks in Japan in 1986, 19 from the United States. In addition, there were 36 foreign securities firms (18 from the United States) versus only 8 in 1983.

In April 1984 the Japanese government allowed foreign-owned banks to deal in Japanese public securities and to underwrite government bonds. In June 1985 it allowed foreign banks to manage Japanese trust and pension funds.

Even with the loosened regulations, foreign banks accounted for only 4 percent of all banking assets in Japan. One of the main reasons is that foreign banks have only a limited access to some popular deposit accounts.

British banks are supervised by the Bank of England. They have much flexibility in entering into various forms of business. The Bank of England serves as a lender of last resort to British banks.

West German banks are overseen by the Federal Banking Supervisory Office and the Bundesbank. Regulation of German banks has increased since the collapse of Herstatt, a major German bank, in 1976. German banks are free to enter into various business activities. Maximum limits are placed on individual loans. The Bundesbank serves as the lender of last resort to German banks.

Due to differences in regulations among countries, some banks are at a disadvantage when competing within the international banking environment. Some governments are directly involved in banking. The French government owns the French banks, while the West German government is a major shareholder of German banks. Banks are more likely to be rescued from any financial problems if their home government serves as a partial or sole owner. The differences in regulation are likely to persist, since each government maintains its own philosophy with regard to its role in regulating the banking industry.

The central banks retain supervisory power over the banks in most European countries, unlike the United States, where other regulatory authorities share a large portion of responsibility. In the Nordic countries, authorities other than the central bank have the primary supervisory role. They conduct on-site examinations to monitor credit policies, foreign activities, and internal control. They also periodically monitor financial reports to assess capital adequacy and risk. The Bank of England analyzes the bank's financial reports but does not conduct on-site examinations. In Germany and Switzerland, auditors are appointed by bank regulators to conduct on-site examinations, addressing a list of detailed questions.

In most countries, banks can establish branches or subsidiaries without approval of their home supervisory authorities. There are some exceptions. Dutch banks must obtain approval to establish foreign branches. Swedish banks are not allowed to establish foreign branches. Italian banks must abide by some restrictions.

Because of international banking, competition will exist within a country even if there is only one local bank. While local bank monopolies are uncommon, many industrialized countries are dominated by a few banks. In France, the Netherlands, Switzerland, and West Germany, three local banks control much of the market. In Canada and the United Kingdom, 10 local banks control much of the industry. The banking industry in the United States is still less concentrated, which is attributed mostly to historical regulations that have either prevented or limited interstate banking. As barriers to interstate banking are eliminated, concentration in the U.S. banking industry should increase, though it will remain far below the level of other industrialized countries. As long as banks are allowed to enter foreign markets, even countries with heavily concentrated local banking will continue to experience strong competition in banking services.

Standardizing Regulations Across Countries

The trend toward globalization in the banking industry is attributed to the recent standardization of regulations around the world. Three of the more significant regulatory events allowing for a more competitive global playing field are (1) the International Banking Act, which placed U.S. and foreign banks operating in the United States under the same set of rules, (2) the Single European Act, which placed all European banks operating in Europe under the same set of rules, and (3) the uniform capital adequacy guidelines, which forced banks of 12 industrialized nations to abide by the same minimum capital constraints. A description of each of these events follows.

INTERNATIONAL BANKING ACT.   Passage of the International Banking Act (IBA) in 1978 restricted foreign-owned banks from accepting deposits across state lines. They were allowed to accept deposits in other states only by establishing Edge Act corporations (discussed earlier in this chapter). U.S.-owned banks were subject to similar restrictions at the time the IBA was passed.

The IBA also required that foreign-owned banks in the United States obtain deposit insurance and adhere to product and service restrictions enforced by the Bank Holding Company Act. In general, the IBA eliminated some comparative advantages of foreign-owned banks in the United States. Recent research by Aharony, Saunders, and Swary has shown that the International Banking Act of 1978 had a strong positive effect on stock returns of the money center banks that were competing with foreign banks on an unequal basis.

SINGLE EUROPEAN ACT.   One of the most significant events affecting the international banking markets is the Single European Act, which was phased in by 1992 throughout the European Economic Community (EEC) countries. Some of the more relevant provisions of the Single European Act for the banking industry are

- Capital can flow freely throughout Europe.
- Banks can offer a wide variety of lending, leasing, and securities activities in the EEC.
- The regulations regarding competition, mergers, and taxes will be similar throughout the EEC.
- A bank established in any one of the EEC countries will have the right to expand into any or all of the other EEC countries.

As a result of this act, the European banks are already consolidating to expand across countries. Efficiency in the European banking markets will increase as banks can more easily cross countries without concern for country-specific regulations that prevailed in the past.

Another key provision of the act is that banks entering Europe receive the same banking powers as other banks there. Similar provisions are allowed for non-U.S. banks that enter the United States.

Even some European savings institutions will be affected by more uniform regulations across European countries. Savings institutions throughout Europe are now evolving into full-service institutions, expanding into services such as insurance, brokerage, and mutual fund management. A merger among Spain's savings institutions will create Spain's biggest financial institution with assets of about $47 billion and 1,650 branches.

UNIFORM CAPITAL ADEQUACY GUIDELINES AROUND THE WORLD. Before 1987, capital standards imposed on banks varied across countries, which allowed some banks to have a comparative global advantage over others. As an example, consider a bank in the Unites States that is subject to a 6 percent capital ratio, which is twice that of a foreign bank. The foreign bank could achieve the same return on equity as the U.S. bank by generating a return on assets that is only one-half that of the U.S. bank. In essence, the foreign bank's **equity multiplier** (assets divided by equity) would be double that of the U.S. bank, which would offset the low return on assets. Given these conditions, foreign banks could accept lower profit margins while still achieving the same return on equity. This would afford them a stronger competitive position. In addition, growth would be more easily achieved as a relatively small amount of capital is needed to support an increase in assets.

Some analysts would counter that these advantages are somewhat offset by the higher risk perception of banks having low capital ratios. Yet, if the governments in those countries are more likely to back banks that experience financial problems, banks with low capital may not necessarily be too risky. Therefore, some non-U.S. banks would have globally competitive advantages over U.S. banks, without being subject to excessive risk. In December 1987, 12 major industrialized countries attempted to resolve the disparity by proposing uniform bank standards. In July 1988 central bank governors of the 12 countries agreed on standardized guidelines. Capital was classified as either Tier 1 ("core") capital, or Tier 2 ("supplemental") capital (Tier 1 capital being at least 4 percent of risk-weighted assets). The use of risk-weightings on assets implicitly created a higher capital ratio for riskier assets, since those assets were assigned lower weights. Off-balance sheet items were also accounted for, so that banks could not circumvent capital requirements by focusing on services (such as letters of credit and interest rate swaps) that are not explicitly shown on a balance sheet. Even with uniform capital requirements across countries, some analysts may still contend that U.S. banks are at a competitive disadvantage because they are subject to different accounting and tax provisions. Nevertheless, the uniform capital requirements represent significant progress toward a more level global field.

IMPACT OF EAST EUROPEAN REFORM ON GLOBAL BANKING

The lifting of the Iron Curtain in November 1989 attracted the attention of commercial banks around the world. The privatization of businesses should result in a substantial need for financing. Some of the more obvious ways in which banks can facilitate the trend towards privatization are (1) providing direct loans to businesses, (2) acting as an underwriter on bonds or stock issued by firms in East Germany, (3) providing letters of credit, and (4) providing consulting services on international trade, mergers, and other corporate activities. While opportunities abound, banks are also wary of the risk. In the past, some banks aggressively pursued loans to Poland, which postponed interest payments in 1982. They aggressively pursued lending to Latin American countries, which was followed by numerous debt reschedulings over the 1980s. More recently, some banks have aggressively financed leveraged buyouts and real estate investment, which could also have serious adverse effects.

Some U.S. banks have been conducting business in Eastern Bloc countries. For example, Chase Manhattan Bank and BankAmerica do business in Moscow, while Citibank does business in Hungary. First Chicago serves as an investment bank and financial advisor to Hungary, the Soviet Union, and Yugoslavia. U.S. banks will likely be somewhat cautious, though, in attempting to capitalize on privatization in East Germany and other Eastern Bloc countries. The lingering problems from the Latin American debt crisis that began in 1982 remind U.S. banks that there may someday be an Eastern Bloc crisis.

The deregulatory momentum in Western Europe and Eastern Europe has precipitated strategic responses by commercial banks. Several banks are forming alliances with other banks to provide customers with reciprocal opportunities. Other banks within particular European countries have merged as a defensive measure to protect their local business. Some European banks are merging with insurance companies.

Even with the actions described above, the European banking industry will continue to be somewhat fragmented. Cross-border mergers between banks have not been as popular as mergers within countries. With the exception of credit cards, bank services will still be offered on a national basis. Cultural differences between countries will prevent some services from being standardized across countries.

Some banks, including those from Japan and West Germany, may feel forced to expand into Eastern Europe in order to maintain relationships with corporate clients that are expanding there. For example, Mitsubishi Bank is considering expansion into Eastern Europe. Tokai Bank established offices in Vienna, where transactions between Eastern and Western Europe take place. Fuji Bank is involved in a joint venture in Hungary. Deutsche Bank, Germany's largest bank, planned on opening 250 new branches in East Germany.

U.S. banks have been less aggressive, as their recent attempts to expand throughout Europe during the 1980s were generally not successful. Yet, as more U.S.-based MNCs establish subsidiaries in Eastern Europe, U.S. banks will likely follow.

SUMMARY

The growth in international banking is largely due to the development of the Eurocurrency market and migration of non-U.S. banks into the United States. The international banking arena should continue to grow as banks attempt to penetrate various foreign markets.

A primary reason for growth in the Eurocurrency market is its lack of regulations. Yet, there have been laws proposed to enforce regulations in this market. Pros and cons of a regulated Eurocurrency market were discussed in this chapter. If regulations are enforced, the activity in this market will likely diminish. Three common forms of risk incurred by a Eurobank are default risk, exchange rate risk, and interest rate risk. There are methods to reduce a Eurobank's exposure to these forms of risk, but it is virtually impossible to totally eliminate them.

QUESTIONS

1. Discuss the motives that led to the growth of international banking.

2. What are IBFs, and how can they serve MNCs?

3. In what ways do banking regulations differ among countries?

4. Describe how a bank can become exposed to exchange rate risk.

5. Describe how a bank can reduce exposure to exchange rate risk.

6. Describe how a bank can become exposed to interest rate risk.

7. Describe how a bank can reduce exposure to interest rate risk.

8. Why did the Eurocurrency market become so popular?

9. What is syndicated lending? Why do banks sometimes prefer this form of lending?

10. Describe the possible differences in risk between a purely domestic bank and an international bank.

11. Why might a venture seem feasible for a Japanese bank, but not for a U.S. bank, even if the cash flows were similar? (Ignore exchange rate effects.)

12. Why might a bank be able to achieve greater economies of scale in Europe now than five years ago?

13. Why did differences in capital requirements give some banks a competitive advantage over others?

14. Even with uniform capital requirements, some banks may have competitive advantage over others because of differences in laws across countries. Explain.

15. Loras Bank planned to establish subsidiaries in various Eastern European countries during the 1990s, even though it did not expect these subsidiaries to be profitable. Its logic was that this action was necessary to retain existing business. Interpret this statement.

Bank of Chicago
Exposure to Exchange Rate and Interest Rate Risk

The Bank of Chicago was a major participant in the Eurocurrency, Eurocredit, and Eurobond markets. Its branches in the Eurocurrency market accepted short-term deposits in nine different currencies. It used these funds to provide short-term or medium-term loans, or to purchase bonds in the Eurocurrency market. About one-third of its funds were allocated to each of these uses of funds. Its philosophy was to always use the same currency deposited to make its investments. In this way, it felt that it would avoid exposure to exchange rate risk. Whenever it needed funds in a particular currency, it would raise its deposit rates on that currency to attract more deposits.

The Bank of Chicago had very strong relations with the French government, but did not have any relations with German or Swiss governments. Therefore, it would often experience a very strong demand for French francs when the French government wanted to borrow funds, but less demand for marks or Swiss francs. Consequently, it would sometimes experience a shortage of French francs, but have excess marks and francs. Whenever it had excess funds, it would loan them out on a daily basis in the interbank market. The annualized return was less than if it could have provided long-term loans with these funds.

The Bank of Chicago was concerned about its exposure to interest rate risk, since some of its assets were less rate-sensitive than its liabilities. It decided to issue notes denominated in British pounds and use the proceeds to invest in British money market securities. As a result, the average rate-sensitivity on all of its liability currencies in aggregate was more closely aligned with the average rate-sensitivity on all of its asset currencies in aggregate.

a) What problems might arise as a result of the Bank of Chicago's philosophy of consistently using the same currency received to make a loan or investment?

b) If the Bank of Chicago did convert some of its excess deposits into francs to accommodate the high demand for franc-denominated loans, would it be very susceptible to large losses resulting from exchange rate risk? Explain.

c) The recent issuance of British notes aligned the rate-sensitivity on both sides of the balance sheet. Is the Bank of Chicago now insulated from interest rate risk? What scenarios could cause the bank to incur losses as a result of its interest rate sensitivities?

1. Once a year, special issues of *Business Week, Forbes*, and *Fortune* review the performance of numerous firms in the previous year. These issues normally come out in April. Find the section in each that is devoted to banking, and assess the performance of the ten largest banks that conduct a significant amount of international business. How did these banks perform relative to smaller banks? Attempt to explain why the international banks did better or worse than the smaller banks.

PROJECT

SUGGESTED READING

Suzanna Andrews. "Banks' Winning Gambits for 1992." *Institutional Investor* (June 1989), pp. 203–207. This article explains how banks are positioning themselves to capitalize on the deregulation throughout Europe.

REFERENCES

Aggarwal, Raj, and Jon Durnford. "Market Assessment of International Banking Activity: A Study of U.S. Bank Holding Companies." *Quarterly Review of Economics and Business* (Spring 1989), pp. 58–67.

Aharony, Joseph, Anthony Saunders, and Itzhak Swary. "The Effects of the International Banking Act on Domestic Bank Profitability." *Journal of Money, Credit and Banking* (November 1986), pp. 493–506.

Aliber, Robert Z. "International Banking: A Survey." *Journal of Money, Credit, and Banking* (November 1984), pp. 661–712.

_____ . "The Integration of Offshore and Domestic Banking Systems." *Journal of Monetary Economics* (October 1980), pp. 509–526.

_____ . "Monetary Aspects of Offshore Markets." *Columbia Journal of World Business* (Fall 1979), pp. 8–16.

Chan, M. W. Luke and D. C. Mountain. "Technological Change and Economies of Scale in Canadian Financial Institutions: A Selection from Competing Hypotheses." *Journal of Economics and Business* (February 1987), pp. 57–66.

Chrystal, K. Alec "International Banking Facilities." *Review* (April 1984), pp. 5–11.

Fieleke, Norman S. "International Lending on Trial." *New England Economic Review* (May–June 1983), pp. 5–13.

————. "International Lending in Historical Perspective." *New England Economic Review* (November–December 1982), pp. 5–12.

Goodman, Laurie S. "Banking Foreign Exchange Operations: A Portfolio Approach." *Journal of Money, Credit, and Banking* (February 1982), pp. 84–91.

Goodman, Laurie S. "The Pricing of Syndicated Eurocurrency Credits." Federal Reserve Bank of New York. *Quarterly Review* (Summer 1980), pp. 39–49.

Grammatikos, Theoharry, Anthony Saunders, and Itzhak Swary. "Returns and Risks of U.S. Bank Foreign Currency Activities." *Journal of Finance* (July 1986), pp. 671–683.

Jain, Arvind K. "International Lending Patterns of U.S. Commercial Banks." *Journal of International Business Studies* (Fall 1986), pp. 73–88.

Jain, Arvind, and Douglas Nigh. "Politics and the International Lending Decisions of Banks." *Journal of International Business Studies* (Summer 1989), pp. 349–359.

Little, Jane Sneddon. "Eurobank Maturity Transformation and LDC Debts." *New England Economic Review* (September–October 1983), pp. 15–19.

Madura, Jeff, Ann Marie Whyte, and Wm. R. McDaniel. "Reaction of British Bank Share Prices to Citicorp's Announced $3 Billion Increase in Loan Loss Reserves." *Journal of Banking and Finance* (forthcoming).

Mahajan, Arvind, and Dileep Mehta. "Strong Form Efficiency of the Foreign Exchange Market and Bank Positions." *Journal of Financial Research* (Fall 1984), pp. 197–207.

Masulka, James, and Michael Hu, "Bankers' Responses to the ETC Act: Attitudes and the Degree of International Involvement," *Journal of Business Research*, (April 1987), pp. 191–200.

Maxwell, Charles E., and Lawrence J. Gitman. "Risk Transmission in International Banking: An Analysis of 48 Central Banks." *Journal of International Business Studies* (Summer 1989), pp. 268–279.

Nigh, Douglas, Kang Rae Cho, and Suresh Krishnan. "The Role of Location-Related Factors in U.S. Banking Involvement Abroad: An Empirical Examination." *Journal of International Business Studies* (Fall 1986), pp. 59–72.

Park, Yoon S., and Jack Zwick. *International Banking in Theory and Practice*. Reading, Mass.: Addison-Wesley Publishing Company, 1985.

Poulsen, Annette B. "Japanese Bank Regulation and the Activities of U.S. Offices of Japanese Banks." *Journal of Money, Credit, and Banking* (August 1986), pp. 366–373.

Putnam, Bluford H. "Controlling the Euromarkets: A Policy Perspective." *Columbia Journal of World Business* (Fall 1979), pp. 25–31.

"Recent Innovations in International Banking: The Policy Implications." *The World of Banking* (July–August 1986), pp. 4–7.

Soenen, Luc A., and Raj Aggarwal. "Banking Relationships and Cash and Foreign Exchange Management: A Study of Companies in the United Kingdom, the Netherlands, and Belgium." *Management International Review*, no. 2 (1988), pp. 56–69.

Swanson, Peggy E. "Compensating Balances and Foreigners' Dollar Deposits in U.S. Banks." *Journal of Financial Research* (Fall 1983), pp. 257–263.

Tschoegel, Adrian. "International Retail Banking as a Strategy: An Assessment." *Journal of International Business Studies* (Summer 1987), pp. 67–88.

CHAPTER 23

The International Debt Crisis and Bank Assessment of Country Risk

T he previous chapter provided a background on the international banking environment. In the early 1980s, this environment was severely affected as several large borrowers experienced difficulty in repaying their international loans on time. This event, often referred to as the international debt crisis (IDC), will have a long-lasting impact on international banking. While the banks have reevaluated their international lending policies as a result of the crisis, they will likely continue to provide international loans. Banks are adjusting their lending policies to insulate themselves from a recurrence of the crisis. A first step in learning from the crisis is to determine its cause, which this chapter addresses. In addition, it explains why some banks were affected by the crisis more than others and why even nonbank MNCs were affected.

Closely related to the IDC is the subject of how banks assess country risk, since an accurate country risk assessment would have indicated in advance the potential debt-repayment problems of borrowers.

THE INTERNATIONAL DEBT CRISIS

During the early 1980s, many less developed countries (LDCs) began to incur large balance of trade deficits, largely because of the global recession that reduced demand by industrialized countries for LDC exports. The large balance of trade deficits caused deteriorated conditions in LDCs. Worsening conditions caused the debt level to rise. By December 1984, Brazil's total debt exceeded $97 billion, Mexico's total debt amounted to $93 billion and Argentina's total debt reached $45 billion. As of that time these LDCs, along with several others, were continuing to work out plans for rebuilding their economies and rescheduling payments on outstanding loans. The sudden emergence of loan-rescheduling requests began in 1980. By 1983 more than 25 countries were victims of the IDC.

A lending bank's task in the negotiation of rescheduling the debtor nations' loan payments is very difficult. If banks are too harsh, this could force LDC loans to default, which would result in a substantial amount of loan losses to the banks. Conversely, being too lenient with any particular LDC could set a precedent for other LDCs that need to reschedule their loan payments.

As a result of the IDC, many critics contend that international lending increases rather than decreases the risk on a bank's loan portfolio. Because the loan rescheduling during the IDC involved not just one but several LDCs, the idea of diversifying to reduce risk has lost some of its allure. During the IDC, it became clear that the economies of many LDCs are highly correlated with each other. Consequently, diversifying loans among them did not significantly reduce a foreign loan portfolio's risk from the banker's point of view.

THE DEBT CRISIS FROM A BANKER'S PERSPECTIVE

To understand the bankers' dilemma during the IDC, consider yourself a chief international loan officer for a bank with millions of dollars lent to each of several LDCs. Assume you receive phone calls from the governments of each of the debtor countries with the message, "We can't pay our outstanding loans, and probably will never be able to unless you help us with additional loans." You, as the chief international loan officer, must determine whether to provide more funds to these countries. If you do not, there is a chance you will never receive repayments on previous loans extended to these countries. However, if you do extend the loans, you still are not guaranteed that the country will generate enough funds to repay them. It is possible that your bad debt will therefore be greater than if you cut off relations now with these debtor countries.

There is no perfect solution to such a problem. Yet, there are some aspects that deserve consideration. First, what are the attitudes of all of the other banks that are in a similar position? If you decide to provide more funds, but the other banks decide not to, these LDCs may have a difficult time rebuilding (since the support from only some of the bankers would be insufficient). Conversely, if you do not extend additional loans while all other bankers do, then there is a better chance the countries will be able to rebuild and someday pay off their debts. In this case, your bank would not be given high priority in terms of loan repayment or future loan requests by the countries, since you declined to provide further assistance when needed.

By meeting with other bankers, you could determine their attitudes toward solving the problem. Bankers did in fact meet frequently to discuss possible solutions during the IDC. Their negotiating ability was strengthened since they acted as a group. Another consideration for an international loan officer faced with this situation is your degree of involvement. A bank with only a very small portion of total loans extended to these countries may prefer to avoid getting further involved and be more willing to write off the outstanding loans as bad debt. Yet, a bank with a large percentage of its total loans provided to these troubled countries has more at stake. It may not be able to afford writing off the outstanding loans. Some of the banks had only a small percentage of loans extended to these LDCs, while other banks were more deeply involved. Such a variety of unique situations among banks caused some intense discussion as to the appropriate solution by bankers as a group.

SHOULD THE U.S. GOVERNMENT INTERVENE IN THE DEBT CRISIS?

In 1983 there was much disagreement as Congress met to determine whether to provide additional funds to the **International Monetary Fund (IMF).** The IMF is an international agency that attempts to facilitate international trade and finance, and help countries experiencing balance of payment difficulties. It could channel funds to LDCs experiencing debt-repayment problems. Most large U.S. banks favored additional IMF funding since they believed it would reduce the LDC's problems. In this case, they hoped that the countries would at some point repay their loans.

Other banks with little exposure to bad debt from foreign loans were generally not as favorable toward Congress appropriating more funds to the IMF. In fact, some of their views reflected the feeling that those banks that extended the loans to these troubled countries should work out their problems without the aid of the government. That is, taxpayers should not be forced to provide the U.S. government with money for the IMF that would later be recycled into the hands of the large banks. Some bankers felt that if the U.S. government was willing to, in a sense, bail out the large banks (by appropriating funds to the IMF), then it should bail out smaller banks that might fail because many of their domestic loans were never repaid.

A possible response to that criticism is that small bank failures do not normally cause massive fear in the banking industry. Large bank failures on the other hand (resulting from bad debt on loans extended to LDCs), could cause bank depositors to withdraw their funds from banks, thereby accelerating a possible collapse in the banking industry. Even though depositors are insured up to a stated maximum amount of funds, there would only be so much money to go around if several large banks did fail. The Federal Deposit Insurance Corporation (FDIC), which insures bank depositors, would not be able to cover all of them.

In November 1983 Congress passed the so-called **IMF Funding Bill,** which called for funds to be sent from the U.S. government to the IMF and then channelled to the LDCs. The IMF provided these funds based on promises by LDCs to improve various aspects of their financial condition, such as their balance-of-trade position. The objective was for the troubled countries to spend more money at home in an effort to stimulate their respective economies. In Argentina's case, for example, the IMF requested an effort to cut the government's budget deficit and reduce its inflation rate. The IMF loans were a key to the LDCs gaining access to additional commercial bank loans.

Under the IMF loan agreement, the IMF can closely monitor the LDCs for progress in meeting their objectives on a short-term basis, rather than wait several years to determine if they have followed through on their longer-term objectives. In this way, deviations from long-term objectives can be more easily detected and corrected under the threat of suspending further credit. Progress can be more easily evaluated in this manner. Brazil, for example, was criticized in 1985 for not complying with its objectives, and the IMF threatened to cut off (at least temporarily) credit to Brazil as a result.

IMPACT OF THE DEBT CRISIS ON NON-BANK MNCs

The IMF package requested LDCs to substantially improve their current account positions. As a result, government authorities imposed import restrictions and currency blockages in an effort to boost spending within these economies. (Currency blockages can be enforced by government authorities to ensure that funds would be spent within the country.) Thus, not only were the large banks with outstanding loans to such countries adversely affected by the crisis, but all MNCs that either export to or maintain subsidiaries within these countries were affected as well. In 1983 some U.S. MNCs simply sold their subsidiaries in Brazil and withdrew. Others struggled to find local supplies for their operations that could serve as a substitute for the supplies they used to import.

The measures taken by the IMF and LDCs affected both the operations and the finances of many MNCs. For example, car sales by plants of the biggest three automobile manufacturers were off by 33 percent in Mexico during the first half of 1983, while truck sales declined 50 percent. Manufacturers in appliances and other industries shut down parts of their normal operations in Mexico. Minnesota Mining and Manufacturing (3M) Company discontinued sales of its video cassettes and copying machines in Latin America. Du Pont's chemical exports to the Southern Hemisphere declined by 20 percent during 1983.

According to Commerce Department statistics, U.S. exports in Latin American countries declined from $39 billion in 1981 to $22.6 billion in 1983 (a 42 percent decrease). While U.S. exports did decline across the world due to the dollar's strength during this period, the decline in other countries was not so substantial. Some industries were affected more than others, although almost all MNCs based in or exporting to Latin America were adversely affected.

Litton Industries discovered that its $1 million on deposit at Mexican banks had been converted by the Mexican government into pesos (the Mexican currency). The peso's weakening over time reduced the dollar value of these deposits. Because the Mexican peso had been very weak throughout the crisis, MNC subsidiaries based in Mexico did not want to finance with other currencies. Their revenues are in pesos and they would have to pay back their loans by converting the weak pesos to whatever currency was borrowed. The Mexican peso weakened against the U.S. dollar by 82 percent from mid-February 1982 to July 1983. Imagine the dollar cost of borrowing to a Mexican subsidiary during that period! To avoid incurring such enormous exchange and financing costs, many Latin American subsidiaries (where local currencies were very weak) began to use local currency financing. With this approach, the revenues received were in the same currency as that needed to pay off loans. However, the interest rates in some of these countries were outrageous. For example, the going interest rate on loans denominated in Brazilian cruzeiros was 205 percent as of July 1983, more than 20 times the prevailing interest rates in developed countries.

The international debt crisis was precipitated by the LDCs' inability to repay their debt. IMF credit was extended with the provision that LDCs show progress toward eventually repaying debt on their own. The import restrictions and currency blockages by governments to satisfy IMF provisions had a negative impact on non-bank foreign operations. Consequently, some non-bank MNCs believed they were affected to a greater degree than those large banks that had billions of dollars in outstanding loans to the LDCs.

IMPACT OF FLOATING EXCHANGE RATES AND LOAN RATES ON THE DEBT CRISIS

The loans to the Latin American countries were largely denominated in dollars. Consequently, loan repayment became more difficult when the dollar strengthened against the borrowers' currencies in the early 1980s. However, the dollar's strength in 1983 and 1984 also had a favorable impact on LDCs, since it encouraged U.S. consumers to purchase goods produced in the LDCs.

Many of the loans to LDCs have floating interest rates (periodically adjusting to some market interest rate). For example, the percentage of floating-rate debt to total debt is provided in Exhibit 23.1 for five individual LDCs. Because the loans were generally of a floating-rate nature, the debt-repayment amount was influenced by changes in the interest rates over time. When interest rates were rising, floating-rate loans became even more difficult to pay off. Due to the influence of prevailing interest rates on the repayment ability, the U.S. government (in particular, the Federal Reserve System) made a special effort to keep U.S. interest rates relatively low. However, this by itself was not sufficient to cure the repayment problem. Stock analysts, rating agencies, and bank examiners continue to monitor bank positions, since the future performance of some banks is highly dependent on the revitalization of the LDCs. The full impact of the IDC on the banking industry is not over yet.

SOLUTIONS TO THE DEBT CRISIS

The ability of debtor nations to cover their debt depends on their ability to export, and to attract foreign investment. However, these nations are unable to attract foreign investment when their existing debt level is perceived to be high. Thus, they must rely on exports to finance their debt. Given that many countries have the same goal in mind, they cannot all attain it. Some countries can be net exporters only if others are willing to be net importers.

To achieve a more favorable balance of trade, governments of LDCs may consider either imposing barriers on imports or intervening in the foreign

EXHIBIT 23.1 Percentage of Loans that Had Floating Rates in Five Different Countries

Country	Floating-Rate Debt as a Percentage of Total Debt
Argentina	66%
Brazil	62
Chile	74
Mexico	78
South Korea	55

SOURCE: Federal Reserve Bank of San Francisco Weekly Letter (September 23, 1983).

exchange market to reduce their home currency value. The former solution commonly causes inefficiencies in local production, as well as retaliation by other country governments. While the latter solution may generate a more favorable trade balance, it can make foreign loan repayments more expensive when loans are denominated in a foreign currency.

BANK MANAGEMENT OF LOAN EXPOSURE SINCE THE DEBT CRISIS

Banks heavily involved in lending to Latin American countries clearly have much at stake. Exhibit 23.2 identifies the amounts owed by some Latin American countries to U.S. banks. The banks were most exposed to the debt of Argentina, Brazil, Mexico, and Venezuela. During the late 1980s, the average exposure of U.S. money center banks to the combined debt of these countries was about 4 percent of their total assets. Exhibit 23.2 shows that other creditors were also exposed to Latin American debt. U.S. banks were responsible for only 17 percent of Argentina's total debt, 23 percent of Brazil's debt, and 25 percent of Mexico's debt.

The claims by U.S. banks on non-OPEC LDCs are shown in Exhibit 23.3. The dollar amount of total claims of all U.S. banks declined since 1982 due to sales of some outstanding loans to some non-bank financial institutions; in addition, some loans have been written off. Note that as of 1985, nine major banks had claims of $62.8 billion, or about 64 percent of the $98.2 billion in claims of all U.S. banks.

The claims as a percent of bank capital are shown in the lower part of Exhibit 23.3. The percentage is clearly highest for the group of nine major banks. For example, in 1985 their claims on LDCs amounted to 265 percent of their capital. Even though the dollar amount of claims on LDCs declined since 1982, the capital level of these banks declined since that time by a greater proportion, causing claims as a percentage of capital to increase.

Although the IDC largely involves LDCs, it also could cause problems in developing countries as LDCs reduce their importing from developing coun-

EXHIBIT 23.2 Debt of Latin American Countries *(billions of dollars)*

	Total Debt	Debt Held by U.S. Banks
Argentina	$ 49.6	$ 8.5
Bolivia	4.2	0.14
Brazil	104.5	23.9
Chile	21.5	5.9
Colombia	13.6	2.6
Ecuador	7.7	2.1
Mexico	97.3	24.8
Peru	14.2	1.65
Uruguay	4.7	0.89
Venezuela	36.5	20.4

SOURCE: *Economic Review*, Federal Reserve Bank of Kansas City (January 1987), p. 25.

EXHIBIT 23.3   Claims of U.S. Banks on LDC Debt

Total Claims of U.S. Banks	All U.S. Banks	Nine Major Banks	Fifteen Major Banks	All Other Banks
1978	$ 52.5 billion	$33.4 billion	$ 9.9 billion	$ 8.9 billion
1982	103.2	64.2	20.2	18.9
1985	98.2	62.8	18.3	17.1
Percent of Capital				
1978	110%	163%	107%	57%
1982	154	227	162	75
1985	168	265	165	71

SOURCE: *Economic Review,* Federal Reserve Bank of Kansas City (January 1987), p. 24.

tries. If the developed countries were severely affected, the large banks would experience further problems since they extend loans in these countries as well.

Sale of LDC Loans

During the international debt crisis, several banks were attempting to reduce their LDC loan exposure and therefore satisfy existing and potential shareholders. Some were willing to swap LDC loans to achieve a more diversified mix (which would reduce their exposure to events in any individual LDC). Foreign loans were sold at a sizable discount. Some Middle Eastern and European banks attempted to sell their entire Latin American loan portfolio. The banks attempting to sell their loans were essentially unwilling to restructure the loan terms and allow time for the LDCs to recuperate. They instead desired to sell the loans cheap and incur the loss immediately. The perceived probability of loan repayment can be assessed by reviewing the discounts on LDC loans sold in the secondary market. Exhibit 23.4 shows the market price for which loans to various countries were selling in the secondary loan market. There are large differences in the value of debt across LDCs. In general, the value of LDC debt generally declined slightly in 1989, but rebounded for some countries in 1990.

Increasing Loan Loss Reserves

In May 1987 Citicorp boosted its loan loss reserves by about $3 billion. This was a major event because it indicated anticipation of large loan losses in the future. Other large banks in the United States followed Citicorp's strategy over the next two months. The stock market seemed to accept the news without any major negative reaction, even though the increased loan loss reserves would depress earnings. Market participants had apparently anticipated that the large banks would need to boost their loan loss reserves well in advance. The banks might have been able to avoid the increase in loan loss reserves temporarily, but eventually the likelihood of some LDC loan defaults would have required it. Perhaps the largest U.S. banks were more willing to

EXHIBIT 23.4 Value of LDC Debt in the Secondary Market

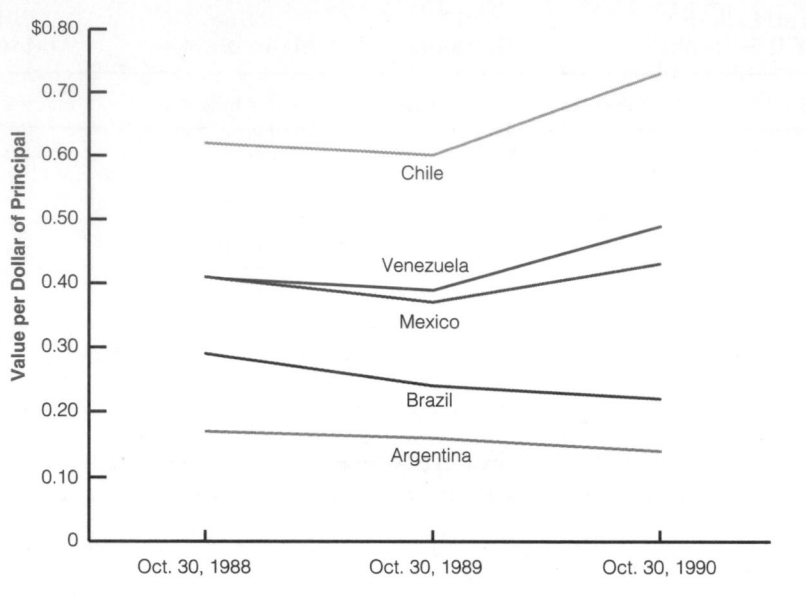

boost loan loss reserves after observing the absence of any negative market reaction to Citicorp's announcement.

In September 1989 another round of increases in loan loss reserves began for some money center banks. The most publicized announcement was J.P. Morgan's increase by $2 billion, which boosted its loan loss reserve account to match its total LDC debt exposure. The total loan loss reserves at other money center banks represented only between 35 and 50 percent of medium- and long-term LDC debt. As a result of its strategy, J.P. Morgan was in a more flexible position, from which it could discontinue negotiations with LDCs and write off the LDC debt.

Use of Debt-Equity Swaps

Many banks and non-bank MNCs have participated in **debt-equity swaps,** which can reduce the amount of LDC debt held by financial institutions in the following manner. A U.S.-based MNC can purchase (at a discount) some of an LDC's outstanding loans in the secondary market. It then trades the debt to the LDC government in exchange for some assets that are being liquidated by the government. Such assets could include airplanes, machinery, buildings, or even land. U.S.-based MNCs such as Allied-Signal Inc., Chrysler Corporation, and General Electric Company have engaged in debt-equity swaps. Allied-Signal has swapped debt for equity investments in Chile. Chrysler and General Electric have swapped debt for companies in Mexico. Many financial institutions that are holding LDC debt have also swapped some of the debt for equity investments. For example, Citicorp has traded debt for an equity investment in gold mining in Chile.

Given sufficient equity investment opportunities in LDCs, MNCs are encouraged to engage in debt-equity swaps. Consequently, the secondary market for LDC debt is more active. If debt-equity swaps were not possible, the only demand for existing LDC loans in the secondary market would be by financial institutions that are willing to assume greater exposure to LDC debt. The existence of debt-equity swaps allows other companies to purchase LDC debt obligations even if they have no plans to hold these obligations. Because debt-equity swaps increase the demand for LDC loans in the secondary market, they reduce the size of the discount on these loans.

While debt-equity swaps enhance a bank's chances of selling LDC debt, they do not necessarily reduce the risk of banks that exchange LDC debt for LDC equity. Some equity investments in LDCs may be just as risky as the LDC loans that were traded in. Furthermore, banks that acquire an equity interest in LDC assets may not have the expertise to manage those assets.

Implementation of the Brady Plan

Over the period from 1985 to 1988, a plan was endorsed as a means of mitigating the LDC debt crisis. The plan was based on voluntary actions by lenders to reduce their exposure. In December 1988 the World Bank proposed a gradual implementation of the plan, along with its commitment to provide loans to LDCs in place of bank loans and impose economic reforms on the LDCs. During 1989 the plan gained momentum as the International Monetary Fund (IMF) signaled its willingness to replace LDC debt maintained by banks. In what then became known as the **Brady Plan,** negotiations between banks and individual LDCs were encouraged in order to provide banks with the option of having their debt replaced by the World Bank and IMF by trading it in at a discount. In July 1989 banks reached an agreement with Mexico in which they were given the following options: (1) agree to a 35 percent cut in the principal or interest on loans, and (2) grant new loans equal to 25 percent of the Mexican loans. Essentially, the trade-off involves either recognizing losses on previous loans while reducing exposure, or increasing investment in LDCs without incurring immediate losses. The agreement could improve Mexico's position, because it reduces the amount Mexico owes on existing debt and also allows for additional loans from banks. In this way, Mexico may be better able to improve its debt-servicing, which would enhance the investor's perceptions of Mexican debt maintained by banks. The agreement between banks and Mexico is encouraging because it could pave the way for agreements with other countries.

A dilemma involved in resolving the crisis is that if all banks prefer to discontinue loans to LDCs by writing off all or a portion of existing loans, the LDCs may be unable to secure adequate financing to improve economic conditions. Their only chance to repay existing loans is by economic reform, which requires more loans. Yet, many banks may feel that providing additional loans is "throwing good money after bad." For this reason, the use of World Bank and IMF funds to assume commercial bank debt at some discounted price could help resolve the ongoing crisis.

In summary, banks have reacted to the international debt crisis by selling some loans, increasing their loan loss reserves, implementing debt-equity swaps, and avoiding new loans to LDCs. All of these strategies reduce a bank's exposure to the debt crisis.

BANK ASSESSMENT OF COUNTRY RISK

A bank's loan evaluation process includes a review of the environment surrounding the applicant. This represents an analysis of country risk. The IDC has convinced large international banks of the need to accurately assess country risk, which, from a banker's perspective, reflects the probability that a country will fail to meet its loan-repayment schedule. A bank's assessment of country risk can affect lending decisions related not only to government requests for loans, but to foreign corporate loan requests as well. Country risk analysis from a bank's point of view will consider political and financial risk factors, similar to a country risk analysis from an MNC's direct foreign investment perspective. However, the manner in which political and financial factors affect a bank can differ substantially from the way they affect an MNC considering direct foreign investment. In addition, the importance attached to the various factors differs.

Country risk measurement by banks involves assessing whether funds will be available to the potential borrower in the future periods of a loan, so any condition that prevents prompt loan repayment can be categorized as a political or financial problem. Thus, a logical approach to country risk analysis involves assessing all relevant political and financial characteristics of a potential borrower.

Political Risk Factors

From a bank lending perspective, the most severe form of political risk would be the refusal to repay loans due to the borrowing country's political relationship with the bank or the bank's home country. However, there are other forms of political risk that are less severe but worth assessing. For example, a change in foreign government tax policy could have a significant impact on a foreign firm's ability to repay outstanding loans. In addition, a foreign government may decide to become the "owner" of a firm. The government's attitude toward fulfilling outstanding loan contracts can differ from that of the firm. A more indirect form of political risk is government blockage of currency convertibility such that a particular currency cannot be obtained to repay loans denominated in that currency.

If the bank is lending funds to a foreign government, it must assess the government's commitment to repay loans. Because government philosophy changes over time, a bank must assess the possibility of a change in governmental ideology that may influence the commitment to repay outstanding loans.

While some assessments of political risk are kept confidential, others are publicly available. The *Institutional Investor* publishes a summary of country risk ratings by 75 to 100 banks. These summaries are revised every six months. The political risk rating scale ranges from a high of 100 (reflecting the highest level of creditworthiness) to a low of zero.

The *Institutional Investor* ratings for several major countries as well as some less-developed countries are displayed in Exhibit 23.5 from 1980 through 1990. Notice that for most industrialized countries, the ratings have been quite stable over time. Yet, they have weakened for some of the LDCs such as Argentina, Brazil, and Mexico. The ideal risk rating system would be able to detect political and financial problems far into the future. It should be

EXHIBIT 23.5 Country Risk Ratings as of:

Country	1980	1981	1982	1983	1984	1985	1986	1987	1988	1989	1990
U.S.	98.2	98.1	97.5	96.1	96.0	95.6	96.3	94.1	91.0	89.8	90.9
Switzerland	98.5	97.0	95.9	95.4	95.4	94.7	95.3	94.2	94.1	94.2	94.6
Japan	95.4	95.2	95.8	95.1	95.1	95.1	95.5	96.0	94.6	94.4	94.8
W. Germany	98.4	96.3	93.9	93.0	92.7	93.1	94.2	94.2	93.1	93.8	93.8
U.K.	91.3	89.9	88.3	88.9	88.6	88.8	88.7	86.7	86.7	87.0	87.0
Canada	93.2	92.0	92.5	87.0	86.7	87.1	88.1	86.5	85.9	85.5	86.7
Norway	88.2	89.5	87.8	86.5	85.7	86.2	87.2	82.2	80.3	77.4	78.6
Netherlands	89.9	89.6	87.2	86.6	85.6	86.3	87.6	87.0	87.0	87.0	87.8
Australia	88.2	90.0	90.2	87.6	83.9	83.9	81.3	76.3	70.7	69.8	71.0
Austria	86.3	85.9	83.9	81.0	81.3	82.5	83.5	83.2	84.1	83.1	84.6
France	92.3	90.2	84.6	80.5	78.8	80.4	82.7	84.1	84.9	85.8	87.2
Singapore	78.6	78.6	78.5	77.6	78.0	79.3	76.7	74.8	75.4	75.6	77.9
Sweden	85.0	83.5	79.8	76.7	76.4	78.7	79.3	79.7	80.8	80.3	81.3
Finland	74.4	77.5	75.1	74.7	74.5	77.2	78.7	77.9	78.5	78.7	79.7
Belgium	87.4	84.4	77.3	72.3	72.3	74.4	75.8	76.7	77.4	77.9	78.9
Saudi Arabia	78.6	73.6	72.9	72.7	72.2	69.6	68.3	60.6	60.3	59.8	60.3
Italy	74.7	74.7	72.4	70.6	71.1	73.5	76.2	79.6	77.6	78.2	80.1
New Zealand	77.2	78.0	75.5	73.0	70.1	70.7	69.1	64.1	65.2	63.7	63.8
Denmark	73.3	73.0	71.7	68.7	69.6	72.2	74.1	72.9	73.0	71.8	72.1
USSR	71.5	69.6	65.5	59.7	61.5	64.5	68.0	65.5	65.4	64.9	62.1
Czechoslovakia	60.7	57.6	51.6	43.1	43.6	46.8	51.8	53.0	54.3	53.0	53.7
East Germany	61.4	58.4	51.9	41.3	43.0	47.6	53.9	56.3	58.4	58.8	57.1
Venezuela	71.2	69.3	63.3	57.4	37.7	36.9	39.7	36.9	35.8	35.1	31.8
Mexico	71.8	71.4	62.8	36.9	36.2	39.1	36.4	28.7	28.0	29.3	32.6
Libya	58.2	51.8	42.8	37.0	33.4	31.4	30.1	29.5	23.2	23.4	25.4
Brazil	58.0	49.7	56.3	48.1	30.0	31.7	31.9	35.5	29.4	29.1	27.2
Israel	47.7	41.4	35.7	32.4	28.3	28.9	28.8	33.0	34.6	34.6	36.4
Chile	52.9	54.4	52.1	44.0	27.3	25.0	24.6	26.0	27.2	31.1	36.1
Turkey	11.4	13.7	17.4	21.9	27.3	34.3	37.3	39.7	40.5	41.0	41.4
Argentina	62.6	63.4	50.5	30.2	25.0	22.0	22.7	24.8	24.8	22.3	18.7
Poland	41.6	32.9	13.0	8.3	10.2	14.1	14.7	16.4	17.8	18.1	19.0

NOTE: On a rating scale of 0–100, where 0 represents the lowest level of creditworthiness and 100 represents the highest level of creditworthiness.

SOURCE: *Institutional Investor*; several issues, reprinted with permission of Institutional Investor Magazine.

emphasized that since the ratings here were conducted by bankers, they are assessed in the context of international lending.

Financial Risk Factors

Country risk assessors must thoroughly evaluate the financial condition of a foreign country, since it influences the probability of loan repayment by both the country's government and corporations. The government of a financially strong country will normally generate sufficient tax revenues to promptly cover its debts. However, a financially weak country will most likely need to spend far more on its people than it taxes them, causing enormous budget deficits. To repay loans at a time like this requires new loans to be used in repaying the maturing loans. Governments may sometimes be reluctant to borrow more money for the purpose of covering maturing debt. It seems unlikely that governments would default on their loans. Yet, the IDC is evidence that even governments are sometimes unable (or unwilling) to meet loan-repayment obligations.

A strong economy in a given foreign country can substantially improve the performance (and therefore ability to repay loans) of firms in that country. For this reason, a bank's country risk assessors evaluate the current and projected economic outlook of all countries where loans are provided. In order to develop a projected economic outlook for a given country, several economic indicators are used, including gross national product (GNP), the unemployment rate, money supply, inflation, and interest rates. Indicators of strong economic growth within a country generally represent favorable news for firms requesting loans within that country. Yet a loan to a particular foreign firm is not safe just because its national economy is strong. Each firm reacts uniquely to economic trends. Consequently, it is critical that banks assess not only the current and projected economy, but also the type and degree of influence that country's economy has on each firm that has requested a loan. This implies there is a two-step process for banks evaluating the economic influence on foreign loan applicants. The first step is to forecast the future economic strength of a country. The second is to forecast the applicant firm's future performance based on the forecast of the economy. This second step requires an understanding of how the firm's sales and profits are influenced by national business cycles.

As with corporate borrowers, country governments that experience cash flow problems have difficulty repaying loans. A bank cannot forecast future national cash flows with perfect accuracy. However, it can set up possible scenarios and develop estimates for cash flows based on each different scenario. This approach generates a distribution of possible cash flow trends that could occur. While the bank does not know with certainty which cash flow trend will actually occur, it can attach probabilities to the various possible trends. Some of the trends would reflect favorable conditions whereby the country would be able to make its loan payments to the bank on time. Other trends would reflect the opposite. From the probability distribution of cash flow trends along with the expected consequence (whether loan payments are expected to be on time), the bank could estimate the overall probability of receiving its payments promptly from the country's government. This financial analysis could be incorporated with political risk analysis to determine whether a country's government is deserving of a loan.

After the Iron Curtain was lifted in November 1989, and subsequent signals of momentum for free enterprise appeared in Eastern Bloc countries, the risk ratings assigned to these countries by commercial banks generally declined. But while the trend to free enterprise was thought to be favorable, most of these countries did not have any clear economic policies. Consequently, there was much uncertainty about future economic conditions. The unfavorable reaction was expected to be only temporary, assuming that these countries would clarify the tax laws and other provisions to be imposed on privately owned firms.

COUNTRY RISK ASSESSMENT PROCEDURE

Assessment of a particular country's risk may involve anywhere from one person to 20 or more people at a particular bank. The assessment usually entails (1) preparation of country studies and reports, (2) use of scoring (or rating) systems where various characteristics of each country are assessed in

RELATED RESEARCH

Using Discriminant Analysis to Identify Characteristics That Affect Country Risk

The technique of discriminant analysis is useful for identifying factors that are distinctly different between two groups. It has historically been used to identify factors that distinguish (or discriminate) between successful and failing firms. It could even be used to identify characteristics that distinguish between good and bad sports teams, or between successful and unsuccessful employees of a firm.

Discriminant analysis is a popular technique for country risk assessment because it can attempt to identify factors that distinguish between those countries experiencing debt repayment problems and countries not experiencing problems. Once these factors are known, they can be closely monitored in the future.

The factors hypothesized to discriminate between two groups must first be identified and they must be numerically measurable. Then historical data are used to measure the factors. Discriminant analysis generates a discriminant function that determines not only which factors distinguish between the two groups, but the type of influence each factor has.

Recent research by Morgan[1] used discriminant analysis to assess the influence of variables on the likelihood that a country would need to reschedule its loan repayments. Morgan found the following characteristics of countries whose loan payments were rescheduled:

- Their total debt to exports ratio was relatively high.
- Their proportion of floating-rate loans (relative to total loans) was relatively high.
- Their real growth rate in gross domestic product (GDP) was relatively low.

While discriminant analysis is useful for identifying characteristics that distinguish countries that rescheduled loans versus those that did not, its accuracy in predicting reschedulings will depend on whether those characteristics continue to have a similar impact on reschedulings. For example, from Morgan's results, one would expect that a country with a greater proportion of floating-rate loans would have a higher probability of experiencing loan-repayment problems. However, if interest rates decrease in the future, countries with a greater proportion of floating-rate loans may be favorably affected.

[1] John B. Morgan, "A New Look at Debt Rescheduling Indicators and Models," *Journal of International Business Studies* (Summer 1986), pp. 37–54.

terms of contribution to risk, and (3) use of rating models that can aggregate the individual risk characteristics of a particular country in order to develop an overall rating. If any one of the techniques is conducted improperly, the overall risk assessment approach will be susceptible to significant errors. For example, inaccurate reporting of a country's current conditions will cause even the most accurate scoring system and rating model to generate incorrect country risk ratings. Each of the three steps to assess country risk is briefly discussed here.

With regard to the accumulation of information about potential borrowers, it is difficult to separate useful data from irrelevant data. For example, is a recent riot involving 500 people in a particular country relevant information to a country risk assessor? If the riot was a one-time event, the information is probably not critical. However, if this small riot could lead to greater tensions and therefore a massive revolt, then the information is valuable. To ascertain whether the event may lead to more critical events is difficult.

The system used for rating individual countries should vary among countries, since the contribution of a particular characteristic to each country's overall risk is different. Thus, the weight of importance attached to, say, outstanding debt as a percentage of total exports should vary, since the reliance on exports varies.

Once a bank has determined what information to incorporate, and how to rate each financial and political characteristic of a country, it must decide how to weigh the contribution of each characteristic. Because there is no perfect solution for any of these decisions, it is understandable that each bank has its own unique approach for assessing country risk. Even if two banks follow the same exact procedure for assessing a particular country, their final decisions on whether to extend loans may differ. This is due to differences among banks regarding willingness to bear risk. An aggressive bank might lend to a borrower rated as a "moderate risk" while a more conservative bank might not.

As of this point in time, banks do not have the capability of detecting substantial increases in country risk several years in advance. To remain free of debt-rescheduling problems, a long-term problem-detection system would be necessary. Such an ideal objective is extremely difficult (if not impossible) to achieve, especially in light of a time lag that renders much of the relevant data somewhat outdated by the time it is published.

There are two common mistakes that can result from country risk assessment: (1) a bank provides a loan it should not have or (2) a bank does not provide a loan it should have. The consequence of the first error is a defaulted loan, while the consequence of the second error is possibly a lost customer. The first error is typically much more damaging to an international bank. Therefore, a common rule of thumb for an international lender may be, if in serious doubt about an international loan applicant's ability to repay loans, do not extend a loan. While the bank may lose that applicant as a customer for other banking services, there are enough other fish in the sea to attract. With this strategy, a bank can reduce loan defaults and boost its image by taking a more conservative approach.

Given the limitations of any country risk assessment approach, banks must recognize that their decisions may turn out to be improper. To reduce the damage caused by providing loans that should not have been provided, banks could place a cap on total volume of loans extended to each particular country. This would limit the sensitivity of the overall loan portfolio to any single country's problems.

If a bank limits its loans to any single country but desires to provide a significant volume of foreign loans, it should diversify its loans among countries. Diversification helps protect the overall loan portfolio from substantially declining in value, since any one country's financial and political problems will affect only a small portion of the portfolio. However, there are some countries whose risk ratings tend to move together. Such countries typically

Example of Country Risk Assessment

The following assessment method was used by a bank to measure country risk. This system was based on four major aspects of a country:

1. *Economic indicators*—to evaluate the country's financial condition
2. *Debt management*—to measure the country's ability to repay debt
3. *Political factors*—to assess political characteristics and political stability
4. *Structural factors*—to measure socioeconomic conditions such as human resource base

Short-term and medium-term models of these four aspects were developed in order to determine an overall short-term rating for a country and an overall medium-term rating. The segmentation into two time horizons was used because a country's economic outlook may vary with the time horizon used.

Each of the four models assigns a score between 0 and 100. Once the four models are complete, the overall rating is determined by weighing the importance of the models. An example of how the overall rating is determined is shown in Exhibit A. Notice that a grade is assigned for both the short- and medium-term horizons. The grades for this hypothetical example were higher in the short term than the medium term. The weight

distribution differed between short- and medium-term horizons, since economic indicators were thought to be more important in the short-term horizon while the political rating was more important for the medium-term horizon.

The overall numerical grade for each horizon can be converted into a rating. The conversion process converts grades into categories similar to Standard and Poor's rating system on securities. Based on the grades shown in Exhibit B, the country's short-term horizon received a rating of A while the medium-term horizon received a grade of BBB.

EXHIBIT B Conversion of a Country's Grade into a Rating

Overall Grade Rating	Rating	
91–100	AAA	Excellent
81–90	AA	
71–80	A	
61–70	BBB	Average quality
51–60	BB	
41–50	B	
31–40	CCC	Low quality
21–30	CC	
11–20	C	
0–10	D	Excessive risk

EXHIBIT A Example of Determining Country Risk Ratings

	Short-term Horizon			Medium-term Horizon		
	Weight	*Grade*	*Weighted Grade*	*Weight*	*Grade*	*Weighted Grade*
Debt management model	.3	80	24	.3	70	21
Economic indicator model	.3	90	27	.2	70	14
Political rating model	.2	60	12	.3	50	15
Structural rating model	.2	75	15	.2	60	12
			78			62

SOURCE: This information was drawn from the article by John B. Morgan, "Assessing Country Risk at Commerce Bank," *Bankers Magazine* (May–June 1985), pp. 23–29.

share a common characteristic, such as oil as their major export, or being located in the same geographical region. A portfolio of loans to such countries exhibits considerable risk since their political and financial conditions tend to move in tandem. International lenders achieve more effective diversification by including countries whose political and financial condition trends are unrelated.

The diversification concept suggests that banks must consider more than a country's individual characteristics. Banks must also assess the contribution of that country risk to the risk of the overall loan portfolio. For example, consider a bank that has extended most of its international loans to countries that are heavy oil importers. The bank is currently assessing the creditworthiness of Country X, another oil importer, and Country Y, an oil exporter. Assume both countries have requested loans. Also assume that based on the individual assessments, Country X deserves a slightly higher individual credit rating. However, the economic conditions of Country X are susceptible to oil price changes in a similar manner as the other countries already within the bank's loan portfolio. Thus, if the market price of oil increases substantially, Country X will be adversely affected along with the other countries in the bank's loan portfolio. Yet, Country Y would probably have benefited from the rise in the market price of oil. From a loan portfolio perspective, a loan to Country Y may be perceived as safer since it may reduce the risk of the overall loan portfolio. This example illustrates why banks must assess a country not only individually, but in terms of its contribution to the overall risk in the bank's loan portfolio.

SUMMARY

Banks are motivated to lend abroad by the potentially higher returns in the international markets that are not available domestically. In addition, penetrating international markets is a way to expand business. The motivation to provide international loans has diminished recently, though, due to the international debt crisis. Yet, large banks have not walked away from the prospects of international lending. While they attempt to resolve the problems faced by LDCs in repayment of loans, they are searching for more effective techniques to determine whether foreign loan applicants are creditworthy.

With regard to assessing foreign creditworthiness, banks must evaluate not only the applicant, but the surrounding environment and the applicant's vulnerability to that environment. For this reason, country risk assessment is incorporated to complement credit analysis. Country risk assessment involves (1) gathering data and distinguishing between relevant versus irrelevant information, (2) using the relevant information to rate the various characteristics of a country that deserve to be assessed, and (3) assigning a degree of importance (weighting by importance) for each of these characteristics and consolidating them to generate an overall country risk rating for each country. While country risk assessment of an individual country will never be perfected, a bank can at least reduce the exposure of its overall loan portfolio to country risk by allocating funds to countries whose risk levels do not move in tandem.

1. Discuss the developments that led to the international debt crisis.

2. Discuss the IMF's role in attempting to resolve the international debt crisis.

3. What does the existence of the international debt crisis suggest about the previous country risk assessments conducted by banks?

4. Identify factors that would likely be used by banks to assess a government's creditworthiness.

5. Identify factors that would likely be used by banks to assess a foreign corporation's creditworthiness.

6. Why are country risk assessments by banks not always accurate?

7. With regard to the international debt crisis, would banks be better off acting as a group or individually in negotiating the rescheduling of loans? Discuss.

8. When a crisis (such as the international debt crisis) develops, should international banks receive any help from their governments to resolve the problem? To what extent should their governments become involved?

9. Why do banks sometimes rate countries differently? That is, what components of the country risk rating procedure can lead to different overall ratings among banks for a particular country?

10. Two common mistakes due to inaccurate country risk assessment by banks are

- Providing a loan it should not have
- Not providing a loan it should have

Which of these mistakes is more critical? Elaborate.

11. There are a variety of statistical techniques (such as discriminant analysis) that are used to identify characteristics that can correctly discriminate between countries that have had debt repayment problems and countries that have not. Explain why such techniques may not correctly predict which countries will experience debt repayment problems in the future.

12. Explain debt-equity swaps and how they increase activity in the secondary loan market.

13. Why do you think the market did not react negatively to money center banks that boosted their loan loss reserves in 1987 and again in 1989? After all, shouldn't the boost in loan loss reserves signal problems involving LDC debt?

14. It has been suggested that the next international debt crisis could result from economic problems in Eastern European countries. Do you think that the Eastern European countries are as exposed to economic problems as the Latin American countries?

15. Briefly describe how the Brady Plan was intended to resolve international debt repayment problems.

Bank of Baltimore
Reducing Exposure to LDC Debt

The Bank of Baltimore presently has $500 million book value in loans to Argentina. Given the recent economic problems experienced by Argentina, the Bank of Baltimore has not received any payments from them lately. It considers selling these loans immediately in the secondary market and believes it would receive 28 cents on the dollar. Alternatively, it is considering a debt-equity swap, in which it would swap the debt in exchange for automobiles owned by the government. It has no direct use of these automobiles but expects that it would be able to sell them for about 1 trillion Austral (the Argentine currency) although it would probably take about one year to complete each of the sales. The exchange rate is presently 4800 Austral to $1. However, the value of the Austral will probably depreciate by about 50 percent within one year.

a) Should the Bank of Baltimore sell the loans in the secondary market, or engage in a debt-equity swap? Defend your answer.

b) Another alternative is to swap the debt immediately for ownership of a privatized business in sheet metal production in Argentina. Based on a comprehensive valuation, the present value of this business is 720 billion Austral. Presently, there are no other competitors bidding for this business. Should the bank choose this alternative?

PROJECT

1. Review the annual report of a large U.S. bank that historically provided loans to less developed countries. Summarize any statements made regarding these loans. Is the bank offering new loans to these countries? Has it reduced its foreign loan exposure by selling loans? Has it increased its loan loss reserves in anticipation that loans may default?

SUGGESTED READING

Ramesh C. Garg. "Exploring Solutions to the LDC Debt Crisis." *Bankers Magazine* (January–February 1989), pp. 46–51. This article explains various strategies that money center banks are using to reduce their exposure to LDC debt.

REFERENCES

Abdullah, Fuad A. "Development of an Advance Warning Indicator of External Debt Servicing Vulnerability." *Journal of International Business Studies* (Fall 1985), pp. 135–141.

Bennett, Barbara A., and Gary Zimmerman. "U.S. Banks' Exposure to Developing Countries: An Examination of Recent Trends." *Economic Review*, Federal Reserve Bank of San Francisco (Spring 1988), pp. 14–29.

Boehmer, Ekkehart, and William L. Megginson. "Determinants of Secondary Market Prices for Developing Country Syndicated Loans," *Journal of Finance* (December 1990), pp. 1517–1540.

Bruner, Robert F., and John M. Simms Jr. "The International Debt Crisis and Bank Security Returns in 1982." *Journal of Money, Credit and Banking* (February 1987), pp. 46–55.

Burton, F. N., and H. Inoue. "An Appraisal of the Early-Warning Indicators of Sovereign Loan Default in Country Risk Evaluation Systems." *Management International Review*, no. 1 (1985), pp. 45–57.

Cline, William R. "External Debt: System Vulnerability and Development." *Columbia Journal of World Business* (Spring 1982), pp. 4–14.

Dale, Richard S. "Country Risk and Bank Regulation." *The Banker* (March 1983), pp. 41–48.

Dennison, Daniel R. "A Pragmatic Model for Country Risk Analysis." *The Journal of Commercial Bank Lending* (March 1984), pp. 29–37.

DeWitt, R. Peter, and Jeff Madura. "How Banks Assess Country Risk." *World of Banking* (January–February 1986), pp. 28–33.

De Lattre, Andre. "Innovative Approaches to the Debt Crisis." *Banker's Magazine* (May–June 1985), pp. 30–37.

Dichtl, Erwin, and Georg Koglmayr. "Country Risk Ratings." *Management International Review*, no. 4 (1986), pp. 4–11.

Dornbusch, Rudiger. "International Debt and Economic Instability." *Economic Review,* Federal Reserve Bank of Kansas City (January 1987), pp. 15–32.

Doukas, John. "Syndicated Euro-Credit Sovereign Risk Assessments; Market Efficiency and Contagion Effects." *Journal of International Business Studies* (Summer 1989), pp. 255–267.

Fieleke, Norman S. "International Bank Lending in Historical Perspective." *New England Economic Review* (November–December 1982), pp. 5–12.

Fratianni, Michele. "International Debt Crisis: Policy Issues." *The Banker* (August 1983), pp. 37–42.

Goodman, Laurie. "Can Risks in LDC Lending Be Diversified?" *Business Economics* (March 1982), pp. 12–19.

Kennedy, John Whitcomb. "Risk Assessment For U.S. Affiliates Based in Less-Developed Countries." *Columbia Journal of World Business* (Summer 1984), pp. 76–79.

Little, Jane Sneddon. "Eurobank Maturity Transformation and LDC Debts." *New England Economic Review* (September–October 1983), pp. 15–19.

Lomax, David. "Sovereign Risk Analysis Now." *The Banker* (January 1983), pp. 33–39.

Mascarenhas, Briance, and Ole Christian Sand. "Country-Risk Assessment Systems in Banks: Patterns and Performance." *Journal of International Business Studies* (Spring 1985), pp. 19–35.

Mathis, John F. "Lessons Learned From International Debt Rescheduling." *The Journal of Commercial Bank Lending,* (January 1983), pp. 15–25.

Merrill, James. "Country Risk Analysis." *Columbia Journal of World Business* (Spring 1982), pp. 88–91.

Miller, Steven. "Is There Life After the Write-Offs?" *Banker's Magazine* (March–April 1988), pp. 32–35.

Morgan, John B. "A New Look at Debt Rescheduling Indicators and Models." *Journal of International Business Studies* (Summer 1986), pp. 37–54.

Morgan, John B. "Assessing Country Risk at Texas Commerce." *Banker's Magazine* (May–June 1985), pp. 23–29.

Morgan, John B. "The Second Wave of LDC Debt Problems." *Banker's Magazine* (July–August 1984), pp. 14–17.

Nagy, Pancras. "Quantifying Country Risk: A System Developed by Economists at the Bank of Montreal." *Columbia Journal of World Business* (Fall 1978), pp. 135–147.

Sabi, Manijeh. "An Application of the Theory of Foreign Direct Investment to Multinational Banking in LDCs." *Journal of International Business Studies* (Fall 1988), pp. 433–447.

ADDRESSES OF MULTINATIONAL CORPORATIONS

Abbott Labs
Abbott Park, Illinois 60064

AFG Industries
18200 Van Karman Avenue
Irvine, California 92715

Allied-Signal
Columbia Road and Park Avenue
Morristown, New Jersey 07960

Aluminum Company of America
1501 Alcoa Building
Pittsburgh, Pennsylvania 15219

AMAX
Amax Center
P.O. Box 1700
Greenwich, Connecticut 06836

Amerada Hess
1185 Avenue of the Americas
New York, New York 10036

American Brands
1700 E. Putnam Avenue
Box 819
Old Greenwich, Connecticut 06870

American Home Products
685 Third Avenue
New York, New York 10017

Ameritech
30 South Wacker Drive
Chicago, Illinois 60606

Amoco
200 E. Randolph Drive
Box 87703
Chicago, Illinois 60680

Anheuser-Busch
One Busch Pl.
St. Louis, Missouri 63118

Apple
20525 Mariana Avenue
Cupertino, California 95014

Armco
300 Interpace Parkway
Parsippany, New Jersey 07054

Ashland Oil
P.O. Box 391
Ashland, Kentucky 41114

Avon
9 W. 57th Street
New York, New York 10019

Baxter Travenol Laboratories
One Baxter Parkway
Deerfield, Illinois 60015

Bell and Howell
5215 Old Orchard Road
Skokie, Illinois 60077

Bethlehem Steel
Bethlehem, Pennsylvania 18016

Black and Decker
701 E. Joppa Road
Towson, Maryland 21204

Boeing
7755 E. Marginal Way S.
Seattle, Washington 98108

Boise Cascade
One Jefferson Square
Boise, Idaho 83728

Borden
277 Park Avenue
New York, New York 10172

Briggs and Stratton
12301 W. Worth Street
Wauwatosa, Wisconsin 53222

Bristol Myers
345 Park Avenue
New York, New York 10154

Brown-Forman
850 Dixie Highway
Louisville, Kentucky 40210

CBS
51 W. 52nd Street
New York, NY 10019

Campbell Soup
Campbell Place
Camden, New Jersey 08101

Chrysler
12000 Chrysler Drive
Highland Park, Michigan 48288

Clark Equipment
100 N. Michigan Street
Box 7008
South Bend, Indiana 46634

Coca-Cola
One Coca-Cola Plaza N.W.
Atlanta, Georgia 30313

ConAgra
One Central Park Plaza
Omaha, Nebraska 68102

Control Data
8100 34th Avenue South
Minneapolis, Minnesota 55440

CPC International
International Plaza
Englewood Cliffs, New Jersey 07632

Data General
4400 Computer Drive
Westboro, Massachusetts 01580

Digital Equipment
146 Main Street
Maynard, Massachusetts 01754

Dow Chemical
2030 Willard H. Dow Center
Midland, Michigan 48674

Dun and Bradstreet
299 Park Avenue
New York, New York 10171

DuPont
1007 Market Street
Wilmington, Delaware 19898

Emerson Electric
8000 W. Florissant Avenue
St. Louis, Missouri 63136

Exxon
1251 Avenue of the Americas
New York, New York 10020

Firestone Tire and Rubber
1200 Firestone Parkway
Akron, Ohio 44317

Ford
The American Road
Dearborn, Michigan 48121

GAF
1361 Alps Road
Wayne, New Jersey 07470

General Dynamics
Pierre Laclede Center
St. Louis, Missouri 63105

General Mills
9200 Wayzata Boulevard
Minneapolis, Minnesota 55440

General Motors
3044 W. Grand Boulevard
Detroit, Michigan 48202

General Signal
High Ridge Park
P.O. Box 10010
Stamford, Connecticut 06904

Georgia Pacific
133 Peachtree Street N.E.
Atlanta, Georgia 30303

Gillette
Prudential Tower Building
Boston, Massachusetts 02199

Goodrich (B F.)
3925 Embassy Parkway
Akron, Ohio 44313

Goodyear Tire and Rubber
1144 E. Market Street
Akron, Ohio 44316

GTE
One Stamford Forum
Stamford, CT 06904

Gulf and Western
One Gulf and Western Plaza
New York, New York 10023

Heinz
600 Grant Street
Pittsburgh, Pennsylvania 15219

Hershey
P.O. Box 814
Hershey, Pennsylvania 17033

Hewlett Packard
3000 Hanover Street
Palo Alto, California 94304

Homestake Mining
650 California Street
San Francisco, California 94108

IC Industries
111 E. Wacker Drive
Chicago, Illinois 60601

Ingersoll-Rand
200 Chestnut Ridge Road
Woodcliff Lake, New Jersey 07675

Inland Steel Industry
30 W. Monroe Street
Chicago, Illinois 60603

Intel
3065 Bowers Avenue
Santa Clara, California 95051

International Business Machines
Old Orchard Road
Armonk, New York 10504

International Paper
Two Manhattanville Road
Purchase, New York 10577

ITT
320 Park Avenue
New York, New York 10022

Johnson and Johnson
One Johnson and Johnson Plaza
New Brunswick, New Jersey 08933

Johnson Controls
5757 N. Green Bay Avenue
Box 591
Milwaukee, Wisconsin 53201

Kraft
Kraft Court
Glenview, Illinois 60025

Litton Industries
360 N. Crescent Drive
Beverly Hills, California 90210

McDonnell Douglas
P.O. Box 516
St. Louis, Missouri 63166

McGraw-Hill
1221 Avenue of the Americas
New York, New York 10020

Minnesota Mining and
Manufacturing
3M Center
St. Paul, Minnesota 55101

Mobil
150 E. 42nd Street
New York, New York 10017

Monsanto
800 N. Lindberg Boulevard
St. Louis, Missouri 63167

Motorola
1303 Algonquin Road
Schaumberg, Illinois 60196

Navistar International
401 N. Michigan Avenue
Chicago, Illinois 60611

Occidental Petroleum
10889 Wilshire Boulevard
Los Angeles, California 90024

Olin
120 Long Ridge Road
Stamford, Connecticut 06904

Owens-Corning Fiberglas
Fiberglas Tower
Toledo, Ohio 43659

Pepsi Company
Purchase, New York 10577

Pfizer
235 East 42nd Street
New York, New York 10017

Philip Morris
120 Park Avenue
New York, New York 10017

Procter and Gamble
One Procter and Gamble Plaza
Cincinnati, Ohio 45202

PPG Industries
One PPG Place
Pittsburgh, Pennsylvania 15272

Quaker State
255 Elm Street
Oil City, Pennsylvania 16301

Reynolds Metals
6601 Broad Street Road
Richmond, Virginia 23261

RJR Nabisco
Corporate Headquarters Building
Box 2959
Winston-Salem, North Carolina
27102

Rockwell International
600 Grant Street
Pittsburgh, Pennsylvania 15219

Scott Paper
Scott Plaza
Philadelphia, Pennsylvania 19113

Smithkline Beecham
One Franklin Plaza
Philadelphia, Pennsylvania 19101

Sun
100 Matsonford Road
Radnor, Pennsylvania 19087

Tektronix
P.O. Box 500
Beaverton, Oregon 97077

Teledyne
1901 Avenue of the Stars
Los Angeles, California 90067

Tenneco
Tenneco Building
Houston, Texas 77002

TRW
1900 Richmond Road
Cleveland, Ohio 44124

Textron
40 Westminster Street
Providence, Rhode Island 02903

United Technologies
United Technologies Building
Hartford, Connecticut 06101

Union Carbide
39 Old Ridgebury Road
Danbury, Connecticut 06817

Upjohn
7000 Portage Road
Kalamazoo, Michigan 49001

USX
600 Grant Street
Pittsburgh, Pennsylvania 15230

Wang Laboratories
One Industrial Avenue
Lowell, Massachusetts 01851

Warner-Lambert
201 Tabor Road
Morris Plains, New Jersey 07950

Western Digital
2445 McCabe Way
Irvine, California 92717

Westinghouse
Six Gateway Center
Westinghouse Building
Pittsburgh, Pennsylvania 15222

Weyerhaeuser
Tacoma, Washington 98477

Xerox
Stamford, Connecticut 06904

Zenith Electronics
1000 N. Milwaukee Avenue
Glenview, Illinois 60025

GLOSSARY

Absolute form of purchasing power parity Also called the law of one price, suggests that prices of two products of different countries should be equal when measured by a common currency.

Accounts receivable financing Exporter provides indirect financing for importer by exporting goods and allowing for payment to be made at a later date.

Agencies Established by banks to provide loans in a particular area (agencies cannot accept deposits or provide trust services).

Agency problem Conflict of goals between a firm's shareholders and its managers.

Airway bill Receipt for a shipment by air, and includes freight charges and title to the merchandise.

All-in-rate Used in charging customers for accepting banker's acceptances, it consists of the discount interest rate plus the commission.

American depository receipts (ADRs) Certificates representing ownership of foreign stocks, which are traded on stock exchanges in the United States.

Appreciation An increase in the value of a currency.

Arbitrage Action to capitalize on a discrepancy in quoted prices; in many cases, there is no investment of funds tied up for any length of time.

Asian dollar market Market in Asia where banks collect deposits and make loans denominated in U.S. dollars.

Ask price Price at which a trader of foreign exchange (typically a bank) is willing to sell a particular currency.

Assignment of proceeds Allows the original beneficiary of a letter of credit to pledge or assign proceeds to an end supplier.

Balance of payments Statement of inflow and outflow payments for a particular country.

Balance of trade Difference between the value of merchandise exports and merchandise imports.

Balance on goods and services Adds to the balance of trade the net amount of payments of interest and dividends to foreign investors and from investment, as well as receipts and payments resulting from

683

international tourism and other transactions.

Bank for International Settlements (BIS) Facilitates cooperation among countries involved in international transactions and provides assistance to countries experiencing international payment problems.

Banker's acceptance Bill of exchange drawn on and accepted by a banking institution—it is commonly used to guarantee exporters that they will receive payment on goods delivered to importers.

Bank letter of credit policy Enables banks to confirm letters of credit by foreign banks supporting U.S. exports.

Barter Exchange of goods between two parties without the use of any currency as a medium of exchange.

Bid price Price that a trader of foreign exchange (typically a bank) is willing to pay for a particular currency.

Bid-ask spread Difference between the price at which a bank is willing to buy a currency versus the price at which it will sell that currency.

Bilateral netting system Netting method used for transactions between two units.

Bill of exchange (draft) A promise drawn by one party (usually on exporter) to pay a specified amount to another party at a specified future date or upon presentation of the draft.

Bill of lading Serves as a receipt for shipment and a summary of freight charges, and conveys title to the merchandise.

Blocked funds Funds that cannot be remitted from the subsidiary to the parent due to host-government restrictions.

Brady Plan Bill intended to provide banks with the option of having some of their LDC debt replaced by the World Bank (and IMF) by trading it in at a discount.

Branches Full-service banking offices that can compete directly with other banks located in that area.

Break-even salvage value Salvage value necessary to achieve a zero net present value for a particular project.

Bretton Woods agreement Conference held in Bretton Woods, New Hampshire in 1944 resulting in agreement to maintain exchange rates of currencies within very narrow boundaries—this agreement lasted until 1971.

Buyer credit policy Permits banks to extend loans to foreign borrowers to purchase U.S. goods.

Capital account Reflects changes in country ownership of long-term and short-term financial assets.

Cash management Optimization of cash flows and investment of excess cash.

Central exchange rate Exchange rate established between two European currencies through the European Monetary System arrangement; the exchange rate between the two currencies is allowed to move within bands around that central exchange rate.

Centralized cash management Consolidates cash management decisions for all MNC units, usually at the parent's location.

Certainty equivalent Value assigned to expected cash flows that reflects the degree of certainty.

Checklist approach Method for evaluation, involving a list of factors that are assigned ratings—used for various assessments (such as country risk assessment).

Coefficient of determination Measures the percentage variation in the dependent variable that can be explained by the independent variables when using regression analysis.

Co-financing agreements Method used by the World Bank in which a portion of the financing is provided to developing countries.

Commercial invoice Exporter's description of merchandise being sold to the buyer.

Commercial letters of credit Trade-related letters of credit.

Comparative advantage Theory suggesting that specialization by countries can increase worldwide production.

Compensation Arrangement in which the delivery of goods to one party is compensated for by buying back a certain amount of the product from that same party.

Compensatory Financing Facility (CFF) Facility that attempts to reduce the impact of export instability on country economics.

Consignment The exporter ships goods to the importer while still retaining title to the merchandise.

Contingency graph As applied to this text, depicts the profit per unit to be earned on a currency option for various possible exchange rate scenarios.

Convertibility clause Clause attached to some Eurobonds that allows them to be converted into a specified number of common stock shares.

Counterpurchase Exchange of goods between two parties under two distinct contracts expressed in monetary terms.

Countertrade The sale of goods to one country is linked to the purchase or exchange of goods from that same country.

Covered interest arbitrage Investment in a foreign money market security with a simultaneous forward sale of the currency denominating that security.

Cross-border factoring Factoring by a network of factors across borders. The exporter's factor can contact correspondent factors in other countries to handle the collections of accounts receivable.

Cross exchange rate Given the values of currencies A and B with respect to a third currency, the cross rate is the exchange rate between currency A and currency B.

Cross-hedging Hedging an open position in one currency with a hedge on another currency that is highly correlated with the first currency. This occurs when for some reason the common hedging techniques cannot be applied to the first currency. A cross-hedge is not a perfect hedge but can substantially reduce the exposure.

Cross-sectional analysis Analysis of relationships among a cross-section of firms, countries, or some other variable at a given point in time.

Cumulative translation adjustment (CTA) account Account used by FASB-52 for capturing translation gains and losses.

Currency call option Grants the right to purchase a specific currency at a specific price (exchange rate) within a specific period of time.

Currency cocktail bond Bond denominated in a mixture (or cocktail) of currencies.

Currency correlation Measurement of the relationship between movements of two currencies.

Currency futures Contracts specifying a standard volume of a particular currency to be exchanged on a specific settlement date.

Currency put option Grants the right to sell a particular currency at a specified price (exchange rate) within a specified period of time.

Currency swap Agreement to exchange one currency for another at a specified exchange rate and date. The banks commonly serve as intermediaries between two parties who wish to engage in a currency swap.

Current account A broad measure of a country's international trade in goods and services.

Debt-equity swap Exchange of a bank's debt (loans) held in return for an equity investment in the borrower's assets; this type of swap was used by commercial banks to reduce their amount of debt owed by less developed countries.

Delphi technique Collection of independent opinions without group discussion by the assessors who provided the opinions—used for various types of assessments (such as country risk assessment).

Dependent variable Referred to in regression analysis to represent the variable that is dependent on one or more other variables.

Depreciation A decrease in the value of a currency.

Direct quotations Exchange rate quotations representing the value measured by number of dollars per unit.

Dirty float Exchange rate system whereby exchange rates are allowed to fluctuate without set boundaries—yet, governments do intervene as they wish.

Double-entry bookkeeping Accounting method in which each transaction is recorded as both a credit and a debit.

Dummy variables Variables used in regression analysis that are classified as either a zero or a one, for qualitative variables.

Economic exposure Degree to which a firm's present value of future cash flows can be influenced by exchange rate fluctuations.

Economies of scale Lower average cost per unit resulting from increased production.

Edge Act corporations Aid corporations that are involved in foreign trade; they are established by banks and can be set up across state borders.

Effective financing rate Cost of financing after considering exchange rate fluctuations—this term is commonly applied to financing with foreign currencies since financing costs will be affected by exchange rate fluctuations.

Effective yield Yield or return to an MNC on a short-term investment after adjusting for the change in exchange rates over the period of concern.

Efficient frontier Set of points reflecting risk-return combinations achieved by particular portfolios (so-called efficient portfolios) of assets.

Efficient market A market in which prices reflect all available information so that excess risk-adjusted returns are not possible.

Equilibrium exchange rate Exchange rate at which the demand for the currency is equal to the supply of the currency for sale.

Equity multiplier Assets divided by equity.

Eurobanks Commercial banks that participate as financial intermediaries in the Eurocurrency market.

Eurobond market Market where bonds are underwritten by international syndicates and sold outside the country of the currency that denominated the bonds.

Eurobonds Bonds sold in countries other than the country represented by the currency denominating them.

Euro-commercial paper Debt securities issued by MNCs for short-term financing.

Eurocredit market Composed of a collection of banks that accept deposits and provide loans in large denominations and in a variety of currencies. The banks that comprise this market are the same banks that comprise the Eurocurrency market; the difference is that the Eurocredit loans are longer-term than so-called Eurocurrency loans.

Eurocurrency market Composed of a collection of banks that accept deposits and provide loans in large denominations and in a variety of currencies.

Eurodollars U.S. dollars deposited in Europe.

Euronotes Unsecured debt securities issued by MNCs for short-term financing.

European Currency Unit (ECU) A unit of account representing a weighted average of exchange rates of member countries within the European Monetary System.

European Monetary System (EMS) Exchange rates of member countries are held together within specified limits, and are also tied to a currency composite called the European Currency Unit (ECU).

Exchange rate Value of one currency with respect to another.

Exercise price (strike price) The price (exchange rate) at which the owner of a currency call option is allowed to buy a specified currency—or the price (exchange rate) at which the owner of a currency put option is allowed to sell a specified currency.

Exposure to exchange rate fluctuations Degree to which a firm can be affected by exchange rate fluctuations; three common types of exposure are (1) transaction exposure, (2) economic exposure, and (3) translation exposure.

Export-Import Bank Attempts to strengthen the competitiveness of U.S. industries involved in foreign trade.

Ex post real interest rate Measures the interest rate after adjusting for inflation in a recent period.

Factor Firm specializing in collection on accounts receivable; exporters sometimes sell their accounts receivable to a factor at a discount.

Factoring Purchase of receivables of an exporter by a factor without recourse to the exporter.

Financial Accounting Standards Board No. 52 Consolidated accounting rules adopted in 1981.

Fixed exchange rate system Exchange rates are either held constant or are allowed to fluctuate only within very narrow boundaries.

Forecast bias Consistent over- or underestimating from forecasting.

Foreign Credit Insurance Association (FCIA) Insures firms against political and credit risk related to international trade.

Foreign exchange market Market composed primarily of banks serving firms and consumers who wish to buy or sell various currencies.

Foreign investment risk matrix Displays financial and political risk by intervals, so that each country can be positioned according to its risk ratings.

Forfaiting Method of financing international trade of capital goods.

Forward contract Agreement between a commercial bank and a client about an exchange of two currencies to be made at a future point in time at a specified exchange rate.

Forward discount Percentage by which the forward rate is less than the spot rate—typically quoted on an annualized basis.

Forward premium Percentage by which the forward rate exceeds the spot rate—typically quoted on an annualized basis.

Forward rate Rate at which a bank is willing to exchange one currency for another at some specified date in the future.

Freely floating exchange rate system Exchange rates are allowed to move due to market forces without intervention by country governments.

Fundamental forecasting Forecasts based on fundamental relationships between economic variables and exchange rates.

General Agreement on Tariffs and Trade (GATT) Allows for trade restrictions only in retaliation against illegal trade actions of other countries.

Hedging Action taken to insulate the firm from exposure to exchange rate fluctuations.

Homemade Diversification Actions by investors to diversify their investments across various types of assets.

Hostile takeovers Acquisitions not desired by the target firms.

IMF Funding Bill Bill passed by Congress in 1983 that called for funds to be sent from the U.S. government to the International Monetary Fund and then channelled to the LDCs.

Imperfect markets theory Suggests that because there are costs to the transfer of labor and other resources used for production, firms may attempt to use foreign factors of production when they are less costly than local factors.

Independent variable Referred to in regression analysis to represent the variable that is expected to influence another (so-called "dependent") variable.

Indirect quotations Exchange rate quotations representing the value measured by number of units per dollar.

Interest equalization tax (IET) Tax imposed by the U.S. government in 1963 to discourage U.S. investors from investing in foreign securities.

Interest rate parity (IRP) Diagonal line depicting all points on a four-quadrant graph that represent a state of interest rate parity.

Interest rate parity theory Suggests that the forward rate differs from the spot rate by an amount that reflects the interest differential between two currencies.

International Bank for Reconstruction and Development (IBRD) Also referred to as the World Bank, it was established in 1944 to enhance economic development by providing loans to countries.

International banking facilities (IBFs) As part of existing banks, they were established to allow for acceptance of deposits or loans to nonresidents of the U.S. Because IBFs are not subject to normal U.S. regulations, they are free from reserve requirements and interest rate ceilings.

International Development Association (IDA) Established to stimulate country development; it was especially suited for less prosperous nations since it provided loans at low interest rates.

International Financial Corporation Established to promote private enterprise within countries; it can provide loans to and purchase stock of corporations.

International Fisher Effect (IFE) line Diagonal line on a graph that reflects points at which the interest rate differential between two countries is equal to the percentage change in the exchange rate between the two respective currencies.

International mutual funds (IMFs) Mutual funds containing securities of foreign firms.

Irrevocable letters of credit Cannot be cancelled or amended without the beneficiary's approval.

Joint venture Venture between two or more firms in which responsibilities and earnings are shared.

Lagging Strategy used by a firm to stall payments, normally in response to exchange rate projections.

Law of one price Also called the absolute form of purchasing power parity (PPP), suggests that prices of two products of different countries should be equal when measured by a common currency.

Leading Strategy used by a firm to accelerate payments, normally in response to exchange rate expectations.

Lease insurance policy Provides insurance coverage to banks and other firms that lease U.S.-manufactured equipment to foreign entities.

Letter of credit Agreement by a bank to make payments on behalf of a specified party under specified conditions.

Licensing A local firm in the host country produces goods in accordance with another firm's (the licensing firm's) specifications; as the goods are sold, the local firm can retain part of the earnings.

Locational arbitrage Action to capitalize on a discrepancy in quoted exchange rates between banks.

Lockbox Post office box numbers to which customers are instructed to send payment.

London Interbank Offer Rate (LIBOR) The interest rate commonly charged for loans between Eurobanks.

Long-term forward contracts Also called long forwards, these contracts state any exchange rate at which a specified amount of a specified currency can be exchanged at a future date (more than one year from today).

Louvre Accord Agreement between countries to attempt to stabilize the value of the U.S. dollar.

Mail float Mailing time involved in payments sent by mail.

Managed float Exchange rate system in which currencies have no explicit boundaries, but central banks may intervene to influence exchange rate movements.

Margin requirements Deposit placed on a contract (such as a currency futures contract) to cover the fluctuations in the value of that contract; this minimizes the risk of the contract to the counter-party.

Market-based forecasting Use of a market-determined exchange rate (such as the spot rate or forward rate) to forecast the spot rate in the future.

Mixed forecasting Development of forecasts based on a mixture of forecasting techniques.

Monetary/nonmonetary approach Used for consolidated accounting rules before 1981, whereby current exchange rates were used to measure monetary assets liabilities, while historic exchange rates were used to measure nonmonetary items.

Money market hedge Use of international money markets to match future cash inflows and outflows in a given currency.

Multi-Buyer policy Administered by the FCIA; provides credit risk insurance on export sales to many different buyers.

Multilateral Investment Guarantee Agency (MIGA) Established by the World Bank, it offers various forms of political risk insurance to corporations.

Multilateral netting system Involves a complex interchange for netting between the parent and several subsidiaries.

Negotiable bill of lading Grants title of merchandise to the holder, which allows banks to use the merchandise as collateral.

Net operating loss carrybacks Applying losses to offset earnings in previous years.

Net operating loss carryforwards Applying losses to offset earnings in future years.

Netting Combining future cash receipts and payments to determine the net amount to be owed by one subsidiary to another.

Net transaction exposure Consideration of inflows and outflows in a given currency to determine the exposure after offsetting inflows against outflows.

New-Export policy Administered by the FCIA; provides coverage on commercial risk defaults to novice exporters.

Nonsterilized intervention Intervention in the foreign exchange market without adjusting for the change in money supply.

Ocean bill of lading Receipt for a shipment by boat, and includes freight charges and title to the merchandise.

Omnibus Act See Trade and Tariff Act of 1984.

Open account transaction The exporter ships the merchandise and expects the buyer to remit payment according to agreed upon terms.

Option look-alikes Have similar characteristics as currency options, but are offered by institutions rather than sold on an exchange.

Options on futures contracts Provide the right to purchase or sell the futures contract of a specified currency at a specified price by a specified expiration date.

Parallel bonds Bonds placed in different countries and denominated in the respective currencies of the countries where they are placed.

Parallel loan Involves an exchange of currencies between two parties, with a promise to reexchange the currencies at a specified exchange rate and future date.

Partial hedge Protects only a portion of foreign currency positions.

Payback period Represents an acceptable period during which the initial investment of a project must be recovered.

Pegged exchange rate An exchange rate whose value is pegged to another currency's value or to a unit of account.

Petrodollars Deposits of dollars by countries which receive dollar revenues due to the sale of petroleum to other countries; the term commonly refers to OPEC deposits of dollars in the Eurocurrency market.

Planned divestment Act of phasing out a portion of business over time—commonly used by MNC's to phase out their overseas investments.

Preauthorized payment Method of accelerating cash inflows by receiving authorization to charge a customer's bank account.

Prepayment Method which exporter uses to receive payment before shipping goods.

Price-elastic Sensitive to price changes.

Private Export Funding Corporation (PEFCO) Provides medium- and long-term funds to importers of U.S. goods and services.

Privatization Conversion of government-owned businesses to ownership by shareholders or individuals.

Product cycle theory Suggests that firms initially establish themselves locally and expand into foreign markets in response to foreign demand for the product; over time, the MNC will grow in foreign markets; after some point, its foreign business may decline unless it can differentiate its product from competitors.

Product differentiation Development of a product that is unique, different from those produced by competitors, in order to maintain or improve market share.

Purchasing power parity (PPP) line Diagonal line on a graph that reflects points at which the inflation differential between two countries is equal to the percentage change in the exchange rate between the two respective currencies.

Purchasing Power Parity (PPP) theory Suggests that exchange rates will adjust over time to reflect the differential in inflation rates in the two countries; in this way, the purchasing power of consumers when purchasing domestic goods will be the same as when purchasing foreign goods.

Quota Maximum limit imposed by the government that is allowed to be imported into a country.

Real cost of hedging The additional cost of hedging when compared to not hedging (a negative real cost would imply that hedging was more favorable than not hedging).

Real exchange rate Quoted exchange rate adjusted for its country's inflation relative to inflation in other countries.

Real interest rate Nominal (or quoted) interest rate minus the inflation rate.

Real net exports Value of inflation-adjusted exports minus inflation-adjusted imports.

Regression analysis Statistical technique used to measure the relationship between variables and the sensitivity of a variable to one or more other variables.

Regression coefficient Measured by regression analysis to estimate the sensitivity of the dependent variable to a particular independent variable.

Relative form of purchasing power parity The rate of change in the prices of products should be somewhat similar when measured in a common currency, as long as transportation costs and trade barriers are unchanged.

Revocable letters of credit Can be cancelled at any time without prior notification to the beneficiary.

Semistrong-form efficient When related to foreign exchange markets, implies that all relevant public information is already reflected in prevailing spot exchange rates.

Sensitivity analysis A technique for assessing uncertainty whereby various possibilities are input to determine possible outcomes.

Simulation A technique for assessing the degree of uncertainty. Probability distributions are developed for the input variables; simulation uses this information to generate possible outcomes.

Single-Buyer policy Administered by the FCIA; allows the exporter to selectively insure certain transactions.

Smithsonian Agreement Conference between nations in 1971 that resulted in a devaluation of the dollar against major currencies, and a widening of boundaries (2 1/4 percent in either direction) around the newly established exchange rates.

Snake Arrangement established in 1972 whereby European currencies were tied to each other within specified limits.

Special Drawing Rights (SDRs) Reserves established by the International Monetary Fund; they are used only for inter-government transactions; the SDR also serves as a unit of account (determined by the values of five major currencies) that is used to denominate some internationally traded goods and services, as well as some foreign bank deposits and loans.

Spot rate Current exchange rate of currency.

Standby letter of credit Used to guarantee invoice payments to a supplier; it promises to pay the beneficiary if the buyer fails to pay.

Sterilized intervention Intervention in the foreign exchange market while retaining the existing money supply.

Strong-form efficient When related to foreign exchange markets, implies that all relevant public information and private information is already reflected in prevailing spot exchange rates.

Structural Adjustment Loan Facility Established in 1980 by the World Bank to enhance a country's long-term economic growth through financing projects.

Syndicated Eurocredit loans Loans provided by a group (or syndicate) of banks in the Eurocredit market.

Systematic risk Risk cannot be diversified away; is common to all firms or countries.

Target zones Implicit boundaries established by central banks on exchange rates.

Tariff Tax imposed by the government on imported goods.

Technical forecasting Using historical prices or trends to develop forecasts.

Time-series analysis Analysis of relationships between two or more variables over periods of time.

Time series models Models that examine a series of historical data; are sometimes used as a means of technical forecasting, by examining moving averages.

Trade and Tariff Act of 1984 Also referred to as the Omnibus Act, established provisions that promote free trade, enacted in 1984.

Transaction exposure Degree to which the value of future cash transactions can be affected by exchange rate fluctuations.

Transferable letter of credit Allows the first beneficiary on a standby letter of credit to transfer all or part of the original letter of credit to a third party.

Transfer pricing Policy for pricing goods sent by either the parent or a subsidiary to a different subsidiary of the MNC.

Translation exposure Degree to which a firm's consolidated financial statements are exposed to fluctuations in exchange rates.

Triangular arbitrage Action to capitalize on a discrepancy where the quoted cross exchange rate is not equal to the rate that should exist at equilibrium.

Umbrella policy Is issued to a bank or trading company to insure exports of an exporter and handle all reporting requirements.

Unilateral transfers Reflect government and private gifts and grants.

Weak-form efficient When related to foreign exchange markets, implies that all historical and current exchange rate information is already reflected in prevailing spot exchange rates.

Withholding tax Commonly refers to a tax imposed by a host country on funds that are remitted from the subsidiary to the parent.

World Bank Established in 1944 to enhance economic development by providing loans to countries.

Writer Seller of an option.

DATA BANK

Quarterly data is provided in this data bank for the following variables:

- Consumer Price Index
- Quarterly Inflation Rates
- Money Market Interest Rates
- Exports by Country
- Imports by Country
- Industrial Share Price Index
- Percentage Change in Industrial Share Prices
- Exchange Rates
- Exchange Rate Percentage Change
- Three-Month Forward Rates

The data were compiled from *International Financial Statistics,* which is published by the International Monetary Fund and is available at many university libraries.

Consumer price index (1980 = 100)

Year	Quarter	Canada	France	Germany	Japan	Netherlands	Sweden	Switzerland	U.K.	U.S.
1972	I	48.8	43.4	66.3	45.8	55.5	46.1	68.4	31.7	50.2
	II	49.2	44.1	67.0	46.7	56.9	46.9	69.2	32.2	50.5
	III	50.2	44.8	68.0	47.2	57.3	47.3	70.2	32.7	51.0
	IV	50.7	45.8	69.1	47.7	58.8	48.1	71.9	33.6	51.4
1973	I	51.7	46.2	70.6	49.1	59.8	49.0	73.7	34.1	52.2
	II	52.8	47.2	72.0	51.6	61.5	49.8	74.9	35.2	53.4
	III	54.3	48.3	72.5	53.2	62.0	50.6	76.0	35.8	54.5
	IV	55.3	49.6	74.0	55.6	63.4	53.1	79.6	36.9	55.8
1974	I	56.6	51.4	75.8	61.1	65.0	53.9	81.4	38.5	57.3
	II	58.5	53.6	77.0	64.0	66.9	54.4	82.0	40.8	58.9
	III	60.3	55.3	77.8	66.4	68.1	55.2	84.0	41.8	60.7
	IV	61.9	57.1	78.8	69.2	70.4	57.6	86.6	43.7	62.4
1975	I	63.2	58.6	80.3	70.6	71.9	58.4	87.9	46.3	63.6
	II	64.6	60.1	81.8	72.6	73.9	59.7	88.9	50.7	64.6
	III	66.9	61.4	82.5	73.2	75.3	61.5	89.5	52.9	66.0
	IV	68.2	62.7	83.2	75.1	77.0	63.0	90.1	54.7	67.1
1976	I	69.1	64.2	84.5	76.9	78.7	64.8	90.4	56.7	67.7
	II	70.2	65.7	85.5	79.4	80.9	66.4	90.3	58.8	68.6
	III	71.2	67.2	85.7	80.2	81.8	67.4	90.7	60.1	69.6
	IV	72.3	69.0	86.2	82.2	83.7	69.0	91.0	62.9	70.4
1977	I	73.8	70.0	87.7	84.0	84.4	70.9	91.4	66.1	71.6
	II	75.5	72.2	88.6	86.3	86.5	73.6	91.6	69.0	73.2
	III	77.2	73.9	88.9	86.6	87.1	76.1	92.0	70.1	74.3
	IV	78.8	75.3	89.3	87.3	88.0	77.9	92.2	71.1	75.1
1978	I	80.3	76.5	90.3	87.7	88.3	80.5	92.4	72.3	76.3
	II	82.2	78.7	91.1	89.4	89.6	81.6	92.8	74.3	78.4
	III	84.4	80.7	91.1	90.1	90.8	82.3	93.0	75.6	80.2
	IV	85.7	82.4	91.4	90.3	91.6	83.5	92.8	76.8	81.8
1979	I	87.6	84.3	93.0	90.0	92.1	85.1	94.2	79.3	83.9
	II	89.9	86.6	94.3	92.3	93.3	86.6	95.1	82.2	86.7
	III	91.7	89.4	95.5	93.2	94.3	88.6	97.0	87.7	89.6
	IV	93.8	91.9	96.3	94.8	95.8	91.3	97.5	90.2	92.2

Consumer price index (1980 = 100) *(continued)*

Year	Quarter	Canada	France	Germany	Japan	Netherlands	Sweden	Switzerland	U.K.	U.S.
1980	I	95.9	95.5	98.2	96.8	97.4	96.4	98.3	94.4	95.8
	II	98.5	99.1	99.9	100.0	99.5	98.2	99.5	99.8	99.3
	III	101.3	99.6	100.5	100.9	101.0	101.3	100.7	102.0	101.1
	IV	104.2	103.1	101.4	102.3	102.2	104.7	101.6	103.9	103.8
1981	I	107.6	107.3	103.8	103.2	103.9	108.8	104.0	106.3	106.5
	II	110.9	110.8	105.7	104.9	105.9	111.1	105.5	111.5	109.0
	III	114.2	115.2	107.2	105.2	107.6	113.5	107.9	113.4	112.1
	IV	117.0	118.9	108.6	106.4	109.6	115.1	108.6	116.2	113.7
1982	I	120.0	122.3	110.0	106.4	111.1	118.6	109.6	118.2	114.7
	II	123.7	126.1	111.3	107.5	112.6	120.6	111.7	121.9	116.4
	III	126.3	127.8	112.7	109.0	113.8	122.3	114.0	122.5	118.6
	IV	128.3	130.2	113.7	108.9	114.6	125.4	114.9	123.4	118.9
1983	I	129.1	133.6	114.4	108.6	114.7	129.1	114.9	124.0	118.8
	II	130.9	137.4	115.0	109.8	115.5	131.1	115.6	126.5	120.3
	III	133.0	140.3	116.2	109.5	116.6	133.6	116.0	128.2	121.7
	IV	134.2	143.0	116.7	110.7	117.8	136.5	117.0	129.6	122.8
1984	I	135.8	145.4	117.7	111.2	118.8	139.7	118.2	130.4	124.1
	II	137.0	148.1	118.3	112.1	119.8	142.3	119.0	133.1	125.5
	III	138.2	150.6	118.3	111.9	120.0	143.8	119.2	134.2	126.9
	IV	139.2	152.7	119.2	113.3	121.3	146.9	120.5	135.9	127.8
1985	I	140.8	154.8	120.5	113.7	121.6	150.9	122.8	137.6	128.6
	II	142.4	157.6	121.2	114.7	122.8	153.7	123.3	142.3	130.2
	III	143.7	159.1	120.9	114.9	122.8	154.0	123.1	142.7	131.1
	IV	145.0	160.1	121.3	115.3	123.4	156.4	124.3	143.4	132.3
1986	I	146.8	160.3	121.3	115.4	123.0	158.9	124.6	144.5	132.6
	II	147.9	161.4	121.0	115.7	123.3	159.7	124.4	146.3	132.3
	III	149.7	162.4	120.4	115.1	122.1	160.4	123.8	146.4	133.3
	IV	151.3	163.5	120.0	115.1	123.2	162.0	124.4	148.4	134.0
1987	I	152.7	165.5	120.7	114.1	121.5	164.5	125.7	150.2	135.5
	II	154.8	166.9	121.1	115.9	122.1	165.1	125.7	152.5	137.3
	III	156.6	167.9	121.1	115.6	122.3	168.0	126.1	152.8	138.8
	IV	157.7	168.7	121.2	115.9	123.1	170.5	126.9	154.5	140.0

Consumer price index (1980 = 100) (continued)

Year	Quarter	Canada	France	Germany	Japan	Netherlands	Sweden	Switzerland	U.K.	U.S.
1988	I	159.0	169.5	121.7	115.3	122.1	172.7	127.8	155.2	140.9
	II	161.0	171.2	122.3	116.1	123.0	175.8	128.2	158.9	142.6
	III	162.9	172.8	122.5	116.3	123.5	177.8	128.3	161.1	144.6
	IV	164.1	173.8	122.9	117.1	123.9	180.5	129.0	164.5	146.0
1989	I	166.1	175.3	124.7	116.6	123.2	183.9	130.6	167.1	147.7
	II	169.0	177.4	125.9	119.3	124.2	187.3	131.9	171.9	150.0
	III	171.4	178.7	125.9	119.4	124.9	189.0	132.4	173.5	151.3
	IV	170.2	180.1	126.8	119.6	124.5	188.9	134.4	172.6	152.8
1990	I	170.3	177.7	127.3	119.8	124.8	197.8	136.8	175.6	152.3
	II	172.5	179.4	128.0	121.5	125.9	202.2	138.1	183.8	153.8
	III	174.3	172.9	128.5	121.5	126.8	206.1	139.7	185.6	156.5
	IV	176.8	N/A	130.8	122.3	128.0	210.0	142.3	187.7	159.0
1991	I	181.8	N/A	N/A	122.4	128.2	219.3	144.9	N/A	160.3

Quarterly inflation rates (percentage change in consumer price index)

Year	Quarter	Canada	France	Germany	Japan	Netherlands	Sweden	Switzerland	U.K.	U.S.
1972	I	N/A	N/A	N/A	N/A	N/A	N/A	N/A	N/A	N/A
	II	.82	1.61	1.06	1.97	2.52	1.74	1.17	1.58	.60
	III	2.03	1.59	1.49	1.07	.70	.85	1.45	1.55	.99
	IV	1.00	2.23	1.62	1.06	2.62	1.69	2.42	2.75	.78
1973	I	1.97	.87	2.17	2.94	1.70	1.87	2.50	1.49	1.56
	II	2.13	2.16	1.98	5.09	2.84	1.63	1.63	3.23	2.30
	III	2.84	2.33	.69	3.10	.81	1.61	1.47	1.70	2.06
	IV	1.84	2.69	2.07	4.51	2.26	4.94	4.74	3.07	2.39
1974	I	2.35	3.63	2.43	9.89	2.52	1.51	2.26	4.34	2.69
	II	3.36	4.28	1.58	4.75	2.92	.93	.74	5.97	2.79
	III	3.08	3.17	1.04	3.75	1.79	1.47	2.44	2.45	3.06
	IV	2.65	3.25	1.29	4.22	3.38	4.35	3.10	4.55	2.80
1975	I	2.10	2.63	1.90	2.02	2.13	1.39	1.50	5.95	1.92
	II	2.22	2.56	1.87	2.83	2.78	2.23	1.14	9.50	1.57
	III	3.56	2.16	.86	.83	1.89	3.02	.67	4.34	2.17
	IV	1.94	2.12	.85	2.60	2.26	2.44	.67	3.40	1.67
1976	I	1.32	2.39	1.56	2.40	2.21	2.86	.33	3.66	.89
	II	1.59	2.34	1.18	3.25	2.80	2.47	-.11	3.70	1.33
	III	1.42	2.28	.23	1.01	1.11	1.51	.44	2.21	1.46
	IV	1.54	2.68	.58	2.49	2.32	2.37	.33	4.66	1.15
1977	I	2.07	1.45	1.74	2.19	.84	2.75	.44	5.09	1.70
	II	2.30	3.14	1.03	2.74	2.49	3.81	.22	4.39	2.23
	III	2.25	2.35	.34	.35	.69	3.40	.44	1.59	1.50
	IV	2.07	1.89	.45	.81	1.03	2.37	.22	1.43	1.08
1978	I	1.90	1.59	1.12	.46	.34	3.34	.22	1.69	1.60
	II	2.37	2.88	.89	1.94	1.47	1.37	.43	2.77	2.75
	III	2.68	2.54	.00	.78	1.34	.86	.22	1.75	2.30
	IV	1.54	2.11	.33	.22	.88	1.46	-.22	1.59	2.00
1979	I	2.22	2.31	1.75	-.33	.55	1.92	1.51	3.26	2.57
	II	2.63	2.73	1.40	2.56	1.30	1.76	.96	3.66	3.34
	III	2.00	3.23	1.27	.98	1.07	2.31	2.00	6.69	3.34
	IV	2.29	2.80	.84	1.72	1.59	3.05	.52	2.85	2.90

Quarterly inflation rates (percentage change in consumer price index) *(continued)*

Year	Quarter	Canada	France	Germany	Japan	Netherlands	Sweden	Switzerland	U.K.	U.S.
1980	I	2.24	3.92	1.97	2.11	1.67	5.59	.82	4.66	3.90
	II	2.71	3.77	1.73	3.31	2.16	1.87	1.22	5.72	3.65
	III	2.84	.50	.60	.90	1.51	3.16	1.21	2.20	1.81
	IV	2.86	3.51	.90	1.39	1.19	3.36	.89	1.86	2.67
1981	I	3.26	4.07	2.37	.88	1.66	3.92	2.36	2.31	2.60
	II	3.07	3.26	1.83	1.65	1.92	2.11	1.44	4.89	2.35
	III	2.98	3.97	1.42	.29	1.61	2.16	2.27	1.70	2.84
	IV	2.45	3.21	1.31	1.14	1.86	1.41	.65	2.47	1.43
1982	I	2.56	2.86	1.29	.00	1.37	3.04	.92	1.72	.88
	II	3.08	3.11	1.18	1.03	1.35	1.69	1.92	3.13	1.48
	III	2.10	1.35	1.26	1.40	1.07	1.41	2.06	.49	1.89
	IV	1.58	1.88	.89	-.09	.70	2.53	.79	.73	.25
1983	I	.62	2.61	.62	+.27	.09	2.95	.00	.49	-.08
	II	1.39	2.84	.52	1.10	.70	1.55	.61	2.02	1.26
	III	1.60	2.11	1.04	-.27	.95	1.91	.35	1.34	1.16
	IV	.90	1.92	.43	1.10	1.03	2.17	.86	1.09	.90
1984	I	1.19	1.68	.86	.45	.85	2.34	1.03	.62	1.06
	II	.88	1.86	.51	.81	.84	1.86	.68	2.07	1.13
	III	.88	1.69	.00	-.18	.17	1.05	.17	.83	1.12
	IV	.72	1.39	.76	1.25	1.08	2.16	1.09	1.27	.71
1985	I	1.15	1.38	1.09	.18	-.25	2.72	1.91	1.25	.63
	II	1.14	1.81	.58	.88	.99	1.86	.41	3.42	1.24
	III	.91	.95	-.25	.17	.00	.20	-.16	.28	.69
	IV	.91	.63	.33	.35	.49	1.56	.97	.49	.92
1986	I	1.24	.13	.00	.09	.09	1.60	.24	.77	.23
	II	.75	.69	-.25	.26	.26	.50	-.16	1.25	-.23
	III	1.22	.62	-.50	-.52	-1.78	.44	-.48	.07	.76
	IV	1.07	.67	-.33	.00	.90	.99	.48	1.37	.53
1987	I	.93	1.22	.58	-.87	-1.38	1.54	1.05	1.21	1.12
	II	1.38	.85	.33	1.58	.49	.36	.00	.67	1.33
	III	1.16	.60	.00	-.26	.16	1.76	.32	.20	1.09
	IV	.70	.48	.08	.26	.65	.89	.63	1.11	.86

Quarterly inflation rates (percentage change in consumer price index) (*continued*)

Year	Quarter	Canada	France	Germany	Japan	Netherlands	Sweden	Switzerland	U.K.	U.S.
1988	I	.82	.47	.41	-.52	-.81	1.29	.71	.45	.64
	II	1.26	1.03	.50	.70	.70	1.78	.29	2.37	1.20
	III	1.15	.92	.20	.20	.40	1.14	.10	1.42	1.37
	IV	.79	.55	.30	.69	.40	1.56	.58	2.11	.99
1989	I	1.22	.91	1.47	-.49	-.60	1.87	1.24	1.55	1.16
	II	1.72	1.17	.97	2.36	.80	1.84	.94	2.88	1.59
	III	1.44	.71	.00	.10	.59	.90	.37	.91	.87
	IV	-.70	.80	.67	.08	-.32	-.05	1.51	-.52	.95
1990	I	.06	-1.33	.39	.33	.24	4.71	1.78	1.74	-.33
	II	1.29	.96	.55	1.42	.88	2.22	.95	4.67	.98
	III	1.04	-3.62	.39	.00	.71	1.92	1.16	.98	1.76
	IV	1.43	N/A	1.79	.66	.94	1.89	1.86	1.13	1.60
1991	I	2.82	N/A	N/A	.08	.15	4.42	1.82	N/A	N/A

Money market interest rates*

Year	Quarter	Canada	France	Germany	Japan	Netherlands	Sweden	Switzerland	U.K.	U.S.
1972	I	3.46	5.11	4.08	5.12	2.84	5.00	5.50	4.36	3.43
	II	3.62	4.64	3.12	4.82	1.50	5.00	3.75	4.70	3.75
	III	3.53	3.80	3.85	4.46	.26	5.00	3.75	5.96	4.24
	IV	3.63	6.26	6.16	4.49	3.10	5.00	3.75	7.15	4.85
1973	I	4.12	7.49	6.38	5.19	1.48	5.00	3.75	8.13	5.64
	II	5.19	7.61	11.05	6.13	2.93	5.00	4.50	7.36	6.61
	III	6.14	9.26	12.06	7.88	9.04	5.00	4.50	10.24	8.39
	IV	6.44	11.27	11.25	9.44	12.29	5.00	4.50	11.50	7.46
1974	I	6.27	12.72	10.39	12.08	10.58	5.00	5.50	11.99	7.60
	II	8.34	12.77	7.49	12.17	9.81	6.00	5.50	11.36	8.27
	III	9.05	13.67	9.31	13.04	8.13	7.00	5.50	11.18	8.28
	IV	7.64	12.48	8.28	12.87	8.29	7.00	5.50	10.96	7.34
1975	I	6.33	10.18	5.60	12.86	7.17	7.00	5.00	10.01	5.87
	II	6.90	7.73	5.03	11.27	2.82	7.00	4.50	9.39	5.40
	III	7.91	7.13	3.44	10.45	1.86	6.00	3.50	10.17	6.33
	IV	8.44	6.62	3.60	8.10	4.83	6.00	3.00	11.13	5.68
1976	I	8.82	7.06	3.50	7.09	3.08	5.50	2.50	9.04	4.95
	II	8.97	7.57	3.60	6.80	4.33	6.00	2.00	10.19	5.17
	III	9.10	8.99	4.30	7.13	12.83	6.00	2.00	11.26	5.17
	IV	8.58	10.62	4.10	6.88	8.88	8.00	2.00	13.99	4.68
1977	I	7.74	9.83	4.50	6.90	6.17	8.00	2.00	11.20	4.62
	II	7.23	9.07	4.30	5.51	2.00	8.00	2.00	7.72	4.83
	III	7.13	8.50	4.10	5.46	2.20	8.00	1.50	6.55	5.47
	IV	7.22	8.88	3.70	4.85	4.82	8.00	1.50	5.26	6.14
1978	I	7.39	9.67	3.40	4.74	5.30	8.07	1.00	5.90	6.41
	II	8.19	8.11	3.50	4.10	4.40	7.47	1.00	8.11	6.48
	III	8.89	7.29	3.40	4.36	4.39	6.33	1.00	9.04	7.32
	IV	10.22	6.55	3.10	4.23	10.87	6.77	1.00	11.00	8.68
1979	I	10.84	6.70	3.70	4.43	7.84	5.67	1.00	11.94	9.36
	II	10.81	7.34	5.30	5.12	7.25	6.77	1.00	11.75	9.38
	III	11.45	10.26	6.20	6.43	8.92	9.43	1.00	13.34	9.63
	IV	13.63	11.86	8.30	7.46	12.12	10.90	2.00	14.87	11.80

Money market interest rates* (continued)

Year	Quarter	Canada	France	Germany	Japan	Netherlands	Sweden	Switzerland	U.K.	U.S.
1980	I	14.10	12.37	8.30	9.18	10.56	11.87	3.00	16.04	13.46
	II	12.37	12.48	9.60	12.47	10.86	12.10	3.00	16.02	10.05
	III	10.50	11.58	9.30	12.06	10.09	12.17	3.00	14.60	9.24
	IV	14.21	10.95	9.00	10.01	9.00	12.53	3.00	13.77	13.71
1981	I	16.71	11.98	11.20	8.59	9.32	15.20	4.00	12.15	14.37
	II	18.20	15.94	13.20	7.44	10.62	15.30	5.00	11.59	14.83
	III	20.15	17.44	12.80	7.50	12.30	13.43	6.00	13.55	15.09
	IV	15.81	15.69	11.20	7.24	11.81	13.48	6.00	14.82	12.02
1982	I	14.59	14.95	10.20	6.64	9.31	12.97	5.50	13.37	12.89
	II	15.50	16.14	9.30	7.27	8.48	13.93	5.50	12.57	12.35
	III	13.89	14.59	8.90	7.38	8.22	14.53	5.00	10.61	9.71
	IV	10.58	13.24	7.20	7.20	6.24	11.74	4.50	9.66	7.93
1983	I	9.33	12.85	5.70	6.92	4.82	9.77	4.00	11.00	8.03
	II	9.18	12.62	5.40	6.69	5.11	11.00	4.00	10.04	8.42
	III	9.27	12.56	5.70	6.79	5.50	10.81	4.00	9.53	9.19
	IV	9.44	12.50	6.30	6.48	5.70	11.84	4.00	9.04	8.79
1984	I	10.03	12.65	6.00	6.31	5.86	10.74	4.00	8.90	9.13
	II	11.33	12.47	6.00	6.26	5.70	10.83	4.00	8.69	9.84
	III	12.29	11.56	6.00	6.34	5.87	13.47	4.00	10.40	10.34
	IV	10.60	11.06	6.00	6.39	5.70	12.03	4.00	9.39	8.97
1985	I	10.39	10.75	6.10	6.41	6.38	12.53	4.00	10.96	8.18
	II	9.54	10.44	5.80	6.35	6.91	14.79	4.00	10.08	7.52
	III	8.92	9.94	4.90	6.40	6.11	15.13	4.00	11.25	7.10
	IV	8.87	9.19	4.80	7.64	5.82	12.94	4.00	10.83	7.13
1986	I	10.76	8.81	4.60	6.22	5.80	11.64	4.00	12.21	6.89
	II	8.55	7.46	4.60	4.75	6.09	10.94	4.00	9.42	6.13
	III	8.31	7.20	4.60	4.63	5.69	9.33	4.00	10.17	5.53
	IV	8.25	7.70	4.70	4.34	5.74	8.68	4.00	10.93	5.34
1987	I	7.11	8.33	4.20	4.15	5.62	10.95	3.22	10.47	5.53
	II	8.19	8.13	3.80	3.77	5.21	8.54	3.21	9.14	5.23
	III	9.09	7.92	3.90	3.68	4.97	8.55	3.09	9.81	6.03
	IV	8.19	8.51	4.10	3.91	4.85	8.61	3.19	9.22	6.00

Money market interest rates* (continued)

Year	Quarter	Canada	France	Germany	Japan	Netherlands	Sweden	Switzerland	U.K.	U.S.
1988	I	8.41	7.94	3.40	3.84	4.05	9.24	1.96	9.01	5.76
	II	8.99	7.75	3.60	3.90	3.70	10.28	2.35	8.39	6.23
	III	9.87	7.66	4.90	4.14	4.95	10.34	3.73	11.33	6.99
	IV	10.66	8.16	5.10	4.44	5.24	10.46	3.99	12.52	7.70
1989	I	11.64	8.97	6.20	4.57	6.02	10.61	5.55	13.06	8.53
	II	12.21	8.83	6.80	4.96	6.60	11.57	6.78	13.46	8.44
	III	12.17	9.15	7.10	5.45	7.12	12.11	6.71	13.93	7.85
	IV	12.20	10.40	8.10	6.52	8.23	11.79	7.38	15.07	7.63
1990	I	12.92	10.97	8.30	7.12	8.47	13.64	8.73	14.82	7.76
	II	13.60	9.83	8.30	7.38	8.10	12.83	8.38	14.79	7.77
	III	12.77	9.87	8.30	7.99	8.06	12.57	8.30	14.86	7.49
	IV	11.95	9.70	8.30	8.20	8.54	14.75	7.86	14.26	7.02
1991	I	9.96	9.58	N/A	N/A	8.95	12.93	7.74	N/A	6.05

*Discount rate used for Switzerland and for Sweden up to the first quarter of 1978.

Exports by country*

Year	Quarter	Canada	France	Germany	Japan	Netherlands	Sweden	Switzerland	U.K.	U.S.
1972	I	4,610	31.25	35.19	1,896	13,053	9,618	6,110	2,320	11.89
	II	5,579	34.81	36.61	2,022	13,626	10,326	6,423	2,440	12.04
	III	4,713	29.69	35.11	2,315	12,864	9,742	6,177	2,050	11.57
	IV	6,047	37.74	42.01	2,574	14,356	12,063	7,304	2,852	13.70
1973	I	5,850	37.97	41.70	2,160	16,824	12,683	6,897	2,828	15.52
	II	6,920	41.54	43.58	2,288	16,751	13,047	7,276	3,075	17.45
	III	6,098	37.41	43.40	2,551	15,657	12,011	7,147	3,056	17.08
	IV	7,569	45.58	48.54	3,032	17,647	15,426	8,470	3,470	20.71
1974	I	7,335	51.98	54.58	3,009	20,420	15,592	8,460	3,583	22.73
	II	8,721	58.67	57.08	3,836	22,815	17,798	9,019	4,199	25.28
	III	8,329	52.69	57.39	4,422	22,071	17,459	8,419	4,216	23.37
	IV	9,078	59.79	61.02	4,953	22,622	19,582	9,094	4,496	27.13
1975	I	8,057	57.73	52.58	3,893	21,492	18,253	7,815	4,559	27.03
	II	9,163	59.25	55.67	3,989	22,487	18,521	8,415	4,915	26.55
	III	8,108	50.40	52.94	4,081	20,043	15,639	7,835	4,837	25.01
	IV	9,334	59.55	60.16	4,609	24,601	19,623	9,242	5,659	28.54
1976	I	9,189	63.35	60.59	4,359	25,356	19,176	8,559	5,848	27.31
	II	10,541	70.77	62.92	4,906	25,933	20,332	9,239	6,459	29.64
	III	9,793	62.91	63.74	5,102	25,387	19,340	8,614	6,309	27.31
	IV	10,409	76.22	69.40	5,564	29,341	21,347	10,603	7,405	30.55
1977	I	10,760	78.19	66.62	5,097	27,130	20,341	9,889	7,809	29.64
	II	12,081	82.84	68.02	5,430	26,788	21,614	10,389	8,463	31.78
	III	11,032	72.30	65.33	5,491	25,204	18,674	10,059	8,486	29.09
	IV	12,277	85.64	73.65	5,641	28,075	25,048	11,674	8,550	30.64
1978	I	12,139	88.04	67.29	5,239	27,398	23,026	10,030	8,756	30.95
	II	14,605	93.87	72.03	5,311	27,082	25,675	10,846	9,626	37.02
	III	13,129	80.04	68.17	4,956	25,603	21,436	9,901	9,031	35.26
	IV	15,365	95.64	77.08	5,062	28,121	28,054	11,031	9,998	40.34
1979	I	15,705	100.48	74.36	4,664	29,911	26,915	10,365	9,097	41.08
	II	16,770	108.88	78.12	5,376	31,716	30,053	11,004	11,068	44.45
	III	16,957	99.76	76.37	5,787	30,957	26,905	10,458	10,606	44.68
	IV	18,836	118.84	85.17	6,705	35,048	34,337	12,253	12,116	51.59

Exports by country* *(continued)*

Year	Quarter	Canada	France	Germany	Japan	Netherlands	Sweden	Switzerland	U.K.	U.S.
1980	I	19,402	121.70	88.80	6,618	38,412	34,368	12,333	12,682	53.02
	II	19,738	127.05	87.52	7,463	36,615	29,831	12,407	12,253	56.59
	III	18,519	110.32	82.91	7,384	33,691	30,448	11,573	11,878	52.99
	IV	21,343	131.48	91.10	7,921	38,042	35,423	13,332	12,698	58.11
1981	I	20,886	134.35	91.20	7,297	40,581	34,200	12,591	11,695	59.74
	II	23,312	148.96	97.18	8,335	42,444	35,600	13,167	12,192	60.76
	III	20,328	137.09	98.79	8,896	41,561	32,238	12,754	12,624	55.15
	IV	22,639	156.27	109.81	8,952	46,477	42,176	14,345	14,188	58.09
1982	I	21,607	154.96	107.62	81.84	46,484	40,582	13,045	13,368	55.31
	II	22,173	160.64	108.27	86.44	44,600	42,328	13,465	13,805	57.03
	III	21,721	143.79	101.34	87.55	40,402	36,810	11,903	13,427	50.24
	IV	21,399	173.69	110.51	88.50	45,365	48,412	14,274	14,940	49.69
1983	I	21,501	166.90	105.59	7,820	46,562	50,853	12,662	14,649	50.08
	II	24,612	184.27	106.12	8,586	46,191	58,503	13,302	14,731	50.51
	III	22,218	167.23	103.41	8,983	43,825	47,064	12,802	14,658	48.38
	IV	26,272	204.67	117.16	9,521	50,027	59,069	14,998	16,545	51.58
1984	I	27,259	206.01	120.06	9,042	53,897	62,538	14,412	16,847	53.79
	II	30,746	214.20	115.12	9,929	52,677	59,521	15,182	16,838	54.90
	III	28,910	197.55	117.97	10,343	47,999	53,056	14,339	16,686	53.28
	IV	30,271	233.18	135.05	11,023	55,807	66,900	16,697	20,140	55.92
1985	I	29,935	226.11	133.84	9,900	59,934	63,383	16,025	20,064	56.15
	II	32,630	236.77	134.01	11,027	57,264	66,679	17,057	20,262	54.32
	III	28,915	206.94	130.76	10,596	52,631	59,573	15,599	18,015	50.34
	IV	32,768	237.11	138.49	10,436	55,739	70,865	17,985	19,990	52.33
1986	I	30,337	218.44	130.28	8,674	54,246	64,482	16,040	17,669	53.66
	II	32,515	222.73	135.02	9,118	51,185	70,131	17,492	18,313	54.47
	III	29,551	199.28	125.94	8,633	45,067	59,617	15,978	16,772	52.83
	IV	32,907	223.90	135.13	8,866	46,479	70,874	17,465	20,263	56.36
1987	I	30,916	212.70	127.26	7,960	46,345	68,034	16,018	19,428	56.15
	II	32,834	219.70	129.33	8,154	46,407	70,966	16,832	19,256	61.69
	III	30,802	209.14	127.47	8,507	44,355	63,114	15,922	19,351	62.22
	IV	35,319	247.91	142.96	8,695	50,467	79,400	18,781	21,681	70.35

Exports by country* (continued)

Year	Quarter	Canada	France	Germany	Japan	Netherlands	Sweden	Switzerland	U.K.	U.S.
1988	I	35,284	239.31	128.21	7,714	48,785	72,420	17,648	19,181	74.86
	II	37,625	253.28	141.21	8,164	50,183	78,770	18,260	20,363	81.86
	III	33,352	234.08	138.86	8,917	49,996	67,600	17,714	20,127	79.08
	IV	38,542	270.99	159.46	9,133	54,765	85,400	20,331	21,806	85.80
1989	I	35,687	284.50	156.19	8,707	56,627	83,400	19,758	21,524	88.87
	II	37,130	293.73	165.25	9,290	58,333	87,600	21,763	22,962	93.80
	III	34,855	260.09	154.38	9,912	53,681	73,900	19,997	22,119	88.70
	IV	35,986	304.65	165.52	9,977	59,320	87,980	22,850	26,599	93.44
1990	I	37,354	308.11	168.88	9,768	60,017	88,090	22,577	25,158	97.37
	II	40,552	295.38	158.74	10,448	58,700	87,800	22,355	26,265	100.74
	III	36,602	265.66	151.90	10,652	56,598	74,100	20,591	24,155	93.88
	IV	39,114	306.75	163.14	10,592	63,606	90,240	22,737	28,054	101.91
1991	I	N/A	299.96	161.96	10,183	N/A	85,110	21,157	N/A	N/A

*The numbers for France, Germany, Japan, and the U.S. are expressed in billions of local currency units. The numbers for the remaining countries are expressed in millions of local currency units.

Imports by country*

Year	Quarter	Canada	France	Germany	Japan	Netherlands	Sweden	Switzerland	U.K.	U.S.
1972	I	4,512	33.58	30.56	1,667	13,767	9,492	7,772	2,717	14.09
	II	5,357	34.68	32.59	1,700	14,049	9,460	8,112	2,732	14.56
	III	4,650	30.15	30.39	1,808	13,273	8,883	7,840	2,550	14.33
	IV	5,428	37.60	34.60	2,055	15,150	10,783	8,593	3,156	15.89
1973	I	5,614	39.35	35.64	2,097	16,713	11,236	8,804	3,569	16.91
	II	6,467	41.79	36.39	2,488	16,591	10,800	8,811	3,723	18.32
	III	5,781	38.56	33.33	2,642	16,986	10,780	8,843	3,940	17.98
	IV	7,058	46.43	39.15	3,177	18,376	13,520	10,090	4,608	20.36
1974	I	7,300	59.89	40.89	4,061	21,209	16,200	10,815	5,332	22.65
	II	8,644	68.34	44.85	4,682	23,668	17,000	11,098	5,995	27.68
	III	8,389	61.58	45.44	4,565	23,067	18,850	10,564	5,762	28.49
	IV	9,471	64.36	46.80	4,758	23,168	19,804	10,434	6,028	29.18
1975	I	8,822	59.90	41.71	4,265	22,616	19,520	9,030	5,807	26.28
	II	9,879	57.30	46.24	4,171	22,073	19,002	8,735	5,813	24.73
	III	8,633	50.61	44.39	4,198	20,778	17,573	8,019	5,991	25.37
	IV	9,499	63.37	50.91	4,540	24,416	19,080	8,459	6,460	27.23
1976	I	9,689	70.29	51.96	4,488	24,771	20,000	8,560	6,847	29.34
	II	10,640	76.12	55.32	4,754	26,827	21,230	8,982	7,927	31.65
	III	9,273	73.45	55.28	4,894	25,487	20,010	9,131	7,874	33.73
	IV	10,124	88.25	59.61	5,093	30,157	24,060	10,201	8,923	34.84
1977	I	10,578	89.03	57.71	4,976	29,501	22,512	10,385	9,217	37.76
	II	12,153	88.94	58.56	4,921	28,868	22,221	10,828	9,766	39.73
	III	10,513	78.91	57.37	4,692	26,884	21,088	10,697	8,964	39.41
	IV	11,478	89.48	61.54	4,540	28,958	24,415	11,022	9,049	40.65
1978	I	11,276	93.96	58.60	4,349	28,640	22,043	10,517	9,791	43.14
	II	14,307	94.07	61.78	4,289	29,017	22,696	11,175	10,616	45.99
	III	12,330	82.02	58.58	3,898	27,870	21,319	9,896	9,995	46.02
1979	I	15,763	105.61	66.53	4,680	30,912	26,415	11,225	10,844	48.25
	II	16,743	111.85	71.66	5,579	33,545	29,750	11,698	12,136	53.23
	III	16,335	109.05	72.89	6,364	33,686	30,040	12,167	11,792	56.35
	IV	17,858	128.20	81.08	7,622	38,542	36,757	13,649	13,286	61.09

Imports by country* *(continued)*

Year	Quarter	Canada	France	Germany	Japan	Netherlands	Sweden	Switzerland	U.K.	U.S.
1980	I	18,067	144.89	86.06	8,043	40,073	36,801	5,590	14,257	65.17
	II	19,031	143.80	85.86	8,655	38,732	32,992	5,086	13,416	64.02
	III	16,678	120.52	81.42	7,588	36,164	34,633	4,691	12,042	59.99
	IV	19,281	150.78	88.04	7,708	40,211	36,210	5,516	11,934	63.82
1981	I	19,931	155.81	91.39	7,528	40,510	34,100	4,568	11,030	68.00
	II	23,170	161.42	90.64	7,904	43,783	34,000	5,081	12,073	69.82
	III	20,389	155.99	91.70	7,847	41,016	34,603	5,198	13,686	66.75
	IV	20,681	181.64	95.50	8,184	43,176	43,015	5,246	14,380	68.78
1982	I	18,693	183.43	96.46	8,307	41,612	40,037	4,160	14,207	64.40
	II	18,331	191.61	95.04	8,008	43,207	39,799	4,696	14,816	63.23
	III	18,481	179.47	89.69	8,021	41,633	40,245	3,943	13,699	65.70
	IV	16,483	203.84	95.28	8,321	45,096	53,851	5,316	14,236	61.55
1983	I	17,941	202.62	93.68	7,413	42,317	48,017	6,497	16,219	60.71
	II	20,245	201.52	95.91	7,213	42,656	47,102	5,471	16,636	66.36
	III	19,698	181.21	95.09	7,307	43,749	47,836	4,700	16,005	69.46
	IV	22,306	214.65	105.52	8,082	48,598	57,391	4,608	17,133	73.35
1984	I	24,194	231.02	108.74	7,999	50,088	53,152	7,318	18,458	82.92
	II	26,744	222.08	106.46	7,872	49,253	53,507	6,949	19,534	84.54
	III	25,354	203.84	105.85	8,211	48,074	50,578	6,778	19,044	90.77
	IV	25,259	243.17	113.16	8,231	52,188	60,400	8,105	21,511	82.95
1985	I	25,505	253.38	120.20	8,335	57,101	62,136	8,425	23,031	87.52
	II	28,804	246.80	115.53	8,097	53,851	62,032	9,277	21,868	92.22
	III	27,334	220.10.	133.23	7,532	52,013	57,028	8,058	19,435	88.68
	IV	28,487	246.86	114.86	7,112	52,502	63,413	9,005	20,267	93.21
1986	I	28,450	231.54	108.05	6,335	49,342	55,444	8,339	20,476	97.13
	II	31,310	235.23	106.98	5,398	46,402	59,197	9,238	21,485	94.91
	III	28,876	204.79	96.55	4,758	42,627	54,181	7,812	21,020	96.75
	IV	29,549	224.34	102.63	5,060	46,420	63,661	8,150	23,194	98.29
1987	I	29,411	232.77	99.48	4,959	45,963	60,981	7,979	22,243	97.11
	II	31,314	238.08	101.58	5,207	44,295	62,823	8,769	23,051	105.12
	III	29,366	220.08	99.54	5,644	44,947	60,729	8,260	23,543	108.45
	IV	32,803	258.85	108.87	5,929	48,933	73,067	20,253	25,178	113.40

Imports by country* *(continued)*

Year	Quarter	Canada	France	Germany	Japan	Netherlands	Sweden	Switzerland	U.K.	U.S.
1988	I	37,304	258.96	103.02	5,688	46,969	67,310	19,378	24,814	110.00
	II	35,001	266.97	107.19	5,918	49,311	68,891	20,493	26,322	114.34
	III	32,054	248.45	107.21	6,280	48,318	65,400	20,572	26,752	114.39
	IV	33,796	288.78	122.34	6,121	51,751	77,660	22,162	28,525	120.55
1989	I	35,623	306.24	120.17	6,516	53,560	75,450	22,291	28,631	117.29
	II	38,352	319.52	130.97	6,969	57,133	80,000	25,082	30,868	124.22
	III	34,547	277.38	120.11	7,542	52,319	68,500	22,749	30,194	123.62
	IV	34,946	327.68	135.40	7,912	57,717	87,280	25,078	31,080	127.18
1990	I	36,637	328.45	132.01	7,941	57,721	81,730	25,390	32,115	124.89
	II	37,745	318.38	130.87	8,391	57,599	78,900	24,947	32,672	124.14
	III	33,078	293.34	132.76	8,364	54,937	73,400	22,640	29,940	129.92
	IV	38,597	333.38	154.93	9,158	58,767	87,320	23,635	30,451	137.20
1991	I	N/A	331.24	156.74	8,243	N/A	74,870	23,477	N/A	N/A

*The numbers for France, Germany, Japan, and the U.S. are expressed in billions of local home currency units. The numbers for the remaining countries are expressed in millions of local currency units.

Industrial share price index (1980 = 100)

Year	Quarter	Canada	France	Germany	Japan	Netherlands	Sweden	Switzerland	U.K.	U.S.
1972	I	53.4	48.3	104.4	45.7	136.8	71.0	125.9	72.6	86.9
	II	55.4	54.5	114.3	54.3	157.7	74.0	131.1	76.4	89.8
	III	58.8	58.2	113.8	64.4	171.7	76.0	132.0	76.0	90.9
	IV	60.8	56.5	110.2	73.9	171.7	76.0	131.6	74.7	94.6
1973	I	64.7	64.5	116.6	83.2	189.8	77.0	131.6	69.1	95.8
	II	61.6	70.0	111.7	76.3	169.2	80.0	122.1	67.9	89.4
	III	64.4	65.7	99.1	77.5	173.1	78.0	115.7	63.3	87.7
	IV	65.0	62.5	93.8	68.9	152.2	76.0	112.8	58.6	85.4
1974	I	63.3	74.0	91.9	67.5	145.1	84.0	107.6	49.0	79.3
	II	56.9	62.9	92.7	70.1	136.1	85.0	97.0	43.9	76.0
	III	49.6	55.0	85.8	64.2	132.6	80.0	87.2	33.5	63.3
	IV	43.3	51.6	82.0	57.5	114.4	77.0	73.2	26.1	57.7
1975	I	48.2	68.5	94.3	62.5	150.4	82.0	81.2	37.1	65.3
	II	51.5	65.6	100.1	68.8	157.9	86.0	85.3	49.3	74.3
	III	52.0	65.7	98.5	65.5	148.9	89.0	79.3	48.5	73.1
	IV	47.7	68.6	104.3	66.1	141.4	93.0	81.7	55.5	74.2
1976	I	53.2	72.5	94.3	71.4	156.4	99.0	91.3	61.1	83.1
	II	54.8	68.1	100.1	72.3	150.4	109.0	90.0	61.1	85.0
	III	52.5	63.7	98.5	74.6	136.8	103.0	92.2	56.1	86.9
	IV	47.0	55.4	104.3	74.7	127.8	92.0	88.1	49.8	85.1
1977	I	48.4	53.9	112.7	79.9	129.3	96.0	93.2	63.1	84.0
	II	47.4	48.6	108.0	79.4	136.8	94.0	95.3	70.3	81.3
	III	46.3	51.8	103.2	80.4	127.8	83.0	96.2	77.7	80.1
	IV	43.7	54.1	97.5	78.1	121.8	78.0	95.8	81.4	76.8
1978	I	44.5	52.4	99.4	81.2	123.3	88.0	95.0	77.0	73.1
	II	47.8	65.7	105.4	86.6	127.8	93.0	92.0	80.0	78.7
	III	53.9	76.6	104.9	89.3	136.8	98.0	90.7	87.0	63.6
	IV	56.3	77.6	106.2	93.0	129.3	92.0	88.7	85.7	80.2
1979	I	63.1	76.7	111.3	95.6	126.3	96.0	104.6	89.1	82.1
	II	69.4	82.0	106.2	94.4	116.8	90.0	106.3	100.9	83.8
	III	77.8	93.8	103.9	94.8	116.2	90.0	106.4	94.3	87.6
	IV	82.7	92.7	100.9	94.9	107.7	90.0	104.8	90.2	87.7

Industrial share price index (1980 = 100) (continued)

Year	Quarter	Canada	France	Germany	Japan	Netherlands	Sweden	Switzerland	U.K.	U.S.
1980	I	100.4	98.2	100.2	97.7	100.6	96.0	104.4	93.3	92.7
	II	96.4	97.4	99.5	98.1	100.5	97.0	100.1	93.8	90.4
	III	103.6	99.0	101.4	100.2	100.6	97.0	97.1	104.0	103.8
	IV	99.6	105.4	99.0	103.9	98.2	109.0	98.4	109.1	112.9
1981	I	103.0	99.0	96.4	107.4	102.6	123.0	94.9	107.5	111.0
	II	104.4	84.3	103.0	117.4	111.9	139.0	93.2	117.7	111.5
	III	93.2	86.0	104.2	123.1	110.8	159.0	90.9	115.7	105.0
	IV	88.9	82.9	98.1	117.4	98.4	175.0	84.9	110.2	101.4
1982	I	78.6	75.6	99.0	118.1	106.4	173.0	86.2	119.3	94.5
	II	68.2	77.5	99.0	114.7	111.7	166.0	89.6	125.2	94.5
	III	71.9	72.0	96.2	111.5	106.2	179.0	87.4	131.0	94.6
	IV	88.3	74.2	101.6	118.9	119.8	222.0	95.5	147.2	113.5
1983	I	101.2	82.9	113.2	124.9	149.1	309.0	107.8	153.1	123.3
	II	114.9	96.5	133.9	133.3	164.5	346.0	113.7	166.2	135.9
	III	114.8	107.3	139.4	141.7	175.3	384.0	116.3	170.6	138.8
	IV	114.7	117.3	147.7	146.1	181.7	397.0	125.8	169.9	138.8
1984	I	111.8	131.8	152.6	164.9	210.0	430.0	131.9	187.6	134.4
	II	103.3	137.5	148.6	173.3	198.0	399.0	131.0	194.7	131.4
	III	106.6	134.7	144.5	168.4	200.8	386.0	131.5	190.7	135.4
	IV	114.5	141.5	155.8	181.7	219.0	355.0	136.1	211.8	137.7
1985	I	126.7	173.2	170.5	201.3	247.2	365	155.8	235.2	147.2
	II	129.6	188.5	185.9	208.6	266.4	350	162.9	239.9	152.2
	III	131.1	178.8	202.6	215.3	293.9	349	173.1	237.3	155.5
	IV	134.4	187.5	240.7	215.6	325.8	404	195.4	256.5	162.9
1986	I	140.8	234.1	273	229.5	383.9	483	218	280.4	180.5
	II	148.7	284.5	273.3	269.1	415.4	592	212.2	308.4	199.4
	III	140.6	294.5	261.7	309.0	453.6	643	197.3	304.5	198.2
	IV	145.3	309.3	273.5	309.4	437.9	678	209.8	308.8	201.3
1987	I	166.4	331.0	246.6	368.6	395.6	650	206.9	366.1	235.1
	II	174.8	344.8	257.1	447.3	401.3	740	211.5	415.1	253
	III	186.5	350.2	278.9	434.7	496.1	834	245.5	452.9	277.5
	IV	144.4	257.7	213.6	401.0	363.5	637	202.5	353	218.3

Industrial share price index (1980 = 100) (continued)

Year	Quarter	Canada	France	Germany	Japan	Netherlands	Sweden	Switzerland	U.K.	U.S.
1988	I	149.7	234.2	188.4	416.3	366.2	710.6	191 8	350.1	221.2
	II	156.8	266.1	199.0	458.4	393.9	776.9	197 5	357.4	226.9
	III	155.4	299.1	214.4	456.7	419.8	817.4	209.7	363.9	228.3
	IV	157.6	337.3	230.4	467.0	423.4	902.1	219.0	358.6	235.4
1989	I	168.3	384.3	244.4	514.9	465.7	1012.6	227.6	396.7	249.7
	II	173.5	407.4	257.6	524.6	499.2	1089.9	241.2	420.9	267.6
	III	186.4	432.5	280.0	546.9	537.0	1215.1	271.9	457.2	290.8
	IV	185.0	428.1	282.2	580.3	523.7	1119.4	258.9	433.2	293.2
1990	I	172.5	N/A	332.2	551.0	513.6	1093.2	250.6	438.0	288.3
	II	163.6	451.0	335.4	485.2	521.7	1148.4	257.1	428.3	303.1
	III	157.3	386.9	300.4	434.2	497.5	1041.7	231.7	416.0	294.7
	IV	148.3	346.8	254.2	368.0	448.5	806.1	206.4	N/A	276.4
1991	I	159.9	362.3	256.0	389.9	468.9	968.1	227.5	N/A	310.3

Percentage change in industrial share prices

Year	Quarter	Canada	France	Germany	Japan	Netherlands	Sweden	Switzerland	U.K.	U.S.
1972	I	N/A	N/A	N/A	N/A	N/A	N/A	N/A	N/A	N/A
	II	3.75	12.84	9.48	18.82	15.28	4.23	4.13	5.23	3.34
	III	6.14	6.79	-.44	18.60	8.88	2.70	.69	-.52	1.22
	IV	3.40	-2.92	-3.16	14.75	.00	.00	-.30	-1.71	4.07
1973	I	6.41	14.16	5.81	12.58	10.54	1.32	.00	-7.50	1.27
	II	-4.79	8.53	-4.20	-8.29	-10.85	3.90	-7.22	-1.74	-6.68
	III	4.55	-6.14	-11.28	1.57	2.30	-2.50	-5.24	-6.77	-1.90
	IV	.93	-4.87	-5.35	-11.10	-12.07	-2.56	-2.51	-7.42	-2.62
1974	I	-2.62	18.40	-2.03	-2.03	-4.66	10.53	-4.61	-16.38	-7.14
	II	-10.11	-15.00	.87	3.85	-6.20	1.19	-9.85	-10.41	-4.16
	III	-12.83	-12.56	-7.44	-8.42	-2.57	-5.88	-10.10	-23.69	-16.71
	IV	-12.70	-6.18	-4.43	10.44	-13.73	-3.75	-16.06	-22.09	-8.85
1975	I	11.32	32.75	15.00	8.70	31.47	6.49	10.93	42.15	13.17
	II	6.85	-4.23	6.15	10.08	4.99	4.88	5.05	32.88	13.78
	III	.97	.15	-1.60	-4.80	-5.70	3.49	-7.03	-1.62	-1.62
	IV	-8.27	4.41	5.89	.92	-5.04	4.49	3.03	14.43	1.50
1976	I	11.53	5.69	-9.59	8.02	10.61	6.45	11.75	10.09	11.99
	II	3.01	-6.07	6.15	1.26	-3.84	10.10	-1.42	.00	2.29
	III	-4.20	-6.46	-1.60	3.18	-9.04	-5.50	2.44	-8.18	2.24
	IV	-10.48	-13.03	5.89	.13	-6.58	-10.68	-4.45	-11.23	-2.07
1977	I	2.98	-2.71	8.05	6.96	1.17	4.35	5.79	26.71	-1.29
	II	-2.07	-9.83	-4.17	-.63	5.80	-2.08	2.25	11.41	-3.21
	III	-2.32	6.58	-4.44	1.26	-6.58	-11.70	.94	10.53	-1.48
	IV	-5.62	4.44	-5.52	-2.86	-4.69	-6.02	-.42	4.76	-4.12
1978	I	1.83	-3.14	1.95	3.97	1.23	12.82	-.84	-5.41	-4.82
	II	7.42	25.38	6.04	6.65	3.65	5.68	-3.16	3.90	7.66
	III	12.76	16.59	-.47	3.12	7.04	5.38	-1.41	8.75	6.23
	IV	4.45	1.31	1.24	4.14	-5.48	-6.12	-2.21	-1.49	-4.07
1979	I	12.08	-1.16	4.80	2.80	-2.32	4.35	17.93	3.97	2.37
	II	9.98	6.91	-4.58	-1.26	-7.52	-6.25	1.63	13.24	2.07
	III	12.10	14.39	-2.17	.42	-.51	.00	.09	-6.54	4.53
	IV	6.30	-1.17	-2.89	.11	-7.31	.00	-1.50	-4.35	.11

Percentage change in industrial share prices (*continued*)

Year	Quarter	Canada	France	Germany	Japan	Netherlands	Sweden	Switzerland	U.K.	U.S.
1980	I	21.40	5.93	−.69	−2.95	−6.59	6.67	−.38	3.44	5.70
	II	−3.98	−.81	−.70	.41	−.10	1.04	−4.12	.54	−2.48
	III	7.47	1.64	1.91	2.14	.10	.00	−3.00	10.87	14.82
	IV	−3.86	6.46	−2.37	3.69	−2.39	12.37	1.34	4.90	8.77
1981	I	3.41	−6.07	−2.63	3.37	4.48	12.84	−3.56	−1.47	−1.68
	II	1.36	−14.85	6.85	9.31	9.06	13.01	−1.79	9.49	.45
	III	−10.37	2.02	1.17	4.86	−.98	14.39	−2.47	−1.70	−5.83
	IV	−4.61	−3.60	−5.85	−4.63	−11.19	10.06	−6.60	−4.75	−3.43
1982	I	−11.59	−8.81	.92	.60	8.13	−1.14	1.53	8.26	−6.80
	II	−13.23	2.51	.00	−2.88	4.98	−4.05	3.94	4.95	.00
	III	5.43	−7.10	−2.83	−2.79	−4.92	7.83	−2.46	4.63	.11
	IV	−22.81	3.06	5.61	6.64	12.81	24.02	9.27	12.37	19.98
1983	I	14.61	11.73	11.42	5.05	24.46	39.19	12.88	4.01	8.63
	II	13.54	16.41	18.29	6.73	10.33	11.97	5.47	8.56	10.22
	III	−.09	11.19	4.11	6.30	6.57	10.98	2.29	2.65	2.13
	IV	−.09	9.32	5.95	3.11	3.65	3.39	8.17	−.41	.00
1984	I	−2.53	12.36	3.32	12.87	15.58	8.31	4.85	10.42	−3.17
	II	−7.60	4.42	−2.62	5.09	−5.71	−7.21	−.68	3.78	−2.23
	III	3.19	−2.04	−2.76	−2.83	1.41	−3.26	.38	−2.05	3.04
	IV	7.41	5.05	7.82	7.60	9.06	−8.03	3.50	11.06	1.70
1985	I	10.66	22.40	9.44	10.79	12.88	2.53	14.48	11.05	6.90
	II	2.29	8.83	9.03	9.03	7.77	−4.11	4.56	1.99	3.40
	III	1.16	5.15	8.98	8.98	10.32	−.29	6.26	−1.08	2.17
	IV	2.52	4.87	18.81	.14	10.85	15.76	12.88	8.09	4.76
1986	I	4.76	24.85	13.42	6.45	17.83	19.56	11.77	9.32	10.80
	II	5.61	21.19	.11	17.26	8.21	22.57	−.26	9.99	10.80
	III	−5.76	3.51	−4.24	14.83	9.20	8.62	−.70	−1.27	−.60
	IV	3.34	5.03	4.51	.13	−3.46	5.44	6.34	1.41	1.56
1987	I	−14.52	7.02	−9.84	19.13	−9.66	−4.13	−1.38	18.56	16.79
	II	5.05	4.17	4.26	21.35	1.44	13.85	−2.19	13.38	7.61
	III	6.69	1.57	8.48	−2.82	23.62	12.70	16.08	9.11	9.68
	IV	−22.57	−26.41	−23.41	−7.75	−26.73	−23.62	−17.52	−22.06	−21.33

Percentage change in industrial share prices (*continued*)

Year	Quarter	Canada	France	Germany	Japan	Netherlands	Sweden	Switzerland	U.K.	U.S.
1988	I	3.67	−9.12	−11.80	3.82	0.74	11.55	−5.28	−0.82	1.33
	II	4.74	13.62	5.63	10.11	7.56	9.33	2.97	2.09	2.58
	III	−.89	12.40	7.74	−0.37	6.58	5.21	6.18	1.82	0.62
	IV	1.41	12.77	7.46	2.26	0.86	10.36	4.43	−1.46	3.11
1989	I	6.78	13.93	6.08	10.26	9.99	12.25	3.93	10.87	6.07
	II	3.09	6.01	5.40	1.88	7.19	7.63	5.98	10.61	7.17
	III	7.37	6.16	8.70	4.25	7.57	11.49	12.73	8.62	8.67
	IV	−.75	−1.02	0.79	6.11	−2.48	−7.88	−4.78	−5.24	0.83
1990	I	−6.75	N/A	18.07	−5.05	−1.92	−2.32	−3.20	1.11	−1.67
	II	−5.16	N/A	.96	−11.94	1.58	5.05	2.59	−2.21	5.13
	III	−3.85	−14.21	−10.43	−10.47	−4.63	−9.29	−9.88	−2.87	−2.77
	IV	−5.72	−10.36	−15.38	−15.20	−9.84	−22.62	−10.92	N/A	−6.21
1991	I	7.82	4.46	.79	5.95	4.55	20.10	10.22	N/A	12.26

Exchange rates* (end of period)

Year	Quarter	Canadian Dollar	French Franc	German Mark	Japanese Yen	Netherlands Guilder	Swedish Kronor	Swiss Franc	British Pound
1972	I	1.0031	.1920	.3157	.003287	.3131	.2094	.2604	2.6158
	II	1.0149	.1999	.3169	.003321	.3152	.2122	.2650	2.4440
	III	1.0169	.1995	.3123	.003321	.3090	.2108	.2631	2.4203
	IV	1.0044	.1951	.3123	.003311	.3100	.2108	.2650	2.3481
1973	I	1.0010	.2202	.3524	.003762	.3397	.2226	.3089	2.4777
	II	1.0016	.2436	.4124	.003769	.3817	.2445	.3378	2.5820
	III	.9942	.2353	.4132	.003764	.3945	.2380	.3309	2.4135
	IV	1.0046	.2124	.3700	.003571	.3541	.2180	.3083	2.3232
1974	I	1.0284	.2099	.3964	.003623	.3724	.2277	.3333	2.3940
	II	1.0286	.2073	.3914	.003520	.3771	.2283	.3336	2.3905
	III	1.0144	.2109	.3769	.003350	.3698	.2242	.3394	2.3323
	IV	1.0089	.2250	.4150	.003323	.3990	.2451	.3937	2.3485
1975	I	.9968	.2372	.4264	.003404	.4176	.2537	.3956	2.4090
	II	.9703	.2475	.4247	.003374	.4098	.2538	.3996	2.1980
	III	.9754	.2205	.3757	.003304	.3655	.2218	.3640	2.0409
	IV	.9839	.2229	.3813	.003277	.3720	.2230	.3817	2.0235
1976	I	1.0161	.2142	.3940	.003337	.3722	.2272	.3946	1.9157
	II	1.0324	.2110	.3885	.003362	.3656	.2247	.4044	1.7813
	III	1.0275	.2030	.4104	.003479	.3893	.2335	.4075	1.6775
	IV	.9909	.2012	.4233	.003415	.4070	.2423	.4081	1.7024
1977	I	.9463	.2012	.4186	.003604	.4013	.2332	.3933	1.7201
	II	.9435	.2033	.4277	.003736	.4044	.2274	.4064	1.7202
	III	.9316	.2039	.4334	.003767	.4071	.2059	.4276	1.7465
	IV	.9137	.2125	.4751	.004167	.4386	.2142	.5000	1.9060
1978	I	.8832	.2183	.4943	.004496	.4622	.2179	.5352	1.8563
	II	.8893	.2221	.4819	.004885	.4479	.2136	.5381	1.8602
	III	.8452	.2309	.5158	.005287	.4747	.2271	.6481	1.9721
	IV	.8432	.2392	.5470	.005139	.5079	.2328	.6173	2.0345
1979	I	.8616	.2327	.5354	.004778	.4965	.2288	.5914	2.0688
	II	.8563	.2334	.5411	.004608	.4926	.2337	.6020	2.1684
	III	.8616	.2439	.5739	.004478	.5177	.2422	.6521	2.1976
	IV	.8561	.2488	.5775	.004172	.5248	.2412	.6329	2.2240

Exchange rates* (end of period) *(continued)*

Year	Quarter	Canadian Dollar	French Franc	German Mark	Japanese Yen	Netherlands Guilder	Swedish Kronor	Swiss Franc	British Pound
1980	I	.8393	.2233	.5150	.004005	.4701	.2244	.5459	2.1668
	II	.8688	.2447	.5688	.004596	.5188	.2409	.6167	2.3620
	III	.8543	.2381	.5521	.004713	.5088	.2402	.6066	2.3883
	IV	.8370	.2214	.5105	.004926	.4696	.2287	.5679	2.3850
1981	I	.8426	.2017	.4758	.004739	.4296	.2177	.5229	2.2442
	II	.8330	.1749	.4183	.004429	.3757	.1967	.4927	1.9428
	III	.8286	.1796	.4306	.004297	.3873	.1786	.5072	1.8005
	IV	.8432	.1740	.4435	.004548	.4051	.1795	.5560	1.9080
1982	I	.8128	.1602	.4142	.004057	.3735	.1680	.5170	1.7817
	II	.7734	.1464	.4065	.003937	.3676	.1641	.4754	1.7383
	III	.8089	.1401	.3956	.003711	.3618	.1590	.4613	1.6927
	IV	.8134	.1487	.4208	.004255	.3810	.1371	.5014	1.6145
1983	I	.8104	.1376	.4121	.004177	.3658	.1332	.4804	1.4790
	II	.8148	.1309	.3934	.004172	.3511	.1308	.4752	1.5304
	III	.8115	.1249	.3789	.004235	.3390	.1278	.4695	1.4957
	IV	.8036	.1198	.3671	.004307	.3263	.1250	.4588	1.4506
1984	I	.7835	.1253	.3861	.004450	.3423	.1296	.4644	1.4426
	II	.7579	.1170	.3592	.004211	.3171	.1222	.4291	1.3527
	III	.7587	.1077	.3305	.004073	.2933	.1165	.4003	1.2480
	IV	.7568	.1043	.3177	.003982	.2817	.1112	.3868	1.1565
1985	I	.7315	.1061	.3233	.003960	.2872	.1125	.3820	1.2430
	II	.7360	.1073	.3267	.004017	.2902	.1136	.3904	1.2952
	III	.7294	.1227	.3746	.004608	.3315	.1240	.4585	1.4010
	IV	.7156	.1323	.4063	.004988	.3608	.1313	.4816	1.4445
1986	I	.7157	.1402	.4315	.005568	.3827	.1366	.5155	1.485
	II	.7211	.1426	.4548	.006061	.4040	.1405	.5569	1.5302
	III	.7202	.1510	.4949	.006510	.4377	.1449	.6104	1.4500
	IV	.7244	.1549	.5153	.006285	.4562	.1467	.6160	1.4745
1987	I	.7662	.1663	.5540	.006859	.4907	.1581	.6640	1.6049
	II	.7512	.1638	.5465	.006802	.4857	.1565	.6579	1.6101
	III	.7639	.1635	.5440	.006833	.4838	.1553	.6540	1.6297
	IV	.8131	.1873	.6309	.008097	.5626	.1709	.7825	1.8716

Exchange rates* (end of period) (*continued*)

Year	Quarter	Canadian Dollar	French Franc	German Mark	Japanese Yen	Netherlands Guilder	Swedish Kronor	Swiss Franc	British Pound
1988	I	.8103	.1778	.6027	.007970	.5368	.1701	.735	1.8798
	II	.8246	.1628	.5491	.007550	.4866	.1599	.6625	1.7093
	III	.8216	.1564	.5320	.007430	.4721	.1554	.6291	1.6855
	IV	.8384	.1650	.5617	.007950	.5001	.1624	.6649	1.8095
1989	I	.8381	.1564	.5283	.007570	.4684	.1557	.6024	1.6888
	II	.8345	.1507	.5122	.006940	.4541	.1534	.5977	1.5502
	III	.8487	.1578	.5352	.007180	.4739	.1550	.6180	1.6252
	IV	.8632	.1727	.5889	.006971	.5220	.1635	.6468	1.6055
1990	I	.8545	.1755	.5903	.006361	.5241	.1632	.6684	1.6428
	II	.8575	.1782	.5980	.006540	.5319	.1656	.7057	1.7418
	III	.8666	.1915	.6411	.007345	.5691	.1739	.7716	1.8812
	IV	.8625	.1962	.6685	.007417	.5937	.1772	.7832	1.9255
1991	I	.8635	.1759	.5951	.007153	.5283	.1641	.6967	1.7616
	II	.8763	.1645	.5584	.007237	.4958	.1540	.6519	1.6351

*Value in U.S. dollars.

Exchange rate percentage change

Year	Quarter	Canadian Dollar	French Franc	German Mark	Japanese Yen	Netherlands Guilder	Swedish Kronor	Swiss Franc	British Pound
1972	I	N/A	N/A	N/A	N/A	N/A	N/A	N/A	N/A
	II	1.18	4.12	.38	1.03	.66	1.36	1.75	-6.57
	III	.19	-.20	-1.44	.00	-1.95	.67	-.71	-.97
	IV	-1.23	2.20	.00	-.30	.31	.03	.72	-2.98
1973	I	-.34	12.86	12.83	13.61	9.58	5.56	16.59	5.52
	II	.06	10.62	17.03	.20	12.37	9.86	9.36	4.21
	III	-.74	-3.41	.21	-.15	3.35	-2.67	-2.05	-6.53
	IV	1.04	-9.73	-10.47	-5.11	-10.23	-8.40	-6.84	-3.74
1974	I	2.37	-1.18	7.13	1.45	5.18	4.44	8.13	3.05
	II	.02	-1.22	-1.25	-2.85	1.24	.29	.07	-.15
	III	-1.38	1.73	-3.69	-4.82	-1.92	-1.79	1.77	-2.43
	IV	-.54	6.67	10.11	-.81	7.88	9.30	15.98	.69
1975	I	-1.20	5.43	2.75	2.43	4.68	3.51	.49	2.58
	II	-2.66	4.34	-.42	-.86	-1.86	.06	1.00	-8.76
	III	.53	-10.93	-11.52	-2.10	-10.02	-12.01	-8.92	-7.15
	IV	.87	1.12	1.49	-.80	1.77	2.79	4.87	-.85
1976	I	3.27	-3.93	3.31	1.82	.07	-.34	3.39	-5.33
	II	1.61	-1.50	-1.39	.77	-1.79	-1.14	2.47	-7.02
	III	-.47	-3.79	5.65	3.46	6.50	3.93	.77	-5.83
	IV	-3.57	-.86	3.13	-1.83	4.54	3.79	.15	1.48
1977	I	-4.50	.01	-1.10	5.51	-1.40	-1.70	-3.62	1.04
	II	-.29	1.02	2.17	3.66	.79	-4.56	3.32	.01
	III	-1.26	.33	1.33	.85	.65	-8.98	5.23	1.53
	IV	-1.92	4.21	9.62	10.60	7.74	3.50	16.92	9.13
1978	I	-3.34	2.72	4.05	7.91	5.38	1.76	7.04	-2.61
	II	.68	1.75	-2.52	8.65	-3.09	.29	.55	.21
	III	-4.95	3.94	7.05	8.22	5.98	3.89	20.43	6.02
	IV	-.24	3.61	6.05	-2.80	6.98	2.53	-4.75	3.16
1979	I	2.19	-2.72	-2.12	-7.02	-2.23	-1.74	-4.20	1.69
	II	-.62	.28	1.05	-3.55	-.79	2.15	1.79	4.81
	III	.62	4.50	6.07	-2.82	5.10	3.65	8.33	1.35
	IV	-.64	2.00	.64	-6.84	1.36	-.42	-2.94	1.20

Exchange rate percentage change (*continued*)

Year	Quarter	Canadian Dollar	French Franc	German Mark	Japanese Yen	Netherlands Guilder	Swedish Kronor	Swiss Franc	British Pound
1980	I	-1.96	-10.24	-10.83	-4.00	-10.41	-6.96	-13.76	-2.57
	II	3.51	9.58	10.45	14.75	10.35	7.39	12.98	9.01
	III	-1.67	-2.68	-2.93	2.54	-1.93	-.31	-1.64	1.11
	IV	-2.03	-7.01	-7.54	4.53	-7.70	-4.79	-6.39	-.14
1981	I	.67	-8.91	-6.79	-8.79	-8.53	-4.78	-7.92	-5.90
	II	-1.14	-13.28	-12.09	-6.55	-12.55	-9.69	-5.78	-13.43
	III	-.52	2.70	2.95	-2.97	3.10	-9.16	2.96	-7.32
	IV	1.76	-3.15	3.00	5.82	4.60	-.48	9.62	5.97
1982	I	-3.61	-7.91	-6.60	-10.79	-7.81	-6.39	-7.02	-6.62
	II	-4.85	-8.60	-1.85	-2.95	-1.56	-2.31	-8.05	-2.44
	III	4.59	-4.33	-2.68	-5.75	-1.59	-3.16	-2.96	-2.62
	IV	.56	6.14	6.35	14.68	5.32	-13.76	8.68	-4.62
1983	I	-.36	-7.49	-2.06	-1.84	-3.99	-2.86	-4.19	-8.39
	II	.54	-4.82	-4.54	-.13	-4.04	-1.75	-1.08	3.48
	III	-.41	-4.64	-3.68	1.52	-3.44	-2.29	-1.18	-2.27
	IV	-.97	-4.06	-3.11	1.68	-3.74	-2.24	-2.28	-3.02
1984	I	-2.51	4.61	5.17	3.34	4.91	3.69	1.22	-.55
	II	-3.26	-6.61	-6.98	-5.39	-7.37	-5.72	-7.60	-6.23
	III	.11	-7.97	-7.97	-3.26	-7.52	-4.65	-6.72	-7.74
	IV	-.26	-3.21	-3.90	-2.23	-3.93	-4.52	-3.37	-7.33
1985	I	-3.34	1.73	1.76	-.55	1.96	1.16	-1.24	7.47
	II	.90	1.31	1.05	1.43	1.04	.97	2.20	4.20
	III	-.89	14.35	14.66	14.71	15.42	9.15	17.44	8.17
	IV	-1.89	7.82	8.46	8.24	8.83	5.89	5.04	3.11
1986	I	.01	5.97	6.20	11.62	6.07	4.04	7.04	2.80
	II	.77	1.71	5.39	8.85	5.56	2.85	8.03	3.04
	III	-.12	5.89	8.82	7.40	8.34	3.14	9.61	-5.24
	IV	.58	2.58	4.12	-3.45	4.22	1.24	.91	1.69
1987	I	5.77	7.35	7.51	9.13	7.56	7.77	7.79	8.85
	II	-1.95	-1.50	-1.35	-.83	-1.01	-1.01	-.91	.32
	III	1.69	-.18	-.18	.45	-.39	-.76	-.59	1.21
	IV	6.44	14.55	15.97	18.49	16.28	10.04	18.74	14.84

Exchange rate percentage change (continued)

Year	Quarter	Canadian Dollar	French Franc	German Mark	Japanese Yen	Netherlands Guilder	Swedish Kronor	Swiss Franc	British Pound
1988	I	-.34	6.28	-4.47	-1.57	-4.59	-.47	-6.07	.44
	II	1.76	-8.44	-8.89	-5.27	-9.35	-6.00	-9.86	-9.07
	III	-.36	-3.93	-3.11	-1.59	-2.98	-2.81	-5.04	-1.39
	IV	2.04	5.50	5.58	7.00	5.93	4.50	5.69	7.36
1989	I	-.04	-5.21	-5.95	-4.78	-6.34	-4.13	-9.40	-6.67
	II	-.43	-3.64	-3.05	-8.32	-3.05	-3.40	-0.78	-8.21
	III	1.70	4.71	4.49	3.46	4.36	3.72	3.40	4.84
	IV	1.70	9.44	10.00	-2.91	10.10	2.88	4.66	-1.21
1990	I	-1.00	1.62	.24	-8.75	.40	1.68	3.33	2.32
	II	.35	1.54	1.30	2.81	1.49	1.47	5.58	6.03
	III	1.06	7.46	7.19	12.31	6.99	5.01	9.34	8.00
	IV	-.47	2.45	4.27	.98	11.62	1.90	1.50	2.35
1991	I	.11	-10.34	-10.98	-3.56	-11.01	-7.39	-11.04	-8.51
	II	1.48	-6.48	-6.17	1.17	-11.83	-6.15	-6.43	-7.18

3-month forward rates* (End of period)

Year	Quarter	Canadian Dollar	French Franc	German Mark	Japanese Yen	Swiss Franc	British Pound
1974	I	1.02988	.20291	.38091	.00337	.32405	2.28820
	II	1.03664	.20220	.39952	.00354	.33662	2.36880
	III	1.01683	.20578	.37924	.00335	.33547	2.30390
	IV	1.01254	.21512	.40999	.00331	.38468	2.29310
1975	I	1.00114	.23667	.43365	.00348	.40639	2.38490
	II	.97177	.24794	.42918	.00341	.40363	2.25620
	III	.97099	.22339	.38559	.00332	.37337	2.06610
	IV	.97969	.22419	.38410	.00326	.38286	1.99820
1976	I	1.00352	.21290	.39296	.00333	.39390	1.92380
	II	1.01881	.20908	.39041	.00334	.41061	1.73480
	III	1.01535	.20081	.40249	.00348	.40861	1.69330
	IV	.97291	.19712	.41990	.00338	.41148	1.63680
1977	I	.94541	.19798	.41886	.00356	.39409	1.68960
	II	.94238	.20043	.42686	.00366	.40390	1.70150
	III	.93011	.20159	.43343	.00376	.42551	1.74310
	IV	.91073	.20548	.46913	.00419	.48834	1.85690
1978	I	.88793	.21054	.49697	.00439	.53703	1.90550
	II	.89181	.21751	.48608	.00474	.54011	1.82210
	III	.85806	.22938	.51453	.00535	.65022	1.94260
	IV	.84996	.23346	.54363	.00524	.61573	1.97920
1979	I	.85112	.23493	.54643	.00492	.61134	2.03110
	II	.85194	.22891	.53683	.00463	.60218	2.09760
	III	.85949	.23824	.56528	.00457	.63809	2.18470
	IV	.85643	.24650	.58508	.00423	.64019	2.19070
1980	I	.86201	.23467	.55399	.00407	.58561	2.20940
	II	.86379	.24152	.56619	.00457	.61884	2.29730
	III	.86166	.24050	.56375	.00467	.62060	2.38130
	IV	.84208	.22351	.52037	.00490	.57966	2.37470
1981	I	.83674	.20294	.47837	.00488	.52989	2.24870
	II	.82852	.17504	.42680	.00458	.49307	2.00280
	III	.82778	.17505	.43158	.00448	.50445	1.83120
	IV	.83812	.17347	.44612	.00465	.55650	1.89680

3-month forward rates* (End of period) (continued)

Year	Quarter	Canadian Dollar	French Franc	German Mark	Japanese Yen	Swiss Franc	British Pound
1982	I	.81767	.16110	.42652	.00424	.54191	1.81480
	II	.78203	.15012	.41891	.00407	.49445	1.77000
	III	.80595	.13902	.40368	.00385	.47716	1.71860
	IV	.80515	.14161	.41702	.00416	.49563	1.61590
1983	I	.81536	.13748	.41996	.00423	.49221	1.48650
	II	.81238	.12909	.39699	.00420	.47984	1.55050
	III	.81294	.12270	.37891	.00416	.46915	1.50010
	IV	.80312	.11848	.36761	.00431	.46242	1.43910
1984	I	.78811	.12360	.38998	.00449	.47411	1.46330
	II	.76721	.11855	.37068	.00434	.44697	1.38650
	III	.76019	.10783	.33556	.00413	.40664	1.26120
	IV	.75635	.10481	.32501	.00406	.39477	1.18510
1985	I	.73201	.10560	.32717	.00450	.38833	1.2653
	II	.73324	.10663	.32848	.00403	.39392	1.2874
	III	.72626	.12202	.37781	.00465	.46226	1.4046
	IV	.70451	.13197	.40932	.00499	.49611	1.4466
1986	I	.71103	.14321	.43439	.00560	.51861	1.4863
	II	.72033	.14515	.45720	.00613	.56026	1.53602
	III	.71615	.15369	.49655	.00656	.61345	1.4456
	IV	.70512	.15793	.51685	.00628	.61960	1.4715
1987	I	.76509	.16572	.55741	.00691	.66930	1.5981
	II	.74838	.16333	.55095	.00687	.66353	1.5982
	III	.75964	.16355	.54883	.00689	.66128	1.6200
	IV	.8082	.1867	.6365	.008256	.7912	1.8642
1988	I	.8062	.1778	.6081	.008121	.7438	1.8704
	II	.8209	.1629	.5538	.007633	.6709	1.7007
	III	.8179	.1567	.5365	.007514	.6356	1.6720
	IV	.8355	.1653	.5667	.008037	.6699	1.7932
1989	I	.8343	.1569	.5334	.007578	.6105	1.6787
	II	.8295	.1511	.5149	.007013	.6002	1.5331
	III	.8427	.1554	.5372	.007242	.6205	1.6041
	IV	.8548	.1702	.5933	.006954	.6454	1.5961
1990	I	.8451	.1745	.5917	.006329	.6661	1.6221
	II	.8443	.1789	.6026	.006583	.7052	1.7207
	III	.8562	.1915	.6409	.007244	.7735	1.8511
	IV	.8556	.1956	.6653	.007426	.7816	1.8975
1991	I	.8564	.1753	.5909	.007133	.6931	1.7362
	II	.8710	.1624	.5543	.007209	.6482	1.6153

*Value in U.S. dollars

INDEX

Movements of Major Currencies against the Dollar

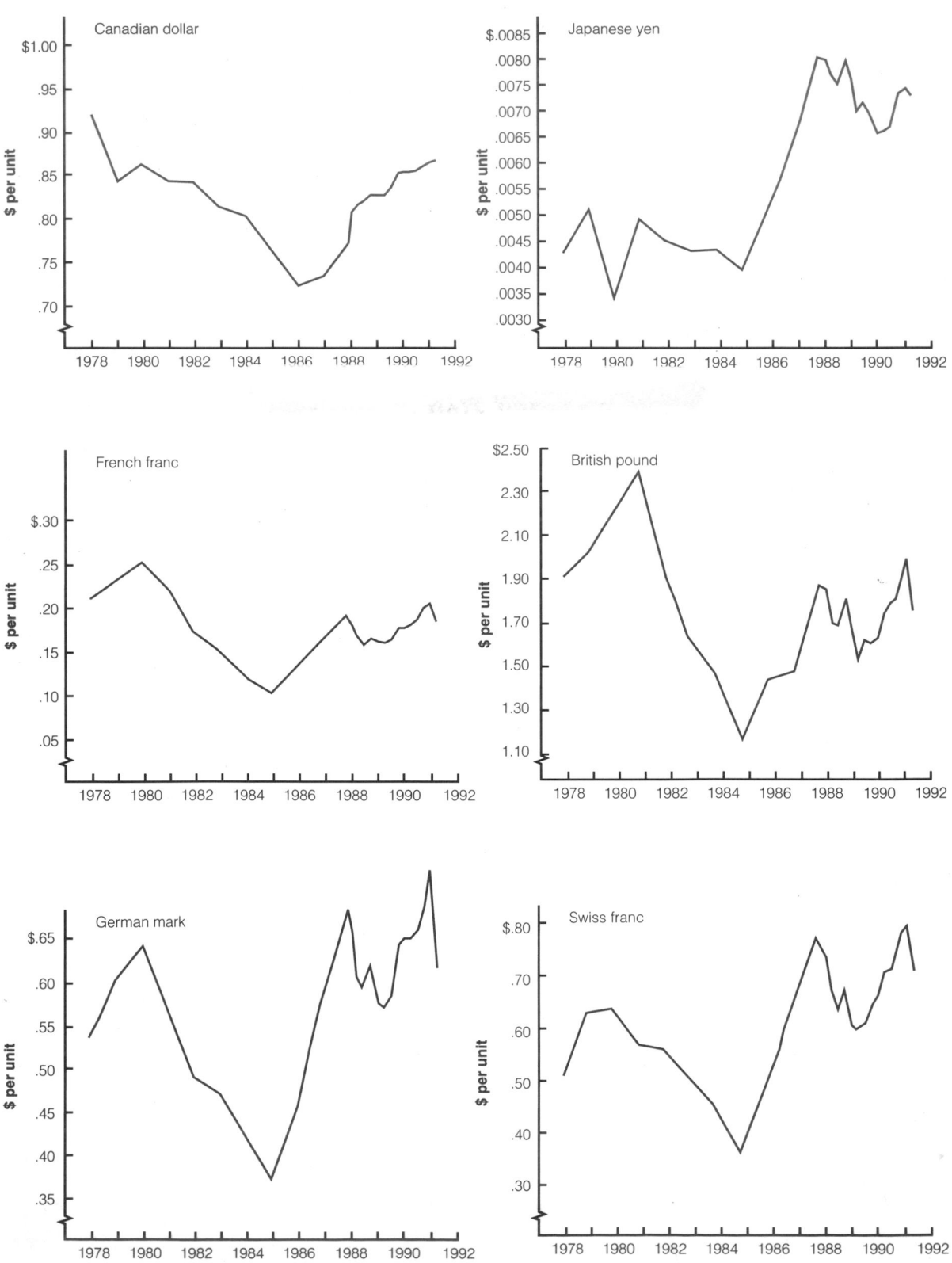